Encyclopedia of the Confederacy

Editorial Advisers

Encyclopedia of the Confederacy

RICHARD N. CURRENT, Editor in Chief
Emeritus, University of North Carolina, Greensboro

Editorial Board

PAUL D. ESCOTT
Wake Forest University

LAWRENCE N. POWELL
Tulane University

JAMES I. ROBERTSON, JR.
Virginia Polytechnic Institute and State University

EMORY M. THOMAS
University of Georgia

Volume 4

SIMON & SCHUSTER
A Paramount Communications Company

New York London Toronto Sydney Tokyo Singapore

Simon & Schuster
Academic Reference Division
15 Columbus Circle
New York, New York 10023

Printed in the United States of America

printing number
3 4 5 6 7 8 9 10

Library of Congress Cataloging-in-Publication Data

Encyclopedia of the Confederacy

Richard N. Current, Editor in Chief; editorial board, Paul D. Escott . . . [et al.].
p. cm..

Includes bibliographical reference and index (p.).
ISBN 0-13-275991-8 (set: alk. paper)
1. Confederate States of America—Encyclopedia.
I. Current, Richard Nelson.

E487.55 1993 973.7'13—dc20 93-4133 CIP

ISBN 0-13-275991-8 (set)
ISBN 0-13-276049-5 (v. 4)

Acknowledgments of sources, copyrights, and permissions to use previously printed materials are made throughout the work.

The paper used in this publication meets the minimum requirements of American National Standard for Information Sciences—Permanence of Paper for Printed Library Materials ANSI Z39.48-1984.

Abbreviations and Symbols Used in This Work

A.D. *anno Domini*, in the year of the (our) Lord
Adj. Gen. adjutant general
Adm. admiral
Ala. Alabama
A.M. *ante meridiem*, before noon
Ariz. Arizona
Ark. Arkansas
b. born; beam (interior measurement of width of a ship)
B.C. before Christ
brig. brigade
Brig. Gen. brigadier general
c. *circa*, about, approximately
Calif. California
Capt. captain
cf. *confer*, compare
chap. chapter (pl., chaps.)
cm centimeters
Col. colonel
Colo. Colorado
Comdr. commander
Como. commodore
Conn. Connecticut
Cpl. corporal
C.S. Confederate States
C.S.A. Confederate States of America, Confederate States Army
CSS Confederate States ship
cwt. hundredweight (equals 772 lbs.)
d. died
D.C. District of Columbia
Del. Delaware
diss. dissertation
div. division
dph. depth of hold
ed. editor (pl., eds.); edition; edited by
e.g. *exempli gratia*, for example
Eng. England
enl. enlarged
Ens. ensign
esp. especially
et al. *et alii*, and others
etc. *et cetera*, and so forth
exp. expanded
f. and following (pl., ff.)
1st Lt. first lieutenant
fl. *floruit*, flourished
Fla. Florida
frag. fragment
ft. feet
Ga. Georgia
Gen. general
Gov. governor
HMS Her Majesty's ship
ibid. *ibidem*, in the same place (as the one immediately preceding)
i.e. *id est*, that is
Ill. Illinois
Ind. Indiana
Kans. Kansas
km kilometers
Ky. Kentucky
l. length
La. Louisiana
lb. pound (pl., lbs.)
Lt. lieutenant
Lt. Col. lieutenant colonel
Lt. Comdr. lieutenant commander
Lt. Gen. lieutenant general
m meters
M.A. Master of Arts
Maj. Major
Maj. Gen. major general
Mass. Massachusetts
mi. miles
Mich. Michigan
Minn. Minnesota
Miss. Mississippi
Mo. Missouri
Mont. Montana
n. note
N.C. North Carolina
n.d. no date
N.Dak. North Dakota
Neb. Nebraska
Nev. Nevada
N.H. New Hampshire
N.J. New Jersey
N.Mex. New Mexico
no. number (pl., nos.)
n.p. no place
n.s. new series
N.Y. New York
Okla. Oklahoma
Oreg. Oregon
p. page (pl., pp.)
Pa. Pennsylvania
pdr. pounder (weight of pro-jec tile in pounds; pl., pdrs.)
pl. plural, plate (pl., pls.)
P.M. *post meridiem*, after noon
Pres. president
pt. part (pl., pts.)
Pvt. private
r. reigned; ruled; river
Rear Adm. rear admiral
regt. regiment
Rep. representative
rev. revised
R.I. Rhode Island
S.C. South Carolina
S.Dak. South Dakota
sec. section (pl., secs.)
2d Lt. second lieutenant
Sen. senator
ser. series
Sgt. sergeant
sing. singular
sq. square
supp. supplement; supplementary
Tenn. Tennessee
Tex. Texas
trans. translator, translators; translated by; translation
U.S. United States
USS United States ship
Va. Virginia
var. variant; variation
vol. volume (pl., vols.)
Vt. Vermont
Wash. Washington
Wis. Wisconsin
W.Va. West Virginia
Wyo. Wyoming
° degress
′ feet; minutes
″ inches; seconds
£ pounds
? uncertain; possibly; perhaps

Key to Map Symbols

Troops, Confederate

Troops, Union

Cavalry, Confederate

Cavalry, Union

Tactical Movement, Confederate

Tactical Movement, Union

Strategic Movement, Confedederate

Strategic Movement, Union

Retreat

Engagement

Artillery

Encampment

Headquarters

Fortifications

Entrenchments

Casemate Ironclad

Gunboat

Monitor

Warship

Trees

Marsh

Elevation

River

Railroad

Unfinished Railroad

Road

State Boundary

Building

Church

Village

Town, Strategic

Town, Tactical

Pontoon Bridge

Bridge

S

(CONTINUED)

SHINPLASTERS. A generic term applied at various times to paper money, especially small-change notes, *shinplasters* also went by the names *shingles, stump tails, red dogs,* and *wildcat* currency. Any term so indiscriminately used probably defies an accurate definition: usually, shinplasters referred to low-value paper money issued by state banks during the free banking era (1837–1863), to virtually all small-change bills, and, during the war in the Confederacy, to any paper money (except of Confederate notes) that circulated at a high rate of depreciation to gold or silver (specie).

Such money, however, was not unusual prior to the free banking era. The scarcity of circulating coin meant that, despite state laws against small-change notes, they circulated widely. Many antebellum Southern cities circulated notes of all types during emergencies, with lottery and railcar tickets also passing as a medium of exchange. In the most general sense, they too constituted shinplasters. During panic times, when banks suspended all specie payments, local businesses and governments issued change scrip in order to continue daily commerce.

Specifically, in the Confederacy, the currency of a number of state banks lost credibility as Federal forces closed in and as the bank specie reserves—already turned over to the Confederate government as backing for bonds or hidden from the government as its policies grew increasingly confiscatory—dwindled. Thus the value of many of those notes dropped to nearly nothing.

One other factor accounted for the depreciation of various notes into shinplasters. After the Emancipation Proclamation, Southerners knew that Federal forces would free slaves as soon as the Union armies occupied an area. To banks, that meant that the collateral for many of their loans had disappeared, thus eroding whatever assets the Southern banks still had.

To alleviate the problem that caused some types of shinplasters, the Confederate Senate, in September 1862, passed a bill to authorize Confederate Secretary of the Treasury Christopher G. Memminger to coin copper tokens of one, five, ten, and twenty-five cents. The Confederate House tabled the measure, and no other small-change law was enacted. Before the war, of course, many individual states had laws prohibiting small notes, but those proved ineffectual even in peacetime.

Neither version of shinplasters—small-change notes or depreciated money—developed owing to any inherent instability in the banking system (North or South). Instead, depreciation of such notes resulted from depreciating bond prices. The shinplaster experience reflected both the confiscatory Confederate policy toward banks and the public's reaction to battlefield events as well as the sudden change in the property status of slaves.

BIBLIOGRAPHY

Hummel, Jeffrey. "Confederate Finance." In *The Encyclopedia of American Business History and Biography: Banking and Finance to 1913.* Edited by Larry Schweikart. Columbia, S.C., 1990.

Pecquet, Gary. "The Tug of War over Southern Banks." In *Durrell Foundation Proceedings.* Berryville, Va., 1992.

Rockhoff, Hugh. *The Free Banking Era: A Reexamination.* New York, 1975.

Rolnick, Arthur J., and Warren E. Weber. "Free Banking, Wildcat Banking, and Shinplasters." *Federal Reserve Bank of Minneapolis Quarterly Review,* Fall 1982, 10–19.

Schweikart, Larry. *Banking in the American South from the Age of Jackson to Reconstruction.* Baton Rouge, La., 1987.

LARRY SCHWEIKART

SHIPYARDS. At war's outbreak the Confederacy seized two U.S. Navy shipyards, Gosport Navy Yard at Norfolk, Virginia, and Pensacola Navy Yard on Florida's Gulf coast.

The Gosport yard converted the frigate *Merrimack* to the ironclad *Virginia,* which battled *Monitor* in Hampton Roads (March 9, 1862). Then advancing Union troops forced Norfolk's abandonment. A similar fate befell Pensacola, and both government yards were lost. The navy established a new yard at Rocketts in Richmond, a site described by one officer as "a shed with 200 or 300 carpenters." Rocketts was active throughout the war, building three ironclads—*Richmond, Fredericksburg,* and *Virginia II*—and maintaining the other ships of the James River Squadron.

Whenever possible, the Navy Department sought to use private industry for wartime manufacturing, including shipbuilding. In the first months of the war both the Confederate and state governments bought commercial steamers and had them converted to warships by private shipyards in Nashville, Savannah, Mobile, and New Orleans. Gunboat contracts were signed with individuals in Mars Bluff and Charleston, South Carolina; Washington and Elizabeth City, North Carolina; Jacksonville and Pensacola, Florida; and Savannah, Saffold, and Early County, Georgia.

When the Navy Department's focus shifted to ironclads, the government continued to rely on independent contractors to build most of the new-style fighting ships. Usually, contractors were forced to create a building site for their project, in effect building their shipyard and then building their ship. Charleston foundry owner James Eason built *Chicora* in a vacant lot behind the post office. To build *Mississippi* at New Orleans, contractors Nelson and Asa Tift first tried to rent the Hughes shipyard at Algiers and then to subcontract the hull to the Harrem and Company or Hyde and Mackey yards. Failing in these efforts, they

SAVANNAH, GEORGIA. Burning of the navy yard at Savannah, December 21, 1864. NAVAL HISTORICAL CENTER, WASHINGTON, D.C.

acquired four acres on the river, installed a sawmill, and opened their own yard. Contractor E. C. Murray rented a lot adjoining that of the Tifts and, in the same way, began building the ironclad *Louisiana*.

Neither New Orleans ironclad survived the capture of the city. Nelson Tift went to Savannah and contracted to convert a blockade runner to the armored *Atlanta* at Henry F. Willink's shipyard. Willink's, one of the few professional shipbuilding facilities left in Confederate control after the spring of 1862, also turned out the ironclads *Savannah* and *Milledgeville* and serviced the rest of the Savannah River Squadron.

By the summer of 1862, with most of the coast and both ends of the Mississippi lost to the South, most Confederate shipbuilding had moved to locations on inland rivers. John Shirley began two ironclads at a steamboat landing below Memphis. When Memphis fell, he burned one and had the other—*Arkansas*—towed up the Yazoo River, where a shipyard was created at the Yazoo City cotton wharf. Gilbert Elliott built the ironclad *Albemarle* in a cornfield at Edwards Ferry, North Carolina. Swampy land at Oven Bluff, Alabama, on the Tombigbee River served as the construction site for three hulls (which were towed to Mobile and never completed).

That contractors had to create their building sites was not a peculiarity of the war. Of the 145 Southern shipyards listed in the 1850 census, the great majority were created for the construction of a single river-going commercial steamer. The wartime experience of shipyards springing up along river banks was just the peacetime practice of Southern shipbuilding gone to war.

Once a yard like Yazoo City or Edwards Ferry was established, other ships were often laid down but rarely completed. Initial construction usually went quickly, as timber was plentiful. But when armor plate and machinery were needed, the work would halt for lack of materials. The ships sat incomplete until advancing Union troops forced the destruction of the vessels and the abandonment of the yard. The Confederate navy contracted for—and saw begun—nearly four times as many ships as were commissioned.

[*See also* Charlotte Navy Yard; Gosport Navy Yard; Tift Brothers.]

BIBLIOGRAPHY

Melton, Maurice. *The Confederate Ironclads.* South Brunswick, N.J., 1968.

Scharf, J. Thomas. *History of the Confederate States Navy.* New York, 1887. Reprint, New York, 1977.

Still, William N., Jr. *Confederate Shipbuilding.* Athens, Ga., 1969.

Still, William N., Jr. "Facilities for the Construction of War Vessels in the Confederacy." *Journal of Southern History* 31 (1965): 285–304.

MAURICE K. MELTON

SHORTER, JOHN G. (1818–1872), Alabama congressman and governor. Born in Monticello, Georgia, John

Gill Shorter graduated from Franklin College (the University of Georgia) in 1837 and then settled in Eufaula, Alabama, where he practiced law and invested heavily in land and slaves. He served briefly in both houses of the Alabama legislature before being elected circuit judge of the Eufaula District in 1852, a position he held until the outbreak of war. Shorter represented Alabama at the Nashville convention in 1850, where he took an early stand in favor of secession. His support of that position grew stronger throughout the 1850s.

When Alabama seceded on January 11, 1861, Shorter was appointed the state's commissioner to the Georgia secession convention. While there he received word that he had been elected to the Confederate Provisional Congress; during his service in Congress, he gave strong support to Jefferson Davis's program. With Governor Andrew B. Moore constitutionally barred from serving a third term, Shorter ran for the office and won easily that fall over Thomas H. Watts.

Little did Shorter realize the magnitude of his prophecy when he warned Alabamians in his inaugural address on December 2, 1861, that they faced "unaccustomed burdens." Within five months Federal troops occupied the state's northern section beyond the Tennessee River, following the Confederate defeat at Shiloh. Shorter had done what he could to support Albert Sidney Johnston, sending him two regiments and a battalion together with five hundred slaves for fortification work. Now one of the areas where he had received his strongest support a year earlier turned bitter as it faced the terrible destruction of war. Caught off guard by the invasion, Shorter delayed two weeks before dispatching four cavalry units to harass the Union forces. When he had to cut short a tour of the region in early 1863 because of pressing business in Montgomery, the people there were further alienated.

Meanwhile Shorter faced a similar threat at the other end of the state. In March 1862 word came that the Confederacy planned to abandon Pensacola. Because Shorter considered it vital to Alabama's coastal defense, he persuaded the Confederacy to postpone the evacuation until May. This gave him time to salvage several cannon and considerable military supplies for use in the defense of Mobile, which appeared threatened following the landing of Federal troops on nearby Ship Island. He also rushed reinforcements to that area, but the Federals moved instead against New Orleans.

Shorter's biggest problem at this time was not lack of manpower but a critical shortage of arms and ammunition. His complaints to the secretary of war went unheeded, so he sought permission from the legislature to impress arms from the citizenry. When this request was turned down, he sent agents throughout the state to bring in militia muskets and buy other arms. Shorter also contracted with local foundries for weapons, but eighteen months later none had made any deliveries.

As problems mounted throughout 1862, securing enlistments became more difficult. Although initially opposed to conscription, Shorter finally accepted it but counseled Confederate officials to postpone its enforcement until after the harvest season, especially in northern Alabama, a rich agricultural region and increasingly a hotbed of dissatisfaction. Armed resistance did indeed break out that fall, forcing Confederate cavalry to move in and restore order. But the problems of resistance and desertion continued to plague the northern hill country and the southeastern corner of the state. When the legislature in October refused Shorter's request that he be allowed to reorganize the state militia with all those from age sixteen to sixty not subject to the draft, the governor turned to volunteers; but the response was disappointing. The legislature finally passed a compromise bill in August 1863 organizing "County Reserves," but this proved generally ineffective.

The legislature was more amenable to Shorter's pleas for assistance for the indigent families of Alabama troops. Many of them were in dire straits, and their condition encouraged desertion by soldiers who felt they were needed at home. The legislature appropriated $2 million for relief in October 1862 to be distributed through county officials who were also encouraged to supplement it through their own efforts. As conditions on the home front worsened, Shorter in November 1863 secured legislative approval for the state to purchase and distribute relief supplies directly. As food shortages mounted and salt became scarce, the governor banned the distillation of alcohol and placed restrictions on cotton production in favor of grain. He established a state salt works and threatened private salt works with confiscation if they overcharged. Exacerbating the situation was a deteriorating railroad system, which handicapped distribution.

Another manpower problem confronting Shorter involved the need for slave labor to work on fortifications and defenses. He had no difficulty in securing 500 slaves in early 1862 to help with Fort Henry; but by October the planters of west central Alabama had become reluctant to let their slaves work on railroad construction because of reports of their neglect and abuse. The governor then persuaded the legislature to give him the power to make requisitions upon the request of military commanders, with the Confederacy reimbursing the owners. With this authorization, he impressed 2,100 slaves to place obstructions on the state's rivers in anticipation of a new invasion. An additional 9,000 were requisitioned in 1863 to work on Mobile's defenses. But reports of abuses mounted in spite of Shorter's protests to the military. When Congress approved the Confederate Impressment Act of March 26, 1863, the governor thought seriously of removing the state from the process but felt honor-bound to continue his cooperation.

Shorter considered this issue, together with his continued strong support of the Davis administration, as the biggest detriment to his reelection. With the state beleaguered on many fronts, Alabamians went to the polls in the fall of 1863 and turned Shorter out of office in favor of his 1861 opponent, Watts, by a margin of three to one. Expressing little bitterness, he retired to his plantation and law practice in Eufaula, appearing only briefly at conservative Reconstruction meetings in Montgomery until his death from tuberculosis in 1872.

BIBLIOGRAPHY

Fleming, Walter L. *Civil War and Reconstruction in Alabama.* New York, 1905. Reprint, Spartanburg, S.C., 1978.

Garrett, William. *Reminiscences of Public Men in Alabama for Thirty Years.* Atlanta, 1872.

Martin, Bessie. *Desertion of Alabama Troops.* New York, 1932.

McMillan, Malcolm C. "Alabama." In *The Confederate Governors.* Edited by W. Buck Yearns. Athens, Ga., 1985.

McMillan, Malcolm C. *The Disintegration of a Confederate State: Three Governors and Alabama's Wartime Home Front, 1861–1865.* Macon, Ga., 1986.

McMillan, Malcolm C., ed. *The Alabama Confederate Reader.* University, Ala., 1963.

William E. Parrish

SHOUP, FRANCIS (1835–1896), brigadier general. The son of a merchant who was active politically and comfortable financially, Francis Asbury Shoup was born March 22, 1835, in Laurel, Indiana. After attending Asbury University briefly, he entered West Point and graduated in 1855. As an artillery officer he saw duty in Florida and campaigned against the Seminoles. He resigned from the army in 1860 to begin the study of law. Shoup established a practice in Saint Augustine, where he became acquainted with E. Kirby Smith.

When war broke out Shoup helped organize a Florida battery, but William J. Hardee quickly summoned him to Fort Morgan to assist in organizing volunteers. He went with Hardee to Arkansas as a trusted subordinate and followed him to Kentucky to become his chief of artillery. In that capacity Shoup served with distinction at Shiloh, helping mass the guns that overwhelmed Benjamin M. Prentiss on the first day. Following Shiloh he served as a staff officer under P. G. T. Beauregard and later under Thomas C. Hindman, winning praise from the latter for his services at Prairie Grove, Arkansas, and recommendation for brigadier general. He was promoted to that rank on September 12, 1862, and took command of a Louisiana brigade at Vicksburg. He was captured there and exchanged. Joseph E. Johnston invited him to Dalton to become chief of artillery of the Army of Tennessee, and in that capacity he served ably throughout the Atlanta campaign. When John Bell Hood became commander of that army, Shoup became his chief of staff.

Following the war Shoup led an active and productive life as a priest in the Episcopal church and as a university professor until his death on September 4, 1896.

BIBLIOGRAPHY

Dickison, J. J. *Florida.* Vol. 11 of *Confederate Military History.* Edited by Clement A. Evans. Atlanta, 1899. Vol. 16 of extended ed. Wilmington, N.C., 1989.

Warner, Ezra J. *Generals in Gray: Lives of the Confederate Commanders.* Baton Rouge, La., 1959.

Nathaniel Cheairs Hughes, Jr.

SIBLEY, HENRY HOPKINS (1816–1886), brigadier general. Sibley was born at Natchitoches, Louisiana, May 25, 1816. He attended West Point and graduated thirty-first in a class of forty-five in 1838. Commissioned a second lieutenant in the Second Dragoons, he saw action in Florida against the Seminoles and fought in Mexico where he was breveted for heroism near Vera Cruz. He spent five years on the Texas frontier, served in Bleeding Kansas, and participated in the 1857–1858 expedition against the Mormons in Utah. Sent to New Mexico Territory, Sibley was with Maj. E. R. S. Canby during the 1860 Navajo campaign.

After resigning from the Federal army in May 1861, Sibley went to Richmond where he convinced President Jefferson Davis of the practicality of seizing New Mexico

Henry Hopkins Sibley. Library of Congress

Territory as a prelude to a Confederate conquest of Colorado and eventually California. Returning to Texas, Sibley assembled a brigade of Texans at San Antonio and set out for Fort Bliss. Pushing up the Rio Grande, Sibley was victorious at Valverde on February 21, 1862, but was turned back at Glorieta Pass near Santa Fe in March and was forced to evacuate the territory. Largely because of his heavy drinking and lack of leadership ability, Sibley was widely blamed for the failure of the campaign. He was sent to Louisiana where he was court-martialed in 1863 following the Battle of Bisland. Although acquitted, he was without a command for the remainder of the war.

After the war, he was recruited into the Egyptian army as a general but was expelled in 1873 for drunkenness. Although well known at one time for his Sibley Tent and Stove Company, he died largely forgotten at Fredericksburg, Virginia, on August 23, 1886.

BIBLIOGRAPHY

Hall, Martin H. *The Confederate Army of New Mexico.* Austin, Tex., 1978.

Hall, Martin H. *Sibley's New Mexico Campaign.* Austin, Tex., 1960.

Thompson, Jerry. *Henry Hopkins Sibley: Confederate General of the West.* Natchitoches, La., 1987.

JERRY THOMPSON

SIGNAL CORPS. The Confederate Signal Corps was, in effect, the creation of a single officer, Edward Porter Alexander, who, while an instructor at West Point, had assisted army surgeon Albert J. Myer in the perfection of his "wig-wag" system of military signaling. After going South in 1861, Alexander was at once put to work organizing, training, and equipping a Signal Corps. Thanks to his skill and energy, the Confederates had a functioning signal service with their forces at First Manassas (July 21, 1861), several months before the confused U.S. War Department could put an effective organization into the field with the Federal armies.

Alexander formed his first signal unit by requesting the detail of some twenty intelligent young privates who could be commissioned if they proved competent. In April 1862 the Confederate government officially established the Signal Service as a branch of its Adjutant General's Department, to consist of one major, ten captains, ten first lieutenants, ten second lieutenants, and twenty sergeants. These men were assigned in small teams to the headquarters of the Confederacy's various field armies, which furnished any needed additional personnel. In 1865 its total strength was approximately 1,500. Its missions were to include signaling, telegraphy, and secret service work.

The Confederate Signal Corps had no distinctive uniform or insignia. Signaling equipment was the same as that used by the Federal Signal Corps, though probably not as complete. The basic items were the signal flags (in the Federal signal service, these were in three sizes—six feet, four feet, and two feet square) and a sixteen-foot staff, made up of four 4-foot sections. The flag commonly used was

SIGNAL STATION NEAR BEVERLEY FORD, VIRGINIA. *FRANK LESLIE'S ILLUSTRATED FAMOUS LEADERS AND BATTLE SCENES OF THE CIVIL WAR*

white, with a red central square, but under some conditions a red flag with a white central square might have greater visibility. A black flag with a white center was used when the ground was snow-covered.

For night signaling, flags were replaced by torches—hollow copper cylinders filled with turpentine or other liquid fuel. Members of the signal detail would carry extra fuel in large round canteens. Torches could be supplemented by a variety of pyrotechnics, such as rockets, flares, and star shells. There were also a variety of improvised methods of communication—fires, signal cannon, and contraptions like the four black-cloth balls that Alexander used for signaling from the Confederacy's one short-lived observation balloon. A Signal Corps officer's most important item of equipment was a powerful telescope or field glasses, essential for reading signals from other stations and observing enemy movements.

The Signal Corps established chains of signal stations, each manned by one or two officers and several enlisted men, from their army's outposts back to its headquarters. These were placed on commanding heights so that each station had a clear line of sight to the stations on either side of it. Where such hills were lacking, tall buildings or specially built signal towers (shaped much like oil derricks) were utilized. The distance between stations depended on the terrain.

Since these stations frequently provided excellent views of the opposing army, the Signal Corps detachments manning them thus had the dual mission of transmitting messages and observing and reporting enemy activities. They also could often observe and copy the messages from the enemy's signal stations. Though all important messages were sent in some type of code, Confederate skills in this art were decidedly inferior to the Federals', who periodically broke Confederate codes and so gained valuable military intelligence. In contrast, the Confederates never were able to read Federal messages, though they occasionally deceived their opponents by sending false information they knew would be intercepted.

One unusual communications function of the Confederate Signal Corps was service aboard blockade runners. Exchanging signals with the Confederate shore defenses, they could obtain the location of close-in Federal warships blockading the seaport and of the safest channels for their ship to use. In 1864 numerous blockade runners reportedly were forced to wait idly in the Bahamas until signal officers could be run out through the blockade to help pilot them in.

The Signal Corps' role in telegraphic communications is not too well recorded. The Confederacy had only limited commercial telegraph service in 1861; there was no unified network to connect Richmond with the various battle fronts and armies. Also, there were relatively few skilled telegraph operators, and telegraph wire was in short supply. The weaknesses of the existing system were aggravated by the damage done to it by Federal raiders—damage that was increasingly difficult to repair as supplies of materials dwindled. (On at least one occasion in 1864 considerable quantities of telegraph wire were stolen by Southern planters for use in baling their cotton.) Though the Signal Corps utilized the existing Southern telegraph systems with their civilian employees and may have somewhat improved and extended them, they never achieved either a nationwide system (such as the North possessed) or a military telegraph service (such as the North had from 1864) to accompany Confederate armies into the field.

The Signal Corps' involvement in "secret service" (a phrase covering what now would be called military intelligence operations) probably grew out of its efforts during the period after First Manassas, when the Confederate outposts were within sight of Washington, D.C., to set up a signal station within that city itself. It was to be managed by a

SIGNAL STATION, JULY 1864.

HARPER'S PICTORIAL HISTORY OF THE GREAT REBELLION

daring spy to whom Confederate sympathizers (including the famous Rose O'Neal Greenhow) would furnish information on Federal forces in the Washington area. This effort failed because the outposts had to be withdrawn, but the Signal Corps continued to be involved in espionage of one sort or another for the duration of the war. It did not have a monopoly on this activity; the Confederate State Department maintained its own intelligence network and practically every Confederate commander utilized his personal contingent of scouts, agents, and spies. (Also there was practically a surplus of enthusiastic amateur spies of both sexes.) This whole business was under no sort of central coordination and control; records of its workings are very incomplete and those available generally exaggerated.

The Signal Corps' one special function in all this seems to have been wire tapping—cutting into Federal telegraph lines and reading the messages being transmitted or inserting their own messages containing false information. Skilled telegraph operators rode with J. E. B. Stuart and John Hunt Morgan on their famous raids; on one occasion Stuart had his operator, a soldier named Sheppard, send the quartermaster general of the U.S. Army a taunting dispatch concerning the poor quality of the mules he had just captured. Other operators infiltrated Federal-occupied territory, tapped wires in some secluded area, and remained there quietly for days recording all messages, as did C. A. Gaston, who was Gen. Robert E. Lee's confidential operator in 1864. Since all important Federal messages were encoded, the amount of valuable information gained from such exploits was minor. But a good many operational messages—such as those directing forces attempting to trap Confederate raiders—were sent "in the clear," and their interception could be highly valuable to the raiders.

Organized hurriedly from scratch, always hampered by shortages of equipment, the Confederate Signal Corps nevertheless rapidly became an effective force. Unfortunately, its services have received little recognition.

[*See also* Alexander, Edward Porter; Balloon; Espionage; Telegraph.]

BIBLIOGRAPHY

Alexander, Edward P. *Fighting for the Confederacy.* Chapel Hill, N.C., 1989.

Coggins, Jack. *Arms and Equipment of the Civil War.* Garden City, N.Y., 1962.

Miller, Francis T. *The Photographic History of the Civil War.* Vol. 8. New York, 1912.

Todd, Frederick P., ed. *American Military Equipage, 1851–1872,* Vol. 2. Providence, R.I., 1977.

JOHN R. ELTING

SIMMS, JAMES PHILLIP (1837–1888), brigadier general. A lawyer before the Civil War, Simms enlisted in the Confederate service in the spring of 1862 as major of the Fifty-third Georgia. He fought in the Peninsular, Seven Days', and Maryland campaigns, and was promoted to colonel on October 8, 1862. In the Battle of Chancellorsville his men served with valor and distinction, capturing the national colors of the Second Rhode Island Volunteers. The regiment took part in the heavy fighting south of the Peach Orchard on the second day of Gettysburg before being transferred west with James Longstreet's command in September 1863.

After leading his regiment in the operations against Knoxville, Simms returned to Virginia, later participating in the Battles of the Wilderness, Spotsylvania, and Cold Harbor. Transferred to the Shenandoah Valley in August 1864, he commanded a brigade at Cedar Creek before returning to the trenches of Petersburg. Promoted to brigadier general on December 8, 1864, Simms took part in the retreat from Richmond but was captured at Sayler's Creek on April 6, 1865. While in prison at Fort Warren, Massachusetts, in April 1865, he was one of a group of officers who wrote to Gen. Ulysses S. Grant expressing their sorrow and outrage over the assassination of Abraham Lincoln.

After the war, Simms resumed his law practice and became a state legislator from Newton County. He strove to improve the prosperity of his constituents until his death in 1888.

BIBLIOGRAPHY

Derry, Joseph T. *Georgia.* Vol. 6 of *Confederate Military History.* Edited by Clement A. Evans. Atlanta, 1899. Vol. 7 of extended ed. Wilmington, N.C., 1987.

Freeman, Douglas S. *Lee's Lieutenants: A Study in Command.* 3 vols. New York, 1942–1944. Reprint, New York, 1986.

U.S. War Department. *War of the Rebellion: A Compilation of the Official Records of the Union and Confederate Armies.* Washington, D.C., 1880–1901. Ser. 1, vol. 25, pt. 1, pp. 833, 837; ser. 1, vol. 27, pt. 2, p. 283; ser. 1, vol. 43, pt. 1, pp. 589–592; ser. 1, vol. 46, pt. 3; p. 787.

MICHAEL G. MAHON

SIMMS, WILLIAM E. (1822–1898), congressman from Kentucky. Simms was as dedicated and fierce a proponent of state rights as any of his colleagues in the Confederate Senate from the lower South. According to historian Jon L. Wakelyn, Simms "was one of the most diligent and able politicians in the Confederate Senate."

Born in Cynthiana, Harrison County, Kentucky, he moved to Bourbon County at an early age. Simms attended local schools, studied law at Transylvania University in Lexington, and entered the bar in Paris, Kentucky, in 1846. Later that year he recruited and commanded a company of the Third Kentucky Infantry, serving in the Mexican War under Gen. Winfield Scott. In 1849 Simms, a Democrat, was elected to one term in the Kentucky House of Representatives. During the political crises of the 1850s he became identified with state rights ideology, practicing law and editing a political newspaper, the *Kentucky State Flag*. In 1858 Simms was elected to the U.S. House of Representatives where he aimed his sharp pro-Southern invective at spokesmen of the new Republican party.

In 1861, after he was defeated for reelection by the more moderate John J. Crittenden, Simms served briefly as a colonel of the First Battalion Kentucky Cavalry in the southwestern Virginia campaign. In November 1861, the Provisional Government of Kentucky appointed Simms a commissioner "with power to negotiate . . . the earliest practicable admission of Kentucky into . . . the Confederate States of America." In 1862 he was elected to the Confederate Senate and served throughout the war. He took on heavy committee responsibilities, including membership in the Accounts, Indian Affairs, Naval Affairs, and Public Buildings committees. In office Simms supported President Jefferson Davis's conscription, exemption, and impressment policies and endorsed arming the slaves. Though once a champion of Davis's military leadership, Simms late in the war favored radical changes in the South's command system.

After Appomattox, Simms went into exile in Canada, not returning to his farm near Paris until 1866. Three decades later, his full political rights were restored.

BIBLIOGRAPHY

Quisenberry, A. C. "The Alleged Secession of Kentucky." *Register of the Kentucky State Historical Society* 15 (1917): 15–32.

Wakelyn, Jon L. *Biographical Dictionary of the Confederacy.* Edited by Frank E. Vandiver. Westport, Conn., 1977.

Warner, Ezra J., and W. Buck Yearns. *Biographical Register of the Confederate Congress.* Baton Rouge, La., 1975.

JOHN DAVID SMITH

SIMPSON, WILLIAM DUNLAP (1823–1890), lieutenant colonel and South Carolina congressman, governor, and supreme court chief justice. Born October 27, 1823, in Laurens District, South Carolina, Simpson graduated from South Carolina College in 1843 and attended Harvard Law School. He read law with Henry C. Young and was admitted to the bar in 1845. He became a planter and served in the state house of representatives (1854–1855, 1858–1859) and the state senate (1860–1863).

During the Civil War Simpson was on the staff of Gen. Milledge L. Bonham (1861) and became major and lieutenant colonel of the Fourteenth South Carolina Infantry (1862–1863). He was elected to Congress to replace Bonham and took his seat on February 5, 1863. He was reelected in October unopposed and served until the end of the war. Simpson usually supported Davis and the central government. He favored few army exemptions, but he proposed that states be permitted to exempt whomever they wished. He backed forced funding of Treasury notes, but did not favor repudiating unfunded notes. He opposed drafting speculators, impressing railroad stock, and suspending the writ of habeas corpus.

In 1868 Simpson attended the Democratic National Convention and was elected to the U.S. Congress. He was disqualified but became lieutenant governor under Wade Hampton in the Redeemer victory of 1876. In 1879 he became governor when Hampton was elected to the U.S. Senate and served until he was elected chief justice of the state supreme court. He remained on the bench until his death on December 26, 1890.

BIBLIOGRAPHY

Biographical Directory of the S.C. Senate, 1776–1985. Edited by N. Louise Bailey et al. Vol. 2. Columbia, S.C., 1986.

Johnson, Allen, and Dumas Malone, eds. *Dictionary of American Biography.* New York, 1935.

A. V. HUFF, JR.

SINGLETON, OTHO ROBARDS (1814–1889), private and congressman from Mississippi. Born in Kentucky and educated there, Singleton moved to Canton, Mississippi, in 1838 after he had gained admission to the bar. Eight years later he began a political career that would intermittently span forty-one years. First, he served in the state house of representatives from 1846 to 1847 and then in the senate from 1848 to 1853. He held a seat in the U.S. Congress from 1853 to 1855, and 1857 to 1861.

In 1858, after controversy had erupted over the subject of admitting Kansas to the Union, Singleton sought to impress upon the Northern members of the House of Representatives that the South would unite to resist change. He accused abolitionists of a "stolid ignorance" if they thought that nonslaveholders would turn their "swords upon their brethren," the slaveholders. He insisted that only "one feeling will animate every heart" and only "one common shout will go up for victory, or one common heap of the slain tell the sad story of defeat."

Of all the members of Mississippi's House delegation in 1859, Singleton was the only one to face opposition. His opponent Franklin Smith ran on a platform strongly opposing secession and supporting Stephen A. Douglas in the event of his nomination. Singleton, on the other hand, unequivocally opposed Douglas and supported immediate secession if any Republican were elected president in 1860, insisting the South must be "up and doing, ready to strike blows." Singleton won two to one.

After the war began, Singleton served briefly as a private in the Confederate army and then was elected to the First

Congress in 1861. He served as chairman of the Committee on Indian Affairs and strictly followed the policies of Jefferson Davis. He rarely contributed debate or advanced any policies of his own. He did express strong feelings about the injustice of the well-to-do being allowed to hire substitutes for army service. Although he served also in the Second Congress, he seldom attended for unknown reasons. Apparently, his frequent absences had nothing to do with any disagreement with the administration's position, which he had advocated from the start of the turmoil.

After the war Singleton worked to return the state to Democratic control. He continued in politics, serving again in the U.S. Congress from 1875 to 1887, two years before his death.

BIBLIOGRAPHY

Alexander, Thomas B., and Richard E. Beringer. *The Anatomy of the Confederate Congress: A Study of the Influences of Member Characteristics on Legislative Voting Behavior, 1861–1865.* Nashville, Tenn., 1972.

Warner, Ezra J., and W. Buck Yearns. *Biographical Register of the Confederate Congress.* Baton Rouge, La., 1975.

RAY SKATES

SKILLED LABOR. *See* Labor, *article on* Skilled Labor.

SLACK, WILLIAM YARNEL (1816–1862), brigadier general. Slack was born August 1, 1816, in Mason County, Kentucky. Three years later his family moved to Boone County, Missouri, settling near Columbia. Slack studied law and opened a practice at Chillicothe. He fought in the Mexican War as captain of the Second Missouri Mounted Volunteers.

When the Civil War began, he was made a brigadier general of the Missouri State Guard by Governor Claiborne F. Jackson. In July he assembled a group in the Fifth District of Missouri, which was later designated the Fourth Division, Missouri State Guard. He fought at Carthage and was severely wounded in the groin at the Battle of Oak Hills on August 10, 1861. He returned to his command in October and took part in the Battle of Elkhorn Tavern, Arkansas, where he led the Second Brigade, Missouri Volunteers. On the morning of March 7 he was marching up the side of Sugar Loaf Mountain when he was wounded again in the groin, almost in the same place as his first injury. He was carried from the field but had to be moved three times to avoid capture by the Federals. Although he seemed to improve slightly, he died on March 21.

Slack was buried in the Roller Cemetery northwest of Gateway, Arkansas, but in 1880 his body was moved to the Confederate Cemetery at Fayetteville. He was promoted to brigadier general on April 17 to date from April 12, 1862—nearly four weeks after his death.

BIBLIOGRAPHY

Pea Ridge National Park. "The Battle of Pea Ridge, 1862." Pamphlet. Rogers, Ark., n.d.

Hughes, Michael A. "A Forgotten Battle in a Region Ignored . . . Pea Ridge, or Elkhorn Tavern, Arkansas—March 7–8, 1862: The Campaign, the Battle, and the Men Who Fought for the Fate of Missouri." *Blue & Gray Magazine* 5 (1988): 8–36.

ANNE J. BAILEY

SLATER, SARAH (1843–c.1880), spy. Known to Union authorities as the mysterious "lady in the veil," Slater, born Sarah Antoinette Gilbert in Middletown, Connecticut, carried Confederate dispatches between Richmond and Canada during the last year of the war. Sometime in 1858 or 1859 Sarah Gilbert moved from Hartford, Connecticut, to North Carolina. She settled in New Bern, where she met and married a music and dancing teacher, Rowan Slater, in 1861.

In January 1865, while in Richmond attempting to obtain a pass to New York, Slater was recruited by Confederate authorities as a spy. A fluent French speaker, she was an ideal candidate for missions to Quebec. In late January she carried information pertaining to the extradition of the St. Albans raiders from Richmond to Montreal. She was escorted back to the South, from New York to Washington, by John H. Surratt, one of the conspirators in the Lincoln assassination plot. In March she made a second trip to Montreal; no further records of her spy activities exist.

Slater's name was raised often in the 1865 Lincoln assassination conspiracy trial and in the 1867 murder trial of Surratt. The first of a handful of witnesses to implicate Slater in the plot was Louis J. Weichmann, a Union war clerk who told Federal authorities he had seen Slater at the Washington, D.C., boarding house of Lincoln conspirator Mary Elizabeth Surratt. Federal authorities searched for Slater through 1867 but were never able to find her or to substantiate the rumor that she was connected to the Lincoln assassination.

BIBLIOGRAPHY

Hall, James O. "The Saga of Sarah Slater." In *In Pursuit Of: Continuing Research in the Field of the Lincoln Assassination.* Clinton, Md., 1990.

ELIZABETH R. VARON

SLAUGHTER, JAMES EDWIN (1827–1901), brigadier general. Slaughter, a great-nephew of President

James Madison, was born on an undetermined date in June 1827 on his father's estate in Culpeper County, Virginia. The site became the center of the battlefield of Cedar (or Slaughters) Mountain. Young Slaughter attended the Virginia Military Institute (1845–1846), but he withdrew to accept a commission as second lieutenant in the U.S. Army at the outbreak of the Mexican War. He was promoted to first lieutenant, August 3, 1852, a rank he held until he resigned at the start of the Civil War.

At the outset of hostilities Slaughter was commissioned a lieutenant and acting inspector general on the staff of Braxton Bragg in the Department of Alabama and West Florida. In the meantime a commission as captain of artillery was dated May 24, 1861, to rank from March 16, although the commission was not confirmed until December 24.

In the bombardment of Pensacola, Slaughter was cited for "patient labor and unceasing vigil given to the organization and instruction of the troops." Promoted to major on November 16, 1861, he was advanced to the temporary rank of colonel on January 10, 1862. A month later, on February 8, he was appointed superintendent of the recruiting service. He was commissioned brigadier on March 18, 1862, and simultaneously was named assistant inspector general under Joseph E. Johnston. After his appointment as inspector general under Bragg on July 17, Slaughter commanded a brigade in William Whann Mackall's division, Department of the Gulf.

In April 1863, Slaughter transferred to Galveston as chief of artillery under John B. Magruder. Subsequently, he commanded the eastern and western subdistricts of Texas. On May 13, 1865, Slaughter commanded Confederate forces in the last engagement of the war, at Palmetto Ranch, near Brownsville, Texas. Although he had heard of Lee's surrender and did not wish to fight, "the enemy advanced upon my forces [and] I attacked and routed them." In announcing the war's end to his troops, Slaughter urged: "Go home and try to make as good citizens as you have soldiers. And do more. I hope that the result will prove that our enemies were right and we were wrong."

Slaughter lived in Mexico after the war, and then moved to Mobile, where he served two terms as postmaster, and finally to New Orleans. He died, January 1, 1901, while visiting Mexico City and was buried there.

BIBLIOGRAPHY

Compiled Military Service Records. James Edwin Slaughter. Microcopy M331, Roll 226. Record Group 109. National Archives, Washington, D.C.

Coyner, Luther. "A Later 'Last Battle of the War.'" *Confederate Veteran* 4 (1896): 416. Reprint, Wilmington, N.C., 1985.

Hotchkiss, Jed. *Virginia.* Vol. 3 of *Confederate Military History.* Edited by Clement A. Evans. Atlanta, 1899. Vol. 4 of extended ed. Wilmington, N.C., 1987.

Warner, Ezra J. *Generals in Gray: Lives of the Confederate Commanders.* Baton Rouge, La., 1959.

West, W. C. "The Last Battle of the War." *Southern Historical Society Papers* 21 (1883): 226–227. Reprint, Wilmington, N.C., 1990.

LOWELL REIDENBAUGH

SLAVE DRIVERS. Drivers were slaves responsible for plantation field production and labor discipline. By the 1830s they were widely employed in the Tidewater rice- and Sea Island cotton-growing areas, the Delta region, and Louisiana sugar parishes, where large agricultural units required close management; many small cotton planters also relied on drivers. On large plantations drivers worked directly under white (and sometimes black) overseers meting out daily work tasks, leading and disciplining work gangs, and managing crop production. On small plantations drivers served as foremen-overseers who reported directly to the master. The staple-crop economy of the plantation South, with its emphasis on regimentation and discipline, meant that the drivers' principal role was to "drive" the slaves by coaxing or coercion. But masters also expected drivers to maintain order in the quarters and to relate the masters' interests to the slaves. Masters rewarded drivers with extra rations, money, access to the local market, and other privileges. Slaves, in turn, suffered drivers so long as they did not abuse their power, kept the masters out of their lives in the quarters, and respected the slaves' community norms. Drivers thus occupied a precarious middle ground between master and slave.

The Civil War fundamentally altered the master-slave relationship, even before emancipation. With the menfolk away, plantation management often was left to planters' wives and "trustworthy" slave drivers. The situation expanded the driver's responsibilities, while paradoxically eroding the structure of bondage on which his power rested. Where drivers had ruled by undue force, embittered slaves retaliated for past abuses by beating and even murdering overseers and drivers, violent acts that were especially widespread in the sugar parishes in 1863 during the Union army advance. Mostly, the unraveling of planter authority forced drivers increasingly to accommodate the slaves' interests to maintain their own authority. Meanwhile, whites at home complained of driver complicity in raiding plantation storehouses (to which drivers often held the keys), aiding runaways, and slowing work, yet planters continued to entrust daily farm management to black drivers and overseers. The trust was not wholly misplaced, for even as drivers lightened slavery's burdens, they tried to maintain minimum levels of production and upkeep. Perhaps more than any other slave, the driver understood that the slaves' physical well-being, and even avoidance of sale, depended on their producing enough foodstuffs and cash crops to keep slaves fed and masters solvent.

Southern whites' postwar accounts of faithful slaves, especially drivers and house servants, protecting the farms and hiding the master's silver from Northern bummers exaggerated the loyalty of slaves but revealed what had bound such "privileged bondsmen" as drivers to the plantations—namely, that they claimed a vested, proprietary interest in the goods and farmsteads they had planted and built. This was most graphically demonstrated on the South Carolina Sea Islands in 1861 when the masters fled their plantations during the Union landing at Port Royal. Before the abolitionists arrived to begin their famous "Port Royal experiment," the drivers already had kept the slaves growing food crops and prevented destruction of farm equipment and buildings.

Immediately after the war some drivers functioned as straw bosses on plantations where owners sought to bind former slaves to long-term contracts in gang-labor systems, but virtually everywhere by the late 1860s sharecropping and tenancy arrangements left no place for drivers. Many former drivers, especially in the Sea Island and Delta areas, parlayed their planting and marketing experience and personal relationships with former masters into access to credit and local markets few other freedmen could command. Their conservative mediating behavior during slavery inclined former drivers toward personal profit and away from politics. Few former drivers held office during Reconstruction. Their public lives had ended with slavery.

BIBLIOGRAPHY

Miller, Randall M. "The Man in the Middle: The Black Slave Driver." *American Heritage* 30 (1979): 40–49.

Mohr, Clarence L. *On the Threshold of Freedom: Masters and Slaves in Civil War Georgia.* Athens, Ga., 1986.

Rose, Willie Lee. *Rehearsal for Reconstruction: The Port Royal Experiment.* New York, 1964.

Thomas, Emory M. *The Confederate Nation: 1861–1865.* New York, 1979.

Van Deburg, William L. *The Slave Drivers: Black Agricultural Labor Supervisors in the Antebellum South.* Westport, Conn., 1979.

RANDALL M. MILLER

SLAVERY. [*This entry is composed of three articles:* Antebellum Slavery *and* Slavery during the Civil War, *which discuss the institution of slavery before and during the war, and* Slave Life, *which discusses the daily lives of slaves and their society and culture. See also* African Americans in the Confederacy; Antislavery; Cotton; Labor; Plantation; Proslavery; Overseers; Slave Drivers; Slave Traders; Sugar; Tobacco.]

Antebellum Slavery

The enslavement of African Americans in what became the United States formally began during the 1630s and 1640s. At that time colonial courts and legislatures made clear that Africans—unlike white indentured servants—served their masters for life and that their slave status would be inherited by their children. Slavery in the United States ended in the mid-1860s. Abraham Lincoln's Emancipation Proclamation of January 1863 was a masterful propaganda tactic, but in truth, it proclaimed free only those slaves outside the control of the Federal government—that is, only those in areas still controlled by the Confederacy. The legal end to slavery in the nation came in December 1865 when the Thirteenth Amendment was ratified. It declared: "Neither slavery nor involuntary servitude, except as a punishment for crime whereof the party shall have been duly convicted, shall exist within the United States, or any place subject to their jurisdiction."

Development of American Slavery

The history of African American slavery in the United States can be divided into two periods: the first coincided with the colonial years, about 1650 to 1790; the second lasted from American independence through the Civil War, 1790 to 1865. Prior to independence, slavery existed in all the American colonies and therefore was not an issue of sectional debate. With the arrival of independence, however, the new Northern states—those of New England along with New York, Pennsylvania, and New Jersey—came to see slavery as contradictory to the ideals of the Revolution and instituted programs of gradual emancipation. By 1820 there were only about 3,000 slaves in the North, almost all of them working on large farms in New Jersey. Slavery could be abolished more easily in the North because there were far fewer slaves in those states, and they were not a vital part of Northern economies. There were plenty of free white men to do the sort of labor slaves performed. In fact, the main demand for abolition of slavery came not from those who found it morally wrong but from white working-class men who did not want slaves as rivals for their jobs.

Circumstances in the newly formed Southern states were quite different. The African American population, both slave and free, was much larger. In Virginia and South Carolina in 1790 nearly half of the population was of African descent. (Historians have traditionally assumed that South Carolina had a black majority population throughout its pre–Civil War history. But census figures for 1790 to 1810 show that the state possessed a majority of whites.) Other Southern states also had large black minorities. (See Table 1.)

Because of their ingrained racial prejudice and ignorance about the sophisticated cultures in Africa from which many of their slaves came, Southern whites were convinced that free blacks would be savages—a threat to white survival. So Southerners believed that slavery was necessary as a means of race control.

Of equal importance in the Southern states was the economic role that slaves played. These states were much more dependent on the agricultural sector of their economies than were Northern ones. Much of the wealth of Delaware, Maryland, Virginia, the Carolinas, and Georgia came from the cash crops that slaves grew. Indeed, many white Southerners did not believe white men could (or should) do the backbreaking labor required to produce tobacco, cotton, rice, and indigo, which were the region's chief cash crops.

As a consequence of these factors, the Southern states were determined to retain slavery after the Revolution. Thus began the fatal division between "free states" and "slave states" that led to sectionalism and, ultimately, to civil war.

Some historians have proposed that the evolution of slavery in most New World societies can be divided (roughly, and with some risk of overgeneralization) into three stages: developmental, high-profit, and decadent. In the developmental stage, slaves cleared virgin forests for planting and built the dikes, dams, roads, and buildings necessary for plantations. In the second, high-profit stage, slave owners earned enormous income from the cash crop they grew for export. In these first two phases, slavery was always very brutal.

During the developmental phase, slaves worked in unknown, often dangerous territory, beset by disease and sometimes hostile inhabitants. Clearing land and performing heavy construction jobs without modern machinery was extremely hard labor, especially in the hot, humid climate of the South.

During the high-profit phase, slaves were driven mercilessly to plant, cultivate, and harvest the crops for market. A failed crop meant the planter could lose his initial investment in land and slaves and possibly suffer bankruptcy. A successful crop could earn such high returns that the slaves were often worked beyond human endurance. Plantation masters argued callously that it was "cheaper to buy than to breed"—it was cheaper to work the slaves to death and then buy new ones than it was to allow them to

TABLE 1. *Comparison of Black and White Populations in the Southern and Border States, 1790–1860*
(Black population, in thousands, to left of asterisk; white population, in thousands, to right of asterisk.)[1]

	1790	1800	1810	1820	1830	1840	1850	1860
Ala.				42 * 85	119 * 190	256 * 335	345 * 427	438 * 526
Ark.				2 * 13	5 * 26	20 * 77	48 * 162	111 * 324
Del.	13 * 46	14 * 50	17 * 55	17 * 55	19 * 58	20 * 59	20 * 71	22 * 91
Fla.					16 * 18	27 * 28	40 * 47	63 * 78
Ga.	30 * 53	60 * 102	107 * 145	151 * 190	220 * 297	284 * 408	385 * 522	466 * 592
Ky.	13 * 61	41 * 180	82 * 324	129 * 435	170 * 519	190 * 590	221 * 761	236 * 919
La.			42 * 34	80 * 74	126 * 89	194 * 158	262 * 255	350 * 357
Md.	111 * 209	125 * 216	145 * 235	147 * 260	156 * 291	152 * 318	165 * 418	171 * 516
Miss.			17 * 23	33 * 42	66 * 70	197 * 179	311 * 296	437 * 354
Mo.			4 * 16	11 * 56	26 * 115	60 * 324	90 * 592	119 * 1,063
N.C.	106 * 288	140 * 388	179 * 376	220 * 419	265 * 473	269 * 485	316 * 553	362 * 630
S.C.	109 * 140	149 * 196	201 * 214	265 * 257	323 * 258	335 * 259	394 * 275	412 * 291
Tenn.	4 * 32	14 * 92	46 * 216	83 * 340	146 * 536	189 * 641	246 * 757	283 * 827
Tex.							59 * 154	183 * 421
Va.	306 * 442	367 * 518	426 * 557	465 * 610	520 * 710	502 * 748	527 * 895	549 * 1,047

[1]No population figures are given for years prior to a state's admission to the Union.

SOURCE: Computed from figures in U.S. Census Office, First through Eighth Census [1790–1860], *Population,* Washington, D.C., 1790–1864.

live long enough and under sufficiently healthy conditions that they could bear children to increase their numbers. During this phase, on some of the sugar plantations in Louisiana and the Caribbean, the life span of a slave from initial purchase to death was only seven years.

The final, decadent phase of slavery was reached when the land upon which the cash crops were grown had become exhausted—the nutrients in the soil needed to produce large harvests were depleted. When that happened, the slave regime typically became more relaxed and less labor-intensive. Plantation owners turned to growing grain crops like wheat, barley, corn, and vegetables. Masters needed fewer slaves, and those slaves were not forced to work as hard because the cultivation of these crops required less labor.

This model is useful in analyzing the evolution of Southern slavery between independence and the Civil War. The process, however, varied considerably from state to state. Those of the upper South—Delaware, Maryland, and Virginia—essentially passed through the developmental and high-profit stages *before* American independence. By 1790, Maryland and Virginia planters could no longer produce the bumper harvests of tobacco that had made them rich in the earlier eighteenth century, because their soil was depleted. So they turned to less labor-intensive and less profitable crops such as grains, fruits, and vegetables. This in turn meant they had a surplus of slaves.

One result was that Virginia planters began to free many of their slaves in the decade after the Revolution. Some did so because they believed in the principles of human liberty. (After all, Virginian slave owners wrote some of the chief documents defining American freedom like the Declaration of Independence, the Constitution, and much of the Bill of Rights.) Others, however, did so for a much more cynical reason. Their surplus slaves had become a burden to house and feed. In response, they emancipated those who were too old or feeble to be of much use on the plantation. Ironically, one of the first laws in Virginia restricting the rights of masters to free their slaves was passed for the protection of the slaves. It denied slave owners the right to free valueless slaves, thus throwing them on public charity for survival. Many upper South slave owners around 1800 believed that slavery would gradually die out because there was no longer enough work for the slaves to do, and without masters to care for them, the ex-slaves would die out as well.

Two initially unrelated events solved the upper South's problem of a surplus slave population, caused slavery to become entrenched in the Southern states, and created what we know as the antebellum South. They were the invention of the cotton gin by Eli Whitney of Connecticut in 1793 and the closing of the international slave trade in 1808.

The cotton gin is a relatively simple machine. Its horizontally crossing combs extract tightly entwined seeds from the bolls of short-staple cotton. Prior to the invention of the gin, only long-staple cotton, which has long soft strands, could be grown for profit. Its soft fibers allowed easy removal of its seeds. But this strain of cotton grew in America only along the coast and Sea Islands of South Carolina and Georgia. In contrast, short-staple cotton could grow in almost any nonmountainous region of the South below Virginia. Before the invention of the cotton gin, it took a slave many hours to de-seed a single pound of "lint," or short-staple cotton. With the gin, as many as one hundred pounds of cotton could be de-seeded per hour.

The invention of the cotton gin permitted short-staple cotton to be grown profitably throughout the lower South. Vast new plantations were created from the virgin lands of the territories that became the states of Kentucky, Tennessee, Alabama, Mississippi, and Arkansas. (Louisiana experienced similar growth in both cotton and sugar agriculture.) In 1810, the South produced 85,000 pounds of cotton; by 1860, it was producing well over 2 billion pounds a year.

There was an equally enormous demand for the cotton these plantations produced. It was so profitable that by 1860 ten of the richest men in America lived not just in the South but in the Natchez district of Mississippi alone. In

TABLE 2. *Value of Cotton Production and Slave Population, 1810–1860, New Orleans Prices*

YEAR	CROP (IN THOUSANDS OF LBS.)	VALUE (IN THOUSANDS)	CROP VALUE PER SLAVE	PRICE OF PRIME FIELD HAND
1810	85,000	$ 12,495	$ 17.94	$ 900
1820	160,000	$ 24,320	$ 26.88	$ 970
1830	331,150	$ 27,817	$ 23.03	$ 810
1840	834,111	$ 75,904	$ 50.34	$1,020
1850	1,001,165	$117,136	$ 59.19	$1,100
1860	2,241,056	$248,757	$101.09	$1,800

SOURCE: Eugene Genovese, ed., *The Slave Economies*, vol. 2, New York, 1973, pp. 202–204.

1810, the cotton crop had been worth $12,495,000; by 1860, it was valued at $248,757,000. (See Table 2.)

Along with this expansion in cotton growing came a restriction on the supply of slaves needed to grow it. The transatlantic slave trade was one of the most savage and inhumane practices in which people of European descent have ever engaged. The writers of the Constitution had recognized its evil, but to accommodate the demands of slave owners in the lower South, they had agreed to permit the transatlantic slave trade to continue for twenty years after the Constitution was ratified. Thus, it was not until 1808 that Congress passed legislation ending the transatlantic trade.

These two circumstances—the discovery of a means of making the cultivation of short-staple cotton profitable throughout the lower South and territories and the restriction on the supply of slaves needed to produce it—created the unique antebellum slave system of the South. It made at least some Southerners very rich and it also made slaves much more valuable. One consequence was that some American slaves were perhaps better treated than those elsewhere in the New World, not because American slave owners were kinder, but because American slaves were in short supply and expensive to replace. The price of slaves increased steadily from 1802 to 1860. In 1810, the price of a "prime field hand" was $900; by 1860, that price had doubled to $1,800. (See Table 2.)

The Slave System in the Nineteenth Century

Slavery in the antebellum South was not a monolithic system; its nature varied widely across the region. At one extreme one white family in thirty owned slaves in Delaware; in contrast, half of all white families in South Carolina did so. Overall, 26 percent of Southern white families owned slaves.

In 1860, families owning more than fifty slaves numbered less than 10,000; those owning more than a hundred numbered less than 3,000 in the whole South. The typical Southern slave owner possessed one or two slaves, and the typical white Southern male owned none. He was an artisan, mechanic, or more frequently, a small farmer. This reality is vital in understanding why white Southerners went to war to defend slavery in 1861. Most of them did not have a direct financial investment in the system. Their willingness to fight in its defense was more complicated and subtle than simple fear of monetary loss. They deeply believed in the Southern way of life, of which slavery was an inextricable part. They also were convinced that Northern threats to undermine slavery would unleash the pent-up hostilities of 4 million African American slaves who had been subjugated for centuries.

Regulating Slavery. One half of all Southerners in 1860 were either slaves themselves or members of slave-holding families. These elite families shaped the mores and political stance of the South, which reflected their common concerns. Foremost among these were controlling slaves and assuring an adequate supply of slave labor. The legislatures of the Southern states passed laws designed to protect the masters' right to their human chattel. Central to these laws were "slave codes," which in their way were grudging admissions that slaves were, in fact, human beings, not simply property like so many cattle or pigs. They attempted to regulate the system so as to minimize the possibility of slave resistance or rebellion. In all states the codes made it illegal for slaves to read and write, to attend church services without the presence of a white person, or to testify in court against a white person. Slaves were forbidden to leave their home plantation without a written pass from their masters. Additional laws tried to secure slavery by restricting the possibility of manumission (the freeing of one's slaves). Between 1810 and 1860, all Southern states passed laws severely restricting the right of slave owners to free their slaves, even in a will. Free blacks were dangerous, for they might inspire slaves to rebel. As a consequence, most Southern states required that any slaves who were freed by their masters leave the state within thirty days.

To enforce the slave codes, authorities established "slave patrols." These were usually locally organized bands of young white men, both slave owners and yeomen farmers, who rode about at night checking that slaves were securely in their quarters. Although some planters felt that the slave patrolmen abused slaves who had been given permission to travel, the slave patrols nevertheless reinforced the sense of white solidarity between slave owners and those who owned none. They shared a desire to keep the nonwhite population in check. (These antebellum slave patrols are seen by many historians as antecedents of the Reconstruction era Ku Klux Klan, which similarly tried to discipline the freed blacks. The Klan helped reinforce white solidarity in a time when the class lines between ex–slave owners and white yeomen were collapsing because of slavery's end.)

The Internal Slave Trade. The factor that made the antebellum system viable was the internal slave trade. White Southerners were embarrassed by the trade, and there is little documentation about how it operated. Slave traders were considered the least reputable of white men. Nevertheless, the genteel aristocrats of the upper South and the aggressive new planters of the lower South both needed slave traders to keep their economic system working. The economy could prosper only because of the transfer of surplus slaves from the upper South to the labor-short, high-profit plantations of the cotton-growing lower South.

The slave trade operated in two forms. The first form of transfer occurred through endowment of heirs. Because states of the upper South still had laws of primogeniture

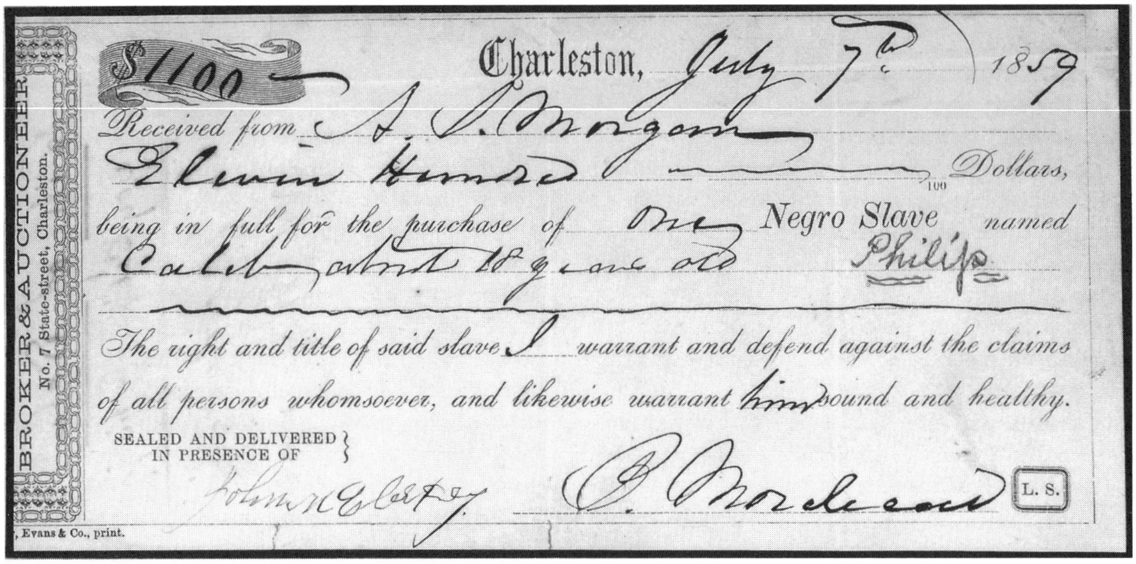
BROKER & AUCTIONEER, No. 7 State-street, Charleston.

$1100 — Charleston, July 7th 1859

Received from A. S. Morgan

Eleven Hundred — 100 Dollars,

being in full for the purchase of One Negro Slave named Caleb about 16 years old Philip

The right and title of said slave I warrant and defend against the claims of all persons whomsoever, and likewise warrant him sound and healthy.

SEALED AND DELIVERED IN PRESENCE OF

L. S.

, Evans & Co., print.

RECEIPT FOR THE SALE OF A SLAVE. GORDON BLEULER

(the eldest son inherited all his father's property), fathers often purchased land for their younger sons in the developing lower South and gave them a number of slaves to work the new land. This meant that some of the caravans of slaves seen by Northern observers traveling southward were, in fact, plantation units composed of intact families being transferred to new locations.

Most historians agree, however, that the second form of slave trade—commercial sale—was by far the most dominant means of transferring slave property from the upper to the lower South. Hundreds of thousands of slaves were sold as individuals, separated from their loved ones through the internal slave trade. Husbands were separated from their wives; children, from their parents. Two million slaves were transferred from one region to the other between 1790 and 1860.

The extent of the interstate slave trade is revealed by figures showing the distribution of the black population between 1790 and 1860. The number of slaves in the upper South grew by 175,000, whereas the number in the lower South increased from 237,000 in 1790 to over 3 million in 1860. Basically, the entire natural increase in the slave population of the upper South was exported to the lower South cotton plantations between 1820 and 1860. Very few slaves born in the upper South grew up there. The antebellum Southern slave economy survived because the upper South—in which fewer slaves were needed because the soil was exhausted—sold its excess slaves to the burgeoning cotton plantations of the lower South.

Slave Labor in the Upper South. If there was a "least bad" place to be a slave in the antebellum South, it was in the towns and on the smaller farms of Virginia and Maryland. When those states turned from growing high-yield crops like tobacco to cultivating crops like grains and vegetables, the change carried some benefits for slaves. The new crops required less intensive labor and permitted some slaves to work under the "task system." Slaves were assigned chores individually or in small groups. They were permitted to work at their own pace, often without direct white supervision. They would be assigned another task upon completion of the first.

The decline in the profitability of slavery appears to have led to a more relaxed and open regime for some slaves in the upper South. Since fewer slaves were needed on plantations, many were allowed by their master to live in town and "hire their own time"—find their own work—paying their masters a portion of their wages, usually two-thirds to three-quarters. This benefited the masters by enabling them to make a profit on an otherwise surplus slave. It was attractive to the slaves because it gave them more independence. Many hoped to save enough from their wages to buy their freedom from their owners.

This more relaxed system extended to other aspects of slave life in the upper South. It appears that most slaves in Virginia and Maryland were allowed to marry and have families, although these families had no legal standing. They existed only through permission of the master. In addition, laws against literacy and holding church services without a white person present were widely ignored or unenforced.

Of course, Virginia slaves were still the property of white masters, to be used as the masters saw fit. To put it bluntly, the chief cash crop of Virginia slave owners after 1807 was the slaves themselves. Historians have been unable to find plantations that openly "bred" slaves for sale, but this does not change the central appalling fact—the number of slaves born in Virginia between 1807 and 1860 was the same number as those sold farther South. So if conditions for slaves *were* better in Virginia, few of those born there grew up to enjoy them there. Indeed, the standard and most effective way to discipline a slave was to threaten to sell him or a loved one to the Deep South.

Slave Labor in the Lower South. The possibility of being "sold south" was no empty threat. Slaves in the lower South were often ill housed, ill fed, and ill cared for. It was more profitable to keep them at work on cotton than allow them time to build decent shelter. It was more profitable to plant every inch of land in cotton than to allot space for growing foodstuffs. Even the little garden plots allowed slaves in the upper South were usually absent in Mississippi. That state, with some of the richest soil in America, was actually a net importer of foodstuffs before the Civil War.

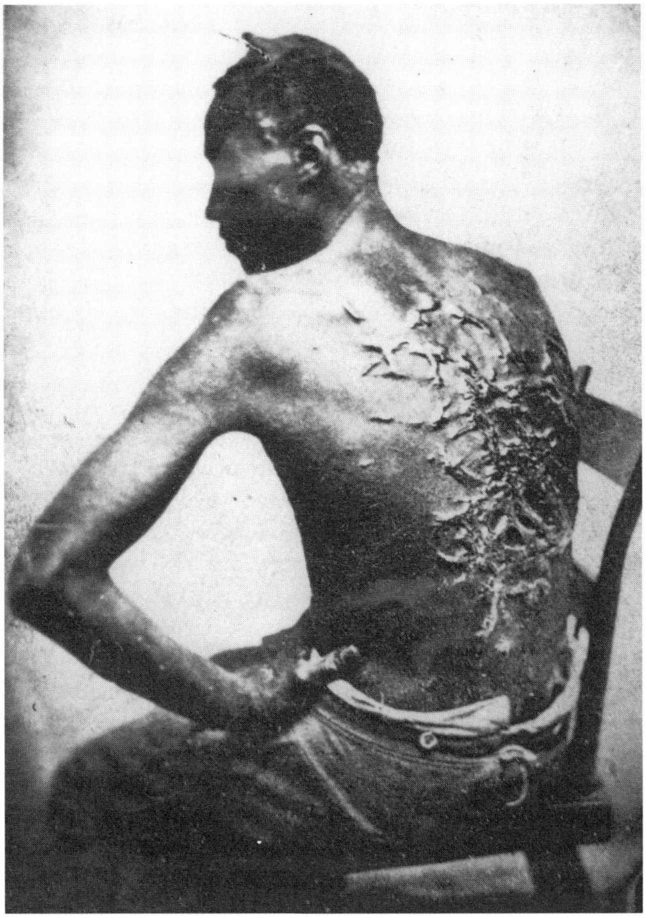

WHIPPED SLAVE. Peter, the slave pictured above, gave the following explanation of his scars when posing for this photograph on April 2, 1863, in Baton Rouge, Louisiana: "Overseer Artayou Carrier whipped me. I was two months in bed sore from the whipping. My master come after I was whipped; he discharged the overseer."
NATIONAL ARCHIVES

Life on the Deep South plantations was also characterized by the impersonality of master-slave relationships. Owners were often absent, and overseers were paid by how much cotton they produced, not by the condition of the slaves they supervised.

On lower South plantations, like those of the upper South, both men and women slaves were expected to toil in the fields from "first light" to "full dark." Because men were stronger and able to work harder, the plantations often had a much larger number of male slaves than female. This made the possibility of marriage problematic for the slave men. Moreover, women were sometimes seen as liabilities because "female problems" such as the menstrual cycle and pregnancy periodically incapacitated them for hard labor. In the cotton and sugar South, slaves were usually worked in gangs supervised by black drivers and white overseers with whips. The pace for plowing, hoeing, weeding, or picking was set by the overseers, and if a worker fell behind, he or she felt the sting of the lash.

Impact of Slavery on the Southern Economy

As the preceding discussion makes clear, slavery in the antebellum South was overwhelmingly a rural phenomenon. This was, in part, because most slave owners believed that slavery would not work well in an urban industrialized environment. Slaves were thought to be too stupid to understand machinery and too careless to be trusted with complex tools.

In fact, however, slaves *were* used successfully in factories such as the Tredegar Iron Works in Richmond. They also labored in the salt mines and turpentine plants of North Carolina, the coal mines of western Virginia, and the sugar mills of Louisiana. Moreover, when, during the Civil War, Southerners confronted a manpower shortage and the need for rapid industrialization, they quickly overcame their prejudices against using slaves in factories.

Objections to Urban Slavery. A major reason for slavery being confined mostly to rural areas in the South concerned its dual purpose for the white population. It was both a means of labor exploitation and a means of race control. It was this second aspect that made the institution problematic in urban areas. Simply put, slaves in cities were much more difficult to supervise.

It was the custom of factory owners to hire slaves from masters rather than purchase them outright. In the upper South, where urban slaves were more common, this allowed slave owners to profit from their excess slaves without having to sell them South. The problem was that industrialists preferred to avoid the burden of overseeing their slave employees outside of the factory, and they tended

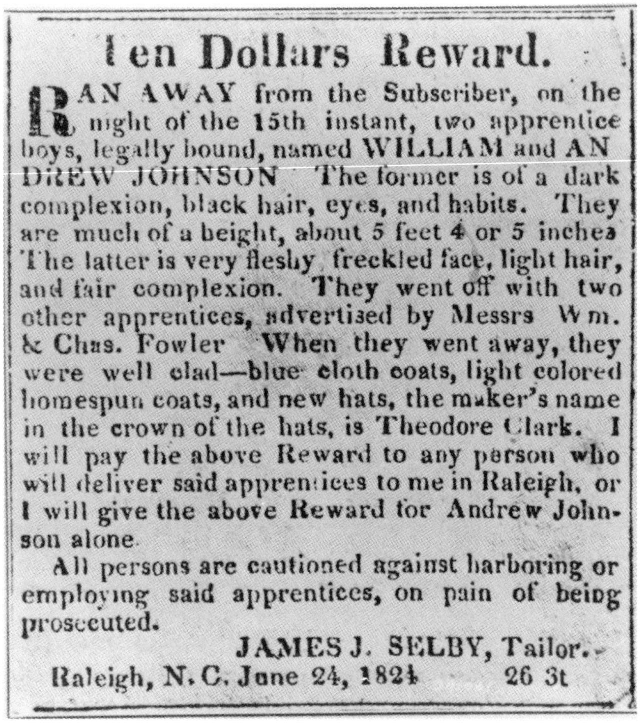
Ten Dollars Reward.

RAN AWAY from the Subscriber, on the night of the 15th instant, two apprentice boys, legally bound, named WILLIAM and ANDREW JOHNSON The former is of a dark complexion, black hair, eyes, and habits. They are much of a height, about 5 feet 4 or 5 inches The latter is very fleshy, freckled face, light hair, and fair complexion. They went off with two other apprentices, advertised by Messrs Wm. & Chas. Fowler When they went away, they were well clad—blue cloth coats, light colored homespun coats, and new hats, the maker's name in the crown of the hats, is Theodore Clark. I will pay the above Reward to any person who will deliver said apprentices to me in Raleigh, or I will give the above Reward for Andrew Johnson alone.

All persons are cautioned against harboring or employing said apprentices, on pain of being prosecuted.

JAMES J. SELBY, Tailor.

Raleigh, N. C. June 24, 1824 26 3t

ADVERTISEMENT FOR RUNAWAY SLAVES. NATIONAL ARCHIVES

to give them stipends to pay for their own housing and board. This enabled urban slaves to live in a varied community that included free blacks, slaves who hired their own time, and white people—some of whom might oppose slavery.

As white Southerners saw it, the urban environment exposed slaves to dangerous ideas about freedom. Most Southern cities were ports that provided access to the outside world where slavery was generally outlawed. Free black sailors and sympathetic white ship captains were known to help slaves escape aboard their vessels.

Cities, therefore, were considered antithetical to effective slave control. White Southerners well remembered that the two largest slave conspiracies (those of Gabriel Prosser in Richmond in 1800 and Denmark Vesey in Charleston in 1822) were urban phenomena. Moreover, both men were free blacks who had persuaded urban slaves to join them in their plots.

Yet another factor militating against urban slavery was the attitudes of workers in antebellum America. Southern white men felt demeaned if they were required to perform the same sort of job as a slave. Moreover, slaves, who received no wages, could do the same labor more cheaply than free white men. White workers—like the caulkers in Baltimore who beat up Frederick Douglass when his master sent him to work in the dockyards—often refused to labor alongside slaves.

So, to maintain better supervision of slaves and assure white solidarity and the status of white laborers, urban slavery in the antebellum South was minimal. The numbers of urban slaves actually declined between 1830 and 1860.

Negative Effects of Rural Slavery. The rural nature of antebellum slavery had unintended negative effects on the Southern economy. The investment of so much capital in land and slaves discouraged the growth of cities and diverted funds from factories. This meant that the South lacked the industrial base it needed to counter the North when the Civil War began. Indeed, in 1860, the South had approximately the same number of industrial *workers* (110,000), as the North had industrial *plants*.

Other detrimental effects arose from the South's devotion to rural slavery. Wealthy planters liked to claim they were living out the Jeffersonian ideal of an agrarian democracy. In truth, the South was agrarian because slave owners found that the best way to maintain their wealth and contain their slaves. Moreover, its "democracy" was very limited because the planters had enormous influence over how white yeomen cast their votes. Except in remote areas of the South with few slaves or plantations, it was the needs and beliefs of the planter class that shaped Southern politics on the local, state, and national levels.

The consequences of this planter dominance was seen in many aspects of the society. The South failed to develop a varied economy even within the agricultural realm. All the most fertile land in the South was owned by slaveholders who chose to grow high-profit staple crops—cotton, tobacco, sugar. That left only marginal land for the vast majority of white farmers. This problem was compounded by the dominance of the planter's image as the social ideal. Alternative means of advancement were unavailable, so yeomen farmers aspired to become planters themselves. They used some of their land to grow food for their family's consumption and devoted the rest to cash crops like cotton. Their hope was to produce enough to save, buy a few slaves, produce yet more, and, ultimately, accumulate the wealth that would elevate them to planter status. For most, this was a futile dream, but they remained committed to it, thereby neglecting other possible avenues for economic advancement.

One reason for the yeomen farmers' lack of aspirations was ignorance. The antebellum South neglected to provide for the education of its people. Planters controlled the governmental revenues that could have financed public education, but they saw no need to do so. Their slaves were forbidden to learn; their own children were educated by private tutors or in exclusive and expensive private academies. As a result, most white yeomen were left without access to education. A few lucky ones near towns or cities could sometimes send their children to fee schools or charity schools, but many were too poor or too proud to use either option.

In a similar vein, the dominating slaveholding class saw no need to create the means to produce inexpensive consumer goods for ordinary whites or to build an infrastructure by which such goods could be moved from production sites to markets in the countryside. Wealthy planters acquired what they wanted by importing expensive European or Northern goods. Thus poor whites were left to their own minimal resources and were deprived of goods they might have bought, had they been available.

This lack of consumer production and markets also retarded the growth of Southern transportation. Highways, canals, and railroads were constructed to move crops to ports and bring in luxury items for the planter class. The need of yeomen farmers to transport their crops to local markets was ignored. As a consequence, it was usually cheaper for plantation owners to import food from the North or upper South than to purchase it from white farmers in the same region. This deficiency in the Southern transportation system proved a serious liability for the Confederacy during the Civil War.

Slavery in the antebellum South, then, made a minority of white Southerners—owners of large slaveholdings—enormously wealthy. At the same time, it demeaned and exploited Southerners of African descent, left the majority of white Southerners impoverished and uneducated, and retarded the overall economic, cultural, and social growth of the region. Slavery was the institution by which the South defined itself when it chose to secede from the Union. But it was the existence of slavery, with its negative impact on politics, economics, and social relations, that fatally crippled the South in its bid for independence.

[*See also* Expansionism in the Antebellum South; Urbanization.]

BIBLIOGRAPHY

Blassingame, John. *The Slave Community.* New York, 1979.

Davis, David Brion. *The Problem of Slavery in Western Culture.* New York, 1966.

Fox-Genovese, Elizabeth. *Within the Plantation Household: Black and White Women in the Old South.* New York, 1988.

Genovese, Eugene. *Roll, Jordan, Roll.* New York, 1974.

Higginbotham, A. Leon. *In the Matter of Color.* New York, 1978.

Morgan, Edmund. *American Slavery, American Freedom.* New York, 1975.

Oakes, James. *The Ruling Race: A History of America's Slaveholders.* New York, 1982.

Rawick, George. *From Sundown to Sunup.* Westport, Conn., 1972.

Scarborough, William K. *The Overseer: Plantation Management in the Old South.* Athens, Ga., 1966.

Stampp, Kenneth. *The Peculiar Institution.* New York, 1956.

Wade, Richard. *Slavery in the Cities.* Oxford, 1964.

Robert Francis Engs

Slavery during the Civil War

Although slavery was at the heart of the sectional impasse between North and South in 1860, it was not the *singular* cause of the Civil War. Rather, it was the multitude of differences arising from the slavery issue that impelled the Southern states to secede.

The presidential election of 1860 had resulted in the selection of a Republican, Abraham Lincoln of Illinois, as president of the United States. Lincoln won because of an overwhelming electoral college vote from the Northern states. Not a single Southern slave state voted for him. Lincoln and his Republican party were pledged only to stop the expansion of slavery. Although they promised to protect slavery where it existed, white Southerners were not persuaded. The election results demonstrated that the South was increasingly a minority region within the nation. Soon Northerners and slavery's opponents might accumulate the voting power to overturn the institution, no matter what white Southerners might desire.

Indeed, many Southern radicals, or fire-eaters, openly hoped for a Republican victory as the only way to force Southern independence. South Carolina had declared it would secede from the Union if Lincoln was elected, and it did so in December 1861. It was followed shortly by the other lower South states of Alabama, Mississippi, Louisiana, Georgia, Florida, and Texas. In February 1861, a month before Lincoln was inaugurated, these states formed a new nation, the Confederate States of America. After the firing on Fort Sumter and Lincoln's call for volunteers to suppress the rebellion, the other slave states of Virginia, North Carolina, Tennessee, and Arkansas joined the Confederacy. The border slave states of Delaware, Maryland, Kentucky, and Missouri remained—not entirely voluntarily—in the Union.

The new republic claimed its justification to be the protection of state rights. In truth, close reading of the states' secession proclamations and of the new Confederate Constitution reveals that it was primarily *one* state right that impelled their separation: the right to preserve African American slavery within their borders. But the white South's decision to secede proved to be the worst possible choice it could have made in order to preserve that right.

There was enormous antislavery sentiment in the North, but such sentiment was also strongly anti-Negro. White Northerners did not wish slavery to expand into new areas of the nation, which they believed should be preserved for white nonslaveholding settlers. This was, in part, why Republicans pledged to protect slavery where it existed. They and their constituencies did not want an influx of ex-slaves into their exclusively white territories, should slavery end abruptly.

Some historians argue that, had the South remained

within the Union, its representatives could have prevented any radical Northern plan for emancipation. By leaving the Union, white Southerners gave up their voice in national councils. Moreover, by seceding, the South compelled the North to realize the extent of its allegiance to a united American nation. Thus, the North went to war to preserve the Union, and the white South went to war for independence so that it might protect slavery. Most participants on both sides did not initially realize that the African American slaves might view the conflict as an occasion that they could turn to their own advantage.

Slaves' Efforts to Undermine the South. In 1861, as the Civil War began, there were four open questions among Northerners and Southerners with regard to the slaves: First, would they rebel? Second, did they want their freedom? Third, would they fight for their freedom? And, finally, would they know what to do with their freedom if they got it? The answer to each question was yes, but in a manner that reflected the peculiar experience of blacks in white America.

First was the question of whether bondsmen would rebel or remain passive. The fear of slave rebellion preoccupied both the Southern slaveholder and the Northern invader. Strikingly, Northerners were as uneasy about the possibility as were Southerners. Initially the Northern goal in the war was the speedy restoration of the Union under the Constitution and the laws of 1861, all of which recognized the legitimacy of slavery. Interfering with slavery would make reunion more difficult. Thus, Union generals like George B. McClellan in Virginia and Henry W. Halleck in the West were ordered not only to defeat the Southern armies but also to prevent slave insurrections. In the first months of the war, slaves who escaped to Union lines were returned to their masters in conformity with the Fugitive Slave Act of 1850.

Concern about outright slave insurrections proved unfounded, however. Slaves were not fools, nor were they suicidal. Mary Boykin Chesnut, the famed Southern diarist and one of the South's most perceptive observers of slavery, understood the slaves' strategy. She wrote from her plantation: "Dick, the butler here, reminds me that when we were children, I taught him to read as soon as I could read myself. . . . But he won't look at me now. He looks over my head. He scents freedom in the air."

Slaves like Dick knew the war was about their freedom, but they were both shrewd and cautious. To rebel on their own was hopeless; the whites were too powerful. But now the Southern whites had an equally powerful outside enemy, and the odds had changed. The slaves, like successful rebels everywhere, bided their time until a revolt could succeed.

Meanwhile, through desertion and noncooperation, they did much to undermine the South long before Union armies triumphed. When the war began, some Confederates claimed that the disparity in white manpower between North and South (6 million potential soldiers for the North versus only 2 million for the South) was irrelevant. The South, Confederates claimed, could put a far higher proportion of their men in the field because they had slaves to do the labor at home.

The South, however, quickly learned that it had what would now be called a "fifth column" in its midst, providing aid and comfort to the enemy. At the beginning of the war, Southern officers took their body servants with them to the front to do their cooking and laundry. A unit of two thousand white soldiers would sometimes depart with as many as a thousand slaves in tow. The custom did not last beyond the first summer of the conflict. The servants deserted at the first opportunity and provided excellent intelligence to Union forces about Southern troop deployments.

In one incident during the early months of the war, Union soldiers on the Virginia Peninsula, stationed at Fort Monroe, repeatedly set out to capture the nearby city of Newport News, but without success. Their inaccurate maps showed the town to be *southwest* of Fort Monroe. Each would-be attack concluded with the troops mired in the swampy land bordering Hampton Roads (the bay between the Virginia Peninsula and Norfolk on the "Southside"). In fact, Newport News was slightly *northwest* of Fort Monroe, and Union forces were unable to find it until an escaped body servant led them there.

Slave Labor with the Confederate Military. Despite such subversion by the slaves, the Confederacy nevertheless successfully used them to advance its war effort. White Southerners, though convinced of the African Americans' inherent inferiority, were far less reluctant about putting the slaves to work militarily than were white Northerners. The Confederate government never used them as soldiers, but it did press them into labor brigades to build fortifications, dig latrines, and haul supplies. Tens of thousands of slaves toiled for the Confederacy in a service both the bondsmen and their owners disliked. For the slave impressed into labor on the frontline, the work frequently was not only harder than that on the plantation but also dangerous. Because of the possibility of escape through Union lines, slaves at the front were much more closely supervised than on their home farms. Moreover, those sent to work with the Confederate army were usually men in their prime, between eighteen and forty. Service with the army denied them their accustomed time with their wife and family.

The slave owners, for their part, were reluctant to send their bondsmen to the front for two reasons. First, they risked the loss of their most valuable property, and, second, because the men were usually overworked and mistreated, they frequently returned to their homes in very poor physical condition. Thus, the owners often contrived to send only their most unmanageable and therefore least marketable slaves to the army. During the war, threatening to send a slave to the front became the disciplinary equivalent of threatening to sell a slave farther South in antebellum days. Ironically, as the South's cause became more desperate, masters were increasingly reluctant to send their slaves to the military. Slavery was dying, yet those with the most to lose hung on tenaciously to their human property, thereby withholding the one remaining resource that might have saved their nation—and them.

The exigencies of war also finally settled the decades-old debate as to whether slaves could be used safely and efficiently in industry. The shortage of white manpower left the South with no other choice than to put slaves to work in its factories and mines. In the Tredegar Iron Works of Richmond alone, thousands of slaves were employed. The Augusta munitions plants of Georgia likewise were primarily staffed by bondsmen. Thousands of others labored in the ultimately futile effort to keep Southern rail lines operating. As with service on the front lines, this labor—especially in extractive industries like the coal mines and salt factories—was harsher than life on the plantation, and slaves resisted it if they could. Many made the long-delayed decision to run away when faced with such dire prospects.

Although their service was extracted involuntarily, slaves in industry and on the battlefield enabled the South to fight on longer than would been possible otherwise. In the final desperate days of the war, the Confederacy even considered using blacks as soldiers, offering emancipation as a reward. The Union had struck that bargain two years earlier. The Southern proposal was made in February 1865 and approved, in part, on March 13 of that year. By then Southerners of both races knew the Confederacy was doomed. Richmond fell less than thirty days later. The provision was never implemented and no slaves officially served as soldiers in the Confederate military.

The Wartime Slave Economy. Just as it did all other aspects of Southern life, the war severely disrupted the slave economy and the market for slaves. The chaos of the period makes an accurate account of change very difficult. Three conclusions, however, can be made about the war years. First, masters tried desperately to protect their investment in slave property to the very end of the war. Second, the slave trade and the antebellum trend of a slave population movement toward the Southwest continued during the war. Third, the prices of slaves rose astronomically (although in inflated currency) during the war even as the security of that form of property became increasingly doubtful.

Slaveholders had seceded and gone to war in the first place to protect their property in human beings, and they adopted various protective measures in the course of that war. Besides resisting the use of their slaves in the Confederate military, they developed another strategy: they transferred their slaves to more secure regions of the Confederacy. Thus, early in the war, thousands of slaves were moved from areas of active conflict or potential invasion—such as Tidewater Virginia and coastal areas along the Atlantic seaboard—to seemingly more secure inland regions. As the war continued to go badly and Northern armies penetrated more deeply into the Confederacy, slave owners moved their bondsmen across the Mississippi to areas in the West, especially Texas.

Their attempt to secure their investment in slave property also resulted in a continuation of the internal slave trade during the war. Owners of healthy young males or of females who were potentially "good breeders" tried to sell them to buyers from more secure regions of the South or simply to those willing to risk their money on Confederate victory. As Union forces triumphed, however, the trade was much disrupted, and it became impossible to move large bands of slaves through areas of possible conflict. The largest slave-trading city, New Orleans, was captured by the North in April 1862. By war's end, only Charleston in the East had an active slave market, although slaves were reportedly still being traded in Richmond on the eve of its fall.

Prices of slaves increased exponentially during the war. A "prime field hand" valued at a thousand dollars in 1860 could fetch ten thousand dollars in 1865. The increased price, however, reflected the inflated Confederate currency. It is impossible to estimate the *volume* of the slave trade during the war. The corresponding value of these prices in gold—from one thousand dollars in 1861 to one hundred dollars in 1865—is evidence of a dramatic price collapse. The inflation of slave prices and the growing insecurity of slave property both grew out of and reinforced the general disintegration of the Southern economy. In the end, it appears that many masters had more faith in the survival of slavery than in Confederate money or bonds. They tried to hold onto their human property until forced to surrender it because of Union victory.

Slave Resistance on the Plantations. When given the option, slaves made it very clear that they wanted *freedom.* The vast majority of slaves, however, remained on their plantations in the countryside. Nevertheless, even these slaves in the Southern interior found ways to demonstrate their desire for freedom. Their behavior could be described as the first massive labor slowdown in American history. They did not cease to work, but they contrived to do considerably less than they had before the war.

Part of the reason for the drop in their industriousness was the South's ill-advised self-imposed cotton embargo. Although this was never official policy, many Southerners believed they could provoke European intervention in the war by refusing to grow or export cotton. This decision changed the nature of Southern agriculture. The region began to emphasize food production, a less intensive form of agricultural labor. But this change did not necessarily reduce the burden on slave laborers. The war cut off many of the South's antebellum sources of food and other goods in the North and abroad. These shortages had to be replaced by what the slaves could produce at home. Their inability to make up the shortfall meant that they, their masters, the soldiers in the field, and the general population all suffered from increasing deprivation as the war went on. Especially problematic were shortages of wool, leather, and salt for the curing of meat, since most of these were diverted for military use. One consequence was the rapid escalation of prices for such necessities. Frugal planters cut back on these supplies for their slaves. Bondsmen did not receive their prewar rations of clothes and shoes, and they had less meat and vegetables in their diet. Even those slaves well removed from the front lines throughout the war recalled it later as a time of great privation.

In addition to the change in the kinds of crops grown and the increasing scarcity of necessities, the quality of management on the plantations changed. Once the war intensified in 1862, there were not enough white men left on the farms and plantations to provide adequate supervision of slave laborers. The Confederacy had attempted to defuse this potential problem through the Ten-Slave Law (later, the Twenty-Slave Law), whereby a percentage of white men were exempted from military service in proportion to the number of slaves in a county or on a plantation. The law clearly favored slaveholders and drew a storm of protest from white yeomen who owned no slaves yet were called upon to defend the Southern cause.

As the war progressed, Southern manpower shortages became acute. In some parts of Georgia, it was reported that there was only one able-bodied white man in a ten-square-mile area. As a result, management of agriculture increasingly fell to white women and their youngest children, elderly fathers, and black slave drivers. All proved less effective taskmasters than the earlier overseers, and the efficiency of Southern farm production declined markedly.

Slaves quickly took advantage of the situation, reducing the pace of their labor, disobeying orders, leaving their farms to visit with friends and relatives. Their perceived "impudence" and "laziness" caused enormous frustration for the white women left to oversee them. Although these women had often been most resourceful managers of household economies in the prewar South, they had never been trained or given experience in day-to-day supervision of farming operations. Many were unequal to the burden and resentful that they were being forced to shoulder it.

One important consequence of this management crisis was the disappearance of even the veneer of paternalism in the master-slave relationship. White women and the few white men left in the countryside viewed the increasingly recalcitrant slaves as a threat, especially the young males. Slave patrols composed of the remaining white men became more energetic and violent in "disciplining" slaves. Those accused or suspected of "misconduct" were brutally punished and sometimes murdered.

Despite these draconian efforts, slaves in the South's interior stepped up their resistance and increasingly worked at a much slower pace. More disturbing yet to the whites around them was their outright refusal to obey orders when they could get away with it. Slaves ran off with greater frequency; they stole food and violated curfew with impunity. They began to hold religious services more openly and even created schools for their children in violation of state laws.

Escaping from Slavery. The second of the four questions preoccupying European Americans, North and South, was: Did the slaves want freedom? Of course they did, as long as they could attain it without losing their lives in the process. The unrest on the plantations clearly indicated their longing for freedom. Even more demonstrable evidence was offered by slaves living on the borders of the Confederacy. Beginning in 1861, and continuing throughout the war, whenever the proximity of Union troops made successful escape likely, slaves abandoned their plantations by the hundreds, even the thousands.

The process of successful slave escapes began in Virginia, in Union-held territory across the Potomac from Washington and around Fort Monroe at the tip of the Virginia Peninsula in Hampton Roads. In May 1861, three slaves fled to the fort and claimed sanctuary because their masters were about to take them South to work on Confederate fortifications. The Union commander there was Gen. Benjamin Butler, a War Democrat from Massachusetts and a perennial thorn in Lincoln's side. Thinking more about the political advantage to be gained among Northern antislavery advocates than about the needs of the fugitives, Butler declared the blacks to be "contraband of war"—enemy property that could be used against the Union. This designation neatly avoided the question of whether or not the escapees were free and turned the Southerners' argument that slaves were property against them. Lincoln reluctantly approved the ruling, and as a consequence, escaped slaves throughout the war were referred to by Northerners as "contrabands."

This legal hairsplitting was of no concern to Virginia slaves. All they knew was that fugitives had gone to Fort Monroe and found sanctuary. Within a month, over 900 had joined those first three. By war's end, there were over 25,000 escaped slaves in and around Fort Monroe. Many of them served in the Union army.

FUGITIVE SLAVES. Crossing the Rappahannock River, Virginia. Photograph by Timothy O'Sullivan, August 1862.

LIBRARY OF CONGRESS

A more massive instance of slaves' defecting occurred the following spring in the Sea Islands off South Carolina. The Union navy landed troops on the islands and the whites fled. Despite efforts by masters—some told the slaves that the Yankees were cannibals—the slaves refused to join their owners and fled to the woods until the Southern whites had left. As a consequence, the Union army suddenly had several thousand contrabands to care for. Interestingly, the first task of the Union commanders on the Sea Islands was to stop the ex-slaves from looting and burning their masters' mansions.

With the fall of New Orleans, also in the spring of 1862, the informal emancipation process expanded into the lower Mississippi valley. It never reached much of the Trans-Mississippi South until war's end because Union forces did not penetrate deeply there.

Throughout the South, the first slaves to escape were typically house servants and skilled craftsmen. They were the people who had the most access to information about Union troop movements (acquired primarily by overhearing their masters' indiscreet conversations around them) and those who had the greatest knowledge of the outside world. Usually the first ones to escape were men. Once they found they would be protected behind Union lines, they returned for their friends and relatives.

The North had not anticipated massive slave escapes. It had no plans about how to care for these black refugees. As a consequence, many escapees found themselves in worse physical conditions than they had known on the plantations. They were herded into camps and given tents and rations in exchange for work. The blacks were put to work in much the way Southern troops were using them, building fortifications, digging latrines, and cleaning the camps. Blacks frequently complained that their Union supervisors treated them worse than their former masters and overseers. In truth, many Union soldiers resented having to serve in the war, especially those who were draftees, and they blamed the blacks for their predicament.

The black refugees in the Union camps usually received no actual income. Most of the money they earned was withheld to pay for their food and clothing, and any remainder was reserved to pay for indigent or crippled escapees who could not work. This was administered by the Quartermaster's Department, a notoriously unreliable branch of any army throughout history. Blacks were defrauded at every turn. Often their rations and clothing were sold on the black market—sometimes to the Southerners—by greedy supply officers.

Hearing of the plight of the contrabands in the camps, Northern benevolent organizations, such as the Freedmen's Aid Societies, and religious groups, such as the American Missionary Association, sent hundreds of missionaries and teachers to the South to aid the blacks. They provided much of the food and clothing that enabled the refugees to survive. They also created the first schools and churches most blacks had ever attended.

It was the blacks themselves, however, who were primarily responsible for their survival in these harsh circumstances. The more enterprising of them earned cash through private work with officers of the camps. Those who fared best struck out from the encampments and squatted on lands abandoned by fleeing Confederates. Frequently they were able to make the land far more productive than it had ever been during slavery.

Lincoln and the Emancipation Proclamation. The extent of slave escapes in the South and the burden it placed upon the Union presented a major dilemma for President Lincoln. From the moment the conflict began at Fort Sumter, Lincoln's foremost goals had been to preserve the Union, to bring the war to an end with a minimum of bloodshed, and to avoid lingering animosity between Northern and Southern whites. If that could best be achieved by preserving slavery, he said, he would do so; if it could be achieved by freeing every slave, he would do that instead. Lincoln despised slavery, but he, like Thomas Jefferson and many others before him, doubted that blacks and whites could ever live in America in a condition of equality.

The spring and summer of 1862 aggravated Lincoln's problem. The slaves, by running away in massive numbers, were freeing themselves. The border slave states of Delaware, Maryland, Kentucky, and Missouri were resisting all of Lincoln's proposals for gradual compensated emancipation. His own schemes to find somewhere outside of the United States where the freed black population could be colonized failed completely.

At the same time, Lincoln was confronted at home by abolitionists who insisted that the war should be one for emancipation. Abroad, he was faced with growing skepticism about Northern war aims. If the Union goal was simply to reunite the country and preserve slavery, then the North was undertaking a war of aggression. The South's claim that it was fighting for its independence, just as the United States had done during the Revolution, was therefore valid, and foreign powers had the right to intervene as the French had done in 1778. All these pressures forced Lincoln to conclude that emancipation would have to become a Union war goal.

The critics of Lincoln and the Emancipation Proclamation are technically correct in observing that the proclamation in January 1863 did not *legally* free a single slave. Slavery's end required a constitutional amendment, which Lincoln advocated and which was ratified as the Thirteenth Amendment in 1865. The *symbolic* importance of the Emancipation Proclamation should not, however, be underestimated. Lincoln thereby silenced his abolitionist critics in the North, defused interventionist sentiment abroad, and energized black slave resisters to continue their efforts in the South.

Lincoln advised his cabinet of his plan in the early summer of 1862. Because the Union cause was not faring well on the battlefield, he delayed its issuance until a Union victory could be attained. He claimed the bloody Battle of Sharpsburg (Antietam), during which Robert E. Lee's first invasion of the North was repulsed, as an appropriate occasion. Slaves in states or territories still in rebellion against the United States on January 1, 1863, would be freed. He hoped, probably only halfheartedly, that this threat would energize Southern moderates and influence them to persuade their leaders to lay down their arms. That was not to be the case.

On January 1, 1863, throughout the Union-occupied areas of the South, contrabands, their Northern white allies, and some Union soldiers gathered to pray, to sing hymns, and to celebrate slavery's demise. (The fact that none of those contrabands had been *legally* freed was irrelevant.) Moreover, the proclamation welcomed all escaping slaves into Union lines and held out the prospect that ex-slaves could volunteer for service in the Union military. African American slaves had tried to make the Civil War one of black liberation. In the Emancipation Proclamation, Abraham Lincoln and the Union appeared to have embraced their cause.

Certainly this was the belief of Southern slave owners. They wrote that both "misbehavior" on the plantations and escape attempts increased significantly after the issuance of the proclamation. Only in the Trans-Mississippi regions of Arkansas, Louisiana, and Texas was the impact of the proclamation minimal. One reminder of that difference is that blacks in that area and their descendants in the Midwest celebrate emancipation not on January 1 but on "Juneteenth," that period in mid-June after the surrender of the last Confederate armies in the West under E. Kirby Smith. Union officers, many now also superintendents of the newly formed Freedmen's Bureau, rode around those western states announcing Lincoln's Emancipation Proclamation to slaves and their masters.

In the eastern half of the Confederacy, slavery had collapsed long before those final western Union victories, in part because of the efforts of former slaves as Union soldiers.

Ex-Slaves in the Union Army. The third of the four questions preoccupying white Americans during the Civil

War was whether blacks would be willing to fight for their freedom. Once again the answer was yes. The fury of the white South when the North decided to make escaped slaves into soldiers is not surprising. What may be more so is the horror with which much of the white North regarded the idea.

Some Northerners, including the editorial board of the *New York Times,* claimed that using black troops would sully the purity of the North's cause. "Better lose the War," it cried, "than use the Negro to win it." A more representative statement was made by a Northern soldier who reflected, "I reckon if I have to fight and die for the nigger's freedom, he can fight and die for it along with me." That was really the point. The Union needed more men, and its efforts to enlist them were encountering increasing resistance among Northern white men. Why not let the black man fight for his own freedom?

In the fall of 1862, with Union victory still doubtful and the Preliminary Emancipation Proclamation already announced, Lincoln yielded to pressure and authorized the formation of the first black army units. African Americans were offered a step toward freedom not because the white North especially wanted them but because the North needed them so much.

The fashion in which black troops were treated was illustrative of Northern white attitudes toward the whole enterprise. At first, black soldiers were confined to service units and not allowed to fight—until white Union casualties became so high that blacks, though often untrained for combat, were simply thrown into the battle. Moreover, until just before the war's end, African American soldiers received unequal pay for the same duty and were denied the enlistment bonuses given to white troops.

The record of one of the most famous black Union regiments illustrates the contributions of ex-slave soldiers in the Confederacy's defeat. The First South Carolina Volunteers was the darling of Northern imagination. It was the first regiment composed entirely of fugitive slaves, organized, as Northerners loved to say, "in the birthplace of treason."

It was at first unclear that the North was entirely serious about this regiment. The unit was supposed to be made up of volunteers, but the first soldiers were acquired by sending white troops on raiding parties into the refugee camps and hauling back any able-bodied black men they could find. Their uniforms were made up of a bright blue jacket, brighter red pantaloons, and a red fez, making them ideal targets for sharpshooters. Nevertheless, the First South Carolina ran up a credible record in Union service. They were, for example, the first known military unit to consistently return from battle with more soldiers than those which with they entered. Slaves on outlying plantations, seeing them in uniform, simply laid down their hoes, picked up discarded guns, and followed the troops back to their camp.

The soldiers of the First South Carolina were only the first of tens of thousands of former slaves who fought for the Union cause. Despite discrimination throughout the war, African American troops distinguished themselves and were instrumental in the North's victory. Overall, about 180,000 blacks served in the Union army, and another 20,000 in the Union navy. Together, they made up about 15 percent of all Northern forces in the war. Of all the Union troops, the African American soldier was fighting for the most tangible of causes—freedom for himself and his people.

The Final Question. The determination with which blacks seized freedom shocked whites, both North and South. In an unanticipated and unplanned war, the African Americans' behavior may have been the element for which both sides were least prepared. In the end, black slaves played a major role in bringing down the Confederacy. They had demonstrated that they wanted freedom and were prepared to fight for its realization.

The fourth question that whites had posed about the slaves—"Would they know what to do with their freedom if they got it?"—would be more candidly phrased—"Would white America let blacks truly exercise their freedom?" That question remains unresolved at the end of the twentieth century. But the limitations that crippled black freedom after Reconstruction did not discourage many African Americans who had been slaves. As one black Union veteran said after the war, "In slavery, I had no worriment. . . . In freedom I'se got a family and a little farm. All that causes me worriment. . . . But I takes the FREEDOM!"

[*See also* African American Forgeworkers; African American Troops in the Union Army, *article on* African Americans in the Confederate Army; Contraband; Emancipation Proclamation; Navy, *article on* African Americans in the Confederate Navy; Thirteenth Amendment.]

BIBLIOGRAPHY

Brewer, James. *The Confederate Negro: Virginia's Craftsmen and Military Laborers, 1861–1865.* Durham, N.C., 1969.

Chesnut, Mary Boykin. *Mary Chesnut's Civil War.* Edited by C. Vann Woodward. New Haven, 1981.

Cornish, Dudley Taylor. *The Sable Arm.* New York, 1966.

Foner, Eric. *Reconstruction: America's Unfinished Revolution.* New York, 1987.

Glatthaar, Joseph. *Forged in Battle: The Civil War Alliance of Black Soldiers and White Officers.* New York, 1990.

McPherson, James. *Abraham Lincoln and the Second American Revolution.* New York, 1991.

McPherson, James. *Battle Cry of Freedom: The Civil War Era.* New York, 1988.

Mohr, Clarence L. *On the Threshold of Freedom.* Athens, Ga., 1986.

Quarles, Benjamin. *The Negro in the Civil War.* New York, 1953. Reprint, New York, 1989.
Taylor, Susie King. *A Black Woman's Civil War Memoirs.* New York, 1988.
Wiley, Bell Irwin. *The Southern Negro, 1861–1865.* New Haven, 1966.

ROBERT FRANCIS ENGS

Slave Life

The African American slave society in the antebellum South (1807–1860) was unique among New World slave systems. In the United States, the slave population not only sustained itself; it expanded exponentially. In other New World nations, slave populations were maintained by continuous importation from Africa. In the American South, however, the slave population grew through natural increase—that is, slave mothers had children who also became slaves. As a result, the vast majority of African Americans in slavery in the United States after 1810 were not African captives but native-born Americans, some of whose ancestors had been in this country nearly as long as the oldest white families.

This longevity of residence in America did not mean that slaves lost all their rich heritage from their African origins. White slave owners, however, were frightened by African customs and behaviors they could not understand. They forced their slaves to give up African means of communication such as their own languages and their drums (a widely used means of "talking" across great distances in West Africa). Indeed, slaves were denied even their original African names and made to accept whatever names their master imposed upon them.

In these circumstances, Southern slaves were forced into syncretism—the process of mixing divergent cultural elements together to create an entirely new culture. They had to combine what they could retain of their African culture with the new European and Native American cultures imposed upon them by their masters. The result was the first genuinely United States culture. It was part African, part European, and part Native American, but refined and developed in a land new to all but one of these groups.

American slaves were able to carve out a unique culture of their own because of the way in which Southern slavery was structured. Most white Southerners did not own slaves. In 1860 only ten thousand Southern white families owned more than twenty slaves, and only three thousand owned more than fifty slaves. Nevertheless, most slaves lived in units of twenty or more. This meant that, on most plantations, blacks far outnumbered whites. They could not all be kept under constant white supervision.

Masters had to evolve a system of rewards and punishments to maintain control over their more numerous slaves. As in any brutal system of unpaid labor, punishment was used more often than reward. As historian Kenneth Stampp has written, the slave owners' strategy in handling their slaves was "to make them stand in fear!" A plantation, however, was not an extermination camp; it was a profit-making enterprise, and blacks had to be given certain rights and privileges to maximize their productivity. They were also valuable pieces of "property." To abuse them too harshly would diminish their value. Slaves seized upon this necessity to create a culture of their own possessing the values that shaped family life, religion, education, and attitudes toward work.

Slave Family Life. The black family in slavery had no legal standing. Slaves and their children were the property of their masters. Slavery was hereditary through the status of the mother; therefore, even children conceived through the rape of a slave woman by a white man (sometimes the woman's master) were still legally slaves. Husbands and wives and their children could be sold apart from one another whenever the desires or economic needs of the master required such sales. Indeed, probably 2 million slaves were sold from the upper South (Virginia, Maryland, and Delaware) to the Deep South between 1800 and 1860. Many of these sales involved the breakup of families.

In the face of the constant threat of separation from loved ones, a strong family system developed. Most slave families in the South were structured like other American families. They were nuclear—that is, they consisted of a father, mother, and their children. The realities of slavery, however, forced the additional creation of an extended family that incorporated all the other slaves on a plantation. This informal family helped protect children (and adults) when a family member was sold away. Thus, every slave child had many honorary aunts, uncles, and cousins who were not biologically related, but who were prepared to assume family roles, should a child be orphaned by the workings of the slave trade.

In the upper South, it was the custom among many slave owners to encourage slave families. The offspring of such unions brought high prices in the lower South's slave markets. In addition, it was an excellent means of slave control. Those slaves most likely to run away were young males between sixteen and thirty. A wife and family might make them more content. Moreover, since successful escape in groups, especially ones including children, was almost impossible, a husband and father was less likely to run away and leave his family behind.

In the lower South, however, cotton profits were so high that some slavemasters had no regard for slave family life. Pregnant women could not pick as much cotton as other field hands. Birth incapacitated mothers for days, and infants or little children were of no use in the fields. Some planters of the lower South thought it cheaper to work their

PLANTATION WORKERS. Newly freed slaves heading for the fields of the James Hopkinson plantation, Edisto Island, South Carolina. Photograph by Henry P. Moore, spring 1862. NATIONAL ARCHIVES

slaves to death and buy more slaves rather than encourage families.

For the slaves, like all other Americans, their families were central to the definition of who they were. Evidence of this truth was demonstrated when the Civil War started and slaves began to desert their plantations in the upper South. To the surprise of whites, both North and South, these escapees often fled *south* rather than to the so-called Freedom Land in the North. They were going in search of loved ones sold through the interstate slave trade.

Religion. Religion was one of the main buttresses that supported the slave family. African American slaves were denied the right to practice the religion of their ancestors. Some African slaves were Muslims; most believed in a variety of forms of ancestor worship that was more similar to Christianity than Europeans understood. Slave owners viewed African religion as a combination of witchcraft and superstition, and they banned its practice, in part, for fear that slaves might use it to put spells or curses on them.

Most slave owners believed that Christianizing their slaves would make them more passive. They also pointed to Christianization as a justification for slavery; they claimed to be uplifting the slaves from their barbarous past. Although the slave owner extracted unpaid labor from his slaves in this life, he ensured their salvation in the next by making them Christians.

Of course, the Christianity taught to slaves by their masters was very different from that which the masters practiced themselves. Omitted were the implicit and explicit messages in the New Testament about individual freedom and responsibility. Instead, slave owners used the Bible selectively. They argued that Africans were the descendants of Ham, who, in the Old Testament, were cursed by Noah to be "servants of servants." From the New Testament, slave owners cited Christ's admonition to "render unto Caesar that which is Caesar's" to justify their right to demand obedience from their slaves. In part to ensure that slaves could not learn all of the other, contrary messages about freedom to be found in the Bible, slavemasters outlawed the teaching of reading and writing to slaves.

Slaves, however, once again combined what they could remember from their old religions with what their masters told them about Christianity and what they learned about Christianity from literate blacks and antislavery whites. From this information they evolved their own form of Christianity, which was a religion of hope and liberation.

In the slaves' version of Christianity, Christ and Moses played almost equal roles as heroes who had led their people to freedom. Black religion was very much anchored in the real world rather than in life after death. Slaves learned to phrase the words of their prayers and spirituals to speak of salvation and freedom in heaven, but, in truth, they were praying and singing about deliverance from slavery in this world, not the next. Thus, a black woman like Harriet Tubman who led dozens of slaves to freedom, used spirituals like "Steal Away to Jesus" to signal plans for escape. She became known, as a result, as "The Moses of Her People."

The burdens of slavery led African Americans to different definitions of God, sin, and even the devil. Slaves did not conceive of God as the stern taskmaster envisioned by their white owners. Rather, they thought of God as an all-forgiving Father who understood the tribulations that his people were suffering and who was planning a better world for them. This vision of the Almighty led, among other things, to a very different style of worship among slaves. As one ex-bondsman tried to explain: "White folks pray powerful *sad.* Black folks pray powerful *GLAD*!"

Slave religion even resulted in a different understanding of sin. It was, for example, a sin to steal from a fellow slave who, like yourself, had nothing. But it was not necessarily a sin to steal food or clothing from the master. He had "aplenty," as the slaves would say, while their children were hungry and naked. God would understand your necessity and forgive you your small transgression.

It was in their conception of the devil that the slaves' remembrance of their African religion was most evident. To white Protestant slave owners, the devil was the Antichrist, the embodiment of evil. To the slaves, however, the devil was just another powerful spirit, albeit a malevolent one. African religions often contained such entities. They were spirits one tried to avoid, but if one was trapped by a devil, African faiths taught that through wit and guile, the spirit could be overcome. Thus, white slave owners were befuddled when a slave, threatened with a whipping or worse, would joke and lie. In the slave's eyes, the man about to punish him was simply possessed by a devil with whom he might be able to negotiate. Sometimes this strategy actually worked. A master would become so exasperated, yet amused, by his slave's excuses and self-deprecation that he would withdraw his threat of punishment. This is only one example of how slaves' African heritage prevented them from making the European distinction between secular and religious behavior. They used their religious vision of the world to help them cope with everyday crises between themselves and their masters.

Education. A scholar once defined education as "all the ways a culture tries to perpetuate itself from one generation to another." Slave owners, in their defense of their peculiar institution, often claimed that slavery was a "school" that helped "civilize" the "savage African." White Southerners proved to be right about slavery being a school, but, much to their surprise and dismay, not the sort they had intended. When emancipation came, they discovered that slavery had taught blacks how to be *Americans* and to demand all the attributes of freedom enjoyed by other Americans.

Slaves were legally denied the foundation of European education—the knowledge to read and write. Nonetheless, thousands of slaves acquired those skills, usually through voluntary or unintentional help from their young masters and mistresses as they were learning their lessons. (Urban slaves like Frederick Douglass sometimes bribed their white playmates or coworkers to teach them.) Literate slaves then tried to pass on their knowledge to others. It was a special goal of older slaves to learn enough to read the Bible before they died.

Because of the peculiar nature of slavery, forms of education within it were frequently unorthodox. One method of education within the slave community clearly had African roots. This was the teaching of survival strategies through folktales, usually ones involving animals. Many of these stories have come down to us as "Br'er Rabbit" tales. Too often, these have been dismissed as merely charming stories to entertain children. They were that, but—in the complex society of slavery—they served other purposes as well. Western African folklore is full of tales about the hare, who is usually a trickster. In the African American stories, Br'er Rabbit is the hero; he is a weak animal in a forest full of larger, more powerful animals that could not be overcome through direct confrontation. The big animals, however, tended to be clumsy and stupid because they never had to work hard to get what they wanted; they also tended to be very greedy. As a result, the smaller animals could sometimes triumph over the larger ones through wit and guile, through tricking the big animals into using their greater strength against themselves.

Slave owners tended to see these tales as harmless. In fact, slave elders were using them to teach their young the all-important skills of "handling master." They should never confront whites directly. But whites were not very bright, as was best proven by their belief that blacks were stupid. It was important never to disabuse the master of that belief. You would thereby be able to get away with things that were otherwise forbidden. For example, if you could convince the master that you were so terrified of the dark that he did not try to make you work late at night, you then had the opportunity to sneak away for a secret prayer meeting or to visit a loved one on another plantation.

Attitudes toward Work. Nowhere were the consequences of this secret education more apparent than in slave work habits on the plantations. There is no doubt that slavery was enormously profitable for large plantation owners. This did not mean, however, that slave labor was efficient. Slaves worked from sunup to sundown in awful conditions. They were usually ill-housed, ill-clothed, and ill-fed. For most slaves, their primary motivation for labor was fear of physical punishment. So, without real incentives to be productive, to take pride in their work, slaves did everything they could to minimize their labor and to do it as poorly as they could without being punished.

Slaves were shrewd in their avoidance of work. They feigned ignorance so that the master could not trust them with livestock or complex machinery. They would claim that illness prevented them from working. They pretended to be superstitious to avoid unpleasant tasks. For example, they might claim a swamp that needed draining was inhabited by "haunts" that would attack them.

All of these tactics were known to slaveowners. They knew that slaves often deliberately lost livestock and sabotaged machinery, but they could seldom prove it. Moreover, they themselves claimed that the slaves were stupid. To acknowledge that the slaves were outwitting them would undermine their authority. Slave owners tried to dismiss the slaves' superstitions, but secretly they shared some of them. They risked even more inefficiency if they tried to force slaves to work when the majority claimed that they were too terrified to do so. Finally, slave owners were completely confounded by slaves' claims of illness. They knew their bondsmen were skilled at faking all kinds of symptoms. They also knew that an unchecked epidemic could sweep through the usually overcrowded and unsanitary slave quarters, incapacitating the entire work force. This could result not only in the loss of the precious cash crop but also in the deaths of equally valuable property: enslaved human beings.

African American slaves, through their commitment to family, their devotion to their religion, their acquisition of education, and their rationing of their labor, forced compromises from their owners. The master unquestionably remained the more powerful force in the relationship. Nevertheless, within the small space that compromises created in the brutal system of bondage, slaves were able to carve out lives that allowed many of them to retain their humanity and courage. When freedom came, they were ready. It was their former masters who were not.

[*See also* Family Life; Labor.]

BIBLIOGRAPHY

Abrahams, Roger D. *Singing the Master: The Development of Afro-American Culture on the Southern Plantation.* New York, 1992.

Berlin, Ira. "Time, Space, and the Evolution of Afro-American Society on the British Mainland of North America." *AHR* (February 1980): 44–78.

Blassingame, John. *The Slave Community.* New York, 1979.

Douglass, Frederick. *Narrative of the Life of Frederick Douglass, an American Slave.* Boston, 1845. Reprint, New York, 1986.

Genovese, Eugene. *Roll Jordan Roll.* New York, 1974.

Gutman, Herbert. *The Black Family in Slavery and Freedom, 1750–1925.* New York, 1976.

Joyner, Charles. *Down by the Riverside: A South Carolina Slave Community.* Urbana, Ill., 1984.

Rawick, George, ed. *The American Slave: A Composite Autobiography.* 31 vols. Westport, Conn., 1972–1978.

Stampp, Kenneth. *The Peculiar Institution.* New York, 1989.

ROBERT FRANCIS ENGS

SLAVE TRADERS. The Confederacy took a pragmatic line on slave trading. Rather than proclaiming the principle of unlimited access to new supplies of slaves, the Confederate Constitution prohibited importation by the African and overseas slave trade. It did this apparently to prevent a drain on funds and because a majority of Confederate states feared that unlimited importation of new slaves into North America would undercut the market values of Southern slaves and threaten overproduction of staple crops. The Confederacy considered, but rejected, a policy of punishing the slave states remaining in the Federal Union by refusing to buy their surplus slaves. Continued importation from this source was probably seen as one way of encouraging mutual ties between slavery interests within and without the Confederacy.

In practice, however, the Civil War must have limited the scale of exportation of slaves from Unionist Missouri, Kentucky, Maryland, and Delaware. And the uncertainties of the war must, compared with the antebellum period, have considerably restricted the interregional slave trade of the South generally. From 1790 to 1860, the interregional traffic had probably carried over three-quarters of a million slaves from the border states and the Carolinas to the importing states. This trade had terminated an estimated one in five marriages of upper South slaves and separated an even higher proportion of parents and children. Evidence from various markets suggests that during the Civil War

SLAVE PEN OF PRICE, BIRCH, AND COMPANY. Two views of the slave pen at Alexandria, Virginia, where slaves from the upper South were held pending their sale in the markets of New Orleans and elsewhere in the lower South. *Above:* interior; *below:* exterior. Albumen photoprints by Andrew Joseph Russell, 1863. NATIONAL ARCHIVES

several hundred traders continued to operate, shipping thousands of slaves. But the volume of trade must have been much below prewar levels, especially after the South's military reverses of 1863.

In late 1860, Richmond slave prices fell by one third. Measured in grossly inflated Confederate currency, the price of male field hands rose massively during the war: $1,160 in late 1861, $1,230 in late 1862, $2,300 a year later, $4,140 in late 1864, and $10,000 in March 1865. Corresponding values in gold, however, were $1,050, $473, $144, $190, and $100—representing a price collapse in real terms. The blockade and the crippling of the cotton market dramatically damaged real slave prices and the slave trade, although the growing need for slave-grown food crops (given the shortage of white labor) gradually moderated this trend somewhat. Military reverses (especially from 1863) hit prices and sales hard. Locally, the planters' policy of evacuating slaves from threatened areas caused major falls in real prices of slaves.

The fall of New Orleans in 1862 removed a major urban slave market that had been unusual in that, because of links with nearby sugar plantations, it had imported more male than female slaves. But many other urban markets continued, as did the main core of the slave traffic, which comprised traders who bought slaves in country areas, took them overland (sometimes by rail), and sold them in the villages and countryside of the lower South. Traders were often men of substantial capital and status. In Charleston, South Carolina, one such dealer was Ziba Oakes. With buying agents in South Carolina and selling agents in several states, he traded throughout the 1850s and well into the Civil War. His status as a leading businessman and citizen in Charleston is shown by his leadership in the city's banking, political, freemason, and Unitarian Church affairs.

The persistence of slave trading during the Civil War is indicated by traders' account books, correspondence, and advertisements, as well as by the reports of contemporary observers. Henry Badgett is an example of a trader operating from at least the early 1840s (especially from North Carolina to Georgia) and still reporting good profits in December 1863. At Savannah, Georgia, one leading trader, "a bitter old rebel," moved his slaves out only as William Tecumseh Sherman approached the city with his Union army in December 1864. In Virginia, Silas and R. F. Omohundro continued until at least 1863 as specialist suppliers of slaves to traders operating out of Richmond. The daybook of Hector Davis, a Richmond auctioneer who sold mainly to traders, shows very extensive activity till early 1863; then for that firm a large decline seems to have occurred. E. H. Stokes continued until at least late 1863 his long-established business of buying slaves in and around Richmond and selling in Georgia and neighboring areas. Robert Lumpkin had also been in the Richmond trade for many years and he continued until the very end. In April 1865, immediately before the fall of Richmond, Charles Carleton Coffin, traveling with the advancing Union army, found Lumpkin shipping out "fifty men, women, and children.... This sad and weeping fifty, in handcuffs and chains, were the last slave coffle that shall tread the soil of America."

BIBLIOGRAPHY

Coffin, Charles Carleton. *Four Years of Fighting.* Boston, 1866. Reprint, New York, 1970.

McElveen, A. J. *Broke by War: Letters of a Slave Trader.* Edited by Edmund L. Drago. Columbia, S.C., 1991.

Tadman, Michael. *Speculators and Slaves: Masters, Traders, and Slaves in the Old South.* Madison, Wis., 1989.

Wiley, Bell Irvin. *Southern Negroes, 1861–1865.* New Haven, 1938. Reprint, Baton Rouge, La., 1965.

MICHAEL TADMAN

SLIDELL, JOHN (1793–1871), U.S. congressman and senator, Confederate commissioner to France. Born into a modest New York City mercantile family, Slidell graduated from Columbia College in 1810 and entered the practice of law. Decline in family fortunes and a touch of scandal involving a duel over the affections of an actress brought him to a new home in New Orleans sometime around 1819.

By the early 1820s he had developed a lucrative legal practice and had become a strong partisan of Andrew Jackson. His work in the campaigns of 1824 and 1828 won him appointment in 1829 as federal attorney for the eastern district of Louisiana, in which position his independence incurred the enmity of Martin Gordon, collector of customs in New Orleans and boss of the Jacksonian forces in the state. Determined to destroy even potential rivals, Gordon turned Jackson against Slidell with false charges of pro-Calhoun nullification sentiments and secret support of the president's foes. Ousted from his position in 1833, Slidell determined to seek vindication through advancement in the Democratic party.

Although defeated repeatedly in bids for a U.S. Senate seat, he won a place in the state house of representatives in 1838 while expanding his fortune through extensive land speculation. In 1840 New Orleans tax rolls showed him as one of the five or six largest property owners in the city. After another unsuccessful try for the Senate in 1843, he won election that same year to the U.S. House of Representatives.

Steeped now in Louisiana politics, he won the state for James K. Polk in the presidential election of 1844 by steamboating Democrats to polls downriver from New

JOHN SLIDELL. NAVAL HISTORICAL CENTER, WASHINGTON, D.C.

Orleans to bypass disfranchisement by Whig commissioners in the city, a gambit denounced by opponents as the Plaquemines Frauds. Perfectly legal, though irregular, the coup brought him national attention and a reputation as an opportunistic political juggler. The ethical taint deepened in later years as he became involved in questionable land deals and various railroad projects in Central America and the South.

In 1845 he was sent to Mexico as the personal emissary of President Polk in an attempt to resolve the disputes that eventually led to war. Mexican authorities refused him an audience, and the mission failed. But increased visibility boosted his strength within Democratic ranks in Louisiana, casting him as a moderate counterbalance to the more radically Southern Pierre Soulé. Soulé's resignation from the U.S. Senate in 1853 to accept a mission to Spain finally gave Slidell the position he had so long coveted and with it domination of Louisiana politics, reinforced by his close ties to Louisiana's other senator, Judah P. Benjamin.

Always the practitioner, never the ideologue, Slidell figured hardly at all in the great political debates of the 1850s. But he consistently tried to dampen what he considered the excesses of Southern radicalism, fearing destruction of the national system he was determined to dominate. Aided by family connections to the banker August Belmont, and with the help of fellow senators James Bayard and John Bright, he moved closer to that objective by masterminding James Buchanan's election to the presidency in 1856. Viewed by contemporaries as the power behind Buchanan's throne, he soon saw his plans for continued national influence threatened by a reopening of the debate over the expansion of slavery into the territories, a push to disruption he now identified as coming not from Southern extremists but from party dissidents like Stephen A. Douglas.

The 1860 presidential campaign, therefore, found him a convert to the radical Southern position he had resisted. Bolting the Democratic convention in Charleston and rejecting Douglas's nomination at Baltimore, he joined the forces backing John C. Breckinridge, convinced that a Republican victory would so change the nation that the South must then indeed secede. Characteristically, he still favored cautious restraint, arguing in November 1860 that withdrawal from the Union might best be effected by joint action of the Southern states. When events took a different course, he unhesitatingly withdrew from the Senate and vigorously supported the independent secession of Louisiana.

He is most widely identified in American history along with James M. Mason as one of the Confederate commissioners seized off the Bahamas from the British mail packet *Trent* by Captain Charles Wilkes of the Union sloop *San Jacinto* in November 1861. Confederate hopes that the incident would result in a diplomatic breach or even war between the United States and England crumbled when President Abraham Lincoln yielded and Slidell was freed to proceed to his post in France. There he enjoyed at first an intimate relationship with Louis Napoleon and Empress Eugénie, as well as with a large coterie of highly placed figures at court and in private circles. But these associations brought little success on the diplomatic front. A small number of commerce raiders built for the Confederacy in French shipyards through his efforts remained blocked in port by diplomatic pressure from the United States, and a Confederate loan based on a European bond issue engineered by him through the French banking house of Erlanger raised only a meager $2,599,000 on a cotton collateral of $45,000,000. Most critical of all, Confederate designs to win French recognition through the promise of cotton exports came to naught because of inability to get shipments through to Europe. Napoleon refused to countenance any French challenge to the United States without backing from the British, and Lord John Russell's opposition to recognition of the Confederacy or any attempt to break the Union blockade of Southern ports never wavered. When it finally became clear as well that Louis Napoleon's hopes of Confederate protection for his protégé Maximilian in Mexico had no basis, Slidell's diplomatic mission collapsed.

Defeat of the Confederacy left Slidell bitter and unreconcilable. He refused to appeal for pardon or restoration of U.S. citizenship and lived out the remainder of his years in Europe, dying in Cowes on the Isle of Wight.

[*See also* Erlanger Loan; Trent Affair.]

BIBLIOGRAPHY

Hendrick, Burton J. *Statesmen of the Lost Cause.* Boston, 1939.

Nichols, Roy F. *The Disruption of American Democracy.* New York, 1948.

Owsley, Frank L. *King Cotton Diplomacy.* Chicago, 1931. Reprint, Chicago, 1959.

Tregle, Joseph G., Jr. "The Political Apprenticeship of John Slidell." *Journal of Southern History* 26 (1960): 57–70.

Willson, Beckles. *John Slidell and the Confederates in Paris (1862–1865).* New York, 1932. Reprint, New York, 1970.

JOSEPH G. TREGLE, JR.

SMALL ARMS. [*This entry contains nine articles that discuss in detail the diverse types of firearms and munitions used in the Confederate army and navy:*

Confederate Long Arms
Confederate Handguns
Captured and Purchased U.S. Small Arms
Alterations to U.S. Small Arms
Imported English Small Arms
Imported English Long-Range Rifles
Imported Austrian, Belgian, and French Small Arms
Naval Small Arms
Munitions

For definitions of small arms terminology and a more general discussion of the impact on military tactics of developments in small arms technology, see Arms, Weapons, and Ammunition. *For a discussion of the swords, bayonettes, and sabers used by Confederate forces, see* Edged Weapons.]

Confederate Long Arms

Over the course of its four-year existence, the Confederacy would produce at most 75,000 long arms for its armies. Considering that the South put 900,000 men into the field during the course of the war, it is easy to see that the bulk of its guns were acquired by other means (primarily from the import of European guns and secondarily from the seizure, capture, and prewar purchase of Federal arms). The quality of the Confederate-produced arms was also below that of arms made in Europe and the North because the South lacked the necessary skilled labor and raw materials. Often inferior materials were substituted (brass for iron) because they were easier to work. With the exceptions of those guns made on the captured Federal machinery at Fayetteville, North Carolina, and Richmond, Virginia, Confederate guns were all practically hand-made, with very little interchangeability of parts.

The fortuitous seizure of the U.S. Arsenal at Harpers Ferry, Virginia, by elements of Virginia state troops the evening of April 18, 1861, provided the tools, machinery, and stock to establish the Virginia Armory in Richmond, later known as the Richmond Armory, and the Fayetteville Armory at Fayetteville, North Carolina. Anticipating just such action, Lt. Roger Jones, commander of Federal forces at Harpers Ferry, set fire to the establishment but was unsuccessful in his efforts to destroy all arms and machinery. The acquisition of this material was the impetus for the most successful Confederate small arms manufactories.

Virginia forces began immediately to salvage material at the arsenal and transport it to Richmond. After initial setup in a tobacco warehouse, the machinery was installed in the empty Virginia Manufactory site and was soon in use to repair damaged arms. The Virginia Armory, as a result of negotiations between the central government and the commonwealth of Virginia, came under the control of the Confederate Ordnance Department on August 23, 1861, for the duration of the war. Thereafter, it was known as the Richmond Armory and arms manufacture began in earnest.

The first arms produced under state auspices were assembled from seized parts and were conventional U.S. models. Subsequently, a modified .58-caliber rifle-musket based on the U.S. model 1855 arm evolved with the same basic configuration and 40-inch barrel. After the central government assumed control, the lockplates were marked "CS" indicating government ownership. The Richmond Armory manufactured long arms from the fall of 1861 until early 1865, when the machinery was sent south. The armory buildings were subsequently destroyed by fire during the evacuation of Richmond on April 3, 1865.

The Armory produced four distinct long arms during its period of operation. These were the model 1855–based rifle-musket, a rifle with 33-inch barrel, a musketoon with 30-inch barrel, and a carbine with 25-inch barrel. All were rifled and .58 caliber with the exception of the musketoon, which was smoothbore and .60 caliber. The rifle-musket, dated 1861 through 1864, is the most commonly encountered. Dates of the others include rifles, 1864; musketoons, 1862 and 1863; and carbines, 1863 and 1864. The musketoon and rifle are quite rare today. The armory managed to produce some 1,500 arms per month once operations got under way, but it never approached its potential because of material shortages. The Richmond Armory manufactured about 45 percent of the long arms produced in the Confederacy during the war, nearly the combined output of

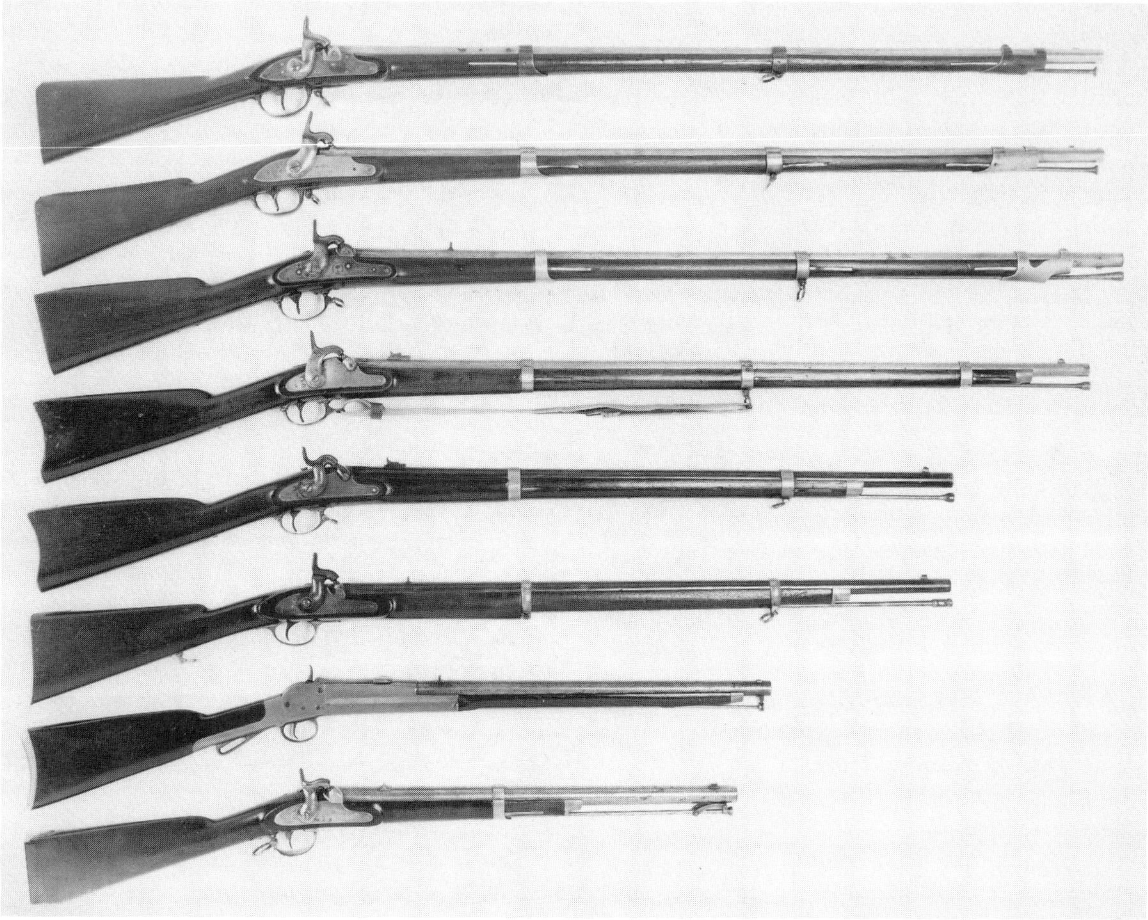

CONFEDERATE LONG ARMS AND ALTERATIONS. Pictured from top to bottom are U.S. model 1816 musket, Confederate alteration to percussion, .69 cal.; Virginia manufactory contract musket, Confederate Barett alteration to percussion, .69 cal.; Glaze-Palmetto Armory model 1842 musket, .69 cal., rifled and sited by Glaze, 1861; Richmond rifle-musket, .58 cal.; Fayetteville late model rifle, .58 cal.; Cook rifle, .58 cal.; Morse breech-loading carbine, .52 cal.; Bilharz, Hall, and Company muzzle-loading carbine, .58 cal.

GLAZE-PALMETTO ARMORY MODEL 1842 MUSKET COURTESY OF JOHN A. CLEVELAND; ALL OTHER ITEMS COURTESY OF RUSS A. PRITCHARD

all private contractors. Total production is estimated to have been about 35,000 arms of all types.

The carbine factory of S. C. Robinson was adjacent to the Richmond Armory. Robinson contracted to make for the government a breech-loading carbine like that produced by Christian Sharps in the North. Although enthusiastic about the project, he ran into problems because of his inexperience. Nevertheless, the company built the machinery and fabricated about 1,900 carbines bearing the Robinson name from December 1862 until March 1, 1863, when the central government took over the operation. Some 3,500 unmarked Sharps carbines were produced under government supervision until the spring of 1864, when the machinery was removed to Tallassee, Alabama, where it was used to make a muzzle-loading carbine. Total production of the Richmond Sharps by Robinson and the government was about 5,400 arms.

Farther south in Virginia was the ordnance complex at Danville that included the establishments of Bilharz, Hall, and Company; Keen, Walker, and Company; Read and Watson; and probably the unknown maker of the Getty brass-framed Sharps carbine.

Bilharz, Hall, and Company early in the war was an established firm, having delivered 100 breech-loading carbines to the Ordnance Department by September 1862. These .54-caliber rising-breech carbines are well made and entirely hand-fitted (they were called rising-breech because the breech literally rose when opened for loading). Later the company produced a copy of the U.S. model 1855 muzzle-loading carbine, .58 caliber. Judging from the surviving serial numbers, it would appear that about 700 of these arms were made. The breech-loading arm is especially rare today. The firm also provided stocks for the Richmond carbine and Richmond Sharps carbine.

Keen, Walker, and Company manufactured brass-framed breech-loading carbines of .54 caliber, which were all delivered at Danville in 1862. Invoices indicate that total production was 282 arms. The company then became involved as a subcontractor with the Read and Watson firm.

Read and Watson made rifles and carbines for the state of Virginia in 1862 and some Virginia state troops in 1863. These are unusual in that components of breech-loading arms were altered to manufacture a muzzle-loading weapon. Two types of alteration have been noted. The first, seen on rifles and carbines, consists of a small brass breechpiece fitted to the barrel with an iron breechplug with cone. The second type of alteration used a much larger brass breechpiece with the iron breechplug and cone. (The breechplug closes the breech of the gun; into it fits the breechpiece, which holds the cone, a nipple on which the hammer falls to strike the percussion cap and ignite the charge.) This method is more substantial and is found only on rifles. The few carbines extant appear to have been manufactured from Hall model 1833 carbines. Rifles were made using parts from both Harpers Ferry and model 1819 contract Hall rifles. The firm's total production is estimated to have been 900 arms of all types.

There is strong circumstantial evidence that the intriguing .52-caliber Getty brass-framed Sharps carbine was also made at or near Danville. This arm utilizes Hall parts in much the same fashion as those of Read and Watson, and it has a brass breechpiece similar to the products of Read and Watson and Keen, Walker, and Company. All three use Roman numeral assembly numbers. Production was very limited, probably less than 100 arms.

The machinery and parts captured at Harpers Ferry were used not only for the Richmond Armory but also for the Fayetteville Arsenal. In early 1862 the machinery for making the U.S. model 1855 rifle, .58 caliber, with 33-inch barrel, was sent to Fayetteville. The shipment included the essential cutting and milling machines together with necessary dies, gauges, and belting with which to run the machines. The material was installed in the old North Carolina Arsenal, and production of a brass-mounted two-band .58-caliber rifle began in January and February 1862. The lack of raw materials continually hampered production, so that the projected output was never achieved. The rifles made at Fayetteville were excellent, however, and production reached about 7,500 arms before the machinery was moved to avoid the advance of William Tecumseh Sherman's army. The vacant arsenal was destroyed on March 14, 1865.

The ordnance complex around Greensboro, North Carolina, was another source primarily for the state. Several companies in the area collaborated in varying degrees to produce a limited number of weapons for North Carolina. All were more or less copies of the U.S. model 1841 rifle, with the exception of a carbine of unique design patented in the Confederacy by Jere H. Tarpley.

Clapp, Gates, and Company near Gibsonville manufactured a relatively crude iron-mounted two-band rifle from 1862 to 1864. Extant specimens are quite scarce, with a total production of probably no more than 200 rifles. Clapp, Gates also furnished components and fittings for other firms. Gillam and Miller at High Point made a very small number of brass-mounted rifles, probably no more than 50. The firm name is stamped in the wood of the stock on one surviving specimen and the arm shows signs of much hand finishing. H. C. Lamb and Company in Jamestown produced good copies of the model 1841 rifle without patchbox (a recessed area in the stock where gun tools are kept). The arms, while handmade and fitted, were substantially built. Production of this .58-caliber rifle was probably about 700 pieces; it is one of the more frequently seen North Carolina contract rifles. Mendenhall, Jones, and Company (Mendenhall, Jones, and Gardner) in Jamestown also made a good brass-mounted copy of the model 1841 rifle. This company was active from late 1861 until the partnership was dissolved in December 1864. During this time they produced some 2,000 serviceable rifles for the state. Searcy and Moore of Greensboro produced about 50 rifles, few of which are extant today. Those that do survive indicate much hand fitting.

A breech-loading brass-frame Tarpley carbine made by J. and F. and E. T. Garrett and Company of Greensboro was sold both commercially and to the state. Between April and September 1863 the state bought some 200 of these .52-caliber arms. One specimen is known to be serial number 421, indicative of a figure near total production. The Tarpley carbine is today one of the Confederate arms most sought after by collectors.

The Asheville Armory produced an excellent .58-caliber copy of the model 1841 rifle. This brass-mounted rifle was fabricated during 1862 and 1863, and some 300 were made before the machinery was shipped to Columbia, South Carolina, during the fall of 1863. The few specimens that survive show good craftsmanship.

George W. Morse produced the most advanced-design long arm used by Southern forces at the State Military Works at Greenville, South Carolina. This brass-frame breech-loading carbine used self-primed, reloadable .50-caliber metallic cartridges. The state ordered 1,000 carbines, which were produced with three variations. The survival rate of these arms is relatively high, indicating the state probably kept them and they were not much used in the field. At the same time Morse developed a simple internal lock that could be adapted for use in any percussion arm. Examples of a .52-caliber rifled carbine and .69-caliber smoothbore musket are known to exist. Utilization must have been very limited with less than 200 arms produced.

The most successful private manufacturer of arms for the

Confederacy was the firm of Cook and Brother founded by two Englishmen, Ferdinand W. Cook and his brother, Francis, in New Orleans in June 1861. The firm produced arms of three basic configurations based on current English patterns—the pattern 1856 short rifle, pattern 1853 artillery musketoon, and pattern 1856 cavalry carbine. All were brass-mounted and .58 caliber with barrel lengths of 33 inches, 24 inches, and 21 inches, respectively. Production, which began in New Orleans, was initially for the state of Alabama. Some 1,000 arms were manufactured before the company had to flee the city ahead of Federal occupation forces. The Cooks managed to save their machinery and unfinished arms and set up shop in Selma, Alabama, where more arms were assembled. The firm relocated to Athens, Georgia, in 1863 and manufactured another 6,500 arms. Total production was about 8,500 arms of all types, the rifle being the most common. Production probably ceased during the summer of 1864 for lack of payment. Maj. Ferdinand Cook was killed in action that year in South Carolina, and after the war, Francis Cook sold the plant to the Athens Manufacturing Company.

The firm of Greenwood and Gray of Columbus, Georgia, manufactured rifles, carbines, and musketoons for both the central government and the state of Alabama. The master armorer was an Englishman named J. P. Murray, whose name appears on many of the locks of arms made by this firm. The company received a contract in 1862 to build 200 rifles and 1,000 carbines of the model 1841 pattern in .58 caliber. Later, the delivery of 262 Mississippi-type rifles and 73 carbines is noted. Total production was less than 1,500 arms of all types. Apparently, not all the carbines were delivered, judging from the number of surviving specimens.

The Georgia Armory at Milledgeville produced a brass-mounted copy of the model 1841 rifle in .58 caliber. Production proceeded from 1862 until November 1864, when the facility was burned by Federal forces. The very few surviving specimens indicate a small operation with total production of less than 100 rifles.

The manufactory of Davis and Bozeman located in Equality, Alabama, built another copy of the model 1841 rifle and a carbine under contract to the state of Alabama. These were well-made .58-caliber arms with brass mountings. Alabama records indicate receipt of 749 rifles and 89 carbines during the period October 1, 1863, to November 1, 1864. State markings on the barrels are identical to those found on the arms of Greenwood and Gray (J. P. Murray) and Dickson, Nelson, and Company.

The Shakanoosa Arms Company (Dickson, Nelson, and Company) was established by Dickson, Nelson, and Sadler at Dickson, Alabama, to manufacture yet another copy of the model 1841 rifle under contract to the state. Fortunes of war forced the firm to move first to Rome, Georgia, then to Adairsville, and finally to Dawson in March 1864. These well-made brass-mounted .58-caliber rifles are marked on the lockplate "Dickson, Nelson & Co." and include the date, either 1864 or 1865. Some 645 rifles were delivered prior to November 1, 1864, under a contract for 5,000 arms. Their carbines are very rare with probably less than 100 completed, but carbine stock blanks found at the armory site after the war indicate there were plans, interrupted when the war ended, to produce a considerable number. Total production was about 750 arms of all types.

The Tallassee carbine was made at Tallassee, Alabama, with machinery sent from the carbine factory in Richmond, formerly the S. C. Robinson Company. These arms were made for the central government rather than a state. The carbine was based on the current English pattern 1856 carbine and was built in .58 caliber. What little evidence survives indicates that 500 carbines were manufactured from June 1864 until April 1865 and that all were still in storage at the arsenal on April 3, 1865. What happened to them after the war is a mystery.

The Pulaski Gun Factory in Pulaski, Tennessee, was in operation during 1861 and 1862 and was the only state armory known to build new arms. These were copies, more or less, of the model 1841 rifle and utilized some sporting arms components. The few surviving specimens are brass-mounted and .54 caliber. Production may have totaled 500 arms.

The only identified major long-arm maker in the Trans-Mississippi theater was the Confederate States Ordnance Works at Tyler, Texas. This facility seems to have produced several different models of iron-mounted rifles and some shorter arms of musketoon length. Calibers varied, .54 and .577 being noted. There was also considerable variation of lock markings. The different models may have been dictated by the availability of used parts and barrels. What few specimens are extant are of consistently poor quality. Total production from October 1, 1863, through March 31, 1865, was about 2,000 arms of all types.

There were other small manufacturers whose arms have not been recognized, but their output was insignificant. A number of entrepreneurs advanced funds for manufacturing but never produced a single firearm. The efforts of the central government and the states to build an ordnance system were sometimes counterproductive and in the end proved to be ineffectual. The Confederate Ordnance Department was unable to influence the outcome of the war.

BIBLIOGRAPHY

Albaugh, William A., III, and Edward N. Simmons. *Confederate Arms.* Harrisburg, Pa., 1957.

Cromwell, Giles. "The Alteration of Virginia Manufactory Weapons, 1818–1863." *Bulletin of the American Society of Arms Collectors,* no. 52 (1985): 25–45.

Flayderman, Norman E. *Flayderman's Guide to Antique American Arms.* 5th ed. Northbrook, Ill., 1990.

Floyd, William B. "The Asheville Armory and Rifle." *Bulletin of the American Society of Arms Collectors,* no. 44 (1981): 21–26.

Fuller, Claud E., and Richard D. Steuart. *Firearms of the Confederacy.* Huntington, W.V., 1944.

Jones, Douglas E. "The Dickson, Nelson Company: Alabama Civil War Gunmakers." *Bulletin of the American Society of Arms Collectors,* no. 60 (1989): 29–37.

Madaus, Howard Michael. "North Carolina Rifle Contracts of the Civil War." *Bulletin of the American Society of Arms Collectors,* no. 54 (1986): 46–53.

Michel, Benjamin P. "The Richmond Armory." *Bulletin of the American Society of Arms Collectors,* no. 33 (1976): 65–74.

Murphy, John M. *Confederate Carbines and Musketoons.* Dallas, Tex., 1986.

RUSS A. PRITCHARD

Confederate Handguns

Handguns were issued to mounted personnel and to officers of all branches of service. Because of their small caliber, limited range, and questionable accuracy, they were considered defensive weapons, with the exception of offensive use by cavalry. In general, the handgun was carried by military personnel who had their hands full performing their primary duties but needed a convenient, accessible weapon in an emergency situation. Weapons of this type had little impact on the conduct of the war.

The great majority of handguns used by the Confederates were in fact various models of the Colt and Remington revolvers captured from Federal forces or seized at Federal installations. A considerable number of weapons were also imported from England, with a lesser number from France. The preponderance of handguns actually manufactured in the South for Confederate forces were the product of only a few concerns: Leech and Rigdon; Rigdon, Ansley, and Company; Spiller and Burr; and Griswold and Gunnison. Their combined production was less than 8,000 firearms. Even if one adds those manufactured by smaller firms, the total production was only about 9,000 pieces at best, thereby accounting for the extreme rarity of these weapons today.

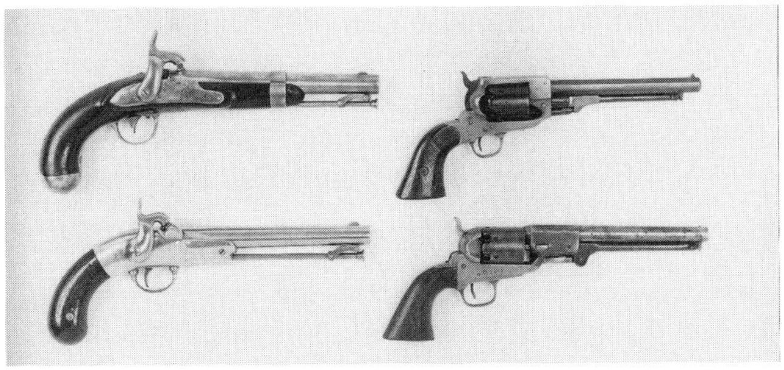

CONFEDERATE HANDGUNS AND ALTERATIONS. Clockwise, from upper left, are U.S. model 1836 pistol, Confederate alteration to percussion, .54 cal.; Spiller and Burr revolver, .36 cal.; Griswold and Gunnison revolver, .36 cal.; Garrett single-shot pistol, .54 cal.

RUSS A. PRITCHARD

The most prolific manufacturer was the firm operated by Samuel Griswold and A. W. Gunnison. Griswold, a Connecticut native, moved south in 1832 to establish a manufacturing facility at what became Griswoldville, Georgia, about ten miles south of Macon. Gunnison was in New Orleans at the beginning of the war and became engaged in revolver manufacture. He escaped Federal occupation troops with his machinery in April 1862 and moved to Macon, joining with Griswold shortly thereafter. Their revolver is a brass-framed copy of the Colt navy revolver, model 1851, .36 caliber, with minor modifications. Deliveries began in October 1862. The earlier revolver has a round barrel housing, which was changed to part octagon around the serial number 1500, probably during July 1863. All Griswold revolvers are remarkably standard, given their hand-finishing by semiskilled slaves. Production ceased in November 1864 when the factory and most of the surrounding structures were demolished by elements of the Tenth Ohio and Third Union Kentucky Cavalry Regiments, part of William Tecumseh Sherman's army on its March to the Sea. Total production was some 3,700 revolvers.

Thomas Leech and Charles H. Rigdon formed a business partnership in Memphis, Tennessee, just before the Civil War, resulting in the firm of Leech and Rigdon, which was closely allied with another enterprise, the Memphis Novelty Works, manufacturers of edged weapons, spurs, musical instruments, and accoutrements. In anticipation of the Federal occupation of the city, the firm moved to Columbus, Mississippi, where a contract for 1,500 revolvers was secured and limited production began. Again moving to avoid Federal interference, the firm settled in Greensboro, Georgia, in March 1863. Focusing on revolver production, the company ceased edged-weapon fabrication, but the partnership was dissolved in December 1863 after production of about 1,000 revolvers. Upon the partnership's dissolution, Rigdon moved the machinery and workers to Augusta, Georgia, site of existing ordnance installations, and continued production under the name of Rigdon, Ansley, and Company, completing the remaining 500 revolvers of the original contract.

This revolver was an iron-framed copy of the Colt navy revolver, model 1851, but with a part-octagon barrel housing like the later Griswold revolvers. The top flat of this barrel housing bears the name "Leech & Rigdon" and the letters "CSA." Revolvers produced by Leech and Rigdon and the successor company are almost identical, since both were made with the same machinery. Minor variations in details exist, however, and the firm name changes as the new company evolves. Markings on arms above serial number 1500 indicate the move to Augusta. Later production revolvers are marked only "CSA" on the barrel flat. Rigdon, Ansley production is identifiable by their twelve-stop cylinder; some 900 were made. Total production of both companies was about 2,500 revolvers.

The next most important manufacturer was the firm founded by Edward N. Spiller of Baltimore and David J. Burr of Richmond, principals, with Lt. Col. James H. Burton, former master armorer at the U.S. Arsenal at Harpers Ferry, then assigned to the Confederate Bureau of Ordnance. The firm secured a contract for 15,000 Colt-style navy revolvers but subsequently bought the Robinson Revolver Factory, which was already tooled to produce a Whitney-style navy revolver. Burton was transferred south to Atlanta in May 1862, and Spiller and Burr left Richmond with him. The trio began delivery of the brass-framed Whitney-type revolver, .36 caliber, at Atlanta in December 1862. Early production had a light Whitney frame prone to fracture. Later revolvers had a heavier frame, but problems continued to plague the company.

The Confederate government, after having received about 840 revolvers, bought the firm in January 1864 and moved the operation to Macon, where an additional 400 revolvers were made. Early specimens are often marked with the firm name on the barrel and the letters "CS" on the left or right side of the brass frame. The firm name was dropped after the government took control. Total production was about 1,250 pieces. These revolvers are very rare, most having been issued to the western armies. (Confederate weapons in the East were often taken into New England after the war by former Union soldiers and preserved as souvenirs. Guns in the West often saw additional action on the frontier, and thus their survival rate was lower.)

The next largest handgun producer of the Confederacy was the firm of J. H. Dance and Bros., also known as Dance and Park, located first in Columbia, Texas, and later in Anderson. The firm was unique in that it furnished both .36- and .44-caliber weapons. The frame configuration of these revolvers was quite different from that of other manufacturers, with the omission of the recoil shield on the frame giving it a somewhat flat, slab-sided appearance. The .36-caliber navy revolver is slightly smaller than the Colt model 1851, and the .44-caliber handgun is actually about dragoon size. Both types are unmarked except for the serial numbers on all major parts. From these numbers it would appear that at least 350 army revolvers and about 135 navy revolvers were produced, no more than a total of 500. Almost all were delivered to the Ordnance Department for issue to Texas mounted units. Many fakes, particularly of the navy model, exist and, like genuine Confederate arms, are very collectible.

The products of the Augusta Machine Works, Augusta, Georgia, constitute an enigma. It is known from several sources that there was a central government–owned revolver factory in the ordnance complex there, but positive identification of its products has never been made. There exists in very limited numbers a well-made iron-framed revolver, a copy of the Colt navy revolver, model 1851, .36 caliber, that has been generally accepted as the product of this establishment, even though none is known to be marked with the firm name. Initial production has a six-stop cylinder like Colt products. Later production appears with a twelve-stop cylinder, a safety feature much like that of the Rigdon, Ansley, and Company revolver. Most specimens extant have letters rather than serial numbers, although there are a few that have single-digit numbers, again indicative of rather limited production. No records exist to determine the start or termination of production. Surviving specimens suggest that over a hundred were produced, and since some are in very good condition, it may be supposed that they were made near the end of the war and did not see sustained combat use. These weapons are particularly well made for Confederate arms and are very scarce and desired by collectors.

The ordnance complex at Columbus, Georgia, was the source of a wide variety of arms and equipment fabricated for the Confederate cause. One of the primary contractors was the firm of Louis Haiman & Bros. Active in the manufacture of edged weapons, Louis and Elias Haiman purchased the Muscogee Foundry and Machinery Company in August 1862 and shortly thereafter set up the Columbus Fire Arms Manufacturing Company. They obtained a contract to furnish 10,000 navy revolvers, copies of the Colt model 1851, .36-caliber arm. Production began slowly, and it is estimated that possibly a hundred revolvers were delivered before the government purchased the factory during the spring of 1864 and integrated it into the Confederate States Armory there. Revolver production was never resumed. These extremely rare handguns are usually marked with the full firm name "Columbus Fire Arms Manuf. Co., Columbus, Ga." on the cylinder and the full firm name or just "Columbus, Ga." on the top flat of the barrel housing. Probably no more than six authentic specimens exist today. So-called unmarked examples are of questionable authenticity.

Besides revolvers made under government contract for military issue, others were made by two more firms—Thomas W. Cofer of Portsmouth, Virginia, and Schneider and Glassick of Memphis, Tennessee. They produced a very small number of weapons for the Southern market, some of which are known to have seen military use.

Cofer patented and produced a unique series of brass-framed, spur-trigger .36-caliber revolvers. All are marked with the Cofer name, patent date, and place of manufacture. There is considerable variation in these handmade revolvers, but there appear to be three major types. The first two require a special cartridge with integral nipple that is reloadable. The first has a two-piece cylinder to facilitate reloading; the second has a one-piece cylinder with an ejector attached to the frame to push fired cartridges out of the cylinder. A third type, possibly the production model, has a conventional percussion cylinder. Less than fifteen of these revolvers survive today. Only double-digit serial numbers have been noted, indicating that less than a hundred were manufactured. These arms are extremely rare.

Firearms production by Schneider and Glassick of Memphis probably began during the fall of 1861 and terminated in March 1862 with the Federal occupation of the city. There are only three known authentic specimens extant. The revolver is a copy of the Colt navy revolver, model 1851, .36 caliber, and has a brass frame similar to that of the Griswold and Gunnison. All are marked with the full firm name on top of the barrel, and serial numbers appear on all major parts. Total production is unknown but certainly very limited.

In addition to these revolvers, a number of obsolete single-shot pistols were manufactured in an effort to arm hard-pressed Confederate units, particularly in the early stages of the conflict. All these weapons were stopgap at best and were manufactured in limited numbers.

One such weapon was the so-called Fayetteville pistol-carbine made of parts captured when Virginia troops occupied the Federal arsenal at Harpers Ferry, Virginia. This was no more than the U.S. model 1855 pistol-carbine, .58 caliber, with the Maynard tape primer system deleted to simplify production. Only those parts captured were assembled into firearms; few if any parts were fabricated. The very few specimens that survive indicate manufacture in 1862.

The other single-shot pistol has tentatively been identified as the product of J. and F. Garrett, Greensboro, North Carolina, also maker of the rare Tarpley carbine. These brass-framed pistols are .54 caliber and utilize at least some surplus parts of the U.S. model 1842 pistol, specifically the barrel, hammer, trigger, and trigger guard. The brass frame follows no known U.S. pattern. Serial numbers extant indicate production of probably 500 pistols.

Although production of single-shot pistols was not seriously undertaken, ordnance records of ammunition delivered during the war would indicate that a substantial number of these arms of .54 and .69 caliber, obviously captured obsolete U.S. models, were pressed into service throughout the war.

Italian-made replicas of some Confederate revolvers began appearing during the centennial in the 1960s, and numerous fakes have been produced over the years. Confederate handguns are in greater demand than ever, and values have increased substantially in recent years.

BIBLIOGRAPHY

Albaugh, William A., III. *The Confederate Brass-Framed Colt and Whitney.* Published privately, 1955.

Albaugh, William A., III, and Edward N. Simmons. *Confederate Arms.* Harrisburg, Pa., 1957.

Albaugh, William A., III, Hugh Benet, Jr., and Edward N. Simmons. *Confederate Handguns.* Philadelphia, 1963.

Albaugh, William A., III, and Richard D. Steuart. *The Original Confederate Colt.* New York, 1953.

Fuller, Claud E., and Richard D. Steuart. *Firearms of the Confederacy.* Huntington, W.Va., 1944.

Gary, William A. *Confederate Revolvers.* Dallas, Tex., 1987.

Wiggins, Gary. *Dance and Brothers: Texas Gunmakers of the Confederacy.* Orange, Va., 1986.

Russ A. Pritchard

Captured and Purchased U.S. Small Arms

At the commencement of hostilities, there was not a single private small arms manufactory in operation in the Southern states. The various state militia units were equipped with mostly obsolete arms. Limited numbers of sporting arms and self-protection handguns were privately owned, as were souvenirs of prior conflicts. There were also thousands of mostly second-class arms (muskets altered from a flintlock to a percussion firing system) in storage at Federal arsenals and other facilities scattered throughout the South.

The organized militias rallied to the new Confederate flag with antiquated flintlocks of various models, smoothbore percussion alterations and muskets, and a number of U.S. model 1841 and 1855 rifles and U.S. model 1855 rifle-muskets. Other men carried sporting arms, double- and single-barrel shotguns, and hunting rifles, which were brought from home or hastily purchased from private sources, all mostly inadequate for their purpose.

The Confederates early in the war seized U.S. arsenals and installations in Southern states at Baton Rouge and New Orleans, Louisiana; Fayetteville, North Carolina; Charleston, South Carolina; Augusta and Macon, Georgia; Mount Vernon, Alabama; Apalachicola, Florida; Little Rock, Arkansas; and San Antonio, Texas. These seizures resulted in the acquisition of about 150,000 arms, primarily obsolete altered flintlocks, and possibly 15,000 rifles of current pattern. Together with arms already in state hands, Confederate forces began the war with at least 220,000 small arms, most of questionable effectiveness.

Early battles until the summer of 1863 were primarily Southern victories. With the battlefields under Southern control, ordnance personnel could gather dropped, surrendered, and damaged weapons of their Federal opponents. This source proved most productive. Over 150,000 small arms of all types were acquired as a result of the Battles

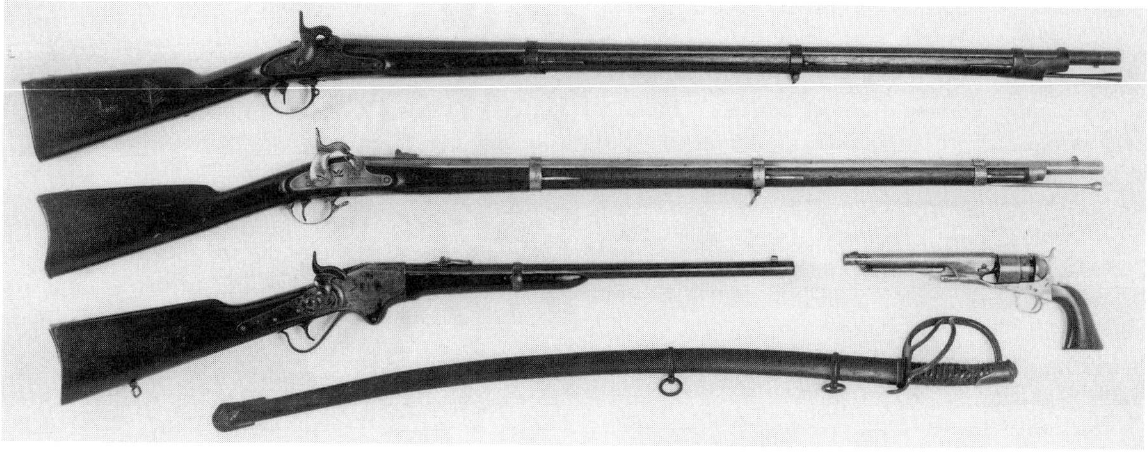

Captured U.S. arms. Pictured from top to bottom are model 1842 musket, .69 cal.; model 1861 rifle-musket, .58 cal.; Spencer breech-loading magazine-fed carbine, .52 cal.; Colt model 1860 army revolver, .44 cal.; model 1860 light cavalry saber. Model 1861 rifle-musket and model 1860 light cavalry saber courtesy of the Civil War Library and Museum, Philadelphia; all other items courtesy of George J. Lincoln III

of First and Second Manassas, the Seven Days' Battles around Richmond, and Fredericksburg, Chancellorsville, and Chickamauga.

Captured Federal weapons, early seizures, and battlefield recoveries amounted overall to over 300,000 arms, second only in importance to imported weapons. By September 1862 Confederate Ordnance could report the manufacture of less than 15,000 arms in recently established Southern arms manufactories.

Arms acquired from Federal repositories varied from nonfunctional or obsolete flintlock muskets to modern breech-loading rifles and multishot revolvers. Ordnance authorities endeavored to alter to a percussion firing system the flintlocks on hand by methods similar to those already used with some success by Federal facilities. But they were never able to develop the expertise to manufacture metallic cartridges used in the more advanced magazine arms and thus were totally dependent on captured ammunition.

The diverse inventory of captured arms included flintlock and altered flintlock muskets and rifles, percussion muskets, rifle-muskets and rifles, a variety of patent breech-loading carbines, and a bewildering array of flintlock, altered flintlock, and percussion single-shot pistols of varying calibers. In all, they were an ordnance department nightmare.

Flintlock muskets were primarily the model 1822 made by various contractors that had not already been percussioned by Federal authorities, and smaller numbers of earlier flintlock arms still in government stores. These antiquated .69-caliber smoothbore arms used a flint and steel ignition system developed in the seventeenth century. The way they were tactically employed acknowledged the inherent inaccuracy of smoothbores: whole regiments of 800 to 1,000 men would fire volleys at opposing formations of a similar size, so that individual accuracy was irrelevant.

Understanding the advantages of rifled and, to a lesser extent, breech-loading arms for special units, U.S. Ordnance began the manufacture of rifles with the model 1803. Subsequent models 1814 and 1817 were produced in limited numbers. The Hall model 1819 breech-loading rifle was purchased by Federal authorities. Rendered obsolete by improved arms, thousands of these, especially Hall models, were stored in Southern repositories.

The Federal ordnance officials also understood the advantages of the percussion system of ignition and adopted the model 1841 rifle and model 1842 musket. The latter retained all the obsolete features of earlier flintlocks with the exception of the ignition system, which made the arm more reliable. Otherwise, it was still the same inaccurate .69-caliber smoothbore arm. The model 1841 rifle, in .54 caliber, was very favorably received and set the stage for acceptance of reduced-bore rifled arms with greater effective range over a decade later. Many thousands of these model 1842 muskets and a lesser number of model 1841 rifles were in Southern hands or seized at the beginning of the war. Confederate forces in April 1861 were armed primarily with these .69-caliber arms, which were already obsolete by U.S. standards.

The U.S. model 1855 rifle-musket, rifle, and carbine were adopted during Jefferson Davis's tenure as U.S. secretary of war. The caliber was reduced from .69 to .58. The rifling of arms increased their effective range from 100 yards to 300 yards. The Maynard tape priming device integral to the rifle and rifle musket proved in humid or inclement weather to be more of a problem than an improvement and was omitted in subsequent models 1861, 1863, and 1864.

With the general acceptance of the percussion system, all obsolete flintlock arms in government stores were categorized in four grades, with first-class serviceable arms to be altered to the percussion system. All model 1816 arms and subsequent models deemed Class I were percussioned, using one of three primary methods. The cone-in-barrel method simply removed the flintlock components from the lock, sealed the vent in the barrel, added a percussion hammer, and placed a percussion cone in a hole drilled on the upper surface of the barrel. This method was both efficient and inexpensive. The patent-breech method was somewhat more elaborate. The breech of the barrel was removed and a new forged bolster with cone was screwed onto the barrel; flintlock components of the lock were removed and replaced by a new percussion hammer. The drum-in-barrel alteration required that a drum with cone be screwed into the side of the barrel over the old vent; the flintlock components were removed from the lock and were replaced by a percussion hammer. Regardless of the method used, the service life of the firearm was extended by these simple, cost-effective modifications, all of which were reasonably satisfactory. A small number of these arms were also rifled and sighted at the time of alteration in a further effort to upgrade their performance. Some few model 1795 and 1808 arms were also altered by the individual states under private contract. The majority of this work took place during the period 1848 to 1852. Thus, thousands of altered muskets and a considerable number of flintlock muskets were stored in Southern Federal repositories when hostilities erupted.

The Militia Act of 1808 had authorized the annual transfer and distribution of Federal arms to the organized military forces of the states. This system had been in effect for decades before the war. Some 115,000 arms in varying condition were sent to Southern Federal arsenals in the year 1860 alone, in accordance with established procedure. These were the arms that were seized so quickly when war began.

In the months immediately preceding hostilities, Southern agents scoured Northern arsenals and supplies held by entrepreneurs, purchasing significant quantities of arms from sources who had no qualms concerning the sale of arms and munitions to a potential belligerent. Numbers of current model Colt, Maynard, Sharps, and Whitney arms were acquired in this manner and shipped to Southern states. Whitney even purchased condemned parts from U.S. armories and other sources to put together weapons to sell to eager agents of both Northern and Southern states. Such commerce continued into the spring of 1861 even after the first shots had been fired.

The early battles were the source of most of the current models acquired by Confederate forces. Frequent captures of the model 1841 and model 1855 rifles and model 1855 rifle-musket greatly added to the limited number of effective arms in the Confederate arsenal. During 1861 and 1862 captures of the Springfield model 1861 and various 1861 contract rifle-muskets were a great boon.

A variety of breech-loading rifles and carbines found their way into Confederate service. It is virtually impossible to calculate the actual numbers seized or captured, but so many of the various models of Colt, Maynard, Merrill, and Sharps arms were in service that Confederate laboratories manufactured specific ammunition for them. Thousands of Burnside and Spencer arms were captured, but again because the Confederates could not manufacture their special metallic cartridges, these arms were relegated to storage arsenals after captured ammunition was expended. Several models of the Hall carbine, the model 1847 carbine, and Musketoon, Cosmopolitan, Jenks, Joslyn, Merrill, and Starr carbines saw service. Calibers ranged from .35 to .72 with almost no ammunition interchangeable.

The vast array of handguns in Confederate service was just as diverse as the long arms with calibers .31, .34, .36, .41, .44, .54, and .69 being used throughout the war. These handguns included current metallic cartridge revolvers of the latest design, such as the Smith and Wesson number 2 army revolver, a popular private-purchase arm, with the other extreme being the obsolete model 1816 and model 1836 single-shot flintlock pistols in .54 caliber, respectively. By far the most common were various Colt and Remington models in .36 and .44 caliber, supplemented by substantial numbers of altered single-shot pistols of .54 caliber and imported revolvers. These percussioned single-shot pistols were received by the states under the 1808 act and were pathetically outdated when compared to the latest revolver of Colt or Remington manufacture. Nevertheless, they were used by Confederate forces, as the manufacture of tens of thousands of rounds of ammunition for them indicates.

The Colt models most commonly encountered were the model 1848 dragoon revolver, .44 caliber; model 1849 pocket revolver, .31 caliber; model 1851 navy revolver, .36 caliber; model 1860 army revolver, .44 caliber; model 1861 navy revolver, .36 caliber; and model 1862 police revolver, .36 caliber. Remington models were primarily the Beals army and navy, .44 and .36 caliber, respectively, and the model 1861 (old model) army and navy revolvers, also .44 and .36 caliber, respectively.

Handguns manufactured by the Massachusetts Arms Company, Allen and Wheelock, Pettengill, Savage Starr, and Whitney in .36 and .44 calibers were obtained by seizure, capture, or private purchase in lesser quantities.

It is easy to see that Confederate forces used just about every American firearm made up to 1861. Regrettably few, if any, of these weapons bear legitimate markings to indicate Confederate use, although there are numerous spurious examples extant. That the Confederate States of America managed to keep nearly a million men of several armies separated by hundreds of miles in the field armed and equipped to conduct war for four years was something of a major accomplishment.

BIBLIOGRAPHY

Cromwell, Giles. *The Virginia Manufactory of Arms.* Charlottesville, Va., 1975.

Edwards, William B. *Civil War Guns.* Harrisburg, Pa., 1962.

The Field Manual for the Use of the Officers on Ordnance Duty. Richmond, Va., 1862. Reprint, edited by Howard Michael Madaus. Arendtsville, Pa., 1984.

Flayderman, Norman E. *Flayderman's Guide to Antique American Arms.* 5th ed. Northbrook, Ill., 1990.

Fuller, Claud E., and Richard D. Steuart. *Firearms of the Confederacy.* Huntington, W.V., 1944.

Lewis, Berkeley R. *Small Arms and Ammunition in the United States, 1776–1865.* Washington, D.C., 1956.

Madaus, Howard Michael. "The Maynard Rifle and Carbine in the Confederate Service." *Bulletin of the American Society of Arms Collectors,* no. 52 (1985): 66–79.

RUSS A. PRITCHARD

Altered U.S. Small Arms

Under the terms of the Militia Act of 1808, a proportionate amount of ordnance was available to the states on an annual basis for arming their militias. Most of the states, both North and South, took advantage of these provisions to obtain field artillery and small arms for issue to the volunteer militia companies. Until 1850, the small arms received were invariably flintlock muskets, either of the muzzle-loading U.S. model 1795 or of the model 1822 pattern; flintlock rifles, either of the muzzle-loading U.S. model 1817 pattern or of the Hall breech-loading model 1819 pattern; or single-shot flintlock pistols, either of the U.S. model 1819 or of the model 1836 pattern.

Between 1820 and 1855, the eleven states that would secede from the Union in 1860 and 1861 received under the 1808 act no fewer than 98,844 smoothbore muskets, 14,954 muzzle-loading rifles (as well as 3,138 of Hall's pattern), 28,935 single-shot pistols, and 17,999 sabers and swords. In addition to those flintlocks supplied by the U.S. government, the Commonwealth of Virginia had manufactured at its state-owned facility in Richmond between 1800 and 1821 a total of 58,400 flintlock muskets, 2,100 flintlock rifles, and 4,200 flintlock pistols. Although many of these arms would be lost to the Southern states owing to general wear and mistreatment by the militia companies, several states retained a significant portion of these obsolete weapons in store at their state arsenals.

At the beginning of 1860, the state arsenals in Virginia stored 51,370 flintlock muskets and 1,020 flintlock rifles. Similarly, Tennessee reported 8,480 flintlock muskets and 350 Hall rifles on hand at its state arsenal in January of 1861. Moreover, when the eight Federal arsenals in the South were seized by the seceding states, they were found to still hold more than 14,500 flintlock muskets, 7,170 flintlock rifles (nearly 7,000 of which were Hall's design), and almost 400 flintlock pistols. Technically obsolete with the introduction of the percussion system, many of these flintlocks were, nevertheless, issued in the South during the arms crisis of mid-1861. Eventually, most of these were recalled and altered to percussion locks during the winter of 1861–1862.

The Confederate states also inherited a large number of U.S. model 1822 muskets already altered from flintlock to percussion at U.S. arsenals and armories. During the twelve years preceding the war, an estimated 7,739 percussion muskets had been transferred to Southern states under the 1808 Militia Act. These were primarily U.S. model 1822 muskets altered from flintlock to percussion. Another 40,000 of these same type muskets (together with 65,000 U.S. model 1842 smoothbore percussion muskets and 10,000 U.S. model 1841 percussion rifles) had been transferred to Southern arsenals in 1860 under orders from Secretary of War (and former Virginia governor) John B. Floyd. Between February and December of 1860, Southern states or their agents purchased no fewer than 11,000 of the altered flintlocks from Southern Federal arsenals, and another 19,050 from Northern Federal arsenals.

These 77,789 muskets had been altered by closing the old vent, crudely cold-forging a cone seat near the breech of the barrel, threading in a percussion nipple, and substituting a percussion hammer for the old flintlock battery. The method was inexpensive but lacked strength. Although at least one contractor in Virginia and another in Alabama copied this system in 1861, most alterations effected in the South instead relied upon a separate bolster for the nipple, either brazed to the side of the breech over the old vent or screwed into an enlarged vent hole. Attaching a percussion hammer in place of the flintlock battery completed the operation.

Of these two systems, the former had been pioneered in South Carolina by William Glaze & Co. in 1852, when Glaze altered 5,960 state-owned flintlocks to percussion; it was championed by Virginia contractors, both for their state and the Confederacy. North Carolina contractors copied Virginia's method of percussioning flintlocks. In the western Confederacy, the use of the drum bolster screwed into the old vent at first predominated; it was found inadequate for muskets but sufficient for old flintlock sporting rifles that were pressed into Confederate service.

Although the Confederacy was able to expand its quantity of usable muskets significantly by altering obsolete flintlocks to percussion, little effort was made to upgrade these smoothbore muskets by rifling and sighting them for long range. Although the flintlock alterations, particularly those altered by the old Federal arsenal method, were generally not suitable for rifling, the smoothbore U.S. model 1842 musket was. In 1861, South Carolina contractor William Glaze rifled and sighted 3,720 of the model 1842 brass-mounted muskets he had made for that state in 1852 and 1853, but the demand for arms in the field, the lack of sights, and limited rifling machinery prevented any mass effort at rifling smoothbore muskets by the South.

The same factors prevented the numerous U.S. model 1841 percussion rifles in the South from being upgraded to "long-range" rifles, although some were at least adapted to accept saber bayonets. The large number of flintlock Hall breech-loading rifles in the South, however, led to numerous attempts to make effective arms of them. Many were percussioned by replacing the flintlock battery with a simple hammer and threading a nipple into the tilting breechblock. Others, notably those in North Carolina, were altered to percussion and then shortened and remodeled into carbines. Perhaps the most interesting attempt to make effective weapons from the Hall breechloaders took place in Virginia, where the firm of Read & Watson salvaged the barrels, some of the furniture, and parts of the stocks from the state's 1808 Militia Act Halls and made between 900 and 1,200 muzzle-loading rifles from them.

BIBLIOGRAPHY

Madaus, Howard Michael. *Warners Collectors Guide to American Longarms.* New York, 1981.

Virginia. *Annual Reports of the Adjutant-General.* Richmond, Va., 1920–1960.

HOWARD MICHAEL MADAUS

Imported English Small Arms

As a result of John Brown's 1859 raid upon the Harpers Ferry Armory, Virginia began in 1860 to seek the means to rebuild the old "Virginia Manufactory of Arms" into a modern factory for the production of a copy of the English pattern 1853 rifle-musket. That plan was altered when the state seized the machinery for the U.S. model 1855 rifle-musket at Harpers Ferry in April of 1861. Prior to this, however, Virginia had arranged through R. H. Maury of Petersburg to import 2,500 of the English rifle-muskets. Payments to Maury in early 1861 indicate that at least some of these were delivered.

In addition to Virginia, four other states made significant purchases of the English pattern 1853 rifle-musket. Between December of 1860 and the end of 1862, South Carolina purchased a minimum of 4,170 (exclusive of the number imported by Charleston speculators, estimated at at least 3,000); Georgia bought at least 5,000; Louisiana acquired about 7,000; and North Carolina imported 2,000 (with another 2,000 following in 1863). Many of these imported English long arms were confiscated by Confederate Ordnance Bureau officers upon their arrival at Southern ports, to the great consternation of the governors of the states that had purchased them from state funds. Although these importations were significant, they were overshadowed by purchases made directly by the agents of the Confederate central government, Capt. Caleb Huse and Maj. Edward C. Anderson.

The Confederacy's prime agent for obtaining ordnance abroad was transplanted New Englander Caleb Huse, who departed for England via Portland, Maine, and Canada, in late April 1861. Initially he would be frustrated in his attempts to acquire small arms. Northern agents from New York and New England arrived in England before him and emptied the market of existing pattern 1853 rifle-muskets. His efforts were further hampered by inadequate and delayed finances, which limited his ability to contract for newly made weapons. With the arrival of Maj. Edward C. Anderson in June, the situation improved dramatically. Together they arranged for the shipment of 10,620 rifle-muskets on the steamer *Fingal,* which arrived in Savannah with Anderson aboard in early November 1861.

Although this first Confederate shipment did little to satiate the demand for small arms (then approaching crisis proportions in the Confederacy), Huse's continued efforts resulted in a dramatic increase in armaments by mid-1862. After several losses to the Union blockade, the Confederate War Department determined not to risk large shipments directly into Southern ports. Instead, shipments from England were diverted to Nassau in the Bahamas. From there the cargoes were transshipped to the Florida coast. The first transshipment of 6,000 rifle-muskets landed there in February of 1862; an equal number arrived the following month. From the end of April until the beginning of August 1862, no fewer than 48,500 English small arms eluded the Union blockade and landed at the ports of Savannah, Georgia; Charleston, South Carolina; and Wilmington, North Carolina. By February 1863, the total importations of English long arms had risen to more than 104,000; 71,000 of these were the latest pattern rifle-muskets and another 9,700 were short rifles. From the end of September 1862 to October 1863, the Confederacy imported another 113,500 small arms, of which 56,800 were of English manufacture. Most of these were received prior to the summer of 1863: from July to October, only 8,200 rifle-muskets and 1,140 carbines of English make were received in Wilmington (the principal blockade-running port from 1863 until December 1864, when it was closed). Another 19,800 English long arms arrived in Wilmington between October 1863 and January 1864, and English imports for 1864 through that city amounted to nearly 26,000 rifle-muskets and 5,900 carbines.

IMPORTED SMALL ARMS. Long arms and edged weapons pictured, from top to bottom: pattern 1842 smoothbore musket, .70 cal.; pattern 1853 Enfield rifle-musket, .577 cal.; triangular socket bayonet, in scabbard, for above; pattern 1856 rifle, .577 cal.; saber bayonet, in scabbard, for above; pattern 1853 artillery musketoon, .577 cal.; pattern 1856 cavalry carbine, .577 cal.; pattern 1853 cavalry saber, in scabbard; Austrian model 1854 rifle, .54 cal. Handguns pictured, from left to right: Kerr revolver, 44 cal.; Beaumont Adams revolver, .44 cal.; Webley wedge frame revolver, .44 cal.; French LeMat revolver, .41 cal., 20 ga. Unless otherwise specified, all weapons are of English manufacture. RUSS A. PRITCHARD

Although gaps in the record (principally in 1862) leave the total number of English arms imported into the South during the war open to some question, it is evident that no fewer than 250,000 and more likely 300,000 long arms of English manufacture entered the Confederate service. These arms principally followed the patterns established for English military service and consisted of eight basic types. The pattern 1853 rifle-musket, in its four variations, was the principal infantry arm of the British service. Its 39-inch-long rifled barrel had a .577-caliber bore and mounted a triangular socket bayonet. The pattern 1851 rifle-musket was the first rifle-musket adopted by the British service, but was quickly supplanted by the pattern 1853. Its 39-inch-long rifled barrel had a .71-caliber bore and mounted a triangular socket bayonet. The five variations of the patterns 1856, 1857 (naval), 1858, 1860, and 1861 rifles had a 33-inch-long rifled barrel, .577-caliber bore, and mounted a saber bayonet with yatagan blade. The pattern 1856 sergeant's rifled fusil had a 33.5-inch-long rifled barrel, a .577-caliber rifled bore, and mounted a triangular socket bayonet. All known examples bear Georgia ownership marks. Up to 500 may have been imported.

The three variations of the patterns 1853, 1858, and 1860 artillery carbines had a 24-inch-long rifled barrel, .577-caliber bore, and mounted the same bayonet as the rifles. A minimum of 1,040 of these were imported by the Confederacy in 1863 and 1864. The patterns 1856 and 1860 carbine were the principal shoulder arms issued to mounted units of the English army. Their 21-inch-long rifled barrel had a .577-caliber bore and took no bayonet. At least 6,040 of these weapons were imported in 1863 and

1864 alone, and another 350 purchased prior to 1863.

The pattern 1842 musket (and rifle-musket) and pattern 1839 musket were the percussion replacements for flintlock muskets of the Napoleonic era. Their 39-inch-long barrels had .75-caliber bores and mounted triangular socket bayonets. The pattern 1842 deviated from the pattern 1838 only in minor differences at the percussion bolster, as the latter had originally been intended to take a flintlock mechanism. More than 21,000 pattern 1851 rifle-muskets, 1842 rifle-muskets or smoothbore muskets, and 1839 muskets were imported into the Confederacy by February of 1863; the majority of these were sent to the western theater.

The pattern 1837 "Brunswick" rifle was considered obsolete by 1860. Its 36-inch-long barrel had a .70-caliber bore rifled with only two grooves for its peculiar belted projectile. A sword bayonet was affixed to two lugs on the right side of the barrel. Only 2,200 of these rifles had reached the Confederacy by February of 1863; many more were captured aboard blockade runners.

Although the prime small arms acquired by the Confederacy in England were muskets and rifles, a number of English-made handguns were also secured. The handgun of choice was the percussion revolver. Three basic types entered the Confederacy.

As a result of long-standing commercial ties between the South and English manufacturers, numerous examples of English-patent belt and pocket revolvers were imported into the South from 1859 until 1861. Nearly all were "double acting": it was not necessary to cock the hammer as a separate action before squeezing the trigger; pulling the trigger both cocked the hammer and in succession discharged the pistol. The most common English double-action revolvers imported prior to hostilities were those made under Adams's, Bently's, Tranter's, and Webley's patents. Unlike the contemporary Colt products, these revolvers exhibited a solid frame with a top strap. This top strap or the barrel were occasionally marked with the name of the Southern agency importing the revolver, particularly on Tranter models.

Although imports of the various English models of revolvers continued into 1861, usually through Charleston, efforts directed by the Confederate Ordnance Bureau and Navy Department concentrated on the acquisition of the Kerr revolver, a product of the London Armory Company, of which James Kerr was superintendent. The Kerr was purchased in quantity through the auspices of Sinclair, Hamilton, & Co. An estimated nine thousand revolvers in .44-caliber (54-bore) were imported into the Confederacy, the final nine hundred arriving on October 31, 1864.

BIBLIOGRAPHY

Anderson, Edward C. *Confederate Foreign Agent: The European Diary of Major Edward C. Anderson.* University, Ala., 1976.

Bailey, D. W. *British Military Longarms.* Harrisburg, Pa., 1972.

Gaidis, Henry L. "The Confederate Kerr Revolver." *Gun Report* 24, no. 8 (January 1979): 14–21.

Huse, Caleb. *The Supplies of the Confederate Army.* Boston, 1904.

Roads, C. H. *The British Soldier's Firearm, 1850–1864: From Smooth Bore to Small Bore.* London, 1964.

Sword, Wiley. *Firepower from Abroad.* Providence, R.I., 1986.

Vandiver, Frank E., ed. *Confederate Blockade Running through Bermuda, 1861–1865: Letters and Cargo Manifests.* Austin, Tex., 1972.

C. A. HUEY and HOWARD MICHAEL MADAUS

Imported English Long-Range Rifles

A full regiment of sharpshooters was authorized by the Confederate Congress in January 1862, but there was no viable source in the Confederacy for a thousand sharpshooter rifles. In fact, the Ordnance Bureau was hard pressed to keep up with the demand for standard rifled percussion muskets. Importation seemed the natural answer. The largest numbers were purchased from Joseph Whitworth of Manchester, England, a world-famous mechanical engineer who perfected his patented hexagonally bored .451-caliber rifle between 1854 and 1858. In highly publicized trials at Hythe, England, in 1857 and 1858, Whitworth's new rifle was shown to be dramatically more accurate than the standard Enfield rifle of .577 caliber.

Confederate Maj. Edward Anderson in July 1861 visited Whitworth's works in Manchester, where he purchased two Whitworth military match rifles. They were dispatched at once to Josiah Gorgas at Richmond and shown to President Jefferson Davis. Agents from the various states also purchased additional Whitworths in 1861. For example, the Eighth North Carolina Infantry was armed with Whitworths at the siege of Charleston. They were very expensive—£25 ($120 in 1860 dollars), cased complete, compared to a standard British rifle-musket at a bit over £3.

After receiving approval in Richmond, Anderson and Maj. Caleb Huse placed an order with Whitworth in September or October 1861 for arms for the Confederacy's sharpshooter service. The gun was to be a less expensive version of the standard Whitworth military match rifle. Savings were made by specifying a musket lock without sliding safety, two standard barrel bands, open elevator rear sight, elimination of the patch box, and a block front sight rather than a globe with screw adjustment. Many of these rifles, however, were equipped with the Davison telescopic sight mounted opposite the lock parallel to the barrel. These weapons, known as the Confederate-contract, second-quality, military-match rifles, were produced from the end of 1861 until late summer of 1862.

The exact number ordered is not known, but it is estimated that the South intended to acquire some fifty cases of twenty rifles each, for a total of one thousand arms. (The serial numbers fall between B500 and C750, a spread of 1,250.) Owing to the limited number of surviving examples, one must conclude that many were never delivered to the Confederacy, having been lost in running the blockade, or that the survival rate was extremely low.

Confederate agents were close to the London Armory Company and its superintendent, James Kerr, who also designed a small-bore rifle with a rifling system similar to Whitworth's but not as acclaimed. Kerr rifles were referred to as Enfield .44s, because their exterior dimensions were the same as a standard .577 musket. Kerr's rifling was a six-groove ratchet form. They had 37-inch barrels, full-sized stocks, three barrel bands, and open long-range sighting, although some had globe front sights, and adjustable wrist-mounted peep sights were available.

Best estimates put Whitworth's at 70 percent of the imported Confederate sharpshooter weapons, Kerr's at 20 percent, and 10 percent other small-bore arms. The majority of the latter were by Thomas Turner of Birmingham and Alexander Henry of Edinburgh, Scotland. Turner's were of .451-caliber five-groove rifling, making one turn in 20 inches. Henry's were of .451-caliber seven-groove rifling, making one turn in 30 inches. Small numbers of Calisher and Terry breech-loading rifles were used, but in much smaller quantities than their carbine. A few J. Rigby rifles of .451-caliber octagonal rifling, making one turn in 18 inches, were reportedly used. Given that at least fifteen types of small-bore Enfields were produced, the Confederates were very selective in keeping the great percentage of their imports to two varieties—Whitworths and Kerrs. All small-bores utilized the standard .442-diameter conical projectiles, which simplified ammunition procurement.

The importation of the English long-range rifles was significant in the Confederate struggle for several reasons. The only combat use of the famous Whitworth weapons occurred during the Civil War. All Whitworth rifles and all but four Whitworth cannons were used by Confederates. Whitworth rifles were capable of striking targets with power at up to 2,000 yards. Numerous mounted officers were hit at ranges of 1,200 to 1,800 yards, a distance considered safe unless Confederate snipers were at work. The morale of the always hard-pressed Confederate army and navy was surely raised by their sharpshooters' use of the finely tooled Whitworths. They had the most accurate long-range rifle in the war. Many a Confederate letter home began proudly, "We have a wonderful new rifle in our army."

BIBLIOGRAPHY

Albaugh, William A., III, and Edward N. Simmons. *Confederate Arms.* Harrisburg, Pa., 1957.

Burton, E. Milby. *The Siege of Charleston, 1861–1865.* Columbia, S.C., 1970.

Edwards, William B. *Civil War Guns.* Harrisburg, Pa., 1962.

Fuller, Claude E., and Richard D. Steuart. *Firearms of the Confederacy.* Lawrence, Mass., 1944.

Hoole, Stanley W. *Confederate Foreign Agent: The European Diary of Major Edward C. Anderson.* Tuscaloosa, Ala., 1976.

Sword, Wiley. *Firepower from Abroad.* Lincoln, R.I., 1986.

Vandiver, Frank E. *Confederate Blockade Running through Bermuda, 1861–1865.*. Austin, Tex., 1947.

C. A. HUEY

Imported Austrian, Belgian, and French Small Arms

Although the bulk of the small arms imported to the Confederacy between 1861 and 1865 originated in England, significant quantities were also purchased on the Continent. These arms were principally of Austrian and Belgian manufacture, the former conforming to the most recent Austrian government model and the latter primarily Liège-made copies or adaptations of French models.

In early 1862, the Confederacy's main European purchasing agent, Caleb Huse, obtained a significant number of Austrian field cannons, paying for them with money borrowed in England. By February of 1863, he had also managed to purchase and deliver to the Confederacy 27,000 Austrian rifles and had another 30,000 in Vienna awaiting payment. Not only were these 30,000 arms eventually secured, but additional arms of the same type were also purchased, allowing the Confederacy to import 56,600 Austrian rifles through Wilmington between July and December of 1863. An additional 4,740 came through the same port in 1864.

All of these nearly 90,000 small arms were of the most recent pattern adopted by Austria in 1854 and known from its designer as the Lorenz. All were rifle-muskets having a 37½-inch-long barrel with a .54-caliber rifled bore and taking a quadrangular socket bayonet. The rifle-musket came with two types of rear sight. Since the greatest number of these arms arrived in 1863, they played a significant role in the rearming of the Army of Tennessee during the winter of 1863–1864.

Although Liège, Belgium, was initially rejected by Huse as a source for small arms in 1861, the evidence is overwhelming that the city served as the South's third most important source of foreign armament during the war. Liège's contacts with the South had begun in 1860 when commercial relations were established with the city during Georgia's industrial fair. As a result of these contacts, efforts were made in 1861 to import Liège-made rifles through New Orleans for the South. These efforts were only partly successful, although at least 820 *rifles à tige* (pillar breech rifles) of Belgian make found their way up the Mississippi to arm a brigade of Confederate Kentuckians. These are believed to have been Liège-made copies of the French model 1846 rifle, whose 34¼-inch-long barrel had a rifled bore of .70 caliber and which accepted a long yatagan saber bayonet on a lug and guide on its right side.

Other purchases of Liège-made small arms trickled through the blockade in 1862. In June, 700 Liège-made rifles were brought through the blockade into Charleston aboard the steamer *Memphis*. Although exact details of the type imported are speculative, these were probably .58-caliber variants of the French model 1859 rifle. Transfer records from the Fayetteville, Richmond, Atlanta, and Montgomery arsenals indicate shipments and issuance of Belgian rifles (and at least 160 smoothbore muskets) from the late summer of 1862 through the spring of 1864. These shipments included at least 218 described as having double-set triggers, which in fact may have been German model 1835 "yager" rifles, tentatively part of a shipment of German rifles that entered Charleston in September 1861 aboard the steamer *Bermuda*. Other shipments of Belgian copies of French arms were less successful in reaching their destinations. The prize court records of the steamers *Ella Warley* (captured in April 1862) and *Columbia* (captured in August 1862) indicate that the former bore at least 280 rifle-muskets of probable Liège manufacture for Louisiana, and the latter 540 Belgian-made .69-caliber rifle-muskets copying the French model 1822 (rifled and altered from flintlocks to percussion ignition) and the French model 1853 (rifled). Clearly Belgian imports were significant, though exact figures remain nebulous.

The Ordnance Bureau also imported in quantity from France a revolver of American design. Jean A. F. LeMat designed and patented a revolver in the United States whose main feature was a hollow cylinder pin that, in conjunction with an adjustment on the hammer, permitted the pistol to serve as a small shotgun or as a revolver at the will of its owner. With the outbreak of the Civil War, LeMat, armed with contracts for his patented revolver, went to Paris to arrange for their manufacture in association with Charles Girard. After production of approximately five hundred revolvers had begun, operations were shifted to England, where another two thousand of the larger .42-caliber–.63-caliber combination revolver-shotguns were made for the army, and about six hundred smaller .32-caliber–.41-caliber revolver-shotguns for the navy.

BIBLIOGRAPHY

Bailey, D. W. *Percussion Guns and Rifles*. Harrisburg, Pa., 1972.

Balace, Francis. *L'Armurerie liégeoise et la guerre de sécession, 1861–1865*. Liège, Belgium, 1978.

Edwards, William B. *Civil War Guns*. Harrisburg, Pa., 1962.

HOWARD MICHAEL MADAUS

Naval Small Arms

Ordnance instructions for the Confederate navy specified a variety of small arms to be carried aboard ship: battle-axes, muskets with bayonets, carbines with bayonets, revolvers, pistols, pikes, and cutlasses, all equipped with appropriate accoutrements. In practice, smoothbore muskets, rifles, and carbines were issued but rarely in combination with one another, and revolvers were often used exclusively in lieu of single-shot, muzzle-loading pistols. The marine guard was usually equipped with weapons apart from those issued the general crew.

Small arms were distributed in combinations based on the crew's duty assignments. Cutlasses were most often issued with pistols or revolvers, and shoulder arms with pikes or battle-axes. Weapons could also be used in other mixtures or alone.

Southern warships were generally well equipped with weapons acquired by early-war seizure of Federal stocks, by capture, by local production, and by import. British-made Enfield muzzle-loading rifles and Kerr revolvers, along with French-made LeMat revolvers, were special favorites in the Confederate navy. Union-made Maynard breech-loading carbines were popular on some ironclads, where cramped space made cumbersome muzzleloaders difficult to handle.

[*See also* Edged Weapons, *article on* Edged Weapons in the Navy.]

BIBLIOGRAPHY

Albaugh, William A., III. *Confederate Edged Weapons*. New York, 1960.

Albaugh, William A., III, and Edward A. Simmons. *Confederate Arms*. Harrisburg, Pa., 1957.

Confederate Navy Department. *Ordnance Instructions for the Confederate States Navy*. 3d ed. London, 1864.

Edwards, William B. *Civil War Guns*. Harrisburg, Pa., 1962.

Sword, Wiley. *Firepower from Abroad: The Confederate Enfield LeMat Revolver*. Lincoln, R.I., 1986.

A. ROBERT HOLCOMBE, JR.

Munitions

The first step toward provisions for ordnance needs was taken by the Confederate government while it was still at Montgomery, when Josiah Gorgas was commissioned as chief of the Ordnance Bureau. Although a number of Federal ordnance facilities would fall into Confederate hands (at Little Rock, Baton Rouge, Mount Vernon, Appalachicola, Augusta, Charleston, Fayetteville, and San Antonio), Gorgas was to find that

> there was little ammunition of any kind, or powder, at the arsenals in the South, and that little relics of the Mexican war, stored principally at Baton Rouge and Mount Vernon arsenals.

I doubt whether there were a million rounds of small-arms cartridges in the Confederacy. Lead there was none in store. Of powder the chief supply was that captured at Norfolk, though there was a small quantity at each of the Southern arsenals, say 60,000 pounds in all, chiefly old cannon powder. The stock of percussion caps could not have exceeded one-quarter of a million.

Immediate steps were taken by the central government and the states to fabricate and procure small arms ammunition. Before the commencement of hostilities, some proprietary rounds for carbines and revolvers were purchased in the North; however, a great reliance was placed on importation from abroad, chiefly from Great Britain (although never with official English sanction).

The Confederacy established nine primary sites for the production of small arms ammunition: Atlanta, Columbus, Macon, and Augusta, Georgia; Charleston, South Carolina; Fayetteville, North Carolina; Lynchburg and Richmond, Virginia; and Selma, Alabama. Other facilities at Columbus and Jackson, Mississippi; Little Rock, Arkansas; Nashville, Tennessee; New Orleans and Baton Rouge, Louisiana; San Antonio and Marshall, Texas; and Savannah, Georgia, had far lower production during the war or were abandoned after operating only briefly.

Gorgas estimated that during the war these manufactories produced 150 million small arms cartridges; half of that number was produced at Richmond alone. Once the facilities were established, the South had ample ordnance workers (mostly women and children for cartridges), but a major continuing concern was the lack of raw materials: lead, paper, gunpowder (niter, sulfur, and charcoal), and copper and mercury for percussion caps.

It was not uncommon for small arms ammunition production to be halted at a laboratory for a month or more for a want of lead for bullets. Gorgas calculated that it required 10 million pounds of lead to produce 150 million cartridges (see accompanying table).

About a dozen small paper mills supplied cartridge paper to the Ordnance Department. By May 1863, and after the accidental burning of the Bath Paper Mills in Augusta, a critical shortage of manila fibers developed and led to curtailed production of ammunition. A heavier reliance was placed on imported English "white-fine" paper for Enfield cartridges.

Pounds of Lead Needed to Produce 150 Million Cartridges

From Trans-Mississippi mines (early in the war)	400,000
From Wytheville, Virginia, mines	2,160,000
On hand at arsenals	140,000
Imported	2,000,000
Recycled from battlefields and civilian donations	5,300,000
Total	**10,000,000**

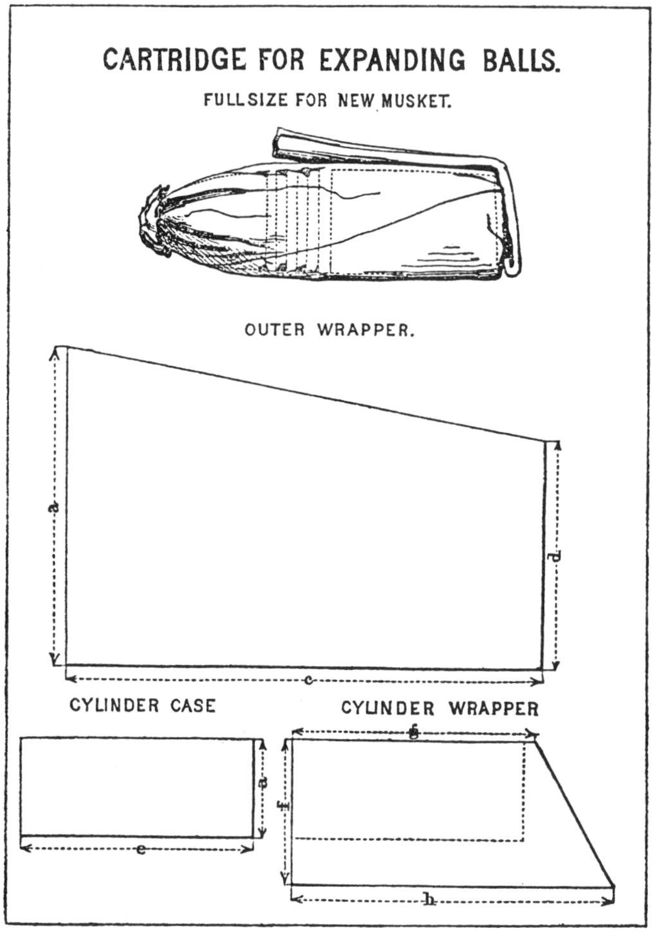

CARTRIDGE FOR EXPANDING BALLS. Illustration reprinted from *Reports of Experiments with Small Arms for the Military Service*, by U. S. Ordnance Department, Washington, D.C., 1856.

CIVIL WAR LIBRARY AND MUSEUM, PHILADELPHIA

In 1861, there were in the South two small private powder mills in Tennessee, two in South Carolina, one in North Carolina, and a little stamping mill in New Orleans. Large orders for powder were sent to the North and, according to Gorgas, "were being rapidly filled at the date of the attack on Fort Sumter." Early on, Jefferson Davis pressed for the erection of a large government powder mill. Under the direction of Col. George W. Rains, the Augusta Powder Works from 1862 to 1865 turned out 2,750,000 pounds of gunpowder. Charcoal was made from cottonwood from the banks of the Savannah River. Several hundred tons of sulfur were found at New Orleans intended for sugar making. Niter from saltpeter was the chief concern. Much was "mined" in bat guano–enriched caves, but most had to be imported. Artificial beds were established throughout the South, but were not fully mature until the war ended.

Percussion cap machinery built in the South was put in operation at Richmond, Atlanta, Augusta, and for a time Columbus, Mississippi. Gorgas also imported English caps. The Union forces' closure of the Ducktown, Tennessee, mines jeopardized the supply of copper, and the casting of bronze field cannons was immediately suspended. An officer was given authority to purchase or impress all copper stills for making turpentine and apple brandy. The commander of the Richmond Arsenal estimated that during the last twelve months of the war all caps there were manufactured from the copper stills of North Carolina. Mercury for the fulminate of mercury explosive in percussion caps came principally from Mexico, although other substitutes also came into use.

Gorgas did not perform these labors alone. In May 1862, John W. Mallet was commissioned superintendent of laboratories to, in his words, "bring order out of the confusion," and also to prepare plans for a Central Ordnance Laboratory to be built at Macon. Here would be produced all the Confederacy's ammunition. Although it was never completed, Mallet performed admirably, overseeing construction, ordering machinery, developing suppliers, and visiting other small arms ammunition sites to maintain quality products. When the visits became too time-consuming, he ordered the facilities to send him monthly samples, which he inspected and reported on to Gorgas and the commanders. He revived an abandoned U.S. Ordnance procedure requiring the quantity, kind, and place and date of manufacture of ammunition to be marked on all packages. This made it easier to track down the source of complaints and make necessary corrections.

The most distinctive Confederate bullet used during the war was the invention of Frederick J. Gardner of Hillsboro, North Carolina. On Mallet's first tour of inspection, he found at the Richmond Laboratory "the simple and effective little machine invented by Mr. Gardner." His patented process saved paper and time. Mallet initially recommended the machine for other laboratories, but complaints from the field about poorly made cartridges led him, in 1863, to work for its elimination from service.

Confederate laboratories and arsenals produced small arms ammunition for all the types of weapons in their service: smoothbore muskets, rifles, rifled muskets, carbines, revolvers, and shotguns. But ordnance officers had to cope with inadequate transportation and severe shortages of raw materials. Nevertheless, William LeRoy Broun, commander of the Richmond Arsenal, was justly proud of his department, stating, "Never was an order received from General Lee's army for ammunition that it was not immediately supplied, even to the last order of sending a train-load of ammunition to Petersburg after the order was received for the evacuation of Richmond."

[*See also* Niter and Mining Bureau; Ordnance Bureau.]

BIBLIOGRAPHY

Confederate Ordnance Bureau. *The Confederate Field Manual.* Richmond, Va., 1862. Reprint, Gettysburg, Pa., 1984.

Thomas, Dean S. *Ready . . . Aim . . . Fire! Small Arms Ammunition in the Battle of Gettysburg.* Gettysburg, Pa., 1981.

Dean S. Thomas

SMALLS, ROBERT (1839–1915), escaped slave, Federal captain, and U.S. congressman. Smalls was born on April 5, 1839, in Beaufort, South Carolina, to Lydia, a slave woman. John McKee was his owner and possibly his father. In 1851 McKee moved to Charleston where Smalls was permitted to hire himself out successively as a waiter, lamplighter, stevedore, rigger, and harbor pilot.

At the onset of the Civil War, the twenty-two-year-old slave was employed as a wheelman on *Planter.* The 150-foot steam-powered ship, capable of transporting 1,400 bales of cotton, was chartered by the Confederacy. Armed with 32- and 24-pound howitzers, the vessel laid torpedoes and

Robert Smalls. National Archives

carried men and supplies for the erection and maintenance of fortifications along the Carolina coast.

Smalls conceived an audacious plan to seize the vessel, liberate its black crew and several family members, and escape to the Union fleet blockading Charleston's harbor. At about 3:00 A.M. on May 13, 1862, while the ship's three white officers spent the night ashore in violation of standing orders, Smalls and seven crewmen fired the boiler and furtively slipped Smalls's wife, daughter, and son aboard, as well as four other women and one child.

Thoroughly familiar with Confederate regulations, Smalls departed the wharf and headed downstream. He donned the straw hat of *Planter*'s captain, C. J. Relyea, and mimicked his familiar walk. The ship slowly steamed past Fort Johnson and Fort Sumter, received a routine acknowledgment from Confederate batteries to proceed, and headed for *Onward,* one of the vessels in the Union blockade. Smalls reportedly informed Union officers that "I thought *Planter* might be of use to Uncle Abe." *Planter* was carrying two hundred pounds of ammunition, four guns, and other supplies destined for Fort Ripley. The crew was later awarded $7,000 in prize money, of which Smalls received $1,500.

The success of Smalls and his coconspirators stunned the Confederacy and astonished Union supporters. Charleston newspapers initially discounted reports of the ship's loss but later demanded that the negligent crewmen be brought to justice. Union flag officer Samuel F. Du Pont praised Smalls. "This bringing out of this steamer, under all the circumstances, would have done credit to anyone." Du Pont added, "This man, Robert Smalls, is superior to any [slaves] who have yet to come into the lines, intelligent as many of them have been." Smalls's feat altered the perceptions of many white Northerners who doubted the capacity of blacks to assume any initiative or to demonstrate any willingness to challenge the authority of the Confederacy. In August Abraham Lincoln and Secretary of War Edwin M. Stanton welcomed Smalls to Washington, and the black hero urged them to employ black troops in the war effort.

Smalls served briefly as a civilian pilot for the U.S. Navy on the ironclad *Keokuk* and was aboard when it was sunk in the Union attack on Charleston on April 7, 1863. He was subsequently commissioned a second lieutenant in Company B of the Thirty-third U.S. Colored Infantry. He spent most of the remainder of the war on *Planter,* which participated in seventeen engagements in the service of the Union army. Smalls's intimate knowledge of Carolina's coastal waters was of critical value. He was promoted to captain in December 1864 after assuming command when the ship's white commander panicked while under a Confederate artillery attack along the Stono River near Charleston. In 1864 Smalls took the ship to the Philadelphia Naval Yard for repairs. On April 14, 1865, he piloted *Planter* at ceremonies held at Fort Sumter commemorating the war's end. But the celebration was marred when Smalls accidentally rammed *Planter* into *Oceanus.*

Smalls went on to enjoy a prominent career in Republican politics in South Carolina. He served in the constitutional conventions in 1868 and 1895 and was elected to the state house in 1868 and the state senate in 1870. He served three terms in the U.S. House of Representatives and was the customs collector at Beaufort from 1897 to 1913. He died on February 22, 1915.

BIBLIOGRAPHY

Christopher, Maurine. *Black Americans in Congress.* New York, 1976.

Quarles, Benjamin. "The Abduction of the 'Planter.' " *Civil War History* 4 (1958): 5–10.

Uya, Okon Edet. *From Slavery to Public Service: Robert Smalls, 1839–1915.* New York, 1971.

WILLIAM C. HINE

SMITH, E. KIRBY (1824–1893), general. Edmund Kirby Smith was born at St. Augustine, Florida, on May 16, 1824. Two years before his birth his New England parents moved to the Florida Territory where his father served as a Federal judge. As a young man Smith attended school in Alexandria, Virginia, before entering West Point where he graduated in 1845, twenty-fifth in a class of forty-one. He fought in the Mexican War under both Zachary Taylor and Winfield Scott and then went on to a career in the U.S. Army. When Abraham Lincoln was elected, Smith was on duty in Texas as part of the Second U.S. Cavalry—the regiment known as Jeff Davis's own, which produced half of the full generals for the Confederate States.

As a young man Smith had gone by the name Ted or Ned, and his elder brother Ephraim Kirby Smith had used E. Kirby Smith. But sometime after the elder Smith died in the Mexican War, the younger brother began signing his name as E. Kirby Smith, and in 1861 this was how he endorsed all official correspondence.

When Texas seceded, Smith was in charge of Camp Colorado in West Texas but evacuated his command on February 26 after surrendering the post to Col. Henry Eustace McCulloch. Smith was in line for promotion when he resigned his commission to join the Confederacy. Upon hearing this Earl Van Dorn wrote the Confederate secretary of war: "Major Smith has always been considered by the Army as one of its leading spirits. . . . He is so well known to the President, however, that it would be superfluous to say anything to call his attention to his merits as an officer."

Although Van Dorn requested that his friend be assigned to him in Texas, Smith was placed in command at Lynchburg, Virginia. But he was soon assigned to Joseph E.

E. KIRBY SMITH. Pictured as a lieutenant general.
CIVIL WAR LIBRARY AND MUSEUM, PHILADELPHIA

Johnston at Harpers Ferry and became the general's adjutant. On June 17, 1861, while at Winchester, Smith was promoted to brigadier general and accompanied Johnston to Manassas. He was slightly wounded in the battle, a bullet striking him near his collarbone, and while recovering from his wound at Lynchburg, he married Cassie Selden. Smith was promoted to major general on October 11 and assigned a division in P. G. T. Beauregard's Potomac District. During the winter Smith was ordered to report to Richmond, and in March he took command of the Department of East Tennessee at Knoxville.

In the summer of 1862 Smith was part of the Confederate plan for a far-reaching offensive in the West. One army under Braxton Bragg would move north toward Kentucky while Smith marched from Knoxville. By September both armies had reached Kentucky where they had a chance to cut the supply line for Don Carlos Buell's army in Tennessee. Over Smith's objections, the two armies met at Frankfort to inaugurate a Confederate governor, but the approach of Federal troops broke up the ceremony. Although the early offenses were successful, the campaign failed because of a lack of cooperation etween the two armies. After the Battle of Perryville on October 8 the Southern armies withdrew to Tennessee, and Smith returned to Knoxville on October 24. Depressed over the recent failures, Smith thought about resigning and entering the ministry, a move he had contemplated before, but on October 26 he learned of his promotion to lieutenant general.

Although still at his post in Knoxville in late December, Smith, early in January 1863, was called to Richmond where he was reassigned to duty west of the Mississippi River. This apparently came as a result of a combination of reasons; the relationship between Smith and Bragg was strained, and President Jefferson Davis needed to appoint a competent commander west of the Mississippi. Robert E. Lee had recently written Davis: "I need not remind you of the merits of General E. K. Smith whom I consider one of our best officers." On January 14, 1863, Smith was ordered to take command of the Southwestern Army, but on February 9, while on his way to Alexandria, Louisiana, he received a second communication that read "The command of Lieut. Gen. E. Kirby Smith is extended so as to embrace the Trans-Mississippi Department." He replaced the unpopular Theophilus H. Holmes and thus entered a new phase of his career.

After the surrender of Vicksburg and Port Hudson in the summer of 1863 the Trans-Mississippi region was virtually isolated from the rest of the Confederacy; operating independently, the area became known as "Kirby Smithdom." Not all the commanders in the region were pleased with Smith's measures. Most important, he had several disagreements about strategy with the influential Maj. Gen. Richard Taylor, who commanded in Louisiana. But President Davis gave Smith a wide range of powers and backed them up by promoting him to the permanent rank of general in the Provisional Army on February 19, 1864.

The greatest threat to Smith's department came in the spring of 1864 when two Federal armies moved toward Shreveport, Louisiana. Nathaniel P. Banks pushed his army up the Red River, being stopped at Mansfield and Pleasant Hill in April, while Frederick Steele marched his army south out of Little Rock toward the same objective. Neither succeeded, but the results of the campaign magnified the differences between Smith and Taylor, and the outcome of this was Taylor's transfer out of the department. Another controversial act was Smith's independent appointment of several Confederate generals, many of whom were later rejected by Richmond.

As the war drew to an end, Smith moved his headquarters from Shreveport to Houston. On June 2 he officially signed a surrender agreement aboard a Federal steamer in Galveston Harbor, but fearing that he might be arrested, he fled to Mexico. He returned to the United States several months later and signed an amnesty oath on November 14 at Lynchburg.

After the war Smith held various positions. Two companies he was associated with, the Accident Insurance Company and the Atlantic and Pacific Telegraph Company, failed. He also served as president of the University of Nashville before moving to Sewanee, Tennessee, in 1875 where he taught at the University of the South. He was the last survivor of the eight full Confederate generals, dying on March 28, 1893. Smith was buried in Sewanee Cemetery.

BIBLIOGRAPHY

Blackwood, Emma Jerome, ed. *To Mexico with Scott: Letters of Captain E. Kirby Smith to His Wife.* Cambridge, Mass., 1917.

Kerby, Robert L. *Kirby Smith's Confederacy: The Trans-Mississippi South, 1863–1865.* New York, 1972.

Johnson, Ludwell H. *Red River Campaign: Politics and Cotton in the Civil War.* Baltimore, 1958.

Parks, Joseph Howard. *General Edmund Kirby Smith, C.S.A.* Baton Rouge, La., 1954.

Anne J. Bailey

SMITH, GUSTAVUS W. (1821–1896), major general and ad interim secretary of war. During the early months of the Civil War, Smith seemed one of the most capable officers the nearly formed Confederate nation could call its own. Forty years old in 1861, he was tall, burly, and unashamedly smug. He had graduated from the U.S. Military Academy near the top of his class in 1842. In the Mexican War, Smith served with distinction and earned a reputation as a talented engineer. He later taught engineering at West Point before leaving the army to pursue a prosperous career in civil engineering. In 1858 Smith became street commissioner of New York City. He still held this position when civil war came to the United States.

From New York, Smith watched the events leading to war closely, sensitive to which side his native state of Kentucky would join. Then circumstances made his choice for him. In April 1861, just before the firing on Fort Sumter, Smith suffered an attack of paralysis. In September his doctor recommended that he go south to Hot Springs, Arkansas, for relief. En route, Smith discovered that the U.S. government, deeming his leaving the North traitorous, had posted a warrant for his arrest. This clinched Smith's decision to join the South. As soon as he was able, he traveled to Richmond and promptly received a commission as major general.

During the next nine months, nothing but praise seemed to surround the name of G. W. Smith. In a letter to President Jefferson Davis, Gen. Joseph E. Johnston referred to Smith as a "man of high ability, fit to command in chief." It seemed great things might come of the tall and confident Kentuckian. The chance for distinction came on May 31, 1862, at the Battle of Seven Pines. Johnston fell severely wounded, and Smith took chief command of the army. But mysteriously, his paralysis again overcame him the next day and made him unfit for duty. Smith's hour of greatness had passed.

Gustavus W. Smith. Library of Congress

When Robert E. Lee became commander of the newly named Army of Northern Virginia, he seemed not to trust Smith's reliability on the field. Lee reassigned Smith to the right wing of the army, which included military responsibility for southeastern Virginia and coastal North Carolina. But uneasiness over Smith's abilities mounted. It was not very long until native North Carolinian Brig. Gen. Robert Ransom, Jr., confided to Lee that he thought Smith was lacking in energy and purpose, and was unfit for his position.

Soon there was overt evidence of the high command's doubts about him. In the fall of 1862 Smith learned that six officers junior to him had received promotion to lieutenant general. He was incensed. Smith believed that the Confederacy had wronged him by failing to appreciate his services and talents. He drafted a letter of resignation and threatened to send it, but was dissuaded temporarily by Secretary of War George Wythe Randolph. He later wrote the secretary, "I would rather have been shot dead than to have had my usefulness in so important a command impaired, if not destroyed, by the recent wholesale overslaughing to which I have been subjected." Smith continued in his post until November 1862, when he briefly acted as secretary of war between the tenures of Randolph and James A. Seddon.

In February 1863 Smith finally resigned in disgust, gave up his commission as major general, and left Virginia. Seeking out those who would appreciate him, he went first to his old army friend Gen. P. G. T. Beauregard to aid in the defense of Charleston, South Carolina. Next, he journeyed farther south to Georgia and assumed the presidency of Etowah Manufacturing and Mining Company. By 1864, Georgia Governor Joseph E. Brown had appointed Smith his aide-de-camp and made him responsible for fortification construction for the defense of the state. When Gen. William Tecumseh Sherman wrought his path of destruction through the heart of Georgia, Smith shuttled state militia forces about in stubborn defiance of Sherman's veterans.

It is ironic that Smith proved himself an able leader in Georgia, most notably during the heated action along the Chattahoochie River before Atlanta and later in defense of Savannah. Although the days of the Confederacy were numbered, Smith's efforts offered some of the strongest resistance Sherman met during the long campaign. On April 20, 1865, Smith surrendered his remaining troops to the victorious Federals in Macon, Georgia.

Smith's commendable performance in Georgia in face of an overwhelming enemy did not expunge his memories of the early war. Through the postwar years, his bitterness lingered. He eventually moved back to New York City and became heavily involved in the fledgling insurance industry. In his spare hours he found time to write numerous articles and books about the war and the part he had played in it. In his *Confederate War Papers,* published in 1883, Smith devoted an appendix of the book to refuting accusations that he had conspired against the United States while serving as a New York City commissioner. He also rehashed the old matter concerning the promotion of the six officers junior to him and included copies of the biting letters exchanged between himself and President Jefferson Davis. He added a section full of favorable appraisals by friends and fellow officers. To the end, Smith remained convinced that he had been unappreciated and misunderstood.

BIBLIOGRAPHY

Evans, Clement A. *Confederate History.* Vol. 1 of *Confederate Military History.* Edited by Clement A. Evans. Atlanta, 1899. Vol. 1 of extended ed. Wilmington, N.C., 1987.

Freeman, Douglas S. *Lee's Lieutenants: A Study in Command.* 3 vols. New York, 1942–1944. Reprint, New York, 1986.

Smith, Gustavus Woodson. *The Battle of Seven Pines.* New York, 1891. Reprint, Dayton, Ohio, 1974.

Smith, Gustavus Woodson. *Confederate War Papers.* New York, 1884.

LESLEY JILL GORDON-BURR

SMITH, JAMES ARGYLE (1831–1901), brigadier general. Smith was born July 1, 1831, in Maury County, Tennessee. In 1853 he graduated from the U.S. Military Academy, forty-fifth in a fifty-two-man class. For eight years he served as a lieutenant in the Sixth U.S. Infantry, resigning May 9, 1861, to join the Confederacy.

Commissioned captain and soon promoted to major, he served on the staff of Maj. Gen. Leonidas Polk before being named lieutenant colonel of Lucius Marshall Walker's Second Tennessee Infantry Regiment, part of the Army of Tennessee. In 1862 the regiment was combined with others to form the Fifth (also called Ninth) Confederate Infantry, and Smith was chosen colonel to command it. He won praise for his performances at Shiloh, Perryville, Murfreesboro, Chickamauga, and Missionary Ridge in 1862 and 1863.

After repeated recommendations from his superiors, Smith was promoted to brigadier general October 1, 1863 (with date of rank set to September 30), and through 1864 commanded a brigade. In the Battle of Atlanta (July 22, 1864) he suffered a painful wound but was back with the army for the Franklin and Nashville campaign. After Maj. Gen. Patrick Cleburne was killed at Franklin on November 30, Smith commanded the division. He was in the Carolinas campaign of 1865 and was paroled at Greensboro, North Carolina, May 1, 1865.

After the war, Smith farmed in Mississippi and in 1877 was elected state superintendent of education. He died December 6, 1901, in Jackson, Mississippi, and was buried there in Greenwood Cemetery.

BIBLIOGRAPHY

Bearss, Edwin C. "James Argyle Smith." In *The Confederate General.* Edited by William C. Davis. Vol. 5. Harrisburg, Pa., 1991.

Warner, Ezra J. *Generals in Gray: Lives of the Confederate Commanders.* Baton Rouge, La., 1959.

RICHARD M. MCMURRY

SMITH, JAMES MILTON (1823–1890), colonel, Georgia congressman and postwar governor. Smith was born into a planter family in Twiggs County, Georgia, on October 24, 1823. His only formal education was at the Culloden School in Monroe County. He studied law, was admitted to the bar in 1846, and moved to Columbus,

Georgia, where he opened a law practice. In 1855 Smith ran for Congress from the state's Third District as an independent state rights Democrat but was defeated by the Know-Nothing candidate Robert P. Trippe.

Though Smith remained Unionist in his sympathies until after Georgia seceded from the Union, he was quick to enlist as a major in the Georgia's Thirteenth Voluntary Infantry. As a result of courageous action in fighting near Richmond, Smith was promoted to colonel. With his regiment, he participated in almost every major engagement in Virginia from First Manassas to Gaines' Mill, where he was seriously wounded in June 1862. During his lengthy recuperation at home, he was elected by a substantial majority to the Second Congress in October 1863.

During his service in Richmond from May 1864 to March 1865, Smith was unsympathetic toward efforts to extend Confederate military measures by arming slaves or increasing specie impressments. His faith in a military victory for the South deteriorated, and he became an avid peace advocate by early 1865. The only bill he introduced before the House was a proposal to discharge from the army all men over forty-five years old and to replace current conscription policy with authorization for governors to call troops for their own state and local defense.

Once the Richmond government dissolved, Smith returned to Columbus, resumed his law practice, and became an outspoken critic of Radical Republican policy in Georgia. He was elected to the state General Assembly in 1870 as part of its first postwar Democratic majority and became Speaker of the House in November 1871. When pressure led to Republican governor Rufus Bullock's resignation and flight from the state in October of that year, Smith was elected to fill his unexpired term, and his assumption of the governorship in January 1872 marked the end of Republican rule in Georgia. He was reelected with almost no opposition to a full term in October of that year. Smith failed in a bid for the U.S. Senate in 1877 and then was named to the first Railroad Commission, which he had been instrumental in establishing. In 1888 he was appointed Superior Court judge for the Muscogee Circuit, a position he held until his death on November 20, 1890.

BIBLIOGRAPHY

Avery, I. W. *History of the State of Georgia from 1850 to 1881.* New York, 1881.

Bell, Hiram P. *Men and Things: Being Reminiscent, Biographical, and Historical.* Atlanta, 1907.

Coleman, Kenneth, and Charles Stephen Gurr, eds. *Dictionary of Georgia Biography.* Vol. 2. Athens, Ga., 1983.

Conway, Alan. *The Reconstruction of Georgia.* Minneapolis, 1966.

Northen, William J. *Men of Mark in Georgia.* Vol. 3. Atlanta, 1908. Reprint, Spartanburg, S.C. 1974.

Telfair, Nancy. *A History of Columbus, Georgia, 1828–1928.* Atlanta, 1929.

Warner, Ezra J., and W. Buck Yearns. *Biographical Register of the Confederate Congress.* Baton Rouge, La., 1975.

JOHN C. INSCOE

SMITH, MARTIN LUTHER (1819–1866), major general and engineer. Born in New York state in 1819, Martin Luther Smith graduated from West Point in 1842 and served in the Mexican War. Although a career officer commissioned in the topographical engineers, he sided with the South during the secession crisis. He had married a Georgian in 1846 and had spent most of his prewar career in the South on surveying assignments in Florida, Georgia, and Texas. Soon after resigning from the U.S. Army on April 1, 1861, he was commissioned a major in the Confederate States Corps of Engineers from Florida.

Smith rose rapidly in the Confederate command structure. He was chosen as colonel of the Twenty-first Louisiana Infantry in February 1862 and was promoted to brigadier general and then to major general in April and November of that year. After brief duty in Virginia, Smith was sent west in early 1862 to plan and construct the river defenses of New Orleans and Vicksburg. While in command at Vicksburg, he supervised the Confederate defenses that repulsed Gen. William Tecumseh Sherman's river-based attack at the Chickasaw bluffs on December 29, 1862. While commanding a division during Ulysses S. Grant's spring offensive against Vicksburg, Smith was captured and later paroled. He served as chief engineer for the Army of Northern Virginia and then the Army of Tennessee from April through October 1864. His last assignment was in Mobile, where he was in charge of the Confederate defenses.

After his surrender at Mobile, Smith returned to Georgia. He died in Savannah in July 1866.

BIBLIOGRAPHY

Nichols, James L. *Confederate Engineers.* Tuscaloosa, Ala., 1957.

Warner, Ezra J. *Generals in Gray: Lives of the Confederate Commanders.* Baton Rouge, La., 1959.

WILLIAM L. BARNEY

SMITH, PRESTON (1823–1863), brigadier general. Smith was born Christmas Day, 1823, in Giles County, Tennessee. He attended Jackson College in Columbia. Later admitted to the bar, he settled in Memphis.

Although he had no prior military experience, Smith in 1861 was commissioned as colonel of the 154th Tennessee. In April 1862, at Shiloh, Smith was severely wounded and did not return to action until the autumn Kentucky campaign. He then commanded a brigade and later Patrick Cleburne's division after Cleburne was wounded at Rich-

PRESTON SMITH. LIBRARY OF CONGRESS

mond. On October 27, 1862, he was promoted to brigadier general.

In August 1863 Smith, along with his brigade, was inside Confederate defenses at Chattanooga. During this time, he had an argument with a Chattanooga man named Moore. Moore's son, who also commanded Confederate infantry, challenged Smith to a duel. But with Union soldiers advancing, a Confederate colonel intervened and kept the duel from taking place.

Following the Confederate retreat from Chattanooga a few days later, Smith commanded a brigade of four Tennessee regiments plus a battalion. During the first day's battle at Chickamauga, Smith crossed the creek with his brigade and took up a position near the center of the Confederate line. In the evening of September 19, Smith's brigade was sent forward to assist with a general assault. In the confusion and growing darkness, Smith rode up to troops he thought were Confederates. When the Federal soldiers recognized him as a Confederate, they fired a volley that killed Smith's aide and mortally wounded the general. Smith died an hour later. He was buried in Atlanta and later reinterred in Memphis, Tennessee.

BIBLIOGRAPHY

Walker, Robert Sparks. "The Pyramids of Chickamauga." *Chattanooga Sunday Times,* August 2, 1936.

Warner, Ezra J. *Generals in Gray: Lives of the Confederate Commanders.* Baton Rouge, La., 1959.

JOHN F. CISSELL

SMITH, ROBERT HARDY (1813–1878), congressman from Alabama and colonel. Smith was born on March 21, 1813, at Edenton in Camden County, North Carolina. He was appointed to the class of 1835 at the U.S. Military Academy at West Point; however, his father's financial reverses forced him to withdraw before graduation. Smith taught school in Virginia before moving to Dallas County, Alabama, in 1834. He continued to teach, studied medicine briefly, and then read law. He was admitted to the Alabama bar in 1837 and opened a practice in Livingston, eventually forming a partnership with William M. Inge.

As a Whig, Smith supported William Henry Harrison for president in 1840 and Henry Clay in 1844. In 1849, he was elected to the Alabama House of Representatives and quickly became one of the leading Whigs in the state. During the 1849 session of the Alabama General Assembly, Smith gave offense to John J. Seibles, who challenged him to a duel. Accepting the challenge, Smith was on his way to meet Seibles when friends intervened and submitted the matter to a board of honor, which settled the dispute to their mutual satisfaction. In 1851 he campaigned for the Alabama Senate, advocating support for the Compromise of 1850 and opposing both the Nashville Convention and state rights Democrats. He was defeated by a single vote.

In 1853 Smith moved to Mobile, Alabama, continued to practice law, and became an active opponent of William Lowndes Yancey and the secession movement. In the 1860 presidential election, Smith actively supported the Constitutional Union party's nominee, John Bell, and worked to ally Bell's supporters with those of Democratic candidate Stephen H. Douglas to defuse the secession movement. Also in 1860 Smith and Isham Warren Garrott were appointed the state's commissioners to confer with North Carolina officials about coordinating the actions of Southern states and forming a confederation should the Southern states secede. Once the sectional crisis destroyed the Whig party, Smith became a Democrat.

Smith's efforts to prevent Alabama's withdrawal from the Union failed, and the state convention voted to secede on January 11, 1861. Once the decision for secession was made, Smith declared his loyalty to Alabama and the South. In January 1861 he was elected as one of two deputies-at-large to represent Alabama in the Provisional Congress meeting in Montgomery, where he was named to the Judiciary Committee and the Committee on Naval Affairs. He also worked with a former law partner, Representative William B. Ochiltree of Texas, to prepare several military options to protect the South from an invasion by Northern troops. The plan was rejected because the Confederacy did not have the resources to implement it.

Smith's most important work was as a member of the committee that drafted the Constitution of the Confederate States of America. He worked diligently on its preparation, stressing the need for a strong national government, a viewpoint that was not shared by his fellow delegates from Alabama. He was determined that the Confederate Constitution be as clear and simple as possible and spent many hours working to clarify and define vague wording. It was Smith who suggested that the terms of office for the provisional government be limited to one year. Afterward he published *An Address to the Citizens of Alabama on the Constitution and Laws of the Confederate States of America* to inform the citizenry of their new form of government and stress his support for the Confederacy.

After the firing on Fort Sumter, Smith proposed that the Confederacy raise a force of independent volunteers that would form the nucleus of a national army to thwart any attack by Federal troops. He broke with President Jefferson Davis, however, over the question of a produce loan to finance the war effort, believing that the measure placed too large a burden on the planter class.

At the end of his first term, Smith declined to seek reelection and raised the Thirty-sixth Alabama Infantry Regiment in the spring of 1862. Although he was elected the regiment's colonel, Smith was forced to resign his commission because of health problems in April 1862. He remained active in the Southern military organization, however, and was appointed president of the military court of Brig. Gen. John Horace Forney's command of South Alabama and West Florida.

After the Civil War, Smith reopened his law practice in Mobile, specializing in constitutional law. He became a well-known litigator, arguing against the validity of a Reconstruction-inspired oath required of attorneys and playing a key role in the impeachment of Richard Busteed, the U.S. District judge for the Southern District of Alabama. Smith's arguments were so convincing that Busteed resigned. Smith also prosecuted the million-dollar case of *Alabama v. The Stanton, Alabama and Chattanooga Railroad*. He died in Mobile on March 13, 1878.

BIBLIOGRAPHY

Brewer, W. *Alabama: Her History, Resources, War Record, and Public Men from 1540 to 1872*. Montgomery, Ala., 1872.

Evans, Clement A., ed. *Confederate Military History*. 12 vols. Atlanta, 1899. Extended ed. in 19 vols. Wilmington, N.C., 1987–1989.

Garrett, William. *Reminiscences of Public Men in Alabama*. Atlanta, 1872.

Owen, Thomas M. *History of Alabama and Dictionary of Alabama Biography*. 4 vols. Chicago, 1921.

Smith, Robert H. *An Address to the Citizens of Alabama on the Constitution and Laws of the Confederate States of America*. Montgomery, Ala., 1861.

Warner, Ezra J., and W. Buck Yearns. *Biographical Register of the Confederate Congress*. Baton Rouge, La., 1975.

PAUL F. LAMBERT

SMITH, THOMAS BENTON (1838–1923), brigadier general. Born February 24, 1838, in Mechanicsville, Tennessee, Smith studied at the Nashville Military Academy. In 1861 he was working for the Nashville and Decatur Railroad.

When Tennessee seceded, Smith was elected a second lieutenant in Company B, Twentieth Tennessee Infantry Regiment. After service in eastern Tennessee and southeastern Kentucky, the regiment joined what became the Army of Tennessee. At the regiment's reorganization on May 8, 1862, Smith was elected colonel.

Smith and his command participated in all the Army of Tennessee's 1862–1863 battles except Perryville (when the regiment was part of a force detached to operate against Baton Rouge, Louisiana). At Murfreesboro, January 2, 1863, Smith was severely wounded. In 1864 his unit fought in the Atlanta campaign, during much of which Smith commanded the brigade, replacing the wounded Brig. Gen. Robert C. Tyler. On August 2, 1864, Smith was appointed brigadier general (with date of rank set to 29 July).

On December 16, 1864, at Nashville, Smith was captured when his position was overrun by attacking Federals. After his capture, he was viciously beaten by a Union officer. Held at Johnson's Island, Ohio, and Fort Warren, Massachusetts, Smith was not released until July 24, 1865.

After the war Smith worked for several railroads and in 1870 made an unsuccessful run for Congress. In 1876 complications arising from his wartime beating led to his admission to a state asylum in Nashville. He remained there until his death May 21, 1923. He was buried in Mount Olivet Cemetery, Nashville.

BIBLIOGRAPHY

Bearss, Edwin C. "Thomas Benton Smith." In *The Confederate General*. Edited by William C. Davis. Vol. 5. Harrisburg, Pa., 1991.

Warner, Ezra J. *Generals in Gray: Lives of the Confederate Commanders*. Baton Rouge, La., 1959.

RICHARD M. MCMURRY

SMITH, WILLIAM DUNCAN (1825–1862), brigadier general. A native Georgian, Smith graduated from West Point in 1846. He fought in the Mexican War and was wounded at Molino del Rey. After garrison and frontier duties in the 1850s as a captain in the Second Dragoons, he resigned his commission on January 28, 1861, to volunteer for Confederate service.

Commissioned colonel of the Twentieth Georgia Infantry in July 1861, Smith was promoted to brigadier general to date from March 7, 1862. He was assigned to the Department of South Carolina and Georgia under Gen. John C. Pemberton and in June was given command of the District of South Carolina at Charleston. Smith's major action in the field occurred at the Battle of Secessionville, South Carolina, on June 16, 1862. Union forces from James Island in Charleston Harbor attacked the Confederate position at Secessionville, a small hamlet on the island. The battle resulted in a Confederate victory that was a sharp setback to Union operations aimed at controlling Charleston Harbor. Smith commanded one wing of the Confederate forces under Gen. Nathan ("Shanks") Evans during the battle. Smith's performance there, in addition to his considerable administrative ability, prompted William Porcher Miles, a Confederate congressman from South Carolina, to recommend that Smith replace Pemberton as the departmental commander. But before any action could be taken on Miles's request, Smith contracted yellow fever and died in Charleston on October 4, 1862.

BIBLIOGRAPHY

Northen, William J., ed. *Men of Mark in Georgia.* Vol. 3. Atlanta, 1908. Reprint, Spartanburg, S.C., 1974.

Warner, Ezra J. *Generals in Gray: Lives of the Confederate Commanders.* Baton Rouge, La., 1959.

William L. Barney

SMITH, WILLIAM EPHRAIM (1829–1890), captain and congressman from Georgia. Smith was born in Augusta, Georgia. Little information is available about his education, though it is known he read law and was admitted to the bar in 1848, at only eighteen years of age. He moved to Albany, Georgia, opened a law practice, and acquired a modest cotton plantation and several slaves. Smith held no elective office prior to the Civil War, though he served Doughtery County in a number of capacities and was solicitor of Georgia's southwestern district before, during, and after the war.

A longtime Whig, Smith initially opposed secession. Once the war broke out, though, he enlisted in the Fourth Georgia Volunteer Infantry as a first lieutenant and was promoted to captain in April 1862. Most of his military service took place in Virginia, where in June 1862, he lost a leg at the Battle of King's School House (also known as the Battle of Oak Grove or the Orchards) during the Peninsular campaign.

He returned home to Albany, where he remained until he was elected to the Second Congress in November 1863, defeating the incumbent Charles James Munnerlyn. In Congress, Smith was active on the Ordnance and Military Affairs Committee. He used the latter position to push for more efficient regimental organization and more thorough procedures in conscripting able-bodied men and engaging noneligible men in civilian war efforts.

After the war, Smith returned to Albany and resumed his law practice. In 1875 he was elected to the first of three terms as a Democrat in the U.S. House of Representatives, serving until 1881. In 1886 he presided over the state Democratic convention as its president and later that year was elected to a single term in the state senate. Smith died in Albany on May 11, 1890.

BIBLIOGRAPHY

Northen, William J., ed. *Men of Mark in Georgia.* Vol. 5. Atlanta, 1908. Reprint, Spartanburg, S.C., 1974.

Wakelyn, Jon L. *Biographical Dictionary of the Confederacy.* Edited by Frank E. Vandiver. Westport, Conn., 1977.

Warner, Ezra J., and W. Buck Yearns. *Biographical Register of the Confederate Congress.* Baton Rouge, La., 1975.

John C. Inscoe

SMITH, WILLIAM "EXTRA BILLY" (1797–1887), major general, Virginia congressman and governor. Smith grew up in a well-to-do, middle-class plantation family near Fredericksburg. He received a sound education at private academies, clerked in several law offices, and in 1818 became a practicing attorney in the upper Piedmont, first at Culpeper and then at Warrenton. He married and started a large family. He did some farming with slave labor and ran a successful mail and coach service that wangled so many extra fees from the post office that he won the enduring nickname "Extra Billy."

An ardent Jacksonian Democrat, he soon became primarily a politician. From 1836 to 1841 he served in the state senate and from 1841 to 1843 in the U.S. House of Representatives. Then the state legislature elected him governor. He served from January 1, 1846, to December 31, 1848, enthusiastically and effectively supporting the war against Mexico. He was especially successful in mobilizing Virginia troops for combat. As soon as his term was over, Smith moved alone to California to recoup his finances, and he prospered by practicing law and speculating in land. In 1853 he returned to his family in Virginia and almost immediately won election again to the U.S. House of Representatives where he served until 1861.

When war erupted the sixty-three-year-old Smith volunteered to serve his state in combat, and Governor John Letcher appointed him colonel of the Forty-ninth Virginia Infantry Regiment. Brave but inexperienced, Colonel Smith was a barely adequate military leader, though he saw much action and was wounded in the Peninsular campaign and more seriously at Sharpsburg in September 1862. Eight months later Brigadier General Smith returned to active duty in time for the Battle of Chancellorsville, but a poor performance at Gettysburg led to his removal from combat command and reassignment to recruiting duties where his gubernatorial experience during the Mexican War proved useful.

During the first two years of the war Smith had also been a member of the Confederate Congress. Since he participated only while on leave from the army, he played a minor role, concentrating on financial and military affairs and generally supporting President Jefferson Davis and the Confederate central government. Then Smith returned to full-time politics by winning a second term as governor of the state. Virginians were distracted by the war, but Major General Smith won a large majority of the army vote, and on January 1, 1864, he began his new administration.

The new governor was elected to serve four years, but the massive Union war machine had already gained a clear advantage over the battered Southern armies. In reality Smith would hold office only a little over fifteen months within the doomed Confederacy.

At first he occasionally bogged down in routine matters, but generally he performed efficiently. Like his predecessor, John Letcher, he followed the practical policy of broadly cooperating with the Confederate government, and, again like Letcher, he urged Virginians to put away for the duration of the war their traditional devotion to state rights, individual freedoms, and strict legalism and to strive even harder for victory. And just like Letcher, he clashed frequently with the increasingly disaffected legislature.

Concerned about Virginia's growing vulnerability, Governor Smith tried to marshal new home defense forces, but the steadily expanding Confederate draft soon drained away manpower from this program. Smith yielded to the draft and called out his few remaining state troops whenever the Confederates made such a request. He also supported Confederate efforts to reduce the number of draft-exempt state and local officials, a scam all over the South, and he especially opposed exempting such officials who had refugeed from enemy-held parts of Virginia, though he did occasionally yield to local protests. He cooperated, too, with Confederate impressment, including the seizure of slave laborers, always an especially sensitive issue. He even ordered state officials to seize uncooperative saltworks in southwestern Virginia, something his predecessor could never quite bring himself to do. And finally Governor Smith acceded to rapidly expanding Confederate control of Virginia's manufacturing facilities and transportation systems. Inevitably these emergency wartime policies led to rising protests that were soon concentrated in the restive legislature, but the pragmatic governor knew that extraordinary, even desperate measures had to be taken if the South was to have any real hope of victory.

A combat veteran, Smith was fully aware of the desperate manpower shortage in the Confederate armed forces. The South still had one great untapped manpower pool—slaves, black Southerners by the hundreds of thousands. Early in 1862 invading Union armies had begun to recruit Southern blacks, and after the Emancipation Proclamation this policy accelerated, so that by the end of the war the Union armed forces had enlisted almost 200,000 blacks, mostly Southerners. Yet even as the war dragged on and Southern casualties soared, the Confederates hesitated to take this final step.

Then in September 1864 Louisiana governor Henry W. Allen's secret call for the use of black troops surfaced. The next month the governors of Virginia, Alabama, Georgia, Mississippi, and the Carolinas met in Augusta, Georgia, and Smith prodded them into issuing a resolution obliquely calling for the use of black troops. Finally, very late in the war, the Davis administration itself moved toward this position.

With Atlanta lost and Abraham Lincoln reelected, Governor Smith in December appealed to the hostile legislature to begin recruiting slaves as soldiers. Conservative Virginia wavered, but when Robert E. Lee called for black troops in January 1865, Smith renewed his appeals, and finally early in March the legislators approved furnishing black Virginians to the Confederate army. In the middle of March the Confederate Congress passed similar legislation, and, thanks in part to continued agitation by Governor Smith, the War Department's new regulations for slave soldiers promised freedom for honorable service. Never in his career had Smith challenged slavery or the assumption of black inferiority upon which it was based, but he saw the desperate need for new manpower and placed contemporary crisis ahead of old dogma. A dramatic, indeed radical change in recruitment finally came, but Virginia and the Confederacy had waited far too long; the war was already lost.

The governor also pushed other sweeping changes during his administration. He early advocated action to control inflation, but the legislature delayed, and the Confederates also failed to restrain the soaring prices that were undermining the Southern economy. After the legislature rejected one of his specific appropriations, the governor tapped his own contingency funds and borrowed more money from a Richmond bank to finance the operation of his state supply system to ease some extreme shortages. A few scarce items began to come in from abroad and from the Deep South, but again it was too little too late as the economy continued to disintegrate.

Early in his administration Governor Smith did gain one large appropriation from the legislature to combat the clothing shortage. He set up a new bureaucracy to obtain cotton and cotton cards to sell to the people at reasonable prices, and he even talked the Confederates into handing over a mill where cotton cloth could be cheaply manufactured. But such stopgap measures could not halt the accelerating decline of Virginia and the Confederacy.

Throughout his administration of slightly more than fifteen months, Governor Smith's best efforts made much sense. He selflessly cooperated with the Confederate central government, convinced that this was the only possible way to win the war against the huge Federal military forces that threatened Virginia on several fronts. But the tide had turned too powerfully against the South. Like Davis and Lee, Smith might delay defeat, but he could not gain victory.

In the last year of the war Union armies knifed deeper and deeper into Virginia's vitals, and finally on April 1, 1865, troops under Ulysses S. Grant overran Lee's massive defenses at Petersburg. On April 3 Smith fled from Richmond just one step ahead of Federal troops. He and a pathetic remnant of the state government fled to Lynchburg and then farther west to Danville. Smith thought about fighting on after Lee surrendered on April 9. He unsuccessfully tried to take command of all remaining Confederate forces in the state and even considered guerrilla warfare. But he soon saw that his people had had enough, and on June 8 he surrendered to Federal officials in Richmond. Five days later he went home to Warrenton and the following month received a pardon from President Andrew Johnson.

Still healthy at sixty-seven, Smith farmed for a living. He remained active in politics and in the mid-1870s served again in the state legislature. On May 18, 1887, he died at home just short of his ninetieth birthday.

BIBLIOGRAPHY

Bell, John W. *Memoirs of Governor William Smith of Virginia: His Political, Military and Personal History.* New York, 1891.

Boney, F. N. "Virginia." In *The Confederate Governors.* Edited by W. Buck Yearns. Athens, Ga., 1985.

Fahrner, Alvin A. "The Public Career of William 'Extra Billy' Smith." Ph.D. diss., University of North Carolina, 1953.

Fahrner, Alvin A. "William ('Extra Billy') Smith: Governor in Two Wars." In *The Governors of Virginia, 1860–1978.* Edited by Edward Younger and James Tice Moore. Charlottesville, Va., 1982.

Fahrner, Alvin A. "William 'Extra Billy' Smith, Governor of Virginia, 1864–1865: A Pillar of the Confederacy." *Virginia Magazine of History and Biography* 74 (1966): 68–87.

F. N. Boney

SMITH, WILLIAM N. H. (1812–1889), congressman from North Carolina. Born September 24, 1812, at Murfreesboro, North Carolina, William Nathan Harrell Smith graduated from Yale University in 1834, studied law there, and commenced practice in his native Hertford County. He was elected as a Whig to the house of commons in 1840 and 1858 and to the state senate in 1848. From 1849 until 1857 he served as district solicitor. In 1859 he won election to the U.S. Congress and came within a few votes of becoming Speaker.

An opponent of secession until Lincoln's call for troops, Smith served in the Provisional Congress and was subsequently elected, without opposition, to the First Congress. Allying himself with the Conservative party, he opposed suspension of habeas corpus, impressment, conscription, and most of the other policies of the Davis administration. After Federal troops captured Roanoke Island and occupied other parts of his coastal district, Smith's critics accused him of neglecting its defense. Although an early supporter of peace negotiations, he believed that the initiative lay with the executive and opposed separate state action. He was reelected in 1863 over two other anti-administration candidates, thus becoming the only North Carolinian to serve in all three Confederate Congresses. Conscientious and energetic, he is regarded as one of wartime North Carolina's most effective representatives.

Smith was active in the Conservative (later Democratic) party after the war, but, nonetheless, agreed to serve as a defense counsel in Republican Governor William W. Holden's impeachment trial in 1870. Appointed chief justice of the state supreme court in 1878, he served there until his death on November 14, 1889.

BIBLIOGRAPHY

Alexander, Thomas B., and Richard E. Beringer. *The Anatomy of the Confederate Congress: A Study of the Influences of Member Characteristics on Legislative Voting Behavior, 1861–1865.* Nashville, Tenn., 1972.

Ashe, Samuel A. *Biographical History of North Carolina.* 8 vols. Greensboro, N.C., 1905–1917.

Wakelyn, Jon L. *Biographical Dictionary of the Confederacy.* Edited by Frank E. Vandiver. Westport, Conn., 1977.

Warner, Ezra J., and W. Buck Yearns. *Biographical Register of the Confederate Congress.* Baton Rouge, La., 1975.

Thomas E. Jeffrey

SMITH, WILLIAM RUSSELL (1815–1896), colonel and congressman from Alabama. Smith was born in Russellville, Logan County, Kentucky, on March 27, 1815. After his father died in 1817, his mother moved the family to Alabama. When she too died in 1823, Smith, his sister, and his brother were distributed among several Tuscaloosa families to be reared, but Smith soon ran away to be with his brother. After his sister married, he went to work in his brother-in-law's tailor shop.

While still a young man, Smith attracted the attention of

George W. Crabb, a prominent citizen. Realizing that Smith was above average in ability, Crabb loaned him money to attend preparatory schools. Smith studied at the University of Alabama from 1831 until 1834, when he ran short of funds and withdrew to read law in Crabb's law office. A year later he was admitted to the Alabama bar and in 1835 opened a practice at Greensboro, Alabama. He became popular in Alabama society, often dressing like a Spanish cavalier, complete with cloak.

When the Creek War broke out in Alabama in 1836, Smith raised a company of mounted infantry, which he commanded as a captain. Smith's Alabama volunteers arrived in the Creek territory too late to take part in the fighting. When he heard of the death of his brother, who had been fighting for the independence of Texas, Smith persuaded his men to follow him to Texas and join the fight. Smith learned of the Texan victory at San Jacinto before his men could reach Texas, however, and the troops disbanded at Mobile.

Smith remained in Mobile for about six months in 1836 and 1837 to edit *The Bachelor's Button: A Monthly Museum of Southern Literature*. Although the periodical was unsuccessful, it marked the beginning of Smith's career as a prolific writer. He published many volumes of poetry, plays, essays, and legal studies over the years. Proud of his literary accomplishments, he was the only member of the Confederate Congress to list his vocation as "writer."

After returning to Tuscaloosa in 1838, Smith resumed his law practice and became active in Alabama Whig politics. He was elected mayor of Tuscaloosa in 1839 and won a seat in the Alabama General Assembly in 1841 and 1842. He fell out with the Whig leadership over policy and left the party in 1843.

Smith then moved to Fayette County, where in 1850 he was elected judge of the Seventh Circuit and a general of militia. He returned to Tuscaloosa that same year and was elected to the U.S. House of Representatives. He resigned his judgeship to assume his seat in Congress.

Smith was reelected in 1852 on a Union Democrat ticket. As a Unionist, he denied the constitutional right of secession but refused to comment on it as a "sovereign" right. In 1854, he joined the American (Know-Nothing) party, and voters returned him to Congress a third time. Later, he became disenchanted with the Know-Nothing party's anti-Catholic and nativist sentiments and split with its leaders.

As a congressman in the 1850s, Smith was opposed to Southern secession and in 1856 declared that "the union of the states is a political indestructibility." His viewpoint was so well received that there was talk of nominating him for vice president in the 1856 election. He lost his bid for a fourth congressional term that same year, however.

During the 1860 presidential election, Smith campaigned for John Bell and the Constitutional Union party. Afterward he was chosen as a delegate to the Alabama secession convention which convened in Montgomery on January 4, 1861. There he espoused Unionism and was characterized as a cooperationist who sought to secure state rights within the Union, and failing that, to maintain them outside the Union. To Smith, allegiance to the state was paramount. Although he refused to sign the ordinance of secession, once it was approved he declared his loyalty to Alabama. Smith's book *History and Debates of the Convention of the People of Alabama . . .*, which was published in 1861, is a principal source for the events that occurred during the Alabama secession convention.

After secession, Smith helped raise the Sixth Alabama Infantry Regiment at Tuscombia in May, and when it was redesignated the Twenty-sixth Alabama, he was elected its colonel. He accompanied the troops to the training camp, but resigned his commission after being elected to the Confederate House of Representatives. Upon taking his seat, Smith was assigned to the Printing Committee, the Flag and Seal Committee, the Foreign Relations Committee, and several special committees. As a member of the Committee on Foreign Relations, Smith opposed reopening the African slave trade, arguing that there were sufficient slaves in the South to fill current needs and that reopening the trade would give credibility to those who said that that had been the main reason for secession.

While in Congress, Smith often found himself at odds with the policies of President Jefferson Davis. He opposed numerous executive appointments as well as many of the administration's tax, commerce, and international relations programs. He supported a ban on hiring slaves to work for the Confederate army and opposed any effort to curtail free trade. He bitterly fought legislation first enacted on February 27, 1862, empowering the president to suspend the writ of habeas corpus and to declare martial law. He also opposed the enactment of conscription legislation.

Smith was reelected to Congress in 1863, but because of his opposition to Davis's administration and his earlier Unionist views, he was not well received by his fellow congressmen. As a result he did not regularly attend sessions. In February 1865 he stopped going altogether when the House of Representatives refused to pass a resolution condemning the *Richmond Sentinel*'s editorial calling any movement for a negotiated peace "treason."

After the war, Smith practiced law in Fayette County and reentered politics, unsuccessfully running for governor in November 1865. In 1870 he was chosen to be the president of the University of Alabama by the Radical Republicans controlling the state government. The university had ceased operations during the war, and when classes resumed in 1865, only one student applied for admission. In the next three years efforts were made to rejuvenate the institution, rebuild its facilities, and replace its equipment. The university reopened in 1868, but because its faculty and president were carpetbaggers, few Southern students entered. The Radical Republicans thus turned to Smith in 1870 in the hope of generating support for the school among Alabama citizens. As a Unionist before the war, but a supporter of the Confederacy after secession, he appeared to be the ideal compromise candidate. In addition, his literary background qualified him as an educator. Unfortunately, Smith faced intractable problems in revitalizing the university, including a continued paucity of students. During his tenure as president only ten students enrolled, and four of them were sons of professors. In addition the Ku Klux Klan became active on campus, and by the time Smith resigned as president in July 1871 there were no students remaining in class.

Smith made one final attempt to reenter politics, seeking election to the U.S. House of Representatives in 1878, but was defeated. He continued to practice law in Tuscaloosa until 1879 when he moved his practice to Washington, D.C. He died there on February 26, 1896, and was buried in Tuscaloosa.

BIBLIOGRAPHY

Brewer, W. *Alabama: Her History, Resources, War Record, and Public Men from 1540 to 1872.* Montgomery, Ala., 1872.

Easley-Smith, Mildred. *William Russell Smith of Alabama: His Life and Works Including the Entire Text of "The Uses of Solitude."* Philadelphia, 1931.

Fleming, Walter L. *Civil War and Reconstruction in Alabama.* New York, 1905.

Garrett, William. *Reminiscences of Public Men in Alabama.* Atlanta, 1872.

Moore, Albert Burton. *History of Alabama and Her People.* New York, 1927.

Pickett, Albert J. *History of Alabama and Incidentally of Georgia and Mississippi from the Earliest Period.* Birmingham, Ala., 1900.

Smith, William Russell. *History and Debates of the Convention of the People of Alabama, Begun and Held in the City of Montgomery, on the Seventh Day of January, 1861; in Which Is Preserved the Speeches of the Secret Sessions and Many Valuable State Papers, 1861.* Montgomery and Atlanta, 1861.

Paul F. Lambert

SNEAD, THOMAS L. (1828–1890), newspaperman, major, and congressman from Missouri. Born in Virginia and educated at Richmond College, Snead graduated from the University of Virginia in 1848. He later moved to Missouri, practiced law, and became associated with the *St. Louis Bulletin.*

Snead used his control of the paper to support vigorously the candidacies of John C. Breckinridge for president in 1860 and that of Claiborne F. Jackson for governor, until the latter announced his support for Stephen A. Douglas in the presidential election. With Abraham Lincoln elected, Snead used the pages of the *Bulletin* to advocate secession and the arming of the state's pro-Southern militia. Failing on both counts, he disposed of the paper in mid-February 1861 and joined Governor Jackson in Jefferson City, becoming the governor's aide-de-camp in May.

After attending the unsuccessful bid for peace known as the Planter's Hotel conference in June, he became assistant adjutant general of the pro-Southern Missouri State Guard the following month with the rank of colonel. Accompanying the Missouri forces into Confederate service along with their leader, Maj. Gen. Sterling Price, later that year, Snead served as Price's adjutant general or, at times, his chief of staff for most of the rest of the war, holding the Confederate rank of major. He participated in the Battles of Booneville, Carthage, Wilson's Creek, and Lexington. In 1864, he was elected by soldiers and refugees from Union-occupied St. Louis to fill one of the state's seats in the Confederate Congress. He remained there for the balance of the war, working to limit Jefferson Davis's executive powers and to retain state control over local militias.

After the war Snead moved to New York City where he edited the *New York Daily News,* practiced law, and authored many articles and *The Fight for Missouri: From the Election of Lincoln to the Death of Lyon* (1886). He was buried in St. Louis.

BIBLIOGRAPHY

Anderson, Galusha. *A Border City during the Civil War.* Boston, 1908.

Snead, Thomas Lowndes. *The Fight for Missouri: From the Election of Lincoln to the Death of Lyon.* New York, 1886.

Warner, Ezra J., and W. Buck Yearns. *Biographical Register of the Confederate Congress.* Baton Rouge, La., 1975.

Steven E. Woodworth

SOCIETY. Tales of military drama dominate the historiography of the Civil War. Only recently have historians shifted their perspective away from the sacrifices on the battlefield and toward the effects of the war on society.

To evaluate Confederate society, one has to question whether it existed as a viable society at all. Many see it as essentially antebellum Southern society in crisis and, thus, a society that was really only changed by the processes of conquest and Reconstruction. Yet the Confederacy itself changed social relations in the South as it geared to fight a war of survival. The desire to preserve a way of life that precluded change was strong enough to wage war over, but paradoxically the war itself forced change upon that way of life.

Early in the Confederacy, white social unity generally prevailed, but as the war continued many white Southerners came to feel that their society had failed them. The societal changes on the home front are fundamental to an understanding of the nature of Confederate society. In the midst of wartime dislocation, the contrasting lifestyles of the planter-lawyer "aristocrats" and the common folks were at the heart of the divisions in the society. Furthermore, black and white relationships changed radically once the war began.

Although the antebellum South is usually considered a homogeneous region, an increasing number of regional and local studies suggest significant differences within the South. Moreover, themes discussed in this essay—planters and aristocracy, poor whites, yeomen, and plain folk, the business and professional classes, slaves and free blacks, and the impact of the war on class unity and class conflict—may or may not be peculiar to the South. How one views these issues depends largely on the interpretation one has of antebellum Southern society.

A young up-country white South Carolinian precisely defined the ramifications of what his society meant to him as he marched off to war: "I go first for Greenville, then for Greenville District, then for the up-country, then for South Carolina, then for the South, then for the United States, and after that I don't go for anything." First and foremost, Southerners understood the unfolding drama through the lens of their own local society. But those societies varied enormously. The aggregate of communities that came together to form the Confederacy were far from a monolith.

Demographics

In 1860, 60 percent of all Southerners were free, but significant deviations existed among the eleven states that would form the Confederacy. In South Carolina 57.2 percent of its population was composed of slaves and in Mississippi, 55.2 percent. Border states had much lower percentages of slave populations; in Arkansas, only a fourth of its population was composed of slaves. Free blacks lived mostly in the northern border regions of the Confederacy, with two-thirds of them in Virginia and North Carolina. Most of the free blacks in Louisiana, the other state with a significant free African American population (18,647), were located in New Orleans (10,689).

The Confederacy was overwhelmingly rural, with only one large city of over 50,000—New Orleans. Cities contained proportionately fewer African Americans than did the Confederacy at large. The black population (free and slave) was disproportionately female in the urban areas. In the Confederacy in general, as in most settled areas, the male-to-female ratio was roughly equal among both black and white. Indicative of a lack of urban industrial centers, relatively few people (37,303) lived in single-member households. Since much of the agricultural labor was provided by slaves, a single white farm laborer had fewer job opportunities in the South. The average free household size of 5.6 members was consistent for most states, North and South, and included boarders.

If household and family size was consistent across the Confederacy, the size of farms was not. Overall, the distribution of farm sizes was fairly wide (see table 1). Half of the farms in the Confederate states, 54.4 percent, fell into the small-farm category of twenty to one hundred acres. Less than 1 percent (4,275) of farms fell in the largest category of a thousand or more acres. The census designations for farms of three acres or more do not distinguish between people who owned farms and those who were tenant farm operators, but some evidence suggests

TABLE 1. *Distribution of Farms by Acreage, 1860*[1]

	Total Farms	3–10 Acres	10–19 Acres	20–49 Acres	50–99 Acres	100–499 Acres	500–999 Acres	1000+ Acres
Alabama	50,064	1,409 (2.8%)	4,379 (8.7%)	16,049 (32.1%)	12,060 (24.1%)	13,455 (26.9%)	2,016 (4.0%)	696 (1.4%)
Arkansas	33,190	1,823 (5.5%)	6,075 (18.3%)	13,728 (41.4%)	6,957 (21.0%)	4,231 (12.7%)	307 (0.9%)	69 (0.2%)
Florida	6,396	430 (6.7%)	945 (14.8%)	2,139 (33.4%)	1,162 (18.2%)	1,432 (22.4%)	211 (3.3%)	77 (1.2%)
Georgia	53,897	906 (1.7%)	2,803 (5.2%)	13,644 (25.3%)	14,129 (26.2%)	18,821 (34.9%)	2,692 (5.0%)	902 (1.7%)
Louisiana	17,281	626 (3.6%)	2,222 (12.9%)	4,882 (28.3%)	3,064 (17.7%)	4,955 (28.7%)	1,161 (6.7%)	371 (2.1%)
Mississippi	37,007	563 (1.5%)	2,516 (6.8%)	10,967 (29.6%)	9,204 (24.9%)	11,408 (30.8%)	1,868 (5.0%)	481 (1.3%)
North Carolina	67,002	2,050 (3.1%)	4,879 (7.3%)	20,882 (31.2%)	18,496 (27.6%)	19,220 (28.7%)	1,184 (1.8%)	311 (0.5%)
South Carolina	28,456	352 (1.2%)	1,219 (4.3%)	6,695 (23.5%)	6,980 (24.5%)	11,369 (40.0%)	1,359 (4.8%)	482 (1.7%)
Tennessee	77,741	1,687 (2.2%)	7,245 (9.3%)	22,998 (29.6%)	22,829 (29.4%)	21,903 (28.2%)	921 (1.2%)	158 (0.2%)
Texas	37,363	1,832 (4.9%)	6,156 (16.5%)	14,132 (37.8%)	7,857 (21.0%)	6,831 (18.3%)	468 (1.3%)	87 (0.2%)
Virginia	86,468	2,351 (2.7%)	5,565 (6.4%)	19,584 (22.6%)	21,145 (24.5%)	34,300 (39.7%)	2,882 (3.3%)	641 (0.7%)
Total	494,865	14,029 (2.8%)	44,004 (8.9%)	145,700 (29.4%)	123,883 (25.0%)	147,925 (29.9%)	15,069 (3.0%)	4,275 (0.9%)

[1]Only farms of three acres or larger are presented in the table. All percentages are rounded to the nearest tenth.
SOURCE: Data taken from U.S. Census Office, Eighth Census [1860], *Agriculture of the United States in 1860*, Washington, D.C., 1864.

that the number of white tenant farmers and landless laborers was increasing in certain areas of the South on the eve of the Civil War. Moreover, many wealthy white Southerners owned several farms or plantations, each of which would be listed individually. In some cases, people in the same households were operating separate farms. Thus, the proportion of householders who were farming three or more acres was overestimated, but it could not have been more than 48 percent. While some of these were town and urban dwellers (professionals and artisans), many Southern whites were landless in a society where land and slaves defined social status.

The distribution of slaveholders by the number of slaves owned (see table 2) correlates with the size of farms. Approximately 25 percent of Southern free families were slaveholders; probably more than three-fourths of all white Southerners lived in nonslaveholding households. Of some 306,300 slaveholders, more than 45 percent held less than five slaves and 85 percent held less than twenty, the number usually considered enough for the owner to be categorized as a planter. "Planter" and "slave owner" were by no means synonymous. Moreover, as with the size of farms, great deviations existed among the Confederate states and within each state. Most slaveholders in Tennessee, Texas, and Arkansas had very few slaves; Alabama (17.9 percent), Mississippi (18.6 percent), and South Carolina (19.9 percent) had the largest share of owners of more than twenty slaves.

These regional differences in slave ownership and size of slaveholdings assumed class overtones with secession. Opposition to secession was strongest in nonslaveholding areas; only after the firing on Fort Sumter did many of these regions take the remarkable step of leaving the Union. Some areas never did, and some Southern whites took an even more extreme position: 100,000 whites from the Confederate states fought for the Union. When one combines that figure with the number of African Americans from the Confederate states who fought for the Union, the term *Civil War* takes on added significance. It was indeed a war between fellow citizens of a nation.

Slavery and Free Blacks in the South

Some historians view secession as a rational act on the part of capitalists to protect their investments; some argue that secession was an act of people determined to preserve their nonbourgeois way of life; others contend that Southern whites were attempting to preserve their republican values as they understood them; and still others assert that extremists whipped citizens into a racist terror. All major historians agree, however, that the Confederacy left the Union between 1860 and 1865 to preserve slavery. "Slavery informs all our modes of life, all our habits of thought, lies at the basis of our social existence, and of our political faith," explained an important South Carolina politico and planter. No less an authority on the war than Robert E. Lee understood that the South was fighting for its society and that slavery was its fundamental underpinning. In 1859, Robert M. T. Hunter argued in Congress that the United States was like an arch "and the very keystone of this arch consists of the black marble cap of African slavery; knock that out, and the mighty fabric, with all that it upholds, topples and tumbles to its fall." Alexander H. Stephens, soon after his inauguration as vice president of the Confederacy, explained that slavery "was the immediate cause of the late rupture and present revolution." Stephens said that "slavery, subordination to the superior race, is his [the African American's] natural and moral condition." Northerners had rejected slavery and now "the stone which

TABLE 2. *Distribution of Slaveholders by the Size of Holdings, 1860*[1]

	Total Slaveholders	Owners of 1–4 Slaves	Owners of 5–19 Slaves	Owners of 20–49 Slaves	Owners of 50–99 Slaves	Owners of 100–499 Slaves	Owners of 500 + Slaves
Alabama	33,730	14,404 (42.7%)	13,295 (39.4%)	4,344 (12.9%)	1,341 (4.0%)	346 (1.0%)	–
Arkansas	1,149	659 (57.4%)	424 (36.9%)	56 (4.9%)	10 (0.9%)	–	–
Florida	5,152	2,233 (43.3%)	2,111 (41.0%)	603 (11.7%)	158 (3.1%)	47 (0.9%)	–
Georgia	41,084	17,534 (42.7%)	17,187 (41.8%)	5,049 (12.3%)	1,102 (2.7%)	211 (0.5%)	1
Louisiana	22,033	10,235 (46.5%)	7,873 (35.7%)	2,349 (10.7%)	1,029 (4.7%)	543 (2.5%)	4
Mississippi	30,943	12,689 (41.0%)	12,359 (39.9%)	4,220 (13.6%)	1,359 (4.4%)	315 (1.0%)	1
North Carolina	34,658	16,071 (46.4%)	14,522 (41.9%)	3,321 (9.6%)	611 (1.8%)	133 (0.4%)	–
South Carolina	26,701	10,017 (37.5%)	11,392 (42.7%)	3,646 (13.7%)	1,197 (4.5%)	441 (1.7%)	8
Tennessee	36,844	19,179 (52.1%)	14,553 (39.5%)	2,550 (6.9%)	335 (0.9%)	47 (0.1%)	–
Texas	21,878	11,342 (51.8%)	8,373 (38.3%)	1,827 (8.4%)	282 (1.3%)	54 (0.2%)	–
Virginia	52,128	25,355 (48.6%)	20,996 (40.3%)	4,917 (9.4%)	746 (1.4%)	114 (0.2%)	–
Total	306,300	139,718 (45.6%)	123,085 (40.2%)	32,882 (10.7%)	8,170 (2.7%)	2,251 (0.7%)	14

[1]All percentages are rounded to the nearest tenth.

SOURCE: Data taken from U.S. Census Office, Eighth Census [1860], *Agriculture of the United States in 1860*, Washington, D.C., 1864.

was rejected by the first builders is become the chief stone of the corner." Slavery was the cornerstone of the Confederacy.

Table 3 ranks the slave states in the order of their date of secession from the Union and includes the proportion of the population that was slave and African American. A nearly perfect correlation exists between the proportion of blacks and the date of leaving the Union. The six states with more than 44 percent of their population black left in the first wave of secession between December 20, 1860, and January 26, 1861. The next five states with an average black population of about 31 percent seceded between February 1 and May 11, 1861. The four slave states with less than a quarter of their population black never seceded. It is apparent what a large part slavery and race played in a state's decision to leave the Union.

Slavery shaped the nature of Southern society; even its few cities and industries were structurally influenced by plantation slavery. White Southerners' liberty and the institution of slavery were linked in their cultural understanding. White Confederates initially believed that slavery would allow more white men to enter the army, for slaves would cultivate the crops and man the industries on the home front. Slaves would also release white soldiers for fighting. Impressed into the army as laborers, they would build fortifications and perform other menial tasks, including cooking and cleaning.

But not all blacks in the South were slaves; a small proportion of them was composed of free African Americans. Some were the descendants of slaves who had gained their freedom during the colonial era. Others had been freed during a brief period of liberalization inspired by the American Revolution. In addition, many light-skinned "free people of color" immigrated to the United States despite bans on what were called "French Negroes." And some antebellum free African Americans derived from the manumission of mulatto children, usually the result of unions between masters and their slave mistresses.

In 1860 about 4.5 million people in the United States were African Americans; 11 percent of them were free blacks, of whom half lived in the North and half in the South. Most free blacks lived in urban areas. They formed associations, such as the Brown Fellowship Society of Charleston, founded urban black churches, and published their own newspapers. Free black artisans lived both in the city and in rural areas. Prosperous free blacks provided a

TABLE 3. *Date of Secession Compared to 1860 Black Population*

	Date of Secession	Slaves	Free Blacks[1]	Total Blacks[2]
		Percentage of Total Population[3]		
South Carolina	Dec. 20, 1860	57.2%	1.4%	58.6%
Mississippi	Jan. 9, 1861	55.2%	0.1%	55.3%
Florida	Jan. 10, 1861	44.0%	0.7%	44.6%
Alabama	Jan. 11, 1861	45.1%	0.3%	45.4%
Georgia	Jan. 19, 1861	43.7%	0.3%	44.0%
Louisiana	Jan. 26, 1861	46.9%	2.6%	49.5%
Aggregate populations of the first six states to secede[4]		48.8%	0.8%	49.6%
Texas	Feb. 1, 1861	30.2%	0.1%	30.3%
Virginia	Apr. 17, 1861	30.8%	3.6%	34.4%
Arkansas	May 6, 1861	25.5%	0.1%	25.6%
Tennessee	May 7, 1861	24.9%	0.7%	25.5%
North Carolina	May 11, 1861	33.4%	3.1%	36.5%
Aggregate populations of the last four states to secede[4]		29.4%	2.0%	31.4%
Kentucky		19.5%	0.9%	20.4%
Maryland		12.7%	12.2%	24.9%
Delaware		1.6%	17.7%	19.3%
Missouri		9.7%	0.3%	10.0%
Aggregate populations of the nonseceding slave states[4]		13.7%	3.8%	17.5%

[1]Includes all free persons of African descent.
[2]Calculated from the aggregate black populations of each state, not the sum of individual percentages.
[3]All percentages rounded to nearest tenth.
[4]Calculated from the aggregate populations of the states listed, not the average of their individual percentages.
SOURCE: Data taken from U.S. Census Office, Eighth Census [1860], *Population*, Washington, D.C., 1864.

model for former slaves building new lives after emancipation. Of those who lived in rural areas, the more economically secure they were, the more likely they resided among white men and women of equal economic status. Some antebellum African Americans owned land and even slaves. A few were antebellum tenant farmers, but most rural free blacks were farm laborers living in poverty.

In certain locales, census takers classified a person as black, mulatto, or white depending on skin color. Some evidence exists that light-skinned African Americans had some choice in whether they integrated into the white world or were part of the black community. In some rural areas, free black men were as likely to marry white women as free black women. Some may have married slaves, which would not have been recorded.

The story of free blacks in the Civil War is complicated, particularly because free African Americans fought on or helped both sides in the conflict. Their loyalties often depended upon their positions within the local society. Before the war free blacks composed a small minority that was often allowed some leeway by a white society unafraid of their privileges. But during the war the situation was especially bad for free African Americans, for the crisis brought them under close scrutiny. The majority concentrated simply on surviving; indeed, black independent farmers and artisans persevered despite white suspicions.

Some Southern states did not allow antebellum free blacks to enter military service at all, and though early in the war some permitted "colored men" to muster into local or state militia units, no Southern state allowed African Americans to serve as regular soldiers. Yet some light-skinned free blacks became "honorary white men" and actually enlisted and fought for the Confederacy. Free blacks in cities like New Orleans, Mobile, Savannah, Richmond, and Charleston joined such services as fire companies or were impressed into labor battalions (as were the slaves) to dig ditches and perform other manual labor. Their families, however, generally were not eligible for even the meager aid furnished to whites by state and local governments.

The war changed the nature of race relations, and even slavery itself changed. As white men left communities to go off with the army, the racial balance of power shifted dramatically in rural areas and on plantations. Fear of slave insurrections pervaded white Confederate society, although in many areas slaves were able to negotiate more freedom and autonomy for themselves and their families as the war continued.

The extent of the changed nature of race relations and slavery can be seen in the last desperate acts of Jefferson Davis. He offered to emancipate slaves in order to obtain recognition and aid from France and England. With the support of Robert E. Lee, Davis also persuaded Congress to arm slaves as Confederate soldiers. Ultimately, of course, the Civil War ended slavery, which constituted the greatest change in Southern society.

Gender Roles in the South

The antebellum South was a society founded upon patriarchy, hierarchy, and tradition. Rich and poor shared these values. A man was patriarch of his home, his family, and his slaves if he had any, and this might be complemented by his dominant position in the local community, the county, the state, or the nation. Patriarchy was pervasive throughout Southern society from the smallest unit, the family, to the largest, the nation. Male domination was cemented by tradition and most of all by community, by familial and organic bonds between rich and poor whites, all knitted together by the racial fears of the consequences of white disunity.

Patriarchy was by definition reciprocal: white men enjoyed the privileges of domination, but they also had the duty to protect slaves, wives, children, kin, and community. Thus the Civil War was about the defense of all that was dear—family, home town, plantation, community, and society.

The role of white women in Southern society cut across class lines. Whether charwoman or chatelaine, the woman was first of all mother, homemaker, and partner in the family economy. Women of all social classes usually bore many children. When a woman was not confined to bed in pregnancy or childbirth, she was responsible for all domestic chores. Of course, her social standing dictated her day-to-day routines. Most women were active partners in the running of plantation, farm, or business. They were administrators and supervisors of complex and busy households. Occasionally a woman was able to show business ability in a man's world, and there are success stories of women paying off their husband's debts and bringing their family through tough financial times.

Prior to the Civil War, white women had no official role in Southern society outside of the family. Within church structures, for instance, they held no leadership positions; they were, however, a powerful force in ensuring the participation of their families, both immediate and extended. Except for church functions, quilting parties, and the like, however, women had few opportunities to gather in rural antebellum society.

This changed during the life of the Confederacy. Whereas white women had expected that in return for wifely devotion and subservience they would receive from the men protection for their families, now they had to fend for themselves, trying to obtain food and supplies and making family decisions. Slaveholding women were fortunate in that they still had slaves for manual labor, but there was now the additional responsibility of controlling and disciplining them, a task that had always been men's work. Southern women had supported patriarchal society before the war, and they blamed the men now for the failure to defend the home against invaders or to provide necessities for the family. Even upper-class Southern women felt betrayed by their husbands, who had abandoned them to unfamiliar plantation duties. They felt that they had upheld their role in the patriarchal social system, but the men had not.

The war necessarily changed the role of women and therefore had a significant impact upon society itself. During the war, women met to sew uniforms, knit socks, pack supplies, and roll bandages. Soldiers' Relief Associations throughout the South included some on boards of directors. With so many men away at war, the number of women relative to the number of men increased, and so did their influence. They found that the exigencies of the war enabled them to make a more substantial contribution to family and community life than they had previously had the opportunity to make. Women ran their farms, businesses, and communities with increasing confidence as the war progressed.

In both North and South women formed a spate of aid associations to raise funds for their local militias. A lasting legacy of these societies was the continued church and community clubs such as the Woman's Christian Temperance Union, missionary societies, library associations, and other voluntary groups. The war increased women's interest in politics as well as their political acumen. At this time some white women envisioned a broader, more active position for themselves in social and political life. But though private diaries demonstrate that women often took pride in their newfound abilities and assertiveness, society as a whole expected women in the postbellum years to return to their old roles in the social order.

The teaching profession did not revert to the prewar situation, offering increased opportunity for women. During the Confederacy women's schools and seminaries were able to stay open, although by 1862 most colleges were closed. Nevertheless, some teaching positions remained, and as men went to war, educated women filled those vacancies. An ideology that the female teacher was a surrogate mother who eased the transition of the child from the home to the community developed and solidified during the war.

The Civil War also opened vocational opportunities in nursing, government agencies, and industry, as women took over traditional male jobs. Prior to the war, only young, unmarried women worked in Southern textile mills, but now adult women joined them, adding to the family income. Thus, to a certain extent, the Confederacy undermined patriarchy.

But after the war the patriarchal system rapidly returned, and most of the new vocational opportunities vanished. Only teaching remained, but the number of applications for teaching was much greater than the number of positions, and the pay was inadequate. The activities of Southern women focused on survival and delayed the reordering of gender roles that was occurring in the North.

Class in the South

Relations among the various classes in the South changed dramatically during the Civil War. Historians have tended to agree that underlying class frictions were kept in check in antebellum Southern society, but that those frictions surfaced when subjected to the pressures of the war. Scholars have never accepted the popular myth of an easy-to-categorize "solid" South. Its society was complex and varied with the region. For the most part, the culture was not dictated by planters, nor was it determined by harmonious communities of yeomen. Unlike New England settlements, Southern locales never had an overarching ideology that defined society. The meaning of each community developed from its everyday behavior, social rituals, and shared experiences. Nevertheless, Southern society exhibited some intriguing similarities among rich and poor whites, free African Americans and slaves. Without exception, the society revered the family, maintaining kinship networks and promoting religious beliefs that glorified domestic life. Both rich and poor connected family values with a sense of personal and regional honor.

Social relationships shaped Southern culture by ordered divisions of domination and subordination: white over black, male over female, wealthy over poor, respected lineage over obscure ancestry, women perceived as "virtuous" over those perceived as "loose," education over illiteracy, age over youth. All whites—men and women—had a societal claim for respect from blacks and from each other. Although wealthy men were at the top of the social ladder, they were expected not to look down on a poorer white man but to play a friendly, paternalistic role. The South's famed diarist Mary Boykin Chesnut provides a delightful vignette of Southern aristocrats paying homage to a muddied, barefoot well-digger.

Face-to-face interactions formed the style of Southern exchange. The poor, the yeoman middle class, and the rich were tied to one another in a multifaceted social network of obligations, trade, and exchanges of labor and services. In agrarian areas people knew and trusted one another; one's word was one's bond. Although in the very few Southern cities, one could find segregation by ethnicity and wealth, in rural towns and the country, whites were not segregated by occupation or income. The landless lived next door to landowning elites and had reciprocal community obligations. The poor often worked for the rich, and small farmers frequently depended upon the help of large planters in getting cotton ginned and to market. Across class lines, families and neighbors got together for cornshuckings, birthday parties, fairs, fish fries, revivals, and prayer meetings. Funerals also brought the community together. Whether in a grand mansion, a log house, or a slave cabin, kin, friends, neighbors, and church members supported one another in times of grief and reinforced the bonds of society.

Kinship ties influenced all segments of the society. Not only did relatives help one another, but people kept close track of each other even when separated by considerable distances, as when family members or acquaintances moved away. Mississippians subscribed to the newspaper of the community from which they had migrated, and letters and visits reinforced ties. Migration patterns often reflected kinship and community. The concept of community extending beyond geographical boundaries was not limited to any one class.

Since nearly everyone farmed, rich and poor alike shared similar concerns about the weather, crop prices, and so on. Neighbors belonged to the same kin networks and the same churches. Because so much of the power in the South was exercised on the plantation, governmental power and social services were limited; the great planters were generally content to let their poorer neighbors live their own lives and manage their own economic and political affairs. The overwhelmingly agricultural plantation South fostered an extremely decentralized system. Thus, instead of the conflicting economic and social interests that developed in Northern society, most social conflict in the South occurred in terms of personal ambitions and personality.

White Southerners' ideas of liberty, linked closely to race and slavery, also diluted class conflict in the South. Freedom depended on personal independence and the wherewithal to take care of one's family. Tragically, even nonslaveholding whites believed that freedom depended on the subjugation of African Americans, and almost all whites were united in racism toward blacks. In 1848 John C. Calhoun characterized the lack of class conflict this way: "With us the two great divisions of society are not the rich and the poor, but white and black; and all the former, the poor as well as the rich, belong to the upper class, and are respected and treated as equals." Slavery was a powerful symbol of degradation, which white yeomen contrasted with their own independence. A society where no one could voice disapproval of slavery demanded community consensus.

Poor Whites. Although groups were not precisely demarcated, white social classes in Confederate society fell into roughly three categories with varying dimensions within each. The line between the poor and the yeomen, for instance, was never very distinct. The poor were landless in an agrarian society that honored landowners. Landless whites accounted for between 25 and 40 percent of the white population. The dividing line between destitution and "respectable" poverty was drawn by different people at different levels. Although some members of white Southern society prejudicially conceived of the white poor as 'ignorant and lazy,' the poor actually shared the values of the larger white society. Some white poor were related to yeomen, and a few to the wealthy. Some actually moved up the social ladder into the ranks of the more prosperous, and some of the more affluent slid from prosperity into the ranks of the poor.

The poor could work as laborers on someone else's farm or could be overseers of someone else's slaves. A small Southern proletariat worked in the few urban areas. Some were employed in antebellum textile mills and lived in segregated mill villages. Fathers usually received all the wages that wives and children made working at the mill. Mill families, like the country people from whom they came, looked to religion as a way of life. As the Civil War progressed, both urban areas and the size of the working class grew. Workers toiled as railroad laborers, sawmill hands, or factory operatives.

Among the very poorest were the inhabitants of poorhouses. These included the blind, deformed, afflicted, epileptic, crippled, and mentally disabled. Southern society did not do much for these people, but they were housed and fed.

The Middle Class and Yeomen. "Middle class" usually connotes merchants and professionals or the bourgeoisie in urban areas. Confederate society had an urban middle class, but it was small. While Northern society industrialized, most people in the South continued to farm. In 1860, less than 10 percent of Southerners lived in urban areas, compared to 25 percent of Northerners. Although within the agrarian South were some commercial-mercantile centers such as Charleston and Richmond, the white labor force remained 80 percent agricultural in the first half of the 1800s. (In the North the labor force changed from 70 percent agricultural to 40 percent.) The South had 15,000 factories with 0.1 million industrial workers. Without cities, Southern society lacked a dynamic urban middle class. The South had no need for the middle-class insurance salesmen, financial agents, and corporate executives whom the North needed for industrialization. The South required only cotton factors to represent the interests of the slaveholding planters.

Although most professional opportunities were in short supply in the agrarian South, attorneys abounded. The legal profession was one of those avenues in the three to four decades preceding the Civil War that white Southern men used for upward mobility. In 1824, noted South Carolinian William Preston had explained, "The object of a Southern man's life is politics and to this end we all practice law."

Doctors also pursued their profession as a springboard into the elite.

The middle class also included schoolteachers and preachers. The latter expanded their roles in Confederate society. Using moral positions to support "the cause," the clergy became vitally important in forging a nationalistic perspective in the Confederacy. At this time Southern preachers also became more professionalized.

For the most part, the middle class was not part of an urban class, but consisted of yeoman farmers. Historian Frank Owsley has called the yeomen the plain folk of the South. Unlike the large planters, nonslaveholding yeomen were more interested in self-sufficiency than in profit. They were staunch believers in family honor, which included patriotism and religion; they tended to be more evangelical than the elite. In contrast to historical stereotypes, the Southern yeoman considered hard work a point of honor. Yeomen were for the most part nonslaveholders. Yet slavery permitted the yeomen a certain degree of independence, as each white male presided over his household and farm.

The Civil War had a major impact on the development of the middle class. As Southern industry expanded to meet the demand for war goods and city populations swelled, business responded. A need for housing stimulated construction, and companies earned huge profits in textiles and the iron industry. Thus, the formation of the Confederacy and the war encouraged the growth of an urban middle class.

The Elite. Ultimately, success in Confederate society meant membership in the landholding elite with wealth invested in slaves. Some have argued that slavery made possible an aristocracy that dominated society and its values and condemned the South to backwardness. The elite is as difficult to define in Confederate society as it is today. It was a continuum rather than a category, and one felt rather than articulated its meaning. It was a recruited aristocracy, and its status was based more on wealth than on kinship and breeding, although the latter two factors played a role. It was not a unified community, but comprised varying economic levels and old- and new-rich factions. Its ranks included planters and those who had worked themselves up from the professions: attorneys, doctors, newspaper editors, political officeholders. Patriciate clans of interlocking kin networks formed political alliances, and the elite controlled newspapers. Military service was another route into the elite, and when war broke out, the ambitious rushed to join the army and take advantage of the opportunity for glory and advancement.

Owners of large slaveholdings composed a unique class that was reared to command and manage large agricultural enterprises. They were inculcated from birth with notions of honor, duty, manliness, and paternalism; duels were part of their way of life.

Social Mobility. Although upward mobility was possible in antebellum society, it was more difficult to become a great planter in the South than to become a great merchant in the North. In the South, one needed both land and slaves. By the time of the American Revolution, only a tenth of Virginia's great planters were self-made men, whereas a third of all Boston merchants were self-made, and that increased to 60 or 70 percent after the Revolution. The South's society was much more unequal than the North's. In the rural South the population was never dense enough or the economy complex enough to require innovative leadership. Democratic forms or institutions might be introduced into government, but community leaders continued to come from slaveholding classes.

Education was a means of social advancement, but in the rural South, where reliable literate workers were rarely in demand, public education was a low priority. The planter elite hired private tutors for their own children and enrolled them in the best academies and colleges (some in the North). Wealthy sons and daughters continued their private education throughout the Civil War. The elite, however, either ignored the campaigns of poorer whites for public schools or actively opposed them, fearing that education would only promote new yearnings for upward mobility and blur the distinction between themselves and the masses. In the South, about 58 percent of the population was literate. Among whites and free blacks, the figure was 83 percent; among slaves, about 10 percent.

Social mobility was not easy in antebellum society, but it was possible. Free blacks could not move up or down the social ladder in the larger community, but they could within their own communities.

Class Conflict during the War

Why class tensions did not convulse antebellum white society is a subject of much historiographical debate. Although the economy and the social structure helped mute class conflict, discrepancies in wealth among whites pointed to the existence of class interests. The conduct of the Civil War brought these interests to the fore.

Even within the white consensus, class conflicts had occasionally occurred, however, and antagonisms erupted during political campaigns. Yeomen tended to be suspicious of people who did not work by the sweat of their brow, lawyers in particular. The antebellum temperance movement focused on the habits of the poor. The middle class and yeomen resented the fact that education was a prerogative of the rich.

Yet with the first call to support a war for Southern independence, white people interpreted the meaning of the conflict from the perspective of their own families, friends, and local society. For most, the war was being fought not simply to secure slavery or protect the planters' way of life;

it was a matter of honor—a fight to protect community values. Initially, many white Southerners saw the Civil War as a test of manhood; a high percentage of young men from the professions enlisted, as did yeomen who had no slaves and little or no wealth. All, however, had a stake in the community and went to war to preserve it. Men who led in the local community were likely to lead on the battlefield, too; they were considered the natural leaders. Thus, the war initially strengthened society's bonds among Confederate men.

In a society founded upon the notion of patriarchy, the absence of large numbers of men created a vacuum of power that would prove problematic. Local communities complained about the scarcity of doctors and, even more, about the lack of skilled craftsmen, such as blacksmiths, tanners, wheelwrights, and carpenters. Food shortages developed quickly, with men not home to plant crops.

At first, the society responded in traditional ways to the needs of families whose menfolk were away at the front. As in the past, kin helped kin in times of want, and the richer helped the poorer. Slaveholding families who retained their labor force of slaves could afford to be generous. But gradually the Confederacy put new demands upon richer citizens. Taxes were increased, slaves were impressed into government service, and the administration sequestered planters' cotton. Many of the rich could no longer provide for the community as they had before, and other wealthy families chose not to.

This breakdown of noblesse oblige led to increasing resentment between classes. Elite women resented queuing in food lines alongside poorer women and tired of the constant stream to their homes of beggars whom they could no longer help. The problem had more serious repercussions for the yeoman class. Poverty became a reality for many for the first time. Yeomen lost their self-sufficiency and with it their social autonomy. They blamed the war, the Confederate government, and, increasingly, their richer neighbors.

Yeomen noticed how easily the rich got exemptions from fighting or acquired safe army jobs behind the lines. Planters justified their exemptions in patriotic terms, proclaiming the importance of aiding the Southern economy. But many of them were growing cotton, not food, and to yeomen and poor whites it appeared that the elite were reneging on their responsibilities of leadership. In turn, these poorer men questioned their previous deference to the elite and began to doubt their reasons for fighting.

Class conflict exploded when the Confederate government failed to provide adequate relief for its citizens and thus to retain their support when it was needed most. For the common people the key element in their discontent was increased economic hardship. Soldiers' income was inadequate, and often they were not paid for months on end. Although prices were initially lowered, they soon became exorbitant. Compounding the difficulties for the South were its comparatively few resources, the fact that most of the fighting took place on its soil, and the increasing effectiveness of the Union blockade. Almost from the beginning there were shortages of foodstuffs, clothing, footwear, medicines, and other necessary items. People resorted to a barter system rather than using the inflated currency. After the destruction of its railroads, the Confederacy increasingly was unable to distribute farm products. The situation was hardest on urban dwellers and the yeomen but, typically, the poorest suffered the worst.

Two hundred fifty thousand Southern refugees compounded the dislocations. Refugees formed a cross-section of society with members of the elite joining the migrations. Most of the aristocrats resented hobnobbing with what they considered to be their social inferiors, and yeoman hosts resented these snobbish guests. Most refugees fled to cities, and Richmond, for one, doubled in size the first year of the Confederacy and, during the remainder of the war, tripled in population. This enormous movement of people necessarily shook society. The flow of refugees produced a new mix of people, altering local societies and making them more cosmopolitan.

But in the midst of want, not everyone suffered. Blockade runners accumulated huge personal fortunes and sometimes even became heroes. Yet, at a time when people were desperate for food, clothes, guns, and ammunition, blockade runners brought in cargoes of needles and pins, buttons and bows. Graft, corruption, and extortion were common in both the North and the South. Some amassed fortunes through speculation, particularly in land. A very few wealthy planters even made money during the war by investing in Northern railroads and other enterprises. Shortages encouraged hoarding and greed. On an individual level, blockade runners, speculators, and merchants were depicted as pariahs and often condemned as outsiders. Yet there was an ambivalent attitude toward such individuals, and many ordinary people were pleased to associate with them as they never would have in the stable prewar social order.

Popular discontent was evident as early as 1861. From Georgia a citizen wrote an open letter:

> Is it right that the poor man should be taxed for the support of the war, when the war was brought about on the slave question, and the slave at home accumulating for the benefit of this master, and the poor man's farm left uncultivated, and a chance for his wife to be a widow, and his children orphans?

The Twenty-Slave Law passed in October 1862 ripped the fabric of white Confederate society. This law allowed the exemption from military service of one white man for every twenty slaves. The law affected only a small number of people, but it was a powerful symbol for the common folk that the war benefited the rich at the expense of the poor. The Twenty-Slave Law was enacted in response to the perceived dangers of slave insurrection in the light of Lincoln's Emancipation Proclamation, but common soldiers and their families saw only that "we poor soldiers . . . are fighting for the 'rich man's negro.' " Southern men resisted conscription at rates that increased dramatically until by 1865 desertion had become epidemic. A hundred thousand Confederates—one out of seven who were inducted into the army—went AWOL at one time or another.

When the war came home to society, some Confederates were more dedicated than others. In local communities, where the war caused a lower standard of living for all, folks noticed who sacrificed the most. Some of the wealthy continued to live well; for them, sacrifice meant giving up some luxuries. For yeomen and the poor, sacrifice meant doing without necessities, and they were galled by the disparity.

The war also intensified class conflict by reserving certain special perquisites for members of the planter class. In North and South huge resentment resulted when the wealthy used the legal and political processes to their own advantage. Yeomen believed conscription was unfair, a burden that fell most heavily on nonslaveholders since they had to work their own farms without the help of slaves. The rich man's ability to hire a paid substitute if he was drafted aroused great popular discontent. Upper-class women who needed jobs used their connections to obtain positions as scribes and clerks in the Confederate government. Taxes to support the war were not equitable, and initially slaves, although considered property, were not taxed.

Inflation and shortages hit the poor much harder than planters, but measures to fight inflation and price gouging were unsuccessful. Provisions to take care of the wives of soldiers were not adequate. When the noblesse oblige of the planter class failed to support them, yeoman women begged for government relief. Desperate letters to the Confederate government spoke of hunger, high prices, and shortages. By mid-1862, survival outranked patriotism as a motivating factor in the South. Some women took revolutionary action and broke into stores demanding food at fair prices in bread riots in Richmond, Augusta, and other cities.

In the midst of hard times, any revelry, a banquet, or the purchase of a fashionable Parisian gown to lift upper-class spirits bordered on treason from the yeoman perspective. On April 4, 1865, as the Confederacy neared its final days, Robert Collins, the son of a wealthy Mississippi cotton planter, married Kate Watts, daughter of the governor of Alabama. Matching bay horses with silver-plated harnesses carried the newlyweds in a luxurious carriage. The bride wore a satin gown that had been brought through the blockade at the expense of food, clothing, weapons, or medicine—this at a time when ordinary Alabamians were desperate. Thousands faced starvation, and near-anarchy reigned. Class antagonism reached a point where large numbers of Southern women came subtly or overtly to war against the war and encouraged their menfolk to desert.

In Alabama internecine warfare broke out between conscription enforcers and people resisting conscription. In parts of Mississippi chaos prevailed. Border areas like Arkansas witnessed merciless bushwhacking and repeated revenge and retaliation. Social order completely collapsed in some areas; in others order was strained but not broken. Late in the war Northern bummers, Union raiders, and Confederate deserters alike roamed the countryside for food, sometimes just destroying wantonly.

A breakdown of civil order followed class lines in Washington County, North Carolina, and social unity declined rapidly as yeoman farmers disagreed with the way planters led recruitment and draft efforts. In June 1862, yeomen with Unionist sympathies combined with tenant farmers and white laborers to confiscate the property of planters who had moved up-country to avoid the Union invasion of the region. Guerrilla war ensued when planters tried to reassert their antebellum level of control. In this area of North Carolina the planter aristocracy had never managed to dominate in either numbers or influence because of geographic and climatic factors that inhibited large-scale plantation farming, and yeoman influence had always remained strong. Now these two groups, who had been united since the 1832 nullification crisis, bitterly split.

In other border states an internal war also threatened to break Confederate control. Dominated by yeoman farmers and poor whites with Union sympathies, guerrilla groups, such as the Heroes of America, were organized. In Piedmont North Carolina, several counties closed their borders against Confederate recruiting agents. Farmers barricaded themselves into hollows in the mountains. Tennessee, Arkansas, and Alabama had organized guerrilla bands. Even the Deep South suffered a crisis of loyalty. Many Southern communities contained disaffected yeoman families who hid male relatives by day and fed and comforted them by night. In what some scholars have interpreted as episodes of class warfare among whites, some areas of the South broke out in guerrilla fighting. One Confederate judge in South Carolina confessed his joy when the Union army of occupation arrived, thereby ending "the civil war" between Confederate deserters and South Carolina militia.

Open Questions about the Confederacy

How much the Confederacy altered Southern society remains unanswered but speaks to gender, class, and race, as well as to both the Old and the New South. Alone among slaveholders of the world, Southern planters thought their system was worth fighting a war. Although only a small minority of the white population was composed of slaveholders, they were able to persuade ordinary Southerners that they had a stake in keeping black people in bondage. For that the majority paid a heavy price because they supplied most of the troops who died for the Confederacy, and their families bore most of the suffering.

Scholars have yet to establish conclusively the specifics on who sacrificed what, who stayed the entire four years, who fought, who deserted, who managed through political connections to serve in the relatively safe state home guards. Scholars still need to separate out those things that persevered, such as family and landownership, and those that changed, such as black and white Southerners' worldviews. If one sees the New South as *different* from the Old in terms of leadership, ideals, and community, Confederate society may be considered the start of this process of change. If, however, one stresses the *continuity* between the Old South and the New, Confederate society appears an aberration, which is the way it probably seemed to the majority of Southerners at the time. The answer will come as more studies of Confederate society focus on long-term continuity and change. Nevertheless, most scholars would agree that the Civil War certainly unleashed pent-up white class conflict in Southern society and that these tensions remained in postbellum society.

[*See also* African Americans in the Confederacy; Civil War, *articles on* Causes of the War, Causes of Defeat, *and* Losses and Numbers; Class Conflict; Community Life; Desertion; Education; Family Life; Foreigners; Honor; Indians; Nationalism; Peace Movements; Plain Folk; Planters; Popular Culture; Population; Poverty; Religion; Slavery; Soldiers' Aid Societies; Urbanization; Women.]

BIBLIOGRAPHY

Ash, Stephen A. *Middle Tennessee Society Transformed, 1860–1870: War and Peace in the Upper South.* Baton Rouge, La., 1988.

Auman, William Thomas. "Neighbor against Neighbor: The Inner Civil War in the Central Counties of Confederate North Carolina." Ph.D. diss., University of North Carolina, 1988.

Burton, Orville Vernon. *In My Father's House Are Many Mansions: Family and Community in Edgefield, South Carolina.* Chapel Hill, N.C., 1985.

Campbell, Randolph B. *A Southern Community in Crisis: Harrison County, Texas, 1850–1880.* Austin, Tex., 1983.

Durrill, Wayne K. *War of Another Kind: A Southern Community in the Great Rebellion.* New York, 1990.

Escott, Paul D. *Many Excellent People: Power and Privilege in North Carolina, 1850–1900.* Chapel Hill, N.C., 1985.

Harris, J. William. *Plain Folk and Gentry in a Slave Society: White Liberty and Black Slavery in Augusta's Hinterlands.* Middletown, Conn., 1985.

Kenzer, Robert C. *Kinship and Neighborhood in a Southern Community: Orange County North Carolina, 1849–1881.* Knoxville, Tenn., 1987.

Krug, Donna Rebecca D. "The Folks Back Home: The Confederate Homefront during the Civil War." Ph.D. diss., University of California, Irvine, 1990.

Massey, Mary Elizabeth. *Refugee Life in the Confederacy.* Baton Rouge, La., 1964.

Palaudan, Philip Shaw. *Victims: A True Story of the Civil War.* Knoxville, Tenn., 1981.

Rable, George C. *Civil Wars: Women and the Crisis of Southern Nationalism.* Urbana, Ill., 1989.

Ramsdell, Charles W. *Behind the Lines in the Southern Confederacy.* Baton Rouge, La., 1944.

Siegel, Frederick F. *The Roots of Southern Distinctiveness: Tobacco and Society in Danville, Virginia, 1780–1865.* Chapel Hill, N.C., 1987.

Wiley, Bell I. *The Plain People of the Confederacy.* Baton Rouge, La., 1944.

ORVILLE VERNON BURTON

SOCIETY OF FRIENDS. At the outbreak of the Civil War, the once-thriving Society of Friends (Quakers) in the South had shrunk to fewer than two thousand members. Concentrated in North Carolina with smaller communities in Virginia, they viewed with alarm the inauguration of hostilities. Unionist, antislavery, and pacifist, Southern Friends were vulnerable in the midst of a war of secession fought in part to preserve slavery.

Around the time of the American Revolution, Quakers had made slaveholding a cause of disownment (expulsion from formal membership but not from the Quaker community) and had repeatedly petitioned the state for its abolition, partly because it frustrated the development of Southern industry. Prevented by state law from freeing their slaves, North Carolina Friends turned title to them over to their yearly meeting (statewide organization) until they could be taken to free territory. After trying to resettle them in Haiti, Africa, and Pennsylvania, the Carolina and Georgia Quakers (working through the North Carolina Manumission Society) took small groups to Ohio and Indiana, where they themselves were moving. The secrecy required to avoid white interference led some Southern Friends, including members of the Coffin family, into the Underground Railroad. Most Quakers deplored the emotional language and violent actions of radical abolitionism.

Although legally exempt from military service in North Carolina, Quakers were often harassed by local Confederate militia. Men were impressed and tortured when they refused to fight, while their families were left to fend for themselves. Some conscripts escaped and went north; others were sent to Southern prison camps. Nereus Mendenhall, the only teacher remaining at the Quaker's New Garden Boarding School in Guilford County, successfully resisted efforts to conscript him and continued to teach throughout the war. A few Southern Friends even fought in the Union army without being disowned.

When destitute Southern Quakers arrived in Baltimore seeking material aid and passage west, the Baltimore Association to Advise and Assist Friends in the Southern

States was established. Association president Francis T. King secured Abraham Lincoln's permission to visit North Carolina in 1864 and 1865. At war's end, the association began channeling funds for relief and development from Northern and British Friends to Southern Quaker communities. It established a statewide school system for Quaker children (Philadelphia Friends oversaw the establishment of schools for freedmen), built a model farm at Springfield (Guilford County), upgraded the boarding school at New Garden to high school and then college level (Guilford College), and used evangelism to increase membership.

Although generally Republican, postwar Southern Quakers deplored aspects of Reconstruction and were ambivalent about the role of blacks in Southern society, including their own religious society. They did not, however, participate in the culture of the Lost Cause. Fernando Cartland's *Southern Heroes* (1895) praised Southern Friends for their witness despite persecution by secessionists. Many Quakers blamed Southern clergymen and Northern abolitionists for having stirred up the sentiment that led to war.

BIBLIOGRAPHY

Cartland, Fernando G. *Southern Heroes; or, The Friends in War Time.* Cambridge, Mass., 1895.

Hilty, Hiram H. *Toward Freedom for All: North Carolina Quakers and Slavery.* Richmond, Ind., 1984.

Hinshaw, Seth B. *The Carolina Quaker Experience, 1665–1985: An Interpretation.* Greensboro, N.C., 1984.

Hinshaw, Seth B. *Mary Barker Hinshaw, Quaker: A Story of Carolina Friends in the Civil War Times.* Richmond, Ind., and Greensboro, N.C., 1982.

Weeks, Stephen B. *Southern Quakers and Slavery: A Study in Institutional History.* Baltimore, 1896.

DAMON D. HICKEY

SOLDIERS. Ordinary men made the Civil War an extraordinary struggle. That war from first to last was a conflict of the plain people. Statesmen and diplomats did their best to plot the struggle; generals did their best to conduct its campaigns; yet the real load of serving, fighting, suffering, and dying was borne by the soldiers in the ranks. Historian Bell I. Wiley summarized them by observing:

> For the most part they were earthy people, in whose natures the fear of God was rivaled by the attraction of the world, the flesh, and the Devil. Among those who donned the uniform, evil, or at least that which was adjudged evil by Americans of a century ago, flourished more freely than righteousness.

Like their Union counterparts, Confederates were volunteer soldiers—civilians in arms who, in many ways, never fully adapted to military life. Fighting they did, to a heroic degree; but at the same time Johnny Rebs tended to be independent, proud, and happy-go-lucky fellows who scoffed at discipline, criticized (often with justification) all facets of army life, fended for themselves much of the time, and displayed the full gauntlet of diversity inherent in the lower classes from which the predominant majority of them sprung.

Southern males became soldiers because they had been caught up in the heated atmosphere and angry words of the day, or they had been moved by fiery oratory, inspiring music, a patriotic call to arms, or the sight of a flag waving defiantly. Products of an unsophisticated age, they went off to combat with dreamy enthusiasm and youthful innocence. The greatest anxiety for many of them was that peace would come before they could get a shot at the enemy or win their "red badge of courage" (a battle wound).

Physical examinations of recruits in the early stages of the war were a sham. The basic if not sole requirement of a potential soldier was whether he possessed all four limbs and most of his sensory organs. A man's performing adequately in any civilian job was proof to most recruiting agents that he was fit for military service. Ease of enlistments and the poor health of many volunteers accepted into the armies were among the primary reasons for the high incidence of sickness and disability among the first waves of men who answered the Confederacy's call.

Following enlistment and muster into an official unit, recruits underwent about two weeks of training at a rendezvous camp. There they faced the awkward process of learning the rudiments of camp life, drill, marches, and discipline. The climax of this basic training period usually came when a delegation—dominated largely by ladies—bestowed an ornate flag upon the new regiment. An officer would accept the flag and pledge in glowing terms that his soldiers would never disgrace the sacred banner.

Foul-ups occasionally turned this solemn ceremony into a comedy. The ladies of Fayetteville, North Carolina, presented a lovingly sewn flag to the Forty-third North Carolina. None of them was willing to make the presentation speech, so they invited a local orator of some reputation to do the honors. The man, quite nervous at his starring role, fortified himself with liquor just before the ceremony. He somehow stumbled through the address; then, in a stupor, he proceeded to give the same speech again. At the end the gentleman sat down and cried—to the mortification of the ladies and the amusement of the soldiers.

The Men's Characteristics. Foreign-born elements composed only 5 percent of the Confederate fighting force since the plantation-dominated antebellum South did not attract immigrants in great numbers. Johnny Rebs were a relatively homogeneous group. A majority of them were rural, Protestant, and single. Less than a fourth of the Southern soldiers possessed slaves or were from slaveholding families.

Four of every five Confederates were between eighteen

and thirty years old, but the age spectrum was wide. Charles C. Hay joined an Alabama regiment at the age of eleven. Texas soldier John M. Sloan lost a leg in battle at thirteen. Fifteen-year-old John Roberts of Tennessee fought in the two-day struggle at Shiloh. Roberts's colonel reported that the lad was twice struck by spent bullets and had his musket blown from his hands, but that he continued to display throughout the contest "the coolness and courage of a veteran." At the same time, a Virginia artilleryman recalled seeing a half-dozen soldiers "over sixty years who volunteered, and served in the ranks, during the war." David Scantlon was almost fifty-two when he became "drummer boy" of the Fourth Virginia. The chaplain of another regiment kept a protective eye on his son, a lieutenant in the unit. In 1862 a substitute named E. Pollard joined a North Carolina detachment. Although he is listed as sixty-two, indications exist that Pollard was over seventy years of age.

Many of the Southern rank and file were men of excellent education, refined and well-read. Outnumbering them at the opposite end, however, were soldiers who were at best semiliterate. Typical of this class was a Tarheel boy who stated in a June 1862 letter: "Mother when you wright to me get somebody to wright that can wright a Plain hand. . . . I cold not read your letter to make sence of it it [was] wrote so bad. I have lurnd to do my one wrading and writing and it is a grate help to me."

Confederates were not as diverse in occupation as Federal troops. Still, more than 100 different occupations are listed on Southern muster rolls. A case in point was the Nineteenth Virginia. Of its original 749 members, 302 were farmers, 80 were laborers, and 56 were machinists. Among the remainder were 10 lawyers, 14 teachers, 24 students, 3 blacksmiths, 2 artists, a distiller, a well-digger, a dentist, and 4 men who classified themselves as "Gentleman."

The advent of Confederate conscription in 1862 brought a different class of men into the army. Volunteers tended to view them, and treat them, with open contempt. "Conscripts" were so often suspect in loyalty and behavior that officers entrusted with getting the draftees to the armies sometimes transported them as if they were prisoners of war. When a group of conscripted recruits arrived at the Army of Northern Virginia in 1864, a veteran snorted: "Some of them looked like they had been resurrected from the grave, after laying therein for twenty years or more."

Supplies. Official manuals described the gray Confederate uniform, but few soldiers had one. What they wore when they left home composed their military dress. A number of soldiers learned to take captured Federal blue uniforms and dye them in a solution of walnut hulls and lye. The result were coats and trousers of a beige color that gave rise to the nickname "Butternuts" for Confederate troops. For those unable to acquire any kind of military attire, raggedness was their lot. Some men complained; others made light of their condition. A Texan wrote from the trenches of Atlanta in 1864: "In this army one hole in the seat of the breeches indicates a captain, two holes a lieutenant and the seat of the pants all out indicates that the individual is a private."

Although Johnny Rebs were supposed to receive eleven dollars monthly, appearances in camp by paymasters were rare. Making matters worse was the galloping inflation in the wartime South, which rendered money of steadily decreasing value. By 1863, for instance, it required six months' pay just to purchase a pair of boots.

The aspect of camp life that produced the most condemnation by soldiers were army rations. One might expect an agricultural South to have had an abundance of foodstuffs, but its major antebellum crops were cotton and tobacco. Even though the Confederacy did produce large amounts of food crops, transportational breakdowns, hoarding, and black marketeering kept much of it from reaching the front. As a result, hunger was a constant companion of the armies. Many men in gray, especially in the last half of the war, went for days without food save for a few grains of corn picked up from the places where the horses fed, stolen apples and peaches, sassafras roots, and the like.

When available, meat and bread were the standard fare of

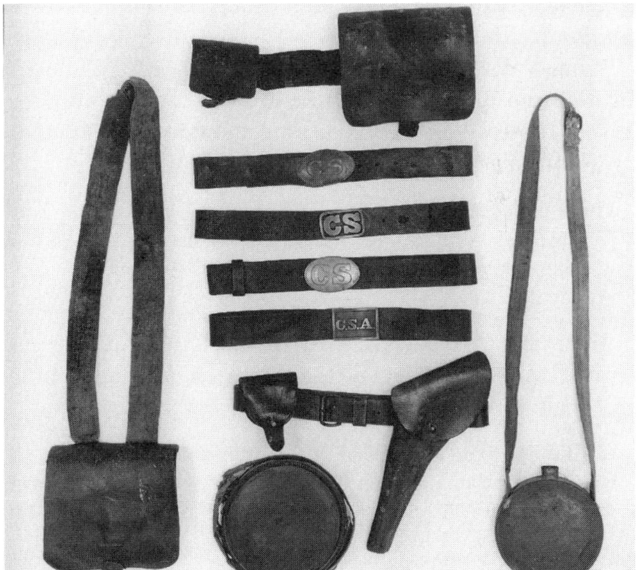

ACCOUTREMENTS. Common items carried or worn by Confederate soldiers during the Civil War. Pictured at left is a cartridge box with a canvas sling. At center, from top to bottom, are a cartridge box and cap box on a waist belt; four various waist belts with brass plates; a revolver holster and cap box on a waist belt; and a wooden drum canteen with a canvas strap. At right is a tin drum canteen with a canvas strap. REVOLVER HOLSTER AND CAP BOX ON WAIST BELT COURTESY OF RUSS A. PRITCHARD; ALL OTHER ITEMS COURTESY OF BENJAMIN P. MICHEL

Southern troops. Quality left a great deal to be desired. Army beef was either fresh or salt-pickled. If chewable, the fresh meat was often eaten raw because it seemed to taste just as good that way as cooked. Preserved meat—"salted horse," the troops called it—was often so tough that a meal of it produced sore teeth. The beef issued to the Confederacy's western army in the war's first year was petrified to the extent that a Louisiana officer threatened to requisition files so that his men could hone their teeth before eating. Later in the war an Alabama soldier complained of his beef being "too old for the conscript law," and a Georgia compatriot described the cows assigned to his regiment for beef as so feeble that "it takes two hands to hold up one beef to shoot it."

Rations became progressively worse as the war continued. From the Petersburg trenches early in 1865 a South Carolinian noted: "We get corn bread now in place of wheat bread. . . . It looks like a pile of cow dung Baked in the sun. I could nock down a cow with a pone of it."

Homesickness and Loneliness. Most men in the Confederate armies were away from home for the first time in their lives. The novelty of army life was short-lived. In its place came homesickness and an overpowering desire to be with loved ones. The plain folk of that era had deep devotion to home and family. Long absence in service produced more anguish than any other aspect of the war. Homesickness crippled morale and filled army hospitals with illnesses baffling to the surgeons.

"I am almost down with histericks to hear from home," an Alabama infantryman wrote in 1863, and his feelings echoed those of thousands of Confederates. A member of the Sixth Mississippi once confided to his wife:

> I have been studying about you and the children all day. oh how I wish I was at home with you this day. it seems as if there is nothing else in this world would please me better than to be with my family.

A number of soldiers tried to mask their loneliness through teasing a loved one at home. In the spring of 1863 a Georgia private "reassured" his wife by stating:

> If I did not write and receive letters from you I believe that [I] would forgit that I was marrid. I don't feel much like a maryed man but I never furgit it sofar as to court enny other lady but if I should you must forgive me as I am so forgitful.

Far more prevalent in the lonely letters of soldiers were such sentiments as those expressed in a May 1863 letter from Alabama cavalryman John Cotton:

> I want to come home as bad as any body can . . . but I shant run away. . . . I dont want it throwed up to my children after I am dead and gone that I was a deserter. . . . I don't want to do anything if I no it will leave a stain on my posterity hereafter.

Accentuating the loneliness was a sentimentality both deep and characteristic of that age. The Civil War brought those two emotions together and created a degree of love not customarily found in the whirlpool that marks life in the late twentieth century. For Confederates in the field, romance became one of life's real treasures. The longer soldiers went without even a glimpse of a woman, the stronger became the yearning. A Virginia private once informed his cousin: "I have not seen a gal in so long a time that I would not know what to do with myself if I were to meet up with one, though I reckon I would learn before I left her."

In love letters, soldiers were temperate in language. Few references were made to the physical aspects of romance. The primary concern of the men in gray was to convey expressions of devotion and hope to receive many like sentiments in return. Quite often they used poetry to enhance their prose. The most frequently used couplets were: "When this you see remember me / Though many miles apart we be," and "My pen is poor my ink is pale / My love for you shall never fail." Georgia soldier William Stillwell wrote many verses to his wife. One closed with the expression: "When silence reigns o'er lawn or lea / Then dearest love I watch for thee."

Camp Life. Every Confederate with the ability to write had something to say about camp life. It was generally negative. A Louisiana soldier told his wife: "Dont never come here as long as you can ceep away, for you will smell hell here." A young Alabama recruit asked his brother to visit him in camp, but to bring a shotgun with him for his own protection.

Much about camp life made it the subject of widespread criticism. Oppressive, stifling heat and constant movements prevailed during the months of activity. With their winter quarters located in tents, drafty log huts, or makeshift shanties, the men spent the cold months trying merely to survive. Any army camp had an overbearing stench. A lack of knowledge about hygienic practices, plus inattention given to latrine procedures and garbage pits, created an always-unhealthy environment. In 1862 a Virginia soldier confided in his diary: "On rolling up my bed this morning I found I had been lying in—I won't say what—something that didn't smell like milk and peaches." The presence of swarms of insects was a natural by-product and additional unpleasantness.

Commanders sought to minimize the stagnation of camp life, and at the same time produce better soldiers, by keeping the men as busy as possible. This meant drill, drill, and more drill, particularly in the first months. Since many officers and men were starting out as complete novices, drill was often akin to the ignorant leading the uneducated. A Virginia recruit observed:

> Maneuvers of the most utterly impossible sort were taught to the men. Every amateur officer had his own system of tactics, and the effect of the incongruous teachings, when brought out in

battalion drill, closely resembled that of the music at Mr. Bob Sawyer's party, where each guest sang the chorus to the tune he knew best.

Green officers trying to give correct instructions while scores of men were attempting to maintain lines and proper cadence during these drills could be a nerve-wracking experience. One day a captain was marching his new company when it rapidly approached a fence. The captain suddenly could not think of the command to give. The closer the column got to the fence, the less his thinking processes functioned. Finally, he frantically called the men to a halt. "Gentlemen!" he then shouted. "We will now take a recess of ten minutes. And when you fall in, please re-form on the other side of the fence!"

The discipline of camp life was irritating to a great many. Disrespect for authority was the most prevalent offense committed by Civil War soldiers. Confederates who had joined the army were products of a new nation dedicated to the ideal that one white man was as good as another. When many of the officers showed themselves to be either as green as the men they were supposed to be leading or know-it-all martinets, troops in the ranks freely displayed or voiced their disgust.

Courts-martial were a daily part of camp life. Usually, insubordination involved verbal attacks. Writings by soldiers reveal such uncomplimentary references to officers as "a vain, stuck-up, illiterate ass," "whore-house pimp," "horse's ass," and the time-honored "son of a bitch." One Johnny Reb classified his colonel as "an ignoramus fit for nothing higher than the cultivation of corn." Similarly, a Florida soldier thought all of his superiors "not fit to tote guts to a Bear."

It was during the two-thirds or three-fourths of each year when Johnny Rebs were in camp that a constant search prevailed for diversions to overcome the tedium and monotony of army routine. Radio, movies, and television, of course, were technologies of the future. There were no army service agencies, post exchanges, lounges, libraries, or camp newspapers. Few entertainment groups visited the troops. Soldiers were left to themselves to provide for their own pastimes. Fortunately for them, their needs and tastes were simple.

The most popular occupation of soldiers was letter-writing. This was the only contact with a loved one back home. Further, the Civil War was the first time in the nation's history when so large a percentage of the male population was pulled away from farms, schools, factories, and shops. As soldiers, they were seeing new things and living an unusual life. They were in a strange world they wanted to share with family and friends, so they wrote letters—untold thousands of letters.

CONFEDERATE CAMP. At the Warrington Navy Yard, Pensacola, Florida, 1861. LIBRARY OF CONGRESS

Thoughts poured forth on paper with little attention to continuity or grammar. They described army life, marches, battles, the merits of commanding officers, and prospects for the future. Interspersed throughout the rambling epistles would be questions about conditions at home. Usually a soldier ran out of paper before he exhausted everything he wanted to write. Many Johnny Rebs developed a sensitivity to gossip or criticism emanating from the home front. In June 1864, a young Confederate responded to muttering from his neighbors about his lack of battle experience by writing to his wife: "The people there that speaks slack of me may kiss my ass. Mollie, excuse the vulgar language if you will."

More than American fighting men of any other time, troops of the 1860s were singing soldiers. Music, next to sending and receiving letters, was the most popular diversion for Johnny Rebs. The Civil War gave rise to more than two thousand new songs. Among the favorite camp tunes were "Home Sweet Home," "Dixie," "Annie Laurie," "Lorena," "Bonnie Blue Flag," "The Girl I Left Behind Me," "Her Bright Eyes Haunt Me Still," "Maryland, My Maryland," "When Johnny Comes Marching Home Again," and dozens of familiar hymns.

Cherished melodies were many, but regimental bands were few. This may have been a blessing. The scarcity of instruments, limited talent among band members, and weariness from campaigning led to inferior renditions on too many occasions. In any sizable group of soldiers, on the other hand, could generally be found someone reasonably proficient with banjo, fiddle, or jew's-harp. That was enough to keep men entertained with such foot-stomping airs as "Arkansas Traveler," "Billy in the Low Ground," "The Yellow Rose of Texas," and "Hell Broke Loose in Georgia."

Physical contests were an integral part of camp life. Boxing, broad-jumping, wrestling, footraces, hurdles, and an occasional free-for-all were common recreations. A new game called baseball was becoming popular. At that time a player had to hit the base runner with a thrown or batted ball to put him out. When the Texas Rangers achieved early championship status in baseball, teams began refusing to play them until a private named Frank Ezell was disqualified. An observer explained that Ezell, a burly Texan, "could throw harder and straighter than any other man. . . . He came very near knocking the stuffing out of three or four of the boys."

Alcohol triggered the most misbehavior in Civil War camps. It is understandable that the men drank, but they also had a tendency to do so excessively. Most of the whiskey smuggled into the armies could be classified as "mean" in those days, "vile" by modern standards. The potency of the liquor is evident from some of the nicknames given to it by Confederates: "Old Red Eye," "Rifle Knock-Knee," "How Come You So," and "Help Me to Sleep, Mother." Whatever the quality of the whiskey, it almost inevitably produced disorder among the imbibers.

The primitive conditions under which the soldiers lived, their lack of immunity to diseases, and insufficient medical treatment combined to make sickness the worst enemy that Confederates faced. More than twice as many men perished from illness and infection as fell in battle. Recruits invariably encountered two onslaughts of sickness. Because so many came from isolated farms, they had been unexposed to childhood diseases when they entered service. Chicken pox, measles, mumps, and whooping cough circulated through camps in epidemic proportions. Next came camp illnesses triggered by impure water, poor food, exposure, insects, and general filth. Such conditions produced the principal killers of the war: diarrhea, dysentery, typhoid fever, pneumonia, and malaria. The smallest abrasion literally opened the door for bacterial infection. With little resistance because of general debilitation, Southern soldiers died daily in camp or in primitive hospitals.

Religious Beliefs. Faith in God became the greatest institution in the maintenance of morale in Confederate as well as Union armies. Because a Louisiana sergeant did not believe "a bullet can go through a prayer," he considered his allegiance to the Almighty a "much better shield than . . . steel armor." Religion also was a connecting link between camp and home. Most devout Johnny Rebs practiced an evangelical faith that was active and expressive. When a soldier prayed or sang a hymn on Sunday, his thoughts could not help but wander far behind the lines to the church where his family was gathering. At such times, a member of the Sixteenth Tennessee confessed, he "had not much hope of ever meeting again the loved ones at home. . . . I thought of earthly home sweet home & cried."

The horrors of war often strained soldiers' beliefs in a merciful God. Some men became embittered from the hell of battle and the loss of friends and compatriots. For the majority, however, war and its uncertainties led to a strengthening of religion. Countless Johnny Rebs would have agreed with the observation by President Abraham Lincoln: "I have often been driven to my knees by the realization that I had nowhere else to go."

Army chaplains were few in number and variable in ability. The good ones were indefatigable in their labors to keep God's love in front of man's evil. Yet for most soldiers faith was an individual matter. Each man worshiped as he saw fit, and the degree of his religion was no one else's business. One Confederate wrote his brother in May 1862: "the greatest pleasure that I have is when I am reading my Bible and praying to my Creator my Heavenly Father for in his car a lon do I feel safe. I som time tak my Bible on the Sabath and go to some grove where I have no on in my way." When a Virginia infantryman was asked to give a testimonial at a prayer service, he succinctly responded: "My

THREE CONFEDERATE PRISONERS CAPTURED AT GETTYSBURG. NATIONAL ARCHIVES

brethren, I'se got nothin' agin nobody, and I hope nobody's got nothin' agin me."

Praying in public was difficult for many men of limited education and simple faith. Nevertheless, they usually managed to convey their thoughts. During one trying period, a North Carolinian intoned: "Oh Lord, we have a mighty big fight down here, and a sight of trouble; and we hope, Lord, that you will take the proper view of the matter, and give us the victory." A fellow soldier, obviously not as devout, once offered this supplication on the eve of battle: "Lord, if you ain't with us, don't be against us. Just step aside and watch the damndest fight you are ever likely to see!"

Motivation and Conduct in Battle. An acute sense of duty was notable among Confederate soldiers. The words *duty* and *honor* appear regularly in their letters. Duty to cause and country were major motivations of most Rebs. They interpreted patriotic duty to be defending their section and their people against Northern invaders who would deny them the inherent right of self-determination, and whose aim was to destroy the South's cherished way of life.

Sergeant John Hagan of a Georgia regiment was one of innumerable Confederates who viewed the Civil War as a struggle parallel to that of the colonists in the 1770s. Hagan stated at one point in 1863:

> I & every Southern Soldier should be like the rebbil blume which plumed more & shinned briter the more it was trampled on. I believe . . . we will have to fight like Washington did, but I hope our people will never be reduced to destress & poverty as the people of that day was, but if nothing elce will give us liberties I am willing for the time to come.

Hagan survived the war. Another Georgia soldier, Robert McGill, told his wife after his first engagement: "I [had] rather die and you be free than live and be slaves. . . . I know that we will be victorious." Gill was killed in an 1864 battle.

The ultimate test of a soldier is battle. All else in warfare is incidental to two armies closing in combat. The Civil War required more raw courage than most conflicts in history. Enormous numbers of men were engaged, yet troops still massed in battle formation with a minimum of support and protection. They charged across open ground against entrenched positions. The advent of the rifle and major improvements in artillery pieces swung the advantage of war from the offense to the defense. Whereas in the old days an attacking column could approach to a hundred yards or less without taking heavy losses, Civil War weapons made it deadly to approach within a quarter-mile of a fixed position. Commanders on both sides nevertheless continued to make massive frontal assaults to the end of the war. Casualties exceeded anything in American history.

Although the men in gray may have left a good deal to be desired in camp and on the march, they more than compensated for those deficiencies by their overall performance on the battlefield. The most prevalent fear among a Civil War soldier was not of being wounded or captured but of "showing the white feather": displaying cowardice that would bring humiliation to himself and his family. Untested soldiers did not know what to expect in their baptism into combat. Battle scenes, they were told, were enough to try men's souls.

Most soldiers were shocked by the noise and trauma. An Arkansas soldier wrote after his first engagement at Murfreesboro, Tennessee: "I cannot use language to Express the nois of this Battle. The Earth seemed to be in perfect commotion as if a heavy Earth Quake was on." Confederate soldier E. D. Patterson wrote in his diary that when he and his comrades assaulted Union works at Gaines' Mill, they met such a concentrated fire "that the whole brigade literally staggered backward several paces as though pushed back by a tornado."

A teenage soldier from Alabama also had deep anxieties over what to expect in combat. Then his regiment was called into its first battle. He responded in the same way as did his fellow soldiers. "My heart beat quick and my lips became dry," he wrote afterward. "My legs felt weak and a prayer rose to my lips. We had barely entered the woods when pandemonium broke loose. The artillery redoubled its fury, the musketry of both sides began to roar like a storm, and I knew I was into it now. Strange to say, the fear passed away, and I no longer realized the danger amid the excitement, and I could face the bullets with perfect indifference." In like vein, a Georgia private proudly told his wife after his first engagement: "our men were turablely Shocked but all acted the part of a Soldier."

Such comments are truly commendable; for in marked contrast to Currier and Ives paintings and other orderly depictions of the Civil War, combat was not clean or easily seen at all. Chaos reigned everywhere. Thick, acrid smoke settled over the field; and in the crash of musketry, the explosions of cannon fire, the shouts and screams of men fighting with clubbed muskets, bayonets, fists, stones, and anything else at hand, a soldier saw only what was directly in front of him. The mass heroism displayed by these citizen-soldiers inspired Winston Churchill to salute them years later with the words: "With them, extraordinary valor became a common virtue."

Maj. James Waddell, in the official report of his Georgia regiment's conduct at Second Manassas, stated that he "carried into the fight over 100 men who were barefoot, many of whom left bloody foot-prints among the thorns and briars through which they rushed, with Spartan courage and jubilant impetuosity, upon the ranks of the foe."

When in an assault and receiving concentrated musketry, soldiers were known to lean forward as if they were moving into the face of a strong wind. Calling for volunteers to perform dangerous tasks would bring a shout of responses. Repeatedly, soldiers jumped atop parapets to yell defiance at the enemy; they begged for the privilege of carrying the colors in front of the ranks; they took command without being told when all the officers were disabled; many refused to leave the field although seriously wounded.

Countless numbers of those men demonstrated fully that they loved their country more than they loved their lives. Before a battle, it became a common practice for soldiers to write their names and addresses on pieces of paper and pin them to their shirts so that burial details afterward could make easy identification. A Louisiana lieutenant was directing the fire of his guns when a Federal shell tore off his left arm at the shoulder. The man grabbed the reins of his horse with his right hand, swung the animal around in an attempt to hide his injury, and shouted: "Keep it up, boys! I'll be back in a moment!" He started riding down a hill and then pitched forward dead.

John Moseley was the youngest member of the Third Alabama. On July 4, 1863, from Gettysburg, he wrote his mother:

> I am here a prisoner of war & mortally wounded. I can live but a few hours more at farthest—I was shot fifty yards [from] the enemy's lines. . . . I have no doubts of the final results of this battle and I hope I may live long enough to hear the shouts of victory yet, before I die. I am very weak. . . . Farewell to you all.

When Gen. William B. Bate concluded his report of the 1863 Battle of Chickamauga, he unknowingly paid a tribute to all troops in every Confederate army when he wrote:

> The private soldier . . . [vied] with the officer in deeds of high daring and distinguished courage. While the "River of Death" shall float its sluggish current . . . and the night wind chant its solemn dirges over their soldier graves, their names, enshrined in the hearts of their countrymen, will be held in grateful remembrance.

Their record of endurance in the nation's darkest hour stands as an eternal monument to their greatness.

[*See also* Artillery, *overview article;* Brothers of War; Cavalry; Chaplains; Civil War, *article on* Losses and Numbers; Conscription; Desertion; Engineer Bureau; File Closers; Food; Foraging; Gambling; Health and Medicine, *particularly articles on* Sickness and Disease *and* Battle Injuries; Infantry; Military Justice; Military Training; Morale; Music; Prisoners of War; Prostitution; Signal

DEAD CONFEDERATE SHARPSHOOTER. In the Devil's Den at Gettysburg, Pennsylvania. Photograph by Alexander Gardner, July 1863.
NATIONAL ARCHIVES

Corps; Substitutes; Trench Warfare; Uniforms, *article on* Army Uniforms.]

BIBLIOGRAPHY

Barton, Michael. *Goodmen: The Character of Civil War Soldiers.*
Daniel, Larry J. *Soldiering in the Army of Tennessee.* Chapel Hill, N.C., 1991. University Park, Pa., 1981.
Linderman, Gerald. *Embattled Courage: The Experience of Combat in the American Civil War.* New York, 1987.
Mitchell, Reid. *Civil War Soldiers.* New York, 1988.
Robertson, James I., Jr. *Soldiers Blue and Gray.* Columbia, S.C., 1988.
Wiley, Bell Irwin. *The Life of Johnny Reb.* Baton Rouge, La., 1971.
Womack, Bob. *Call Forth the Mighty Men.* Bessemer, Ala., 1987.

JAMES I. ROBERTSON, JR.

SOLDIERS' AID SOCIETIES. Soldiers' aid societies, variously named, came into existence throughout the Confederacy as a part of army mobilization in the summer of 1861. They continued to exist throughout the war. They were essentially local organizations, usually for a town, city, or county. Their main concern was to furnish soldiers from the area with clothing, but they sometimes furnished food, medicines, and hospital supplies. Some of them helped any troops in need in their area, regardless of where the troops were from.

The societies made all sorts of clothing: underwear, shirts, uniforms, overcoats, scarfs, socks, and blankets. If there were local tailors, as there were in many towns, they might help the ladies. For instance, in Athens, Georgia, the tailors cut the heavy cloth for the uniforms, and the ladies then sewed the garments.

These societies were made up of women of the locality who did the sewing themselves or had their household seamstresses do it if they had such people among their servants. Some of the members met together to sew on certain days and thus made a social affair of their work. Other members worked individually in their homes. Members could knit socks and other items while visiting, traveling, or at home.

Soldiers' aid societies were generally made up of middle- and upper-class women. Poorer women made clothing on an individual basis for their relatives and also sent them food when they had it to spare. As the main effort was for soldiers from the locality, it was frequently possible to make garments for specific individuals and thus to have sizes correct as well as give the ladies a feeling of personal service for their friends and relatives.

Cloth for the clothing was sometimes furnished by the states, sometimes by the local government, sometimes by contribution of local citizens, sometimes by contributions by local textile mills, and sometimes by purchase by the societies. The societies frequently held entertainments, auctions, and other functions to raise funds to buy the needed supplies. Some of the societies probably aided the families of poor soldiers who were in need, but this also might be done by other local organizations—churches, government, individuals, or a combination of these. Since such efforts were often essentially local, there was a great deal of variation in who did these things and how they were financed.

Because of the shortage of manufacturing establishments for ready-made clothing in the Confederacy, the work of these societies was of great value. Many soldiers would have been considerably less well clothed or supplied without their efforts. Besides the aid to the soldiers, the societies were good for the morale of their members and of those who contributed supplies and money for the work of the societies. Thus they could encompass all types of Confederates and made a real contribution to the war effort and to military and civilian morale.

[*See also* Beauvoir; Uniforms.]

BIBLIOGRAPHY

Coleman, Kenneth, ed. "Ladies Volunteer Aid Association of Sandersville, Washington County, Georgia, 1861–1862." *The Georgia Historical Quarterly* 52 (1968): 78–95.

Coulter, E. Merton. *The Confederate States of America.* Vol. 7 of A History of the South. Baton Rouge, La., 1950.

Massey, Mary Elizabeth. *Bonnet Brigades.* New York, 1966.

Patton, James W., ed. *Minutes of the Proceedings of the Greenville Ladies Association in Aid of the Volunteers of the Confederate Army.* Durham, N.C., 1937.

Simkins, Francis Butler, and James Welch Patton. *The Women of the Confederacy.* Richmond,Va., and New York, 1936.

Kenneth Coleman

SOLDIERS' HOMES. Throughout the Civil War various residences scattered across the South served as makeshift convalescent homes for wounded veterans of Southern armies. But these "soldiers' homes" were relatively small-scale endeavors supported wholly by private means, and they ceased operating soon after the war ended. The previous year, in February 1864, President Jefferson Davis vetoed a bill that would have established a national Confederate soldiers' home with a board of managers appointed by the governors of the then-existing Confederate states. Although recognizing that disabled ex-Confederate soldiers and sailors were "peculiar objects of governmental benevolence," Davis objected to the act on constitutional grounds, arguing that control and management of the institution properly belonged to the central government in Richmond.

The first state-supported Confederate soldiers' home, chartered in Louisiana in March 1866, was soon abandoned after a Radical Republican–dominated legislature cut off funding. Seventeen years later, however, two strong Confederate veterans' benevolent societies headquartered in New Orleans cosponsored the establishment of what would later become the Camp [Francis T.] Nicholls Confederate Soldiers' Home of Louisiana. Also among the first homes founded by and for Confederate veterans was the R. E. Lee Camp Soldiers' Home of Virginia, established in 1884. Inspired by the success of these two examples in Louisiana and Virginia, Confederate veterans' groups in several other states joined the soldiers' home movement. Numerous ex-Confederate generals—including Joseph E. Johnston, E. Kirby Smith, James Longstreet, Clement A. Evans, Fitzhugh Lee, Bradley Tyler Johnson, John B. Gordon, Lawrence Sullivan Ross, and Joseph Wheeler, as well as the wives and daughters of Gens. Robert E. Lee, Thomas J. ("Stonewall") Jackson, and A. P. Hill, among others—participated in and gave their pledges and influence to the benevolence activity. By 1929, sixteen homes were founded, one in each of the eleven states that had composed the Confederacy, plus Maryland, Kentucky, Oklahoma, Missouri, and even California.

Originally, only honorably discharged and poor Confederate veterans (and in some cases veterans' wives, but only when accompanied by their husbands) were admitted as inmates to Confederate soldiers' homes. Funding for the homes came from private contributions and, predominantly, state revenues, but never from the Federal government; and unlike their national counterparts, Confederate soldiers' homes from the outset excluded veterans of other wars. In all, an estimated twenty thousand indigent and disabled Confederate veterans resided in the sixteen homes, where they were given food, medical care, and shelter. Some of the men died at the homes and were buried in nearby cemeteries. But a majority resided temporarily, in many cases for less than a year, before leaving. Initiated during a period of rampant ex-Confederate activity, the soldiers' homes also served the larger public; there, Southerners of all ages could congregate on special occasions to help celebrate and relive the achievements of the Lost Cause with the men who had fought during the war.

Most of the Confederate soldiers' homes remained open until the 1930s, when the last veteran died, and the surviving widows and daughters were transferred to other institutions. But a few of the homes continued operating until the mid- to late 1950s. Today, several of the original buildings of the Virginia home in Richmond are extant, the Alabama home site located near Montgomery is open to the public, and the Jefferson Davis Memorial Home for Confederate Soldiers and Sailors at Biloxi, Mississippi—built on the grounds of the ex-president's beloved estate, Beauvoir—continues to attract thousands of tourists each year.

[*See also* Beauvoir.]

BIBLIOGRAPHY

Lashley, Tommy G. "Oklahoma's Confederate Veterans Home." *Chronicles of Oklahoma* 55 (1977): 34–45.

Poole, Herbert. "Final Encampment: The North Carolina Soldiers' Home." *Confederate Veteran* 26 (1987): 10–17.

Rosenburg, R. B. "Living Monuments: Confederate Soldiers' Homes in the New South." Ph.D. diss., University of Tennessee, 1989.

Williams, Emily J. " 'A Home . . . for the Old Boys': The Robert E. Lee Camp Confederate Soldiers' Home." *Virginia Cavalcade* 28 (1979): 40–47.

R. B. ROSENBURG

SONS OF LIBERTY. *See* Copperheads.

SORREL, GILBERT MOXLEY (1838–1901),

brigadier general. Sorrel was the grandson of a colonel of engineers in the French army and brother-in-law of Gen. W. W. Mackall. He was born February 23, 1838, in Savannah, Georgia, where he worked before the war as a clerk in the banking department of the Georgia Central Railroad.

When the war broke out, Sorrel saw service at Fort Pulaski and Skidway Island as a member of the Georgia Hussars. Thereafter, however, he grew impatient over the delay of the Hussars' acceptance into Confederate service and went to Virginia where he was a volunteer aide to James Longstreet at First Manassas. In time he became adjutant of Longstreet's division and ultimately chief of staff of the First Corps. Promotions came quickly for Sorrel: he was commissioned captain, September 11, 1861; major, May 5, 1862; and lieutenant colonel, June 18, 1863.

Sorrel was instrumental in healing the breach between Longstreet and A. P. Hill in early 1862. He helped with the guns at Sharpsburg (where he was severely wounded) and performed admirably in the Wilderness. In the 1864 engagement, Sorrel led three brigades in a successful flanking attack against Winfield Scott Hancock, a movement that drew Longstreet's praise for his "skill, promptness and address." Longstreet also recommended Sorrel's promotion to brigadier general. With similar endorsements by Richard Anderson and Robert E. Lee, Sorrel received his wreathed three stars, October 27, 1864. He also was given command of Ambrose Ransom Wright's old brigade in William Mahone's division.

GILBERT MOXLEY SORREL. Late or post-Civil War photograph.
NAVAL HISTORICAL CENTER, WASHINGTON, D.C.

In the closing months of the war Sorrel was wounded in the leg near Petersburg and shot through the lung at Hatcher's Run. The Federals were so confident that the second wound was mortal that his obituary was published in the *New York Herald*. Sorrel recovered, but Lee surrendered before he could rejoin his command.

Described by a fellow officer as "bad tempered and inclined to be overbearing," Sorrel was depicted by historian John Warwick Daniel as "tall, slender and graceful with a keen, dark eye, a trim military figure and an engaging countenance."

After receiving his parole at Lynchburg, May 20, 1865, Sorrel returned to Savannah, where he became manager successively of the Ocean Steamship Company and of the Georgia Export and Import Company. He also served on the city council and was vice president of the Georgia Historical Society for twelve years. Sorrel died August 10, 1901, at the home of his brother, Dr. Francis Sorrel, near Roanoke, Virginia. He was buried in Savannah.

BIBLIOGRAPHY

Dawson, Francis W. *Reminiscences of Confederate Service, 1861–1865.* Charleston, S.C., 1882.

Goree, Thomas Jewett. *The Civil War Correspondence of Thomas Jewett Goree.* Vol. 1. Bryan, Tex., 1981.

Obituary. *Atlanta Journal,* August 17, 1901.

Sorrel, Gilbert Moxley. *Recollections of a Confederate Staff Officer.* Jackson, Tenn., 1958.

Warner, Ezra J. *Generals in Gray: Lives of the Confederate Commanders.* Baton Rouge, La., 1959.

LOWELL REIDENBAUGH

SOULÉ, PIERRE (1801–1870), U.S. diplomat and provost marshal of New Orleans. Born in the French Pyrenees, Soulé fled to America in 1825 to avoid imprisonment for antimonarchical activities. He prospered in New Orleans and defeated John Slidell for a U.S. Senate seat in 1848, becoming a leader of the state rights Democrats after the death of John C. Calhoun.

A flamboyant character, Soulé was involved in controversial episodes throughout his life. His principal historical notoriety stems from his role as U.S. minister to Spain from 1853 to 1855, when his eagerness to annex Cuba provoked international confrontations in the *Black Warrior* and Ostend Manifesto affairs. He also injured the French ambassador in a duel. Repudiated, he resigned, returned to law practice, defended Nicaraguan filibusterer William Walker, and played a hand in the projected Central American isthmian canal.

Although initially opposed to secession, Soulé joined the government of New Orleans as provost marshal and confidant of Mayor John T. Monroe. After Union troops captured the city, he clashed with Gen. Benjamin F. Butler and was arrested on April 28, 1862, for "plotting treason" and for writing "insolent letters" to David Farragut. Imprisoned at Fort Lafayette, New York, until November 1862, he was paroled in Boston but fled back to the Confederacy by way of the Bahamas and Cuba.

He served as an honorary brigadier general on the staff of P. G. T. Beauregard in the defense of Charleston and also attempted to recruit troops abroad, but Jefferson Davis refused to confirm his rank or give him an active command. After the war, he dabbled in an abortive plan to settle Confederate veterans in the Mexican province of Sonora under French protection. He died in New Orleans on March 26, 1870.

BIBLIOGRAPHY

Malone, Dumas, ed. *Dictionary of American Biography.* New York, 1935.

Moore, J. Preston. "Pierre Soulé: Southern Expansionist and Promoter." *Journal of Southern History* 21 (May 1955): 203–223.

JAMES J. HORGAN

SOUTH CAROLINA. In 1860 the population of South Carolina was 703,708. About 30 percent was concentrated in the coastal region, or low country, and some 70 percent in the rest of the state, or the up-country. South Carolina ranked as the tenth most populous state in the South and eighteenth in the nation. There were 291,300 whites, 402,406 African American slaves, and 10,002 free nonwhites. Slaves comprised 57.2 percent and free blacks 1.4 percent of the population, or together 58.6 percent. This black majority represented the highest proportion of African Americans to whites of any state in the nation.

The slaves were employed in the agricultural economy of South Carolina, producing its two main cash crops, cotton and rice. More than one-third of the slaves were located in the state's coastal region—its low country and Sea Islands—from Georgetown to the Savannah River where they cultivated rice and long-staple or Sea Island cotton. Black majorities predominated in the low-country districts in 1860 with the percentage of slaves ranging from a low of 77 percent of the population in Colleton, to 81 percent in Beaufort, to a high of 85 percent in Georgetown.

Over 440 planters using slave labor each raised more than 20,000 pounds of rice annually in the coastal region, while in Georgia, the second most productive rice state, only 88 planters cultivated the crop. South Carolina's Sea Islands in 1859 also produced 43 percent of the long-staple cotton grown in the United States.

Charleston was the social and cultural center of the low country, the state's manufacturing center, and its principal and most cosmopolitan city. With a population of some 40,522 in 1860, it was the second largest city after New Orleans in those states that subsequently left the Union, and it was the twenty-second largest urban center in the nation. Charleston's annual industrial output was exceeded only by Mobile and New Orleans in the South. It ranked eighty-fifth nationwide. An excellent railroad system linked Charleston with the up-country. According to the eighth Federal census, Charleston contained 5.8 percent of the state's population in 1860.

The African American population of Charleston was 17,146 and constituted approximately 42 percent of the

SOUTH CAROLINA DELEGATION TO THE U.S. CONGRESS. This group attended the Thirty-sixth Session of the U.S. Congress, March 4, 1859, to March 3, 1861. They left after South Carolina passed its ordinance of secession on December 20, 1860. Pictured in the top row, from left to right, are Rep. Lawrence Keitt, Rep. John McQueen, and Rep. Milledge L. Bonham. In the middle row are Sen. James Chesnut and Sen. James H. Hammond. In the bottom row are Rep. W. W. Boyce, Rep. John D. Ashmore, and Rep. William Porcher Miles.

HARPER'S PICTORIAL HISTORY OF THE GREAT REBELLION

city's population. Of these, 34 percent or 13,909 were slaves, and 3,237 free persons of color made up 8 percent of the city's population in 1860; about 75 percent of the latter were mulattoes. The city's free blacks accounted for about one-third of South Carolina's entire free African American population. Approximately 3 percent of Charleston's free people of color constituted a mulatto aristocracy. Some were slaveholders themselves. Their position locally was unequaled in numbers and status elsewhere in the state.

In other ways Charleston was an anomaly in South Carolina and the nation. The inequality in the distribution of wealth in the city was enormous by comparison to Northern cities. About 10 percent of the 4,644 free heads-of-households owned 77 percent of the city's wealth; the top 3 percent owned approximately half of the assets in Charleston and were at the top of the pyramid of wealth in the city, state, and nation.

Most Charlestonians owned neither land nor slaves. Some of the poorest whites in the city were recent immigrants. Two-fifths of the laboring class were white people and about 60 percent foreign-born in 1860. The well-to-do were concerned that these propertyless classes represented a threat to their society and institutions. Charleston's middle class included small merchants, teachers, and craftsmen, but visitors to the city reported they saw only two classes: rich and poor. Poor white farmers across the low country produced some grain, hogs, and cattle on the least desirable land.

The production of short-staple cotton grown in South Carolina's up-country increased enormously during the first half of the nineteenth century. This cotton boom opened opportunities for small farmers to become slave owners, and by 1860 there were black majorities in about half of the up-country districts of South Carolina. The numbers of middle-class farmers multiplied. About 80 percent of these rural whites and more than 45 percent of all slaves came to live on small or medium-sized farms. Indeed, counting slave assets the per capita wealth of South Carolina in 1860 was $864, the third highest in the nation and behind only Mississippi and Louisiana. By this date the wealth production of the low country and up-country was approximately equal.

There were, however, vast imbalances in the geographic distribution of wealth throughout the state. For instance, the ten wealthiest districts had black majorities, whereas the ten districts with white majorities ranked among the poorest in the state. The per capita wealth was approximately $1,000 in the plantation districts of the state's lower cotton belt and was sharply less in the districts with white majorities in the upper Piedmont, sandhills, and pine barrens. Wealth, then, was unevenly distributed in the up-country and skewed especially toward the wealthiest one-fifth of households, but approached the existing inequalities elsewhere in the nation. Indeed, the widespread ownership of property tended to mitigate any popular concerns over the uneven distribution of wealth in the Carolina up-country.

The Move Toward Secession

The vast inequalities in wealth in South Carolina did not appear to give rise to any class-based opposition to the movement for secession. Although the well-planned attack by the antislavery extremist John Brown on the Federal arsenal at Harpers Ferry in October 1859 failed, it shocked whites of all classes. Brown's abortive raid played into the hands of radical secessionists who had long advocated separate state action like Robert Barnwell Rhett, Sr., the Charleston lawyer, planter, politician, and owner of the disunionist paper, the *Mercury*.

Meanwhile, Charleston's Christopher G. Memminger, leader of South Carolina's cooperationists (those who sought a united secession movement among the other Southern states) visited Virginia in December to urge a joint call for disunion, but Virginia preferred to wait; subsequently, South Carolina's Governor William H. Gist urged governors of the Deep South to secede together.

In April 1860 the Democratic National Convention met in Charleston, but in a few days the convention divided into Northern and Southern wings and disbanded. Later, in Baltimore, the Northern Democrats nominated Stephen A. Douglas and the Southerners, meeting in Richmond, put forward John C. Breckinridge. When the national Republican party nominated Abraham Lincoln for president, Charleston disunionists formed the "1860 Association," which became the South's leading publisher of pamphlets calling for secession. Disunion sentiment spread rapidly across South Carolina. The sectional split in the Democratic party facilitated Lincoln's election in November.

With Lincoln's victory, the movement for secession peaked, uniting planters and plain folk alike in South Carolina. One interpretation is that the remarkable unity and enthusiasm for such revolutionary, separate state action was precipitated by a crisis of fear of slave insurrections and abolitionism; secession was deemed necessary for race control. Another interpretation is that both yeoman farmers and planters rose together since they believed that only secession could protect their liberty and economic independence from powerful external forces. White unity was founded on the old "country-republican" ideal of personal independence, which was reinforced by the use of black slaves as the mudsill class.

In sum, despite the occasional incidents of class conflict and the historic hostility of up-country toward low country, South Carolina was more of one mind than ever before and more so than any other Southern state in 1860. Within a deferential society plain folk and planters nevertheless were

PALMETTO STATE SONG. Sheet music cover commemorating the signing of the South Carolina ordinance of secession. Lithograph by A. Hoen and Company, published by Henry Siegling, Charleston, South Carolina, 1861. LIBRARY OF CONGRESS

bound together by ties of ethnicity, culture, personal relationships, self-interest, and racism. They were convinced that their property and way of life were threatened, and Lincoln's election provided the catalyst for the revolutionary act of secession.

When news of Lincoln's victory arrived, the legislature issued a call for elections to a secession convention. Now cooperationists like Memminger and Gist joined advocates of separate state action like the radical secessionist Rhett. Within days Rhett lost a bid for the governorship when the state legislature picked the more moderate candidate, Francis W. Pickens. Still there were few who dissented from the movement for secession. The old up-country Unionist Benjamin F. Perry was defeated in his bid for election to the convention; in Charleston, Unionist James L. Petigru, who did not actively oppose secession, wrote Perry: "why should one put himself to the pains of speaking to the insane if he has not the power of commanding a strait jacket for them?"

Following an outbreak of smallpox in Columbia, the secession convention reconvened in Charleston on December 20. The 169 delegates, mostly a wealthy, middle-aged, native-born, slaveholding elite of planters and lawyers, unanimously adopted an ordinance of secession, which dissolved South Carolina's union with the United States. The Palmetto Republic now stood alone.

The secession convention also adopted a set of resolutions written by the fire-eater Rhett proposing a convention of seceded states to meet in Montgomery, Alabama, in early February 1861 to adopt a constitution for a Southern confederacy. Commissioners were dispatched to alert all slaveholding states to the meeting. In touch with radicals throughout the South, Rhett planned for the rapid creation of a Southern nation and a concerted program that would appeal to cooperationists. Rhett has been called the "father of disunion."

Fort Sumter

While the secession convention met in Charleston, Maj. Robert Anderson, commanding the U.S. garrison at Fort Moultrie on nearby Sullivan's Island, quietly moved his eighty-two soldiers to Fort Sumter, a more defensible site in Charleston Harbor. Though the fort was still unfinished, its guns could command the shipping channel and fire on the city.

Governor Francis W. Pickens immediately began raising troops and ordered the occupation of federal properties in and around Charleston. The few Federal soldiers holding Fort Moultrie, Castle Pinckney, and the U.S. Arsenal offered no resistance when, in the first military encounter of the war, South Carolina troops quickly seized all three. They hauled down the Stars and Stripes and hoisted a flag with a new moon and a palmetto tree—the South Carolina flag.

As tensions increased, Charleston's mulatto aristocracy was harassed and threatened. Some left the city at great personal loss, but others volunteered to assist in its defense.

In January 1861 President James Buchanan sent a merchant vessel, *Star of the West,* to reinforce Major Anderson in Fort Sumter. On January 9 it was fired on from Morris Island and, following orders, turned back. Major Anderson had not returned the fire from the shore batteries because he was awaiting orders from Washington.

Governor Pickens, regarding the Federal occupation of Fort Sumter as a threat to South Carolina, asked Buchanan to cede it to the state. Sentiment was rising to storm the fort and criticism of Pickens mounted, but he refused to be stampeded by firebrands. Meanwhile, the legislature passed an act creating a regular army for the Palmetto Republic.

When the Montgomery convention opened in February, the South Carolina delegation included Memminger and Rhett, who was disappointed when he was not elected president of the new Confederate States of America estab-

BOMBARDMENT OF FORT SUMTER. Floating battery during the bombardment of Fort Sumter, South Carolina.

FRANK LESLIE'S ILLUSTRATED FAMOUS LEADERS AND BATTLE SCENES OF THE CIVIL WAR.

lished there. Memminger chaired the committee that drafted the Provisional Constitution and subsequently was appointed secretary of the treasury.

The Palmetto delegation demanded that the assembly either accept the Fort Sumter problem as a common one or allow South Carolina forces to attack the fort. The new Congress accepted the responsibility, and in March Gen. P. G. T. Beauregard was sent to take command of all Southern military forces in the Charleston area. He redeployed the troops there and rearranged the growing ring of batteries around the harbor.

On March 7 Lincoln took the oath of office in Washington as president and promised to "hold, occupy, and possess the property and places belonging to the government." South Carolinians knew this meant Fort Sumter.

On April 7 a naval expedition sailed for Charleston to reprovision the fort. The following day a representative of the U.S. State Department delivered a message to Governor Pickens informing him of the expedition. The governor passed the information to General Beauregard, who asked for instructions from Jefferson Davis, president of the Confederacy. Davis thought war was inevitable, but he had hoped to avoid firing the first shot. Now he saw no alternative.

On April 10 Beauregard was instructed by telegraph to demand the surrender of Fort Sumter or to reduce it. When Major Anderson refused to surrender, Beauregard ordered the bombardment of the fort on April 12. After a fierce shelling from Confederate shore batteries and with food and ammunition running low, Anderson surrendered the following day. Celebrations erupted in Charleston as Confederate soldiers occupied Fort Sumter and its Federal garrison departed for the North.

The final catalyst for war had come in Charleston Harbor. President Lincoln now called for 75,000 volunteers from the loyal states and a blockade of Southern ports. States in the upper South that had initially hesitated now joined the Confederacy.

South Carolina in the War

The Confederate government requested Pickens to dispatch troops to Virginia, as the South Carolinians were better prepared than similar units in other Southern states. When he sent these volunteer units to fight at First

Manassas, he was roundly criticized. He also became unpopular for requisitioning slaves as laborers, and foodstuffs and medicines for South Carolina troops.

Gen. Robert E. Lee arrived in Charleston on November 6 to take command of the Military Department of South Carolina, Georgia, and Florida. The following day Hilton Head Island, Port Royal, and Beaufort fell to a force of 12,000 Union soldiers who planned to use the area as a base for military operations and headquarters of the blockading fleet. Here the first South Carolina slaves were mustered into the Union army. Eventually, 5,462 black South Carolinians entered Federal service.

The invasion struck panic in white citizens, and they blamed Pickens for inadequate coastal defenses. South Carolina's secession convention was reconvened. Action was taken to improve the defenses around Charleston and a new Executive Council was created. The governor was furious since the council assumed almost unlimited powers. But when the new body began requisitioning slaves, declaring martial law, and recruiting troops for the Confederate government, its popularity waned among the independent-minded South Carolinians. Now the council was branded as dictatorial.

After the initial rush to the colors, recruitment of troops for both home defense and Confederate quotas proved difficult. In March 1862 the council passed a conscription plan for white males between the ages of eighteen and forty-five. The Confederate Congress enacted a similar law to enlist men between eighteen and thirty-five. South Carolina then organized two militia corps of men over thirty-five for home defense, and the council gave to Confederate draft officials the rolls that were to be used by the state for conscription. In September 1862, when the Confederate government passed a law to draft all men between eighteen and forty-five, South Carolina's plans for defending the state were disrupted. The state now was forced to enact a law calling up all men between the ages of sixteen and sixty-five. That same month the legislature abolished the Executive Council and nullified its acts.

During most of 1862 thousands of South Carolina troops were rushed into fierce fighting in Virginia, Maryland, Mississippi, Kentucky, and Tennessee. The following year they were in the thick of the battles at Chancellorsville, Gettysburg, and Chickamauga. They suffered heavy losses.

When Pickens's term as governor ended in December 1862, a joint session of the legislature elected Milledge L. Bonham as the state's new chief executive. Bonham, a former brigadier general in the Confederate army, had been serving as a representative from South Carolina in the Confederate Congress. He pledged to continue the policy of supporting the Confederacy but soon faced the same problems that had plagued his predecessor.

General Beauregard, who now commanded the Department of South Carolina and Georgia, believed that a minimum of 30,000 troops were needed for the defense of South Carolina alone. But in January 1863 there were only 10,000 Confederate soldiers available in the entire state.

Union strategists were determined to seize Charleston, "the cradle of secession," to stop the daily manufacture of cartridges in the former U.S. arsenal there and the building of ironclad vessels, and to stem the flow of vast amounts of military supplies and luxury goods brought in by blockade runners. Anticipating an attack, Beauregard ordered all noncombatants out of Charleston in February and appealed to Bonham for armed forces. Reluctantly, Bonham ordered all white males sixteen to eighteen and forty-five to fifty years of age to be called up for the defense of Charleston. Three regiments were mustered, but arming and supplying them was problematic since the state had turned over most of its supplies to the Confederacy. Nevertheless, by April, Beauregard had under his command a poorly equipped force of 22,648 men thinly stretched from Charleston to the Savannah River, with 12,856 occupying the fortifications in the city and on the nearby islands.

The first attack came in June when 6,000 Union troops landed southeast of the city and a fierce firefight took place on James Island. Casualties were heavy on both sides and the Union forces retreated. On April 7 Federal ironclads under the command of Commo. Samuel L. Du Pont attempted to destroy Fort Sumter. They were forced to withdraw, however, owing to Confederate fire and the threat of mines or submarine torpedoes, a naval weapon developed by the Confederate Torpedo Bureau that inaugurated a new era in naval warfare. The third attack, a joint army-navy operation, began in July.

Six thousand Federal troops under Gen. Quincy A. Gillmore quickly occupied most of Morris Island. But heroic and costly assaults by African American troops failed to overrun the Confederate strong point, Fort Wagner, which withstood fifty-eight days of fierce bombardment. This prevented the navy from executing its role in the operation, since the batteries around the harbor and the well-placed torpedoes remained formidable obstacles. Gillmore dug in on Morris Island and trained his long-range rifled guns on Fort Sumter, which was soon reduced to rubble though it remained garrisoned. One 200-pounder Parrott rifled gun was aimed at Charleston some four miles away. On August 21 Gillmore demanded that Beauregard evacuate Fort Sumter and Morris Island. When Beauregard refused, Gillmore ordered the bombardment of Charleston. It would continue for the next 587 days. Charlestonians were angry and frightened. Those in the city who could afford the fare took the next train or carriage to safer communities.

The Union occupation of Morris Island and the increased surveillance by the Union navy severely curtailed blockade running while Federal land forces inched closer to the city.

In Charleston and across the state, Confederate money depreciated and the costs of goods and services soared. A few speculators in foodstuffs made huge profits, but destitution was widespread.

By mid-1863 war-weariness had grown to alarming proportions in South Carolina. Rhett's newspaper, *Mercury*, attacked President Davis's ability to wage war successfully. Among the poor, resentment flared against speculators and Confederate and state conscription laws that permitted the well-to-do to evade the draft. Some embittered soldiers took up the cry, "It's a rich man's war and a poor man's fight." Deserters swarmed through the western regions of the state terrorizing the citizenry. Governor Bonham called on the Confederate War Department to provide protection against deserters as well as the new threat in early 1864 posed by Union cavalry in the region. But Bonham lost this argument and another with the Confederate secretary of war when Beauregard was ordered to release most of his cavalry for duty in Virginia in March 1864.

By late 1864 Gen. William Tecumseh Sherman with 60,000 battle-hardened veterans had marched across Georgia and now posed a threat to South Carolina. In the entire state there was a mere 22,000 regular and irregular troops to oppose the Union forces. Bonham recommended that the state assume more responsibility for its defense and urged the new legislature to pass a conscription law to be carried out by state officials rather than Confederate authorities. Bonham had cooperated with the Confederacy until near the end of his term when he believed that his state faced a crisis. After his term ended in late 1864, the legislature once more became a champion of state rights and nullified most important Confederate laws. This anti-Confederate attitude was also that of the new governor, Andrew G. Magrath, a Charlestonian and former Confederate district judge.

The legislature passed acts permitting Magrath to exempt from Confederate service whomever he wished and restricting the Confederacy's authority to impress slaves in South Carolina. At the same time Magrath repeatedly asked the Richmond government for assistance, but to little avail.

Magrath concluded that the state could no longer depend on the Confederacy and that the only way to save it was to convince North Carolina and Georgia to cooperate militarily. Any such plan collapsed in early February 1865 when Sherman invaded South Carolina, which his army referred to as "the Hellhole of Secession."

After a feint toward Charleston and Augusta, Sherman's army continued its strategy of total war and cut a wide swath of destruction across the state. Sherman's real destination was Columbia, the state capital. The army lived off the land and plundered the countryside; within three weeks planters' homes, churches, and a dozen villages went up in flames. Governor Magrath called on South Carolinians to destroy or carry away anything that might be of value to the enemy.

With his supply lines cut and Union troops closing in, Gen. William J. Hardee, the commanding officer at Charleston, decided that the city was no longer defensible. On the evening of February 17–18 he ordered military equipment and supplies set afire, and the city's 10,000 defenders left the city, retreating northward across the Santee River. As the Union forces entered Charleston, one citizen observed, "Total ruin is staring us in the face."

Governor Magrath fled Columbia when Sherman's army reached the state capital. As they had done in other towns, Sherman's soldiers set it afire, although one Ohio lieutenant claimed that "*whiskey done it* and *not the* soldiers." About one-third of Columbia was destroyed. When the army marched away from the city and toward North Carolina, Sherman's soldiers burned and pillaged portions of Camden, Winnsboro, Lancaster, Chesterfield, and Cheraw.

Meanwhile, the governor's office was a rolling entourage moving from one town to another. In April Magrath met with a few members of the legislature in Greenville and apprised them of the near anarchy in the state. Several days later he fled to Columbia when Union cavalry seized Greenville. By late May the government of the state had collapsed, Magrath had been captured and imprisoned, and Union forces were in control of South Carolina.

South Carolina's battlefield casualties were among the highest of any state in the Confederacy. Approximately 75,000 white, male South Carolinians entered the field as regulars and another 10,000 served in the home guard. Of these some 40,000 were killed or gravely wounded, which was a rate of loss sharply higher than the average of about 10 percent for other states in the Confederacy. This high casualty rate resulted from the fact that South Carolina units were among the best prepared for combat and therefore were rushed into some of the early, bloodiest battles of the war.

South Carolina's countryside was devastated, its villages and cities were in ruins. The economic, labor, and social system of the state was no more. Once enslaved African Americans were now free and they exuberantly embraced their new freedom. Many left their farms and plantations and streamed into the cities. But in these urban centers and the countryside there was starvation among blacks and whites alike. One member of the South Carolina white elite observed, "The war has ruined us." Most whites who had survived were demoralized and dispirited.

A Northern reporter who toured Charleston a few months after the war ended described it as "a city of ruins, of desolation, of vacant homes, of widowed women, . . . of weed-wild gardens, . . . of grass-grown streets." He could have been describing many South Carolina cities in 1865.

[*For further discussion of South Carolina cities and battles, see* Carolinas Campaign of Sherman; Charleston, South Carolina; Columbia, South Carolina; Fort Wagner, South Carolina; Port Royal, South Carolina. *See also* Fort

Sumter, South Carolina, *biographies of numerous figures mentioned herein, and* Appendix *for the texts of South Carolina's secession ordinance and the Declaration of the Immediate Causes of Secession.]*

BIBLIOGRAPHY

Cauthen, Charles Edward. *South Carolina Goes to War, 1860–1865.* Chapel Hill, N.C., 1950.

Channing, Steven A. *Crisis of Fear: Secession in South Carolina.* New York, 1970.

Coclanis, Peter A., and Lacy K. Ford. "The South Carolina Economy Reconstructed and Reconsidered: Structure, Output, and Performance, 1670–1985." In *Developing Dixie: Modernization in a Traditional Society.* Edited by Winfred B. Moore, Jr., Joseph F. Tripp, and Lyon G. Tyler, Jr. New York, 1988.

Doyle, Don. *New Men, New Cities, New South: Atlanta, Nashville, Charleston, Mobile, 1860–1910.* Chapel Hill, N.C., 1990.

Edmunds, John B., Jr. "South Carolina." In *The Confederate Governors.* Edited by W. Buck Yearns. Athens, Ga., 1985.

Ford, Lacy K., Jr. *Origins of Southern Radicalism: The South Carolina Upcountry, 1800–1860.* New York, 1988.

Fraser, Walter J., Jr. *Charleston! Charleston!: The History of a Southern City.* Columbia, S.C., 1989.

Glatthaar, Joseph T. *The March to the Sea and Beyond: Sherman's Troops in the Savannah and Carolinas Campaigns.* New York, 1985.

Johnson, Michael P., and James L. Roark, eds. *No Chariot Let Down: Charleston's Free People of Color on the Eve of the Civil War.* Chapel Hill, N.C., 1984.

Thomas, Emory M. *The Confederate Nation: 1861–1865.* New York, 1979.

Wallace, David Duncan. *A Short History of South Carolina, 1520–1948.* Chapel Hill, N.C., 1951.

WALTER J. FRASER

SOUTHERN EXPRESS COMPANY. Privately owned companies that hauled freight and delivered mail expanded their businesses during the Civil War. Many small shippers, some with a single wagon and team of horses, carried goods locally and over short intercity distances. Before the war, five companies monopolized the interstate trade, but only one of these, the Adams Express Company, with origins in 1840 and consolidations in 1854, stretched into the South.

With the onset of war, the Confederate government threatened to confiscate the assets of Northern businesses within its borders. To protect itself, the Adams Express transferred its Southern branches to company superintendent Henry B. Plant. Plant, a Connecticut man who had expanded the company into the South in 1854, felt the need to "prove" his allegiance to the Confederacy in order to conduct business. He reorganized the company under a group of Southern stockholders and renamed it the Southern Express Company. On May 1, 1861, Plant petitioned the Georgia legislature for a charter, which was granted on July 5. Plant met with Jefferson Davis, swore his loyalty to the Confederacy, and negotiated to become an adjunct to the Confederate Quartermaster Corps. Plant's express was the largest private company to transport supplies for Southern armies and collect tariffs for the government. Secretary of the Treasury Christopher G. Memminger exempted express workers from military service because of their critical duties as civilian contractors. Often, commanders detailed soldiers for temporary service with the company.

Headquartered at Augusta, Georgia, the Southern Express Company continued its established weekly routes to New Orleans, Richmond, Nashville, Vicksburg, Charleston, and other major cities from the eastern seaboard to Texas. It made large profits shipping payrolls, munitions, and supplies, transporting millions of packages to soldiers in hospitals, prisons, or camps, and delivering letters to widely located rural homes. For most of the war, the company carried soldiers' mail free of charge. It provided an alternative to the Confederate Post Office, which handled mostly letters, and it helped sustain the morale of Confederate soldiers by bringing them packages from home and conveying battlefield souvenirs and pay to their families.

The company carried happy packages from home as well as the saddest of all shipments—coffins with dead soldiers. There are no figures on the costs of transporting a body. Generally, it cost twenty-five cents to send a letter within the South and fifty cents to mail it north. Many packages cost one dollar per pound, but as Confederate money lost value, company agents refused script in favor of barter items, including chickens, pigs, corn, and other commodities.

The Southern Express never really severed itself from the Adams Express Company; its name change and charter were chimerical political moves to divert criticism and maintain profits. As rival armies moved along the battlefront, the Southern Express cooperated with Adams at various points to keep packages flowing across the lines. When Confederate armies advanced, the Southern occupied Adams's offices and freely used its wagons and supplies. Confederate retreats brought Adams's employees back to their old stations. Since the U.S. Post Office refused to deliver mail to and from the Confederate states, the two express companies filled the void.

Many Southerners questioned the patriotism of Plant and the company. Although some editors challenged the company's motives, insisting it had not broken from Adams and charging it with treason, most agreed with an Augusta editor that the Southern Express was "a powerful auxiliary to the Government and of incalculable benefit to the soldiers in the field, and to commerce generally." Nevertheless, the company operated first for profits and second to help the Confederacy.

BIBLIOGRAPHY

Confederate Papers Relating to Citizens or Business Firms. Microcopy M346. Record Group 109. National Archives, Washington, D.C.

Harlow, Alvin F. *Old Waybills: The Romance of the Express Companies.* New York, 1934.

Martin, S. Walter. "Henry Bradley Plant." In *Georgians in Profile: Historical Essays in Honor of Ellis Merton Coulter.* Edited by Horace Montgomery. Athens, Ga., 1958.

Smyth, G. Hutchinson. *The Life of Henry B. Plant: Founder and President of the Plant System of Railroads and Steamships and also of the Southern Express Company.* New York, 1898.

Wells, Henry. *Sketch of the Rise, Progress, and Present Condition of the Express System.* Albany, N.Y., 1864.

RUSSELL DUNCAN

SOUTHERN HISTORICAL SOCIETY. Devoted to the preservation of Confederate history, the Southern Historical Society was organized in New Orleans in 1869. Led by former officers and supporters of the Confederacy, the society sought to mobilize Southerners to preserve a "true history" of the Civil War, one that established the honor and nobility of the Confederate cause. The society met with very little response, however; probably no more than a hundred people joined. In hopes of increasing interest, the society in 1873 met at White Sulphur Springs, West Virginia. There a group of Virginians, led by former Confederate general Jubal Early, took control of the organization. The society then moved its headquarters to Richmond and in 1876 began to publish the *Southern Historical Society Papers.*

Under the leadership of Early, an irascible fellow never reconciled to the Confederacy's defeat, and J. William Jones, a Baptist minister with similar attitudes who served as editor of the *Papers,* the Southern bias of the SHS became even more pronounced. At times, its partisans appeared to be refighting the war (Early once referred to an article as a bomb delivered against the enemy) and clearly hoped to revive the culture of the Old South and the Confederacy. To rally the South to this cause, the SHS dispatched agents and sought to establish auxiliary societies in other states. A few short-lived auxiliary groups formed, but for the most part the SHS never boasted a large following in the South. The *Papers* had only a little over fifteen hundred subscribers and encountered repeated financial problems. Publication, which had initially been monthly, became annual with the 1885 volume.

The *Papers* nevertheless became the most important legacy of the SHS. These volumes not only preserved reports, reminiscences, and other historical material about the Confederacy but helped develop interpretations that became central to the Lost Cause mythology and to the modern historiography of the Civil War. Articles published in the *Papers* provided evidence to support a growing Southern conviction that the Confederacy had succumbed only to the North's overwhelming numbers and resources. Others celebrated the military genius of Robert E. Lee, helping establish him as the South's premier hero, and accused Gen. James Longstreet of tardiness during the second day at Gettysburg, implying that his failure there had lost the war.

Much of this contribution had been made by 1887, when Jones resigned and financial difficulties overtook the SHS. R. A. Brock, another Virginia veteran and secretary of the Virginia Historical Society, became the new editor of the *Papers.* The originality of contributions declined, and after 1910, with Brock ill, Confederate veterans dying off, and the SHS all but defunct, volumes appeared only sporadically. In 1926, Douglas Southall Freeman, the distinguished Lee biographer, and a few of his friends in Richmond took over the SHS and saw through to publication additional volumes of the *Papers,* which printed the proceedings of the Confederate Congress. After Freeman's death in 1953, the Virginia Historical Society received all of the society's assets and completed the publication of the proceedings. The final volume of the *Papers,* the fifty-second, appeared in 1959.

[*See also* Lost Cause, *overview article.*]

BIBLIOGRAPHY

Connelly, Thomas L. *The Marble Man: Robert E. Lee and His Image in American Society.* New York, 1977.

Coulter, E. Merton. "What the South Has Done about Its History." *Journal of Southern History* 2 (February 1936): 3–28.

Foster, Gaines M. *Ghosts of the Confederacy: Defeat, the Lost Cause, and the Emergence of the New South, 1865 to 1913.* New York, 1987.

Piston, William Garrett. *Lee's Tarnished Lieutenant: James Longstreet and His Place in Southern History.* Athens, Ga., 1987.

Wilson, Charles Reagan. *Baptized in Blood: The Religion of the Lost Cause, 1865–1920.* Athens, Ga., 1980.

GAINES M. FOSTER

SOUTHERN ILLUSTRATED NEWS. *See* Magazines, *article on* Southern Illustrated News.

SOUTHERN LITERARY MESSENGER. *See* Magazines, *article on* Southern Literary Messenger.

SOUTH MOUNTAIN, MARYLAND. This slope, two miles east of Harpers Ferry, was the site of a battle, fought on September 14, 1862, as a result of the Federals' inadvertent discovery of Gen. Robert E. Lee's campaign plans (Special Order 191) on September 13.

In the order, issued September 9 at Frederick, Maryland, the unorthodox Lee divided his forces, directing three columns to attack and capture the Federal garrison at Harpers Ferry, while the remainder of the army awaited reunion of the detached forces west of South Mountain near Boonsboro, Maryland. Although outnumbered two to one, Lee considered Army of the Potomac commander George B. McClellan a minimal threat since the Union army remained in a defensive stance protecting the approaches to Washington and Baltimore.

But when McClellan arrived at Frederick on September 13, two Indiana soldiers discovered Special Order 191 wrapped around three cigars in an abandoned Confederate camp east of Frederick. The "lost order" arrived at McClellan's headquarters before noon on the thirteenth, and the ecstatic Federal commander wired President Lincoln: "I think Lee has made a gross mistake. I have all the plans of the rebels and will catch them in their own trap." McClellan subsequently ordered an advance against South Mountain on the fourteenth "to cut the enemy in two and beat him in detail."

South Mountain commences at the Potomac River two miles east of Harpers Ferry, and it runs north into Pennsylvania. Its precipitous, wooded slopes range from eight hundred to nearly two thousand feet, and with the exception of three gaps near its southern end, South Mountain presents a formidable barrier.

McClellan's strategy drove three wedges into South Mountain. At Crampton's Gap, six miles northeast of Harpers Ferry, McClellan ordered Maj. Gen. William B. Franklin and his twelve-thousand-man corps to relieve the besieged Harpers Ferry garrison and entrap seven thousand isolated Southerners in Pleasant Valley. Six miles north of Crampton's, McClellan directed Maj. Gen. Jesse L. Reno's corps to strike at Fox's Gap. One mile farther north at Turner's Gap, the corps of Maj. Gen. Joseph Hooker was to advance. By smashing through Fox's and Turner's Gaps, McClellan expected to slice the retreat routes of Lee and the remaining Confederates in Maryland—James Longstreet's and John Bell Hood's divisions at Hagerstown and D. H. Hill's division near Boonsboro.

McClellan failed to accomplish any of his objectives. Delays in marching and deployment, extravagant Federal exaggerations about the number of Confederate defenders, and the rugged mountain terrain all conspired in General Lee's favor. At Crampton's Gap, five hundred Southerners behind a stone wall near Burkittsville at the eastern base of the mountain held off Franklin's corps for three hours. Crampton's Gap finally was seized at dark, but too late to rescue the Harpers Ferry garrison, which surrendered on the morning of the fifteenth, thus allowing the Confederates in Pleasant Valley to escape south of the Potomac. At Fox's Gap, Samuel Garland, Jr.'s, brigade of a thousand North Carolinians bruised the head of a Federal corps and held the gap long enough to allow reinforcements to arrive from Hill and Hood. North of Turner's Gap, Robert Rodes's Alabama brigade of eleven hundred stalled Hooker's corps, and the one thousand Georgians of Alfred H. Colquitt's brigade stopped the Union Iron Brigade advance along the National Pike. About 10:00 P.M. on the night of the fourteenth, Lee ordered a withdrawal from Fox's and Turner's Gaps toward Sharpsburg, but he had gained the extra time needed to force Harpers Ferry's surrender and to reunite his army along the Antietam Creek.

Federal casualties in the battle include 1,821 wounded, 87 missing, and 438 killed; Maj. Gen. Jesse L. Reno was mortally wounded at Fox's Gap. The Confederates lost 1,768 wounded, 1,279 missing, and 387 killed (including Brig. Gen. Samuel Garland, Jr.).

BIBLIOGRAPHY

Cox, Jacob D. "Forcing Fox's Gap and Turner's Gap." In *Battles and Leaders of the Civil War.* Edited by Robert U. Johnson and C. C. Buel. Vol. 2. New York, 1888. Reprint, Secaucus, N.J., 1982.

Hill, Daniel Harvey. "The Battle of South Mountain or Boonsboro." In *Battles and Leaders of the Civil War.* Edited by Robert U. Johnson and C. C. Buel. Vol. 2. New York, 1888. Reprint, Secaucus, N.J., 1982.

Murfin, James V. *The Gleam of Bayonets.* New York, 1964.

Priest, John Michael. *Before Antietam: The Battle for South Mountain.* Shippensburg, Pa., 1992.

Sears, Stephen. *Landscape Turned Red.* New York, 1985.

U.S. War Department. *War of the Rebellion: A Compilation of the Official Records of the Union and Confederate Armies.* Ser. 1, vol. 19, pts. 1–2. Washington, D.C., 1888.

DENNIS E. FRYE

SPAIN. With its strategic Cuban colony, Spain loomed as an important factor in the American Civil War. Recognizing the special advantages that might accrue from Spanish recognition, the Confederate commissioners in Europe, in June 1861, requested authority to represent the Confederacy at the court of Spain. On August 24 Secretary of State Robert M. T. Hunter instructed them to proceed to Madrid and seek recognition, observing that an independent Confederacy, with a social system similar to that of Cuba, would be a friendly power in North America rather than a formidable and dangerous rival.

Commissioner Pierre A. Rost reached Madrid in March 1862 and received a cordial reception from the Spanish secretary of foreign affairs. Rost assured the secretary that Spain and the Confederacy were natural allies with many mutual interests in the New World. He quickly concluded that Spain considered Cuba to be vulnerable to Northern power, rendering any departure from the policies of Britain and France an unacceptable risk. Regarding his presence in Madrid useless as well as an insult to the Confederacy, Rost left the country.

In the spring of 1863 John Slidell, the Confederate commissioner in Paris, convinced that France would never act alone, sought special permission to promote a possible Franco-Spanish axis in Madrid favorable to the Confederacy. He received the desired instructions, but reported on May 23 that the conditions that prompted his request no longer existed. The Spanish minister in Paris, Francisco de Isturiz, had informed him that his country under no circumstances would pursue a policy antagonistic to that of the United States. Finally in August 1863 Slidell suggested to Isturiz that Spain take the initiative on recognition; France would follow. The minister assured Slidell that Spain would act if France took the lead in recognition. But Napoleon looked to England, not to Spain, for the protection of French interests, and England had no intention of meddling in American affairs.

BIBLIOGRAPHY

Crook, David Paul. *The North, the South, and the Powers, 1861–1865.* New York, 1974.

Owsley, Frank Lawrence. *King Cotton Diplomacy: Foreign Relations of the Confederate States of America.* Revised by Harriet Chappell Owsley. Chicago, 1959.

NORMAN A. GRAEBNER

SPARROW, EDWARD (1810–1882), congressman from Louisiana. Born in Dublin, Ireland, on December 29, 1810, Edward Sparrow was taken by his parents as an infant to Columbus, Ohio, where as a young man, according to family tradition, he attended Kenyon College. After studying law for several years, he was admitted to the Ohio bar. In 1831, he moved to Vidalia, Louisiana, where he again took up the study of law and gained admission to the Louisiana bar. Sparrow's lengthy record of public service began in 1833 when he was elected clerk of court of Concordia Parish. One year later he was elected sheriff, a position he held until 1840. Sparrow continued to practice law until 1852 when he moved to Carroll Parish and established his plantation, Arlington, on the shore of Lake Providence.

In 1860, Arlington boasted 460 slaves, and Sparrow's total estate was valued at $1,248,050. Like several other members of the Louisiana delegation to the Confederate Congress, Sparrow ranked among the largest slaveholders in the South, and his great wealth gave him the distinction of being the richest member of Congress. Although he had always been active in the Whig party (he ran for lieutenant governor in 1846), Sparrow, during the secession crisis of 1861, voted for immediate secession at the January Louisiana convention. After serving as a member of the Provisional Congress in Montgomery, Alabama, Sparrow, together with Thomas Semmes, was chosen by the Louisiana legislature to represent the state in the Senate. He continued to hold this office until the end of the war.

Throughout his four and a half years of service to the Confederacy, Sparrow maintained a strong nationalist approach to the objectives of winning the war and achieving independence. In the Provisional Congress his committee assignments included Military Affairs, Indian Affairs, and Flag and Seal, as well as the committee to draft the Confederate Constitution. Once in the Senate, Sparrow played his most significant role as chairman of the Senate Committee on Military Affairs. From this vantage point, he exercised his belief in the unlimited war powers of the Congress as well as those of the commander in chief, the president. His nationalist outlook led him to support such policies as suspending habeas corpus, allowing appointed commissioners to determine market and impressment prices in order to curb speculation, and expanding conscription laws to include younger and older men to serve in the reserve corps of each state. This last policy was designed to allow more men of prime age to serve in the Confederate army.

In keeping with his resolve to win the war at all costs, and in contrast to the rest of the senators from the wealthy lower South states, Sparrow opposed the exemption of corporations and farmers from double taxation on property and income. His only concession to state rights philosophy was his belief that exemptions from the draft ought to be left as a power of the states. But, at the same time, he also supported legislation that toughened the exemption laws to ensure that only overseers on plantations with fifteen or more slaves owned by either a feme sole (a woman granted the legal right of self-representation) or by a man absent in the service of the Confederacy would be exempt from military service. Support of such legislation testifies to his planter background, but in general Sparrow tended to place the interests of the nation as a whole before those of the individual.

Although Sparrow generally supported the nationalist policies of the Davis administration, he shared in the animosity that developed between most members of the Louisiana congressional delegation and the president. The roots of this conflict lay in the controversy surrounding Gen. P. G. T. Beauregard's public criticism of Davis following First Manassas. Jefferson Davis's decision to remove Beauregard, a Louisianan, from the command of the Army of the West following the defeat at Shiloh provoked the Trans-Mississippi delegates to petition for Beauregard's restoration to his command. Senators Sparrow and Semmes presented the petition personally to Davis, who reportedly read the petition aloud, all the while making negative comments in the senators' presence. Contrary to the desires of the Trans-Mississippi delegates, Davis transferred Beauregard to Charleston and appointed Gen. Braxton Bragg, considered to be Davis's "pet," to the western command. Davis's handling of the matter succeeded in alienating the western delegates, many of whom continued to harbor a personal hostility toward the president, manifesting itself in the anti-Bragg faction within Congress.

Although Sparrow joined with the other delegates from his region in supporting Beauregard and opposing Bragg, by 1865 he was willing to go against the interests of his own region by favoring the surrender of the Trans-Mississippi Department, most of which was already under Union control. Sparrow's own plantation, Arlington, had been seized by Federal troops and used as housing during Ulysses S. Grant's Vicksburg campaign. His willingness to relinquish his own land in the hope of saving the remnant of the Confederacy demonstrates Sparrow's continued belief in the righteousness of the Confederate cause.

After the war's end, Sparrow returned to Arlington, which had been spared by the Federals, and attempted to rebuild his ruined estate. He remained there until his death on July 4, 1882.

BIBLIOGRAPHY

Alexander, Thomas B., and Richard E. Beringer. *The Anatomy of the Confederate Congress: A Study of the Influences of Member Characteristics on Legislative Voting Behavior, 1861–1865.* Nashville, Tenn., 1972.

Wakelyn, Jon L. *Biographical Dictionary of the Confederacy.* Edited by Frank E. Vandiver. Westport, Conn., 1977.

Warner, Ezra J., and W. Buck Yearns. *Biographical Register of the Confederate Congress.* Baton Rouge, La., 1975.

Yearns, Wilfred B. *The Confederate Congress.* Athens, Ga., 1960.

LESLIE A. LOVETT

SPAR TORPEDOES. The spar torpedo was an offensive naval weapon consisting of a watertight explosive charge attached to a movable shaft mounted on the forward end of a vessel near its waterline. Equipped with multiple pressure-sensitive fuses, it was designed to be rammed and detonated against the underside of an enemy ship. Such an apparatus was conceived as early as 1810 when Robert Fulton submitted to Congress a harbor and coastal defense scheme based on underwater warfare.

The idea was revived in the South during the Civil War. In October 1862, army Capt. Francis D. Lee received permission to build a torpedo ram armed with a spar torpedo of his own design, for which he later received a patent. Robert E. Lee's successful demonstration of the weapon's destructive power against a hulk the following winter spurred interest in the device. As a result, the ironclads *Chicora* and *Palmetto State* and a small fleet of rowboats at Charleston were the initial vessels equipped with spar-mounted explosive charges. One of the latter, crewed by seven men commanded by navy Lt. William T. Glassell on March 18, 1863, attacked the USS *Powhaten* in the first combat use of the weapon. The effort failed when one of the crew panicked, throwing the boat off target.

Subsequent unsuccessful attempts by man-powered torpedo boats prompted the development of small steam-driven craft designed specifically for the purpose. The first of these was *David,* a semisubmersible, cigar-shaped vessel forty-eight and one-half feet long and five feet in diameter. Commanded by Glassell, *David* struck USS *New Ironsides* with a spar torpedo on October 5, 1863. The explosion caused considerable damage but failed to sink the massive ironclad. As many as six additional *David*-type torpedo boats were built at Charleston and another five at Savannah, but none achieved the success of the original.

At Richmond, steam-powered torpedo launches were constructed and operated as part of the James River Squadron. One, *Squib,* made a daring assault on USS *Minnesota* off Newport News, Virginia, after stealing down the James and through the Union fleet. Little damage was inflicted when the torpedo exploded too near the water's surface. Additional torpedo launches designed by Naval Constructor William A. Graves were planned for construc-

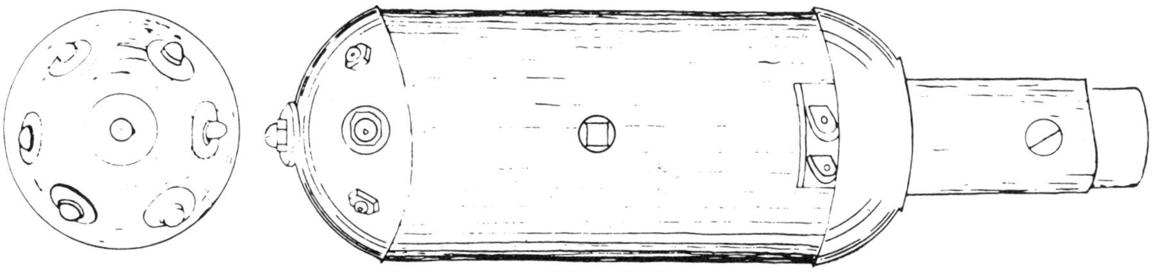

SPAR TORPEDO. Confederate spar torpedo used with *David*-class torpedo boat.

NAVAL HISTORICAL CENTER, WASHINGTON, D.C.

tion late in the war at Richmond; Columbus, Georgia; on the Peedee River, South Carolina; and elsewhere. Others were to be built in Britain and shipped through the blockade.

The most successful use of the weapon occurred February 17, 1864, when the ill-fated hand-powered submarine *H. L. Hunley* exploded its spar torpedo against USS *Housatonic* off Charleston Harbor. As a result of the explosion the Union vessel quickly sank with the loss of five lives—the first warship destroyed in combat by a spar torpedo. The *Hunley* failed to return from this mission and was lost with all hands, presumedly a victim of her own torpedo.

Spar torpedoes were ultimately fitted to all manner of craft, from small tugboats to huge ironclads, at most major Confederate ports. The torpedoes employed varied from small copper cylinders to large wooden barrels containing 50 to 150 pounds of powder. As many as seven pressure-sensitive fuses were screwed into the forward and upper surfaces of the torpedo. The most commonly utilized fuse was a chemical ignitor developed by Captain Lee. It consisted of a small glass vial containing sulfuric acid enclosed within a thin three-inch-long lead tube containing a mixture of chlorate of potassa (now called potassium chlorate), powdered sugar, and rifle powder. When crushed by impact, the acid ignited the compound, which in turn exploded the torpedo.

Although the Confederates never achieved the results desired, they clearly demonstrated the potential of offensive torpedo warfare. Moreover, the psychological impact on the enemy was considerable. The fear of torpedo attacks forced the Federal blockading fleets to adopt drastic precautionary measures that often restricted their ability to perform their primary function of maintaining the blockade.

[*See also* Davids; Hunley, H. L.; Torpedoes and Land Mines.]

BIBLIOGRAPHY

Barnes, John S. *Submarine Warfare, Offensive and Defensive.* New York, 1869.

Burton, E. Milby. *Siege of Charleston, 1861–1865.* Columbia, S.C., 1970.

Glassell, W. T. "Torpedo Service in Charleston Harbor." *Confederate Veteran* 25 (1917): 113–114. Reprint, Wilmington, N.C., 1985.

Parker, William H. *Recollections of a Naval Officer, 1841–65.* New York, 1883.

Perry, Milton F. *Infernal Machines: The Story of Confederate Submarine and Mine Warfare.* Baton Rouge, La., 1965.

A. Robert Holcombe, Jr.

SPECIAL UNITS. Confederate elite units were many in number, spanning both the western and eastern theaters of operations, as well as the inland water navy, the high seas navy, and coastal defense units.

In the western theater of operations the infantry division of Maj. Gen. Patrick Cleburne stands out as such a unit, as do the First Missouri Brigade and the Kentucky Orphan Brigade. Nathan Bedford Forrest's cavalry and his artillery under the command of Capt. John Morton were outstanding in every respect. An elite Confederate western artillery unit was the Fifth Company, Washington Artillery of New Orleans, also known as Slocum's Battery. Other units included John Hunt Morgan's cavalry, and Capt. John Dickinson's guerrillas who operated in Florida. Another special unit, the Davis Guards, received medals (the only ones awarded by the Confederacy) for their heroic stand at Sabine Pass, Texas, in 1863.

The eastern theater of operations saw an abundance of elite ground forces. Foremost were the Stonewall Brigade and John Bell Hood's Texas Brigade, both of which were models of courage, discipline, and esprit de corps. In addition, A. P. Hill's Light Division and the Louisiana Tiger Brigade were exceptionally fine units, as was Wade Hampton's Legion, formed early in the war. The First Virginia Infantry Regiment, which traced its origin to George Washington in the French and Indian War, spearheaded George E. Pickett's charge at Gettysburg. Composing an elite unit that was not a regular part of the Army of Northern Virginia were the Virginia Military Institute cadets who gained immortality at the Battle of New Market in 1864. The Army of Northern Virginia included the famed Washington Artillery of New Orleans, the Rockbridge Artillery of the Stonewall Brigade, the Richmond Howitzers, and John Pegram's and William T. Pougue's Artillery Battalions.

Like the western theater, the Confederate cavalry in the eastern theater contained many elite units. Their names ring across the years: Turner Ashby's cavalry, John S. Mosby's Rangers, the Laurel Brigade, and J. E. B. Stuart's Cavalry Corps. Accompanying the latter was the elite Stuart Horse Artillery under John Pelham.

On the high seas the Confederacy was equally well served. Such vessels as *Alabama* and *Shenandoah* were renowned. In the inland water navy, elite units manned *Virginia* and *Tennessee.* The volunteer crew of *Hunley,* the first submarine that sank a warship, manned an experimental vessel whose previous crews had drowned during test voyages. Such courage could be found only among the finest of fighting units.

[*See also entries on the numerous biographical figures, military units, and ships mentioned herein.*]

BIBLIOGRAPHY

Connolly, Thomas L. *Army of the Heartland: The Army of Tennessee, 1861–1862.* Baton Rouge, La., 1967.

Connolly, Thomas L. *Autumn of Glory: The Army of Tennessee, 1862–1865.* Baton Rouge, La., 1971.

Freeman, Douglas S. *Lee's Lieutenants: A Study in Command.* 3 vols. New York, 1942–1944. Reprint, New York, 1986.
Jones, Virgil Carrington. *The Civil War at Sea.* 3 vols. New York, 1960–1962. Reprint, Wilmington, N.C., 1990.
Roth, David. "The Battle of Sabine Pass, Texas." *Blue and Gray Magazine* 4, no. 1 (August–September 1986): 7–24.

KIM BERNARD HOLIEN

SPECULATION. Both real and imagined, speculation hit all Southerners at one point or another during the war and created bitterness and anger toward the perpetrators. Moreover, it precipitated a decline in living standards and thus affected morale.

From the beginning of its existence, the Confederacy faced the problem of how to pay for the war effort. Secretary of the Treasury Christopher G. Memminger tried a number of plans, but by the midpoint of the war, his office was forced to rely upon the printing press and loans to pay for the war. The increased circulation of paper currency produced inflation. At first, the general commodity price index stood at antebellum levels, but by 1863 it had skyrocketed to levels twenty-eight times higher than those of 1861.

The increased cost of manufactured goods and agricultural products hit people hard, especially those living in the urban centers. Residents of Richmond and Atlanta, for example, saw the cost of foodstuffs grow prohibitive: in 1864, flour was sold for $250 a barrel—when it could be had; sweet potatoes garnered $16 a bushel; and meat commanded over $2 a pound. Discontent increased in proportion to the rise in prices, and most Southerners began to seek a cause for the exorbitant cost of necessities. Initially, they blamed the Commissary Department for buying up goods for the army and thus creating shortages on the home front which led to higher prices. Soon, manufacturers were also targeted: editorials and diarists argued that the factories charged higher prices on goods for the public in order to compensate for the loss they took producing for the government at lower fixed prices. Before long, merchants and traders were also pilloried in the press and in private. Such accusations often became anti-Semitic in tone, as Confederates began equating all traders with Jews and all Jews with Shylock-like practices.

Some Southerners, mostly women, refused to accept inflation and speculators without protest. The year 1863 witnessed a number of food riots throughout the urban Confederacy. Women, beaten down by high prices, took matters into their own hands in Richmond, Atlanta, Salisbury and High Point, North Carolina, and other places and demanded relief. These outbursts of violence can be interpreted as manifestations of unrest motivated by the perception and reality that speculation and speculators caused inflation and shortages, and hence deprivation.

The extent of real speculation in the Confederate South is difficult to assess. Basically, anyone who bought food, clothing, or other goods and held them for a period of time could expect to make a profit as money became increasingly cheaper. Still, some did not realize as great a profit as critics alleged. Though a merchant or manufacturer might hold an item off the shelves for a while to realize a profit, that profit was gained in inflated currency and was probably less than the original price of the good.

Speculators did exist in the Confederacy from the very beginning. Their practices were time-honored: buy a commodity in bulk to corner the market, float rumors of shortages, and then raise prices and sell at a profit. Most speculators dealt in such goods as cotton, salt, and meat; others dealt in necessities like shoes and clothing.

Confederate state governments could not ignore the problem of speculation—public outrage as inflation grew made some type of action imperative. Governors Andrew B. Moore of Alabama and Zebulon Vance of North Carolina published denunciations of speculators and extortioners (the words were usually used synonymously) and threatened to take drastic action. But Governor Joseph E. Brown of Georgia admitted laws against speculation were largely meaningless because speculators would find a way to evade them by continuing to withhold goods from the market or by refusing to sell goods to military authorities. Brown's comments to the General Assembly of Georgia in April 1863 epitomize the kind of language used to describe speculators: They are "a class . . . who remain at home preying upon the vitals of society, determined to make money at every hazard, who turn a deaf ear to the cries of the soldiers' families and are prepared to immolate even our armies and sacrifice our liberties upon the altar of mammon." Brown saw to it that Georgia taxed those speculating in needed commodities, but like other legislation aimed at speculators, it had little effect.

Although it is true that many did seek private gain at public expense, the real reasons for inflated prices and shortages of goods lay elsewhere. Many farmers found that government policies of impressment and the tax-in-kind hurt them; consequently, they withheld food from the market or planted less, which added to the inflationary spiral. Other farmers who did produce for both the people and the army had to cope with a transportation system that was woefully inadequate: often food would rot at depots awaiting transportation to markets or the front. Finally, the Union blockade stopped the flow of European goods, adding to the shortages and inflated prices. The net effect of all these factors—poor transportation facilities, the blockade, government policies, and the unscrupulous efforts of some who sought to reap profits during wartime—created inflated prices and led to charges of speculation and extortion.

There is no doubt that speculation—real and imagined—had a tremendous impact on the Confederate nation. Diaries, newspaper editorials, and public pronouncements against speculation demonstrate that Southerners detested the problem and the culprits. Disgust with unsavory practices and the inability to obtain needed goods for survival caused many Confederates to lose faith in a government that seemed ill equipped and unprepared to deal with the problem. The net result of inflation and speculation was a noticeable decline in support for the Confederate cause.

[*See also* Bread Riots; Extortion; Inflation.]

BIBLIOGRAPHY

Escott, Paul D. *After Secession: Jefferson Davis and the Failure of Confederate Nationalism.* Baton Rouge, La., 1978.

Escott, Paul D. *Many Excellent People: Power and Privilege in North Carolina, 1850–1900.* Chapel Hill, N.C., 1985.

Lerner, Eugene. "Inflation in the Confederacy." In *Studies in the Quantity Theory of Money.* Edited by Milton Friedman. Chicago, 1956.

Thomas, Emory. *The Confederate Nation, 1861–1865.* New York, 1979.

Todd, Richard Cecil. *Confederate Finance.* Athens, Ga., 1954.

MARY A. DECREDICO

SPENCER, CORNELIA PHILLIPS

SPENCER, CORNELIA PHILLIPS (1825–1908), journalist and education advocate. Born in Harlem, New York, on March 20, 1825, Spencer moved with her family to North Carolina at the age of one year when her father became a professor at the University of North Carolina. Spencer, unlike her two brothers, could not attend the university because of her gender, but she studied on her own. From 1855 to 1861, she lived in Clinton, Alabama, with her husband, James Monroe Spencer, and when he died, returned to her parents' home in Chapel Hill with her only child.

During the war, Spencer gave private lessons in Latin and Greek, but the Civil War and the defeat of the South led her to question how North Carolina could improve itself in order to compete successfully with other states. Her articles on this issue brought her to the attention of the Reverend Charles Force Weems, who persuaded her to write articles for his magazine, the *Watchman,* describing the final weeks of the war in North Carolina. Using the recollections of friends and veterans, Spencer related the chaos, bravery, and despair that accompanied the Northern armies' march through the state as the war drew to a close. The articles were published in 1866 as *The Last Ninety Days of the War in North Carolina.*

Spencer after the war became a champion on behalf of the University of North Carolina, lobbying vigorously for its funding. In 1894 she moved to Cambridge, Massachusetts, with her daughter's family and died there on March 11, 1908.

BIBLIOGRAPHY

Chamberlain, Hope S. *Old Days in Chapel Hill.* Chapel Hill, N.C., 1926.

James, Edward T., ed. *Notable American Women: A Biographical Dictionary.* Cambridge, Mass., 1971.

CHRISTINE A. LUNARDINI

SPIES

SPIES. *For discussion of Confederate and Federal spies, see* Espionage, *articles on* Confederate Military Spies *and* Federal Secret Service.

SPOTSYLVANIA CAMPAIGN

SPOTSYLVANIA CAMPAIGN. Spotsylvania Court House, Virginia, a county seat approximately nine miles southwest of Fredericksburg, became for a two-week period in May 1864 the focus of a series of engagements between the Army of Northern Virginia and the Army of the Potomac commanded respectively by Gens. Robert E. Lee and George G. Meade. When the opposing armies began to depart the area on the evening of May 20, the Confederates had sustained between 9,000 and 10,000 casualties here and the Federals more than 18,000.

Following two days of fighting in the Wilderness on May 5 and 6, Union General in Chief Ulysses S. Grant, who accompanied Meade's army in this summer campaign, ordered the army commander to move his force southeast twelve miles to the vicinity of Spotsylvania Court House. The movement began after dark on May 7. Lee also decided to move his First Corps to the same location during the night. The Confederates arrived just before the Federals, and the opposing advanced forces collided one and a half miles northwest of the village on the morning of May 8. Throughout the remainder of the day additional units from each army arrived and became engaged, with the Confederates maintaining their original position.

During the campaign Lee was operating at a disadvantage concerning two of his key subordinates. His ablest corps commander, Lt. Gen. James Longstreet, had been seriously wounded by friendly troops in the Wilderness fighting. Lee selected Maj. Gen. Richard Heron Anderson to command his First Corps until "Old Pete" returned. On the morning of May 8 Third Corps commander Maj. Gen. A. P. Hill was too ill to mount his horse. Maj. Gen. Jubal Early, a division commander in Maj. Gen. Richard S. Ewell's Second Corps, was chosen to replace Hill.

On May 9 the Union Ninth Corps, commanded by Maj. Gen. Ambrose E. Burnside, advanced south from the area of Chancellorsville and assumed position east of the courthouse with its left lying on the Fredericksburg-Spotsylvania

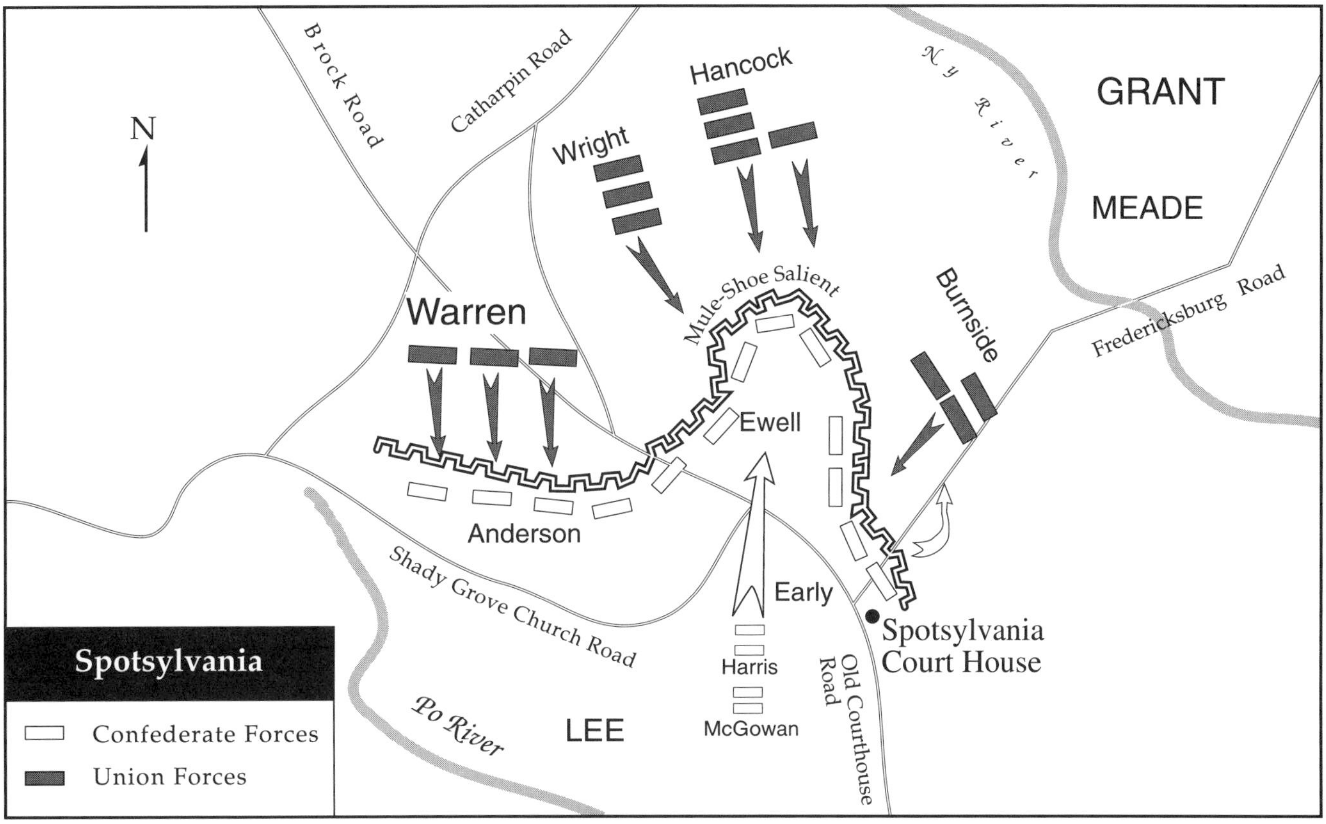

Court House Road. As a result, when Early's Third Corps arrived, Lee placed it opposite Burnside's troops immediately east of the village. In the morning a Confederate sharpshooter killed the commander of the Union Sixth Corps, Maj. Gen. John Sedgwick. On this day, the Union's chief of cavalry, Maj. Gen. Philip Sheridan, led most of the Federal cavalry corps from the area on a raid south toward Richmond. Lee dispatched his chief of cavalry, Maj. Gen. J. E. B. Stuart, with Maj. Gen. Fitzhugh Lee's division to pursue the Federal horsemen. Two days later Stuart was mortally wounded in an engagement at Yellow Tavern, immediately north of Richmond. This was a crippling loss to the Confederacy.

At Spotsylvania the Confederate battle line consisted of Anderson's First Corps on the left and Ewell's Second in the center; both of these units faced north. Early's Third Corps manned the right of the line facing east. The center of the line occupied by Ewell's troops bulged forward to the north in the form of a salient, or "mule-shoe."

On May 10 the Federals executed attacks all along the line but were unable to coordinate them. Union Maj. Gen. Winfield S. Hancock's Second Corps advanced beyond Anderson's left flank, but darkness fell before the Northerners were prepared to assault that vulnerable flank. Late in the afternoon twelve Union regiments commanded by Col. Emory Upton succeeded in penetrating a segment of Ewell's line along the western face of the salient and captured nearly a thousand Confederates. The Unionists were not supported, however, and were pushed back by Confederate reserve forces. Upton's temporary success gave Grant an idea. The twelve regiments had been massed compactly and had penetrated the Southern position with relative ease. Grant ordered Meade to move Hancock's entire Second Corps from the right of the Union line to the center opposite Ewell and with it attack the tip or apex of the Confederate salient at first light on May 12.

On May 11 General Lee, evaluating certain Union activities behind their lines such as reconnaissance missions and the repositioning of supply wagons, erroneously concluded that the Federals were preparing to break contact that night and move east to Fredericksburg and thence south toward Richmond. If this occurred, the Southern commander was determined to attack the Federals in transit. He ordered his artillery corps commanders to move rearward after dark any batteries that would be difficult to relocate rapidly once a movement by the army had been determined. Thus, many of the guns positioned along the apex of the salient were withdrawn.

As Hancock's troops moved into position for the attack, they were heard by Ewell's pickets who immediately reported these sounds. Ewell was eventually persuaded by one of his division commanders, Maj. Gen. Edward ("Allegheny") Johnson, whose division was positioned along the apex of the salient, to recall the artillery pieces that had been withdrawn. The recall order did not reach the artillerymen in the rear until 3:40 A.M.

Visibility on the morning of May 12 was reduced to fifty yards by ground fog. Hancock's troops began their advance at 4:35 A.M. Their number totaled 19,000 with the two leading divisions consisting of 11,000. "Allegheny" Johnson's division of 4,000 infantrymen would bear the brunt of this onslaught with little artillery support. Some Confederate pickets were captured. Others fired a hasty round and took to their heels. They warned their comrades manning the main line of the mass of Federals approaching, but the troops could only wait until the Bluecoats became visible about a hundred yards in front. At this time the orders to fire were given. Rain had fallen intermittently during the night, and much of the Southern powder was damp and did not ignite. The Northerners poured over the works in overwhelming numbers. The returning artillery pieces arrived at this time and were overrun and captured. A few gun crews were able to fire a round or two before surrendering.

Many of the Federals continued to advance southward inside of the salient in disorganized groups. These were stopped and driven back to the outside of the works by Confederate reserves. Approximately 3,000 Southerners including "Allegheny" Johnson were captured in the attack along with twenty pieces of artillery.

With most of Johnson's division gone, a considerable segment of the line was unoccupied on the inside by any Confederate troops. To correct this, Lee forwarded two brigades from the Third Corps during the morning. These were Brig. Gen. Nathaniel H. Harris's Mississippi Brigade and the South Carolinians of Brig. Gen. Samuel McGowan's brigade who arrived on the scene at 7:30 A.M. and 9:30 A.M., respectively. These troops upon arrival drove the Federals away from the outside of the works and reoccupied a portion of the trench line formerly held by Johnson's troops. McGowan was wounded in the advance to the front line and was superseded in command by Col. Joseph N. Brown. By noon the entire Federal Sixth Corps, now commanded by Brig. Gen. Horatio G. Wright, had been moved opposite Harris's and McGowan's positions.

These opposing forces—Harris's and Brown's brigades inside the works, and the Union Sixth Corps and portions of Hancock's Second outside—retained their relative positions along the northern face of the salient front and maintained continuous fire of varying intensity until 4:00 the following morning. At times the antagonists were only twenty yards apart. Occasionally an impulsive surge forward by a hundred or so Northerners would carry over the works and be immediately hurled back in bloody hand-to-hand fighting. Rain fell intermittently during the afternoon.

While this desperate fighting occurred, other Confederates were constructing a new defensive line of works across the base of the salient nearly one mile to the rear. Finally, at 4:00 A.M., Harris's, Brown's, and the remaining Confederate troops in position along the sides of the salient were permitted to retire to the new line. Thus ended what was probably the most intense twenty-three-hour period of land warfare in a confined area up to that time.

The operations conducted during the remaining ten days of the campaign were anticlimactic. The Army of the Potomac joined the Ninth Corps east of the village where its line lay in a north-south direction facing west. The Confederates changed their relative alignment accordingly. The opposing forces departed the vicinity of Spotsylvania Court House on May 21 and May 22. They would meet again at the North Anna River.

Assuming that Lee's objective in the campaign was to keep the enemy out of central Virginia by holding the line of the Rapidan River, the Battle of Spotsylvania can be considered a strategic defeat. After the Wilderness fighting on May 7 and again on May 21, Lee was unable to prevent the Federals from moving their forces in the direction they desired. This had not happened before in northern Virginia during the war.

The Army of Northern Virginia had once again inflicted severe casualties upon its old antagonist, but its own losses were in some respects more damaging. On May 12 alone Lee lost the services of one major general and seven brigadier generals. During the two weeks of Spotsylvania, 4,600 troops from Ewell's Second Corps became prisoners. Lee could not readily replace these losses.

Spotsylvania was only one of the many series of battles that swept across Virginia in May and early June of 1864. It took a heavy toll of experienced officers and invaluable enlisted men from the Army of Northern Virginia. These losses contributed significantly to the weakening of the Confederacy's military capabilities.

[*See also* Yellow Tavern, Virginia.]

BIBLIOGRAPHY

Brown, Varina D. *A Colonel at Gettysburg and Spotsylvania.* Columbia, S.C., 1931.

Freeman, Douglas S. *Lee's Lieutenants: A Study in Command.* 3 vols. New York, 1942–1944. Reprint, New York, 1986.

Humphreys, Andrew A. *The Virginia Campaign of '64 and '65.* New York, 1883.

Johnson, Robert U., and C. C. Buel, eds. *Battles and Leaders of the Civil War.* 4 vols. New York, 1887–1888. Reprint, Secaucus, N.J., 1982.

Matter, William D. *If It Takes All Summer: The Battle of Spotsylvania.* Chapel Hill, N.C., 1988.

U.S. War Department. *War of the Rebellion: A Compilation of the Official Records of the Union and Confederate Armies.* Washington, D.C., 1880–1901. Ser. 1, vol. 36, pts. 1–3; ser. 1, vol. 51, pts. 1–2.

The Wilderness Campaign, May–June, 1964. Papers of the Military Historical Society of Massachusetts, no. 4. Boston, 1905. Reprint, Wilmington, N.C., 1989.

WILLIAM D. MATTER

STAFFORD, LEROY A. (1822–1864), brigadier general. Born near Cheneyville, Louisiana, on April 13, 1822, Stafford became a wealthy planter and sheriff of Rapides Parish. A Mexican War veteran, he opposed secession but raised a company of infantry when war began.

Stafford was elected lieutenant colonel of Richard Taylor's Ninth Louisiana Volunteers and became colonel upon Taylor's promotion to brigadier general. During the 1862 Shenandoah Valley campaign Stafford earned a reputation for gallantry at Winchester and Port Republic. He later was described by Gen. Edward Johnson as being the bravest man Johnson ever met. Stafford briefly commanded Taylor's First Louisiana Brigade during the Seven Days' campaign and was then transferred to the Second Louisiana Brigade. At the Second Battle of Manassas he temporarily commanded William E. Starke's brigade and defended an exposed part of the line. There the brigade earned widespread fame by defending its position with rocks after ammunition ran out. A few weeks later Stafford again led the brigade at Sharpsburg. In thirty minutes of combat he lost almost three hundred men and was forced out of action himself during the day by a painful foot bruise he received from a shell fragment.

Rejoining the First Louisiana Brigade, Stafford's regiment participated in the attack at Salem Church on May 4, 1863. Stafford was captured when the brigade was repulsed, but he was exchanged in time to fight at Gettysburg. Promoted to brigadier general on October 8, 1863, he was given command of the Second Louisiana Brigade and handled it well at Payne's farm on November 27. On May 5, 1864, Stafford led his brigade into the Wilderness and was shot through the spine. He died in Richmond on May 8.

BIBLIOGRAPHY

Jones, Terry L. *Lee's Tigers: The Louisiana Infantry in the Army of Northern Virginia.* Baton Rouge, La., 1987.

Stafford, G. M. G. *General Leroy Augustus Stafford, His Forebears and Descendants.* New Orleans, La., 1943.

TERRY L. JONES

STAMPS. The Confederate government was continually frustrated in its attempts to supply citizens with postage stamps—either in the quantity or of the quality to which they had become accustomed under Federal postal jurisdiction. Making use of experienced specialists in stamp design and production would have answered this need, but these printers were located in the North, and any hope of contracting with Union publishers to produce Confederate stamps ended when the war began. On occasion, the Confederacy would try importing its stamps, but the blockade eventually choked off such trade. As for homemade products—when there were enough artists available to design them and sufficient ink and paper to print them—they were invariably inferior to anything available in the North or abroad. What one period observer remarked about the new nation's currency might as easily have been

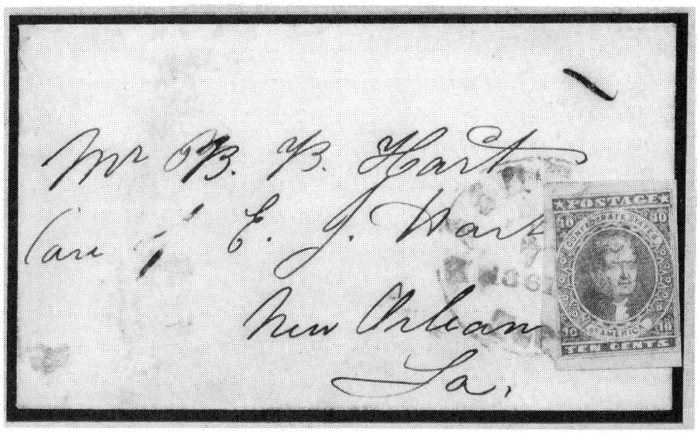

TEN-CENT BLUE THOMAS JEFFERSON STAMP. Lithographed on stone by Hoyer & Ludwig, Richmond, Virginia. The envelope, postmarked Nashville, Tennessee, February 7, 1861, was actually mailed in 1862 to B. B. Hart, care of E. J. Hart, New Orleans, Louisiana. GORDON BLEULER

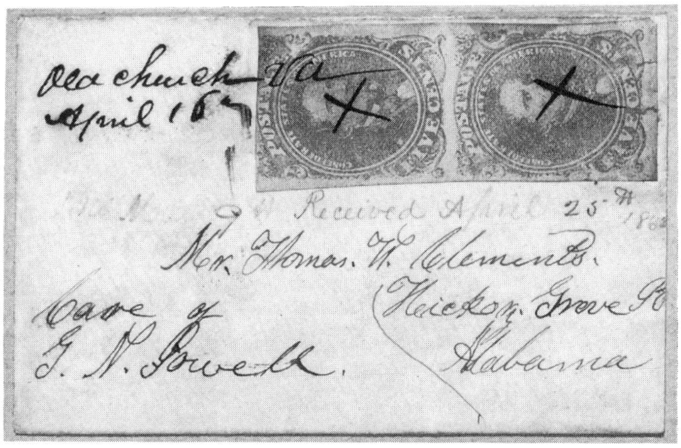

PAIR OF FIVE-CENT BLUE JEFFERSON DAVIS STAMPS. Lithographed on stone by Hoyer and Ludwig, Richmond, Virginia. The envelope was postmarked by hand at the Old Church Post Office in Hanover, Virginia, April 16, 1862, and is addressed to Mr. Thomas W. Clements, Hickory Grove Post Office, Alabama, care of G. A. Powell. GORDON BLEULER

Two-cent green Andrew Jackson stamp. Lithographed on stone by Hoyer and Ludwig, Richmond, Virginia. This stamp, for circular use, is one of the scarcest of the Confederate regular issues. The envelope, postmarked Lynchburg, Virginia, October 4, 1862 or 1863, is addressed to Henry St. George Husier, Esq., Virginia Mills, Buckingham County, Virginia. Gordon Bleuler

said of its postage stamps: "Neither in material nor in execution would they have reflected credit on a village printing-office."

Southern-born heroes like George Washington had long adorned Federal postage stamps, and with the establishment of the Confederate Post Office Department in 1861, officials determined to maintain this tradition. The government awarded the first contract to produce stamps to Hoyer & Ludwig, Richmond-based publishers best known for their parlor prints and songsheet covers. (The awarding of such priority contracts all but ended the production of decorative prints for the remainder of the war; firms like Hoyer & Ludwig were virtually ordered to focus on what one journalist called "needed articles," and it was not unusual for the government to transfer artists from other firms, or from the army, to assist with official orders.)

By April 1861 Hoyer & Ludwig had supplied John H. Reagan, postmaster general of the Confederacy, with their first "samples of postal stamps," explaining: "The ten-cent stamps represent the C. S. Flag, which we have engraved. The two- and five-cent stamps we only made the drawings of, which we intend to make if the order should be given to us. The twenty we would like to make with President Davis's portrait, in which case you would have to furnish us with a good likeness, if you should favor us with the contract for making the stamps." Hoyer & Ludwig still found it necessary to add their hope that they would receive "preference" over "Northern houses."

By the time their designs were under review, Fort Sumter had been taken and the war was underway; "Northern houses" were no longer competing. But the problems facing the Richmond publisher were obvious from their first letter: they did not even have on hand a likeness of the new president on which to model a portrait.

Hoyer & Ludwig got their contract, but not for engraved stamps, which were too expensive to produce. Instead they

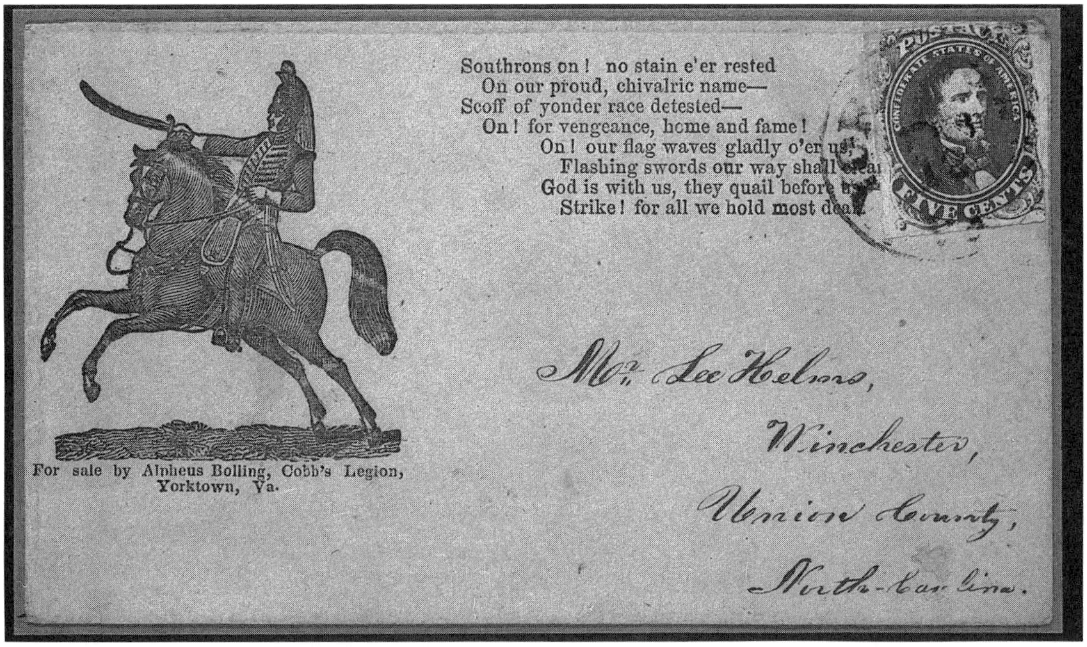

Five-cent green Jefferson Davis stamp. Lithographed on stone by Hoyer & Ludwig, Richmond, Virginia. The patriotic envelope is postmarked Yorktown, Virginia, and addressed to Mrs. Lee Helms, Winchester, Union County, North Carolina. Gordon Bleuler

issued lithographed five-cent stamps in sheets of one hundred each. These first stamps were not perforated; users had to cut them apart themselves. A portrait of Jefferson Davis was evidently obtained and copied, for the new stamps featured a blurry, if familiar prewar likeness of the president. The stamps were on sale by October 1861, when the *Richmond Daily Dispatch* generously praised the "very excellent bust of President Davis," adding of the stamps: "Their introduction supplies a want which has heretofore seriously taxed the public endurance." Prior to the issue of these first stamps, local postmasters had been left to their own initiative. They had marked postal rate, town, and cancellation by hand or had used provisional hand stamps. Some postmasters had even prepared their own postage stamps for local sale and use.

Hoyer & Ludwig continued to manufacture stamps for the Confederacy for the duration of the war. One artist remembered that the firm's twelve presses were on line "most of the time," usually for the production of stamps and currency. "At first my output was 200 sheets per day," he added, shedding light on the human side of stamp production in the Confederacy. "But I soon got it up to a ream—480 sheets. You see, I was getting $5.00 a week in Confederate money, with a bonus for all over 200 sheets pulled per day."

The very month the Hoyer & Ludwig stamps first appeared, Postmaster General Reagan was already searching for an alternative to the homemade products. He authorized a government agent traveling to England in search of arms imports to arrange also for the creation of higher-quality stamps. A contract was signed with Thomas De La Rue & Co. of London, which commissioned an artist named Jean Ferdinand Joubert de la Ferte to engrave a Davis likeness for a new stamp, a vast improvement over the Richmond models. In February 1862 De La Rue exported the finished plates, along with 2 million stamps, to the Confederacy. But even this huge supply was quickly depleted, and the blockade made it difficult to continue relying on such imports.

That year, Reagan contracted with another Richmond firm, Archer & Daly, to make their own stamps directly from the De La Rue plates. Native paper and ink, however, proved inferior to the British variety, and so did native skill with the presses. The results from Archer & Daly were wildly inconsistent, and one infamous run proved so flawed it made President Davis appear to be wearing a long white tie. The "white cravat" Davis stamp eventually became one of the most coveted among postwar collectors.

On July 1, 1862, the Confederacy doubled its basic postal rate to ten cents, requiring new issues. The De La Rue company was hired to make new plates, but apparently did little more than burnish out the "five cents" inscription on the old plates, replacing it with the new rate. These stamps were issued in a rose-colored hue, supplanting the "five cent blues" that had become familiar to Confederates, flaws notwithstanding. De La Rue also supplied some 400,000 copies of a one-cent stamp depicting John C. Calhoun and intended for less expensive mailings, such as circulars and

Confederate Regular Postal Issues

Date	Denomination/ Color	Portrait	Notes
1861	5¢ green	Jefferson Davis	
1861	10¢ blue	Thomas Jefferson	
1862	2¢ green	Andrew Jackson	
1862	5¢ blue	Jefferson Davis	
1862	50¢ rose	Thomas Jefferson	
1862	1¢ orange	John Calhoun	Printed in England, never placed in use.
1862	5¢ blue	Jefferson Davis	Printed in England.
1862	5¢ blue	Jefferson Davis	
1863	2¢ brown	Andrew Jackson	
1863	10¢ blue	Jefferson Davis	Denomination is spelled "Ten," no number is shown. Stamp has a distinct shade of blue.
1863	10¢ blue	Jefferson Davis	A heavy frame line was ruled between each of the stamps in the pane of 100 units (10 × 10).
1863	10¢ blue	Jefferson Davis	Type I: outer scrolls show up clearly. Vast range of shades.
1863	10¢ blue	Jefferson Davis	Type II: outer scrolls have been filled in completely around borders of stamp. Vast range of shades.
1863	20¢ green	George Washington	

Source: Skinner, Hubert C., Erin Gunter, and Warren H. Sanders, *Dietz CSA Catalog and Handbook*, Miami, Fla., 1986.

PAIR OF FIVE-CENT BLUE JEFFERSON DAVIS STAMPS. Electrotype plates by Thomas De La Rue & Company, London, England; printed by Archer & Daly, Richmond, Virginia. The bottom stamp of this pair is a "white cravat" stamp, one of the most coveted by postwar collectors. A flaw in the printing makes it appear as if Davis is wearing a white tie (see arrow on illustration). The handmade envelope, constructed from wallpaper owing to a shortage of traditional materials, is postmarked Navasota, Texas, October 7, 1863, and is addressed to Mrs. A. J. McCarty, Rockwall, Kaufman County, Texas, from William McCarty, 3d Regiment, Texas State Infantry, Camp Lane, Fannan County, Texas. GORDON BLEULER

newspapers. By the time these stamps arrived, the circular rate had increased to two cents; as a result, the stamps were never released for sale or use. The Confederacy also managed to issue a ten-cent stamp (from Hoyer & Ludwig) depicting Thomas Jefferson, and a two-cent "green" featuring a horribly smudged portrait of Andrew Jackson. It was not unusual for the colors of these issues to vary as markedly as the quality of their portrait likenesses.

Whatever their shortcomings, Confederate postage stamps after the war became highly desirable collectibles, not only in unused states, but affixed to patriotic envelopes or even canceled on everyday mail. The rage inspired its share of bogus reissues from surviving plates and stones, as well as out-and-out fakes, including a clever Stonewall Jackson ten-cent issue that in all likelihood originated no earlier than 1867. One scholar of the Confederate postal service and its stamp issues has estimated that nearly a quarter of the examples he has inspected have been forgeries.

BIBLIOGRAPHY

Dietz, August, Sr. *The Postal Service of the Confederate States of America.* Richmond, Va., 1929.

Green, Brian M. *The Confederate States Five-Cent Blue Lithograph.* New York, 1978.

Green, Brian M. *The Confederate States Ten-Cent Rose Lithograph.* New York, 1978.

Green, Brian M. *The Confederate States Two-Cent Green Lithograph.* New York, 1977.

Green, Brian M. *The Typographs of the Confederate States of America: Postal Stamps and Postal History.* New York, 1981.

Neely, Mark E., Jr., Harold Holzer, and Gabor S. Boritt. *The Confederate Image: Prints of the Lost Cause.* Chapel Hill, N.C., 1977.

HAROLD HOLZER

STANLEY, HENRY MORTON (1841–1904), Confederate private, Union artillerist and sailor, journalist, and explorer. Born in Wales, John Rowlands immigrated to the United States in 1859. He found employment in New Orleans with a cotton broker, Henry Morton Stanley, whose name he took.

In 1861, swept along by the emotion and enthusiasm of the moment, he enlisted with the Sixth Arkansas Infantry (Dixie Grays), a decision he later considered a "grave blunder." His *Autobiography* contains a highly critical account of the hardships endured by the Grays during their "seasoning" and a compelling and graphic description of the fighting at Shiloh where Stanley was made a prisoner.

Confined at Camp Douglas, near Chicago, Stanley was unable to endure the privations of prison life. Thus, after two months, he enrolled in the U.S. Artillery Service, motivated not by conversion to the Northern cause but by "a fear of being incarcerated for years." When he arrived at Harpers Ferry, dysentery and fever overcame him and led to his discharge on June 22, 1862. In August 1864 he joined the U.S. Navy. He served as a ship's writer and witnessed the attacks on Fort Fisher, North Carolina, in January 1865. Northern newspapers welcomed his vivid accounts of the action, and this launched him on a journalistic career.

After the war, Stanley distinguished himself as a correspondent for the *New York Herald* and achieved international fame for finding missionary David Livingstone in central Africa. Subsequently he returned to Britain and became a member of Parliament.

BIBLIOGRAPHY

Hohenberg, John. *Foreign Correspondence: The Great Reporters and Their Times.* New York, 1964.

Stanley, Henry Morton. *The Autobiography of Sir Henry Morton Stanley.* Edited by Dorothy Stanley. New York, 1937.

Stanley, Henry Morton. *My Early Travels and Adventures in America and Asia.* 2 vols. London, 1895.

CHARLES MCARVER

STANLY, EDWARD (1810–1872), Union military governor of North Carolina. A Whig congressman from an eastern North Carolina district (from 1837 through 1843, and from 1849 through 1853) Stanly moved to San

Francisco, California, in 1853 to practice law. There he was the new Republican party's unsuccessful candidate for governor in 1857. He spoke out strongly in favor of the Union in 1861 and against those who wished to establish a separate Pacific republic. In April 1862, Abraham Lincoln appointed him military governor of North Carolina and peace emissary, with the duty of reestablishing federal authority in his native state.

Stanly arrived in New Bern on May 26, 1862, and soon learned that he faced an impossible task. On the one hand, North Carolina Confederates regarded him as a traitor and renegade, and pent up within the Union lines along the coast, he could get no hearing; on the other, his refusal to approve a school for blacks at New Bern aroused the ire of Northern abolitionists. Stanly viewed a Free Labor movement among nonslaveholding whites as a serious threat to his conciliation policy. He ordered a congressional election in North Carolina's Second District on January 1, 1863, but the House of Representatives refused to seat the winner, Jennings Pigott.

Stanly resigned his abortive "mission of love" on January 15, 1863, after Lincoln issued his final Emancipation Proclamation. He warned the president it would do "infinite mischief" and crushed "all hope of making peace by any conciliatory measures." The resignation took effect on March 1, 1863, and Stanly returned to California. Lincoln named no successor, and Presidential Reconstruction in North Carolina was abandoned until after the war.

BIBLIOGRAPHY

Brown, Norman D. *Edward Stanly: Whiggery's Tarheel "Conqueror."* University, Ala., 1974.

Brown, Norman D. "A Union Election in Civil War North Carolina." *North Carolina Historical Review* 43 (October 1966): 381–400.

Stanly, Edward. *A Military Governor among Abolitionists: A Letter from Edward Stanly to Charles Sumner.* New York, 1865.

NORMAN D. BROWN

STAPLES, WALLER R. (1826–1897), congressman from Virginia. In the 1850s, Waller Redd Staples became a leading lawyer and large slaveholder in Montgomery County, Virginia, which he represented in the lower house of the state legislature in the 1853–1854 session. In 1861, he opposed secession until President Abraham Lincoln's call for troops in April.

After Virginia joined the Confederacy, the secession convention chose him as one of the state's four delegates to the Provisional Congress. The voters subsequently elected him to the First and Second Congresses, so that he served throughout the war. He tended to follow the path of the majority in Congress, from, for example, opposing significant taxes early in the war to supporting the Confederacy's arming of slaves in the winter of 1864–1865. As he struggled with the problems of how best to prosecute the war, he favored the impressment of tobacco and cotton but not of corn and other food crops.

After the war, Staples returned to the practice of law in Montgomery County. A prewar Whig, he became a postwar Democrat. The first legislature to meet under the Constitution of 1870 elected him to a twelve-year term as a judge of the Virginia Supreme Court of Appeals, but the Readjuster legislature defeated his bid for reelection in 1882. For much of the rest of his life, he was senior partner in a Richmond law firm with Beverly B. Munford. In addition, he served as one of three commissioners who produced the Virginia State Code of 1887, and he served for a year as president of the Virginia State Bar Association.

BIBLIOGRAPHY

"Judge Staples Dead." *Richmond Dispatch,* August 21, 1897.

Warner, Ezra J., and W. Buck Yearns. *Biographical Register of the Confederate Congress.* Baton Rouge, La., 1975.

PETER WALLENSTEIN

STARKE, PETER BURWELL (1815–1888), brigadier general. With the exception of such battles as Brandy Station or Brice's Cross Roads, most cavalrymen in the Civil War spent their time on raids, reconnaissance, and other expeditions, or on garrison duty at various outposts. Starke commanded a cavalry regiment on such routine service for nearly three years and was one of the last officers promoted to brigadier general under Nathan Bedford Forrest.

Starke, younger brother of Confederate Gen. William E. Starke, was born in Brunswick County, Virginia, in 1815. He settled in Mississippi and served in both houses of the state legislature through the 1850s. When the Twenty-eighth Mississippi Cavalry organized in February 1862, Starke became its colonel.

He spent most of his Confederate career in his adopted state, serving in the defenses at Vicksburg in 1862 and at such outposts as Canton and Panola through 1863. During William Tecumseh Sherman's Meridian campaign in early 1864, Starke commanded a brigade and was praised for his performance by his superiors. He was transferred with his regiment to the Army of Tennessee for the Atlanta campaign that summer and then to Tennessee for the Franklin and Nashville campaigns in the fall of 1864. He was recommended for advancement while serving with Forrest in Tennessee and was promoted on November 4, 1864. His brigade returned to Mississippi in early 1865 and surrendered at Columbus.

Starke lived in Mississippi and his native Virginia after

the war. He died near Lawrenceville, Virginia, on July 13, 1888.

BIBLIOGRAPHY

Compiled Military Service Records. Peter B. Starke. Microcopy M331, Roll 235. Record Group 109. National Archives, Washington, D.C.

Hooker, Charles E. *Mississippi.* Vol. 7 of *Confederate Military History.* Edited by Clement A. Evans. Atlanta, 1899. Vol. 9 of extended ed. Wilmington, N.C., 1987.

J. TRACY POWER

STARKE, WILLIAM EDWIN (1814–1862), brigadier general. Starke was born in Brunswick County, Virginia, the brother of Confederate general Peter B. Starke. He worked as a cotton broker in New Orleans before the war.

Starke returned to Virginia at the beginning of the Civil War and served as an aide to Brig. Gen. Robert S. Garnett during Garnett's fatal western Virginia campaign in 1861. After Garnett's death, Starke was commissioned colonel of the Sixtieth Virginia Infantry and led it through the Seven Days' Battles. He was promoted to brigadier general effective August 6, 1862, and was given command of the Second Louisiana Brigade in Thomas J. ("Stonewall") Jackson's forces. Being an outsider, Starke was at first resented by his men but his leadership eventually won their confidence and loyalty. He refused to allow straggling on the march, even to the point of arresting officers who failed to keep their men in line. At the Battle of Groveton, Starke was heavily engaged and temporarily took command of the division when Brig. Gen. William Booth Taliaferro was wounded. On August 29 he continued to command the division at the Second Battle of Manassas and once personally led his men in a counterattack that captured two enemy cannons.

During the Maryland campaign, Starke was back in command of his brigade and participated in the capture of Harpers Ferry. At the Battle of Sharpsburg on September 17, 1862, he again took command of the division when Brig. Gen. John Robert Jones was wounded. While leading the Louisiana Brigade in a counterattack, Starke was shot three times and died soon afterward. During the Sharpsburg campaign civilians in Frederick had accused some of Starke's men of theft, and Jackson had ordered the brigade back to town. Starke knew his men were innocent and refused to obey. He was ordered arrested by Jackson, but died before being brought to trial. Starke is buried in Richmond's Hollywood Cemetery.

BIBLIOGRAPHY

Jones, Terry L. *Lee's Tigers: The Louisiana Infantry in the Army of Northern Virginia.* Baton Rouge, La., 1987.

Hotchkiss, Jed. *Virginia.* Vol. 3 of *Confederate Military History.* Edited by Clement A. Evans. Atlanta, 1899. Vol. 4 of extended ed. Wilmington, N.C., 1987.

TERRY L. JONES

STAR OF THE WEST. After Maj. Robert Anderson moved his garrison from Fort Moultrie to Fort Sumter in Charleston Harbor on December 26, 1861, he continued to face the threat of attack from hostile South Carolinians. President James Buchanan considered sending a warship to relieve Anderson, but Gen. Winfield Scott persuaded Buchanan instead to send a merchant vessel with concealed troops and armament so as to assure secrecy and avoid the appearance of coercion. Accordingly, the administration chartered for $1,500 a day the side-wheeler *Star of the West,* which left New York ostensibly for New Orleans on January 5, 1861. Buchanan's secretary of the interior, the North Carolinian Jacob Thompson, surreptitiously telegraphed warnings to Charleston, but Buchanan neglected to notify Anderson.

When *Star of the West* approached the entrance to Charleston Harbor early on the morning of January 9, the battery on Morris Island opened a cannonade, scoring a couple of hits but causing no serious damage. Major Anderson withheld his fire. He had orders to remain "strictly on the defensive," and in any case the Morris Island battery was beyond the reach of the Sumter guns. Receiving no support, the captain of the *Star* decided to steam away.

Anderson then dispatched a messenger to inquire of South Carolina Governor Francis W. Pickens whether he had authorized the firing and to notify him that unless he "disclaimed" it Anderson would "regard it as an act of war." Pickens replied that Anderson himself had committed a warlike act when he recently transferred his garrison from Fort Moultrie to Fort Sumter and that Buchanan must have known that his attempt to reinforce Sumter would be viewed as another such act. Pickens insisted that the firing was "perfectly justified."

While depressing morale in the North, the incident buoyed the confidence of the Southerners. The South Carolina governor called upon his military experts to get ready to "reduce that fortress," and they began to construct additional batteries to surround Sumter and command the approaches to it. Authorities in other seceding states, having been encouraged to believe they could do so with impunity, hastened to seize the forts and other Federal properties within the respective state boundaries.

BIBLIOGRAPHY

Stern, Philip Van Doren. *Prologue to Sumter.* Bloomington, Ind., 1961.

STAR OF THE WEST. Approaching Fort Sumter, South Carolina. *THE SOLDIER IN OUR CIVIL WAR*

Swanberg, W. A. *First Blood: The Story of Fort Sumter.* New York, 1957.

RICHARD N. CURRENT

STATE DEPARTMENT. Diplomacy could not ensure the Confederacy's independence, but it could open channels of communication to the major powers of Europe and encourage the assertion of foreign interests that favored the Southern cause. With the formation of the Confederate State Department on February 21, 1861, Jefferson Davis selected Robert Toombs, a leading Georgia Whig and recent member of the U.S. Senate, as secretary. Toombs's detailed instructions of March 16, 1861, to the Confederate commissioners—William Lowndes Yancey, Pierre A. Rost, and A. Dudley Mann—inaugurated the Confederate quest for European recognition. To aid the commissioners Toombs provided a full rationale for Southern secession and delineated all the political and moral reasons why the Confederacy merited membership in the family of nations.

While the commissioners made their way to London, Toombs lost interest in the department. His staff was small, and except for writing occasional instructions, he found little to occupy his time. He once refused to accept additional assistants, explaining, in the words of the *Daily Richmond Examiner,* that he "carried the business of the State Department around in his hat." In May 1861 the Confederate government moved from Montgomery to Richmond. There the State Department acquired offices, as did the president, on the upper floor of a spacious granite building known as the Federal Customs House. In July, Toombs, long preferring a military career, sought and obtained an appointment as brigadier general. He fought at Manassas and Sharpsburg in 1862, resigned, and returned to Georgia in 1863.

President Davis named Robert M. T. Hunter of Virginia as Toombs's successor. During his long political career Hunter had remained a Democrat and a strong defender of slavery and its expansion. In 1861 he was, like Toombs, a member of the U.S. Senate. Hunter was far more learned and methodical than Toombs, however, and had a better grasp of public affairs. His elaborate instructions to James M. Mason and John Slidell, commissioned to London and Paris, respectively, in September 1861, embodied the grand policy of the Confederacy toward the European powers. Hunter argued again that the Confederacy was not a coalition of rebellious states but a country presenting itself to the world "through a Government competent to discharge its civil functions, and strong enough to be responsible for its actions to the other nations of the earth." He emphasized the ineffectiveness of the Federal blockade and its contravention of the Treaty of Paris (1856), which declared that blockades, to be legal, had also to be effective.

Hunter saw the immense danger to Confederate interests in Europe's refusal to challenge the blockade; it permitted the North, with a minimum of naval power, to seriously curtail the Southern war effort. Despite his determination to enlist European support, Hunter was powerless to capitalize on the South's victory at Manassas in July 1861 and the *Trent* affair of November and December. The decision of Union naval captain Charles Wilkes to remove two Confederate leaders from the British mail-steamer *Trent* unleashed a seething anger in Britain and, for expectant Southerners, the specter of war and a British-Confederate alliance. But Lincoln and Secretary of State William H. Seward acknowledged Wilkes's error, freed the Confederates, and quickly terminated the crisis. Hunter left the State Department in March 1862 to become a senator from Virginia, a position he held until the end of the war. Beyond Europe's acknowledgment of Confederate belligerency in May 1861, Confederate diplomacy had achieved nothing.

During March, as the Confederacy's permanent government went into effect, President Davis faced the task of reconstituting his generally unpopular cabinet. Among its least popular members was Judah P. Benjamin, then temporary secretary of war. Benjamin, who had the appearance of a stocky, prosperous shopkeeper, was renowned for his wit and intelligence, his strong yet ingratiating personality, and a fatalism that attributed importance only to the present. A New Orleans lawyer of major repute, he had won election to the U.S. Senate in 1852 and, like Toombs and Hunter, was a member of that body in 1861. Benjamin had entered the cabinet in February 1861 as attorney general, a position too confining for his energy and ambition. His open criticism of the Southern war effort led him to the War Department, where Secretary Leroy P. Walker had found the challenge of organizing and directing the Confederate army beyond his capabilities. Upon Walker's resignation in September, the president appointed Benjamin acting secretary of war. Benjamin brought order to the department, but made mistakes and carried the blame for the army's reverses after Manassas. Nevertheless Davis appointed him secretary of state in the permanent cabinet.

Benjamin inherited from Hunter his assistant secretary, William M. Browne, a former Washington newspaperman. Browne, a man of considerable talent and totally acceptable to Benjamin, resigned in April to become a member of President Davis's personal staff. Benjamin did not fill Browne's position but relied rather on the department's chief clerk, Lucius Quinton Washington, formerly an editorial writer for the *Richmond Examiner*. Washington, who had entered the department in November 1861, remained at his post until April 1865. The other members of the State Department staff consisted of three clerks, a messenger, and a laborer—Philip Green, a hired slave. A Northern visitor described Benjamin's office in 1864 as unattractive, with maps and battle plans on the walls, a tier of shelves loaded with books in one corner, and a green-baize-covered desk, littered with papers, in the middle of the room.

Years later Washington recalled Benjamin's high competence as secretary of state:

> He was a man of wonderful and varied gifts, rare eloquence and accomplishments, a great lawyer, senator, and man of affairs. He could despatch readily and speedily a very large amount of business. I have known him to compose a most important State paper of twenty pages or more at a single sitting in a clear, neat chirography, and hardly a single word interlined or erased. His style was a model of ease and perspicuity.

President Davis set great value on Benjamin's services and friendship. Their offices were separated by only a hundred feet, permitting Benjamin to visit the president almost every day to discuss the problems confronting the Confederacy.

Benjamin was determined to succeed where his predecessors had failed. In letters to Mason and Slidell on April 8, 1862, he launched an attack on the legitimacy of the blockade by listing over a hundred vessels that had passed between Southern and foreign ports during November, December, and January. Seven European nations including the five great powers had, in the Treaty of Paris, adopted the principle that blockades "to be binding, must be effective—that is to say, maintained by a force sufficient really to prevent access to the coast of the enemy." The Confederation had accepted that principle.

Then on February 11, 1862, British foreign minister Earl Russell explained to Lord Lyons in Washington:

> Her Majesty's government . . . are of opinion that, assuming that the blockade was duly notified and also that a number of ships is stationed and remains at the entrance of a port sufficient really to prevent access to it, *or to create an evident danger of entering it or leaving it,* and that these ships do not voluntarily permit ingress or egress, the fact that various ships may have successfully escaped through it . . . will not of itself prevent the blockade from being an effectual one by international law.

Benjamin observed that the underscored words in Russell's statement did not appear in the Treaty of Paris and seemed to be an abandonment of its principles. He noted additionally that Russell's defense of the British decision hinged on the premise that the ships stationed at the entrance of a port were sufficient to prevent access or at least to render it dangerous. The fact that vessels moved freely through the blockade challenged the validity of the British assumption. "The absurdity of pretending that 2,500 miles of seacoast are guarded by the United States 'by a force sufficient really to prevent access,' " he wrote, "is too glaring to require comment; yet it is for this extravagant assumption that the United States claim and neutral powers accord respect." By

Russell's definition, Benjamin added, any blockade could be rendered effective if, by common consent, no nation chose to challenge it.

Benjamin simultaneously assaulted Europe's refusal to recognize the Confederacy as a separate nation. Nonrecognition, he reminded Mason, merely sustained an unnecessary war by perpetuating the notion that conquest of the South was possible. But recognition, as the verdict of an impartial jury, Benjamin predicted, would lead to "the immediate organization of a large and influential party in the Northern States favorable to putting an end to the war." Thus Britain, with little effort or detriment to its interests, could end the desolating struggle in America.

Benjamin's special appeal for French recognition focused on material considerations. He offered that country a Southern commercial dependency by instructing Slidell to propose a treaty under which the South would accept French products free of duty for a specified period of time in exchange for France's abandonment of its policies regarding recognition and the blockade. Benjamin suggested that the Confederacy supply French merchant vessels in designated ports 100,000 bales of cotton, worth enough to "maintain afloat a considerable fleet for a length of time quite sufficient to open the Atlantic and Gulf ports to the commerce of France." Benjamin wanted the French, like the British, to understand that the continuance of the war was "attributable in no small degree to the attitude of the European powers in abstaining from the acknowledgement of our independent existence as a nation of the earth."

Emboldened by the Confederate military successes of June and July 1862, especially in Virginia, Benjamin framed a new approach to break Europe's neutrality. During July Mason and Slidell, on their own, agreed to demand recognition as a matter of right, but concluded that such a course, without the leverage of additional Confederate victories, would produce only further European alienation. On August 14, however, Benjamin advised A. Dudley Mann, assigned to Brussels in September 1861 with the appointments of Mason and Slidell, that further communications with foreign governments would presume the unquestioned justice of the Confederate cause. Earlier Confederate efforts to explain the South's right to secede may have been proper, Benjamin conceded, but when common sense had failed to elicit any response but a timid neutrality, he concluded, "we prefer speaking in other tones and insisting that an admission into the family of nations is a right which we have conquered by the sword." In November Benjamin instructed L. Q. C. Lamar, commissioner to Russia, that he should not maintain the Southern right of secession unless the czar's government should inquire about it, but rather insist that the Confederacy had won its right to recognition in war.

In August 1863, convinced that Britain would never grant recognition or modify its attitude toward the blockade, Benjamin ordered Mason to conclude his mission and withdraw from London unless the British cabinet revealed a changed attitude. After receiving Benjamin's instructions on September 21 and conferring with Slidell, Mason departed for Paris. For more than a year Benjamin had argued that breaking the blockade would enhance British commerce and that recognition would bring peace, but he failed to convince the British ministry.

In September 1863 Benjamin turned to France, reminding the emperor of the damage that Europe's recognition of the Federal blockade had imposed on the South. He instructed Slidell to urge the French government to stop giving countenance "either to the validity of the pretended blockade, . . . or to the innovations and modifications which the Government of Great Britain has attempted to engraft on the declaration of Paris in derogation . . . of the rights of all other parties." In November the French minister, Édouard Drouyn de Lhuys, declared that France was not responsible for Europe's decision on the blockade and that the vulnerability of French interests in Europe and Mexico ruled out any policy that might antagonize the governments in London and Washington. In the end Benjamin revealed only contempt for French behavior, troubled by the contrast between the emperor's perennial professions of sympathy for the Southern cause and his persistent subservience to the anti-Confederate policies of Britain and the United States.

In a dispatch to Slidell on December 27, 1864, Benjamin lamented the contribution that the neutral powers had made to the Union cause. Why, he wondered, had the Europeans refused to recognize the Confederacy? He concluded that the elusive element had been the South's failure to offer a program of emancipation. He dispatched Duncan F. Kenner, congressman from Louisiana, to convey such a proposal to Mason and Slidell in Paris. In March 1865 the French emperor assured Slidell that the offer of emancipation would not have influenced his decision regarding recognition; in London Prime Minister Lord Palmerston offered the same response to Mason.

Before Benjamin could receive the assurance that slavery had not damaged the Southern cause in Europe, the Confederacy no longer existed. The secretary had acknowledged often enough that the experience on the battlefield would determine the success of Southern diplomacy no less than the future of the Confederacy itself. His quest for recognition and foreign cooperation failed because he could never convince Europe's leaders that Confederate arms would triumph. With the fall of Richmond, Benjamin, in a variety of disguises, fled to the Florida coast and made his way to Europe. Throughout the war his wife and family had resided in Paris. Benjamin chose, however, to move to England where he became a distinguished member of the

English bar, leaving behind the trials of his Confederate years as if they had never occurred.

[*See also* Blockade, *overview article;* France; Great Britain; Mexico; Russia; Spain; Trent Affair; *and biographies of numerous figures mentioned herein.*]

BIBLIOGRAPHY

Evans, Eli N. *Judah P. Benjamin: The Jewish Confederate.* New York, 1988.

Hendrick, Burton J. *Statesmen of the Lost Cause.* Boston, 1939.

Meade, Robert Douthat. *Judah P. Benjamin: Confederate Statesman.* New York, 1943.

Owsley, Frank Lawrence. *King Cotton Diplomacy: Foreign Relations of the Confederate States of America.* Revised by Harriet Chappell Owsley. Chicago, 1959.

Patrick, Rembert W. *Jefferson Davis and His Cabinet.* Baton Rouge, La., 1961.

Phillips, Ulrich Bonnell. *The Life of Robert Toombs.* New York, 1913.

Washington, L. Q. "Confederate States State Department." *Southern Historical Society Papers* 29 (1901): 341–349. Reprint, Wilmington, N.C., 1991.

NORMAN A. GRAEBNER

STATE NAVIES. Seven Southern states—South Carolina, Georgia, Florida, North Carolina, Louisiana, Alabama, and Texas—established state navies following secession and prior to joining the Confederacy. Each state had a different conception of its navy's function. Georgia floated the Naval Coast Guard; Florida called its service the Marine Police; and North Carolina operated a force of small steamers dubbed the Mosquito Fleet.

Although each state gave its navy a different name, all had similar characteristics. They were makeshift forces comprising former Federal vessels and merchant steamers. The ships flew the state flag, performing coastal patrols. They served as much for peace of mind as for action against the enemy. Officers were commissioned in state service at the rank held in the U.S. Navy or Revenue Cutter Service.

South Carolina was the first state to create a navy; it also commissioned the largest fleet. It seized vessels and armed them, making them serviceable. On December 30, 1860, ten days after declaring secession, South Carolina took over the revenue schooner *William Aiken* at Charleston. In the following weeks a lighthouse tender schooner, a coastal passenger side-wheeler, and two coast survey schooners were added to the South Carolina State Navy. The state purchased the iron propeller tug *James Gray* at Charleston, armed it, and renamed it *Lady Davis.* The large coastal passenger side-wheeler *Marion* was seized and armed.

The Georgia State Navy arose from a resolution of the Georgia state convention on January 25, 1861, six days after secession, authorizing the navy to procure three steamers to defend the state. The first officer appointed was Lt. John McIntosh Kell of Darien. On February 25, Kell purchased the side-wheel steamer *Everglade,* which was armed and renamed *Savannah.* Three days later, Capt. Josiah Tattnall became senior flag officer. *Savannah* reported ready for service March 7. The 500-ton side-wheel steamer *Huntress* was bought at New York by a "Mr. Hall" and armed. The U.S. steamer *Ida* was seized by the state. The Georgia navy was absorbed into the Confederate States Navy in mid-April 1861. *Savannah* and *Ida* were both taken into the navy under the same names. They operated in the Naval Coast Guard squadron primarily on the Georgia coast. *Huntress* later became the blockade runner *Tropic.*

Florida seized the coast survey schooner *F. W. Dana,* used it briefly, and released it. The state also seized the U.S. war steamer *Fulton* under repair at the Pensacola Navy Yard. The state employed the schooner *Judah* as a vessel of the Florida Marine Police.

North Carolina's Mosquito Fleet acquired the 207-ton passenger steamer *J. E. Coffee,* armed it, and renamed it *Winslow.* Four river tugs rounded out the fleet. *Winslow* captured sixteen prizes while operating out of Hatteras Inlet. It was lost while attempting to rescue a shipwrecked crew. When North Carolina joined the Confederacy, the entire flotilla entered the navy. It fought in several battles in the sounds of North Carolina.

The state of Louisiana likewise seized revenue service vessels: the schooner *Robert McClelland* and the brig *Washington* at New Orleans on January 26. The state also seized the armament of the cutter *Lewis Cass,* using it to arm other vessels.

Alabama seized two Federal vessels for the state. The revenue cutter service schooner *Lewis Cass,* and the lighthouse tender schooner *Alert* were taken on January 30, 1861, at Mobile. *Lewis Cass* was later transferred to the Confederate States Navy.

The commander of the decrepit revenue service schooner *Henry Dodge,* armed with one pivot gun, turned it over to the state of Texas on March 2, 1862, at Galveston. Texas operated a Marine Department throughout the war as an adjunct of the Confederate forces. The department was instrumental in the recapture of Galveston in 1864, seizing seven vessels in the process.

State leaders appear to have expected that the state navies would be subsumed into the national service. As anticipated, all were taken into the Confederate States Navy and served as regional coastal forces. The state navies served a valuable purpose—as an interim force until a Confederate navy could be created.

[*See also entries on particular states.*]

BIBLIOGRAPHY

d'Antignac, Munroe. *Georgia's Navy.* Griffin, Ga., 1944.

Brown, Alexander Crosby. *Juniper Waterway: A History of the Albemarle and Chesapeake Canal.* Charlottesville, Va., 1981.

Scharf, J. Thomas. *History of the Confederate States Navy.* New York, 1887. Reprint, New York, 1977.

KEVIN J. FOSTER

STATE RIGHTS. Secession was based on the idea of state rights (or "states' rights," a variant that came into use after the Civil War). This exalted the powers of the individual states as opposed to those of the Federal government. It generally rested on the theory of state sovereignty—that in the United States the ultimate source of political authority lay in the separate states. Associated with the principle of state rights was a sense of state loyalty that could prevail over a feeling of national patriotism. Before the war, the principle found expression in different ways at different times, in the North as well as in the South. During the war it reappeared in the Confederacy.

From Colonies to Constitution. The idea of state rights antedated the U.S. Constitution. During the colonial period the people of each colony showed an attachment to their own and often an antagonism toward other colonies. Intercolonial jealousies prevented union when, in 1754, Benjamin Franklin proposed the Albany Plan for combining to meet a threat from the French and their Indian allies. The same sentiments hampered intercolonial cooperation during the ensuing French and Indian War. Traveling through the middle settlements in 1759 and 1760, the Englishman Andrew Burnaby was struck by the disparities he observed: "Fire and water are not more heterogeneous than the different colonies in North America. Nothing can exceed the jealousy and emulation which they possess in regard to each other." Burnaby thought the colonies differed so much in culture and in economic interests that "were they left to themselves, there would even be a civil war."

Their shared hostility to the British government enabled the colonies to join in the Continental Congress and, as states from 1776 on, to win the Revolutionary War. Their rivalries continued, however, and delayed the adoption of the Articles of Confederation until 1781. The second of the Articles affirmed: "Each state retains its sovereignty, freedom and independence, and every Power, Jurisdiction and right, which is not by this confederation expressly delegated to the United States, in Congress assembled." The separate states retained, among other powers, the exclusive power to tax. All had to approve before the Articles could be amended. When New York refused to approve an amendment giving Congress the power to levy customs duties, it failed to be adopted.

Alexander Hamilton and other "nationalists" desired a stronger government, and since they could not amend the Articles, they undertook to replace them. At the Philadelphia Convention of 1787, delegates from the various states drew up a new plan of government, which its "father" James Madison said was "in structure, neither a national nor a federal Constitution, but a composition of both." Indeed, it was the result of compromises between nationalists and state-rightists, and it evaded a number of issues that might have prevented any agreement. Still, the new Constitution gave much greater power to the central government than the Articles of Confederation had given.

The Constitution was to be ratified by separate state conventions and was to go into effect among the ratifying states when nine of them had acted. Antinationalists, who called themselves "Antifederalists," opposed ratification. To reassure them, Madison wrote in one of the Federalist Papers (later gathered in *The Federalist*) that the document was to be ratified "by the people, not as individuals composing one nation; but as composing the distinct and independent States to which they respectively belong." Before the end of 1788 eleven states had ratified, but some had done so only on the understanding that certain amendments would soon be added. Two others (North Carolina and Rhode Island) still held out, waiting to see what would happen.

All were satisfied by the ten amendments proposed by the new Congress at its first session. These amendments further limited the powers of the central government, and the tenth provided: "The powers not delegated to the United States by the Constitution, nor prohibited by it to the States, are reserved to the States respectively, or to the people." Thus amended, the Constitution was more nearly balanced between national and state rights tendencies—and was more ambiguous.

Hamiltonians and Jeffersonians. The Constitution could be interpreted in opposite ways. In its clause giving Congress all powers "necessary and proper" for carrying the specified powers into effect, Alexander Hamilton as secretary of the treasury found ample authorization for his financial program, including a national bank. In the Tenth Amendment, however, Thomas Jefferson as secretary of state discovered a bar to congressional legislation of that kind: no power to establish a bank having been delegated to Congress, that power must have been reserved to the states. As president, George Washington sided with Hamilton and signed the bills that Congress passed to enact Hamilton's plan. Eventually Jefferson withdrew from the Washington administration and, with Madison, organized an opposition to it. Thus, in the 1790s, originated the two parties, Federalist and Republican, the one willing to exploit the "implied powers" of the Constitution, the other demanding a "strict construction" of the document.

The Republicans, already convinced that much of the

Federalist legislation was unconstitutional, were further outraged when, in 1798, Congress passed the Alien and Sedition Acts. The Sedition Act—providing for the fining and imprisoning of those who uttered anything "false, scandalous, and malicious" against the government, the Congress, or the president—seemed flagrantly to violate the First Amendment, which stated that Congress should pass no law abridging freedom of speech or of the press.

What agency should decide the question of constitutionality? The Constitution did not, in so many words, give the Supreme Court the power to decide, and the Republicans denied that the Court could rightfully assume the power. Their leaders, Jefferson and Madison, arguing that the state legislatures should decide, ably expounded their views in two sets of resolutions, one written (anonymously) by Jefferson and adopted by the Kentucky legislature (1798–1799) and the other drafted by Madison and approved by the Virginia legislature (1798).

These Kentucky and Virginia Resolutions asserted the following propositions: The Federal government had been formed by a "compact" or contract among the states. It was a limited government, possessing only specific delegated powers. Whenever it attempted to exercise any additional, undelegated powers, its acts were "unauthoritative, void, and of no force." The parties to the contract, the states, must decide for themselves when and whether the central government exceeded its powers. The state legislatures must serve as "sentinels" to watch out for unconstitutional acts. And "nullification" by the states was the "rightful remedy" whenever the general government went too far. The resolutions urged all the states to join in declaring the Alien and Sedition Acts null and void and in demanding their repeal at the next session of Congress, but none of the other states went along with Virginia and Kentucky.

State rights and strict construction were usually the arguments of the party out of power (and so they were to be throughout American history). As long as the Republicans were outsiders, they remained strict constructionists, but once they had become insiders, with Jefferson as president, they used the full powers of the Federal government to further the agrarian interests they represented. Indeed, they used much more than the rightful and constitutional powers, according to the Federalists, who now adopted the state rights point of view.

The Jefferson administration bought Louisiana from France in 1803 even though the Constitution gave Congress no explicit power to acquire new territory. On the constitutionality of the purchase Jefferson himself had serious doubts but managed to overcome them. The administration also imposed an embargo in 1807 forbidding American ships to leave American ports, though the Constitution allowed Congress only to regulate interstate and foreign commerce, not to prohibit it. In anger against the Louisiana Purchase, a few extreme Federalists, the Essex Junto, conspired to bring about the secession of New England. In condemning the embargo, a much larger number resorted to the doctrine of state rights. The young New Hampshire Federalist Daniel Webster, for one, paraphrased the Virginia and Kentucky Resolutions: "The Government of the United States is a delegated, *limited* Government."

During the presidency of Jefferson's friend and successor James Madison, the New England state rights men gained their largest following in opposition to the War of 1812. In Congress, Webster attacked and helped defeat a conscription bill. "The operation of measures thus unconstitutional and illegal ought to be prevented by a resort to other measures which are both constitutional and legal," he declared, hinting at nullification by New Hampshire. "It will be the solemn duty of the state governments to protect their own authority over their own militia and to interpose between their citizens and arbitrary power." In fact, some of the New England states, by refusing to support the war, virtually nullified the war effort of the Federal government. New England state-rightism and sectionalism reached a climax in the Hartford Convention (1814–1815), which demanded changes in the Constitution and threatened secession if they were not made.

Some of Jefferson's followers had turned against him when, as they saw it, he departed from his own principles. His distant cousin and (before 1804) House leader John Randolph of Roanoke organized within the Republican party a state rights faction known as the Quids. Randolph remained a fanatical defender of Virginia rights. John Taylor of Caroline, an equally consistent but more original thinker than Randolph, led the Virginia School, which included St. George Tucker and Spencer Roane. These men rationalized resistance to the centralizing trend, especially to the work of the Supreme Court under Virginian John Marshall. Jefferson, after his retirement from the presidency, joined in opposing the Federalist-minded judges as "sappers and miners" who were undermining the Constitution. The Georgia state rights men, whose leader was William H. Crawford, had their own quarrel with Marshall, who ruled against them when the state undertook to evict its Indians from their tribal lands.

Calhoun's Contribution. John C. Calhoun was a latecomer to the state rights cause, but he developed the theory more fully than anyone else. In Congress he had favored the War of 1812 and had advocated protective tariffs, internal improvements at Federal expense, and a national bank. By 1828 he was convinced that a protective tariff was not only harmful to his state, South Carolina, but was also contrary to the Constitution. He then began to work out his system for state resistance to unconstitutional laws.

Calhoun refined and elaborated the doctrine of sentinel-

JOHN C. CALHOUN. NATIONAL ARCHIVES

ship that Madison and Jefferson had presented in the Virginia and Kentucky Resolutions. He based his theory on the assumption that the people (not the government) in each state were sovereign and, in their sovereign capacity, had ratified and thus given validity to both the state constitution and the U.S. Constitution. They had done so, he argued, through their delegates in specially elected conventions. In this ratification process he discovered the procedure for dealing with questions of constitutionality. A state convention—not the state legislature as in Madison's and Jefferson's proposal—could nullify a Federal law. That law would remain null and void within the state until three-fourths of all the states had ratified a constitutional amendment specifically giving Congress the power in question. If they should ever do so, the nullifying state would still have a recourse—secession. Just as a state could "*ac*cede" to the Union by ratifying the Constitution, it could "*se*cede" by repealing its ordinance of ratification.

South Carolina put nullification to the test in 1832, when a state convention declared all protective tariffs, particularly those of 1828 and 1832, to be null and void within the state. Calhoun having resigned the vice presidency, the nullifiers sent him to the Senate to present their case. Debating him was Daniel Webster, now a senator from Massachusetts, who had switched from a state rights position to a nationalist one while Calhoun was doing the reverse. "The truth is," Webster contended, "and no ingenuity of argument, no subtlety of distinction, can evade it, that, as to certain purposes, the people of the United States are one people." According to the new Webster, a state might secede from the Union, but only on the basis of the right of revolution, not on the basis of any constitutional right. While remaining in the Union, however, a state could not nullify congressional acts, for nullification was no right at all, he maintained.

President Andrew Jackson, agreeing with Webster, denounced nullification as treason and asked Congress for authority to use the army and the navy to enforce the laws. Though the nullificationists had sympathizers in other Southern states, not one of those states officially endorsed the South Carolina stand. Calhoun claimed a victory for nullification when Congress passed and Jackson signed a compromise bill for gradually lowering the tariff. But nullification had not really worked the way Calhoun had intended. It had not been generally accepted as a legitimate and constitutional procedure. Calhoun came to realize that a single state, unaided, was powerless to interpose against Federal authority. So he set about cultivating a spirit of unity among all the slave states.

Slavery, according to Calhoun, occupied a special place in the Constitution, and certainly it occupied a special place in his theory of state rights. It was, he insisted, the only kind of property that the Constitution specifically recognized (though, in fact, the document did not mention slaves or slavery by name; it referred only to "free Persons" and "all other Persons" and to a "Person held to Service or Labour"). Therefore, nullification could be used to defend or strengthen slavery but not to attack or weaken it. Calhoun strenuously objected when, after 1842, several free states tried their own brand of nullification by adopting "personal liberty" laws that forbade state authorities to assist in the enforcement of the Federal Fugitive Slave Act of 1793.

Calhoun was further outraged when the House, though not the Senate, passed the Wilmot Proviso in 1848, which aimed to exclude slavery from all territories to be acquired in consequence of the Mexican War. Then, when the Compromise of 1850 proposed to admit California as a free state and thus to upset the balance of free and slave states, he thought the time had come for the slave states to resort to their ultimate redress, secession.

Taney and the Territories. During the 1850s the doctrine of state rights became a dogma of state powers—powers that extended beyond the boundaries of the states themselves. The development of this dogma was occasioned by the question of slavery in the territories.

Many Northerners held that Congress could exclude slavery, as it had done with respect to the Northwest Territory in the Northwest Ordinance (1787, 1789) and with respect to part of the Louisiana Purchase in the Missouri Compromise (1820–1821). Some advocated "popular sovereignty," or "squatter sovereignty," which would allow the settlers themselves to decide whether to permit slavery in a particular territory, and this principle was embodied in the Kansas-Nebraska Act of 1854. But proslavery Southerners insisted that any prohibition of slavery in a territory, whether by Congress or by the local people, was unconstitutional.

From the proslavery point of view, the sovereign states had delegated to Congress only the power to make routine "rules and regulations" for the territories, not the power to make basic policies for them. When dealing with the subject, the Federal government must act merely as a trustee for the states and must give effect to their laws, particularly the laws respecting slavery. State rights was no longer just a defense of local self-determination; it had become a means of imposing a state's laws on people outside the state.

The theory now called for an enlargement rather than a reduction of Federal authority, at least in regard to the territories, though this authority could be exercised only to protect slavery. As President Franklin Pierce said in 1855, the Federal government was "forbidden to touch this matter in the sense of attack or offense" and could do so only "in the sense of defense." Proslavery advocates looked to the Supreme Court for an endorsement of their new theory of state sovereignty. The Court obliged in the *Dred Scott* case (1857) with an obiter dictum declaring unconstitutional the Missouri Compromise prohibition of slavery in part of the Louisiana Purchase. Chief Justice Roger B. Taney said: "The Government of the United States had no right to interfere for any other purpose but that of protecting the rights of the [slave] owner."

For the time being, the strongest assertion of state rights in defiance of Federal authority came not from any Southern state but from Wisconsin, which invoked the doctrine to oppose slavery rather than to support it. When a Federal court convicted Sherman Booth of violating the Fugitive Slave Act of 1850, the Wisconsin Supreme Court repeatedly (1854–1855) issued writs of habeas corpus to release him on the ground that the act was unconstitutional. Booth and fellow antislavery radicals made state rights a test of orthodoxy in the newly formed Republican party; they demanded that the party's candidates endorse the principles of the Virginia and Kentucky Resolutions of 1798 and 1799. In the case of *Ableman* v. *Booth* (1859) Taney and the Supreme Court again upheld the Southern as opposed to the Northern state rights position. They overruled the supreme court of Wisconsin.

The Wisconsin governor then reasserted the sovereignty of his state. As commander in chief of the state militia, he challenged the president as commander in chief of the U.S. Army and Navy. "It is reported," a Wisconsin official notified the captain of one of the militia companies, ". . . that you have stated that, in the possible contingency of a conflict between the U.S. authorities and those of this State, you . . . would obey a call for your company to turn out, made by the U.S. authorities, but would *not* obey a call by your superior officials under the State laws." When the captain replied that he would consider it treason to disobey a presidential order, the governor dismissed him and disbanded his company. That was in 1860, only months before South Carolina began the secession of the Southern states.

Secession and the Confederate Constitution. Some advocates of secession justified it as a revolutionary right, but most of them based it on constitutional grounds. The 1860 South Carolina Declaration of the Causes of Secession quoted the state's 1852 declaration, which said that "the frequent violations of the Constitution of the United States by the Federal Government, and its encroachments upon the reserved rights of the States," would justify the state in withdrawing from the Union. The South Carolina secession ordinance, following the procedure that Calhoun had prescribed, simply repealed the state's ratification of the Constitution and subsequent amendments. The secession ordinances of other states did the same.

The Confederate Constitution proved to be somewhat inconsistent in regard to state rights. It contained no provision for secession, though its preamble averred that each Confederate state was "acting in its sovereign and independent character." One article (like the Tenth Amendment of the U.S. Constitution) affirmed that the "powers not delegated" were "reserved to the States." The states, however, were limited in important ways. For example, they could not (just as the states of the Union could not) pass any law "impairing the obligation of contracts." They could not get rid of slavery, for the citizens of each state were to "have the right of transit and sojourn in any State . . . with their slaves."

Congress was forbidden to impose duties or taxes "to promote or foster any branch of industry" but in some ways was given even greater powers than the U.S. Congress. The ambiguity regarding territories and slavery was removed. The Confederacy could "acquire new territory," and Congress could "legislate" (not merely make "rules and regulations") for the territories. In all of them "the institution of negro slavery" was to be "recognized and protected by Congress and by the territorial government." Congress could make all laws "necessary and proper" for carrying out its specified powers. If this or any other clause should lead to a dispute over the constitutionality of a law, the Confederate courts (rather than state legislatures or conventions) would presumably decide the issue. This was implied by the following provision: "The judicial power shall extend to all cases arising under the Constitution."

In sum, the new Constitution was more *national* than the old one with regard to slavery, which it guaranteed as a nationwide institution. The document provided no more basis for nullification or secession than its predecessor had done—despite the preamble's reference to the member states as "sovereign" and "independent." Nevertheless, there remained room for the reassertion of state rights in the Confederacy.

State Rights in the Confederacy. To win its independence, the Confederacy needed a government strong enough to make the most of all the available human and material resources, but some of the state leaders were no more willing to concede power to the Confederate government than they had been to the Federal government. Appealing to the principle of state rights, they resisted the efforts of the Jefferson Davis administration to control blockade running and manufacturing, to impress slaves and other property, and even to raise troops. Georgia was the locus of the greatest recalcitrance, Joseph E. Brown the most obstreperous of the governors, and Vice President Alexander H. Stephens the busiest fomenter and philosopher of resistance. North Carolina, under Governor Zebulon Vance, was the next most important center of obstructionism, but practically all the states had some occasion for expressing opposition to Confederate measures.

The most serious question was the constitutionality of the conscription acts (April/September 1862, and February 1864). Davis justified the legislation on the basis of the constitutional clause giving Congress the power to raise and support armies. But Brown and Stephens argued that the Confederate government could raise troops only by making requisitions upon the states, which alone, they said, had the constitutional power to impose a draft. Stephens declared: "The citizen of the State owes no allegiance to the Confederate States Government . . . and can owe no 'military service' to it except as required by his own State." Brown protested to Davis that conscription was a "bold and dangerous usurpation by Congress of the reserved rights of the States."

To enforce conscription, Congress authorized the president to suspend the privilege of the writ of habeas corpus. To Stephens, this seemed as bad as conscription itself. He denounced the suspension in resolutions which the Georgia legislature passed and which, along with speeches by Brown and Stephens's half-brother Linton Stephens, were printed and widely circulated. The legislatures of North Carolina and Mississippi adopted similar resolutions.

The question of constitutionality could not be referred to a Confederate supreme court, for there was none. In 1861 the Provisional Congress provided for such a court, with the power of judicial review, but the permanent Congress established only a system of lower tribunals. When Congress considered adding a supreme court in 1863, opponents objected to the potential subordination of the state supreme courts. These consequently were left to go on deciding the

ALEXANDER H. STEPHENS. Confederate vice president and state rights advocate. *HARPER'S PICTORIAL HISTORY OF THE GREAT REBELLION*

constitutionality of both state and Confederate laws. The supreme court in Georgia and in every other state except North Carolina upheld the Confederate conscription acts. "When Congress calls for the military service of the citizen," the Texas judges ruled, ". . . the right of the State government must cease or yield to the paramount demand of Congress."

Despite the pro-Confederate decisions of state courts, conflicts between the Confederate government and the state governments persisted. Texas objected to giving up control of state troops, as did Alabama, Mississippi, and all the Gulf states except Florida. A Florida judge, however, issued an injunction against Confederate officers who were ordered to take up some of the track of the Florida Railroad—and who disregarded the injunction.

More serious obstruction came from North Carolina, where Governor Vance took pains to "preserve the rights and honor of the State." He said it was "mortifying" to see North Carolinians "commanded by strangers"—that is, by men from other states—and he demanded that their officers be North Carolinians. Operating a state-owned blockade runner, *Advance,* he objected to the Confederacy's claim to half of the cargo space. He warehoused uniforms, shoes, and blankets for the exclusive use of North Carolina troops at a time when Robert E. Lee's army in Virginia was suffering from the want of such supplies. State officials being exempt from the draft, he appointed thousands of men to state jobs to keep them out of the Confederate army.

Governor Brown of Georgia went even further in making unnecessary state appointments. Then, after enrolling ten thousand militiamen, he refused to allow them to enter the Confederate service even when in 1864 Davis attempted to requisition them—as Brown had previously said the president had a right to do. Brown now insisted he was protecting his state against both "external assaults and internal usurpations." The Confederate secretary of war compared him to the New England governors who had resisted the war effort during the War of 1812. Brown rejected the Richmond authorities' references to "refractory Governors" and "loyal States." Such remarks were "utterly at variance with the principles upon which we entered into this contest in 1861," he said. The Confederate government was "the agent or creature of the States," and its officers had no business "discussing the loyalty and disloyalty of the sovereign States to their central agent—the loyalty of the creator to the creature."

The right of secession followed logically from such Calhounian doctrine. Vance, however, would not hear of it when disaffected North Carolinians talked of calling a secession convention in 1863. Brown and Stephens declined when, after taking Atlanta, Gen. William Tecumseh Sherman proposed a meeting to discuss Georgia's leaving the Confederacy and making a separate peace. But Stephens wrote privately: "Should any State at any time become satisfied that the war is not waged for purposes securing her best interests . . . she has a perfect right to withdraw." By early 1865, at least one Georgia planter had come to suspect that Stephens and his associates were plotting to "withdraw if possible this and two other States from the Confed. and set up for themselves."

In fact, none of the states ever came close to seceding from the Confederacy, and most of them avoided an extreme state rights position all along. Nevertheless, Davis had ample cause for complaint. In a private letter of December 15, 1864, he wrote that his difficulties had been "materially increased by the persistent interference of some of the State Authorities, Legislative, Executive, and Judicial, hindering the action of the Government, obstructing the execution of its laws, denouncing its necessary policy, impairing its hold upon the confidence of the people, and dealing with it rather as if it were the public enemy than the Government which they themselves had established for the common defense, and which was the only hope of safety from the untold horrors of Yankee despotism."

Historians have differed about the importance of state rights as a cause of Confederate defeat. One writer has gone so far as to suggest that the following words should be engraved on the Confederacy's tombstone: "Died of State Rights." Others minimize its effects, pointing out that it was a symbol of more fundamental grievances (as, indeed, it had been throughout American history). Some have even argued that it was an asset rather than a liability to the Confederate cause, since, they say, it served as a safety valve for possibly disruptive discontent.

The doctrine may have influenced the outcome through its effect on Davis personally and directly. He prided himself on being a state-rightist and a strict constructionist, and though his state rights opponents accused him of dictatorship, he was generally careful to confine himself to the letter of the Confederate Constitution. The *Times* of London said in 1865 that one reason for the defeat of the Confederacy was his reluctance to "assume at any risk the dictatorial powers" that were "alone adapted to the successful management of revolutions."

Afterward Davis agreed with Stephens about the basic issue of the war. In *A Constitutional View of the Late War between the States* (1868–1870) Stephens maintained: "It was a strife between the principles of Federation, on the one side, and Centralism, or Consolidation, on the other." In *The Rise and Fall of the Confederate Government* (1881) Davis held that the Confederates had "fought for the maintenance of their State governments in all their reserved rights and powers." Both men forgot that the preservation of slavery had been the object of state sovereignty, state rights, secession, and the formation of the Confederacy.

[*See also* Civil War, *article on* Causes of the War; Compromise of 1850; Conscription; Constitution; Dred Scott Decision; Fugitive Slave Law; Habeas Corpus; Judiciary; Kansas-Nebraska Act; Nullification Controversy; Secession; Wilmot Proviso; *and entries on particular states and biographies of numerous figures mentioned herein.*]

BIBLIOGRAPHY

Bestor, Arthur. "State Sovereignty and Slavery: A Reinterpretation of Proslavery Constitutional Doctrine, 1846–1860." *Journal of the Illinois State Historical Society* 54 (1961): 147–178.

Current, Richard N. *John C. Calhoun.* New York, 1963.

Escott, Paul D. *After Secession: Jefferson Davis and the Failure of Confederate Nationalism.* Baton Rouge, La., 1978.

Freehling, William W. *Prelude to Civil War: The Nullification Controversy in South Carolina.* New York, 1966.

Merriam, Charles E. *A History of American Political Theories.* New York, 1926.

Moore, Albert B. *Conscription and Conflict in the Confederacy.* New York, 1924.
Owsley, Frank L. *State Rights in the Confederacy.* Chicago, 1925.
Schlesinger, Arthur M. "The State Rights Fetish." In *New Viewpoints in American History.* New York, 1922.

RICHARD N. CURRENT

STATE SOCIALISM. The Confederacy was founded on the premise of state rights, but during the course of the war, this ideology underwent many changes. Indeed, one of the most obvious ways in which state rights and limited government were abandoned was in the economic sphere. The government took an increased role in the economic life of the nation, an action that led to government control of shipping and war industry. These endeavors are reflective of the Confederacy's embrace of state socialism, a system approximating the central government's control of the economy at the expense of state sovereignty.

The need for armaments, ammunition, and other accoutrements of war was great in 1861. Initially, the Ordnance Bureau under the direction of Josiah Gorgas relied upon war matériel stockpiled in Federal arsenals that was seized once the Southern states seceded. This was obviously not enough, so Gorgas also endeavored to purchase goods from abroad. Soon he deemed this source too risky because of the Union naval blockade of Southern ports. Undaunted, he set out to tap domestic sources. Gorgas contracted with private factories and established government works in virtually every Confederate state. The results were impressive: Gorgas estimated that, by 1863, the Confederacy was self-sufficient in war matériel.

In the process of negotiating contracts, and as the war's scope grew ever larger, Gorgas, with government approval, had to exert increased control over private enterprises. In essence, all firms with government contracts were forced to sell their full output to War Department agents. In some instances (and the Tredegar Iron Works of Richmond is the most famous case), key factories were taken over by government agents.

The government's seizure or impressment of factories with war contracts was not limited to firms producing arms and ammunition. Similar actions took place in the textile manufacturing sector. There, quartermaster agents saw to it that all firms with government contracts for uniforms, blankets, tents, and the like produced almost solely on government account if they were not to lose their sources of raw materials and labor.

The other area in which the government assumed a role approximating state socialism was in shipping. After President Jefferson Davis realized that the self-imposed embargo on cotton was not going to produce European intervention, he changed the policy and encouraged private shipping companies and individuals to run the Union blockade. This policy served to enrich the blockade runners, both Southern and European, because they found that lucrative profits could be made from the importation of luxuries. At Davis's request, Congress passed a law in 1863 that radically altered the private enterprise aspect of blockade running: beginning in that year, all vessels running the blockade had to carry one-third to one-half of their inbound and outbound cargoes on government account. In other words, those ships had to carry government cotton out and bring war supplies in. Congress enacted a supplemental law in 1864 that outlawed the importation of luxuries and the exportation of cotton, tobacco, military supplies, and other goods.

Many individuals—state governors who were also running the blockade on state accounts, and private citizens—protested these measures, but Davis stood firm. With the government involved in shipping, the rate of success running the blockade was very high. The cotton that reached Europe played a crucial role in boosting Confederate credit abroad. It is not too much to say that had the government taken control of shipping sooner, the military outcome of the war might have been different.

Historians have debated the extent to which the Confederacy truly became a "socialistic" nation. The earliest treatment of state socialism, Louise B. Hill's monograph, noted that there is no conclusive evidence that Southern leaders consciously embraced the economic theories of European socialists. Rather, these individuals pushed for and oversaw the centralization of the Southern economy because it seemed the most efficacious way to mobilize and fight the war. For Hill, the embrace of state socialism by men untrained and implicitly uninterested in socialist economic theory demonstrates that exigencies developed talent and the desire to innovate in the economic realm in order to win the war.

Other scholars have echoed this assessment, though several have pushed the interpretation one step further. Most agree that the Confederacy created a "quasi-nationalized" economy, but they differ as to the reason the Confederacy embraced such a position. For some historians, the Confederacy's state-managed economy was a logical reaction to the need for raw materials and manufactured goods; for others, centralization or state socialism was necessary because "there was too little time for a class of industrial entrepreneurs to . . . flower 'naturally.' "

There is no doubt that the Confederacy did, by 1863, direct the production and distribution of war materials. Nor is there any doubt that legislation directing impressment and shipping regulations led to increased government involvement in the economy. Still, the Richmond government stopped short of totally directing the economic affairs of the nation. It did not, for example, nationalize the

Southern railroad system in the manner it did Confederate shipping. This failure was probably one of the most disastrous: the South depended on its rail network for supply and troop deployments, but railroad managers resisted any attempts to regulate rates, schedules, or routes, and the Confederate government allowed them to have their way. Consequently, railroad affairs remained in the hands of the managers who pursued policies more beneficial to their companies. This situation remained unchanged until the very end of the war, and it undoubtedly contributed to Confederate defeat.

In the final analysis, the Confederacy's control of the economy, though not total, was, indeed, the nearest thing to a socialistic system that existed in the nineteenth century. The South's regulation of most sectors of the wartime economy indicates once again the way in which Southerners compromised or dispensed with the ideology of laissez-faire and limited government when events demanded it. Confronted with the need to fight a war and supply the troops, the Confederate government adopted a number of expedients that would have been considered anathema in 1860.

[*See also* Naval Ordnance Works; New Plan; Ordnance Bureau; Quartermaster Bureau; Railroads; State Rights; Textile Industry; Tredegar Iron Works.]

BIBLIOGRAPHY

Hill, Louise B. *State Socialism in the Confederate States of America.* Charlottesville, Va., 1936.

Luraghi, Raimondo. "The Civil War and the Modernization of American Society: Social Structure and Industrial Revolution in the Old South before and during the War." *Civil War History* 18 (September 1972): 230–250.

Owsley, Frank L. *State Rights in the Confederacy.* Chicago, 1925.

Thomas, Emory M. *The Confederate Nation, 1861–1865.* New York, 1979.

MARY A. DECREDICO

STEELE, WILLIAM (1819–1885), brigadier general. Born in Albany, New York, Steele graduated from West Point in 1840. An officer in the Second U.S. Dragoons, he fought in the Seminole and Mexican Wars and afterward served for a time in Texas.

When the Civil War began, Steele resigned his commission in the Dragoons (then stationed at Fort Leavenworth) and returned to Texas. He accepted a commission as a colonel in the Seventh Texas Cavalry assigned to Gen. Henry H. Sibley, Army of New Mexico. He fought in Sibley's unsuccessful campaign in New Mexico and Arizona (1861–1862). After being promoted to brigadier general on September 12, 1862, he took command of the Confederate forces in Indian Territory in December. Here Steele complained of a tired and inefficient force as well as a lack of supplies. Steele left Indian Territory in December 1863 convinced "that with a few exceptions, the Indians are wholly unreliable as troops of line." Although sent to the District of Texas, he was ordered to reinforce Gen. Richard Taylor when Nathaniel P. Banks advanced up the Red River. Steele commanded a brigade in Gen. Thomas Green's division during the Red River campaign of 1864 and fought at Mansfield (April 8), Pleasant Hill (April 9), and Blair's Landing (April 12). Steele took command of the division upon Green's death at Blair's Landing, but he was soon replaced by John Austin Wharton.

After the war Steele took up permanent residence in Texas, serving in state government. He died in San Antonio in 1885.

BIBLIOGRAPHY

Hall, Martin Hardwick. *Sibley's New Mexico Campaign.* Austin, Tex., 1960.

Kerby, Robert L. *Kirby Smith's Confederacy: The Trans-Mississippi South, 1863–1865.* New York, 1972.

THOMAS J. LEGG

STEPHENS, ALEXANDER H. (1812–1883), vice president, and postwar Georgia congressman and governor. The son of a yeoman farmer of modest fortune, Alexander Stephens, sickly from birth to death and cursed with a

ALEXANDER H. STEPHENS. NATIONAL ARCHIVES

freakish, spectral appearance, never weighed more than ninety pounds. His myriad physical ailments and the early death of his father doubtless contributed to a crippling melancholy that plagued Stephens for most of his life. Despite these handicaps in a society that put a premium on physical prowess, he parlayed driving ambition, substantial intelligence, spellbinding oratorical talents, and prodigious capacity for work into one of the antebellum South's most illustrious political careers.

After a short, unhappy stint as a teacher upon graduation from Franklin College at Athens, Georgia, in 1832, Stephens took up the practice of law in his hometown of Crawfordville, Georgia. His success as a lawyer led him, in 1836, into politics, his first and last love. He never married, but throughout his life he maintained an extraordinarily close relationship with his half-brother Linton.

Elected to the U.S. Congress in 1843 as a Whig, he soon assumed a position of leadership in the party. When the Whigs foundered on the shoals of the Compromise of 1850—which he vigorously supported—Stephens pursued an independent course until 1855, when he became a Democrat rather than espouse Know-Nothingism. The year before, he had played a pivotal role in the passage of the Kansas-Nebraska Act in the House. Although he served as a key administration operative in the unsuccessful attempt to gain acceptance of the proslavery Lecompton constitution for the admission of Kansas, he did not break with Stephen A. Douglas and the Northern Democrats on the issue. Worn out and disgusted, he retired from the House in 1859. Deploring the split of the Democratic party in 1860, he supported Douglas in the election. After Abraham Lincoln's election, he opposed secession as a hasty and ill-advised movement undertaken without sufficient provocation. Nonetheless, he bowed to the wishes of his state when it seceded.

The Georgia secession convention then selected him as a delegate to the Montgomery convention. There he played a leading role in the shaping of the Confederate Constitution, especially the provision allowing the future admission of free states. As the most prominent opponent of secession in the South, Stephens was a logical choice for executive office in the new Confederate government. Impelled by a desire to balance competing factions in the South, to appeal to the border states, and to present a united front to the world, the convention elected Jefferson Davis, a moderate secessionist and old Democrat, provisional president and Stephens, cooperationist and old Whig, as provisional vice president of the Confederacy on February 9, 1861. (They were elected, without opposition, to their permanent positions in national elections on November 6, 1861.)

Although the working relations between these two proud men began amicably enough, they were deteriorating even before the war started. Davis regarded Stephens's extolling of slavery as the "cornerstone" of the Confederacy in a widely reported speech at Savannah as heedless of the paramount issue at stake between the Federal and Confederate governments: state versus national sovereignty. Ironically, the future split between Davis and Stephens turned on this issue within the Confederacy itself.

Stephens grew increasingly disenchanted with his office. In Montgomery, the president had consulted with him frequently, had dispatched him as commissioner to Virginia before that state seceded, and had offered other important assignments. In early summer, the vice president diligently undertook an extensive speaking tour on behalf of the produce loan to raise money for the government, and he faithfully attended to his official duties. But things had changed by early 1862. For months Stephens had been systematically ignored by Davis and the cabinet. For a man of ability once secure in his power and influence, this inactivity was a bitter pill. With little to do but preside over the Senate where he could neither speak nor vote, Stephens saw no point in spending much time in the capital. He began staying at home for long periods of time.

After months of frustration, Stephens moved to more overt opposition against the government with passage of the first Confederate Conscription Act in April 1862. He regarded conscription as a dangerous and unconstitutional centralization of power, counter to the whole reason the Confederacy existed: to be a bastion of both state sovereignty and personal liberty. Accordingly, he approved of Georgia Governor Joseph E. Brown's long public argument with Davis on the subject and under a pseudonym in September 1862 denounced the draft himself in a public letter. Shortly thereafter, in another public letter, he denied that martial law even existed under the Constitution.

Contrary to his detractors, who contended that he was at heart a Unionist, Stephens remained devoted to the cause of Southern independence. But he differed sharply with the administration over the means to achieve the end. For example, from the beginning and throughout the war he was one of the few to espouse stiff taxation in lieu of issuance of Treasury notes to finance the war. For this reason, Confederate financial policy, which rested on the highly inflationary expedient of printing money to finance its debts, never met his approval. He had similarly urged, to no avail, that the government use cotton as credit to back its bonds and finance the purchase of war matériel abroad. And although not theoretically averse to impressment—indeed, he sanctioned a broad reading of the Constitution to reach the taxable property of the wealthy—he deplored the capricious way in which the law operated.

Far more than Davis, Stephens heeded political currents in the North and was willing to court them to achieve independence. The best time to extend peace feelers, he thought, was during times of relative quiescence on the battlefields. Accordingly, in June 1863, following Robert E. Lee's great victory at Chancellorsville and with the North discontented over the passage of conscription there, he placed a proposal before Davis. He would undertake a mission to the North to reestablish the cartel for the exchange of prisoners that had broken down amid bitter threats of mutual retaliation on innocent prisoners after the Emancipation Proclamation in January. Such a conference, Stephens hinted, might afford him the opportunity to address the larger issue of a general settlement. Davis, who knew as Stephens did not that Lee was invading the North, accepted the offer.

Upon his arrival in Richmond, Stephens discovered to his horror that the president wanted him to accompany Lee's army north. The president thought this would improve Stephens's chances of being received. Stephens emphatically disagreed, but at the urging of cabinet and president, he consented to undertake the mission. According to his instructions, its purpose was "humanitarian" with "no political aspect." Rainy weather, which made roads impassable, dictated that Stephens travel to Washington by steamer. As he had anticipated, the venture came to naught. Stephens arrived at Newport News, Virginia, at noon on July 4, 1863. After keeping the Confederate envoy waiting for two days, the Lincoln government, buoyed by the victories at Gettysburg and the fall of Vicksburg, refused to let him proceed. Disgusted that his advice had once again been disregarded, Stephens returned to Georgia.

Except for a few speeches trying to encourage his countrymen in the wake of the midsummer disasters, Stephens kept his peace for the balance of 1863. But he had not retreated an inch from his convictions about the course the Confederacy should take. He could barely find words to express his abhorrence of the notion in some quarters that the South appoint a dictator to rule the country during the war. The only way to preserve "constitutional liberty," his umbrella term for individual and state rights, was to preserve constitutional limits on authority. Preserving the purity of that document was the war's chief object; even independence was secondary. "Nothing could be more unwise than for a free people," he told Howell Cobb, "at any time, under any circumstances, to give up their rights under the vain hope and miserable delusion that they might thereby be enabled to defend them."

Stephens dallied over returning to Richmond for the opening of the congressional session in November 1863; first one thing and then another delayed his leaving Georgia. Meanwhile, Governor Brown was seriously considering calling the Georgia legislature into special session to formally protest government policies as well as broach the subject of peace negotiations with the Federal government. Stephens dissuaded Brown from doing so until Congress had acted on some of the vexatious issues. And from his sickbed, he penned a long letter to the president warning that it would be impolitic to suspend again the writ of habeas corpus and to extend conscription; he also reasserted the evils of the present impressment machinery, to no avail. In mid-February, the Congress authorized another six-month suspension of the writ and extended conscription.

The events in Richmond spurred Brown to go ahead with his plans: he called the Georgia Assembly into special session on March 10, 1864. The vice president and his brother Linton, a member of the legislature, both advised Brown about how the protest should be handled. In accordance with these plans, Brown delivered a scalding message on Confederate policy on the heels of which Linton Stephens offered two sets of resolutions. The first condemned the suspension of the writ; the second proposed that the South proffer peace negotiations to the North after every victory it won in the field. Although he had not intended to become publicly identified with the protest for obvious reasons of propriety, the vice president yielded to the entreaties of his brother to come to Milledgeville, the capital, when it appeared that the resolutions might fail.

There, on the night of March 16, Stephens delivered an impassioned address in support of the resolutions. He branded both conscription and suspension of the writ as unconstitutional and unwise. The latter act also presented a grave danger to public liberty: the legislature should request its immediate repeal and its constitutionality should be tested in the courts. Stephens dismissed the notion that Davis would be circumspect about using the power. Abuses would inevitably arise from the military authorities who would enforce the law. Stephens took pains to deny that he desired a counterrevolution. What he wanted was to keep the present revolution on the right track. The best way to prevent a counterrevolution was for the state to speak out. The truest supporters of the government and the troops in the field upheld the fundamental law.

After a fierce struggle, the Georgia Assembly passed the resolutions two days later but accompanied them with another expressing undiminished confidence in Davis. Stephens had long since lost such confidence, but with palpable self-delusion, he also denied any personal antipathy to the president. In fact, he had always considered Davis unfit for the presidency, and although he professed in March 1864 to believe Davis "a man of good intentions," their ensuing relations would prove just how corrosive Stephens's suspicions of him had become.

As the war dragged on into the summer of 1864, an increasing number of prominent Confederates both in and outside of Congress began broaching various plans for peace. Stephens, too, was vitally interested in the subject. One of his enduring beliefs from the beginning of the war was that the political, economic, and cultural ties between the South and the Old Northwest could be used to further the cause of the Confederacy. Consequently, he believed that the Confederacy should do all it could to influence Northern elections, should offer to negotiate on the basis of state sovereignty, and, if need be, should accept an offer to negotiate on the basis of reunion. With a friendly government in place, the South could obtain an armistice through negotiation, which, in Stephens's opinion, would inevitably lead to its independence.

Davis, though he sanctioned covert aid to anti-Lincoln elements in the North, did not believe the Confederacy should be involved with foreign elections. Nor should it court negotiation with the enemy save only on one unalterable basis: Confederate independence. The surest way of securing independence in his view was to demonstrate the futility of subduing the South by force. This fundamental difference of opinion led to the final breach between the Confederacy's two top executives.

Davis had already publicly misrepresented Stephens's futile 1863 mission as an illustration of the North's intractability on the peace issue. This enraged the vice president, who was even more upset when in a speech at Columbia, South Carolina, in October 1864 the president repeated the charge and barely alluded to the Northern elections. Stephens found it incomprehensible that the Confederate government did not respond favorably to the peace plank in the platform of the Northern Democrats in 1864, which demanded a cessation of hostilities so that "at the earliest moment peace may be restored on the basis of the Federal Union." Contrary to what many thought, the vice president did not favor any scheme for separate state action for peace—indeed, for any course of action that bypassed the Richmond government. As the fortunes of the Confederacy became increasingly desperate, many in the South, including Governor Brown and Linton Stephens, came to favor this course. Stephens opposed them all, arguing that under the Constitution only the central government was empowered to conclude treaties. Even a general convention of the states would have to be acceded to by Richmond and Washington.

Partly to further legitimate peace initiatives and partly to oppose additional draconian war measures being proposed by the government, Stephens returned to Richmond in December 1864. Almost immediately he engaged in an acrimonious exchange of letters with Davis over the latter's remarks in Columbia. Shortly thereafter, his considerable dignity wounded when the Senate refused to allow him to speak on the habeas corpus issue, Stephens decided to resign his office. Only the importuning of the president pro tem of the Senate, Robert M. T. Hunter, dissuaded him.

To Stephens's surprise, however, on January 6, 1865, the Senate invited him to address it after adjournment. He spoke for two hours, urging a complete revision of policy to reanimate the people: an end to conscription and impressment, friendship toward the Northern Democrats (i.e., agreement to a general convention of the states), and a revamped military policy. Although typically unrealistic, it had not been a gloomy speech. Stephens gave up his idea of returning home for the moment and continued to aid those in Congress who were trying to force the president's hand on peace negotiations. Several resolutions to do this (a couple framed by Stephens) had been introduced in the Congress.

It was largely to forestall these plans that Jefferson Davis entertained a proposal that had been carried down from Washington, with Lincoln's blessing, by Francis P. Blair. Blair suggested that the two sides cease fighting and join forces against the French in Mexico. Lincoln did not subscribe to this idea, but he was willing to talk "informally" to secure peace "to the people of our common country." Davis, for political reasons of his own, seized the opportunity. Not only was peace sentiment strong and increasing among congressmen, press, and people, but several states, including Georgia, threatened separate state action for peace. By responding favorably to Blair's initiative, Davis, who knew Lincoln's terms but felt fairly sure that a Confederate delegation would be received and fail, saw the chance to silence his critics and rally the populace to the government again.

At the urging of Georgia Senator Benjamin H. Hill, Davis appointed Stephens (along with Hunter and John A. Campbell) to the Confederate delegation. Unknown to Davis, Hill had struck a deal with Stephens: the support of Georgia's delegation for peace resolutions in Congress in exchange for the vice president's help in restraining Brown from initiating separate state action for peace in Georgia. Fearful of being hamstrung by his instructions, Stephens tried to avoid serving on the commission, but he could not. As he had feared, the object of the mission spelled out in the official commission was "an informal conference . . . for . . . securing peace to the two countries."

The three Confederate commissioners met with Lincoln and U.S. Secretary of State William Seward on board a steamer at Hampton Roads, Virginia, on February 3, 1865. Although Stephens tried to steer discussion to the Blair proposal, Lincoln would have none of it and insisted on reunion and an end to the rebellion. After four hours, the conference ended. All that had been decided was that the war would continue, although Stephens did secure Lincoln's promise to release his nephew from a Federal prisoner of war camp.

Stephens returned to the capital and stayed only long enough to write his report of the conference. The result at Hampton Roads, besides engendering a final upsurge of warlike resistance in the South, had effectively silenced

Davis's congressional critics. In his last interview with Davis, Stephens said he would return home and say nothing further. On May 11, 1865, Stephens was arrested by Union troops and two weeks later was incarcerated at Fort Warren in Boston Harbor. He was released on parole in early October.

Elected to the U.S. Senate by the Georgia legislature in 1866, Stephens, like many other ex-Confederates, was prevented from taking his seat. Thus barred by the provisions of Reconstruction and extremely poor health from participation in public life in the immediate postwar period, Stephens devoted his time to writing. His ponderous two-volume work, *A Constitutional View of the Late War between the States,* published from 1868 through 1870, presented a detailed justification of secession and the antebellum Southern interpretation of the Union. It has been judged the ablest defense of the Southern position ever made.

With his political disabilities removed, Stephens in 1873 assumed his familiar position as representative of Georgia's Eighth District in the U.S. House. He remained there until 1882 when he was elected governor of Georgia. Stephens died in office the next year, barely one hundred days into his term.

Less understood than labeled, Alexander Stephens has not been treated kindly by most historians. Although guilty of many of the sins they have accused him of—naiveté, pettiness, narrowness, rashness—Stephens does not deserve the reputation of either a closet Unionist or traitor to the Confederate cause. His critics often overlook or excuse the obstinate refusal of Davis to countenance criticism from any source and his political ineptness in dealing with a host of other antagonists. Stephens represented a widespread segment of Southern opinion. He was hardly alone in his passionate concern for individual liberties and state rights against what was widely perceived as encroachments by a powerful central government. But at no time during the conflict did Stephens ever counsel resistance to government authority except through lawful, constitutional means: the courts and Congress.

Stephens's critics also ignore clear evidence of the vice president's commitment to Confederate independence. It never wavered throughout the war. Whether the remedies to the Confederacy's ills that Stephens proposed would have worked is not the question. A better question might be whether anyone who opposes a government's policy in the midst of war is likely to get a fair hearing—then or later.

[*See also* Cornerstone Speech; Hampton Roads Conference; Vice Presidency.]

BIBLIOGRAPHY

Avary, Myrta Lockett, ed. *Recollections of Alexander H. Stephens: His Diary Kept When a Prisoner at Fort Warren, Boston Harbor, 1865; Giving Incidents and Reflections of His Prison Life and Some Letters and Reminiscences.* New York, 1910.

Cleveland, Henry. *Alexander H. Stephens in Public and Private: With Letters and Speeches, before, during, and since the War.* Philadelphia, 1886.

Escott, Paul D. *After Secession: Jefferson Davis and the Failure of Confederate Nationalism.* Baton Rouge, La., 1978.

Johnston, Richard Malcolm, and William Hande Browne. *Life of Alexander H. Stephens.* Philadelphia, 1878.

Schott, Thomas E. *Alexander H. Stephens of Georgia: A Biography.* Baton Rouge, La., 1988.

Stephens, Alexander H. *A Constitutional View of the Late War between the States: Its Causes, Character, Conduct and Results, Presented in a Series of Colloquies at Liberty Hall.* 2 vols. Philadelphia, 1868–1870.

Von Abele, Rudolph. *Alexander H. Stephens: A Biography.* New York, 1946.

THOMAS E. SCHOTT

STEPHENS, LINTON (1823–1871), lieutenant colonel and Georgia state legislator. Linton Stephens was the younger and much beloved half brother of Alexander H. Stephens, the vice president of the Confederacy. He graduated from Franklin College in 1843 and the University of Virginia Law School in 1845. After some months at Harvard, he assumed the practice of law in Hancock County, Georgia. The extraordinarily close relationship between the two brothers reveals much about Linton Stephens: they were virtually political twins for almost thirty years. But the younger brother was always the more volatile of the two.

Stephens began his political career as a state legislator in 1853. Swept out of office by the Know-Nothings in 1855 and unsuccessful in a subsequent bid for Congress, he regained prominence in 1859 when he was appointed to the bench of the Georgia Supreme Court by Governor Joseph E. Brown. The political alliance that developed between Brown and Stephens carried over into the war. Like Alexander, Linton opposed secession, but he enlisted in the Fifteenth Georgia Regiment of Robert Toombs's brigade after the firing on Fort Sumter and was quickly elevated to the rank of lieutenant colonel and a staff position. Impatient with inaction and scornful of army leaders, he resigned his commission in December 1861. During William Tecumseh Sherman's Georgia campaign, he raised a company of cavalry for the Georgia state guard, but it didn't see action and Stephens soon returned to civilian life—and to his virulent opposition to Jefferson Davis and all his works.

Stephens disapproved of Davis from the moment of his election, and by the end of the war he hated him with passionate intensity. Like his brother, he opposed conscription, basing his opposition on state rights grounds, and he abetted Joseph E. Brown's protracted opposition to the Davis administration on the matter. As the war continued,

Stephens professed to discern in conscription and other government war measures, such as impressment and suspension of the writ of habeas corpus, a concentrated attempt by Davis to impose a military despotism on the Confederacy.

From his position as representative in the Georgia assembly he played a key role in the state's protest movement against the administration in March 1864. On the heels of a heated message from the governor, Stephens introduced a set of resolutions endorsing a plan of offering negotiations for peace to the North after Confederate victories and denouncing suspension of the writ of habeas corpus as unconstitutional. Largely at Linton's instigation, his brother endorsed these resolutions in an impassioned address before the lawmakers on the evening of March 16, 1864. After a fierce struggle, the assembly passed the resolutions three days later.

Stephens spent the balance of the war promoting, often in concert with Brown, various plans for achieving peace through separate action by Georgia and other states. The vice president did not support this position: it was their only serious disagreement during the war. Though of little importance as an individual, Linton Stephens as a key agent of his brother and political protégé of Joseph E. Brown personified the strict constructionist, anti-Davis, state rights segment of the educated Confederate populace.

Following the war, Stephens returned to his law practice in Sparta, Georgia. Both he and his brother opposed the Reconstruction Acts, the Fourteenth and Fifteenth Amendments, and the Republican state government in Georgia. In December 1870 Linton ran afoul of Governor Rufus Bullock when he instigated the arrest of several voters and election managers in Sparta. Charges stemming from the incident were later quashed, but not before his arrest and appearance before a federal magistrate in Macon. Linton Stephens died after a brief illness in July 1871 and is buried beside his brother in Crawfordville, Georgia.

BIBLIOGRAPHY

Johnston, Richard Malcolm, and William Hand Browne. *Life of Alexander H. Stephens*. Philadelphia, 1878.

Schott, Thomas E. *Alexander H. Stephens of Georgia: A Biography*. Baton Rouge, La., 1988.

Waddell, James D. *Biographical Sketch of Linton Stephens Containing a Selection of His Letters, Speeches, State Papers, Etc.* Atlanta, 1877.

THOMAS E. SCHOTT

STEUART, GEORGE HUME (1828–1903), brigadier general. Born in Baltimore on August 24, 1828, Steuart was only nineteen when he graduated next to last in his West Point class. Routine cavalry service on the frontier with the Second Dragoons ended with Steuart's April 22, 1861, resignation from the army.

GEORGE HUME STEUART. LIBRARY OF CONGRESS

Hailed as "one of Maryland's gifted sons," he labored vigorously but in vain to bring his native state into the Confederacy. Initially a captain of cavalry, Steuart soon became lieutenant colonel of the newly formed First Maryland Infantry. He succeeded to regimental command after First Manassas. According to a fellow officer, Steuart's "rigid system of discipline quietly and quickly conduced to the health and morale of this splendid command."

On March 6, 1862, Steuart received promotion to brigadier general and command of a brigade composed of four Virginia regiments and his own Maryland unit. At Cross Keys, Steuart received a shoulder wound that disabled him for several months. He was conspicuous again at Gettysburg; yet on May 12, 1864, he and most of his brigade were captured in the fighting at Spotsylvania's "Bloody Angle." Steuart was imprisoned at Hilton Head, South Carolina, until his exchange. He then led a brigade in Pickett's division through Appomattox.

Steuart divided his time after the war between Maryland farming and rising to state command of the United Confederate Veterans. He died November 22, 1903, and was buried in Baltimore's Green Mount Cemetery.

Because his surname was so often misspelled, and to distinguish him from cavalry commander J. E. B. Stuart, Confederates always referred to him as "Maryland" Steuart.

BIBLIOGRAPHY

Goldsborough, William W. *The Maryland Line in the Confederate States Army.* Baltimore, 1869. Reprint, Gaithersburg, Md., 1983.

Howard, McHenry. *Recollections of a Maryland Confederate Soldier and Staff Officer under Johnston, Jackson and Lee.* Baltimore, 1914. Reprint, Dayton, Ohio, 1975.

McKim, Randolph. *A Soldier's Recollections.* New York, 1910.

JAMES I. ROBERTSON, JR.

STEVENS, CLEMENT HOFFMAN (1821–1864), brigadier general. Stevens was born in Norwich, Connecticut, August 14, 1821, the son of a naval officer. Raised in Florida and South Carolina, he joined a Charleston banking firm at age twenty-one. His wife, Ann, was the sister of Barnard E. Bee, a future Confederate general. Following the secession of South Carolina, Stevens designed the "Iron Battery," an innovative fortification with a slanted wooden front covered with railroad iron, which was useful in the reduction of Fort Sumter.

Stevens was seriously wounded at First Manassas, where he served as a volunteer aide to his brother-in-law. A capable officer, he was commissioned colonel of the Twenty-fourth South Carolina Infantry in the spring of 1862 and saw action at Secessionville, South Carolina, on June 16. After serving briefly at Wilmington, his regiment was ordered to Mississippi to relieve Vicksburg in May 1863. Transferred with his regiment to the Army of Tennessee, Stevens fought at Chickamauga where he was again severely wounded and had two horses shot from under him. His superior, Gen. W. H. T. Walker, commended him as "the gallant Stevens."

He was promoted to brigadier general effective January 20, 1864, and served throughout the Atlanta campaign until the Battle of Peachtree Creek on July 20. There, during the attack by William J. Hardee's corps, he was struck by a rifle ball and died July 25. Stevens is buried in St. Paul's Episcopal Church Cemetery, Pendleton, South Carolina, beside General Bee.

BIBLIOGRAPHY

Obituary. *Daily Constitutionalist* (Augusta, Ga.), July 27, 28, Aug. 4, 1864.

Capers, Ellison. *South Carolina.* Vol. 5 of *Confederate Military History.* Edited by Clement A. Evans. Atlanta, 1899. Vol. 6 of extended ed. Wilmington, N.C., 1987.

STEPHEN DAVIS

STEVENS, WALTER HUSTED (1827–1867), brigadier general. Born in Penn Yan, New York, August 24, 1827, Stevens graduated from the U.S. Military Academy in 1848, ranking fourth in a class of thirty-eight that also included George Hume ("Maryland") Steuart and Nathan ("Shanks") Evans.

Assigned to the Corps of Engineers, Stevens spent virtually all his prewar years in the South, where he married a sister of future Confederate Gen. Louis Hébert. His work during this period consisted of engineering duties on rivers and harbors, four years as lighthouse inspector, and supervisor of fortifications at Galveston and New Orleans. He was promoted to first lieutenant in 1855, a rank he held when he resigned on March 2, 1861.

Initially, Stevens was commissioned a major in the Confederate army and reported to Braxton Bragg at Pensacola as chief engineer. On June 12, 1861, however, he was commissioned a captain in the Corps of Engineers and was ordered to report to P. G. T. Beauregard, on whose staff he served during the First Manassas campaign.

The Compiled Service Records list Stevens as a lieutenant colonel on January 31, 1862, when he was ordered to report to Robert E. Lee in Richmond. Curiously, in midyear his rank is given as major and his title as chief engineer for the Army of Northern Virginia. From August 25, 1862, to August 1864 Stevens was in Richmond as the chief of the Engineer Department, Department of Northern Virginia.

On December 5, 1862, J. F. Gilmer, chief of the Engineer Bureau, recommended Stevens for promotion "in consideration of his great zeal, abilities, and services—the importance of the works committed to his direction, and the vast labor and responsibility involved." Stevens was commissioned a colonel, March 3, 1863. Shortly thereafter Arnold Elzey recommended further advancement for Stevens. On April 14, 1864, Bragg added a mysteriously worded endorsement: "but one objection ever existed as far as I know . . . and I hope from what I learned and from recent observation that no longer exists." Four months later Lee endorsed the same document, noting, "I see no evidence of the objection referred to by Genl. Bragg." The brigadiership was dated August 28, 1864.

When Richmond fell in April 1865, Stevens allegedly "turned back into the flames of the burning bridge over which the troops were marching in order that he might be the last soldier to leave the city" (*Dictionary of American Biography,* 1908).

Paroled at Appomattox, Stevens went to Mexico where he became superintendent-engineer of the Imperial Railroad. He died at Vera Cruz, November 12, 1867, and was buried in Hollywood Cemetery, Richmond.

BIBLIOGRAPHY

Compiled Military Service Records. Walter Husted Stevens. Microcopy M331, Roll 236. Record Group 109. National Archives, Washington, D.C.

Hotchkiss, Jed. *Virginia.* Vol. 3 of *Confederate Military History.*

Edited by Clement A. Evans. Atlanta, 1899. Vol. 4 of extended ed. Wilmington, N.C., 1987.

Warner, Ezra J. *Generals in Gray: Lives of the Confederate Commanders.* Baton Rouge, La., 1959.

LOWELL REIDENBAUGH

STEVENSON, CARTER (1817–1888), major general. Carter Littlepage Stevenson was born September 21, 1817, in Fredericksburg, Virginia. In 1838 he graduated from the U.S. Military Academy—a lowly forty-second in a forty-five-man class—and was commissioned into the Fifth Infantry. In 1861, when he "went south," he was a captain.

Stevenson was commissioned into the Confederate army and served briefly as colonel of the Fifty-third Virginia Regiment and as assistant adjutant general of the Army of the Northwest. On March 6, 1862, he was appointed brigadier general and sent to the Department of East Tennessee. In the fall of that year, he served with the East Tennessee army of Maj. Gen. E. Kirby Smith during the Kentucky campaign.

In October 1862, Stevenson was promoted to major general and assigned to command a division that was soon sent to Mississippi. Captured at Vicksburg in July 1863, he was paroled and put in command of a camp of paroled prisoners of war at Demopolis, Alabama. That fall, after his exchange, he resumed command of his division.

Sent to Georgia in 1864, Stevenson and his division joined the Army of Tennessee and fought with that army through the Atlanta, Franklin and Nashville, and Carolinas campaigns. On May 1, 1865, after the surrender of the Army of Tennessee, Stevenson was paroled at Greensboro, North Carolina.

CARTER STEVENSON. LIBRARY OF CONGRESS

After the war Stevenson worked as a civil and mining engineer. He died August 15, 1888, and was buried in the Fredericksburg city cemetery.

BIBLIOGRAPHY

Hewitt, Lawrence L. "Carter Littlepage Stevenson." In *The Confederate General.* Edited by William C. Davis. Vol. 6. Harrisburg, Pa., 1991.

Warner, Ezra J. *Generals in Gray: Lives of the Confederate Commanders.* Baton Rouge, La., 1959.

RICHARD M. MCMURRY

STEWART, ALEXANDER P. (1821–1908), lieutenant general. A native of Rogersville, Tennessee, Alexander Peter Stewart was born October 2, 1821. In 1842 he graduated from the U.S. Military Academy, standing twelfth of fifty-six in his class. Commissioned a second lieutenant of artillery, he resigned on May 31, 1845, to teach mathematics and natural and experimental philosophy (physics) at Cumberland University and then at the University of Nashville.

After Tennessee's secession, Stewart was commissioned major of artillery, first in the state army and then in the Confederate forces. He served in western Tennessee and Missouri in 1861 and 1862. On November 8, he became a brigadier general and assumed command of a brigade in what eventually became the Army of Tennessee. A very competent officer, Stewart was promoted to major general in June 1863, to command a division. On June 23, 1864, he was named lieutenant general and assigned to the corps command left vacant by the death of Leonidas Polk.

Stewart commanded his corps through the Atlanta, Franklin and Nashville, and Carolinas campaigns. Surrendering with Confederate forces in North Carolina, he was paroled in May 1865 at Greensboro. He had suffered two slight wounds during the war—one at Chickamauga (September 1863), and one at Ezra Church (July 1864).

After the war Stewart taught, engaged in business in St. Louis, served as chancellor of the University of Mississippi (1874–1886), and was a member of the commission that planned Chickamauga-Chattanooga National Military Park. He died in Biloxi, Mississippi, August 30, 1908, and was buried in Bellefontaine Cemetery, St. Louis.

BIBLIOGRAPHY

Wingfield, Marshall. *General A. P. Stewart: His Life and Letters.* Memphis, Tenn., 1954.

Warner, Ezra J. *Generals in Gray: Lives of the Confederate Commanders.* Baton Rouge, La., 1959.

RICHARD M. MCMURRY

ST. JOHN, ISAAC M. *The biography of Isaac M. St. John is alphabetized as if his last name were spelled* Saint John.

STONE, KATE (1841–1907), diarist. Sarah Katherine ("Kate") Stone was born at Mississippi Springs, Hind County, Mississippi, on January 8, 1841. As a young girl, she moved with her parents to Stonington Plantation near Delta, Louisiana. In 1861 Stone was living with her widowed mother, five brothers, and a younger sister at Brokenburn, a 1,260-acre cotton plantation about thirty miles northwest of Vicksburg, Mississippi, in present-day Madison Parish, Louisiana. They were a wealthy family, owning about 150 slaves.

In May 1861, Stone began keeping a journal, recording the activities of her neighbors. As her younger brothers and many local men left to join the fighting and $20,000 worth of her mother's cotton was burned, Stone's hatred of the North grew. She provides a vivid description of the Federal assault on nearby Vicksburg and the arrival of Union troops in Madison Parish. Eventually her family fled the fighting and sought refuge in Lamar County, Texas, in July 1863. Her journal describes the trip and the condition of the Southern refugees. The sight of unshaven men and hoop-skirted but barefoot women living in primitive log cabins increased her despair. Late in 1863 the family resettled in Tyler, Texas, where they remained until the spring of 1865.

After the war, the family returned to find Brokenburn "overflowed and rank with weeds" and spent the next two years attempting to recoup its lost fortunes. Her journal provides a firsthand account of the hardships endured by many Confederate families during the conflict and the destruction of the Southern economy at the end of the war. Stone's original journal was kept daily between May 1861 and November 1865. She added summary sketches to the journal in 1867 and 1868. In 1900 Kate copied her original journal into two large ledger books without making any corrections to the original manuscript. The journal was passed on to Kate's daughter, Amy J. Holmes, who in turn allowed John Q. Anderson to publish the journal for the first time in 1955. Stone died at Talluah, Louisiana, on December 28, 1907.

BIBLIOGRAPHY

Anderson, John Q., ed. *Brokenburn: The Journal of Kate Stone, 1861–1868.* Baton Rouge, La., 1955.

PAUL F. LAMBERT

STONEMAN'S RAIDS. Union Maj. Gen. George Stoneman, Jr., campaigned in both the eastern and the western theaters of the war. As chief of cavalry of the Army of the Potomac, his first foray behind Confederate lines began on April 12, 1863, when Maj. Gen. Joseph Hooker ordered him across the Rappahannock River to flank Gen. Robert E. Lee's Army of Northern Virginia, cut the supply lines south to Richmond, and block Lee's anticipated retreat.

Stoneman was slow getting started and a spring freshet soon made the Rappahannock unfordable. It was April 29 before the river subsided enough for him to cross at Kelly's Ford. Orders from Hooker diverted half his column westward to engage Confederate cavalry stationed at Culpeper Court House, while Stoneman continued south with 3,500 men and six pieces of artillery.

Crossing the Rapidan River at Raccoon Ford, he struck the Virginia Central Railroad at Louisa Court House, wrecking eighteen miles of track. Meeting only feeble opposition, he closed to within a few miles of Richmond, damaging sections of the Richmond, Fredericksburg, and Potomac Railroad and destroying several wagon bridges across the North and South Anna rivers, the Chickahominy, and the James. The raid caused considerable consternation in the Confederate capital, but the trains were running again by the time Stoneman recrossed the Rappahannock on May 8.

Stoneman suffered only 200 casualties, but his absence deprived Hooker of the cavalry to screen his flanks and scout his advance. Lee deliberately kept his own cavalry close at hand and these troopers discovered Hooker's exposed right flank, enabling Lee to win a stunning victory at the Battle of Chancellorsville (May 2–3, 1863). Stoneman was made a scapegoat and relieved.

Reassigned to the western theater as chief of cavalry of the Army of the Ohio, he commanded a division during Union Maj. Gen. William Tecumseh Sherman's Atlanta campaign. On July 25, 1864, Sherman outlined plans to cut the last railroad supplying the city's beleaguered defenders. Stoneman was to lead his division and one commanded by Brig. Gen. Kenner Dudley Garrard around the east side of the city; Brig. Gen. Edward Moody McCook would bring two others around from the west. The two columns, 9,400 strong, were to meet at Lovejoy's Station, twenty-five miles south of Atlanta, and tear up the Macon and Western Railroad while Sherman's Fifteenth, Sixteenth, and Seventeenth Corps moved in a shorter arc around the west side of the city to capture the railroad junction at East Point.

The day before the raid was scheduled to begin, Stoneman asked Sherman for permission to make a dash southward after cutting the railroad to liberate 32,000 Union prisoners of war held at Macon and Andersonville. Sherman admitted there was something "captivating" about the idea and gave the scheme his blessing, telling Stoneman it would be "an achievement that will entitle you and the men of your command to the love and admiration of the whole country."

Stoneman marched at dawn on July 27, 1864. Leaving Garrard's division at Flat Rock to keep Maj. Gen. Joseph Wheeler's Confederate cavalry at bay, he crossed the headwaters of the Ocmulgee River with 2,200 men and two pieces of artillery and moved down the east bank. Unable or unwilling to recross the Ocmulgee, Stoneman failed to keep his rendezvous with McCook and marched straight to Macon, where he confronted 2,000 Georgia militia and Confederate convalescents commanded by Maj. Gen. Howell Cobb on July 30. Unable to breech the city's defenses, Stoneman retraced his steps northward.

By this time, Wheeler had turned back Garrard, overtaken McCook, and dispatched Brig. Gen. Alfred Iverson, Jr., after Stoneman. Iverson's three small brigades intercepted the Federal column nineteen miles northeast of Macon and, after a day-long struggle at Sunshine Church on July 31, forced Stoneman and 500 of his men to surrender. The abortive raid, combined with Wheeler's defeat of McCook at the Battle of Newnan, Georgia, on July 30, cost Sherman almost a third of his cavalry and prolonged the outcome of the campaign.

Exchanged in October 1864, Stoneman returned to duty as second in command of the Army of the Ohio, over the strident objections of Secretary of War Edwin M. Stanton, who characterized him as "one of the most worthless officers in the service." Eager to salvage his reputation, Stoneman proposed to destroy the railroad and saltworks in southwest Virginia.

Leaving Knoxville, Tennessee, on December 10, 1864, he led a mounted column of 5,500 men and four guns across the Holston River at Kingsport and into Virginia. Following the line of the East Tennessee and Virginia Railroad, his troopers drove forces led by Brig. Gen. Basil W. Duke and John C. Vaughn through Bristol, Abington, Marion, and Mount Airy, Virginia, burning the trestles, rolling stock, and depots from Bristol to ten miles beyond Wytheville. After sending a detachment to destroy the lead mines near Wytheville, Stoneman doubled back toward Marion, defeating 1,000 Confederates led by Maj. Gen. John C. Breckinridge on December 17 and 18. He captured the saltworks at Saltville on December 20 and destroyed the Confederacy's most important source of this valuable commodity before returning to Knoxville on December 29.

His reputation restored, Stoneman was given command of the District of East Tennessee in February 1865. Acting on orders from Lt. Gen. Ulysses S. Grant, on March 21 he mounted a raid across the Blue Ridge, feinting toward Salisbury, North Carolina, and then turning north into Virginia to pick up where he had left off in December. By April 5, his 3,000 troopers had wrecked the East Tennessee and Virginia Railroad from Wytheville to Lynchburg. Turning south, Stoneman's columns cut the Richmond and Danville Railroad and rampaged unchecked through western North Carolina, destroying the railroads from Greensboro to Salisbury and west to the Catawba River. The raid ended any hope of a junction between the armies of Robert E. Lee and Joseph E. Johnston and hastened the end of the war.

BIBLIOGRAPHY

Mathews, Byron H., Jr. *The McCook-Stoneman Raid.* Philadelphia, 1976.

Starr, Stephen Z. *The Union Cavalry in the Civil War.* 3 vols. Baton Rouge, La., 1979–1985.

Van Noppen, Ina Woestemeyer. *Stoneman's Last Raid.* Raleigh, N.C., 1961.

David Evans

STONES RIVER, TENNESSEE. *See* Murfreesboro, Tennessee.

STONEWALL. The French-built ironclad ram CSS *Stonewall* displaced 900 tons, was 171 feet long, and had a draft of 14½ feet. The submerged iron-sheathed ram protruded under water from the bow. The armor was three-quarter-inch iron backed by two-feet-thick solid oak. It had a 300-pound Armstrong cannon on the bow and two 70-pounders to the rear. Square-rigged, the ship had twin parallel engines that could generate 300 horsepower, attaining a speed of 12 knots; by reversing the twin screw propellers, it could turn within its length.

Stonewall was designed by Confederate naval agent James Dunwoody Bulloch and Lucien Arman, a Bordeaux shipbuilder. The contract was signed July 16, 1863, before news of Vicksburg and Gettysburg reached Europe. The ironclad ram was designed for American coastal and river waters to break the Union blockade and open Southern ports to foreign trade. Changing fortunes of war, French intervention in Mexico, revival of the French cotton industry, and U.S. diplomatic remonstrances led the French government to forbid delivery to the Confederate navy.

Arman arranged to sell the ironclad, then called *Sphinx,* to Denmark. The Danish war with Prussia delayed delivery until peace was established, when Denmark renamed it the *Staerkodder* and happily sold her back to Arman who changed her name to *Olinde.* He arranged with Bulloch to place a Confederate crew aboard in French waters.

Under Capt. Thomas J. Page, the ironclad was renamed CSS *Stonewall.* After a stop in Ferrol, Spain, for repairs, Page faced down two U.S. ships—*Niagara* and *Sacramento*—and sailed *Stonewall* across the Atlantic Ocean and into Havana Harbor for fuel and repairs. There he learned the war had ended. On May 19, 1865, he sold her to the Spanish authorities for $16,000 to pay off his crew.

CSS *Stonewall*. Engraving of the ship leaving Lisbon Harbor, Portugal, March 1865. From *Harper's Weekly*, May 13, 1865.
Naval Historical Center, Washington, D.C.

The U.S. Navy acquired the ship for the same price and sold it to the shogun of Japan ($400,000), who renamed her, first *Kotetsu* and then *Adzuma*. As a Japanese vessel, she was in commission for thirty more years. The ship of six names proved more effective in Japanese than in American waters.

BIBLIOGRAPHY

Bulloch, James D. *The Secret Service of the Confederate States in Europe*. Vol. 2. Liverpool, 1883. Reprint, New York and London, 1959.

Case, Lynn M., and Warren F. Spencer. *The United States and France: Civil War Diplomacy*. Philadelphia, 1970.

Kennet, Lee. "The Strange Career of the *Stonewall*." *United States Naval Institute Proceedings* 94 (February 1968): 74–85.

Spencer, Warren F. *The Confederate Navy in Europe*. University, Ala., 1983.

Warren F. Spencer

STONEWALL BRIGADE. One of the most famous battle units in American history, the Stonewall Brigade achieved a record for marching, fighting, and sacrifice rarely equaled in the annals of war. Writers over the years have likened it to Caesar's Tenth Legion, Charlemagne's Paladins, and Napoleon's Old Guard. The brigade's original members were in the initial wave of volunteers who answered Virginia's call to arms. All the soldiers in the unit were from the Shenandoah Valley and adjacent areas.

In the spring of 1861, the Second, Fourth, Fifth, Twenty-seventh, and Thirty-third Virginia Infantry Regiments, plus the Rockbridge Artillery Battery, were organized into a brigade. Their commander was Gen. Thomas J. Jackson. The unit was Virginia's First Brigade until July 21, 1861, when, at the Battle of First Manassas, it and its general received the nickname "Stonewall." Jackson left his regiments in the autumn for higher command, but the Stonewall Brigade remained under him, was always his favorite unit, and became the brigade on whom he called as a pacesetter both on the march and in combat.

The brigade's mobility in the 1862 Shenandoah Valley campaign (particularly a fifty-seven-mile march in fifty-one hours) earned it the title "Jackson's foot cavalry." It, along with Jackson's forces, joined the Army of Northern Virginia on the eve of the Seven Days' Battles. Thereafter, from Mechanicsville to Appomattox, the brigade participated in every major battle in the East. It took especially heavy losses at First Manassas, Kernstown, Cedar Mountain, Groveton, Second Manassas, Chancellorsville, Gettysburg, and Spotsylvania. On May 30, 1863, following Jackson's death, the Confederate War Department officially designated the unit as the Stonewall Brigade. It was the only large command in the Southern armies to have a sanctioned nickname.

After vicious 1864 combat at Spotsylvania's Bloody Angle, so few troops remained in the brigade that it ceased to exist as a separate command. Its survivors, along with those of other equally decimated units, were reorganized into a loose brigade. Over 6,000 men served in the Stonewall Brigade during the course of the Civil War. At Appomattox, after thirty-nine engagements, only 210 ragged and footsore soldiers were left—none above the rank of captain.

Jackson's successors as brigade commander were Gens. Richard B. Garnett and Charles S. Winder, Col. William S. H. Baylor, Gens. Elisha Franklin Paxton, James Alexander Walker, and William Terry. Not one of those six officers lived, or escaped serious wounds long enough, to be promoted to higher command.

The original Stonewall Brigade had a makeup and personality unique among Confederate units. Two of every three of its members were farmers, blacksmiths, masons, or machinists. An unusually high percentage of non-English, foreign-born men were in the ranks; Irish and Scotch-Irish were the largest ethnic groups. Few slaveholders were members of the brigade. In addition, the five regiments were typically a family affair, with numerous companies consisting of fathers, sons, brothers, uncles, and cousins.

The brigade came to possess a combination of Jackson's iron discipline and a feeling of confidence gained from repeated successes. It was always an independent-minded unit: a brigade that was outstanding and knew it.

BIBLIOGRAPHY

Frye, Dennis E. *Second Virginia Infantry.* Lynchburg, Va., 1984.

Reidenbaugh, Lowell. *Thirty-third Virginia Infantry.* Lynchburg, Va., 1987.

Robertson, James I., Jr. *Fourth Virginia Infantry.* Lynchburg, Va., 1982.

Robertson, James I., Jr. *The Stonewall Brigade.* Baton Rouge, La., 1963.

Wallace, Lee A., Jr. *Fifth Virginia Infantry.* Lynchburg, Va., 1988.

James I. Robertson, Jr.

STOUT, SAMUEL HOLLINGSWORTH

(1822–1903), physician and hospital administrator. A native of Nashville, Tennessee, Stout was educated at the University of Nashville (A.B., 1839; A.M., 1842) and the University of Pennsylvania Medical School (M.D., 1848). After briefly practicing medicine in Nashville, Stout in 1850 moved to Giles County, Tennessee, the home of his wife's family, where he had previously taught school. By the outbreak of the Civil War he owned a substantial plantation and conducted a successful medical practice there.

After Tennessee joined the Confederacy, Stout in May 1861 became regimental surgeon for the Third Tennessee Regiment, partly composed of his Giles County neighbors. His hospital was used for demonstrations for new field surgeons. In November 1861 Stout was ordered to Nashville to take charge of the Gordon Hospital, where he instituted and enforced military hospital regulations until the fall of Nashville in February 1862 forced the evacuation of the hospitals. Stout's next assignment, post surgeon at Chattanooga, Tennessee, placed him in charge of two small hospitals, but because of Chattanooga's strategic position as a railroad crossroads, the city soon became an important hospital center. Stout's administrative abilities so impressed Gen. Braxton Bragg, commander of the Army of Tennessee and a noted stickler for military regulations, that in August 1862 Bragg placed Stout in charge of all the Army of Tennessee hospitals in the Chattanooga area. In mid-1863 Stout became medical director of hospitals for the entire Army of Tennessee, a position he held for the rest of the war.

As medical director for the Army of Tennessee hospitals behind the lines (he never directed any field hospitals), Stout held an enormously responsible position. He assigned doctors, stewards, and matrons to specific hospitals, delegated responsibilities to them, mediated their quarrels, and disciplined or transferred them as necessary, supervising several hundred doctors and several thousand other subordinates at any given time. Stout selected hospital sites and sometimes designed the structures to be built on them. In addition, he prodded medical purveyors, commissaries, and quartermasters who were often slow to supply hospitals, oversaw general obedience to Richmond's orders, and made sure that his subordinates completed their extensive paperwork properly. Stout managed the largest hospital district in the Confederacy with, for example, more than sixty facilities in Georgia and Alabama in September and October 1864.

Gen. William Tecumseh Sherman's Union troops, marching through Georgia in 1864, complicated Stout's numerous administrative responsibilities because the hospitals had to move frequently to stay out of Sherman's way, a task made even more difficult by the supply and transportation shortages of the declining Confederacy. Despite these problems, Stout was able to keep at least some of his hospitals functioning until the end of the war.

Financially ruined after the war, Stout moved to Atlanta where he briefly served on the faculty of the Atlanta Medical College, helped establish the public school system, and practiced medicine, with no particular financial success. In 1882 he moved his family to Texas where he again engaged in educational and medical pursuits. He wrote a number of articles on medical subjects and his Civil War experiences, but he never completed his intended three-volume study of the Army of Tennessee medical department, based on the 1,500 pounds of hospital records he had preserved. He died in Clarendon, Texas.

BIBLIOGRAPHY

Cunningham, Horace H. *Doctors in Gray: The Confederate Medical Service.* Baton Rouge, La., 1958. Reprint, Gloucester, Mass., 1970.

Emmons, Julia. "The Medical Career of Samuel H. Stout." *Journal of the Medical Association of Georgia* 69 (November 1980): 904–910; 70 (March 1981): 169–177.

Schroeder-Lein, Glenna Ruth. "Waging a War behind the Lines: Samuel Hollingsworth Stout and Confederate Hospital Administration in the Army of Tennessee." Ph.D. diss., University of Georgia, 1991.

Stout, Samuel H. "Outline of the Organization of the Medical Department of the Confederate Army and Department of Tennessee." Edited by Sam L. Clark and H. D. Riley, Jr. *Tennessee Historical Quarterly* 16 (1957): 55–82.

Stout, Samuel H. "Some Facts of the History of the Organization of the Medical Service of the Confederate Armies and Hospitals." *Southern Practitioner* 22–25 (November 1900–October 1903).

GLENNA R. SCHROEDER-LEIN

STOVALL, MARCELLUS AUGUSTUS (1818–1895), brigadier general. Born September 18, 1818, in Sparta, Georgia, Stovall received much of his early education in Massachusetts. In 1835 he joined a Georgia unit for service against the Seminole Indians. He attended the U.S. Military Academy in 1836 and 1837 but dropped out because of illness. Settling in Augusta, Georgia, he went into the mercantile business. In 1846 he moved to Floyd County in northwestern Georgia.

Active in a local military organization, Stovall was a captain of artillery in 1861, and upon Georgia's secession, he became a colonel of artillery in the state militia. On December 31, 1861, he was appointed lieutenant colonel of the Third Georgia Infantry Battalion (with date of rank set to October 8) and entered the Confederate army. After brief service in Virginia and North Carolina, he and his battalion were sent to eastern Tennessee. The unit was eventually absorbed into the Army of Tennessee.

After participating in the Battle of Murfreesboro, Stovall was promoted to brigadier general on April 23, 1863 (to rank from January 20). His father's death in late 1863 and a severe bout with rheumatism kept him away from the army for some time, but he was back in command of his brigade in 1864 for the Atlanta and Franklin and Nashville

MARCELLUS AUGUSTUS STOVALL. LIBRARY OF CONGRESS

campaigns. In 1865 he was with the Confederate force in the Carolinas campaign.

Paroled May 9, 1865, Stovall returned to Augusta where he was a cotton broker and operated the Georgia Chemical Works, which manufactured and sold fertilizer. He died in Augusta August 4, 1895, and was buried in the city cemetery.

BIBLIOGRAPHY

Snellgrove, Benjamin E. "Marcellus Augustus Stovall." In *The Confederate General.* Edited by William C. Davis. Vol. 6. Harrisburg, Pa., 1991.

Warner, Ezra J. *Generals in Gray: Lives of the Confederate Commanders.* Baton Rouge, La., 1959.

RICHARD M. MCMURRY

STRAHL, OTHO FRENCH (1831–1864), brigadier general. Strahl was born in McConnelsville, Ohio, June 3, 1831. After attending Ohio Wesleyan University, he moved to Tennessee and was practicing law in Nashville when the state seceded.

Strahl entered Confederate service in what was to become the Fourth Tennessee Infantry Regiment, and when that regiment organized, he was chosen its lieutenant colonel. The regiment became part of Brig. Gen. Alexander P. Stewart's brigade in the Army of Tennessee. Strahl participated in most of that army's major battles. In April 1862 he was promoted to colonel.

In February 1863 the field officers of the brigade presented a document attesting to Strahl's *"sterling worth"* and declaring that "as a tactician we recognize no superior; as an officer, but few equals; and as a gentleman, none more worthy, or better qualified for promotion." In recommending Strahl's promotion, Stewart called him "one of the best officers of his grade in this army" and noted that he was a native of Ohio, "but of Virginia parentage." On July 28, 1863, Strahl was named brigadier general to command the brigade (Stewart had been promoted to division command).

In late 1863 and 1864 Strahl performed with competence. He was wounded in the fighting around Atlanta in August 1864 but returned to his brigade for the Franklin and Nashville campaign. At Franklin, November 30, 1864, he was killed in an attack upon a strong Federal position. Buried first at Ashwood, Tennessee, his body was later moved to Old City Cemetery in Dyersburg, Tennessee.

BIBLIOGRAPHY

Bearss, Edwin C. "Otho French Strahl." In *The Confederate General.* Edited by William C. Davis. Vol. 6. Harrisburg, Pa., 1991.

Warner, Ezra J. *Generals in Gray: Lives of the Confederate Commanders.* Baton Rouge, La., 1959.

RICHARD M. MCMURRY

STRATEGY. *See* Civil War, *article on* Strategy and Tactics. *See also entries on particular battles.*

STRICKLAND, HARDY (1818–1884), congressman from Georgia. Strickland was born into a modest planter family in Jackson County, Georgia, in 1818. His only education came from private tutors and some local schooling. When gold fever struck the northern Georgia mountains, Strickland and his brother moved to nearby Forsyth County, where they operated a successful mining operation. With the profits from this venture, Strickland acquired a plantation and slaves while continuing to supervise the Strickland brothers' gold mine. In 1847, he was elected without his knowledge to represent Forsyth County in the state legislature, where he served all but one term until 1858.

Strickland was an active supporter of John Breckinridge's Southern Democratic ticket in the 1860 election and attended Georgia's secession convention in Milledgeville as a strong proponent of immediate secession. During the war's early months, he served in Virginia with Howell Cobb's regiment. In November 1861, he was elected to represent Georgia's Ninth District in the First Confederate House of Representatives. He did not play a particularly active role as congressman, but like many of his colleagues from Georgia, he generally supported Davis administration policies over the state rights opposition of Governor Joseph E. Brown. Strickland pushed unsuccessfully for activating the mint at Dahlonega, Georgia, for the coinage of Confederate gold currency, and he took an interest in efforts to improve sanitation conditions in army hospitals. Strickland chose not to run for reelection in 1863 owing to severe rheumatism, but he agreed to serve as quartermaster for the state reserves for the duration of the war.

Within a few years, his rheumatism confined Strickland to a wheelchair. He died in 1884 at his home in Ackworth.

BIBLIOGRAPHY

Alexander, Thomas B., and Richard E. Beringer. *The Anatomy of the Confederate Congress: A Study of the Influences of Member Characteristics on Legislative Voting Behavior, 1861–1865.* Nashville, Tenn., 1972.

Temple, Sarah B. *The First Hundred Years: A Short History of Cobb County, Georgia.* Atlanta, 1935.

Warner, Ezra J., and W. Buck Yearns. *Biographical Register of the Confederate Congress.* Baton Rouge, La., 1975.

JOHN C. INSCOE

STUART, J. E. B. (1833–1864), major general. Born February 6, 1833, at Laurel Hill in Patrick County, Virginia, James Ewell Brown ("Jeb") Stuart spent his youth in a large family possessed of political and social influence, but lacking comfortable wealth. At age twelve Stuart took an oath at his mother's knee that he would never drink alcohol—very likely a commentary upon Elizabeth Letcher Pannill Stuart's rectitude and Archibald Stuart's fondness for creature comforts. Young Stuart attended Emory and Henry College and then secured an appointment to West Point, where he became "Beauty" Stuart because his classmates considered him anything but.

Despite a penchant for fistfights, Stuart enjoyed success at West Point. His pattern of attaching himself to successful people began now, and he counted such disparate cadets as Custis Lee, son of academy Superintendent Robert E. Lee, and Oliver Otis Howard, at the time a stereotypical Yankee prig, among his friends. In 1854 Stuart graduated thirteenth in his class of forty-six and secured a commission in the cavalry. By this time he was committed to a career as a "bold dragoon."

Following a short tour of duty in western Texas, Stuart joined the First Cavalry at Fort Leavenworth, Kansas. There he met and married (November 14, 1855) Flora Cooke, daughter of the post commander, Phillip St. George Cooke. The couple named their firstborn son Phillip St. George Cooke Stuart.

Stuart saw action against Cheyenne warriors in Kansas

J. E. B. STUART. NAVAL HISTORICAL CENTER, WASHINGTON, D.C.

and once survived a pistol ball fired at him at point-blank range. Fortunately for Stuart, the powder charge was too small, and he suffered only a flesh wound. While on the frontier Stuart served at Forts Leavenworth and Riley in Kansas and at Fort Wise, Colorado. In 1856, while involved in a peacekeeping force attempting to staunch civil unrest in Bleeding Kansas, Stuart encountered radical abolitionist John Brown, an incident that later rendered Stuart the only person at Harpers Ferry able to identify the insurgent "Mr. Smith" as Brown.

Alert to ways of improving his fortune, Stuart spent time during the winter months on the plains tinkering with inventions. He developed something he called "Stuart's Lightening Horse Hitcher" and in the fall of 1859 secured leave to go to Washington to try to sell the War Department a device designed to assist cavalrymen to mount and dismount while armed with sabers.

By coincidence Stuart was at the War Office when the first reports of trouble at Harpers Ferry arrived. He volunteered to help quell the disturbance and served as aide to Robert E. Lee, who commanded the marines sent to Harpers Ferry. Very early on the morning of October 18, 1859, Stuart delivered Lee's demand for surrender to the raiders, who were barricaded in a fire engine house with thirteen hostages. When the engine house door opened a crack, Stuart recognized John Brown pointing a carbine at him. Brown tried to bargain—hostages for freedom—but Stuart in accord with Lee's orders gave a signal to the storming party of marines, and they soon overwhelmed Brown and his followers. Stuart acquired Brown's Bowie knife and some local notice from the event.

As the secession crisis deepened during 1860 and 1861, Stuart vowed to "go with Virginia" but otherwise remained essentially apolitical. When Virginia seceded, Stuart resigned his U.S. commission and secured first a Virginia, later a Confederate, commission as colonel of cavalry. He commanded the First Virginia Cavalry at Harpers Ferry initially under the command of Thomas J. ("Stonewall") Jackson and then in the army of Joseph E. Johnston.

Soon Stuart emerged as a master teacher of cavalry tactics, and he trained his regiment by toying with the then less competent Union horsemen. Stuart grasped the essentials of the mission of mounted troops in the mid-nineteenth century. He had intuited that cavalry charges against massed infantry were doomed relics of Napoleon's day, and although he once said that he wanted to die at the head of a cavalry charge, he never led a charge against an enemy prepared to receive such an assault. Cavalry, Stuart realized, had to dominate the ground between major armies, discern the enemy strength, disposition, and intentions, and deny such information about friendly forces to the enemy. Cavalry could raid, wreck, and disrupt enemy supply and communications; but the first function of horsemen in this conflict was reconnaissance, and to this purpose Stuart schooled his soldiers.

In the campaign that produced the first major battle of the war, Stuart and his three hundred men were appropriately active. He screened the movement of Johnston's army from the Shenandoah Valley to Manassas Junction and then rejoined Johnston for the battle on Bull Run. The First Virginia did charge some disorganized New Yorkers during fighting on July 21, 1861, but for the most part Stuart directed artillery and guided troop units during the conflict. It was Stuart who led Jubal Early and his brigade to the position on the Federal flank at the critical moment in the battle. Early's appearance provoked the Federal withdrawal and the Confederate rush that won the day for the Southerners.

Promoted to brigadier general on September 24, 1861, Stuart commanded the cavalry attached to the Confederacy's primary eastern army. A massed mounted command gave Stuart the advantage over Federal cavalry, which then operated in smaller units dispersed throughout the Union army. Stuart rode in strength, confident of his capacity to overwhelm his adversaries, and so he continued his control of the space between field armies in Virginia. He cultivated his reputation as a "jolly centaur," recruited musicians for his retinue, and seemed to have wonderful fun playing at war.

In June of 1862 Stuart expanded his fame and became known throughout the United States and the Confederacy. Union Gen. George B. McClellan and his huge army threatened Richmond from the suburbs of the Confederate capital. Stuart's West Point superintendent and Harpers Ferry superior Robert E. Lee assumed command of the Army of Northern Virginia and, intending to attack the Federal right flank and rear, dispatched Stuart upon the crucial mission of reconnaissance beyond the Confederate left. On June 12, 1862, Stuart roused his staff at 2:00 A.M. with the proclamation, "Gentlemen, in ten minutes every man must be in his saddle!" and led 1,200 troopers behind the Federal right flank to discover what Lee needed to know. Then he continued his ride completely around the Union army, covering one hundred miles in three days and causing considerable destruction of enemy property and frustrated embarrassment for the Federals—all at the cost of only one Confederate casualty.

Stuart's only regret regarding his Ride around McClellan, or Pamunkey raid, was not encountering his father-in-law in combat. Most of Stuart's in-laws in some way served the Confederacy; Flora Cooke Stuart's cousin John Esten Cooke, for example, served periodically on Stuart's staff. But Phillip St. George Cooke remained with the U.S. Army. "He will regret it [his decision] but once," Stuart remarked, "and that will be continuously." Stuart also directed that his son no longer bear the name of this loyal traitor; Phillip St. George Cooke Stuart became James Ewell Brown Stuart, Jr. During the Ride around McClellan, Cooke commanded the Union cavalry reserve, but he was too slow and cautious to intercept Stuart's horsemen.

Stuart's success enhanced his legendary fame. But the jingling spurs, plumed hat, and fiddle music were in a sense a façade concealing hard work and meticulous planning. Stuart had dispatched John S. Mosby to scout this region days before his ride, and Stuart had consulted with his spies before he ever left camp. He knew what he would find on his reconnaissance before he made his scout. And he carefully placed in his ranks men familiar with the ground over which he would ride and brought them forward as guides at the appropriate times. Stuart was indeed a calculating cavalier.

Lee's army made good use of Stuart's intelligence in the Seven Days' campaign and drove McClellan from Richmond. In the aftermath of victory Stuart became a major general (July 25, 1862), and his cavalry played important roles in the series of victories subsequently achieved by the Army of Northern Virginia. In addition Stuart led a raid on Catlett's Station (August 22, 1862), purloining Union Gen. John Pope's uniform and dispatch book, and he seized 1,200 horses during the Chambersburg raid (October 10–12, 1862). With each new adventure Stuart's fame expanded, giving rise to stories, songs, and poems about him.

In the spring of 1863 Stuart discovered the exposed flank of Joseph Hooker's Union army near Chancellorsville and guided Stonewall Jackson's corps on the flank march to launch the Southern assault. Stuart was at hand when Jackson suffered his mortal wound, and thereafter Stuart took command of Jackson's infantry corps. Stuart handled his sudden assignment quite well and managed the crucial reconnecting with Lee's lines at the same time that he pounded Hooker's with massed artillery. Once more Lee won a significant victory, with Stuart playing an important part.

By June 1863, Stuart commanded almost 10,000 horsemen as Lee's army concentrated for a thrust into Pennsylvania. On June 9, however, Union Gen. Alfred Pleasonton sent an equal number of Federal troopers, plus infantry, against the unsuspecting Stuart at Brandy Station. The Federals achieved surprise and compelled the Confederates to fight for their lives. Brandy Station was the largest, exclusively cavalry battle of the war—indeed, the largest ever in North America—and Stuart held his own only with immense difficulty. His enemies had served notice that they could fight him on equal terms. Still, Stuart claimed victory, although most Southerners knew otherwise.

As Lee persisted with his campaign into Pennsylvania, Stuart dutifully screened the army's march. Then, however, he determined again to ride around another Union army and began his own march north by circling east of the Federal force. En route Stuart captured 150 supply wagons, and this baggage impeded his capacity to move and scout. Thus, on the eve of the Gettysburg campaign, Stuart somehow lost contact with two huge armies, friend and foe, and failed in his vital obligation of reconnaissance.

"Well, General Stuart, you are here at last," were Lee's reported words when Stuart finally joined the army at Gettysburg on the second day of the battle. Stuart's tardiness left Lee uninformed about the strength of his enemy, but he knew the location of George G. Meade's Federals by this time; on the third and climactic day of Gettysburg he sent a massive infantry charge at the center of Union lines on Cemetery Ridge. As George Pickett led the assault that bears his name, Stuart mounted his own charge against Federal cavalry a mile or two from the infantry action. Both Stuart's and Pickett's charges failed; had they succeeded, Stuart would certainly have shared the glory of having slashed Meade's army into fragments. As he had done after Brandy Station, Stuart attempted to compensate for his errors in the field with a bombastic report of his actions. Unfortunately, he confused fantasy and reality, in much the same way he confused fame with greatness, because he lacked the depth and maturity to know the difference.

Stuart nevertheless was a great cavalry commander, arguably the best in the war. He had proved capable of leading a large mounted force, of cooperating and contributing within a major field army, and of carrying out raids and reconnaissance with equal facility.

By 1864, though, his horsemen were outnumbered and outmounted. He served Lee well in the Wilderness campaign, but then had to confront a thrust against Richmond by Union Gen. Philip Sheridan. The Federal commander planned to lure Stuart away from Lee's army and destroy him. On May 11, at Yellow Tavern, only six miles from Richmond, Stuart confronted Sheridan's 10,000 men with a force less than a third its size. In the battle Stuart suffered a wound that proved mortal. Carried to Richmond, he lay in pain as well-wishers, including Jefferson Davis, visited him. At 7:38 P.M. on May 12 Stuart died; his legend, though, still lives.

[*See also* Stuart's Raids.]

BIBLIOGRAPHY

Blackford, W. W. *War Years with Jeb Stuart.* New York, 1945.

Davis, Burke. *Jeb Stuart: The Last Cavalier.* New York, 1957.

Freeman, Douglas S. *Lee's Lieutenants: A Study in Command.* 3 vols. New York, 1942–1944. Reprint, New York, 1986.

McClellan, H. B. *The Life and Campaigns of Major-General J. E. B. Stuart.* Boston and New York, 1885.

Thomas, Emory M. *Bold Dragoon: The Life of J. E. B. Stuart.* New York, 1986.

Thomason, John W., Jr. *Jeb Stuart.* New York, 1930.

EMORY M. THOMAS

STUART'S RAIDS. James Ewell Brown ("Jeb") Stuart and his cavalry disrupted Union supply lines and gathered significant intelligence for Robert E. Lee in support of operations of the Army of Northern Virginia throughout 1862.

Stuart's most spectacular expedition occurred on June 12 through 15 in the Peninsular campaign. As a prelude to his plan to relieve Northern pressure upon Richmond, Lee instructed the twenty-nine-year-old Stuart to "make a secret movement to the rear of the enemy" to determine the practicability of striking the Federal army's right wing north of the Chickahominy River. Subsequently at 2:00 A.M. on the twelfth, Stuart ordered 1,200 troopers from four Virginia regiments into the saddle, and the half-mile-long column began moving northwest toward Hanover Court House.

Breaking bivouac early on the thirteenth, Stuart shifted his direction from north to east, heading for Old Church Crossroads. With the exception of a brief encounter with a Fifth U.S. Cavalry detachment, in which Capt. William Latané of the Ninth Virginia Cavalry was killed, Stuart met with no opposition. (The *Burial of Latané,* an 1864 oil painting by William Washington, idealized Southern womanhood and soldierly valor and became a central icon of the postwar Lost Cause movement.)

Arriving at Old Church on the afternoon of the thirteenth, Stuart's semicircular route had carried him thirty-five miles from Richmond and behind George B. McClellan's army. He had discovered McClellan's right was vulnerable, but the Confederate cavalier now became concerned about his own rear. Reasoning that the Federals would intercept his return, Stuart decided upon "the quintessence of prudence," turning his mounts south in an attempt to ride completely around McClellan's army. "There was something of the sublime in the implicit confidence and unquestioning trust of the rank and file," Stuart later informed Lee, "in a leader guiding them straight . . . into the very jaws of the enemy."

Nine miles south at Tunstall's Station, on the York River Railroad, Stuart seized and burned supply wagons and nearly captured a train. By midnight of the fourteenth, the column reached the Chickahominy, but its rain-swollen swamps prevented easy passage. Stuart ordered a bridge constructed, and his troopers crossed the river just ahead of pursuing Federals, commanded by Stuart's father-in-law, Brig. Gen. Philip St. George Cooke. Stuart then headed for the James River, returning to Richmond on June 15 after nearly a hundred miles of riding. He had captured 165 prisoners and 260 mules and horses during his journey around 105,000 Union soldiers, and he had learned that McClellan's right flank was "in the air." McClellan likewise observed this vulnerability, and he began moving his base of supplies and his army south toward the James.

Following the Seven Days' campaign and the Union decision to withdraw McClellan from the Virginia Peninsula, Lee turned north to encounter John Pope. On August 22, while sparring with Pope along the Rappahannock, Stuart received approval to strike the enemy's rear. With 1,500 men and two guns, Stuart crossed the Rappahannock at Waterloo Bridge and proceeded toward Catlett's Station on the Orange and Alexandria Railroad. Reaching Catlett's after dark on the twenty-second, Stuart surprised Pope's headquarters camp and seized Pope's uniform and dispatch book. The Confederates failed to sever Pope's supply line, however, as the railroad bridge across Cedar Run had become saturated during a terrific thunderstorm. In addition to Pope's personal baggage, Stuart captured over three hundred prisoners during this one-day raid.

Three weeks after the conclusion of the Sharpsburg campaign, Lee and McClellan remained stationary about sixty miles northwest of Washington. On October 8, in an effort to determine the Federals' "position, force, and probable intention," Lee ordered Stuart to embark on an expedition into western Maryland and southern Pennsyl-

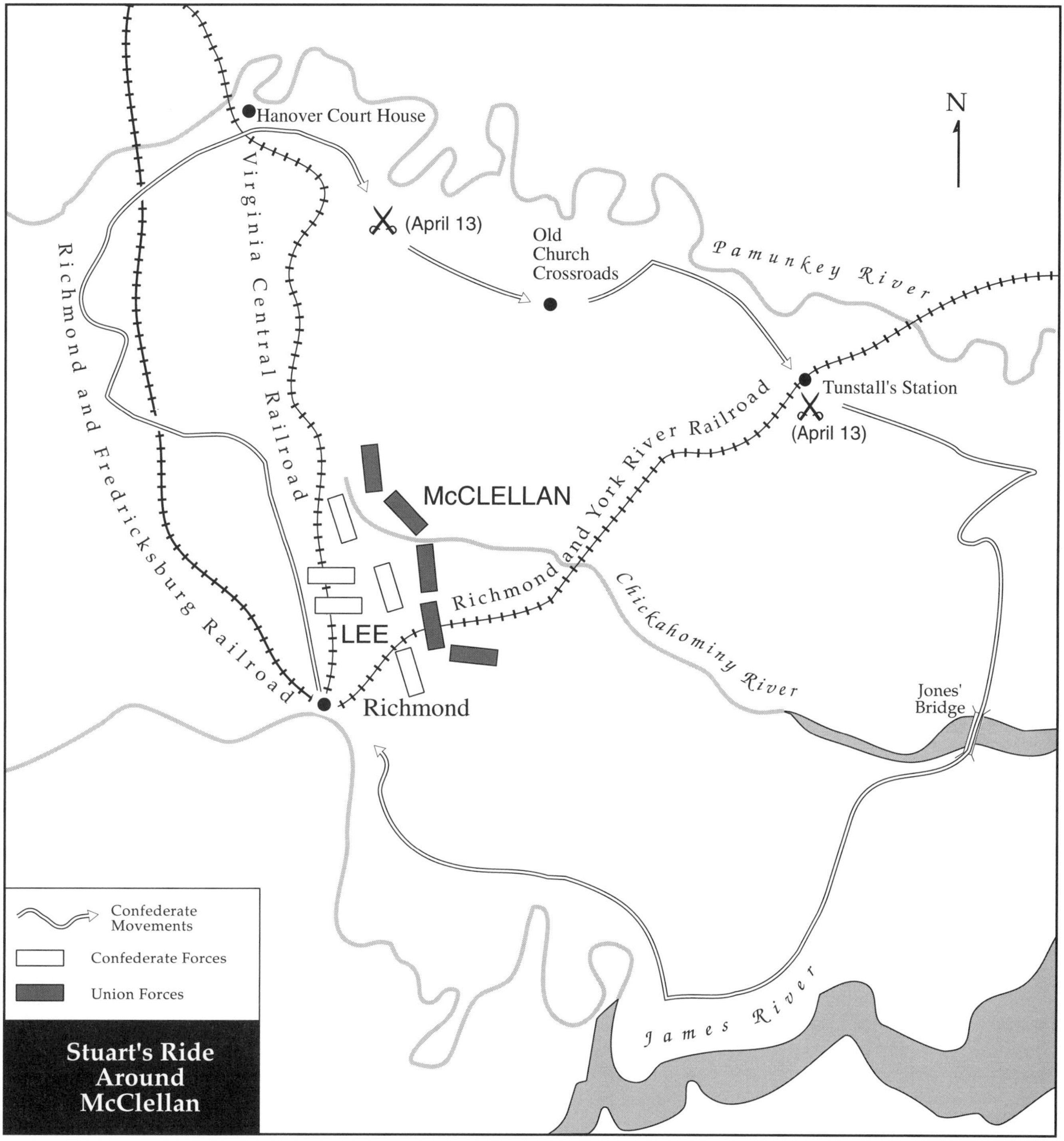

vania. Lee specifically instructed Stuart to slice McClellan's main supply line by destroying the Conococheage bridge of the Cumberland Valley Railroad near Chambersburg. Lee also asked Stuart to arrest "citizens of Pennsylvania holding State or government office . . . [so] that they may be used as hostages, or the means of exchange." Lee also granted Stuart permission to round up horses from Maryland and Pennsylvania farmers.

Execution of Stuart's Pennsylvania raid commenced during the night of October 9–10 when a force of 1,800 cavalry and four guns left Darkesville near Opequon Creek. When the Confederate crossing of the Potomac began about

3:00 A.M. at McCoy's Ferry, Union cavalry detected the movement and quickly spread the word. Meanwhile, Stuart rode swiftly north, arriving at Chambersburg at dark. The Confederates had ridden forty miles without opposition.

While at Chambersburg, Stuart's men failed to destroy the iron trestle of the Conococheague bridge, but the Southerners did torch the railroad's extensive machine shops and depot buildings. In addition, about five thousand muskets were destroyed, and 280 wounded Federals paroled.

As Stuart headed east toward Gettysburg on the eleventh, Union authorities plotted to seal off his escape routes. "Not a man should be permitted to return to Virginia," insisted General in Chief H. W. Halleck. McClellan responded by sending infantry divisions north and west of the Potomac and cavalry to the east. As McClellan declared, "I hope we may be able to teach them a lesson they will not soon forget."

Stuart, anticipating the Union clamp, kept the Federal chasers off guard with deceptive cross-country maneuvers. Finally he recrossed the Potomac at White's Ford near Poolesville late in the morning on the twelfth.

In three days, Stuart's command had traveled 180 miles, 80 in the last twenty-four hours of the raid. The Confederates captured over 1,200 horses and suffered no men killed and only one wounded. In addition to detecting the position of the enemy and causing a political fallout for the Lincoln administration, Stuart concluded that "the consternation among property holders in Pennsylvania beggars description."

Stuart's final behind-the-enemy raid of 1862 occurred following the Confederate victory at Fredericksburg in mid-December. On Christmas Day, Stuart led 1,800 men and four guns across the Rappahannock at Kelly's Ford and then in the direction of Dumfries and the Occoquan River. His purpose was to seize the Telegraph Road and destroy any trains supplying Ambrose Burnside's Army of the Potomac.

Stuart discovered Dumfries too well defended by Federal infantry and little traffic on the Telegraph Road. His command did capture nearly a hundred prisoners at Greenwood Church near the Occoquan before moving northwest toward the Orange and Alexandria Railroad. At Burke's Station, Stuart seized the telegraph and wired the quartermaster general of the United States to complain about the poor quality of the Federal mules he had lately captured. His command then destroyed the railroad bridge over the Accotink River before proceeding north and west toward Fairfax Court House and Loudoun County. Stuart returned to Fredericksburg on New Year's Day with more than two hundred prisoners and twenty-five wagons, with a loss of only one killed and six wounded.

[*See also* Brandy Station; Gettysburg Campaign.]

BIBLIOGRAPHY

Blackford, W. W. *War Years with Jeb Stuart.* New York, 1945.

Davis, Burke. *Jeb Stuart: The Last Cavalier.* New York, 1957.

McClellan, H. B. *The Life and Campaigns of Maj. Gen. J. E. B. Stuart.* Richmond, Va., 1985.

Thomas, Emory M. *Bold Dragoon: The Life of J. E. B. Stuart.* New York, 1988.

DENNIS E. FRYE

SUBMARINES. The Union blockade of Southern ports forced Confederates to develop a variety of weapons to counter it: the ironclad, the rifled cannon, the torpedo, the semisubmersible torpedo boat, and, most remarkably innovative, the submarine.

Experiments with submarines had been made as early as the American Revolution; Robert Fulton was among the first inventors. The Civil War concentrated and accelerated efforts that had previously been merely speculative.

By the late summer of 1861, submarine development got underway at Tredegar Iron Works in Richmond and along the James River. The major effect was psychological, for the Union fleet at Hampton Roads was unnerved by rumors and false sightings of what later came to be known as an "infernal machine." A strong possibility exists that the Confederacy also built other submarines for which no conclusive evidence exists. Federal reports placed submarines in the James River, Virginia, at Houston, Texas, and Shreveport, Louisiana.

The dreaded threat of a submarine strike did not become reality until February 17, 1864, when USS *Housatonic* became the first ship sunk in battle by a submarine—*H. L. Hunley* in Charleston Harbor. That single triumph had been hard bought by a New Orleans group composed of inventor J. R. McClintock and investors H. L. Hunley, R. F. Barrow, Henry L. Leovy, Baxter Watson, and J. K. Scott.

The men first constructed *Pioneer* at Leeds Foundry in a civilian for-profit operation. *Pioneer* was commissioned as a privateer, and the group applied for a letter of marque to attack Union shipping. The risks were great, but so were the potential returns on their investment.

Pioneer served as a prototype for the more famous *Hunley*. The cigar-shaped craft was thirty-four feet long, with a cabin four feet by four feet by ten feet. The crew could sight through circular windows on the sides, and a manhole on the conning tower above provided access to the vessel. This earliest design of a submarine carried a crew of two, one to man a hand crank that turned the propeller and the other to steer the sub beneath a ship and screw a clock torpedo (mine) to the hull. Tests conducted in Lake Pontchartrain were successful, but New Orleans fell to Adm. David Farragut's fleet before *Pioneer* could inflict any

PRIVATEER SUBMARINE *PIONEER*. Photographed on April 24, 1957, while being moved to an exhibition site in the Presbytere Arcade, Louisiana State Museum, New Orleans. NAVAL HISTORICAL CENTER, WASHINGTON, D.C.

damage on Union vessels. It was destroyed to avoid capture. (The submarine currently preserved at the Louisiana State Museum in New Orleans is believed not to be *Pioneer*, but some other, unknown vessel.)

Hunley, Watson, and McClintock moved their operation to Parks and Lyon's Foundry in Mobile, where they constructed *American Diver,* with dimensions thirty-six feet long by three feet wide by four feet deep. Because the cylindrical ends of *Pioneer* had created steering problems, twelve feet of hull on each end were tapered. An expensive effort to develop an electromagnetic engine was abandoned in favor of four crewmen cranking the propeller shaft. Foul weather prevented *American Diver* from attacking the Mobile blockaders, but Hunley's group, now joined by army engineers Lts. W. A. Alexander and G. E. Dixon, was determined to launch a fully operational submarine.

H. L. Hunley was a larger, nine-man version of previous ships at 40 feet long by 3½ feet wide by 4 feet deep. Ballast tanks at either end of the hull could be flooded for submersion and pumped out to ascend. A heavy iron keel plate supplied ballast, but could be released by loosening bolts inside the hull should an emergency ascent be necessary. Eight men cranked the propeller. In addition to the manhole in the conning tower and the round windows, this sub had more sophisticated equipment: two hollow pipes with stop cocks that extended above the surface as a kind of snorkle, a mercury depth gauge, and a compass. A candle served the dual purpose of providing light and warning of dangerously low oxygen.

The original design called for *Hunley* to pass under a ship with a cylinder torpedo in tow. Once the sub had cleared the hull, the torpedo would detonate on contact. Because this tactic would not work against a ship in shallow water, this design was replaced by a spar torpedo.

Reports of *Hunley* distressed the Union blockaders but so impressed Gen. P. G. T. Beauregard that he ordered it transferred from Mobile Harbor to Charleston, where the need for such a weapon was more critical. In August 1863, the submarine was raised and sent with priority scheduling through the rail system to Charleston. Test runs immediately got underway with the help of veteran pilots who knew the slightest variations of wind and tide in the harbor. Even so, a navy crew promptly sank the "New Fangled boat," which was beginning to earn another name: "peripatetic coffin."

Hunley was summoned from Mobile, with Dixon, Alexander, and Thomas Parks, to train a crew and manage the sub. On October 15, Hunley, Parks, and six crewmen were lost when they were unable to raise the ship in an emergency. Partially turned bolts on the keel plate, a cock inadvertently left open, and the death agonies apparent in the bodies of the crew were painful evidence of the risks of the new technology.

Despite Beauregard's refusal to allow further risk of life, Dixon assembled a crew and soon was conducting further training, including submersion for increasingly longer periods. Once, when they remained submerged for more than an hour, anxious observers mistakenly gave them up for dead and left the wharf.

Sinking *Housatonic* after more than two years of labor became, then, an immense achievement for the Confederacy. The event was all *Hunley*'s inventors and crew might have imagined. Just after 8:00 P.M., the officer of the deck glimpsed what appeared to be a log floating toward his ship; he shouted a warning, the drummer beat to quarters, and in another moment the giant ship was lifted out of the water by an exploding torpedo.

At dawn, Union rescue boats found many crewmen perched in the ship's rigging, for it had settled into the relatively shallow harbor. *Hunley,* however, was nowhere to be found. The effect of the threat remained, for Union blockaders thought it had been concealed or even returned to Mobile. Alexander, Beauregard, and the rest knew better. Dixon, his crew, and *Hunley* had vanished. Years later, a diver found the little craft, which apparently had been trapped beneath the hull of the sinking *Housatonic*.

The Confederacy had repeated a familiar chapter in its naval history: inventive, persistent, heroic, and ultimately futile—except in this sense: future navies would successfully adapt the technology that claimed the lives and fortunes of history's first submariners.

BIBLIOGRAPHY

Civil War Naval Chronology, 1861–1865. 6 vols. Washington, D.C., 1961–1965.

Kloppel, James E. *Danger beneath the Waves.* College Park, Ga., 1987.

Perry, Milton F. *Infernal Machines: The Story of Confederate Submarine and Mine Warfare.* Baton Rouge, La., 1965.

Robinson, William H., Jr. *The Confederate Privateers.* New Haven, 1928.

MAXINE TURNER

SUBSTITUTES. [*This entry discusses the use by Confederate citizens and soldiers of substitutes for previously available goods that became unavailable as the Civil War progressed. For discussion of the hiring of military substitutes to avoid conscription into the Confederate army, see* Conscription.]

The establishment of the Confederate nation produced many changes in the daily life of the average Southerner. Very early in the conflict Southerners discovered that the common things they had taken for granted in the past had become scarce or nonexistent. The increased effectiveness of the Union blockade and the South's shortage of essential—and nonessential—raw materials and finished goods forced Southerners to develop substitutes. In this realm, they proved to be resourceful and ingenious.

One of the most common complaints was the lack of certain foods and beverages, especially coffee. Southerners became adept at creating substitutes for that favorite drink. Many women submitted recipes to local newspapers calling for such ingredients as chicory, okra, crushed acorns, or rye. Confederate soldiers, too, argued the merits of various nut and fruit concoctions that produced a dark liquid reminiscent of coffee—at least in color. Sugar for that coffee or for baking was also in short supply. Southerners turned to sorghum or honey or boiled down fresh fruits to make a thick, sweet syrup.

Clothing shortages affected everyone. The South's textile base was virtually monopolized by the demands of the Quartermaster Bureau. Consequently, civilians were often forced to make do with old clothes. People recycled old material to create everyday clothing. Many women pulled spinning wheels out of the attic and began to manufacture homespun, or they utilized their sewing skills to convert draperies, carpets, and bed sheets into usable clothing for their families. The loss of wool supplies from areas overrun by Federal troops produced severe shortages of that commodity. In its place, Southerners combined cotton with rabbit or raccoon fur to make warmer garments. In order to render these homemade pieces more attractive, people turned to nature for dyes: berries, bark, and the like produced colors that helped hide the makeshift nature or origin of the piece. Shoes, however, were the scarcest item, and it took every bit of ingenuity to devise usable substitutes. Generally, families recycled old bits of leather, but some used wood and heavy canvas duck to create shoes.

On both the battle front and the home front the shortage of medicine had potentially dire consequences. In this realm, the blockade had a far-reaching effect, as did the cessation of trade with the Northern states. Shortages of quinine, morphine, and other necessary drugs were common. Home remedies enjoyed some popularity, but for many ailments, there was no adequate substitution. Substitutes for quinine were tried and found to be effective—cottonseed tea and dog fennel, for example. But for other drugs, such as chloroform or morphine, no makeshift sufficed, so Southerners were forced to rely upon the contraband trade in drugs.

Although most shortages affected mainly the civilian population behind the lines, other people, more directly related to the war effort, also encountered difficulties. For example, many war contractors found that shortages of raw materials hampered their production for the government. These entrepreneurs tried myriad experiments with substitute items. When supplies of oil for engines and lubrication ran short, railroad engineers discovered that lard oil, peanut oil, and castor oil worked just as well. Those manufacturing artillery or cavalry harnesses substituted oak or hickory wood splints for leather. People made ropes for battlefield or farm use by weaving moss, grasses, cotton, or okra stalks into twine.

It is safe to say that shortages of goods affected all Confederates at one time or another, and the dearth of everyday items probably took a toll after a while. Wax for good-quality candles was lacking; paper and ink for letters and newspapers disappeared; lost buttons became irreplaceable. Through it all, Southerners adapted. But as ingenious as they were, they never fully solved the problem. Shortages, and the adoption of substitutes, testifies to how dependent the region was upon foreign and domestic importations for the most common goods.

[*See also* Clothing; Food; Health and Medicine, *article on* Medical Treatments; Sugar; Uniforms.]

BIBLIOGRAPHY

Coulter, E. Merton. *The Confederate States of America, 1861–1865.* A History of the South, vol. 7. Baton Rouge, La., 1951.

Massey, Mary Elizabeth. *Ersatz in the Confederacy.* Columbia, S.C., 1952.

Thomas, Emory M. *The Confederate Nation, 1861–1865.* New York, 1979.

MARY A. DECREDICO

SUGAR. The sugar industry of the antebellum South was largely concentrated in south Louisiana (95 percent) with some small production in Texas, coastal South Carolina and Georgia, and south Florida. In the 1850s the annual crop averaged about 150,000 tons (300,000 hogsheads of 1,000 pounds). Sugar planters shipped their product to the southern Mississippi valley and to eastern cities where it was consumed largely as raw sugar rather than refined. Southern sugar production supplied one-third to one-half of total U.S. consumption. The remainder was imported from the West Indies.

Ideal conditions for the growth of sugar cane include a temperature averaging 75° F year-round with no freezes, an annual rainfall of sixty inches well distributed, and a fertile soil that drains rapidly and thoroughly. The Southern sugar region possessed most of these characteristics, but it was subject to cold weather and freezes, which threatened the crops.

Sugar cane is planted from seed cane taken from the preceding year's crop. Southern cane planters took only three crops from a field before replanting, in contrast to the many years cane was allowed to ratoon (sprout from the roots) in tropical areas. Cane, planted in rows of five to seven feet in width, was cultivated mainly by mule-driven plows by the 1850s, although hoe cultivation was still used from time to time.

The large farm or plantation was the dominant agricultural unit in the Southern cane region; farms of fewer than a hundred acres were neither numerous nor important in the output of sugar. The working force included planter-owners, overseers, sugar makers, and from time to time hired skilled laborers. But the major part of the labor force was made up of slaves, who by 1860 composed 60 percent of the population of the Louisiana sugar region.

The harvesting season began in mid- or late October when the slaves, working with huge knives, began the cutting, which was completed in late December or early January. Once the juice was crushed from the cane with steam-driven rollers, the process of making sugar began. Most common was the open-kettle process utilizing a set of six cast iron kettles. The heated juice was ladled from one to another as impurities were removed, water evaporated, and the juice clarified. When the juice reached the last kettle, the temperature was extremely hot and the syrup was ready for granulation; after the crystals had formed, the sugar was packed into hogsheads and the remaining syrup allowed to drain.

Southern sugar houses produced raw sugar of varying quality that was usually consumed in that form. By the 1850s, greatly improved apparatus for sugar making had been developed by Norbert Rillieux, a distinguished black creole of Louisiana who had studied physics and mechanics in France and was familiar with developments in the manufacture of beet sugar. The advanced equipment utilized vacuum pan evaporators, which produced a sugar that was of more uniform consistency and whiter and dryer than open-kettle sugar.

The Texas and Florida sugar areas escaped the ravages of war, but the Louisiana area was not so fortunate. Life in that region experienced abrupt changes when Federal troops arrived in 1862. As the troops extended their control, great numbers of blacks left the plantations in order to join the Northerners. Both planters and newly freed blacks attempted to adjust to the altered situation in 1862 and 1863, but neither group was satisfied with the new relationship. In order to ensure an adequately disciplined labor force, especially during the harvesting season, planters sought to regulate both the working and nonworking hours of the cane cutters. Many of the blacks viewed their efforts as tantamount to a reimposition of slavery.

In January 1863 Gen. Nathaniel P. Banks, commander of the Department of the Gulf, issued orders dealing with the operation of plantations. Planters were to provide "food, clothes, proper treatment, and just compensation" for the blacks. Workers were to receive one-twentieth of the proceeds of the crop at the end of the year or a fixed monthly compensation of two dollars for field hands and three dollars for mechanics and sugar hands.

Early in 1864 General Banks, attempting to respond to dissatisfaction by both planters and sugar cane workers, issued new orders, which increased wages, regulated the workday, and guaranteed just treatment, healthy rations, clothing, quarters, medical attention, and education for children. Workers could choose their employers, but contracts were to remain in force for one year. In order to ensure completion of the year, one-half of a worker's wages could be withheld until the end of the year. Contracts based on these stipulations were entered into throughout the sugar region in 1864 and 1865.

After the Confederates lost control of the Mississippi River and the sugar region of south Louisiana in 1862, the sugar supply almost entirely disappeared from Mississippi to Virginia. Only the small amounts arriving by blockade-runners and that cultivated in Florida and Georgia were available. Substitute sweeteners such as honey, maple syrup, and especially sorghum cane syrup were used instead.

Under the disordered conditions of the war years, it was impossible to grow, harvest, manufacture, and market the sugar crop successfully. From a record 460,000 hogsheads (230,000 tons) of sugar valued at $25 million, the crop declined steadily until the cumulative effect of an inadequate labor force and widespread destruction of capital equipment resulted in an 1864 crop of only 10,000 hogsheads valued at less than $2 million. Although more than 1,200 plantations in twenty-four parishes had produced sugar in 1861, in 1864 only 175 plantations in sixteen parishes were still making sugar.

The collapse of the industry can be seen in its capital losses. In 1861 the total capital invested in the industry was estimated at $194 million of which $100 million was in slave property, $25 million in land, and $69 million in capital equipment and rolling stock. With the investment in slave property wiped out, capital equipment largely destroyed, and a drastic decline in the value of sugar lands, the industry was worth only $25 million in 1865.

With the end of the Civil War, sugar planters and workers alike had to adjust to a new order of society, which demanded abandonment of old habits, convictions, and prejudices.

BIBLIOGRAPHY

Heitmann, John. *Modernization of the Louisiana Sugar Industry, 1830–1910.* Baton Rouge, La., 1987.

Prichard, Walter. "The Effects of the Civil War on the Louisiana Sugar Industry." *Journal of Southern History* 5 (1939): 315–332.

Roland, Charles P. *Louisiana Sugar Plantations during the American Civil War.* Leiden, Holland, 1957.

Sitterson, J. Carlyle. *Sugar Country: The Cane Sugar Industry in the South, 1753–1950.* Lexington, Ky., 1953.

Sitterson, J. Carlyle. "The Transition from Slave to Free Economy on the William J. Minor Plantations." *Agricultural History* 17 (1943): 216–224.

J. Carlyle Sitterson

SUMNER, CANING OF. On May 22, 1856, Preston Brooks, a congressman from South Carolina, entered the chambers of the upper house and beat Senator Charles Sumner of Massachusetts senseless with a cane. This event, which came at a time when the struggle over slavery in Kansas was creating powerful tensions between the North and the South, further polarized the sections, contributed to the rapid rise of the Republican party, and was an important landmark on the road to the Civil War.

Sumner had been elected to the Senate in 1851; by that date he was already well known in Massachusetts as a leading critic of slavery. In 1855 he had helped organize the Republican party, which was pledged to stop the expansion of slavery into the western territories. On May 19 and 20, 1856, he delivered a carefully prepared speech in the Senate on "The Crime against Kansas" in which he lashed out at slavery and the South. Sumner launched scathing attacks on individual Southerners, including his fellow senator Andrew P. Butler of South Carolina, who was absent at the time Sumner spoke. Butler, Sumner charged, had taken "the harlot, Slavery" as "his mistress to whom he has made his vows," and Sumner contended that if the whole history of South Carolina were blotted out of existence "civilization might lose . . . little." Most who heard the speech were

"THE SYMBOL OF THE NORTH IS THE PEN; THE SYMBOL OF THE SOUTH IS THE BLUDGEON."— Henry Ward Beecher.
TOOMBS
DOUGLAS
CRITTENDEN
KEITT
BROOKS

"ARGUMENTS OF THE CHIVALRY." Northern interpretation of the beating of Senator Charles Sumner of Massachusetts (seated at right) by Representative Preston S. Brooks of South Carolina (standing above him with raised cane). In the foreground, at left, Senators Robert Toombs of Georgia and Stephen A. Douglas of Illinois look on approvingly. Facing them stands Representative Lawrence Keitt of South Carolina with a cane and pistol to ward off any interference. In the background Senator John J. Crittenden of Kentucky is restrained by an unidentified man. Above them is a quote from Henry Ward Beecher, delivered at a New York rally in support of Sumner nine days later: "The symbol of the North is the Pen; the symbol of the South is the bludgeon." Lithograph by Winslow Homer.

LIBRARY OF CONGRESS

appalled at Sumner's language, and Congressman Brooks, who was a cousin of Butler's, was outraged. Two days after Sumner had concluded his remarks, Brooks assaulted him.

News of Sumner's caning rapidly swept the nation. In the North, even conservatives who were critical of Sumner's antislavery views and vituperative speeches were infuriated by Brooks's assault. Their anger mounted as it became evident that Southerners, rather than condemning Brooks, revered him for defending the honor not only of his relative but of the whole section. Constituents showered him with new canes; merchants of South Carolina sent him one inscribed with the words "hit him again." Southern votes prevented the House from expelling Brooks, who resigned anyway but was triumphantly reelected by his constituents. A fine of three hundred dollars levied by a Washington court proved to be his only punishment.

At the very time news of Sumner's caning reached the North, word came from Kansas that a proslavery mob had attacked the homes, shops, and newspapers of free-state advocates in Lawrence. Republicans, whose party had just been formed and whose future seemed uncertain, were quick to exploit Northern anger at both these actions, characterizing them as proof of Southern willingness to assault free institutions in order to defend slavery. This contention proved popular with many Northerners who were not particularly concerned about the issue of slavery but were worried about defending freedom of speech and press from Southern attack.

Sumner's caning, rather than the sack of Lawrence, provided the Republicans with their most effective image of Southern arrogance. Widespread indignation at the deed led many moderates and conservatives who had previously joined the newly formed American, or Know-Nothing, party to join them instead, and in the 1856 presidential election the Republicans almost defeated the Democratic candidate.

Sumner did not return to the Senate until December 1859, and his empty seat was a constant reminder to the North of Brooks's deed. His critics argued that the senator was feigning illness, but his injuries, complicated by posttraumatic syndrome, had truly disabled him. In 1860 the Republicans took the White House, thereby precipitating the secession of the lower South. Sumner's caning, by arousing the North and helping to make the Republican party a major political force, had proved to be a long step toward war.

[*See also* Bleeding Kansas.]

BIBLIOGRAPHY

Donald, David. *Charles Sumner and the Coming of the Civil War.* New York, 1960.

Gienapp, William. "The Crime against Sumner: The Caning of Charles Sumner and the Rise of the Republican Party." *Civil War History* 25 (1979): 218–245.

RICHARD H. ABBOTT

SUMTER. The wooden cruiser *Sumter* was converted from *Havana,* a sail-steam packet ship that ran between Havana and New Orleans. It was built in 1859 in Philadelphia by the Vaughn and Lynn Company. The conversion at James Martin's Atlantic Dry Dock in Algiers, across the river from New Orleans, was under the direction of *Sumter*'s designated captain, Commdr. Raphael Semmes.

Semmes added a birth deck, strengthened the main deck to support the cannon, changed the two-masted rigging to square sails, added space for crew and officer quarters, and rigged the smokestack so it could be lowered while under sail only. These changes lengthened the ship from 152 to 184 feet, increased the width from 27 to 30 feet, and reduced the draft from $12\frac{1}{2}$ to 12 feet. *Sumter*'s greatest deficiency as a cruiser was a small coal bin (only eight days' steaming capacity) and the stationary propeller that created drag when under sail only. Her top speed under steam and sail was no more than ten knots. The converted *Sumter* retained *Havana*'s scroll head and round stern, which gave her, as Semmes wrote, "a sort of saucy air." *Sumter*'s arms were four 32-pounders mounted broadside and one 8-inch cannon pivot-mounted amidships so that it could fire from both port and starboard sides.

Despite delays in receiving needed materials, the conversion was completed in less than two months, from April 23 to June 3, 1861. The crew consisted of twenty-three officers and ninety-two seamen of various nationalities recruited from the New Orleans waterfront. The officers, most of

SUMTER. Running the blockade of New Orleans, Louisiana, past USS *Brooklyn,* June 30, 1861. Lithograph by Netherclift from *The Cruise of the "Alabama" and the "Sumter,"* by Raphael Semmes, London, 1864. NAVAL HISTORICAL CENTER, WASHINGTON, D.C.

whom had served in the U.S. Navy, included Marine Lt. B. Howell, brother-in-law to Jefferson Davis.

Sumter departed New Orleans on June 18, 1861, but not until June 30, in an exciting race with USS *Brooklyn,* could Semmes run the Union blockade into the Gulf of Mexico. She was the first Confederate ship to carry the flag onto high seas and into foreign ports. Her first capture (July 2) was *Golden Rocket* out of Brewer, Maine. Semmes condemned the vessel and burned her. But he felt it to be "a painful duty to destroy so noble a ship" and later attempted to bully weak neutrals into adjudicating his captures in their port. In two days off Cuba, *Sumter* captured seven ships. *Sumter* cruised the Gulf of Mexico, the Caribbean Sea, and down the South American coast to Brazil. At the port of St. Pierre, Martinique, *Sumter* was blocked by USS *Iroquois.* By cleverly dodging into the shadow of a large rock and suddenly changing course, *Sumter* evaded the more powerful Union vessel. She then headed for Cadiz, Spain, for repairs. Frustrated there by a "bull-head, stupid official," Semmes sailed *Sumter* into the harbor of Gibraltar where he received coal and made some repairs. Blockaded by three U.S. warships, Semmes abandoned *Sumter.*

During her career in the Confederate navy in slightly over six months (June 30, 1861, to January 18, 1862), *Sumter* captured altogether eighteen ships, burned seven with their cargoes, released two on bond, lost eight to Cuban internment, and had two recaptured by the enemy. While awaiting her fate, *Sumter* was the scene of a murder when Acting Master's Mate Joseph Goodwin Hester shot and killed Midshipman William Andrews. This was the ship's only fatality. Bought at auction by a Liverpool merchant on December 19, 1862, and renamed *Gibraltar,* she made several successful runs into the South with cargoes of arms and munitions.

BIBLIOGRAPHY

Kell, John McIntosh. *Recollections of a Navy Life Including the Cruises of the Confederate States Steamers "Sumter" and "Alabama."* Washington, D.C., 1900.

Semmes, Admiral Raphael. *Memoirs of Service Afloat during the War between the States.* Baltimore, 1869. Reprint, Secaucus, N.J., 1987.

Spencer, Warren F. *The Confederate Navy in Europe.* University, Ala., 1983.

Summersell, Charles Grayson. *The Cruise of C.S.S. Sumter.* Tuscaloosa, Ala., 1965.

WARREN F. SPENCER

SWAN, WILLIAM G. (1821–1869), congressman from Tennessee. Born in Alabama, Swan graduated from East Tennessee College in 1838, read law in Knoxville, and practiced in Knox and surrounding counties, prior to serving as state attorney general (1851–1854) and as a Democratic mayor of Knoxville (1855–1856). On the eve of the war, his estate amounted to approximately $70,000, with investments in real estate, railroads, utilities, and publishing, but reportedly no slaves.

Contrary to what has been written, Swan, an original secessionist, was not a candidate for Congress in August 1861 and therefore did not lose to Unionist Horace Maynard, who defeated J. H. Shields. The election had been, in effect, a referendum on secession in eastern Tennessee, with Maynard receiving more votes for the U.S. Congress than Shields did for the Provisional Confederate Congress. (Maynard later made his way to Washington and was seated, while Shields refused to claim his seat in Richmond.) Meanwhile, Swan enlisted in the army and served as a private, until he was elected in November 1861 by about a two-to-one margin over John Baxter to represent Tennessee's Second District in the First Confederate Congress. While in Richmond, Swan resided at the home of his friend, John Mitchel, the Irish patriot, with whom he had published a newspaper in Knoxville in the late 1850s.

The Davis administration had an ally in Swan, who was reelected in 1863. A member of the important Military Affairs Committee, he voted in favor of all three major conscription bills, as well as the December 1863 measure abolishing substitution, and he was reluctant to grant draft exemptions. Keenly interested in the war in eastern Tennessee, he urged Jefferson Davis to adopt an aggressive strategy and often requested military information and battle reports in the region. Moreover, he was with Gen. Braxton Bragg and later Gen. James Longstreet during the campaign against Knoxville (November 1863). In March 1862 and again in April of the following year, he proposed the recall of the Confederate commissioner to Great Britain for that country's refusal to extend diplomatic relations to the Confederacy. On economic matters, however, Swan was less cooperative, opposing the general revenue measure of April 24, 1863, which levied both a direct tax and license fees on the Confederate populace.

After the war ended, Swan resided and practiced law for several months in Macon and later Columbus, Georgia, but he soon moved to Memphis, where he remained until his death and where he was buried.

BIBLIOGRAPHY

Amnesty File. William G. Swan. Microcopy M1003, Roll 50. Record Group 94. National Archives, Washington, D.C.

Bryan, Charles F., Jr. "The Civil War in East Tennessee: A Social, Political, and Economic Study." Ph.D. diss., University of Tennessee, 1978.

Green, John W. *Bench and Bar of Knox County, Tennessee.* Knoxville, Tenn., 1947.

Journal of the Congress of the Confederate States of America, 1861–1865. 7 vols. Washington, D.C., 1904–1905.

Warner, Ezra J., and W. Buck Yearns. *Biographical Register of the Confederate Congress.* Baton Rouge, La., 1975.

R. B. ROSENBURG

T

TACTICS. *See* Civil War, *article on* Strategy and Tactics. *See also entries on particular battles.*

TALIAFERRO, WILLIAM BOOTH (1822–1898), major general. Born into the Tidewater aristocracy in Gloucester County, Virginia, Taliaferro graduated from William and Mary in 1841, attended Harvard Law School, and fought as a captain in the Eleventh and as a major in the Ninth U.S. Infantry during the Mexican War. From 1850 to 1853, Taliaferro represented Gloucester County in the Virginia legislature. In November 1859, he commanded the state's militia at Harpers Ferry in the aftermath of John Brown's raid.

Commissioned a colonel on May 1, 1861, Taliaferro participated that day in the engagement at Gloucester Point. Two months later he fought at Carrick's Ford. He was a strict disciplinarian and his manner alienated many of his men, one of whom physically assaulted him. Serving under Thomas J. ("Stonewall") Jackson in 1862, Taliaferro rankled Jackson by appealing to his political friends in Richmond to support W. W. Loring's protest over Jackson's tactics and winter quarters. Jackson resigned, reconsidered, and protested Taliaferro's promotion to brigadier general in March 1862, but he still had confidence in the military abilities of his mutinous subordinate.

Taliaferro proved himself during the Shenandoah Valley campaign of 1862 and took command of the Stonewall Division after the death of Gen. Charles S. Winder at Cedar Mountain on August 9, 1862. Wounded at Groveton, Taliaferro recovered in time to help repulse the Union attack at Fredericksburg.

In February 1863 Taliaferro was in charge of the military district of Savannah before being assigned to command Fort Wagner on Morris Island, where on July 18 he repulsed the charge of the Fifty-fourth Massachusetts Infantry and other Federal units. Subsequently, Taliaferro served on James Island, in Florida, and at Savannah. Promoted to major general on January 1, 1865, Taliaferro surrendered with Joseph E. Johnston on April 26.

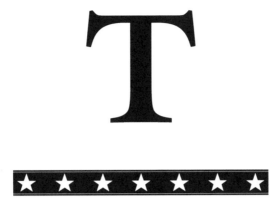

WILLIAM BOOTH TALIAFERRO. LIBRARY OF CONGRESS

He returned to Virginia, where he served as county judge and state legislator until his death in 1898.

BIBLIOGRAPHY

Krick, Robert K. *Stonewall Jackson at Cedar Mountain.* Chapel Hill, N.C., 1990.

Taliaferro, William B. "Jackson's Raid around Pope." In *Battles and Leaders of the Civil War.* Vol. 2. Edited by Robert U. Johnson and C. C. Buel. New York, 1888. Reprint, Secaucus, N.J., 1982.

Tanner, Robert G. *Stonewall in the Valley.* Garden City, N.Y., 1976.

RUSSELL DUNCAN

TALLAHASSEE, FLORIDA. The small town of Tallahassee was the only Confederate capital east of the Mississippi not captured and occupied by Union forces during the entire war. Located halfway between St. Augustine and Pensacola, it was twenty miles north of its cotton port of St. Marks on the Gulf of Mexico. Throughout the war Tallahassee was isolated from much of the state and the rest of the Confederacy by inadequate roads, bridges, and ferries and an incomplete railroad system, although a good railroad and parallel plank road joined the capital to Port St. Marks. One east-west railroad, the Pensacola and Georgia, had its western terminus 40 miles west on the Apalachicola River but 160 miles from the vital port of Pensacola. Eastward the railroad passed through Tallahassee to join, in late 1861, the Florida Atlantic and Gulf Coast at Lake City, giving the capital rail access to the Atlantic port of Jacksonville. There was no track north of Jacksonville into Georgia. Thus Florida's thousands of troops, if they were not coming from the vicinity of Pensacola, had to leave the state on foot to reach the rest of the Confederacy. Regular transportation north from Tallahassee was by stagecoach.

This frontier capital's streets were unpaved and unnumbered, with very little public lighting. The public water supply consisted of three open wells in the center of town. Human waste removal was not a responsibility of the village, nor did it have a police force. Two years before the war the town got its first telegraph line.

In 1861 the capital had a population of 1,932 individuals equally divided by race—997 whites, 889 slaves, and 46 free persons of color. Of the town's 241 heads of households, 143, or 60 percent, owned slaves. The ethnic and cultural background of the free population was predominantly native-born white, Anglo-Saxon, and Protestant. The small foreign-born element was made up of Scottish, Irish, English, German, and French immigrants.

Wartime Tallahassee had no industrial capacity. The town's chief business before and during the war was supplying the wealthiest plantations in the state with the necessities of a cotton-growing region. At the beginning of the war fifty thousand bales of cotton were being shipped out annually from St. Marks until the Union navy's blockade closed both St. Marks and Jacksonville in 1862. The town had six churches within its city limits—two Methodist (one for blacks and one for whites), one Presbyterian, one Episcopal, one Baptist, and one Catholic. There were two newspapers. The larger, the Democratic-oriented *Floridian and Journal,* was owned by Charles Dykes and James Carlisle. Edwin Hart owned the smaller Whig-oriented *Florida Sentinel,* which ceased operation in December 1863 owing to wartime shortages. The higher education center of the state of Florida was Tallahassee's West Florida Seminary and Female Academy (forerunner of Florida State University), which granted B.A. degrees.

Because of its isolation, lack of industrial capacity, and the blockade of its only gulf port, Tallahassee had less strategic value than many other Southern cities. But the efficient wartime governor John Milton and his Tallahassee legislature made up for much of the shortfall by organizing the provision, throughout the war, of a constant supply of Florida beef to the Confederacy. The Tallahassee legislature also raised more troops, over 13,000, than were registered voters in the entire state of Florida. Among them was Brig. Gen. Theodore W. Brevard, the last general officer appointed by Jefferson Davis at the end of the war. The city also supplied eleven colonels and twenty-three captains as well as six army surgeons. All of Florida's infantrymen in the east were brigaded together in the Army of Northern Virginia and called, successively, the Florida, Perry, and Finegan Brigade. Tallahassee's most notable casualty of the war was planter Col. George T. Ward, who died leading

Tallahassee Area Troops

UNIT		OFFICERS	MEN
1st Fla. Inf.	(Co. A)	8	69
" " "	(Co. D)	12	165
2d Fla. Inf.	(Co. D)	10	102
" " "	(Co. M)	11	99
5th Fla. Inf.	(Co. C)	7	102
" " "	(Co. K)	5	85
8th Fla. Inf.	(Co. C)	6	92
1st Fla. Cav.	(Co. F)	7	69
2d Fla. Cav.	(Co. D)	4	125
" " "	(Co. E)	4	101
5th Fla. Battn. Cav.	(Co. C)	4	93
Dykes Light Arty.		5	86
Gambles Light Arty.		6	147
Totals		89	1,340

SOURCE: Mary W. Keen, "Some Phases of Life in Leon County during the Civil War," *Tallahassee Historical Society Annual* 4 (1939): 20–47.

the Florida Brigade at the Battle of Williamsburg, May 5, 1862.

No serious Union attempt was ever made to capture the capital. In February 1864 a Union army of about 5,000 men led by Brig. Gen. Truman Seymour marched west out of Jacksonville along the Florida Atlantic and Gulf Coast Railroad toward Tallahassee. Their objective, however, was not the capital but the Suwanee River where they hoped to cut Florida's supply links with Confederate forces farther north. The Union troops were defeated February 20 at the Battle of Olustee, or Ocean Pond, near Lake City, by an equal number of mostly Georgia regulars under Gen. Joseph Finegan and Gen. Alfred H. Colquitt. For the Union this was the third bloodiest battle of the war in terms of percentage of losses per unit.

A year later Tallahasseans braced themselves for what they thought was to be an assault on their capital. In February 1865 around 1,000 troops, led by Maj. Gen. John Newton, disembarked near the St. Marks lighthouse and marched northward along the St. Marks River toward Newport so as to flank the target of the expedition, Port St. Marks. The Tallahassee militia hastily built a large square earthwork, Fort Houston, on the southern edge of town, at the juncture of the plank road from Newport, to repel the Union men. On February 28 over 2,000 Confederate regular and militia troops under Maj. Gen. Samuel Jones met and defeated 893 black troops at the Battle of Natural Bridge ten miles southeast of the capital. Sixty cadets from West Florida Seminary, led by Col. George W. Scott, participated in the battle.

On April 1, 1865, Governor Milton, despondent over Confederate reverses elsewhere, left Tallahassee and killed himself near his home in Marianna, Florida. On May 10, the Union cavalry general Brig. Edward M. McCook, riding in advance of 500 troops, entered the capital to receive its surrender from Major General Jones. On May 20, with acting Governor Abraham K. Allison presiding, the Union flag was raised over the old capitol building. The only military fortification of the Civil War today in Tallahassee is a remnant of Fort Houston.

[*See also* Olustee, Florida.]

BIBLIOGRAPHY

Groene, Bertram. *Antebellum Tallahassee.* Tallahassee, Fla., 1981.

Keen, Mary W. "Some Phases of Life in Leon County during the Civil War." *Tallahassee Historical Society Annual* 4 (1939): 20–47.

Robertson, Fredric L. *Soldiers of Florida in the Seminole Indian, Civil and Spanish-American Wars.* Live Oak, Fla., 1909. Reprint, Macclenny, Fla., 1983.

Rogers, William. "A Great Stirring in the Land and Leon County in 1860." *Florida Historical Quarterly* 64 (1985): 148–160.

BERTRAM HAWTHORNE GROENE

TALLAHASSEE. Built in 1864 as *Atalanta* by John and William Dudgeon of Millwall, London, for Stringer, Pembroke, and Company, the iron-hulled, schooner-rigged, twin-screw blockade runner was 500 tons burden and measured 202.7 feet long, 23.6 feet in beam, and 12.5 feet in depth of hold. Each of its two-cylinder, direct-acting engines powered an independent screw propeller, giving a top speed of 14.13 knots. By July 1864 *Atalanta* had run the blockade eight times.

The Confederate navy purchased *Atalanta* at Wilmington, North Carolina, renamed it CSS *Tallahassee,* and placed Lt. John Taylor Wood in command. *Tallahassee* was armed with a 100-pounder rifle, a 32-pounder rifle, a 30-pounder Parrot rifle, and a brass howitzer. In August 1864 it raided coastal shipping along the New England coast, capturing and destroying twenty-six vessels and releasing five on bond. The cruise created panic in seaboard New England. *Tallahassee* took on coal at Halifax, Nova Scotia, and was forced to return to Wilmington. The name was changed again, to CSS *Olustee,* with Lt. William H. Ward, the former executive officer, succeeding to command. *Olustee* made a second cruise in early November 1864 during which it captured six more large vessels. It was sighted near the mouth of Chesapeake Bay and chased by four Union gunboats back to Wilmington.

The Confederacy desperately needed army supplies and so converted *Olustee* back to a blockade runner. Its papers were whitewashed to allow the vessel to sail as a merchant ship, and its name was changed again, appropriately to *Chameleon.* Capt. John Wilkinson commanded the ship on its last blockade-running voyage on January 19, 1865, from Bermuda with a load of provisions for the armies in Virginia. Wilkinson ran the blockade but discovered that Fort Fisher had been captured. *Chameleon* escaped the Union fleet and carried the news to Nassau. It then ran to Charleston but found that that port too was closed. *Chameleon* returned to Great Britain where it was seized by the British government.

It was reregistered under its original name *Atalanta* and sold at auction. U.S. Consul Thomas Haines Dudley sued for possession, and the ship, now named *Amelia,* was turned over to the United States, which auctioned it at Liverpool. Renamed *Haya Maru* and rerigged as a brig, it plied the Japanese coast from March 1867 until it wrecked on the coast of Honshu June 17, 1868.

BIBLIOGRAPHY

O'Driscoll, Patricia E. "Ship with Seven Names." *Sea Breezes* n.s. 19, no. 110 (February 1955): 134.

Scharf, J. Thomas. *History of the Confederate States Navy: From Its Organization to the Surrender of Its Last Vessel.* New York, 1976.

Shingleton, Royce Gordon. *John Taylor Wood: Sea Ghost of the Confederacy.* Athens, Ga., 1979.
Wise, Stephen. *Lifeline of the Confederacy: Blockade Running during the American Civil War.* Columbia, S.C., 1989.

KEVIN J. FOSTER

TAPPAN, JAMES CAMP (1825–1906), brigadier general. Tappan was born in Franklin, Tennessee, on September 9, 1825. He graduated from Yale University in 1845, studied law in Vicksburg, Mississippi, and was admitted to the bar in 1846. Subsequently he moved to Arkansas, where he served in the legislature and as a circuit judge prior to the outbreak of the war.

With the secession of Arkansas, Tappan offered his services to the Confederate government. Commissioned colonel of the Thirteenth Arkansas Infantry Regiment, he led the unit at Belmont and in the Battle of Shiloh where he and his men repeatedly charged the Hornet's Nest. Tappan's unit, as part of Braxton Bragg's invasion of Kentucky, fought in the Battles of Richmond and Perryville. On November 5, 1862, he was promoted to brigadier general and transferred to the Trans-Mississippi Department.

Assigned to Gen. Sterling Price's command, Tappan led Thomas Churchill's Arkansas division with distinction at Pleasant Hill and during the Red River campaign. Upon Churchill's return, his brigade participated in Gen. E. Kirby Smith's operations against Gen. Frederick Steele at Jenkins's Ferry, Arkansas. In July 1864 his brigade participated in the poorly conducted defense of Little Rock. Price's mismanagement of the battle gave the city to the Federals and nearly cost the Confederacy two divisions. Tappan's poise and bravery was amply demonstrated as he helped rally the Confederates after this debacle.

With the surrender of Kirby Smith's command, Tappan returned to his law practice in Helena, Arkansas, and was sent to the state legislature in the 1870s. He died March 19, 1906.

Tappan was an ambitious, aggressive leader who displayed great ability in his short tenure as division commander. Unfortunately, Richmond felt that the Trans-Mississippi was already glutted with senior staff, and the War Department never offered a permanent divisional command to this extremely competent officer.

BIBLIOGRAPHY

Thomas, David Y. *Arkansas in War and Reconstruction, 1861–1874.* Little Rock, Ark., 1926.
Warner, Ezra J. *Generals in Gray: Lives of the Confederate Commanders.* Baton Rouge, La., 1959.

ROY R. STEPHENSON

TATTNALL, JOSIAH (1795–1871), naval officer. Born at his family estate of Bonaventure near Savannah, Georgia, Tattnall entered the U.S. Navy as a midshipman in 1812. He rose steadily until appointed flag officer and commander of the East India Squadron in 1857. Two years later his squadron assisted an Anglo-French naval force in attacking Chinese forts. His excuse for ignoring American neutrality was that "blood is thicker than water."

JOSIAH TATTNALL. From a photograph of an earlier portrait.
NAVAL HISTORICAL CENTER, WASHINGTON, D.C.

During the secession crisis, Tattnall resigned his commission and accepted appointment as flag officer in command of the Georgia State Navy. In March he became a captain in the Confederate navy and was placed in command of the naval defense of Georgia and South Carolina. In the fall of 1861 Tattnall's force of four small vessels cooperated in the unsuccessful defense of Port Royal.

In March 1862 Tattnall was ordered to James River to take command of the ironclad *Virginia* to replace the wounded Frank Buchanan. He was in charge of the squadron less than three months. In April he attempted unsuccessfully to lure *Monitor* into combat. The same month, the Federal blockading force tried to bring *Virginia* to combat, but Tattnall refused to engage the Union warships. On May 9 Norfolk was occupied by Federal troops. Two days later *Virginia* was blown up to prevent her capture, and the small wooden gunboats in the squadron retired up the James River. Tattnall was court-martialed for *Virginia*'s destruction but was acquitted. In July he returned to Savannah. He initially commanded both the Savannah Naval Station and forces afloat in the Savannah River. In March 1863 he was relieved of the squadron's command, but he headed the station for the remainder of the war.

After the war, Tattnall lived in Nova Scotia, Canada, for four years. In 1868 he returned to Savannah as port inspector. He died in that city on June 14, 1871.

BIBLIOGRAPHY

Jones, Charles C., Jr. *The Life and Services of Commodore Josiah Tattnall.* Savannah, Ga., 1878.

Lawrence, Alexander A. *A Present for Mr. Lincoln: The Story of Savannah from Secession to Sherman.* Macon, Ga., 1961.

WILLIAM N. STILL, JR.

TAXATION. Taxation supplied only a fraction of all government revenues, state and Confederate, in the Civil War South. Throughout the war, the Confederate government issued Treasury notes, from which it derived half of all its revenue (in current dollars), and sold bonds, which generated another one-fourth of the total. In addition, it impressed, or seized, vast quantities of supplies and thus obtained 17 percent of its aggregate purchasing power. That left only 7 percent of all Confederate national revenue secured through taxation. That increment of taxation permitted the Confederacy to purchase some supplies on the open market, while also offering a means of absorbing a minor portion of the Confederacy's redundant currency.

Only gradually did the Confederacy adopt direct taxes. At first, members of the new national government anticipated either no war or only a short one. Moreover, given the pervasive unpopularity of direct taxes, the Provisional Congress enacted only import and export duties. But the war came, expenditures grew, and the Federal blockade curtailed revenues from duties. Therefore, in August 1861, the Congress imposed direct taxes payable in Treasury notes. The new tax, at one-half of 1 percent of assessed property valuation, relied on the fiscal machinery of the state governments and ultimately generated $17.4 million. Reflecting the structure of the tax base across the South, the new tax derived 35 percent of that amount from slaves and another 33 percent from real estate. Most states took advantage of a provision that permitted a state to pay its citizens' share of the tax by April 1, 1862, at a 10 percent discount. Similarly, most states borrowed to obtain that money and then failed to tax their citizens to retrieve the amount paid over to the Confederacy. Thus the national tax took the form of state debt.

Only in April 1863 did the Confederacy enact a comprehensive tax law. It levied taxes on occupations, income, and produce as well as on property. Like the 1861 act, which had exempted any head of family whose taxable property was valued at less than $500, the new law was designed to secure purchasing power, on a graduated (or at least proportional) basis, only from those families who likely had some surplus to contribute. The statute placed license taxes ranging from $50 to $500 on many occupations, levied a graduated tax on annual incomes of more than $500, taxed at 8 percent all naval stores, money, and agricultural products "not necessary for family consumption," and imposed a tax-in-kind of 10 percent of annual agricultural productions beyond an allowance for subsistence. Subsequent measures in February 1864, June 1864, and March 1865 raised these rates.

The Confederate system of direct taxes, such as it was, carried several unmanageable burdens. For one, though reliance on taxation became greater in the second half of the war, the aggregate value of supplies seized through impressment dwarfed the revenue achieved through taxation, and nothing guaranteed anything remotely resembling fiscal fairness in the activities of the impressment agents. Heedless of local needs or of producers' ability to pay, those agents gathered supplies, instead, according to local availability and government need. For another, the issue of Treasury notes generated seven times the purchasing power that taxation did, three times the amount raised through impressment, and twice the combined total of impressment and taxation. The tax system simply failed to absorb a sufficient quantity of the Treasury notes from circulation. Inflation raced ahead of revenues.

With four years of war, state and local governments, too, faced huge demands. Their revenue systems, however, were already in place and fully functional in 1861, though the war forced major adjustments in their operations. The states varied widely in particulars of their wartime fiscal behavior, yet they tended to share a number of general features. They typically resorted at first to huge bond issues and then moved primarily to the issue of Treasury notes. They maintained the core of their prewar tax systems throughout the war, but rates on traditional objects of taxation climbed, and new measures tapped new objects.

Though taxation supplied only a small fraction of each state's wartime revenue, taxation provided an even smaller share of the Confederate government's total income. In contrast to both Confederate and state governments, counties generated little long-term debt, as they typically paid for large portions of their expenditures by issuing certificates of indebtedness, which they then called back in by means of taxes payable in those certificates. The larger political units mostly ignored calls that they do likewise. Nobody thought that wartime taxes should fully match public expenditures, whether by the states or the Confederate governments, but, though bonds offered a means of making long-term loans, many Southerners argued that a larger fraction of Treasury notes should be called in for taxes than was the case.

Georgia offers one model of fiscal change in the Confederate South. On the eve of the war, its state tax system relied on a general property tax that, with low (and even declining) rates, supplied all the tax revenue that expenditures required. A poll tax more or less offset a standard deduction against the property tax. The state poll tax stayed unchanged through the war, while state property taxes multiplied by almost sixteen between 1860 and 1864. That increase was greater than any other state displayed, but virtually every state substantially hiked its rates on property.

Georgia also illustrates another major facet of the Confederate South's fiscal experience. On the tax side of the state budget, Georgia favored its less wealthy citizens. Across the South, public authorities sought to cushion the smaller farmers and other less wealthy white families from the full force of the tax rate increases. Exemptions from the property tax grew for Confederate soldiers' families who held property of only modest valuation. Thus new exemptions characterized Southern tax systems at the same time that much higher general property tax rates did. Moreover, Georgia left its poll tax rates unchanged throughout the war, and by 1863 it suspended even those rates for all soldiers with only small holdings.

On the spending side, too, Georgia proved a representative state in offering benefits to small farmers that it denied the more wealthy. State and local authorities recognized early on that winning the war depended on retaining in the army the tens of thousands of soldiers from farm families who had little economic cushion. As one Mississippi soldier wrote his governor, "we are poor men and are willing to defend our country but our families first and then our count[r]y." Soldiers would, and did, desert the battlefront to head back home when they believed their loved ones to be suffering from inadequate supplies of food and other necessities.

Authorities therefore made commitments to allocate enormous sums for the support of soldiers' families. At first, the counties acted, particularly when it became clear that calls for voluntary contributions drew uneven—and thus unequal and insufficient—amounts of aid. Counties responded by resorting to the coercion of the tax system to obtain the funds (or the provisions) that they needed. But then it became clear that the counties most in need often had the least resources, and thus the state stepped in. Georgia's state government, matching its own direct military expenditures almost dollar for dollar through the war, supplied huge sums for the support of soldiers' families. Throughout much of the South, state and local authorities alike allocated large, even major, portions of their budgets to the distribution of cash or such commodities as salt, corn, and bacon.

In these ways, the Georgia experience demonstrates how Southern state and local governments became more progressive during the war, and how authority and responsibility grew more centralized. The tax system became more progressive as rates on the wealthy rose at the same time that the less wealthy gained exemptions. And, on the spending side, the state government taxed planters in the black belt to generate funds with which to acquire food to supply soldiers' families in the nonplantation counties. The huge increases in state tax rates midway through the war reflected, in part, an assumption by the state of responsibilities that the counties had undertaken in the first two years of the war.

In these various ways, state and local authorities demonstrated that they acted with one eye on the home front and one eye on the battlefront. And they supplied tangible benefits to constituents whose support was essential if the war was to be prosecuted with much chance of success. As part of a wartime agenda, the higher taxes—first at the county level, then at the state—could be seen to be purchasing real goods for real constituents. Governments at the state and local levels revealed themselves as in the business of caring for civilians as much as they were covering the costs of rifles, tents, and boots for the troops. Such could not be said for Confederate national spending policies. These facets of state and local operations may help explain why the men who set state and local taxes felt that they could demand escalating taxes—why they may have detected less resistance to higher and higher taxes than their national counterparts seemed to perceive.

Yet all such considerations highlight, too, the differences, by class and by region within each state, that separated the larger slaveholders from their less prosperous fellow citizens. The differences were real, and they emerged in struggles over tax policy. Indeed, a central issue in parts of the South related to the taxes on planters' slaves. In North Carolina, for example, perhaps the leading issue in state politics in the 1850s had been whether slave property should carry a larger share of the state tax burden. On the eve of the war, small farmers had finally achieved success, they thought, in demanding that planters carry a larger share, but their victory proved illusory, even in the crucible of war. In Virginia in 1861, by contrast, planters from the eastern half of the state offered the small farmers of the west a major concession—higher taxes on slaves—in hopes of cementing their support for the Confederacy. Though the concession was real, much of that support evaporated, as West Virginia went its separate political, military, and fiscal way.

By late 1864 and early 1865, the Confederacy's war effort was winding down, and for more reasons than a shortage of military manpower in a war of attrition. Real shortages and runaway inflation each help explain why the Confederacy lost. Tax rates climbed much higher than ever before, yet they played only a minor role in the Confederate government's efforts to finance its operations, and they proved too low to absorb enough of the endless supply of state and Confederate Treasury notes. Though state and local governments clearly treated their citizens on the bases of ability to pay and nature of need, the Confederacy's heavy reliance on impressment could operate to vitiate those policies. In any case, the logistical problems of distributing aid to civilians proved as great as the logistical problems of moving battalions of troops. The Confederacy ran too low on food and clothing, on the means of purchasing them, and on the means of distributing them. The fiscal system failed. And the war ended.

[*See also* Currency, *overview article;* Impressment; State Socialism; Tax-in-Kind.]

BIBLIOGRAPHY

Ball, Douglas B. *Financial Failure and Confederate Defeat.* Urbana, Ill., 1991.

Bettersworth, John K. *Confederate Mississippi: The People and Policies of a Cotton State in Wartime.* Baton Rouge, La., 1943. Reprint, Philadelphia, Pa., 1978.

Butts, Donald C. "A Challenge to Planter Rule: The Controversy over Ad Valorem Taxation of Slaves in North Carolina, 1858–1862." Ph.D. diss., Duke University, 1978.

Ramsdell, Charles W. *Behind the Lines in the Southern Confederacy.* Baton Rouge, La., 1944. Reprint, New York, 1969.

Ringold, May Spencer. *The Role of the State Legislatures in the Confederacy.* Athens, Ga., 1966.

Todd, Richard Cecil. *Confederate Finance.* Athens, Ga., 1954.

Wallenstein, Peter. *From Slave South to New South: Public Policy in Nineteenth-Century Georgia.* Chapel Hill, N.C., 1987.

PETER WALLENSTEIN

TAX-IN-KIND. The Confederate States of America tried from its inception to develop a system to provide revenue for its treasury. Resistant to enacting an income tax, Confederate Treasury Secretary Christopher G. Memminger and the Congress proposed and passed into law other initiatives. One of the most unpopular was the tax-in-kind, enacted in April 1863.

Secretary Memminger designed the tax-in-kind to serve as an alternative to the impressment of agricultural products. The Treasury and War departments, the chief administrators of the tax-in-kind, enumerated items that agents, or "T.I.K. men," would collect in each locality. The list of goods included wheat, oats, corn, rice, potatoes, fodder, sugar, cotton, wool, tobacco, and rye. Each farmer was to retain for his or her own use fifty bushels of sweet potatoes, either one hundred bushels of corn or fifty bushels of wheat, and twenty bushels of peas or beans; from what remained, the farmer was required to donate 10 percent to government agents. Southern agriculturalists were also required to pay in kind on bacon and pork, based upon a 10 percent tax on all hogs slaughtered during 1863. The agents would assess the value of the farms' products and notify the farmers of the amount they were required to tithe. If the assessor's estimate varied greatly from the farmer's, a mediator would make the final determination of the value of the goods. Farmers who failed to pay their tithe were subject to a stiff penalty. The agents collected the goods and funneled them to local and district-level quartermasters who were supposed to ensure that the items reached the armies in the field.

The tax-in-kind proved to be one of the most, if not *the* most, unpopular acts the Confederate Congress ever passed. Farmers resisted the quotas, especially since they were based on the gross value of crops, not on profits, and they loathed the T.I.K. men who pressed them for payment. A serious problem with the tax lay in its collection and distribution: often crops would rot at depots before quartermasters could transport them to the army. The program was also plagued by phony agents who swindled farmers out of their produce.

It is difficult to determine how much the Treasury gained from the tax-in-kind. Confederate agents estimated that about $6 million in produce was collected by the end of 1863; by late winter of 1864, the figure stood at $40 million. Public outcry against the tax led to its amendment. In December 1863, Congress allowed the tax on sweet potatoes to be paid in cash. By February 1864, Congress was extending exemptions on the collection of the tax-in-kind for soldiers' families and small farmers; by 1865, the act barely resembled its 1863 version: individuals could substitute cash payments for payments in farm produce.

The criticisms of and alterations to the tax-in-kind indicate that Congress was not oblivious to the flaws of the original act. Despite the chorus of protest, however, the tax-in-kind did help supply and feed the Confederate armies during the final two years of the war.

BIBLIOGRAPHY

Ball, Douglas B. *Financial Failure and Confederate Defeat.* Urbana, Ill., 1991.

Coulter, E. Merton. *The Confederate States of America, 1861–1865.* A History of the South, vol. 7. Baton Rouge, La., 1951.

Goff, Richard. *Confederate Supply.* Durham, N.C., 1969.

Todd, Richard Cecil. *Confederate Finance.* Athens, Ga., 1954.

MARY A. DECREDICO

TAYLOR, RICHARD (1826–1879), lieutenant general. A Confederate general with no formal military education, Taylor served with distinction and in 1865 surrendered the last organized Confederate force east of the Mississippi.

Born in Kentucky, the son of President Zachary Taylor, Richard studied at Harvard, Edinburgh, and Yale, before becoming a Louisiana sugar planter. Elected colonel of the Ninth Louisiana Infantry at the war's outset, he and his regiment reached Virginia too late for the First Battle of Manassas. Taylor was a brother-in-law of President Jefferson Davis, and rumor had it that in the fall of 1861 he was offered the post of quartermaster general of the Confederate army. If so, he declined it, but from time to time throughout the war he continued to be the beneficiary of Davis's favoritism. In October he was promoted to brigadier general and given command of a Louisiana brigade that became part of Richard S. Ewell's division.

Taylor served with distinction in the Shenandoah Valley campaign during the spring of 1862 but was kept out of the Seven Days' Battles by rheumatoid arthritis. Recovering within a few weeks, he was promoted to major general and was assigned to command of the District of Western Louisiana in August 1862. Although dreaming of retaking New Orleans, he generally found himself falling back before Federal forays such as Maj. Gen. Nathaniel P. Banks's April 1863 Bayou Teche expedition. At the urging of Trans-Mississippi commander E. Kirby Smith, who was himself under pressure from Richmond, Taylor moved against Ulysses S. Grant's supply lines on the west bank of the Mississippi opposite Vicksburg. The attempt was a failure, and Grant's campaign culminated in the capture of that key Confederate stronghold.

Taylor was forced to fall back before Banks's Red River expedition in the spring of 1864 but defeated Banks at the Battle of Mansfield, Louisiana, south of Shreveport, on April 8, 1864. Outnumbered twelve thousand to nine thousand in troops engaged, Taylor inflicted double his own casualties and captured twenty cannons and two hundred supply wagons. Although defeated the next day at Pleasant Hill and ordered by Smith to fall back temporarily on Shreveport, he had succeeded in forcing the withdrawal of Banks's ill-fated expedition.

Rewarded with a promotion to lieutenant general, Taylor was nevertheless bitter toward Smith, blaming him for Banks's escape. He thus welcomed orders to take his troops across the Mississippi for service in the East. Finding the river too heavily patrolled by the U.S. Navy, he had to remain in the Trans-Mississippi until August 22, 1864, when he was ordered to go east personally to take command of the Department of Alabama, Mississippi, and Eastern Louisiana.

On January 23, 1865, Taylor was named as successor to John Bell Hood as commander of the remnants of the Army of Tennessee, which Hood had wrecked at Franklin and Nashville. As such, Taylor's prime role was shipping his units off to the Carolinas to oppose William Tecumseh Sherman. On May 4, 1865, he surrendered to Gen. E. R. S. Canby at Citronelle, Alabama.

After the war, Taylor was active in Democratic party politics in Louisiana, opposing the Reconstruction regime. In 1879, the year of his death, he published his reminiscences of the war, *Destruction and Reconstruction,* one of the best of the memoirs of the conflict's participants.

BIBLIOGRAPHY

Parrish, T. Michael. *Richard Taylor: Soldier Prince of Dixie.* Chapel Hill, N.C., 1992.

Taylor, Richard. *Destruction and Reconstruction.* New York, 1879. Reprint, edited by Charles P. Roland. Waltham, Mass., 1968.

STEVEN E. WOODWORTH

TAYLOR, THOMAS HART (1825–1901), colonel. By the time the Civil War began, Kentuckian Taylor had graduated from college, fought as a private in the Mexican War, traveled to and from California, and managed a business in Memphis. When war came, Taylor was not the sort of man to avoid the fight, but his experiences in the Confederate army, although varied, were never as colorful as those of his prewar years.

Taylor's first appointment was as captain in the Confederate army and lieutenant colonel of the First Kentucky Infantry in the Provisional Army. He led his fellow Kentuckians through the Battle of First Manassas and the Peninsular campaign. When the regiment disbanded in 1862, Taylor transferred to the western theater to command a mixed unit of Alabama and Mississippi regiments at Cumberland Gap and in the 1862 Kentucky campaign. Although Taylor acted as a brigadier general, President Jefferson Davis never approved his promotion, and most references do not recognize him as such. Taylor next served as provost marshal under John C. Pemberton during the ill-fated defense of Vicksburg, Mississippi. Captured at Vicksburg, he was exchanged and returned to the army to become head of the District of South Mississippi and East Louisiana. He later resumed his duties as provost marshal, this time under Gen. Stephen D. Lee. Taylor spent the last days of the war as post commander at Mobile, Alabama.

After the war ended, he utilized his provost marshal experience to become deputy U.S. marshal and chief of police in Louisville.

BIBLIOGRAPHY

Faust, Patricia, ed. *Historical Times Illustrated Encyclopedia of the Civil War.* New York, 1986.

Johnston, J. Stoddard. *Kentucky.* Vol. 9 of *Confederate Military History.* Edited by Clement A. Evans. Atlanta, 1899. Vol. 11 of extended ed. Wilmington, N.C., 1988.

Warner, Ezra. *Generals in Gray: Lives of the Confederate Commanders.* Baton Rouge, La., 1959.

LESLEY JILL GORDON-BURR

TELEGRAPH. The Civil War was the first war in which the electric telegraph played a major role. It was used by both sides at both the tactical and strategic levels, though much more effectively by the Union. Indeed, it can be said with some justification that the way that Union forces used telegraph communications was a major factor in determining the outcome of the war.

The simple and rugged American telegraph design was well suited to battlefield use. For transmitting, the operator used a "key" to make and break electrical contact and to send short and long pulses of current from a battery over the wire (only a single wire was needed; connections were made to the ground at each end, and the ground performed the function of a second wire to complete the circuit.) At the receiver the current activated an electromagnet, which pulled against a lever to make short and long clicking noises—"dots" and "dashes" that in combinations represented letters and numbers.

Samuel F. B. Morse, a portrait painter, had invented this form of telegraphy in the 1830s. With money from Congress and practical assistance from Alfred Vail, he constructed a successful demonstration line between Baltimore and Washington in 1844. When no further interest was shown by the government, he licensed private individuals to develop the system. The result was a rapid expansion over the next decade and a half (including competition from non-Morse systems), culminating in a transcontinental line that was completed in the fall of 1861. A transatlantic cable was momentarily successful in 1858, but it failed before it could be placed in commercial operation and was not replaced until 1866.

On the eve of the war there thus existed an infrastructure of tens of thousands of miles of wire, about 10 percent of it in the states of the Confederacy. These latter lines lay along two major routes reaching to New Orleans: in the east, from Washington through Richmond, Petersburg, Raleigh, Columbia, Augusta, Macon, Montgomery, and Mobile (with side links to Charleston, Savannah, and Atlanta); in the west, along two competing lines from Nashville, one by way of Vicksburg and Natchez, the other through Florence and Jackson. Along with the advantage in miles of wire, the Union had a comparable advantage in numbers of trained operators. The North also, apparently, had a better sense of the value of this form of communications. The Union established a military telegraph service, which constructed and operated fifteen thousand miles of lines during the war; individual Confederate forces established a total of one thousand miles. Furthermore, Union forces used codes to protect their messages; the Confederates, in general, did not.

The significance of these communications systems had thus far been told only in anecdotal form. At the Battle of First Manassas, for instance, P. G. T. Beauregard used the telegraph to call for reinforcements; Theophilus H. Holmes arrived in time to be a decisive factor in the outcome. Another account tells that C. A. Gaston, Robert E. Lee's confidential operator, was able to wiretap Ulysses S. Grant's line for six weeks during the siege of Richmond and Petersburg. Among the unciphered messages was one telling of the impending arrival of 2,536 head of beef at Coggins' Point. A timely raid captured the entire herd. On another front, John H. Morgan's success has been attributed in considerable part to the skill of his operator in intercepting messages and in sending false and misleading messages. Similar stories have been told about virtually every major battle of the war.

Use of the telegraph dramatically altered the manner in which commanders exercised their authority. No longer did they have to be close to the battlefield, and they could be aware of all aspects of a conflict, no matter how large. Thus, during the Wilderness and Atlanta campaigns both Grant and Lee were in almost hourly contact with the various elements of their troops. During the period before and during the battle at Gettysburg, Abraham Lincoln followed the action closely from the War Department office in Washington, where he spent much of his time. By telegraph before the conflict he relieved Joseph Hooker of command and replaced him with George G. Meade. In the aftermath he unsuccessfully urged Meade to pursue Lee to prevent him from escaping across the Potomac River.

The significance of the telegraph in the American Civil War (during which 6.5 million messages are estimated to have been sent by the Union side alone) was not lost on military planners elsewhere. Every regular army in Europe soon had its telegraph corps, and every war fought since then has depended on electrical communications for command and control systems.

BIBLIOGRAPHY

Beringer, Richard E., et al. *Why the South Lost the Civil War.* Athens, Ga., 1986.

Harlow, Alvin F. *Old Wires and New Waves.* New York, 1936.

Plum, William R. *The Military Telegraph during the Civil War in the United States.* Chicago, 1882. Reprint, New York, 1974.

Scheips, Paul J., ed. *Military Signal Communications.* New York, 1980.

Thompson, Robert L. *Wiring a Continent.* Princeton, N.J., 1947. Reprint, New York, 1972.

BERNARD S. FINN

TEMPLE, OLIVER PERRY (1820–1907), Tennessee attorney, Unionist, and historian. Born near Greeneville, Tennessee, Temple graduated from Tennessee's Washington College in 1844 and was admitted to the bar in 1846. A Whig, he challenged unsuccessfully Congressman Andrew Johnson in 1847 and developed a close friendship with "Parson" William G. Brownlow, editor of the *Knoxville*

Whig. Temple moved to Knoxville in 1848 to practice law; on the Civil War's eve he was counted among the city's wealthier inhabitants. In 1860, he served first as a delegate to the convention of the Constitution Union party and then canvassed East Tennessee as a Bell-Everett elector. Following Abraham Lincoln's election, he gave the first pro-Union speech in the state.

Opposed to Tennessee's secession, Temple helped organize the Knoxville and Greeneville Conventions (May 30–31, June 17–20, 1861), which petitioned for the creation of a separate state of East Tennessee loyal to the Union; he headed the commission to present this proposal before an unsympathetic Tennessee legislature. Returning to Knoxville, he defended Unionists and others arraigned before Confederate justice. His most famous clients were the Andrews Raiders, who were accused of espionage for stealing the locomotive General and attempting to burn North Georgia bridges. Their trial was adjourned when Ambrose Burnside's army threatened Knoxville. Following the city's return to Federal control, Temple created the East Tennessee Relief Association, which raised over $250,000 to aid the region's destitute inhabitants.

Temple helped shape Tennessee's postwar Republican party, promoted the New South philosophy of agricultural-industrial diversity, and as an education leader played the seminal role in creating the University of Tennessee's agricultural college. Besides these activities, he also wrote two histories: *East Tennessee and the Civil War* (1899) and *Notable Men of Tennessee from 1833 to 1875* (published posthumously, 1912).

[*See also* Knoxville and Greeneville Conventions.]

BIBLIOGRAPHY

Bailey, Fred Arthur. "Oliver Perry Temple, New South Agrarian." M.A. thesis, University of Tennessee, Knoxville, 1972.

Needham, Joseph Wade. "Oliver Perry Temple: Entrepreneur, Agrarian, and Politician." Ph.D. diss., University of Tennessee, 1990.

Pittenger, William. *The Great Locomotive Chase: A History of the Andrews Raid into Georgia in 1862.* New York, 1893.

Temple, Mary. Introduction to *Notable Men of Tennessee from 1833 to 1875,* by Oliver Perry Temple. New York, 1912.

FRED ARTHUR BAILEY

TENNESSEE. One of only three states to cast its electoral ballots for Constitutional Unionist John Bell in the 1860 presidential election, Tennessee resisted secession until after the fall of Fort Sumter and did not officially leave the Union until June 8, 1861. With a population of 1,109,801 (of whom 275,719 were slaves and 7,300 were free blacks), the state provided 140,000 men to the Confederate army. Internal divisions and Federal military occupation, however, limited Tennessee's contributions to the Confederate cause and encouraged at least 51,000 other Tennesseans, white and black, to join the Union army.

From beginning to end, Tennessee's experience was unique among the Confederate states. The last state to secede, it was also the only one to leave the Union by means of a legislative "declaration of independence" rather than a secession ordinance adopted by a special convention, the only one to experience large-scale *Confederate* military occupation and martial law, the only one wholly exempted from the Emancipation Proclamation, the only one fully under Federal control before the war ended, the only one with a reconstructed state government with uncontested political authority operating before the end of the war, and the only one that freed its own slaves.

Geography profoundly influenced the course of events in Tennessee from 1860 to 1865. The state's three "grand divisions" are physically distinct, and in the antebellum decades they diverged socially and economically. In eastern Tennessee, a relatively isolated region of hills and mountains, there evolved a yeoman-dominated society marked by small, self-sufficient farms and little reliance on slavery; in 1860 only 9 percent of eastern Tennessee's 301,056 inhabitants were slaves. Western Tennessee, a flat alluvial plain, developed an economy resembling the staple-producing plantation system of the Deep South; over 33 percent of its 304,311 inhabitants were slaves. Middle Tennessee, a lush basin surrounded by highlands, produced corn and livestock on commercial farms of middling size; 29 percent of its 504,434 inhabitants were slaves. Though the state was overwhelmingly rural, each grand division boasted an important urban center: Memphis in the west, Nashville in the middle, and Knoxville in the east. Three major rivers—the Mississippi, Tennessee, and Cumberland—provided access to western and middle Tennessee and would assume great importance in Civil War military strategy.

Secession Crisis in Tennessee

Two-party politics persisted in Tennessee even after the collapse of the national Whig party in the 1850s. A strong opposition party, composed mostly of former Whigs, provided a solid base for Unionism in the state—in contrast to the Deep South, where Democratic hegemony fostered secessionism. In 1860 Tennessee oppositionists endorsed middle Tennessean John Bell, a strong Unionist, for president. Bell quickly attracted a national following among voters who rejected the sectionalism embodied by the three other presidential contenders (Stephen A. Douglas, the Northern Democratic candidate; John C. Breckinridge, representing Southern Democrats, especially the fervent state rights advocates; and the Republican Abraham Lincoln, representing antislavery Northerners). In the November election Bell won Tennessee with 69,710 votes, a plurality of 48 percent. Breckinridge (65,053 votes) and Douglas (11,394) split the Democratic vote (Lincoln was not on the ballot in Tennessee). The election was not a clear-cut referendum on secession in Tennessee: for one thing, the voting closely mimicked the traditional Whig-Democratic pattern of the antebellum years; and, too, many devoutly Unionist Democrats—including Andrew Johnson of eastern Tennessee—supported Breckinridge. Nevertheless, the combined Bell-Douglas total suggests that a solid majority of Tennessee voters favored a conservative approach to the sectional issue.

That conservatism was reaffirmed in the months that followed. The election of Lincoln provoked the secession of South Carolina in December and gave Tennessee's secessionist minority, led by Governor Isham G. Harris, hope that Tennessee might follow South Carolina's lead. Harris called the legislature into session on January 7, 1861, and asked it to authorize a secession convention. The legislature approved a referendum to be held February 9, in which Tennessee voters would decide whether a convention should be held and would also elect delegates.

By February 9 the Deep South states had all seceded, but in Tennessee, Unionism was triumphant that day. The call for a convention was defeated by 69,675 to 57,798, figures that understate the Unionist majority, because many Unionists voted for a convention in the hope that it would decisively reject secession. In fact, the votes amassed by declared Unionist candidates for delegate exceeded those of secessionist candidates by nearly four to one. Nevertheless, the election results indicated an incipient political realignment in the state. Western Tennesseeans voted 74 to 26 percent in favor of a convention, eastern Tennesseans 81 to 19 percent against, and middle Tennesseans 51 to 49 percent against, a pattern reflecting a stronger correlation between slaveholding and secessionism than in the November election.

Secession had thus been rejected in Tennessee, but events were to show that (except in the eastern section) Tennessee Unionism was contingent on a conciliatory policy toward the South on the part of the incoming administration. When Lincoln called for troops to suppress the rebellion following the bombardment of Fort Sumter on April 12, Unionism in middle and western Tennessee evaporated. Forced now to take sides in a civil war, most citizens outside eastern Tennessee chose to join the Deep South. John Bell himself, who since November had urged support of Lincoln, now reluctantly renounced his Unionism.

Again Governor Harris put himself at the head of the secession movement and this time led it to victory. Having informed the Lincoln administration that "Tennessee will not furnish a single man for purposes of coercion but 50,000 if necessary for the defence of our rights and those of our Southern brothers," Harris called the legislature into session. When it met on April 25, the governor asked for a declaration of independence based on the right of revolution. The legislature obliged, by a vote of twenty to four in the Senate and forty-six to twenty-one in the House, stipulating that the declaration be submitted to a popular vote on June 8.

By that time traditional party lines had broken down almost completely, and regionalism had emerged as the most important voting determinant. Eastern Tennessee held fast to the Union even as the other two sections went over to secession. (Of the twenty-five legislators who voted against the declaration of independence, all but seven were eastern Tennesseans.) As old-line Whigs and Democrats jumped on the secession bandwagon in middle and western Tennessee, those in eastern Tennessee joined hands to resist the secessionist onslaught. Several hundred Unionists held a convention in Knoxville on May 30 and 31, where they heard speeches by longtime political foes T. A. R. Nelson and Andrew Johnson and then adopted resolutions denouncing secession.

In the June 8 referendum, which officially took the state out of the Union by a vote of 104,913 to 47,238, eastern Tennesseans voted 69 to 31 percent against secession, whereas western Tennesseans voted 83 to 17 percent in favor and middle Tennesseans 88 to 12 percent in favor. On July 22 Tennessee formally joined the Confederate States of America.

Even before the June 8 referendum, however, Governor Harris had taken steps to prepare the state for war and ally it with the Confederacy. On April 20 he dispatched an official envoy to the Confederate government. On May 7 he endorsed a military pact with the Confederacy, which the state legislature immediately ratified. He also granted the Confederacy permission to build a defensive work at Memphis and began raising and arming troops. Before the legislators adjourned on May 9 they and Harris had approved legislation creating a 55,000-man state military force, which was turned over to the Confederacy in July and formed the nucleus of the Army of Tennessee. In these and subsequent actions Harris proved himself an ardent Confederate and a tireless administrator who cooperated wholeheartedly with the Confederate government.

Most eastern Tennesseans refused to acquiesce in the state's secession even after the June 8 referendum. The Unionist convention that had met in Knoxville reassembled in Greeneville from June 17 through 20 and approved a resolution asking the legislature to grant separate statehood to eastern Tennessee. (The legislature declined to act on the matter.) Governor Harris initially adopted a conciliatory policy toward the restive eastern Tennessee Unionists, hoping to win them over. Confederate military authorities (who stationed troops in eastern Tennessee to guard the strategic Cumberland Gap and the vital railroad linking

Virginia and the Deep South) likewise treated the citizens with kid gloves. They even permitted the prominent Knoxville newspaper editor William G. Brownlow to continue his vehemently pro-Union editorializing unmolested.

Eventually, however, the stiff-necked defiance of the eastern Tennessee Unionists wore down the patience of Harris and the Confederates. The results of the August 1861 state elections particularly perturbed Harris. Though he swept middle and western Tennessee and easily won another two-year term as governor over his opponent, William H. Polk, Harris lost eastern Tennessee by a considerable margin. Moreover, Unionists there nominated and elected *Federal* congressmen in every congressional district in the region.

Thereafter, state and Confederate authorities tightened the screws. For example, they forced Brownlow to shut down his newspaper and flee Knoxville; later he was jailed and eventually exiled to the North. Resistance persisted, however. A Unionist leader traveled secretly to Washington and obtained official approval of a plot to burn the railroad bridges in eastern Tennessee. The deed was supposed to be carried out in conjunction with a Federal military invasion of the region and a mass uprising of Unionists. On the night of November 8, 1861, Unionists burned five bridges. But the promised Federal invasion failed to materialize, the uprising fizzled, and most of the bridge burners were arrested; several were hanged.

Subsequently, Confederate authorities adopted an even harsher policy in eastern Tennessee, including martial law, mass arrests, forced loyalty oaths, and confiscation of Unionist property. By the spring of 1862, ten thousand Confederate troops were posted in the region as a virtual army of occupation. Thousands of eastern Tennesseans fled to Kentucky, where many joined the Union army. Others who stayed at home took up arms as guerrillas against the Confederacy.

In the meantime, however, Confederate military reverses in middle and western Tennessee had resulted in the dissolution of the state government. The legislature met in the summer of 1861 and again from October to December. When next it met, in January 1862, Union armies were threatening the state. When the Cumberland River defenses fell in February, the legislators fled Nashville and reassembled in Memphis. A short session there in March 1862 proved to be the legislature's last.

With Federal forces occupying middle and western Tennessee and the state government defunct, Governor Harris attached himself to the Army of Tennessee as a staff officer, though he continued to exercise what few official gubernatorial functions remained. He even insisted on carrying out another state election in August 1863. Harris himself declined to run again for office, however, and the vote was miniscule. Because the state legislature could not meet, the winning gubernatorial candidate, Robert Looney Caruthers, was never inaugurated.

Military Action in Tennessee

Tennessee's strategic location made it the focus of military operations in the western theater for much of the war. Among the states, only Virginia was the scene of more battles and skirmishes than Tennessee. All three of Tennessee's grand divisions were prime targets of the Federal armies, and all three were in Federal hands well before the war's end.

Control of the Mississippi River, a major Union objective, was impossible without possession of western Tennessee. Middle Tennessee and lower eastern Tennessee had to be held to allow Union armies to invade the Confederate heartland by way of the Nashville-Chattanooga-Atlanta corridor, the second major Federal objective in the West. Furthermore, middle Tennessee was a rich food-producing region; Nashville was an important Confederate manufacturing center and military supply depot; the Cumberland-Tennessee River region near the Kentucky border boasted some of the South's largest ironworks; and the mines of eastern Tennessee produced lead, copper, and saltpeter. Moreover, eastern Tennessee had vast human resources—the loyal Unionists—that the North hoped to pry from the Confederacy's grip.

The campaigns and battles in Tennessee were, with few exceptions, disappointments or disasters for the Confederacy. When Gen. Albert Sidney Johnston assumed command of Confederate forces defending Tennessee in September 1861, he faced an overwhelming task. In the preceding months Confederate authorities had concentrated on the Mississippi River defenses, neglecting the Tennessee and Cumberland. The works defending the latter two rivers, Forts Henry and Donelson, were still unfinished when Union Gen. Ulysses S. Grant led army and naval forces against them early in 1862. Fort Henry fell on February 6, leaving the Tennessee River open to Federal penetration. Fort Donelson surrendered on February 16, leaving middle Tennessee unprotected. Nashville was captured February 25 by a second Union army under Don Carlos Buell.

Johnston retreated into northern Mississippi, whence he launched an attack on Grant, who had moved up the Tennessee River to Pittsburg Landing, just north of the Mississippi state line. The attack precipitated the bloody Battle of Shiloh (April 6–7, 1862), which turned in Grant's favor after reinforcements from Buell arrived. Meanwhile a third Union army advanced down the Mississippi River, capturing the Confederate fort at Island Number 10 on April 7 and thus endangering Memphis, which fell to Union forces in June.

Johnston was killed at Shiloh. His successor, Braxton Bragg, led the Army of Tennessee on an abortive invasion of Kentucky in the fall of 1862, in which he was joined by the Confederate troops defending eastern Tennessee, commanded by E. Kirby Smith. This offensive forced Buell's army to evacuate middle Tennessee temporarily, though a strong garrison retained control of Nashville. Bragg soon retreated into middle Tennessee, where at year's end he attacked the Federals (now commanded by Buell's successor, William S. Rosecrans). In the ensuing Battle of Murfreesboro or Stones River (December 31, 1862–January 2, 1863), success again eluded the Confederates. Bragg then withdrew into the southeastern corner of middle Tennessee.

Thus, by early 1863 all of western Tennessee and most of middle Tennessee were in Union hands. The exploits of the brilliant Confederate cavalry commanders Nathan Bedford Forrest and John Hunt Morgan, who roamed the state destroying isolated Union detachments and disrupting enemy communications, were the only bright spots in the generally dismal Confederate military record in Tennessee up to that time.

The year 1863 brought more Confederate failures. Rosecrans's Tullahoma campaign that summer maneuvered Bragg out of middle Tennessee without a fight. Bragg retreated into northern Georgia, where he finally bested Rosecrans in September at the Battle of Chickamauga with the aid of troops under James Longstreet sent from the Virginia front. Rosecrans withdrew northward to Chattanooga; Bragg followed and laid siege. Grant then arrived to take command of the Federal forces and in the Battles of Lookout Mountain (November 24, 1863) and Missionary Ridge (November 25) drove Bragg back into Georgia.

BRAXTON BRAGG. Commander of the Army of Tennessee.
THE SOLDIER IN OUR CIVIL WAR

Meanwhile Longstreet had marched northeastward to oppose a Federal army under Ambrose Burnside that had invaded eastern Tennessee in August 1863 and had occupied Knoxville in September. In the Battle of Fort Sanders (November 29, 1863) Longstreet failed to crack Knoxville's defenses. He then withdrew his troops toward the northeast and in the spring of 1864 returned to Virginia, leaving Union forces in undisputed control of the entire state of Tennessee.

Late in 1864 the Army of Tennessee, now under John Bell Hood, made a last desperate attempt to recapture the state. Hood marched into middle Tennessee from Georgia, where he had recently lost Atlanta to William Tecumseh Sherman's Union army. Sherman dispatched troops to Gen. George H. Thomas in Tennessee to stop Hood. At the Battles of Franklin (November 30, 1864) and Nashville (December 15–16) Thomas's forces dealt crushing blows that destroyed the Army of Tennessee as an effective fighting force and ended the Confederate hope of redeeming Tennessee.

Union Occupation

Soon after Fort Donelson fell, Abraham Lincoln had appointed Andrew Johnson military governor of Tennessee. Johnson, a stalwart Unionist and the only senator from a seceding state who had stayed at his post in Washington, arrived in Nashville in March 1862. His position was somewhat anomalous. He was expected to oversee the reestablishment of a loyal civil government in the state, but he was also given military rank as a brigadier general and was granted broad powers, including suspension of habeas corpus. Moreover, he was initially cut off from his natural constituency—the eastern Tennessee Unionists, who remained under Confederate domination until the autumn of 1863. Thus, for the first year and a half of his administration, Johnson's only allies were the Unionists of middle and western Tennessee, a tiny minority of the populace and (being mostly former Whigs) longtime political adversaries of Johnson's. Furthermore, the fact that his military governorship functioned side by side with the Federal army command in Tennessee inevitably provoked conflicts of authority.

At the time he assumed his duties, Johnson shared Lincoln's belief that the majority of the South's citizens were really Unionists at heart who had been duped or browbeaten by secessionist demagogues. He also shared Lincoln's desire to restore the South to the Union quickly and without revolutionary social or economic upheaval. Consequently, Johnson adopted a policy of suppressing the hard-core secessionist leaders while encouraging the "erring and misguided" masses to renounce secession and take a hand in the speedy political reconstruction of the state.

In Nashville Johnson summarily arrested or banished a number of prominent secessionists, including the mayor and city councilmen and certain newspaper editors, wealthy planters, and clergymen. But he received a shock in his first attempt to get the reconstruction process underway. In an election for circuit judge in middle Tennessee in May 1862, the voters defiantly rejected the Unionist candidate and elected a secessionist. Johnson permitted the winner to take office but then had him arrested.

That incident, along with other evidence of persistent secessionism and rabid antipathy to Johnson in middle and western Tennessee, forced the military governor to rethink his policy. He concluded that only original Unionists, not oath-taking ex-Confederates, could be relied on to help rebuild the state government. Furthermore, by 1863 Johnson (like Lincoln) adopted a more radical, punitive approach toward the rebellious South.

Johnson's conversion to radicalism split the Tennessee Unionists, many of whom continued to favor a mild reconstruction policy that would restore the status quo ante bellum. The conservative Unionists were especially alarmed by emancipation, which Johnson eventually advocated,

ANDREW JOHNSON. Union military governor of Tennessee.
HARPER'S PICTORIAL HISTORY OF THE GREAT REBELLION

even though Lincoln exempted Tennessee from the Emancipation Proclamation. The division in the Unionist ranks became very evident in August 1863, when conservative Unionists insisted on holding a gubernatorial election despite the refusal of Johnson, who wanted to wait until eastern Tennesseans could participate. The conservatives elected their candidate, William B. Campbell, only to have Lincoln reject the election. The president deplored the Unionist factionalism in Tennessee, but in this and other instances he consistently supported Johnson and the radical wing.

Lincoln's Proclamation of Amnesty and Reconstruction in December 1863 gave Johnson a method by which to bring Tennessee back into the Union; but he considered it too lenient, for it granted political rights to any citizen who took a simple oath of allegiance. As a prerequisite to participating in the county elections he planned for March 1864, Johnson devised his own oath, which required voters "to ardently desire" and "heartily aid" the defeat of the Confederacy. This effectively disfranchised not only most of the former secessionists who had taken Lincoln's amnesty oath but also some conservative Unionists, who protested loudly but unavailingly. The turnout in the county elections was, not surprisingly, quite meager.

Another controversy arose as the November 1864 presidential election neared. Conservative Unionists supported the Democratic nominee, but Johnson was determined that the state's electoral ballots would go to the Lincoln ticket, on which he himself was the vice-presidential candidate. Consequently he demanded from each voter an oath opposing any negotiated peace with the Confederacy—which was a key plank of the Democratic platform. Naturally the Lincoln-Johnson ticket won in Tennessee; Congress, however, rejected the Tennessee vote.

The reconstruction of the state's civil government finally got underway in January 1865, when some five hundred Unionists, mostly radicals, gathered in convention in Nashville. Ignoring objections that the convention was unrepresentative and its proceedings irregular under Tennessee law, the delegates approved a state constitutional amendment abolishing slavery and a series of resolutions that repudiated Tennessee's declaration of independence, voided all acts of the Confederate state government, and called for state elections. These actions received Johnson's endorsement and then were ratified by popular referendum on February 22, 1865. On March 4 the voters elected a governor and state legislature. The new governor was William G. Brownlow, who had returned to Knoxville after its capture by Federal troops. The March turnout was small (about 25,000 votes), but it was large enough to satisfy the Ten Percent Clause of Lincoln's December 1863 proclamation. Thus the reconstructed Tennessee state government was acceptable in Washington. The new legislature met in

Nashville and inaugurated Brownlow on April 5, 1865, ten days before Johnson succeeded Lincoln as president.

The abolition of slavery by state constitutional amendment merely gave legal imprimatur to an accomplished fact. Ironically, slaves in Tennessee—the only Confederate state wholly exempted from the Emancipation Proclamation—found more opportunities to free themselves from bondage than did slaves in any other Confederate state. The early Federal military conquest of Tennessee was of course the key factor.

No sooner did Union troops invade the state than slaves began running off to the army camps seeking refuge. Despite the initial conservatism of the Federal commanders, the army soon began welcoming runaways as laborers and rebuffing the attempts of masters to reclaim them. Eventually the army became an active agent of emancipation and established "contraband camps" across the state to care for fugitive slaves. After military recruitment of blacks became Federal policy in 1863, over twenty thousand Tennessee blacks volunteered as Union soldiers. In addition to freedom and military service, blacks in Tennessee seized other opportunities during the war that blacks in most other parts of the South would not have until the postwar Reconstruction period, including contract labor, education, and political activity.

To be sure, black Tennesseans also experienced hardships and mistreatment during the war at the hands of Northern soldiers as well as Southern slaveholders, but they could at least revel in their newfound freedom. Most white Tennesseans, on the other hand, found nothing at all to celebrate about their wartime experience. Whether they lived in towns or with the great majority in the countryside, they suffered severely, for military invasion brought in its wake immense property destruction, harsh military rule, and violence and privation on a previously unimaginable scale.

Tennessee's three major cities and many of its towns were held by large Union garrison forces during much of the war, even after the main field armies moved on to Georgia. These occupation troops seized buildings for their own use, dug mountains of fortifications, and enforced strict army and Treasury Department edicts governing disloyalty, travel, and trade. Moreover, the huge influx of soldiers, runaway slaves, white refugees, Northern speculators and humanitarians, and others into the occupied cities and towns led to overcrowding, unemployment, inflation, food and fuel shortages, and disease.

Rural Tennesseans were less often directly under the thumb of the Federal occupiers than urbanites were, but they nonetheless encountered extreme hardship. The Union army depended on Tennessee's farms for supplies of all sorts and thus ruthlessly seized crops, stored food, livestock, and fencing, not to mention slaves. Military impressment and pillaging were so frequent and so devastating in some sections of the state that many farmers abandoned their homesteads and fled to the Deep South or to the occupied towns. Those who stayed at home had to endure not only privation but also anarchy and violence. With local government suspended by the Federal invasion, and battles, skirmishes, and guerrilla warfare ravaging the countryside, communal institutions disintegrated and law and order collapsed. Banditry was widespread by 1864, and the rural areas remained places of danger and disorder until peace was restored in the spring and summer of 1865.

The enormous destruction and suffering, combined with the incontrovertible Federal control of the state, withered Confederate morale in Tennessee. Well before the war's end, the great majority of Tennessee's Confederates resigned themselves to defeat and emancipation. They did not, however, resign themselves to Unionist political predominance nor to equal rights for the freedmen. Thus, the stage was set for Tennessee's postwar Reconstruction era, which would prove to be quite as unique as its Confederate experience.

[*For further discussion of battles and campaigns fought in Tennessee, see* Chattanooga, Tennessee, *article on* Chattanooga Campaign; Chickamauga Campaign; Forrest's Raids; Franklin and Nashville Campaign; Henry and Donelson Campaign; Knoxville Campaign; Morgan's Raids; Murfreesboro, Tennessee; New Madrid and Island Number 10; Shiloh Campaign; Wheeler's Raids. *For further discussion of Tennessee cities, see* Chattanooga, Tennessee, *article on* City of Chattanooga; Memphis, Tennessee; Nashville, Tennessee. *See also* Knoxville and Greeneville Conventions *and biographies of numerous figures mentioned herein.*]

BIBLIOGRAPHY

Alexander, Thomas B. *Political Reconstruction in Tennessee.* Nashville, Tenn., 1950.

Ash, Stephen V. *Middle Tennessee Society Transformed, 1860–1870: War and Peace in the Upper South.* Baton Rouge, La., 1988.

Bryan, Charles F., Jr. "A Gathering of Tories: The East Tennessee Convention of 1861." *Tennessee Historical Quarterly* 39 (1980): 27–48.

Bryan, Charles F., Jr. " 'Tories' Amidst Rebels: Confederate Occupation of East Tennessee, 1861–63." *East Tennessee Historical Society's Publications* 60 (1988): 3–22.

Cimprich, John. *Slavery's End in Tennessee, 1861–1865.* University, Ala., 1985.

Connelly, Thomas L. *Civil War Tennessee: Battles and Leaders.* Knoxville, Tenn., 1979.

Crofts, Daniel W. *Reluctant Confederates: Upper South Unionists in the Secession Crisis.* Chapel Hill, N.C., 1989.

Hall, Kermit L. "Tennessee." In *The Confederate Governors.* Edited by W. Buck Yearns. Athens, Ga., 1985.

Maslowski, Peter. *Treason Must Be Made Odious: Military Occupation and Wartime Reconstruction in Nashville, Tennessee.* Millwood, N.Y., 1978.

Parks, Joseph H. "Memphis under Military Rule, 1862 to 1865." *East Tennessee Historical Society's Publications* 14 (1942): 31–58.

Patton, James Welch. *Unionism and Reconstruction in Tennessee, 1860–1869.* Chapel Hill, N.C., 1934.

STEPHEN V. ASH

TENNESSEE. One of the most powerful ironclads built in the Confederacy, *Tennessee* was 217 feet long and 48 feet wide, and drew 14 feet of water. Its 2-foot thick, angled wooden casemate was armored with 6 inches of iron plate on its forward end and 5 inches on its sides and after end. Four inches of iron protected the warship's waterline, and 2 inches covered its exterior decks. Six Brooke rifled cannon provided the vessel's main offensive punch. Two 6.4-inch guns were mounted on each broadside, and a single 7-inch gun was pivot-mounted at each end of the casemate and designed to fire from one of three gunports. A reinforced, armored bow formed another potential and much-feared weapon, the ram. Secondhand, high-pressure steam machinery, often attributed to the riverboat *Alonzo Child* but probably from the Mississippi River steamer *Vicksburg,* turned a single propeller through a series of gears and provided *Tennessee* with a speed of six knots.

A near-sister of ironclads *Columbia* and *Texas, Tennessee* was built from plans developed by Chief Naval Constructor John L. Porter. Construction commenced October 1862 at the Selma, Alabama, Navy Yard under the immediate supervision of Acting Naval Constructor Joseph Pierce. When launched February 26, 1863, *Tennessee* struck and demolished a brick warehouse as it slid from the ways—its first and only experience as a ram. The unfinished vessel was then towed down the Alabama River to Mobile where it was completed and placed into service under the command of Lt. James D. Johnston on February 16, 1864. To get the heavy-draft ironclad over the Dog River bar and into lower Mobile Bay, its primary operating grounds, caissons were laboriously fitted to the ship's sides and pumped free of water in order to reduce its draft. This task was successfully accomplished on May 18, and four days later Adm. Franklin Buchanan, highest ranking officer in the Confederate navy and commander of the Mobile Squadron, hoisted his flag on *Tennessee.*

SURRENDER OF *TENNESSEE.* *Tennessee,* at center in foreground, surrounded by Federal ships at the battle of Mobile Bay, August 5, 1864. Etching by J. O. Davidson. NAVAL HISTORICAL CENTER, WASHINGTON, D.C.

Buchanan immediately began preparations to counter Union Adm. David G. Farragut's anticipated attack on the Confederate defenses at the mouth of the bay. When this assault took place on August 5, *Tennessee,* with sidewheel wooden gunboats *Gaines, Morgan,* and *Selma,* placed a deadly raking fire on the eighteen-ship Federal fleet as it fought its way past Fort Morgan. Although Farragut suffered heavy casualties and lost the monitor *Tecumseh* and nearly its entire crew to a torpedo, he successfully entered Mobile Bay and came to anchor. Determined to inflict additional damage on the Federals, Buchanan quickly followed them up the bay and attacked. A terrific combat ensued, pitting *Tennessee* against the entire enemy fleet, including three monitors. Numbers ultimately told; with its smokestack riddled and broken off, its steering chains shot away, three of its guns rendered inoperative because of jammed port shutters, and Buchanan wounded, *Tennessee* was reluctantly surrendered by Johnston after an hour's battle. Remarkably, only two Confederates were killed and nine wounded.

Immediately commissioned into Federal service, the ex-Confederate ironclad assisted in the assault and capture of Fort Morgan and then was sent west where it performed useful duty on the Mississippi River. Following the close of the war *Tennessee* was decommissioned at New Orleans August 19, 1865, and sold for scrap November 27, 1867.

BIBLIOGRAPHY

Johnston, James D. "The Ram *Tennessee* at Mobile Bay." In *Battles and Leaders of the Civil War.* Edited by Robert U. Johnson and C. C. Buel. Vol. 4. New York, 1888. Reprint, Secaucus, N.J., 1982.

Scharf, John Thomas. *History of the Confederate States Navy.* New York, 1887. Reprint, New York, 1977.

Still, William N., Jr. *Iron Afloat: The Story of the Confederate Armorclads.* 2d ed. Columbia, S.C., 1985.

A. Robert Holcombe, Jr.

TERRELL, ALEXANDER W. (1827–1912), colonel, acting brigadier general, and U.S. plenipotentiary to Turkey. Terrell was born on November 23, 1827, in Patrick County, Virginia. In 1832 he and his family moved to Missouri. There Terrell attended the University of Missouri and subsequently studied law before moving to Texas in 1852. He was serving as a district judge in Texas when the Civil War began.

Terrell was appointed major of the First Texas Cavalry Regiment, Arizona Brigade. He helped raise a unit that became known as Terrell's Texas Cavalry Battalion and was named its lieutenant colonel. After his promotion to colonel he was allowed to expand the unit to a regiment, which he commanded throughout the Red River campaign in 1864. The men participated in the Battles of Mansfield and Pleasant Hill and later in the operations against Nathaniel Banks's forces in Louisiana. Gen. E. Kirby Smith assigned Terrell as a brigadier general on May 16, 1865, in the Trans-Mississippi Department. (These orders were published after the Richmond government had collapsed and therefore were never confirmed officially.)

When the Trans-Mississippi Department surrendered, Terrell fled to Mexico and fought with the forces of Maximilian. After his return to Texas, he served in the legislature for sixteen years and sponsored a number of bills aimed at reforming regulation of railroads and improving the state university. President Grover Cleveland later appointed Terrell plenipotentiary to Turkey. He died in Mineral Wells, Texas, on September 8, 1912.

An extremely efficient recruiter, organizer, and administrator, Terrell was apparently a mediocre commander. Although he and his unit are cited in the military record of the Red River campaign, he does not receive a citation for bravery or leadership.

BIBLIOGRAPHY

Roberts, O. M. *Texas.* Vol. 11 of *Confederate Military History.* Edited by Clement A. Evans. Atlanta, 1899. Vol. 15 of extended ed. Wilmington, N.C., 1989.

Terrell, Alexander Watkins. *From Texas to Mexico and the Court of Maximilian in 1865.* Dallas, Tex., 1933.

Roy R. Stephenson

TERRILL, JAMES BARBOUR (1838–1864), brigadier general. Barbour was born February 20, 1838, on a farm near Warm Springs, Virginia. An 1858 graduate of Virginia Military Institute, Terrill was practicing law in Warm Springs when war came. He entered Confederate service as major of the Thirteenth Virginia, the unit with which he was associated throughout his military career.

Terrill was in every battle in the East from First Manassas through Spotsylvania. As of May 15, 1863, he was the colonel of his regiment. Terrill led by example. One of his men called him "that unflinching, hard fighter"; Gen. Jubal Early observed that Terrill and his men were "never required to take a position that they did not take it, nor to hold one that they did not hold it."

On May 31, 1864, the Confederate Senate confirmed Terrill's promotion to brigadier general. Tragically, the previous day, Terrill had been shot in the head and killed at Bethesda Church. He remained buried where he fell until his father secured Terrill's body, took it home, and placed it in the same grave with his brother William, a Union brigadier who had been slain at Perryville, Kentucky.

James Terrill was one of those fighting colonels who repeatedly sustained the high reputation of the Army of

Northern Virginia. An admirer wrote of the young commander:

> His clarion voice, encouraging his men, was frequently heard above the din of battle; and when asked by his friends (as he frequently was) how it was that he acted so fearlessly in time of action, his reply invariably was, "I never think on such occasions of being killed."

BIBLIOGRAPHY

Buck, Samuel D. *With the Old Confeds.* Baltimore, Md., 1925.

Riggs, David F. *Thirteenth Virginia.* Lynchburg, Va., 1988.

Walker, Charles D. *Memorial, Virginia Military Institute.* Philadelphia, 1875.

JAMES I. ROBERTSON, JR.

TERRY, WILLIAM (1824–1888), brigadier general and U.S. congressman. The last and least colorful general who commanded the Stonewall Brigade, Terry nevertheless achieved the admiration of his soldiers and acquired an unusual number of battle wounds. Born August 14, 1824, in Amherst County, Virginia, he graduated in 1848 from the state university. A brief teaching career ensued, after which Terry studied law and established a practice in Wytheville. He also founded the *Wytheville Telegraph* and was active in the local militia.

Terry entered Confederate service in 1861 as a lieutenant in the Fourth Virginia. Promotion to major came the following year. So did his first battle wound at Manassas. He led the Fourth Virginia at Chancellorsville in fighting that cost the regiment half of its strength. Three-fourths of the survivors were casualties at Gettysburg. In September 1863, Terry received promotion to colonel. The following May, at Spotsylvania's Bloody Angle, Terry re-formed his lines on his own initiative and thereby staved off further disaster to Robert E. Lee's army. Terry received two slight wounds in that engagement.

On May 19 he was promoted to brigadier general and given a brigade consisting of pieces of fourteen regiments. The five regimental scraps from the Stonewall Brigade were included. The slightly built, unassuming brigadier with gray-streaked hair picked up additional battle injuries at Winchester and at Fort Stedman.

In the postwar years Terry resumed his law practice, served two terms in the U.S. Congress, and was a delegate to the 1880 Democratic National Convention. On September 3, 1888, while attempting to ford rain-swollen Reed Creek near his home, he slipped into the water and drowned. Terry is buried in Wytheville.

BIBLIOGRAPHY

Robertson, James I., Jr. *Fourth Virginia Infantry.* Lynchburg, Va., 1982.

Robertson, James I., Jr. *The Stonewall Brigade.* Baton Rouge, La., 1963.

Terry, William. "The 'Stonewall Brigade' at Chancellorsville." *Southern Historical Society Papers* 14 (1886): 364–370. Reprint, Wilmington, N.C., 1990.

JAMES I. ROBERTSON, JR.

TERRY, WILLIAM RICHARD (1827–1897), brigadier general. Terry was born at Liberty (now Bedford), Virginia, March 12, 1827. After graduating from the Virginia Military Institute in 1850, he became a gentleman farmer. When war came in 1861, he enlisted and was elected captain of a volunteer company of cavalry.

Terry's company fought with distinction at First Manassas, and in September, he received promotion to colonel and command of the Twenty-fourth Virginia Infantry. He led the unit in most of the major battles of the Army of Northern Virginia for the next three years, winning the reputation of being one of the hardest-charging officers in the army, always at the head of his troops. He was seriously wounded three times (not seven, as some sources report). At the Battle of Williamsburg (May 5, 1862) he was shot through the face, a wound that left him paralyzed on the right side of his face the rest of his life. On July 3, 1863, at Gettysburg, Terry was with James Lawson Kemper's brigade in Pickett's Charge. When Kemper was mortally wounded, Terry took command and led the brigade over the stone wall near the Angle supporting Lewis Armistead's brigade. After Armistead fell, Terry was the highest-ranking officer still standing, and he deserves the credit for finally ordering the few pitiful survivors back to Confederate lines. Although wounded in the charge himself, he succeeded to command of Kemper's brigade. He commanded that unit in an acting capacity until permanently promoted to brigadier in August 1864. After Gettysburg, he was assigned to the Department of North Carolina and Southern Virginia where he fought in the campaign against New Bern and the stand against Benjamin Butler on the south side of the James River. He was wounded a third time at Dinwiddie Court House (March 31, 1865) and surrendered what was left of his men at Appomattox.

After the war Terry returned to Bedford, representing his district in the state legislature for eight years beginning in 1869 and then was appointed superintendent of the state penitentiary and, finally, commandant of the Soldier's Home in Richmond. He died on his farm in Chesterfield County, March 28, 1897, and was buried in Hollywood Cemetery in Richmond.

BIBLIOGRAPHY

Gunn, Ralph W. *Twenty-fourth Virginia Infantry.* Lynchburg, Va., 1987.

Hotchkiss, Jed. *Virginia.* Vol. 3 of *Confederate Military History.* Edited by Clement A. Evans. Atlanta, 1899. Vol. 4 of extended ed. Wilmington, N.C., 1987.

James, C. F. "Battle of Sailor's Creek." *Southern Historical Society Papers* 24 (1896): 83–88. Reprint, Wilmington, N.C., 1991.

Loehr, Charles T. "Battle of Drewry's Bluff." *Southern Historical Society Papers* 19 (1891): 100–105. Reprint, Wilmington, N.C., 1990.

Mayo, Joseph C. "Pickett's Charge at Gettysburg." *Southern Historical Society Papers* 34 (1906): 327–335. Reprint, Wilmington, N.C., 1991.

"The Soldier's Home, Richmond (From Richmond *Dispatch,* Nov. 27, 1982)." *Southern Historical Society Papers* 20 (1892): 323–324. Reprint, Wilmington, N.C., 1990.

RICHARD SELCER

TEXAS. In the election of 1860 Texas favored Southern Democrat John C. Breckinridge with 75 percent of its votes over Constitutional Unionist John Bell and then moved to secede on February 1, 1861. From a population of 604,215 (420,891 white and 182,921 black), the Lone Star State sent perhaps 90,000 troops to serve in the Confederate military.

On the eve of the Civil War, Texas ranked ninth among future Confederate states in population. Within the white population, settlers from the upper South provided a majority in North and Central Texas counties, and migrants from the lower South formed a majority in East Texas counties. German immigrant families, concentrated mostly in Central Texas and in larger towns, represented over 7 percent of free Texans; Hispanics in South Texas formed between 3 and 5 percent. The 182,566 slaves, primarily on East Texas farms and plantations, composed 30 percent of the total population. There were only 355 free blacks, since state laws had limited their number. Settlement in 1860 had advanced one or two counties beyond San Antonio, Austin, and Fort Worth, with the exception of El Paso in the Trans-Pecos region. Native Americans, primarily Apaches and Comanches, controlled much of West Texas.

Cotton formed the major export crop with 431,000 bales in 1860, and some grain crops and over 3 million cattle were raised primarily for subsistence. Trade flowed through Galveston, the major port with a population of 7,307, slightly smaller than San Antonio. The state contained only 3,449 workers in industry, 306 miles of railroads, and a few banks.

As Texans approached the election of 1860, the Unionist sentiment that had carried Sam Houston to the governorship in 1859 weakened, and passions rose as many Texans attributed fires in the summer of 1860 to slaves and abolitionists. Houston, a national Democrat, received some consideration as a nominee for president by the Constitutional Union party, but he failed to gain enough support. Texans cast 47,548 votes for the state rights Democrat Breckinridge and 15,438 votes for Constitutional Unionist Bell. With the election of Republican Abraham Lincoln, several leading Democrats in Texas, fearing Northern dominance and slave unrest, urged separation. Despite opposition from Houston, a convention met and on February 1, 1861, easily passed a secession ordinance, which received ratification later that month with 46,153 in favor and 14,747 opposed. Several counties in North and Central Texas and one in East Texas produced majorities against secession.

SAM HOUSTON. Unionist governor of Texas at the time of the state's secession. NATIONAL ARCHIVES

The secession convention also established a Committee of Public Safety for the purpose of assuming control over the Federal forts in Texas. To accomplish that goal the committee called for volunteer troops. Ben McCulloch led 500 men who captured the department commander, David Twiggs, and 160 U.S. soldiers at his headquarters in San Antonio on February 16, 1861. John S. ("Rip") Ford directed another force that seized Fort Brown near the entrance to the Rio Grande, while Henry Eustace McCulloch and a third group occupied frontier posts. The Texans captured extensive supplies, weapons, and ammunition as well as 2,700 Federal troops. Most of the soldiers were allowed to depart by ship, but 600 who remained after the firing on Fort Sumter became prisoners of war at Camp Verde.

Texans on the War Front

To counter Lincoln's call for troops, Texas joined the other Confederate states in recruiting soldiers. Early enthusiasm led 25,000 men to enlist during 1861. By 1865 the number of men enrolled in Confederate units from Texas had grown to possibly 90,000. The first troops left amid fiery speeches after receiving flags sewn by ladies of their communities. Their weapons ranged widely from rifles to shotguns and other types of firearms. Because of a strong volunteer military tradition based on service in the Texas Revolution, the war with Mexico, and frontier ranger companies, two out of three among the almost ninety regiments enlisted as cavalry, a reversal of the pattern in other states. The need for greater numbers of infantry led to the dismounting of fifteen Texas cavalry regiments, which at least temporarily hurt morale in each unit. Texans also raised forty-three batteries of artillery. The strong frontier military tradition meant that about half of the thirty-seven Texas generals had volunteer experience, but only about one-fourth had been professional soldiers, also the reverse of patterns in most states. The Confederacy with its small population introduced military conscription in 1862, which stimulated volunteering in Texas as in other states.

Many of the first regiments from Texas hurried across the Mississippi River to join the major Confederate armies defending against Union attacks in Virginia and Tennessee. Three Texas infantry regiments developed a tough combat reputation as Hood's Brigade in the Army of Northern Virginia. They participated in almost every major battle in the East from the Seven Days' Battles in 1862 to Appomattox in 1865. Among the 4,350 men of the regiments 62 percent were wounded, killed, or captured.

Greater numbers of Texans served in the Army of Tennessee defending the region from the Appalachian Mountains to the Mississippi River. Albert Sidney Johnston, a former officer in the armies of the Republic of Texas and of the United States, became a full general and the Confederate commander in Tennessee. His effort to surprise and defeat Ulysses S. Grant at Shiloh in April 1862 ended when Johnston died in the battle. The Eighth Texas Cavalry, called Terry's Rangers, fought with Johnston's army and later with Joseph Wheeler's cavalry corps over a span of four years. Four Texas cavalry regiments, some with early combat experience, crossed the Mississippi River in 1862 and became known as Ross's Brigade in Mississippi and later in the Atlanta and Nashville campaigns of 1864.

The Army of Tennessee also included several Texas infantry units. The Second Texas Infantry Regiment saw action at Shiloh in Tennessee and Corinth in Mississippi during 1862 before being captured, along with Thomas Neville Waul's Texas Legion, after defending Vicksburg for several weeks in 1863. Four dismounted cavalry regiments fought at Murfreesboro, Chickamauga, Atlanta, Nashville, and Mobile as Ector's Brigade. Other Texas infantry and dismounted cavalry regiments were consolidated after they had been captured at Arkansas Post and exchanged. They became best known as Granbury's Brigade during service in the Chattanooga, Atlanta, and Nashville campaigns. John Bell Hood, former commander of the Texas Brigade in Virginia, led the Army of Tennessee in the Atlanta and Nashville campaigns without success.

Many Texans protected their state in fighting around its borders. In 1861 the Eleventh Texas Cavalry occupied Federal forts above the Red River in the Indian Territory (now Oklahoma). The Forty-sixth Texas Cavalry held the posts on the western fringe of Texas settlement, though Comanche Indian raids drove back the frontier in many areas. At Dove Creek in 1865 a band of Kickapoo Indians drove off a Confederate attack in the largest frontier engagement of the war. From Texas a cavalry brigade under Henry H. Sibley advanced toward New Mexico and Arizona in the winter of 1861–1862. After a victory at Valverde in February 1862, Sibley occupied Albuquerque and then Santa Fe. A defeat at Glorieta Pass in March forced a retreat into Texas with heavy losses by summer.

To defend the coast, district commanders of Texas, first Earl Van Dorn and then Paul O. Hébert, formed artillery units and began to entrench Galveston and other ports in 1861. After raiding Corpus Christi and Sabine Pass, the Federal blockading fleet occupied Galveston in October 1862. A new district commander, John B. Magruder, planned a successful counterattack to retake the port with cottonclad river steamers as well as army troops on January 1, 1863. At Sabine Pass a small artillery battery under Dick Dowling drove off a Union attempt to land troops on September 8, 1863. Federal troops under Nathaniel P. Banks did occupy Brownsville and the coast from the Rio Grande to Matagorda Bay in the fall and winter of 1863. John S. Ford led a Confederate recapture of the Rio Grande Valley in 1864. Because they captured Union soldiers along the coast, Confederates built two military prisons, Camp Ford at Tyler and Camp Groce near Houston.

Union advances into Arkansas, the Indian Territory, and Louisiana also appeared threatening to Texans. Ben McCulloch led Confederate troops including some Texans who defeated a Federal force at Wilson's Creek in Missouri during 1861. While directing one wing of the Confederate army at Elkhorn Tavern, Arkansas, early in 1862, McCulloch died in action. After helping recapture Galveston, Sibley's cavalry regiments marched into Louisiana where they became known as Green's Brigade while holding back Union forces with the help of Major's Brigade of Texas cavalry in 1863. Several Texas cavalry regiments, usually called Parsons' Brigade, defended Arkansas during 1862 and 1863. Gano's Brigade of Texas cavalry helped protect

BEN MCCULLOCH. Confederate general. *FRANK LESLIE'S ILLUSTRATED FAMOUS LEADERS AND BATTLE SCENES OF THE CIVIL WAR*

against Union movements into the Indian Territory. Walker's Division, three brigades of Texas infantry, served in Arkansas during 1862 and in Louisiana during 1863. Additional infantry, best known as Polignac's Brigade, also defended Louisiana in 1863. The commander of the Trans-Mississippi Department, E. Kirby Smith, brought these units together in early 1864 to turn back the Union Red River expedition. Further support came from Bee's Division, two Texas cavalry brigades drawn from the Gulf coast. Thomas Green, the most successful of the Texas cavalry officers and commander of all mounted units in the Red River campaign, died in the fighting that spring. Little combat occurred in or near Texas during the final months of the war, though small units skirmished at Palmito Ranch in the Rio Grande Valley on May 13, 1865, shortly before the surrender of the Trans-Mississippi Department on June 2.

The Home Front

Not all the conflict took place on the battlefield. Once the war began, those who had opposed secession faced difficult decisions. Some like James Throckmorton served the Confederacy but urged restraint in the use of government power. Others who were old enough to avoid military service, such as former governors Sam Houston and Elisha M. Pease, left the field of politics. But when the Confederacy adopted a military draft in 1862, the option of neutrality disappeared for younger men. Many German immigrants on the edge of settlement in Central Texas had tried to serve only for frontier defense. Confederate authorities created a military court in San Antonio to hear charges of disloyalty and imprisoned or exiled those who were convicted. When a company of German Unionists left home for Mexico to avoid harassment, Confederate cavalry intercepted them at the Nueces River in August 1862, killing wounded prisoners, though others escaped. Confederate troops entered Mexico to capture and hang Unionist William Montgomery. Edmund J. Davis and Andrew Jackson Hamilton successfully departed from Texas to become Union generals. They recruited two Federal cavalry regiments, half of whom were German immigrants and Tejano troops.

Unionists in North Texas began to meet privately to consider alternatives to conscription. Their actions stirred fears among Confederates who seized numerous suspects in the fall of 1862. An unofficial jury in Cooke County, under mob pressure, offered none of the normal opportunities for a legal defense before ordering the execution of forty-seven men. Of the several men arrested in Wise, Denton, and Grayson counties only six were executed, as the authorities there exercised more restraint. Unionists killed two prominent Confederates in retaliation.

Both the Confederate and Texas governments sought to support the war effort, but the state rights and limited-government views of 1861 increasingly came into conflict with wartime exigencies. Confederate Senator Louis T. Wigfall had strongly supported state rights before the war, but now became a proponent of the military draft. John H. Reagan represented Texas in the Confederate cabinet as postmaster general. Political parties dissolved in Texas as in other Confederate states, though factions and individuals struggled over power and position. When Houston refused to accept secession, Lieutenant Governor Edward Clark completed his term. Francis R. Lubbock then led the state from 1861 to 1863 and cooperated well with Confederate authorities.

When better known political leaders joined the army, Pendleton Murrah won the election for governor in 1863 and served until Confederate surrender in 1865. He soon clashed with Magruder, the district commander, on two issues. Murrah wanted to retain control over 6,000 state troops, though many fell within the draft ages set by the Confederate government. In a compromise he agreed the army could assume command of the units in a military crisis, such as the Red River campaign of 1864, though cooperation even then proved less than perfect.

The governor and the general confronted each other again over government roles in the cotton trade. The Texas State Military Board, created in 1862, found it could not compete well with private speculators for cotton to pay for military supplies. The Confederate army and Treasury Department sought to regulate the trade with little success, which led E. Kirby Smith to create a Cotton Bureau in 1863 for impressment of cotton. The Confederate and state governments continued to clash over the trade until Murrah and Smith reached an agreement favoring the Confederacy in 1864.

During the war Texans at various levels of government also entered into new areas of activity. The Confederate government created its own shops and arsenals in Texas and elsewhere to produce weapons and supplies. Texas used its prison to manufacture cloth. Counties limited liquor production to save grain for food. City and county governments aided disabled soldiers and war widows.

Although the Texas government faced some economic problems during the conflict, the state's economy fared better than those of most Confederate states. Foreign trade continued on a more elaborate scale in Texas because most commerce shifted to flow south by wagon across the Rio Grande into Mexico, where shippers at Matamoros sent a significant amount on to Europe or even to the Union states. Through that pattern of trade over 300,000 bales of cotton left the state, about two-thirds being shipped to England and the rest to New York. Because of the civil war in Mexico, shifts in political control of the border could alter or slow the flow of goods. Benito Juárez and the republicans favored the Union, while Maximilian, the French-supported emperor, preferred the Confederates. Santiago Vidaurri, who governed Nuevo León and Coahuila during 1862 and 1863, also traded with the Confederates. Rio Grande Valley merchants profited enough from the trade to develop major landholdings such as the great ranch of Richard King.

Lesser amounts of goods came and went via blockade runners at Galveston and other Gulf ports. Federal warships in the Gulf tightened their watch on the coast but captured only about two hundred ships during some fifteen hundred attempts to run the blockade. But it was small sailing ships carrying no more than forty bales of cotton on each voyage that conducted most of the risky commerce. Thus the total trade through the blockade amounted to only twenty-five thousand to fifty thousand bales during the war.

Given the reduction in the exchange of cotton for manufactured goods, the Texas government sought to encourage industry. The number of manufacturers chartered by the state increased from six in 1861–1862 to thirty-three in 1863–1864; nevertheless, they remained too few to meet the variety of needs.

Because of the Mexican outlet for cotton and the limited Union invasions of Texas, agriculture suffered less disruption than in most Confederate states. Planters and slaveholding farmers lost part of their wealth, however, as a result of emancipation in 1865. Texans who committed themselves to Confederate currency also felt the pinch of reduced capital after the Confederates' defeat.

Conflict brought change to Texas society as it did in the economy. Shortages of various products resulted in makeshift substitutions. Inflation pushed the prices of food and other necessities to three or four times their prewar levels. Civilian frustrations led to food riots at San Antonio in 1862 and at Galveston in 1864. As the Union army advanced through Arkansas and Louisiana refugees from those states flooded into East Texas. Citizens of Galveston moved to Houston seeking escape from bombardment or occupation. Some stayed with friends or relatives, and others received aid from churches. Growing bands of deserters dominated some rural areas in spite of efforts by local law officers and the Confederate army to apprehend them.

To meet problems created by the war, churches sent chaplains to the army where they aided wounded and disabled soldiers as well as the families of those who died. With so many men leaving home for military service, their mothers, wives, and daughters assumed new roles. Some took over farms and businesses, others raised money or sewed uniforms, and still others nursed the wounded or taught in schools for the first time.

Slavery retained more stability in Texas than in most states of the Confederacy because of the limited Union movements into the state. The slave population continued to grow rapidly because some refugees from nearby states brought their slaves with them. By 1865 probably 250,000 slaves labored in Texas. The army's need for laborers, especially to dig entrenchments along the coast, led to the impressment of several hundred slaves. Some bondsmen continued to escape to Mexico, and others sought freedom with the Federal forces in the Indian Territory or on the coast. White fears of revolt resulted in arrests and executions of slaves. In 1864 some Texas officers and political figures favored freeing individual slaves if they agreed to fight for the Confederacy, but opposition from other government leaders and several editors delayed any serious effort. Confederate defeat brought freedom for all slaves when the Union army landed at Galveston on June 19, 1865, which became the date of Texas emancipation celebrations in following years.

Texans felt the impact of the Civil War in every aspect of society. Military campaigns resulted in thousands of men killed or disabled and some destruction in coastal areas. To conduct the war, every level of government expanded its activities, which led to numerous conflicts. Lingering differences over secession added further tensions. Some economic dislocations and inflation left the state poorer, but more diverse in its range of economic activities. Deaths, shortages, and refugee problems created social disorder. On the other hand, the expanded roles for women and emancipation for slaves represented positive steps amid the tragedy of war.

[*For further discussion of battles and campaigns fought in Texas, see* Andrews Raid; Brownsville, Texas, *article on* Battle of Brownsville; Galveston, Texas, *article on* Battle of Galveston. *For further discussion of Texas cities, see* Austin, Texas; Brownsville, Texas, *article on* City of Brownsville; Galveston, Texas, *article on* City of Galveston. *See also* Hood's Texas Brigade *and biographies of numerous figures mentioned herein.*]

BIBLIOGRAPHY

Ashcraft, Allan C. *Texas in the Civil War: A Résumé History.* Austin, Tex., 1962.

Betts, Vicki. *Smith County, Texas, in the Civil War.* Tyler, Tex., 1978.

Buenger, Walter L. *Secession and the Union in Texas.* Austin, Tex., 1984.

Campbell, Randolph B. *An Empire for Slavery: The Peculiar Institution in Texas.* Baton Rouge, La., 1989.

Marten, James. *Texas Divided: Loyalty and Dissent in the Lone Star State, 1856–1874.* Lexington, Ky., 1990.

Oates, Stephen B. "Texas under the Secessionists." *Southwestern Historical Quarterly* 67 (1963): 167–212.

Winsor, Bill. *Texas in the Confederacy: Military Installations, Economy, and People.* Hillsboro, Tex., 1978.

Wright, Marcus J. *Texas in the War, 1861–1865.* Hillsboro, Tex., 1965.

ALWYN BARR

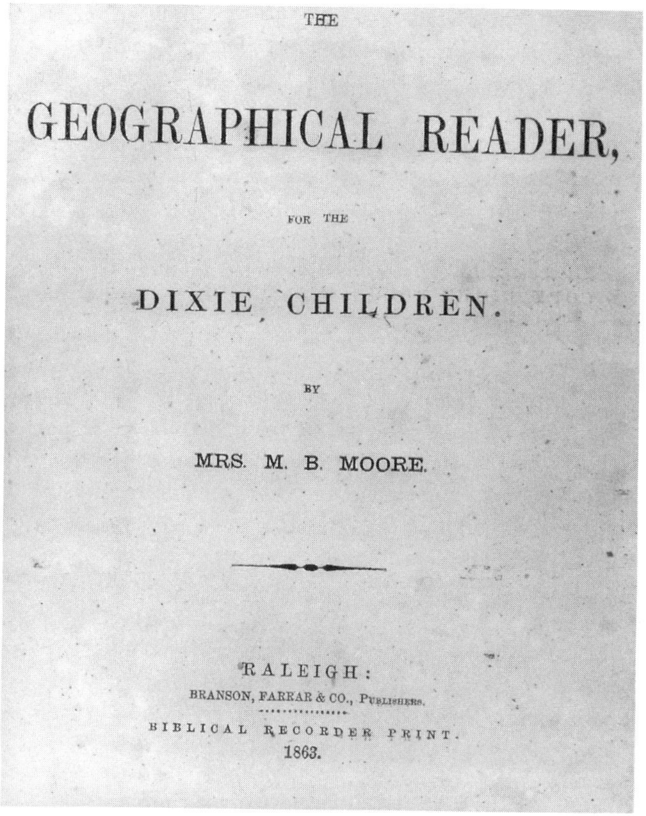
THE

GEOGRAPHICAL READER,

FOR THE

DIXIE CHILDREN.

BY

MRS. M. B. MOORE.

RALEIGH:

BRANSON, FARRAR & CO., PUBLISHERS.

BIBLICAL RECORDER PRINT.

1863.

CONFEDERATE GEOGRAPHY PRIMER.

CIVIL WAR LIBRARY AND MUSEUM, PHILADELPHIA

TEXTBOOKS. Confederate schools faced many problems throughout the war: a lack of funds, waning public support, a shortage of quality teachers, decreasing enrollments, and dwindling supplies. Perhaps the greatest problem, however, was in procuring sufficient and distinctly regional textbooks. Northern publishers had traditionally supplied Southern schools, but with less than satisfactory results. The volumes, many believed, slighted Southern sensibilities and themes, were subtly abolitionist, and were sometimes obscure, using vocabulary and colloquial expressions foreign to Southern readers. In response, many Northern companies further aggravated the situation by charging more for shipments to the South, substituting title pages on standard editions so as to imply revisions had been made, or defacing books to remove or obscure passages on life and labor in the South offensive to Southerners. Locally produced texts such as the Reverend Calvin H. Wiley's *North Carolina Reader* were simply too few to make a substantial difference.

With the outbreak of war, however, Jefferson Davis spoke for many in remarking that the production of textbooks "commands my fullest sympathy, and has, for many years, attracted my earnest consideration." A Mobile, Alabama, bookseller, S. H. Goetzel, offered funds toward a convention to consider the matter. The *Atlanta Daily Intelligencer* called for new books "by the time we satisfy the North that we are superiors in arms," and the *Baptist Banner* warned that "when this war is over, we must no longer look to the abolition North for the books we place in the hands of our children." An 1861 Atlanta conference of teachers recommended a more widespread use of blackboards to alleviate any school's dependence on Northern books and urged that teachers ration still-suitable titles, and that schools help hasten the production of replacement textbooks.

Individual states such as Georgia and North Carolina formed committees to develop uniform texts and to establish both bounties and sponsorships for suitable materials. The Virginia Educational Association instead voted to support the best books, whether they be new, foreign editions or even reprints of the least offensive Northern titles. To meet the need, and eyeing the profits that had traditionally accrued to Northern competitors, many Confederate printers turned to regional and local textbook publishing. For example, two Greensboro, North Carolina, teachers, Richard Sterling and James Campbell, joined with a local printer, James W. Albright, to produce a number of books; a Macon, Georgia, press successfully printed the *Confederate Spelling Book;* and a New Orleans company issued the locally used speller, *Exercices de Cacographie.*

Considering the difficulties the Confederacy faced in procuring enough materials, qualified printers, and experienced textbook authors, problems were to be expected. *The World in Miniature,* a geography textbook, appeared so quickly after the first wave of secessions that four eventual Confederate states were listed as in the Union. The *Dixie Primer for the Little Folks,* printed in Raleigh by Branson and Farrar, also suffered from hasty production; like many books, its pages were off-center and its ink barely decipherable. Several others—such as *The Confederate Primer, The Southern Confederacy Arithmetic,* and the *Geographical Reader for the Dixie Children*—brimmed over with the authors' arcane knowledge, such as mathematical formulas or obscure economic statistics, or were only revisions of long-popular Northern or even foreign texts.

Occasionally books were so obviously plagiarized that authors openly admitted they had "availed themselves of all the assistance they could obtain from the labors of their predecessors." The Reverend Robert Fleming of Thomasville, Georgia, in his reprint of a standard Noah Webster speller, simply added "Bible Readings on Domestic Slavery," and the author of *Smith's Revised English Grammar,* published in 1863, merely substituted Confederate for Northern names in its examples. The latter had sold over twenty thousand copies by March 1865. *A Complete Grammar of the French Language* was, in fact, merely a Confederate version of an Edinburgh imprint in its fifteenth edition. In short, as Charles W. Smythe admitted in his grammar text, "We are compelled to undertake these things at our own risk and under great disadvantages, and hope therefore to receive aid and encouragement from the friends of education."

Perceived as integral to the war effort, the books bristled with national purpose. The *Oral Catechism,* published as a denominational periodical for young children and the illiterate, was "admirably adapted to the Slave population, for whose benefit it was especially prepared." *The Confederate Spelling Book* defined a soldier as "a man who fights for his country." And, assuming victory, the *Southern Pictorial Primer* included Arizona and New Mexico among the Confederacy's territories. The Reverend George B. Taylor of Staunton, Virginia, was still at work on a "child's history of the war" as late as the spring of 1865. Charles E. Leverett's *Southern Confederacy Arithmetic* asked students to calculate the years between momentous dates in U.S. history and the firing on Fort Sumter, and the 1864 *Geography for Beginners* described the election of Abraham Lincoln as an "attempt to subjugate the Southern States by military occupation." Mathematical problems were particularly adaptable; one posed the problem that if the "United States commander in Fort Sumter had 2 lb. of bread per day for each soldier, for 10 days; but, by private dispatches, learning that his government would relieve him soon, he wishes to stave off surrender 15 days: to do that, what must be the daily allowance, say to 80 men?"

Confederate schoolbooks were often uninspired, borrowed, or heavily supplemented in their content. Moreover, textbook publishing persistently suffered from scanty supplies, a lack of widespread printing expertise, sometimes woeful and uninviting book designs, poor production quality, and formidable distribution problems. Nevertheless, Southern schoolbooks represented one of the Confederacy's most widespread and innovative adaptations to wartime conditions. And with defeat and deprivation, Southern schools had no choice but to continue using many of the outmoded textbooks well into the postwar years, in the end winning a victory of sorts for a regional school literature.

BIBLIOGRAPHY

Kennerly, Sarah Law. "Confederate Juvenile Imprints: Children's Books and Periodicals Published in the Confederate States of America, 1861–1865." Ph.D. diss., University of Michigan, 1956.

Parrish, T. Michael, and Robert M. Willingham, Jr., comps. *Confederate Imprints: A Bibliography of Southern Publications from Secession to Surrender.* Austin, Tex., and Katonah, N.Y., 1987.

Stillman, Rachel Bryan. "Education in the Confederate States of America, 1861–1865." Ph.D. diss., University of Illinois at Urbana-Champaign, 1972.

Weeks, Stephen B. *Confederate Text-Books: A Preliminary Bibliography.* Washington, D.C., 1900.

EDWARD D. C. CAMPBELL, JR.

TEXTILE INDUSTRY. The South's cotton textile industry was called upon to play an active role in the Confederacy's war mobilization. Although the states of the Confederacy did not build any new mills, many of those that existed at the outbreak of hostilities expanded production dramatically in order to meet the demand for war matériel.

When the Southern states seceded in 1860 and 1861, they contained 143 "cotton goods establishments." These mills represented 164,840 spindles and 4,013 looms. The vast majority of textile establishments were located in Georgia, North Carolina, South Carolina, and Alabama, and they relied upon water for their motive power. These mills became the primary suppliers for the Confederate Quartermaster Bureau.

For many Southern mill owners, the outbreak of war was a godsend: it meant that they would receive lucrative war contracts that would allow them to expand the Southern industrial base. They also hoped that the need for manufactures would encourage those uninterested in manufacturing to support such endeavors. Mill entrepreneurs eagerly sought government contracts for the production of uniforms, tents, blankets, and other cotton goods. Most mills produced only the cloth: material such as kerseys or osnaburgs. This material would then be farmed out to private or government-sponsored shops where a mixed work force of men and women would fashion the cloth into uniforms or blankets. In many ways, the Confederacy's wartime textile industry resembled a preindustrial cottage system: some factories could produce finished goods, and others were dependent on outside workers.

Textile managers found that the government was a voracious consumer of cotton and woolen goods. Initially, textile owners realized huge profits: government profit ceilings stood at 75 percent. But the government changed these generous terms in 1862: profit ceilings were lowered to 33⅓ percent and draft exemptions for workers were made contingent upon the factory's furnishing the government with a minimum of two-thirds of its output. These stringent controls enabled the Confederate government to attain a virtual monopoly on all textile products produced in the South.

Most of the Confederacy's textile factories were destroyed by retreating Southerners or invading Northerners. Only the establishments in the Augusta, Georgia, area remained relatively untouched, but many of them had deteriorated as a result of increased wartime demands. Nonetheless, those who had been the leaders in wartime textile manufacturing would reorganize and refurbish their companies. They would survive the unsettled financial conditions of the postwar South and would lay the groundwork for the expansion of the region's textile industry in the late 1870s and 1880s.

[*See also* Clothing; Uniforms.]

BIBLIOGRAPHY

Coulter, E. Merton. *The Confederate States of America, 1861–1865.* A History of the South, vol. 7. Baton Rouge, La., 1951.

DeCredico, Mary A. *Patriotism for Profit: Georgia's Urban Entrepreneurs and the Confederate War Effort.* Chapel Hill, N.C., 1990.

Goff, Richard. *Confederate Supply.* Durham, N.C., 1969.

MARY A. DECREDICO

THEATER. Despite often presenting abysmal material, performed by actors of widely varying abilities, in auditoriums threatened by both shortages and encroaching armies, the Confederate theater throughout the war remained a vibrant and popular facet of Southern culture. Though to some observers the productions were immoral, sordid entertainments, for others the very existence of Confederate theatrical arts was a defiant act of independence, evidence that Southern life continued unabated by war. "It strikes us impolitic in the military authorities," commented the *Southern Punch* in 1864, "to close the Theatre, for the reason it tells against at the North." It was more important that, as one wartime broadside proclaimed, "notwithstanding the many difficulties against which the Management have had to contend," the theater every night offered "brilliant and attractive programmes, diversified by choice selections from the most sterling productions of the Dramatic Repertory."

Behind the optimistic declarations, however, lurked numerous difficulties. The theaters, for example, no matter what they presented, attracted large and boisterous audiences. The demand for entertainment was so high, in fact, that theater managers often sacrificed quality in an effort to stage as many productions as possible. Soldiers on leave, civil servants, industrial workers, and an assortment of troublemakers all flocked to plays and musicales, filling the saloons and cheaper seats in the upper tiers and firing pistols, shouting, and otherwise offending the more refined ticket buyers below. The situation was severe enough that managers in their advertising assured their customers that "elite audiences" did indeed attend the theater. Perhaps no matter. Sources of amusement were so scarce, there were few alternatives. Besides, as Gen. Joseph E. Johnston remarked in 1863, "I never saw so many beautiful women together. I hardly saw the actors, and do not remember the play. It would have taken very good acting," he added, "to have held my eyes from that 'drama of fair women.' "

Still, conditions were bad enough that the "reading and reflective class" of Confederate society sometimes held its own productions. In Richmond in 1864, for example, Mrs. J. C. Ives presented a performance of *The Rivals* in her own home. Charity productions were also common: in Montgomery in 1862, enthusiastic amateurs presented Joseph Hodgson's *The Confederate Vivandiere; or, The Battle of Leesburg* as a benefit for the First Alabama Cavalry.

In the war's first years, theaters flourished in most Southern cities. Until its capture by Union forces in 1862, New Orleans was home to the most theaters; thereafter, Richmond was. The Confederate capital included the Broad Street, Metropolitan, and Varieties, but the most popular was the New Richmond—the only theater built in the South during the war. Even bigger than the New Richmond was Thalian Hall in Wilmington, North Carolina. Built in 1858 as a wing of the city hall, the theater housed nearly a thousand seats, a stage measuring forty-two by fifty-seven feet, and lighting provided by some two hundred gas burners. There were active theaters in Atlanta, Augusta, Macon, Memphis, Mobile, Montgomery, and Nashville. There were also a number of traveling stage companies, such as the enormously popular W. H. Crisp troupe—its male members all honorably discharged Confederate veterans—which plied the smaller towns and army camps.

Assembling a cast was never easy. As theater manager John Hill Hewitt admitted in 1861, too often "the best of the profession fled North, thinking it the safest ground to stand upon—for actors are cosmopolites and claim citizenship nowhere." Many male actors eventually had to flee the draft, and by 1864 women increasingly filled in for them. Other casts were simply overworked keeping up with the demand. Worse, as the *Southern Illustrated News* pointed out in 1864, the few performers available insisted that each "glitter in the firmament as a *star* of the first magnitude, before which all others must pale."

Some deserved such recognition. Ida Vernon, "the South's greatest star," after several unsuccessful attempts finally ran the blockade to reappear on the Confederate stage. Ella Wrenn, "the Mocking Bird of the South," was especially popular in Montgomery and Savannah. Both Jessie Clark and Cecilia Crisp were favorites in Mobile. Eloise Bridges, Edmond R. Dalton, Walter Keeble, Charles Morton, Richard D'Orsay Ogden, and Jennie Powell were well known throughout the South. The older, Irish-born divorcée Clementina DeBar was one of the Confederacy's most accomplished actors. Certainly as popular was Harry Macarthy, who presented his new song, "The Bonnie Blue Flag," at a Jackson, Mississippi, show in 1861.

Far too many productions were, as the *Southern Illustrated News* remarked, little more than "illegitimate and spectacular drama," too affected by poor acting, greedy theater managers, and declining public taste. Of the more than four hundred productions staged in Richmond during the war, more than sixty were supposedly new works. Most, with a few notable exceptions, were hardly worth the bother: the *Southern Illustrated News* and *Southern Punch* repeatedly agreed that more often than not "the dialogue is stupid, the incidents are stale, and the plot ridiculous." The public, however, sometimes disagreed. Capt. G. W. Alexander's *The Virginia Cavalier,* for example, was so atrocious that "literary gentlemen groaned inadvertently, and despondingly moved towards the door," yet it became the Confederacy's greatest stage success. James D. McCabe's *The Guerrillas* was "enthusiastically received" and a considerable commercial success. *Love's Ambuscade; or, The Sergeant's Stratagem* by J. J. Delchamps also did well, as did John Hill Hewitt's operetta *The Artist's Wife.* Hewitt was also known for his "blood and thunder" melodramas such as *Ben Bolt* and *The Courier; or, The Siege of Lexington.* William Gilmore Simms's *Benedict Arnold,* though never staged, did at least appear serially in the *Magnolia Weekly.*

Theater managers also presented familiar favorites. There were numerous productions of Shakespeare's work; the New Richmond Theater in particular frequently mounted productions of *Macbeth.* John Maddison Morton's farces such as *Slasher and Crasher* and *Box and Cox* were popular throughout the region. Audiences filled theaters to see "the criminal sensations" of William H. Ainsworth's *Jack Sheppard,* William Lemon Rede's *Sixteen String Jack, the Gallant Highwayman,* or Charles Selby's *The Devil in Paris.* Sir Walter Scott's *Mary Queen of Scots, Lady of the Lake,* and *Rob Roy* provided traditional, romantic fare. There were even operas. But with little funding and few musicians, *Daughter of the Regiment, Il Trovatore,* and *William Tell* were all produced without music.

Characterized as but a "brief candle," Confederate theater nevertheless stubbornly lasted until the end. The New Richmond Theater on April 1, 1865, presented a double bill, the next day closed as the Confederate army evacuated Richmond, and two days later reopened—with a special invitation extended to officers of the occupying army.

BIBLIOGRAPHY

"Civil War Theater." *Civil War History,* special issue 1 (September 1955): 204–304.

Dorman, James H. "Thespis in Dixie: Professional Theater in Confederate Richmond." *Virginia Cavalcade* 28 (Summer 1978): 4–13.

Harwell, Richard Barksdale. *Brief Candle: The Confederate Theatre.* Worcester, Mass., 1971.

Parrish, T. Michael, and Robert M. Willingham, Jr., comps. *Confederate Imprints: A Bibliography of Southern Publications from Secession to Surrender.* Austin, Tex., and Katonah, N.Y., 1987.

Rulfs, Donald J. "The Professional Theatre in Wilmington, 1858–1870." *North Carolina Historical Review* 28 (April 1951): 119–136.

EDWARD D. C. CAMPBELL, JR.

THIRTEENTH AMENDMENT. Drawing on the antislavery belief that slavery destroyed an inherent right to self-ownership, Republican members of Congress, in late 1863 and early 1864, introduced several bills to abolish slavery by constitutional amendment. The precise wording of those bills elicited an intense and protracted debate. Some argued that the amendment should specify only that slaves be freed from physical restraint; others said it should vest blacks with certain rights, including the right to own property, testify in court, and sign marriage contracts. Charles Sumner declared that the amendment should state that "all persons are equal before the law." In the end, after intense lobbying by President Abraham Lincoln, a final version passed the House of Representatives on January 31, 1865, by a vote of 119 to 56, two votes more than the necessary two-thirds. The proposed amendment read simply: "Neither slavery nor involuntary servitude, except as a punishment for crime whereof the party shall have been duly convicted, shall exist within the United States, or any place subject to their jurisdiction." Section 2 said that "Congress shall have power to enforce this article by appropriate legislation."

During the final months of the Civil War, most white Southerners recognized that slavery was doomed. Nevertheless, after the war, when the amendment was submitted for ratification to Southern states now under President Andrew Johnson's newly formed governments, some former Confederates worked to defeat the article. The question, they argued, was not whether chattel slavery was dead but whether Congress should be granted the power to intrude into the "domestic affairs" of a state. When the Mississippi legislature rejected the amendment by a vote of 45–25 in the fall of 1865, a writer for the *Jackson Clarion,* reflecting the views of other whites in the lower South, proclaimed that to adopt the amendment would be tantamount to surrendering "all of our rights as a State to the Federal Congress." He and others refused "to sharpen the sword" that would "sever the arteries of our political life." The Alabama legislature ratified the amendment, but only after declaring that its approval did not extend to the second section.

President Johnson, however, pressed the former Confederate states to ratify the amendment as one precondition for restoration to the Union, assuring them that an end to slavery meant essentially that freedmen and women should be at liberty to work and enjoy the fruits of their labor. With such assurances and the backing of the president, the amendment was ratified by three-fourths of the states on December 18, 1865.

In proposing the amendment, neither Congress nor the framers envisioned a radical change in the relationship between the states and the Federal government; nor did they seek to endow newly freed slaves with citizenship rights. Nevertheless, Article 13 was the first amendment designed to accomplish a national reform, the first to grant Congress power of execution, and the first of the Reconstruction era. During the next few years Congress passed several civil rights laws and the nation ratified two additional constitutional amendments—the Fourteenth Amendment (1868) granting citizenship rights to former slaves, and the Fifteenth Amendment (1870) extending the franchise to freedmen. Thus, the passage of the amendment ending slavery began a process that would fundamentally alter the legal position of blacks in the United States and increasingly shift the responsibility for the protection of former slaves to the Federal government.

BIBLIOGRAPHY

Belz, Herman. "The Constitution and Reconstruction." In *The Facts of Reconstruction: Essays in Honor of John Hope Franklin.* Edited by Eric Anderson and Alfred A. Moss, Jr. Baton Rouge, La., 1991.

Belz, Herman. *Emancipation and Equal Rights: Politics and Constitutionalism in the Civil War Era.* New York, 1978.

Berry, Mary Frances. *Military Necessity and Civil Rights Policy: Black Citizenship and the Constitution, 1861–1868.* Port Washington, N.Y., 1977.

Buchanan, G. Sidney. *The Quest for Freedom: A Legal History of the Thirteenth Amendment.* Houston, Tex., 1976.

Harris, William C. *Presidential Reconstruction in Mississippi.* Baton Rouge, La., 1967.

Malz, Earl M. *Civil Rights, the Constitution, and Congress, 1863–1869.* Lawrence, Kans., 1990.

LOREN SCHWENINGER

THOMAS, ALLEN (1830–1907), brigadier general and diplomat. Thomas, born December 14, 1830, in Howard County, Maryland, graduated from Princeton in 1850. He studied law, later practicing in Howard County before moving to Louisiana and becoming a planter.

At the beginning of the war, he organized an infantry battalion and was appointed major. It was later expanded into the Twenty-eighth Louisiana and Thomas became colonel on May 3, 1862. His unit served during the Vicksburg campaign, with particular gallantry at the Battle of Chickasaw Bluffs. After the siege and surrender of Vicksburg, he was paroled and given the task of collecting and helping reorganize the other parolees.

Appointed brigadier general on February 4, 1864, he was placed in command of a brigade of troops from Louisiana and assigned to Lt. Gen. Richard Taylor's department. When Maj. Gen. Camille J. Polignac returned to France, General Thomas was given command of his division. After the surrender, he was paroled at Natchitoches, Louisiana, on June 8, 1865.

He again became a planter at New Hope on the Mississippi River after the war. He was a presidential elector in 1872 and 1880 but declined a nomination for Congress. Thomas was a member of the board of supervisors of Louisiana State University and a professor of agriculture from 1882 to 1884. Following this, he was a coiner at the mint in New Orleans until moving to Florida in 1889. In January 1894, he was commissioned consul and later minister to Venezuela. Thomas returned to Florida in 1897 and then moved to Waveland, Mississippi. He died on December 3, 1907, and is buried at Donaldsonville, Louisiana.

BIBLIOGRAPHY

Dimitry, John. *Louisiana.* Vol. 10 of *Confederate Military History.* Edited by Clement A. Evans. Atlanta, Ga., 1899. Vol. 13 of extended ed. Wilmington, N.C., 1988.

Johnson, Allen, ed. *Dictionary of American Biography.* Vol. 9. New York, 1964.

Warner, Ezra J. *Generals in Gray: Lives of the Confederate Commanders.* Baton Rouge, La., 1970.

CHRIS CALKINS

THOMAS, BRYAN MOREL (1836–1905), brigadier general. Twenty-five-year-old Thomas was four years out of West Point and serving on the western frontier when his native state of Georgia seceded from the Union. When war seemed imminent in early April 1861, Thomas resigned from the U.S. Army to return South and offer his services to the Confederacy.

Initially commissioned a lieutenant to teach drill to raw recruits at Fort Gaines, Alabama, Thomas soon joined the staff of Brig. Gen. Jones Mitchell Withers. Thomas achieved the rank of major and remained on Withers's staff through the battles of Shiloh, Corinth, Munfordville, Perryville, Murfreesboro, and Chickamauga. His competence as a staff officer earned him promotion to colonel and the opportunity for field command in the spring of 1864. After briefly heading a reserve unit of Alabama cavalry, he became a brigadier general August 14, 1864. Thomas's brigade of Alabama infantry, mixed with Louisiana, Mississippi, and Tennessee batteries, participated in the Confederacy's last desperate battles at Spanish Fort, Fort Blakely, and Mobile. Thomas was captured at Mobile and imprisoned until late June 1865.

His life as a soldier ended, Thomas returned to Georgia to become a planter, deputy U.S. marshal, and school superintendent.

BIBLIOGRAPHY

Caldwell, A. B. "Thomas, Bryan Morel." In *Men of Mark in Georgia.* Vol. 3. Atlanta, 1908. Reprint, Spartanburg, S.C., 1974.

"General B. M. Thomas." *Confederate Veteran* 13, no. 9 (1905): 424–425.

LESLEY JILL GORDON-BURR

THOMAS, EDWARD LLOYD (1825–1898), brigadier general. Born in Clarke County, Georgia, March 23, 1825, Thomas graduated from Emory College in 1846 and enlisted as a private in a Georgia cavalry regiment for the Mexican War. In the Battle of Huemaretta, he captured the son of the ex-emperor who was a member of Santa Anna's staff. In recognition of the feat, the Georgia legislature adopted resolutions in 1848 commending Thomas for his gallantry. At the close of hostilities, Thomas was offered a commission in the regular army, which he declined. While in Mexico, Thomas also captured a sword that led to bitter feelings between Thomas and his immediate superior, Capt. George Thomas ("Tige") Anderson. On their return to Georgia, Anderson apparently represented the sword as his personal trophy of war. Intense acrimony resulted and a duel was threatened before mature judgment intervened. The pair subsequently became close friends.

At the start of the Civil War, Thomas recruited a regiment, which became the Thirty-fifth Georgia Infantry, with Thomas as its colonel. When the regiment marched onto the field at Seven Pines, it was, according to historian Joseph T. Derry, "armed with the old remodeled flint-lock guns, the very best that the majority of the Southern soldiers could procure; but when it came out it was provided with the very best arms of the enemy."

Thomas opened the Battle of Mechanicsville as a part of A. P. Hill's division. Though wounded in the engagement, he took part in the remaining battles of the Seven Days' campaign. When brigade commander Joseph R. Anderson was knocked unconscious by a blow to the forehead at Frayser's Farm, Thomas, as senior colonel, assumed command of the brigade.

He also participated in all the subsequent battles fought by the Army of Northern Virginia with the exception of Sharpsburg. During that engagement Thomas was on detached duty at Harpers Ferry supervising the removal of captured property. On November 1, 1862, he received his brigadier's commission, which was confirmed April 22, 1863.

Paroled at Appomattox, Thomas returned to his plantation where he lived quietly for twenty years. He returned to public life in 1885 when President Grover Cleveland appointed him to an office in the Land Department. In Cleveland's second administration Thomas was named agent to the Sac and Fox in the Oklahoma Territory, a post he resigned when William McKinley became president. Thereafter Thomas participated actively in veteran affairs until his death, March 8, 1898, at South McAlester in present-day Oklahoma. He was buried in Kiowa, Oklahoma.

BIBLIOGRAPHY

Compiled Military Service Records. Edward Lloyd Thomas. Microcopy M331, Roll 245. Record Group 109. National Archives, Washington, D.C.

Derry, Joseph T. *Georgia.* Vol. 6 of *Confederate Military History.* Edited by Clement A. Evans. Atlanta, 1899. Vol. 7 of extended ed. Wilmington, N.C., 1987.

"Gen. Edward L. Thomas." *Confederate Veteran* 6 (1989): 191. Reprint, Wilmington, N.C., 1985.

Jed Hotchkiss Papers. Library of Congress, Washington, D.C.

Warner, Ezra J. *Generals in Gray: Lives of the Confederate Commanders.* Baton Rouge, La., 1959.

LOWELL REIDENBAUGH

THOMAS, JAMES HOUSTON (1808–1876), congressman from Tennessee. Thomas was born in Iredell County, North Carolina, but moved with his parents at an early age to Columbia, Tennessee. Admitted to the bar in 1831, Thomas became James K. Polk's law partner, and they kept up a steady correspondence while Polk was in Washington. Like Polk, Thomas was an admirer of Andrew Jackson and became a leader in the Democratic party. He was elected district attorney general in 1836 and then served three terms in Congress—from 1847 to 1851 and from 1859 to 1861.

Thomas, addressing Congress on January 17, 1861, expressed a desire to remain in the Union if he could with dignity, but he chided the North for its aggressiveness toward the South and its institutions. "The Southern states have a common interest and a common destiny," he told House members, adding that Southerners would protect their interests, "peacefully if we can but forcibly if we must." The speech was printed and widely circulated in Tennessee and several Southern states.

Thomas supported Governor Isham G. Harris in bringing about Tennessee's secession and then was elected to the Provisional Congress from the Sixth District. His voting record was that of a strong Southern nationalist, but he did not play a major role in the Congress and returned to Columbia after one term. He disappointed some colleagues when he attempted to dissociate himself from the Confederate cause after the Federals took Nashville and middle Tennessee.

After his return to Columbia he lived in semiretirement until his death on August 4, 1876. He was buried at the St. John Cemetery, in the Ashwood Community, about six miles west of Columbia.

BIBLIOGRAPHY

Journal of the Congress of the Confederate States of America, 1861–1865. 7 vols. Washington, D.C., 1904–1905.

Thomas, James Houston. *Speech of Honorable James H. Thomas of Tennessee, in the House of Representatives, January 17, 1861.* Pamphlet. Washington, D.C., 1861.

Turner, William Bruce. *History of Maury County, Tennessee.* Nashville, Tenn., 1955.

Warner, Ezra J., and W. Buck Yearns. *Biographical Register of the Confederate Congress.* Baton Rouge, La., 1975.

Weaver, Herbert, and Paul Bergeron. *Correspondence of James K. Polk.* 2 vols. Nashville, Tenn., 1969–1972.

ROBERT E. CORLEW

THOMAS, JOHN J. (1813–1895?), congressman from Kentucky. Thomas served only two months in the Confederate Congress and played an insignificant role in its proceedings. He sat on no committees. Thomas best represents Kentucky's small planters who determined to side with the South for reasons of class and race.

Born in Albemarle, Virginia, Thomas was a distant relative of Thomas Jefferson and, according to one source, graduated from the University of Virginia. In the 1820s Thomas settled in Christian County, Kentucky, where he became a surveyor and planter. During the Polk administration Thomas worked as a clerk in the U.S. Post Office Department. In 1851 he served one term in the Kentucky legislature before returning to his farm in Christian County.

In December 1861, Thomas was appointed by the governor and executive council of Kentucky's Confederate government to the Provisional Congress from the Second District. He was the largest slaveholder among Kentucky's Confederate congressional delegation; in 1860 he owned fifty slaves as well as real estate valued at $70,000. During his short tenure in Congress, Thomas supported President Jefferson Davis but attempted to deny him authority over home guard units along the Kentucky-Tennessee frontier. Electing not to run for a seat in the First Congress, Thomas served on the staff of Gen. John Stuart Williams for the duration of the war. He saw service in the Department of East Tennessee and in the western Virginia campaigns.

After Appomattox, Thomas worked as a tobacco broker in Clarksville, Tennessee, and as a tobacco inspector in New York City. In 1878 he settled in Paducah, Kentucky, as a tobacco dealer. Thomas's place and date of death remain unknown, though historians suspect it occurred in Camden, Arkansas, in 1895.

BIBLIOGRAPHY

Quisenberry, A. C. "The Alleged Secession of Kentucky." *Register of the Kentucky State Historical Society* 15 (1917): 15–32.

Wakelyn, Jon L. *Biographical Dictionary of the Confederacy.* Edited by Frank E. Vandiver. Westport, Conn., 1977.

Warner, Ezra J., and W. Buck Yearns. *Biographical Register of the Confederate Congress.* Baton Rouge, La., 1975.

JOHN DAVID SMITH

THOMAS, WILLIAM HOLLAND (1805–1893), colonel. A western North Carolina merchant, businessman, and advocate for the local Cherokee Indians, Thomas served as a Whig politician in the state senate (1848–1861) and in that state's secession convention.

Loyalty to his region and to the Indians prompted Thomas to assume a military career at the age of fifty-six. A civilian volunteer, he raised a company of one hundred Cherokees and twelve white men who entered the Confederate army on April 9, 1862. Stationed near Knoxville at Strawberry Plains, Tennessee, Thomas used his Indians and Highlanders to guard the railroads and mountain passes against a Union invasion and to defend the Confederates against Unionist natives. He accepted more volunteers until in September 1862, by order of Gen. John P. McCown, Thomas was named colonel of a legion including two infantry companies of Cherokees. They saw action at Baptist Gap, Tennessee (September 13–15, 1862); at Sevierville, Tennessee (November 1863); and at Deep Creek, North Carolina (February 1864). But Thomas's divided command functioned primarily as a home guard in eastern Tennessee and western North Carolina.

Thomas was no favorite of Governor Zebulon Vance or Gen. Alfred Eugene Jackson. Both men thought he was useless as a military commander and Vance considered him a political rival. Thomas was therefore court-martialed three times for taking in deserters, who were often Indians, but Jefferson Davis pardoned him. Thomas surrendered at Waynesville on May 7, 1865. Broken in health and reduced in fortune, Thomas never recovered from the war. He died in a mental hospital at Morganton, North Carolina.

BIBLIOGRAPHY

Crow, Vernon H. *Storm in the Mountains: Thomas' Confederate Legion of Cherokee Indians and Mountaineers.* Cherokee, N.C., 1982.

Finger, John R. *The Eastern Band of Cherokees, 1819–1900.* Knoxville, Tenn., 1984.

Godbold, E. Stanly, Jr., and Mattie U. Russell. *Confederate Colonel and Cherokee Chief: The Life of William Holland Thomas.* Knoxville, Tenn., 1990.

Inscoe, John C. *Mountain Masters, Slavery, and the Sectional Crisis in Western North Carolina.* Knoxville, Tenn., 1989.

E. Stanly Godbold, Jr.

THOMASON, HUGH FRENCH (1826–1893), congressman from Arkansas. Thomason was born in Tennessee on February 22, 1826. His family moved to Arkansas in 1829 and settled in the state's northwest. Prior to the Civil War Thomason lived in Van Buren, Arkansas, where he was an attorney and an active politician. He was aligned politically with the Know-Nothing party in the 1850s and in 1860 was a Unionist. In March 1861 Thomason attended the state secession convention, where he helped prevent secession during the first session. With other Unionists, however, he converted to secession after the firing on Fort Sumter, and he signed the ordinance of secession when the convention reconvened in May 1861.

The convention elected Thomason to the Provisional Congress. There he was an active member, helping to develop the new government's tax laws, create a judiciary, and formulate Indian treaties. He vigorously supported the army, introducing a measure to arm troops with pikes, lances, spears, and shotguns. On economic measures he generally opposed strengthening the power of the central government, however. In November 1861, he ran for reelection to the First Congress, but was defeated by Felix I. Batson in a campaign that focused on Thomason's original Unionism. He then returned to Arkansas.

Following the war Thomason practiced law, supported railroad development, and was active in Democratic politics. He participated in the overthrow of Republican rule in the state in 1874. He died at Van Buren on July 30, 1893.

BIBLIOGRAPHY

Shinn, J. L. *Pioneers and Makers of Arkansas.* Washington, D.C., 1908.

Warner, Ezra J., and W. Buck Yearns. *Biographical Register of the Confederate Congress.* Baton Rouge, La., 1975.

Carl H. Moneyhon

THOMPSON, JACOB (1810–1885), U. S. congressman, U.S. secretary of the interior, Confederate colonel, and agent for the Confederacy. Born and raised in North Carolina, Jacob Thompson graduated from the University of North Carolina in 1831 and was admitted to the bar in 1835. He moved to Mississippi where he married well, practiced law, became a planter, and was politically active. A Democrat, he served six terms (1839–1851) in the U.S. House of Representatives but lost a bid to become U.S. senator from Mississippi in 1855. Active in national party politics, Thompson supported Franklin Pierce in 1852 and worked for the nomination and election of James Buchanan in 1856. Buchanan made Thompson secretary of the interior, and he was an energetic department head.

With regard to the intensifying sectional controversy, Thompson insisted that Southern grievances were legitimate. The central issue in his view was Northern unwillingness to vouchsafe "the rights of Southern men in their slave property." Although defending secession as an inherent right of the states, he was not eager to see the South withdraw from the Union and took a cooperationist stance on the matter. Following Abraham Lincoln's election in November 1860, Thompson hoped that the Buchanan administration could preserve the peace in the crucial months before Lincoln's inauguration and thereby provide an opportunity for the success of compromise efforts that were underway within and without Congress. During cabinet sessions, Thompson counseled restraint in dealing with the secessionists and, if necessary, acceptance of disunion. While still a member of the cabinet and with the acquiescence of the president, Thompson visited the legislature of North Carolina as a formal representative of Mississippi to discuss a cooperationist strategy in the event of drastic provocation on the part of the Federal government. Upon learning of the presidential decision that dispatched *Star of the West* with reinforcements and supplies for Fort Sumter, Thompson resigned his cabinet post.

During the early years of the war, Thompson served with the Confederate army in Tennessee and Mississippi and was also a member of the Mississippi legislature. He accepted an assignment from Jefferson Davis in the spring of 1864 to head a mission to Canada for the purpose of exploiting and encouraging discontent and peace sentiment throughout the North. To finance the undertaking, Davis authorized Thompson to spend as much as $1 million at his own discretion. Clement C. Clay of Alabama agreed to serve with Thompson, and they traveled to Wilmington, North Carolina, where they slipped through the blockade to Bermuda and took passage to Halifax, Nova Scotia. Thompson's usual base of operations while in Canada was Toronto, and Clay operated from St. Catharines, Ontario. Thompson coordinated activities with Clay and had the services of agents sent from the Confederacy. Thompson also enlisted the cooperation of Confederate soldiers who had escaped from Northern prisons, Southerners residing in Canada, and sympathetic Northerners.

He invested considerable time and money in efforts to wreak havoc in the North. He joined with leaders of the Order of the Sons of Liberty during the summer of 1864 in plotting armed uprisings timed to coincide with the return of Clement L. Vallandigham to Ohio from exile and with the Democratic National Convention at Chicago. These plots collapsed amid the hesitation, indecision, and disorganization of the Sons of Liberty. In another scheme, Thompson helped lay plans for armed insurrections in Chicago and New York City on election day, November 8, 1864. The work of spies brought the arrest of key leaders in Chicago, and rumors of trouble in New York prompted the Federal government to send ten thousand soldiers to patrol the city during the canvass. After the troops withdrew, the conspirators, with Thompson's sanction, undertook a plan to burn the city by simultaneously setting fires in several buildings. The resulting blazes created panic but produced little property damage. Various schemes forcibly to release Confederate soldiers held as prisoners of war at Camp Douglas and Johnson's Island also came to naught.

Not all the plans Thompson laid involved violence. He contributed money to the political campaign of the Democratic candidate for governor of Illinois. He gave financial backing to a feeble effort to undermine the Federal currency by converting greenbacks to gold and shipping the gold to England where it was converted to sterling bills of exchange with which to purchase more U.S. gold for export to England. Through repeating the process, the conspirators managed to send $2 million in gold out of the country before ending the operation out of fear of detection and arrest. Thompson also worked to obtain the release of fellow conspirators in the custody of either Canadian or U.S. authorities.

As the mission to Canada drew to a close, Thompson recognized that his efforts had been largely unsuccessful. He attributed his failures to the frustration of his plans by Federal spies who managed to obtain crucial information and to arrest important leaders. He also cited the presence of large numbers of Federal troops who made organization of disaffected citizens impossible. Thompson did not realize that his failures were also due to a misreading of Northern public opinion. Contrary to his assumptions, Northerners who were weary of the war and unhappy with the Lincoln administration were not necessarily Confederate sympathizers or willing to aid in the dismemberment of the Union. On the other hand, Thompson rightly contended that his mission successfully brought consternation and fear in the North.

The assignment ended when Edwin Gray Lee reached Canada early in 1865 at the behest of the Confederate government to relieve Thompson. As instructed, Thompson gave some of the funds entrusted to him to Lee and deposited about $400,000 to the credit of the Confederacy in a British financial institution. Prior to departing Canada for Europe, he learned of President Andrew Johnson's proclamation of May 2, 1865, naming Thompson as one of the conspirators in the assassination of Lincoln. The charge was utterly false, as Thompson declared in a public letter sent to a New York newspaper. He remained out of the United States until 1869 when he returned only to find his property in northern Mississippi devastated. Shunning politics, he went into business in Memphis, Tennessee, and was residing there at the time of his death.

BIBLIOGRAPHY

Kinchen, Oscar A. *Confederate Operations in Canada and the North.* North Quincy, Mass., 1970.

Nelson, Larry E. *Bullets, Ballots, and Rhetoric: Confederate Policy for the Presidential Election of 1864.* University, Ala., 1980.

Robbins, Peggy. "The Greatest Scoundrel." *Civil War Times Illustrated* 31, no. 5 (November–December 1992): 54–59, 89–90.

LARRY E. NELSON

TIBBS, WILLIAM HENRY (1816–1906), congressman from Tennessee. Tibbs was born in 1816 in Appomatox, Virginia, and moved with his parents to Smith County, Tennessee, in 1819. As a young adult, he settled in Cleveland (Bradley County) and engaged in business and political affairs. Strongly interested in education, he was instrumental in the formation of an academy for women.

His primary interest was politics, and he became a leader in the formation of the Whig party in Bradley County. In 1853, he served in the state house of representatives, but lost a race in 1859 for the state senate when election results were challenged. A strong secessionist, he won a seat in the Confederate Congress from the Third District in 1861.

As a congressman, Tibbs was a firm nationalist and supporter of President Jefferson Davis. He urged that men from the ages of seventeen to fifty-five be drafted for military service and complained that conscription was not enforced properly in Tennessee. He was greatly alarmed when the Federals took Forts Donelson and Henry, and he joined with other congressmen in the creation of a committee to investigate "the disasters."

After the Federals tightened their grip on Tennessee, Tibbs fled to Georgia and by 1866 had established himself in several business enterprises, including hotel management. He also bought land and farmed for the next forty years. A newspaper account published in Dalton shortly before his death described him as the operator of "a large cattle ranch that is among the most valuable properties in . . . the state."

BIBLIOGRAPHY

Journal of the Congress of the Confederate States of America, 1861–1865. 7 vols. Washington, D.C., 1904–1905.

Lillard, Roy G. *Bradley County, Tennessee.* Memphis, Tenn., 1980.

McBride, Robert, and Dan M. Robison. *Biographical Directory of the Tennessee General Assembly.* Vol. 1. Nashville, Tenn., 1975.

Report of the Select Committee to Whom Was Referred the Claims of William H. Tibbs to a Seat in the Senate from the Eighth Senatorial District. Pamphlet. Nashville, Tenn., 1859.

Warner, Ezra J., and W. Buck Yearns. *Biographical Register of the Confederate Congress.* Baton Rouge, La., 1975.

Robert E. Corlew

TIFT BROTHERS. Natives of Connecticut, Confederate shipbuilders Asa Forsythe Tift (1812–1889) and Nelson Tift (1810–1891) moved south in their youth. Asa ultimately settled in Key West, Florida, where he engaged in warehousing, wrecking, and other maritime enterprises, and Nelson settled in southwestern Georgia, where he established the town of Albany and pursued shipping, planting, and other business and political interests.

When the Civil War broke out both brothers espoused the Southern cause. In the summer of 1861 Nelson devised a novel ironclad warship design whereby all of the vessel's surfaces were either flat or angular, thus eliminating intricately curved hull frames and the need for skilled shipwrights to construct them. Offering to build the vessel as agents of the Navy Department with no compensation other than travel expenses, the Tifts quickly gained approval from Navy Secretary Stephen R. Mallory and left for New Orleans to construct the unorthodox craft. In mid-October the brothers laid the keel of the formidable 260-foot *Mississippi,* launching the Confederacy's most ambitious attempt to build a man-of-war. Following the April 1862 loss of New Orleans and the resulting destruction of the unfinished *Mississippi,* the Tifts moved to Savannah where they successfully converted the blockade runner *Fingal* into the ironclad *Atlanta.*

Afterward the Tifts returned to Albany by order of the Navy Department where they erected a slaughterhouse, bakery, barrel factory, tannery, and extensive grain mills. These works provided provisions to the army and Federal prisoners at Andersonville as well as the navy. On October 1, 1864, Nelson was appointed assistant paymaster in the Confederate navy.

After the war Asa returned to his business interests in Key West where he died February 7, 1889. Nelson remained in Albany and became one of the dominant forces in the development of the region. He died November 21, 1891.

BIBLIOGRAPHY

Coleman, Kenneth, and Charles S. Gurr, eds. *Dictionary of Georgia Biography.* Vol. 2. Athens, Ga., 1983.

Dufour, Charles L. *The Night the War Was Lost.* Garden City, N.Y., 1960.

Jones, Virgil Carrington. *The River War.* Vol. 2 of *The Civil War at Sea.* New York, 1961. Reprint, Wilmington, N.C., 1990.

Still, William N. *Confederate Shipbuilding.* 2d ed. Columbia, S.C., 1987.

Still, William N. *Iron Afloat: The Story of the Confederate Armorclads.* 2d ed. Columbia, S.C., 1985.

A. Robert Holcombe, Jr.

TILGHMAN, LLOYD (1816–1863), brigadier general. Tilghman was born on January 18, 1816, at Rich Neck Manor, Maryland, and graduated from the U.S. Military Academy in 1836. He resigned from the army that same year and became a railroad construction engineer, working throughout the South in that field and settling in Kentucky in 1852. He interrupted his career to serve in the Mexican War with the Maryland and District of Columbia battalion and on the staff of Gen. David E. Twiggs.

Tilghman entered the Confederate army in 1861 and was assigned duty as inspector of Forts Henry and Donelson. He was later appointed commander of Fort Henry, and as an engineer, reported on its poor location. But he decided to defend it against Ulysses S. Grant's army because the construction of a fort at a better location (Fort Heiman) had scarcely begun. When Fort Henry was attacked by Commodore Andrew H. Foote's ironclad gunboats, Tilghman realized that it could not withstand the bombardment and dispatched the majority of his forces to Fort Donelson before Grant could arrive and invest the work. Staying with the rear guard, Tilghman fought until the heavy guns were dismounted and then surrendered the fort to Commodore Foote. The Union held him prisoner until exchanging him in the fall of 1862.

Tilghman assumed command of the First Brigade of W. W. Loring's division in Earl Van Dorn's army fighting at Corinth, Mississippi. During the Confederate retreat from Holly Springs to Grenada, Tilghman commanded the rear guard. On May 16, 1863, while he was directing artillery during the Battle of Baker's Creek, a shell fragment hit and killed him. He is buried in Woodlawn Cemetery in New York.

Tilghman was personally brave, but proved indecisive and dilatory when preparing the defense of Fort Henry. His procrastination contributed to an easy Union victory at the fort and the Confederate loss of northern Tennessee.

BIBLIOGRAPHY

Cooling, Benjamin Franklin. *Forts Henry and Donelson: The Key to the Confederate Heartland.* Knoxville, Tenn., 1987.

Manakee, Harold R. *Maryland in the Civil War.* Baltimore, 1961.

Warner, Ezra J. *Generals in Gray: Lives of the Confederate Commanders.* Baton Rouge, La., 1959.

ROY R. STEPHENSON

TIMROD, HENRY (1828–1867), poet.

TIMROD, HENRY (1828–1867), poet. Son of a bookbinder and minor poet, Timrod was born December 8, 1828. He was educated in Charleston and at the University of Georgia (1845–1846) and read law (1847–1849) with James L. Petigru. He began contributing verse to Charleston newspapers in 1846 and to Southern magazines in 1849. In 1859, *Poems,* the only collection published during his lifetime, appeared.

At the beginning of the war, then, Timrod was known chiefly for his conventional lyrics on love and nature and for his essays on poetry and culture published in periodicals. His reputation was mostly local and southeastern. The publication in 1861 of "Ethnogenesis" and "The Cotton Boll," however, soon established him as the poet of the Confederacy. Irregular odes in a traditional sense, these laureatelike lyrics celebrate the qualities of the new nation and prophesy its future. In spite of his literary success, his poor health, and his earlier opposition to secession, he volunteered for military service three times in 1862 and 1863, but his tubercular condition could not sustain active duty. Consequently, he devoted himself to journalism and to the composition of such patriotic poems as "A Cry to Arms," "Carolina," "Charleston," and "Carmen Triumphale," thereby consolidating his position as unofficial laureate of the Confederacy. Other pieces of the same period like "Christmas," "Spring," "The Unknown Dead," and, later, the memorial "Ode" of 1866 confirmed his stature as a significant American lyricist.

Timrod served irregularly in editorial posts for Charleston and Columbia newspapers during the war and afterward. Concurrently, he became increasingly poverty-stricken, and his precarious health deteriorated steadily. He died on October 7, 1867, before he could fully realize the promise evident in his poetry and criticism.

BIBLIOGRAPHY

Hayne, Paul H., ed. *Poems of Henry Timrod.* New York, 1872.

Hubbell, Jay B., ed. *The Last Years of Henry Timrod, 1864–1867.* Durham, N.C., 1941.

Parks, Edd Winfield. *Henry Timrod.* New York, 1964.

Parks, Edd Winfield, ed. *The Essays of Henry Timrod.* Athens, Ga., 1942.

Parks, Edd Winfield, and Aileen Wells, eds. *The Collected Poems of Henry Timrod: A Variorum Edition.* Athens, Ga., 1965.

RAYBURN S. MOORE

TISHOMINGO CREEK, MISSISSIPPI. *See* Brice's Cross Roads, Mississippi.

TOBACCO. Native Americans cultivated tobacco in North America before the first English settlers arrived in Jamestown in 1607. The Indians believed that native tobacco had both religious and medicinal importance. Its use, for example, had great ritual significance for the Indians in the Chesapeake region. Native Americans often smoked tobacco in a pipe to cement a peace accord.

Colonists at Jamestown were the first Europeans on the North American mainland to cultivate tobacco. As early as 1610 John Rolfe shipped a cargo to England for sale. But the naturally occurring tobacco plant in the Chesapeake region *(Nicotiana rustica)* was considered too bitter and harsh, and in 1611 Rolfe obtained seeds of the milder *Nicotiana tabacum* from the Spanish West Indies, Venezuela, and Trinidad for the Jamestown colonists. Thereafter, tobacco production increased rapidly in the Chesapeake Bay area, soon spreading to Maryland. Production continued to increase throughout the colonial period and by the middle of the eighteenth century, Maryland and Virginia were shipping nearly 70 million pounds of tobacco a year to Britain.

Some colonial aristocrats in both Britain and the American colonies believed that tobacco smoking was evil and hazardous to the health. This had little effect in halting the spread of the practice. By the eve of the Revolutionary War, tobacco had become the leading cash crop produced by all the colonies, North and South. Exports rose to over 100 million pounds a year, constituting half of all colonial export trade with Britain.

The methods used for cultivating and curing tobacco have changed over time and varied from region to region. Initially, planters in the Chesapeake region cured tobacco by gathering the plant on the ground and letting the sun dry the leaves, but sun-curing was soon given up in favor of a technique known as air-curing. Tobacco workers gathered leaves in parcels called "hands" and placed them over polls five feet in length. Then the hands were hung inside an open barn to complete the curing process. When fully dried, the tobacco was packed into large containers called hogsheads for shipping. Air-curing, popular in the Piedmont and tidewater regions until the early nineteenth century, resulted in a milder-tasting leaf.

Methods of curing tobacco by heat were known in the 1700s, but the process did not become popular until the early nineteenth century. In the 1820s the bright tobacco leaves of North Carolina and eastern Virginia, and later Kentucky and middle Tennessee, were cured by using enclosed smoking-sawdust fires to dry the tobacco hung in small barns. Although the modern method of flu-curing tobacco using charcoal heat was invented in 1839 in North Carolina, this method was not widely used until after the Civil War.

Both tobacco cultivation and manufacturing are labor-intensive activities. Initially, the Virginia Company of London used white indentured servants to harvest the crop, but they were soon replaced by African slaves. The presence of a large slave population engaged in the cultivation and curing of tobacco tied the growth of slavery to the rise of the plantation system. By 1860, 350,000 slaves were cultivating tobacco. It was, however, an exploitive crop that quickly exhausted the soil, requiring constant clearing of new land. The system also worked against the establishment of urban industrial centers in the colonial and antebellum South.

Throughout the colonial period commercial production of tobacco had centered in Northern port cities, but by the antebellum period, as a result of a surplus of slave labor and the great supply of raw material, commercial manufacturing shifted to the tobacco-growing regions in the South. Virginia dominated the industry with factories located at Richmond, Petersburg, Lynchburg, and Danville, and the border states of Kentucky, Tennessee, and Missouri also became tobacco-manufacturing centers.

The differing ways of consuming tobacco have often mirrored larger cultural trends. Tobacco has been smoked in pipes, cigars, and cigarettes, and also chewed and taken as snuff. Pipe smoking was the most prevalent form of tobacco consumption in the colonial period, although in the late 1700s taking snuff became popular among the elite who were emulating the European aristocracies. Chewing was distinctly American and became popular on the expanding frontier. After the Mexican War cigar smoking became the fad, but during the Civil War people returned to pipes and began rolling cigarettes for the first time.

As in so many other areas of Southern life, the Civil War seriously disrupted the South's tobacco growing and manufacturing. The tobacco-rich states of Virginia, North Carolina, and Tennessee sided with the Confederacy; the success of their crop rose and fell with that of the rebel nation. The tobacco-producing border states of Missouri, Kentucky, and Maryland fell early to Union control. Under the pressure of war, tobacco manufacturing, located in the South throughout the antebellum period, shifted quickly to the North. New York city became the North's tobacco-manufacturing center, servicing the area once dominated by Virginia tobacco planters. Like New York, Louisville also profited by the war's disruption of Southern market towns, becoming the center of tobacco trade in the West.

Confederate policy and military campaigns in the heartland of the South's tobacco regions devastated Southern tobacco planting and manufacturing. In an attempt to encourage the planting of foodstuffs, the Confederate Congress in March 1862 passed a joint resolution recommending that Confederate states refrain from planting tobacco. Planters often ignored Congress's suggestions, however. The Virginia Assembly also attempted to limit tobacco growing with a law passed in March 1863, and renewed planting restrictions again in February 1864. Other tobacco-growing states passed similar legislation during the war. In addition, local newspapers such as the *Edgefield Advertiser* of South Carolina also exhorted their readers to switch from the planting of tobacco to desperately needed foodstuffs.

Union control of the Mississippi from mid-1863, combined with the naval blockade, restricted the export and manufacturing of tobacco products, as did the shift of factories to manufacturing war matériel. In Richmond, after the First Battle of Manassas, several tobacco warehouses were converted into prisons for Union soldiers. The tobacco-rich county of Louisa, Virginia, saw the kind of physical destruction typical of regions exposed to intense military activity. Intermittent Union raids into the county and one of the war's largest cavalry battles at Trevillian's Depot destroyed not only the crops and livestock but also the county's infrastructure. Every Confederate and border state saw a decline in tobacco production in the 1860s.

The tobacco town of Danville, Virginia, however, took advantage of the vicissitudes of war. In the late 1850s its tobacco industry was in decline, and the community was reluctant to answer the call to arms in 1861. Nevertheless, Danville prospered during the war. Located safely behind enemy lines along a major railroad to Richmond, Danville became a lucrative place for the activities of merchants and manufacturers. Through their investments, the town and the surrounding county saw a revival in the tobacco industry. As a result of its returning prosperity, Danville citizens opposed attempts by Confederate soldiers to destroy the rail connection with Richmond in order to stop the Union advance. Local businessmen also looked favorable upon the Union takeover on the ground that it would bring peace and stability to the region.

While the war made it difficult for the public to obtain tobacco, both Confederate and Union soldiers found it plentiful. Since much of the fighting took place in the tobacco-rich regions of the South, soldiers often helped themselves. For years the U.S. Navy had supplied its sailors with tobacco rations. In February 1864 the Confederate government followed suit and included tobacco as part of the army's rations. Often, in the quiet moments between battle, Confederate and Union soldiers would exchange goods. The traditional swap was Northern coffee for Southern tobacco. Tobacco habits also revealed class distinctions in the South. Confederate officers did not receive the tobacco rations granted to soldiers. Nevertheless, Confederate officers favored the more fashionable smoking of cigars.

Tobacco had a profound influence on the history of the South. Early cultivation brought prosperity and helped ensure the economic survival of the colonies. The development of the tobacco plantation system, however, helped establish slavery in the South to a degree not found in the North. Because tobacco cultivation quickly wore out the soil, planters were constantly clearing new land, leading to the expansion of slavery and tobacco growing. The slave plantation system also worked to slow urban industrial development in the South. Moreover, the early opponents of tobacco use have been proven correct in their argument that it is hazardous to one's health. Thus, at best, tobacco has been a mixed blessing for the South.

BIBLIOGRAPHY

Gates, Paul. *Agriculture and the Civil War.* New York, 1965.

Gray, Lewis Cecil. *History of Agriculture in the United States to 1860.* 2 vols. New York, 1941.

Hilliard, Sam Bowers. *Atlas of Antebellum Southern Agriculture.* Baton Rouge, La., 1984.

Kulikoff, Allen. *Tobacco and Slaves: The Development of Southern Cultures in the Chesapeake, 1680–1800.* Chapel Hill, N.C., 1986.

Rachleff, Peter J. *Black Labor in the South: Richmond, Virginia, 1865–1890.* Philadelphia, 1984.

Robert, John C. *The Story of Tobacco in America.* Chapel Hill, N.C., 1967.

Seigel, Frederick F. *The Roots of Southern Distinctiveness: Tobacco and Society in Danville, Virginia, 1780–1865.* Knoxville, Tenn., 1982.

Shifflett, Crandall A. *Patronage and Poverty in the Tobacco South: Louisa County, Virginia, 1860–1890.* Knoxville, Tenn., 1982.

ORVILLE VERNON BURTON and HENRY KAMERLING

TODD, GEORGE (1838?–1864), Missouri guerrilla. According to legend, George Todd escaped to Canada after killing a man in his native Scotland. His family moved to Independence, Missouri, shortly before the Civil War, where he worked as a bridge mason for his father, a contractor. He was round-faced, taciturn, and by reputation sullen and sadistic. Although his motivations for doing so are unclear, Todd, by the end of 1861, had joined with the already notorious William Clarke Quantrill, for whom he served as a chief lieutenant. Quantrill's band ravaged the land on both sides of the Kansas-Missouri border, in the vicinity of Kansas City. On October 21, 1863, Todd was one of the approximately 450 guerrillas under Quantrill who sacked and burned the Union stronghold of Lawrence, Kansas, killing about 150 unarmed civilian men and boys.

Todd remained with Quantrill longer than did most of the other guerrillas, who eagerly set up on their own, but he finally left Quantrill in the summer of 1864 to lead his own band. At times he joined his men to other commands, including those led by John Thrailkill and William ("Bloody Bill") Anderson. In October 1864, during the big and spectacularly unsuccessful Confederate raid up into Missouri, Todd's men served as scouts for Generals Sterling Price and Joseph O. Shelby. After the Confederate army fled southward, Todd's band remained isolated in northern Missouri, where the citizens were beginning to turn their backs on what increasingly appeared to be a lost cause. On October 21, 1864, Todd was shot through the neck by a Union sniper and died within an hour.

BIBLIOGRAPHY

Brownlee, Richard S. *Gray Ghosts of the Confederacy: Guerrilla Warfare in the West, 1861–1865.* Baton Rouge, La., 1958.

Castel, Albert. *William Clarke Quantrill: His Life and Times.* New York, 1962.

Connelley, William Elsey. *Quantrill and the Border Wars.* Cedar Rapids, Iowa, 1909. Reprint, New York, 1956.

Fellman, Michael. *Inside War: The Guerrilla Conflict in Missouri during the American Civil War.* New York, 1989.

MICHAEL FELLMAN

TOMBS, JAMES H. (1800–1900), naval engineer and torpedo expert. Born in Florida, Tombs declined appointment as third assistant engineer in the U.S. Navy and accepted the same position in the Confederate States Navy on June 21, 1861. He served on CSS *Jackson* and CSS *McRae* at New Orleans in 1861 and 1862, and on board the ironclad CSS *Louisiana* at Forts Jackson and St. Philip, where he was captured on April 28, 1862. He was confined at Fort Warren until exchanged August 5. Tombs then served aboard the ironclad CSS *Chicora* and the converted blockade runner CSS *Juno* on the Charleston station. There he was promoted to second assistant engineer on September 5, 1862, and first assistant engineer on August 15, 1863.

On September 18, 1863, Tombs volunteered for duty as engineer of the special service detachment under Lt. William T. Glassell, with orders to place mines and attack blockaders with explosive-armed rowboats. Later he served as engineer of the experimental steam torpedo boat *David.* On October 5, 1863, *David* attacked the ironclad USS *New*

Ironsides. The torpedo explosion partially flooded *David*, and the crew abandoned ship. When *David* did not sink, Tombs and another man climbed back aboard and guided it to port. On June 2, 1864, he was nominated for promotion "for gallant and meritorious conduct" to chief engineer in the Provisional Navy, effective from the date of the exploit. He was then given command of *David*. On March 6, 1864, *David* attacked USS *Memphis;* on March 14 it unsuccessfully attacked the frigate *Wabash*. Afterwards Tombs was assigned to special torpedo service in the Savannah Squadron, where he mined approaches to the city in advance of William Tecumseh Sherman's troops. He was paroled May 16, 1865, at Tallahassee, Florida.

BIBLIOGRAPHY

Navy Department. *Register of Officers of the Confederate States Navy, 1861–1865*. Washington, D.C., 1931.

Perry, Milton F. *Infernal Machines: The Story of Confederate Submarine and Mine Warfare*. Baton Rouge, La., 1965.

KEVIN J. FOSTER

TOMPKINS, SALLY L. (1833–1916), captain and nurse. On November 9, 1833, Sally Tompkins was born at Poplar Grove in Matthews County, Virginia, and lived in Richmond from the age of five. When troops from the Battle of First Manassas overwhelmed the city's medical facilities, President Jefferson Davis appealed to the citizens to establish private hospitals.

Responding to his call, Tompkins received permission from Judge John Robertson to utilize his home on Third and Main streets as a hospital. Established on July 31, 1861, the Robertson Hospital opened under her supervision. Within weeks, it was evident that too many patients lingered in Richmond well past their recovery, and Davis ordered all private hospitals to be placed under military personnel. With the help of Judge W. W. Crump, assistant secretary of the treasury, Tompkins met with Davis in an attempt to retain control of Robertson Hospital. To circumvent the military order rule, the president commissioned Tompkins a captain of cavalry (unassigned) in charge of her hospital. When signing her commission, Tompkins noted underneath her name that she "would not allow my name to be placed upon the pay roll of the army."

Tompkins operated Robertson Hospital until June 13, 1865, using her family's money and government rations. Among the 1,333 patients who passed through her hospital, only 73 died. It primarily served the most seriously wounded and earned the distinction of having the highest rate of soldiers returning to action.

In postwar Richmond, the woman described by her contemporaries as "not over 5 feet, hardly a Southern beauty, with a splendid face, her dark eyes [shining] out under smooth hair parted squarely in the middle," continued to be active in charity work and religious activities. Affectionately referred to as "Captain Sally," she regularly attended Daughters of the Confederacy and veterans' meetings. In 1905, she retired to the Confederate Women's Home in Richmond, where having exhausted her resources, she remained as a guest until her death on July 25, 1916.

As an honorary member of the R. E. Lee Camp of the Confederate Veterans, she was buried with full military honors in Matthews County. In the Confederate Women's Home, her room became a hospital ward. Four chapters of the United Daughters of the Confederacy are named in her honor. On September 10, 1961, a stained glass window depicting her many works was dedicated at the church she attended, St. James's Episcopal in Richmond.

BIBLIOGRAPHY

Dabney, Virginius. *Richmond: The Story of a City*. New York, 1976.

Richmond News Leader, July 26, 1916; January 29, 1959; September 9, 1961; July 21, 1966.

Richmond Times Dispatch, July 26-27, 1916; October 4, 1942.

Tompkins, Sally. Papers. Museum of the Confederacy, Richmond, Virginia.

Tompkins, Sally. Papers. The Valentine Museum, Richmond, Virginia.

SANDRA V. PARKER

TOOMBS, ROBERT (1810–1885), U.S. congressman, Confederate secretary of state, and brigadier general. Wilkes County, Georgia, was the first and last home of Robert Toombs, who was born there in comfortable economic circumstances on July 2, 1810. Toombs seemed to enjoy a tempestuous youth that presaged his mercurial life and career. He attended Franklin College (which became the University of Georgia) but suffered expulsion on the eve of his graduation in 1828. Legend has it that Toombs appeared at the ceremony anyway, stood beside an oak tree outside of the college chapel, and delivered his own graduation oration. He did graduate from Union College in Schenectady, New York, and then studied law for a year at the University of Virginia. He returned to Georgia in 1830, married Julia Ann Dubose, and gained admittance to the Georgia bar.

Toombs, a large man, lived on an equally large scale. He was six feet tall and weighed over two hundred pounds. A brilliant courtroom lawyer, he was famous for his speeches to juries. He possessed inherited wealth and augmented his inheritance with the profits from his law practice and speculations in land and slaves. Toombs lived in a Greek Revival mansion in Washington, Georgia, and at various times owned plantations in Stewart County, Georgia; Desha County, Arkansas; and Tarrant County, Texas.

ROBERT TOOMBS. Photographed in 1861.
NAVAL HISTORICAL CENTER, WASHINGTON, D.C.

Elected to the Georgia House of Representatives six times (1837–1843), Toombs then won election to the U.S. Congress for four consecutive terms (1844–1851). He became a Whig in Georgia and national politics and voted for the tariff and against war with Mexico. Agitation over slavery alarmed Toombs, however, and in the course of supporting the Compromise of 1850, he helped form the Constitutional Union party as a haven for dissident Whigs. In 1855 Toombs became a Democrat and thereafter counted himself a strong Southern rights advocate, if not a fire-eater. By this time Toombs was in the Senate (1852–1861), where he was one of the leading Southern radicals.

Although he had serious second thoughts about secession following the election of Abraham Lincoln to the presidency, Republican rejection of the Crittenden Compromise drove Toombs into the front ranks of the immediate secessionists. And when delegates from seceded states convened in Montgomery to form the Confederacy, Toombs was a serious candidate for president of the new republic.

Toombs, however, seemed too radical to many of the delegates, and according to fellow Georgian Alexander H. Stephens, he sealed his fate with his fondness for the grape in Montgomery. Stephens wrote that Toombs was "tight every day at dinner" and on one evening shortly before the election became "*tighter* than I ever saw him." Whatever the reason, Toombs lost to Jefferson Davis and did not much like it. He did accept Davis's offer to name him secretary of state, though, and began his Confederate career in what was supposed to be an exalted post.

Toombs wrote out the instructions for the Confederacy's unofficial foreign ministers before they left to try to secure recognition in Europe. But then he had nothing left to do. He was secretary of state in a nation with no foreign relations, and he chafed at his inactivity and at what he perceived to be a lack of influence in the Davis administration. When pressed by a would-be bureaucrat for a job in his department, Toombs removed his hat and informed the supplicant that his entire department was inside. He resigned his position in July 1861, used his influence to secure an appointment as a brigadier general, and tried to contribute to the war effort.

General Toombs was a poor soldier made worse because he was entirely unaware of how unsuited he was for the military. He resented professional officers and carried on his own campaign against "West Pointers" in the Southern army. He derided the defensive strategy to which the Davis government resorted out of necessity. After the Seven Days' campaign (June 25–July 1, 1862), Toombs challenged D. H. Hill, his immediate superior, to a duel; Hill declined and pointed out that they might better spend their energy killing the enemy. At Sharpsburg on September 17, Toombs and his brigade fought well and Toombs himself was wounded. For this service he demanded a promotion; when it was not forthcoming, he resigned his commission.

Back home in Georgia, Toombs devoted most of the remainder of his Confederate career to criticizing Davis and the Richmond government. In his enterprise he joined Georgia Governor Joseph E. Brown and Vice President Alexander H. Stephens. Brown in 1864 made Toombs a colonel of Georgia troops and gave him a cavalry regiment in the effort to thwart Gen. William Tecumseh Sherman's invasion. Like everyone else, Toombs was ineffective.

When the Confederacy collapsed, Toombs fled to Europe and lived in Paris until 1867. He then returned home, resumed his practice of law in Washington, Georgia, and regained much of his antebellum influence in state politics. He never asked for a pardon—"Pardon for what? I haven't pardoned you all yet!" he supposedly said—and so was never able to hold national office again. Nevertheless he furthered the efforts of white conservatives for "home rule" and also supported some protopopulist causes such as state regulation of railroads and other corporations.

Toombs's health declined rapidly during the 1880s, and he died December 15, 1885. He remained very much unreconstructed to the end. Local lore in Wilkes County has Toombs at the telegraph office in town during the Great Chicago Fire of 1870. When he emerged, a crowd gathered to hear the news, and Toombs described the heroic efforts of the many fire companies to stem the spread of the flames. Firemen and volunteers from miles around Chicago were doing their best. "But the wind," Toombs added, "is in our favor."

BIBLIOGRAPHY

Freeman, Douglas S. *Lee's Lieutenants: A Study in Command.* 3 vols. New York, 1942–1944. Reprint, New York, 1986.

Patrick, Rembert W. *Jefferson Davis and His Cabinet.* Baton Rouge, La., 1944.

Phillips, Ulrich B. *The Life of Robert Toombs.* New York, 1913.

Phillips, Ulrich B., ed. "The Correspondence of Robert Toombs, Alexander H. Stephens, and Howell Cobb." In *Annual Report of the American Historical Association.* Vol. 2. Washington, D.C., 1911.

Thompson, William Y. *Robert Toombs of Georgia.* Baton Rouge, La., 1966.

EMORY M. THOMAS

TOON, THOMAS FENTRESS

TOON, THOMAS FENTRESS (1840–1902), colonel and acting brigadier general. Born in Columbus County, North Carolina, on June 10, 1840, Toon was a student at Wake Forest College in 1861. At the outset of the Civil War, Toon left school and enlisted in the Twentieth North Carolina Infantry. He then returned to school to complete his studies. When he rejoined his company in June the men elected him first lieutenant and then its captain a month later.

His bold leadership in the fighting at Seven Pines, the Seven Days' Battles, South Mountain, and Fredericksburg led to his promotion to colonel on February 26, 1863, and command of the regiment. Wounded on the second day at Chancellorsville, he returned to direct his regiment at Gettysburg, Bristoe Station, and Mine Run. In the Battles of the Wilderness and Spotsylvania his regiment performed admirably, eliciting praise from Robert E. Lee, and when Robert D. Johnston fell wounded on May 12, Toon assumed command of the brigade. Appointed temporary brigadier general in May 1864, he led the brigade during Jubal Early's march on Washington, D.C. In August Johnston returned, and Toon reverted to colonel in command of his old regiment. He then took part in the fighting at the Third Battle of Winchester, Fisher's Hill, and Cedar Creek. Transferred to Petersburg a short time later, he was wounded in the attack on Fort Stedman in March 1865.

After the war Toon had a career as a North Carolina state legislator and teacher. In 1901 he was elected superintendent of public instruction, a position he held until his death on February 19, 1902.

BIBLIOGRAPHY

Freeman, Douglas S. *Lee's Lieutenants: A Study in Command.* 3 vols. New York, 1942–1944. Reprint, New York, 1986.

Gallagher, Gary W. *Stephen Dodson Ramseur: Lee's Gallant General.* Chapel Hill, N.C., 1985.

Spencer, James. *Civil War Generals.* Westport, Conn., 1986.

U.S. War Department. *War of the Rebellion: A Compilation of the Official Records of the Union and Confederate Armies.* Washington, D.C., 1880–1901. Ser. 1. Vol. 25, pt. 1, p. 987; vol. 36, pt. 2, p. 989; vol. 43, pt. 2, pp. 912, 927.

MICHAEL G. MAHON

TORIES

TORIES. In Confederate usage, "tories" were white men from the Confederacy who served in the Union army. At the end of the war the U.S. adjutant general credited Tennessee with thirty-three Federal regiments, West Virginia with almost as many, and every state of the Confederacy with at least one except for Virginia, Georgia, and South Carolina. (Virginia provided troops that were credited to West Virginia; Georgia furnished a battalion of its own; and South Carolina contributed men to units from other states.) The official count of enlistments came to slightly more than 86,000.

In addition, many Southerners joined units from Northern and border states and were included in the totals credited to those states. About 7,000 Tennesseeans and more than 1,000 Arkansans did so, according to the Tennessee and Arkansas adjutant generals. In most parts of the South, especially in hilly or mountainous areas, Union officers found willing recruits. For instance, Benjamin F. Butler in New Orleans enlisted more than 1,200 to fill the ranks of his regiments, and Abel D. Streight in northern Alabama added 400 Alabamians to his Fifty-first Indiana Regiment. Also, five regiments of Confederate prisoners, "galvanized Yankees," were organized for U.S. service on the frontier. All together, the Southerners in the Union army probably totaled at least 100,000.

Members of Southern regiments usually served in or near their home states, though some of the units, such as the First Alabama Cavalry, U.S.A., took part in distant campaigns. Many of the men, whether in Northern or in Southern regiments, were deserters from the Confederate army and faced the threat of death if captured and recognized. George E. Pickett saw to the hanging of twenty-two men from the Second North Carolina Infantry, U.S.A., on the grounds of desertion. Whether deserters or not, Southerners fighting for the Union risked harsher treatment from Confederates than Northerners did.

Nathan Bedford Forrest was no more inclined to show mercy to the "Tennessee Tories" in Fort Pillow than he was to the black troops there.

[*See also* Galvanized Yankees; Unionism.]

BIBLIOGRAPHY

Current, Richard N. *Lincoln's Loyalists: Union Soldiers from the Confederacy*. Boston, 1992.

Hoole, William S. *Alabama Tories: The First Alabama Cavalry, U.S.A., 1862–1865*. Tuscaloosa, Ala., 1960.

Lowe, Richard. *Republicans and Reconstruction in Virginia*. Charlottesville, Va., 1991.

RICHARD N. CURRENT

TORPEDOES AND MINES. *Torpedo* is a generic term for a variety of naval and land mines employed mainly by the Confederacy. The word derived from the Latin name for an electric ray fish whose sting numbs its prey; it was first used to describe a weapon in 1776. Disapproved on moral grounds because targets were struck without warning, the torpedo satisfied the Confederacy's urgent need to make technology compensate for its inferior strength of arms.

Torpedoes destroyed more Union vessels than all other actions: forty-three were sunk or damaged, according to the best estimate. The psychological effect in naval and military action is incalculable. Yet only one Confederate vessel fell victim to a Union torpedo: the ironclad *Albemarle* in Lt. William B. Cushing's famous raid.

As early as June 1861, Matthew Fontaine Maury initiated experiments to design and test torpedoes in the James River. Working with him were Lt. Hunter Davidson and Lt. William L. Maury. As with other naval technologies that the

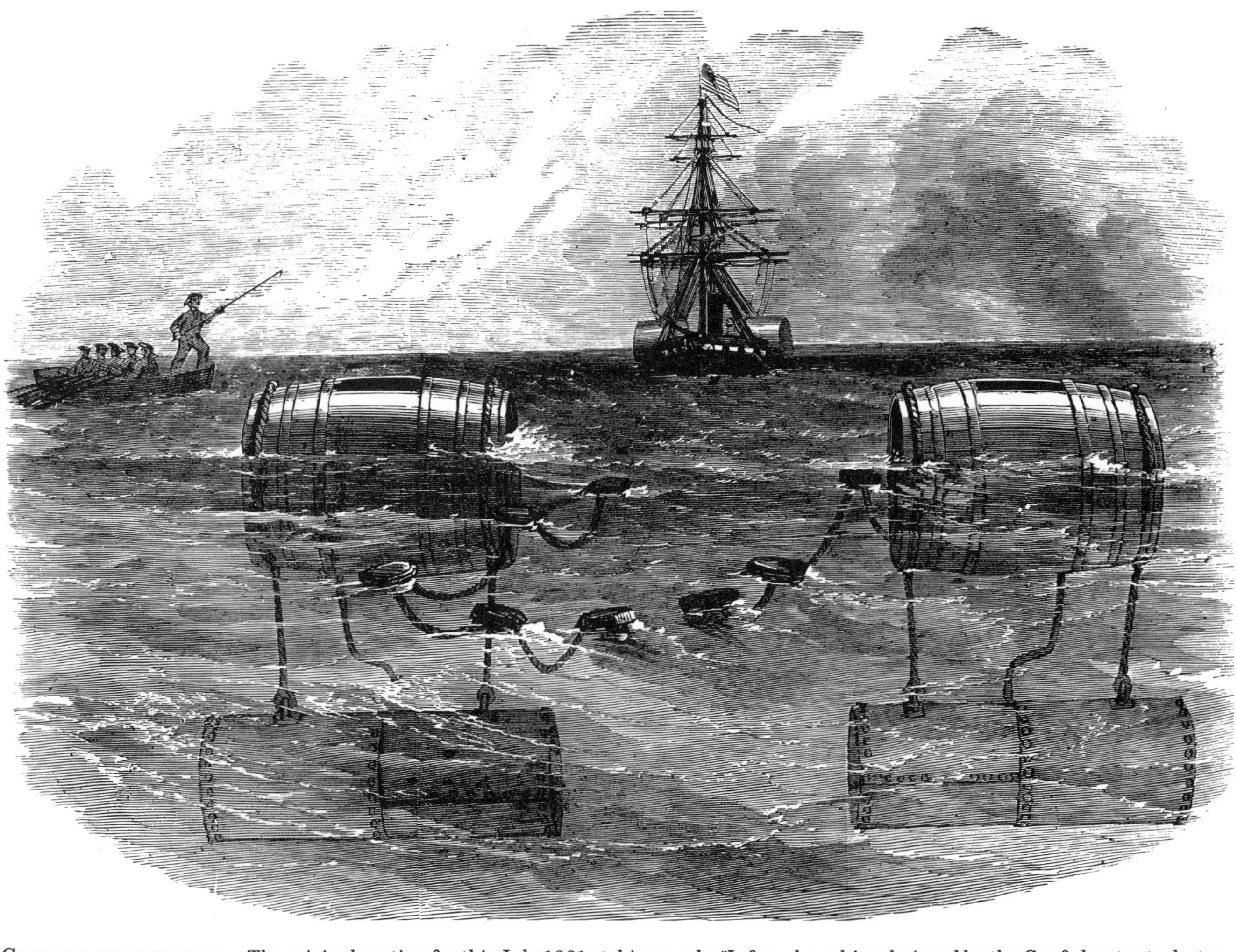

CONFEDERATE TORPEDOES. The original caption for this July 1861 etching reads: "Infernal machine designed by the Confederates to destroy the Federal Flotilla in the Potomac, discovered by Captain Budd of the steamer 'Resolute'."

FRANK LESLIE'S ILLUSTRATED FAMOUS LEADERS AND BATTLE SCENES OF THE CIVIL WAR

Confederacy refined, primitive torpedos had been used as early as the Revolution and the Crimean War.

Maury, who was past fifty and crippled by old injuries from a carriage accident, continually placed himself at risk in experimental attempts to torpedo ships in the James. Partly because of these circumstances, the Confederate authorities sent him to England in 1862 to procure supplies and test his designs under safer conditions. Davidson succeeded Maury as commander of the newly formed Naval Submarine Battery Service, a unit of the Bureau of Ordnance and Hydrography. From the James, use of torpedoes quickly spread southward, not only in large harbors like Charleston and Mobile, but on the inland waters of rivers like the St. Johns and Tennessee.

In addition to major factories such as Tredegar in Richmond and the Augusta Powder Works, many small facilities around the South were engaged in manufacturing torpedoes. In Atlanta, wives of naval personnel at the Atlanta Naval Arsenal were employed in this work. An array of moorings, floats, kegs, boilers, springs, triggers, and levers was utilized in various torpedo manufactures. Each type presented three basic design problems—how to deliver the torpedo to the target, how to keep the powder dry, and how to detonate the charge—problems that were addressed in a variety of ways.

Some torpedoes were set adrift in a river current or on a rising tide to strike a ship's hull in random collisions. Others were anchored by grapnels or on weights to float just beneath the surface. In more shallow waters in slower currents, stationary frames held "plantations" of torpedoes. On one such frame, the torpedoes were set at a 45-degree angle facing downstream. This arrangement gave Confederate vessels unobstructed passage over the frame, but Union ships traveling upstream would trigger explosions on contact.

The most daring means of delivering a torpedo to its target was the spar torpedo. This device was fixed at the end of a movable spar attached to the prow of a small, semisubmersible ship, which approached the target ship at such close range that a ten- or twenty-foot spar could reach the ship's hull below the waterline. When these small armored Davids were not available, open canoes fitted with a boom and spar carried out the same mission.

Very large barrels floating just beneath the surface or large boilers resting on a riverbed and loaded with many hundreds of pounds of powder were formidable—if the powder was kept dry. Thus, watertight casing was essential. Wooden kegs and demijohns were available, as were ships' boilers and lengths of pipe. Tin was frequently used to fabricate cones, cylinders, or lantern-shaped casings.

The crux of torpedo design was the triggering device. Some were detonated mechanically by means of a percussion fuse or a trigger pulled on a lanyard. Detonating a torpedo on a thirty-fathom lanyard or a ten-foot spar involved considerable danger. Setting torpedoes adrift or planting an unmanned stand of torpedoes involved a considerable element of chance. A ship might not collide with the weapon or might "sweep" and destroy them. Powder and fuses deteriorated swiftly in the water, or live torpedoes created a peril for Confederates.

If precise, reliable electrical firing devices could be designed, a very large torpedo in a channel could be linked to a station on shore by insulated wire and then fired by an operator at the moment a Union ship was over the torpedo. Developing the technology to do that obsessed Maury. And even when he could address the problem in principle, supplies were scarce. Galvanic batteries were inefficient if they were available at all. A Wallaston battery used in the earliest trials consisted of eighteen pairs of ten-by-twelve-inch zinc plates in thirty-six-gallon vats of sulfuric acid. Acid was requisitioned in the small lots kept in pharmacies and soon cost twenty-five dollars per gallon. In one operation, twenty-one batteries were networked in sheds along the James River.

Only a few miles of insulated wire were available in the Confederacy and only a few feet of fine platinum wire needed for fuses. These fuses combined both modern and ancient supplies. Electricity passed through the insulated copper wire to a short length of platinum wire run through the center of a short quill. The quill formed a little vial filled with fulminate of mercury, sealed with beeswax, and enclosed in a cartridge pouch of rifle powder. The electric current melted the platinum wire and set off a chain reaction, which ignited the charge.

CONFEDERATE TORPEDO. Wooden torpedo recovered from Light House Inlet, Charleston, South Carolina. Photographed at the U.S. Military Academy Museum, Highland Falls, New York, 1950.

NATIONAL ARCHIVES

Torpedoes were to take many configurations, for their production was limited only by ingenuity and available supplies. The term was applied not just to floating mines studded with percussion fuses; the "coal torpedo," for instance, could probably be classified as a booby trap, for it was a bomb disguised as a lump of coal and hidden in coal bunkers. Shoveled into a Union ship's boiler, it had a devastating effect. A "clock torpedo" smuggled aboard a ship at City Point on the James functioned like a time bomb to create one of the most spectacular and costly explosions of the war.

Ships, military and naval personnel, and civilians were imperiled by stray torpedoes after the war. But by 1865 they had become an established and accepted mode of warfare.

[*See also* Davids; Hand Grenades and Land Mines; Spar Torpedoes.]

BIBLIOGRAPHY

Perry, Milton F. *Infernal Machines: The Story of Confederate Submarine and Mine Warfare.* Baton Rouge, La., 1965.

Scharf, J. Thomas. *History of the Confederate States Navy from Its Organization to the Surrender of Its Last Vessel.* New York, 1887. Reprint, New York, 1977.

Stern, Philip Van Doren. *Secret Missions of the Civil War.* New York, 1990.

MAXINE TURNER

TRACY, EDWARD DORR (1833–1863), brigadier general. Born and raised in Macon, Georgia, Tracy moved to Huntsville, Alabama, in the 1850s, where he practiced law. In the election of 1860, he was selected as an alternate elector for the state at large and stumped the state for Southern Democratic presidential candidate John C. Breckinridge (later a Confederate major general).

At the outbreak of war, Tracy was chosen captain of a company from Madison County, which soon became part of the Fourth Alabama Volunteer Regiment of Infantry. Offered the position of major with the Twelfth Alabama, he declined and fought with the Fourth Alabama at the First Battle of Manassas. On October 12, 1861, he was named lieutenant colonel of the Nineteenth Alabama, under Joseph Wheeler. At the Battle of Shiloh, Tracy had a horse shot out from under him. He was then transferred to eastern Tennessee with John P. McCown's division and was promoted to brigadier general in August 1862.

In the spring of 1863, Tracy's brigade of five Alabama regiments was sent to the Vicksburg theater in Mississippi, where he was assigned to Carter Stevenson's division. Tracy's brigade, along with another under Brig. Gen. William Edwin Baldwin, was ordered to move south to assist in the defense of Port Gibson, thirty miles south of Vicksburg, and attached to John Stevens Bowen's division. On May 1, the four brigades engaged two-thirds of Ulysses S. Grant's entire army several miles south of Port Gibson. Hopelessly outnumbered, the Confederate troops fought stubbornly and lost 787 men in the day-long battle, 272 in Tracy's brigade alone. While leading his men along the front line, Tracy was struck in the chest and died almost instantly. His remains were returned to Macon for burial.

BIBLIOGRAPHY

Carter, Samuel, III. *The Final Fortress: The Campaign for Vicksburg, 1862–1863.* New York, 1980.

Faust, Patricia, ed. *Historical Times Illustrated's Encyclopedia of the Civil War.* New York, 1986.

Warner, Ezra J. *Generals in Gray: Lives of the Confederate Commanders.* Baton Rouge, La., 1959.

CHRISTOPHER PHILLIPS

TRANS-MISSISSIPPI DEPARTMENT. The Trans-Mississippi region included Texas, Arkansas, Missouri, Indian Territory, that part of Louisiana west of the Mississippi River, and the Arizona Territory (about two-fifths of the modern states of New Mexico and Arizona). Although there were numerous minor campaigns and battles in this area, none affected the war's outcome. The Trans-Mississippi was made a separate department in May 1862, but because President Jefferson Davis's primary concern was Virginia and Tennessee, he relegated the region to secondary importance. The surrender of Vicksburg assured the area's virtual isolation, and for all practical purposes the department was out of the war after 1863. Nevertheless, the Trans-Mississippi contributed significant numbers of men to the armies serving east of the river, and provided the Confederacy with a considerable quantity of food and supplies. Moreover, the small Army of the Trans-Mississippi forced the Union to retain a military presence in the region, thus tying up Federal soldiers that could have been used elsewhere.

Although the Trans-Mississippi was not part of the main war effort, the area west of the river comprised a notable portion of the total land mass of the Confederate states. From the Mississippi River to the California border and from Iowa to the Gulf of Mexico, the region covered around 600,000 square miles, but realistically Texas, Arkansas, and West Louisiana (thirty-one complete parishes and parts of six others) became the nucleus of the western limits of the Confederate nation. In 1860 the population of these three states included about 908,000 whites, around 5,500 free blacks, about 543,000 slaves, and 600 Indians. In addition, the Indian Territory reported about 58,000 Indians, whites, and free blacks and over 7,000 slaves. That Missouri did not secede and join the Confederacy was significant because, with 1 million white citizens, it was the second-largest slave state, ranking only behind Virginia.

The area was the fastest growing in the South and rich in many commodities. The inhabitants raised a variety of agricultural products, including cotton in the river valleys of Louisiana and Texas. Missourians produced more corn than in any other Southern state and harvested impressive quantities of wheat and oats. Missouri also counted more swine than any other slave state and ranked only behind Kentucky in the number of horses. Texas led the nation in the production of beef: the census reported over 3.5 million cattle in the state. The Trans-Mississippi's geographic location, too, offered advantages. Texas was the only Confederate state to border on a neutral foreign nation, Mexico, and an international waterway, the Rio Grande; thus it gave the South a link to the outside after the Union blockade became effective along the coastline. The region was also the gateway to any dreams of a Confederate empire in the Far West.

The states that composed the Trans-Mississippi had the same problems that plagued other agrarian areas in wartime. The population was widely scattered; there were few towns of any size, and even these were very small. Some of the largest population centers were San Antonio with 8,235, Galveston with 7,307, Little Rock with 3,727, and Shreveport with 2,190. The department had few railroads, almost no industrial facilities, and inadequate telegraph lines. Moreover, it was the only part of the Confederacy that had an Indian problem; the region had some 50,000 to 60,000 "hostile" Indians. The frontier in Texas retreated east after the able-bodied men joined the army, and the dangerous situation in West Texas added to the troubles facing the state authorities.

Early Military Operations

When the war began there was neither an overall military plan for the area nor an intention to make it into one department. In 1861 Louisiana belonged to Department No. 1 and parts of Arkansas belonged to Department No. 2. A separate Department of Texas was created on April 21 and placed under Col. Earl Van Dorn, who soon after capturing *Star of the West* at Galveston was promoted to brigadier general. Van Dorn left the state in September, briefly transferring command to Col. Henry Eustace McCulloch, but on September 18 Brig. Gen. Paul O. Hébert assumed command. In theory, Confederate commanders worked with state officials to organize and equip the army. Each state raised troops, and each seized Federal arsenals and forts within its boundaries. This arrangement obviously led to difficulties between state and Confederate authorities, and in Missouri it provoked armed conflict.

Missouri was the only state in the department that never officially seceded, and throughout the war it had two rival governments. In May 1861 pro-Confederate Governor Claiborne F. Jackson tried to lead the state out of the Union, but in St. Louis this effort had been thwarted by Union Capt. Nathaniel Lyon, who organized a force and seized the state militia at Camp Jackson. The ensuing riot had left many civilians dead and persuaded the popular Unionist Sterling Price to throw his support to the South. This led to an armed conflict between the pro-Southern forces of Jackson and Price, on one hand, and the pro-Union army of Lyon, on the other. When the two sides met at Wilson's Creek, Missouri, on August 10, 1861, Lyon was killed. Price tried to take advantage of the victory by moving into Missouri, but Union soldiers forced him back into southwestern Missouri and finally into northwestern Arkansas. Missouri, in effect, had two governors. The pro-Union legislature replaced Jackson with Hamilton R. Gamble and voted to remain within the Union. Jackson, ignoring this, joined the Confederacy and moved his headquarters south.

There were also plans to establish a Confederate empire in the West. In June 1861 Col. John R. Baylor led Confederate troops up the Rio Grande into the New Mexico Territory. In August he claimed Arizona and made himself governor of the territory. Brig. Gen. Henry Hopkins Sibley also moved into the region and early in 1862 defeated Federal forces at Valverde before taking Albuquerque and Santa Fe. After a loss at Glorieta Pass in March, however, Sibley retreated to San Antonio, and the dreams of a Confederate empire in the West vanished.

The first major clash in the Trans-Mississippi came along the Missouri-Arkansas border. In December 1861 Brig. Gen. Samuel R. Curtis took command of the Union Army of the Southwest and early in 1862 advanced toward Springfield, Missouri. The friction between Sterling Price, commanding the Missouri State Guard, and Brig. Gen. Ben McCulloch, commanding Confederate troops, was rectified on January 10, 1862, with the creation of the Trans-Mississippi District of Department No. 2. This district contained the Indian Territory, that portion of Louisiana north of the Red River, and all of the counties of Missouri and Arkansas except those located between the St. Francis and Mississippi rivers. Maj. Gen. Earl Van Dorn was placed in command; he arrived late in January and led the Confederate Army of the West at Elkhorn Tavern, Arkansas, in March. Van Dorn planned to stop Curtis's move south, and the two armies met in the Boston Mountains near Fayetteville. Although the Federals were outnumbered, around 11,000 to Van Dorn's almost 17,000, Van Dorn's plan to split his army and attack from two directions failed. During the fighting on March 7 McCulloch and Brig. Gen. James McIntosh were killed, leaving no one in charge of one wing of the assault. On the second day of the battle, Curtis's men were able to drive the Confederates from the field. Van Dorn moved south toward the Arkansas River and then received orders to join the Confederate army under Gen. Albert Sidney Johnston in Mississippi. Although he did not reach his destination in time to take part in the Battle of Shiloh, he left Arkansas virtually defenseless.

Elkhorn Tavern was the first major battle in which Indians from the Five Civilized Tribes participated. The early fighting in the Indian Territory had consisted mainly of skirmishes between pro-Confederate and pro-Union Indians. When the war began Confederate representatives had negotiated alliances with the five tribes—the Chickasaws, Creeks, Cherokees, Choctaws, and Seminoles. Eventually, the pro-Union Indians retreated to Kansas and left the region briefly under Confederate control. The Indians who fought at Elkhorn Tavern returned to the Indian Territory when Van Dorn crossed the Mississippi River, and by 1863 many had become disillusioned with the Confederacy; both Creeks and Choctaws talked of resuming relations with the United States. Cherokee Stand Watie, who commanded an Indian cavalry brigade in the Army of the Trans-Mississippi, was the only Indian to attain the rank of brigadier general in the Confederate army, and the last general officer to surrender at the end of the war, June 23, 1865.

Creation of the Trans-Mississippi Department

After the disaster at Elkhorn Tavern the Confederate government recognized that something drastic had to be done. Faced with the serious situation of having Curtis's army positioned in northwestern Arkansas and with no way to defend the region, the Confederate government finally created a separate territorial organization, the Trans-Mississippi Department on May 26, 1862. General Order No. 39 stated that the department would embrace the states of Missouri and Arkansas, including the Indian Territory, that part of Louisiana west of the Mississippi River, and the state of Texas. On May 31 Maj. Gen. Thomas C. Hindman was appointed commander, and he did an excellent job of organizing an army and defending Little Rock. Hindman, however, argued with Albert Pike in the Indian Territory. Partly because of this argument (Pike was a friend of Jefferson Davis) and partly because Hindman's draconian measures to instill discipline and order in the army were unpopular, Hindman was replaced by Maj. Gen. Theophilus H. Holmes, another of Davis's personal friends. On July 16, 1862, Holmes was ordered to Little Rock, and he assumed command on July 30. On August 20 the department was divided into districts: the District of Texas was composed of the state of Texas and the territory of Arizona and remained under Hébert; the District of West Louisiana was under the command of Maj. Gen. Richard Taylor; and the District of Arkansas, which included the states of Arkansas and Missouri and the Indian Territory, was under Hindman.

But as overall department commander Holmes was a poor choice; he was difficult to get along with and was sometimes excessively rude. Holmes thought in terms of what best served his own department rather than what might be best for the Confederate nation. When asked to send reinforcements to Vicksburg, he delayed and used his personal friendship with Davis to frustrate the movement of troops out of his department. Not only did he keep his soldiers in the Trans-Mississippi, never providing any real assistance to Vicksburg, but he never satisfactorily defended his own borders. In December, Hindman in northwestern Arkansas was defeated by Federal Brig. Gens. James Blunt and Francis Herron at Prairie Grove, and in early January 1863 Arkansas Post in the southeast surrendered to a superior Union force.

Certainly there were serious problems in the Trans-Mississippi when Holmes took over, but his actions did nothing to improve the situation. Citizens living in the Trans-Mississippi felt abandoned, which created perilous morale problems throughout the department. Holmes, as early as October 1862, had asked Richmond to relieve him. In January 1863 the government was ready to agree. Secretary of War James A. Seddon reported in March that "the most deplorable accounts reached Richmond of the disorder, confusion, and demoralization everywhere prevalent, both with the armies and people of that State." Holmes, he claimed, had "lost the confidence and attachment of all," and the result was "fearful."

The Trans-Mississippi under E. Kirby Smith

On January 14, 1863, Lt. Gen. E. Kirby Smith was assigned to the command of the Southwestern Army, "embracing the Departments of West Louisiana and Texas." The order made it clear that the geographical limits of this "new department" would be separate and distinct from the Trans-Mississippi Department. But Holmes wanted out and urged his friend Davis to find a replacement for him. On February 9 Smith took command of all Confederate forces west of the Mississippi River and made Alexandria, Louisiana, headquarters of the Trans-Mississippi Department. On March 18, Holmes was officially relieved, although he remained in charge at Little Rock.

At the time of Smith's arrival the department still comprised several districts, although some of the commanders had changed since the summer. Holmes took over the District of Arkansas and held this position until he resigned on March 16, 1864. Taylor continued in the District of Western Louisiana and, though he and Smith frequently disagreed, remained in command until late 1864. Brig. Gen. William Steele headed the District of the Indian Territory until replaced by Brig. Gen. Samuel Bell Maxey; and Maj. Gen. John B. Magruder commanded Texas, New Mexico, and Arizona. Magruder had arrived in Texas in October 1862 and promptly recaptured Galveston from the

Union forces on January 1, 1863. Magruder, known as "Prince John," would remain in this position until transferred to Arkansas near the war's end. Texas was divided into three subdistricts: Brig. Gen. James E. Slaughter headed the Eastern Sub-District; Brig. Gen. Hamilton P. Bee, the Western Sub-District; and Brig. Gen. Henry McCulloch, the Northern Sub-District. Upon his arrival, Smith complained, "There was no general system, no common head; each district was acting independently."

The department also encountered problems keeping its men fit and in camp. Sickness took a heavy toll, and it was difficult to procure medicine. Desertion was another serious problem, with men going home and returning to the army at will. The extent of the problem is indicated by the figures reported after an inspection of the department in February 1864. In the District of Arkansas there were 10,354 troops present for duty, 25,623 aggregate present and absent; in the District of Western Louisiana, 10,657 troops present, 21,808 aggregate present and absent; in the District of Texas, 7,574 troops present, 12,992 aggregate present and absent; among state troops, 1,529 present, 3,960 aggregate present and absent; and in the District of the Indian Territory, 1,666 troops present, 8,885 aggregate present and absent. Overall, counting various other commands, it was reported the total present for duty in the department was 31,780, aggregate present and absent, 73,268.

Supplying these troops was a formidable task. It was imperative, Smith thought, to begin "general systematizing and development of the departmental resources." When Smith arrived, the Quartermaster's Bureau, recently established, reported on hand almost $17 million, but only $12,350 was in money. The remainder was in drafts, which the chief quartermaster complained he could not cash. "The want of funds to meet the necessities of the army embarrasses to a great degree the efficiency of my department," he noted. Moreover, the head of the Clothing Bureau clamored for funds to outfit his men. Hats and shoes were manufactured at several locations, and the Huntsville penitentiary turned out cloth, cotton jeans, woolen plaids, and woolen jeans. But money was needed to meet other pressing demands: many soldiers had not been paid for months.

Kirby Smithdom. The Trans-Mississippi was isolated, with the U.S. Navy making it difficult for troops and supplies to cross the Mississippi River. With Smith in charge, the region became known as "Kirby Smithdom." Powerful Texans believed the Confederate government had abandoned their state by surrendering it to Smith's control. Even Richard Taylor complained that Smith worried too much about "the recovery of his lost empire, to the detriment of the portion yet in his possession," and Taylor believed that "the substance of Louisiana and Texas was staked against the shadow of Missouri and Northern Arkansas." Smith, in fact, assumed exceptional power, but Jefferson Davis supported him, declaring that his "confidence in the discretion and ability of General Smith assures me that I shall have no difficulty in sustaining any assumption of authority which may be necessary."

Governors and state officials met in the late summer of 1863 and agreed that the department must become self-sustaining. They called for public support and closed with a vote of confidence in Smith. Soon after, Smith organized the Cotton Bureau for the purchase, collection, and disposition of government-owned cotton. Bureaucrats hoped that cotton taken to Mexico could be exchanged for weapons and supplies desperately needed by the South. Although the plan did supply many essential goods, the work of the bureau was hampered by private speculators, currency problems, and an inability to convince Texans of the need to cooperate. Illicit commerce flourished, particularly along the Red River, as Southern cotton made its way to New England factories with the knowledge and support of government officials on both sides. But by mid-1864 most of the available cotton was gone, and Smith, who had come to depend upon this source of revenue, realized his department was in danger of financial collapse. Therefore, without official sanction from Richmond, he ordered the bureau to buy or impress one-half of all cotton grown, thus keeping the trade going until the war's end.

The Trans-Mississippi was unique in the Confederacy in that a Union attack was not the only danger it faced. In the summer of 1863 a serious threat to the region came from the Indians. Comanches and Kiowas began to raid closer to large settlements—at one point just west of Fort Worth. Many families left their homes, moved in together, and built small forts. Confederate soldiers, receiving letters from home, became alarmed; many deserted to check on their families, although most returned when assured that their homes were safe. Texas's governors, first Francis R. Lubbock and then Pendleton Murrah, did their best to control the situation. Henry McCulloch, in command of the Northern Sub-District with headquarters at Bonham, had to deal with Indian war parties roaming along the frontier.

In addition, the frontier was alive with deserters, outlaws, and Unionists. Even the notorious Confederate William Quantrill plagued Texans when he moved south out of Missouri. McCulloch never had enough men to deal with all the problems, and in 1864 the authorities finally closed the frontier in an effort to protect the citizens.

Yet another burden was the sizable number of refugees that flooded Texas. Many Southerners with friends or relatives in the Trans-Mississippi fled other states to escape Federal armies. It is impossible to estimate accurately the number of people who relocated in Confederate-held regions. Women and children often brought slaves with them in order to avoid confiscation of their property, and as many as 200,000 blacks may have entered Texas during the last years of the war. The drain on the department created by these exiles placed a severe strain on Smith's resources, and contributed to the war-weariness that pervaded the region after 1863.

Military Operations of 1863. While Smith wrestled with domestic matters, he had also to cope with the military situation. Davis and the War Department had directed him to give top priority to defending Confederate-held territory along the Mississippi River. Throughout the spring and early summer of 1863, he tried to furnish aid to both Port Hudson and Vicksburg. In an attempt to draw Federal troops away from Vicksburg, Smith authorized an invasion of Missouri in April. Confederates under Brig. Gen. John Sappington Marmaduke tried unsuccessfully to take Cape Girardeau on the Mississippi River and quickly retreated into Arkansas. This strategy to assist Vicksburg failed, and Ulysses S. Grant continued his movement south. Although Holmes had resisted any efforts to send troops from the Trans-Mississippi to Vicksburg while he was department commander, Smith did order Confederates from Arkansas to reinforce Richard Taylor in Louisiana. Also as a diversion to help the Vicksburg defenders, Holmes authorized an attack on the Federal stronghold of Helena, Arkansas, on July 4. But in a mismanaged affair the Confederates were quickly repulsed with heavy losses on their side. Moreover, all attempts to aid Vicksburg from the west side of the river failed, and the town surrendered on July 4, 1863. Port Hudson fell five days later, and with the Union taking control of the river, the Confederacy was split in two.

On July 17, Federal troops decisively defeated the Confederates at the Battle of Honey Springs (or Elk Creek), the largest single engagement of the Civil War in the Indian Territory. Late in August Federal forces headed toward Little Rock, and in southern Louisiana Taylor made preparations for an attack. Texans, especially in the Rio Grande valley, feared an invasion. The situation in Mexico provided diplomatic reasons to control Texas; Napoleon III, the French ruler who was openly pro-Southern, had taken advantage of the weakened U.S. government and backed a puppet monarchy in Mexico. Moreover, Abraham Lincoln was not unaware of the interest that New Englanders had in Texas cotton. And yet the important decision of where the assault should be made along the Texas coast was left to the incompetent political general Nathaniel P. Banks.

Banks decided to strike at the mouth of the Sabine River, the boundary between Louisiana and Texas. A surprise assault at Sabine Pass would give access to the port of Beaumont. Moreover, the Confederates manning the pass were not adequately armed and made an easy target for the Union fleet. A combined force under Banks and Adm. David Farragut left New Orleans and sailed for Sabine Pass. On September 8, 1863, they faced the guns of Lt. Dick Dowling and forty-two men of the Davis Guard, a rowdy group composed primarily of Irishmen from Houston. The determined Confederates, members of the First Texas Heavy Artillery Regiment, turned their cannons on the naval force under Maj. Gen. William B. Franklin. About 4:00 P.M. *Sachem* was struck in the boilers and *Clifton* was grounded; both ships soon surrendered. The attack lasted less than an hour, and Federal losses were substantial, including the two gunboats. Dowling and his men, who fired their artillery over a hundred times, were unscathed. As a result of this impressive Confederate victory, Lincoln watched Northern morale fall and the stock market temporarily drop. Davis called it "the greatest military victory in the world," and Franklin took his place in American military history as the first general to lose part of his fleet to land batteries alone.

While Banks unsuccessfully struck at Texas, the Federals were victorious in Arkansas. On September 10, 1863, Little Rock fell to Union forces under Maj. Gen. Frederick Steele, and the Confederates fled the city. As Little Rock became the headquarters of the Union Department of Arkansas, another Union expedition under Brig. Gen. James G. Blunt drove Brig. Gen. William Steele from Fort Smith into the Indian Territory. On September 1, the Federals moved into Fort Smith, and Arkansas was divided in half on an east-west line that ran from Helena on the Mississippi to Little Rock and across to Fort Smith. Even Pine Bluff fell to the Union advance, and the Confederates controlled only a strip of land in the southern part of Arkansas. Moreover, except for scattered skirmishes, the Indian Territory was virtually out of the war.

Lincoln, however, still wanted to capture locations on the Texas coast. A new force invaded the Rio Grande valley in November and occupied Brownsville, forcing the Confederates to reroute the cotton crop heading for Mexico. The Union troops continued to move up the coast, and Magruder had to work hard to quell rumors that he had abandoned South Texas. In December, when a threat to Galveston developed, he asked that the Texas cavalry in Louisiana under Brig. Gens. Thomas Green and James Patrick Major be returned to the coast. But the Union released its grip, except at the Rio Grande, when the authorities realized it was impossible to hold the entire shoreline. Washington now turned to strategy for the 1864 spring campaign.

Union Offensive of 1864. As the new year opened, Union authorities plotted a major offensive in the Trans-Mississippi. As spring approached Lincoln's government planned to invade Arkansas and Louisiana in an effort to move into the rich cotton land of East Texas. Banks was to march up the Red River from Alexandria and meet Steele's advance from Little Rock at Shreveport. Neither army would have to march very far to reach Smith's headquarters. Once they had taken this Red River port, it would be easy to move into Texas. Moreover, victories in this part of the Confederacy could eliminate Arkansas and Louisiana from the war. Perhaps more important, Lincoln needed a meaningful military victory, for the fall election was only months away.

The two-pronged invasion began in March. Banks's force, increased by 10,000 men on loan from William Tecumseh Sherman's army and assisted by Porter's fleet, numbered around 22,000. He easily took Fort DeRussy on the Red River and headed for Shreveport. Smith and Taylor disagreed on how to respond to the columns moving north. Taylor started the campaign with around 6,000 men, and reinforcements from Texas and Arkansas increased the number to about 12,000. With this disparity in numbers, Smith urged caution, but Taylor was eager to strike quickly. On April 8 Taylor hit the strung-out Federal army near the little town of Mansfield. Banks's advance force fell back on their long wagon train, and a complete rout would have occurred if reinforcements had not arrived in time. The next day the Confederates hit Banks's army at Pleasant Hill. Although Taylor did not defeat Banks, the Federal army pulled back to Grand Ecore. Taylor then asked Smith for permission to pursue the disorganized Union army, but Smith refused; he had to shift some of Taylor's troops north to prevent the Federals from succeeding in Arkansas.

The second prong of the Federal advance started in a more promising fashion. Sterling Price had around 8,000 men in Arkansas, along with some recently arrived cavalry from the Indian Territory, to oppose Frederick Steele's 10,000 to 12,000 troops. While Banks pushed up the Red River, Steele advanced south toward Washington, Arkansas. He occupied the town of Camden by the time that Smith had shifted troops back to Arkansas. In late April Confederate forces captured a supply train coming from Pine Bluff. The Battle of Poison Spring was notable because the loss of the supply train was a major factor in Steele's decision to retreat, but it was also a controversial battle in which many black soldiers died. Both sides claimed victory, but Steele withdrew to Little Rock.

The Confederate Trans-Mississippi Department had survived. As Steele fell back to Little Rock, Banks retreated to Alexandria. The politician-turned-general had to use all of his ingenuity to save the army, and Porter was fortunate to maneuver his fleet down the falling river. A Wisconsin soldier suggested that the navy build a dam to raise the water level; the river, having fallen to three feet in some places, was too shallow for the passage of the gunboats. When Banks escaped, Smith and Taylor had another serious disagreement, and Taylor was replaced in Louisiana by Maj. Gen. John G. Walker.

Final Confederate Operations. In August Taylor took command of the Department of East Louisiana, Mississippi, and Alabama, and crossed the river. In fact, Jefferson Davis told Kirby Smith to send any units he could spare to help at Mobile, and Smith received specific orders to have several Trans-Mississippi brigades join the campaigns in the East. He protested that the loss of troops would seriously damage the morale of the department, and when the men learned of the proposed plans they threatened to mutiny rather than fight. As the plan bogged down in controversy, it was dropped. Taylor maintained this was because too many gunboats had arrived at the crossing point to allow such an operation to succeed, but Davis later claimed he had never really planned to cross huge numbers. In fact, Taylor revealed that many men had decided to desert rather than comply. Smith hotly denied this, charging that because of his disagreements with Taylor, the Louisiana general was trying to discredit him. For whatever reason, the scheme to shift Trans-Mississippi troops across the Mississippi failed.

While all of this was occurring in Louisiana, Kirby Smith and Sterling Price were planning a raid into Missouri—the last major campaign in the Trans-Mississippi. Price, who had succeeded Holmes in command of the District of Arkansas, had been a politician before the war, and he was aware of the advantage to be gained by successfully invading his home state before the November presidential election. He personally hoped to take control of regions of the state long enough to elect a new governor and legislature. By taking command of the expedition, however, Price was forced to relinquish command of the District of Arkansas, and he was replaced by Maj. Gen. John B. Magruder. Price headed for Missouri with only cavalry from Arkansas organized into three divisions under Maj. Gen. James Fleming Fagan and Brig. Gens. Joseph O. Shelby and John S. Marmaduke. Price and his 12,000 men entered Missouri in September; he hoped to gain recruits and supplies as he went along. The raid, which covered over 1,500 miles and took three months, turned into a disaster; Price and his badly beaten army returned to Arkansas in early December.

In the winter of 1864–1865 morale plummeted throughout the department. Smith was always fearful that Richmond might order his troops to fight in the East, and he could ill-afford a drain on his manpower; the army was already badly depleted by desertion as many men on leave failed to return. Trade with Mexico was at a wartime low, and much of the gunpowder coming in from that country was of such poor quality it would not fire. Although the states in the department suffered less from shortages than other Southern states, inflation hit hard by winter. Moreover, the Texas frontier was rife with rumors of Indian raids, and large bands of deserters and bushwhackers tried to take over areas where the military had little control.

When Lee surrendered in April 1865, Kirby Smith, along with military and civil authorities, issued calls for the people

VOLUNTARY DISPERSION OF THE ARMY OF THE TRANS-MISSISSIPPI. E. Kirby Smith's troops are depicted at Shreveport, Louisiana, May 1865. *FRANK LESLIE'S ILLUSTRATED FAMOUS LEADERS AND BATTLE SCENES OF THE CIVIL WAR*

of the Southwest to continue the fight. The last battle of the war occurred in the Trans-Mississippi deep in South Texas where Col. John S. ("Rip") Ford and the Second Texas had not learned that the end was near. Three hundred Federal troops from the island of Brazos Santiago under Col. T. H. Barrett landed on the mainland and headed toward Confederate-held Fort Brown. Barrett, whose command was mostly black soldiers, met a detachment of Ford's regiment at Palmito Ranch near Brownsville, but after a brief skirmish both sides withdrew. The following day, May 13, Ford struck at the Union soldiers; 113 surrendered and 30 were killed or wounded. The Texans learned from their prisoners that Lee and Johnston had surrendered in April.

In May military units in the department began to disband, and by the end of the month Smith had only a few scattered troops left in Texas and Louisiana. Lt. Gen. Simon Bolivar Buckner, acting Brig. Gen. Joseph L. Brent, and Maj. Gen. Sterling Price headed for New Orleans to negotiate terms, and on May 25 the military and naval forces of the Trans-Mississippi surrendered to Maj. Gen. E. R. S. Canby. The next day Buckner signed the official terms of surrender, which paroled the Trans-Mississippi soldiers and allowed them to return home unmolested. Kirby Smith, who decided to transfer his headquarters from Shreveport to Houston, arrived there on May 27 only to find he was a general without an army. On June 2 he boarded a Federal steamer in Galveston Harbor and placed his signature on the completed agreement, officially surrendering the Trans-Mississippi Department.

[*See also* Arkansas Campaign of 1864; Brownsville, Texas; Elkhorn Tavern, Arkansas; Galveston, Texas; Glorieta Pass, New Mexico; Little Rock, Arkansas; Mansfield, Louisiana; Port Hudson, Louisiana; Prairie Grove, Arkansas; Price's Missouri Raid; Red River Campaigns; Sabine Pass, Texas; Wilson's Creek Campaign; *and biographies of numerous figures mentioned herein.*]

BIBLIOGRAPHY

Bragg, Jefferson Davis. *Louisiana in the Confederacy.* Chapel Hill, N.C., 1952.

Johnson, Ludwell H. *Red River Campaign: Politics and Cotton in the Civil War.* Baltimore, 1958.

Josephy, Alvin M., Jr. *The Civil War in the American West.* New York, 1991.

Kerby, Robert L. *Kirby Smith's Confederacy: The Trans-Mississippi South, 1863–1865.* New York, 1972.

Nichols, James L. *The Confederate Quartermaster in the Trans-Mississippi.* Austin, Tex., 1964.

Oates, Stephen B. *Confederate Cavalry West of the River.* Austin, Tex., 1961.

Parks, Joseph Howard. *General Edmund Kirby Smith, C.S.A.* Baton Rouge, La., 1954.

Thomas, David Y. *Arkansas in War and Reconstruction, 1861–1874.* Little Rock, Ark., 1926.
Wooten, Dudley G., ed. *A Comprehensive History of Texas, 1865 to 1897.* 2 vols. Dallas, Tex., 1898.

ANNE J. BAILEY

TRANSPORTATION. Transportation routes in the antebellum South developed mainly to get cash crops out to the seaports, to bring in manufactured goods from the Northeast, and to bring in grain from the Middle West. Transportation was geared more toward providing access to local markets than toward binding sections of the country together or facilitating rapid transport of military forces, as the great highways of the Roman Empire had done.

In the early days drovers would move herds of cattle and hogs along trails and primitive roads over the mountains to eastern markets, negotiating with farmers along the way to allow the animals to feed in their cornfields. Later the railroads took over most of this business. But the greatest stimulus to railroad building in the South came from the competition of seaport cities whose merchants were anxious to improve their trade.

Major rivers carried products from the hinterlands to the sea, and roads and railroads tended to supplement that movement without major redirections of the flow of traffic. Few major interstate highways were to be found. The South for the most part resisted the canal-building craze that spread across the North. It participated to an extent in the great railroad building of the 1850s, but only on a small fraction of the scale and still with few long-distance lines.

In 1850 if a man wanted to travel from Richmond to New Orleans, for instance, he could go by a series of railroads from Richmond to Wilmington, North Carolina, in twenty-one hours for $8.40. From Wilmington he would take a steamboat for a sixteen-hour voyage to Charleston at a fare of $6.00. Thence he would take a railroad train to Atlanta, with a change in Augusta. There he would have to take a stagecoach for twenty-four hours to the town of Chehaw on the Alabama border and then a railroad again to Montgomery. Now came a long leg of 200 miles that took thirty-six hours by stagecoach to reach Mobile. He would make the final leg of 175 miles to New Orleans by steamboat. The whole trip of about 1,460 miles would take seven days at a cost of about $56.00.

In 1861 it was possible to go by rail all the way from Richmond to New Orleans by way of Abingdon, Knoxville, Chattanooga, Decatur, Alabama, and Corinth and Jackson, Mississippi. But there still was no rail connection between Texas and the Mississippi, and none for Arkansas except a short line from Madison.

Similar obstacles blocked travel by highways and waterways, although in 1850 one could travel by main roads and turnpikes from Washington to New Orleans or from Nashville to Augusta. Improvements of the waterways went little beyond clearing snags from the rivers.

The attitude in the South was one of hostility toward internal improvements at the expense of the general government. In 1856, when Congress passed an internal improvements bill that included $100,000 for clearing impediments to navigation on the Mississippi, and another $50,000 for the Tennessee, it was over the strong opposition of Southern leaders who insisted that the locales and the users should pay for their own improvements.

Indeed the Confederate Constitution forbade appropriations for internal improvements. It stated: "Neither this, nor any other clause contained in the Constitution, shall ever be construed to delegate the power to Congress to appropriate money for any internal improvement intended to facilitate commerce." The only exceptions were for lights and buoys on the coasts, the improvement of harbors, and the removal of obstructions in the rivers, but in all cases the users were to be taxed to pay the costs.

When war came in 1861, the whole Southern transportation system suffered and then broke under the strain. The advance of Federal armies and river flotillas gained control of the Cumberland and Tennessee rivers and then of the Mississippi for its entire length. In his campaign to Atlanta and then the marches to Savannah and to Goldsboro, William Tecumseh Sherman wrought havoc with the railroads in his path. Cotton could not be moved out to market, and many farmers planted corn instead. But much of what did not fall to the enemy remained in the granaries for want of horses and wagons and railroads and boats. Local roads fell into such disrepair as to be almost impassable for wagons, but most of the wagons and horses were with the armies anyway.

Railroads deteriorated further with each month of war. There was no iron to repair the tracks. There were no new cars or locomotives to replace worn rolling stock. The army itself was hard pressed to keep up supplies of food, ammunition, and replacement weapons with the altogether insufficient means of transportation in the country to support it.

The U.S. Congress in 1862 passed an act that authorized the president to take possession of the railroads whenever he considered that the situation demanded it. The Confederates were reluctant to do this. Not until February 28, 1865, did the Confederate Congress approve such a measure, and then it was a broad one. Although coming at a time when it could have little practical effect, it gave the secretary of war power to put navigation and railroad companies under military officers and to provide assistance to secure their efficiency.

[*See also* Horses and Mules; Railroads; Roads; Waterways.]

WINTER HUTS AND CORDUROY ROADS. NATIONAL ARCHIVES

BIBLIOGRAPHY

The American Heritage Pictorial Atlas of United States History. New York, 1966.

Black, C. F. *The Railroads of the Confederacy.* Chapel Hill, N.C., 1952.

Dunbar, Seymour. *A History of Travel in America.* Indianapolis, 1915.

Hunter, Louis C. *Steamboats on the Western Rivers.* Cambridge, Mass., 1969.

Parsons, Lewis B. *Rail and River Army Transportation in the Civil War.* St. Louis, Mo., 1899.

Randall, J. G., and David Donald. *The Civil War and Reconstruction.* Boston, 1961.

Turner, George Edgar. *Victory Rode the Rails.* Indianapolis, 1953.

JAMES A. HUSTON

TRAPIER, JAMES H. (1815–1865), brigadier general. James Heyward Trapier was born near Georgetown, South Carolina, on November 24, 1815. He attended West Point, graduating third in the 1838 class of forty-five, and for several years served as an engineer officer, primarily building and repairing seacoast forts. Following the Mexican War, Trapier left the army to become a planter. During his retirement he was active in the South Carolina militia; as chief of ordnance, he helped arm the state, including the purchase of many of the heavy ordnance pieces used on April 12, 1861, to bombard Fort Sumter.

On October 21, 1861, Trapier became a brigadier general in the Confederate army and took command of the Department of Middle and Eastern Florida. Unhappy in this administrative position, he applied for field duty and in March 1862 received assignment to the western army to command the Fourth Brigade in Jones Mitchell Withers's division. When Withers went on sick leave in April 1862, Trapier took temporary command of the division, proving himself a poor infantry officer during the siege of Corinth. Gen. Braxton Bragg found Trapier so lacking in ability that he requested Trapier's removal from the Army of Tennessee. In November 1862 Trapier returned to his home state, where he served in subordinate positions for the remainder of the war.

Trapier died on December 21, 1865, and is buried in Georgetown, South Carolina, at the Church of St. George, Winyah.

BIBLIOGRAPHY

Capers, Ellison. *South Carolina.* Vol. 5 of *Confederate Military History.* Edited by Clement A. Evans. Atlanta, 1899. Vol. 6 of extended ed. Wilmington, N.C., 1987.

Manigault, Arthur Middleton. *A Carolinian Goes to War: The Civil War Narrative of Arthur Middleton Manigault, Brigadier General, C.S.A.* Edited by R. Lockwood Tower. Columbia, S.C., 1983.

JUDITH LEE HALLOCK

TREASURY DEPARTMENT. The Confederate Treasury Department was created by the Provisional Congress on February 21, 1861, at Montgomery, Alabama. The department then moved to Richmond, Virginia. Its operations in Richmond were hindered because, from 1863 on, all the able-bodied men were frequently called out for military duty. At such times, the dispatch of business slowed to a crawl. The department ceased to exist after the evacuation of Richmond on April 2, 1865.

Next to the War Department, the Treasury was the most important arm of the government. It not only collected and dispersed all the government's funds, but its payment or nonpayment of the War Department's bills meant the difference between success and defeat.

The department was a copy of that existing in Washington. It comprised the secretary, the assistant secretary, the chief clerk, the treasurer, the register, the comptroller, an auditor, and their staffs. This force totaled roughly one hundred persons at the seat of government and seven hundred more at the ports and mints. Many of these persons had Washington experience, and some brought with them sets of the Federal Treasury forms. Thus, within a few weeks, the Confederate Treasury was organized with an invaluable continuity of bureaucratic procedure and experience. By 1864, the Treasury had one thousand employees in Richmond and two thousand in the field offices.

The key figure in the department was the secretary, an office occupied by Christopher G. Memminger from February 21, 1861, until June 15, 1864, when he was succeeded by George Trenholm. The secretary was responsible for his department's efficient operation, and he had to prepare for Congress the government's recommendations for financial legislation.

The assistant secretary was the department's special projects officer and the acting secretary in the absence of his chief. This post was filled in February 1861 by Philip Clayton, who had been Howell Cobb's assistant secretary. His unbusinesslike practices forfeited the confidence of his chief, and he was dismissed in 1863. He was replaced by William W. Crump, who served until 1865.

The Office of the Treasurer was headed by Edward C. Ellmore from March 1861 until October 1, 1864, when he was succeeded by John N. Hendren. The treasurer received, held, and dispersed Confederate government funds, signed all but the post office warrants, and kept records of all receipts and disbursements. He signed, together with the register, the first Confederate notes.

The treasurer also supervised the Treasury Note Bureau. This bureau was headed by Thompson Allen until it was split into two parts in May 1862; one division, which printed the notes, moved to Columbia, South Carolina. The other, which signed, numbered, clipped, packed, and shipped the notes, remained in Richmond. The Columbia bureau was headed by Joseph Daniel Pope until April 1863, when he was succeeded by Charles F. Hanckel. The Richmond bureau was headed by Sanders G. Jamison until September 1864, when the two parts were reunited in Columbia and Jamison resumed sole control. The bureau broke up with the fall of Columbia in February 1865.

The printers required close supervision because they were short of men and supplies and were far more interested in their profits than in the proper execution of their contracts. In addition, there were obstructions to getting treasury notes and securities to Richmond because of a shortage of trains and couriers. This delayed the preparation and distribution of the treasury notes, which in turn prevented the government from making urgently needed military payments.

The Treasury Note Bureau in Richmond had to number and sign twice over eighty million notes, requiring a staff of nearly three hundred clerks. Because of the manpower shortage, Secretary Memminger hired women to perform these tasks.

A related bureau was the Office of the Register, headed by Alexander B. Clitherall in early 1861 and subsequently by Robert Charles Tyler, from August 13, 1861, on. The register was responsible for appointing individuals to countersign the treasury notes and to keep registers of those emitted and canceled. The register's staff had to number every Confederate bond and to sign the coupons on each of over 800,000 bonds. In 1864 the register's signature was printed on each coupon. The register was also required to sign all warrants, transfer drafts, coupon bonds, registered bonds, and call certificates. This paperwork load resulted in the designation of Charles T. Jones, Tyler's chief clerk (another Washington veteran), as acting register and the appointment of two assistant registers in early 1863.

The duty to audit claims and accounts devolved upon the comptroller. This office was occupied throughout the war by Louis Cruger, who had held a similar position in Washington. In performing his duties, Cruger was required to adjust and preserve the public accounts, to examine all accounts and certify the balances to the register, to countersign all the warrants drawn by the secretary, to report the collection of the customs and export duties to the secretary, and to provide for the payment of all moneys collected. Finally, he was to sue delinquent officers or debtors and to rule on all claims made against the Confederacy. To perform these tasks, Cruger was furnished with twenty clerks and one messenger. His work force had increased to thirty-two clerks by 1864, in five sections: those covering civil expenses, the War Department, canceled treasury notes, deceased soldiers' claims, and the bookkeepers.

The first auditor of the treasury, Bolling Baker, who had held that post in Washington, was initially responsible for auditing all the government's accounts. By 1864 he had fifty-three employees who were assigned to six divisions covering the customs service, the navy, the interest on the public debt, taxes, funding, and a miscellaneous section.

To reduce Baker's work load, the office of second auditor was created on March 16, 1861, and Walter H. S. Taylor, a former U.S. Treasury clerk, was appointed to the post. He was responsible solely for the War Department's accounts. To perform this duty, he was assigned 40 clerks, which by 1864 had become 158 persons working in seven divisions—bookkeeping, claims, pay, ordinance, engineer and medical, quartermaster, and subsistence expenses.

In 1864, the position of third auditor was created. That officer dealt exclusively with the voluminous post office accounts.

The Lighthouse Bureau was a small office carried over from the Federal government. It supervised the operation of lighthouses in twenty-nine districts from Tappahannock, Virginia, to Padre Island, Texas. The outbreak of hostilities and the suppression of most of the lighthouses left this bureau largely dormant.

There were two bureaus created after the war began. The first of these was the Produce Loan Bureau. The Produce Loan Bureau was supervised during the provisional government by James D. B. De Bow. The register then took over until May 1, 1863, when Archibald Roane became Produce Loan Bureau manager. He supervised produce loan agents in each state and insured that all government cotton was safeguarded and all food products were handed over to the army commissary department.

The office of the commissioner of taxes was created in 1863. This position was filled by Thompson Allen, another man with Washington experience. In addition to supervising his staff both in Richmond and the field offices, he issued regulations, advised the secretary in tax matters and furnished the Congress with reports and recommendations.

In addition to the officials located at Richmond, there were officials located throughout the Confederacy. The Treasury was fortunate that the personnel at the mints and customs houses stayed at their posts after secession. The secretary therefore did not have to train employees to perform routine government functions. The field offices were located at three sites: the lighthouses, the customs houses, and the mints.

The customs houses were mostly located along the coast and the Mexican border. This service was divided into twenty-five districts, employing approximately six hundred officials. With the proclamation of the blockade and the loss of several ports, there were considerable reductions in this work force. At the same time, because of the increase of trade with Mexico, more officials were posted to that frontier. The remaining officials found it difficult to regulate trade or collect a revenue from it. For example, the export duty on cotton was collected on only a fifth of the bales that left the ports or went overland to Mexico.

A large prewar force was employed by the mints at New Orleans, Dahlonega, and Charlotte. The Confederacy did not have a Bureau of the Mint to coordinate mint activities, and the shortage of supplies needed for minting operations resulted in Charlotte and Dahlonega being reduced to the status of assay offices. The mint in New Orleans was captured on April 25, 1862.

If the previously existing field offices atrophied, new branches burgeoned. The receipt and payment of vast sums for taxes, loans, and government expenses necessitated an expansion of the treasurer's offices. Anthony J. Guirot, formerly the treasurer of the New Orleans mint, was made assistant treasurer on May 11, 1861. Forced to flee from New Orleans in 1862, he was driven from one city to another, ending up at Mobile.

A second assistant treasurer's office was created in Charleston. Later, because of the siege, it relocated to Columbia.

In addition to the two assistant treasurers, there were depositories located throughout the Confederacy. Although there was usually only one office per city, multiple offices existed in Richmond, Wilmington, Charleston, Mobile, and Jackson. There were two kinds of depositories: those that paid out funds ("pay depositories" of which there were usually only two or three per state), and those used only to fund notes ("funding depositories").

Secretary Memminger was slow to establish depositories prior to 1863. The 1864 funding records suggest that had a comprehensive system of depositories been set up in 1861, a considerably larger amount of currency would have been funded at an earlier date.

Most of the depositaries were bank officers, but in Florida, Arkansas, Mississippi, and Texas, the Treasury hired local financiers. There were approximately two hundred depositories, and the Confederate government's ability to supervise their operations or furnish them with standardized forms was limited. For example, after the loss of the Mississippi Valley, the secretary of the treasury was cut off from the Trans-Mississippi Department. As a result, in November 1864, the Treasury was largely ignorant of the names and locations of its agents in that area.

In 1861, when the produce loan idea was first broached, large numbers of citizens volunteered to serve as agents. But there were no agents west of the Mississippi River, and the government put this volunteer effort on a more professional basis in early 1862. Agents were given formal appointments and commissions on subscriptions allowed.

When the Confederate Congress authorized the secretary to purchase cotton with bonds under the act of April 14, 1862, the government created the Produce Loan Bureau, appointing one full-time agent with a staff for each state. These agents collected and safeguarded the produce subscribed, donated, or later collected as part of the tithe tax. These duties proved increasingly onerous as Federal armies captured or compelled the destruction of the government's cotton. The absence of proper bagging and the collapse of the transportation system resulted in much waste.

The last group of field offices were those of the Confederate tax collectors. Under the war tax of August 19, 1861, the secretary was authorized to appoint a chief collector for each state, who in turn appointed a collector and one or more assessors for each county. These persons were to secure appraisals or declarations on all property and then forward a consolidated local report to the chief collector, who furnished a statewide valuation to the Treasury.

The tax machinery created in 1861–1862 then lapsed, and a new tax collection system had to be created for the act of April 24, 1863. Under that law, collectors were appointed for each congressional district, with a collector having one or more assistants. This tax force came to less than five hundred persons.

Taken as a whole, the Treasury Department proved reasonably efficient. The deficiencies of Secretary Memminger, however, particularly in fiscal policy formulation, his governance of the Treasury printers, his mismanagement of the Produce Loan Bureau, and his refusal to collect a specie reserve, reduced the department's effectiveness.

[*See also overview article on* Currency; Produce Loan; Taxation; *biographies of Christopher G. Memminger and George Trenholm.*]

BIBLIOGRAPHY

Capers, Henry D. *The Life and Times of C. G. Memminger.* Richmond, 1893.

Ryan, Carmelita S., comp. *Preliminary Inventory of the Treasury Department Collection of Confederate Records.* Washington, D.C., 1967.

Todd, Richard C. *Confederate Finance.* Atlanta, 1954.

Douglas B. Ball

TREDEGAR IRON WORKS. The Tredegar Iron Works in Richmond, Virginia, the largest industrial base in the South at the beginning of the Civil War, was the only facility capable of producing major ordnance, iron plate, and iron products in 1861. During the war, other ironworks were developed in the lower South, but Tredegar remained the leading ordnance producer and served as a model for further Southern industrialization.

Francis B. Deane, a Richmond businessman, with a group of partners combined a forge, rolling mill, and foundry in the mid-1830s, initiating the Tredegar operations. The company was officially incorporated by the Virginia legislature on February 27, 1837. (Its name derives from ironworks in Tredegar, Wales.) In 1841, sluggish sales and indebtedness induced company directors to accept a proposal by Joseph Reid Anderson that he become the company's commercial agent. Anderson, a West Point graduate and a state engineer for turnpike construction, brought in new investments and provided favorable sales management. He became a leaseholder of the entire company in 1843, and after five years he purchased the company outright from stockholders for $125,000.

In the 1850s the Tredegar Iron Works increased in capacity, and Anderson maintained high quality in order to secure U.S. government contracts for its products. The company diversified its output and used varied partnerships for its different operations in an attempt to promote good management and increase expertise. By 1859, Anderson had merged with an adjacent munitions works run by his in-laws, bought off some old partners, and consolidated remaining ones as Joseph R. Anderson and Company. By this time also, the Tredegar Works was attracting wider markets in the South and was recognized as the largest industrial complex south of the Potomac River.

When the Confederacy was established, Anderson and his partners supported it wholeheartedly. The company severed all trade and sales in the North and concentrated on supplying orders from seceding states for ordnance and munitions. By the end of 1861 Tredegar's work force had grown from 350 free and slave laborers in 1853 to nearly 1,000 men, of whom 10 percent were slaves.

Labor problems in the company had existed since its early days. Anderson in the 1840s increased the firm's use of slave labor, which in 1847 precipitated a strike of white workers who sought to eliminate their black competition. Their demands were overridden by Anderson, and the black labor force—some free, some slave—continued to increase with Tredegar's expansion. But since slaves had to be fed, clothed, and housed on the premises, their use failed to reduce production costs significantly. Nevertheless, black labor proved more and more essential as some Northern and foreign workers departed the company at war's start, and by early 1863, with more skilled labor drawn away for military duty, blacks constituted one-half of Tredegar's 2,000 workers.

As the war got underway, longer-term contracts between the Tredegar Iron Works and the Confederacy's War and Navy departments took the place of orders from individual states, although those from the private railroad system continued. The Confederacy never took over railroads, but very early it moved to centralize and coordinate the securing of war supplies. Steady orders from the government prompted the expansion of Tredegar's rolling mill and ordnance facilities and was further encouraged by the Confederacy's promise of annual financial backing. What the government could not do was live up to its promise to supply all the pig iron and coal that Tredegar's operations needed. In April 1862 the Confederate Congress allowed the War and Navy departments to provide loans to Tredegar to expand the company's pig iron and fuel sources, and new blast furnaces were opened up. Further assistance proved to be very limited, however, and despite Tredegar's wartime growth, its operations remained at only one-third its full capacity throughout the war.

By the years 1863 and 1864 new ironworks at Selma, Alabama, and elsewhere in the lower South, as well as facilities set up by Confederate bureaus, created further difficulties for Tredegar by competing for scarce resources. The Confederacy's industrial thrust, as expansive as it seemed, was slowed by the lack of raw materials. This disadvantage, coupled with the poor distribution service of its rail system, was an ominous portent for the government's survival.

At the outset of the war Joseph Anderson had offered to turn the Tredegar Works over to the Confederate government for lease or purchase, which was rejected in favor of sustaining private business. Increasingly, Anderson and his partners, whose commitment to Southern independence never faltered, complained that the government's control over the prices it would pay for war supplies left Tredegar with no profit margin. The situation worsened in the last year of the war as government payments fell short. In April 1865, the government still owed almost $1 million to the Tredegar Iron Works.

The company had in the early years fulfilled much of its industrial potential, supplying the big guns for the Confederacy before 1863, as well as iron plate for ironclads (e.g., *Merrimac*'s conversion to *Virginia*), munitions, and other war products. It had even participated in experimental developments of submarines and torpedoes and the modernization of naval weapons and machine guns. But by war's end, the insurmountable problems of skilled labor shortages, the depletion of basic raw materials, and the failure to obtain adequate provisions for Tredegar workers had drastically hampered the firm's high-quality productivity.

Near the end of the war Anderson once again offered the Tredegar Works for lease to the government, but it was too late. The Tredegar Battalion, a militia of employees established in 1861, guarded the company's physical plant against rampage when the Confederacy collapsed in April 1865. With the fall of Richmond the Tredegar Iron Works remained intact, though occupied by Union troops for a short while. The company partners feared confiscation of the firm's property under Federal law, and Anderson immediately sought a way to resume operations, underscoring Tredegar's readiness for production and employment. Private meetings with President Andrew Johnson resulted in personal pardons for Anderson and his partners in September 1865. The company reorganized in 1867 with Anderson continuing as president.

Anderson earlier had hedged against future loss or collapse by engaging in blockade running for consumer goods from Europe. Profit from those sales had provided him with the means to maintain a separate London bank account. The London sterling deposits plus additional investments, including some from Northern financiers, enabled the Tredegar Works to move from the leading wartime producer of ordnance for the Confederacy to peacetime operations assisting in the renewal of the South's commerce and industry.

But Tredegar's heyday as the South's major industrial complex was over. Financial ties with a failing New York railroad operation during the panic of 1873 forced the company into receivership, with Joseph Anderson serving as receiver until 1879. Moreover, iron production was rapidly giving way to steel production, and Tredegar could not afford to shift operations to steel. What had once been a great model for Southern industrialization had receded to a more modest operation, which was carried on at the site until 1958.

BIBLIOGRAPHY

Beringer, Richard E., Herman Hattaway, Archer Jones, and William N. Still, Jr. *Why the South Lost the Civil War.* Athens, Ga., 1986.

Bruce, Kathleen. *Virginia Iron Manufacture in the Slave Era.* New York, 1931.

Daniels, Larry J. "Manufacturing Cannon in the Confederacy." *Civil War Times Illustrated* 12 (November 1973): 4–10, 40–46.

Dew, Charles B. *Ironmaker to the Confederacy: Joseph R. Anderson and the Tredegar Iron Works.* New Haven, Conn., 1966.

Tredegar Company Records. Virginia State Library, Richmond, Virginia.

FREDERICK SCHULT

TRENCH WARFARE. *For discussion of the development of trench warfare during the Civil War and its effects on the course of particular battles and on the war as* *a whole, see* Forts and Fortifications, *article on* Field Fortifications and Trench Warfare.

TRENHOLM, GEORGE (1807–1876), merchant and secretary of the treasury. George Alfred Trenholm was born on February 25, 1807, at Charleston, South Carolina. After his father's death in 1822, he went to work for John Fraser and Company, a firm engaged in shipping and factoring Sea Island cotton. Trenholm's progress was rapid. In 1836, he succeeded his employer as a director of the Bank of Charleston, the largest bank in South Carolina. He was elected to the legislature (1852–1856), and by 1860 he was a rich man. His personal assets, and those of his firm, consisted of plantations, slaves, warehouses, wharves, ships, and substantial investments. The company had branches in New York (Trenholm Brothers) and Liverpool (Fraser, Trenholm). Trenholm's reputation for integrity assured him of almost unlimited credit.

In a private capacity, Trenholm faithfully served the Confederacy. He built and donated to South Carolina the gunboat *Chicora.* In addition, he worked on the Board of Commissioners fortifying Charleston. He also expanded his fleet until by 1864, his firm either owned or held under charter fifty ships. He used these not to import high-priced luxury goods for profit but to bring in urgently needed military supplies and items for the Confederate civilian market. When James M. Mason and John Slidell, the Confederate commissioners, were unable to get out of Charleston because of the blockade, Trenholm personally leased a ship at half price to convey the two diplomats to Havana.

Nor did his services end there. A personal friend of Secretary of the Treasury Christopher G. Memminger, he provided both practical aid and sound advice in the management of the Confederacy's financial affairs. Starting in April 1861, the firm of Fraser, Trenholm became the government's financial agent in Europe. That office furnished cash advances to the Confederate procurement agents, who otherwise would have been seriously delayed in securing supplies for the army. This relationship was formalized by an act dated November 26, 1861.

Recognizing the importance of furnishing the government with the means for exporting its own produce and importing urgently needed supplies, Trenholm sent his son William to Montgomery in May 1861 to propose the purchase by the government of one or both of two available British shipping lines. The cabinet and President Jefferson Davis rejected this idea, thereby doing serious injury to the Confederate cause.

Trenholm was frustrated on other blockade-related issues. He strongly urged the government to stop the Committees of Safety from inhibiting cotton exports. The government, however, refused to confront the committees, preferring instead to deal with the situation one problem at a time. Trenholm also tried to lease ships on the government's behalf, but his efforts to promote exports of Treasury-owned cotton failed because Memminger blocked the procurement of the requisite cotton.

Trenholm also advised Memminger that it was vital to make treasury notes the South's currency. With that aim in view, Trenholm organized and attended a bankers' convention in June 1861. The meeting was adjourned to Richmond from July 24 to 26, 1861, when the banks agreed to receive and pay out Confederate treasury notes, thereby ensuring a nationwide demand for them.

Moreover, Trenholm was also behind the series of laws passed in February 1864 that provided for stringent controls over imports and exports, the acquisition of government ships, and the preemption of cargo space on the government's account to export cotton and import supplies needed by the army. Had this program been enacted in 1861, as Trenholm had originally proposed, the Treasury would have been strengthened, the army better supplied, and the Confederacy's economic deterioration mitigated.

Disgusted by the uncooperative attitude of the Confederate Congress and its mismanagement of the economy, Trenholm urged Memminger to resign, which he did on June 15, 1864. Much to Trenholm's surprise, President Davis then offered to appoint him secretary of the treasury. Trenholm reluctantly accepted this position on July 18, 1864.

At the time he took office, Trenholm confronted a bankrupt Treasury. He tried to educate the public and win the respect of the congressmen. But he was unable to induce them to pass better legislation, and this soon led to disaster. In November 1864, Trenholm found that the Treasury was over $360 million in arrears in its payments for the army. These arrears undermined the troops' morale and resulted in mass desertions. Trenholm did his best to prevent this by selling off government coin and cotton and even donated $200,000 himself.

Evacuating Richmond on April 2, 1865, Trenholm fled south. By April 27, however, he was so ill he had to resign his post. Accompanied by his son William, Trenholm rejoined his family in Columbia. There he remained under house arrest until June 21, when he was instructed to report to the provost marshal at Charleston.

Arriving with a valise containing the assets of his firm, which he planned to give to its trustees, Trenholm and William were arrested and escorted to jail. There he was told he was to be imprisoned and his assets sequestered. Ordered to leave, William calmly walked out with the bag containing the John Fraser assets. The elder Trenholm went to Fort Pulaski, from which, on October 11, 1865, he was released on parole.

The remaining eleven years of Trenholm's life were devoted to salvaging his personal affairs. The U.S. government sued Fraser, Trenholm for the former Confederate assets the firm had used to offset its claims against the Confederacy. Defeated in the British courts and assessed costs, the Federal government then filed immense claims against Trenholm and his firm in Charleston, seeking penalties and interest for nonpayment of customs dues. As a result of this and bad cotton crops, Trenholm's firms went bankrupt. Nonetheless, by 1874, he was once more a wealthy man. As a token of respect, Charlestonians lowered their flags to half-mast following his death on December 10, 1876.

BIBLIOGRAPHY

Patrick, Rembert W. *Jefferson Davis and His Cabinet.* New York, 1961.

Todd, Richard Cecil. *Confederate Finance.* Atlanta, 1954.

DOUGLAS B. BALL

***TRENT* AFFAIR.** On October 12, 1861, newly appointed Confederate commissioners James Mason and John Slidell boarded the steamer CSS *Theodora* in Charleston, South Carolina. Their mission was to secure recognition for the Confederate States of America in both England and France and find military supplies and negotiate commercial trading agreements that would support the newly declared country. *Theodora* carried Mason and Slidell safely through the Union blockading squadron off Charleston and then to Nassau in the Bahamas. Unable to find immediate passage to Europe from Nassau, the Confederate commissioners were taken on to Cuba aboard *Theodora.* After several weeks of socializing and being entertained by the governor of Cuba, Mason and Slidell booked passage to England on the royal mail steamship *Trent* on November 8, 1861. Both men assumed their voyage on *Trent* would be protected by international laws that guaranteed the sovereignty of every nation's vessels. As a consequence they made no effort to conceal their plans.

When word of their voyage reached Capt. Charles Wilkes aboard USS *San Jacinto* at Cienfuegos, he decided to intervene. After a serious examination of the potential consequences and consultation with the U.S. consul general, Wilkes decided to intercept *Trent* and capture Mason and Slidell. On November 8, Captain Wilkes discovered the British steamer 240 miles east of Havana. Against legal council Wilkes fired a shell across *Trent*'s bow, forcing the ship to stop, and brought *San Jacinto* alongside. Over the protests of Capt. James Moir, an armed crew from *San Jacinto* forcibly removed Mason and Slidell. As *Trent* steamed on to St. Thomas, Captain Wilkes headed for Hampton Roads, Virginia. There he took on coal and telegraphed the secretary of the navy of his intent to sail for Boston. Upon arrival there Wilkes received orders from Secretary of State William H. Seward to take the prisoners to Fort Warren in Boston Harbor for detention.

News of Wilkes's seizure of the Confederate commissioners was greeted with enthusiasm throughout the Union. At a time when the fortunes of war appeared to favor the Confederacy, the event was perceived as something of a military victory over the South if not also Great Britain. Northern newspapers generally reflected the public opinion. With the exception of newspapers in some northeastern cities that would be vulnerable in the event of hostilities with Great Britain, most viewed the incident as Wilkes's victory and glossed over or denied the impact of potential political repercussions. Regardless of international consequences, the press expressed a consensus that the captives should not be surrendered. Many editorialized that Captain Wilkes had not done anything more serious than the British had on numerous occasions. The *Philadelphia Sunday Dispatch* commented that Britain could hardly protest "a good old English practice" of search and seizure. Union leaders, however, were divided in their feelings. Seward was reported to be "elated," but Abraham Lincoln was concerned that the British reaction would provide political support for the Confederacy. It was clear that the Union was in no position to risk angering the European community. At the same time Lincoln did not want to dampen much-needed enthusiasm in the North. Instead of adopting an antagonistic position, he waited for Britain to officially react to the incident.

In the Confederacy Wilkes's forcible removal of Mason and Slidell was received with both indignation and satisfaction. Southerners were outraged by the United States's blatant disregard for the sovereignty of a British vessel and the seizing of duly appointed commissioners of the Confederate States of America. At the same time they appear to have been as elated about the incident as Northern supporters of Wilkes. Many felt that the affair would advance the South's cause by generating support for British recognition of the Confederacy. Southern newspapers were as vocal on the issue as those of the North. The *Richmond Enquirer* stated that Great Britain would find it impossible to accept the "disgrace," and the *Atlanta Southern Confederacy* called the *Trent* affair "one of the most fortunate things for our cause." Secretary of War Judah P. Benjamin agreed with the *Southern Confederacy.* Many officials felt the crisis would lead Great Britain into a war with the United States and thus assist the Confederate bid for independence.

Relations between Great Britain and the United States had frequently been strained prior to the Civil War. The rebellion in Canada; disputed boundaries between Maine, Oregon, and Canada; the acquisition of Texas and California; competing interests in Central America; and American reaction to British recruiting in the United States during the Crimean War all contributed to the impression that Americans were a disagreeable sort at best. Lincoln's selection of William H. Seward to head the State Department had reinforced British apprehension, as Seward was on occasion highly antagonistic toward Great Britain. The situation did not improve when Queen Victoria issued a proclamation of neutrality in May 1861. The seizure of Mason and Slidell appeared to bring many festering issues to a head. Though British newspapers admitted that "the honor of England" was "tarnished" and the injustice should be resolved, some were willing to admit that the United States had done nothing more than Great Britain had on previous occasions.

Richard B. Pemell, the second Lord Lyons and Her Majesty's minister to the United States, suggested possible courses of action. The first was to clearly establish that Britain would not condone violations of its sovereignty. Lord Lyons also suggested that the threat of war warranted the reinforcement of Canada and the strengthening of naval squadrons in the Atlantic, Pacific, and West Indies. He was of the opinion that Britain should act in concert with France in responding to the affair and to resist offering aid to the South but not reject their envoys. The French minister of foreign affairs, Antoine Édouard Thouvenel, confirmed that though France was not directly involved, the government viewed the incident as a breach of international law.

The gravity of the *Trent* affair was evident in the creation of a War Committee in the British cabinet. The committee members considered their options and, after determining that Wilkes's act was illegal, contemplated preparing for war with the United States. At the same time they approved a dispatch drafted by Lord John Russell to be delivered in Washington by Lord Lyons. Great Britain was willing to concede that Wilkes may have acted on his own or had misunderstood his orders, but the prisoners had to be released and a public apology issued. For Britain the matter was one of national honor. Lord Lyons was to give Lincoln and his government seven days to respond to the communication. If a satisfactory answer was not received within that time, Lyons was to break off relations with the United States and return with his staff to England.

President Lincoln's initial reaction to the British note was immediate rejection. News of it set off waves of public protest and heated debate in Congress. In spite of intense popular opinion and congressional pressure, Lincoln eventually yielded to Seward's argument that the United States could not risk war with Great Britain at a time when suppression of the rebellion and major financial problems were paramount. After lengthy consideration of the matter, Lincoln and his cabinet agreed that the prisoners must be released and a satisfactory apology issued to Great Britain. Seward drafted a complex and rambling document that affirmed that Wilkes had indeed acted without orders and that by "voluntarily" intercepting *Trent* he had committed an illegal act for which Britain justifiably deserved reparations. On January 1, 1862, amid public protests, Slidell and Mason were released and transported aboard HMS *Rinaldo* to Bermuda, where they boarded the vessel *La Plata* and continued their voyage to Britain. The *Trent* crisis had been resolved after an intense two months of negotiations and compromise. In Great Britain and France, Mason and Slidell served the Confederate States of America until the end of the war, but failed to secure official recognition of the new government.

RICHARD B. P. LYONS. Lord Lyons was the British minister to the United States from December 1858 to February 1865. Photograph by Mathew Brady. NATIONAL ARCHIVES

The *Trent* affair was the most serious crisis of diplomacy faced by the United States during the Civil War. Although resolved to the mutual satisfaction of the United States and Great Britain, the issues associated with the affair complicated diplomacy well into the twentieth century. The problems of neutral and belligerent rights, search and seizure at sea, the nature of contraband and government dispatches, the legal status of mail ships, transport of military and civilian belligerents, and diplomatic privileges and immunities demanded international consideration but defied immediate and concise definition.

[*See also* Mason, James M.; Slidell, John.]

BIBLIOGRAPHY

Adams, Ephram Douglass. *Great Britain and the Civil War.* 2 vols. New York, 1958.

Callahan, James Morton. *Diplomatic History of the Southern Confederacy.* Springfield, Mass., 1957.

Cullop, Charles P. *Confederate Propaganda in Europe, 1861–1865.* Coral Gables, Fla., 1969.

Ferris, Norman B. *Desperate Diplomacy: William H. Seward's Foreign Policy, 1861.* Knoxville, Tenn., 1976.

Ferris, Norman B. *The Trent Affair: A Diplomatic Crisis.* Knoxville, Tenn., 1977.

Jenkins, Brian. *Britain and the War for the Union.* 2 vols. Montreal, Canada, 1974, 1980.

Owsley, Frank Lawrence. *King Cotton Diplomacy: Foreign Relations of the Confederate States of America.* 2d ed. Chicago, 1959.

Warren, Gordon H. *Fountain of Discontent: The* Trent *Affair and Freedom of the Seas.* Boston, 1981.

GORDON WATTS

TRÉVIGNE, PAUL (1825–1908), newspaper editor. In the fall of 1862 black creole Paul Trévigne, the editor in chief of *L'Union,* a new French-language newspaper founded by free men of color, challenged presidential policy. While condemning slavery and race prejudice, Trévigne angrily denounced President Abraham Lincoln's proposal to resettle African Americans in Central America. He pointed to events in the French Caribbean in 1848 when free blacks and slaves had achieved political equality in the wake of the Second Republic's emancipation and enfranchisement decrees. He demanded full citizenship rights for black Americans. Trévigne's bold vision owed as much to his black creole heritage as to his awareness of black gains in the French revolution of 1848.

During the 1850s, Trévigne, a French-speaking native New Orleanian of African descent whose father, a Spaniard, had fought in the War of 1812, taught languages and mathematics at the Institution Catholique des Orphelins Indigents, a free black school founded in 1848 by black creole leaders under the auspices of the Catholic church. At the school, Trévigne worked with the free black community's foremost romantic literary artists as well as leading proponents of spiritualism, a radical new religious sect.

With the Federal occupation of the city in the spring of 1862, Trévigne and his colleagues mobilized the black creole community. In *L'Union,* they attacked slavery and urged their readers to support the Union cause. At the same time, they waged an unrelenting campaign for racial equality. In 1864, after black creole Dr. Louis Charles Roudanez reorganized *L'Union* and renamed the paper the *New Orleans Tribune,* Trévigne became the editor of the first black-owned daily newspaper in the United States.

After he and his *Tribune* colleagues spearheaded a civil rights movement that led to the desegregation of New Orleans public schools during Radical Reconstruction, Trévigne served on the New Orleans school board. Following his ouster from the board after the collapse of the Republican regime in 1877, Trévigne joined other prominent black leaders in a struggle against forced segregation that culminated in the 1896 Supreme Court case, *Plessy v. Ferguson.*

BIBLIOGRAPHY

Blassingame, John W. *Black New Orleans, 1860–1880.* Chicago, 1973.

Desdunes, Rodolphe Lucien. *Our People and Our History.* Edited by Dorothea Olga McCants. Baton Rouge, La., 1973.

Hirsch, Arnold R., and Joseph Logsdon. *Creole New Orleans: Race and Americanization.* Baton Rouge, La., 1992.

Houzeau, Jean-Charles. *My Passage at the New Orleans "Tribune."* Edited by David C. Rankin. Baton Rouge, La., 1984.

Roussève, Charles B. *The Negro in Louisiana.* New Orleans, La., 1937.

CARYN COSSE BELL

TRIMBLE, ISAAC (1802–1888), major general. Regarded as the most prominent soldier contributed by Maryland to the Southern cause, Isaac Ridgeway Trimble was born May 15, 1802, in Culpeper, Virginia. He graduated from West Point in 1822 and spent ten years as an artillery officer. Trimble then left the army and devoted almost three decades to railroad construction, much of it in his adopted state of Maryland.

In April 1861, as commander of Baltimore defenses, Trimble burned a number of bridges north of the city to impede passage of Federal troops en route to Washington. The next month he accepted a colonelcy of engineers in Virginia forces and helped in the construction of Norfolk's defensive works. Following his appointment on August 9, 1861, as a Confederate brigadier general, Trimble took command of a brigade in Richard S. Ewell's division. He was, a fellow officer stated, "a veteran in years but with the fire and aggressiveness of youth."

Dependable service in Jackson's Shenandoah Valley and the Seven Days' campaigns ended momentarily at Second Manassas when a Federal bullet shattered Trimble's left knee. On January 17, 1863, while still recuperating from his wound, Trimble received advancement to major general. He

ISAAC TRIMBLE. LIBRARY OF CONGRESS

returned to duty, but on July 3, 1863, while leading two North Carolina brigades in the Pickett-Pettigrew charge, Trimble again was shot in the left leg. Dr. Hunter McGuire amputated the limb the next day. Unable to travel, Trimble surrendered to Union authorities. He endured imprisonment at Johnson's Island and Fort Warren before his February 1865 release.

After the war, and equipped with an artificial leg, Trimble resumed his engineering work. He resided in Baltimore, where he died January 2, 1888. He is one of five Confederate generals buried in that city's Green Mount Cemetery.

BIBLIOGRAPHY

Grace, William M. "Isaac Ridgeway Trimble: The Indefatigable and Courageous." M.A. thesis, Virginia Polytechnic Institute and State University, 1984.

Manakee, Harold R. *Maryland in the Civil War.* Baltimore, Md., 1961.

Trimble, Isaac R. "The Civil War Diary of General Isaac Ridgeway Trimble." *Maryland Historical Magazine* 18 (1922): 1–20.

JAMES I. ROBERTSON, JR.

TRIPLETT, GEORGE WASHINGTON

TRIPLETT, GEORGE WASHINGTON (1809–1894), major and congressman from Kentucky. Triplett joined the Confederate Congress late in the war and brought with him valuable experience in equipping and supplying troops in the field. Once in office he adopted a conservative state rights view that, according to historians Ezra J. Warner and W. Buck Yearns, "put him out of step with the more nationalist Kentucky [congressional] delegation."

Triplett was born in Franklin County, Kentucky, descended from Virginians who had distinguished themselves as officers in the American Revolution. Educated locally, Triplett in the 1820s worked as a teacher and surveyor. In 1833 he moved to Daviess County, Kentucky, where he surveyed, farmed, and worked as a merchant. He held the post of county surveyor for seventeen years. In 1840 Triplett, a Whig, was elected to the Kentucky House of Representatives and, in 1848, to the Kentucky Senate, serving until 1852.

Once the Civil War broke out, Triplett joined the Confederate army, serving as a captain in the First Kentucky Cavalry. Later he was promoted to the rank of major in the Quartermaster Corps and served on the staffs of Gens. Benjamin Hardin Helm, Earl Van Dorn, and Nathan Bedford Forrest. In 1862 he joined the staff of Gen. John C. Breckinridge as chief quartermaster. In February 1864, Triplett was elected from the Second District to the Confederate House of Representatives. He served on the Claims Committee, and as a former quartermaster officer, he not surprisingly voted to supply and equip the Confederate forces. But Triplett objected to Jefferson Davis's centralization policies, opposing the destruction of private property in the path of the enemy and the conscription of farmers and mechanics.

Following Appomattox, Triplett farmed and served many terms as a judge in Daviess County.

BIBLIOGRAPHY

Wakelyn, Jon L. *Biographical Dictionary of the Confederacy.* Edited by Frank E. Vandiver. Westport, Conn., 1977.

Warner, Ezra J., and W. Buck Yearns. *Biographical Register of the Confederate Congress.* Baton Rouge, La., 1975.

JOHN DAVID SMITH

TRIPPE, ROBERT PLEASANT (1819–1900), private and congressman from Georgia. Trippe was born in Jasper County, Georgia, on December 21, 1819; his family moved soon afterward to a plantation in Monroe County, where Trippe grew up. At fifteen, he attended Randolph-Macon College in Virginia and two years later entered the University of Georgia, where he graduated with honors in 1839. After a year reading law in Athens, Trippe was admitted to the bar and opened a practice in Forsyth, Georgia. He was elected to the Georgia General Assembly in

1849 and 1851, and to the U.S. House of Representatives in 1855, where he served two terms.

Originally a Whig, Trippe turned to the Democratic party in the late 1850s. His opposition to secession led him into the Constitutional Union party, and he attended its 1860 convention in Baltimore. He actively campaigned in Georgia for its presidential candidate, John Bell, and was elected as a Unionist to the state's secession convention in January 1861. Though he voted against Georgia's ordinance of secession, he pledged his loyalty to the Confederacy and entered its army as a private. He served only until November 1861, when he was elected over his commanding officer, Judge E. G. Cabaniss, to represent Georgia's Seventh District in the First Congress.

During his term in Richmond, he supported an aggressive war effort and strong army, but unlike other members of Georgia's delegation, he did not support conscription as the best means of achieving these goals. From his position on the Commerce Committee, he pushed for more efficient and equitable tax-collection procedures. But because he favored Davis administration policies over those of Governor Joseph E. Brown on most other issues, he lost support within his district and declined to run for reelection in 1863. When his term ended, he reenlisted in the Confederate army, again as a private. There is little information about his military service during the war's final two years.

Trippe resumed his law practice in Forsyth after the war but refused to get involved in politics. Nevertheless, in 1872, his old friend Governor James Milton Smith appointed him associate justice to the state supreme court. He served until 1875 when he resigned and moved his law practice to Atlanta. He died there on July 22, 1900.

BIBLIOGRAPHY

Northen, William J., ed. *Men of Mark in Georgia.* Vol. 3. Atlanta, 1908. Reprint, Spartanburg, S.C., 1974.

Wakelyn, Jon L. *Biographical Dictionary of the Confederacy.* Edited by Frank E. Vandiver. Westport, Conn., 1977.

Warner, Ezra J., and W. Buck Yearns. *Biographical Register of the Confederate Congress.* Baton Rouge, La., 1975.

JOHN C. INSCOE

TUBMAN, HARRIET (1820 or 1821–1913), Union spy and abolitionist. Tubman was born on a plantation in Dorchester County, Maryland. One of the eleven children born to her slave parents, Harriet Green and Benjamin Ross, she was given the name Araminta. The young slave girl suffered whippings and beatings and sustained a life-threatening head injury in her teens. At the age of twenty-three she married a free black, John Tubman.

In 1849 when her owner died, she escaped into freedom (leaving her husband behind when he refused to accompany her), took the name Harriet Tubman, and found work in Philadelphia. Within a year, she was involved in rescue attempts to free other family members and became an invaluable asset to the movement organized to assist slaves escaping to freedom. Braving the dangers, Tubman became one of the most intrepid conductors on the Underground Railroad. She moved to Canada in 1852, having made a total of eleven trips in three years, rescuing several dozen slaves.

Given the title "General Tubman" by abolitionist John Brown, Tubman became even more active when the Civil War broke out. For this reason, slave owners put a steep price on her head, and she was perhaps the most wanted woman in the Confederacy. Despite this threat, Tubman made nineteen more trips, leading nearly three hundred runaways out of the South. She worked out of Fortress Monroe, Virginia, before being sent to Beaufort, South Carolina, by the governor of Massachusetts. Under the command of Maj. Gen. David Hunter, Tubman was a scout and spy. During the summer of 1863 she assisted Col. James Montgomery in military campaigns designed to terrorize civilians and stir slaves into rebellion along the Combahee River. They were able to liberate nearly eight hundred slaves and effectively undermine Confederate morale in the South Carolina low country.

Tubman remained relatively impoverished, receiving only three hundred dollars for her three years of service to the Union. After the war she retired to Auburn, New York, and opened a Home for Indigent and Aged Negroes. She died in 1913 in relative obscurity, unheralded as a war hero until the modern era.

BIBLIOGRAPHY

Conrad, Earl. *Harriet Tubman.* Washington, D.C., 1990.

Sterling, Dorothy, ed. *We Are Your Sisters: Black Women in the Nineteenth Century.* New York, 1984.

CATHERINE CLINTON

TUCKER, JOHN RANDOLPH (1812–1883), naval officer. This thirty-five-year veteran of the U.S. Navy "went South" with his home state of Virginia in April 1861. As skipper of *Patrick Henry* in 1861 and 1862, he commanded a small flotilla of gunboats on the James River and fought in the Battles of Hampton Roads and Drewry's Bluff. In September 1862, he took charge of the ironclad ram *Chicora* at Charleston, South Carolina, where the following March he became flag officer of the squadron.

Under Commodore Tucker, Charleston became a showcase for Confederate contributions to naval technology, including mines, torpedo boats, and the first submarine *(H. L. Hunley)* to sink a ship in combat. After the evacuation of Charleston in February 1865, Tucker commanded the naval batteries on the James River near Richmond. His naval battalion of some four hundred sailors and marines, which joined the rear guard of the Army of Northern Virginia as it retreated toward Appomattox, distinguished itself at the Battle of Sayler's Creek. In this final major field engagement of the Civil War, Tucker was the last of Lee's commanders to surrender.

In 1866, Tucker became a rear admiral in the Peruvian navy. He introduced Confederate naval technology to the combined fleet of Peru and Chile, which he commanded for eight months in a war against Spain. As president of Peru's Hydrographic Commission of the Amazon (1867–1874), Admiral Tucker and his handpicked team of former Confederate officers charted the headwaters of the Amazon River for steam navigation. He died at Petersburg, Virginia.

BIBLIOGRAPHY

Rochelle, James Henry. *Life of Rear Admiral John Randolph Tucker.* Washington, D.C., 1903.

Werlich, David P. *Admiral of the Amazon: John Randolph Tucker, His Confederate Colleagues, and Peru.* Charlottesville, Va., 1990.

DAVID P. WERLICH

TUCKER, WILLIAM FEIMSTER (1827–1881), brigadier general. Tucker was born May 9, 1827, in Iredell County, North Carolina. He attended Emory and Henry College in Virginia; upon graduation he moved to Houston, Mississippi. Tucker won election as probate judge of Chickasaw County in 1855. He was subsequently admitted to the bar and was practicing law when the Civil War began.

Tucker fought in a number of important campaigns during the war. In May 1861, he entered the army in Lynchburg, Mississippi, gaining a commission as captain of Company K of the Eleventh Mississippi Infantry. He served in the Shenandoah Valley and fought at First Manassas under Gen. Barnard E. Bee. Shortly thereafter he was transferred west and named colonel of the Forty-first Mississippi on May 8, 1862. His regiment fought at the Battles of Perryville, Murfreesboro, Chickamauga, and Chattanooga. He led a brigade at Missionary Ridge and during the Atlanta campaign, gaining the rank of brigadier general in March 1864. On May 14, Tucker sustained a severe wound at Resaca, Georgia, and saw no additional field action. At the end of the war, he was commander of the District of Southern Mississippi and Eastern Louisiana.

Tucker returned to Chickasaw County, working as an attorney and serving in the legislature in 1876 and 1878. He was killed at Okolona, Mississippi, on September 14, 1881, the victim of an angry plaintiff in a misappropriation-of-funds suit Tucker had pending. The former general was buried in Okolona.

BIBLIOGRAPHY

Connelly, Thomas L. *Army of the Heartland: The Army of Tennessee, 1861–1862.* Baton Rouge, La., 1967.

Connelly, Thomas L. *Autumn of Glory: The Army of Tennessee, 1862–1865.* Baton Rouge, La., 1971.

Spencer, James, comp. *Civil War Generals: Categorical Listings and a Biographical Directory.* New York, 1986.

Warner, Ezra J. *Generals in Gray: Lives of the Confederate Commanders.* Baton Rouge, La., 1959.

MARVIN SCHULTZ

TUPELO, MISSISSIPPI. In the spring of 1864, Gen. William Tecumseh Sherman was pushing his forces toward Atlanta and was concerned about his supply line, which ran through middle Tennessee. The supplies for his 100,000 men traveled over the Nashville and Chattanooga Railroad; its security had to be preserved. His primary fear was Gen. Nathan Bedford Forrest and his successful cavalry, then operating in Mississippi under the command of Gen. Stephen D. Lee. Forrest had a reputation for raiding and defeating formidable forces with limited resources.

Sherman respected Forrest's skill and in May deployed Gen. Samuel D. Sturgis from Memphis to seek out Forrest. Sturgis returned to Memphis when he could not locate the general, who was replenishing his forces in Tupelo, Mississippi, a town in the northeast part of the state. Forrest, under orders from Lee, soon left Tupelo to attack Sherman's supply lines. He did not get far before Sherman again ordered Sturgis to find and destroy him. This time, on June 10, Sturgis's cavalry commander, Gen. Benjamin H. Grierson, met Forrest at Brice's Cross Roads, about thirty miles north of Tupelo. By noon, Forrest's outnumbered cavalry, armed with six-shot Colt revolvers, had defeated Grierson decisively, and the Federal troops fled, abandoning their supplies.

Now Sherman became even more determined to keep Forrest from interfering with his plans. This time he sent Gen. A. J. Smith, who happened to be in the same area as Forrest. Smith's orders were to "bring Forrest to bay and whip him if possible." Smith collected a force of 14,000 men, made up of two infantry divisions, Grierson's cavalry, and a brigade of African American troops. They moved south July 5 on two parallel roads. Two days later the force was intercepted by troops sent out by Forrest. This time, the Southerners fled, and Smith moved toward Pontotoc, a town about twenty miles directly west of Tupelo.

The Confederate commanders, Generals Lee and Forrest, with a combined force of 8,000 men (about half the number commanded by Smith), hoped to choose the site for a battle while slowing the march of Smith's column with skirmishes. At Okolona, south of Pontotoc and Tupelo, the Confederates had deployed on a hill behind a swamp that was further obstructed by fallen trees. One of their brigades, under James Roland Chalmers, attacked the Federal forces east of Pontotoc. Because Lee and Forrest felt secure in Okolona, they wanted Smith to continue to move south. Smith hesitated after the attack. The Confederates thought he was starting a retreat and abandoned their secured location to pursue him. Smith, however, surprised them on July 13 by turning east toward Tupelo rather than continuing south toward Okolona. Actually, Smith had plans to secure Tupelo and gain possession of the Mobile and Ohio Railroad, which had been completed just before the war.

Forrest, with Hinchie P. Mabry's Mississippi Brigade, attacked Smith's rear on the Tupelo road. Lee, with Chalmers's and Abraham Buford's divisions, moved parallel to, but south of, Smith's troops. Twice on July 13, Lee attacked Smith's flank. The Confederate attacks were not well coordinated; Smith's brigade of African American troops, acting as a rear guard, successfully deflected Forrest's attempts, and Lee's flank attacks were ineffectual. Smith was able to position his troops for battle in Tupelo.

On the fourteenth, Lee ordered an assault. His troops attacked from the front while Forrest moved on the Union left and rear. Forrest later commented that Smith's fortifications were "almost impregnable." The Confederates made little progress against the enormous firepower of the Union forces. Soldiers repeatedly charged the fortifications only to meet bayonets and volleys at close range. The Mississippi summer heat also took a heavy toll. Yet Lee's forces continued to fall back, rally, and attack again and again, "yelling and howling like Comanches," according to Smith. About 1:00 Lee ordered the Confederates to fall back. They then withdrew and built a fortified position out of rails, logs, and bales of cotton. In the fighting many were killed or wounded. Forrest reported 210 killed, 1,116 wounded; in Mabry's Mississippi Brigade, all the commanders were killed or wounded. Smith suffered fewer casualties—77 killed, 559 wounded, and 38 missing. The Confederates would not give up; they attempted a rear attack and a late night attack at 11:00 P.M. Nothing was successful. Smith's forces remained in position.

Despite his success, Smith did not take the initiative. Forrest was able to rally his troops, and Smith began withdrawing toward Memphis because of a shortage of supplies. Forrest's men pursued and attacked at Old Town Creek. His cavalry outfought Grierson's, but the Confederates could do little against Smith's infantry. In the fighting Forrest received a "painful wound" and had to withdraw. Smith continued his retreat to Memphis, pursued by Confederate soldiers.

The Confederate forces suffered enormous losses; in Forrest's words, the battle would "furnish the historian a bloody record." He consoled himself, however, with the belief that Lee's forces had spared northeastern Mississippi an enormous amount of destruction that Smith would have inflicted had he been able to remain in the area. Also, Forrest was still capable of harassing the Union men.

The battle nevertheless was a costly draw. The Confederates suffered heavy casualties, but Smith failed to destroy Lee's and Forrest's army.

When Gen. Ulysses S. Grant heard of Smith's retreat and the Confederate loss, he wrote Sherman that the Union forces must "keep a close watch on Forrest, and not permit him to gather strength and move into Middle Tennessee." General Sherman was on his way to Atlanta when he got word of the results. Disappointed that Forrest was still capable of fighting and could still attack his supply line, he commanded Smith to "keep after Forrest."

BIBLIOGRAPHY

Bearss, Edwin C. *The Tupelo Campaign, June 22–July 23, 1864: A Documented Narrative and Troop Movement Maps.* Washington, D.C., 1969.

Lee, Stephen D. "The Battle of Tupelo." *Publications of the Mississippi Historical Society* 6 (1902): 38–52.

U.S. War Department. *War of the Rebellion: A Compilation of the Official Records of the Union and Confederate Armies.* Ser. 1, vol. 39, pts. 1–2. Washington, D.C., 1892.

RAY SKATES

TURNER, JOSEPH A. (1826–1868), editor and publisher. Before the war, Turner managed his plantation near Eatonton, Georgia, served in the state legislature, published a manual for planters and some poetry, and contributed to several Southern literary journals. In 1860 he published *Plantation: A Southern Quarterly Journal,* which was noted as much for its vigorous defense of slavery as for its literary content. Because of a physical disability, Turner did not enter the Confederate military, but he contributed to the cause by delivering speeches to departing troops and publishing several wartime articles in the *Milledgeville Southern Recorder.*

In March 1862 Turner launched the *Countryman,* a weekly magazine whose purpose was to create distinctive Southern literature. In addition to Turner's own poetry and essays, it included articles on a variety of topics and some essays by Joel Chandler Harris. The magazine served as an unofficial journal of record for the Confederacy, containing weekly summaries of war news, messages and speeches by public officials, military orders, and announcements by President Jefferson Davis and state governors. Turner's editorials in the *Countryman* consistently stressed the necessity of cooperation if Southerners hoped to win the war. Always a strong supporter of Davis, Turner frequently criticized Georgia Governor Joseph E. Brown and once wrote a farce about the governor's speedy evacuation from Milledgeville shortly before the arrival of Union troops in 1864. Turner argued that Union military successes were in large part due to Brown's persistent opposition to Davis's policies.

In early 1866 Turner's antisubmission editorials antagonized Federal authorities, and when they placed what he regarded as limits on his freedom of expression, Turner discontinued the *Countryman.*

BIBLIOGRAPHY

Bain, Robert, ed. *Southern Writers: A Biographical Dictionary.* Baton Rouge, La., 1979.

Flanders, Bertram Holland. *Early Georgia Magazines.* Athens, Ga., 1944.

Hubbell, Jay B. *The South in American Literature, 1607–1900.* Durham, N.C., 1954.

Huff, Lawrence. "Joseph Addison Turner: Southern Editor during the Civil War." *Journal of Southern History* 29 (February-November 1963): 469–485.

Huff, Lawrence. "The Literary Publications of Joseph Addison Turner." *Georgia Historical Quarterly* 46 (1962): 223–234.

CHARLES MCARVER

TURNER, JOSIAH (1821–1901), captain and congressman from North Carolina. Born in Hillsborough, North Carolina, on December 27, 1821, Turner attended the University of North Carolina but left without graduating. After studying law, he was admitted to the bar in 1845. A Whig in politics, he represented Orange County in the House of Commons in 1852 and 1854 and 1855. He was defeated in a bid for the state senate in 1856 but was elected in 1858 and 1860. Although a successful attorney and the son of the second largest landowner in Orange County, he owned an estate valued at only $5,000 in 1860 and possessed only four slaves.

During the crisis of 1860–1861, Turner was an outspoken opponent of secession—a doctrine that he attributed to the unconstitutional and unpatriotic teachings of Thomas Jefferson and his successors in the Democratic party. An admirer of Alexander Hamilton and Daniel Webster, he surpassed most Southern Whigs in his unabashed nationalism and his condemnation of "the poison of state sovereignty." Denying that a state could constitutionally withdraw from the Union, he acknowledged the right of the Federal government to use military force to compel a recalcitrant state to obey its laws. Following the secession of South Carolina, he introduced a resolution into the state senate, declaring it the duty of the Federal government to collect the revenue duties, "peaceably if it could, forcibly if it must." In January 1861, after a group of citizens seized Forts Johnson and Caswell on the Cape Fear River, he sponsored another resolution denouncing the action and praising Governor John W. Ellis for returning the forts to Federal custody. He opposed the bill calling for a state convention and resisted efforts to arm the state militia. Even after Abraham Lincoln's call for troops, he voted against a resolution commending Governor Ellis for putting the state on a firm military footing.

Once hostilities had actually commenced, however, Turner remained loyal to his native state and initially supported the goal of Southern independence in order "to avoid the humiliation which follows subjugation." After joining the Guilford Grays and then serving in Fort Macon, he raised a company of cavalry and was elected its captain. At the Battle of New Bern in March 1862, he sustained a wound that effectively ended his military career. He resigned his commission the following November.

Despite his military service, Turner remained adamantly hostile toward the secessionists in the Democratic party, whom he blamed for starting the war. In November 1861 he campaigned for a seat in the First Confederate Congress but lost to Democrat Archibald Hunter Arrington. Running in a predominantly Democratic district in the northern Piedmont, he carried only one county and received less than 30 percent of the vote.

Two years later, however, he managed to win the congressional seat by capitalizing upon widespread disenchantment with the Jefferson Davis administration and upon Arrington's unpopular vote in favor of exempting overseers from the draft. Running as a Conservative, he denounced the tax-in-kind and other administration policies, promised to "exert himself to maintain the civil law against the usurpations of the military power," and received a commanding 60 percent of the vote. Although the Conservative party in North Carolina was bitterly divided over the propriety of entering into direct peace negotiations with the North, Turner successfully cultivated the support of both factions, and after the election each group claimed him as one of its own.

Once in Congress, where he served on the Foreign Affairs and Indian Affairs committees, Turner quickly aligned himself with the extreme opponents of the Davis administration. He voted against virtually all of its economic and military policies, including conscription, impressment, the suspension of the writ of habeas corpus, and proposals to draft slaves into the army. He also became prominently associated with the peace movement. Although he did not play an active role in the gubernatorial election of 1864, he apparently supported William W. Holden, who was urging North Carolina to undertake unilateral negotiations with the North, over incumbent governor Zebulon Vance, who believed that the initiative lay with the president and Congress. During the second session, which commenced in November 1864, he became a leader in the movement to force President Davis into opening peace negotiations and introduced a resolution to that effect on December 16. Acting upon "the firm conviction that we were whipped," he was one of only a handful of congressmen to advocate peace on the basis of reconstruction of the Union. During the final weeks of the Virginia campaign, he worked unsuccessfully to convene the North Carolina General Assembly in order to make a separate peace.

Despite his strong ties to the peace movement, Turner broke with its leader, William W. Holden, soon after the war and played a central role in bringing about the provisional governor's defeat in the election of November 1865. Their estrangement apparently resulted from Holden's refusal to endorse his application for a presidential pardon—a long and rambling tirade against the leaders of the antebellum Democratic party, which the governor (himself a Democrat) indignantly characterized as "a bill of indictment against the Democracy." Prevented by the Radical Republicans from assuming the seat in the U.S. Congress to which he was elected in 1865, he was appointed president of the North Carolina Railroad and served in that position until 1868, when he became editor of the *Raleigh Sentinel.*

As a newspaper editor, Turner quickly gained notoriety for his caustic attacks on Congressional Reconstruction and on Governor Holden and the Republican-dominated General Assembly. His arrest and imprisonment on Holden's orders in 1870 was one of the major factors leading to the governor's impeachment. Indeed, he is frequently credited with being the person singly most responsible for the overthrow of Reconstruction in North Carolina. Nonetheless, his erratic and combative personality ultimately alienated his former allies and, ironically, he ended his political life as a Republican. While his talents as a partisan propagandist were formidable, Turner's career both in the Confederate Congress and in the postwar period largely corroborates the assessment of his contemporary, Samuel A. Ashe, that he "was good to pull down, but not to build up." He died at his home near Hillsborough on October 26, 1901.

BIBLIOGRAPHY

Alexander, Thomas B., and Richard E. Beringer. *The Anatomy of the Confederate Congress: A Study of the Influences of Member Characteristics on Legislative Voting Behavior, 1861–1865.* Nashville, Tenn., 1972.

Ashe, Samuel A. *Biographical History of North Carolina.* 8 vols. Greensboro, N.C., 1905–1917.

Hamilton, Joseph G. de Roulhac, and Max R. Williams, ed. *The Papers of William Alexander Graham.* 7 vols. to date. Raleigh, N.C., 1957–.

Wakelyn, Jon L. *Biographical Dictionary of the Confederacy.* Edited by Frank E. Vandiver. Westport, Conn., 1977.

Warner, Ezra J., and W. Buck Yearns. *Biographical Register of the Confederate Congress.* Baton Rouge, La., 1975.

THOMAS E. JEFFREY

TUSCALOOSA. A 500-ton bark, *Tuscaloosa* was formerly the merchantman *Conrad* of Philadelphia. Bound from Buenos Aires to New York with a cargo of wool in June of 1863, *Conrad* was overhauled by the Confederate commerce raider *Alabama,* commanded by Raphael Semmes. Instead of burning his prize as was his usual practice, Semmes converted *Conrad* into a tender to *Alabama,* renaming it *Tuscaloosa.* He appointed one of his officers, John Low, as acting lieutenant, commanding two other officers and at least a dozen sailors. (Low himself later listed twenty-three men who served aboard *Tuscaloosa.*). Transferred aboard the tender were three 12-pounder cannon, small arms, and provisions.

While cruising toward the Cape of Good Hope, Low captured and bonded an American merchantman, but because of the scarcity of U.S. merchant vessels, this became *Tuscaloosa*'s only capture during its six-month cruise. After a brief stay at Simon's Bay, South Africa, *Tuscaloosa* rendezvoused with *Alabama* at Angra Pequeña, southwest Africa. At its next port of call, Santa Catarina, Brazil, authorities ordered *Tuscaloosa* to leave immediately. A frustrated Low brought his ship back to Simon's Bay, only to have it seized by British authorities for alleged violation of Britain's neutrality. They rejected Low's contention that since *Tuscaloosa* had not been challenged during its previous visit, it had been recognized as a legitimate warship.

Three weeks after *Tuscaloosa* was seized, Low paid off and discharged his crew and left for England. Authorities at Simon's Bay, meanwhile, waited for the original owners to claim their ship. Since none appeared, however, the ship was subsequently turned over to the United States.

BIBLIOGRAPHY

Low, John. *The Logs of the CSS Alabama and CSS Tuscaloosa, 1862–1863 by John Low, CSN.* Edited by William Stanley Hoole. University, Ala., 1976.

Official Records of the Union and Confederate Navies in the War of the Rebellion. Washington, D.C., 1894–1927. Ser. 1, vol. 2.

Semmes, Raphael. *Memoirs of Service Afloat during the War between the States.* Baltimore, 1869. Reprint, New York, 1987.

NORMAN C. DELANEY

TWIGGS, DAVID E. (1790–1862), major general. Born in 1790 in Richmond County, Georgia, David Emanuel Twiggs had a distinguished career in the regular army; he fought in the War of 1812 and in the Black Hawk and Seminole wars. When the Mexican War began, he was colonel of the Second Dragoons, was promoted to brigadier general, and earned a brevet to major general at Monterey. Twiggs was not a West Pointer and was not popular with his officers and men. In 1858 he was court-martialed for a

DAVID E. TWIGGS. LIBRARY OF CONGRESS

breach of military discipline and briefly relieved of his command of the Department of Texas. He was back in charge, however, when the secession crisis began.

Twiggs wrote Winfield Scott in December 1860 and again in January 1861 asking what he should do in the event of the state's secession. Col. C. A. Waite was ordered to relieve him, but before he could do so, Ben McCulloch, a future Confederate brigadier general, raised a force of 500 volunteers and marched on Twigg's headquarters at San Antonio. Twiggs, with only 160 troops, surrendered February 18, 1861, without a shot being fired. For this action, he was dismissed by President James Buchanan "for treachery to the flag of his country" on March 1, 1861. On May 22 he was appointed a major general in the Confederate army and assigned to command the District of Louisiana. He was, however, unable to perform his duties very long. He returned to Georgia where he died July 15, 1862.

Twiggs is buried at the family home near Augusta. His daughter was married to the first Confederate quartermaster general, Col. Abraham C. Myers.

BIBLIOGRAPHY

"An Episode in the Texas Career of General David E. Twiggs." *Southwestern Historical Quarterly* 41 (1937): 167–173.

Brown, Russell K. "An Old Woman with a Broomstick: General David E. Twiggs and the U.S. Surrender in Texas, 1861." *Military Affairs* (1984): 57–61.

Brown, Russell K. "David Emanuel Twiggs." *Richmond County History* (1983): 12–26.

Brown, Russell K. "The Twiggs Swords." *Richmond County History* (1982): 22–31.

ANNE J. BAILEY

TYLER, JOHN (1790–1862), governor of Virginia, U.S. president, president of the 1861 Washington peace conference, and congressman from Virginia. The only former U.S. president to serve in the Confederate Congress, Tyler was born March 29, 1790, at Greenway, Charles City County, Virginia, the sixth child of John and Mary Marot (Armistead) Tyler. The younger John Tyler entered the College of William and Mary at age twelve and graduated five years later. After reading law with his father, he was admitted to the Virginia bar in 1809. In 1811 he was elected to the Virginia House of Delegates as a representative from Charles City County; he held this seat for five years until his elevation to the Virginia Council. During the War of 1812 he served as a captain of volunteers protecting the state capital. On March 29, 1813, he married Letitia Christian of New Kent County.

In 1816 Tyler was elected to the U.S. House of Representatives, where he showed himself a strict constructionist and opposed the Missouri Compromise. Poor health, which plagued him much of his life, forced him to resign in 1821. Two years later the citizens of Charles City County again sent him to the House of Delegates. In 1825 and 1826 he served one-year terms as governor. Following the completion of Tyler's second term, anti-Jackson forces in the General Assembly elected him to the U.S. Senate, where he remained until he was forced to resign in February 1836 after a dispute over legislative instructions. He retired briefly to Williamsburg to practice law. During the election of 1836 he was nominated for the vice-presidential slot on two of the four regional Whig tickets as the running mate of both William Henry Harrison and Hugh L. White, but he did no campaigning. He returned to the Virginia House of Delegates in the April 1838 election.

An attempt to regain his seat in the U.S. Senate in 1839 was abortive, but Tyler was named as the running mate of William Henry Harrison of Ohio at the Whig National Convention in December. The "log cabin and hard cider" campaign of 1840 swept the Harrison-Tyler ticket into office. When the sixty-eight-year-old Harrison died one month after his inauguration, Tyler settled the question of the status of a vice president who assumes executive duties on the death of the president. Instead of becoming acting president, Tyler became president in his own right and thus established the precedent for future generations.

Tyler's strict constructionism had always made his association with the Whigs an uneasy one, and his accession to the presidency ruptured his alliance with Henry Clay. Tyler's effort to sustain the delicate balance of factions by not immediately introducing a program allowed Clay, who was seeking to secure absolute control of the Whig party and to ensure his own election to the White House in 1844, to seize the initiative. Tyler had made it clear that he would support repeal of Martin Van Buren's Independent Treasury but left it to the special session of Congress that had been called by his predecessor to propose a new banking plan, though he reserved the right of veto.

When it became clear that Clay intended to revive the Bank of the United States, Tyler indicated his preference for a district bank. Clay maneuvered several amendments to the presidential plan that rendered it unacceptable to Tyler, who vetoed it on August 16. Unable to override the presidential veto, Clay tried vainly to introduce an amendment to the Constitution that would allow presidential vetoes to be overturned by a simple majority vote. On September 9 Tyler vetoed a second bank bill. In a move engineered by Clay in hopes of forcing Tyler to step down, the entire cabinet, with the exception of Secretary of State Daniel Webster, resigned on September 11. Two days later, Tyler was publicly read out of the Whig party.

For the next two years of his administration, Tyler faced a hostile Whig Congress that delighted in passing bills that the president routinely vetoed as unconstitutional. Several House committees recommended at various times that he be impeached for impeding the operation of government. Of necessity, low-key domestic policy characterized the last years of the administration. Tyler's most lasting contribution—aside from the precedent set by his accession to power—was the annexation of Texas.

Seeking an issue on which to found a third major political party centered on himself, Tyler settled as early as October 1841 on adding Texas to the Union. Downplaying the issue of the expansion of slavery, a specter that raised its head each time talk of Texas was introduced, Tyler and his secretary of state, Abel P. Upshur of Virginia, entered into secret negotiations with Sam Houston, the president of Texas. Midterm elections in 1842 had returned a Democratic majority to the House and reduced the Whig dominance in the Senate, so by the time the finishing touches were being put on the treaty of annexation in February 1844, Tyler was confident of winning congressional approval.

On February 28, however, Secretary of State Upshur and seven others were killed when a bow cannon called the "Peacemaker" exploded on the frigate *Princeton* while on a pleasure cruise on the Potomac. Tyler intimate Henry A. Wise of Virginia made a public pronouncement that Tyler would name John C. Calhoun to succeed Upshur. Backed into a corner, Tyler turned the delicate negotiations over to Calhoun. When the annexation treaty went to the Senate, Calhoun sent along copies of two official letters he had written to the British minister in Washington, stating that annexation was imperative to protect Southern slaveholders and the national security of the United States from the danger of British abolitionists working to eradicate the peculiar institution in the independent Texas nation. By resurrecting the slavery issue, Calhoun took the treaty down to defeat.

In the meantime, Tyler used his nascent third party to great advantage. On the same day that the Democratic convention met in Baltimore to nominate its presidential candidate for the 1844 election, Tyler followers convened in the same city to nominate their incumbent with the rallying cry "Tyler and Texas." Apprehensive of the potential pulling power of Tyler's state rights, strict constructionist stand and manipulated by Calhoun loyalists, the Democratic convention ignored front-runner Martin Van Buren, who was on record as opposed to annexation, and gave the nod to dark-horse candidate James K. Polk on a platform that included a call for the annexation of Texas. In August Tyler endorsed Polk rather than Clay, the Whig nominee. When Polk won the White House in the November election, Tyler announced that the Democratic victory had been a mandate on the annexation issue. Because a two-thirds majority in the Senate favoring ratification of the treaty was unlikely, Congress passed a joint resolution calling for the annexation of Texas, which Tyler signed into law on March 1, 1845, three days before his term expired.

Tyler retired to Sherwood Forest, a plantation near his birthplace in Charles City County that he had purchased during his presidency, and settled down to the life of a gentleman planter. His wife, Letitia, long partially paralyzed from a stroke, had died on September 10, 1842, while Tyler was in the White House. During his last year in office, on June 26, 1844, the president had married New York belle Julia Gardiner. (He was the first president to marry while in office.) Her father, David, had been one of those killed on board *Princeton;* indeed, both she and Tyler had been present on the fatal Potomac cruise.

Tyler's annexation of Texas exacerbated sectional tensions. Bitter debates over the expansion of slavery into the territories won during the Mexican War seized the national stage. From the peace of Sherwood Forest, Tyler commented on the Compromise of 1850, the Kansas-Nebraska Act, and the *Dred Scott* decision and was even occasionally mentioned as a presidential candidate.

Fearing slave rebellion in Charles City County in the

wake of John Brown's raid on Harpers Ferry, Tyler collected firearms at Sherwood Forest and became captain of the Silver Greys, a cavalry unit that would serve as the second line of defense in the event of an uprising.

In the spring of 1859 he supported Henry Wise and his own son, Robert Tyler, for the 1860 Democratic presidential nomination, but by July he was being prodded by moderates such as James D. B. De Bow of *De Bow's Review* to make himself available as a compromise candidate at the upcoming Democratic convention. Tyler believed that the worst mistake the party could make would be to adopt a platform of any sort and criticized the withdrawal of some of the Southern delegates at Charleston as a strategic blunder. During the ensuing campaign he backed Southern Democrat John C. Breckinridge, although he hoped that the election would in fact give none of the candidates a majority in the electoral college and that the election would be thrown to the House of Representatives, where he was sure that Joseph Lane of Oregon would win approval as president.

When sectional tensions mounted after the election of Abraham Lincoln, Tyler called on December 14, four days before South Carolina seceded, for a peace convention of the twelve border states. The Virginia General Assembly responded the next month by proposing a convention of all the states, a move Tyler considered abortive because it would involve both abolitionist and fire-eater extremists. Tyler won appointment as one of the five representatives the Old Dominion sent to the Washington peace conference. Simultaneously, he was also named as Virginia's special commissioner to James Buchanan with instructions to persuade the lame-duck president to take no action against the seceded states until the peace conference had convened on February 4. Three days later, Tyler was elected to represent Charles City, James City, and New Kent counties in the emergency Virginia convention that was to assemble in Richmond on February 13.

The peace conference unanimously chose Tyler president on February 5. As he had feared, because of the secession of the lower South, there were twice as many free states represented at the conference as there were slave states. Tyler divided his time between chairing the conference and beseeching Buchanan to abandon Fort Sumter and thus avoid a showdown with the hotheads in South Carolina. During the critical period between the convening of the peace conference and the reporting by the resolutions committee chaired by James Guthrie of Kentucky, Tyler abandoned his moderate Unionist stand. Previously he had been a conditional Unionist—one who supported the preservation of the Union but not at the cost of emancipation, even a compensated one. By February 15, Tyler no longer believed that a political solution to the sectional crisis was possible. Instead, he believed that Virginia should leave the Union. The Old Dominion's secession would force the withdrawal of the border states, Pennsylvania, New York, and New Jersey, thus crippling the North, which would not be able to retaliate militarily. In Tyler's view, Virginia's secession would allow the South to battle to a stalemate without a shot being fired.

Tyler's change in view, and his despondency after he and several other commissioners to the peace conference met with Lincoln on February 23, led him to support James A. Seddon's minority report to the peace conference, which reiterated the right of any state to secede from the Union and which would have guaranteed the South control of executive appointments below the old Missouri Compromise line. He consistently voted against the Guthrie resolutions but passed them along to Congress as instructed after they carried by narrow margins.

On the last day of February, Tyler returned to Richmond, condemned the results of the peace conference, and advocated the immediate secession of Virginia. Taking his seat in the state convention, he rose on March 13 and 14 to deliver a set piece calling for secession if Lincoln did not abandon the Federal forts, recognize the Confederate States of America, and begin treaty negotiations with the new nation. In the roll calls on April 3, 15, and 17, he cast his vote for secession.

After the firing on Fort Sumter and Virginia's decision to leave the Union, Tyler served on the Virginia commission that negotiated joining the Confederacy and drafted the resolution placing the commonwealth's military forces under the command of Jefferson Davis. Citing poor health, he declined nomination to the Provisional Confederate Congress while it met in Montgomery but accepted his unanimous election by the Virginia state convention once the Confederate government relocated to Richmond.

In the Confederate House of Representatives elections of November 1861, Tyler handily defeated William H. Macfarland and James Lyons in Virginia's Third Congressional District but had little opportunity to serve his constituents. He died January 18, 1862, at the Exchange Hotel in Richmond after a brief illness. His express wish that he be buried simply at Sherwood Forest was ignored. Tyler's body lay in state in the Confederate Congress on January 20. After an elaborate service the next day at St. Paul's Episcopal Church, he was interred in Hollywood Cemetery near the grave of former president James Monroe.

On May 7, 1864, black troops under the command of Brig. Gen. Edward A. Wild occupied Sherwood Forest. A month later Wild turned possession of the house over to two of the Tyler family slaves. The plantation was looted and the ground floor turned into a school. Although furniture was destroyed, a death mask of Tyler smashed, and outbuildings and fences burned, the former president's papers and most of the family silver and portraits were saved, all having been removed to Richmond for safekeeping in April (ironically, most of the papers were destroyed during the evacuation fire in 1865). In spite of Tyler's position as the only former U.S. president to have advocated secession and served in the Confederate government, his widow successfully lobbied Congress in 1881 for an annual Federal pension of $1,200, an amount increased to $5,000 in March 1882 after the assassination of President James A. Garfield.

BIBLIOGRAPHY

Gunderson, Robert G. *Old Gentlemen's Convention: The Washington Peace Convention of 1861.* Madison, Wis., 1961.

Morgan, Robert J. *A Whig Embattled: The Presidency under John Tyler.* Lincoln, Nebr., 1954.

Peterson, Norma Lois. *The Presidencies of William Henry Harrison and John Tyler.* American Presidency Series. Lawrence, Kans., 1989.

Seager, Robert, II. *and Tyler too: A Biography of John & Julia Gardiner Tyler.* New York, 1963.

Tyler, Lyon Gardiner. *The Letters and Times of the Tylers.* 3 vols. Richmond, Va., 1884–1896.

SARA B. BEARSS

TYLER, ROBERT CHARLES (c. 1833–1865), brigadier general. Evidence is scarce about Tyler's prewar life. Apparently born in Baltimore in 1833 and raised there, he took part in William Walker's filibustering expedition to Nicaragua in 1856. He lived in Memphis at the start of the war, volunteering for Company D, Fifteenth Tennessee Infantry, on April 18, 1861. Promoted to captain, Tyler was present at the Battle of Belmont and then elevated to lieutenant colonel on December 26. He led the Fifteenth on the first day of Shiloh until he was seriously wounded.

Commissioned colonel of the regiment soon thereafter, Tyler also served briefly in the fall of 1862 as supply officer and provost marshal for Braxton Bragg's Army of Tennessee. He led the consolidated Fifteenth and Thirty-seventh Tennessee at Hoover's Gap, June 24, 1863, and Chickamauga, where he performed particularly well and was slightly wounded. At Missionary Ridge, November 25, Tyler commanded Bate's Brigade. While trying to rally his men after the Union breakthrough, he was again severely wounded; his left leg was subsequently amputated.

Though promoted to brigadier general to date from February 23, 1864, Tyler never returned to the army. Convalescing at West Point, Georgia, he took charge of local defense at the approach of James H. Wilson's Union raiders on April 16, 1865. Tyler was shot and killed while defending a small earthwork fort named for him. He is buried in Pinewood Cemetery, West Point.

BIBLIOGRAPHY

Slatter, W. J. "Last Battle of the War." *Confederate Veteran* 4 (1896): 381–382. Reprint, Wilmington, N.C., 1985.

Warner, Ezra J. "Who Was General Tyler?" *Civil War Times Illustrated* 9 (October 1970): 15–19.

STEPHEN DAVIS

TYSON, BRYAN (1830–1909?), Unionist. An anti-Confederate political activist from central North Carolina, Tyson promoted reunionism and the peace movement in the Tarheel state between 1862 and 1864, and the cause of the Northern Democrats in the 1864 presidential election. Son of Aaron Tyson, a wealthy farmer and physician, Bryan was raised on a farm in Brower's Mills, a rural community in southern Randolph County. When the war erupted, Tyson, owner of four slaves, was the proprietor of a farm and a farm implement manufacturing firm in northern Moore County.

Tyson, an old-line Whig, was a staunch Unionist during the secession crisis. Repelled by the Confederate Conscription Act passed in April 1862, Tyson began writing a reunionist tract entitled *A Ray of Light; or, A Treatise on the Sectional Troubles Religiously and Morally Considered,* which was published clandestinely in August in Raleigh. Tyson warned readers that the Confederacy must arrange an armistice and negotiate a return to the Union while it still had the power to do so. Otherwise the South would surely be defeated and subjected to Republican rule. Tyson pointed out that although the Northern Democrats opposed Confederate nationhood, they were willing to compromise with the South and work for reunion with a constitutional guarantee of slavery for the returning Southern states. He urged his readers to cooperate with the Northern Democrats in their drive to reconstruct the Union peacefully.

Tyson was arrested and imprisoned because of his disloyal publications. While in jail, he wrote a short "reunion circular" advocating reunion on the basis offered by the Northern Democrats. It was later printed in Raleigh and circulated through the mails. With the help of influential friends and family members, he managed to gain release from jail and a deferment from the draft.

Tyson mailed copies of his book and circular to Jefferson Davis, Alexander H. Stephens, and select members of the Confederate Congress. He was arrested again but released when he promised that he would no longer try to circulate his writings. Tyson became a wanted man when he broke his pledge and sent copies of his publications to 150 members of the North Carolina General Assembly.

Rather than face arrest and prison a third time, Tyson fled to the Union lines and then to Washington, D.C., where he was rewarded for his loyalty to the Union with a clerkship in the Treasury Department. He sent copies of his reunionist political tracts to Abraham Lincoln, who ignored his request that the president assist him in the publication of a pro-Union propaganda tract to be distributed to Confederate prisoners of war in the North.

Tyson's political activism finally bore fruit in the peace movement that swept North Carolina in the summer of 1863, when peace advocates began to call openly for peace and reunion on the basis suggested by the Northern Democrats. In August, Tyson sent a circular to North Carolina for peace advocates to copy and distribute. In this "Day-Star Circular," Tyson urged North Carolina "to take her position under the stars and stripes; and, one star plucked from the Confederacy, the remaining states would soon follow."

In October 1863, Tyson published a Democratic political tract entitled *The Institution of Slavery in the Southern States, Religiously and Morally Considered in Connection with Our Sectional Troubles.* In it, he pleaded with Northerners to encourage the Unionist-led peace movement in the South by assuring Southerners that the war was being waged only to defend the Constitution and to preserve the Union—not to destroy slavery in the Southern states. Influential Republicans had Tyson dismissed from his job in the Treasury Department for publishing the pamphlet.

In support of George B. McClellan's bid for the presidency in 1864, Tyson wrote another tract entitled *Object of the Administration in Prosecuting the War,* which was endorsed by the National Democratic Resident Executive Committee. Tyson accused the Lincoln administration of deliberately sabotaging all efforts made by Southern Unionists to overthrow the Confederacy and reestablish the Union. Radical Republicans, he charged, feared that a coalition of Democrats, moderate Republicans, and Southern Unionists might achieve reunion short of emancipation. Tyson urged Northerners to vote for McClellan, who as president would return the South to the Union on a "strictly Constitutional basis"—that is, with the institution of slavery left intact.

As 1864 ended, Tyson saw all he had worked for during the past three years fall into ruins. His archenemies, both the secessionists and the Radical Republicans, had bested him. The secessionists, largely through military repression, had thwarted the peace advocates of North Carolina in their political campaign of 1863 and 1864 to carry the Old North State out of the Confederacy and back into the Union; the Radicals, in addition to helping quash McClellan's bid for the White House, had refused to encourage or aid Southern peace advocates, indirectly contributing to the movement's political demise.

BIBLIOGRAPHY

Auman, William Thomas. "Bryan Tyson: Southern Unionist and American Patriot." *North Carolina Historical Review* 62 (1985): 257–292.

Zuber, Richard L. *Jonathan Worth: A Biography of a Southern Unionist.* Chapel Hill, N.C., 1965.

William Thomas Auman

U

UNIFORMS. [*This entry is composed of two articles that discuss the design, production, and distribution of uniforms for the Confederate armed services:* Army Uniforms *and* Navy and Marine Uniforms. *For further discussion of the uniforms of particular branches of the Confederate armed services, see* Artillery, *overview article;* Infantry; Marine Corps; Medical Department; *and* Signal Corps. *See also* Clothing; Medals and Decorations.]

Army Uniforms

Within the Confederate army, from beginning to end, simply clothing the troops consistently took precedence over achieving uniformity. This fact is central to an understanding of both the variety and the uniformity of Confederate clothing. Also crucial is a grasp of the two main systems the Confederate government employed to get clothing to the troops, the commutation system and the issue system.

The commutation system, decreed by the Confederate Congress at the beginning of the war, was intended to save precious government resources by requiring the 100,000 volunteers of the Provisional Army to clothe themselves. They were to be paid fifty dollars a year per man in commutation money for the use of the clothing. Although the money sometimes was paid to the states, a few of which provided clothing according to state uniform regulations, most went to the captains of companies or the men themselves. With no uniform regulations to follow, the clothing the volunteers obtained was as varied as the hundreds of companies in Confederate service.

The uniform regulations issued by the Confederate government in May 1861 were intended only for the Confederate Regular Army, an organization of about 6,000 men. These regulations were inspired by Austrian Jager and French officers' uniforms and for both officers and enlisted men consisted of cadet gray double-breasted frock coats trimmed in a color indicating the wearer's branch of service, sky blue trousers (dark blue for field and general officers), and branch-color kepis. Only the quality of the uniforms and the insignia distinguished officers from enlisted men. Very few of the enlisted uniforms were actually made, but eventually most officers of both the Regular and Provisional armies adopted versions of the Regular Army uniform.

Confederate insignia was one of the few areas where the Regular Army regulations took a firm hold, in part because it was based on the old U.S. Army system. Branch colors were as follows: infantry, sky blue; artillery, red; cavalry, yellow; medical, black; and staff, buff. These colors were used to trim collars, cuffs, and the fronts of coats and were also the body color of the kepi. Noncommissioned-officer rank insignia was based on chevrons on each sleeve in the branch color, worn points down, two for corporals and three for sergeants. First sergeants wore a lozenge within the angle of the chevrons, ordnance sergeants a star, quartermaster sergeants a tie, and sergeants major an arc. Their trousers were trimmed with branch-color stripes in widths based on rank. Privates wore no insignia, but did wear branch trim on their coats.

Officers' rank insignia was based on the Austrian system of stars or bars worn on the collar, and the French sleeve braid system known as "galons." Line officers—second lieutenants, first lieutenants, and captains—wore one, two, or three bars, respectively, on each side of the collar, with lieutenants wearing one strand of sleeve braid and captains two. Field officers—majors, lieutenant colonels, and colonels—wore one, two, or three stars, respectively, and three strands of sleeve braid. General officers wore three stars surrounded by a wreath and four strands of sleeve

ENLISTED MAN'S JACKET. Jacket of Pvt. E. Courtney Jenkins, Company B, Twenty-First Virginia Infantry. At least three Confederate companies privately procured these jackets manufactured by Kent, Paine, and Company, of Richmond, Virginia. While they were not standard jackets issued from Confederate army depots, their style is typical of those used by enlisted men. Photograph by Katherine Wetzel.

THE MUSEUM OF THE CONFEDERACY, RICHMOND, VIRGINIA

OFFICER'S FROCK COAT. Double-breasted frock coat of Brig. Gen. James Conner, C.S.A. Photograph by Katherine Wetzel.

THE MUSEUM OF THE CONFEDERACY, RICHMOND, VIRGINIA

braid. The number of sleeve braids was repeated on the kepi. There was also a system of trouser stripes of different widths of gold braid based on rank. Buttons were of brass, sometimes gilt, with a spread eagle for staff officers, a German *E* for engineer officers, and a block *A, I,* or *C* for artillery, infantry, and cavalry.

Waistbelt plates were not specifically uniform items, but rather parts of ordnance-supplied accoutrements. Although regulations specified that the device would be the "Arms of the Confederate States," such arms were never designed. This, plus the fact that officers procured their own sword belts, resulted in a wide variety of plates being worn, some with "CS" or "CSA" on the face, others plain brass, and still others in a buckle form; state seal plates also saw wide use. The most common forms actually used were probably the brass frame buckle, iron roller buckles, or captured U.S. belt plates.

Although the commutation system was intended to avoid both the stockpiling of uniforms and the need for making them, as early as the summer of 1861 there were reports of ragged Confederate troops in the field. The Confederate Quartermaster's Department discovered that much of the clothing the volunteers had purchased was of inferior quality. Far from home, these men now had no way to replenish their supply. As a result, the department sought and obtained congressional sanction to issue clothing. By the fall of 1861 the department had established clothing manufactories in several Southern cities and began to issue clothing to troops in need. This system was considered successful enough by October 1862 that it officially replaced the commutation system, although the changeover took some time to accomplish.

The issue system resulted in large quantities of simple jackets, trousers, shirts, drawers, shoes, and socks being issued, and lesser quantities of hats, caps, overcoats, and blankets. Each depot produced its own patterns and developed its own sources of supply, usually utilizing materials such as gray woolen jeans produced by local mills and supplemented, particularly later in the war, by large quantities of imported English cadet gray cloth. Thus, though each depot's product had some uniformity of its own, there was pattern variation between the depots. The quantity was usually sufficient for overall issue, but the quality of the clothing sometimes left much to be desired.

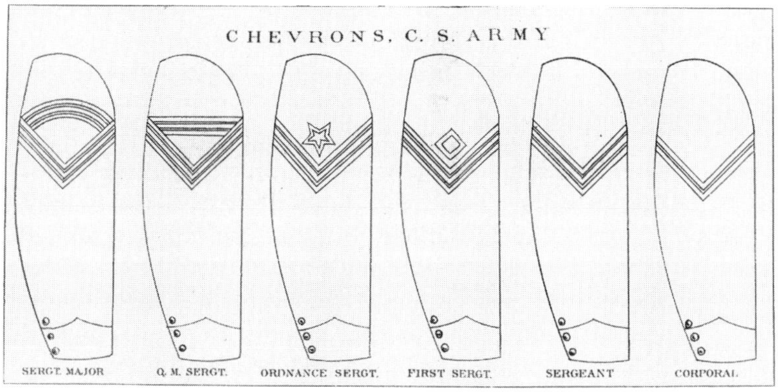

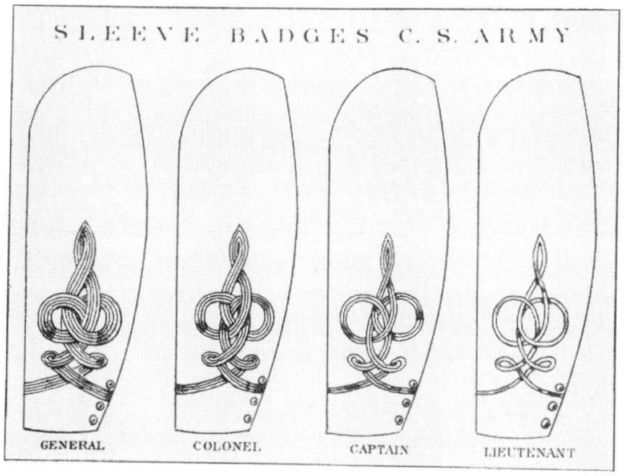

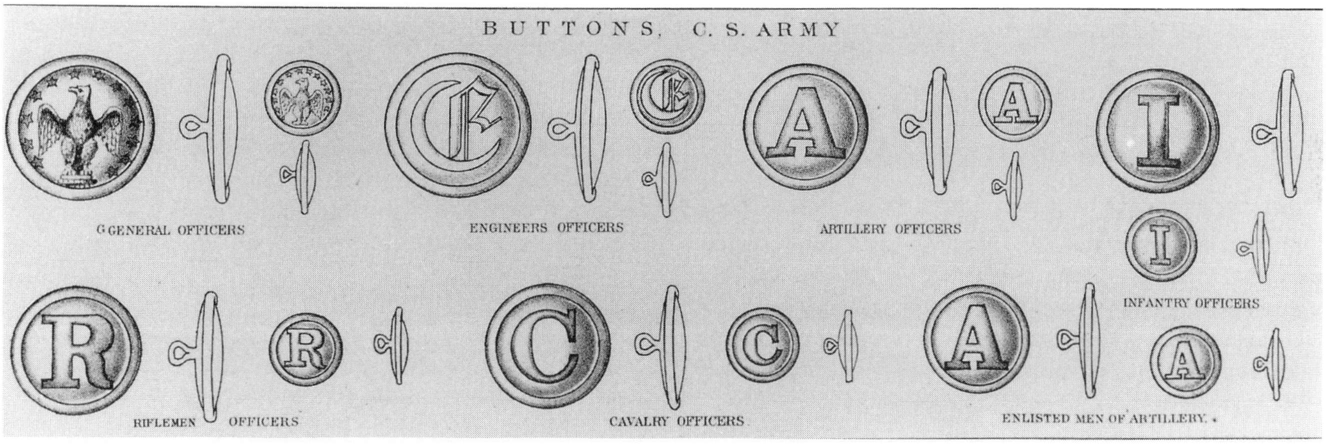

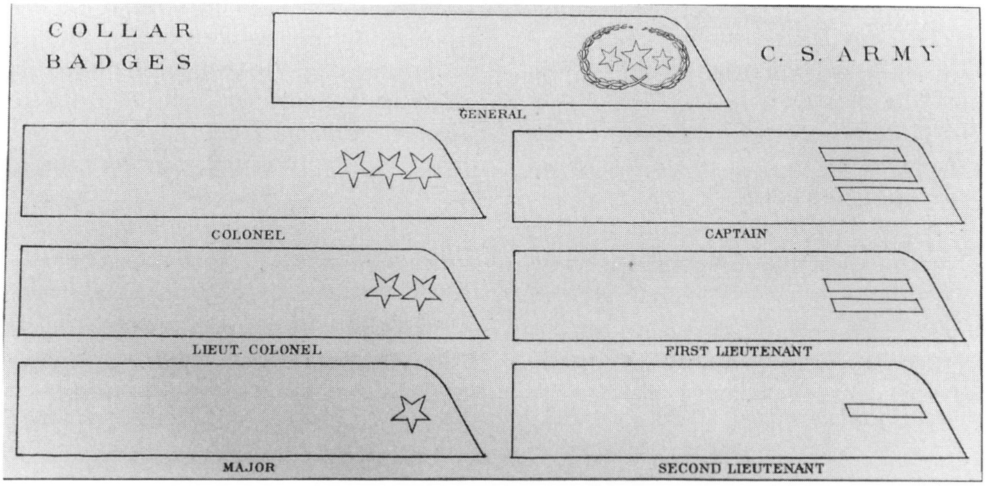

INSIGNIA AND BUTTONS. Chevrons, sleeve badges, buttons, and collar badges used in the Confederate army. The button shown for enlisted men of artillery is the same as the buttons worn by all other enlisted men, except that those buttons contained the number of the regiment, in figures, rather than the letter *A*. Illustrations taken from *Atlas to Accompany the Official Records of the Union and Confederate Armies,* compiled by Calvin D. Cowles, Washington, D.C., 1891–1895, plate 170. CIVIL WAR LIBRARY AND MUSEUM, PHILADELPHIA

Moreover, baths and the washing of clothing in the field was infrequent or nonexistent, which resulted in an accelerated wearing out of what should have been a sufficient supply. Often the issue clothing was supplemented by contributions from home or by captured Federal items. Occasionally, this captured clothing was dyed to conceal the blue color. When combined with the Confederate soldier's propensity to affect an individual look, these varied sources and styles resulted in a lack of uniformity in the Confederate ranks.

BIBLIOGRAPHY

Hill, Tucker, ed. *Catalogue of Uniforms, the Musuem of the Confederacy*. Richmond, Va., 1987.

Jensen, Leslie D. "A Survey of Confederate Central Government Quartermaster Issue Jackets." *Military Collector & Historian* 41, nos. 3–4 (1989).

Todd, Frederick P. *American Military Equipage, 1851–1872*. Vol. 2. Providence, R.I., 1977.

LES JENSEN

Navy and Marine Uniforms

Both the Confederate navy and the Marine Corps were small organizations, and although they faced shortages like the army, their size often allowed them to achieve a degree of uniformity in clothing that the army lacked.

Unlike the army, the Confederate navy issued clothing to its sailors from the beginning of the war. The initial supply came from captured U.S. Navy uniforms obtained from the Gosport Navy Yard in Norfolk, Virginia; soon after, this supply was supplemented by clothing purchased in England. In both cases, the uniforms were largely dark blue, and most of the navy wore this color through at least 1862. Confederate naval officers also wore dark blue uniforms, often old U.S. Navy clothing with the insignia changed.

Sometime in 1862, the Navy Department issued uniform regulations changing the basic color to gray. The change was not universally liked, many officers objecting on the basis that no navy in the world wore gray. By 1863, however, the changeover had largely been accepted.

The regulations seem to have been based mainly on the U.S. Navy's 1852 regulations, with the exceptions that there were no dress uniforms and a considerably different and complicated system of rank insignia was adopted. Officers wore double-breasted frock coats of steel gray cloth with rolling collars, gray trousers, and gray visored caps; enlisted ranks wore gray jackets or gray frocks with white duck collars, gray pants, and black or gray visorless caps in winter and white duck frocks with blue collars and cuffs, white pants, and gray or white visorless caps in summer. Officers wore rank insignia on the sleeves and shoulder straps; seamen wore it on their sleeves.

The Confederate Marine Corps was never officially allowed more than ten companies, and only six were recruited during the war. These companies never served together as a unit, instead operating as small detachments on board ship or at naval stations. No Marine Corps uniform regulations are known to exist, and it is probable, given the small size of the corps, that none were issued. Marine uniforms were therefore subject to variations based on local supply situations; yet some elements seem to have been common to most, if not all uniforms. Marine officers appear to have worn navy gray frock coats, double-breasted and cut in either the rolling collar navy style or the standing collar army style. Rank insignia was often the army sleeve braid, although distinctive marine shoulder knots were also sometimes worn.

Enlisted uniforms were probably based on the U.S. Marine Corps 1859 regulations. Enlisted men probably wore double-breasted gray frock coats or single-breasted jackets like the army's. At least in 1862, the style was distinctive and different from the Army's. Rank chevrons were probably worn points up rather than down as in the army. But the fact that there are no known photographs of Confederate enlisted marines, no known surviving enlisted uniforms, and no known regulations make specifics very difficult to establish.

BIBLIOGRAPHY

Donnelly, Ralph W. *The History of the Confederate States Marine Corps*. Washington, D.C., 1976.

Todd, Frederick P. *American Military Equipage, 1851–1872*. Vol. 2. Providence, R.I., 1977.

LES JENSEN

UNIONISM. In simplest terms Unionism describes the attitude of those white Southerners who opposed the Confederacy because they favored the Union. That simple definition, however, does not do justice to the diversity of Unionist sentiments and the changes in its meaning over time. Southern Unionism, after all, has a history older than the Confederacy. Decades before secession took place, Southerners and Northerners were denominating certain white Southerners as Unionists. In those earlier times it usually meant opposition to state rights, as during the nullification crisis, or, later, opposition to the advocacy of secession.

The term is also complicated in that among the states of the United States, only Southern states seceded. That singularity meant that only white Southerners were confronted with the necessity of calculating their degree of commitment to the United States. We will never know, as we do about white Southerners, the depth or intensity of Unionism among Northerners; they were never asked to make a choice between region and nation. Indeed, simply because eleven Southern states seceded and formed the Confederacy, it is often assumed that the existence of Southern Unionism needs to be explained. In fact, it is secession that requires explanation since it was accomplished in a region that during the era of the great Virginian presidents—Jefferson, Madison, and Monroe—was probably the most Unionist section in the nation. And when South Carolina in 1832 challenged the national authority over the tariff issue, it was a Southern-born president, Andrew Jackson, who forced the state to rescind its act of nullification. Significantly, too, no Southern states offered support to South Carolina's position and some fiercely denounced the idea of nullification. Even as late as 1850 and 1851, Southern candidates who supported the Unionist Compromise of 1850 won election across the region. Southern Unionism during the Confederacy, in short, had deep roots in the Southern past. As a result, Unionism helped shape the way secession itself took place.

Unionism during the Election of 1860. One measure of the strength of Unionist sentiment during the election campaign of 1860 was the almost instantaneous creation of the Constitutional Union party. Although national in aims and intention, the party was really a Southern organization, which sought to escape the conflict over slavery by simply asserting the value of keeping the Union intact. Its presidential candidate, John Bell of Tennessee, a large slaveholder and prominent Whig politician, was a well-known and fervent opponent of secession. (He had been Unionist enough to vote against the Kansas-Nebraska Act.) Although many of the South's leading politicians threatened to support secession if Abraham Lincoln were elected in November, both Bell and his new party made no such threats. The election statistics measured how close the Constitutional Union party had come to reflecting the sentiments of the voters of the South. When the Confederacy went to war in April 1861, 49 percent of its voting population less than six months before had supported candidates (Bell, with 40.3 percent, and Stephen A. Douglas, with 8.6 percent) who opposed secession and the formation of the Confederacy. Even John C. Breckinridge, the Southern Democratic candidate, did not advocate secession; he merely was prepared to accept it.

The objection to secession during the election of 1860 was clearly an outgrowth of Southern history, particularly the two-party politics of the antebellum years, and the geographical distribution of slaveholding. Both help account as well for the persistence of Southern Unionism during the Confederate years. Although the Whig party was officially dead throughout the nation by 1860, among Southerners the nationalist or Unionist sentiments that had been the hallmark of the party over the years persisted. Statistical analyses of voting patterns reveal a high correlation between those counties in the South that had voted Whig in the 1840s and those that supported Bell and Douglas in 1860. Surprisingly, many of those counties were in the plantation areas of the Deep South, which had long been Whig. The ballots may have been cast against secession, but the motive was not necessarily enduringly Unionist, as the reaction of these areas showed, once Lincoln won the election.

Unionism during the Secession Crisis. The first real test of the South's commitment to Unionism came soon after the election of Lincoln in November. Within three months seven states of the Deep South had seceded, an alacrity that some historians later thought measured the secessionists' fear that once the excitement of the election had faded Southern Unionist sentiment would revive and stop secession in its tracks. And it is true that, of those seven, only Texas, the last Deep South state to secede, permitted a popular vote on the issue of secession. (Other states voted on the issue, but they were in the upper South.) In any case, even if in fact a majority of white Southerners in the seven states did endorse secession, most historians agree that the margin of those supporting secession was at most only paper-thin. Even in South Carolina prominent figures resisted the call for secession, openly declaring their wish to remain with the Union. Among them were James L. Petigru and Benjamin Perry, both of whom had proclaimed their Unionism during the nullification crisis almost thirty years before. Neither Petigru nor Perry, it is worth noting, left the South once the Confederacy was established. Indeed, Perry worked to recruit soldiers for the Confederate army during the war.

More vocal and powerful opposition to secession was voiced in the conventions of Georgia, Florida, Alabama, and Louisiana, but it would be a mistake to see that as a sign of the strength of Unionism in the Deep South, where slaveholdings were concentrated. The great majority of the delegates to the conventions in the Deep South who fought against secession were really cooperationists—that is,

U.S. Regiments of White Southerners

State	No. of Regiments	No. of Volunteers
Alabama	1	2,578
Arkansas	10	8,289
Florida	2	1,290
Louisiana	10	5,224
Mississippi	1	545
North Carolina	4	3,156
Tennessee	33	31,092
Texas	4	1,965
West Virginia	37	31,872
Total	102	86,011

men who wanted their individual states to secede only in conjunction with other states. As one Alabama cooperationist newspaper wrote, "Before Lincoln's election we were against disunion . . . but now the die is cast, the last feather has been placed on the camel's back, and our only salvation is in secession." In sum, the cooperationists' Unionism did not deny the right of secession, merely the practicality of it.

A stronger Unionism was apparent in the four states of the upper South that joined the Confederacy later: Arkansas, North Carolina, Tennessee, and Virginia. They seceded neither with the election of Lincoln nor with the creation of the Confederacy in February 1861. Instead, that same month, the people of North Carolina and Tennessee voted down calls for conventions to decide on secession. In Tennessee the vote was 68,000 against, 59,000 for. In Arkansas and Virginia conventions were convened, but their delegates were strongly opposed to secession. Indeed, the Arkansas convention soon voted against secession (39–35) and adjourned just three weeks before Fort Sumter was fired on. Virginia's convention, on the other hand, stayed in session until it became clear that the Lincoln administration intended to use force against those states that had seceded. It was only then that the decision was taken to secede. Lincoln's call for state troops to suppress the rebellion also tested and found wanting the Unionist majority in Arkansas, North Carolina, and Tennessee, all of which then joined the Confederacy. For many Unionists, like former Whig politician Jonathan Worth of North Carolina, the choice was difficult. Worth as a state senator had led the fight against his state's secession, working to have the decision submitted to the people, but to no avail. His private remarks on the eve of North Carolina's vote to secede captured the inner conflict felt by many Unionists as the fighting began. "I think the annals of the world furnish no instance of so groundless a war," he wrote, "but as our nation will have it—if no peace can be made—let us fight like men for our own firesides."

Unionism in the Confederacy. Generally speaking, the more enduring Unionism of the upper Southern states can be related to their lesser dependence on slavery than the states of the Deep South. Nowhere does this connection become more telling than in the creation in 1863 of the state of West Virginia out of the mountainous region of western Virginia. There slavery was almost nonexistent, and dissatisfaction with the slaveholders' long domination of the state's politics had frequently been heard. Of the fifty-five members of the Virginia convention who had voted against secession, half came from the part of the state that became West Virginia.

Mountainous eastern Tennessee, which like western Virginia counted few slaves, had also resisted the movement toward secession. When a popular vote was taken in the state on dissolving Tennessee's connection with the Union, the people in the eastern part voted to stay with the United States by a majority of two thousand. This was also the area within the South in which unconditional Unionism during the Confederacy reached its height in numbers and intensity. Although that region, unlike the rest of the state, counted few slaveholders, its Unionism was rooted in opposition not to slavery but to the wealth that slaves represented and to the Democratic politics of their owners. The small farmers of East Tennessee had long been staunch Whigs. One native historian of the region has described the hostility of the Unionists toward the Tennessee Confederates as exhibiting signs of a "class struggle as well as a political and military contest." One measure of the threat the Unionists posed to the Southern war effort was the often brutal reprisals that the Confederate authorities mounted against Unionists whose destruction of bridges was especially damaging to the military effort. Dozens of Unionist sympathizers were executed and their bodies left hanging in public as a warning to others. Nevertheless, in 1862, Confederate conscription in eastern Tennessee was brought to a halt by the Unionist resistance. Significantly, the best known Unionist leaders of the state came from both parties. Perhaps the most notorious was William G. Brownlow, a former Whig newspaper editor whose slashing Unionist propaganda caused him to flee the state until U.S. military force could protect him. The leading Democratic Unionist was Andrew Johnson, the only U.S. senator from a seceding state to refuse to abandon his seat in Washington. Later he became the military governor of Tennessee after U.S. troops had conquered portions of the state. His committed Unionism earned him the post of running mate with Abraham Lincoln in 1864.

Wherever slavery was weakly established, as in the mountainous counties of northern Alabama, northwestern Arkansas, and western North Carolina, there, too, Unionist sentiment and overt resistance to the Confederate war effort persisted throughout the life of the Confederacy. Thirty-three members of the Alabama secession convention refused to sign the secession ordinance; by the fall of 1862 the first U.S. regiment of white Alabama troops had been organized, reaching a complement of two thousand men by war's end. The unit even served with William Tecumseh Sherman in his drive across Georgia. Counties in the Ozark Mountains of Arkansas also displayed a continuing resistance to the Confederacy, usually in the form of peace societies, which the Confederate authorities took pains to suppress. By 1863 Union officials were easily recruiting hundreds of Arkansans into the Federal army. The mountain Unionists of North Carolina organized a secret society, the Heroes of America, to sabotage and undermine the Confederate war effort. At the height of the war, in 1863, the Heroes' guerrilla attacks compelled the Confederacy to send six army companies into western North Carolina in an attempt to suppress the society, the membership of which one historian has estimated may have reached ten thousand.

The willingness of white Southerners to fight against their fellow Southerners was undoubtedly the ultimate test of the depth of Unionist conviction. Thousands of white Southerners from eight states passed that test. As one might anticipate, eastern Tennessee supplied more men by far to the Union army than any other Confederate state. More than 31,000 men, organized in 33 regiments, fought for the Union from Tennessee. All told, more than 86,000 white Southerners served in the invading forces, among which were more than a hundred officers of general or admiral rank who had been born in what became the Confederate States of America. (This figure of 86,000 is a minimum; it is known that several thousand white Southerners are uncounted because they served in Northern regiments.) More white men from Tennessee, Florida, Arkansas, and Alabama served in the armed forces of the United States than blacks from those states.

Although the most extensive areas of Unionist sentiment were located in the mountain regions, substantial numbers of individual Union sympathizers were active in the plantation areas, among them some of the wealthiest slaveholders. The counties along the Mississippi River in Mississippi had been conspicuous in their resistance to secession and in their support of cooperation when the state was considering its response to Lincoln's election. Once the Union forces arrived in that region, some of the wealthiest planters gave voice to their Unionist sentiment by freely supplying the invading armies. Especially notable was John Minor of Mississippi who contributed $64,000 worth of supplies to the U.S. military during the war. Another planter of the same state, implacable old Whig William Sharkey, immediately took the oath of allegiance to the United States in 1863 when Federal troops occupied Natchez. After the war he was recompensed some $2,000 for his contributions to the Union military cause.

Former Whig planters of substance in Louisiana also contributed heavily to the Federal army. Conspicuous among them was William Bailey, one of the wealthiest men in the state and the owner of scores of slaves. James Madison Wells, another Louisiana planter of considerable wealth—he owned ninety-six slaves in 1860—denounced secession in 1861 and, once the war began, became a guerrilla leader and highly successful recruiter of troops for the Union army.

Although a number of individual slaveholding or wealthy supporters of the United States in the course of the war can be identified, the significance of this class of Unionists depends upon how numerous they were. Fortunately, thanks to the records of the Southern Claims Commission which Congress set up after the war, some measure, albeit imperfect, of the extent of wealthy, usually slaveholding Unionists in the South can be gained. Because of the stringent criteria Congress specified to substantiate a claim, the number of Southerners who finally received compensation from the U.S. government for their contributions to the Union military victory probably represented only a fraction of the actual number. As it was, almost 7,000 claimants received recompense; 22,000 persons had submitted claims. Those who were reimbursed received a total of $4.6 million. These Unionists differed markedly from those of the mountain regions, besides their being considerably less numerous: these were men of property, which was primarily what they contributed to the Union cause.

Since the claims of these wealthy Unionists were broken down into classes of amounts, it is possible to obtain some idea of the extent to which planters supported the Union during the war. At a time when $5,000 was a substantial amount of money (the annual salary of the chief justice of the United States was $6,000), 1,500 white Southerners asserted that they had contributed $5,000 or more to the Federal war effort. Of those 1,500, almost half filed claims of $10,000 or more. About 80 percent of these claimants were large slaveholders; each of them owned, on the average, fifty-four slaves. (In 1860 only about 68,000 people in the whole South owned as many as fifteen or more slaves.) And despite the especially stringent requirements for substantiating a claim of $10,000, almost 200 of the claimants received recompense. Of the 786 claims for amounts between $5,000 and $10,000, 224 obtained reimbursement. In sum, literally hundreds of the planters in the South, many of whom had been Whigs and cooperationists in 1860 and 1861, had persisted in their Unionism throughout a war that was supposed to be defending slavery, the source of their wealth.

Some slaveholders opposed secession simply because they thought it would hasten the end of slavery, as in fact it did. By staying in the Union, these men reasoned, the Southern slaveholders would have at least the Federal government behind them inasmuch as the Constitution upheld slavery. Outside the Union the South would be at the mercy of a world increasingly opposed to slavery.

For many wealthy Unionists, the operative point was that secession was a radical step, as people at the time frequently remarked. One North Carolinian Whig remembered in 1868, "I never was in favor of anything that was radical. I was opposed to abolition because it was radical. I was opposed to secession because it was radical." It is not accidental that students of the secession conventions have found that the younger delegates tended to favor secession and that delegates of an older generation tended to oppose withdrawal from the Union. By its nature, Unionism, like the Union itself, was traditional, the creation of the Founding Fathers; it was the established way of thinking.

The natural tendency of men and women of wealth was to keep things as they were. To change them was to threaten the existing order and the success and comfort it had brought these people. In contrast, the nonslaveholders, the former Whigs, men of the backcountry and mountain regions, also favored the traditional Union but because it was threatened by their old enemies, secession-minded planters who dominated the Democratic party.

Southern Unionism needs to be seen not only as varying in degrees as the differences between the sections deepened but also as an underground sentiment that resurfaced as the war progressed and the likelihood of defeat for the Confederacy mounted. The most notable example of this phenomenon was the growth of peace societies, the one in North Carolina under the leadership of William Holden being the most prominent and successful. Holden himself offers special insight into the ambiguities inherent in Unionism. Before 1860, the *North Carolina Standard,* of which Holden was editor, had been a strong advocate of secession, but once the war began Holden and the *Standard* increasingly called for peace and a return to the Union. His opposition to the war in the name of peace became sufficiently strong in 1863 to provoke a sacking of the *Standard*'s offices in Raleigh; Holden himself fled into the countryside for a spell. After the war he became the first Republican governor of North Carolina. As the fortunes of the Confederacy waned in 1864 and 1865, peace movements that were thin disguises for a reviving Unionism emerged in other states as well.

The persistence of Unionism not only serves to document once again the diversity within the South and therefore within the Confederacy; it also exposes a significant source of social and political division that persisted long after the Confederacy died at Appomattox. Many of those white Southerners who had been Unionists during the war became the scalawag leaders and rank-and-file supporters of Reconstruction.

[*See also* Compromise of 1850; Constitutional Union Party; Cooperationists; Election of 1860; Heroes of America; Kansas-Nebraska Act; Missouri Compromise; Nullification Controversy; Peace Movements; Tories; Whig Party; *and entries on particular states.*]

BIBLIOGRAPHY

Auman, William T., and David D. Scarboro. "The Heroes of America in Civil War North Carolina." *North Carolina Historical Review* 58 (October 1981): 327–363.

Crofts, Daniel W. *Reluctant Confederates: Upper South Unionists in the Secession Crisis.* Chapel Hill, N.C., 1989.

Degler, Carl N. *The Other South: Southern Dissenters in the Nineteenth Century.* New York, 1974.

Harris, William C. *William Woods Holden: Firebrand of North Carolina Politics.* Baton Rouge, La., 1987.

Klingberg, Frank W. *The Southern Claims Commission.* Berkeley, Calif., 1955.

Patton, James Welch. *Unionism and Reconstruction in Tennessee, 1860–1869.* Chapel Hill, N.C., 1934.

Tatum, Georgia Lee. *Disloyalty in the Confederacy.* Chapel Hill, N.C., 1934.

CARL N. DEGLER

UNION OCCUPATION. [*This entry serves only as an introduction to the Union occupation of Confederate territory. For a more detailed examination of specific areas under occupation, see entries on particular states and cities. See also* Contraband.] Large sections of the Confederacy, including a number of important cities, fell under Union control during the Civil War. By mid-1862 the following areas were in Federal hands: northern, southeastern, and western Virginia, including Alexandria and Norfolk; middle and western Tennessee, including Nashville and Memphis; southeastern Louisiana, including New Orleans and Baton Rouge; and several points along the coasts of North and South Carolina and northeastern Florida. By the end of 1863 more territory had been conquered: the remaining cities along the Mississippi River, including Natchez and Vicksburg; the section of Alabama north of the Tennessee River; the northern half of Arkansas; and eastern Tennessee. The final year of the war saw the capture of Atlanta, Savannah, Charleston, and Wilmington.

Military occupation of the South confronted the Union army and government with vast and unprecedented military, political, economic, and social problems. Holding towns and protecting communication lines in the midst of a mostly hostile population required tens of thousands of troops and constant vigilance. Spying, smuggling, guerrilla attacks, and other forms of civilian resistance plagued the occupiers.

Federal commanders imposed martial law in the occupied regions and endeavored not only to subdue resistance but also to assume the functions of municipal government. Moreover, in four states—Tennessee, Louisiana, North Carolina, and Arkansas—President Lincoln appointed military governors to oversee occupation and political reconstruction. Before the war's end, civil governments controlled by native Unionists were established in Tennessee, Louisiana, Arkansas, and Virginia. The military governors and state officials had frequent conflicts of authority with army commanders and with Treasury Department agents who supervised wartime trade.

Foremost among the transformations wrought by Union occupation was the dissolution of slavery. Wherever Federal forces invaded the South, slaves flocked to their lines. Most military commanders initially declined to tamper with the institution of slavery, but eventually they welcomed runaways as laborers. As the Union government's slavery policy moved from conservative to radical, the army became an active agent of emancipation. Military officials established "contraband camps" to shelter black fugitives, oversaw contracts between black laborers and white employers, and enlisted black recruits. Northern humanitarians went south to organize schools for the freedmen.

Federal actions against slavery were just one aspect of the revolutionary upheaval precipitated by Union occupation. To a far greater extent than in the regions held by the Confederacy, society in the occupied South fractured along its fault lines. Slaves by the hundreds of thousands defied their masters, liberated themselves, and took control of their own lives, even where military authorities were conservative or where the Emancipation Proclamation did not apply. Poor whites likewise seized opportunities to challenge the hegemony of the South's ruling elite. Southern Unionists struck back at the secessionist majority who had tyrannized them. This social turmoil was aggravated by widespread devastation, privation, and institutional disruption.

Facing extreme hardship and unchallengeable Federal power, Confederate sympathizers in the occupied regions soon forsook their cause. Well before Appomattox, most resigned themselves to defeat and grudgingly accepted black emancipation.

BIBLIOGRAPHY

Belz, Herman. *Reconstructing the Union: Theory and Policy during the Civil War.* Ithaca, N.Y., 1969.

Capers, Gerald M. *Occupied City: New Orleans under the Federals, 1862–1865.* Lexington, Ky., 1965.

Durrill, Wayne K. *War of Another Kind: A Southern Community in the Great Rebellion.* New York, 1990.

Futrell, Robert J. "Federal Military Government in the South, 1861–1865." *Military Affairs* 15 (1951): 181–191.

Gerteis, Louis S. *From Contraband to Freedman: Federal Policy toward Southern Blacks, 1861–1865.* Westport, Conn., 1973.

Stephen V. Ash

URBANIZATION. The role of cities in the antebellum and Confederate South exhibited a paradox. On the one hand, the cities of the future Confederacy were crucial to the existence of the plantation economy, linking it to the international markets that had created it and the flow of capital and supplies that sustained its growth. In the Confederacy, cities became even more vital as administrative centers, supply depots, and manufacturing points. Yet at the same time cities were marginal to the antebellum South, seriously constricted in their range of functions and in their vitality. In an age when American cities outside the region were developing integrated networks of cities and towns and launching on a process of self-sustaining and mutually reinforcing growth, the urban centers of the future Confederacy remained largely tethered to their hinterlands, on the one hand, and to the great centers of international commerce and credit, on the other. Their inadequacies, like those of other components of Southern society, would be glaringly revealed in the harsh light of war.

Urbanization in the Antebellum South

That the process of urbanization in the future Confederate states lagged behind that of the future Union states is apparent from the summary statistics. As table 1 shows, in 1790 less than 2 percent of Southerners lived in incorporated places of at least 2,500 people, the current census definition of an "urban place." To be sure, the difference from the North was not striking; the young Republic north of the Potomac was at that time only 7 percent urban. By the time of secession, however, nearly a quarter of the Union's population counted as city people; less than 7

Table 1. *Percentage of Urban Population, 1790–1860*

Year	Future CSA[a]	Virginia	Non-CSA
1790	1.97	1.78	6.99
1800	2.36	2.62	8.15
1810	3.18	3.63	9.38
1820	3.34	3.78	9.12
1830	3.87	4.82	11.21
1840	5.05	6.92	13.45
1850	5.86	7.97	19.33
1860	6.89	9.50	24.72

[a]Includes the eleven states of the future Confederate States of America; West Virginia is excluded from the Future CSA and Virginia totals. Future CSA totals for 1790 include the states of Virginia, North Carolina, South Carolina, Georgia, and Tennessee; later additions are Alabama and Mississippi (1800), Louisiana and Arkansas (1810), Florida (1830), and Texas (1850).

Source: Computed from figures in *U.S. Census of Population: 1970*, Washington, D.C., 1970. Vol. 1, pt. 1, sec. 1, tables 8 and 18.

TABLE 2. *Relative Urbanization Indexes, 1790–1860*

YEAR	FUTURE CSA[a]	VIRGINIA	CSA WITHOUT VA., LA.[b]
1790	.384	.346	.419
1800	.389	.431	.359
1810	.439	.500	.270
1820	.465	.525	.293
1830	.442	.551	.262
1840	.468	.640	.220
1850	.383	.522	.227
1860	.349	.481	.224

[a]"Future CSA" is defined as in Table 1. The "relative index of urbanization" is calculated by dividing the relevant subunit's share of U.S. urban population by its share of total population.
[b]This column is designed to illustrate urbanization in the future Confederacy when the anomalous cases of Virginia and New Orleans (Louisiana) are excluded. Because New Orleans's hinterland was considerably larger than Louisiana alone, excluding Louisiana understates the extent of antebellum Southern urbanization. However, because New Orleans's hinterland included extensive non-Southern territory as well, and because the Crescent City's role as interregional entrepôt made it unique among Southern cities, including it in Southern urbanization statistics is equally distorting in the other direction.
SOURCE: Computed from figures in *U.S. Census of Population: 1970*, Washington, D.C., 1970. Vol. 1, pt. 1, sec. 1, tables 8 and 18.

TABLE 3. *Principal Cities of the Future Confederacy, Populations and Ranks*

	1800		1820		1840		1860	
City	Pop.	Rank	Pop.	Rank	Pop.	Rank	Pop.	Rank
New Orleans			27,176	1	105,400[a]	1	179,598[b]	1
Richmond	5,737	3	12,067	3	20,153	3	40,703[c]	2
Charleston	18,924	1	24,780	2	29,261	2	40,522	3
Mobile					12,672	5	29,258	4
Norfolk[d]	6,926	2	8,478	4	17,397	4	24,116	5
Memphis							22,623	6
Savannah	5,166	4	7,523	6	11,214	6	22,292	7
Petersburg	3,521	6	6,690	7	11,136	7	18,266	8
Nashville					6,929	9	16,988	9
Alexandria	4,971	5	8,218	5	8,459	8	12,654	10
Augusta					6,403	10	12,493	11

[a]Includes Lafayette. [b]Includes Algiers and Jefferson. [c]Includes Manchester. [d]Includes Portsmouth in 1840 and 1860.
SOURCE: *U.S. Census of Population*, Washington, D.C., 1800–1860.

TABLE 4. *Number of Urban Places, 1790–1860*

YEAR	FUTURE CSA[a]	VIRGINIA	OUTSIDE VIRGINIA	U.S.[b]
1790	2	1	1	24
1800	6	4	2	33
1810	7	4	3	46
1820	7	4	3	61
1830	16	6	10	90
1840	22	8	14	131
1850	33	8	25	236
1860	52	9	43	392

[a]Includes all incorporated places, excluding suburbs (Lafayette, Louisiana, in 1840 and 1850; Algiers and Jefferson, Louisiana, in 1860; Manchester, Virginia, in 1860).
[b]Figures include the future Confederacy.
SOURCES: Urban places in future Confederacy compiled from *U.S. Census of Population*, Washington, D.C., 1790–1870. U.S. figures from Allan Pred, *Urban Growth and City-Systems in the United States, 1840–1860 (Cambridge, Mass., 1980), p. 23.*

percent of the Confederacy's population did. Of the 102 American cities of over 10,000 people in 1860, the Confederacy, with 29 percent of the old Union's total population, contained only 11. If a more sophisticated measure, the index of relative urbanization (see table 2), is used to trace Southern urbanization over time, it reveals that the region, while generally less than half as urban as the nation as a whole, urbanized at a slightly faster rate than the larger nation until 1840 and then dramatically lost ground in the late antebellum period.

The summary statistics mask enormous variation, for there was no single kind of "Southern city," nor was there a coherent urban hierarchy in the region before secession. Looming large in the summary statistics was New Orleans (see table 3). Entering the Union through the Louisiana Purchase in 1803, it was immediately the fifth largest American city, maintaining that rank throughout the antebellum period. The development of the western river steamer after the War of 1812 allowed the city to burgeon as the great entrepôt (intermediary center of trade and transshipment) of the Mississippi valley as well as the leading cotton and sugar port, so that by 1840 it contained nearly 40 percent of the total urban population of the future Confederacy. Its growth slowed dramatically after 1840, though, as the canals and railroads of the later transportation revolution increasingly directed the trade of the Old Northwest toward the Northeast.

Another anomalous case was the state of Virginia. Relatively nonurban in 1790, the Old Dominion (here not including the future West Virginia) by 1840 was, after Louisiana, the South's most urban state, containing eight of the region's twenty-three cities, including the third largest, Richmond, and over a quarter of its urban population. A complex of factors contributed to Virginia's relatively rapid urbanization. The agricultural shift from tobacco to wheat encouraged a vigorous grain trade, increasingly supplemented by the manufacture and export of flour. Changes in tobacco marketing concentrated the trade in Richmond, Petersburg, and Lynchburg and fed their burgeoning tobacco factories. Norfolk and Portsmouth became entrepôts for both Virginia and nearby North Carolina, while Richmond and Petersburg became the South's only true manufacturing cities. After 1840, though, as the pace of urbanization picked up in the North, Virginia lost relative ground, and in 1860 it was less than half as urban as the nation as a whole; except for Richmond, its cities grew slowly, and only one new center, the Shenandoah Valley town of Staunton, appeared in the late antebellum period.

With minor exceptions, notably the western outfitting and provisioning center of Nashville, virtually every other significant Southern city was at least in part the product of the cotton trade, and cotton largely defined the Southern urban character. Dominating the lower South as far north as Tennessee and North Carolina were the cotton ports, which in addition to New Orleans included Charleston, Savannah, Mobile, and Memphis. These cities performed variably during the years before 1860. Charleston, the major city of the South in 1790, stagnated but remained the second city in 1860. As the cotton belt pushed westward, Mobile and, later, Memphis arose, first as outfitting centers for settlers and then as outlets for their staple production. To the interior of these centers there developed a string of much smaller towns, usually on rivers at or near the fall line. In late antebellum times interior points proliferated; the number of incorporated towns in the region tripled between 1840 and 1860 (see table 4). Generally, though, cotton belt urbanization lagged badly; outside of Virginia and Louisiana only 4.4 percent of the region's people lived in cities.

Behind these and other indicators of antebellum urban underdevelopment lay the failure of most Southern cities to transcend their original roles as entrepôts for the plantation staple economies of their hinterlands. All U.S. cities originated as colonial outposts, funneling settlers and supplies to expanding frontiers and exporting primary products abroad. In the nineteenth century, however, cities outside the future Confederacy launched on a path of self-sustaining and mutually reinforcing growth while at the same time drawing strength from relatively densely populated hinterlands generating strong and diverse demand. Southern cities, though, traded little with each other and engaged in little innovative growth; dealing chiefly in one major staple, cotton, these centers did not have much to offer each other. Accordingly, no Southern *system* of cities developed; major centers with their hinterlands developed independently of each other, maintaining their principal trading links with the rising metropolises of western Europe and the American Northeast. Like their colonial forebears they served the undemanding needs of the plantations and the narrowly focused desires of a distant metropolitan core, with profound and deleterious consequences for their development.

The most striking structural feature of Southern urban systems, especially in the cotton belt, was their *primate* character—that is, relative to the North, local centers in the hinterlands of cotton ports were few and underdeveloped, so that the central city largely monopolized both population and urban services. Charleston comprised 83 percent of South Carolina's urban population in 1860, and Mobile 60 percent of Alabama's; New Orleans (with its suburbs) and Memphis together contained 87 percent of the urban dwellers in Louisiana, Mississippi, Arkansas, and western Tennessee. Because cotton and other plantations oriented their production toward outside markets, and because modern means of transportation and communication were slow to develop in the region, planters needed to move their crops to a seaport or one of the larger river towns. Lacking adequate marketing information, they needed the services of agents in those few points enjoying adequate contact with the outside world. Accordingly, the staple trade, and the factors, buyers, and bankers who controlled it, concentrated at very few points, chiefly on the edge of the region, where shipping facilities could be located and where fast, reliable information was most readily available.

The central figures in antebellum Southern urban commerce were commission merchants called *factors*. Specializing in a specific staple, factors served planters as sales agents, offering their strategic locations and specialized knowledge to interior producers seeking advantageous prices. The same advantages encouraged factors to become all-purpose commercial intermediaries for their clients, purchasing and shipping supplies, providing short- and long-term loans, and vouching for credit. Primarily serving the needs of factors, Southern banks were few in number, relatively large in scale, and highly concentrated in location; in 1860 nine of the eighteen banks in South Carolina were located in Charleston. Buyers similarly clustered around factorage centers, as did merchants catering to the planting trade. Because of the slow pace of these urban outposts, and because factors' businesses relied heavily on personal relationships with their clients, the tone of business life was unhurried and social; Charleston, in particular, had a reputation for being almost as much a resort as a business center. Factors typically forged close alliances with their planter clients, and probably a majority were native Southerners. There was a significant non-Southern presence in the trade, however, especially among buyers and agents for northeastern or English houses; Scotch-Irish merchants became powerful in early nineteenth-century Charleston, and in the newer southwestern ports New Yorkers and Englishmen, often part-time residents, played major commercial roles.

Whatever the origins of urban merchants, they worked within a system that left them dependent for markets, capital, and services on cities outside the region. Although Southern banks became increasingly prominent in late antebellum times, many financial services were obtained from the banks, insurance companies, merchants, and shippers of England and the great northeastern ports. Of the latter, New York became increasingly dominant, in large part because of its success in organizing the international cotton trade. Most shipping was controlled by outside interests; moreover, the pattern of shipping that developed enhanced dependence. Southern ports were typically heavy exporters but light importers; accordingly, to minimize backhaul unit costs on the westbound Atlantic voyage, New York shippers established a triangular trade, carrying cotton directly to England, manufactured goods and immigrants to New York, and manufactured goods south. Although Southern urban spokesmen complained loudly of the tribute they thus had to pay the Northerners, no Southern city save New Orleans could sustain direct European trade on its own, and attempts, notably through the commercial convention movement, to foster a cooperative effort at establishing direct Southern ties to Europe ran chronically afoul of urban rivalries within the region.

The low level of imports through Southern cities was, in turn, primarily a product of the low density of demand in their outlying areas. The very lack of a significant urban population with its characteristic abandonment of rural habits of domestic production was part of the problem, as was the large proportion of poor, thinly populated mountain and pine barren land in the region. The most critical inhibitor of demand for goods, though, was the plantation system itself. Its large units helped reduce population density in the Southern countryside relative to that in the North. More important, the economic logic of the slave plantation system led it to minimize outside consumption. Slaves were underutilized in staple crop production, but as "fixed capital" they were available year-round to perform a variety of provisioning and domestic manufacturing operations at little marginal cost. Because they were slaves, it was to the interest of their masters to keep their consumption, especially of high-value goods, to a minimum. Since planters served as purchasing agents for their slaves and dealt chiefly with factors in the nearest major city, plantations provided little stimulus to the development of smaller commercial centers, reinforcing the primate character of the urban system. To be sure, between two-thirds and three-quarters of the white Southern rural population lived in nonslaveholding households, but the plain folk lived plainly. Fearing the risks of commercial agriculture, they involved themselves little in staple production and either produced for themselves or obtained what they needed through local trade. In any case, they lived disproportionately in up-country regions well away from the predominantly coastal major centers, regions made accessible only near the very end of the antebellum period. Whether planter, slave, or yeoman, then, rural Southerners were generally poor customers for urban importers.

Likewise, they were poor customers for urban manufacturers. Although American cities generally were mercantile in character as late as 1840, manufacturing became increasingly associated with cities over the next twenty years—but not in the South. In 1860, the eleven future Confederate cities with populations of over ten thousand employed proportionately less than half as many workers in manufacturing as did their non-Southern counterparts. Of the 102 American cities for which the statistics were reported, Charleston and Mobile had the lowest proportions, 2.1 percent and 2.3 percent, of the nonsuburban incorporated places; with Norfolk, Savannah, and New Orleans, they composed half of the bottom ten, and Memphis followed three ranks further down.

A yet greater deficiency for the long term was the structure of Southern urban manufacturing. Most Southern industry was designed to process raw materials for shipment (tobacco, lumber), supply commercial services (printing and publishing), or provide cheap slave cloth (cotton textiles). On the other hand, in contrast to the factories and shops of cities in the contemporary West, Southern cities developed few of the varied consumers' and producers' goods industries that would lay the groundwork for the subsequent rise of smokestack America. Not only was consumer demand inhibited, but the crude techniques of plantation agriculture and the ability of planters to extend their operations simply by adding more slaves (contrasting with the limited labor available to family farmers in the free states) smothered the development of a large-scale agricultural implement industry. With thin demand in the countryside and poorly developed trading links between cities within the region, few Southern cities could reach the threshold of demand required to sustain urban industrial production.

Finally, Southern cities were handicapped by a dearth of cheap energy sources; usually neither fossil fuels nor water power was available in the coastal zones where Southern cities arose. Petersburg and Richmond, the major exceptions to this rule among cities of over ten thousand in 1860, were likewise the only ones specializing in manufacturing, 17.0 percent and 19.7 percent of their populations being so employed. The two Virginia cities were at or near tidewater, but were endowed with ample water power by virtue of their location on the fall line and had access to nearby deposits of coal. The two cities became leading centers of tobacco manufacture; Petersburg developed extensive cotton mills, and Richmond milled flour and tapped supplies of pig iron that had been floated down the James River and Kanawha Canal from the Great valley to develop a sizable ironworking industry, epitomized by the famous Tredegar Iron Works. Other manufacturing developed at smaller interior points, chiefly along the fall line; the cities of Fayetteville, North Carolina, and Augusta and Columbus, Georgia, became important textile centers, and Lynchburg, up the James River from Richmond, flourished as a tobacco center. Generally, though, the urban manufacturing sector was poorly developed and poorly balanced, and moreover operated under severe handicaps; Tredegar, the flagship iron maker, suffered from high costs, inadequate supplies of pig iron, and poor markets, depending heavily (and, for the Confederacy, fortunately) on Federal ordnance contracts for much of its prewar sustenance.

Southern cities, then, even in relatively favored Virginia, were handicapped in their development by a host of structural disabilities, most of them imposed by the constricted role assigned them by the plantation slave economy. Although the dynamic impulse in antebellum Southern urbanization was weak by comparison with that further north, it was by no means absent. Cities were almost always dominated by a commercial-civic elite, a core of merchants and their commercial allies that commanded not only the central economic institutions of the city but also its press and its government. As with booster elites elsewhere in the country, Southern urban leaders identified their own aspirations with those of the town, and vice versa. To facilitate their common business they organized banks and insurance companies and developed port facilities. Through franchised private companies and municipally owned enterprises they worked to extend city services such as water, gas, paved streets, police and fire protection, and public amenities such as markets and parks; undertaken to enhance the city's attractions as a business location and improve the quality of life for the elite, these services were unevenly distributed, being concentrated in the business district and the better residential neighborhoods.

Most important, Southern urban boosters sought to extend and consolidate their trade through transportation projects. Economic and geographic expansion in the nineteenth century sparked increasing rivalry among American cities generally, and Southern cities were no exceptions, ardently seeking ways to exploit new opportunities and protect themselves from their competitors. A brief canal boom in the 1820s brought few lasting benefits outside Virginia, but new opportunities appeared with the advent of the railroad. Worried about the constriction of its hinterland by its rival Savannah, Charleston capitalists completed the South Carolina Railroad to Hamburg, opposite Augusta, in 1833; 136 miles in length, it was at the time the longest railroad in the world. In later years other major cities, notably those of Virginia and Georgia, took up the challenge. But Southern railroads suffered from the same lack of hinterland demand and unbalanced traffic flows afflicting their terminal cities, and expansion was slow until the 1850s, when a major building boom tripled Southern mileage.

Financed by combinations of private, municipal, state, and outside investment, Southern railroads were planned and operated in accordance with what one historian has termed a developmental strategy; each city's system served to define and extend its hinterland, encourage market production, and channel shipments down the line to the primate city. Accordingly, railroad systems long remained isolated from each other, maintaining separate terminals, refusing connections, and using different gauges. Even as late as 1860, interconnections between city systems were rare and roundabout; with numerous unfilled gaps and dead ends, the Southern rail network was far less articulated than its Northern counterpart (no model of organization itself). Designed to serve the restricted needs of a staple-producing periphery, Southern railroads were thus poorly equipped to support the Confederacy in its struggle for existence.

Some moves toward articulation, though, began to appear late in the antebellum period. Several major cities nursed regional, and even interregional, aspirations; though none successfully met the competition of northeastern ports for the western trade, these larger ambitions began to create embryonic long-haul systems by the 1850s, drawing overland shipments from the Deep South and Southwest into South Atlantic ports. Of major future consequence for Southern urbanization was the resulting rise of a new kind of urban place, the interior railroad city. Most of them were still small in 1860; Atlanta, the future regional rail hub, had fewer than ten thousand inhabitants, despite mushroom-like growth since its incorporation in 1843. But the appearance on the scene of cities such as Atlanta and Chattanooga, and the rail-induced expansion of older centers such as Nashville, portended a revolution in the character and spatial distribution of Southern cities. Improved transportation and telegraphic communication not only encouraged interior economic development but undercut the economic monopoly of the factorage system, on which rested the primacy of the cotton ports, and created new centers with vested interests in breaking free of coastal domination. Interior merchants had long sought to dispense with the factor's expensive services, and direct, ready access to the centers of international markets and finance offered opportunities they were eager to exploit. As a result, the Southern urban landscape would look quite different in 1900 than it did in 1860.

Demographics

However commercial they were, Southern cities were hardly mere nodes of merchants, and the great bulk of their inhabitants were of far humbler status than the commercial-civic elites. Inevitably in a slave society, a large number of city dwellers were slaves; the proportion ranged widely, though only rarely exceeding 50 percent. Some slaves were in town as personal servants of their owners; most worked in the commercial economy, chiefly in unskilled work but in numerous skilled trades as well. Slaves provided the principal work force for the tobacco factories, flour mills, and ironworks of Virginia. In contrast to the countryside, slave hiring was common in the cities, especially in manufacturing centers, where the majority were hired. Despite legal restrictions, many of these hired slaves managed their own employment, paying their owners for the privilege. A minority, again larger in manufacturing centers and again despite legal prohibitions, were allowed to live apart from either owner or user. As this evidence suggests, slavery could be easily adapted to the needs of an urban society, and city growth does not appear to have been inhibited by the institution's inflexibility. Nonetheless, slavery was less important in cities, where there were alternative sources of labor, than it was on the plantation, where the advantages of forced labor were much clearer. Accordingly, urban slave populations tended to drop proportionately over time and in the cotton boom of the 1850s frequently dropped absolutely. Because it encouraged planters to use their chattels in relatively lucrative rural pursuits, plantation slavery thus imparted a structural anti urban bias to the population distribution of the Old South.

Free blacks constituted a small group in Southern cities (usually less than 10 percent of the population), but they were far more urban in their residence than either native whites or slaves; in the upper South one-third of free blacks, and in the lower South a majority, were urbanites, disproportionately concentrated in larger cities. In Virginia, where they constituted 10 percent of all blacks, urban free blacks engaged largely in unskilled pursuits; farther south, where they were fewer in number, they were more likely to be skilled. Typically, skilled workers tended to be of mixed blood and to be heavily concentrated in personal-service occupations catering to whites, such as barbering. The most successful of these artisans were able to establish themselves as a "colored aristocracy." Other free blacks engaged in petty retailing and other services to fellow blacks, free and slave, and over the course of the antebellum period developed institutions, notably the black church, that would lay the foundation for racial consciousness and solidarity after emancipation.

A majority of residents in most cities, as in the region generally, were white, but white urbanites differed in striking respects from those in the countryside. A great many propertyless white poor congregated in the cities, producing greater extremes of wealth and poverty than existed even in the plantation districts; in particular, single or widowed females sought employment in the factories of cities such as Petersburg. Native white males tended to concentrate in white-collar occupations and in skilled pursuits such as printing. The most unusual characteristic of the Southern white urban population, though, was its large foreign-born component. Although few antebellum immigrants chose to settle in the South, most who did moved to the larger cities; sizable minorities of city populations were foreign-born, and non-natives not uncommonly dominated the white male working class. Many of these immigrants, the Irish in particular, were relegated to unskilled work, often substituting for slaves; many more, though, especially among the Germans, provided a number of essential skills and developed vigorous petty entrepreneurial communities. With immigrant people came immigrant culture; Judaism and (outside Louisiana) Roman Catholicism established their principal beachheads in the major cities, ethnic social and mutual-aid institutions became important to urban life and commerce, and the Irish in places like New Orleans left an enduring imprint on local accents. Finally, it was in cities that class consciousness and class conflict were most likely to arise. These took the usual forms (labor unions and strikes) appearing in other American cities, but the presence of slave and free black workers, along with an official ideology of white supremacy, added peculiar twists and complexities to class relationships among whites, leading in particular to increased pressure on vulnerable free black communities in the 1850s.

In contrast to the countryside, cities were crowded, and social relations were characterized by relative anonymity and fluidity, enhancing the concerns of the elite over their ability to control social turmoil. As was underscored by the abortive slave uprising planned by Denmark Vesey and others in Charleston, urban black populations could not be constrained as easily as rural ones. Accordingly, municipalities assumed much of the task of domination handled on plantations by the individual slave owner, and inevitably in the name of the white race rather than the slaveholding class. Thus many of the institutions associated with postwar segregation appeared in antebellum times, although racial separation was explicitly harsher on both slaves and free blacks. The white working class could not be treated so bluntly; nonetheless, the influx of immigrants, in particular, heightened elite concerns over social control, and the visibility of the white urban poor stirred consciences among an elite wedded both to white supremacy and to Whiggish notions of moral stewardship. Cities thus became centers of social benevolence, creating orphanages, hospitals, public and private relief agencies, and, toward the end of the antebellum period, the first genuine public schools in the South. In many of these endeavors the lead was taken by societies of middle-class women assuming roles as "civic housekeepers," in the process beginning a redefinition of their constricted sphere that would prove of long-term significance.

Cities during Secession and the Confederacy

As the antebellum period progressed, especially into the 1850s, the sectional conflict increasingly brought a variety of pressures on cities, and they in turn played a significant role of their own in the events leading up to secession. Engaged as they were in commerce, the Southern commercial-civic elites valued stability and maintained close business and personal ties with their northeastern correspondents. Moreover, their desires for commercial and industrial development, frequently with government aid, had traditionally clashed with the free-trade proclivities of rural Southerners. They had traditionally been inclined to Whiggery, regretted the rise of radicalism in both North and South, and thus in the 1860 election tended to support Constitutional Union party candidate John Bell. Moreover, immigrant workers, in particular, were questionable loyalists to the cause of Southern rights; in 1860, in large part because of their vote, Democratic Stephen A. Douglas, otherwise scarcely a factor in the South, scored heavily in cities such as Memphis, Mobile, and New Orleans.

On the other hand, Southern cities were intellectual centers for the ideology of Southern rights; the leading fire-eaters tended to be young, ambitious urbanites of the sort that generally take the lead in developing nationalist movements, and cities such as Charleston became hotbeds of secessionist sentiment. Moreover, the close ties binding Southern cities to the northeastern metropolises generated frustration over their continued dependency and fears that a Federal government in the hands of the North would distribute internal improvement aid inequitably. Industrialists such as Tredegar's Joseph R. Anderson dreamed that an independent South would provide them a huge protected market. Finally, white Southern urbanites were, above all, white Southerners; when the stark choice was posed between secession and "submission" to a "tyrannical" Federal government, secession won easily.

For many cities the Confederate period was brief, as their strategic importance made them early targets of Union advances. Alexandria, Virginia, nominally the tenth largest Confederate city, was under Federal control from the beginning; within little more than a year after the firing on Fort Sumter, Memphis, Nashville, Norfolk, Portsmouth, and the major urban prize of New Orleans had passed behind enemy lines, spending the remainder of the war chafing under hostile occupation but prospering from the military supply trade and from illicit commerce between the two sides.

For the remaining cities, however, war brought unprecedented importance. Although the expanding Union blockade effectively shut down some ports, notably Savannah, others, such as Charleston (until the summer of 1863), Wilmington, and to a lesser extent Mobile, became major centers of blockade running, thanks not only to their harbors but to their financial and entrepreneurial communities. Richmond, the Confederate capital, swelled to 128,000, over three times its prewar size, with the burgeoning of the Confederate wartime bureaucracy. Manufacturing and supply operations doubled the populations of cities in interior Georgia. Industrial demands brought a flood of new entrepreneurs into manufacturing, along with the Confederate government itself, which established important facilities at, among other locations, Augusta, Georgia, and Selma, Alabama. Military authorities developed urban infrastructure, such as sewers, in the interest of preserving the health of their troops; the Confederate government filled in critical gaps in the rail network, notably between Greensboro, North Carolina, and Danville, Virginia, an action that would have a major impact on future Southern urban patterns.

In the end, though, the war lent little enduring impetus to urbanization. The operations of critical manufacturing firms such as Tredegar were hampered by supply bottlenecks, and the monopolization of scarce industrial capacity by military production left little opportunity for city building; indeed, the Southern infrastructure deteriorated in the course of the conflict. War-induced growth was hothouse growth, and enterprises begun to satisfy a single tolerant customer were ill equipped to satisfy many demanding ones. Indeed, all told, the war's significance to Confederate cities lay less in its benefits than in the intense strains it placed on them. Cities became bloated with workers and refugees. The deurbanization of slavery was reversed, as numbers of slaves were impressed for military work, brought to town by refugee owners, or simply abandoned by hard-pressed masters and mistresses. Municipal efforts to counter increased slave independence were largely dead letters, and the institution showed clear signs of decay well before formal emancipation. The swelling numbers of propertyless employees, especially women whose men were in military service, were peculiarly vulnerable to the rampant inflation tearing through the Confederate economic fabric; it has been estimated that real wages dropped by 60 percent in the course of the war. Blockade-running ports such as Charleston and Wilmington enjoyed a diseased prosperity, as runners and merchants profited from trade in military supplies and luxuries that clogged supply lines and sent the cost of living soaring. Despite efforts at expanding poor relief, inflation, impressment, and the inadequacies of the Confederate distribution system left poorer urbanites in an increasingly serious plight and generated enormous social tensions, usually directed against speculators. These tensions culminated in a number of bread riots, frequently led by women, the greatest number of which occurred in the spring of 1863.

Confederate cities generally managed to withstand social tensions, but the powerful Union offensives beginning in the summer of 1864 began to tear the urban system apart. Cities, notably Richmond, had long been important Union objectives; by the end of the summer the capital and nearby Petersburg were under siege, and in early 1865 the last major ports east of Texas, Mobile and Wilmington, were sealed by the Union navy. Moreover, beginning in 1864 the deliberate destruction of cities and the transportation links tying them together became integral to a policy of crippling the Confederate war-making capacity. After capitulating in the summer, Atlanta was burned by Gen. William Tecumseh Sherman in November as he embarked on his March to the Sea and the capture of Savannah; in February 1865 Columbia shared Atlanta's fate, although Sherman's culpability in the burning of the South Carolina capital remains in dispute. Gen. James H. Wilson's cavalry, on its sweep through the Deep South in the spring of 1865, destroyed the war-industry centers of Selma and Columbus, aided in the looting of the Georgia city by slaves and women workers. Other cities, such as Charleston, Richmond, and Petersburg, suffered severe damage incidental to military action in the course of the war.

Above all, the end of the war brought the end of the system of plantation slavery that had shaped the character of Southern cities. To be sure, its legacy would continue to influence Southern urban development in profound ways, some still discernible today. Nonetheless, the destruction of the slave regime would fundamentally alter the course of urbanization in the region. From the ashes of the Confederacy would arise a different and more dynamic Southern urban order.

[*See also* Bread Riots; Foreigners; Free People of Color; Inflation; Poor Relief; Poverty; Railroads; Textile Industry; and entries on the numerous cities mentioned herein.]

BIBLIOGRAPHY

Amos, Harriet E. *Cotton City: Urban Development in Antebellum Mobile.* University, Ala., 1985.

Coclanis, Peter A. *The Shadow of a Dream: Economic Life and Death in the South Carolina Low Country, 1670–1920.* New York, 1989.

DeCredico, Mary A. *Patriotism for Profit: Georgia's Urban Entrepreneurs and the Confederate War Effort.* Chapel Hill, N.C., 1990.

Goldfield, David R. *Cotton Fields and Skyscrapers: Southern City and Region, 1607–1980.* Baton Rouge, La., 1982.

Goldfield, David R. *Urban Growth in the Age of Sectionalism: Virginia, 1847–1861.* Baton Rouge, La., 1977.

Goldfield, David R., and Blaine A. Brownell, eds. *The City in Southern History: The Growth of Urban Civilization in the South.* Port Washington, N.Y., 1977.

Goldin, Claudia Dale. *Urban Slavery in the American South, 1820–1860.* Chicago, 1976.

Gutman, Herbert G., and Ira Berlin. "Natives and Immigrants, Free Men and Slaves: Urban Workingmen in the Antebellum American South." *American Historical Review* 88 (1983): 1175–1200.

Meyer, David R. "The Industrial Retardation of Southern Cities, 1860–1880." *Explorations in Economic History* 25 (1988): 366–386.

Wade, Richard C. *Slavery in the Cities: The South, 1820–1860.* New York, 1964.

Woodman, Harold D. *King Cotton and His Retainers: Financing and Marketing the Cotton Crop of the South, 1800–1925.* Lexington, Ky., 1968.

David L. Carlton

V

VALLEY, SHENANDOAH. *See various entries under* Shenandoah Valley, *including entries on* Shenandoah Valley Campaign of Jackson *and* Shenandoah Valley Campaign of Sheridan.

VANCE, ROBERT BRANK (1828–1899), brigadier general and U.S. congressman. Vance, the older brother of North Carolina's governor, Zebulon Vance, was born in Buncombe County, North Carolina. He engaged in mercantile and agricultural businesses and served as county clerk until the Civil War started.

In 1861 Vance organized a company, the Buncombe Life Guards. When the company joined the Twenty-ninth North Carolina Infantry Regiment, he was elected colonel. The regiment guarded a railroad in eastern Tennessee until February 1862, when it was assigned to Gen. Carter Stevenson's command at Cumberland Gap. As part of Gen. James Edwards Rains's brigade Vance's regiment saw action at Cumberland Gap in March, followed by minor actions at Tazewell and Baptist Gap.

At Murfreesboro Rains led the brigade forward with Vance's regiment on the left in an attack that outflanked the Union right. When the brigade was caught in a crossfire, Rains was shot and killed. Although Vance was wounded and his horse was shot, he took command of the brigade, leading it to safety in the cedar woods. Gen. John P. McCown reported that Vance "bore himself gallantly" in this action. Vance commanded the brigade briefly at Shelbyville, Tennessee, until becoming ill.

Vance had been promoted to brigadier general on March 4, 1863, and upon recovering from his illness he was assigned to western North Carolina, where he struggled to organize his command and repulse Union raids. On January 14, 1864, Vance raided toward Sevierville, Tennessee, with a small cavalry force. During his return he stopped to rest at Crosby Creek, Tennessee. No rear guard was stationed, and Union pursuers surprised the Confederates, capturing Vance and his staff. Vance spent the rest of the war in Union prison camps and was detailed to assist Gen. William N. R. Beall in buying clothing for Confederate prisoners. He was exchanged on March 14, 1865.

After the war Vance served in both the North Carolina legislature and the U.S. Congress (1873–1885). He died in Asheville, North Carolina, in 1899.

BIBLIOGRAPHY

Clark, Walter. *Histories of the Several Regiments and Battalions from North Carolina in the Great War, 1861–1865.* Vol. 2. Raleigh, N.C., 1901.

Hill, D. H., Jr. *North Carolina.* Vol. 4 of *Confederate Military History.* Edited by Clement A. Evans. Atlanta, 1899. Vol. 5 of extended ed. Wilmington, N.C., 1987.

U.S. War Department. *War of the Rebellion: A Compilation of the Official Records of the Union and Confederate Armies.* Washington, D.C., 1880–1901. Ser. 1, vol. 20, pt. 1, pp. 753, 755; ser. 1, vol. 30, pt. 4, p. 656; ser. 1, vol. 31, pt. 3, p. 759; ser. 1, vol. 32, pt. 1, pp. 73–77; ser. 2, vol. 8, pp. 188–190, 241, 359.

CHARLES M. SPEARMAN

VANCE, ZEBULON (1830–1894), colonel, governor of North Carolina, and U. S. senator. Zebulon Baird Vance was born on May 13, 1830, in the Reems Creek community of Buncombe County, North Carolina. A comfortable childhood ended in 1844 when his father died and the family farm and slaves had to be sold. This ended Vance's formal education until 1851 when he studied law at the University of North Carolina. In 1852, he passed the bar examination and was elected solicitor of the Buncombe County court.

In 1854, he was elected to the state legislature as a Whig and soon after became an editor of the *Asheville Spectator*. When the Whig party collapsed, Vance joined the Know-Nothings. He won a special election for the U.S. Congress in 1858 and was reelected the next year. Vance's success was largely due to his popular speaking style, which combined skilled partisan rhetoric with bawdy good humor.

Although Vance was a firm advocate of slavery, he was a strong defender of the Union during the secession crisis. He campaigned for the John Bell presidential ticket during the election of 1860, and in Congress he supported many compromise proposals to end the crisis. During February 1861, Vance campaigned as a Union supporter in the secession referendum held in North Carolina. His stand was vindicated when a large majority of the state's voters rejected the call for secession. Because Vance had been assured by William H. Seward that Abraham Lincoln would withdraw the troops from Fort Sumter, he felt betrayed by the attempt to resupply the fort and Lincoln's call for troops.

Vance's career as a Confederate officer was not distinguished. He helped organize the "Rough and Ready Guards" of Buncombe County and was elected company captain. Before the unit saw action, however, he was elected colonel of the Twenty-sixth North Carolina Volunteer Regiment. Vance was poor at organizing a military unit, and only the presence of Henry King Burgwyn, Jr., as second in command ensured that the regiment learned elemental military tactics. During the Battle of New Bern on March 14, 1862, Vance's regiment was placed on the extreme right of a weak Confederate line. An attack by General Ambrose Burnside's much larger army shattered the Confederate line and forced Vance and his men into rapid retreat. The regiment joined the Army of Northern Virginia and took part in the Seven Days' Battles around Richmond. Vance and his regiment participated in the final and unsuccessful assault on Malvern Hill on July 1, 1862.

Vance's military career ended in 1862 when he reentered politics. On June 15, he became the Conservative party's gubernatorial nominee. That party was formed by the Whig party leadership and William W. Holden, a former leader of North Carolina Democrats. Vance's opponent was William Johnston, the candidate of the original secessionists who now called themselves Confederates. Vance won the August election overwhelmingly by gaining the support of those who opposed the war and those who thought that the Confederate party was responsible for the inadequate defense of the state. Since Vance was the candidate of the dissatisfied, many observers expected him to challenge the Confederacy. Starting with his inaugural address in September 1862, however, he proclaimed his allegiance to the Southern nation.

Although Vance never repudiated his support of the Confederacy, he was more than willing to defend his state and challenge Confederate policies. When North Carolina Supreme Court justice Richmond Pearson ruled that the state militia could not enforce conscription and that men who had hired substitutes could not be subsequently conscripted, Vance refused to override these rulings despite frequent requests from Confederate authorities to do so. Vance defended Pearson despite his personal disagreement with Pearson's findings. Vance's commitment to North Carolina's welfare had many other manifestations. He initiated a very successful state blockade-running plan that predated that of the Richmond government. In addition, he pushed a state program to clothe the North Carolina troops, a salt procurement program, and a series of measures to provide more food for the poor.

During this same period, Vance frequently clashed with James A. Seddon and Jefferson Davis. Among his most common complaints were that North Carolina officers were not being promoted as rapidly as those from other states, that Confederate troops were abusing North Carolina civilians, and that the Confederate government was trying to conscript state officials. The correspondence was often heated, and at one point, Davis attempted to break off further communication with Vance. Despite the rather sharp rhetoric in the letters, Vance rarely impeded the war effort and publicly defended conscription and unpopular Confederate tax policies. As late as October 1864, Vance was a moving force in the Confederate governor's conference held in Augusta, Georgia, that reaffirmed the allegiance of the states to the Confederacy.

A significant minority of North Carolinians opposed Vance and the Confederacy. From the beginning of the war, Unionists in all parts of the state resisted Confederate conscription. Despite the use of force in such disparate areas as Washington County, Randolph County, and the Shelton Laurel community, Vance's Home Guards and the Confederate army were unable to eliminate this persistent opposition. By the summer of 1864, there were an estimated ten thousand Unionists enrolled in the Heroes of America. Many other North Carolinians also began to withdraw their commitment to the Confederacy. As early as 1862, yeoman farmers were outraged that those who owned twenty slaves were exempted from conscription. After Confederate defeats at Gettysburg and Vicksburg, Vance's political ally William W. Holden issued a call for peace meetings throughout the state to bring an end to the fighting.

The North Carolina peace movement was the most vocal in the Confederacy. During July and August 1863, about a hundred public meetings were held urging a peaceful end to the war. Vance reluctantly broke with Holden and issued a proclamation on September 7, 1863, that ended the public demonstrations. In the congressional elections of 1863, the peace candidates were successful in a majority of districts.

Following up on this victory, Holden urged peace advocates to demand a state convention where delegates could negotiate a truce with Northern political leaders. Vance challenged Holden's program when he opened his reelection campaign in February 1864. After Holden announced his candidacy, Vance stumped the state attacking him and claiming that the peace program would involve North Carolina in a war with the Confederacy. Vance also attacked Davis's use of the writ of habeas corpus. The strategy was successful, and Vance was reelected by an overwhelming majority in August.

Vance tried unsuccessfully to prevent the collapse of the Confederacy in North Carolina after his election. He sought to collect supplies for the Confederate army and to return deserters to Robert E. Lee's army; he rushed the state militia to Wilmington to assist in the defense of Fort Fisher. A month later, Vance refused to take part in an attempted coup against Jefferson Davis engineered by William A. Graham and other members of Congress. When William Tecumseh Sherman's large army entered North Carolina in April 1865, Vance arranged for the surrender of Raleigh before attending one last meeting with the fleeing Davis. On May 13, 1865, Vance was arrested in Statesville, North Carolina, and transported to Washington where he was placed in the old Capitol prison. On July 6, he was paroled to his home in North Carolina.

During Reconstruction, Vance resumed the practice of law and moved to Charlotte. In 1870, he was elected to the U.S. Senate, but the Republican majority refused to remove his political disabilities and Vance had to relinquish his seat. The Democrats nominated Vance as their gubernatorial candidate in 1876. The outstanding rhetorical abilities of Vance and his Republican opponent, Thomas Settle, and their debates across the state made this the most famous campaign in North Carolina's history. Vance's narrow victory over Settle ended Republican Reconstruction in North Carolina. Vance was elected to the U.S. Senate in January 1879, but his Senate career was frustrating and largely unproductive.

Starting in 1889, Vance suffered from failing health, and he died in Washington on April 14, 1894. His death prompted a massive outpouring of grief in North Carolina where scores of memorial services honored the state's war governor. He is still regarded as the most popular public figure in North Carolina history.

BIBLIOGRAPHY

Barrett, John G. *The Civil War in North Carolina.* Chapel Hill, N.C., 1963.

Davis, Archie K. *Boy Colonel of the Confederacy: The Life and Times of Henry King Burgwyn, Jr.* Chapel Hill, N.C., 1985.

Dowd, Clement. *The Life of Zebulon Vance.* Charlotte, N.C., 1897.

Johnston, Frontis K., ed. *The Letters of Zebulon Baird Vance.* Vol. 1. Raleigh, N.C., 1963.

Kruman, Marc W. *Parties and Politics in North Carolina, 1836–1865.* Baton Rouge, La., 1983.

McKinney, Gordon B., and Richard M. McMurry, eds. *The Papers of Zebulon Vance.* Frederick, Md., 1987.

Tucker, Glenn. *Zeb Vance: Champion of Personal Freedom.* Indianapolis, 1966.

Yates, Richard E. *The Confederacy and Zeb Vance.* Tuscaloosa, Ala., 1958.

GORDON B. MCKINNEY

VAN DORN, EARL (1820–1863), major general. Van Dorn was born September 20, 1820, near Port Gibson, Mississippi, the son of a local magistrate and great-nephew of Andrew Jackson. After almost being dismissed from West Point for excessive demerits, Van Dorn graduated fifty-second out of fifty-six. Van Dorn, whose friends called him "Buck," served on the frontier and was seriously wounded in a battle with the Comanches. In Mexico he was wounded again and won two brevets for gallantry. In the mid-1850s he joined the Second U.S. Cavalry and served in Texas.

Van Dorn resigned from the Federal army on January 31, 1861, and offered his services to his home state. He was made a brigadier general of the Mississippi state troops,

EARL VAN DORN. LIBRARY OF CONGRESS

second only to Maj. Gen. Jefferson Davis. The two were good friends, and Van Dorn eventually succeeded Davis in command. On March 26, 1861, Van Dorn joined the Confederacy as a colonel and took over the forts below New Orleans. On April 11 he was made commander of the Department of Texas and on June 5 was promoted to brigadier general. He was elevated to major general on September 19 and transferred to Virginia where he led a division.

When a disagreement in the West between Sterling Price, commander of the Missourians, and Brig. Gen. Ben McCulloch made coordination almost impossible there, Van Dorn was ordered to the District of the Trans-Mississippi, Department No. 2. He assumed command over the disputatious men and led the Confederates in his first battle as an army commander. At Elkhorn Tavern, Arkansas, poor planning and inadequate management turned the battle into a series of disasters. After this loss Van Dorn took his Army of the West across the Mississippi River but was too late to participate in the Battle of Shiloh. In March 1862 he was appointed district commander and in late June took over the defense of Vicksburg. When Van Dorn attacked William S. Rosecrans at Corinth on October 3 through 4, 1862, he was defeated. Mississippians had already become disenchanted with Van Dorn, partly because of his scandalous private life and partly because of his unpopular decision to implement martial law. Following the loss at Corinth, President Davis had John C. Pemberton promoted to lieutenant general over Van Dorn, and he assumed command of the cavalry. Van Dorn is best remembered for his destruction of Ulysses S. Grant's supply depot at Holly Springs, Mississippi, in December 1862, which halted the Union move on Vicksburg.

Van Dorn might have become a first-class cavalry leader, but he was murdered in his headquarters at Spring Hill, Tennessee, on May 7, 1863. A jealous husband, Dr. George B. Peters, claimed that Van Dorn had "violated the sanctity" of his home, although Van Dorn's numerous friends denied the validity of this charge. Van Dorn had the reputation of being a "horrible rake." He was described as a "small, elegant figure," whom women found attractive. One soldier observed that Van Dorn looked "more like a dandy than a general of an army." Jefferson Davis's brother observed that "when Van Dorn was made a general, it spoiled a good captain." He is buried at Port Gibson, Mississippi.

BIBLIOGRAPHY

Ferguson, John L. *Arkansas and the Civil War.* Little Rock, Ark., 1964.

Hartje, Robert G. *Van Dorn: The Life and Times of a Confederate General.* Nashville, Tenn., 1967.

ANNE J. BAILEY

VAN LEW, ELIZABETH (1818–1900), Union spy. An outspoken opponent of slavery, Van Lew ran a Union spy ring in her hometown of Richmond, Virginia, during the war. At Van Lew's behest, Mary Elizabeth Bowser, a former servant of the Van Lews, gained employment as a domestic in the Confederate White House. There Bowser gathered military information and passed it on to Van Lew, who in turn transmitted it to Union forces.

Van Lew frequently visited Federal prisoners in Libby Prison in Richmond to bring them food, books, and clothing; she is rumored to have helped some escape. In April 1864 she arranged for the clandestine reburial of Union hero Col. Ulric Dahlgren, whose body was mutilated and secretly buried by Confederate forces after he was killed leading a surprise raid on Richmond in March.

Although Van Lew was under close surveillance by Confederate agents during the war, she was never caught at espionage work; her bizarre dress and behavior, which earned her the name "Crazy Bet," was her ploy to divert suspicion. During the last year of the war, her intelligence operations included a network of five relay stations from Richmond to Federal headquarters downriver. When Union forces occupied her native city in 1865, Van Lew raised the first American flag to be seen there since 1861.

After the war President Ulysses S. Grant appointed Van Lew postmistress of Richmond, an office she held until 1877. In her last years she became an advocate of women's suffrage, paying her taxes under protest. In 1900, after enduring years of social ostracism from ex-Confederates, she died and was buried in Richmond.

BIBLIOGRAPHY

Bailey, James H. "Crazy Bet, Union Spy." *Virginia Cavalcade* 1 (1952): 14–17.

Kane, Harnett T. *Spies for the Blue and Gray.* Garden City, N.Y., 1954.

Turney, Catherine. "Crazy Betty." *Mankind: the Magazine of Popular History* 3 (1971): 58–64.

ELIZABETH R. VARON

VAUGHAN, ALFRED JEFFERSON, JR. (1830–1899), brigadier general. Born in Dinwiddie County, Virginia, Vaughan graduated from the Virginia Military Institute in 1851 and headed west. After traveling to Missouri and California, he settled in Marshall County, Mississippi. Although initially opposed to secession, Vaughan in 1861 raised a company of volunteers, which he took to Tennessee where it was mustered in as Company F of the Thirteenth Tennessee Infantry. He was elected lieutenant colonel of the regiment.

Vaughan's first taste of combat came on November 7 at Belmont, Missouri, where the Thirteenth Tennessee occupied the extreme left of the Confederate line. Assuming the rank of colonel, Vaughan led his regiment in capturing a six-gun battery at Shiloh. Following Maj. Gen. E. Kirby Smith into Kentucky in August 1862, the Thirteenth Tennessee fought at the Battle of Richmond during which Vaughan was temporarily placed in command of his brigade when Brig. Gen. Preston Smith was hospitalized. As the year drew to a close, Vaughan led the brigade into action at Murfreesboro, where it suffered the highest casualty rate of all brigades in Maj. Gen. B. Franklin Cheatham's division.

When Smith returned, Vaughan rejoined his regiment and oversaw its consolidation with the 154th Tennessee. At Chickamauga, Vaughan participated in a confused evening attack that almost led to his death when the brigade mistakenly marched into Federal lines. Smith was killed, but Vaughan's regiment captured the colors of the Seventy-seventh Pennsylvania along with three hundred prisoners. Vaughan was again given command of the brigade and, following the battle, drove Federal troops off Missionary Ridge. He was promoted to brigadier general on November 10.

In the summer of 1864 Vaughan participated in Gen. Joseph E. Johnston's attempt to stop William Tecumseh Sherman from seizing Atlanta. On July 4, after turning back the federals at Kennesaw Mountain, Vaughan was severely wounded in the left foot by an exploding artillery shell at Vining Station. The foot was amputated, ending Vaughan's service.

After the war Vaughan returned to Mississippi and concentrated on farming. In 1872, he moved to Tennessee, where he was elected six years later to serve as clerk of the criminal court for Shelby County. In 1897, Vaughan was given command of the Tennessee Division of the United Confederate Veterans. He died in Indianapolis, Indiana.

BIBLIOGRAPHY

Bearss, Edwin C. "Alfred Jefferson Vaughan, Jr." In *The Confederate General.* Edited by William C. Davis. Vol. 6. Harrisburg, Pa., 1991.

Porter, James D. *Tennessee.* Vol. 8 of *Confederate Military History.* Edited by Clement A. Evans. Atlanta, 1899. Vol. 10 of extended ed. Wilmington, N.C., 1987.

Warner, Ezra J. *Generals in Gray: Lives of the Confederate Commanders.* Baton Rouge, La., 1959.

ALAN C. DOWNS

VAUGHN, JOHN CRAWFORD (1824–1875),

brigadier general. Born in Roane County, Tennessee, Vaughn was a merchant and volunteer soldier who fought in the Mexican War with the Fifth Tennessee Infantry. In April 1861, he was in Charleston for the bombardment of Fort Sumter, and he quickly returned home to East Tennessee to raise a Confederate regiment in what was predominantly a Unionist area of the South. On June 6, 1861, he was commissioned colonel of the Third Tennessee Infantry.

JOHN CRAWFORD VAUGHN. LIBRARY OF CONGRESS

Vaughn's regiment soon fought under Gen. Joseph E. Johnston at First Manassas in July 1861. After an assignment in eastern Tennessee in the spring of 1862, Vaughn was promoted to brigadier general on September 22, 1862. He was transferred to the western theater, where he led his brigade during the Vicksburg campaign. Captured at Vicksburg and subsequently paroled, he was given a new command of mounted troops in eastern Tennessee and southwestern Virginia. His brigade took part in Confederate actions against Gen. David Hunter's Union offensive in the Shenandoah Valley in 1864. Vaughn was at the Battle of Piedmont on June 5, 1864, and later accompanied Gen. Jubal Early on his move against Washington in July 1864. After recovering from a wound received near Martinsburg, West Virginia, Vaughn was placed in command of Confederate forces in eastern Tennessee. At the end of the war he was with Johnston's army in North Carolina, and his brigade accompanied Jefferson Davis on his southward flight from Richmond.

Vaughn was a merchant and planter after the war, and he served in the Tennessee senate before his death in 1875.

BIBLIOGRAPHY

Civil War Centennial Commission. *Tennesseans in the Civil War.* Part I. Nashville, Tenn., 1964.

Warner, Ezra J. *Generals in Gray: Lives of the Confederate Commanders.* Baton Rouge, La., 1959.

WILLIAM L. BARNEY

VENABLE, ABRAHAM WATKINS (1799–1876), congressman from North Carolina. Venable was born in Prince Edward County, Virginia. He attended both Hampton-Sidney College and Princeton College, graduating in 1816 and 1819, respectively. Forsaking an initial interest in medicine, Venable studied law and was admitted to the Virginia bar in 1821. Practicing first in his native state, he moved to North Carolina, settling in Granville County in 1829.

As a respected lawyer, Venable ventured into the world of politics and was chosen to be an elector on the Democratic tickets in 1832 and 1836. He was elected to the U.S. Congress in 1846 and served in the House of Representatives for three terms. There he spoke out in opposition to the admission of California to the Union and the desire by some to annex Cuba—arguing in both cases that each would be detrimental to Southern interests. Losing a bid for reelection in 1852, Venable returned to North Carolina and resumed his law practice.

Never far from the political scene, Venable became an active secessionist and served as an elector on the Democratic ticket of Breckinridge and Lane in 1860. Following North Carolina's secession from the Union, the former congressman was elected to the House of Representatives of the Provisional Confederate Congress. He was appointed to serve on both the Committee on Naval Affairs and the Committee on Foreign Affairs, but was excused from the latter at his own request. Venable generally voted to support the policies of the administration. During the debate over the bill to authorize the issuance of Treasury notes and to provide a war tax for their redemption, Venable moved unsuccessfully to remove the death penalty for convicted counterfeiters and substitute a ten- to fifteen-year prison term. He lost his bid for election to the First Congress and returned to North Carolina. He died in Oxford.

BIBLIOGRAPHY

Biographical Directory of the American Congress, 1774–1971. Washington, D.C., 1971.

Journal of the Congress of the Confederate States of America, 1861–1865. 7 vols. Washington, D.C., 1904–1905.

Wakelyn, Jon L. *Biographical Dictionary of the Confederacy.* Edited by Frank E. Vandiver. Westport, Conn., 1977.

Warner, Ezra J., and W. Buck Yearns. *Biographical Register of the Confederate Congress.* Baton Rouge, La., 1975.

ALAN C. DOWNS

VEST, GEORGE G. (1830–1904), congressman from Missouri. Born in Kentucky and educated at Centre College and Transylvania University, Vest came to Missouri as a young lawyer and set up his practice first at Georgetown and later at Booneville.

In 1860 Vest was a presidential elector on the ticket of Stephen A. Douglas, who carried the state. Vest also ran successfully for a seat in the Missouri House of Representatives, and there soon became chairman of that body's Committee on Federal Relations. As such he took an active role in attempting to secure the state's secession from the Union. He authored a series of resolutions, known as the "Vest Resolutions" and passed by the Missouri legislature, opposing Federal coercion of Southern states claiming to have seceded. He also played a leading role in the legislature's denunciation of the seizure of pro-Southern forces at Camp Jackson, outside St. Louis, by Federal forces under Nathaniel Lyon. He may have drafted the ordinance of secession adopted by the state's orphaned Confederate government at Neosho in the fall of 1861. That government then selected him to serve in the Confederate Congress, where he sat on the Committee on the Judiciary.

In January 1865 he resigned to accept a seat in the Confederate Senate. Although he had supported the presidential administration in hopes of a reconquest, Vest was ready to force a reform in the cabinet and command of the war. He continued, nonetheless, to support emergency legislation.

Vest submitted to the Ironclad Oath after the war and practiced law. Relocating in Kansas City, he served from 1879 to 1903 in the U.S. Senate. Vest died in Sweet Springs, Saline County, and was buried in St. Louis.

BIBLIOGRAPHY

McElroy, John. *The Struggle for Missouri.* Washington, D.C., 1909.

Meyer, Duane G. *The Heritage of Missouri.* St. Louis, 1970.

Snead, Thomas Lowndes. *The Fight for Missouri: From the Election of Lincoln to the Death of Lyon.* New York, 1886.

STEVEN E. WOODWORTH

VICE PRESIDENCY. The provisions of the Confederate Constitution concerning the office of the vice president mirrored those of the U.S. Constitution except for its duration of one six-year term. The vice president's only stipulated duty was to serve as president of the Senate, without a vote except in case of ties. Alexander H. Stephens served as provisional and permanent vice president of the Confederacy.

Lacking confidence in Stephens, President Jefferson Davis and his cabinet largely ignored him after the first few months of the war. By war's end, Davis and Stephens were almost completely estranged, and the vice president played no official role in shaping Confederate policy. He did undertake several special missions at Davis's request, most notably the Hampton Roads conference in 1865. But he spent most of the war away from Richmond in self-imposed exile at his Georgia home. Increasingly disillusioned with the administration's war measures, he abetted Georgia governor Joseph E. Brown and Davis's congressional foes in opposing them. In early 1865, he actively assisted in the framing of several peace plans in the House. Overall, however, his influence in the Congress was minimal, although he retained the friendship and respect of several administration backers, especially Senator Herschel V. Johnson.

As a prominent embodiment of the South's state rights philosophy and particularist approach to the Constitution, the vice president stirred intense feelings in the public. Administration supporters disliked and distrusted him, but thousands of common people suffering from the war, especially in Georgia, revered him as their spokesman.

[*See also* Stephens, Alexander H.]

BIBLIOGRAPHY

Escott, Paul D. *After Secession: Jefferson Davis and the Failure of Confederate Nationalism.* Baton Rouge, La., 1978.

Schott, Thomas E. *Alexander H. Stephens of Georgia: A Biography.* Baton Rouge, La., 1988.

Thomas, Emory. *The Confederate Nation, 1861–1865.* New York, 1979.

THOMAS E. SCHOTT

VICKSBURG CAMPAIGN.

The city of Vicksburg, Mississippi, located on the east bank of the Mississippi River midway between Memphis and New Orleans, was the site of a key Confederate river defense and the focal point of Maj. Gen. Ulysses S. Grant's operations in the West from October 1862 to July 1863. The surrender of its fortifications and a garrison of 29,500 men on July 4, 1863, was a severe psychological blow to the Confederacy and, combined with the simultaneous defeat of the Army of Northern Virginia at Gettysburg, loss of manpower that the South could ill afford.

In 1861, Vicksburg's population of nearly five thousand was the second largest in the state. Its economy was prospering, thanks to the city's status as a commercial center and transportation hub for Mississippi and Louisiana planters. To the east, the Southern Railroad of Mississippi linked Vicksburg and Jackson and connected the former to other lines including the northward-running Mississippi Central Railroad. To the west, the Vicksburg, Shreveport and Texas Railroad went as far as Monroe, Louisiana, giving planters in the bottomlands access to the river and New Orleans. Riverboats of all shapes and sizes docked at the city's wharves and took cargoes of cotton and passengers south to the Crescent City.

When the war began, Vicksburg took on an even greater significance. It became one of the key links between the eastern Confederacy and the Trans-Mississippi South, serving as a transit point for troops and as a port of entry for Louisiana salt, sugar, and molasses, the latter two frequently exchanged for meat for the armies. Efforts to safeguard the city became crucial in the spring of 1862 when Memphis and New Orleans fell to Federal forces. Vicksburg remained the only railhead on the east bank of the river and as such provided the last direct link between the two "halves" of the Confederacy. Its maintenance also effectively blocked Federal waterborne communications down the river.

In May 1862, three thousand troops, evacuated from New Orleans, arrived in Vicksburg along with their commander, Brig. Gen. Martin Luther Smith. They were joined by companies from Mississippi and Louisiana, turning the city into a garrison. Smith concentrated on fortifying the city's river approaches, where he was aided by the natural features of the area. Vicksburg sat in a cluster of hills two hundred feet above the river opposite De Soto Peninsula—ideal defensive terrain. Seven batteries were erected on the bluffs just in time for the arrival of USS *Oneida,* which on May 20 fired upon the city, commencing the thirteen-month-long campaign for Vicksburg.

Early Federal Moves against Vicksburg. Throughout the rest of May and into June, ships from Flag Officer David Farragut's deepwater fleet multiplied in the river south of Vicksburg, reinforced by mortar schooners under Commdr. David D. Porter. On June 27, work began on a plan to bypass the Confederate river defenses by using troops and impressed slaves to dig a canal across the base of the peninsula created by the river's bend. The following day, Farragut's fleet conducted an early morning run past Vicksburg's gauntlet of batteries and linked up with Flag Officer Charles H. Davis's gunboat flotilla north of the river's bend out of range of Confederate guns. But the Federal navy was unable to develop a plan to force the city's capitulation and reverted to bombarding Vicksburg while continuing construction on the canal.

Farragut's fortunes took a turn for the worse in July when Porter was transferred east, the subsiding waters of

VICKSBURG, MISSISSIPPI. View from the hills to the north of the city. *HARPER'S PICTORIAL HISTORY OF THE GREAT REBELLION*

the Mississippi threatened to leave his oceangoing fleet stranded upriver for the remainder of the year, and the Confederate ram *Arkansas* created havoc by sailing into the Federal fleet on July 15. Unable to destroy *Arkansas,* Farragut took his ships out to sea on July 25 while Davis steamed north to Helena, Arkansas. It was clear that the U.S. Army would play the predominant role in subduing Vicksburg, and Major General Smith, aware of this, focused on building up the city's fortifications.

On June 28, Maj. Gen. Earl Van Dorn had arrived in the city to assume command. Van Dorn continued to strengthen the defenses of Vicksburg and of the stretch of river south of the city by fortifying Port Hudson. With the departure of the Federal fleet, Van Dorn turned his attention to enemy troops in northern Mississippi and western Tennessee under the command of Grant. The resulting fiasco at Corinth cost Van Dorn five thousand troops and left Vicksburg exposed. Grant now suggested to Maj. Gen. Henry Halleck that he be allowed to conduct "a forward movement against Vicksburg."

While Van Dorn was engaging Federal troops at Corinth, the Confederate War Department appointed Maj. Gen. John C. Pemberton to head a military district comprising the state of Mississippi and that part of Louisiana east of the Mississippi River. Pemberton assumed command on October 14, establishing his headquarters in Jackson. His assignment was part of a large-scale administrative change that placed all Confederate forces west of the Alleghenies and east of the Mississippi River under Gen. Joseph E. Johnston. Johnston, lukewarm about his new assignment, argued that the ambiguities inherent in President Jefferson Davis's new command arrangements made his role purely "nominal" and that he possessed little authority but great responsibility. Although he established his headquarters at Chattanooga, however, Johnston did not ignore Vicksburg.

Grant Takes Command. Grant's campaign to capture the city officially began on November 2 when he assembled an army of thirty thousand at Grand Junction, Tennessee, and began moving in three columns down the line of the Mississippi Central Railroad toward Holly Springs, twenty miles south. Pemberton's initial response was to fortify the south bank of the Tallahatchie River. But turning movements on both flanks threatened the Confederate rear and forced Pemberton to withdraw to the south bank of the Yalobusha River at Grenada.

Grant, with Halleck's approval, now detached Maj. Gen. William Tecumseh Sherman to lead a waterborne operation. His plan called for simultaneous advances south by his army and Sherman's, forcing Pemberton to divide his resources and fight on two fronts.

Although well conceived, Grant's operation fell victim to Confederate cavalry attacks against the vulnerable Federal lines of communication. Brig. Gen. Nathan Bedford Forrest's destruction of sixty miles of rail lines in western Tennessee caught Grant by surprise. Most damaging of all was a December 20 strike by Van Dorn (now commanding Pemberton's cavalry) against the Federal supply depot at Holly Springs. Grant lost the supplies necessary to continue his half of the two-pronged operation and, thanks to Forrest, could not replace them. By the time Sherman heard of Grant's withdrawal northward he was already committed to proceeding with his own attack. On December 26 and 27, Sherman's expeditionary force of 32,000 men disembarked from transports near Chickasaw Bayou on the Yazoo River and assaulted the city's northernmost defenders under

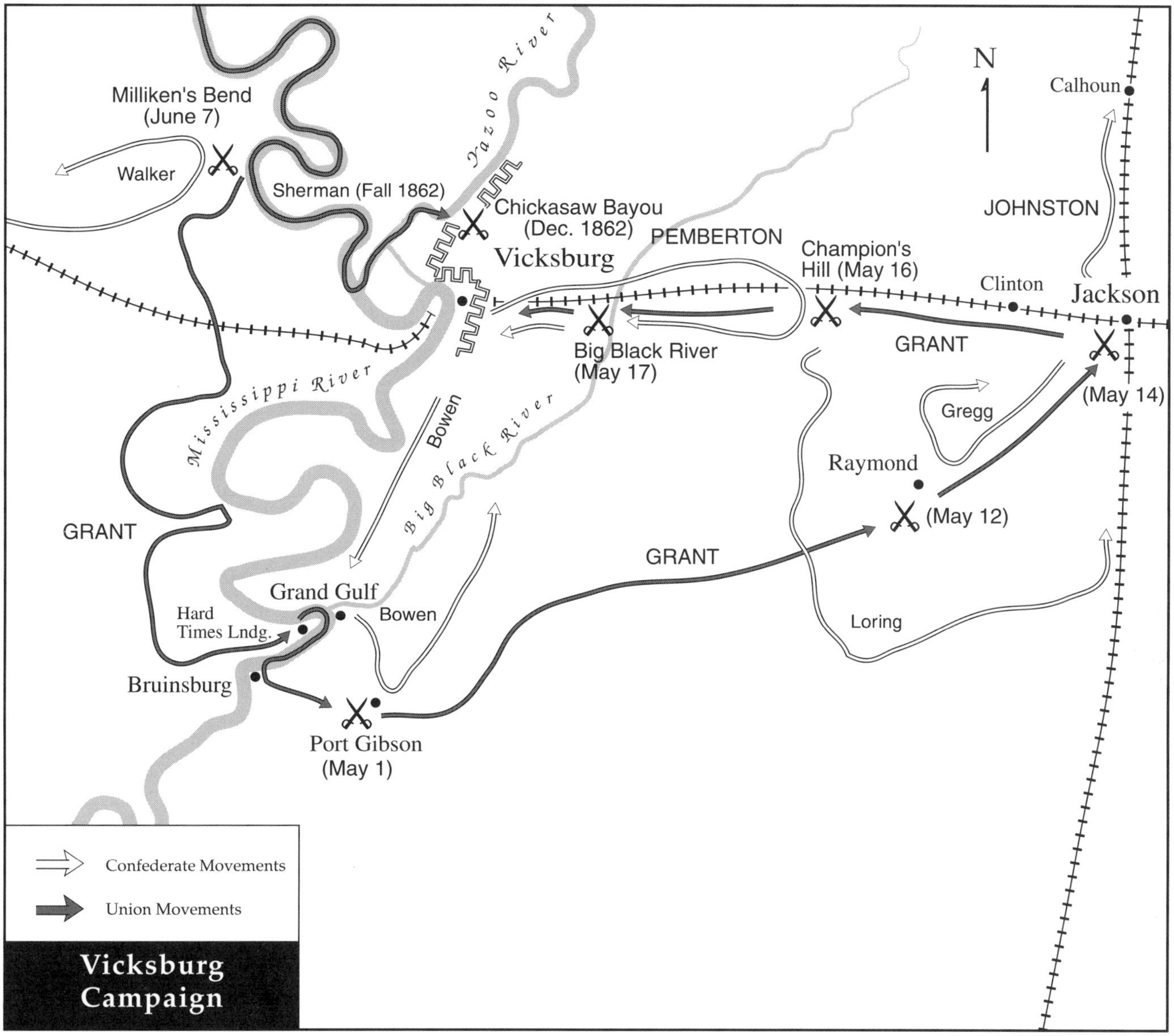

Brig. Gen. Stephen D. Lee. The three-day battle proved to be a Federal disaster, and Sherman withdrew on January 2.

By the end of January, Grant's new objective was to isolate the city by severing its rail link to Jackson. To accomplish this, he planned to execute a turning movement from the north and east. Realizing that movement along the railroad would leave him vulnerable to attack, he chose to forgo land communications and use the Mississippi as his main line of operations. The Mississippi route was secure from enemy attacks thanks to the return of Union gunboats now under the command of Porter, but lacked sufficient dry ground for offensive operations. The ideal terrain for Grant's army was south of the city, but getting vulnerable transport ships south past the batteries would be difficult at best.

Grant's efforts to get his army on dry ground south and east of the city led to several unorthodox maneuvers. Initially, he considered using the transpeninsula canal begun the previous year, but it was turning into a quagmire. He then thought of creating a southerly route to the river south of the city by using a combination of lakes, bayous, and streams west of the Mississippi, including Lake Providence, a six-mile-long body of water that was once part of the river. Grant, however, grew disenchanted with the project after a February 4 inspection trip to the lake and looked for yet another solution.

An alternative was already materializing on the east bank

of the river. Grant was notified that by destroying a levee at Yazoo Pass, fifty miles below Memphis, vessels could pass through an old channel to the Coldwater River, enter the Tallahatchie, and steam down the Yazoo River to the rear of Vicksburg. Pemberton quickly caught on to Grant's scheme after the levee was opened on February 2 and responded by sending two thousand troops under Maj. Gen. W. W. Loring to block the movement. Loring constructed a stronghold called Fort Pemberton out of cotton bales and sand, and armed it with thirteen guns, including a 6.5-inch rifled cannon. Between March 11 and 16, a Federal expedition led by Lt. Commdr. Watson Smith and Brig. Gen. Leonard Fulton to reduce the fort was foiled by the ineffectiveness of the gunboats, the accuracy of the Confederate's rifled cannon, and the fort's inaccessibility from land. An operation begun on March 14 by Porter and Sherman up Steele's Bayou in an effort to enter the Yazoo below Fort Pemberton was transformed by Grant into another would-be solution to his problem. Instead of moving to help Smith and Fulton, Porter was ordered to operate against Vicksburg itself with the goal of deploying Sherman's troops northeast of the city. After battling obstructions and sharpshooters, Porter abandoned the operation on March 20 and returned to the Mississippi. On April 4, Grant recalled the Yazoo Pass expedition and prepared to try something else.

Grant's new plan originated out of his earlier designs for Lake Providence and the success in February of two vessels in running past the Vicksburg batteries. His idea was to move the majority of his army down the west side of the Mississippi River below Vicksburg and then run Porter's gunboats and empty transports southward past the Confederate defenses to Hard Times, where they would rendezvous with the awaiting army. The vessels could then ferry the army across the river, allowing Grant to begin his campaign against the city and the rail line. Sherman's corps would initially stay behind to conduct demonstrations near Vicksburg. Col. Benjamin H. Grierson's 1,700 cavalrymen would undertake an extensive raid into Mississippi to disrupt Confederate communications and draw attention away from Grant's operation.

Federal troops began moving south on March 31, and twenty-eight days later two corps had reached Hard Times. On April 16, eleven out of the twelve boats (including two transports) assigned by Porter completed a midnight run past the Vicksburg batteries and proceeded south to join Grant. The next day, Grierson's troopers left their camp in southwest Tennessee and headed south toward the railroads, supply depots, and plantations of eastern Mississippi. On April 22, five more transports and six barges successfully ran the gauntlet. By April 29, Grant was prepared to ferry his army across the river. From April 30 through May 1, while Sherman conducted his diversion north of Vicksburg, 23,000 Federal troops disembarked at Bruinsburg on the east bank of the Mississippi. Grant was now on dry soil, and the final phase of the campaign for Vicksburg was about to begin.

For Pemberton, the flurry of Federal activity across the river in early April was indicative of a withdrawal. After assuring Davis and Johnston that Grant was abandoning his operations against Vicksburg, Pemberton went so far as to prepare to send reinforcements to Gen. Braxton Bragg's Army of Tennessee, the next logical target of a Federal western offensive. But on April 17, Johnston and Adj. Gen. Samuel Cooper learned from Pemberton that Grant's army was not leaving after all. Nevertheless, Pemberton chose to focus his attention upon Grierson's raid rather than on determining Grant's intentions, deploying an infantry division to try and trap Grierson's cavalry. Johnston, a proponent of maneuverability, informed Pemberton from Tennessee that he should unite his whole force to beat Grant, remarking "Success will give back what was abandoned to win it." Davis, on the other hand, sent Pemberton instructions to hold both Vicksburg and Port Hudson—evacuation ran counter to the president's strategic principles. Thus Pemberton, who had never commanded an army in combat, received conflicting instructions and chose to comply with the president's and his own preference for holding fortifications.

The Confederate indecision and confusion allowed Grant to pursue his strategy at will. After landing at Bruinsburg, he moved quickly against Brig. Gen. John Stevens Bowen's small and divided force at Port Gibson and Grand Gulf, forcing the latter's evacuation on May 3. The line of march chosen by Grant out of now Federally controlled Grand Gulf was in part dictated by the general's original plan to move on Vicksburg from the east after first securing the Southern Railroad of Mississippi. A second factor was the 100-mile-long Big Black River that ran from the center of the state above Jackson southwestwardly to Grand Gulf. Crossing the river and moving directly north toward Vicksburg could be risky if his force was challenged, and the broken terrain between the Big Black and the city favored Pemberton. Therefore, Grant chose to move north and east, threatening both Vicksburg and Jackson. His army advanced in three columns: Maj. Gen. John McClernand's corps on the left, with instructions to "hug the river [the Big Black]," the recently arrived Sherman in the center, and Maj. Gen. James McPherson on the right.

The first major Confederate resistance to the march occurred on May 12 near Raymond, fourteen miles southwest of Jackson. Brig. Gen. John Gregg brought his brigade out of the capital and struck the vanguard of McPherson's corps, led by Maj. Gen. John A. Logan. The Confederates held for six hours before being forced to retire. Grant now knew that Southern troops might be concentrating in

Jackson. He decided therefore to take advantage of his central position between two Confederate forces, sending McPherson northeast to Clinton where he was to destroy the railroad and move east to the capital. Sherman was to move his corps through Raymond toward Jackson. McClernand was ordered to be in position to reinforce either of the other two corps and to watch for an advance by Pemberton from the west.

On the same day that Grant issued these orders, Johnston arrived in Jackson to assume command of Confederate forces in Mississippi and learned the full magnitude of the situation: Grant was between Jackson and Vicksburg and Pemberton had not concentrated his forces. Johnston was too late to execute the speedy concentration of force that he had hoped to use against Grant. The railroad and telegraph lines were cut and any union of Pemberton's army and Johnston's gathering reinforcements would have to be coordinated from a distance using unreliable communications. For his part, Pemberton and 17,500 troops ventured out of the Vicksburg defenses on May 12 and advanced as far as Edwards Station, a railroad town east of the Big Black and halfway to Jackson. Aware of Pemberton's general location and seeing an opportunity to strike Grant while his army was divided, Johnston sent word via three couriers for Pemberton to strike the rear of the Federal force on the railroad at Clinton.

On May 14, with only 6,000 troops available in Jackson and inadequate earthworks to use as protection, Johnston evacuated the capital and moved north toward Calhoun. Dispatches were sent east and south to inform incoming reinforcements of the situation. By midafternoon, Federal troops had successfully fought their way through the Confederate rear guard and entered Jackson where they remained until May 16. Pemberton meanwhile pondered Johnston's instructions and held a council of war with his subordinates. Although the majority of his officers favored compliance with Johnston's directive, the council nevertheless decided to move southeast to cut Grant's supply line to the Mississippi. Thus Pemberton decided essentially to send his army away from rather than toward a unification with Johnston's. When the latter was informed of this development, he quickly sent another message urging conformity to his original instructions. By that time it was too late. Grant, learning Johnston's intentions from a Northern sympathizer who happened to be one of the Confederate general's original three couriers, was rapidly moving westward to confront Pemberton.

The two forces clashed on May 16 at Champion's Hill, eighteen miles east of Vicksburg. In an all-day fight, Pemberton displayed little tactical skill and was eventually defeated. In his report to Johnston, Pemberton stated that his current position was too vulnerable, and he felt compelled to withdraw back to the safety of Vicksburg. Consequently, after attempting to slow the Federal advance across the Big Black River on May 17 and losing Loring's division when it was separated from the main body of the army, the majority of Pemberton's troops returned to the city with Grant's entire army in pursuit.

Johnston sent word to Pemberton instructing him to evacuate Vicksburg and march to the northeast. For the commanding general, the object of the campaign was the defeat of Grant's army, not the retention of a geographic point. By now, the strategic significance of Vicksburg was at best questionable. The value of the Mississippi River to the Confederacy had been drastically reduced ever since the capture of New Orleans and Memphis and the resulting loss of two of the three most important rail termini on the river. After Porter's gunboats successfully ran past the batteries in April, steamboats could no longer safely reach the railhead at Vicksburg, thus severing the Trans-Mississippi supply line. The only remaining significance of Vicksburg was political and psychological. Davis had promised his fellow Mississippians that Vicksburg would not fall. Moreover, from his point of view, he could ill afford to lose this symbol of Confederate control on the Mississippi.

In response to Johnston's request for an evacuation, Pemberton held a second council of war and this time received, according to his own account, unanimous support for remaining in the city. He wrote Johnston that "I still conceive it to be the most important point in the Confederacy." The decision made, he prepared to turn away the approaching Federals.

The Siege of Vicksburg. Grant, eager to take Vicksburg and avoid a protracted siege, attacked the city's defenses on May 19 and again three days later. Both assaults were repulsed with heavy casualties. He was now forced to resort to a siege and instructed his engineers to begin encircling the nine miles of Confederate entrenchments. Once completed, the twelve-mile-long Federal line paralleled the Confederate earthworks at an average distance of six hundred yards and was anchored at both ends on the Mississippi River. By the end of May, 50,000 men surrounded the city; two weeks later 27,000 more were on hand.

Through May and into June, Johnston, focusing on raising an army sufficient to lift the siege or at least open a hole long enough for Pemberton to escape, wrote repeatedly to the War Department requesting troops from all available sources. On June 1, Johnston reported he had 24,053 effectives and needed more. He, along with Lt. Gen. James Longstreet and Gen. P. G. T. Beauregard, suggested to the War Department that an operation in middle Tennessee might draw Federal troops away from Pemberton. Longstreet and Beauregard also suggested that reinforcements from Virginia be used to aid Bragg in a strike against Maj. Gen. William Rosecrans, followed by an advance to the Ohio valley, but Gen. Robert E. Lee's aversion to reinforcing the West undermined the plan. Little help would be coming from the Trans-Mississippi either, as Maj. Gen. John G. Walker's division attempted too late to destroy Grant's supply base at Milliken's Bend. Consequently, on June 15, Johnston informed the War Department that saving Vicksburg was "hopeless."

Grant, however, was conscious of Johnston's potential ability to disrupt Federal operations if allowed to go unchecked, so he took measures to ensure his army's safety. He had already destroyed the railroads around Jackson, so that Johnston would have to rely upon an insufficient number of wagons to move his army. Likewise, the Federal army thoroughly foraged the countryside, making it difficult for Johnston's troops to sustain themselves within striking distance of Grant's army without an adequate supply line. Most important, Grant was concerned about his central position between two Confederate forces and posted Sherman and 34,000 men on a defensive line fifteen miles east of Vicksburg to protect his rear.

Although often the subject of historical debate, Johnston's military options were very limited. Ideally, he could cooperate with Pemberton in a simultaneous assault against Grant and Sherman. In this scenario, neither Federal army would easily be able to reinforce the other, and the Confederates could hope for a blunder that might open a window of opportunity for success. In order for this plan to work, however, timing, organization, and numerical superiority were critical. With the uncertainty and delays necessarily associated with the courier system, neither general could depend upon timing or be certain about organization. Moreover, both Pemberton and Johnston would have to launch assaults against a numerically superior, entrenched army. Johnston therefore chose another option. By June 28, he had pieced together over 31,000 troops and sent a courier to Pemberton informing him of one last hope—he would make a diversionary attack on July 7 designed to allow the Vicksburg garrison to cut its way out. (Pemberton had earlier informed him that he could hold the city until July 10.) Johnston's message never arrived.

The situation within the city was rapidly deteriorating. Citizens sought shelter from daily bombardments by hiding in basements or digging caves into the hillsides. Water became scarce and the meat supply dwindled. By the end of June mule meat was substituted for bacon and bread rations were reduced. After questioning his senior officers on the status of their men, Pemberton decided that his garrison was too weakened by the forty-six-day siege to undertake the rigors of the field. Accordingly, on July 3, Pemberton met Grant between the lines and arranged to surrender the following day. All told, he surrendered 2,166 officers, 27,230 enlisted men, 115 civilian employees, 172 cannons, and 60,000 long arms. The symbolic bastion on the Mississippi was now in Federal hands. Port Hudson surrendered five days later, freeing the river of all major Confederate resistance. "The Father of Waters," President Abraham Lincoln observed, "again goes unvexed to the sea."

Johnston heard the news of Vicksburg's surrender on July 5 and, after a brief skirmish with Sherman, fell back from his position on the east bank of the Big Black to Jackson. Eleven days later, the general evacuated the capital city and headed east, first to Brandon and then to Morton, Mississippi. For Grant, the capture of the river fortress vaulted him into national prominence; his martial abilities were confirmed five months later at Chattanooga. For the Confederacy, the first week of July 1863 proved to be a major turning point in the war. The defeats at Gettysburg and Vicksburg did not guarantee ultimate Federal victory, but many Southerners now realized that the Confederacy was running out of manpower and time.

[*See also* Corinth, Mississippi; Holly Springs, Mississippi; Jackson, Mississippi, *article on* Battle of Jackson; Port Gibson, Mississippi; Port Hudson, Louisiana.]

BIBLIOGRAPHY

Bearss, Edwin C. *The Vicksburg Campaign.* 3 Vols. Dayton, Ohio, 1985–1986.

Ballard, Michael B. *Pemberton: A Biography.* Jackson, Miss., 1991.

Carter, Samuel, III. *The Final Fortress: The Campaign for Vicksburg, 1862–1863.* New York, 1980.

Govan, Gilbert E, and James W. Livingood. *A Different Valor: The Story of General Joseph E. Johnston, C. S. A.* New York, 1956.

McFeely, Mary D., and William S. McFeely, eds. *Memoirs and Selected Letters: Ulysses S. Grant.* New York, 1990.

Miers, Earl Schenck. *The Web of Victory: Grant at Vicksburg.* New York, 1955. Reprint, Baton Rouge, La., 1984.

Walker, Peter F. *Vicksburg: A People at War, 1860–1865.* Chapel Hill, N.C., 1960.

Woodworth, Steven E. *Jefferson Davis and His Generals: The Failure of Confederate Command in the West.* Lawrence, Kans., 1990.

Alan C. Downs

VIDEO. *See* Film and Video.

VILLEPIGUE, JOHN BORDENAVE (1830–1862), brigadier general. A native of South Carolina and West Point graduate, Villepigue served seven years as a dragoon in the U.S. Army before resigning in March 1861 to join the Confederate army.

First commissioned a captain of artillery, Villepigue soon became colonel of the Thirty-sixth Georgia Infantry. During

JOHN BORDENAVE VILLEPIGUE. LIBRARY OF CONGRESS

the Federal bombardment of Fort McRee in Pensacola Harbor, Villepigue proved himself a stalwart fighter and skilled officer. Gen. Braxton Bragg praised his "coolness and self-possession" during the fight. But he had suffered a serious wound during the battle, which kept him out of active service for several weeks. When he recovered, he joined Bragg's staff as chief of engineers and artillery. He later returned to his post at Pensacola, followed by a brief assignment at Mobile, Alabama. Promoted to brigadier general on March 13, 1862, Villepigue next took command of Fort Pillow on the Mississippi. Stubbornly defending the fort, he refused to yield to the enemy's overwhelming land and naval attacks until ordered to retreat by his superiors. Villepigue next fought at Corinth in Gen. Earl Van Dorn's Army of Mississippi.

Great things might have come of the young officer, but his stubbornness contributed to his premature death. At Port Hudson in November, Villepigue became violently ill with fever. He refused to leave his command and death came quickly. The loss of Villepigue for the war effort was, in Bragg's words, a "severe one." Bragg maintained that Villepigue's fighting ability had been "by all odds [John C. Pemberton's] ablest support, and was fully equal, I think, to the best young men in the service."

BIBLIOGRAPHY

Capers, Ellison. *South Carolina.* Vol. 5 of *Confederate Military History.* Edited by Clement A. Evans. Atlanta, 1899. Vol. 6 of extended ed. Wilmington, N.C., 1987.

Warner, Ezra. *Generals in Gray: Lives of the Confederate Commanders.* Baton Rouge, La., 1959.

LESLEY JILL GORDON-BURR

VILLERÉ, CHARLES JACQUES (c. 1828–1899), congressman from Louisiana. Villeré was born in St. Bernard Parish, Louisiana. Raised as a Roman Catholic, he was educated at St. Mary's College, Baltimore, and studied law in New Orleans until he was admitted to the bar in 1849. Like many future Confederate congressmen, Villeré combined his law practice with actively managing a plantation in Plaquemines Parish. His ownership of eighty-nine slaves placed him among the ranks of the large slaveholders of the South. From 1854 to 1858 Villeré, a Democrat, served two terms in the state legislature.

Strongly supporting secession in 1861, Villeré organized a company of cavalry for the Confederate army and was appointed as an aide to his brother-in-law, Gen. P. G. T. Beauregard. In November 1861, he was elected from Louisiana's First Congressional District to the House of Representatives and was reelected in 1863. While serving in Congress, Villeré was noted for being a strong nationalist, but he exhibited a personal animosity toward the Davis administration. After Jefferson Davis removed General Beauregard as commander of the Army of Tennessee, Villeré retaliated with a published attack on the president. He also took part in the anti–Braxton Bragg faction and voted no confidence in Secretaries Stephen R. Mallory and Christopher G. Memminger. Villeré's committee assignments included Claims, Commerce, and Military Affairs in his first term and Impressments and Military Affairs in his second.

After the war, Villeré returned to southern Louisiana, where he remained a sugar planter until his death on January 7, 1899.

BIBLIOGRAPHY

Alexander, Thomas B., and Richard E. Beringer. *The Anatomy of the Confederate Congress: A Study of the Influences of Member Characteristics on Legislative Voting Behavior, 1861–1865.* Nashville, Tenn., 1972.

Wakelyn, Jon L. *Biographical Dictionary of the Confederacy.* Edited by Frank E. Vandiver. Westport, Conn., 1977.

Warner, Ezra J., and W. Buck Yearns. *Biographical Register of the Confederate Congress.* Baton Rouge, La., 1975.

Yearns, Wilfred B. *The Confederate Congress.* Athens, Ga., 1960.

LESLIE A. LOVETT

VIRGINIA. In the second year of the Civil War, a Southern newspaperman editorialized: "If the Confederacy loses Virginia it loses the backbone and right arm of the war." Noted historian Bruce Catton later asserted: "The new Southern nation that was struggling to be born [in 1861] needed Virginia as a man needs the breath of life."

These were not exaggerations. Without Virginia, the young Confederacy could not hope to win its fight for independence. With Virginia, the Southern attempt had a chance. Few events in American history were more momentous than the secession of the Old Dominion, for it turned the simple suppression of a rebellion into a four-year upheaval that shook the nation to the depths of its being.

That Virginia was among the last states to secede was evidence of its strong ties with the Union. The Old Dominion had been the mother state of the nation. Its sons played many leading roles in the birth and formative years of the Republic. Eight of the first eleven presidents were Virginians. In addition to such Founding Fathers as George Washington, Thomas Jefferson, James Madison, and James Monroe, far-visioned men like Patrick Henry, Richard Henry Lee, George Mason, and John Marshall had plotted the course of democracy in the New World. Other native sons had made marks elsewhere: Stephen F. Austin, founder of Texas, and Sam Houston, its first president; statesmen Henry Clay of Kentucky and William H. Crawford of Georgia; Ephraim McDowell, a pioneer in abdominal surgery; Cyrus McCormick, inventor of the mechanical reaper; plus nine governors of states and twelve governors of territories. It is inconceivable to think of the creation of the United States of America without Virginians participating.

Debate over Secession. By the first months of 1861, however, the state found itself literally in the middle of approaching hostilities between North and South. The issue of the day was slavery, yet three-fourths of all white Virginians were nonslaveholders. For most citizens of the Old Dominion, the *Richmond Examiner* asserted, "the cause . . . the whole cause, on our part, is the maintenance of the sovereign independence of these States."

Both sides looked anxiously to Virginia for support. Sharply divided sentiment existed inside the Old Dominion. Governor John Letcher was a moderate; his predecessor, Henry A. Wise, was an outspoken fire-eater. Secession sentiment was concentrated in the Tidewater and Piedmont regions, with their slave-based economies of tobacco and other crops. Most residents of the mountainous western third of the state felt a closer attachment to the Washington government.

Although Unionist voices were strong throughout the state, their expressions ran counter to Unionist feeling elsewhere. Virginia conservatives opposed the secession of their state, not secession itself. They preferred to work for a solution to the national dilemma from within the national framework; secession was a last-resort measure. But at the same time Virginia Unionists were of one voice in their

THE CAPITOL AT RICHMOND.
HARPER'S PICTORIAL HISTORY OF THE GREAT REBELLION

opposition to coercion of seceded states by the Federal government.

Sharply divided feelings led Governor Letcher in January 1861 to ask the state legislature to convene a secession convention of 152 delegates in order to gauge public opinion. The convention met and quickly voted against Virginia leaving the Union. Debate grew more heated. One conservative explained his position by declaring that "the desire of some for change, the greed of many for excitement . . . seems to have unthroned the reason of men, and left them at the mercy of passion." A Richmond newspaper labeled such spokesmen "old fogies" and "conceited old ghosts who crawled from a hundred damp graves to manacle their state and deliver her up as a husbandman to the hideous chimpanzee from Illinois [Abraham Lincoln]."

In the face of sharply divided opinion and seven states already out of the Union, Virginia moderates continued to work for peace. The Virginia General Assembly invited delegates from twenty-one Northern and Southern states to meet early in February in a concerted effort to avoid a major catastrophe. Venerable ex-president John Tyler presided over the Peace Convention. It drew up a conciliatory plan that basically would have restored the Missouri Compromise line to the Pacific Ocean, thus protecting slavery in the lower half of the nation. Extremists on both sides opposed the plan, victorious Republicans would give it no support, and the measure died in the U.S. Congress.

On April 4, the Virginia convention by an almost 2–1 vote again rejected secession. The delegates, however, agreed to remain in session to await further developments. Letcher dispatched a Virginia delegation to Washington on April 13 in a last-minute effort to avert war. Fort Sumter surrendered that day after a heavy Confederate bombardment. Virginian Edmund Ruffin, a grim, humorless old fire-eater, had fired one of the first cannon shots at Sumter.

War and Secession. Lincoln then issued a call on all Union states for troops to force the belligerent Confederates back into the Union. The Union president, a Richmond editor angrily retorted, "demands a quota of cutthroats to desolate Southern firesides." Virginia could no longer remain neutral. Its people had watched and waited, with the thin hope that the North and Deep South might somehow find a solution for the crisis. The thin hope was now dead. Stronger ties with Southern sister-states, decades of abolitionist denunciations of the region, repeated Northern assaults on state sovereignty in the face of Virginia's deep-rooted belief in local self-government, an 1859 invasion of Virginia by the abolitionist John Brown, and now Lincoln's call for force to coerce the South—all propelled Virginia to the decision it had to make.

"The war is not a civil war," a Virginia newspaper stated. "It is a war of two countries divided by geographical lines and interests. It is a quarrel of patriotism and not of opinion." For the majority of Virginians, jubilation greeted the news that warfare had begun. Crowds in Richmond filled the downtown. Everyone "seemed to be perfectly frantic with delight," a participant declared. "I never in all my life witnessed such excitement."

The day after Lincoln called on Virginia to furnish eight thousand troops as its quota in the confrontation, Letcher responded with a bitterly worded telegram. "Your object is to subjugate the Southern States," the governor stated, "and a requisition made upon me [for troops] for such an object . . . will not be complied with. You have chosen to inaugurate civil war."

In an atmosphere of frenzied emotion, the Virginia convention met on April 17 and took its third vote on the question of secession. The result was eighty-eight for, fifty-five against. Of the affirmative votes, fifty-five came from east of the mountains, ten from the central and northern part of the Shenandoah Valley, eighteen from the southwest peninsula, and five from the northwest mountainous region. The convention adjourned after solemnly resolving that "all acts of the General Assembly of this State ratifying, or adopting amendments to [the U.S. Constitution] are hereby repealed and abrogated; [and] the union between the State of Virginia and other States under the Constitution is hereby dissolved." For all practical purposes, Virginia joined the Confederacy with that pronouncement. The state had been driven against its will to seek independence.

"The great event of our lives has at last come to pass," one Virginia newspaper intoned. "A war of gigantic proportions . . . is on us, and will affect the interests and happiness of every man, woman, or child, lofty or humble, in this country called Virginia. . . . The hour for action is on us."

Events occurred with lightning speed thereafter. During April 18 through 21, state militia seized the arsenal at Harpers Ferry and the navy yard at Norfolk. Robert E. Lee, whom Army General in Chief Winfield Scott called "the very best soldier I ever saw in the field," arrived in Richmond on April 22 to take command of all state military forces. Lee had cast his lot with his native state because he could not "raise my hand against my relatives, my children, my home."

At an April 25 meeting in Richmond, Letcher and the Virginia convention concluded an alliance with Confederate officials that permitted Southern troops to enter the state and placed Virginia regiments under Confederate authority. Southern leaders expressed appreciation two days later by naming Richmond as the new capital of the Confederacy. Virginia's secession was also a powerful influence in the departure from the Union of three more states: Tennessee, Arkansas, and North Carolina. Late in May, in a fait accompli, Virginians went to the polls and approved the ordinance of secession by a 4–1 margin.

West Virginia formed. The Old Dominion's withdrawal from the Union proved doubly traumatic, for it became the only state to lose territory as a direct result of civil war. In 1861 Virginia was the size of New England. Population west of the Blue Ridge Mountains was ninety thousand greater than in the Piedmont and Tidewater. The western counties, however, had been at odds with the eastern section for decades. When Virginia left the Union, westerners began to talk about leaving Virginia—a threat that came as no real surprise to Richmond officials.

In the summer of 1861, a small Federal force entered the mountainous area and, without great difficulty, defeated the ragtag Confederate defenders. The presence of Union soldiers there afforded the necessary protection to enable mountain Unionists to organize their own state of West Virginia. On June 20, 1863, it received recognition from the Northern government. This secession from a seceded state reduced Virginia's size by a third.

Contributions to the Confederacy. From the moment of its 1861 alignment with the Confederate States, Virginia held the pivotal position. It was the most northern, and most exposed, of all the Southern states. Only the Potomac River divided it from the Federal capital at Washington; on three of its four sides lay enemy territory. The very shape of the state was like a spear thrusting itself toward the heart of the Union.

Additionally, Virginia's heritage and immense prestige were unrivaled. The state was the largest, richest, and most populous of the seceded states. It had more white inhabitants (1,105,000), more slaves (496,000), and more military-age whites (196,500) than any other state at war with the North. Virginia's 5,400 manufacturing establishments were nearly as great as those of the seven original Confederate states combined. A third of the South's nonagricultural goods came from Virginia. The iron yield of the Old Dominion was three times greater than that of the next Southern state. Twenty percent of the Confederacy's nine thousand miles of railroads lay in Virginia. The longest of these lines—the only thing in the South akin to a trunk system—ran from Richmond to Lynchburg, Bristol, and on to Chattanooga, Corinth, Jackson, and New Orleans. This railroad provided an unbroken connection between the Confederate capital and the Mississippi River.

Virginia possessed other assets critical to Southern war efforts. The Shenandoah Valley became the "Breadbasket of the Confederacy" because of its abundance of grain fields, livestock herds, and fruit orchards. Most of the South's coal, salt, and lead came from mines in the isolated southwestern part of the state. The southern region was the nation's major producer of tobacco. Northern Virginia enjoyed a world-famous reputation for its horses. Norfolk was a principal seaport as well as the site of the largest navy yard in the Confederacy.

Richmond was not merely the capital of a state and a country; it was the closest thing to a manufacturing center existing in the lower half of America. The city could boast of business firms that included fourteen iron foundries, six rolling mills, fifty metal works, fifty-two tobacco companies, and eight flour mills (among which was the world's largest). In addition to being an international seaport and the eastern terminus of a two-hundred-mile canal connecting it with the valley of Virginia, Richmond was also the converging point for five railroads. Had the metropolis itself been a Confederate state, it would have ranked in the upper half of the states in production.

Gen. Robert E. Lee faced an ominous task in the first weeks of war. He had to create a fighting machine from little or nothing. A Richmond newspaper voiced the truth in asserting: "The state's public means of resistance is simply nil. Virginia has a few serviceable arms and scarcely any powder." Weapons and gunpowder came with the seizures of Harpers Ferry and the Gosport Navy Yard. As for manpower, Lee demonstrated within three months his great creative abilities. He displayed the hard work and proficiency that had made him famous and organized Virginia units totaling forty thousand soldiers. Absorbed into Confederate forces, these troops enabled the South to have a major army in the field when the first offensive against Richmond began that summer.

The Old Dominion's contributions to Southern leadership were unmatched. Robert M. T. Hunter, Alexander H. H. Stuart, and William Preston Ballard were powerful figures in the political arenas of the Confederacy. Both George Wythe Randolph and James A. Seddon served as secretary of war. Matthew Fontaine Maury, the "Father of Oceanography," superintended the river defenses that protected Richmond for the entirety of the war.

A fourth of the 425 Confederate generals were Virginians. Included in the number were Robert E. Lee, Joseph E. Johnston, Thomas J. ("Stonewall") Jackson, A. P. Hill, J. E. B. Stuart, Jubal Early, Turner Ashby, Edward Johnson, James Lawson Kemper, James Lane, William Mahone, John McCausland, and Robert Rodes. (Seventeen Virginia officers, Winfield Scott and George H. Thomas among them, became Federal generals.) Other native sons such as Archibald B. Fairfax, French Forrest, Sidney Smith Lee, William F. Lynch, Arthur Sinclair, and William C. Whittle made indelible marks in Confederate naval history.

Virginians by the tens of thousands flocked to answer their state's 1861 call to arms. From the mountains to the flatland, from cities, counties, and colleges, they came forward to defend their home. All of them felt a patriotism expressed by one of the recruits: "Noble, grand old state! I love her dearer in her days of tribulation than in her prosperity, and while life is spared me I will fight in [Virginia's] behalf so long as a foe is on her soil."

Fully a fourth of the Army of Northern Virginia, the Confederacy's premier fighting machine, consisted of sons of the Old Dominion. The state came in time to boast of a host of outstanding units: the Stonewall Brigade, Old First Regiment, Pickett's Division, Stuart's Horse Artillery, Richmond Howitzers, Mosby's Rangers, Pegram's Artillery Battalion, to name but a few. In all, Virginia contributed to its defense 104 batteries of artillery, 27 regiments and 22 battalions of cavalry, 62 regiments and 11 battalions of infantry, plus local defense troops, state rangers, home guards, reserves, and militia.

Virginia as a Battleground. Every man was needed. For four years the state in general and Richmond in particular were principal targets of Union military might. Virginia felt the brutal hand of war as no other region of America ever has. Irony and tragedy both exist in the fact that one of the last states to join the Confederacy became the principal battlefield in its struggle with the Union.

The major reasons for this were military thinking and geography. European strategists had long taught that the capture of the enemy's capital brought checkmate-victory in the chess game of war. The early stages of the American struggle therefore became "a tale of two cities." Richmond and Washington were barely a hundred miles apart. To the Federals, who necessarily were on the offensive, Richmond was an inviting objective.

Confederate officials were aware that a mere four-day march could bring Federal forces to the outskirts of Richmond. Such a march, however, would be extremely costly for an invader. If shore guns or naval batteries could keep Union warships out of Virginia's large rivers while land troops controlled the mountain passes no more than 150 miles to the west, any Federal army would have to advance south through a relatively narrow corridor. Dense forests, open expanses, swampy areas, and a half-dozen

THE VICINITY OF RICHMOND.

HARPER'S PICTORIAL HISTORY OF THE GREAT REBELLION

major streams running west to east, would impede any advance on Richmond from the north.

The distance and terrain between the two river capitals lay with the defense. A resourceful Southern general could almost choose his battleground and strike back at the enemy at his pleasure. As long as the opposing armies bore any relation to one another in size, the Northern battle cry "On to Richmond!" was in essence a siren's song—a lullaby of death—for Union soldiers. The capture of Richmond and the neutralization of rich resources at Virginia's perimeters became the overriding Northern war goals.

Vying for control of the state's far western area brought 1861 clashes at Philippi, Rich Mountain, Carnifex Ferry, and Cheat Mountain. Confederates proved more successful on the other end of Virginia by routing a Federal probe at Big Bethel. The North's opening drive on Richmond produced at Manassas the first major land battle of the Civil War. Another Southern victory came in the autumn at Ball's Bluff on the upper Potomac.

War struck Virginia in 1862 with staggering force. The first engagement between ironclad ships occurred in March at Hampton Roads. It was a prelude to the Union's second attempt to capture the Confederate capital. The resultant Peninsular campaign of Gen. George B. McClellan brought heavy fighting at Williamsburg, Drewry's Bluff, Seven Pines, Mechanicsville, Gaines' Mill, Savage's Station, Frayser's Farm, and Malvern Hill. Commensurate with the start of that series of battles east of Richmond, Stonewall Jackson started a separate campaign in the Shenandoah Valley that resulted in defeat for three Union armies. Major actions were at Kernstown, McDowell, Front Royal, Winchester, Cross Keys, and Port Republic.

A summer invasion of north-central Virginia by Gen. John Pope's Federal army resulted in major engagements at Cedar Mountain, Groveton, Second Manassas, and Ox Hill. The Union garrison at Harpers Ferry was bombarded into surrender. Lee closed the 1862 fighting with a lopsided victory at Fredericksburg.

Despite successes in the field, Confederate morale declined slowly as war sapped the resources of the South. More than 30 percent of the Confederate soldiers were absent without leave during the winter of 1862–1863. Many men left the armies because of families starving and freezing at home.

The following year saw army contests at Chancellorsville, Second Fredericksburg, Salem Church, Second Winchester, Stephenson's Depot, Bristoe Station, Rappahannock Station, and Mine Run. Cavalry engagements of a major nature took place at Kelly's Ford, Brandy Station, Aldie, Upperville, and Leesburg. Union efforts to secure southwestern Virginia failed after sharp actions at Wytheville and Bristol.

Virginia was badly battered as the 1864 onslaughts produced the worst pounding of the war. Union horsemen slashed through southwestern Virginia again in an effort to neutralize the Virginia and Tennessee Railroad and the rich salt and lead mines of that area. Confederates put up stiff but ultimately futile resistance at Cloyds Mountain, Wytheville, New River Bridge, Saltville, Abingdon, and Bristol. Gen. Ulysses S. Grant, with the huge Army of the Potomac, began a southbound campaign that produced heavy fighting at the Wilderness, Spotsylvania, North Anna River, Cold Harbor, and the eastern outskirts of Petersburg. Simultaneously, Federal Gen. Benjamin F. Butler's army advanced westward up the James River before it was stopped less than twenty miles from Richmond after bitter clashes around Drewry's Bluff and Bermuda Hundred.

Grant then began a ten-month siege of Richmond and Petersburg. That triggered battles at Jerusalem Plank Road, Weldon Railroad, the Crater, Globe Tavern, Reams's Station, Peeble's Farm, Fort Harrison, Burgess's Mill, and Stony Creek Station. Meanwhile, after mounted fighting at Yellow Tavern and Trevilian Station, Union cavalry destroyed much of the agricultural productivity in the country north and west of Richmond. The summer and autumn of 1864 saw three Federal generals in succession trying to end Confederate resistance in the Shenandoah Valley. Combat ensued at New Market, Second Kernstown, Piedmont, Lexington, Lynchburg, Hanging Rock, Opequon Creek, Tom's Brook, Fisher's Hill, and Cedar Creek. At the end of October, Union Gen. Philip H. Sheridan wired Grant: "The whole country from the Blue Ridge to the North Mountains has been made untenable." The great valley was a veritable wasteland, its citizens at the mercy of Federal occupation forces.

The winter of 1864–1865 found Lee's dwindling army facing every adversity in the trenches at Petersburg. Federal Gen. Butler would later state with unconcealed admiration: "The fact is incontestable that a soldier of our army would have quite easily starved on the rations . . . served out to the Confederate soldiers before Petersburg."

Fighting in front of Petersburg continued in 1865 with engagements at Hatcher's Run, Fort Stedman, White Oak Road, Dinwiddie Court House, and Five Forks. On the Confederate retreat westward, fighting occurred at High Bridge and Sayler's Creek that cost Lee a third of what was left of his army. Palm Sunday at Appomattox saw the end of Confederate resistance in the Old Dominion. By then, over two hundred engagements had taken place within the state. A half-million men had been killed, wounded, or captured on Virginia soil. The state had stood firm and defiant in the Civil War until little else remained. The Southern Confederacy experienced defeat when Virginia experienced destruction.

Prisons and Hospitals. In addition to being the major battleground of the Civil War, Virginia also had two other sad claims of distinction. It contained the largest concentration of prisoner-of-war compounds and the greatest number of soldier-hospitals of any state in that conflict.

Richmond's military prisons became notorious in the first half of the war for their terrible conditions. At one time, four thousand Federal officers were crammed into a warehouse known as Libby Prison. Over ten thousand enlisted men fought exposure, hunger, and sickness on Belle Isle directly in front of downtown Richmond. Hundreds of other captured soldiers huddled in smaller compounds such as Castle Thunder.

When Grant's army began pushing hard against the capital in 1864, many of the Federal prisoners there were transferred to six tobacco warehouses in Danville. Their crowded conditions, shortages of food and clothing, and an epidemic of smallpox only heightened the incidence of death. Smaller prisoner-of-war camps were located at Petersburg, Lynchburg, and several other cities around the state.

What to do with tens of thousands of sick and wounded soldiers was a problem that the hard-pressed Confederacy never adequately solved. In the course of the war, improvised military hospitals were established at every major city at or near a railroad. Danville, Charlottesville, Gordonsville, Staunton, Petersburg, Culpeper, Warrenton, Winchester, and Fredericksburg were among forty Virginia towns with at least one large soldier hospital. Lynchburg became a virtual hospital city with at least two dozen first-aid stations. Yet Richmond quickly became the major medical complex of the Confederacy.

Trainloads of wounded men arrived at the capital beginning with the aftermath of the Battle of First Manassas. Some sixteen thousand Confederate soldiers in bloody bandages poured into the capital by wagon, carriage, and on foot following the 1862 Battle of Seven Pines. The flood rarely lessened thereafter. Accommodations were swamped; businesses, warehouses, churches, and private homes became makeshift hospitals. Richmond eventually contained twenty-eight soldier hospitals, including Winder and Chimborazo, the two largest ever constructed. Three of every five ill Confederate soldiers passed through one of Richmond's medical facilities at some point in the war. Wagons and hearses bearing lifeless soldiers made daily trips to Oakwood and Hollywood cemeteries. The mournful strains of the "Dead March" seemed so prolonged that a local matron said, "It comes and it comes, until I feel inclined to close my eyes and scream."

The Home Front. One of the great myths in American history is the idea that the Confederacy was a patriotic medley of magnolias, mint juleps, and muskets. In reality, and especially in Virginia, the epic of the Southern nation was the story of disorganization and destitution, shortsightedness and sickness, anxiety and misery.

The Davis administration sought throughout the war to centralize the national government as a means of strengthening Southern unity. Such a move, however, ran counter to the state rights principle underlying the existence of the Confederacy. Bitterness between Confederate authorities and state governments quickly developed. Many state officials throughout the South complained that Virginia had more generals in the field and received more partial treatment from the Confederate government than did other members of the Southern nation. Moreover, critics sneered, Virginians never missed an opportunity to remind everyone of their superior status. Overlooked, of course, was the fact that the alleged favoritism of Confederate officials toward Virginia made the state the principal battlefield of the Civil War.

Although Virginia's John Letcher was the governor with whom Davis enjoyed the closest friendship and cooperation, Letcher was unable to join Davis in any nationalistic effort. He and the Virginia legislature were mutually distrustful.

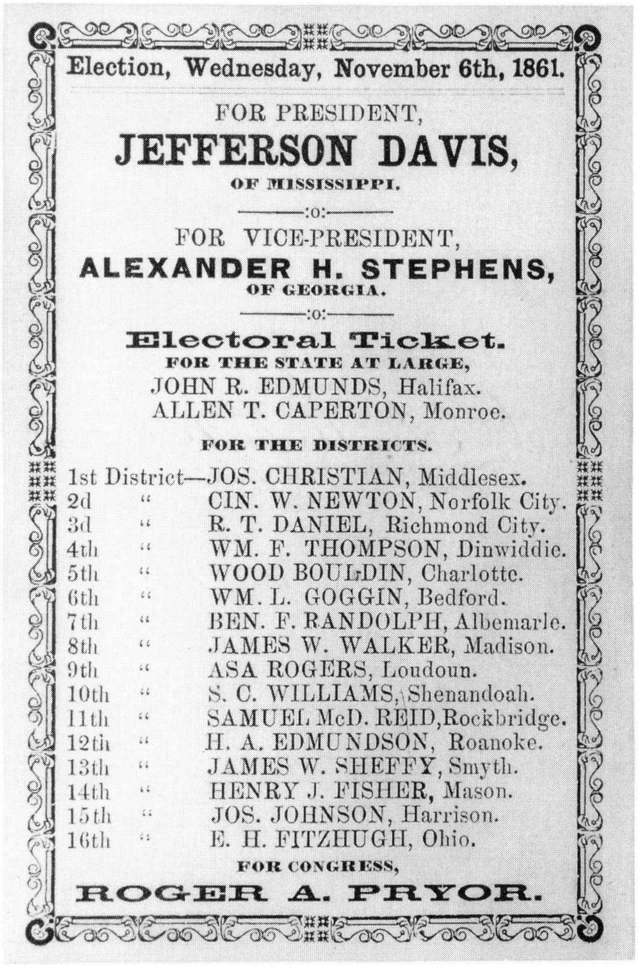

Election, Wednesday, November 6th, 1861.

FOR PRESIDENT,

JEFFERSON DAVIS,

OF MISSISSIPPI.

:o:

FOR VICE-PRESIDENT,

ALEXANDER H. STEPHENS,

OF GEORGIA.

:o:

Electoral Ticket.

FOR THE STATE AT LARGE,

JOHN R. EDMUNDS, Halifax.

ALLEN T. CAPERTON, Monroe.

FOR THE DISTRICTS.

1st District—JOS. CHRISTIAN, Middlesex.
2d " CIN. W. NEWTON, Norfolk City.
3d " R. T. DANIEL, Richmond City.
4th " WM. F. THOMPSON, Dinwiddie.
5th " WOOD BOULDIN, Charlotte.
6th " WM. L. GOGGIN, Bedford.
7th " BEN. F. RANDOLPH, Albemarle.
8th " JAMES W. WALKER, Madison.
9th " ASA ROGERS, Loudoun.
10th " S. C. WILLIAMS, Shenandoah.
11th " SAMUEL McD. REID, Rockbridge.
12th " H. A. EDMUNDSON, Roanoke.
13th " JAMES W. SHEFFY, Smyth.
14th " HENRY J. FISHER, Mason.
15th " JOS. JOHNSON, Harrison.
16th " E. H. FITZHUGH, Ohio.

FOR CONGRESS,

ROGER A. PRYOR.

HANDBILL FOR THE ELECTION OF NOVEMBER 6, 1861.

GORDON BLEULER

Their inability to work together during the war years left Virginia citizens to fend for themselves most of the time. Government instability became the order of the day. So did social chaos as a result.

Civilian populations increasingly became hungry and ill-clad. Hoarding, black marketeering, price-fixing, and speculation became rampant. In January 1863, an angry Governor Letcher told the General Assembly that "a reckless spirit of money making seems to have entire possession of the public mind.... avarice has become a ruling passion.... patriotism is second to love of 'the almighty dollar.' "

Inflation zoomed as food, clothing, firewood, soap, cloth, metal goods, and other necessary items became scarce. Transportational facilities deteriorated steadily. Life inside Confederate Virginia, especially among the lower classes, slowly devolved into an ordeal of survival. Many families lived in one room because they could not afford coal or wood to heat their entire home. A Richmond matron told of taking her money to the market in a basket and bringing home the purchases in her pocketbook. War Department clerk J. B. Jones wrote in his diary during the winter of 1863–1864 that "we are in a half-starving condition." A few months later, he added, "We are a shabby looking people now—gaunt and many in rags."

As battles raged over the countryside and enemy soldiers occupied communities, destruction was a by-product. In Norfolk, for example, all trade by 1863 had ceased, schools were closed, newspapers nonexistent, streets filled with potholes, filth everywhere. Richmond's population swelled to three times its 1860 figure. No town in the path of war bore any resemblance to its antebellum tranquillity.

Virginia's large black population, both slave and free, pursued two different courses in the war years. Many blacks continued to serve the Confederacy. They labored on fortifications at Richmond and elsewhere; they were employees in ordnance, quartermaster, and commissary departments; they served as teamsters, blacksmiths, carpenters, and cooks; they mined coal, manned riverboats, maintained railroads, and ministered to sick soldiers in hospitals.

Other blacks took the first opportunity to flee into Union lines. "In many cases," one historian has stated, "the flow was so great that it carried away the bulk of the male slave population." Shirley Plantation below Richmond suffered such a fate. By war's end, 5,700 Virginia blacks were soldiers in the Union armies.

Lawlessness was prevalent throughout the war years in every sector of Virginia. Federal occupation forces were rarely known for good behavior. Guerrilla bands roamed the countryside and preyed indiscriminately on the innocent. It was dangerous to walk the crowded streets of a city even in daytime. Because there was no gas or lamp oil for streetlights, those who ventured forth after dark risked their lives.

RUINS OF RICHMOND. Main Street, April 1865. *HARPER'S PICTORIAL HISTORY OF THE GREAT REBELLION*

In that environment, needy citizens often took matters into their own hands. A half-dozen bread riots occurred in the wartime South. By far the worst came on April 2, 1863, when a predominantly female mob of a thousand people poured through Richmond's streets in quest of food and ransacked stores for any items of value.

By April 1865, Virginians looked out at devastation. Countless homes and businesses had been destroyed, fields ruined, farms put to the torch, crops and livestock confiscated, streams contaminated, bridges wrecked, railroads decimated. The Shenandoah Valley would never regain its prewar productivity. A Northern visitor that spring described the region from Alexandria to Manassas as showing "no sign of human industry, save here and there a sickly, half-cultivated corn field. . . . the country for the most part consisted of fenceless fields abandoned to weeds, stump lots and undergrowth."

Virginia's urban areas lay in shambles. All of Fredericksburg, much of Lexington, and the center of Richmond were in ashes; Petersburg was gutted from months of Federal bombardment; Norfolk was an abandoned ghost town; Manassas, Bristol, Wytheville, Saltville, Dublin, Winchester, and scores of small towns bore the scars of war. A half-dozen college campuses appeared beyond repair. Warrenton, Culpeper, Lynchburg, Danville, and many other communities had a general air of neglect and filth. Worst of all, of the 170,000 Virginians who had served in the Confederate armies, over 15,000 were dead and an enormous number crippled or impaired. The state was bankrupt, its governmental agencies all but nonexistent, its constitutional powers suspended. Military occupation would be its lot for years to come. A bleak future loomed for the proud old commonwealth.

John Esten Cooke, a Virginian who had been among the foremost of Confederate writers, begged the victorious Federals to allow Virginians to keep their memories. "Leave us that, at least," Cooke implored. "Leave us the poor consolation of recalling the grand figures and bright hours of the past!"

Virginia has remembered. Preserved battlefields and scores of monuments, museums, and roadside markers exist to a degree found in no other state. The Old Dominion has become the New Dominion, industrialized and progressive. Virginia moves forward with optimism; it looks back with pride.

Colonel G. F. R. Henderson of the British army studied the American conflict in depth. He concluded:

> Far and wide between the mountains and the sea stretches the fair land of Virginia, for which Lee and Jackson and their soldiers, one equal temper of heroic hearts, fought so well and unavailingly. Yet [Virginia's] brows are bound with glory, the legacy of lost children; and her spotless name, uplifted by their victories and manhood, is high among the nations. Surely she must rest content, knowing that so long as men turn to the records of history will their deeds live, giving to all time one of the noblest examples of unyielding courage and devotion the world has known.

[*For further discussion of battles and campaigns fought in Virginia, see* Appomattox Campaign; Ball's Bluff, Virginia; Beefsteak Raid; Big Bethel, Virginia; Bristoe Station, Virginia; Buckland Mills, Virginia; Cedar Mountain, Virginia; Chancellorsville Campaign; Cloyds Mountain, Virginia; Cold Harbor, Virginia; Early's Washington Raid; Fredericksburg Campaign; Gettysburg Campaign; Kelly's Ford, Virginia; Kilpatrick-Dahlgren Raid; Lynchburg, Virginia; Manassas, First; Manassas, Second; Mine Run Campaign; New Market, Virginia; Peninsular Campaign; Petersburg Campaign; Piedmont, Virginia; Seven Days' Battles; Shenandoah Valley; Spotsylvania Campaign; West Virginia Operations; Wilderness Campaign. *For further discussion of Virginia cities, see* Danville, Virginia; Norfolk, Virginia; Richmond, Virginia. *See also* Bread Riots; Hospitals; Prisons; Virginia Military Institute; West Virginia; *and biographies of numerous figures mentioned herein.*]

BIBLIOGRAPHY

Dabney, Virginius. *Virginia, The New Dominion.* Garden City, N.Y., 1971.

Hotchkiss, Jed. *Virginia.* Vol. 3 of *Confederate Military History.* Edited by Clement A. Evans. Atlanta, 1899. Vol. 4 of extended ed. Wilmington, N.C., 1987.

Robertson, James I., Jr. *Civil War Sites in Virginia: A Tour Guide.* Charlottesville, Va., 1982.

Robertson, James I., Jr. *Civil War Virginia.* Charlottesville, Va., 1991.

Wallace, Lee A., Jr. *A Guide to Virginia Military Organizations, 1861–1865.* Lynchburg, Va., 1986.

JAMES I. ROBERTSON, JR.

VIRGINIA. Built on the hull of the ex-Union steam frigate *Merrimack,* the ironclad ram *Virginia* measured 262 feet in length, 51 feet in width, and 22 feet in draft of water. Its 195-foot-long casemate, angled on sides and ends at thirty-five degrees to better deflect projectiles, carried four inches of iron plate backed with two feet of wood. Within the casemate were ten guns: six 9-inch Dahlgren smoothbores and two 6.4-inch Brooke rifles in broadside, and a 7-inch Brooke rifle pivot-mounted at each end. A crew of 320 was required to operate *Virginia.*

Faced with insurmountable odds in the form of an established and rapidly expanding U.S. Navy, Confederate Navy Secretary Stephen R. Mallory early recognized the potential of armorclad warships in offsetting the numerical disadvantage under which the South labored. After first attempting to purchase an ironclad in Europe, Mallory decided to construct an armored vessel in the Confederacy. On June 22, 1861, following consultations with Lt. John M. Brooke, Naval Constructor John L. Porter, and Chief Engineer William P. Williamson, the secretary accepted a plan submitted by Brooke and directed that suitable machinery be found with which to power it. Three days later, finding no acceptable engines and boilers and determining that the time entailed in constructing them would be too great, the three officers, on the recommendation of Williamson, suggested that instead the remains of USS *Merrimack* be altered into the desired armor-plated warship.

Mallory agreed and immediately ordered Porter to produce plans based on the previously accepted design and supervise the conversion. Williamson was to refurbish the steam machinery, and Brooke was to arrange the armor and ordnance. Accordingly, *Merrimack,* which had been burned at Gosport Navy Yard in Norfolk, Virginia, the previous April by retreating Union sailors, was raised and placed into dry dock, and on July 11, Mallory ordered the conversion to proceed with all possible dispatch. These orders not only produced one of the most celebrated warships in naval history but launched an acrimonious debate among the officers involved, particularly Brooke and Porter, over who should receive credit for *Virginia*'s design. Although this controversy has been carried over into modern times by devotees of each, the evidence indicates that Brooke, Porter, and Williamson each made significant contributions to the vessel's plan.

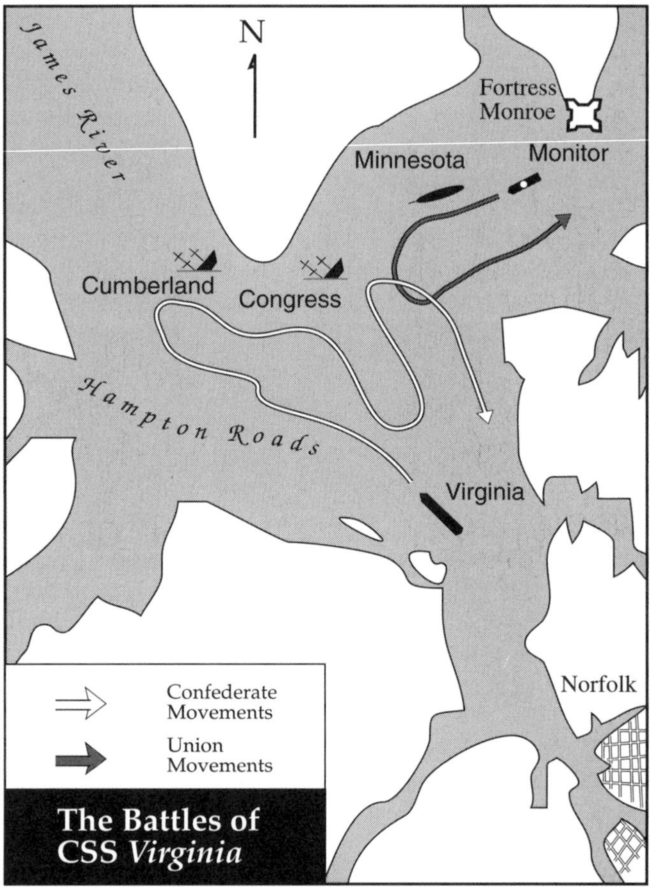

The Battles of CSS *Virginia*

In a race to finish the conversion of *Merrimack* before the completion of the Union turreted ironclad *Monitor,* known by the Confederates to be under construction at New York, the huge ironclad was floated in dry dock February 17, 1862, and commissioned *Virginia.* Under the command of Commo. Franklin Buchanan, with Lt. Catesby Jones as ordnance and executive officer, *Virginia* sortied March 8, 1862, from the navy yard into Hampton Roads to assault the Union fleet. Fearing its rifled cannon, Buchanan first attacked the sloop-of-war *Cumberland.* After exchanging broadsides, *Virginia* rammed and sank the Union warship but lost its cast-iron prow in the process. Turning to *Congress, Virginia* pounded the helpless frigate into submission with gunfire and then set it afire with hot shot. During the course of this action Buchanan was wounded by musket fire from shore, and command of *Virginia* passed to Jones. Darkness brought an end to the first day's fighting with the steam frigate *Minnesota* aground in shallow water just out of reach of the Confederates' guns.

Intending to renew combat with *Minnesota* and other Federal warships the following morning, Jones was confronted instead by *Monitor,* which had arrived dramatically the night before by the glow of the burning *Congress.* The ensuing four-hour combat between the two armor-plated antagonists was furious but inconclusive. Finally, a well-placed shot by *Virginia*'s stern rifle hit *Monitor*'s pilot house, temporarily blinding its captain and causing the ironclad to veer off. Low on ammunition and faced with a falling tide, *Virginia* returned to the navy yard. Although neither vessel inflicted serious damage on the other, the remainder of the Federal fleet in Hampton Roads was saved and the blockade was preserved.

Placed under the command of Capt. Josiah Tattnall, *Virginia* was repaired and continued to operate as a threat to Union forces in the area. The Confederate evacuation of Norfolk resulted in the destruction of *Virginia* by its crew on May 11, 1862, when its excessive draft prevented removal up the James River. In 1867 and again from 1874 through 1876, portions of the shattered *Virginia* were recovered and scrapped. A drive shaft and an anchor with chain, currently at the Museum of the Confederacy in Richmond, and a few other relics scattered in museums around the country are all that remain of the once-mighty ironclad.

Virginia's actions in Hampton Roads had worldwide implications. The destruction of *Cumberland* and *Congress*

NAVAL BATTLE AT HAMPTON ROADS. Contemporary lithograph of the March 9, 1862, battle between USS *Monitor,* in foreground, and CSS *Virginia,* directly behind. The other ships depicted in the background, left to right, are USS *Cumberland,* USS *Newport News,* CSS *Jamestown,* CSS *Yorktown,* USS *Congress,* USS *Swell's Point,* and USS *Minnesota.* Cumberland and Congress had, in fact, been sunk by *Virginia* the previous day and were not present as depicted. NAVAL HISTORICAL CENTER, WASHINGTON, D.C.

symbolically ended the centuries-long reign of the wooden, sail-powered warship, and its battle with *Monitor* presaged the modern era, adding impetus to a technological revolution in naval warfare already underway.

BIBLIOGRAPHY

Baxter, James P., III. *The Introduction of the Ironclad Warship.* Cambridge, Mass., 1933. Reprint, Cambridge, Mass., 1968.

Brooke, George M., Jr. *John Mercer Brooke: Naval Scientist and Educator.* Charlottesville, Va., 1980.

Daly, R. W. *How the Merrimac Won: The Strategic Story of the C.S.S. Virginia.* New York, 1957.

Davis, William C. *Duel between the First Ironclads.* New York, 1975.

Flanders, Alan B. *The Merrimac: The Story of the Conversion of the U.S.S. Merrimac into the Confederate Ironclad Warship, C.S.S. Virginia.* Portsmouth, Va., 1982.

A. ROBERT HOLCOMBE, JR.

VIRGINIA MILITARY INSTITUTE. After the War of 1812, the Commonwealth of Virginia had a quantity of arms and munitions that needed to be protected and maintained. As a result, the legislature authorized in 1816 the creation of three arsenals, one of which was to be located west of the Blue Ridge Mountains. The site chosen, originally a tract of slightly less than eight acres, was located in Lexington, Virginia, a beautifully situated village in the upper end of Virginia's famed Shenandoah Valley. The arsenal property was to be garrisoned by twenty militiamen and a captain. Because of disturbances and several incidents created by the soldiers at the arsenal, the Virginia state government created the Virginia Military Institute to replace the soldiers with young men whose education was to be combined with military training and guard duty at the arsenal.

Patterned after the Ecole Polytechnique of France and the U.S. Military Academy at West Point, VMI was organized several months before it officially opened on November 11, 1839, when the first cadet sentinel, John B. Strange, mounted the guard at the old arsenal. Largely the brainchild of John Thomas Lewis Preston, a Lexington lawyer and graduate of neighboring Washington College (later Washington and Lee), VMI was brought into being by

VIRGINIA MILITARY INSTITUTE CADET. NATIONAL ARCHIVES

an organizing board but governed by a board of visitors with a superintendent to oversee the daily operations. The first president of the board was Col. Claudius Crozet, a graduate of the Ecole Polytechnique, former artillery officer under Napoleon and professor of engineering at West Point, and state engineer of Virginia. Professor (later Maj. Gen.) Francis Henney Smith, distinguished graduate of West Point, was named the first superintendent.

Smith found the arsenal to be thoroughly inadequate for the new institute. He worked for nearly a decade formulating plans for a new barracks, parade ground, mess hall, and residences. New York architect Alexander Jackson Davis was employed to carry out Smith's plans. Davis, who was to become one of the foremost American architects of the nineteenth century, designed the first of the institute's buildings in the Gothic revival style, a style which influenced every other building on the VMI Post. The first of the new buildings was opened in September 1851. The other buildings of the pre–Civil War period were completed during the 1850s.

Unlike West Point, which had as its educational goal the training of cadets to be professional officers in the American military, VMI focused first on leadership in civil life, but also trained its cadets for service as citizen-soldiers in time of war or national emergency. VMI, from the beginning, has maintained that the best way to achieve its educational goal is within a military framework and a system of individual discipline and guidance based on an honor system.

At the outbreak of the Civil War nearly 300 of the 348-man Corps of Cadets were sent to Richmond to help drill and instruct the thousands of recruits who were daily pouring into the Confederate capital. Estimates vary, but it has been suggested that the recruits drilled by the cadets ranged in number from 25,000 to 50,000. At the beginning of the war there had been 1,217 matriculates at the institute, and another 813 enrolled during the war, bringing the total to 2,030. Of these, 1,902 were living at the commencement of hostilities, and 1,796 (94 percent) went into Confederate service. Of this total, 259 (14.5 percent) died, either killed outright or by wounds or disease. Small wonder, then, that VMI has been referred to as the "West Point of the South" or that Superintendent Francis H. Smith was prompted to say in 1877 that the Institute "left more of its alumni on the battle-field among the slain in the civil war of 1861–65 than West Point in all the wars of the United States since 1802, when the United States Military Academy was established."

The institute gave to the Confederacy 3 major generals, 17 brigadier generals, 92 colonels, 64 lieutenant colonels, 107 majors, 306 captains, and 221 lieutenants. Nor were the casualties or volunteers confined to the ranks filled by cadets or former cadets. The VMI faculty contributed its share. Among these were Lt. Gen. Thomas J. ("Stonewall")

Jackson, Maj. Gen. Robert Rodes, Col. Stapleton Crutchfield, Brig. Gen. John McCausland, Lt. Scott Shipp, and more than a dozen others.

Probably the most dramatic moment in VMI history came in May of 1864 when the Corps of Cadets was called out to help repel the invasion of the Shenandoah Valley by Federal Gen. Franz Sigel. The cadets, some 241 in number under the command of Scott Shipp, joined Confederate Gen. John C. Breckinridge's command near New Market, Virginia, in time to participate in the rout of the Union army. The charge of the cadets across a muddy field in the face of determined musketry and artillery fire brought undying fame to the institute; in the course of that brief action ten cadets were killed or mortally wounded and another forty-five wounded. Today, six of the slain, known as New Market Cadets, lie buried on the VMI grounds beside Moses Ezekiel's statue "Virginia Mourning Her Dead." (Ezekiel himself was a New Market Cadet, class of 1866.)

VMI was shelled, needlessly sacked, and burned on June 12, 1864, by Federal Gen. David Hunter. The library was scattered across the grounds and put to the torch along with other property, and many items that belonged to cadets or townspeople, including a replica of Houdon's statue of Washington, were carted off as souvenirs. Had it not been for the tireless efforts of Gen. Francis H. Smith and other members of the faculty, the VMI might never have reopened its doors as it did on October 17, 1865. In 1916 the U.S. government awarded it $100,000 for damages sustained during the war, part of the claim VMI had pressed as a result of property loss during Hunter's raid.

Superintendent Smith continued to lead the institute during the postwar years until his resignation and death in 1890, whereupon Scott Shipp became VMI's second superintendent. Counted among its faculty or the Corps of Cadets during the latter part of the nineteenth century were Matthew Fontaine Maury, Gen. George C. Marshall, Gen. John A. Lejeune, Richard Evelyn Byrd, Jr., and Charles E. Kilbourne. Two national fraternities were founded by or at VMI—Alpha Tau Omega (1865) and Sigma Nu (1869). In the time-honored tradition, VMI continues to educate citizen-soldiers who serve their state and country.

BIBLIOGRAPHY

Couper, William. *One Hundred Years at Virginia Military Institute.* Richmond, Va., 1939.

Couper, William. *The V.M.I. New Market Cadets.* Charlottesville, Va., 1933.

Smith, Francis H. *History of the Virginia Military Institute.* Lynchburg, Va., 1912.

Wise, Henry. *Drawing Out the Man: The V.M.I. Story.* Charlottesville, Va., 1980.

Wise, Jennings Cropper. *The Military History of the Virginia Military Institute, 1839–1865.* Lynchburg, Va., 1915.

TERRENCE V. MURPHY

VOLCK, ADALBERT (1828–1912), artist. His only biographer claimed that "what Thomas Nast . . . was to do for the North, Volck . . . did for the South." In truth, this gifted artist was all but unknown to Confederate audiences because during the war his works could not be shipped through the lines into the South. After peace was restored, however, Volck had an enormous impact on the culture of the Lost Cause through the circulation of his brilliantly conceived and crafted etchings.

Born in Bavaria, Volck learned to draw at artists' colonies near Nuremberg. After the Revolutions of 1848 he fled to America, settling in Baltimore and there earning a degree in dental surgery in 1852. Six years later he joined the Allston Association, a devoutly pro-Southern art league.

When war broke out and Baltimore was occupied, Volck was inspired to produce a series of incisive etchings variously vilifying the North and lauding Southern virtues. His first collection, *Ye Exploits of Ye Distinguished Attorney and General B. F. B. (Bombastes Furioso Buncombe)* assailed Union Gen. Benjamin F. Butler. His *Comedians and Tragedians of the North* viciously lampooned such Union leaders as Henry Ward Beecher, whom Volck portrayed as a black man.

Volck's greatest work was his *Sketches from the Civil War in North America,* first published in 1863 under the thinly veiled pseudonym "V. Blada" (the first five letters of his given name spelled backward). Although it bore a London imprint, like his previous works it was published secretly in Baltimore and distributed to only two hundred fellow Confederate sympathizers there.

In several editions of the portfolio, Volck expanded his vitriolic pictorial assault on Northern policies and leaders, particularly Abraham Lincoln, and portrayed Union generals as Hun-like plunderers. By contrast, the artist celebrated Southern life by depicting bathetic but inspiring scenes, which fellow artists overlooked. His *Making Clothes for the Boys in the Army* and *Cave Life in Vicksburg,* for example, poignantly celebrated brave and selfless Southern women. *Slaves Concealing Their Master from a Searching Party* illumined the myth of the eternally loyal slave. And both *Offering of Church Bells to be Cast into Cannon* and *[Prayer] Scene in Stonewall Jackson's Camp* suggested a holy aspect to the Confederate struggle.

After the war, Volck's etchings at last were circulated in the South, where they became immensely popular and helped define the myth of the Lost Cause. Volck himself stayed active, producing several canvases of Robert E. Lee for adaptation into chromolithographs, but he never again approached the brilliance he displayed as an underground artist in wartime.

Although Volck never recanted his pro-Confederate sympathies, he did confess regret at directing "ridicule at that great and good Lincoln." Otherwise, he insisted that his works had shown Civil War events "as truthfully as my close connections with the South enabled me to get at them."

BIBLIOGRAPHY

Anderson, George McCullough. *The Works of Adalbert Johann Volck, 1828–1912.* Baltimore, 1970.

Foley, Gardner P. H. "Adalbert Volck, Dentist and Artist." *Journal of the American College of Dentists* 16 (March 1949): 60–66.

Halstead, Murat. "Historic Illustrations of the Confederacy." *Cosmopolitan* (August 1890): 496–507.

Neely, Mark E., Jr., Harold Holzer, and Gabor S. Boritt. *The Confederate Image: Prints of the Lost Cause.* Chapel Hill, N.C., 1987.

HAROLD HOLZER

W

WADDELL, JAMES (1824–1886), naval officer. Waddell was born in Pittsboro, North Carolina. Appointed a midshipman in the U.S. Navy in 1841, he was wounded in a duel with another midshipman the same year. Waddell served in the Mexican War, both afloat and ashore, and later on ships worldwide. He resigned from the U.S. Navy in November 1862 while at St. Helena Island, but returned with his ship to New York, where his resignation was accepted.

Waddell traveled to Richmond and obtained a commission as lieutenant in the Confederate navy, March 27, 1862. He served briefly on the ironclad CSS *Mississippi,* scuttling the ship to prevent its capture during the withdrawal from New Orleans. He next served as ordnance officer at the battle between the Union fleet and Confederates at Drewry's Bluff on the James River, Virginia. He later commanded special defenses at the port of Charleston. Waddell was ordered to Great Britain in March 1863, probably to officer one of the Laird rams. When the British government seized the rams, the officers who were intended for them took up other duties.

Waddell's most important service came when he was placed in command of a commerce raiding voyage against the Union whaling fleet in the northern Pacific Ocean. Matthew Fontaine Maury, who had charted the sailing routes used by whalers, assisted Waddell in planning the cruise. Waddell left Liverpool, with other Confederate naval officers and men, on October 8, 1864, aboard the Confederate supply steamer *Laurel.* They met the auxiliary steamer *Sea King* at Funchal, Madeira, in the Azores and transshipped *Laurel*'s cargo of arms and supplies to that vessel. On October 20, 1864, Waddell commissioned his new raider CSS *Shenandoah,* shipped a crew, and mounted the guns. He sailed for Melbourne, Australia, taking eight prizes on the way.

In Melbourne, the Union consul petitioned government representatives to prevent *Shenandoah* from making repairs, but Waddell successfully argued his case. The ship repaired mechanical defects on a private slip and took on supplies. Waddell also illegally augmented his crew with a number of stowaways before heading north toward the Pacific whaling grounds. After further successes against the whaling fleet, and while headed for a raid against San Francisco, Waddell learned of the war's end from a British ship. He ordered *Shenandoah*'s armament dismantled and stored in the hold, and headed back around Cape Horn for England. *Shenandoah* entered Liverpool on November 6, 1865, flying the Confederate flag, the last military unit to do so.

Because he was abroad during the surrender of other Confederate military units, Waddell was not covered by any surrender terms and stayed abroad until 1875. In that year he returned and commanded the large new Pacific Mail Company liner *San Francisco* briefly until the ship was lost on an uncharted Mexican reef. In the early 1880s, Waddell moved to Annapolis, Maryland, where he commanded the state regulatory oyster navy. He died in Annapolis on March 15, 1886.

BIBLIOGRAPHY

Bulloch, James Dunwoody. *The Secret Service of the Confederate States in Europe; or, How the Confederate Cruisers Were Equipped.* 2 vols. New York, 1884. Reprint, New York, 1959.

Horan, James D., ed. *C.S.S. Shenandoah: The Memoirs of Lieutenant Commanding James I. Waddell.* New York, 1960.

Hunt, Cornelius E. *The Shenandoah; or, The Last Confederate Cruiser.* New York, 1866.

Kevin J. Foster

WALKER, HENRY H. (1832–1912), brigadier general. Born October 15, 1832, Henry Harrison Walker was a graduate of the U.S. Military Academy, finishing in the bottom fifth of his class of 1853. After an unspectacular prewar career on the plains, Walker joined the Fortieth Virginia Infantry as its lieutenant colonel in November 1861. He spent a short time on detached duty with another unit in early 1862, but by that summer he was back with his Virginians. On June 27, 1862, Walker was twice wounded at the Battle of Gaines' Mill, effectively disabling him for further duty during the year. He resigned his post with the Fortieth Virginia in August and went on general staff duty.

Walker returned to the army in July 1863 after receiving promotion to brigadier general. He commanded a sadly depleted brigade of Virginians that included his old unit, the Fortieth. The man whom he replaced, Col. John Mercer Brockenbrough, attributed Walker's promotion to the new general's "puerile exertions." From late July 1863 until May 1864, Walker led his brigade through a few minor campaigns and then fought in the Battle of the Wilderness. Shortly thereafter, on May 10, his foot was blown off by an artillery round while he was leading his men in fighting near the Po River at Spotsylvania Court House. Once again he was forced into administrative duty, and he finished the war guarding a railroad.

HENRY H. WALKER. LIBRARY OF CONGRESS

Walker emigrated from the South after the war, relocating to Morristown, New Jersey, where he died March 22, 1912, and is buried. The general was known in the Confederate army as "Mud" Walker, but the origin of that peculiar nickname remains unknown.

BIBLIOGRAPHY

Compiled Military Service Records. Henry H. Walker. Microcopy M331, Roll 257. Record Group 109. National Archives, Washington, D.C.

Evans, Clement A., ed. *Confederate Military History.* 12 vols. Atlanta, 1899. Extended ed. in 19 vols. Wilmington, N.C., 1987–1989.

Freeman, Douglas S. *Lee's Lieutenants: A Study In Command.* 3 vols. New York, 1942–1944. Reprint, New York, 1986.

ROBERT E. L. KRICK

WALKER, JAMES ALEXANDER (1832–1901), brigadier general and U.S. congressman. Few Virginia leaders were more stormy, or more lovable, than "Stonewall Jim" Walker. He was born August 27, 1832, in the Shenandoah Valley's Augusta County. In 1852, only weeks from graduation from the Virginia Military Institute, and ranked at the top of his class, Walker became embroiled in a classroom argument with Professor Thomas J. Jackson. Walker was expelled from the institute, and the future Stonewall Jackson declined the youth's challenge to a duel.

Walker obtained a law degree from the University of Virginia. When civil war came, he was a practicing attorney in Pulaski County. The VMI training served Walker well. He served successively as a captain in the Fourth Virginia, colonel of the Thirteenth Virginia, and brigadier general (as of May 13, 1863) of the famed Stonewall Brigade. Walrus-like in appearance, with profanity and short temper in keeping with his fighting prowess, Walker participated in more than fifty engagements while serving first under Jackson and later under Robert E. Lee. A shattered elbow in the fierce action at Spotsylvania blocked his almost-certain promotion to major general.

After the war he gained a seat in the Virginia legislature in 1871. Election to lieutenant governor followed six years later. Cast aside for governor by fellow Democrats, Walker angrily joined the Republican ranks and ultimately won two terms in the U.S. Congress. A gunfight following another, contested election left Walker crippled. He died October 20, 1901, and was buried in Wytheville, Virginia.

Walker's daughter stated of the colorful soldier-politician: "Though in every great fight of his life, he lost,

JAMES ALEXANDER WALKER. LIBRARY OF CONGRESS

he never recognized defeat nor knew malice, and always bore about him the manner of a conqueror."

BIBLIOGRAPHY

Caldwell, Willie Walker. *Stonewall Jim: A Biography of General James A. Walker, C.S.A.* Elliston, Va., 1990.

Riggs, David F. *Thirteenth Virginia Infantry.* Lynchburg, Va., 1988.

Robertson, James I., Jr. *The Stonewall Brigade.* Baton Rouge, La., 1963.

JAMES I. ROBERTSON, JR.

WALKER, JOHN GEORGE (1822–1893), major general. Although he had no formal military education, Walker rose quickly to division commander and served in four different theaters during the war. Born in Cole County, Missouri, on July 22, 1822, Walker served fifteen years in the U.S. Army, rising to captain after enlisting at age twenty-four during the Mexican War. Walker joined the Confederacy relatively late, waiting until July 31, 1861 (ten days after First Manassas), before resigning from the U.S. Army.

After serving with the Eighth Texas Cavalry, Walker received his brigadier star on January 9, 1862, but he experienced little action until the September 1862 Maryland campaign. As part of Special Order 191, Robert E. Lee assigned Walker a dual task: blowing up the Chesapeake and Ohio Canal aqueduct spanning the Monocacy River and seizing Loudoun Heights, an eleven-hundred-foot mountain overlooking Harpers Ferry and the Shenandoah River. Walker's two-thousand-man division failed to destroy the aqueduct, but he occupied Loudoun Heights without resistance on September 13. The next day, in cooperation with Thomas J. ("Stonewall") Jackson, Walker's cannoneers opened the bombardment, and on the fifteenth, Harpers Ferry surrendered. Walker then rushed to Sharpsburg, where he drove back the Federals during the West Woods attack on September 17.

On November 8, 1862, Walker became a major general, commanding the Texas infantry division in the Trans-Mississippi Department. After the Red River campaign, he controlled the District of West Louisiana, and at war's end, he commanded a division in the District of Texas, New Mexico, and Arizona. Walker died July 20, 1893, and was buried in the Stonewall Cemetery at Winchester, Virginia.

BIBLIOGRAPHY

Walker, John G. "Jackson's Capture of Harpers Ferry." In *Battles and Leaders of the Civil War.* Edited by Robert U. Johnson and C. C. Buel. Vol. 2. New York, 1888. Reprint, Secaucus, N.J., 1982.

Warner, Ezra J. *Generals in Gray: Lives of the Confederate Commanders.* Baton Rouge, La., 1959.

DENNIS E. FRYE

JOHN GEORGE WALKER. LIBRARY OF CONGRESS

WALKER, LEROY P. (1817–1884), secretary of war and brigadier general. Leroy Pope Walker was born in Huntsville, Alabama, the son of U.S. Senator John Williams Walker. He attended the universities of Alabama and Virginia in preparation for a career in law. After his admission to the bar in 1837, he practiced law in several Alabama towns before settling in Huntsville in 1850. In 1843 Walker was elected to the Alabama House of Representatives where, as a Democrat, he subsequently played an important role in the formulation of the extremely proslavery Alabama Platform protesting the Wilmot Proviso and threatening secession. His efforts in defense of Southern rights and slavery led to his election in 1847 as Speaker of the Alabama House of Representatives and his reelection in 1849. During the 1850s he became one of the leading attorneys in the state.

In 1860 Walker served as William Lowndes Yancey's chief lieutenant in the Alabama legislature in reaffirming the state's commitment to a strong Southern rights position. He chaired the state's Democratic delegation that bolted the national convention at Charleston, and during the campaign he canvassed northern Alabama for Southern Democratic candidate John C. Breckinridge. When Abraham Lincoln won the election, he called for the immediate secession of the state. During the winter of 1860–1861 Walker served as a state commissioner to secure Tennessee's support for secession.

LEROY P. WALKER. LIBRARY OF CONGRESS

After the Confederacy was formed, President Jefferson Davis, desiring to have every state represented in his cabinet, looked to Alabama for his secretary of war. Both Clement C. Clay and Yancey, the state's most prominent political leaders, declined the appointment and instead recommended Walker for the position. Although Davis did not know Walker personally, he selected him for the War Department. Despite the fact that the new secretary had no military or even administrative experience, the Southern press, which, like Davis, actually knew little about Walker, applauded the appointment. Astute observers, however, privately predicted that Walker would be only a man of straw for President Davis who would exercise his well-known love for military affairs and control the War Department. They were largely correct.

Walker's term as Confederate secretary of war, extending from February 21 to September 16, 1861, was a brief and troubled one. Beginning with the Fort Sumter crisis, it was clear that Walker would not have an important role in the formulation of policy. Although he participated in the cabinet meetings on Fort Sumter, he did little more than dispatch Davis's messages to Gen. P. G. T. Beauregard at Charleston. It was Walker who wired the fateful order of April 10 for Beauregard to demand the evacuation of Fort Sumter, "and if this is refused proceed, in such manner as you may determine, to reduce it." After the bombardment and surrender of the Federal garrison, Walker gained notoriety in the North when he predicted that "in a few months more the flag of the Confederate States would wave over the capitol at Washington." This rash statement outraged Northerners and helped rally Union support for the war.

Although Davis gave Walker little authority over the planning and conduct of military operations, he did delegate to his secretary the main responsibility for raising the armies and providing the means for them to fight. This task would have taxed the ingenuity and energy of the ablest administrator. Nevertheless, Walker and his subordinates in the War Department managed by September to raise a force of 200,000 men. Although one of the Confederate armies won a stunning victory at Manassas in July, Walker's inability to provide sufficient arms, ammunition, and equipment for Southern forces made him a convenient target for critics.

Walker also received more than his share of blame for the continued vulnerability of coastal defenses. When Fort Hatteras fell to a Federal assault in August, shocking Confederates everywhere, he was severely criticized. His lack of a military background increasingly hurt him among those who wanted a professional army officer in charge of the War Department. Jealous of his prerogative and realizing the necessity for a unified command, Walker became embroiled with state rights–obsessed governors like Joseph E. Brown of Georgia in a conflict over the recruitment and control of troops. His failure to grant commissions to friends of governors created further opposition from powerful politicians.

For a variety of reasons, Davis by the late summer of 1861 had lost confidence in Walker. The president, who had a fetish for administrative detail, became upset when Walker did not maintain a similarly high standard of administration. Walker's periodic absences from the War Office contributed to Davis's concern that the secretary was not doing his job. In early September a conflict over military policy occurred between the two men. The president became irritated when Walker directed Gen. Leonidas Polk to withdraw from Columbus, Kentucky. Although the occupation of Columbus violated Kentucky's neutrality, Davis countermanded the order and indicated his general displeasure with Walker. On September 10, Walker submitted his resignation and asked the president for a military command in Alabama. Davis appointed him a brigadier general and placed him in charge of three regiments of Alabama troops, none of which was properly armed or equipped. Failure was certain, and on January 27, 1862, Gen. Braxton Bragg, an old nemesis, removed Walker from command.

Returning to his law practice in Huntsville, Walker defended Unionists accused of treason against the Confederate government. Although he had reached the conclusion by 1863 that the Confederate cause was hopeless, he accepted an appointment as presiding judge of the Military Court of North Alabama, a position he held until the surrender.

During Reconstruction Walker was one of the Democratic leaders in the overthrow of Republican rule in Alabama, and in 1875 he served as president of the state convention that reversed important and, on the whole, progressive provisions of the so-called Radical Constitution of 1867. He died in Huntsville on August 23, 1884.

BIBLIOGRAPHY

Eaton, Clement. *Jefferson Davis.* New York, 1977.

Harris, William C. *Leroy Pope Walker: Confederate Secretary of War.* Tuscaloosa, Ala., 1962.

Patrick, Rembert W. *Jefferson Davis and His Cabinet.* Baton Rouge, La., 1944.

William C. Harris

WALKER, LUCIUS MARSHALL (1829–1863), brigadier general. Born October 18, 1829, in Columbia, Tennessee, Walker was a nephew of former president James K. Polk and brother-in-law of Brig. Gen. Frank Crawford Armstrong. He graduated from West Point in 1850, fifteenth out of forty-four but resigned the regular army two years later and moved to Memphis.

Walker joined the Fortieth Tennessee Infantry when the Civil War began and was elected colonel on November 11, 1861. He was made commander at Memphis and promoted to brigadier general to date from March 11, 1862. He was not at Shiloh but served under Braxton Bragg at Corinth. Walker and Bragg had a misunderstanding that prompted Bragg to say that Walker was not "safe" to entrust with any command. When Walker applied for a transfer to the Trans-Mississippi Department, Bragg speedily approved it. He arrived in Arkansas in 1863, and E. Kirby Smith gave him command of a cavalry brigade. Walker fought in the Battle of Helena on July 4, 1863, but as soon as the fight had ended, Brig. Gen. John Sappington Marmaduke criticized Walker's handling of the affair and declared that he would no longer serve with him. Angered, Walker challenged Marmaduke to a duel. In spite of the fact that the Federal army was threatening Little Rock, the two men met on September 6, 1863. Walker was mortally wounded and died the next day. Sterling Price placed Marmaduke under arrest but soon released him because of the pending battle; Little Rock fell four days after the duel. Walker was buried in Memphis.

BIBLIOGRAPHY

Bailey, Anne J. *Between the Enemy and Texas.* Fort Worth, Tex., 1989.

Huff, Leo E. "The Last Duel in Arkansas: The Marmaduke-Walker Duel." *Arkansas Historical Quarterly* 23 (1964): 36–49.

Kerby, Robert L. *Kirby Smith's Confederacy: The Trans-Mississippi South, 1863–1865.* New York, 1972.

Anne J. Bailey

WALKER, REUBEN LINDSAY (1827–1890), brigadier general. Born May 29, 1827, in Albemarle County, Virginia, Walker graduated from the Virginia Military Institute in 1845, but made no immediate use of his military education. He worked as an engineer and farmed before the war. Walker received an artillery commission in 1861 and led the Purcell Artillery for a few months. His superiors recognized Walker's aptitude for artillery, and he advanced slowly but steadily through the ranks, becoming brigadier general of artillery on February 18, 1865. His duties from 1862 onward, however, had been commensurate with those of a higher rank.

"Old Rube" Walker served with A. P. Hill throughout the war, working for months as Hill's chief of artillery for the division and then advancing to supervision of the Third

REUBEN LINDSAY WALKER. LIBRARY OF CONGRESS

Corps artillery. He was a model of consistency. Rarely did he deserve criticism and he was usually present for duty, in part because he escaped the war without being wounded.

Although Hill and others found little fault with Walker, he inspired colorfully insulting descriptions from at least two subordinates. One thought him a "perfect nincompoop"; another found "Old Rube" to be a man of "sloth and uxoriousness." In contrast, Gen. William N. Pendleton lauded him as "zealous, bold, and vigorous."

Walker surrendered with his guns at Appomattox and resumed his prewar occupations. He lived in several states after the war, including Texas where he supervised construction of the state capitol building in Austin. Walker died in Virginia on June 7, 1890, and is buried at Richmond's Hollywood Cemetery.

BIBLIOGRAPHY

Compiled Military Service Records. Reuben Lindsay Walker. Microcopy M331, Roll 257. Record Group 109. National Archives, Washington, D.C.

Evans, Clement A., ed. *Confederate Military History.* 12 vols. Atlanta, 1899. Extended ed. in 19 vols. Wilmington, N.C., 1987–1989.

Freeman, Douglas S. *Lee's Lieutenants: A Study In Command.* 3 vols. New York, 1942–1944. Reprint, New York, 1986.

ROBERT E. L. KRICK

WALKER, RICHARD WILDE (1823–1874), congressman from Alabama. Born on February 16, 1823, in Huntsville, Alabama, Walker was educated at Spring Hill College, Mobile, the University of Virginia, and Princeton University, from which he graduated with honors in 1841. He returned to Huntsville, read law, and was admitted to the bar in 1844. In 1845 he settled in Florence, Alabama, where he was district solicitor until 1848, and served in the Alabama legislature in 1851 and 1855. In 1859 he was appointed to fill a vacancy on the Alabama Supreme Court and was elected to that post in 1860.

A close personal ally of cooperationalist Alexander H. Stephens of Georgia, Walker differed with the views of his brother, Leroy P. Walker, a supporter of John C. Breckinridge in 1860 and the first Confederate Secretary of War. Richard Walker represented Alabama in the Provisional Confederate Congress, serving on the Commercial and Financial Independence, Foreign Affairs, and Provisional and Permanent Constitution committees. A supporter of President Jefferson Davis in the Provisional Congress, Walker had come to oppose Davis by 1863, when he replaced Clement Claiborne Clay in the Second Confederate Senate. There he served on the Joint Commerce, Engrossment and Enrollment, Judiciary, Post Office and Post Roads, and Public Buildings committees and firmly opposed increased powers for the Confederate central government. After the war he resumed his law practice in Huntsville, where he died June 16, 1874.

BIBLIOGRAPHY

McMillan, Malcolm C. *The Alabama Confederate Reader.* University, Ala., 1963.

Owen, Thomas McAdory. *History of Alabama and Dictionary of Alabama Biography.* 4 vols. Chicago, 1921.

Thornton, J. Mills, III. *Politics and Power in a Slave Society: Alabama, 1800–1860.* Baton Rouge, La., 1978.

Wakelyn, Jon L. *Biographical Dictionary of the Confederacy.* Edited by Frank E. Vandiver. Westport, Conn., 1977.

Warner, Ezra J., and W. Buck Yearns. *Biographical Register of the Confederate Congress.* Baton Rouge, La., 1975.

SARAH WOOLFOLK WIGGINS

WALKER, W. H. T. (1816–1864), major general. Born in Augusta, Georgia, Walker attended West Point, where he graduated in 1837 near the bottom of his class. After an active military career, "Old Shot Pouch" Walker resigned from the U.S. Army and was appointed a major general of Georgia volunteers on April 25, 1861. One month later he received a commission as a brigadier general in the Confederate army. Serving first at Pensacola, Florida, Walker was sent to Virginia in August 1861 and given command of a brigade in Gen. Joseph E. Johnston's Army of the Potomac. With the reorganization of the army in

October, Walker was transferred to the First Brigade of Maj. Gen. E. Kirby Smith's division. Seven days later he resigned, possibly owing to dissatisfaction either with this rearrangement or with the Davis administration's management of the war. Clearly health was not as big a factor as he claimed, for the following month he accepted Georgia Governor Joseph E. Brown's invitation to serve as a brigadier general commanding the Third Brigade of Georgia state troops.

Walker returned to Confederate military service in March 1863 as a brigadier general in the Department of South Carolina, Georgia, and Florida and was appointed to a board of officers charged with examining the defenses of Savannah and its approaches. On May 5, Walker's brigade was ordered to Mississippi to reinforce Johnston at Vicksburg. The brigade saw minor action during the ill-fated defense of Jackson on May 14. On Johnston's recommendation, Walker was promoted to major general on May 23 and sent with his division to Yazoo City to fortify it. After Johnston's unsuccessful attempt in late June and early July 1863 to break the Federal investment of Vicksburg, Walker's division participated in a second defense of the Mississippi capital until forced to withdraw on July 16.

In August, Johnston, now in Morton, Mississippi, detached two divisions, including Walker's, to reinforce Gen. Braxton Bragg's Army of Tennessee at Chattanooga. At the Battle of Chickamauga, Walker commanded the Reserve Corps and attacked the Federal left on September 20. During the ensuing siege of Chattanooga, Walker controlled all troops west of Chattanooga Creek until he went on leave November 12. Returning to duty in January 1864, Walker reported to Johnston in Dalton, Georgia, where he became embroiled in the controversy over Maj. Gen. Patrick Cleburne's proposal to enlist slaves in the army. Walker objected, privately labeling Cleburne a traitor and publicly stating that "further agitation of such sentiments and propositions would ruin the efficacy of our Army and involve our cause in ruin and disgrace."

Walker's division participated in the Army of Tennessee's movement toward Atlanta in 1864. Walker died on July 22 when he was shot during the opening phases of the Battle of Atlanta. Two days later his division was disbanded.

BIBLIOGRAPHY

Connelly, Thomas L. *Autumn of Glory: The Army of Tennessee, 1862–1865.* Baton Rouge, La., 1971.

Derry, Joseph T. *Georgia.* Vol. 6 of *Confederate Military History.* Edited by Clement A. Evans. Atlanta, 1899. Vol. 7 of extended ed. Wilmington, N.C., 1987.

Mosser, Jeffrey. "I Shall Make Him Remember." *Civil War Times Illustrated* 32, no. 1 (1993): 24, 49, 52–57, 60–62.

Warner, Ezra J. *Generals in Gray: Lives of the Confederate Commanders.* Baton Rouge, La., 1959.

Alan C. Downs

WALKER, WILLIAM (1812–1899), brigadier general. Walker, born in Pittsburgh, Pennsylvania, on April 13, 1822, was raised in Washington by his uncle, Mississippi Senator Robert J. Walker. After school, Walker enlisted in the U.S. Army and fought in the Mexican War as a lieutenant. He won a captain's brevet at Chapultepec for gallantry and meritorious conduct. Mustered out in 1848, he was recommissioned in 1855 as colonel of the First U.S. Cavalry, which he resigned in May 1861 when the South seceded.

In March 1862 Walker was promoted to colonel, Inspector General's Office, charged with mustering and inspecting the troops in the Department of South Carolina and Georgia. On October 30, 1862, Walker was promoted to brigadier general under P. G. T. Beauregard. In early 1863 he received command of the Third Military District between the Ashepou and Savannah rivers, and the following April, temporary command of N. G. Evans's brigade at Weldon, North Carolina. In May the brigade joined Beauregard's forces around Richmond.

On the afternoon of May 20, 1864, Walker led a daring charge against Benjamin F. Butler's Union forces at Ware Bottom Church, when the Federals counterattacked to retake entrenchments lost to the Confederates earlier. Walker became separated from his troops and in the confusion blundered into Federal lines, where he was fired upon while trying to escape. Walker's horse was killed and the general's left arm was pierced and right leg shattered. He was sent to Fort Monroe, where his leg was amputated after he dictated death-bed letters to family and friends. He survived, however, and was exchanged in October. After partially recovering, Walker returned to the field and was given command of the forces at Weldon, North Carolina, in October 1864. He surrendered there in April 1865.

After the war, Walker moved to Georgia and became a businessman. He died in Atlanta on June 7, 1899, and was buried in Oakland Cemetery.

BIBLIOGRAPHY

Sisfakis, Stewart. *Who Was Who in the Civil War.* New York, 1988.

Warner, Ezra J. *Generals in Gray: Lives of the Confederate Commanders.* Baton Rouge, La., 1959.

Kenneth L. Stiles

WALLACE, WILLIAM HENRY (1827–1901), brigadier general. Wallace was born March 24, 1827, in Laurens District, South Carolina, and graduated from South Carolina College in 1849. He began his career as a planter, newspaper publisher, and lawyer. In 1860 he was elected to the South Carolina legislature as a secessionist. Rather than run again, he enlisted in the Eighteenth South Carolina Infantry, a regiment in N. G. Evans's brigade, as a private, though he was soon named its adjutant.

In May 1862 Wallace was elected the regiment's lieutenant colonel, and in July the unit was sent to Virginia. At Second Manassas, Wallace took command of the Eighteenth on August 30 when its colonel was killed. Wallace commanded the regiment through the Sharpsburg campaign and went with the Eighteenth when it was transferred to the Charleston defenses in late 1862. The next year Wallace and the unit were sent back to Virginia, where in 1864 they took part in the Petersburg campaign. At the Battle of the Crater four companies were blown up in the initial blast, and the Union attack engulfed what was left of the Eighteenth. That September Wallace was promoted to brigadier general and given command of Elliott's Brigade. Bushrod Rust Johnson urged that Wallace be given temporary command because he was "the officer best qualified in the brigade for the position [and] . . . the efficiency of the brigade [would] be improved." During the Appomattox campaign the brigade dropped from 1,300 men on March 29 to 350 on April 2. Wallace was given command of Johnson's division (2,200 men) on April 9, just before the surrender.

After the war, Wallace returned to his life as a plantation owner and lawyer. He ran as a Democrat for the state legislature in 1872 and served three terms. In 1877 he was appointed a circuit court judge. Retiring from the court in 1893, he died in Union, South Carolina, on March 20, 1901.

BIBLIOGRAPHY

Faust, Patricia L., ed. *Historical Times Illustrated Encyclopedia of the Civil War.* New York, 1986.

U.S. War Department. *War of the Rebellion: A Compilation of the Official Records of the Union and Confederate Armies.* Washington, D.C., 1880–1901. Ser. 1, vol. 11, p. 962; ser. 1, vol. 19, pt. 1, p. 947; ser. 1, vol. 28, pt. 2, p. 587; ser. 1, vol. 42, pt. 2, p. 1232.

Warner, Ezra J. *Generals in Gray: Lives of the Confederate Commanders.* Baton Rouge, La., 1959.

KENNETH L. STILES

WALLS, JOSIAH

WALLS, JOSIAH (1842–1905), U.S. congressman from Florida. Born a free black in Westchester, Virginia, Walls was pressed into valet service to a Confederate artillery battery. Captured by Union troops in the Battle of Yorktown in 1862, he was given a year's schooling in Harrisburg, Pennsylvania. In 1863, he enlisted as a private in the Third Regiment, U.S. Colored Infantry, at Camp William Penn near Philadelphia. Fighting at Fort Wagner, South Carolina, and at St. Johns Island and Jacksonville, Florida, Walls was promoted to sergeant major. At Jacksonville he was assigned instructor in light and heavy artillery. Mustered out in Florida in November 1865, he settled in Alachua County, Florida.

During Reconstruction, Walls became a farmer, plantation owner, real estate dealer, lawyer, and politician in Alachua County. Elected to Florida's constitutional convention in 1868, he served in both state legislative houses before his election as Florida's sole representative to the U.S. Congress in 1871. On March 9, 1871, his seat was challenged and Democrat Silas Niblack was declared Florida's representative, January 28, 1873. Walls then defeated Niblack and served a full term in the Forty-third Congress. Reelected, Walls served from 1872 to 1876. Unseated by Democrat Jesse Johnson Finley, Walls failed to secure another nomination. Party conflicts and questionable election activities led to both electoral defeats.

Walls served as assistant superintendent of farms at the State Normal and Industrial College for Colored Students (the present-day Florida Agricultural and Mechanical University). He died in Tallahassee.

BIBLIOGRAPHY

Congressional Globe. 42d Cong., 3d Sess., 1873. Pt. 2.

Congressional Record. 44th Cong., 2d Sess., 1876. Vol. IV, pt. 3.

Klingman, Peter D. *Josiah Walls: Florida's Black Congressman of Reconstruction.* Gainesville, Fla., 1976.

Maxwell, Grace Rushing. "Josiah Thomas Walls, Florida's Black Congressman: His Quest for Economic Independence." *Florida Agricultural and Mechanical University Research Bulletin* 81 (1981): 30–39.

Richardson, Joe M. *The Negro in Reconstruction of Florida, 1865–1877.* Tampa, Fla., 1973.

GRACE RUSHING MAXWELL

WALTHALL, EDWARD CARY

WALTHALL, EDWARD CARY (1831–1898), major general and U.S. senator. Born in Richmond, Virginia, Walthall moved to Holly Springs, Mississippi, where he read law and was admitted to the bar in 1852. In 1861 he helped organize the Yalobusha Rifles, which on June 6 became Company H, Fifteenth Mississippi Infantry. Promoted to lieutenant colonel, Walthall was sent to eastern Tennessee and then to Kentucky, where he saw action at Camp Wildcat in October and at Mill Springs in January. Walthall commanded the regiment at the latter battle, where it suffered the highest casualty rate of all Confederate regiments engaged.

On April 11, 1862, Walthall was elected colonel of the Twenty-ninth Mississippi and assigned to James Ronald Chalmers's brigade. Following the evacuation of Corinth, the regiment moved to Tupelo and Chattanooga, before marching north into Kentucky. On September 14, in an attempt to seize the Louisville and Nashville Railroad, Chalmers's brigade unsuccessfully attacked Federal earthworks at Munfordville, later occupying the site after Federal forces withdrew.

On November 17, Walthall was given command of his

own brigade and promoted to brigadier general the following month. Absent on sick leave, he was unable to lead his troops at Murfreesboro. In July 1863, he was stationed in Atlanta before leaving in September to participate in the Battle of Chickamauga. The brigade captured 411 prisoners and two batteries at Alexander's Bridge on September 19. Having pursued the retreating Federals to Chattanooga, Walthall's Mississippians were posted on the west side of Lookout Mountain near the northern slope. Despite a desperate effort, the brigade was unable to repel Maj. Gen. Joseph Hooker's assault up the mountain on November 24 and withdrew to Missionary Ridge, only to meet the same fate the following afternoon. Although wounded in the foot, Walthall oversaw the evacuation of his troops southward toward Chickamauga Creek that evening.

In 1864, Walthall participated in the campaign in northern Georgia to stop Maj. Gen. William Tecumseh Sherman from seizing Atlanta. After his brigade performed well in the face of heavy fire at Resaca and Cassville, Walthall assumed command of Brig. Gen. James Cantey's division and successfully defended Big Kennesaw on June 27. He was promoted to major general on July 6. Outside Atlanta, Walthall's division fought in the Battles of Peachtree Creek and Ezra Church before evacuating the city with Gen. John Bell Hood and heading north to Tennessee. There, at the Battles of Franklin and Nashville, Walthall led his men in losing efforts against overwhelming odds. Walthall's division, now seriously depleted, covered the retreat of Hood's army through Alabama to Tupelo.

The war ended for Walthall in North Carolina, as his division joined Johnston for an attack against one wing of Sherman's advancing army on March 19 near Bentonville. Stiff Federal resistance nullified some initial success and Johnston was forced to retreat to Greensboro, and he surrendered to Sherman on April 26. Walthall was paroled on May 2 and returned to Mississippi. He died in Washington, D.C., after serving as a U.S. senator for twelve years.

BIBLIOGRAPHY

Bearss, Edwin C. "Edward Cary Walthall." In *The Confederate General.* Edited by William C. Davis. Vol. 6. Harrisburg, Pa., 1991.

Hooker, Charles E. *Mississippi.* Vol. 7 of *Confederate Military History.* Edited by Clement A. Evans. Atlanta, 1899. Vol. 9 of extended ed. Wilmington, N.C., 1987.

Warner, Ezra J. *Generals in Gray: Lives of the Confederate Commanders.* Baton Rouge, La., 1959.

ALAN C. DOWNS

WAR CORRESPONDENTS. Throughout the war Southern newspapers attempted to provide their readers with firsthand accounts of military activities. In some cases editors such as John Forsyth of the *Mobile Advertiser,* William T. Thompson of the *Savannah Morning News,* and James Sledge of the *Athens Southern Banner* went to the front to gather news. Most papers, however, depended on volunteers, officers, and sometimes enlisted men, who sent telegrams and letters from the field. One of these amateur journalists was John E. Cooke whose sometimes highly colored accounts of the Army of Northern Virginia revealed the talent that later made him a successful novelist.

Among the more than a hundred Southern reporters covering the war at various times were a number of "specials" (paid correspondents), most of whom provided copy for several papers and frequently wrote under various pseudonyms. The most famous was Peter Alexander who worked for several Georgia papers including the *Savannah Republican* as "P. W. A." or "A.," and for the *Mobile Advertiser* and the *Richmond Dispatch* as "Sallust." Alexander built a reputation for accurate and reliable combat reporting. In addition, he stressed the privations of the ordinary soldiers and frequently criticized officers and medical personnel for incompetence.

Felix Gregory de Fontaine, "Personne" of the *Courier,* led Charleston's talented corps of correspondents. He provided South Carolinians with lively descriptions of Confederate military life but gained greater notoriety for his graphic portrayals of Robert E. Lee, Thomas J. ("Stonewall") Jackson, and other commanders. "The poet laureate of the Confederacy," Henry Timrod, briefly covered the Confederate Army of the West for the *Mercury.* Also on the *Mercury* staff were Timrod's close friend Dr. John Bruns, William Courtenay, and Leonidas Spratt, who after reporting on First Manassas was subsequently briefly detained on suspicion of spying—a hazard of the profession.

Serving the Richmond reading public well were the *Dispatch*'s Dr. William Shepardson ("Bohemian"), James B. Sener, and occasionally Alexander. The *Mobile Register* aggressively covered the war with several competent reporters, one being Henry Watterson (possibly under the name "Shadow"), who served on the staffs of Leonidas Polk, Albert Sidney Johnston, and John Bell Hood. Other *Register* agents included Albert Street ("N' Importe"), Israel Gibbon, the ubiquitous Samuel Reid ("Ora"), and Shepardson ("Evelyn").

The peripatetic *Memphis Appeal* assembled an army of specials. John Linebaugh followed the Army of Tennessee as "Ashantee" and may also have been "Shadow" in the early years of the war. Reid filed reports as "Sparta" while also working for the *Atlanta Intelligencer* as "290." Others whose real names are unknown included "Vesper," who wrote a description of the siege of Vicksburg, and "Quel Qu' Un," who reported on the Army of Tennessee.

Papers unable to afford specials relied heavily on the Confederate Press Association's correspondents. These men had instructions to be objective, avoid rumors and secondhand information, and never to be scooped by specials. The most notable association newsmen were Bartholomew Riordan; John Hatcher; Jonathan Albertson, attached to the Army of Northern Virginia; W. O. Woodson, with the Army of Tennessee; and A. J. Wagner, who concentrated on southern Mississippi.

Working for low pay, frustrated by restrictions placed on their activities by commanders, and subject to the hazards of combat, Confederate journalists valiantly endeavored to keep the public informed on military matters.

[*See also* Newspapers.]

BIBLIOGRAPHY

Andrews, J. Cutler. *The South Reports the Civil War.* Princeton, N.J., 1970.

Carter, Hodding. *Their Words Were Bullets: The Southern Press in War, Reconstruction and Peace.* Athens, Ga., 1969.

Chester, Thomas M. *Thomas Morris Chester, Black Civil War Correspondent: His Dispatches from the Virginia Front.* Edited by R. J. Blackett. New York, 1989.

Griffith, Louis Turner, and John Erwin Talmadge. *Georgia Journalism, 1763–1950.* Athens, Ga., 1951.

Harwell, Richard Barksdale. "John Esten Cooke, Civil War Correspondent." *Journal of Southern History* 19 (1953): 501–516.

Charles McArver

WAR DEPARTMENT. The largest and most important department of the Confederate government, the War Department, was founded with the creation of the Confederacy. Established by an act of Congress on February 21, 1861, it was given charge of all matters pertaining to the army (and Indian tribes), subject to the general direction of the president. Its offices were located in an abandoned warehouse, known as Government House, which shared space with other departments in Montgomery, Alabama, then the capital. Here the military establishment of the South was born, as hundreds of officeseekers appeared and thousands of army commissions and officers' assignments were issued. After Virginia joined the Confederacy in late May, the capital was moved to Richmond, a city of forty thousand people.

The War Department was served by five secretaries and one ad interim appointee during the life of the Confederacy: Leroy Pope Walker (February 21 to September 16, 1861); Judah P. Benjamin (acting secretary starting September 17, official secretary from November 21, 1861, to March 17, 1862); George Wythe Randolph (March 18 to November 15, 1862); Gustavus Woodson Smith (ad interim secretary, November 17 to 20, 1862); James A. Seddon (November 21, 1862, to February 5, 1865); John C. Breckinridge (February 6 to May 3, 1865).

Organization of the War Department

The mission of the department was to raise and arm men for the defense of the South. On March 6, Congress authorized recruitment of 100,000 men, twelve-month volunteers, for a provisional army. State militia and volunteers were mustered into national service, despite a critical deficiency in weapons, uniforms, and equipment. In April, following the opening of hostilities at Fort Sumter, tens of thousands of enthusiastic volunteers thronged Southern towns and cities, only to find the government unable to equip them. Early efforts to purchase war matériel in the North (the Raphael Semmes mission) were terminated with the outbreak of war; similar missions to Europe (those of Maj. Caleb Huse and Capt. James D. Bulloch) were not productive until November 1861 when the blockade runner *Fingal* arrived, carrying ten thousand Enfield rifles from England. Seizure of Federal arms stored in the South, plus the limited resources of state authorities and privately held weapons, provided most of the means for the first battles.

Walker, the new secretary of war, undaunted, requested authorization from Congress in July of 560 regiments, and the following month was granted power to enlist up to 400,000 men, again for only twelve months' service. By September, the department had armies in the field totaling 200,000 men.

The War Department in Richmond was located in an old brick building at Ninth and Franklin streets, which once had housed the Mechanics Institute. All other government departments also occupied this building except the Treasury and State departments. To reach the secretary's office, a visitor had to climb a gas-lighted stairway and traverse a long, gloomy corridor. In the outer room one found clericals pouring over the details of administration (among these, the *Rebel War Clerk* diarist J. B. Jones). Off in one corner (by October 1862) was the assistant secretary, former U.S. Supreme Court justice John A. Campbell, conferring with war leaders. At other desks, paymasters explained arrears in pay to some field officer, while soldiers plied officials for furloughs, and couriers, often mud-splattered, occasionally rushed in and were immediately brought before the secretary. Other callers waited, talking, chewing, speculating (as a foreign visitor noted in mid-1862). The appointments blackboard seldom seemed empty, owing to the department's genial, personal way of doing business. When finally shown into the secretary's presence, a visitor would find a room that breathed austerity. The walls bore no paint or decoration; the floor was without covering. Here, six hours daily, and often late into the night, the secretary waded through the routine of appointments, correspondence, consultation, planning, forwarding telegrams, signing commissions, and advising on the myriad details of running a war.

By the time of the first secretary's resignation in the fall of 1861, the department had become a going concern. Although the leaders of the Confederacy had originally contemplated a small military organization, by the fall of 1862 a comprehensive system of bureaus staffed by military officers had come into being. In addition to an assistant secretary there was an adjutant and inspector general, the Confederacy's ranking officer Samuel Cooper. A professional soldier and intimate of Jefferson Davis, Cooper was responsible for departmental orders, army records, and the inspection of army personnel. But his purview of power broadened as he became the essential tie between commanders in the field and the civilian administration. His name routinely appeared on all general orders emanating from the department to the armies throughout the South and often on many specific orders to key generals at the front.

Within the War Department were nine bureaus, including Cooper's office. These were staffed by some of the ablest and one or two of the most mediocre officers in the South. Col. Abraham C. Myers was quartermaster general and Col. Lucius B. Northrop, commissary general of subsistence. These two were responsible for furnishing the armies with food, clothing, and all other supplies except munitions. In time, perhaps more from the nature of their task than their personal conduct, they were subjected to increasingly harsh criticism. Myers, victimized by a personal quarrel with the president, was replaced by Gen. Alexander R. Lawton in August 1863. Northrop, because he was a personal friend of Davis's, remained in office until almost the end of the war. To most he seemed hopelessly incompetent and, in the estimation of most historians, the least qualified man for the critical position he held.

Munitions was the responsibility of the Confederacy's ordnance genius, Col. Josiah Gorgas, who at first headed both the Engineer and the Ordnance bureaus. Later, Capt. Alfred L. Rives and Col. Jeremy P. Gilmer alternately served as chief engineer. Gorgas was the outstanding bureau chief of the department. Thanks to his singular drive and pertinacity, by 1862 the armies of the agricultural South were never without arms or powder.

Related to the Ordnance Bureau was the Niter and Mining Bureau, headed by Isaac M. St. John. Its chief was one of the minor figures in the Confederate hierarchy whose invaluable services made possible its well-equipped armies. In February 1865 his talents were recognized when he was promoted to brigadier and commissary general, to succeed the hapless Northrop.

The Medical Department was first headed by Surgeon General David Camden De Leon, previously a surgeon in the U.S. Army. He served briefly from May 6 to July 12, 1861, then resigned to serve in the field for the remainder of the conflict. On July 30 Samuel Preston Moore, a surgeon before the war, was appointed in De Leon's place. Described as a "venerable, dandyish old fellow," Moore was competent and resolute, with the harrying task of providing medical supplies and overseeing maintenance of military hospitals. His whole medical corps had 3,237 medical officers (23 of whom served with the navy), or less than 4 doctors for every thousand men. There were 6 medical officers on duty in the surgeon general's office.

Two other bureaus completed the original organization of the department, that of Indian Affairs and the Bureau of War, which was the coordinating office of the department. After Seddon's appointment, two additional bureaus were created—the Signal Corps and the Conscription Bureau. The latter was headed successively by two generals, Gabriel J. Raines (until May 1863) and John S. Preston. The secretary worked diligently with them, and with the many conscript officers stationed throughout the South, on the problems of manpower procurement. The Signal Corps, headed by Maj. William Norris, was given authority to supervise the operations of the Confederacy's military communications and the Southern Telegraph Company, a privately owned system. In 1864 this resourceful officer worked intimately with the secretary in the shadowy realm of espionage and secret service activities behind Northern lines.

The War Department bureaus were organized in such a way that each was independent in its own sphere, and the secretary gave the respective heads a wide latitude of authority. Requisitions for special services or for ordnance or quartermaster supplies passed directly from the field commanders to the bureau concerned, and only when the system broke down or specific criticisms were raised did the secretary of war intervene. With the exceptions of criticisms of Northrop and conscription and impressment officers in the field, few complaints were lodged against War Department officials by Confederate commanders or the press. The most important bureaus were, of course, those directly concerned with the maintenance of the armies—the Commissary, Quartermaster, Ordnance, and Conscription bureaus. Each was subjected to excessive demands and responsibilities, which only Gorgas was able to fulfill completely in his own sphere.

Subordinate to the secretary in the daily routine was the collection of clerks and messengers who constituted the Bureau of War. It was headed by a young Virginia captain, Robert Garlick Hill Kean. Although a strong Randolph partisan who disliked Davis, Kean came to view Seddon and Assistant Secretary Campbell with admiration and respect. He worked closely with the latter in coordinating the administrative functions of the department and was directly concerned with keeping the overall operations of his office functioning smoothly. As supervisor of a large clerical staff, Kean was responsible for directing the vast flow of correspondence in the bureaucratic empire. He observed much policy-making at first hand and was a good judge of his superiors and colleagues. He was in a key position to sympathize with the plight of the grossly overworked department and its chiefs, much of which he recorded in his valuable diary (which is often more reliable and perceptive than the more quoted diary of J. B. Jones).

The Department in Action

The first secretary of war, Leroy P. Walker, an Alabama aristocrat, planter, and politician, was selected by Davis to represent his state in the seven-member cabinet. He was "a pure civilian," as Thomas Cooper DeLeon characterized him, "a shrewd lawyer, of great quickness of perception, high cultivation, and grasp of mind." In his initial months, he worked successfully with military and civilian leaders (despite state rights problems with several governors), although he was slow to perceive the dimensions and length of the war. His relations with Davis were harmonious. When Walker left office to seek service in the field, the military establishment of the Confederacy was a fait accompli, even if on delicate foundations. Its armies had won victories east and west, and some part of the credit for these achievements must rest with this civilian leader.

The second secretary of war, Judah P. Benjamin, held office for a brief stormy period. A brilliant lawyer and solid friend of Davis and his wife, he possessed a keen intellect and qualities of statesmanship that earned him the soubriquet "the brains of the Confederacy." But he was often lacking in patience with stiff military protocol and at times was insensitive of the egos and ambitions of army men. Too often he sided, uncritically, with Davis. His efforts to obtain from the Congress long-term enlistment laws for the armies failed, though his measures to encourage manufacturing in the South were fruitful. Much of his usefulness was overshadowed by public clashes with several generals. Blame for military reverses (Forts Henry and Donelson, Roanoke Island) he took upon his own shoulders, thus shielding Davis from his critics and, more important, concealing the internal military weakness of the Confederacy. Benjamin was a dedicated public servant but a failure as war secretary.

His successor, George Wythe Randolph, was popular with military leaders, and they expected much of him. But his term was too brief for him to accomplish much. His greatest service was the achievement of the first military draft in America, in April 1862, when the Conscription Act was adopted to meet the Confederacy's manpower needs. Randolph also had a try at grand strategy. By mid-1862 he saw that the weak point in the South's defenses was in the West, and he proposed a strong autonomous Department of the West, with a commander who could coordinate the disparate forces within the region. Differences with Davis over implementation of the plan worsened relations between the two, and Randolph resigned in November after eight months in office.

His successor, James A. Seddon, was a vigorous man, a clear thinker, and a tough-minded, dedicated worker. He was also a Southern zealot respected by similar men and much of the press of the South, yet above all a man possessed of tact and diplomacy, and a close friend of the hypersensitive president.

The new secretary's initial months in office saw his efforts to invigorate the Confederate cause by an active prosecution of the war in Virginia, increased support for the Atlantic coastal defenses, and new strategic considerations for the western theater (with the appointment of Joseph E. Johnston to its supreme command). He persuaded Davis to travel to the West, conciliate the commanders there, and rally the people and soldiers against the invaders. He urged the use of internal lines for supply and troop reinforcement, favoring the shifting of men from one theater to another as needs or opportunity suggested. He kept a close eye on unfolding developments, down to the double crisis of Gettysburg and Vicksburg in midsummer 1863. While his concern centered on the two major fronts, the daily activities of the department were focused upon food needs of the armies, the shortage of horses for the cavalry, the deteriorating railroads, the need for regulation of the overall transport system, and better use of blockade runners for supplies from abroad (a small fleet of ships was soon hired by the department, at Seddon's insistence). Another problem was financial. Desperate measures were necessary to replace depreciated currency, and the department began to use cotton as a medium of exchange. The staple was shipped through the blockade almost daily, and a steady stream of war matériel, uniforms, and rations soon poured into the Confederacy. In 1864 authorization was granted to exchange cotton for meat and other foodstuffs with the Federals in the Trans-Mississippi theater. The starvation that had stalked areas of the South since the second year of the war—the armies were on half-rations—justified such measures.

Manpower needs were reaching a crisis by 1863. In the remaining months of that year, the department had to deal with declining manpower resources, large-scale desertions, and obstructions from the governors of Georgia and North Carolina in matters of conscription and impressment. Defeatism, by early 1864, was rampant in many parts of the South.

Deficiency in military strength was matched by the lack of workers in industry and government bureaus. The low salary scale did not attract employees unless they also received exemption from military duty. After passage of the Third Conscription Act, a system of detail from field duty was put into effect by which soldiers were assigned to service in offices or as industrial or railroad workers. This system succeeded in obtaining laborers at low costs, but military leaders complained that it stripped their commands of fighting men.

The War Department was directly involved in the development and operation of munitions and arms works, mining establishments, and clothing factories. Instead of turning to private industries for most of its needs, the government had created its own war enterprise. During Seddon's tenure, attempts were made to expand almost every segment of the military-industrial organization. It was in the scope and magnitude of these government-owned industries that the civil administration of the South differed most from that of the North. Almost all industries in the Union remained in private hands.

Of 70,000 civil employees in the service of the Confederate government, 57,124 were employed by the War Department. The Engineer Bureau and Niter and Mining Bureau alone employed 17,000 persons, which included many blacks (both free and impressed slaves), women, and some children. At the close of 1863, Gorgas reported that the Ordnance Bureau was operating seventeen arsenals, armories, foundries, depots, and powder mills. In Richmond, the department controlled and supervised ordnance shops, munitions plants, foundries, medical laboratories, and uniform and shoe factories.

The department's staff continued to grow as the war progressed. There were, in 1864, twelve major officials (four of them civilians) and 265 clerks and messengers. But unlike the U.S. government, there was no chief of staff, only a military adviser to the president, Gen. Braxton Bragg, and instead of three assistant secretaries such as Edwin M. Stanton had at his service, Seddon had only one, the invaluable Campbell. Lacking these important posts, the War Department suffered much unnecessary inefficiency. The most unsuccessful bureau, Conscription, was dissolved in February 1865 and its duties delegated to the generals of reserve forces in the individual states. The overall governmental machinery at Richmond was frequently inadequate, yet somehow many of the needs of the fighting South were provided by this overworked and pathetically small bureaucracy.

Foreign imports continued to provide the mainstay needs of the department from 1864 until the end of the war. A special agent, Colin J. McRae, sent by Seddon to England to supervise purchasing operations there, was working near-miracles. A thoroughgoing businessman, he is to be credited with the astute use of funds (especially from the Erlanger cotton loan). In March, Col. Thomas L. Bayne of the Ordnance Bureau was made head of the newly created Bureau of Foreign Supplies and was granted control of the importation of all war matériel that was to be paid for with exported cotton. All vessels operated by the department were now transferred to his control. Working both sides of the Atlantic, McRae and Bayne supervised the blockade traffic for the remainder of the war. The reports of the secretary and of various bureau heads, as well as letters and dispatches from Fraser, Trenholm, and Company of Liverpool and foreign service correspondence in the Library of Congress, testify to large returns from the department's system. Millions of pounds of meat, coffee, lead, and saltpeter, more than 500,000 pairs of shoes, 316,000 blankets, 2,600 packages of medicines, 69,000 rifles, 43 cannons, and large amounts of other articles came into the Confederacy between October 26, 1864, and January 2, 1865. Vast quantities of cotton shipped out of Southern ports, together with funds on deposit or being created in Europe, completed this bold enterprise.

The last great issue before the department and its leaders and the Southern people in late 1864 was the question of arming the slaves. As the number of troops was drastically reduced by deaths and desertions (Seddon had admitted earlier that one-third of Confederate armies were AWOL in November 1863), it was clear to many that the last great untapped manpower resource of the South must be used. Some military and civil leaders had advocated such a radical policy at different turns in the war, and in November 1864 a conference of Southern governors went on record favoring it. The War Department had long used blacks (free and slave) in menial roles, especially as workmen on coastal defenses; in earthworks about Charleston, Atlanta, and Richmond; and in various parts of the western theater. Blacks had also been in service in all Confederate armies since the beginning of the war as teamsters, cooks, and body servants to officers. Seddon, strongly influenced by his friend Robert M. T. Hunter, held back. Gorgas, Campbell, and others in the war office, however, were in support. Finally when Robert E. Lee, Benjamin, and Davis came out publicly in favor, Congress acted early in February 1865. The department's mission was to implement the policy. Orders quickly were passed down the line, as recruiting officers began to receive volunteers. Two companies of Confederate blacks soon appeared in Richmond—too late to effect the outcome of the struggle.

Early in 1865, as a sense of gloom overshadowed much of the Confederacy, Congress recommended that Davis restructure his cabinet in the hope of restoring public confidence in the cause. Seddon took personal umbrage at this motion and abruptly resigned. The president failed to persuade him to withdraw his resignation, and a popular successor was sought. In John C. Breckinridge, former U.S. vice president and Confederate general, the fifth secretary of war was found. He presided over the department for less than four months—largely, it seems, to terminate its life preparatory to ending the war. He immediately took stock of its health (results mostly negative) and urged the president to seek peace. In this he was strongly supported by Campbell. Both men felt that the only course was an honorable surrender. Breckinridge organized the government's evacuation of the capital on April 2 and accompanied the president and cabinet on its flight to Danville, Virginia. Here efforts were made *not* to surrender but to restructure the administration. Two weeks later, the "government on wheels" was in further flight south—to Charlotte, North Carolina, and finally Washington, Georgia, where the last official cabinet meeting was held. Here the final disintegration occurred. The War Department ceased to exist as the secretary and other cabinet heads fled. Cooper, who had taken charge of its physical remains, namely its archives, surrendered these valued records to the Federal authorities.

The history of the Confederate War Department is yet to be written. It is contained in the tens of thousands of documents in the "Rebel War Archives" of the National Archives and in related papers in the Library of Congress. Mastery of these materials may reveal the unromantic, yet herculean labors of this body of bureaucrats who helped form the backbone and substance of the Confederate army. When these records are searched, and the odds against which its employees struggled are weighed, the resulting annals will show that the Confederate War Department worked marvels with meager means.

[*See also* Army; Commissary Bureau; Conscription; Engineer Bureau; Espionage, *article on* Confederate Secret Service; Impressment; Medical Department; New Plan; Ordnance Bureau; Quartermaster Bureau; Signal Corps; *and biographies of numerous figures mentioned herein.*]

BIBLIOGRAPHY

DeLeon, Thomas Cooper. *Four Years in Rebel Capitals.* Mobile, Ala., 1892.

Evans, Eli N. *Judah P. Benjamin: The Jewish Confederate.* New York, 1988.

Harris, William C. *Leroy Pope Walker: Confederate Secretary of War.* Tuscaloosa, Ala., 1962.

Jones, J. B. *A Rebel War Clerk's Diary at the Confederate States Capital.* 2 vols. Philadelphia, 1866. Reprint, edited by Earl Schenck Miers. New York, 1958.

O'Brien, G. F. J. "James A. Seddon: Statesman of the Old South." Ph.D. diss., University of Maryland, 1963.

Patrick, Rembert W. *Jefferson Davis and His Cabinet.* Baton Rouge, La., 1944.

Shackelford, George Green. *George Wythe Randolph and the Confederate Elite.* Athens, Ga., 1988.

Younger, Edward, ed. *Inside the Confederate Government: The Diary of Robert Garlick Hill Kean.* New York, 1957.

JOHN O'BRIEN

WARD, GEORGE TALIAFERRO (1810?–1862),

congressman from Florida and colonel. Little is known of Ward's early years. He was born in Fayette County, Kentucky, and it appears that he attended Transylvania University in Lexington in 1824 and moved to Tallahassee, Florida, later that decade. During the 1830s, he became a prominent Episcopalian planter and Whig party leader in Leon County and during the 1840s was a director of the Union Bank of Tallahassee. In 1852, he was the last Whig to run for governor and was defeated by Democrat James E. Broome. The Whig party collapsed in 1854, and moderates like Ward found themselves unable to counter the drive for secession by radical Democrats. A Constitutional Unionist, he worked for John Bell during the 1860 election and attempted to delay secession at the Florida convention in 1861.

When the war began Ward became a loyal Confederate and was appointed to the Provisional Confederate Congress in May 1861 after James Patton Anderson resigned. He served actively on the Military Affairs, Claims, Public Lands, and Commercial and Financial Independence committees, but resigned in February 1862 in order to serve in the Confederate army. As a colonel, he served at Yorktown under Gen. John B. Magruder and A. P. Hill. He was killed during the Peninsular campaign while commanding the Second Florida Regiment near Williamsburg on May 5, 1862.

BIBLIOGRAPHY

Alexander, Thomas B., and Richard E. Beringer. *The Anatomy of the Confederate Congress: A Study of the Influences of Member Characteristics on Legislative Voting Behavior, 1861–1865.* Nashville, Tenn., 1972.

Sifakis, Stewart. *Who Was Who in the Civil War.* New York, 1988.

Wakelyn, Jon L. *Biographical Dictionary of the Confederacy.* Edited by Frank E. Vandiver. Westport, Conn., 1977.

ARCH FREDRIC BLAKEY

WARLEY, ALEXANDER FRAZER (c.1820–1896),

navy lieutenant. The son of a South Carolina legislator, Warley was born in Bartholomew Parish. He was one of the talented young Annapolis graduates who joined the Confederate navy, where his duty assignments involved him in significant actions.

He commanded the ironclad *Manassas* in the defense of Head of the Passes below New Orleans. As one of the earliest ironclads, the ship was an engineering curiosity that also required considerable skill to manage. In one of those coincidences so common to the Civil War, Warley's command rammed and damaged *Mississippi,* on which he had served earlier during a round-the-world voyage.

He saw action on another of the early ironclads, *Louisiana,* and with the fall of Forts St. Philip and Jackson he was among those captured and later exchanged in the summer of 1862. His next assignment at Charleston placed him on *Chicora* when that ship and *Palmetto State* attacked a small Union force on Morris Island at Charleston.

For a time in 1864, Warley was assigned to the blockade runner *Harriet Lane.* His most famous exploit, however, was as commander of *Albemarle* when Lt. William B. Cushing sank the ironclad in a daring torpedo attack.

Little is known of his postwar life except that he died in New Orleans in 1896.

BIBLIOGRAPHY

Civil War Naval Chronology, 1861–1865. 6 vols. Washington, D.C., 1961–1965.

Register of Officers of the Confederate States Navy, 1861–1865. Washington, D.C., 1931.

Still, William N., Jr. *Iron Afloat: The Story of the Confederate Armorclads.* Nashville, Tenn., 1971.

MAXINE TURNER

WASHINGTON PEACE CONFERENCE. In response to a call of the Virginia General Assembly, the Washington Peace Conference met February 4–27, 1861, in the Willard Hotel's Dancing Hall in Washington, D.C. The purpose of the meeting was to seek constitutional guarantees that might hold the border slave states in the Union and ease tensions between the states that had seceded and those dominated by the Republican party whose candidate was soon to occupy the presidential office. Virginia had suggested that the proposals introduced in the Senate by John J. Crittenden of Kentucky in December 1860, though they had been rejected in committee, could be the basis for a resolution of the controversy between slave and free states.

Former president John Tyler, one of Virginia's five commissioners to the conference, had wanted to invite only the border states. Knowing that the Deep South states would not attend, he feared that Northerners would control the meeting. But the General Assembly opted to invite all the states. Eventually 133 commissioners from twenty-one of the existing thirty-four states attended, though only 60 men from eleven states had arrived by the opening day.

In spite of Virginia's plea to all concerned to avoid acts that might lead to war, representatives of six Deep South states met in Montgomery, Alabama, to organize a Southern government on the same day the Peace Conference convened. Those states, as well as one other that had seceded, sent no delegates, nor did Arkansas, Minnesota, Michigan, Wisconsin, California, or Oregon.

Dubbed the "Old Gentlemen's Convention" of "political fossils" by Horace Greeley's *New York Tribune,* the assemblage nevertheless included the "best and the brightest" their states could offer. The delegates selected John Tyler as president of the conference and decided that each state would have one vote and that the proceedings would be kept secret.

Moderates had high hopes of resolving the issue, but the opposing sides made success seem unlikely. Most Republicans had no intention of budging from the Chicago platform that called for a ban on any further extension of slavery in the territories. Southern radicals, for their part, sought extreme measures that had no chance of acceptance. The legislatures of Ohio and Indiana had instructed their commissioners to seek adjournment of the conference at least until after the inauguration of the new president. Ohio had also instructed its delegates that no concessions to the South were necessary. Indiana's governor appointed as delegates only those persons who had convinced him by their answers to a written questionnaire that they likewise would make no concessions.

The Resolutions Committee submitted its report on February 15 after several postponements because of the late arrival of many delegations. Confused debate then ensued over the committee's report and several minority reports. Some delegates defended slavery; others attacked it. All impugned each other's motives. On February 22 the conference agreed to limit debate to ten minutes for each person and got down to business.

The Resolutions Committee had reported seven provisions as a proposed amendment to the Constitution. The first would extend the Crittenden Compromise line of 36° 30′ to the Pacific, with involuntary servitude permitted below the line and prohibited above it during territorial status. States subsequently would be admitted on either side of the line as their constitutions directed. The chief argument concerned Virginia's demand that slavery in any territories acquired in the future should be protected, but the conference adopted a substitute resolution that limited the protection of slavery to present territory.

Other sections of the final report provided that major acquisitions of new territory would have to be approved by a majority of all senators from both the free and the slave states and that Congress would have no control over slavery in the District of Columbia without the owners' and Maryland's (but not Virginia's) consent. The slave trade would continue to be prohibited in the District of Columbia and the interstate slave trade protected, at least to a degree. Congress was to prohibit the importation of slaves and of Chinese laborers forever. Congress would compensate an owner when authorities were prevented from recovering a fugitive slave, but the person would lose ownership of the slave by accepting compensation. Key provisions of the proposals and of the existing U.S. Constitution could never be amended or abolished in the future without the agreement of all the states.

Virginia delegates had sought to prohibit blacks from

voting and to gain the right to acquire territory for colonization of blacks. They had also hoped to secure condemnation of personal liberty laws, the strengthening of the Fugitive Slave Law, and a declaration of the constitutionality of secession.

The final package, which was not voted on as a whole, satisfied almost no one. William C. Rives had declared that "Virginia steps in to arrest the country on its road to ruin"—but Virginia voted against the key section (which carried by only one vote) and three others. Two states opposed all seven propositions adopted by the conference, one state opposed six, and four states opposed five. New York deadlocked on every vote and Kansas on all but one, though four Northern states and four border states were on the winning side every time. Had Michigan, Wisconsin, and Minnesota participated, the Peace Conference would have no doubt been totally paralyzed.

Tyler submitted the report as a proposed thirteenth amendment to the Constitution, but with a lukewarm endorsement, and departed for Virginia, where he soon urged his state's secession. It was February 27, less than a week before Lincoln's inauguration and the scheduled adjournment of Congress. Many Southern congressmen had returned to their states, and the remaining representatives were probably less interested in compromise than they had been two months before. The Senate voted against the proposals, 28–7. The House refused to suspend its rules to receive them. The Peace Conference had failed. Once South Carolina had seceded, it was probably too late to arrest the march to war, for Southern secessionists and Northern Republicans had fixed on a collision course.

BIBLIOGRAPHY

Crittenden, Lucius E. *Report of the Debates and Proceedings of the Peace Convention Held at Washington, D.C., 1861.* New York, 1864. Reprint, New York, 1971.

Gunderson, Robert G. "The Old Gentlemen's Convention." *Civil War History* 7 (1961): 5–12.

Gunderson, Robert G. *Old Gentlemen's Convention: The Washington Peace Conference of 1861.* Madison, Wis., 1961.

Keene, Jesse L. *The Peace Convention of 1871.* Confederate Centennial Studies no. 18. Tuscaloosa, Ala., 1961.

Morrison, Samuel E. "The Peace Convention of February, 1861." *Proceedings of the Massachusetts Historical Society* 73 (1961): 58–80.

LYON G. TYLER

WATERHOUSE, RICHARD (1832–1876), brigadier general. Born in Rhea County, Tennessee, Waterhouse ran away as a young boy to fight in the Mexican War. After the war his family relocated to Texas, and he went to work in the family business.

Upon the outbreak of the Civil War he organized a regiment and received a colonel's commission in the Nineteenth Texas Infantry, which was assigned to Henry Eustace McCulloch's corps in the Army of the Trans-Mississippi Department. He saw his first action in Arkansas. In 1863 his regiment participated in the effort to relieve the Confederate garrison at Vicksburg; he led an assault against a Union force near Milliken's Bend on June 7, 1863. McCulloch said that Waterhouse "behaved in the most gallant manner." In 1864 he commanded a regiment (William R. Scurry's brigade) during the Red River campaign and fought at Mansfield (April 8) and Pleasant Hill (April 9), winning the praise of both Scurry and Gen. Richard Taylor. On May 13, 1864, Gen. E. Kirby Smith promoted Waterhouse to brigadier general to date from April 30, 1864. By this time the Trans-Mississippi was cut off from the East, and Waterhouse was not confirmed until the last day the Confederate Senate met in session, March 17, 1865.

RICHARD WATERHOUSE. LIBRARY OF CONGRESS

After the war Waterhouse lived in San Augustine and Jefferson, Texas, where he was an active land speculator. He died in 1876.

BIBLIOGRAPHY

Kerby, Robert L. *Kirby Smith's Confederacy: The Trans-Mississippi South, 1863–1865.* New York, 1972.

Roberts, O. M. *Texas.* Vol. 11 of *Confederate Military History.* Edited by Clement A. Evans. Atlanta, 1899. Vol. 15 of extended ed. Wilmington, N.C., 1989.

U.S. War Department. *War of the Rebellion: A Compilation of the Official Records of the Union and Confederate Armies.* Washington, D.C., 1880–1901. Ser. 1, vol. 41, pt. 4, pp. 1016–1019; ser. 1, vol. 48, pt. 1, pp. 1428–1430.

THOMAS J. LEGG

WATERWAYS. The Southern states were surrounded by navigable waterways, indeed by protected waterways where small craft could carry the commerce and the forces of the Confederacy. On the northeast was the Chesapeake Bay and the Potomac River; then on the north the great Ohio, and on the west the mighty Mississippi with its tributaries, the Arkansas and the Red River, connecting it with Arkansas and Texas. All along the Atlantic coast, from Virginia to Florida, with some interruptions, a protected waterway, hospitable to shallow-draft steamboats and smaller vessels, ran between the mainland and strings of offshore islands; it continued for most of the way along the Gulf coast, around Florida to Pensacola and on to New Orleans, and then for much of the way along the Texas coast.

There were no great rivers flowing in an east-west direction that could have connected the Confederacy at its heart. But in all the states major rivers drained a rich hinterland to the sea and provided a means of getting crops to seacoast markets and of getting manufactured goods into the interior: the James River gave an outlet from Lynchburg and Richmond to Hampton Roads and Norfolk; the Roanoke from central Virginia to the Carolina coast; the Cape Fear from Fayetteville to Wilmington, North Carolina; the Pee Dee River and the Santee from central South Carolina to Charleston; the Savannah from Augusta to Savannah; the Chattahoochee and the Flint from Atlanta to the Gulf of Mexico; the Alabama from Montgomery to Mobile; in Mississippi the Pearl River from Jackson to the approaches to New Orleans; in the north, the New River connecting the Great Appalachian Valley from western Virginia to the Ohio; the Tennessee connecting the Great Valley, around Knoxville, with Chattanooga and northern Alabama thence across western Tennessee and Kentucky to the Ohio; and the Cumberland connecting northern Tennessee with the Ohio. And the beltway of coastal waterways and major rivers connected them all. It was like a great geopolitical wheel, with the spokes, radiating from the interior, joined by the rim of coastal waterways and peripheral rivers.

Control of this water beltway surely was a key to the solvency of the Southern states and even to the Confederacy's success in the war. But from the outset Federal forces began slowly but inexorably to constrict it. Seizure of Harpers Ferry by Federal forces assured Northern control of the upper Potomac, and George B. McClellan's first action, a relatively minor campaign in western Virginia in July 1861, assured Northern control of the upper Ohio. Before the year was out U.S. forces captured Hatteras Inlet, North Carolina; Port Royal Sound, commanding the waterway between Charleston and Savannah; Tybee Island on the Georgia coast; and Biloxi, Mississippi, on the Gulf of Mexico.

In February 1862, Ulysses S. Grant, with the support of a flotilla of river gunboats under David Farragut, captured Fort Henry on the Tennessee and Fort Donelson on the Cumberland River, and other U.S. forces captured Roanoke Island, North Carolina. Succeeding weeks saw the occupation of Jacksonville, Florida; the neutralization of the ironclad *Virginia* by the *Monitor* in Hampton Roads; the fall of New Orleans on April 25; the loss of Norfolk, Virginia, and Pensacola, Florida, and, on June 6, the loss of Memphis on the Mississippi. The great belt waterway, the rim of the wheel, was being broken all along its course. Surely the fall of Vicksburg on the Mississippi in July 1863 was as much a turning point of the war as was the Battle of Gettysburg going on at the same time in Pennsylvania.

The waterways could have been of utmost advantage to the South in carrying commerce and supporting military forces if all or most of its segments could have been controlled. Commerce-raiding cruisers, such as *Alabama, Shenandoah,* and *Georgia,* were a nuisance and a menace to Northern shipping, but they could have no influence on the outcome of the war. On the other hand, if the Confederate States somehow could have gained and maintained command of the rivers, particularly the Ohio and Mississippi, and the adjacent seas of the Atlantic and the Gulf of Mexico, their success at arms scarcely could have been denied. Great flotillas of gunboats would have been more valuable than great armies without adequate means of support, and a high-seas fleet plus shallow-draft gunboats capable of breaking the Northern blockade would have been more valuable than scores of commerce raiders. It may not be without symbolic significance that the Federals named their armies (with some exceptions) for the rivers—the Army of the Potomac, the Army of the James, the Army of the Ohio, the Army of the Cumberland, the Army of the Tennessee—whereas the Confederates (with a few exceptions) named theirs for states or regions—the Army of Northern Virginia, the Army of Tennessee.

During the first half of the nineteenth century watercraft of many kinds had appeared on the interior rivers. A common one for downstream trips was the flatboat, about twenty feet long and ten feet wide, with a hull rising three feet or so above the water, a little house or shelter in the middle, and a sweep or long oar at the stern to guide it.

Rivermen would transport cargoes of grain, salted meat, or other products, then sell the boat as well as the cargo and walk or find wagons or stages back for another boat. Families sometimes would move with all their belongings downstream on a flatboat and then use the boat for lumber at their destination. Pirogues were large, flat-bottom boats with oars and poles to enable them to move upstream. Scows were large flatboats, sometimes referred to as arks. Broadhorns were like scows, but with sweeps both on bow and stern for steering downstream. Similar to the scows were the batteaux, especially significant on the James River. The skiff was a small flat-bottom boat used for local traffic and sometimes carried in tow by larger boats for side trips to the shore. Keel boats were built with heavy timber keels down the center; these had the advantage of being able to absorb the shock of collisions with obstacles in the rivers. Barges were bigger boats, thirty to seventy feet long, equipped with a passenger cabin and oars and sails to move upstream as well as down on the big rivers. Packet boats were larger barges.

A canal-building boom in the Northern states between 1820 and 1850 did not extend into the South. The major exceptions were in Virginia. The Chesapeake and Ohio Canal, a cooperative effort of Virginia, Maryland, and the Federal government, after many years of effort was completed in 1850 between Alexandria, Virginia, and Cumberland, Maryland. When war came this was beyond the reach of the Confederacy, however. More important for its purposes was the James River canal that was completed from the fall line at Richmond 146 miles to Lynchburg in 1840 and to Buchanan in 1856. Plans to extend it to Covington were interrupted by the war. A canal of twenty-three miles connected Deep Creek and Joyce's Creek and the Dismal Swamp area.

Except for one major obstacle the Tennessee River was navigable for large boats for the full 650 miles from Knoxville to Paducah, Kentucky. The obstacle was a series of rapids known as Muscle Shoals in northern Alabama. Attempts to bypass the shoals by a canal ended in failure. Connection of the upper and lower Tennessee valley had to depend on the Tuscumbia and Decatur Railroad, completed in 1834. There were some short connecting canals in Georgia and the Carolinas, but they were in large part abandoned before the war.

The decade preceding the Civil War saw the apogee of the steamboat on the rivers. That also was the decade of great expansion of the railroads that would lead to the steamboat's decline. The first steamboat on the western rivers was *New Orleans,* built at Pittsburgh in 1811. It descended to New Orleans, but never made it back from that city. Others, appearing in subsequent years, were bigger and more powerful; *Eclipse,* built in 1852, reached a length of 363 feet, a width of 76 feet, and carried a crew of 121 men (the smallest steamers might have a crew of only 4 or 5). Most of the early steamboats were driven by sidewheels, but later sternwheelers came to be favored. Many carried passengers above and freight below, although sometimes bales of cotton were piled so high on the deck that it was necessary to light candles or lamps in the cabins. Most of the boat building for the Mississippi valley was on the upper Ohio; the one boat-building center within the South was at Nashville on the Cumberland.

In 1845 there were 332 steamboat arrivals and departures at Nashville and 580 in 1860. Steamboat arrivals at New Orleans numbered 3,024 in 1847 and 3,566 in 1860. The 1,600 steamboats that plied the Mississippi before the war represented an investment of perhaps $60 million.

Coastal shipping still depended to a considerable extent on wooden sailing vessels, although paddlewheel steamers were coming into use. River-type boats could be used on the inner coastal waterways.

During the war rivers were not subject to sabotage and destruction to the extent that railroads were. The Federal forces, however, gained control of key points or entire segments of the peripheral waterways, and without the rim, the spokes were of little use—and beyond that, in many places, the spokes too were broken. The waterways could have been critical for Confederate success; the foresight and resources were not there to take advantage of them.

BIBLIOGRAPHY

The American Heritage Pictorial Atlas of United States History. New York, 1966.

Dunbar, Seymour. *A History of Travel in America.* Indianapolis, 1915.

Hunter, Louis C. *Steamboats on the Western Rivers.* Cambridge, Mass., 1969.

Meyer, B. H. *A History of Transportation in the United States before 1860.* Washington, D.C., 1917.

Nevins, Allan. *The War for Union.* 4 vols. New York, 1959–1960.

Parsons, Lewis B. *Rail and River Army Transportation in the Civil War.* St. Louis, Mo., 1899.

Randall, J. G., and David Donald. *The Civil War and Reconstruction.* Boston, 1961.

Semple, Ellen Churchill. *American History and its Geographic Conditions.* Boston, 1903.

James A. Huston

WATIE, STAND (1806–1871), brigadier general and principal chief of the Confederate Cherokees. Born at Oothcaloga in the Cherokee Nation, Georgia, on December 12, 1806, Stand Watie's Cherokee name was De-ga-ta-ga, or "he stands." He also was known as Isaac S. Watie. He attended Moravian Mission School at Springplace, Georgia, and served as a clerk of the Cherokee Supreme Court and Speaker of the Cherokee National Council prior to removal.

As a member of the Ridge-Watie-Boudinot faction of the Cherokee Nation, Watie supported removal to the Cherokee Nation, West, and signed the Treaty of New Echota in 1835, in defiance of Principal Chief John Ross and the majority of the Cherokees. Watie moved to the Cherokee Nation, West (present-day Oklahoma), in 1837 and settled at Honey Creek. Following the murders of his uncle Major Ridge, cousin John Ridge, and brother Elias Boudinot (Buck Watie) in 1839, and his brother Thomas Watie in 1845, Stand Watie assumed the leadership of the Ridge-Watie-Boudinot faction and was involved in a long-running blood feud with the followers of John Ross. He also was a leader of the Knights of the Golden Circle, which bitterly opposed abolitionism.

At the outbreak of the Civil War, Watie quickly joined the Southern cause. He was commissioned a colonel on July 12, 1861, and raised a regiment of Cherokees for service with the Confederate army. Later, when Chief John Ross signed an alliance with the South, Watie's men were organized as the Cherokee Regiment of Mounted Rifles. After Ross fled Indian Territory, Watie was elected principal chief of the Confederate Cherokees in August 1862.

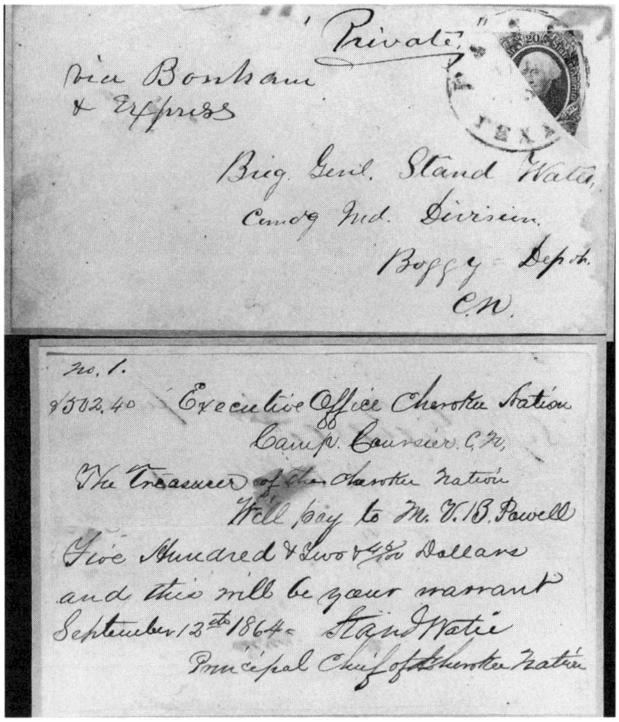

Private

Via Bonham & Express

Brig. Genl. Stand Watie, Comdg Ind. Division. Boggy Depot C.N.

No. 1.
$502.40 Executive Office Cherokee Nation
Camp Council C.N.
The Treasurer of the Cherokee Nation
Will pay to Mr. V. B. Powell
Five Hundred & Two & 40/100 Dollars
and this will be your warrant
September 12th 1864. Stand Watie
Principal Chief of the Cherokee Nation

TREASURY WARRANT. Written and signed by Stand Watie, 1864.
GORDON BLEULER

STAND WATIE. LIBRARY OF CONGRESS

A portion of Watie's command saw action at Oak Hills (August 10, 1861) in a battle that assured the South's hold on Indian Territory and made Watie a Confederate military hero. Afterward, Watie helped drive the pro-Northern Indians out of Indian Territory, and following the Battle of Chustenahlah (December 26, 1861) he commanded the pursuit of the fleeing Federals, led by Opothleyahola, and drove them into exile in Kansas. Although Watie's men were exempt from service outside Indian Territory, he led his troops into Arkansas in the spring of 1861 to stem a Federal invasion of the region. Joining with Maj. Gen. Earl Van Dorn's command, Watie took part in the Battle of Elkhorn Tavern (March 5–6, 1861). On the first day of fighting, the Southern Cherokees, which were on the left flank of the Confederate line, captured a battery of Union artillery before being forced to abandon it. Following the Federal victory, Watie's command screened the Southern withdrawal.

Watie, or troops in his command, participated in eighteen battles and major skirmishes with Federal troops during the Civil War, including Cowskin Prairie (April 1862), Old Fort Wayne (October 1862), Webbers Falls (April 1863), Fort Gibson (May 1863), Cabin Creek (July 1863), and Gunter's Prairie (August 1864). In addition, his men were engaged in a multitude of smaller skirmishes and meeting engagements in Indian Territory and neighboring states. Because of his wide-ranging raids behind Union lines, Watie tied down thousands of Federal troops that were badly needed in the East.

Watie's two greatest victories were the capture of the federal steamboat *J. R. Williams* on June 15, 1864, and the seizure of $1.5 million worth of supplies in a Federal wagon supply train at the Second Battle of Cabin Creek on September 19, 1864. Watie was promoted to brigadier general on May 6, 1864, and given command of the First Indian Brigade. He was the only Indian to achieve the rank of general in the Civil War. Watie surrendered on June 23, 1865, the last Confederate general to lay down his arms.

After the war, Watie served as a member of the Southern Cherokee delegation during the negotiation of the Cherokee Reconstruction Treaty of 1866. He then abandoned public life and returned to his old home along Honey Creek. He died on September 9, 1871.

BIBLIOGRAPHY

Abel, Annie H. *The American Indian as a Participant in the Civil War.* Cleveland, Ohio, 1919.

Franks, Kenny A. *Stand Watie and the Agony of the Cherokee Nation.* Memphis, Tenn., 1979.

Knight, Wilfred. *Red Fox: Stand Watie's Civil War Years in Indian Territory.* Glendale, Calif., 1988.

KENNY A. FRANKS

WATKINS, WILLIAM W. (1826–1898), congressman from Arkansas. Born on April 1, 1826, in Tennessee, William Wirt Watkins moved to Arkansas as a child. Before the war he was a lawyer in Carrollton, Boone County. Watkins, a Unionist in 1860, was elected to represent his district in the Arkansas secession convention of 1861. In the first session in March, he proposed that the state send delegates to a border state convention at Frankfort, Kentucky; the meeting had been proposed by Virginia and Missouri to secure cooperation among the slave states. With other Unionists he prevented his state convention from taking Arkansas out of the Union during its first session. Following the firing on Fort Sumter, however, Watkins shifted his position and supported secession in the reconvened convention in May 1861.

The secession convention selected Watkins to serve in the Provisional Congress. He was not an active member of the Congress. Generally he opposed measures designed to strengthen the power of the Confederate government, although he did back measures that increased control over commerce and military affairs. Watkins did not run for reelection to the First Congress in the November 1861 elections. He returned to his home in Boone County and remained there during the rest of the war.

Following the war Watkins was active in state politics. He died on January 15, 1898.

BIBLIOGRAPHY

Warner, Ezra J., and W. Buck Yearns. *Biographical Register of the Confederate Congress.* Baton Rouge, La., 1975.

Woods, James M. *Rebellion and Realignment: Arkansas's Road to Secession.* Fayetteville, Ark., 1987.

CARL H. MONEYHON

WATSON, JOHN W. C. (1808–1890), congressman from Mississippi. John William Clark Watson, a native Virginian, graduated from the University of Virginia Law School. After practicing law in Abingdon, Virginia, from 1831 to 1845, he moved to Holly Springs, Mississippi. He had already developed an interest in politics in Virginia and had run as a Whig candidate for Congress. In Mississippi he remained a Whig and as a member of the 1851 state convention, expressed strong opposition to secession.

In 1860 he established a newspaper in Holly Springs to advocate the wisdom of preserving a unified nation. But the tide in the state was running strongly toward secession, especially after the election of Abraham Lincoln, and he was defeated for a seat at the Mississippi secession convention of 1861. Watson, seeing the state drifting away from the Union, modified his position and supported the Confederate cause. He defeated James Phelan, a staunch secessionist, in 1863 for a senatorial seat in the Second Congress. In the Senate, Watson continued to equivocate on the issues. On the one hand, he advocated peace negotiations, and on the other, he voted to suspend habeas corpus and to arm slaves.

By the end of the war, Watson had become a peacemaker, trying to avoid antagonizing the Federal government—a position he supported at both the 1865 and 1868 Reconstruction conventions in Mississippi. He resigned from the 1868 body, however, when he realized that it was framing a constitution that would bar from office anyone who had had any connection with the Confederacy. Subsequently, he campaigned against its adoption.

The last twenty years of Watson's long life were spent as a circuit court judge and as a lawyer. He once represented Mississippi before the U.S. Supreme Court in a successful case concerning rate regulation by the Mississippi Railroad Commission.

BIBLIOGRAPHY

Alexander, Thomas B., and Richard E. Beringer. *The Anatomy of the Confederate Congress: A Study of the Influences of Member Characteristics on Legislative Voting Behavior, 1861–1865.* Nashville, Tenn., 1972.

Warner, Ezra J., and W. Buck Yearns. *Biographical Register of the Confederate Congress.* Baton Rouge, La., 1975.

RAY SKATES

WATTS, THOMAS H. (1819–1892), colonel, attorney general, and governor of Alabama. Watts was born near Butler Springs in western Conecuh County (present-day Butler County), Alabama Territory, on January 3, 1819. As a young man, he arranged with his father to exchange any inheritance for a classical education. When he was sixteen, he enrolled in Airy Mount Academy, in Dallas County, Alabama, and graduated with distinction from the University of Virginia in 1840. In 1841, he was admitted to the bar and opened a practice at Greenville, Alabama, moving in 1847 to Montgomery. He became recognized as one of the best legal minds in the state and was a well-known orator.

Entering politics, Watts was elected to the Alabama House of Representatives four times in the 1840s and to the Alabama Senate in 1853. He served as a presidential elector for Zachary Taylor in 1848. During the 1860 presidential election he supported the Constitutional Union party and campaigned for John Bell.

Although Watts was a strong Unionist and a supporter of the U.S. Constitution, he joined the secession movement upon the election of Abraham Lincoln in 1860. Along with William Lowndes Yancey, he represented Montgomery County in the secession convention in January 1861, where he was appointed chairman of the Committee on the Judiciary. During the debate over Alabama's withdrawal from the Union, Watts, who staunchly believed in state rights and the constitutional right of a state to secede, argued that "the power of the convention to interfere with the constitution was confined to such changes as were necessary to the perfect accomplishment of secession." Realizing that secession would probably mean war, he urged the convention to give the Alabama General Assembly power to confiscate the property of alien enemies and to suspend the payment of debts to them. In August 1861 he ran for governor but was defeated by a narrow margin by John G. Shorter.

With the outbreak of war, Watts was elected colonel of the Seventeenth Alabama Infantry Regiment, which was organized in Montgomery in August 1861. In November the regiment was transferred to Pensacola where it saw action that month and in January 1862. Watts's military career ended on March 18, 1862, when he was appointed attorney general for the Confederate States of America to replace Judah P. Benjamin, who had resigned. He was honorably discharged from the service on March 27 and left for Richmond to assume his new post. A strong supporter of state rights, Watts served until October 1, 1863, when he resigned after being elected governor of Alabama by a large majority over Governor Shorter. He was the second native-born governor of Alabama and in the election carried every county in the state except one.

Inaugurated in December 2, 1863, Watts was faced with growing internal dissatisfaction with the national government. He maintained his staunch state rights ideas, however, and during his term the state militia clashed with Confederate conscription officers attempting to enforce the draft laws in Alabama. He also opposed the impressment of private property, which he viewed as a violation of state sovereignty. Watts also supported the demands of Alabama business leaders and other Southern governors who opposed the central government's restriction of trade. Watts however, spent most of his time trying unsuccessfully to stem a Federal invasion of the state.

In July 1864 a force of 1,300 Federal cavalry raided eastern Alabama, destroying much property. In August, Union troops, supported by naval vessels commanded by Adm. David G. Farragut, launched an offensive against the coast of Alabama. They seized Dauphin Island and later captured Fort Gaines and Fort Morgan. After consolidating their gains, the Federals, led by Edward R. S. Canby, marched out of Fort Morgan and seized Mobile in April 1865. At the same time another Federal force invaded northern Alabama, capturing Selma on April 2 and Montgomery on April 12. On May 4, Gen. Richard Taylor surrendered all Confederate forces in the state.

After capturing the capital, Federal troops removed Watts from office. He was later arrested, sent north, and briefly imprisoned. He was finally pardoned by President Andrew Johnson in 1868.

A prominent planter, Watts had owned 250 slaves who worked a large plantation producing as much as 200 bales of cotton annually. Most of his property was destroyed by Federal troops who, when they seized his plantation, burned 250 bales of cotton and 3,000 bushels of corn awaiting distribution to starving civilians. As a result Watts was forced into bankruptcy. He resumed his legal practice, however, and discharged all his debts in the postwar era. He also joined the Democratic party and was active in several presidential elections. He was reelected to the Alabama House of Representatives from Montgomery County in 1880 and served as president of the Alabama Bar Association in 1889 and 1890. Watts died in Montgomery on September 16, 1892.

BIBLIOGRAPHY

Brewer, W. *Alabama: Her History, Resources, War Record, and Public Men from 1540 to 1872.* Montgomery, Ala., 1872.

Evans, Clement A., ed. *Confederate Military History.* 12 vols. Atlanta, 1899. Extended ed. in 19 vols. Wilmington, N.C., 1987–1989.

Garrett, William. *Reminiscences of Public Men in Alabama.* Atlanta, 1872.

Pickett, Albert J. *History of Alabama and Incidentally of Georgia and Mississippi from the Earliest Period.* Birmingham, Ala., 1900.

PAUL F. LAMBERT

WAUL, THOMAS NEVILLE (1813–1903), congressman from Texas and brigadier general. Born in South Carolina on January 5, 1813, Waul studied at South Carolina College (later the University of South Carolina). After teaching in northern Alabama, he read law in Vicksburg and became an attorney in Mississippi. In 1850 he migrated to Texas and became a planter near Gonzales (owning forty-five slaves by 1860) and practiced law in New Orleans. Waul represented Bexar County, Texas, at state conventions of the Democratic party in 1856 and 1857. He lost an election for congressman from West Texas in 1859, but the next year Texas Democrats made him a statewide presidential elector.

When the Texas secession convention met in January 1861, its members selected Waul as one of seven Texas representatives to the convention in Montgomery, Alabama, that created the Confederate government and became the Provisional Congress. He served on the committees for Commercial Affairs and for Indian Affairs and drew upon his legal training to help draft many of the laws passed by Congress. To launch the new nation he offered several bills aimed at immediate problems such as the creation of Confederate courts, and the organization of military supply and intelligence efforts, as well as local protection from attacks. He proposed, unsuccessfully, a clause in the Confederate Constitution allowing the importation of slaves from other parts of the Americas. In the area of trade he opposed governmental controls, especially in the case of cotton exports.

Waul ran for election as a Confederate senator from Texas in 1861 but was defeated. Early the next year he began to raise troops for a unit called Waul's Legion, a command that encompassed infantry, cavalry, and artillery. He received the rank of colonel on May 17 and completed the creation of his unit that summer in Washington County near Houston.

During the fall of 1862, Waul led his men across the Mississippi River to help defend Mississippi against a Union invasion. He advanced his legion to protect the withdrawal of the Confederate army under Gen. Earl Van Dorn after its defeat at Corinth in October. During the winter of 1862 to 1863 Waul and his men built Fort Pemberton on the Tallahatchie River and held it against Federal attack. In the spring, orders separated his cavalry battalion from the legion, while most of the infantry and artillery moved south with Waul in May to defend against a Union crossing of the Big Black River from the east as Gen. Ulysses S. Grant advanced to attack Vicksburg. After Federal successes forced the Confederate army back into Vicksburg, Waul and his men helped drive back an attack aimed at the railroad redoubt on May 22 and continued to defend their section of the trench line until the Vicksburg garrison surrendered on July 4 and received paroles.

Once the exchange process allowed his return to duty, Waul received advancement to brigadier general on September 18, 1863. During the fall he returned to his home state with orders to reorganize and expand his legion into a mounted brigade for service east of the Mississippi River. Before he could do so, however, Waul replaced J. M. Hawes in February 1864 as commander of an infantry brigade in John G. Walker's Texas Division stationed in Louisiana to defend the Trans-Mississippi Department. When Gen. Nathaniel P. Banks led a Union army up the Red River in March to seize cotton and invade Texas, Gen. Richard Taylor pulled back his Confederate troops including Waul's brigade toward Shreveport. After reinforcements arrived from Texas, Waul and his men joined in Taylor's attack against Banks at Mansfield, Louisiana, on April 8 and defeated the Federals. At Pleasant Hill the next day a second assault by Walker's entire division failed, though Banks again retreated back toward the Mississippi River following the battle. Gen. E. Kirby Smith, commander of the Trans-Mississippi Department, then sent the division north to assist Gen. Sterling Price in halting a Union army advancing south from Little Rock, Arkansas, to join Banks. At Jenkins's Ferry, Arkansas, on April 30, Waul again led his brigade in a charge that helped drive Federal forces under Gen. Frederick Steele back across the Saline River. In the fighting Waul fell wounded and soon after the battle received a furlough home to Texas.

Following the conflict Waul ran successfully to represent Gonzales County at the Texas constitutional convention in 1866. From 1868 to 1895 he established himself as a leading attorney at Galveston. He went into retirement in rural Hunt County of northern Texas where he died on July 28, 1903. His daughter buried him in Fort Worth.

BIBLIOGRAPHY

Warner, Ezra J., and W. Buck Yearns. *Biographical Register of the Confederate Congress.* Baton Rouge, La., 1975.

Winkler, Ernest William. *Platforms of Political Parties in Texas.* Austin, Tex., 1916.

Bearss, Edwin C. *Texas at Vicksburg.* Austin, Tex., 1961.

Blessington, J. P. *The Campaigns of Walker's Texas Division.* Austin, Tex., 1968.

Brown, John Henry. *Indian Wars and Pioneers of Texas.* Austin, Tex., 1896.

ALWYN BARR

WAYNE, HENRY CONSTANTINE (1815–1883), brigadier general. A West Point graduate of the class of 1838, Wayne served on the frontier and later taught artillery, cavalry, and infantry tactics at the military academy. He took part in the Mexican War, earning a promotion to major, and in 1855 participated in the army's experiment in using camels to transport supplies in the West.

Wayne resigned from the army in December 1860, and soon after, Georgia Governor Joseph E. Brown appointed him adjutant and inspector general of state troops. He became a brigadier general in the Confederate service on December 16, 1861, assigned to command in Virginia, but he resigned four weeks later to resume his state duties. His primary responsibility was raising troops for Georgia, but he also took part in fortifying the state's defenses. In April 1863 Wayne directed troops to the northwestern part of the state to suppress a disturbance caused by disgruntled citizens. Gen. Joseph E. Johnston appealed to him in early 1864 to have the governor reform the management of the Western and Atlantic Railroad, stating that the army would have to retreat back to its supplies if conditions were not improved. During William Tecumseh Sherman's March to the Sea, Wayne commanded the state troops defending the Oconee River bridge, west of Savannah, but had to retire before superior Federal forces. He surrendered the state troops under his command on May 8, 1865.

After the war, Wayne worked in the lumber business in Savannah.

BIBLIOGRAPHY

Bryan, T. Conn. *Confederate Georgia.* Athens, Ga., 1953.

U.S. War Department. *War of the Rebellion: A Compilation of the Official Records of the Union and Confederate Armies.* Washington, D.C., 1880–1901. Ser. 1, vol. 23, pt. 2, pp. 737–738; ser. 1, vol. 32, pt. 2, p. 552; ser. 1, vol. 44, pp. 877–878, 892–894, 897.

MICHAEL G. MAHON

WEAPONS. *See* Arms, Weapons, and Ammunition.

WEBB.

When *William H. Webb* arrived at New Orleans in May 1861, it received a privateer's commission but performed transport duty until mid-January of 1862 when Maj. Gen. Mansfield Lovell converted it into a formidable ram. The 656-ton side-wheeler measured 195 feet by 31 feet 6 inches, had a draft of 9 feet 6 inches, and traveled between fifteen and twenty-five knots. Its armament usually consisted of one heavy rifled cannon and two field pieces. With two exceptions, *Webb* avoided Union gunboats.

About 9:45 P.M. on February 24, 1863, *Webb* and two other vessels attacked USS *Indianola,* anchored near New Carthage, Mississippi. Manned by soldiers under Maj. J. L. Brent, *Webb,* with its second ramming, disabled *Indianola* and started several leaks; the most formidable vessel in the West sank in shallow water.

Lt. Charles W. Read then took command of *Webb* in the Red River on March 30, 1865. Readied for privateer duty, *Webb* started for the Gulf. At 8:30 P.M. on April 23, it passed three vessels blockading the river's mouth. Making twenty-five knots, *Webb* successfully passed and outdistanced every Union vessel. Flying the U.S. flag at half mast for Abraham Lincoln as a deception, *Webb* passed New Orleans about midnight on April 24, where it received three hits that destroyed the spar torpedo. Under the Confederate flag, *Webb* encountered USS *Richmond* twenty-five miles downriver, and Read grounded and ignited his ship. The entire crew was soon captured in the neighboring swamps.

BIBLIOGRAPHY

Dufour, Charles L. *Nine Men in Gray.* Garden City, N.Y., 1963.

Still, William N., Jr. *Iron Afloat: The Story of the Confederate Armorclads.* Nashville, Tenn., 1971.

LAWRENCE L. HEWITT

WEISIGER, DAVID ADDISON (1818–1899),

brigadier general. Born in Chesterfield County, Virginia, Weisiger lived in Petersburg at the outbreak of the Mexican War and assisted in raising a company for the First Regiment of Virginia Volunteers. He became a second lieutenant in this company and, in 1848, was appointed adjutant of the regiment, which saw arduous service in Mexico, but no battles. Afterward he became colonel of Petersburg's Thirty-ninth Regiment of militia.

In January 1861, he was elected major to command the Fourth Battalion of Virginia Volunteers, composed of Petersburg's uniformed volunteer militia companies. The battalion, mustered into service in April, was expanded into the Twelfth Regiment of Virginia Infantry with Colonel Weisiger in command. He led the regiment at Seven Pines,

DAVID ADDISON WEISIGER. LIBRARY OF CONGRESS

through the Seven Days' Battles, and at Second Manassas, where he was given command of the brigade after the wounding of Brig. Gen. William Mahone. In the same battle Weisiger himself was seriously wounded and hospitalized. In the reorganization following the wounding of General Longstreet at the Wilderness, Weisiger was again put in command of Mahone's brigade. He was appointed on June 7, 1864, as a temporary brigadier general. For his gallantry at the Battle of the Crater in the Petersburg campaign, he was commissioned permanently as a brigadier general on November 1, 1864, to date from July 30, the day of the battle. When he was paroled at Appomattox Courthouse, he had been in over twenty battles and had been wounded three times.

Weisiger became a Petersburg banker and later moved to Richmond, where he resided until his death. He was buried in Blandford Cemetery at Petersburg.

BIBLIOGRAPHY

Bernard, George S. *War Talks of Confederate Veterans*. Petersburg, Va., 1892.

Evans, Clement A., ed. *Confederate Military History*. 12 vols. Atlanta, 1899. Extended ed. in 19 vols. Wilmington, N.C., 1987–1989. Weisiger's name is erroneously given as "Daniel Adams Weisiger" in his biographical sketch.

Henderson, William D. *Twelfth Virginia Infantry*. Lynchburg, Va., 1984.

Lee A. Wallace, Jr.

WELCH, ISRAEL VICTOR (1822–1869), private and congressman from Mississippi. Welch, born in Alabama, moved to Wahalak, Mississippi, when he was twelve years old. For many years he practiced law in Macon, and in 1858 he was elected to the state house of representatives. Welch was a strong advocate of secession, and as a member of the Mississippi convention of 1861, he voted for the state's leaving the Union. When war broke out, Welch enlisted as a private in the Confederate army. His unit, Company F, Noxubee Rifles, of the Eleventh Regiment of Mississippi Infantry, took part in the Battle of First Manassas.

Welch left the army in 1862 to run for election to the First Congress. He won that campaign and was reelected in 1863. Throughout his tenure, Welch supported the policies of the administration and was primarily interested in issues concerning manpower. He favored a strong, fair draft with limited and regulated exemptions, strongly opposed the policy of allowing substitutes to be hired for military service, and fought for a draft of 100,000 slaves to fight for the Confederacy.

After the war, Welch returned to his law practice for the last four years of his life. Although he had spent only one year in the army, the inscription on his gravestone lists his company's name; no other details of his life are mentioned.

BIBLIOGRAPHY

Alexander, Thomas B., and Richard E. Beringer. *The Anatomy of the Confederate Congress: A Study of the Influences of Member Characteristics on Legislative Voting Behavior, 1861–1865.* Nashville, Tenn., 1972.

Warner, Ezra J., and W. Buck Yearns. *Biographical Register of the Confederate Congress*. Baton Rouge, La., 1975.

Ray Skates

WELLS, JAMES MADISON (1808–1899), Unionist governor of Louisiana. Although Wells was born to a well-to-do planter family in Rapides Parish, Louisiana, he was orphaned at the age of eight and spent most of his childhood with relatives or in schools in Kentucky, Connecticut, and Ohio. In 1830, he returned to Louisiana, where he eventually owned five Rapides Parish plantations and nearly one hundred slaves.

Wells had acquired a strongly nationalistic outlook during his days in Cincinnati, where he studied law with Charles Hammond, an outspoken Federalist and abolitionist. Throughout the decades leading up to the Civil War, Wells played an active role in local Whig politics; he supported Stephen A. Douglas in the 1860 presidential campaign and led the fight against secession in upstate Louisiana. His Unionism proved to be unconditional, and after the firing on Fort Sumter he spoke widely against the conflict as a "rich man's war and a poor man's fight." In 1862 and 1863, Wells escaped persecution by taking to the heavily wooded "Bear Wallow," from which he led poor whites and Confederate deserters in attacks against the South's supply lines. Confederate efforts to arrest him—apparently renewed when he criticized Gen. Thomas J. ("Stonewall") Jackson after the latter's death—forced him to find refuge in New Orleans late in 1863.

Wells's uncompromising Unionism and wealth made him a natural candidate in the turbulent politics of occupied Louisiana. Nominated for lieutenant governor by the radical as well as the conservative factions of Unionists for the fall 1864 elections, he became governor when the gubernatorial victor, Michael Hahn, went to the U.S. Senate in early 1865. Despite his initial affiliation with the radicals' Free State party, Wells as governor promulgated a conservative program for a number of reasons. Though he had long resided in the North, he resented Northern intervention in Louisiana. And as a planter, he was less than sympathetic to the cause of racial equality and rather contemptuous of the Union officers and agents sent to reconstruct Louisiana. Wells hoped to lead his state through the sort of quick, relatively painless Reconstruction later advocated by President Andrew Johnson. To that end, the governor appointed former Confederates to state and parish offices and opposed granting the vote to or providing public education for freedmen. These actions helped reelect Wells as the National Democrat nominee for governor in the fall of 1865.

Shortly thereafter, however, Wells's alliance with the conservative-controlled legislature was threatened when he opposed their more drastic measures—he vetoed a particularly harsh vagrancy law—and became embroiled in conflicts over political patronage. The final break came when Wells announced his support for black suffrage and the Fourteenth Amendment in the spring of 1866. Wells's turnaround on black suffrage—he had earlier opposed it because he believed the freedmen would remain loyal to their former masters—was consistent with his Unionism. As his own wartime loyalties became a political liability and as former Confederates began to reestablish control over the state government, Wells sought a way to prevent the seizure of the government by unreconstructed ex-Confederates. He came to believe this could be accomplished only by forming an alliance with the Radical Republicans and winning the electoral support of the blacks being victimized by the Black Codes passed by the conservative legislature. His ploy failed, and by the time Gen. Philip Sheridan removed him from office in July 1867, Wells had become as hated by the conservatives as he had previously been by the radicals.

Wells never held an elective office again, although he served for several years as surveyor of customs for the port of New Orleans, influenced Republican patronage in Louisiana for decades, and, as chairman of Louisiana's infamous "Returning Board," helped give the state's electoral votes to Rutherford B. Hayes in the disputed election of 1876. He died at his Lecompte Plantation in Rapides Parish at the age of ninety-one.

BIBLIOGRAPHY

Lowrey, Walter McGehee. "The Political Career of James Madison Wells." *Louisiana Historical Quarterly* 31 (1948): 995–1123.

Taylor, Joe Gray. *Louisiana Reconstructed, 1863–1877.* Baton Rouge, La., 1974.

Tunnell, Ted. *Crucible of Reconstruction: War, Radicalism, and Race in Louisiana, 1862–1877.* Baton Rouge, La., 1984.

JAMES MARTEN

WEST VIRGINIA. For Virginians who lived in what became West Virginia the Civil War was a painful experience. Many of them had strong ties to Virginia, but most of the 357,678 white residents, who were chiefly of English, Scotch-Irish, and German extraction, had an even deeper attachment to the Union. In 1860 the 16,401 slaves made up slightly more than 4 percent of the population, and the 2,742 free blacks constituted less than 1 percent. For political, economic, and psychological reasons, both the Union and the Confederacy strove to control this borderland, where communities and even families were divided and brother often fought against brother.

On the eve of the Civil War a spirit of moderation prevailed in western Virginia. In 1860 Virginia gave its electoral vote to John Bell, the Constitutional Unionist, and Southern Democrat John C. Breckinridge was second in popular votes. But in the western part of the state Breckinridge led with 21,961 votes, followed by Bell with 21,175. Stephen A. Douglas, the Northern Democrat, trailed with 5,112, and Abraham Lincoln won about 1,200. With the support of the party organization, press, and leaders, Breckinridge carried the normally Democratic counties of Virginia, including present-day West Virginia, where party loyalty apparently remained intact. Moreover, many voters evidently believed that neither Douglas nor Bell could win the election and that Breckinridge offered the best assurance of defeating Lincoln and preserving the Union.

During the crisis that followed the secession of South Carolina and other states, most western Virginians opposed any hasty action by their state. A large gathering at Parkersburg declared that national well-being and prosperity depended upon preservation of the Union and that the election of Lincoln was no reason to abandon "the best Government ever yet devised by the wisdom and patriotism of men." A Union meeting at Lick Creek, in Greenbrier County, considered it "unwise, impolitic, and unpatriotic not to give Mr. Lincoln a fair trial before we either secede from the Union or condemn his administration."

Following the firing upon Fort Sumter and Lincoln's call for troops, forces of moderation lost ground. On April 17, 1861, the Virginia convention adopted an ordinance of secession by a vote of eighty-eight to fifty-five. Of the forty-seven delegates from present-day West Virginia, thirty-two voted against secession, eleven voted for it, and four did not vote. (Two of those opposing secession and two who did not vote later signed the ordinance.) A popular referendum on the matter was set for May 13.

Western delegates opposed to secession hastened home to organize resistance movements. A mass meeting at Clarksburg, assembled on April 22 by John S. Carlile, initiated steps that led to the First Wheeling Convention on May 13 through 15. The Wheeling gathering, also essentially a mass meeting, had 436 irregularly chosen or self-appointed participants from twenty-seven counties. All but one county became part of West Virginia, and all but four were located west of the Alleghenies and north of the Kanawha River. Carlile favored an immediate proclamation of separate statehood. Waitman T. Willey, John J. Jackson, and others urged another convention, to meet in June after the results of the referendum were known. In the referendum, popular support for secession in eastern Virginia was strong, but almost 65 percent of the voters in present-day West Virginia opposed it.

The Second Wheeling Convention, which met in regular session on June 11, 1861, had 105 delegates from thirty-eight counties, two of which never became part of West Virginia. Fifteen trans-Allegheny counties, later included in the state, sent no delegates. The convention declared all state offices vacant and set up a Reorganized Government of Virginia at Wheeling, on the basis of loyalty to the Union. It chose Francis H. Peirpoint governor, arranged for a complement of state officials, and filled the U.S. Senate and congressional seats vacated by Virginia Confederates. The Senate seats of Robert M. T. Hunter and James M. Mason went to Willey and Carlile.

Meanwhile, twenty-one men represented West Virginia counties or delegate districts in the Richmond legislature, and eight represented senatorial districts embracing forty-six West Virginia counties. Allen T. Caperton of Monroe County became a member of the Confederate Senate. Alexander R. Boteler of Shepherdstown, Albert Gallatin Jenkins of Cabell County, Robert Johnston of Clarksburg, Samuel Augustine Miller of Charleston, and Charles Wells Russell of Wheeling served in the Confederate House of Representatives.

The number of West Virginians who fought for the Confederacy and the Union has not been ascertained. Older histories give figures ranging from 28,000 to 36,000 Union troops and 9,000 to 12,000 Confederate troops. But a recent challenge to these statistics substantially reduces the number of Union troops and increases that of Confederates.

Military Actions in the Region. At the outset of the war the military picture in western Virginia was confused, with Union and Confederate volunteers drilling in many of the same towns. The U.S. secretary of war added the part of the region north of the Kanawha to the Department of Ohio, under Gen. George B. McClellan. Col. George A. Porterfield, the Confederate commander in the Monongahela valley, occupied Grafton, a key junction on the Baltimore and Ohio Railroad, and ordered bridges destroyed between that point and Wheeling. At McClellan's direction, Col. Benjamin F. Kelley occupied Fairmont, forced Porterfield to withdraw from Grafton to Philippi, and on June 3, 1861, routed the Confederates from Philippi in what has sometimes been called the first land battle of the Civil War. McClellan then forced Brig. Gen. Robert S. Garnett, who replaced Porterfield, from defensive positions at Rich Mountain Pass near Beverly and Laurel Hill near Belington, which were within striking distance of the Baltimore and Ohio, and into battle at Corricks Ford, where Garnett lost his life. The Confederates were left with no important positions in the Monongahela valley.

The Confederate hold upon the Kanawha valley, where Gen. Henry A. Wise had 2,700 men, seemed more secure. In July 1861, however, Gen. Jacob D. Cox, with Federal troops from Ohio, advanced up the Kanawha and engaged the Confederates in an indecisive battle at Scary Creek, about fifteen miles west of Charleston. Believing that Cox was receiving reinforcements, Wise abandoned Tyler Mountain and Charleston and withdrew by way of the James River and Kanawha Turnpike to White Sulphur Springs. Cox pursued the Confederates and occupied Gauley Bridge at the junction of the New and Gauley rivers.

Confederate authorities directed Gen. John B. Floyd to reoccupy the Kanawha valley, a plan that threatened Cox at Gauley Bridge and Gen. William S. Rosecrans, who had succeeded McClellan in the Monongahela Valley. Failure of Floyd and Wise to cooperate, however, wrecked the plan, and Federal forces defeated the Confederates in the Battle of Carnifex Ferry. With northwestern Virginia under Federal control, the Reorganized Government at Wheeling could continue its work unmolested and the West Virginia statehood movement could proceed.

Keenly aware of the importance of his crumbling mountain front, Gen. Robert E. Lee undertook "a tour of inspection and consultation." He found the Confederates "too wet and too hungry" to dislodge Union forces from Cheat Mountain and their camp at Elkwater, but on December 13 they beat back an attack on their own position at Allegheny Mountain. Meanwhile, angered by the feud between Floyd and Wise, President Jefferson Davis ordered Wise to turn over his command to Floyd, who was instructed to move via the Coal River to the Kanawha and cut Cox's communications with Ohio. Gen. W. W. Loring was directed to push Rosecrans back toward Clarksburg. Wise's men proved too demoralized to provide assistance, and the initiative passed to Rosecrans.

In the eastern panhandle much of the military activity centered around the Baltimore and Ohio Railroad, with Romney as its focal point. In 1861 Thomas J. ("Stonewall") Jackson, West Virginia's most distinguished Confederate officer, harassed Federal troops and destroyed tracks between Harpers Ferry and Martinsburg, appropriating the rails to Southern use. Jackson also urged a vigorous defense of Harpers Ferry, with its armory and arsenal, but Gen. Joseph E. Johnston regarded it as indefensible.

Jackson then proposed to sweep across the Alleghenies, complete the destruction of the Baltimore and Ohio, and recover northwestern Virginia. He forced Kelley out of Romney, which he placed under Loring before going into winter quarters at Winchester. Chafing under his assignment, Loring engaged in machinations that induced Secretary of War Judah P. Benjamin to direct Jackson to give up Romney and move Loring to Winchester. The distraught

Confederate battery at Harpers Ferry. Erected on the heights overlooking the town, the battery commanded the railroad bridge and the canal.

The Soldier in Our Civil War

Jackson sent a letter of resignation to Governor John Letcher but was persuaded, with great reluctance, to withdraw it.

In order to stop Jackson's devastations in the valley of Virginia and the Potomac valley, Lincoln in 1862 placed John C. Frémont in charge of the newly created Mountain Department, with headquarters at Wheeling. Frémont's plans failed, and Jackson dealt him such a defeat that he resigned his command. Meanwhile, Confederate Gen. Henry Heth, in expectation of an attack upon the Virginia and Tennessee Railroad, dispatched troops to Flat Top Mountain and to Muddy Creek, near Lewisburg, on the James River and Kanawha Turnpike. After indecisive action around Princeton, the Confederates fell back toward Lewisburg, which Gen. George Crook attacked on May 12. Fearing that he himself might be cut off, Crook withdrew to Meadow Bluff, and Cox declined to attack the Virginia and Tennessee line. By then, it was said, "the long shadow of Stonewall Jackson reached even to the banks of the New and Greenbrier rivers."

The Confederates achieved other successes in 1862. Preparatory to an invasion of the Kanawha valley, Brig. Gen. Albert Gallatin Jenkins made a sweeping raid with about six hundred cavalry through the southeastern and central parts of West Virginia. Loring then moved from Fayetteville into the Kanawha valley, forcing Gen. Joseph A. J. Lightburn to give up Gauley Bridge and Charleston and to withdraw toward the Ohio River. Loring, however, disobeyed orders to use the Kanawha valley as a base and attack the Cheat Bridge with part of his troops. In doing so, he threw away Confederate gains, allowing the Federals under Cox to regain control of the Kanawha valley.

The most spectacular Confederate actions in West Virginia in 1863 were daring raids. The Jones-Imboden raid, which covered much of north-central West Virginia, resulted in the destruction of twenty-one railroad bridges and a tunnel, turnpike bridges, oil and oil field equipment, and military installations and supplies; the taking of about five thousand cattle and two thousand horses; and recruitment of about four hundred men for Confederate service. Federal forces under Gen. William W. Averill, however, defeated the Confederates under Gen. John Echols at Droop Mountain and extended the area under Federal control to roughly the eastern boundaries of West Virginia.

Confederate raids also punctuated the fighting in 1864. Gen. John McCausland, a West Virginian, dashed into Pennsylvania and burned the town of Chambersburg. Federal counterstrikes included a raid on Dublin and the Battle of Cloyds Mountain in Virginia. In February 1865 Capt. John McNeill of Hardy County and his son Jesse struck into Maryland and captured Union generals Crook and Kelley in their hotel rooms in Cumberland.

The Creation of West Virginia. Federal military dominance of the trans-Allegheny region allowed the creation of West Virginia, toward which the first steps had been taken at the adjourned session of the Second Wheeling Convention in August 1861, to proceed without serious interruption. A constitutional convention, which met from November 26, 1861, until February 18, 1862, drew up a framework of government and defined boundaries approximating those of the present state. Slavery hung like a shadow over the convention. Gordon Battelle, a Methodist minister and educator, introduced resolutions forbidding the entry of additional slaves into the proposed state and providing for gradual emancipation of those already there. Failing in that, he introduced other resolutions, one of which, calling for a popular referendum on gradual emancipation, failed by a single vote. A compromise provided that no free person of color should be brought into the state for permanent residence.

To comply with a requirement of the U.S. Constitution that a new state must have the approval of the state from which it is carved, the makers of West Virginia turned to the Reorganized Government of Virginia at Wheeling, already known to be friendly to the idea. Since a popular referendum on the question had already resulted in 18,862 votes in favor of statehood and only 514 votes against it, the Virginia General Assembly readily gave its approval on May 13, 1863, and Governor Peirpoint signed the measure.

The West Virginia statehood bill encountered unexpected opposition in the U.S. Senate when Carlile, an original champion of statehood and a member of the Senate Committee on Territories to which the statehood question was referred, drafted a bill calling for the addition of fifteen counties, a new constitutional convention of sixty-three counties (many of them known to be opposed to statehood), and the gradual abolition of slavery. With statehood teetering on the brink of failure, Senator Willey, with help from Senator Benjamin F. Wade of Ohio, saved the bill with an amendment whereby slaves under twenty-one years of age on July 4, 1863, would become free upon attaining that age. Carlile made yet another vain effort to kill the statehood bill by requiring popular ratification of gradual emancipation by a majority of the registered voters in the proposed state; in the end he refused to vote in favor of the new state. President Lincoln, after much consideration, signed the statehood bill, and on June 20, 1863, West Virginia entered the Union as the thirty-fifth state. The Reorganized Government of Virginia, which was still recognized by Lincoln and the U.S. Congress as the government of Virginia, thereupon moved to Alexandria. At the close of the war, when the Confederate government of the state fell, it moved to Richmond. Wartime animosities gradually receded, and questions regarding the constitutionality of the methods by which West Virginia achieved statehood became academic. For its people, the new state, won at such a frightful cost in human and material resources, stood as the central achievement of the war and as an assurance that they would share in the new economic and social order presaged by the victorious Union.

[*For further discussion of battles and campaigns fought in West Virginia, see* Early's Washington Raid; Gettysburg Campaign; Sharpsburg Campaign; Shenandoah Valley, *articles on the campaigns of Jackson and Sheridan;* West Virginia Operations. *See also* Chambersburg, Pennsylvania; Cloyds Mountain, Virginia; Harpers Ferry, West Virginia; Loring-Jackson Incident; Virginia; *and biographies of numerous figures mentioned herein.*]

BIBLIOGRAPHY

Ambler, Charles H., and Festus P. Summers. *West Virginia, The Mountain State.* 2d ed. Englewood Cliffs, N.J., 1958.

Curry, Richard Orr. *A House Divided: Statehood Politics and the Copperhead Movement in West Virginia.* Pittsburgh, 1964.

McGregor, James C. *The Disruption of Virginia.* New York, 1922.

Moore, George E. *A Banner in the Hills: West Virginia's Statehood.* New York, 1963.

Rice, Otis K. *West Virginia: A History.* Lexington, Ky., 1985.

Summers, Festus P. *The Baltimore and Ohio in the Civil War.* New York, 1939.

Williams, John Alexander. *West Virginia: A Bicentennial History.* New York and Nashville, 1976.

OTIS K. RICE

WEST VIRGINIA OPERATIONS.

[*This entry is composed of two articles,* Operations of 1861 *and* Operations of 1862 and 1863.]

Operations of 1861

When the Civil War began on April 12, 1861, after the Confederate bombardment of Fort Sumter in Charleston, South Carolina, many Southerners loyal to the U.S. government were unwilling to side with the secessionist cause. This was particularly true in border states, as well as areas such as eastern Tennessee and western Virginia.

The Commonwealth of Virginia seceded from the Union on April 17, 1861, but the citizens of the state were radically divided on the issue. In the trans-Allegheny region, the majority of the mostly nonslaveholding, small-farm Virginians were extremely pro-Union, their culture and economy long tied more to that of Ohio and Pennsylvania to their north, while the generally politically powerful landed slaveholding class in the Tidewater and Piedmont sections of the state was, by and large, vehemently pro-Confederacy. Western Virginians felt they were very much underrepresented in the legislature and severely overtaxed, receiving little public assistance from the state; to add insult to injury, they felt looked upon as inferior mountain dirt farmers by the well-heeled eastern planter elite. With the state split in two and the population of one section adamantly opposed to the politics of the other, it is not surprising that the outcome was the formal parting of western Virginia from the eastern region of the state.

Upon learning of Virginia's ordinance of secession, the citizenry of the trans-Alleghenies began holding mass pro-Union meetings stating their refusal to secede from the Federal government and, in some cases, raising armed militia for the Union. And with Virginia's separation from the Federal government, the people of the western counties of the state reacted violently and bitterly against any of their fellow citizens—and there were a sizable number of them—who advocated Confederate secession. (This rancor and viciousness would last throughout the war and, in some cases, for generations to come.)

For Washington, the western part of Virginia was of vital strategic importance because of the long stretch of the Ohio River on its border and the Baltimore and Ohio Railroad. The latter tied East Coast cities to western destinations such as Louisville, Indianapolis, and St. Louis, enabling Federal troops and supplies to be shuffled quickly to where they were most needed. The Alleghenies protected Ohio and Pennsylvania, as well as western approaches to the Shenandoah Valley. The mountains also covered eastern Tennessee. One other advantage in holding this area for the Union lay in the fact that many men who might enter the Confederate army would now be available to fight for the North.

Twenty thousand Northern troops from the Department of the Ohio under the command of Gen. George B. McClellan soon came to the aid of the western Virginians, routing a small party of Confederate bridge burners at Philippi on June 3, one of the first actual field combats of the Civil War. Meanwhile, Southern troops from eastern Virginia and Georgia were moving into the mountains. These men were under the command of Gen. Robert S. Garnett, and Garnett had entrenched his troops on Laurel Hill and nearby Rich Mountain in June. On July 6, 1861, McClellan advanced his soldiers, who began skirmishing with Garnett's Confederates on July 7. Then on July 11, after four days of parrying, McClellan's Ohio troops assaulted and defeated the Confederate forces on Laurel Hill.

Meanwhile, on the same day, a Federal brigade commanded by Gen. William Rosecrans attacked up the steep slopes of Rich Mountain in a rainstorm, swiftly overpowering the weak 1,300-man force and four fieldpieces—under the command of Lt. Col. John Pegram—left there by Garnett to defend that mountain. These victories secured for the Union an important crossroads of the Parkersburg-Staunton Turnpike at Beverly in the Tygart River valley, fifty miles west of the Shenandoah Valley. Holding this road and these two mountains assured the Union victors of the

ability to control access to northwestern Virginia. At his disposal for these two relatively minor actions, McClellan had about 15,000 soldiers—not all of whom actually fought—while Garnett could field only some 4,500 men.

After the small battles at Laurel Hill and Rich Mountain, Garnett retreated across Cheat Mountain into the Cheat River valley, while Indiana and Ohio troops in Gen. Thomas A. Morris's brigade pursued over difficult roads and in a driving rain. On July 13, at midday, Morris's men overtook Garnett's Confederates at Carrick's Ford and opened fire, chasing them back to another ford a couple of miles distant. There, fighting resumed until the Confederates were defeated and routed. During this action, while directing his skirmishers, Garnett was killed by Federal gunfire. Total casualties were very light on both sides, however.

With such decisive—but greatly exaggerated—victories in quick succession, George McClellan became a national hero in the North and was called to Washington to assume greater responsibilities. Two weeks later, Gen. Robert E. Lee would come to the Alleghenies in a futile bid to control these western counties.

Politically, meanwhile, the people of the area had been taking every step to become independent from eastern Virginia. On June 11, 1861, delegates from thirty-four northwestern counties—representing four-fifths of the population in the mountainous area—convened in Wheeling and demanded to remain in the Union. The intention of the convention was not to secede from the state of Virginia, but rather to proclaim itself the legitimate government of the commonwealth and to declare the secession of the state illegal.

The plans espoused by this convention were hardly practical, however, and two months later ordinances were adopted by the delegates that effectively made West Virginia—initially called Kanawha—a separate state, with Francis H. Peirpoint its governor. In November, a convention was held to draft a new state constitution, and it was ratified by citizens loyal to the Union on April 2, 1862. On May 13, the West Virginia legislature petitioned the U.S. government for admission to the Union, and after much political wrangling, and an agreement by Wheeling for the eventual abolition of what little slavery existed there, West Virginia became a state on June 20, 1863.

BIBLIOGRAPHY

Cohen, Stan. *The Civil War in West Virginia: A Pictorial History.* Missoula, Mont., 1976.

Moore, George E. *A Banner in the Hills.* New York, 1963.

Smith, Edward Conrad. *The Borderland in the Civil War.* New York, 1927.

Stutler, Boyd B. *West Virginia in the Civil War.* Charleston, W.Va., 1963.

WARREN WILKINSON

Operations of 1862 and 1863

Military activity in West Virginia in 1862 and 1863 centered in the upper Potomac valley and along the Allegheny front, which extended from Flat Top Mountain northward to Cheat Mountain. The upper Potomac front was one of great fluidity. Confederate objectives there included control of its section of the Baltimore and Ohio Railroad and of the lower part of the Shenandoah Valley, which was commonly regarded as the gateway into Virginia and the Confederacy. Towns along the railroad changed hands frequently. Romney, for instance, passed back and forth fifty-six times during the war.

In order to achieve its goals, the Confederacy created its Shenandoah District and placed Thomas J. ("Stonewall") Jackson in command of the 8,500 troops in the region. Jackson immediately undertook to drive Union forces out of his district and to destroy the Baltimore and Ohio Railroad between Harpers Ferry and Martinsburg. Later he organized his winter march against Romney, which he considered one of the most important towns on the railroad. He also believed that if the Confederacy were to move against northwestern Virginia, it must do so in the winter of 1861–1862.

Although he was confident that Federal officers in Romney would not expect an attack in midwinter, Jackson did not march directly from his Winchester headquarters to Romney. Instead, he made use of a feint by marching north to Berkeley Springs and from there into Maryland. Jackson encountered some resistance, but on January 17, 1862, he captured Romney with only minimal difficulty.

Jackson's success in the Shenandoah Valley, especially his deftness in striking and then eluding forces under Nathaniel Banks, influenced Abraham Lincoln's decision to create the overarching Mountain Department in March 1862. He ordered Gen. John C. Frémont, the commander, who had 35,000 troops at Wheeling, to destroy the Virginia and Tennessee Railroad, but before Frémont could do so, Lincoln sent him to assist in efforts to trap Jackson in the Shenandoah Valley.

Union strength in the Kanawha valley was also reduced when Brig. Gen. Jacob D. Cox, with headquarters at Gauley Bridge, was ordered to the defense of Washington, D.C. The defense of the Kanawha valley then fell to Brig. Gen. Joseph A. J. Lightburn, who was at Gauley Bridge with six regiments of infantry, one of cavalry, and some local organizations left him by Cox. Aware of Union vulnerability in the Kanawha valley, Confederates believed that the time was propitious for an offensive against northwestern Virginia. They hoped to destroy western sections of the Baltimore and Ohio Railroad, harass the Unionist government of Restored Virginia, obstruct the West Virginia statehood movement, and recruit for the Confederate army.

Fearing that any escape down the Kanawha might be cut off, Lightburn moved his headquarters to Charleston and later to Ohio. W. W. Loring followed him down the Kanawha, but he prepared for any confrontation by sending Gen. Albert Gallatin Jenkins on a wide-ranging raid into territory north and south of the Kanawha River. Their movements dealt Union forces their most severe setback in West Virginia up to that time.

By 1863 the Confederates, as well as the Federals, had reassessed their military objectives and strategies. Confederates thereafter placed less emphasis on moving armies across mountains than in well-executed raids and strikes, as well as moves against Unionist Restored Virginia. The most spectacular and effective military move in 1863 was the William E. Jones–John D. Imboden raids, which covered a vast area of north-central West Virginia. They destroyed large segments of the Baltimore and Ohio Railroad, netted the Confederacy large numbers of cattle and horses, resulted in recruitment of men for the Confederate service, wrecked oil production on the Little Kanawha, and spread panic across the state. Such successes helped to mitigate disasters on other fronts.

By the end of 1863 Confederate military and political objectives in West Virginia were no longer attainable. West Virginia had become a state, and Union armies occupied most of the territory within its boundaries. Confederate forces were decimated by deserters, large numbers of whom joined guerrilla bands or became bushwhackers. Although many of these irregulars continued to profess Confederate sympathies, they were no longer a reliable fighting force and constituted no threat to Union supremacy. Prospects for Confederate success had, in fact, vanished forever.

BIBLIOGRAPHY

McKinney, Tim. *Robert E. Lee at Sewell Mountain: The West Virginia Campaign.* Charleston, W.Va., 1990.
Moore, George Ellis. *A Banner in the Hills: West Virginia's Statehood.* New York, 1963.
Rice, Otis K., and Stephen W. Brown. *West Virginia: A History.* 2d ed. Lexington, Ky., 1993.
Stutler, Boyd B. *West Virginia in the Civil War.* Charleston, W.Va., 1963.

OTIS K. RICE

WHARTON, GABRIEL COLVIN (1824–1906), brigadier general. Born in Culpeper, Virginia, Wharton stood second in the Virginia Military Institute's class of 1847. A civil engineer in Arizona before the Civil War, Wharton became the major of the Forty-fifth Virginia in July 1861 and the next month the colonel of the Fifty-first Virginia. During the summer and fall of 1861, Wharton fought in western Virginia. He then headed west at the beginning of 1862 and helped garrison Fort Donelson, Tennessee. Commanding a brigade, Wharton fought his way out of Donelson on February 15, which earned him the accolades of his superiors.

Wharton's brigade returned to Virginia in the spring of 1862 and occupied the Kanawha Valley the following September. Though a promotion for Wharton was in order, he still remained a colonel. His slow promotions throughout the war resulted from a stormy relationship with Jefferson Davis. Not until Wharton commanded the Shenandoah Valley District in July 1863 did he receive a brigadier generalship on the eighth of the month. Wharton's brigade was transferred to Gen. James Longstreet's command in eastern Tennessee that fall. He reported to Gen. John C. Breckinridge in April 1864, and fought at New Market (May 15) and Cold Harbor (June 3). Wharton also participated in Jubal Early's raid on Washington, D.C. (June 27–August 7). He led a division in the 1864 Shenandoah Valley campaign but never received the appropriate rank of major general. Though official recognition rarely came from Richmond authorities, his superiors in the army demonstrated their confidence in Wharton by assigning him responsibilities above his rank.

After the war he devoted himself to mining enterprises in southwestern Virginia. He died on May 12, 1906.

BIBLIOGRAPHY

Hotchkiss, Jed. *Virginia.* Vol. 3 of *Confederate Military History.* Edited by Clement A. Evans. Atlanta, 1899. Vol. 4 of extended ed. Wilmington, N.C., 1987.
Wert, Jeffry D. *From Winchester to Cedar Creek.* Carlisle, Pa., 1987.
Wharton, J. U. H. "Maj. Gen. Gabriel C. Wharton." *Confederate Veteran* 8 (July 1990): 320. Reprint, Wilmington, N.C., 1985.

PETER S. CARMICHAEL

WHARTON, JOHN AUSTIN (1828–1865), major general. Born July 3, 1828, near Nashville, Tennessee, Wharton as a child was brought to Galveston, Texas. He attended South Carolina College (later the University of South Carolina) and married the governor's daughter. He opened a law practice in Brazoria, Texas, and in 1861 was a member of the secession convention.

When the Civil War began, Wharton left for Virginia but fell ill and returned home. He joined Col. Benjamin Franklin Terry's Texas Rangers (Eighth Texas Cavalry) as a company captain. Eventually he succeeded to command of the regiment and led it at Shiloh where he was wounded. He took part in the Kentucky campaign in 1862 and was

JOHN AUSTIN WHARTON. LIBRARY OF CONGRESS

promoted to brigadier general on November 18, 1862. Wharton served under Nathan Bedford Forrest and Joseph Wheeler and distinguished himself at Murfreesboro and Chickamauga. He was promoted to major general in November 1863. In April 1864, while on leave from the Army of Tennessee, Wharton arrived at Shreveport, Louisiana, where he was asked to take command of Richard Taylor's cavalry after the death of Brig. Gen. Thomas Green. He fought in the final days of the Red River campaign and remained in the department for the rest of the war. On April 6, 1865, Wharton died at John B. Magruder's headquarters at Houston after Col. George W. Baylor, claiming that Wharton had struck him in the face and called him a liar, drew his pistol and shot him, though he was unarmed. Wharton is buried in Austin.

BIBLIOGRAPHY

Blackburn, James Knox Polk. *Reminiscences of the Terry Rangers.* Austin, Tex., 1919.

Giles, Leonidas B. *Terry's Texas Rangers.* Austin, Tex., 1911.

Jeffries, C. C. *Terry's Rangers.* New York, 1961.

"Statistics About Gen. Wharton." *Confederate Veteran* 5 (1893): 530. Reprint, Wilmington, N.C., 1985.

Wright, Marcus J., comp., and Harold B. Simpson, ed. *Texas in the War, 1861–1865.* Hillsboro, Tex., 1965.

ANNE J. BAILEY

WHEELER, JOSEPH (1836–1906), major general and U.S. congressman. Born September 10, 1836, in Augusta, Georgia, Wheeler spent much of his childhood in Connecticut. In 1859, he graduated from West Point and received the rank of second lieutenant in the regiment of mounted rifles stationed at Fort Craig, New Mexico Territory. On April 22, 1861, Wheeler resigned his commission to join the Confederate army as a first lieutenant of artillery.

By 1862, West Point officers were in great demand in the South, and Wheeler received a quick promotion to colonel, leading the Nineteenth Alabama Infantry into combat at Shiloh. Afterward, he transferred to the cavalry. Gen. Braxton Bragg, now in command of the Army of Mississippi, named Wheeler his cavalry chief. In this capacity he led the mounted arm of the Confederate armies of Mississippi and later Tennessee throughout the rest of the war.

During Bragg's invasion of Kentucky, Wheeler was notable for his daring leadership of the Southern horsemen, earning promotion to brigadier general on October 30, 1862. He received the rank of major general on January 30, 1863, and later was recommended for, but not confirmed as lieutenant general. Wheeler ably commanded Bragg's cavalry in the Murfreesboro, Tullahoma, and Chattanooga campaigns. By May 1864, he was the ranking Confederate cavalry leader.

During the Atlanta campaign, Wheeler gained additional notoriety by raiding Union Gen. William Tecumseh Sherman's supply and communications lines. After the fall of Atlanta, Wheeler's troopers were the only organized opposition to Sherman's march through Georgia, and the Confederate cavalrymen fared badly. By the end of the year, the corps had earned a reputation for lack of discipline. Wheeler continued to lead the cavalry in the Carolina campaigns until superseded by Lt. Gen. Wade Hampton.

During the course of the war, Wheeler fought in 127 battles; he was wounded three times, had sixteen horses shot out from under him, and had thirty-six staff officers fall by his side. His active style of fighting led to his sobriquet "Fighting Joe." Though he was somewhat disappointing as an independent commander, his true genius was displayed when his cavalry covered the movements of the main army. In 1863, he published *Cavalry Tactics,* a manual for use by the mounted arm.

Wheeler was captured by Federal troops in May 1865 and imprisoned temporarily at Fort Delaware. After his release, he moved first to New Orleans and then in 1868 to Wheeler Station, Alabama, where he started a law practice and a plantation. In 1881, he entered politics, serving eight terms in the U.S. House of Representatives. During the Spanish-American War, Wheeler joined the U.S. Army, serving with the rank of major general of volunteers. He led a division of troops at the Battles of El Caney and Kettle Hill, Cuba, and later served in the Philippines. He retired from the service on September 10, 1900, with the rank of brigadier general of regulars. Wheeler died on January 25, 1906, in Brooklyn, New York.

[*See also* Wheeler's Raids.]

BIBLIOGRAPHY

Dyer, John Percy. *"Fightin' Joe" Wheeler.* Baton Rouge, La., 1941.

Dyer, John Percy. *From Shiloh to San Juan.* Baton Rouge, La., 1961.

Lawson, Lewis A. *Wheeler's Last Raid.* Greenwood, Fla., 1986.

DONALD S. FRAZIER

WHEELER'S RAIDS. As commander of the cavalry corps of the Army of Tennessee, Joseph Wheeler, Jr., enjoyed only limited success as a raider. His first expedition, reminiscent of J. E. B. Stuart's famous ride around McClellan, came during the Battle of Murfreesboro, December 31, 1862 to January 2, 1863. With 1,100 men, Wheeler rode around the opposing Army of the Cumberland, not once, but two and a half times, destroying a thousand wagons and capturing hundreds of horses, mules, and prisoners.

A week later, he captured five transports and a gunboat on the Cumberland River, northwest of Nashville. Some of his men also swam the icy river and burned an enormous supply depot at Ashland, Tennessee, on January 12, 1863, which, combined with the losses at Murfreesboro, virtually immobilized the Army of the Cumberland for the next six months.

The exploit earned Wheeler a promotion to major general and a vote of thanks from the Confederate Congress. It also roused the ire of older, more experienced subordinates, such as Nathan Bedford Forrest, John Hunt Morgan, and John Austin Wharton, who resented taking orders from "that boy."

After the Confederate victory at the Battle of Chickamauga left the Army of the Cumberland besieged in Chattanooga, Wheeler led 3,700 men across the Tennessee River forty miles east of the city on September 29, 1863. Sweeping over Walden's Ridge, he intercepted a heavily laden supply train in the Sequatchie Valley on October 2, destroying an estimated eight hundred to one thousand wagons, but Federal horsemen hounded him so closely he was unable to inflict any lasting damage on the vital railroad linking Chattanooga and Nashville. Blue-coated cavalry overtook him near Farmington, Tennessee, and drove him across the Tennessee River at Muscle Shoals, Alabama, on October 9 with the loss of 2,000 men.

During the Atlanta campaign, Confederate newspapers and politicians were sharply critical of Wheeler for failing to cut the Western and Atlantic Railroad, the sole source of supply for Union Maj. Gen. William Tecumseh Sherman's advancing armies. Wheeler was eager to try, but the Army of Tennessee was so badly outnumbered his cavalry was compelled to fight on foot alongside the infantry.

Not until the army reached Atlanta and withdrew inside the city's formidable defenses was Wheeler given free rein. Between July 27 and 31, 1864, he pursued, caught, and defeated three raiding columns bent on wrecking the Macon and Western Railroad, putting Sherman's cavalry corps out of action for almost a month.

This enabled Wheeler to leave Covington, Georgia on August 10, 1864, with 4,000 men and the long-awaited orders to cut Sherman's supply line. He tore up a few sections of track between Atlanta and Chattanooga and captured a herd of beefs, but when high water kept him from crossing the rain-swollen Tennessee River near Chattanooga, he wandered into the strategically barren highlands of eastern Tennessee. Eventually he swung west, cutting the railroads south of Nashville before being chased across the Tennessee River at Florence, Alabama, on September 9. The damage was quickly repaired, and despite his glowing reports, Wheeler's last raid did little more than deprive the Army of Tennessee of half its cavalry during a critical stage of the Atlanta campaign.

BIBLIOGRAPHY

Dodson, William C. *Campaigns of Wheeler and His Cavalry, 1862–1865.* Atlanta, 1899.

Dubose, John W. *General Joseph Wheeler and the Army of Tennessee.* New York, 1912.

Dyer, John P. *"Fightin' Joe" Wheeler.* Baton Rouge, La., 1941.

Lawson, Lewis A. *Wheeler's Last Raid.* Greenwood, Fla., 1986.

DAVID EVANS

WHIG PARTY. Disturbed by Andrew Jackson's increasing executive power and his opposition to governmental economic activism, opponents organized a coalition of National Republicans, conservative Democrats, and Anti-Masons. Jackson's opponents eventually adopted the name "Whig" as a symbol of resistance to tyranny, since they believed Old Hickory far too powerful an executive who consulted too frequently with personal friends rather than with cabinet members confirmed by Congress. Originally derived from Whiggamore, a Scot who marched on Edinburgh in 1648 to oppose the court party, and applied by extension to those who opposed the royal prerogative in Britain, the name Whig had been adopted by American revolutionaries during the war for independence before its use in the 1830s.

Until the controversy over the expansion of slavery into the territories tore the Whig party apart in the 1850s, the Democratic and Whig parties remained quite evenly balanced in the South. The Whigs dominated in North Carolina, Kentucky, and Tennessee, holding at the same time competitive strength in Virginia and Georgia. The competition offered by the Whigs promoted voter participation and broadened the scope of politics.

Strong party leadership developed in the Southern states. Notable among the Whig luminaries were Alexander H. Stephens and John M. Barrien of Georgia, John Bell and Ephraim Foster of Tennessee, and Henry Clay and John J. Crittenden of Kentucky.

Countering Jackson's general opposition to Federal promotion of economic development, Clay proposed the American System. The Kentuckian offered a protective tariff, distribution of money from sale of Federal lands, construction of roads and canals, and the rechartering of the Second Bank of the United States. As conservatives, the Whigs expected to avoid economic leveling through growth and increased opportunity.

Clay's program did not prove uniformly attractive to Southerners. Proposals for public roads and canals attracted certain well-placed commercial interests. Some, however, opposed internal improvements because they feared the Federal government would fund such projects through revenue from the protective tariff, which bore most heavily on the South. The southeastern Whigs generally opposed the construction of a national road, but many in the Southwest supported it.

At the same time, Whig principles appealed to many evangelical Protestants. Profoundly influenced by the Second Great Awakening, the Southern Whigs proudly stood for religion, morality, paternalism, and duty. Accusations of adultery against Jackson and Secretary of War John Eaton drew denunciations of the two men from moralistic Whigs. Whigs promoted public education, prison and mental hospital reform, and social justice. Even Southern frontiersman Davy Crockett opposed the theft of Cherokee lands.

In practice, the Whigs remained viable competitors until the 1850s. They did well in congressional elections during the 1840s, controlling the House from 1841 through 1842 and from 1847 through 1850. They lost the presidential elections of 1832 and 1836, but succeeded in electing two Virginia-born war heroes—William Henry Harrison (then of Ohio) in 1840 and Zachary Taylor (who grew up in Kentucky but lived in Louisiana) in 1848.

After Whig presidential candidate Winfield Scott's decisive 1852 defeat, the demoralized party failed to mend the growing rift over slavery between its two great sectional wings. Northern Whigs generally opposed slavery and its expansion into the territories, whereas Southerners defended it as a positive good. As the division over slavery deepened, many Southern Whigs like Stephens swallowed their pride and moved into the Democratic party.

When Southern states began to secede, many old Whigs like Stephens opposed the breakup of the Union. As businessmen, professionals, and planters tied to a national market, they had little to gain from disruption or war. Nevertheless, loyal to their section, they went along when their states seceded.

As a ticket-balancing measure, Stephens was elected vice president of the Confederacy to complement Mississippi Democrat Jefferson Davis. The Confederacy repudiated some Whig principles by prohibiting protective tariffs and appropriations for internal improvements. The Confederate Constitution offered a sop by proposing congressional seats for cabinet members, but the Congress failed to approve implementing legislation. Although organized political parties failed to emerge in the Confederacy, ex-Whigs tended to show less enthusiasm for military and executive power than did ex-Democrats. Whigs enjoyed a resurgence in some Southern states during the war because of their defense of constitutionalism and compromise. In the Georgia legislature, for instance, Stephens's brother Linton secured the passage of resolutions calling for an armistice followed by plebiscites on joining the Union or Confederacy. The party did not reemerge after the Civil War, and though some former Southern Whigs joined the Republican party, most became Democrats.

BIBLIOGRAPHY

Alexander, Thomas B. *Sectional Stress and Party Strength: A Study of Roll-Call Voting Patterns in the United States House of Representatives, 1836–1860.* Nashville, Tenn., 1967.

Brown, Thomas. *Politics and Statesmanship: Essays on the American Whig Party.* New York, 1985.

Howe, Daniel Walker. *The Political Culture of the American Whigs.* Chicago, 1979.

McCormick, Richard P. *The Second American Party System: Party Formation in the Jacksonian Era.* Chapel Hill, N.C., 1966.

Sellers, Charles Grier, Jr. "Who Were the Southern Whigs?" *American Historical Review* 59 (January 1954): 335–346.

THOMAS G. ALEXANDER AND TRACY L. ALEXANDER

WHITE, DANIEL PRICE (1814–1890), congressman from Kentucky and military surgeon. Kentuckian Daniel P. White served as a Confederate congressman for only six weeks and played an insignificant role in Congress's proceedings. He was born in Greensburg, Green County, Kentucky, attended Centre College of Kentucky, and studied medicine both at Transylvania University's renowned medical department and in Cincinnati. In 1837 he established a successful medical practice in Greensburg but eventually abandoned medicine in favor of farming and politics. A Democrat, White was elected in 1847 to the Kentucky House of Representatives, where he served many terms. In 1857 he became Speaker of the House.

In 1860 White attended the Democratic National Convention in Charleston, South Carolina, and in the November election was an elector-at-large for Stephen A. Douglas. Following Abraham Lincoln's election, White favored Kentucky's secession, and after war broke out, he transported his twelve slaves to Yell County, Arkansas, for safety. In 1861 White served as a surgeon in an unofficial capacity for Kentucky volunteers who assembled at Camp Boone. In December 1861, White was elected from the Fifth District to the Provisional Congress. During his brief tenure he served on no committees. Though White fought to retain the prerogative of Kentucky's Confederate governor in terms of military appointments, on other issues he supported Jefferson Davis's centralization measures. For example, he did not oppose the utilization of Kentucky's home guards by the central government. Like Kentucky's other representatives, he favored an invasion of the commonwealth to liberate the state from Union troops. White declined to stand for election to the First Congress in 1862. He served the remainder of the war as a voluntary surgeon with units, including the First Kentucky Brigade, attending to the troops at Shiloh, Prairie Grove, Poison Spring, and Jenkins' Ferry.

After Appomattox, White became a partner in a tobacco business in Louisville.

BIBLIOGRAPHY

Quisenberry, A. C. "The Alleged Secession of Kentucky." *Register of the Kentucky State Historical Society* 15 (1917): 15–32.

Wakelyn, Jon L. *Biographical Dictionary of the Confederacy.* Edited by Frank E. Vandiver. Westport, Conn., 1977.

Warner, Ezra J., and W. Buck Yearns. *Biographical Register of the Confederate Congress.* Baton Rouge, La., 1975.

JOHN DAVID SMITH

WHITE HOUSE. No official residence was ready for President Jefferson Davis when he arrived in Richmond with his family in May 1861. City officials quickly purchased the Brockenbrough Mansion on Clay and Twelfth streets for $35,000 (plus $7,894.97 for furnishings). Davis refused to accept the house as a gift, so the Confederate government leased it from the city, and the Davis family moved in on July 29.

Designed by Robert Mills, the stately neoclassical mansion dated to 1818. The two-story hillside house was extensively remodeled by subsequent owners. A third floor was added, along with ornate Victorian details.

"We . . . began to feel more at home when walking through the old-fashioned terraced garden or the large airy rooms in the seclusion of family life," Varina Howell Davis recalled. Although her husband kept his formal office in a nearby government building, he also had a study and reception room in their new home. Although "the rooms are comparatively few," Mrs. Davis wrote of the mansion, the effect was of a "very large house." She did not mention it, but one of its features, a newspaper reported, was "a well-appointed bathroom on the second floor."

Mrs. Davis entertained often and lavishly in her new surroundings and gave birth to two children there. But life in the mansion had its dark side. Their son Joseph was killed there in 1864, plunging over a banister into the brick courtyard in the rear. And servants periodically fled, once setting fire to the house during a levee. "Constant robberies, servants coming and going daily to the Yankees, carrying over silver etc.," observed Richmond diarist Mary Boykin Chesnut, "does not conduce to make a home happy."

The Confederate White House was abandoned altogether when the president sent his family south in March 1865, giving his wife little time even to pack. When Union forces occupied the mansion they found "all the furniture . . . undisturbed in the house of the traitor chief." By 1867 the house had become headquarters of Military District No. 1

CONFEDERATE WHITE HOUSE, RICHMOND, VIRGINIA. Now adjacent to the Museum of the Confederacy, the building has been designated a national historic landmark. NATIONAL ARCHIVES

under Reconstruction. It was returned to the city of Richmond in 1870, but authorities then inexplicably auctioned off its historic contents. Later that year the house reopened as a school. Not until 1889 did the Confederate Memorial Ladies' Association raise $31,000 to purchase it and convert it into the Confederate Museum in 1896.

In the late 1980s the Museum of the Confederacy, as it was then known, undertook a $4.5 million renovation. Today the old Davis mansion has been restored as closely as possible to its wartime appearance—including its exterior color. Despite its nickname, the "White House of the Confederacy" was painted Confederate gray.

BIBLIOGRAPHY

Davis, Varina Howell. *Jefferson Davis, Ex-President of the Confederate States of America: A Memoir.* 2 vols. New York, 1890.

Hill, Tucker. *Victory in Defeat: Jefferson Davis and the Lost Cause.* Richmond, Va., 1986.

Holzer, Harold, and Mark E. Neely, Jr. "America's Other White House." *Antique Trader Weekly,* August 16, 1989, 58–61.

Holzer, Harold, and Mark E. Neely, Jr. "The Miserable First Ladies." *Civil War* 21 (December 1989): 8–14.

HAROLD HOLZER

WHITFIELD, JOHN WILKINS (1818–1879), U.S. congressional delegate from Kansas and brigadier general. Whitfield was born on March 11, 1818, in Franklin, Tennessee. Raised and educated in his home state, he left to serve as captain of the First Tennessee Infantry and lieutenant colonel of the Second Tennessee Infantry during the Mexican War. In 1853 he migrated to Missouri, briefly serving as an Indian agent. In 1854, Whitfield won election as delegate to the U.S. Congress from Kansas Territory. He held the seat in Congress until 1857, although the House of Representatives declared the seat vacant for a brief time in 1856. Afterward, Whitfield became register of the land office at Doniphan, Kansas, from 1857 to 1861.

With the outbreak of the Civil War, Whitfield entered Confederate service as captain of the Twenty-seventh Texas Cavalry Regiment, receiving subsequent promotions to major and colonel. He fought at Elkhorn Tavern, Arkansas, on March 7 and 8, 1862, and on September 19 served under Maj. Gen. Sterling Price at the Battle of Iuka, where he was severely wounded. Attached to Maj. Gen. Earl Van Dorn's command in the spring of 1863, Whitfield received a promotion to brigadier general on May 9. He fought under Gen. Joseph E. Johnston in the Vicksburg campaign and commanded a brigade under Brig. Gen. William Hicks Jackson in Mississippi. On June 29, 1865, he was paroled at Columbus, Texas.

Whitfield remained in Texas, farming and raising stock in Lavaca County. He represented the county in the state legislature and died near Hallettsville, Texas, on October 27, 1879.

BIBLIOGRAPHY

Biographical Dictionary of the American Congress, 1774–1984. Washington, D.C., 1984.

U.S. War Department. *War of the Rebellion: A Compilation of the Official Records of the Union and Confederate Armies.* Washington, D.C., 1880–1901. Ser. 1, vol. 17, pt. 1, pp. 128–129.

Warner, Ezra J. *Generals in Gray: Lives of the Confederate Commanders.* Baton Rouge, La., 1959.

BRIAN S. WILLS

WHITFIELD, ROBERT HENRY (1814–1868), congressman from Virginia. A native of Nansemond County, Virginia, Whitfield attended Randolph-Macon College and graduated from the University of Virginia. He began to practice law in the town of Smithfield in Isle of Wight County. He married Rebecca Ann Peebles, and they had five children. Although he failed to win an election to the House of Representatives, in the next year, 1852, he was elected commonwealth attorney for Isle of Wight and served until 1860.

A Unionist member of the 1861 Virginia convention, Whitfield nevertheless advocated secession if the Washington peace conference failed. Like other Unionists at the convention, he was against secession on the first ballot and for it on the second. He refused to take the oath of loyalty in 1862 when Northern troops occupied Smithfield and was briefly arrested but then released. He won election in 1863 to the Second Congress where he served on the Patents and Naval Affairs committees. His attendance was poor throughout, and he resigned in March 1865 just before the legislature's last meeting. As a congressman he opposed the administration in economic matters but did not wish to limit government military authority.

He returned to his Smithfield plantation after the war and struggled to recoup his serious financial losses. Whitfield died on October 5, 1868.

BIBLIOGRAPHY

Gaines, William H., ed. *Biographical Register of Members, Virginia State Convention of 1861, First Session.* Richmond, Va., 1969.

Wakelyn, Jon L. *Biographical Dictionary of the Confederacy.* Edited by Frank E. Vandiver. Westport, Conn., 1977.

Warner, Ezra J., and W. Buck Yearns. *Biographical Register of the Confederacy.* Baton Rouge, La., 1975.

NELSON D. LANKFORD

WHITING, W. H. C. (1824–1865), major general. William Whiting, a native of Biloxi, Mississippi, was born March 22, 1824. He graduated from West Point in 1845 and entered the Engineer Corps in 1858. In this capacity he worked on fortification construction and on river and harbor improvements.

When the war began, Whiting resigned his commission in the U.S. Army and was appointed major and chief engineer in the Confederate service. On July 21, 1861, he was promoted to brigadier general for his service in transferring troops to the battlefield of Manassas. In 1862 he saw action at Seven Pines, in Jackson's Shenandoah Valley campaign, and in the Seven Days' Battles at Richmond. Following these engagements, Whiting was ordered to Wilmington, North Carolina, where he developed Fort Fisher on the Cape Fear River.

He was appointed major general on April 22, 1863, and in the spring of 1864 was sent to the Petersburg, Virginia, area to fight against Union Gen. Benjamin Butler's forces in the Bermuda Hundred campaign. His poor performance in the action at Walthall Junction on May 16 led to accusations of his being intoxicated. He asked to be relieved of command and returned to North Carolina.

On January 15, 1865, after a prolonged naval bombardment and land assault, Fort Fisher fell to Union forces. In the hand-to-hand fighting, Whiting, while in the act of tearing down a Federal flag, received two wounds. He was carried as a prisoner of war to Fort Columbus on Governor's Island, New York, where he died on March 10, 1865. He is buried in Oakdale Cemetery at Wilmington.

BIBLIOGRAPHY

Gragg, Rod. *Confederate Goliath: The Battle of Fort Fisher.* New York, 1991.

Hill, D. H., Jr. *North Carolina.* Vol. 4 of *Confederate Military History.* Edited by Clement A. Evans. Atlanta, 1899. Vol. 5 of extended ed. Wilmington, N.C., 1987.

Lamb, William. *Story of Fort Fisher.* Carolina Beach, N.C., 1966.

Warner, Ezra J. *Generals in Gray: Lives of the Confederate Commanders.* Baton Rouge, La., 1959.

CHRIS CALKINS

WHITTLE, WILLIAM C. (1805–1878), naval officer. Whittle, who was born in Norfolk, Virginia, was appointed a midshipman on May 10, 1820. He participated in the Seminole War and was wounded at the Battle of Tuxpan during the Mexican War. He resigned his commission as a commander on April 20, 1861, and was immediately appointed a captain in the Virginia State Navy and charged with the defense of the York River.

On June 11, Whittle was appointed a commander in the Confederate navy, to date from March 26. Despite his controversies with army officers (about which Robert E. Lee commented, "Petty jealousies . . . when carried so far as to interfere with the effectiveness of a command, become both criminal and contemptible"), Whittle remained in charge of the three batteries that guarded the York River. In January 1862, he commanded the naval forces at Columbus, Kentucky, but Federal activity in the Gulf of Mexico brought about his transfer to New Orleans. There, on March 29, he took charge of the naval station and three gunboats on Lake Pontchartrain. Although never in command of all the naval forces on the lower Mississippi River, nor responsible for completing the ironclad *Mississippi,* Whittle became something of a scapegoat after the fall of New Orleans. Although involved in various investigations in 1862, he was promoted to captain on October 23, to date from February 8. Assigned to Richmond in 1863, he apparently remained there awaiting orders until the end of the war.

Whittle died in Virginia in 1878. His son, William C. Whittle, Jr., was the first lieutenant aboard CSS *Shenandoah.*

BIBLIOGRAPHY

Scharf, J. Thomas. *History of the Confederate States Navy from Its Organization to the Surrender of Its Last Vessel.* New York, 1887. Reprint, New York, 1977.

Whittle, W. C. "The Opening of the Lower Mississippi in April, 1862—A Reply to Admiral Porter." *Southern Historical Society Papers* 13 (1885): 560–572. Reprint, Wilmington, N.C., 1990.

LAWRENCE L. HEWITT

WICKHAM, WILLIAMS CARTER (1820–1888), brigadier general and congressman from Virginia. Wickham was born in Richmond September 21, 1820. After attending the University of Virginia, he practiced law in his home county of Hanover. Prior to the war he was a member of the Virginia House of Delegates (1849) and Senate (1859) and was a justice in Hanover County. In November 1859 he formed the Hanover Light Dragoons, a mounted militia company. Wickham was elected by Hanover County to attend the Virginia state convention on secession. He was a Unionist initially, but when the convention's outcome was clear, he went along with his colleagues and offered the services of his militia company.

At First Manassas, the Hanover Dragoons pursued the Federals as they retreated across Bull Run to Centreville. On September 18, 1861, Wickham was appointed lieutenant colonel of the Fourth Virginia Cavalry, and when it was reorganized in April 1862, he was elected colonel. On May 4, 1862, during the Battle of Williamsburg, Wickham was sabered in the side, but remained saddled until the battle was over and the open field before Fort Magruder was secured. While recuperating from his wound at his home in Ashland, Wickham was captured by Federal troops on May 29. He was paroled on the spot, promising not to bear arms until his exchange. Though he was ready to rejoin his

WILLIAMS CARTER WICKHAM. LIBRARY OF CONGRESS

regiment in a month, he had to wait until August when he was exchanged for his wife's kinsman, Lt. Col. Thomas Kane of Pennsylvania.

Throughout 1862, Wickham and the Fourth Virginia Cavalry participated in all the major campaigns undertaken by Robert E. Lee's Army of Northern Virginia. During J. E. B. Stuart's raid on Catlett's Station (August 22–23), Wickham was praised for being "energetic and thorough-going" by the general. Wickham's regiment was one of the first units to occupy Manassas Junction on August 26, and the men "supplied themselves with all they could carry away." As they had a year earlier at Manassas, Wickham's men pursued the fleeing Federals after the Second Battle of Manassas was fought on August 30. From September 5 until September 19, Wickham's regiment was continually engaged with Federal troops during the Sharpsburg campaign. The 259-man regiment also rode with Stuart on October 10 on his raid into Chambersburg, Pennsylvania. When the Army of Northern Virginia moved back to the Rapidan-Rappahannock River line late in October, Wickham commanded the brigade for the disabled Fitzhugh Lee. On November 3, while protecting A. P. Hill's troops as they moved by Ashby's Gap, the Fourth Virginia engaged Federal cavalry forces at Upperville. The regiment, fighting dismounted, slowly withdrew before the Union forces. The pike was contested all the way to the gap, where the Fourth held the Federals at bay until all the infantry had passed. During this fight, Wickham was wounded in the neck and was praised by Stuart for "great zeal, ability, and bravery."

In April 1863, Wickham ran for and won a seat in the House of Representatives, but he would delay taking his seat until November 1864. During the Chancellorsville campaign, Wickham and the Fourth Virginia were actively engaged covering the army's flanks, capturing some 250 prisoners from April 28 until May 5. At Kelly's Ford, on June 9, the Fourth experienced its worst defeat. Coming up to support the Second South Carolina Cavalry near Stevensburg, the Fourth was overrun, suffering 43 casualties, despite Wickham's efforts to rally his men. Wickham thought the affair so disgraceful he kept his report short, not trying to explain the matter, but leaving it to Stuart to decide if an inquiry should be undertaken. After this humiliation, Wickham and the Fourth redeemed themselves during the Battle of Aldie on June 17 when they held back a much larger Federal force. Wickham commanded his regiment throughout the Gettysburg campaign when it accompanied Stuart. On September 1, with the reorganization of Stuart's cavalry, Wickham was promoted to brigadier general and given command of four cavalry regiments of Fitz Lee's division. The promotion may have been an effort to keep him from leaving the army for Congress—he was apparently promoted over Thomas Munford of the Second Virginia Cavalry. Lee wrote on September 4, "Genl. Wickham still continues in the service, but I fear is getting tired of it."

In February 1864 Wickham's brigade helped counter the Federal raid into Albemarle County, and during the spring and summer, it played a major role in all the battles around Richmond. During the pursuit of Philip Sheridan from Spotsylvania Court House to Yellow Tavern, the brigade led the harassment of the Federal's rear guard. At one point Wickham led his old regiment, the Fourth Virginia, in a headlong charge into the Union ranks, shouting "Give them hell, boys! Damn 'em, give them hell!" In August Wickham's brigade was ordered to the Shenandoah Valley to support Gen. Jubal Early. At Winchester, after Wickham took command of the division for the wounded Fitz Lee, his brigade covered Early's rear during the withdrawal up the valley, pushing back the Federal pursuers along the Luray Pike and preventing Early from being outflanked. When Sheridan began withdrawing down the valley in late September, Wickham's brigade led the Confederate pursuit, engaging in battles at Bridgewater, Mt. Crawford, Brock's Gap, Tom's Brook, and Cedar Creek.

On November 9, 1864, Wickham resigned his commission

in the Army of Northern Virginia and took his seat in Congress. He had run his 1863 campaign on a platform of seeking peace, and when he won by a large margin, his election was seen as a "rebuke of the administration," as a Richmond paper put it. He was appointed to the Military Affairs Committee and generally opposed the Davis administration. He saw little hope for victory by late 1864 and wanted to end the suffering and sacrifice of the war. He was against extensions of emergency laws and giving the president additional powers. He worked to settle citizens' claims against the Confederate government, to relieve the hardships of areas under Federal occupation, to exchange prisoners, to exempt men from military service, and to improve the lot of the common soldier. In February 1865 his Bill to Increase the Efficiency of the Cavalry was passed by Congress. This bill required the government to supply horses to cavalry units operating outside of their home states; when cavalrymen lost their horses, good soldiers were to receive remounts and the "unfit" were to be reassigned. In January Wickham wrote, "The house of cards maintained by Davis and Company [is] crumbl[ing]." His actions culminated in his support for the Hampton Roads peace conference of February 3, 1865.

After the war, Wickham joined the Republican party, alienating many of his comrades, and became president of the Virginia Central Railroad. In 1883 he was elected to the Virginia Senate, where he served until his death on July 23, 1888. In 1891, a statue of General Wickham was dedicated in Monroe Park, Richmond. Wickham wrote to a friend after the war in a letter reflecting his early Unionist sentiments, "I have often said to those with whom I was on terms of friendship that I never saw the United States flag, even when approaching it in battle, that I did not feel arising those emotions of regard for it that had been wont to inspire. I have in like manner said that one of the most painful sights I had ever seen was on the night of the first battle of Manassas, when I saw an officer trailing the flag in the dust before a regiment of the line."

BIBLIOGRAPHY

Dowdey, Clifford, and Louis H. Manarin, eds. *The Wartime Papers of R. E. Lee.* New York, 1961.

Hotchkiss, Jed. *Virginia.* Vol. 3 of *Confederate Military History.* Edited by Clement A. Evans. Atlanta, 1899. Vol. 4 of extended ed. Wilmington, N.C., 1987.

Warner, Ezra J. *Generals in Gray: Lives of the Confederate Commanders.* Baton Rouge, La., 1959.

Wright, Marcus Joseph. *General Officers of the Confederate Army.* New York, 1911.

KENNETH L. STILES

WIGFALL, LOUIS T. (1816–1874), brigadier general and congressman from Texas. Louis Trezevant Wigfall was born April 21, 1816, to Levi Durand and Eliza

LOUIS T. WIGFALL. LIBRARY OF CONGRESS

(Thomson) Wigfall, in Edgefield, a frontier district of South Carolina. Both his parents' families had been among the first to arrive in South Carolina and were socially prominent. As a boy and a student at a private military academy, the University of Virginia, and South Carolina College, Wigfall came to believe in a society led by the planter class and based on black slavery and the chivalric code. Politically, he became an avid spokesman for state rights and secession, drawing on his classical education in oratory, history, literature, and Latin.

Wigfall's brief experiences in military school and in the Seminole War helped him get an appointment as a South Carolina militia colonel. He became known for pistol marksmanship, reckless courage, and a thin-skinned sense of honor. He also earned a reputation for drinking, gambling, and financial carelessness while neglecting the law practice his brother had left to him.

In the 1840 South Carolina gubernatorial campaign that pitted two aristocratic cliques against each other, Wigfall supported John P. Richardson out of dislike for the Brooks family, who supported James H. Hammond, Richardson's principal rival. Wigfall's contribution to the campaign was to take over covert editorship of the *Edgefield Advertiser,* turning the newspaper's support from Hammond to Richardson. In well-reasoned editorials, Wigfall helped win the state for Richardson.

When it became known that Wigfall had written the editorials, some of the Brooks family attacked him personally. Over the next five months, Wigfall was involved in a fistfight, three near-duels, two actual duels, and a shooting with the Brooks family—all of which left one man dead and two, including Wigfall, wounded. In the shooting incident, Wigfall fired upon and killed a young man who had shot at him first. In one of the duels, Wigfall and another Brooks family member missed on their first shots and were persuaded to accept an arbitrated settlement favorable to Wigfall. In the last duel, both men were wounded, Wigfall in the thigh and Preston Brooks in the hip. (This wound may have been the reason Brooks carried the cane he later used to beat Senator Charles Sumner of Massachusetts on the floor of the Senate.)

Although Wigfall remained a firm believer in the dueling, this was his last duel. His reputation for violence persisted, however, and he did nothing to discourage false stories about his dueling exploits. Rather, he capitalized on his purported willingness to shoot people who disagreed with him, intimidating political opponents who were fearful of triggering his temper.

Governor Richardson appointed Wigfall aide-de-camp for his services in the 1840 election campaign, but his first foray into politics and newspaper editing had been costly. Although a grand jury failed to bring in an indictment for the killing of the young man and murder charges were dropped, many people in the community still blamed Wigfall. His neglected law practice dwindled further, and despite his marriage to his respected second cousin, Charlotte Cross, Wigfall was nearly ruined socially, professionally, and financially. Their first son's serious illness became an additional drain on their finances.

But even as his son lay dying and his debts mounted, Wigfall became more interested than ever in politics. As a delegate to the state Democratic convention, he helped draw up resolutions for the 1844 campaign. At the convention, Wigfall spoke in favor of the annexation of Texas in order to maintain the right of slavery, and against protective tarriffs, seeing them as a threat to Southern civilization. John C. Calhoun argued only for nullification to oppose the tariffs, but Wigfall, sixteen years ahead of most South Carolinians, said the state should secede, alone if necessary.

Unable to rebuild his standing in South Carolina, Wigfall moved Charlotte and their three children to Texas in 1846, a year after it joined the Union. He opened a law office in Marshall, Texas, building a practice and a reputation as a lawyer. Nevertheless, his first concern was still politics, and he was never financially solvent for more than a few weeks at a time.

Wigfall headed a committee that formulated resolutions reiterating the state rights argument and condemning the Wilmot Proviso and the concept of "squatter sovereignty" to prevent expansion of slavery into territories. Speaking for the resolutions, Wigfall asserted that the Federal government was a creation of the states, not of the people, and that each state had the right to leave the Union if it acted "unconstitutionally." Although the resolutions passed, Wigfall expressed sorrow that Texas would not take the lead in seceding.

Named in 1850 to the Texas House of Representatives, Wigfall attacked Sam Houston, then a U.S. senator and strongly pro-Union, as a recreant to Texas and the South and denounced him for voting for the Compromise of 1850. Wigfall played a major role in organizing Texas Democrats to oppose Houston and the Know-Nothings in 1855 and 1856. He led a successful fight in the Texas legislature to pass a resolution censuring Houston for his opposition to the Kansas-Nebraska Act and was widely credited with Houston's defeat for the governorship in 1857, which put an end to Houston's influence in the U.S. Senate. Now recognized in Texas as the leader of the radical state rights Democrats, Wigfall was elected to the Texas Senate in 1857 and had a strong voice in the 1858 state Democratic convention, which adopted a state rights platform.

With the breakup of the Know-Nothings, however, many moderates moved back into the Democratic party, and it appeared that Wigfall's radicalism was repudiated. He chose this time, however, to push two of his ultraradical proposals: the revival of the foreign slave trade and filibustering in Cuba, Mexico, and farther south for more slave territory. When these proposals split Texas Democrats, Wigfall had to abandon them. Nevertheless, he was elected to the U.S. Senate in 1859, with the inadvertent help of John Brown. By capitalizing on the fear engendered by Brown's Harpers Ferry raid, Wigfall defeated more moderate candidates.

Wigfall was the most pugnacious of the radical members of the Thirty-sixth Congress, who were intensifying the sectionalism that was leading to war. As a freshman senator, Wigfall was in the forefront of the Southern fire-eaters, earning a reputation for eloquence, witty but bitter debate, acerbic taunts, and a readiness for personal encounters. And his debates did not end on the Senate floor; he frequented bars and gaming rooms, always seeking out adversaries. In opposing the Homestead Act, partly on the ground that 160 acres was too small for a plantation with slaves, Wigfall lampooned it as a bill that would provide land for the landless and homes for the homeless, but not "niggers for the niggerless," as he put it. It is not surprising that he failed to obtain Federal funds for Texas to defend its frontiers against Indian attacks and to build the Southern Pacific Railroad into the state. He assured his fellow senators that the South would never accept a Black Republican as president. Let war come, he declared, "and if we do not get into Boston . . . before you get into Texas, you may shoot me."

In the campaign of 1860, Wigfall helped discredit Stephen A. Douglas and split the Democratic party. After Abraham

Lincoln was elected president, Wigfall coauthored the Southern Manifesto, declaring that any hope for relief within the Union was gone and that the honor, safety, and independence of the Southern people required the organization of a Southern confederacy. The manifesto was widely quoted in the Deep South, and even Southern moderates seemed to give up any idea of remaining in the Union.

Wigfall contributed greatly to thwarting compromises to save the Union. Although he occasionally expressed hope that separation would be peaceful, most of the time he equated it with war, avowing that the concluding treaty would be signed in Boston's Faneuil Hall. Wigfall stayed in the U.S. Senate even after Texas left the Union. He spied for the South, baited Northern senators, raised and trained troops in Maryland and sent them to South Carolina, and bought revolvers and rifles for Texas Confederates through July 1861, when he was finally expelled from the Senate well after the war started.

Typically, Wigfall had made his presence felt when the Civil War began at Fort Sumter in April, rowing under fire to the fort and dictating unauthorized surrender terms to the Federal commander. Many Southern newspapers hailed the recklessness and gallantry of Senator Wigfall, calling him the Confederate man of the hour. He refused an offer of the Texas governorship and became instead an aide to President Jefferson Davis, a Texas colonel, a Confederate colonel, and a member of the Confederate Provisional Congress, for a time concurrently while he was still a U.S. senator.

Wigfall initially was a friend and supporter of Davis and helped him become president. Most fire-eaters had wanted Barnwell Rhett, but Wigfall helped persuade Rhett to support Davis. Wigfall was influential with Davis, prevailing upon him to select Leroy P. Walker as the Confederacy's first secretary of war. The Davises and Wigfalls were together a great deal during May and June 1861. And in early July, Gen. P. G. T. Beauregard, in command of the Confederate troops at Manassas, wrote to Wigfall, seeking his assistance in presenting his grievances to Davis.

In early July, Wigfall became commander of the Texas troops, now a battalion, near Richmond. Since the command was not a large one, his appointment carried only a lieutenant colonelcy. Wigfall had hoped to be named a general, but the battalion was being mustered into Confederate service, and more troops from Texas were slow in coming.

Because Wigfall's battalion was in a train wreck on the way to the First Battle of Manassas, it did not arrive until the morning after the fighting. Nevertheless, Wigfall criticized the Confederates' failure to march on to Washington after the victory. Gen. Joseph E. Johnston said his army had been unable to press the attack because of a shortage of food supplies—a shortage he attributed to the failure of Davis's commissary general, Lucius B. Northrop, to deliver them. Wigfall sided with his friend Johnston, and apparently Davis considered criticism of Northrop to be criticism of himself.

Wigfall also took Johnston's side in the controversy over his rank, agreeing with his friend that he should be the highest ranking Confederate general because he was the highest to leave the U.S. Army. The controversy began when Robert E. Lee, then Davis's military adviser, ordered a new adjutant general into Johnston's headquarters. Johnston, certain he outranked Lee, protested repeatedly to the War Department. Even Lee was uncertain of his rank and position. But instead of clarifying their positions, Davis simply marked Johnston's letters "Insubordinate."

Wigfall soon had his own disagreement with Davis over rank. Prominent Texas friends recommended that Wigfall be moved up two steps to brigadier general. But Davis in August nominated him to move up only one step, to colonel, and Congress confirmed it immediately. The number of Texas troops was increasing to brigade level, however, and Davis nominated Wigfall for a brigadier generalcy in November. Wigfall was then still devoting part of his time to serving as Texas senator in the Permanent Congress. About the time Congress confirmed his generalcy in December, Wigfall resigned it to devote full time to Congress in order to press for military legislation.

During the optimistic period of February 1862 until May 1863, Congress debated many important military topics but took little action on them. During these months, Wigfall was a pro-administration militarist if not a nationalist. He backed almost all legislation that Davis favored and introduced several administration bills, including a proposal for the first conscription system in American history. One of the few staunch state rights advocates to support the measure, Wigfall argued that there should be only Confederate armies under Confederate generals, a stance that put him at loggerheads with other Texas delegates, who wanted to retain soldiers in their own state to protect its borders. Texas colleague W. P. Ballinger said that some of his friends thought Wigfall was a ruthless man.

During the Peninsular campaign, Wigfall blamed Gen. George B. McClellan's threat to Richmond on Davis's failure to order an invasion of Maryland. To a friend, Wigfall confided that he regretted ever having tried to move such a "dish of skimmed milk" to honorable action. Davis for his part said he lost confidence in Wigfall because of his drunkenness and his antipresident speeches in hotels. In the Peninsular campaign's Battle of Seven Pines, Wigfall cared for the wounded and became an aide to Gen. James Longstreet and a good friend of his and Lee's. They and other Confederate generals considered him their champion in pleading their needs to Congress and Davis.

Both Davis and Wigfall considered themselves expert

military strategists, and this was the focus of many of their quarrels. Nevertheless, they agreed on the need for widespread conscription to defend the Confederacy. This issue brought Wigfall into conflict with many of his colleagues in Congress. By 1863 when others were coming to agree with him, Wigfall was still ahead of them, proposing extending the original age limits of eighteen through thirty-five to sixteen through sixty. Both houses accepted his basic bill, though lowering the upper age to fifty. And yet Wigfall seemed surprised when his own sixteen-year-old son Halsey ignored advice to stick to his schoolbooks and instead volunteered and saw extensive action as a member of J. E. B. Stuart's cavalry.

Wigfall used the argument of military necessity to pass a bill he had tried to get through the U.S. Senate, calling for the construction of a railroad through Texas. This would connect Richmond with key positions in the West and South. Texas would have played a greater role in the war effort had it not been so remote and cut off by the Federal sea blockade. Ten days after the bill was enacted, however, New Orleans fell to Union troops and Texas was effectively separated from the rest of the Confederacy. Wigfall led the legislative struggle that established the government's power to impress private railroads and finally, in February 1865, to take control of all railroads in the Confederacy.

Although Wigfall was consistent with his earlier state rights arguments in insisting that Confederate courts had no right to override the decisions of state courts, he generally worked to provide the central government with enough powers to sustain itself. Concerned that state rights were hampering the military, Wigfall introduced a resolution in May 1864, seeking to define Confederate and state jurisdiction over civil rights. Wigfall defined a federal rather than a confederate system of government and even introduced a successful bill providing for military impressment of private property as needed to sustain the army.

When many conscripts defied the draft law and were protected by state judges who readily released them by issuing writs of habeas corpus, Wigfall responded to another Davis plea. He introduced and helped pass a bill in Congress to authorize the president to suspend the writ when necessary to ensure viable Confederate armies.

In arguing for suspension of the writ of habeas corpus, Wigfall assured his colleagues that Davis could be trusted to use the power wisely. Nevertheless, Wigfall did not trust the president to appoint army staff. In October 1862, he persuaded both houses to pass a bill limiting Davis's power of appointment and providing generals with staffs of their own choosing. The president vetoed the bill. Nor did Wigfall trust the president to appoint heads of armies. Wigfall's covert efforts forced Davis to replace Gen. Braxton Bragg with Joseph Johnston as head of the Army of Tennessee, but Wigfall could not induce Davis to provide Johnston with adequate support. Announcing his loss of trust in Johnston, the president replaced him with John Bell Hood, with ruinous results. Wigfall admired Hood's bravery and probably encouraged the close relationship that developed in his home between his fifteen-year-old daughter and the Texas general while he recuperated there from serious battle wounds. But the senator predicted Hood's fiasco at Atlanta.

Having lost all faith in Davis, Wigfall decided that the Confederacy's only hope lay in leadership by Senate hegemony. During the last two years of the war, Wigfall waged a four-pronged public and conspiratorial campaign against the president's power and popularity in an effort to bend him to the Senate's will: the Senate rejected his unwise appointments; Wigfall fixed responsibility for military losses on Davis, where he thought they belonged; Congress tried to force the president to observe the Constitution and hemmed him in with restrictions; and Wigfall and others belittled Davis in public to destroy the people's confidence in him. A positive relationship between Wigfall and Davis might have made it possible for the executive and legislative branches to collaborate, extending the life of the Confederacy. But neither the president nor the senator was willing to compromise, even as the Confederacy was facing destruction.

Probably Wigfall's policies were more sound than Davis's, and it is not surprising that several of the best generals looked to Wigfall for legislation and to plead their cases. But he rejected their pleas to strengthen their armies by arming slaves. Wigfall was willing to lose the war rather than admit that African Americans were worthy of being soldiers.

After the fall of the Confederacy, Wigfall fled to England where he tried to foment war between Britain and the United States, hoping to give the South an opportunity to rise again. He returned to Texas in 1872, died in Galveston in 1874, and was buried there in the Episcopal Cemetery.

BIBLIOGRAPHY

Chesnut, Mary Boykin. *Mary Chesnut's Civil War.* Edited by C. Vann Woodward. New Haven, Conn., 1981.

Clay-Clopton, Virginia. *A Belle of the Fifties.* New York, 1904.

Eaton, Clement. *Mind of the Old South.* Baton Rouge, La., 1964.

Hofstadter, Richard. *Paranoid Style in American Politics.* New York, 1965.

King, Alvy L. *Louis T. Wigfall: Southern Fire-Eater.* Baton Rouge, La., 1970.

Ledbetter, Billy D. "The Election of Louis T. Wigfall to the United States Senate, 1859: A Reevaluation." *Southwestern Historical Quarterly* 77 (1973): 241–254.

Russell, William H. *My Diary North and South: The Civil War in America.* London, 1863. Reprint, New York, 1954.

Wright, Louise Wigfall. *A Southern Girl in '61.* New York, 1905.

ALVY L. KING

WILCOX, CADMUS MARCELLUS (1824–1890), military author and major general. Wilcox was born May 29, 1824, in North Carolina and grew up in Tennessee, entering the U.S. Military Academy from the latter state in 1842. He was in the bottom quarter of his class in both grades and conduct during his four years at West Point and ranked fifty-fourth among fifty-nine graduates in 1846. Despite his weak academic standing, Wilcox later displayed scholarly tendencies by writing two important military books: a treatise on rifle practice, published in 1859, and a massive (711 pages) history of the Mexican War, published posthumously.

Lieutenant Wilcox fought through the Mexican War and won a brevet for conduct at Chapultepec. During nearly fifteen years in the U.S. Army, he advanced only from second lieutenant to captain, and that rank came on the day that South Carolina seceded from the Union. Wilcox was in New Mexico at the time; his resignation from his Federal commission was not final until June 8, 1861.

Wilcox's first Confederate position was as colonel of the Ninth Alabama Infantry, effective July 9. He was present at First Manassas, though not heavily engaged. Despite a lack of battle experience, Wilcox received promotion to brigadier general on October 21, 1861. He fought at Williamsburg, at Seven Pines, and through the Seven Days' Battles with marked success in each instance. By the summer of 1862, Wilcox was acting as commander of a three-brigade division, but in the formal alignment of divisions and corps that fall he did not win promotion, probably because of lack of support from corps commander James Longstreet, whom Wilcox loathed.

General Wilcox performed his most famous service to the army, and his greatest feat of the war, during the Chancellorsville campaign. He had been left in an isolated position near Banks Ford to observe Federals on the opposite bank. When he saw the opportunity, Wilcox moved southward aggressively toward the fighting near Fredericksburg that had resulted in penetration of Robert E. Lee's rear guard under Jubal Early. Wilcox skillfully thwarted the Federal advance near Salem Church on May 3, allowing Lee to complete his great victory. The army reorganization in May 1863 again bypassed Wilcox, though he was considered for division command. His promotion to major general finally came after the Battle of Gettysburg.

Wilcox took over the division that had belonged to William Dorsey Pender and led it for the rest of the war. He established a solid, workmanlike record without displaying any of the brilliance that might have prompted talk of further promotion. At both the Wilderness and Spotsylvania his division performed ably. The division fought tenaciously along the Orange Plank Road in the Wilderness, providing one-half of the Confederate strength there on May 5, 1864. At Spotsylvania it defended the Confederate right near the crucial courthouse crossroads. During the long siege of Richmond and Petersburg, Wilcox remained steadily at his post; his division held Lee's rear during the evacuation on April 2, 1865. Wilcox surrendered with Lee at Appomattox, having carved out an admirable record of achievement that earned him wide respect.

He lived after the war in Washington with his brother's widow. After rejecting offers of military commissions in Korea and Egypt, Wilcox held a Federal post given him by President Cleveland from 1886 until his death in 1890.

BIBLIOGRAPHY

Evans, Clement A., ed. *Confederate Military History.* 12 vols. Atlanta, 1899. Extended ed. in 19 vols. Wilmington, N.C., 1987–1989.

Wilcox, Cadmus M. *History of the Mexican War.* Washington, D.C., 1892.

Wilcox, Cadmus M. *Rifles and Rifle Practice.* New York, 1859.

Robert K. Krick

WILCOX, JOHN A. (1819–1864), congressman from Texas. A native of North Carolina, John Alexander Wilcox was born on April 18, 1819. He moved to Mississippi sometime prior to 1845 and served as a lieutenant of the Second Mississippi Infantry in the Mexican War. After the war he was secretary of the Mississippi State Senate and was a Unionist member from Mississippi to the House of Representatives in the U.S. Congress (1851–1853). He moved to San Antonio, Texas, in 1853. Wilcox practiced law and was active in Know-Nothing politics in his new home. In January 1861, he was a delegate to the state secession convention from Bexar County and was a member of the committee that drafted the ordinance of secession.

In February 1861, Wilcox was commissioned by the Texas Committee on Public Safety, authorized by the state convention, to raise a military company that became part of Ben McCulloch's force of state troops. Wilcox accompanied McCulloch to San Antonio to demand the surrender of U.S. troops stationed there and was one of the chief negotiators in the proceedings that led to the Federal evacuation of San Antonio and the surrender of arms and munitions to the state.

In November 1861, Wilcox was elected to the House of Representatives of the First Congress. He chaired the Committee on Territories and Public Lands. In the Congress Wilcox usually supported President Jefferson Davis's administration. He was an advocate of conscription, although he also voted for extensive exemptions. Between sessions he returned to Texas and served on the staff of Gen. John B. Magruder in the Battle of Galveston in January 1863.

He returned to Richmond for the sessions of the Second Congress but died of apoplexy on February 7, 1864.

BIBLIOGRAPHY

Estill, Mary S., ed. "Diary of a Confederate Congressman." *Southwestern Historical Quarterly* 38 (April 1935): 270–301; 39 (July 1935): 33–65.

Warner, Ezra J., and W. Buck Yearns. *Biographical Register of the Confederate Congress.* Baton Rouge, La., 1975.

CARL H. MONEYHON

WILDERNESS CAMPAIGN. The Wilderness, a region in Orange and Spotsylvania counties in northern Virginia, gave its name to a major battle fought in its tangled thickets on May 5 and 6, 1864. The battle pitted Robert E. Lee against Ulysses S. Grant in the opening stage of the overland campaign that eventually led to the siege of Richmond and Petersburg. Lee had wintered his Army of Northern Virginia in Orange County, west of the Wilderness, while the Federal Army of the Potomac camped across the Rapidan River in Culpeper County. Grant, newly appointed commander in chief of all Federal armies, took his headquarters into the field with the Army of the Potomac in March. Gen. George G. Meade remained in nominal command of that army for the rest of the war, but Grant exerted his authority over all substantive decisions. During the Wilderness, for instance, Meade had no control over one of the army's four corps, Burnside's Ninth.

The Army of the Potomac began its move south over the Rapidan early on May 4, crossing primarily at Germanna Ford, with nearly 120,000 men in the ranks. That number seemed to Grant to be operationally appropriate to begin the campaign. He also could draw on virtually limitless replacements. Lee's army counted about 65,000 troops, with only limited reserves in prospect, and those available only at the cost of stripping other threatened points. Grant and Meade hoped to march straight through the Wilderness in the direction of Spotsylvania Court House without hindrance, moving past Lee's right flank before he could respond effectively and thus interposing between the Confederate army and Richmond.

Lee responded to the threat by moving swiftly eastward toward the Wilderness, camping on the night of May 4 within easy striking distance of the roads Grant had to use on his projected southward march. The Confederate army moved on two roads that ran through the Wilderness on roughly parallel courses and that eventually joined east of the ground that became the battlefield. The old Orange Turnpike was about two miles north of the newer Orange Plank Road at the longitude of the heaviest fighting. No means of ready communication between the two roads existed. As a result the Battle of the Wilderness was fought in two discrete halves that remained remarkably isolated from each other. Richard S. Ewell's Second Corps marched east on the turnpike while A. P. Hill's Third Corps paralleled it on the Plank Road. The other corps of Lee's army, the First under James Longstreet, began its march unfortunately far to the southwest in the vicinity of Boswell's Tavern in Louisa County. Lee's incaution in leaving so large a force so far from his other units, combined with a slow and confused march to action by the First Corps, would have a major impact on the conduct of the battle.

Fighting broke out first on the turnpike on the morning of May 5. The advance brigades of Ewell's force clashed with Federals marching south past the vicinity of Wilderness Tavern. Union Gen. G. K. Warren's Fifth Corps turned west onto the turnpike to face Ewell's men. Northern troops rolled over the first opposition they met and Confederate Brig. Gen. John M. Jones was shot from his horse. Elements of the division commanded by Robert Rodes restored order for the Confederates, who took up a line perpendicular to the turnpike in woods at the western edge of a large clearing straddling the pike known as Saunders Field. Fighting in this northern sector of the Wilderness on both days of the battle centered on the turnpike and especially on Saunders Field. Grant and Meade established their headquarters on a knoll just north of the pike and a mile east of the field. Warren made his headquarters just across the road from his two superiors at the Lacy house, Ellwood, which is the only building on the battlefield that survives today. Fighting ebbed and flowed around Saunders Field during May 5 as the rest of Ewell's Second Corps arrived and the Federal Fifth Corps, supported by most of the Sixth, deployed to face it. The Confederates lost Brig. Gen. Leroy A. Stafford, who was mortally wounded in one fierce localized attack by the Sixth Corps.

Meanwhile the Confederate column on the Plank Road had approached its intersection with the north-south Brock Road, on which Grant was moving south, and fighting broke out in that zone. Confederate control of the intersection would break Grant's attenuated army into two pieces and leave it susceptible to destruction in detail. During May 5 Hill came up against stout resistance from Union Gen. W. S. Hancock's Second Corps, supported by one division of the Sixth Corps under George W. Getty. Most of the fighting raged in the thickly overgrown woodland on either shoulder of the Plank Road not far west of the intersection. The only clearing of note along the road in the battle area was the meager subsistence farm of a widow named Catharine Tapp, and that lay west of the front lines during the first day of the battle.

As darkness closed the fighting on May 5, the Southern position near the turnpike remained along the western edge of Saunders Field and extended beyond the field on both sides in a straight line, particularly northward, to counter

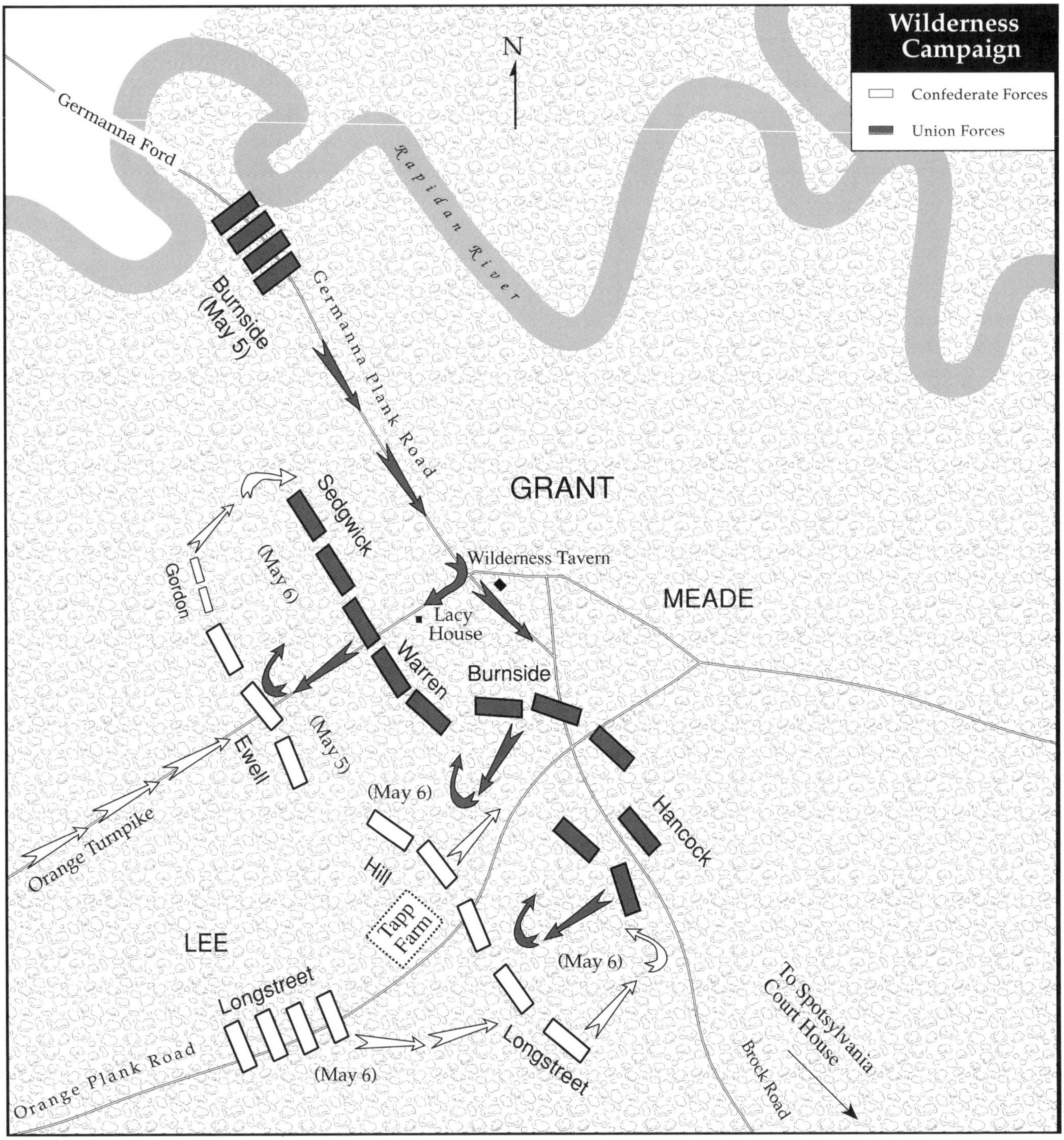

Federal threats. All over the battlefield the soldiers of both sides energetically threw up earthworks reinforced with logs; the era of major entrenchments had arrived to stay and would reach unprecedented levels during the next two weeks. On the Plank Road front, Hill's brigades maintained a tenuous grip on ground fairly close to the crucial intersection with the Brock Road. They had been fought to a frazzle, however, and lay haphazardly in the thickets without adequate connection between units. Hill's subordinates desperately petitioned the corps commander to fall back and regroup. He refused on the premise that Longstreet's men would be on hand by morning as reinforcements and insisted that the weary soldiers be allowed to rest.

Early on May 6 a massive assault arranged by the capable Hancock rolled irresistibly over Hill's tattered remnants and threatened to destroy the Army of Northern Virginia. According to Edward Porter Alexander and James Fitz Caldwell, Lee rode among his fleeing troops, asking one veteran brigade why it was "fleeing like wild geese" and atypically expressing himself "rather roughly." At this critical moment, probably the most desperate in the army's career to date, the first units of Longstreet's First Corps finally began arriving on the field. Hancock had smashed through the woods to the Widow Tapp's clearing, where a battalion of Confederate artillery had been parked. The artillery of both armies accomplished little during the battle because of dense ground cover that rendered cannon less important here than in any other major action in the Virginia theater. These reserve guns suddenly became Lee's last line of defense, however, while Longstreet's men deployed. When the veteran Texas Brigade (three Texas and one Arkansas regiments) moved past the guns and into the breach, Lee attempted to lead them forward in an episode that became instantly famous and eventually grew larger than life in later years. Fearing for Lee's safety, the men of the brigade turned him back and then rushed forward in an attack that left half of them casualties.

Longstreet's reinforcements gradually stabilized the front along the Plank Road. The tide turned when a broadly mixed Confederate task force—four brigades from four divisions—moved secretly through the woods south of the road to an unfinished railroad bed that provided them with a corridor to use in creeping past the far left Federal flank. When the flanking column spread out into line and then dashed north, it routed the Union troops who had been flushed with success, rolling up the line "like a wet blanket," in Hancock's phrase. As the victorious Confederate attackers dashed northward toward the Plank Road, Longstreet and his subordinates led their men east on that road to exploit Hancock's collapse. But some of the Confederates in the woods, apparently of William Mahone's Virginia Brigade, fired at the group of horsemen along the road and with that volley ruined their army's chance for a great success. The volley killed Gen. Micah Jenkins and severely wounded Longstreet. In the shocked aftermath, the movement lost its momentum. Later in the day, Lee directed a renewal of the attack toward the intersection, but it resulted in a costly repulse after surging close to its goal.

May 6 on the Orange Turnpike front featured more fighting over and around Saunders Field. The exposed Federal right north of the field offered a tempting target, but corps commander Ewell timidly refused suggestions to exploit the opening. Finally, near dusk, Georgian John B. Gordon led a column that smashed the Federal right, just as Longstreet had destroyed the Federal left earlier in the day. Gordon captured hundreds of prisoners, including two brigadier generals, and pushed the Union right back through an arc of nearly ninety degrees in the gathering darkness.

The two armies faced each other from behind steadily deepening earthworks on May 7. Then Grant moved south in a race for the next crucial crossroads, a race that resulted in a two-week battle around Spotsylvania Court House. The Wilderness battlefield meeting between Lee and Grant had cost the Federal army about eighteen thousand casualties. Lee's losses, which cannot be computed precisely for this stage of the war, totaled at least eight thousand and probably reached near ten thousand. Lee's tactical skill had thwarted the intentions of an army twice the size of his own. Grant had quickly discovered the difference between fighting Lee and toying with Braxton Bragg. At the Wilderness Grant's army earned the distinction of having both of its exposed flanks abruptly turned and crumpled, the only such result in any of the war's battles in the Virginia theater. Nonetheless he pushed steadily on from the Wilderness toward Richmond. The war had turned its final corner in the Wilderness, and now it would grind inexorably by means of attrition through eleven months of steady fighting to Appomattox.

BIBLIOGRAPHY

Dowdey, Clifford. *Lee's Last Campaign.* Boston, 1960.

Kelley, Dayton. *General Lee and Hood's Texas Brigade at the Battle of the Wilderness.* Hillsboro, Tex., 1969.

Schaff, Morris. *The Battle of the Wilderness.* Boston, 1910.

Steere, Edward. *The Wilderness Campaign.* Harrisburg, Pa., 1960.

Trudeau, Noah André. *Bloody Roads South.* Boston, 1989.

ROBERT K. KRICK

WILEY, CALVIN H. (1819–1887), educator and superintendent of common schools for North Carolina. Wiley, who was born February 3, 1819, in Guilford County, North Carolina, graduated from the University of North Carolina in 1840. He was admitted to the bar the next year and opened a practice in Oxford, South Carolina, where he also edited the *Oxford Mercury.* A writer, Wiley published a number of novels and educational books in the 1840s and 1850s and established the *Common School Journal* in 1856, which later became the *North Carolina Journal of Education.*

Wiley returned to North Carolina and served in the state legislature as a Whig from 1850 to 1852. Involved in improving the state's common education system, Wiley pushed through legislation creating a superintendent of common schools, to which he was appointed on January 1, 1853. He held the position until April 26, 1865, when all state offices were terminated by Reconstruction officials.

With the outbreak of the Civil War, Wiley fought to prevent chaos in the state's common school system as male teachers left to join the services. When he learned that county courts throughout the state were ordering the diversion of public school funds from educational purposes to the war effort, Wiley organized a massive mailing campaign to convince public officials of the importance of preserving school funds for education. He was especially instrumental in helping to protect North Carolina's Literary Fund. Largely through his efforts the state's public school system functioned throughout the fighting; by 1863, however, it was reduced to a core of 875 teachers, who received an average monthly salary of twenty-five dollars to hold school for three- and four-month terms.

Wiley was also a leader in slave reform in the South, urging the expansion of educational opportunities to slaves. He constantly worked for the repeal of laws forbidding slaves to read and write and pressed for legislation to legalize slave marriages, prevent the sale of young children from their mothers, and allow the testimony of slaves in court. Wiley's work, *Southern Negroes, 1861–1865,* was a classic on the economic decline of slavery brought on by the inflation of Confederate currency. His statistics show that while the price of slaves, when valued in Confederate currency, continued to rise after 1862, their actual value in relation to gold dollars decreased and continued downward throughout the war.

After the war, Wiley, who had been ordained in the Presbyterian church in 1866 but never held a charge, worked with the American Bible Society in several Southern states. Eventually he settled in Winston, North Carolina, where he died on January 11, 1887.

BIBLIOGRAPHY

Eaton, Clement. *A History of the Southern Confederacy.* New York, 1954.

Noble, M. C. S. *A History of the Public Schools of North Carolina.* Chapel Hill, N.C., 1930.

Wiley, Calvin Henderson. Papers. North Carolina State Department of Archives and History, Raleigh, N.C.

PAUL F. LAMBERT

WILKES, PETER SINGLETON (1827–1900), private and congressman from Missouri. Born in Maury County, Tennessee, in 1827, Wilkes spent his youth in Miller County, Missouri. Listed as a student in the 1850 Miller County census, Wilkes apparently ended his collegiate career in 1852. Shortly after, he was elected Miller County's representative to the Missouri General Assembly (1852–1854). Wilkes reportedly was an editor of the *Springfield Advertiser* in 1856, and he is known to have practiced law in the Springfield, Missouri, area from 1857 to 1861.

Vehemently pro-Southern, the secessionist Wilkes had served as a vice president of the 1860 Democratic state convention. After the outbreak of the Civil War, Wilkes recruited troops for the Confederate cause. In 1862 he joined the Third Missouri Cavalry as a private and served in the commissary department. He vowed never to accept a rank higher than private because he did not want the men he recruited to think him overly ambitious.

Wilkes was elected to the Second Congress in May 1864. Continually supportive of the Davis administration's policies, he served on the Post Office and Indian Affairs committees. During the last months of the war, Wilkes advocated providing Davis with every necessary power to prolong hostilities, except using slaves in the army.

When the war ended, Wilkes settled in Mazatlán, Mexico. In the 1870s he migrated to Stockton, California, where he again took up the practice of law. He died in Stockton on January 2, 1900.

BIBLIOGRAPHY

Machir, John. Papers. Western Historical Manuscripts Collection. University of Missouri, Columbia.

Obituary. *Stockton Mail* (California), January 2, 1900.

Wakelyn, Jon L. *Biographical Dictionary of the Confederacy.* Edited by Frank E. Vandiver. Westport, Conn., 1977.

Warner, Ezra J., and W. Buck Yearns. *Biographical Register of the Confederate Congress.* Baton Rouge, La., 1975.

JAMES GOODRICH

WILKINSON, JOHN (1821–1891), naval officer. Wilkinson was born on November 6, 1821, in Amelia County, Virginia. His father was a career naval officer and young Wilkinson followed in his footsteps. After appointment as a midshipman in 1837, he was assigned to several ships and cruised the South Atlantic and the Pacific. In the years between the Mexican War and the Civil War, Wilkinson made lieutenant and was assigned duty aboard the steamers *Southern Star* and *Corwin.* As commander of *Corwin,* Wilkinson spent a valuable year charting the waters of the Florida Keys and the Bahamas.

When Virginia seceded from the Union, Wilkinson submitted his resignation to the U.S. Navy and offered his services to the Confederacy. At first he was detailed to Fort Powhatan on the James River and later to batteries on Acquia Creek, as there were no billets ashore or afloat for Confederate naval officers. That situation changed in June 1861 when Wilkinson was offered a rank as first lieutenant in the Confederate navy and dispatched to New Orleans to command the steamer *Jackson* and later the ironclad *Louisiana.* When the U.S. Navy forced passage of the Confederate defenses on the Mississippi River below New Orleans, Wilkinson burned the ironclad to prevent its

JOHN WILKINSON. From a photograph by S. M. Gault.
NAVAL HISTORICAL CENTER, WASHINGTON, D.C.

falling into enemy hands. While attempting to escape, he and several others were captured and sent to Fort Warren in Boston Harbor for imprisonment.

On August 5, 1862, Wilkinson was exchanged after three months in prison, and within a week he was ordered to Europe with Maj. Ben Ficklin to secure a steamer for the War Department. That vessel was to be used to run supplies through the Union blockade of Confederate ports. Ficklin and Wilkinson negotiated the purchase of the powerful steamer *Giraffe* from the firm of Alexander Collie and Company. After the steamer was loaded with ordnance and medical and lithographic supplies, Wilkinson took command and sailed for Puerto Rico. There he secured a crew and cleared for Charleston, South Carolina. After finding bad weather and low visibility off Charleston, Wilkinson ran on to Wilmington and entered the Cape Fear River after the pilot ran *Giraffe* aground.

Upon arriving in Wilmington, Wilkinson rechristened the vessel *Robert E. Lee.* During the next eleven months he ran the blockade twenty-one times, bringing in cargoes for the War Department and developing tactics for blockade running that were adopted by other Confederate vessels. In all *Robert E. Lee* carried seven thousand bales of cotton valued at $2 million through the blockade. The War Department then selected Wilkinson to lead another risky operation. He was to organize and lead a group of naval personnel in a raid on the Union prison on Johnson's Island at the entrance of Sandusky Bay on Lake Erie. Wilkinson's plan required that his raiders capture the steamer USS *Michigan* and use the vessel to overwhelm the prison garrison. After delivering the Confederate prisoners to Canada, Wilkinson and his crew would use *Michigan* to destroy U.S. merchant shipping on the Great Lakes with impunity, for the aging iron steamer was the only U.S. warship permitted on the lakes in accordance with a treaty with Canada. Wilkinson was forced to abandon the enterprise when his plans were discovered.

After returning to Wilmington, North Carolina, in command of the blockade runner *Whisper,* Wilkinson was ordered to Richmond, where he was assigned the task of planning a raid to release twenty thousand Confederate prisoners held at Point Lookout, Maryland. Like the raid on Johnson's Island, the project was discovered and Wilkinson returned to Wilmington. He worked on a system to improve blockade running by establishing signal and range lights at the entrances to the Cape Fear River and organizing an office to assign pilots and signalmen to each vessel.

Late in the summer of 1864, Wilkinson assumed command of the blockade runner *Edith,* which had been recently confiscated by the Confederate government. Wilkinson armed and fitted out the vessel for commerce raiding under the name CSS *Chickamauga.* Because of the ship's dependency on coal, Wilkinson's cruise lasted only twenty days, but seven U.S. merchant vessels were burned or bonded. Upon his return he took command of the steamer CSS *Tallahassee* and, after changing the name to *Chameleon,* ran the ship out to Bermuda for provisions much needed by the Army of Northern Virginia. The fall of Fort Fisher on January 15, 1865, closed the port of Wilmington before *Chameleon* arrived and Wilkinson was almost trapped by Union warships in the harbor. After a daring escape Wilkinson took the blockade runner to Nassau and, in concert with Capt. John N. Maffitt of the *Owl,* attempted to reach Charleston. Both Maffitt and Wilkinson took their vessels to Liverpool and in April 1865 turned them over to Comdr. James D. Bulloch, the Confederate agent in England attempting to close out European affairs.

After Wilkinson was discharged, he took up residence in Halifax, Nova Scotia, for several years before returning to Amelia County, Virginia, to engage in surveying and open a small boarding school for women. Wilkinson's enterprises in Amelia County all failed, and he died virtually destitute in Annapolis, Maryland, on December 29, 1881.

BIBLIOGRAPHY

Bradlee, Francis B. *Blockade Running during the Civil War and the Effect of Land and Water Transportation on the Confederacy.* Philadelphia, 1974.

Hearn, Chester G. *Gray Raiders of the Sea.* Camden, Me., 1992.
Scharf, J. Thomas. *History of the Confederate States Navy.* New York, 1887. Reprint, New York, 1977.
Wise, Stephen R. *Lifeline of the Confederacy: Blockade Running during the Civil War.* Columbia, S.C., 1988.

GORDON WATTS

WILLIAM H. WEBB. *See entry on the ship* Webb.

WILLIAMS, JOHN S. "CERRO GORDO" (1818–1898), brigadier general and U.S. senator. John Stuart Williams was born on July 10, 1818, in Montgomery County, Kentucky. An 1838 graduate of Miami University (Oxford, Ohio), he studied law and was admitted to the Kentucky bar in 1843. He volunteered for the Mexican War, entering service as a captain. Commissioned colonel of the Fourth Kentucky Volunteers, he was assigned to Maj. Gen. Winfield Scott's command. His dashing conduct at the Battle of Cerro Gordo (April 17–18, 1847) won for him the sobriquet "Cerro Gordo." After the war, Williams farmed and practiced law. A Whig in politics, he was elected to the Kentucky lower house in 1851 and 1853.

JOHN S. "CERRO GORDO" WILLIAMS. LIBRARY OF CONGRESS

At the outbreak of the Civil War, Williams offered his services to the Confederacy and was commissioned colonel of the Fifth Kentucky Infantry on November 16, 1861. The next year, on April 16, he was promoted to brigadier general, serving under Gen. Humphrey Marshall in eastern Kentucky and southwestern Virginia. Later he was assigned command of the Department of East Tennessee and in the fall of 1863 opposed the advance of Federal Gen. Ambrose Burnside against Knoxville. He aided in the defeat of a Federal attack on the all-important saltworks at Abingdon, Virginia. In 1864 his command was attached to Joseph Wheeler's cavalry corps, but he ended the war employed in the defense of southwestern Virginia.

Williams returned to central Kentucky after the war, reentered farming, served two terms in the state legislature, ran unsuccessfully for governor, and won election to the U.S. Senate in 1878. In later years he promoted railroad building in the mineral regions of Kentucky and is credited with growing the first commercial crop of white burley tobacco in the United States. He died on July 17, 1898, and is buried in Winchester, Kentucky.

BIBLIOGRAPHY

O'Rear, Edward C. *History of the Montgomery County (Ky.) Bar.* Mt. Sterling, Ky., 1912.
Warner, Ezra J. *Generals in Gray: Lives of the Confederate Commanders.* Baton Rouge, La., 1959.

TERRENCE V. MURPHY

WILLIAMSBURG, VIRGINIA. The former colonial capital of Williamsburg became the scene of fierce fighting on May 4 and 5, 1862, as Confederate Gen. Joseph E. Johnston abandoned his positions at Yorktown under pressure from Maj. Gen. George B. McClellan's Union army. Despite having committed his forces to elaborate siege preparations and being plagued by poor weather conditions, McClellan responded relatively quickly and sent troops in pursuit of the retreating Confederates. Much of the pursuit and the ensuing fighting would be carried out in a driving rain.

The Southerners assumed defensive positions in a line of earthworks constructed earlier by Confederate Maj. Gen. John B. Magruder two miles east of Williamsburg. Fort Magruder stood at the center of this line of fourteen redoubts, some of which the Confederates did not occupy.

Elements of Brig. Gen. J. E. B. Stuart's cavalry were the first Confederates to clash with their Union opponents near Williamsburg, as they attempted to screen the Southern retreat. This pressure quickly convinced Johnston of the need for a strong rearguard defense. He left this defense to

Maj. Gen. Lafayette McLaws, while the bulk of the Confederate army attempted to make further progress along the muddy roads.

On the night of May 4, Maj. Gen. James Longstreet's division replaced that of McLaws, taking up positions in Fort Magruder and most of the redoubts along the line. The next morning, two Union divisions under Maj. Gen. Joseph Hooker and Brig. Gen. William F. ("Baldy") Smith faced the Confederates. At 7:30 A.M., Hooker launched an assault, which pressured the Southerners severely enough for Longstreet to recall more troops for the rearguard defense, including his old brigade, now under the command of Brig. Gen. A. P. Hill. Hill brought his men into position on the Confederate right, and when Longstreet ordered a counterattack, Hill personally led them against Hooker's Federals, recapturing ground Hooker had taken earlier that morning. For seven hours of grueling combat, the opposing forces grappled with each other until the Confederates, their ammunition nearly exhausted, pulled back. Nevertheless, Hill had helped stabilize the Southern line at a critical moment in the battle when a collapse would have endangered the Confederate army.

In the meantime, Johnston reached the field and decided to send for Maj. Gen. D. H. Hill's division to support Longstreet. Federal attempts to strike both Confederate flanks necessitated the move. Although the Union force sent to hit the Southern right stalled, another part of Smith's division, under Brig. Gen. Winfield S. Hancock, successfully reached the Confederate left flank and promptly seized some unoccupied redoubts. Hancock's action threatened to enfilade the Southern line. The Union fire was severe enough to endanger the occupants of Fort Magruder and the surrounding earthworks.

When Hill arrived on the field, he found Longstreet hard pressed by the intense Union fire. Brig. Gen. Jubal Early led the first of Hill's brigades into the fighting. Both he and the division commander were eager to attack Hancock, but in their haste they launched a piecemeal assault that became disorganized in the broken terrain. Only two of Early's four regiments advanced against the Federals, and although temporarily successful, they withered under heavy Union volleys. The valiant Confederate attack proved costly. Early's two attacking regiments, the Twenty-fourth Virginia and the Fifth North Carolina, suffered casualties of 50 percent and 85 percent, respectively, and Early himself was hit in the shoulder by a minié ball.

Despite the arrival of McClellan and additional Union troops, the fighting gradually subsided. Then, with nightfall, the Confederates retreated from their hard-fought positions and continued their withdrawal toward Richmond. The fighting at Williamsburg cost both sides heavily. The Federals lost 468 killed, 1,442 wounded, and 373 captured or missing, while the Confederates lost 288 killed, 975 wounded, and 297 captured or missing. Two infantry regiments—the Seventieth New York and the Fifth North Carolina—lost 80 and 85 percent of their strength, respectively.

BIBLIOGRAPHY

Freeman, Douglas S. *Lee's Lieutenants: A Study in Command.* 3 vols. New York, 1942–1944. Reprint, New York, 1986.

Hastings, Earl C., and David S. Hastings. "'Encounter in the Rain': The Battle of Williamsburg, 1862." *Virginia Cavalcade* 22 (Winter 1973): 20–27.

Johnson, Robert U., and C. C. Buel, eds. *Battles and Leaders of the Civil War.* 4 vols. New York, 1887–1888. Reprint, Secaucus, N.J., 1982.

Longstreet, James. *From Manassas to Appomattox: Memoirs of the Civil War in America.* Philadelphia, 1896.

Robertson, James I., Jr. *General A. P. Hill: The Story of a Confederate Warrior.* New York, 1987.

BRIAN S. WILLS

WILLIAMSON, WILLIAM P. (1810–1870), engineer-in-chief of the navy. Born in Norfolk, Virginia, Williamson studied mechanical engineering in New York City in his youth. Afterward he worked at the Gosport Navy Yard and by 1842 had charge of the machine works there. On October 20, 1842, he was appointed chief engineer in the U.S. Navy and became one of the ranking officers of that newly formed corps. When he refused to take the oath of allegiance after the outbreak of the Civil War, he was imprisoned and then dismissed from the service.

After brief duty in the Virginia navy, Williamson entered the Confederate navy on June 11, 1861, as its senior engineer. With Lt. John M. Brooke and Naval Constructor John L. Porter he quickly became involved in formulating plans for an armor-plated vessel. It was Williamson who first proposed converting the charred remains of USS *Merrimack* into the ironclad *Virginia* and then successfully refurbished its troublesome engines. In the fall of 1861 he assumed responsibility for planning, constructing, and installing all naval steam machinery in the South. On September 17, 1862, he was promoted to engineer-in-chief of the navy, a rank commensurate with his duties. Initially hampered by inadequate industrial facilities, Williamson established naval works at Richmond, Virginia, Charlotte, North Carolina, and Columbus, Georgia, and by war's end reliable marine machinery was being produced for the Confederacy's warships.

After his parole at Greensboro, North Carolina, May 1, 1865, Williamson obtained a position at the Vulcan Iron Works in Baltimore building steam engines. He returned to Norfolk in 1870 to take charge of the Atlantic Iron Works but died soon afterward on October 20.

BIBLIOGRAPHY

Bennett, Frank M. *The Steam Navy of the United States.* Pittsburgh, Pa., 1896.

Still, William N. *Confederate Shipbuilding.* 2d ed. Columbia, S.C., 1987.

Still, William N. *Iron Afloat: The Story of the Confederate Armorclads.* 2d ed. Columbia, S.C., 1985.

A. Robert Holcombe, Jr.

WILMINGTON, NORTH CAROLINA. Situated on the Cape Fear River twenty-eight miles from the river's mouth, Wilmington in 1860 was North Carolina's largest city. Its population was 9,542, which was made up of 2,722 white males, 2,480 white females, 244 free black males, 329 free black females, 1,882 male slaves, and 1,895 female slaves. A deep-water port, the city was known for its beautiful churches and impressive homes, and it boasted a theater in the town hall run by a local Thalian Association.

At the start of the war most of Wilmington was not considered a major port; however, it did have excellent internal communications through three railroad lines: the Wilmington and Manchester, which connected the port to Charleston and Columbia, South Carolina; the Wilmington and Weldon, which ran north to Virginia; and the unfinished Wilmington, Charlotte, and Rutherford, which extended into North Carolina's interior. The city also had daily steamboat service up the Cape Fear River to Fayetteville and was connected by steamships to Charleston and New York. Wilmington's main exports were turpentine, resin, tar, lumber, rice, corn, and flour.

Wilmington could be reached through two channels that connected the Cape Fear River to the Atlantic. The main channel, which led out to the southwest, was called Old Inlet. It had a treacherous, shifting bar that varied in depth from ten to fifteen feet. The second entrance, called New Inlet, had been formed in 1761, when a hurricane cut a northeast channel through Federal Point Peninsula. The new pass was more shallow than the main channel but was quite navigable for small and medium-sized vessels.

From 1860 until the end of the war, Wilmington's mayor was John Dawson, a local businessman. At the start of the secession crisis, citizens of Wilmington formed the Cape Fear Minutemen and on January 10, 1861, seized Forts Caswell and Johnston at the mouth of the Cape Fear River; since North Carolina had not yet seceded, however, the governor ordered the forts returned the next day. Three months later, on April 13, 1861, militia with proper authorization recaptured the forts.

Considered to be a secondary port by the Federal navy, Wilmington was not blockaded until July 21, 1861, nearly two months after blockades were set up off Charleston and Savannah. For the first few months of the war, Wilmington's shipping trade stagnated and the city's economy entered into a depression. Some businessmen made profits from the production of salt, which soon became a major wartime industry. A few owners of schooners and brigs continued a small coastal trade, and some sailing ships undertook the 570-mile voyage to Nassau or the 674-mile trip to Bermuda in search of profits.

At the beginning of the war, only a few steam blockade runners used Wilmington. One of these, *Kate,* brought with it yellow fever. From early September until November 11, 1862, the town suffered 1,500 cases and 700 deaths, 15 percent of the town's population. After the epidemic, city and military authorities undertook an extensive quarantine program to keep such a severe outbreak from occurring again.

In the fall of 1862, the head of the Confederate Ordnance Bureau, Josiah Gorgas, chose Wilmington as the port of entry for his bureau's line of blockade runners. The steamers, operating out of St. George, Bermuda, some 674 miles away, brought immense amounts of military supplies to Wilmington and carried away government cotton. In charge of the Ordnance Bureau's operations at Wilmington was James M. Sexias. The Ordnance Bureau's runners were soon joined by private runners who also saw the advantages of using Wilmington, and in July 1863, after the Federal attack on Charleston effectively closed down blockade running there, Wilmington became the South's primary port.

Like other ports, Wilmington gained little from the supplies being unloaded at its docks; most went inland. As a result, goods grew scarce and prices went up. Conditions quickly became bad, and soon the prewar society was forced out by the influx of speculators, sailors, and other individuals associated with blockade running. Prostitution became rampant, and other citizens were reduced to begging. Some civic groups and individuals, such as the Ladies Relief Society operated by Miss Mary Ann Buie, tried to help those in need, but their activity was often lost among the fast-living blockade runners who came to dominate the town. As one commentator reported, Wilmington was the meanest place in the Confederacy. The presence of sailors, speculators, businessmen, and the other elements of a wartime port was a necessary evil, however, for after July 1863, Wilmington became the most important element in the Confederate supply system. Before the war ended, blockade runners made over three hundred round trips to Wilmington—more than all the other Confederate ports combined.

Because of its vital importance to the Confederacy, Wilmington was guarded by a number of fortifications. An outer ring guarded New and Old Inlets while other forts lined the Cape Fear River, and the city was encircled by a line of trenches. Its major fortifications were Fort Caswell at Old Inlet and Fort Fisher at New Inlet. Since most blockade runners preferred New Inlet, Fort Fisher, under the command of Col. William Lamb, became the most important and largest fort in Wilmington's defenses.

For most of the war Wilmington's commander was Brig. Gen. W. H. C. Whiting, who worked to make Wilmington one of the best defended cities in the Confederacy. Besides coordinating the area's defenses, Whiting controlled blockade running through the issuance of strict regulations. No vessel could leave the port without permission from the army. Curfews were established in Wilmington, and the army assigned the blockade runners with their signalmen and pilots. All vessels were inspected, and captains were required to keep an accurate list of their vessel's cargo, crew, and passengers. In March 1864, after a disastrous fire burned nearly one thousand bales of cotton worth $691,000, Whiting ordered that all runners had to be towed into the river before firing their engines. To help enforce these regulations, the army purchased the former blockade runner *Flora,* which they renamed *Cape Fear,* to use as an armed transport.

Whiting's tight regulations often caused friction with Wilmington's naval commander, Flag Officer William F. Lynch, who commanded a small squadron of wooden gunboats. On one occasion, in February 1864, the army and navy nearly came to blows over a cargo of naval cotton. The matter was settled in Richmond, and Lt. John Wilkinson was sent to Wilmington to assist blockade running and secure harmony between the military authorities.

During the war the casemated ironclads *Raleigh* and *North Carolina* were completed at Wilmington. *North Carolina* was plagued with mechanical problems and spent most of its career moored off Smithville near the mouth of the Cape Fear River where it eventually sank owing to a worm-eaten bottom. *Raleigh* made a foray from New Inlet against the Federal blockaders on the evening of May 6, 1864, but the next morning ran aground off Smithville and became a total loss. A double-ended, twin-tower ironclad called *Wilmington* was started late in the war, but was unfinished at the war's end.

In July 1864, the Confederate navy purchased the twin-screw-propeller blockade runner *Atalanta* and renamed it *Tallahassee;* in September another twin-screw runner, *Edith,* was purchased, and in October, under the name *Chickamauga,* it joined the *Tallahassee,* now called *Olustee.*

Though these raiders carried out various missions and returned safely, many government officials feared their use as commerce raiders would result in a tightened blockade and lead to an attack on Wilmington. Their complaints stopped further raids, and none of the ships ever again ventured out as warships, except *Olustee,* which later went out as a blockade runner under the name *Chameleon.*

During the war Wilmington served as the port not only for the Ordnance Bureau vessels but for all east-coast blockade runners operating under contracts with the Confederacy. It was also used by the vessels owned by the states of North Carolina, Virginia, and Georgia, as well as private companies. During the war numerous Confederate agents passed through Wilmington on their missions, including Rose O'Neal Greenhow, who drowned when her blockade runner, *Condor,* ran aground near New Inlet on September 30, 1864. She was later buried in Wilmington with full military honors.

During 1864, the blockade-running trade at Wilmington greatly increased as the South's demand for overseas goods grew. Though luxury items continued to arrive, the Confederacy placed tighter restrictions on the blockade runners, which resulted in the importation of vast amounts of military goods. Besides munitions, Wilmington was also the receiving point for the Army of Northern Virginia's meat rations. Gen. Robert E. Lee, knowing the reliance of his army on the supplies coming into Wilmington, reported that should the port fall, he would be unable to maintain his troops.

Throughout the war the North attempted to keep Wilmington under a tight blockade, but the port's widely spaced entrances forced the Union navy to split its warships into two squadrons that could not support each other. This division of strength coupled with the power of the Confederate forts stymied any effective blockade. Though active operations against Wilmington had been considered as early as the summer of 1862, the North was unable to put together a combined army and navy expedition against Fort Fisher until December 1864. Two assaults were made against the fort, and it, along with Whiting and Lamb, was captured on January 15, 1865.

The fall of Fort Fisher ended Wilmington's role as a blockade-running port and effectively cut the Confederacy's lifeline to Europe. Though the Confederates, under Gen. Braxton Bragg, continued to resist Northern advances against Wilmington for another month, the city's fate as well as that of the Confederacy was sealed, and on February 22, 1865, while a rear guard destroyed government property and records, Bragg evacuated Wilmington. On March 14, in order to show Wilmington's new loyalty and encourage business, Mayor Dawson organized a mass celebration called the Grand Rally, which celebrated the return of Wilmington to Federal control.

[*See also* Fort Fisher, North Carolina.]

BIBLIOGRAPHY

Johns, John. "Wilmington during the Blockade." *Harper's New Monthly Magazine* 33 (September 1866): 497–503.

Sprunt, James. *Tales and Traditions of the Lower Cape Fear, 1661–1898.* Raleigh, N.C., 1916.

Watson, Alan D. *Wilmington: Port of North Carolina.* Columbia, S.C., 1991.
Wood, Richard E. "Port Town at War: Wilmington, North Carolina, 1860–1865." Ph.D. diss., Florida State University, 1976.

STEPHEN R. WISE

WILMOT PROVISO. During an 1846 debate over a $2 million appropriation for the acquisition of California and New Mexico, Pennsylvania Congressman David Wilmot proposed a prohibition on slavery in any territory acquired in the Mexican-American War that was then underway. Wilmot's motivations for offering the proposal were mixed. As a Northern Democrat he supported the war effort and Manifest Destiny but opposed the expansion of slavery and the settlement of free blacks in the territories. He told the Congress that the proviso would create territories where "my own race and own color can live without the disgrace" of "association with negro slavery." By offering the proviso, Wilmot hoped to finesse the issue—coming out both for the war and against the expansion of slavery. This would allow Northern Democrats to resist Whig attacks on them as doughfaces who always appeased the South.

The House adopted Wilmot's proviso by a vote of 83 to 64 in the face of almost unanimous Southern opposition, but the Senate adjourned before taking action on the appropriations bill to which it was attached. In 1847 the House attached the proviso to a $3 million appropriation despite unanimous Southern opposition in that body. In the Senate a few Northerners joined their unanimous Southern colleagues to defeat the proviso. Southern members of Congress unanimously rejected both the goal of the proviso—to prohibit slavery in the new territories—and its implication that Southern institutions (and thus Southerners) were too immoral to enter the new territories. The debate over the proviso revealed the danger to the South posed by a Congress increasingly polarized over slavery. The change of one vote in the Senate could prevent slaveholders from taking their slaves into Mexican Cession territory.

The proviso was a radical departure from American politics before the Mexican War. From the Northwest Ordinance (1787) until 1846, American politics had institutionalized the notion that the Southern territories were open to slavery and the Northern ones were not. The proviso threatened this balance, and in the process put the South on the defense in a new and dramatic way. A resolution of the Virginia legislature, adopted in February 1850, illustrates how the proposal of the proviso helped shape Southern thought and served as a prelude to secession. After asserting that Virginia's "loyalty to the Union . . . is stamped upon every page of her history," the legislature declared, "in the event of the passage of the Wilmot proviso . . . Virginia will be prepared to unite with her sister slaveholding states, in convention or otherwise" to consider "measures . . . for their mutual defence."

While the proviso inspired Southern fears and secessionist stirrings, it inspired an entire political party in the North, the Free-Soil party. The new party was a coalition of forces, including political abolitionists and former Liberty Party members, antislavery (conscience) Whigs, and antislavery Democratic negrophobes who were fed up with Southern domination of their party. The main platform of the party was the proviso and a demand for keeping slavery (and blacks) out of the territories. Although the party did poorly in 1848, the idea behind the proviso remained strong and reemerged as part of the main slogan of the Republican party in 1856, "Free Soil, Free Labor, Free Speech, Free Men."

[*See also* Compromise of 1850; Kansas-Nebraska Act; Missouri Compromise; Republican Party.]

BIBLIOGRAPHY

Bestor, Arthur. "State Sovereignty and Slavery: A Reinterpretation of Proslavery Constitutional Doctrine, 1846–1860." *Journal of the Illinois State Historical Society* 54 (1961): 117–180.
Freehling, William W. *The Road to Disunion: Sectionalism at Bay, 1776–1854.* New York, 1990.
Morrison, Chaplin. *Democratic Politics and Sectionalism: The Wilmot Proviso Controversy.* Chapel Hill, N.C., 1967.

PAUL FINKELMAN

WILSON, CLAUDIUS CHARLES (1831–1863), brigadier general. Wilson was born in Effingham County, Georgia, on October 1, 1831. He graduated from Emory College in Oxford, Georgia, and was admitted to the bar in Savannah in 1852.

By the late 1850s, Wilson was working for the U.S. court system but resigned in 1860. When war broke out, he entered Confederate service as commander of Company I, Twenty-fifth, Georgia. Before the year ended, he was elected colonel. Wilson and his regiment spent most of 1862 along the coasts of South Carolina and Georgia, and he became known for his ability to organize and lead men in combat. In 1863, the regiment served at Vicksburg, returning to Georgia when the city fell under Federal control.

During the Chickamauga campaign, Wilson commanded a brigade in W. H. T. Walker's reserve corps, which found itself in the thick of fighting. On September 18, the corps tried to secure Alexander's Bridge as a crossing for Confederate troops, but it was too well defended. Walker's corps then moved north to cross the Chickamauga at Byram's Ford. The following morning, while bivouacked at the Alexander house, Wilson's brigade, in response to Nathan Bedford Forrest's call for infantry, was sent forward to meet Union infantry near Jay's Mill. In the confused fighting that took place in the thick woods and fields near the Chickamauga Creek, Wilson's brigade distinguished itself. Before the battle ended, the brigade had lost nearly 50 percent of its numbers.

Wilson survived Chickamauga but became ill during the siege of Chattanooga. He died in Ringgold, Georgia, on November 27, 1863. He was promoted to brigadier general posthumously on February 17, 1864, in recognition of his services at Chickamauga.

BIBLIOGRAPHY

Derry, Joseph T. *Georgia.* Vol. 6 of *Confederate Military History.* Edited by Clement A. Evans. Vol. 7 of extended ed. Atlanta, Ga., 1899.

Warner, Ezra J. *Generals in Gray: Lives of the Confederate Commanders.* Baton Rouge, La., 1959.

JOHN F. CISSELL

WILSON, WILLIAM SYDNEY (1816–1862), congressman from Mississippi and lieutenant colonel. Wilson was born in Maryland into a political family. His father, Ephraim, was a U.S. congressman from 1827 to 1831, and his brother, also named Ephraim, was a U.S. senator from 1885 until his death in 1891. After becoming a lawyer, William Wilson moved to Mississippi, where he had relatives in the Natchez area. From Claiborne County, he was elected to two terms in the state legislature—in 1858 and 1860.

In Mississippi, on January 7, 1861, a convention was called to consider the relationship between the U.S. government and the state. After the convention passed the Mississippi ordinance of secession, revised the state constitution, and formed a military organization, it elected delegates to a convention to be held in Montgomery, Alabama, in February. Wilson was one of seven elected. The meeting was originally called to consider a Confederate constitution but then declared itself the Provisional Confederate Congress. Wilson, who apparently opposed this shift, resigned on April 29 and was replaced by Jehu Amaziah Orr.

He then returned to Claiborne County and recruited the Claiborne Volunteers, an infantry company that became Company F of the Second Mississippi Battalion. The company participated in the Battle of Seven Pines in the 1862 peninsula campaign and in the campaign in northern Virginia. Wilson was wounded at the Battle of Sharpsburg, September 17, 1862; it is likely that his death on November 3 was a result of his injury. In the course of his military career, he was promoted from captain to lieutenant colonel.

BIBLIOGRAPHY

Alexander, Thomas B., and Richard E. Beringer. *The Anatomy of the Confederate Congress: A Study of the Influences of Member Characteristics on Legislative Voting Behavior, 1861–1865.* Nashville, Tenn., 1972.

Warner, Ezra J., and W. Buck Yearns. *Biographical Register of the Confederate Congress.* Baton Rouge, La., 1975.

RAY SKATES

WILSON'S CREEK CAMPAIGN. The Planter's House conference had failed. The meeting between Unionists Brig. Gen. Nathaniel Lyon and Congressman Frank Blair and secessionists Governor Claiborne F. Jackson and Maj. Gen. Sterling Price had represented the last chance to quell the unrest growing in Missouri. On June 11, 1861, after hours of fruitless discussion, Lyon terminated the meeting by declaring war on the state of Missouri. The campaign that culminated in the Battle of Oak Hills (or Wilson's Creek) began two days later.

Lyon left St. Louis, marching with one column of Union troops up the Missouri River to capture Jefferson City, the state capital. Aware that Confederate troops were organiz-

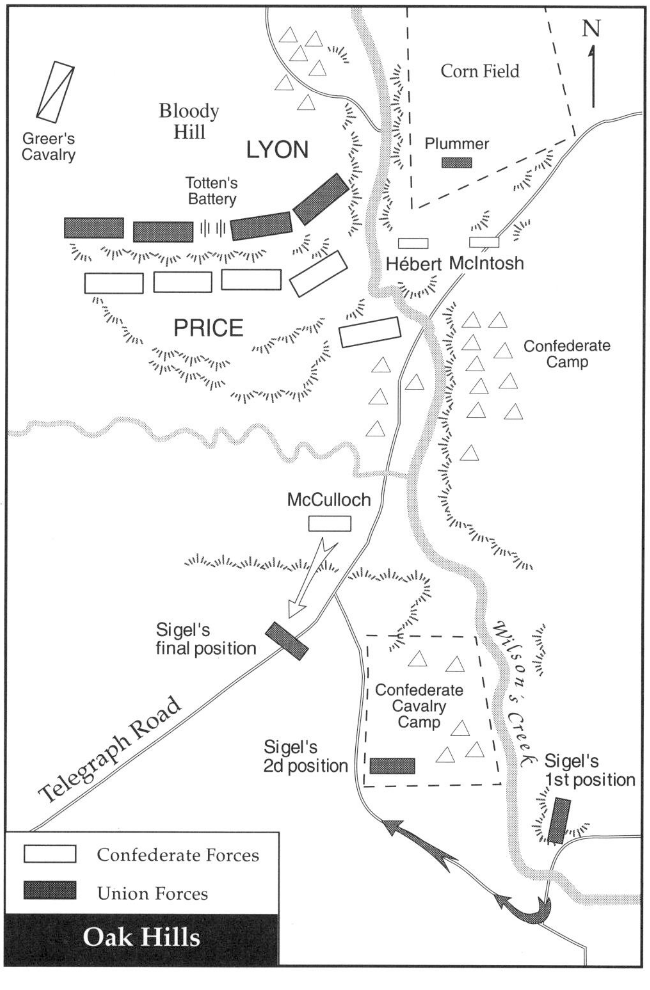

ing in northern Arkansas, a logical rendezvous point for the pro-Confederate Missouri State Guard and Confederate troops, he directed Brig. Gen. of Missouri Volunteers Thomas Sweeny to lead a column to southwestern Missouri.

On June 15, as Lyon neared Jefferson City, Jackson abandoned the capital and moved up river to Boonville. The Federals secured the capital, pursued Jackson, and defeated him in a skirmish on the seventeenth. Jackson and his troops retreated southwest, while Lyon concentrated his efforts on establishing Union control of the vital Missouri River. Meanwhile, Sweeny's column easily secured the route from St. Louis to Springfield.

While Jackson marched south with elements of the state guard, Price moved to the southwestern corner of the state and selected Cowskin Prairie as the rendezvous point for the state guard. Camped just across the state line, in Arkansas, were the troops of Gens. Ben McCulloch and N. Bart Pearce. On July 1, a portion of Sweeny's column led by Col. Franz Sigel marched west from Springfield in an attempt to block Jackson and Price from joining forces. As Jackson's column moved south, however, thousands of Missourians joined him. Sigel was outnumbered four to one, and his command of a thousand men was defeated in the Battle of Carthage on July 5. The Federals retreated to Springfield, while Jackson continued south and joined forces with Price.

Lyon, having secured the Missouri River, began marching south. On July 7, his command was reinforced by Maj. Samuel Sturgis's troops from Fort Leavenworth, Kansas. Two days later, Lyon received word of Sigel's defeat at Carthage, and he ordered an immediate forced march to Springfield. After four grueling days during which the Federals marched over a hundred miles and crossed three major rivers and numerous streams, they arrived in Springfield on the thirteenth.

Although Lyon's force now numbered about seven thousand effectives, the Army of the West faced numerous problems. The men were in need of food and supplies, and still more worrisome were three Southern forces camped to the southwest. If they united and moved against Lyon, he would be outnumbered almost two to one. Nevertheless, Gen. John C. Frémont in St. Louis repeatedly denied Lyon's requests for reinforcements. In addition, most of Lyon's army was composed of ninety-day enlistees whose terms of service were coming to an end. By mid-August, the army would be reduced to a skeleton force facing a growing Southern army.

On July 31, Lyon's fears became a reality. At the town of Cassville, about fifty miles southwest of Springfield, McCulloch, Price, and Pearce rendezvoused. Their twelve-thousand-man force began its march up Telegraph Road toward the enemy on the first of August. Lyon learned of the advance, but mistakenly thought the Southerners were moving in three separate columns and would unite near Springfield. He knew that once united, the larger Southern army could defeat his command and force him to abandon the region's pro-Union population. To avert this, Lyon led a column of more than 5,800 down Telegraph Road, planning to engage each column separately.

The next day, when advance elements of both armies fought a brief skirmish at Dug Springs, the victorious Federals learned that the Confederates were now united. Lyon ordered his men back to Springfield. The Southern army followed and went into camp where Telegraph Road crossed Wilson's Creek, only ten miles from the city.

By August 9, both armies had decided on similar plans of action. The Confederates planned to advance up Telegraph Road and strike the Federals at dawn on the tenth. But a light rainfall and the threat of a downpour canceled the operation. The majority of Southerners were without cartridge boxes, and heavy rain would disarm them. Lyon planned to leave a small force in Springfield, while he led 4,200 men out to attack the Confederate encampment from the north. At the same time Sigel, with 1,200 soldiers, would attack from the south. The element of surprise would be critical to the success of the operation.

To Lyon's great fortune, the Southern pickets had not returned to their posts after the night march was canceled, and the dawn attack was a success. The Federals overran several camps and drove the enemy south. The Union column advanced about one mile, reaching a ridge crest later called "Bloody Hill." From the east and across Wilson's Creek, a Confederate battery opened fire and stalled the advance. Price seized the opportunity to organize elements of the state guard into line of battle and ordered them up the hill's south slope to repulse the Federals.

As the Federals advanced down the west side of Wilson's Creek, Lyon, realizing his left flank was vulnerable to any force on the east side of the stream, ordered Capt. Joseph Plummer across the creek with a small force to advance in conjunction with the main column and guard the flank. After crossing the creek, Plummer observed the Confederate artillery's effect on the Federals on Bloody Hill and immediately moved against the battery. But two Confederate regiments blocked Plummer in John Ray's cornfield. In a brief, violent fight the Federals were routed and retreated across the stream. Plummer's defeat secured this section of the battlefield for the Southerners.

About a mile and a half south of Bloody Hill, Sigel had heard Lyon's attack and ordered his artillery to open fire on the main Southern cavalry camp. The Confederates abandoned their camp and retreated to the protection of nearby woods, leaving the way unopposed for Sigel's Federals to cross to the west side of Wilson's Creek, advance north, and take a position on a hill where they overlooked the cavalry camp and blocked Telegraph Road. Despite the strength of this position, Sigel was attacked and routed by Southern infantry led by McCulloch. The rear of the Confederate army was now secure, and all its efforts could be concentrated on Bloody Hill.

By 6:30 A.M. the battle lines had been drawn on Bloody Hill. The Federals held the crest and Price's Missourians the south slope. Between 7:30 and 10:00 A.M., the state guard assaulted the Union line twice, failing in each attempt. During the second attack Lyon was wounded but continued to direct his command. Around 9:30 Lyon ordered the Second Kansas and First Iowa Infantry regiments forward to reinforce the line, and the Southern attack stalled. But while leading the Second Kansas into position Lyon was killed by a musket ball.

As Price's attack lost its momentum, Confederate cavalry launched an assault on the Union right and rear. This diversion of the Federals' attention permitted Price to disengage his troops and fall back down the hill. As the cavalry closed on the enemy's line, musket volleys and artillery broke the charge, turning it back.

After Lyon's death, Sturgis, as senior officer, assumed command of the Union forces. Realizing that Price was organizing for a third assault, Sturgis reinforced his line to meet the attack. Around 10:30, some five to six thousand Confederates surged up the hill, and the fighting raged unabated for thirty minutes. At one point Southern infantry closed to within twenty paces of the Union-held crest, and battle smoke from both lines formed one huge cloud on the south slope. The Federal line was hammered along its entire length, but it did not break. By 11:00 Price realized the attack had failed and withdrew to the base of the hill.

During this lull Sturgis learned that Sigel had been routed and that the troops on Bloody Hill were dangerously low on ammunition. Deciding he could not withstand a fourth assault, Sturgis began withdrawing his forces, and by 11:30 the Federals had abandoned Bloody Hill. Unaware of Sturgis's move, the Southerners launched a fourth assault. Upon reaching the crest, they observed the Union rear guard and main column retreating to Springfield. Exhausted by almost five hours of combat, low on ammunition, lacking in experience, and misled by rumors of Federal reinforcements approaching Springfield, the Confederates chose not to pursue their adversaries.

The Battle of Oak Hills was over. Of the 5,400 Federals on the field, 1,317 were casualties with 258 killed, 873 wounded, and 186 missing. The Southerners suffered 1,222 losses, with 277 dead and 945 wounded out of 10,125 effectives. Losses totaled 24.5 percent for the Federals and 12 percent for the Confederates.

The campaign marked the beginning of the war in Missouri and the Trans-Mississippi. Afterward the Federal army withdrew to Rolla, Missouri, leaving the Southerners in possession of most of the southwestern region of the state. McCulloch and Pearce returned to Arkansas, and Price and the Missouri State Guard advanced north toward Lexington, where, on September 20, they captured the Union garrison. With victories at Wilson's Creek and Lexington, Confederate hopes in the state reached new heights. In October, Governor Jackson led his exiled state government out of the Union, and Missouri became the twelfth Confederate state. Meanwhile, pro-Union Missourians organized a loyal government in Jefferson City. Throughout the remainder of the war, Missouri never politically reunited.

BIBLIOGRAPHY

Adamson, Hans Christian. *Rebellion in Missouri: 1861.* Philadelphia, 1961.

Bearss, Edwin C. *The Battle of Wilson's Creek.* 3d ed. Bozeman, Mont., 1988.

Brown, Dee Alexander. "Wilson's Creek." *Civil War Times Illustrated* 11, no. 1 (April 1972): 8–18.

Holcombe, Return I., and W. S. Adams. *An Account of the Battle of Wilson's Creek, or Oak Hills, Fought between the Union Troops, Commanded by Gen. N. Lyon, and the Southern, or Confederate Troops, under Command of Gens. McCulloch and Price, on Saturday, August 10, 1861, in Greene County, Missouri.* Springfield, Mo., 1883. Reprint, Springfield, Mo., 1985.

Monaghan, Jay. *Civil War on the Western Border, 1854–1865.* Boston, 1955.

Phillips, Christopher. *Damned Yankee: The Life of General Nathaniel Lyon.* Edited by William E. Foley. Columbia, Mo., 1990.

Snead, Thomas L. *The Fight for Missouri: from the Election of Lincoln to the Death of Lyon.* New York, 1886.

Ware, Eugene F. *The Lyon Campaign in Missouri. Being a History of the First Iowa Infantry and of the Causes which Led up to Its Organization, and How It Earned the Thanks of Congress, which It Got. Together with a Birdseye View of the Conditions in Iowa Preceding the Great Civil War of 1861.* Topeka, Kans., 1907.

RICHARD W. HATCHER III

WILSON'S RAID ON SELMA. *See* Selma, Alabama, *article on* Wilson's Raid on Selma.

WINCHESTER, VIRGINIA. Located at the northern, or lower, end of the Shenandoah Valley, Winchester played a vital role in three campaigns—Thomas J. ("Stonewall") Jackson's Valley campaign of 1862, the Gettysburg campaign of 1863, and Philip Sheridan's Valley campaign against Jubal Early in 1864. The first two battles (May 25, 1862, and June 14–15, 1863) resulted in Southern victories, but the final one (September 19, 1864) proved the beginning of the end of Confederate control of its eastern granary.

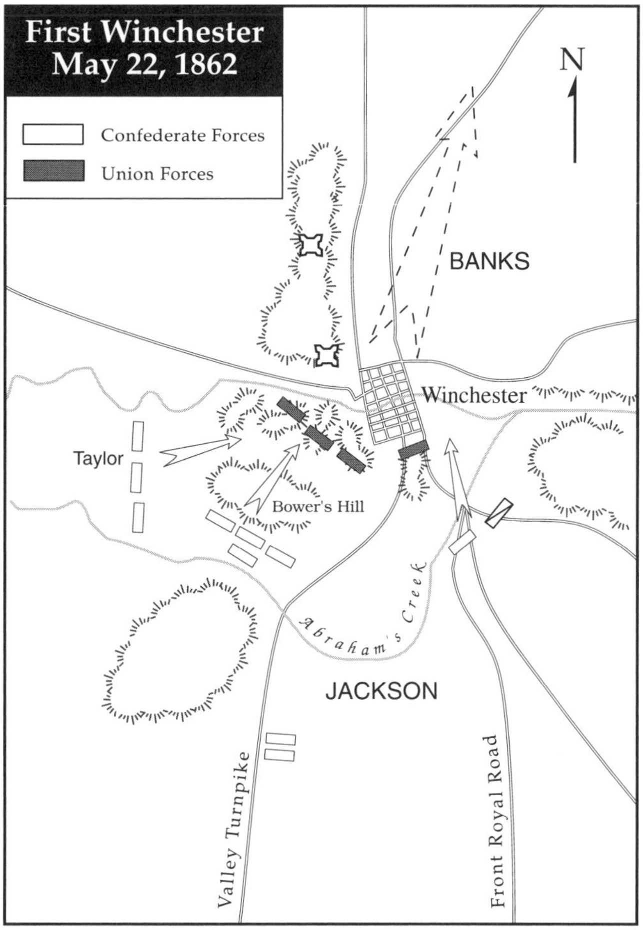

Founded in 1743, Winchester sat at an important juncture of roads and rail. The Valley Turnpike, a macadamized road that ran from Staunton to Martinsburg, split the town. The Winchester and Potomac rail line connected with the Baltimore and Ohio Railroad at Harpers Ferry, thirty-two miles away. The town lay on the invasion route the South or North would choose as a flanking movement around Washington or Richmond. Control of Winchester allowed the South to threaten Washington and some of the Union's logistical communications with the West. And the town provided an entry into the Shenandoah Valley, one of the most productive agricultural regions in the Confederacy. Winchester and the lower valley consequently saw numerous small engagements, as well as battles of larger proportion and meaning on three occasions.

Battle of 1862. The first came on May 25, 1862, when 17,000 Confederates under Maj. Gen. Thomas J. ("Stonewall") Jackson overwhelmed between 7,000 and 8,000 Union soldiers under Maj. Gen. Nathaniel P. Banks. The First Battle of Winchester came at the end of a three-day running fight that had begun on May 23 when the Confederates defeated a thousand-man force at Front Royal. Jackson forced his men on long marches to chase the retreating Federals and captured a number of wagons and supplies at Newtown on May 24. His men made a particularly exhausting march to bring them to the vicinity of Winchester, with Jackson distributing his troops in two groups—one along the Front Royal road to the southeast and the main attack column on the Valley Turnpike to the southwest.

Jackson wanted his men to take high ground to the west of the Valley Turnpike to dislodge Union troops who had formed on Bowers Hill. Because every second counted, the strictly religious Jackson laid aside his usual reservations about fighting on a Sunday and pressed his troops to take hills about four hundred yards from the Union forces. Federal artillery pummeled the Confederates, causing Jackson to order Louisianans under Brig. Gen. Richard Taylor to flank the enemy's left by marching northwest along Abraham's Creek. While a brigade held Union attention on the Front Royal Road, Taylor's men marched under fire across a plain and swept the Union forces from the high ground.

Poor leadership—particularly on the part of Brig. Gen. George Hume Steuart—kept the cavalry far from the action, botching the chance to inflict even more damage on Banks's men as they abandoned the town and retreated across the Potomac at sundown. As it was, the Union sustained the loss of nearly half its force, with 3,030 captured along with 9,300 small arms, 2 field guns, and supplies valued by Jackson at $125,185. This came at a cost of only 400 Confederates over the three days. More important, the action halted the advance of 40,000 Union troops from Fredericksburg to the peninsula where Maj. Gen. George B. McClellan threatened Richmond.

Battle of 1863. The Second Battle of Winchester, like the first, also occurred on the Sabbath. The action on June 14, 1863, pitted the Army of Northern Virginia's Second Corps under Lt. Gen. Richard Ewell against 6,900 Union soldiers of the Second Division, Eighth Corps, led by Maj. Gen. Robert H. Milroy. Ewell's men led the advance of the army under Gen. Robert E. Lee that began in early June and culminated in the Battle of Gettysburg (July 1–3, 1863). The garrison at Winchester blocked the Southern advance and threatened Lee's communications. Intelligence had warned the Union commander about the Southern threat, but Milroy discounted the information and also failed to withdraw on the night of the thirteenth after brushing with the vanguard of the Southern army as it moved into position for an attack.

Winchester was protected on the north and northwest by three unfinished earthworks. Confederates focused on the one farthest west called West Fort. Ewell wanted a division under Maj. Gen. Edward Johnson to demonstrate on the road to Front Royal from the southeast while Maj. Gen.

Jubal Early led his division on a flank march to Little North Mountain west of town. Early left a brigade under Brig. Gen. John B. Gordon to hold the crest of Bowers Hill to the southwest and by 4:00 P.M. on June 14 had three brigades on Little North Mountain. Shortly after 6:00 P.M., Confederate artillerists wheeled out twenty guns and opened a crushing fire on West Fort. Forty-five minutes later, Hays's Louisianans led the successful assault on the fort. A counterattack failed. Milroy decided to evacuate the town at 1:00 A.M. on June 15, but Johnson's force cut him off near Stephenson's Depot, four miles from Winchester on the way to Martinsburg.

The Union commander escaped with a small force but lost nearly 3,500 men, most of them captured. He was later exonerated of blame by a board of inquiry. Confederates sustained light casualties, totaling 269. The attack cleared the path for the rest of the army to advance and alerted Northerners that the Southern army had eluded the Army of the Potomac.

Battle of 1864. The Third Battle of Winchester, September 19, 1864, became the first of three losses that cost the South control of the Shenandoah Valley. Operating in the valley since mid-June, Jubal Early had managed to save Lynchburg, threaten Washington, D.C., and force Union commander Ulysses S. Grant to divert troops from the siege against Lee at Petersburg. And since August 10, Early had made a nuisance of himself in the lower valley.

Grant visited the theater and approved of Union Maj. Gen. Philip Sheridan's plans to attack Early's army at Winchester. Federals consistently estimated the Confederate force at around 20,000, but Early had at best 12,500 men as opposed to Sheridan's 35,000 infantry and artillery, plus 8,000 cavalry. Unfortunately for Early, he had weakened his force shortly before Sheridan's attack by returning an infantry brigade under Maj. Gen. Joseph B. Kershaw to Lee at Petersburg. Unlike the prior two battles, most of the fighting at Third Winchester took place to the east and northeast of town.

Preliminary maneuvers featured mistakes by both sides. On September 18, Old Jube sent a cavalry brigade and divisions under Maj. Gen. Robert Rodes and Maj. Gen. John B. Gordon to Martinsburg to check rumors of work crews on the Baltimore and Ohio Railroad. Another division under Maj. Gen. Dodson Ramseur guarded the Berryville Pike. Early's best defensive position was miles to the south of Winchester, but his scattered divisions forced him to reconcentrate his army near town or face piecemeal destruction. Sheridan blundered by launching his attack through Berryville Canyon, a narrow, two-mile-long gorge east of Winchester that became clogged with 20,000 infantrymen and bought the Confederate army precious time in which to position itself.

When the attack began at 11:40 A.M., Ramseur's division bore the brunt of the fighting until Rodes and Gordon returned and launched two major counterattacks. Gordon's division nearly smashed the Nineteenth Corps. And as the Sixth Corps advanced, a gap occurred in the Union lines when soldiers followed the Berryville Pike, which slanted southward away from the main line of advance. Rodes's men struck at the gap and nearly split the Union forces in two. Rodes was killed during the assault, which Union veterans finally managed to stop. Late in the day, a final surge by Brig. Gen. George Crook's Eighth Corps, supported by cavalry, broke the Confederate left. Early's men retreated through town and headed south.

The Confederates had fought stubbornly all day, but they were outnumbered three to one and they lost 1,707 killed and wounded and another 1,800 missing. Sheridan's Army of the Shenandoah sustained just over 5,000 total casualties. Perhaps more important to the Confederates was the sting of defeat—for the first time, the Second Corps of Lee's army retreated from ground it had held.

Sheridan followed his victory with another success on September 22, 1864, at Fisher's Hill near Strasburg, twenty-some miles south of Winchester. The battles left Winchester in Union hands for the remainder of the war and opened much of the Shenandoah Valley to the Federals, allowing Sheridan to begin the massive destruction of crops that residents referred to as "The Burning." The victories, along with others at Atlanta and Mobile, Alabama, helped turn the tide for Northern morale and ensure the reelection of Abraham Lincoln.

BIBLIOGRAPHY

Freeman, Douglas S. *Lee's Lieutenants: A Study in Command.* 3 vols. New York, 1942–1944. Reprint, New York, 1986.

Gallagher, Gary W., ed. *Struggle for the Shenandoah: Essays on the 1864 Valley Campaign.* Kent, Ohio, 1991.

Nye, Wilbur Sturtevant. *Here Come the Rebels!* Baton Rouge, La., 1965.

Tanner, Robert G. *Stonewall in the Valley: Thomas J. "Stonewall" Jackson's Shenandoah Valley Campaign, Spring 1862.* New York, 1966.

Wert, Jeffry D. *From Winchester to Cedar Creek: The Shenandoah Campaign of 1864.* Carlisle, Pa., 1987.

WILLIAM ALAN BLAIR

WINDER, CHARLES S. (1829–1862), brigadier general. Member of a prominent Maryland family, Charles Sidney Winder was born October 7, 1829, in Talbot County. He was an 1850 graduate of West Point. Four years later, Winder was on a troop ship bound for Panama when a hurricane wrecked the vessel. His heroism in the ordeal brought instant promotion and made Winder the youngest captain then on duty.

Strong Southern feelings led to his April 1, 1861,

CHARLES S. WINDER. LIBRARY OF CONGRESS

resignation from the army. Winder traveled to Montgomery, Alabama, and received appointment as a major of artillery. On July 8, 1861, following participation in the Fort Sumter bombardment, he became colonel of the Sixth South Carolina. Winder saw no battle action before his March 1, 1862, promotion to brigadier. He was then assigned to command of Thomas J. Jackson's old unit, the Stonewall Brigade.

For the tall, thin, graceful, and immaculately dressed Marylander, it was not a pleasant post. Winder succeeded the highly popular but ousted Richard B. Garnett; regimental colonels inside the brigade resented an outsider no more qualified than they for brigade command; and Winder's rigid system of discipline grated on the carefree and confident airs held by Jackson's favorite troops.

In spite of the hostility, Winder led his men well in Jackson's Shenandoah Valley campaign and through the Seven Days'. On August 9, 1862, he was directing artillery fire at Cedar Mountain when he was struck and mortally wounded by a cannon shell. A saddened Jackson wrote his wife: "I can hardly think of the fall of Brigadier-General C. S. Winder without tearful eyes." Winder was buried near Easton, Maryland.

BIBLIOGRAPHY

Casler, John O. *Four Years in the Stonewall Brigade.* Guthrie, Okla., 1893. Reprint, Dayton, Ohio, 1971.

Howard, McHenry. *Recollections of a Maryland Confederate Soldier and Staff Officer under Johnston, Jackson and Lee.* Baltimore, Md., 1914. Reprint, Dayton, Ohio, 1975.

Robertson, James I., Jr. *The Stonewall Brigade.* Baton Rouge, La., 1963.

JAMES I. ROBERTSON, JR.

WINDER, JOHN H. (1800–1865), provost marshal general of Richmond and Confederate commissary general of prisons. Winder was born February 21, 1800, at the family plantation, Rewston, in Somerset County, Maryland. Admitted to West Point in 1814, he arrived there just as his father, Gen. William Henry Winder, was being routed at the Battle of Bladensburg, August 24, 1814. Determined to redeem the family reputation, Winder graduated in 1820 and served with distinction in the old army (he was twice brevetted during the Mexican War, finishing as lieutenant colonel), but he was not satisfied with his military rank or status in 1861 and resigned to join the Confederacy.

Too old for field command, Brigadier General Winder served from 1862 to 1864 as provost marshal general of Richmond, where he was much resented because of his strict enforcement of martial law. Simultaneously, he was placed in control of Union prisoners (1861–1865) and finished his career as commissary general of prisoners, a position that blackened his reputation ineradicably. Criticized as a tyrant in the Southern press and vilified as the "inhuman fiend of Andersonville prison" in the North, he was damned no matter what he did. Had he not died of a heart attack on February 6, 1865, he might have suffered the same fate as his subordinate, Henry Wirz, who was tried and executed for war crimes.

Winder was not the cruel villain long portrayed in the history books. He performed thankless tasks as ably as he could, and the ultimate tragedy is that no one in the Confederacy could have done any better.

BIBLIOGRAPHY

Blakey, Arch Fredric. *General John H. Winder, C.S.A.* Gainesville, Fla., 1990.

Thomas, Emory M. *The Confederate State of Richmond: A Biography of the Capital.* Austin, Tex., 1971.

ARCH FREDRIC BLAKEY

WIRZ, HENRY (1823–1865), commandant of Andersonville Prison. Wirz was born Heinrich Hermann Wirz in Zurich, Switzerland, on November 25, 1823, the son of a tailor. He received elementary and some secondary schooling. Although he was interested in medicine, his father insisted on mercantile training. He later claimed to be a physician and assisted doctors in America, but he almost certainly had no medical degree. While in Europe, he married and had two children, but legal troubles led to brief imprisonment followed by divorce. Immigrating to America in 1849, he lived in Massachusetts and then Kentucky, where he married a widow. At the start of the Civil War he was living in Milliken's Bend, Louisiana. He enlisted in the Fourth Louisiana Infantry and became a sergeant. At the Battle of Seven Pines, he incurred a wound above his right wrist, which left him partially incapacitated and in pain for the rest of his life.

Wirz was then assigned to the Confederate military prisons at Richmond headed by Gen. John H. Winder. On June 12, 1862, he was promoted to captain and became one of Winder's adjutants. He was then sent to supervise prisoners farther south and for a time headed the prison at Tuscaloosa, Alabama. On December 19, 1862, he was furloughed to go as a representative of President Jefferson Davis on a mission to Paris and Berlin.

Returning to the Confederacy in February 1864, he was ordered on March 27 to Andersonville Prison in Georgia, where he was given command of the prison's interior. Faced with problems largely created by his supervisors, who crammed prisoners into the ill-supplied stockade, Wirz vainly attempted to reorganize the prison. He had only limited authority over most of the personnel, however, and to strengthen his position, he sought promotion. Though supported by superiors and sometimes referred to as "major," he never received that rank. As conditions deteriorated at Andersonville, Wirz was blamed by the prisoners for their suffering. Inmates of earlier prisons had often been amused at his manner, but those at Andersonville described him as a brutal tyrant. Observers commented negatively on his German accent, his frequent use of profanity, and his outbreaks of rage. By war's end, he and General Winder were among the most notorious Confederate prison officials. When Winder died of a heart attack, Wirz was left to bear the brunt of Northern outrage.

Perhaps because of naiveté or lack of understanding of the North's anger over prison conditions, Wirz did not join other prison officers who fled. Instead he stayed on at Andersonville, where he was arrested and taken to Washington, D.C. There, beginning August 23, 1865, he was tried by a military commission on charges of murder and mistreatment of prisoners. The hostile commission permitted Wirz only a limited opportunity to defend himself, and it heard much testimony, often conflicting, against both Wirz and his superiors. The commission found him guilty, and when clemency was denied, he was hanged on November 10 in the yard of the Old Capitol Prison.

The published record of his trial became a leading source for postwar anti-Confederate propaganda. Nonetheless, some former Confederates and even ex-prisoners defended Wirz. In 1909, the Georgia chapter of the United Daughters of the Confederacy unveiled at Andersonville a memorial shaft to the only Confederate executed in the aftermath of the Civil War.

[*See also* Andersonville Prison.]

EXECUTION OF HENRY WIRZ. Washington, D.C., November 10, 1865. Etching from *Frank Leslie's Illustrated Newspaper,* November 25, 1865. NATIONAL ARCHIVES

BIBLIOGRAPHY

Blakey, Arch Fredric. *General John H. Winder, C.S.A.* Gainesville, Fla., 1990.

Futch, Ovid. *History of Andersonville Prison.* Gainesville, Fla., 1968.

Hesseltine, William B. *Civil War Prisons: A Study in War Psychology.* Columbus, Ohio, 1930. Reprint, New York, 1964.

Parker, Sandra V. *Richmond's Civil War Prisons.* Lynchburg, Va., 1990.

FRANK L. BYRNE

WISE, HENRY A. (1806–1876), U.S. diplomat, governor of Virginia, and brigadier general. Born on December 3, 1806, and reared in Drummondtown, Virginia, Henry Alexander Wise was graduated with honors in 1825 from Washington and Jefferson College in Washington, Pennsylvania. Admitted to the bar after studying law for two additional years, Wise practiced the legal profession in Virginia and Tennessee. A successful farmer, Jacksonian Democrat, and outspoken champion of slavery and state rights, he was elected to the U.S. House of Representatives in 1835, serving in that body and vehemently espousing the Southern way of life until 1843. In 1844, Wise was named U.S. minister to Brazil. Wise was too candid with his views to ever succeed as a diplomat, however, and in 1847 he resigned his post and returned to Virginia. Elected governor of Virginia in 1855 by the Democrats, he served as chief executive of that state from 1856 until 1860. After John Brown was convicted for his 1859 attempt to seize the U.S. Arsenal at Harpers Ferry, Wise oversaw Brown's hanging, even visiting him before his execution.

After the start of the Civil War, Wise helped engineer the capture of Harpers Ferry in the spring of 1861. On June 5, 1861, Henry Wise, with much political clout but absolutely no military experience, was commissioned a brigadier general in the Confederate army. His first assignment was commanding the Confederate Army of the Kanawha in present-day West Virginia. A failure in all respects, Wise was soon replaced by Gen. John B. Floyd, an equally inept political soldier with whom Wise could not and would not get along. After an unqualified defeat at Carnifix Ferry in September and a disastrous November campaign, Wise and his brigade, known as Wise's Legion, were ordered to North Carolina.

On February 7, Union Gen. Ambrose Burnside made a successful amphibious assault on Roanoke Island, North Carolina, and the following day his troops defeated the Confederate forces there. Wise was in overall command of the island, and his son was killed during the battle. Posted next with Gen. Robert E. Lee's Army of Northern Virginia, he and his men saw action during the Seven Days' fighting as Union Gen. George B. McClellan battled up the Virginia Peninsula in a disastrous attempt to capture Richmond. Remaining in the Richmond defenses for about a year following the Peninsular campaign, Wise was sent to command the Sixth Military District of South Carolina from October 1863 until returning to the Army of Northern Virginia to take part in the Battle of Drewry's Bluff on May 16, 1864. There, the Confederate forces under Gen. P. G. T. Beauregard effectively sealed up the Union army of Gen. Benjamin Butler at Bermuda Hundred.

Commanding a district at Petersburg, Virginia, Wise served with Lee's army during the ten-month-long siege there. When Petersburg fell to the Union forces on April 2, 1865, Wise joined the Confederate retreat to Appomattox, fighting with his troops at the Battle of Sayler's Creek on April 6. Present at Lee's surrender at Appomattox Courthouse three days later, Wise took his parole, but never applied for amnesty for his role in the Confederate service.

Following the war, he resumed his career in law until he died in Richmond on September 12, 1876.

BIBLIOGRAPHY

Patterson, Richard. "Schemes and Treachery: The 1861 Plot to Seize the Arsenal at Harpers Ferry." *Civil War Times Illustrated* 28, no. 2, April, 1989.

Simpson, Craig M. *A Good Southerner: The Life of Henry A. Wise of Virginia.* Chapel Hill, N.C., 1985.

Wise, Barton H. *The Life of Henry A. Wise of Virginia, 1806–1876.* N.p., 1899.

Wise, Henry A. *Seven Decades of the Union.* Philadelphia, 1871.

WARREN WILKINSON

WITHERS, JONES MITCHELL (1814–1890), major general. Withers was born in Madison County, Alabama. He attended West Point, graduating in 1835, but served in the army less than a year before returning to Alabama, where he became a lawyer, merchant, and politician. He reenlisted during the Creek War of 1836 and again during the Mexican War, rising to colonel of the Ninth Infantry.

In 1861 Withers, now mayor of Mobile, joined the Confederate army and was elected colonel of the Third Alabama Infantry, which he accompanied to Norfolk, Virginia. In July he was promoted to brigadier general and placed in charge of the defenses of Mobile. In March 1862 Withers joined the army gathering in western Tennessee to counter the Union invasion. At Shiloh, his first major battle, Withers led a division of three brigades on the Confederate right. In the confusion Withers struggled to control his troops but was swept up in the fight for the Union center. On the second day of battle he fought an effective rearguard action and was praised by Braxton Bragg, who said his division "performed service rarely surpassed."

Withers was promoted to major general on April 6, 1862. During the Perryville campaign his brigades helped capture Munfordville, Kentucky. At Murfreesboro on December 31, 1862, Withers led his division for the last time in a major battle. Because of a reorganization by Gen. Leonidas Polk just before the battle, Withers's attacks were poorly coordinated, resulting in high casualties and failure to capture a Union strongpoint, the Round Forest (a half acre of mature hardwoods along the Nashville and Chattanooga Railroad held by Gen. Thomas Crittenden). Despite this, Bragg praised him for "valor, skill, and ability."

Plagued by illness, Withers left the army after the Tullahoma campaign in the summer of 1863 to assume the less arduous duties of organizing and stationing forces in Alabama. For the remainder of the war he commanded the Alabama reserves and sent troops to threatened areas in the state, especially Mobile.

After the war Withers returned to Mobile, where he was again elected mayor in 1867 and served as editor of the *Mobile Tribune*.

BIBLIOGRAPHY

Brewer, Willis. *Alabama: Her History, Resources, War Record and Public Men*. Montgomery, Ala., 1872.

The National Cyclopaedia of American Biography. Vol. 11. New York, 1897.

U.S. War Department. *War of the Rebellion: A Compilation of the Official Records of the Union and Confederate Armies*. Washington, D.C., 1880–1901. Ser. 1. Vol. 6, pp. 738, 815; vol. 10, pt. 1, pp. 532–536; vol. 20, pt. 1, pp. 753–758; vol. 23, pt. 2, p. 925; vol. 32, pt. 2, pp. 685–686; vol. 39, pt. 2, pp. 711, 730.

Wheeler, Joseph. *Alabama*. Vol. 7 of *Confederate Military History*. Edited by Clement A. Evans. Atlanta, 1899. Vol. 8 of extended ed. Wilmington, N.C., 1987.

CHARLES M. SPEARMAN

WITHERS, THOMAS (1804–1865), congressman from South Carolina. Born at Ebenezer, near Rock Hill, South Carolina, Withers graduated from South Carolina College in 1823. In 1825 he became editor of the *Columbia Telescope* and warmly supported nullification. Admitted to the bar in 1828, he began the practice of law in Camden. He was elected circuit solicitor in 1832 and a common law judge in 1846. In the secession crisis of 1851, Withers was a cooperationist. By the time of the Civil War, he owned twenty-three slaves and property valued at $107,000.

In 1860 Withers was elected to the state secession convention and subsequently to the Provisional Congress. Rumored to have been snubbed by Jefferson Davis long before, Withers nevertheless supported strong military and financial measures. A determined advocate of state rights, he proposed omitting the words "We, the people" from the Constitution, making the powers of Congress "delegated," not "granted," and preventing a foreign citizen from suing a state. He supported laws to identify state ownership of former U.S. property and to allow states to govern river navigation and administer sequestered property.

In June 1861, after the second session of the Provisional Congress, Withers resigned his seat because it was proposed that a supreme court be established and given appellate jurisdiction over the state courts. He resumed his judicial duties in South Carolina. His wealth destroyed by the war, he died almost penniless on November 7, 1865.

BIBLIOGRAPHY

Cyclopedia of Eminent and Representative Men of the Carolinas of the Nineteenth Century. Vol. 1. Madison, Wis., 1892.

Warner, Ezra J., and W. Buck Yearns. *Biographical Register of the Confederate Congress*. Baton Rouge, La., 1975.

A. V. HUFF, JR.

WITHERSPOON, JAMES HERVEY (1810–1865), colonel and congressman from South Carolina. Born in Lancaster District, South Carolina, on March 23, 1810, Witherspoon graduated from South Carolina College in 1831 and became a planter. In 1837 he became district commissioner in equity, serving until 1864. He also served as district ordinary. In 1860 he owned twenty-two slaves and property valued at $120,000.

In 1861 Witherspoon volunteered as a private in the Lancaster Greys. A year later he became colonel of the Eighth South Carolina Reserves, and in 1863 colonel of the Fourth South Carolina Regiment. He saw no military action.

In October 1863 Witherspoon defeated John McQueen for Congress. He served on the Foreign Affairs, Ordnance and Ordnance Stores, and Post Office and Post Roads committees. He supported central authority over all but local matters and congressional, not executive, authority over army manpower and taxation. He backed destruction of property to prevent its capture, central control of cargo space on state-owned vessels, and the right of impressment. He opposed suspension of the writ of habeas corpus and arming slaves.

After the war, Witherspoon returned to Lancaster where he died on October 3, 1865.

BIBLIOGRAPHY

Wardlaw, Joseph G., comp. *Geneology of the Witherspoon Family*. Yorkville, S.C., 1910.

Warner, Ezra J., and W. Buck Yearns. *Biographical Register of the Confederate Congress*. Baton Rouge, La., 1975.

A. V. HUFF, JR.

WOFFORD, WILLIAM TATUM (1824–1884), brigadier general. The grandson of a Revolutionary War colonel, Wofford was born June 28, 1824, in Habersham County, Georgia. After graduating from Franklin College, he studied law in Athens, was admitted to the bar in 1846, and practiced in Cassville. In 1847, he raised a cavalry company for the Mexican War. He was subsequently cited for his services in a resolution by the Georgia General Assembly. Wofford served in the state house of representatives for four years and as clerk of the house for two years. At the same time he developed a prosperous plantation and helped establish the weekly *Cassville Standard.*

As a member of the state convention in 1861, Wofford voted against secession. When Georgia left the Union, however, he immediately offered his services to the state. Initially commissioned a captain, he was later elected colonel of the Eighteenth Georgia Infantry upon the organization of that regiment.

Following duty in North Carolina, Wofford transferred to the Army of Northern Virginia and participated in the Seven Days' campaign. He was at Second Manassas, South Mountain, and Sharpsburg, after which he was praised by John Bell Hood for "gallant conduct" and "conspicuous bravery."

After the death of Thomas R. R. Cobb at Fredericksburg, Wofford took command of the brigade and was promoted to brigadier general January 17, 1863. He led the brigade at Chancellorsville and Gettysburg, accompanied James Longstreet to eastern Tennessee, and was in the Overland campaign of 1864, during which he was wounded twice. Later he took part in Jubal Early's Valley campaign of 1864. In July of that year, Wofford was recommended twice for promotion, but there was no vacancy and he continued a brigadier.

WILLIAM TATUM WOFFORD. LIBRARY OF CONGRESS

At the request of Governor Joseph E. Brown of Georgia, Wofford was placed in charge of the Department of Northern Georgia in January 1865. In that capacity, he raised seven thousand troops to defend against the invaders. He surrendered at Resaca, Georgia, May 2, 1865.

In the postwar years, Wofford helped organize two railroad lines, served as a trustee of the Cherokee Baptist College, and donated land and money for the establishment of Wofford Academy. He was elected to Congress in 1865, but was denied his seat. He also served as an elector on the Greeley ticket of 1872 and the Tilden ticket of 1876. Wofford died near Cass Station, Georgia, May 22, 1884, and was buried in Cassville Cemetery.

BIBLIOGRAPHY

Compiled Military Service Records. William Tatum Wofford. Microcopy M331, Roll 272. Record Group 109. National Archives, Washington, D.C.

Conyos, Lucy J. *The History of Bartow County, Georgia.* Jefferson, Ga., 1933.

Derry, Joseph T. *Georgia.* Vol. 6 of *Confederate Military History.* Edited by Clement A. Evans. Atlanta, 1899. Vol. 7 of extended ed. Wilmington, N.C., 1987.

Warner, Ezra J. *Generals in Gray: Lives of the Confederate Commanders.* Baton Rouge, La., 1959.

LOWELL REIDENBAUGH

WOMEN. As the secession movement spread across the South, it encompassed nearly three million adult women, white and black, living in many different situations.

White Women in the Confederacy

Those who were most visible to publicists at the time and to historians since composed a minority: daughters and wives of successful planters in the old black belt or the newer cotton and sugar lands to the west and their counterparts in the urban elite. We know a great deal about these women because at least some of them were highly literate and much given to writing letters and journals.

Some were planters in their own right. From early times a not inconsiderable number of Southern women had owned plantations; of the 440 South Carolinians who owned one hundred slaves or more on a single estate, for example, more than 10 percent were women, many of them married. Across the South scores of such women directed planting operations themselves.

In every town and city there were a few "leading families," whose women set the pace for the urban middle class. In places like Charleston, Savannah, Montgomery, and New Orleans, a small but highly visible group, made up of wives of lawyers and politicians, played an informal but vigorous and sometimes influential part in politics themselves. Mary Boykin Chesnut, Virginia Clay, and Varina Howell Davis were among the best known. Public policy and the men who made it were central to their interests.

With the election of Abraham Lincoln in November 1860 more women began to take part in political discussion, as the debate over a response to the election took shape. In Alabama women proposed a boycott of Northern goods, modeled on the boycotts of British goods in the 1770s. Many spoke out strongly in defense of slavery and the Southern ideology. Others wrote for their local papers or regional journals such as *DeBow's Review*. When fighting began, a surprising number made a strenuous effort to understand, and record, the military progress of the war.

Though these two elite groups shared economic and social status, their experiences, once war began, were quite different. Women on plantations, large or small, often had to take over as planters when their husbands were called to serve in the government or the army. Despite the Confederate law that permitted owners of twenty slaves to avoid military service on the grounds that they were indispensable to food production and to keeping the peace, the countryside was gradually drained of white men. Many areas took on the aspect of a matriarchy. Women had to learn or improve their knowledge of agricultural and financial management and struggle with the management of slaves. Some handled these responsibilities very well while keeping up the fiction that they were only following advice from absent spouses. Those who had reliable overseers or trusted slave managers or who had been managers behind the scene all along were lucky. Others found the task too much to bear and complained bitterly of their burdens. The woman who described her state as "anxiety about something to eat, something to wear and anxiety about everything" or the one who wrote her husband "I tell you candidly all this attention to farming is uphill work. . . . I am heartily tired" had plenty of company.

But however much some might complain, there was no one else to do the job. In the end it was largely women who kept the plantations going and managed the difficult but essential shift from cotton to food production. A South Carolina senator's daughter remarked in 1865 upon the strange turn of events that meant that women could not count on men to help them. She added that the men, when asked for advice, were apt to say that since they knew not what to advise, the women must simply do their best and get away from the Yankees if possible.

Somewhere in the middle of the social ladder, and not so visible in the record, were a large number of white women who lived on small farms or small plantations (those with ten slaves or less). For these the demands were even more strenuous than those resting on large planters' wives. Since they were less likely than their more prosperous sisters to keep records, it has been easy to overlook their response to the challenge of the Civil War. But a handful of surviving records indicates that these women functioned much as farmers had for generations: overseeing planting and plowing whether the actual labor was done by slaves or family members, growing gardens, and raising chickens, pigs, and sheep for home use, and selling or bartering the surplus.

The diary of Emily Lyles Harris provides the most detailed picture of a woman's life on this kind of farm. Though carrying on as a highly competent farmer, she was exceedingly self-critical, fretting about her children, worrying as slaves became more restive and, by her lights, impudent, and wondering what wickedness of her own had brought her to such a pass. Emily Harris can stand for thousands of women who filled the evangelical churches on Sundays, went to revival meetings when they could, raised numerous children, and kept the economy going for the four years of war. Few had her skill with a pen, though most shared her profound religious commitment. Her support for the war was lukewarm from the first and diminished each time her husband went off to the army. She thought the Confederate government woefully mismanaged and once wrote that she would as soon get rid of the men who ran it as the Yankees. The isolation and localism of her experience, in the South Carolina Piedmont, emerges vividly in her diary entries and was doubtless characteristic of many people in her situation.

Further down the social scale were families who had barely managed to survive in peacetime and faced the real possibility of starvation when the men went off to war. Some of these fell into that dim category of "poor whites" or "sand hillers" or "crackers"—people for whom a combination of poor land and poor health dictated a marginal existence.

Effects of the War

Women of childbearing age—rich or poor, country or town—whose husbands went off to war enjoyed a welcome reprieve from constant pregnancy; for this reason visits to or from the patriarch were often viewed with mixed emotions. On the other hand, thousands of women—presumably those too old to have little children—risked considerable danger to follow the army. Wives of officers sometimes felt it better to be where they could know what was going on than to stay at home waiting for uncertain mail, so they set up housekeeping as near to army camps as they could. Other women followed the army—as women always have—to earn a living by washing or cooking, and some, of course, by prostitution.

Once the war was actually under way, spirited young women began to wonder, why should men have all the excitement? The most daring dressed as men and enlisted in the army, sometimes serving for years before they were found out. Others found adventure that peacetime seldom provided by undertaking espionage work for the Confederacy. The best known of these spies was Belle Boyd, only seventeen in 1861, who by the following year had become a heroine in the South and a most-wanted character in the North. She served intermittently throughout the war, despite several terms in Northern prisons. Her final mission took her on a ship to England. The ship was captured, and she was exiled to Canada, but she eventually married the captain whose ship had intercepted her. A man of similar exploits would probably have been executed early on.

Next to spying, the most demanding service women could undertake was that of acting as volunteers in army hospitals. Many women, mostly single or widowed, offered their services as nurses and—despite the extreme reluctance of the male doctors to accept them—performed admirably; a number finally took charge of hospitals. An official report to the Confederate Senate contains evidence that mortality rates in hospitals run by women was about half that in those run by men.

Working long hours under uncomfortable conditions, the nurses sometimes allowed themselves the luxury of pouring scorn on their less adventurous sisters. One remarked with heavy sarcasm that a woman who thought her reputation could be ruined by serving her country had obviously not much reputation to lose. Another, listening to a younger woman say she had often wished to volunteer, commented laconically, "I wondered what hindered her." Along with the well-known nurses (Phoebe Pember, Kate Stone, Sally Tompkins, Louisa Cheves McCord, Ella King Newsome) were thousands of nameless women who staffed and supplied wayside hospitals in nearly every community along railroad lines to take care of wounded soldiers trying to get home. These functioned until the very end of the war when supplies ran so short they could no longer carry on.

Urban women, more dependent on the market than those in the country, were the first to feel the pinch of shortages, a pinch that would develop into a vise by the end of the war and that in time would encompass much of the countryside as well. Women brought astonishing ingenuity to bear on the problem of shortages: salt was retrieved from smokehouses, old clothes were unraveled and reknitted, carpets were transformed into blankets, herbs and edible plants were gathered, and every family had its coffee substitute, though no satisfactory one was ever devised. By 1865 in many places it was no longer a matter of finding substitutes but of finding any food at all. Black-eyed peas and corn kept people alive, but widespread malnutrition laid the groundwork for postwar epidemics.

Once-pampered women worked all day, seven days a week, as spinning wheels and looms were dragged from attics and goods once routinely bought were made at home. Mistress and slave worked in tandem. We have Mary Chesnut's word for it that she rarely saw a woman without knitting in her hand.

The Confederacy from the first was in dire need of all kinds of supplies for the army, and women turned to supplying soldiers as they had long supplied their families. Every town and hamlet had its soldiers' aid society, and more than a thousand took shape across the South to provide uniforms, medical supplies, tents, sandbags for fortifications, and fresh food (to ward off scurvy) for the Confederate army. Working every day, not excluding Sundays, some of these voluntary associations developed primitive systems of mass production and turned out extraordinary quantities of goods. If it were not for their meticulous record keeping, the amount of materials Southern women transformed into uniforms, shirts, hospital supplies, and the like would defy belief. In addition to supplying the needs of soldiers—most often those from their own communities—women's societies took on responsibility for the indigent families of men in the army and those who had been killed.

While women who could afford to do so supported the war effort with their labor, poorer women, suffering from inflation and extortion, were the major players in urban food riots. In 1863 such riots occurred in several North Carolina, Georgia, and Alabama towns, as wives of soldiers, working-class women, and others who found it impossible to feed their families intimidated merchants and carried away flour, molasses, and salt. In Richmond women who had perhaps read of women in other Southern cities demanding that merchants sell them goods at government-established prices met to consider their own situation. The following day more than two thousand took to the streets, and though they began in good order, anger took over and riot ensued. The women made off with flour, bacon, shoes, brooms, and whatever else they had found too scarce or too expensive to buy. Mayor Joseph Mayo came out to plead with them, and the governor threatened to shoot them all. The women went home, and in due course the city council set up a system of food distribution for soldiers' families.

In addition to the vast amount of volunteer work, many women, usually out of necessity, found paying jobs. Only 7 percent of Southern teachers had been women before the war; by 1865 they constituted 50 percent of the teaching force. Other women went to work as clerks for the government in Richmond (paid half what their male counterparts received) or in state and local governments.

Women replaced men in stores, shops, sawmills, and any other place where the need was great.

The war propelled women into public life in other ways. As time went by, an astonishing number from every social class all across the South wrote letters or petitions to various government bodies, proposing improvements in the way the government was doing things or asking that their husbands be promoted or sent home because their families were starving. At one end of the social spectrum was author Augusta Jane Evans who wrote long letters of unsolicited advice on the conduct of the war to J. L. M. Curry; at the other end were the almost illiterate women whose letters of complaint poured into Raleigh or Montgomery.

As these letters and many private ones make clear, women's support for the war diminished steadily as casualties mounted and life at home became one continuous struggle for existence. At the beginning virtually everybody who talked openly exhibited vigorous patriotism; young women, in particular, were famous (or infamous) for insisting that men they knew should enlist. In private, opinion was less unanimous. Surviving diaries and letters show that some women from the beginning doubted that separation from the Union was possible or that the war would be as short as the leaders seemed to think. One doubter wrote scornfully of men "drunk with passion and women who share their frenzy." But however they felt at the beginning, as the war stretched on, more and more women decided that the price of independence was too high. Women who visited battlefields came home convinced that nothing could justify such carnage. Those who at the start felt confident that God would not allow the Confederacy to be defeated began to realize that they could not count on divine protection. For some this meant a gradual change in the nature of their religious convictions.

Women in the path of either army often suffered traumatic experiences. The loss of possessions and the shock of discovering the worst side of human nature could be devastating. Neither white hair nor pregnancy provided protection against Sherman's soldiers who, toward the end of his march through Georgia, were often out of control. Deserters and outlaws from the Confederate army were not much better, and even ordinary hungry Southern soldiers had little respect for the goods and crops of wealthy planters.

Those who could get away before invaders arrived became refugees, sometimes for the rest of the life of the Confederacy. Living with friends, relatives, or strangers, sometimes farming on borrowed land, these people usually joined, at least in their minds, the peace party.

Some women, the subject of much comment, could not bear to give up their accustomed luxuries and provided a market for blockade runners who were willing to put profit before patriotism. Mary Chesnut's diary offers plenty of evidence of an "eat, drink, and be merry" spirit in Richmond in the final years. But counterbalancing this image is that of the many others described by a contemporary as women "with coarse, lean and brown hands . . . women with scant, faded cotton gowns and coarse leather shoes . . . who silently and apathetically packed the boxes [for soldiers] looking into them with the intense and sorrowful gaze that one casts into a tomb."

Black Women in the Confederacy

Alongside the white women of the Confederacy were perhaps a million adult black women, most of them slaves. Of all the women who went through the Confederate experience these are the least well recorded from their own perspective. Evidence from their owners is more plentiful, but far from perceptive.

Like white women, slave women did not comprise a homogeneous group. Their individual life experiences were largely shaped by the economic situation and the character of their owners. The range from best to worst was very wide. For slave women life continued to be principally endless hard work, shadowed by the insecurity of family ties, the ever-present danger of being sold away from husband, children, kin, and friends. Some few who were the property of humane planter families—we have no way of knowing how many—had carved out for themselves within the humiliating confines of servitude a life of some comfort and satisfaction. Even the luckiest, however, were always at the mercy of some turn of fate over which they had no control.

The war brought with it a host of rumors, and whenever word spread that the Northern army was near, some slaves seized the opportunity to run away. Few things are more ironic than the dismay of a mistress when a favorite ("pampered" was the word often used) slave woman was one of the first to leave. Such sisterhood as the plantation system had permitted evaporated when the promise of freedom reached the land. Among those who stayed—especially on plantations or farms being run by women—insubordination grew. As little groups of slaves planned ways to take advantage of the new situation, women often turned out to be the leaders.

Slave women did their share of the hard work of supplying the Confederate army, spinning, weaving, and sewing for those who were fighting to keep them in servitude.

When the Union army liberated an area, its black women suddenly found themselves free. In Memphis these newly freed women, working in the existing black churches, moved at once to form their own voluntary associations to provide help for their own people. In the South Carolina Sea Islands, where Northerners came to teach the freed people, women among the thousands of slaves who had been abandoned by their owners flocked to school to learn to read. Similarly, in the Hampton Roads area of Virginia, thousands of slaves seeking freedom with the Union army gathered. A free black woman, Mary Peake, who had conducted illegal classes before the war took the lead in meeting the pressing demand for schooling.

Life after the Confederacy

For women as for men, after the brief failed experiment with independence and four years of bloody warfare, life would never be the same again. For white women who had been adults in 1861 the Civil War became the central event of their lives, shaping their self-images and fantasies ever after. Those who had succeeded in unaccustomed responsibilities were among those whose response to Reconstruction amazed Northern and Southern observers alike. Caroline Merrick, writing in Mississippi, noted that "in these days of awful uncertainties when men's hearts failed them, it was the woman who brought her greater adaptability and elasticity to control circumstances, and to lay the foundation of a new order." An Alabama woman wrote that "the women, the courageous women, everywhere were busy reorganizing lives, building up new homes out of the wrecks." Northern journalists made similar comments, and in 1891 a native Southerner, writing on the way the war had affected women, said flatly that it was the women who had set the South going again after the war, "filling the stronger sex with utter amazement at the readiness and power with which they began to perform duties to which they had never been used before." (He seemed not to notice any irony in his characterization of men as the stronger sex.) Attitudes, self-images, were changed. An amusing memoir of one South Carolina woman recounts her effort to conceal from her returned soldier-husband all the things she was now able to do for herself, lest his self-esteem be damaged. She was wittier than most, but there is no reason to think her unique.

Years later, Thomas Dabney, a great planter from Mississippi who had lost everything in the war, wrote to one of his daughters: "That you and Ida are quite able to take care of yourselves I entertain no doubt, but still it does me good to find you asserting the fact with so much boldness. Of all the principles developed by the late war, I think the capability of our Southern women to take care of themselves was by no means the least important."

The most dramatic change, of course, came to black women who at last had their freedom, if not much more. For them the end of the Confederacy was the first step toward a new life, a life not fully attained even yet.

For white women the long-term consequences were various: women expanded their role in the educational structure; some continued to work for wages in the postwar years; widows struggled to carry on plantations with free labor; younger women faced a generation in which the number of available husbands was very small. It took a generation before the full effect of the changes the war had wrought in the South were manifested in the lives of women. But by the 1890s many perceptive observers had come to realize the import of what Cornelia Phillips Spencer had written in 1870: "with the strongest conservative principles it is impossible to believe that women will continue to move in the same narrow ruts as heretofore." Rebecca Latimer Felton, in 1915, contrasted the postwar world with the prewar years when a woman's only chance lay "in finding herself a good master." By the 1890s the new woman, born in the Confederacy, growing up during Reconstruction, was everywhere appearing in the South.

[*See also* Bread Riots; Civil Service; Cold Water Parties; Courtship; Diaries, Letters, *and* Memoirs; Education, *article on* Women's Education; Espionage, *article on* Confederate Military Spies; Family Life; Feminism; Hospitals; Marriage and Divorce; Nursing; Plantation Mistress; Prostitution; Refugeeing; Soldiers' Aid Societies; *and biographies.*]

BIBLIOGRAPHY

Crabtree, Beth Gilbert, and James W. Patton, eds. *Journal of a Secesh Lady: The Diary of Catherine Ann Devereux Edmonston, 1860–1866.* Raleigh, N.C., 1979.

Cumming, Kate. *Gleanings from the Southland.* Birmingham, Ala., 1895.

Faust, Drew Gilpin. "Altars of Sacrifice: Confederate Women and the Narratives of War." *Journal of American History* 76, no. 4 (1990): 1200–1228.

Friedman, Jean E. *The Enclosed Garden.* Chapel Hill, N.C., 1990.

Harwell, Richard Barksdale, ed. *Kate: The Journal of a Confederate Nurse.* Baton Rouge, La., 1959.

Lebsock, Suzanne. *Virginia Women, 1600–1945.* Richmond, 1987.

Patton, James, and Francis Butler Simkins. *The Women of the Confederacy.* Richmond, 1936.

Pember, Phoebe Yates. *A Southern Woman's Story.* New York, 1879.

Perdue, Charles L., Jr., Thomas E. Barden, and Robert K. Phillips, eds. *Weevils in the Wheat: Interviews with Virginia Ex-Slaves.* Charlottesville, Va., 1976.

Rable, George. *Civil Wars: Women and the Crisis of Southern Nationalism.* Urbana, Ill., 1989.

Racine, Philip N., ed. *Piedmont Farmer: The Journals of David Golightly Harris, 1855–1870.* Knoxville, Tenn., 1990.

Scott, Anne Firor. *The Southern Lady: From Pedestal to Politics.* Chicago, 1970.

White, Deborah Gray. *Ar'n't I a Woman? Female Slaves in the Plantation South.* New York, 1985.

Woodward, C. Vann, ed. *Mary Chesnut's Civil War.* New Haven, 1981.

Anne Firor Scott

WOOD, FERNANDO (1812–1881), Northern politician and Southern sympathizer. Born in Philadelphia,

Pennsylvania, on June 14, 1812, Wood moved to New York City with his family in 1822. He eventually earned a large fortune in various business enterprises, especially maritime shipping. Wood entered politics in 1834 and rose to leadership in Tammany Hall. Backed by tenement dwellers and recent immigrants, he served in the U.S. House of Representatives from 1841 to 1843 and as mayor of New York City from 1855 to 1858.

In 1858 he lost the backing of Tammany Hall and was defeated for a third term but continued his political activities. He helped finance Stephen A. Douglas's senatorial campaign against Abraham Lincoln, and in 1859 he urged Virginia Governor Henry A. Wise to send John Brown to prison rather than make a martyr of him through execution. With backing from his brother Benjamin, who owned the *New York Daily News,* Wood in 1860 was returned to office as mayor of New York City. Later that year he led an anti-Douglas delegation to the Democratic convention in Charleston, to work for a pro-South candidate, but his delegation was not seated.

During the secession crisis, Wood suggested that New York City secede from the state of New York and become a free city. After the firing on Fort Sumter, however, he proposed a million-dollar appropriation to outfit Northern regiments. Defeated for another term as mayor, Wood was elected to the U.S. House of Representatives and served from 1863 to 1865. During the 1864 presidential campaign he and his brother supported Clement L. Vallandigham and helped him prepare the Democratic party's peace platform.

After the war Wood served in the House from 1867 to 1881, where he was a critic of Republican Reconstruction. A canny politician with a knack for organization, Wood owed his longevity in politics to his understanding of New York voters.

BIBLIOGRAPHY

Mushkat, Jerome. *Fernando Wood.* Kent, Ohio, 1990.

Pleasants, Augustus S. *Fernando Wood of New York.* New York, 1948.

STEPHEN R. WISE

WOOD, JOHN TAYLOR (1830–1904), naval officer, colonel. Well connected and with a spirit of adventure, Wood consistently secured assignments he liked best—raiding the enemy. Born August 13, 1830, at the army outpost of Fort Snelling, Iowa Territory (now Minnesota), Wood was a grandson of Zachary Taylor, his mother being Taylor's eldest daughter, Anne Mackall (Taylor). Lt. Jefferson Davis married Taylor's second daughter, Sarah Knox (Taylor), which made the future president of the Confederacy Wood's uncle.

Wood's naval service began in 1847 and consisted of periodic stints at the new Naval Academy at Annapolis mixed with training at sea. He graduated second in his class at Annapolis on June 10, 1853, and then shipped to the Mediterranean. Back at Annapolis as assistant commandant, he was commissioned a lieutenant as of September 16, 1855. After further service with the Mediterranean squadron, he became a professor of gunnery and tactics at Annapolis in 1860.

At the onset of war, Wood's father, an army surgeon from Rhode Island, remained loyal to the Union and served as assistant surgeon-general. A younger brother, Robert C. Wood, Jr., went south and rode with John Hunt Morgan. Wood resigned from the U.S. Navy April 21, 1861, and went to Richmond where Jefferson Davis appointed him a lieutenant in the Confederate navy effective October 4, 1861. Wood's first major duty was aboard the CSS *Virginia,* where he was instrumental in recruiting and training gunners for the ironclad and commanded the aft gun. In March 1862 he participated in the famous battle with USS *Monitor.*

The naval supremacy held by the Federals prompted Wood to strike in a series of cutting-out expeditions in Virginia and North Carolina rivers. Moving his boarding cutters overland on wagons by day, Wood and his men would suddenly emerge from unexpected places at night to board and capture enemy vessels. These daring raids proved Wood to be a remarkable fighter, although he was modest and rather cultivated in demeanor. His captures often involved hand-to-hand combat and included armed gunboats; especially arduous was the destruction of USS *Underwriter* at New Bern, North Carolina. The raids earned Wood promotion to commander effective August 23, 1863, and a resolution of thanks on February 15, 1864, from the Confederate Congress. As commander of CSS *Tallahassee,* Wood in August 1864 steamed out of Wilmington, North Carolina, and during the next three weeks captured thirty-three Union merchant vessels off the North Atlantic coast.

Between raids Wood served on Davis's staff with the rank of colonel of cavalry. One of the few men to hold dual rank, he wielded considerable influence in the Confederate government by inspecting ship construction and coastal fortifications and acting as liaison officer between the army and navy.

Captured with Davis in Georgia in May 1865, Wood escaped to Florida. In company with a small band of ex-Confederates including John C. Breckinridge, Wood traveled down the east coast of the state amid a series of adventures involving Indians, Union blockaders, and pirates. In a small open boat the party survived a crossing of the Gulf Stream in a storm to arrive in Cuba. From there Wood journeyed to Halifax, Nova Scotia, where he lived out his life with his family as an expatriate, engaging in shipping and marine insurance. Wood died in Halifax of muscular rheumatism on July 19, 1904.

BIBLIOGRAPHY

Scharf, J. Thomas. *History of the Confederate States Navy.* Albany, N.Y., 1894. Reprint, New York, 1977.

Shingleton, Royce. *John Taylor Wood: Sea Ghost of the Confederacy.* Athens, Ga., 1979.

ROYCE SHINGLETON

WOOD, STERLING ALEXANDER MARTIN

(1823–1891), brigadier general. Wood, a native of Alabama, was born March 17, 1823. He graduated from the Jesuit College of St. Joseph's in Bardstown, Kentucky, in 1841. After practicing law in Tennessee, he moved to Alabama where he became solicitor of the Fourth Judicial District of that state. In 1857, he was elected to the Alabama legislature and in 1860, became editor of the *Florence Gazette.* He was a strong supporter of John C. Breckinridge for president. When war broke out, he entered Confederate service as captain of the Florence Guards.

First assigned with his regiment to Florida, Wood moved north early in 1862 to join Albert Sidney Johnston in Kentucky. He was wounded at Perryville while serving as commander of Simon Bolivar Buckner's Fourth Brigade.

The following year at Chickamauga, Wood's brigade was attached to Patrick Cleburne's division, which was in the thick of the fighting, especially on the second day. During the late morning hours of September 20, Cleburne ordered part of Wood's brigade forward near the Poe House. As it advanced toward the LaFayette Road, it met with heavy rifle and artillery fire from the left and right. The Confederate line withdrew but not before five hundred men were killed or wounded in just a few minutes. Wood was mentioned in Cleburne's report on the battle but not praised as the other brigade commanders were. Although it is not known exactly why Wood resigned his commission on October 17, 1863, it may have been related to this report. Wood then returned to Alabama to practice law, joining his family in Tuscaloosa where they had sought refuge from the war.

Following the hostilities, Wood again served in the Alabama legislature and was a member of the law faculty at the University of Alabama. He died on January 26, 1891, and is buried in Tuscaloosa.

BIBLIOGRAPHY

Purdue, Howell, and Elizabeth Purdue. *Pat Cleburne: Confederate General.* Hillsboro, Tex., 1973.

Warner, Ezra J. *Generals in Gray: Lives of the Confederate Commanders.* Baton Rouge, La., 1959.

JOHN F. CISSELL

WRIGHT, AMBROSE RANSOM "RANS"

(1826–1872), major general. No Georgian, it was written, "was more highly honored or more universally beloved" than "Rans" Wright, born in Louisville, Jefferson County, April 26, 1826. A Democrat, Wright supported the Bell-Everett ticket in 1860 and, as an ardent advocate of state rights, voted for secession. After Georgia left the Union, Wright was appointed a commissioner to Maryland, where he attempted to induce that state to follow Georgia's example.

In April 1861, Wright enlisted as a private in the Confederate Light Guards, which, when it became a company in the Third Georgia Infantry, elected him colonel. After service in North Carolina, Wright was promoted to brigadier and transferred with his command to the Army of Northern Virginia. He fought in the Seven Days' campaign and at Second Manassas before he was wounded in the breast and leg while defending the Sunken Road at Sharpsburg.

Wright's brigade gained the crest of Cemetery Ridge on the second day at Gettysburg but was forced to relinquish the ground for lack of support. In August 1863, Wright was charged with "disobedience of orders, disrespect towards superior officers" in connection with his actions at Gettysburg. He was acquitted by a court-martial presided over by Henry Heth.

In November 1863, Wright was a successful candidate for the Georgia State Senate. He resumed command of his brigade after the legislature adjourned.

Wright, described by biographer Bernard Suttler as "a man of commanding appearance [who] . . . looked the soldier," participated in the battles of early 1864 and then moved to the defenses of Petersburg. While there, he was forced by illness to relinquish his command. He returned to Georgia where he was given command of the post at Augusta. On November 26, 1864, he was promoted to major general and placed in command of a division in Savannah under William J. Hardee. He was present at the siege of and retreat from Savannah and moved with Joseph E. Johnston into North Carolina, where he surrendered.

Returning to Augusta, Wright found the city gripped by a mob of former soldiers who, enraged by privations, threatened to plunder the business houses in search of food. The general's eloquent and forceful appeal for law and order dispersed the mob.

Impoverished by the war, Wright reopened his law office and became editor of the *Augusta Chronicle and Sentinel.* By his own popularity and aggressive efforts he soon put the moribund publication on a profitable basis. Defeated in a bid for the U.S. Senate in 1871, Wright won a seat in the U.S. House of Representatives in 1872. Death intervened, however, on December 21, 1872. He was buried in City Cemetery, Augusta.

BIBLIOGRAPHY

Derry, Joseph T. *Georgia.* Vol. 6 of *Confederate Military History.* Edited by Clement A. Evans. Atlanta, 1899. Vol. 7 of extended ed. Wilmington, N.C., 1987.

Northen, William J. *Men of Mark in Georgia.* Vol. 3. Atlanta, 1906. Reprint, Spartanburg, S.C., 1974.

Warner, Ezra J. *Generals in Gray: Lives of the Confederate Commanders.* Baton Rouge, La., 1959.

LOWELL REIDENBAUGH

WRIGHT, AUGUSTUS ROMALDUS (1813–1891), congressman from Georgia and colonel. Wright was born in Wrightsboro, Georgia (near Augusta), on June 16, 1813, the son of one of the area's earliest settlers and wealthiest planters. He was educated at the University of Georgia, where he was a classmate and became a close friend of Alexander H. Stephens. Wright studied law in Litchfield, Connecticut, and was admitted to the Georgia bar in 1835. He practiced law for a year in Crawfordville and for several years in Cassville in the state's newly opened Cherokee country, where he was appointed circuit judge for the superior court from 1842 to 1849. During those years he ran twice unsuccessfully for Congress as a Whig. In 1849, Wright moved to nearby Rome, Georgia, and returned to private law practice. In 1856 he was elected to Congress as a Democrat and served a single term.

In 1860, Wright was a Unionist and a strong supporter of Stephen A. Douglas in the presidential election. As a delegate to the state's secession convention in Milledgeville in January 1861, he joined Stephens, Benjamin H. Hill, and others in actively opposing secession. But like them, once the majority carried Georgia out of the Union, Wright pledged his support for the new Confederacy and the war effort. He was elected to its Provisional Congress and reelected to the First Congress. Through the early months of the latter, Wright advocated a strong central government and supported Jefferson Davis's attempts to control Confederate military strength. He introduced a bill to allow the president to bypass state governors to call up to 100,000 troops for special duty. But by late 1862, Wright had become disillusioned with the government's management of the war and opposed conscription and impressment, which he felt were violations of personal and property rights.

He began pushing for peace negotiations as early as February 1864, long before William Tecumseh Sherman's invasion led other Georgia leaders to support such measures. When in October of that year, Sherman offered Georgians the opportunity to make a separate peace, Wright went to Washington and met privately with Abraham Lincoln and members of his cabinet in an attempt to win terms acceptable to enough Georgians to allow their state to reenter the Union. Lincoln purportedly offered Wright the provisional governorship of the reconstructed state, an offer Wright declined.

Wright did not run for reelection to the Second Congress, but devoted his attention during the war's closing months to Wright's Legion, a company in Georgia's Thirty-eighth Infantry that he had earlier raised and equipped and briefly led as colonel. After the war, Wright resumed his law practice in Rome, where he built a large estate, Glenwood. In 1877 he served as a member of Georgia's constitutional convention. He died on March 31, 1891.

BIBLIOGRAPHY

Battey, George. *A History of Rome and Floyd County.* Atlanta, 1922.

Northen, William J., ed. *Men of Mark in Georgia.* Vol. 3. Atlanta, 1908. Reprint, Spartanburg, S.C., 1974.

Warner, Ezra J., and W. Buck Yearns. *Biographical Register of the Confederate Congress.* Baton Rouge, La., 1975.

JOHN C. INSCOE

WRIGHT, JOHN V. (1828–1908), colonel and congressman from Tennessee. Resigning his seat as a third-term Democrat in the U.S. Congress in March 1861, Wright, who was the brother of Gen. Marcus Joseph Wright, returned home to McNairy County, Tennessee. There he recruited a company known as "Wright's Boys," which together with other companies from the West Tennessee area comprised the Thirteenth Tennessee Infantry; the men chose Wright as their colonel. Still not fully recovered from a twisted knee sustained when his horse fell on him during the Battle of Belmont, Colonel Wright was elected in November 1861 as Tenth District representative to the First Congress.

Although admitted to the House in March 1862, Wright did not have a committee assignment until some six months later, after the start of the second session, when he was appointed to the Ordnance and Ordnance Stores Committee. Even then, owing to extended illness in his family, he did not attend regularly, twice receiving a leave of absence, and there is no record of his having participated in any debate on the floor of Congress. His role in the Second Congress, to which he was easily reelected in June 1863, was just as undistinguished. Serving on the Naval Affairs Committee, he again was absent most of the time, missing much of May 1864 and the last two months of the final session in 1865. When he was in attendance, his voting tended to favor conscription and impressment measures, but was somewhat cool toward suspending the writ of habeas corpus.

After the war he resided in Alabama for a few years before returning to Tennessee, where he served variously as a circuit court judge, chancellor, and state supreme court judge in the 1870s. Afterward he held an Interior Department post in Washington.

BIBLIOGRAPHY

Hughes, Nathaniel C., Jr. *The Battle of Belmont: Grant Strikes South.* Chapel Hill, N.C., 1991.

Journal of the Congress of the Confederate States of America, 1861–1865. Washington, D.C., 1904–1905.

Porter, James D. *Tennessee.* Vol. 8 of *Confederate Military History.* Edited by Clement A. Evans. Atlanta, 1899. Vol. 10 of extended ed. Wilmington, N.C., 1987.

Wright, John V. Papers. Southern Historical Collection. University of North Carolina, Chapel Hill.

R. B. ROSENBURG

WRIGHT, MARCUS JOSEPH (1831–1922), brigadier general and historian. Marcus Joseph Wright was a native of Purdy, Tennessee, but spent most of his adult years in Memphis. He studied law and became a clerk of common law and chancery court. He also served as lieutenant colonel of a state militia regiment.

After the war started, Wright was appointed military governor of Columbus, Kentucky, and served until it was evacuated. He fought in the Battles of Belmont and Perryville and was wounded at Shiloh. On December 13, 1862, he was promoted to brigadier general and led a Tennessee brigade in the Chickamauga and Chattanooga campaigns. At Chickamauga, 27 percent of the men in his brigade were casualties. Through much of the latter part of the war, he commanded the posts of Atlanta, Macon, North Mississippi, and West Tennessee. Wright ended his military career under the command of Gen. Richard Taylor, son of Zachary Taylor. He was paroled in May 1865 and returned to Memphis to practice law.

During the postwar years, Wright was a government agent in the navy yard at Memphis. He also wrote a number of articles and books. One of his most notable tasks was his involvement beginning in the late 1870s with the collection of Confederate war records for the Federal government's publication, *War of the Rebellion: A Compilation of the Official Records of the Union and Confederate Armies.* He was praised for his fairness and objectivity in preparing the documents.

Wright died in Washington, D.C., on December 27, 1922, at the age of ninety-two.

BIBLIOGRAPHY

Warner, Ezra J. *Generals in Gray: Lives of the Confederate Commanders.* Baton Rouge, La., 1959.

Wright, Marcus J. "Diary." *William and Mary Quarterly* 15 (1935): 89–95.

JOHN F. CISSELL

WRIGHT, WILLIAM BACON (1830–1895), congressman from Texas. Wright, who was born at Columbus, Georgia, on July 4, 1830, may have studied at Princeton University before he became an attorney in Georgia. He settled in Eufaula, Alabama, around 1850, but migrated to Texas during 1854 and established his legal office at Paris. The Democratic party had attracted his support over the American party by 1856. Texas Democrats selected Wright in 1860 as an alternate for presidential elector. He favored separation by late 1860 and, after Texas seceded, ran successfully during the congressional races in the fall of 1861.

In the Confederate Congress (1862–1864), Wright, a member of the committees for Indian affairs and for patents, preferred short speeches and efficient procedures. He favored a tax-in-kind over other forms of taxation, yet he usually supported President Jefferson Davis in his conduct of public affairs. Wright's greatest impact on legislation came in one proposal that the conscription act exclude state troops protecting the frontier and in another that the army not requisition bondsmen used entirely in the production of grain crops. Following his defeat for reelection in 1863, he accepted a commission as major for the quartermaster service in early 1864.

Following the war Wright resumed his legal career at Clarksville and Paris. At the 1875 state constitutional convention he helped shape the judiciary article. After practicing law in Dallas during the 1880s, he became an attorney and banker in San Antonio until his death on August 10, 1895.

BIBLIOGRAPHY

Journal of the Congress of the Confederate States of America, 1861–1865. 7 vols. Washington, D.C., 1904–1905.

Warner, Ezra J., and W. Buck Yearns. *Biographical Register of the Confederate Congress.* Baton Rouge, La., 1975.

Winkler, Ernest William. *Platforms of Political Parties in Texas.* Austin, Tex., 1916.

ALWYN BARR

Y, Z

YAHOLA, OPOTHLE. *See* Opothleyahola.

YANCEY, WILLIAM LOWNDES (1814–1863), diplomat and congressman from Alabama. Renowned in his lifetime as the most fiery and eloquent orator for Southern independence, Yancey was born in Warren County, Georgia, in 1814. His father died of yellow fever a year later, and in 1821 his mother married the Reverend Nathan Beman, the headmaster of a Presbyterian academy in Georgia, which the young Yancey attended. After selling his wife's slaves, Beman, a native New Englander, moved his family to Troy, New York, in 1823 and soon took up the cause of abolitionism. Beman's relations with Carolina, Yancey's mother, were stormy, and the adolescent Yancey bitterly resented what he saw as the hypocritical and cruel self-righteousness of his abolitionist stepfather. Indeed, throughout his public career Yancey would attack the abolitionists in much the same terms as he had denounced the values of his stepfather.

In 1833 Yancey returned to the society and culture his stepfather had rejected. He left Williams College in Massachusetts before graduating and moved to South Carolina. He read law in Greenville under Benjamin Perry, the leader of the up-country Unionists during the nullification crisis, and, like his mentor, defended the Union against the Calhounite state rights enthusiasts. Marriage in 1835 to Sarah Caroline Earle, the daughter of a wealthy slave owner, brought with it thirty-five slaves and instant elevation to planter status. Yancey abandoned his law practice and moved in 1836 to Dallas County in the Alabama black belt where he rented a plantation. In 1838, while on a return trip to Greenville, Yancey killed his wife's uncle, Dr. Robinson Earle, in a brawl that stemmed from an exchange of personal insults. Although convicted of manslaughter, Yancey exulted in the affair as a vindication of his honor. Far more damaging to his career than any notoriety in the wake of the killing of Earle, however, was the economic loss occasioned by accidental poisoning of his slaves in 1839. Already suffering financially from low cotton prices after the panic of 1837, Yancey was now forced to return to law for the funds needed to rebuild his estate.

Yancey entered politics for a second time in 1840, and, in a marked reversal of his earlier attitudes, he returned as a committed state righter. He edited a newspaper and backed Martin Van Buren for the presidency in 1840. After serving in the Alabama house in 1841 and 1843, he was elected to fill a vacant seat in Congress in 1844 and was reelected in 1845. But Yancey had neither the taste nor the talent for the compromising posture that was necessary for effective party politics at the congressional level, and he resigned his seat in 1846. Before he did so, he fought a duel (ending in a harmless exchange of shots) with Congressman Thomas Lanier Clingman of North Carolina, a future Confederate general. Clingman challenged Yancey in response to a congressional speech that Clingman believed had sullied his honor.

Yancey held no other political office before the outbreak of the Civil War. His fame and influence rested on his oratory. He had a beautifully clear speaking voice that could hold an audience enraptured while he espoused the cause of Southern rights. Yancey first became identified in the public mind as the champion of the South against the antislavery North as the result of the Alabama Platform of 1848, a set of resolutions passed by the Alabama legislature denying the right of Congress to prevent slavery from expanding into the Federal territories. Reveling in the role of a sectional agitator in the 1850s, he spread the message of secession as a legal right of individual Southern states in hundreds of speeches. He helped make secession possible by

WILLIAM LOWNDES YANCEY. LIBRARY OF CONGRESS

first making it conceivable. In a famous publicized letter of 1858 to James S. Slaughter, a letter that Yancey insisted was meant to be private, he called for committees of safety to "fire the Southern heart" in defense of liberties allegedly being trampled by a hostile North.

His oratory won him a reputation as the "prince of the fire-eaters," and it was only fitting that he led the Southern delegates who bolted the National Democratic Convention at Charleston in 1860 over the party's refusal to endorse the old Alabama Platform of 1848 with its demand for the right of slavery to expand into the territories. Yancey went on a Northern speaking tour in support of John C. Breckinridge, the nominee of the Southern state rights Democrats in 1860. When the election resulted in Abraham Lincoln's victory, Yancey capped his career as a fire-eater by leading the secessionist forces in the state convention of January 1861 that took Alabama out of the Union.

Yancey's reputation and career peaked in the flush of enthusiasm over the success of secession. Yet neither he nor the other leading fire-eaters were to be entrusted with positions of power in the new Confederate government. He received scant support for the presidency of the Confederacy from the delegates assembled at Montgomery, Alabama, in February 1861. Indeed, Yancey himself was not even chosen as a delegate. The founders of the Confederacy wanted to project an image of careful moderation, and Yancey was considered far too radical and headstrong for such politically delicate tasks as persuading the upper South, especially Virginia, to join the lower South in leaving the Union.

Yancey's oratorical skills as an agitator and his influence in Alabama politics, however, made him a potential disruptive threat to the fledgling Davis administration, were he denied any position or office. Jefferson Davis moved to counteract the threat by offering Yancey his choice of either the relatively minor cabinet post of attorney general or leadership of a three-man diplomatic mission to Europe. Against the advice of his fellow radical, Robert Barnwell Rhett, Sr., of South Carolina, Yancey accepted the diplomatic assignment in March 1861 and sailed for England in early April with the other commissioners, Pierre A. Rost of Louisiana and A. Dudley Mann of Georgia.

Yancey's diplomatic mission was a failure, but it is hard to see how it could have succeeded in its goal of securing official recognition of the Confederacy. One problem was Yancey himself. His quick temper, impatience with temporizing, and rhetorical outbursts were precisely those personality traits most ill-suited to effective diplomacy. Moreover, and as Rhett had forewarned him, he brought very little leverage to his discussions with the British and French. Contrary to Rhett's urgings, Davis did not empower Yancey to offer long-term commercial treaties in exchange for diplomatic recognition. Without this power, Yancey could not make any direct appeal to the economic self-interest of his European adversaries. All he could do was argue for the legitimacy of the Confederate cause and hint at a cotton embargo in the event of European nonrecognition.

Lord John Russell, the British foreign secretary, coldly distanced himself from Yancey's diplomatic team. He did grant a brief interview on May 3 and an even shorter one on May 9, but he refused to commit himself. In response to Lincoln's proclamation of a Union blockade of the Southern coast, the British issued a proclamation of neutrality in mid-May conferring on the Confederacy the rights of a belligerent, but they withheld official diplomatic recognition. Meanwhile, Napoleon III of France, although professing sympathy for the Confederate cause, made it clear that he would not move unless Britain took the first step toward recognition. By the late summer, after Lord Russell had cut off personal interviews with the Confederate commissioners and limited contact with them to formal, written statements, Yancey was ready to leave for home. Requested to stay until the arrival of James Mason of Virginia, the newly appointed Confederate commissioner to England, Yancey was still in London when news of the *Trent* affair reached England in late November. This Union seizure of two Confederate diplomats from a British mail packet ignited a crisis in Anglo-American affairs that gave Yancey one last chance to make his case for British assistance to the Confederacy.

In a letter of November 30 Yancey repeated his argument that the British were not bound by international law to recognize a Union blockade that was both ineffective and harmful to European commercial interests. He declared that the Confederacy would never be subdued by the blockade and urged the British to reopen their access to the cheap, abundant cotton supplies of the South. Lord Russell was unmoved and on December 7 informed Yancey, Rost, and Mann that "he must decline to enter into official communication with them." This was the final insult for Yancey, and he sailed for home once Mason arrived in January.

Yancey was chastened and angry when he returned to the South in February 1862. Shortly after disembarking in New Orleans, he told a crowd of well-wishers that the Confederacy could count on no friends abroad. He blamed the prevalence of antislavery public opinion in England for the failure of his diplomatic mission and confessed that it was naive to believe that the power of King Cotton could force European recognition of the Confederacy. The South's salvation, he concluded, could be achieved only through military victories that subjugated the Northern enemy.

Yancey had passed on word from England that he would gladly consent to serve as a senator in the First Regular Confederate Congress. So elected in his absence by the Alabama legislature, Yancey took his seat in Congress in April 1862. He soon became entangled in a contest of wills with Davis. Now believing, as Rhett had from the very beginning, that Davis had played him for the fool on the abortive European mission, Yancey was quick to find fault with Davis's handling of the war effort.

Having been forced to borrow funds in London to pay for his passage home, Yancey knew from personal experience that Confederate diplomats and foreign agents suffered from a lack of timely financial assistance. In a thinly veiled criticism of the administration's conduct of its foreign affairs, he wrote Davis in early April outlining missed opportunities for arms purchases by Confederate agents in Europe. Davis's reply was cool but tactful. He was stung more deeply by a letter of April 21 written by Yancey and his Alabama colleague in the Senate, Clement C. Clay. The senators lodged an official protest over Davis's appointment policy for generals. They cited figures showing that Alabama had forty regiments in the field but only five brigadier generals. After hinting that Davis was guilty of political favoritism in his appointments, they submitted the names of five regimental commanders of Alabama troops for promotion to brigadier general. Offended by what he viewed as a blatant challenge to his constitutional prerogatives, Davis indignantly responded that the charges were unfair and unworthy of any further consideration.

Yancey's early clashes with Davis were symptomatic of the ideological rift that soon developed in the Confederacy between the Davis administration and the more radical secessionists, men such as Yancey, Rhett, and Louis T. Wigfall of Texas. Yancey, like his fellow fire-eaters, was willing enough to support essential war measures. For example, he voted for the first Conscription Act in April 1862. He set aside his constitutional misgivings over granting such a power to the national government in consideration of the overriding military necessity of retaining in the field the original twelve-month volunteers raised through the action of the individual states. By the same token, he generally backed the economic measures of the increasingly unpopular Treasury Department. For Yancey and other radicals, however, the Confederate bid for independence rested above all else on the individual rights and liberties of the Southern (white) people. He was thus quick to see in the broadening powers of Davis and Confederate officials a pattern of executive tyranny that endangered the very liberties he believed the Confederacy had been created to protect.

Consistent with the prewar stand that had won him fame as a fire-eater, Yancey the senator repudiated party ties and institutional loyalties for the role of agitator. He used his position in the Senate as a forum to warn fellow Confederates of the despotic threats of a distant, centralizing government controlled by President Davis. He granted the military need for such government programs as the impressment of private goods to supply Confederate armies but argued in vain that such seizures should be pegged to the market value of the impressed property in order to be fair and equitable. Despite his early rebuff by Davis on the issue of appointing generals, Yancey continued to accuse Davis of damaging army morale through a policy that slighted the pride and valor of state troops in its selection of brigadier generals. In particular, Yancey still believed that Davis was ignoring the rightful claims of Alabamians to top commands. In September 1862, at a time when Virginia had twenty-four brigadier generals and Alabama but four, he introduced a bill setting up a quota system for the nomination and appointment of brigadier generals based upon the number of troops furnished by each state. The bill was defeated, in part because many senators felt that Yancey was engaging in a personal vendetta against Davis.

One of the clearest expressions of Yancey's conceptions of the Confederate experience came during a debate over an amendment offered by Senator William T. Dortch of North

Carolina to the Conscription Act in the late summer of 1862. Dortch proposed that the Confederate government be authorized to draft justices of the peace. Benjamin H. Hill of Georgia, a leading spokesman for the Davis administration in the Senate, supported Dortch's amendment by claiming that the war-making powers of Congress extended to the conscription of civil officials. For Yancey, this claim smacked of the heretical nationalism of the hated Lincoln government. He feared that such a nationalist belief, what he called the fallacy of a "national life," would supersede and submerge individual and state liberties and thus negate the constitutional freedoms Southern armies were fighting to uphold. "The province of this government, its sole province," he insisted, "is to defend Constitutional government—the Constitutional liberties of States and of the people of States. There is no National life to defend." The unwarranted power of the national government to draft civil officials, he warned, was the power to destroy state governments, and it was a form of despotism that he feared "more than a million Yankee bayonets."

In his unsuccessful attempts to liberalize the access of the press to Senate debates and to loosen the rules by which the Senate often sat in secret sessions, Yancey continued to portray himself as the champion of the Southern people against a national government that shrank from full public accountability for its actions. His last major battle for what he construed as endangered Southern liberties culminated in the most celebrated episode of his Senate career when Benjamin Hill hurled two glass inkstands at him on February 4, 1863. Hill hit Yancey flush on the right cheekbone with the first inkstand. The two men had been exchanging personal insults for days. Before a bleeding Yancey could attack the Georgian, fellow senators restrained the combatants. Yancey, but not Hill, was officially censured by the Senate for his part in the affair.

The Yancey-Hill clash erupted in the context of a debate over Hill's bill to establish a Confederate supreme court with appellate jurisdiction over state supreme courts. Yancey led the floor fight against the bill, and his state rights arguments were by now familiar to his colleagues: "When we decide that the state courts are of inferior dignity to this Court, we have sapped the main pillar of this Confederacy." He conceded to supporters of the bill that the First Congress of the United States under the venerable George Washington had established a supreme court in 1789, but, in a remarkable statement, given the near deification of Washington's generation in Southern political rhetoric, he claimed that "we are wiser than the men of those days." The Founding Fathers, he noted, could only speculate as to the impact of their legislation. The founders of the new Southern republic, however, should have known from bitter experience how the implied centralizing powers of a federal government could be used to sap individual liberties.

Yancey may have been bloodied by Hill, but he won the court battle. The Confederacy never did have a supreme court. In addition to Yancey's success in arousing fears of centralization, the Davis administration decided there was no pressing need for such a court in light of the generally favorable treatment of Confederate legislation by the existing state courts.

Yancey did not live to see the death of the Confederacy that his oratory had been so instrumental in bringing to life. Already plagued by the late 1850s with a severe case of neuralgia, he suffered through increasingly poor health during his years of Confederate service. Bladder and kidney ailments reduced him to a bedridden invalid by the summer of 1863, and he died at his farmhouse near Montgomery on July 27. In a final tribute to the prince of the fire-eaters, a magnificent funeral procession accompanied the body from the Presbyterian church to its interment in the city cemetery.

BIBLIOGRAPHY

Denman, Clarence P. *The Secession Movements in Alabama.* Montgomery, Ala., 1933.

Draughon, Ralph B. "The Young Manhood of William L. Yancey." *Alabama Review* 19 (1966): 28–37.

DuBose, John Witherspoon. *The Life and Times of William Lowndes Yancey.* 2 vols. Birmingham, Ala., 1892. Reprint, New York, 1942.

Thornton, J. Mills, III. *Politics and Power in a Slave Society: Alabama, 1800–1860.* Baton Rouge, La., 1978.

Walther, Eric H. *The Fire-Eaters.* Baton Rouge, La., 1992.

William L. Barney

YELLOW TAVERN, VIRGINIA. Six miles outside Richmond, J. E. B. Stuart's Confederate cavalry corps met Philip Sheridan's force on May 11, 1864. The fierce battle took its toll on both armies, but the Southerners suffered an irreplaceable loss—the death of J. E. B. Stuart.

At the beginning of May, the Army of the Potomac crossed the Rapidan and began thrusting southward. From the densely covered terrain of the Wilderness to the crossroads at Spotsylvania Court House, the Federals engaged the Army of Northern Virginia in desperate and bitter fighting while inching ever closer to the Confederate capital.

Philip Sheridan, the commander of the Federal cavalry corps, had brashly told Gen. George Meade that, given the chance, he could beat J. E. B. Stuart. Meade conferred with Ulysses S. Grant, and on May 8 Sheridan received orders to move southward, "engage Stuart, and clean him out." Sheridan hoped to find Stuart in an isolated position, cut off from Robert E. Lee's infantry.

Early on the morning of May 9, Sheridan set out with

seven brigades, totaling nearly ten thousand troopers, to meet Stuart. That same day, Stuart received the news that Sheridan and his force were moving down Telegraph Road in the direction of Richmond. The Confederate general mobilized his three brigades to pursue the Union cavalry.

Sheridan veered his men southwest from Telegraph Road until they reached Beaver Dam, a Confederate supply base. There the Union troops destroyed precious rations and medical supplies and liberated over three hundred prisoners before continuing toward Richmond.

Arriving at Beaver Dam the next morning, Stuart surveyed the damage and tried to anticipate Sheridan's next move. He had information that Sheridan was traveling with an enormous number of soldiers; hence Stuart supposed that he planned to take Richmond. Yet Sheridan also might strike the Richmond, Fredericksburg, and Potomac Railroad. To ascertain Sheridan's real objective, Stuart sent one brigade to follow the Union troops while he took his remaining two brigades to rush toward Richmond in an attempt to place himself between the Confederate capital and the enemy.

That night, following on the heels of the Federal troops, Stuart and his men reached Hanover Junction where they briefly stopped to rest. At 1:00 A.M., they began moving again in the direction of Ashland, which they found in a shambles. During the night Sheridan's cavalry had torn up six miles of the railroad, destroyed several railroad cars, and burned Confederate storehouses.

Stuart forged ahead, and at 8:00 A.M. on May 11 he reached Yellow Tavern ahead of the Federal troops. Yellow Tavern sat at the junction of Mountain Brook Road from Louisa, Telegraph Road from Fredericksburg, and Brook Turnpike, which led into Richmond. There Stuart chose to wait for the Federals.

In the hours before Sheridan arrived, Stuart planned his strategy. He pondered whether to confront Sheridan's corps outright or rely on help from Braxton Bragg, the commanding officer in Richmond, and attempt to flank the Federals. Stuart sent a messenger to Bragg to ask him if he could hold Richmond, manned only by local troops.

At 11:00, before Bragg had time to answer Stuart's inquiry, Sheridan's troops began positioning themselves in front of the Confederate lines. Stuart chose to place his men, unmounted, along Mountain Road and hope for the best from Richmond. The Confederates held off the waves of Federal attacks through the afternoon. At 2:00 P.M. the messenger returned with Bragg's answer; he felt he could defend the capital with his four thousand local men. Stuart breathed easier.

After a lull in the fighting in the late afternoon, the Federals launched a coordinated attack at 4:00. They simultaneously struck both the center and the left of Stuart's line. On the extreme left, George Armstrong Custer's troops hit Lunsford Lindsay Lomax's brigade particularly hard. Stuart rode to the left to lend encouragement to Lomax's men. Another wave of Federals advanced on the Confederates. In the ensuing melee the Southerners rallied and beat Custer's men back behind the Union lines.

Though the Confederates had managed to repel the latest Northern attack, a retreating Federal shot Stuart in his right side; the ball pierced his abdomen and lodged in his body. Stuart's corps continued to repulse Sheridan's division until dark as an ambulance carried Stuart to his brother-in-law's home in Richmond. He died the next day.

At Yellow Tavern, Stuart's cavalry succeeded in resisting the Federal move on the Confederate capital. Sheridan abandoned his position around Richmond and then moved east and down the Chickahominy River. He later stated that he chose not to enter Richmond because he would have lost five hundred to six hundred soldiers in the process, and he did not have sufficient strength to hold the city. Besides, he had already accomplished what he set out to do—beat J. E. B. Stuart.

BIBLIOGRAPHY

Freeman, Douglas. *Lee's Lieutenants: A Study in Command.* 3 vols. New York, 1942–1944. Reprint, New York, 1986.

Thomas, Emory M. *Bold Dragoon: The Life of J. E. B. Stuart.* New York, 1986.

JENNIFER LUND

YORK, ZEBULON (1819–1890), brigadier general. Born on October 10, 1819, in Avon, Maine, York moved to Louisiana and became one of the state's wealthiest planters. When the war began he raised a company of infantry and was elected major of the Fourteenth Louisiana Volunteers. He later was promoted to lieutenant colonel and fought well at the Battle of Winchester, Virginia, where he was wounded.

Widely known as a very brave but profane officer, York became colonel of the regiment in August 1862 and was wounded again at Second Manassas. After serving at Sharpsburg and Fredericksburg, he spent much of 1863 in Louisiana recruiting and drilling conscripts. During the Wilderness campaign the First and Second Louisiana Brigades were consolidated under the overall command of Gen. Harry Thompson Hays. York was given command of the Second Brigade but apparently was absent at the Battle of Spotsylvania. When Hays was wounded at Spotsylvania, York was promoted to brigadier general on June 2, 1864, (to date from May 31) and given command of the consolidated brigade. He was the only Polish-American to become a Confederate general.

York's brigade participated in Jubal Early's raid on Washington and played a major role in his victory at

Monocacy, where York's casualties ran at almost 50 percent. At the Third Battle of Winchester, York again was in the thick of the fighting and received a wound that led to the amputation of his arm. He ended his military career in Salisbury, North Carolina, trying unsuccessfully to gather recruits from the disillusioned German and Irish Union prisoners held there.

After the war, York moved to Natchez, Mississippi. Financially ruined by the war, he operated the York House until his death on August 5, 1890.

BIBLIOGRAPHY

Jones, Terry L. *Lee's Tigers: The Louisiana Infantry in the Army of Northern Virginia*. Baton Rouge, La., 1987.

Uminski, Sigmund H. "Poles and the Confederacy." *Polish-American Studies* 22 (1965): 99–106.

TERRY L. JONES

YORKTOWN, VIRGINIA. Throughout most of the month of April and early May 1862, Confederates under Maj. Gen. John B. Magruder held a much larger Federal army under Maj. Gen. George B. McClellan at bay along defensive lines established near Yorktown, Virginia. McClellan had landed at Fortress Monroe in March, planning to sweep up the Virginia Peninsula and threaten Richmond. Magruder had less than fifteen thousand men on the Yorktown line to oppose him, but Federal intelligence reports, offered in part by Allan Pinkerton, exaggerated that number.

Advance elements of the Union army reported the presence of the Confederate line of fortifications early on April 5. Rather than aggressively testing the strength of these defenses, McClellan chose to move cautiously. Marshy ground, muddy roads, and rainy conditions further compounded the Union general's problems.

Under these circumstances and lacking the cooperation he expected from the navy, McClellan decided to undertake siege operations. This was the type of military operation with which he was familiar, having participated in the Crimean War at the siege of Sevastopol as an observer from the United States. McClellan believed that this style of fighting was the surest way to prevent the heavy loss of life he had witnessed in frontal assaults against well-entrenched opponents. Early in the siege, he clearly expressed his desire to avoid "the faults of the Allies at Sebastopol."

Shortly after beginning the siege of Yorktown, McClellan received word that President Abraham Lincoln had decided to retain Maj. Gen. Irvin McDowell's corps in northern Virginia. The Union commander was outraged, seeing this as a sign of the lengths to which his political enemies would go to discredit him. McClellan was convinced that, should he fail to deliver a victory for the Union cause, the blame would lie with the president who he thought had sabotaged his campaign from the start.

Actually, Lincoln spent most of his time encouraging McClellan to act or attempting to bolster his confidence. He carefully stroked the general's ego, but added on one occasion, "you must act." Finally, on May 1, an exasperated President Lincoln inquired, "Is anything to be done?"

Magruder was responsible for some of McClellan's indecision and caution. He shrewdly deceived the Union commander by moving his minimal forces from point to point to magnify their numbers. At the same time, he desperately hoped that Gen. Joseph E. Johnston would arrive with the rest of the Confederate forces before McClellan found his nerve. Johnston shifted his forces and arrived himself at Yorktown late in April. He immediately determined that he would not be able to hold the Yorktown line against McClellan's larger army.

On May 3, the twenty-ninth day of the siege, McClellan sounded a depressed note to his wife, noting that he expected to be relieved of duty at any time. For weeks his men had dug entrenchments and dragged siege weapons into place through the mud. McClellan planned to unleash the full force of over one hundred heavy guns and mortars, but Johnston denied him the opportunity by pulling his 56,000 men out of their positions on the night of May 3–4. By midday on May 5, McClellan accepted the fact that his adversary had withdrawn and set his army in motion in pursuit.

BIBLIOGRAPHY

Cullen, Joseph P. *The Peninsula Campaign, 1862: McClellan & Lee Struggle for Richmond*. Harrisburg, Pa., 1973.

Marks, J. J. *The Peninsular Campaign in Virginia; or, Incidents and Scenes on the Battlefields and in Richmond*. Philadelphia, 1864.

Sears, Stephen W. *George B. McClellan: The Young Napoleon*. New York, 1988.

Sears, Stephen W. *To the Gates of Richmond: The Peninsula Campaign*. New York, 1992.

BRIAN S. WILLS

YORKTOWN. *See entry on the ship* Patrick Henry.

YOUNG, PIERCE MANNING BUTLER (1836–1896), major general and U.S. congressman. Young was born November 15, 1836, at Spartanburg, South Carolina, the son of a doctor. The family moved to Bartow County, Georgia, in 1839. Young graduated from the Georgia Military Academy in 1856 and the next year secured an appointment to the U.S. Military Academy. He

PIERCE MANNING BUTLER YOUNG. LIBRARY OF CONGRESS

resigned from the academy, however, when Georgia seceded from the Union.

Young immediately cast his lot with the Confederacy, entering the army as a second lieutenant in the First Georgia Regiment. He was soon promoted to lieutenant colonel and put in command of the cavalry in Cobb's Legion, which was attached to Wade Hampton's brigade, J. E. B. Stuart's cavalry corps, Army of Northern Virginia. Young performed gallantly during the Sharpsburg campaign of 1862, especially at South Mountain. After another fine performance at Brandy Station a year later, he was promoted to brigadier general on September 28, 1863. The next year he was temporarily placed in command of Hampton's division and sent to Georgia to defend against William Tecumseh Sherman. On December 30, 1864, Young was promoted to major general. He spent the last months of the war under Hampton's command resisting Sherman's march through the Carolinas. He surrendered in North Carolina and was paroled in May 1865.

After the war Young returned to Georgia. He became a planter, politician, and diplomat. A Democrat, he served in the U.S. House of Representatives for two terms, 1870 to 1875, and filled diplomatic posts in Russia, Guatemala, and Honduras. Young died in New York City on July 6, 1896, and is buried in Cartersville, Georgia.

BIBLIOGRAPHY

Northen, William J., ed. *Men of Mark in Georgia.* 6 vols. Atlanta, 1911. Reprint, Spartanburg, S.C., 1974.

Wakelyn, Jon L. *Biographical Dictionary of the Confederacy.* Edited by Frank E. Vandiver. Westport, Conn., 1977.

Warner, Ezra J. *Generals in Gray: Lives of the Confederate Commanders.* Baton Rouge, La., 1959.

JOHN G. BARRETT

YOUNG, WILLIAM HUGH (1838–1901), brigadier general. Born in Booneville, Missouri, Young spent his childhood in Texas before leaving to attend college. After graduating from the University of Virginia in July 1861, Young remained in the state to study military tactics at a school affiliated with his alma mater. Returning to Texas the following September, Young organized a company of volunteers and was elected its captain. As part of the Ninth Texas Infantry, the company participated in the Battle of Shiloh, where the regiment suffered devastating losses. Upon its reorganization after the battle, the regiment elected Young its new colonel.

His regiment participated in the invasion of Kentucky and saw limited action at the Battle of Perryville before Young's major engagement at Murfreesboro, Tennessee, on December 31. There, after failing to hear orders to retreat, the commander of the Ninth Texas led his regiment in an advance against the Federal right. Col. Alfred Jefferson Vaughan, Jr., commanding the Fourth Brigade during the battle, reported that Young "seized the colors of his regiment in one of its most gallant charges." He was wounded in the shoulder during the engagement.

Young and his regiment traveled to Mississippi in May 1863 to participate in Gen. Joseph E. Johnston's attempt to lift the siege of Vicksburg. The Ninth Texas was transferred to Georgia in August and ultimately took part in the Battle of Chickamauga, where Young was again wounded. The brigade then went back to Mississippi until receiving orders to return to Georgia in May 1864. Young saw duty as an "observing officer on the mountain" at Little Kennesaw on June 28. On July 27, he took charge of the First Brigade, replacing its wounded commander. Young was subsequently promoted to brigadier general on August 16.

William Young's last taste of combat occurred on October 5, 1864, when his brigade was ordered by Gen. John Bell Hood to attack a Federal position at Allatoona, Georgia. After almost losing his left foot to an artillery projectile, the severely wounded brigadier general was left behind by the retreating Confederates and was captured by Federal cavalry.

Young finished the war as a prisoner at Johnson's Island, Ohio. Released on July 24, 1865, he returned to Texas and focused his attention on the legal profession and real estate. He died in San Antonio.

BIBLIOGRAPHY

Hewitt, Lawrence L. "William Hugh Young." In *The Confederate General*. Edited by William C. Davis. Vol. 6. Harrisburg, Pa., 1991.

Roberts, O. M. *Texas*. Vol. 11 of *Confederate Military History*. Edited by Clement A. Evans. Atlanta, 1899. Vol. 15 of expanded ed. Wilmington, N.C., 1989.

U.S. War Department. *War of the Rebellion: A Compilation of the Official Records of the Union and Confederate Armies*. Washington, D.C., 1880–1901. Ser. 1, vols. 16, 17, 20, 22, 23, 30, 32, 39; ser. 2, vol. 8.

Wakelyn, Jon L. *Bibliographical Dictionary of the Confederacy*. Edited by Frank E. Vandiver. Westport, Conn., 1977.

Warner, Ezra J. *Generals in Gray: Lives of the Confederate Commanders*. Baton Rouge, La., 1959.

ALAN C. DOWNS

YOUNGER BROTHERS. Thomas Coleman ("Cole") Younger (1844–1916) and James ("Jim") Younger (1848–1901) were noted Missouri pro-Confederate guerrillas and postwar bandits. In the summer of 1861, a band of Kansas Jayhawkers (antislavery Unionists, some enrolled in the militia, some freebooters) robbed the wealthy Harrisonville, Missouri, landowner and livery stable owner, Henry W. Younger, of four thousand dollars' worth of carriages and wagons and forty saddle horses. Following this incident, Younger's strapping eighteen-year-old son, Cole, joined the guerrilla band of William Clarke Quantrill. In 1862, a Union captain shot Henry in retaliation for vicious guerrilla deeds.

After the deaths of several of the young female kin of these guerrillas, including two of Cole's cousins, in a collapsed Kansas City jail, Cole served as a Quantrill lieutenant in the August 21, 1863, raid on Lawrence, Kansas, in which approximately 450 guerrillas killed about 150 unarmed men and boys. After going to Texas with Quantrill late in 1863, Cole joined the regular Confederate army, served as a recruiter in New Mexico, and then sat out the rest of the war in California. At age sixteen, late in 1864, Jim joined Quantrill on a raid into Kentucky, where he was captured and imprisoned in March 1865.

After the war, Cole and Jim, joined later by their younger brothers, Bob (1854–1889) and John (1856?–1874), teamed up with the famous bank and train robbers, Frank and Jesse James. John was killed by Pinkertons in 1874, and the other three brothers were captured in 1876, following a Northfield, Minnesota, bank heist. Bob died in prison of tuberculosis, and Jim committed suicide shortly after he and Cole were released from prison in 1901. Cole, who subsequently joined with Frank James in a wild west show and lectured widely on the topic "Crime Does Not Pay," died in his sleep in 1916.

THE YOUNGER FAMILY. Clockwise from left: James Younger, his sister Rhetta, and their brothers Robert and Cole.
LIBRARY OF CONGRESS

BIBLIOGRAPHY

Brant, Marley. *The Outlaw Youngers: A Confederate Brotherhood.* Lanham, Md., 1992.

Brownlee, Richard S. *Gray Ghosts of the Confederacy: Guerrilla Warfare in the West, 1861–1865.* Baton Rouge, La., 1958.

Croy, Homer. *Last of the Great Outlaws.* New York, 1956.

Settle, William A., Jr. *Jesse James Was His Name: or, Fact and Fiction Concerning the Careers of the Notorious James Brothers of Missouri.* Columbia, Mo., 1966.

Younger, Coleman. *The Story of Cole Younger by Himself.* Chicago, 1903.

MICHAEL FELLMAN

FELIX K. ZOLLICOFFER. LIBRARY OF CONGRESS

ZOLLICOFFER, FELIX K. (1812–1862), U.S. congressman and brigadier general. Zollicoffer went down in Southern history as an early martyr to the cause. Of Swiss descent, he was born in Tennessee May 19, 1812, into the planter class and attended college for a year. As a newspaper editor, he rose in state political circles. In 1835 he was named state printer and served in the Second Seminole War. In the 1840s Zollicoffer edited the *Nashville Republican Banner,* the major Whig journal, which made him a political king-maker in the state. He served in the state senate and helped elect a governor and carry Tennessee for Winfield Scott in the 1852 presidential contest. He won a seat the same year in the U.S. House of Representatives, which he held for three terms. In 1860 he supported John Bell for president and later became a Unionist delegate to the Washington peace conference of 1861.

Abraham Lincoln's call for troops in April created a crisis of loyalties for this political moderate. Zollicoffer (nicknamed "Zollie") stood by his state and accepted a general's commission from Governor Isham G. Harris. In July he became a Confederate brigadier and was ordered to eastern Tennessee, where it was hoped his name would rally Unionists to the support of the state. Here his great opportunity came—and ended tragically.

In November he moved his small command to the Cumberland and then crossed the river into Kentucky. There he was encamped, the river at his rear, when Maj. Gen. George B. Crittenden, his immediate superior, arrived. With Union forces advancing on January 19, 1862, the two Confederates rushed to attack at Mill Springs. In the lead of his men, Zollicoffer was instantly killed by a Union volley. Had he ridden impulsively directly into enemy fire? This brave leader, like so many others, was cut down at the outset of a promising military career and became one of the might-have-beens of history. His body, graciously, was sent across the lines by his opponent, Gen. George H. Thomas. His name subsequently became the subject of much verse and memorialization in the wartime South: "A name in song and story—'He died on the field of glory.' "

BIBLIOGRAPHY

Connelly, Thomas L. *Army of the Heartland: The Army of Tennessee, 1861–1862.* Baton Rouge, La., 1967.

Horn, Stanley F. *The Army of Tennessee.* Indianapolis, 1941.

Myers, Raymond E. *The Zollie Tree.* Louisville, Ky., 1964.

Woodworth, Steven E. *Jefferson Davis and His Generals: The Failure of Confederate Command in the West.* Lawrence, Kans., 1990.

JOHN O'BRIEN

Back Matter

Synoptic Outline of Contents
Appendices:
Appendix 1. South Carolina's Ordinance of Secession
Appendix 2. Declaration of the Immediate Causes of Secession
Appendix 3. Constitution of the Confederate States of America
Appendix 4. Cornerstone Speech
Appendix 5. Parole of Robert E. Lee and Staff
Appendix 6. Robert E. Lee's Farewell to the Army of Northern Virginia
Appendix 7. Parole of Joseph E. Johnston and Troops
Appendix 8. Parole of Richard Taylor and Troops
Appendix 9. Parole of E. Kirby Smith and Troops
Index

Synoptic Outline of Contents

The outline presented here is designed to provide an overview of the conceptual scheme of this encyclopedia. It is divided into six parts:

Union and Disunion
Government and Politics
Military
Economics
Society and Culture
Confederate Legacy

Each of these parts is divided into a variety of subsections. Because these subsections are not necessarily mutually exclusive, certain entries in the encyclopedia are listed more than once.

I. UNION AND DISUNION

PRINCIPAL ARTICLES

Confederate States of America
Civil War
  Names of the War
  Causes of the War
  Strategy and Tactics
  Causes of Defeat
  Losses and Numbers
Expansionism in the Antebellum South
Secession
Unionism
State Rights
Nationalism

SUPPORTING TOPICS

American Party
Antislavery
Baltimore Riot
Bleeding Kansas
Bluffton Movement
Butler's Woman Order
Compromise of 1850
Constitutional Union Party
Cooperationists
Copperheads
Cornerstone Speech
Crittenden Compromise
Declaration of Immediate Causes
Democratic Party
Dred Scott Decision
Election of 1860
Fire-eaters
Fugitive Slave Law
Galvanized Yankees
Georgia Platform
Hampton Roads Conference
Harpers Ferry, West Virginia
  John Brown's Raid
Heroes of America
Jones County, Mississippi
Kansas-Nebraska Act
Knoxville and Greeneville Conventions
Lincoln, Abraham
  Image of Lincoln in the Confederacy
Mason-Dixon Line
Missouri Compromise
Montgomery Convention
Northwestern Conspiracy
Nullification Controversy
Oath of Allegiance
Peace Movements
Proslavery
Republican Party
Sumner, Caning of
Thirteenth Amendment
Tories
Union Occupation
Washington Peace Conference
Whig Party
Wilmot Proviso

UNION AND DISUNION *(cont.)*

RELATED BIOGRAPHIES

Brockenbrough, John Mercer
Brownlow, William G.
Calhoun, John C.
Fitzhugh, George
Hammond, James H.
Helper, Hinton Rowan
Holden, William W.
Johnson, John Lewis
Petigru, James L.
Ruffin, Edmund
Temple, Oliver Perry
Tyson, Bryan
Van Lew, Elizabeth

II. GOVERNMENT AND POLITICS

PRINCIPAL ARTICLES

Politics
Constitution
Presidency
Congress
Judiciary
Governors
Cabinet

CONFEDERATE BUREAUCRACY

Civil Service
Commissary Bureau
Medical Department
Navy
  Navy Department
Niter and Mining Bureau
Ordnance Bureau
Patent Office
Post Office Department
Quartermaster Bureau
State Department
Treasury Department
Vice Presidency
War Department

RELATED BIOGRAPHIES

Benjamin, Judah P.
Bragg, Thomas
Breckinridge, John C.
Browne, William M.
Campbell, John A.
Davis, George
Davis, Jefferson
Ellet, Henry T.
Gorgas, Josiah
Hunter, Robert M. T.
Keyes, Wade
Lawton, Alexander R.
Mallory, Stephen R.
Memminger, Christopher G.
Moore, Samuel Preston
Myers, Abraham C.
Northrop, Lucius B.
Randolph, George Wythe
Reagan, John H.
St. John, Isaac M.
Seddon, James A.
Smith, Gustavus Woodson
Stephens, Alexander H.
Toombs, Robert
Trenholm, George
Walker, Leroy P.
Watts, Thomas H.

DIPLOMACY

Alabama Claims
Blockade
  An Overview
Canada
Cuba
Diplomacy
Enchantress Affair
France
Great Britain
Imperialism
Index
Mexico
Monroe Doctrine
Nicaragua
Propaganda
Russia
Spain
State Department
Trent Affair

RELATED BIOGRAPHIES

Bledsoe, Albert T.
Hotze, Henry
Lamar, L. Q. C.
Leon, Edwin de
Mann, A. Dudley
Pickett, John T.
Rost, Pierre A.
Slidell, John

CONGRESSMEN AND CONGRESSIONAL DELEGATES

Akin, Warren
Anderson, Clifford
Anderson, James Patton
Arrington, Archibald Hunter
Ashe, Thomas S.
Atkins, J. D. C.
Avery, William Waighstill
Ayer, Lewis Malone
Baker, James McNair
Baldwin, John B.
Barksdale, Ethelbert
Barnwell, Robert W.
Barry, William Taylor Sullivan
Bartow, Francis S.
Bass, Nathan
Batson, Felix I.
Baylor, John R.
Bell, Caspar Wistar
Bell, Hiram Parks
Blandford, Mark Hardin
Bocock, Thomas S.
Bonham, Milledge L.
Boteler, Alexander R.
Boudinot, Elias C.
Boyce, W. W.
Bradford, Alexander Blackburn
Bradley, Benjamin Franklin
Branch, Anthony Martin
Breckinridge, Robert J., Jr.
Bridgers, Robert R.
Brockenbrough, John White
Brooke, Walker
Brown, Albert Gallatin
Bruce, Eli M.
Bruce, Horatio Washington
Burnett, Henry C.
Burnett, Theodore Legrand
Callahan, Samuel Benton
Campbell, Josiah A. Patterson
Caperton, Allen T.
Carroll, David W.
Caruthers, Robert Looney
Chambers, Henry Cousins
Chambliss, John Randolph, Sr.
Chesnut, James
Chilton, William P.

Chrisman, James Stone
Clark, John B.
Clark, William W.
Clay, Clement C.
Clayton, Alexander M.
Clopton, David
Cluskey, M. W.
Cobb, Howell
Cobb, T. R. R.
Collier, Charles Fenton
Colyar, A. S.
Conrad, Charles M.
Conrow, Aaron H.
Cooke, William Mordecai
Craige, Francis Burton
Crawford, Martin J.
Crockett, John Watkins
Cruikshank, Marcus H.
Currin, David M.
Curry, Jabez L. M.
Darden, Stephen Heard
Dargan, E. S.
Davidson, Allen Turner
Davis, George
Davis, Nicholas
Davis, Reuben
Dawkins, James Baird
de Clouet, Alexandre
de Jarnette, Daniel C.
DeWitt, William H.
Dickinson, James Shelton
Dortch, William Theophilus
Dupré, Lucien Jacques
Echols, Joseph Hubbard
Elliott, John Milton
Ewing, George Washington
Farrow, James
Fearn, Thomas
Foote, Henry S.
Ford, Samuel Howard
Forman, Thomas Marsh
Foster, Thomas J.
Freeman, Thomas W.
Fuller, Thomas C.
Funsten, David
Gaither, Burgess S.
Gardenhire, E. L.
Garland, Augustus Hill
Garland, Rufus K.
Garnett, Muscoe Russell Hunter
Gartrell, Lucius Jeremiah
Gentry, Meredith Poindexter
Gholson, Thomas Saunders
Gilmer, John A.
Goode, John, Jr.
Graham, Malcolm D.
Graham, William A.
Gray, Henry
Gray, Peter W.
Gregg, John
Hale, Stephen Fowler
Hanly, Thomas B.
Harris, Thomas A.
Harris, Wiley Pope
Harrison, James Thomas
Hartridge, Julian
Haynes, Landon Carter
Heiskell, J. B.
Hemphill, John
Henry, Gustavus Adolphus
Herbert, Caleb C.
Hill, Benjamin H.
Hilton, Robert B.
Hodge, Benjamin Louis
Hodge, George Baird
Holcombe, James P.
Holder, William Dunbar
Holliday, Frederick William Mackey
Holt, Hines
House, John F.
Hunter, Robert M. T.
Ingram, Porter
Jemison, Robert
Jenkins, Albert Gallatin
Johnson, Herschel V.
Johnson, Robert W.
Johnson, Thomas
Johnson, Waldo
Johnston, Robert
Jones, George Washington
Jones, Henry Cox
Jones, Robert McDonald
Jones, Thomas McKissick
Keeble, Edwin A.
Keitt, Lawrence
Kenan, Augustus Holmes
Kenan, Owen Rand
Kenner, Duncan F.
Lamkin, John Tillman
Lander, William
Leach, James Madison
Leach, James T.
Lester, George N.
Lewis, David Peter
Lewis, David W.
Lewis, John W.
Logan, George Washington
Lyon, Francis Strother
Lyons, James
McCallum, James
McDowell, Thomas David Smith
MacFarland, William H.
Machen, Willis Benson
McLean, James Robert
McMullen, Fayette
McQueen, John
McRae, Colin J.
McRae, John Jones
Macwillie, Marcus H.
Marshall, Henry
Marshall, Humphrey
Martin, John Marshall
Mason, James M.
Maxwell, Augustus Emmett
Memminger, Christopher G.
Menees, Thomas
Miles, William Porcher
Miller, Samuel Augustine
Mitchel, Charles Burton
Monroe, Thomas Bell
Montague, Thomas Latane
Moore, James William
Morehead, John Motley
Morgan, Simpson Harris
Morton, Jackson
Munnerlyn, Charles James
Murray, John Porry
Nisbet, Eugenius Aristides
Norton, Nimrod Lindsay
Ochiltree, William B.
Oldham, Williamson S.
Orr, James L.
Orr, Jehu Amaziah
Oury, Granville H.
Owens, James B.
Perkins, John, Jr.
Peyton, Robert Ludwell Yates
Phelan, James
Preston, Walter
Preston, William Ballard
Pryor, Roger A.
Pugh, James Lawrence
Puryear, Richard C.
Ralls, John Perkins
Ramsay, James Graham
Read, Henry English
Reade, Edwin Godwin
Reagan, John H.
Rhett, Robert Barnwell, Sr.

GOVERNMENT AND POLITICS *(cont.)*

Rives, William C.
Robinson, Cornelius
Rogers, Samuel St. George
Royston, Grandison D.
Ruffin, Thomas
Russell, Charles Welles
Rust, Albert
Sanderson, John Pease
Scott, Robert Eden
Seddon, James A.
Semmes, Thomas
Sexton, Franklin B.
Shewmake, John Troupe
Shorter, John G.
Simms, William E.
Simpson, William Dunlap
Singleton, Otho Robards
Smith, James Milton
Smith, Robert Hardy
Smith, William Ephraim
Smith, William "Extra Billy"
Smith, William N. H.
Smith, William Russell
Snead, Thomas L.
Sparrow, Edward
Staples, Waller R.
Stephens, Alexander H.
Strickland, Hardy
Swan, William G.
Thomas, James Houston
Thomas, John J.
Thomason, Hugh French
Tibbs, William Henry
Toombs, Robert
Triplett, George Washington
Trippe, Robert Pleasant
Turner, Josiah
Tyler, John
Venable, Abraham Watkins
Vest, George G.
Villeré, Charles Jacques
Walker, Richard Wilde
Ward, George Taliaferro
Watkins, William W.
Watson, John W. C.
Waul, Thomas Neville
Welch, Israel Victor
White, Daniel Price
Whitfield, Robert Henry
Wickham, Williams Carter
Wigfall, Louis T.
Wilcox, John A.
Wilkes, Peter Singleton
Wilson, William Sydney
Withers, Thomas
Witherspoon, James Hervey
Wright, Augustus Romaldus
Wright, John V.
Wright, William Bacon
Yancey, William Lowndes

STATES AND TERRITORIES

Alabama
Arizona
Arkansas
Border States
Florida
Georgia
Indian Territory
Kentucky
Louisiana
Mississippi
Missouri
New Mexico
North Carolina
South Carolina
Tennessee
Texas
Virginia
West Virginia

STATE GOVERNORS

Allen, Henry W.
Allison, Abraham K.
Bonham, Milledge L.
Brown, Joseph E.
Brownlow, William G.
Caruthers, Robert Looney
Clark, Charles
Clark, Edward
Clark, Henry T.
Ellis, John W.
Flanagin, Harris
Fletcher, Thomas
Gillem, Alvan C.
Hahn, Michael
Harris, Isham G.
Hawes, Richard
Jackson, Claiborne F.
Johnson, Andrew
Johnson, George W.
Letcher, John
Lubbock, Francis R.
Magoffin, Beriah
Magrath, Andrew G.
Milton, John
Moore, Andrew B.
Moore, Thomas O.
Murphy, Isaac
Murrah, Pendleton
Peirpoint, Francis H.
Perry, Madison S.
Pettus, J. J.
Pickens, Francis W.
Rector, Henry M.
Reynolds, Thomas C.
Shepley, George F.
Shorter, John G.
Smith, William "Extra Billy"
Stanly, Edward
Vance, Zebulon
Watts, Thomas H.
Wells, James Madison

CITIES AND OTHER GEOGRAPHIC REGIONS

Atlanta, Georgia
 City of Atlanta
Austin, Texas
Baton Rouge, Louisiana
Black Belt
Brownsville, Texas
 City of Brownsville
Charleston, South Carolina
 City of Charleston
Charlotte and Mecklenburg County, North Carolina
Chattanooga, Tennessee
 City of Chattanooga
Columbia, South Carolina
Danville, Virginia
Galveston, Texas
 City of Galveston
Greensboro, North Carolina
Jackson, Mississippi
 City of Jackson
Jones County, Tennessee
Little Rock, Arkansas
Macon, Georgia
Memphis, Tennessee
Mobile, Alabama
 City of Mobile
Montgomery, Alabama
Nashville, Tennessee
New Orleans, Louisiana
 City of New Orleans
Norfolk, Virginia

Raleigh, North Carolina
Richmond, Virginia
Savannah, Georgia
City of Savannah
Selma, Alabama
City of Selma
Shenandoah Valley
An Overview
Tallahassee, Florida
Wilmington, North Carolina

OTHER SUPPORTING TOPICS

Antislavery
Censorship
Citizenship
Civil Liberties
Confiscation
Conscription
Cornerstone Speech
Democratic Party
Direct Tax Act
Election of 1863
Extortion
Fast Days
Flags
Freedom of the Press
Habeas Corpus
Hampton Roads Conference
Heroes of America
Impressment
Knoxville and Greeneville Conventions
Mason-Dixon Line
Montgomery Convention
Peace Movements
Proslavery
Provost Marshal
Public Finance
Speculation
Stamps
State Socialism
Taxation
Tax-in-Kind
Urbanization
Whig Party

III. MILITARY

Army

PRINCIPAL ARTICLES

Army
Confederate Army
Manpower
Army Departments
African Americans in the Confederate Army
Army of Northern Virginia
Army of Tennessee
Trans-Mississippi Department
Soldiers

SPECIAL ARMY UNITS

Barksdale's Mississippi Brigade
Hampton's Legion
Hood's Texas Brigade
Louisiana Tigers
Mosby's Rangers
Orphan Brigade
Special Units
Stonewall Brigade

OTHER SUPPORTING TOPICS

Artillery
An Overview
Cavalry
Commissary Bureau
Engineer Bureau
Forts and Fortifications
Infantry
Medical Department
Niter and Mining Bureau
Ordnance Bureau
Quartermaster Bureau
Signal Corps
War Department

CONFEDERATE GENERALS AND ACTING GENERALS

Adams, Daniel Weisiger
Adams, John
Adams, William Wirt
Alexander, Edward Porter
Allen, Henry W.
Allen, William Wirt
Anderson, George B.
Anderson, George Thomas "Tige"
Anderson, James Patton
Anderson, Joseph R.
Anderson, Richard Heron
Anderson Robert
Anderson, Samuel Read
Archer, James Jay
Armistead, Lewis A.
Armstrong, Frank Crawford
Ashby, Turner
Bagby, Arthur P.
Baker, Alpheus
Baker, Laurence Simmons
Baldwin, William Edwin
Barksdale, William
Barringer, Rufus
Barry, John Decatur
Barton, Seth Maxwell
Bate, William Brimage
Battle, Cullen Andrews
Beale, Richard Lee Turberville
Beall, William N. R.
Beauregard, P. G. T.
Bee, Barnard E.
Bee, Hamilton P.
Bell, Tyree Harris
Benning, Henry L.
Benton, Samuel
Blanchard, Albert Gallatin
Boggs, William Robertson
Bonham, Milledge L.
Bowen, John Stevens
Bragg, Braxton
Branch, Lawrence O'Bryan
Brandon, William Lindsay
Brantly, William Felix
Bratton, John
Breckinridge, John C.
Brevard, Theodore Washington
Brown, John Calvin
Browne, William M.
Bryan, Goode
Buckner, Simon Bolivar
Buford, Abraham
Bullock, Robert
Butler, Matthew Calbraith
Cabell, William Lewis
Campbell, Alexander William
Cantey, James
Capers, Ellison
Carroll, William Henry
Carter, John Carpenter
Chalmers, James Ronald
Chambliss, John Randolph, Jr.
Cheatham, B. Franklin
Chestnut, James
Chilton, Robert Hall
Churchill, Thomas James
Clanton, James Holt
Clark, Charles
Clark, John B., Jr.
Clayton, Henry DeLamar

MILITARY *(cont.)*

Cleburne, Patrick
Clingman, Thomas Lanier
Cobb, Howell
Cobb, Thomas R. R.
Cocke, Philip St. George
Cockrell, Francis Marion
Colquitt, Alfred H.
Colston, Raleigh Edward
Conner, James
Cook, Philip
Cooke, John Rogers
Cooper, Douglas Hancock
Cooper, Samuel
Corse, Montgomery Dent
Cosby, George Blake
Cox, William Ruffin
Crittenden, George B.
Cumming, Alfred
Daniel, Junius
Davidson, Henry Brevard
Davis, Joseph Robert
Davis, William George Mackey
Dearing, James
Deas, Zachariah Cantey
DeBray, Xavier B.
de Lagnel, Julius Adolph
Deshler, James
Dibrell, George Gibbs
Dockery, Thomas Pleasant
Doles, George Pierce
Donelson, Daniel Smith
Drayton, Thomas F.
DuBose, Dudley McIver
Duke, Basil Wilson
Duncan, Johnson K.
Dunovant, John
Early, Jubal
Echols, John
Ector, Matthew Duncan
Elliot, Stephen, Jr.
Elzey, Arnold
Evans, Clement A.
Evans, Nathan "Shanks"
Ewell, Richard S.
Fagan, James F.
Featherston, Winfield Scott
Ferguson, Samuel Wragg
Field, Charles W.
Finegan, Joseph
Finley, Jesse Johnson
Floyd, John B.
Forney, John Horace
Forney, William Henry
Forrest, Nathan Bedford
Frazer, John Wesley
French, Samuel G.
Frost, Daniel Marsh
Fry, Birkett Davenport
Gano, Richard Montgomery
Gardner, Franklin
Gardner, W. M.
Garland, Samuel Jr.
Garnett, Richard Brooke
Garnett, Robert S.
Garrott, Isham Warren
Gartrell, Lucius Jeremiah
Gary, Martin Witherspoon
Gatlin, Richard Caswell
Gholson, Samuel Jameson
Gibson, Randall Lee
Gilmer, Jeremy Francis
Girardey, Victor Jean Baptiste
Gist, States Rights
Gladden, Adley Hogan
Godwin, Archibald Campbell
Goggin, James Monroe
Gordon, B. Frank
Gordon, George Washington
Gordon, James Byron
Gordon, John
Gorgas, Josiah
Govan, Daniel Chevilette
Gracie, Archibald, Jr.
Granbury, Hiram Bronson
Gray, Henry
Grayson, John Breckinridge
Green, Martin Edwin
Green, Thomas
Greer, Elkanah Brackin
Gregg, John
Gregg, Maxcy
Griffith, Richard
Grimes, Bryan
Hagood, Johnson
Hampton, Wade
Hanson, Roger
Hardee, William J.
Hardeman, William Polk
Harris, Nathaniel Harrison
Harrison, James Edward
Harrison, Thomas
Hatton, Robert Hopkins
Hawes, J. M.
Hawthorn, Alexander Travis
Hays, Harry Thompson
Hébert, Louis
Hébert, Paul O.
Helm, Benjamin Hardin
Heth, Henry
Higgins, Edward
Hill, A. P.
Hill, Benjamin Jefferson
Hill, D. H.
Hindman, Thomas C.
Hodge, George Baird
Hogg, Joseph Lewis
Hoke, Robert Frederick
Holmes, Theophilus H.
Holtzclaw, James Thadeus
Hood, John Bell
Huger, Benjamin
Humes, William Young Conn
Humphreys, Benjamin Grubb
Hunton, Eppa
Imboden, John D.
Iverson, Alfred
Jackman, Sidney D.
Jackson, Alfred Eugene
Jackson, Henry Rootes
Jackson, John King
Jackson, Thomas J. "Stonewall"
Jackson, William Hicks
Jackson, William Lowther "Mudwall"
Jenkins, Micah
Johnson, Adam Rankin "Stovepipe"
Johnson, Bradley Tyler
Johnson, Bushrod Rust
Johnson, Edward
Johnston, Albert Sidney
Johnston, George Doherty
Johnston, Joseph E.
Johnston, Robert Daniel
Jones, David Rumph "Neighbor"
Jones, J. R.
Jones, John M.
Jones, Samuel
Jones, William Edmondson "Grumble"
Jordan, Thomas
Kelly, John Herbert
Kemper, James Lawson
Kennedy, John Doby
Kershaw, Joseph B.
King, William H.
Kirkland, William Whedbee
Lane, James

Lane, Walter Paye
Law, Evander McIvor
Lawton, Alexander R.
Leadbetter, Danville
Lee, Edwin Gray
Lee, Fitzhugh
Lee, George Washington Custis
Lee, Robert E.
Lee, Stephen D.
Lee, William Henry Fitzhugh
Leventhorpe, Collett
Lewis, Joseph Horace
Lewis, Levin M.
Lewis, William Gaston
Liddell, St. John Richardson
Lilley, Robert Doak
Little, Lewis Henry
Logan, Thomas Muldrup
Lomax, Lunsford Lindsay
Long, Armistead Lindsay
Longstreet, James
Loring, W. W.
Lovell, Mansfield
Lowrey, Mark Perrin
Lowry, Robert
Lyon, Hylan Benton
McCausland, John
McComb, William
McCown, John P.
McCulloch, Ben
McCulloch, Henry Eustace
McGowan, Samuel
McIntosh, James McQueen
Mackall, William W.
McLaws, Lafayette
Maclay, Robert P.
McNair, Evander
McRae, Dandridge
MacRae, William
Magruder, John B.
Mahone, William
Major, James Patrick
Maney, George Earl
Manigault, Arthur Middleton
Marmaduke, John Sappington
Marshall, Humphrey
Martin, James Green
Martin, William Thompson
Maury, D. H.
Maxey, Samuel Bell
Mercer, Hugh Weedon
Miller, William
Moody, Young Marshall
Moore, John Creed
Moore, Patrick Theodore
Morgan, John Hunt
Morgan, John Tyler
Mouton, Jean Jacques Alfred Alexander
Myers, Abraham C.
Nelson, Allison
Nicholls, Francis
Northrop, Lucius B.
O'Neal, Edward Asbury
Page, Richard L.
Palmer, Joseph Benjamin
Parsons, Mosby Monroe
Paxton, Elisha Franklin
Payne, William Henry Fitzhugh
Peck, William Raine
Pegram, John
Pemberton, John C.
Pender, William Dorsey
Pendleton, William N.
Perrin, Abner Monroe
Perry, Edward Aylesworth
Perry, William Flank
Pettigrew, J. Johnston
Pettus, Edmund Winston
Pickett, George E.
Pike, Albert
Pillow, Gideon
Polignac, Camille J.
Polk, Leonidas
Polk, Lucius Eugene
Posey, Carnot
Preston, John Smith
Preston, William
Price, Sterling
Pryor, Roger A.
Quarles, William Andrew
Rains, Gabriel J.
Rains, James Edwards
Ramseur, Dodson
Randal, Horace
Randolph, George Wythe
Ransom, Matt Whitaker
Ransom, Robert, Jr.
Reynolds, Alexander Welch
Reynolds, Daniel Harris
Richardson, Robert Vinkler
Ripley, Roswell Sabine
Roane, John Selden
Roberts, William Paul
Robertson, Beverly Holcombe
Robertson, Felix Huston
Robertson, Jerome Bonaparte
Roddey, Philip Dale
Rodes, Robert
Ross, Lawrence Sullivan
Rosser, Thomas Lafayette
Ruggles, Daniel
Rust, Albert
St. John, Isaac M.
Sanders, John Caldwell Calhoun
Scales, Alfred Moore
Scott, Thomas
Scurry, William R.
Sear, Claudius Wistar
Semmes, Paul J.
Sharp, Jacob Hunter
Shelby, Joseph O.
Shelley, Charles Miller
Shoup, Francis
Sibley, Henry Hopkins
Simms, James Phillip
Slack, William Yarnel
Slaughter, James Edwin
Smith, E. Kirby
Smith, Gustavus W.
Smith, James Argyle
Smith, Martin Luther
Smith, Preston
Smith, Thomas Benton
Smith, William Duncan
Smith, William "Extra Billy"
Sorrel, Gilbert Moxley
Stafford, Leroy A.
Starke, Peter Burwell
Starke, William Edwin
Steele, William
Steuart, George Hume
Stevens, Clement Hoffman
Stevens, Walter Husted
Stevenson, Carter
Stewart, Alexander P.
Stovall, Marcellus Augustus
Strahl, Otho French
Stuart, J. E. B.
Taliaferro, William Booth
Tappan, James Camp
Taylor, Richard
Taylor, Thomas Hart
Terrell, Alexander W.
Terrill, James Barbour
Terry, William
Terry, William Richard
Thomas, Allen
Thomas, Bryan Morel

MILITARY *(cont.)*

Thomas, Edward Lloyd
Tilghman, Lloyd
Toombs, Robert
Toon, Thomas Fentress
Tracy, Edward Dorr
Trapier, James H.
Trimble, Isaac
Tucker, William Feimster
Twiggs, David E.
Tyler, Robert Charles
Vance, Robert Brank
Van Dorn, Earl
Vaughan, Alfred Jefferson, Jr.
Vaughn, John Crawford
Villepigue, John B.
Walker, Henry H.
Walker, James Alexander
Walker, John George
Walker, Leroy P.
Walker, Lucius Marshall
Walker, Reuben Lindsay
Walker, W. H. T.
Walker, William
Wallace, William Henry
Walthall, Edward Cary
Waterhouse, Richard
Watie, Stand
Waul, Thomas Neville
Wayne, Henry Constantine
Weisiger, David Addison
Wharton, Gabriel Colvin
Wharton, John Austin
Wheeler, Joseph
Whitfield, John Wilkins
Whiting, W. H. C.
Wickham, Williams Carter
Wigfall, Louis T.
Wilcox, Cadmus Marcellus
Williams, John S. "Cerro Gordo"
Wilson, Claudius Charles
Winder, John H.
Wise, Henry A.
Withers, Jones Mitchell
Wofford, William Tatum
Wood, Sterling Alexander Martin
Wright, Ambrose Ransom "Rans"
Wright, Marcus Joseph
York, Zebulon
Young, Pierce Manning Butler
Young, William Hugh
Zollicoffer, Felix K.

Navy

PRINCIPAL ARTICLES

Navy
  Confederate Navy
  Navy Department
  Manpower
  African Americans in the Confederate Navy
Sailors
Blockade
  An Overview
  Blockade Running
  Blockade Runners

SHIPS

Advance
Alabama
Albemarle
Alexandra
Arkansas
Atlanta
Banshee
Camilla
Chattahoochee
Chickamauga
Colonel Lamb
Commerce Raiders
Cottonclads
Davids
Don
Eastport
Florida
Georgia
Harriet Lane
H. L. Hunley
Ironclads
Jackson
Jefferson Davis
Laird Rams
Missouri
Nashville
Neuse
Patrick Henry
Pee Dee
Privateers
Rams
Rappahannock
Robert E. Lee
Savannah
Shenandoah
Star of the West
Stonewall
Submarines
Sumter
Tallahassee
Tennessee
Tuscaloosa
Virginia
Webb

OTHER SUPPORTING TOPICS

Alabama Claims
Charleston Squadron
Charlotte Navy Yard
Columbus Naval Iron Works
Enchantress Affair
Gosport Navy Yard
James River Squadron
Laird Shipyards
Marine Corps
Mobile Squadron
River Defense Fleet
Savannah Squadron
State Navies
Naval Stations
Shipyards
Spar Torpedoes
Torpedoes and Mines

BIOGRAPHIES OF NAVAL FIGURES

Beall, John Y.
Brooke, John M.
Brown, Isaac Newton
Buchanan, Franklin
Bulloch, James Dunwoody
Carter, Jonathan H.
Cooke, James W.
Davidson, Hunter
Elliott, Gilbert
Farrand, Ebenezer
Forrest, French
Gift, George W.
Glassell, William T.
Graves, William A.
Guthrie, John J.
Hollins, George N.
Hunley, Horace
Ingraham, Duncan N.
Jones, Catesby
Kell, John McIntosh
Lamar, Gazaway B.
Loyall, Benjamin P.

Lynch, William F.
Maffitt, John N.
Maury, Matthew Fontaine
Maury, William L.
Mitchell, John K.
North, James H.
Parker, William
Porter, John L.
Randolph, Victor M.
Read, Charles W.
Rousseau, Lawrence
Scharf, John Thomas
Semmes, Raphael
Tattnall, Josiah
Tift Brothers
Tombs, James H.
Tucker, John Randolph
Waddell, James
Warley, Alexander Frazier
Whittle, William C.
Wilkinson, John
Williamson, William P.
Wood, John Taylor

Campaigns and Battles

Andrews Raid
Appomattox Campaign
Arkansas Campaign of 1864
Atlanta, Georgia
Atlanta Campaign
Averasboro, North Carolina
Ball's Bluff, Virginia
Beefsteak Raid
Belmont, Missouri
Bentonville, North Carolina
Big Bethel, Virginia
Brandy Station, Virginia
Brice's Cross Roads, Mississippi
Bristoe Station, Virginia
Brownsville, Texas
Battle of Brownsville
Buckland Mills, Virginia
Burnside's Expedition to North Carolina
Carolinas Campaign of Sherman
Cedar Creek, Virginia
Cedar Mountain, Virginia
Centralia Massacre
Chambersburg, Pennsylvania
Chancellorsville Campaign
Charleston, South Carolina
Bombardment of Charleston
Chattanooga, Tennessee
Chattanooga Campaign
Chickamauga Campaign
Cloyds Mountain, Virginia
Cold Harbor, Virginia
Corinth, Mississippi
Cross Keys and Port Republic, Virginia
Dalton, Georgia
Drewry's Bluff, Virginia
Early's Washington Raid
Elkhorn Tavern, Arkansas
Fisher's Hill, Virginia
Forrest's Raids
Fort Fisher, North Carolina
Fort Harrison, Virginia
Fort Pickens, Florida
Fort Pillow Massacre
Fort Pulaski, Georgia
Fort Stedman, Virginia
Fort Sumter, South Carolina
Fort Wagner, South Carolina
Franklin and Nashville Campaign
Frayser's Farm, Virginia
Fredericksburg Campaign
Front Royal, Virginia
Gaines' Mill, Virginia
Galveston, Texas
Battle of Galveston
Gettysburg Campaign
Glorieta Pass, New Mexico
Harpers Ferry, West Virginia
Battle of 1862
Henry and Donelson Campaign
Holly Springs, Mississippi
Iuka, Mississippi
Jackson, Mississippi
Battle of Jackson
Kelly's Ford, Virginia
Kennesaw Mountain, Georgia
Kentucky Campaign of Bragg
Kilpatrick-Dahlgren Raid
Knoxville Campaign
Lynchburg, Virginia
Malvern Hill, Virginia
Manassas, First
Manassas, Second
Mansfield, Louisiana
March to the Sea, Sherman's
Mechanicsville, Virginia
Meridan Campaign
Mill Springs, Kentucky
Mine Run Campaign
Mobile, Alabama
Battle of Mobile Bay
Mobile Campaign
Morgan's Raids
Munfordville, Kentucky
Murfreesboro, Tennessee
New Madrid and Island Number 10
New Market, Virginia
New Orleans, Louisiana
Capture of New Orleans
Olustee, Florida
Paducah, Kentucky
Peninsular Campaign
Perryville, Kentucky
Petersburg Campaign
Piedmont, Virginia
Port Gibson, Mississippi
Port Hudson, Louisiana
Port Royal, South Carolina
Prairie Grove, Arkansas
Price's Missouri Raid
Red River Campaigns
Sabine Pass, Texas
Saltville Massacre
Savannah, Georgia
Savannah Campaign
Selma, Alabama
Wilson's Raid on Selma
Seven Days' Battles
Seven Pines, Virginia
Sharpsburg Campaign
Shenandoah Valley
Shenandoah Valley Campaign of Jackson
Shenandoah Valley Campaign of Sheridan
Shiloh Campaign
South Mountain, Maryland
Spotsylvania Campaign
Stoneman's Raids
Stuart's Raids
Tupelo, Mississippi
Vicksburg Campaign
West Virginia Operations
Operations of 1861
Operations of 1862 and 1863
Wheeler's Raids
Wilderness Campaign
Williamsburg, Virginia
Wilson's Creek Campaign
Winchester, Virginia
Yellow Tavern, Virginia
Yorktown, Virginia

MILITARY *(cont.)*

Other Military Entries

ARMS, WEAPONS, AND AMMUNITION

Arms, Weapons, and Ammunition
Arsenals and Armories
Artillery
Edged Weapons
Hand Grenades and Land Mines
Harpers Ferry, West Virginia
 Arsenal and Armory
Naval Guns
Naval Ordnance Works
Palmetto Armory
Powder Works
Selma, Alabama
 Selma Naval Ordnance Works
Small Arms
Spar Torpedoes
Torpedoes and Mines

ESPIONAGE

Baxley, Catherine Virginia
Booth, John Wilkes
Boyd, Belle
Copperheads
Espionage
 Confederate Secret Service
 Federal Secret Service
 Confederate Military Spies
Ford, Antonia
Greenhow, Rose O'Neal
Harrison, Henry Thomas
Hart, Nancy
Heroes of America
Lincoln, Abraham
 Assassination of Lincoln
Moon Sisters
Morris, Augusta Hewitt
Roman, André Bienvenu
Slater, Sarah
Thompson, Jacob
Tubman, Harriet
Van Lew, Elizabeth

PRISONS

Andersonville Prison
Belle Isle Prison
Castle Thunder Prison
Fort Delaware Prison
Johnson's Island Prison
Libby Prison
Point Lookout Prison
Prisoners of War
Prisons
Salisbury Prison
Wirz, Henry

MEDICINE

Beers, Fannie
Duke, Basil C.
Health and Medicine
Hospitals
Jones, Joseph
McCord, Louisa Cheves
Moore, Samuel Preston
Newsom, Ella King
Nursing
Pember, Phoebe Yates
Stout, Samuel Hollingsworth
Tompkins, Sally L.

SUPPORTING TOPICS

African American Troops in the Union Army
Army
 African Americans in the Confederate Army
Balloon
Battles, Naming of
Brothers of War
Bummers
Civil War
Conscription
Dahlgren Papers
Desertion
Education
 Military Education
File Closers
Foraging
Galvanized Yankees
Guerrilla Warfare
Impressment
Joe Brown's Pikes
Loring-Jackson Incident
Medals and Decorations
Military Justice
Military Training
Monuments and Memorials
 Battlefields
Provost Marshal
Rules of War
Tories
Uniforms

RELATED BIOGRAPHIES

Anderson, William
Benavides, Santos
Dallas, Moses
Hotchkiss, Jedediah
James Brothers
Jomni, Henry
McLean, Wilmer
Mosby, John S.
Opothleyhahola
Quantrill, William Clarke
Rivers, Prince
Smalls, Robert
Stanley, Henry Morton
Thomas, William Holland
Todd, George
Wirz, Henry
Younger Brothers

IV. ECONOMY

PRINCIPAL ARTICLES

Economy
Treasury Department
Public Finance
Labor
 An Overview
 Skilled Labor
Slavery
 Antebellum Slavery
 Slavery during the Civil War
Plantation

SUPPORTING TOPICS

Anglo-Confederate Purchasing
Banking
Bonds
Bread Riots
Cotton
Counterfeiting
Currency
Debt
Direct Tax Act
Erlanger Loan
Extortion

Farming
Food
Free Markets
Horses and Mules
Impressment
Inflation
Lead
Mining
New Plan
Poor Relief
Poverty
Produce Loan
Railroads
Rice
Roads
Salt
Saltpeter
Shelby Iron Company
Shinplasters
Slave Traders
Southern Express Company
Speculation
State Socialism
Substitutes
Sugar
Taxation
Tax-in-Kind
Telegraph
Textile Industry
Tobacco
Transportation
Tredegar Iron Works
Waterways

V. SOCIETY AND CULTURE

PRINCIPAL ARTICLES

Society
Community Life
Population
Morale
Nationalism
Slavery
  Antebellum Slavry
  Slavery during the Civil War
  Slave Life
Urbanization

SLAVERY

Antislavery
Compromise of 1850
Contraband
Cornerstone Speech
Dred Scott Decision
Emancipation Proclamation
Fugitive Slave Law
Harpers Ferry, West Virginia
  John Brown's Raid
Juneteenth
Kansas-Nebraska Act
Missouri Compromise
Overseers
Proslavery
Slave Drivers
Slave Traders
Sumner, Caning of
Thirteenth Amendment
Wilmot Proviso

ETHNICITY

African American Forgeworkers
African Americans in the Confederacy
Cherokees
Chickasaws
Choctaws
Creeks
Creoles
Foreigners
Free People of Color
Germans
Indians
Irish
Jews
Miscegenation
Navy
  African Americans in the Confederate Navy
Osages
Quapaws
Seminoles
Senecas
Shawnees

FAMILY, CLASS, AND GENDER

Class Conflicts
Courtship
Education
  Women's Education
Family Life
Marriage and Divorce
Plantation Mistress
Women

RELIGION

Baptist Church
Bible Societies
Chaplains
Episcopal Church
Fast Days
Jews
Lutheran Church
Mennonites
Methodist Church
Moravian Church
Presbyterian Church
Religion
Roman Catholic Church
Sermons
Society of Friends

EDUCATION

Citadel, The
Education
Georgia Military Institute
Louisiana State Seminary and Military Academy
Textbooks
Virginia Military Institute

ARTS AND LETTERS

Book Publishing
Broadsides
Burial of Latané
Censorship
Currency
  Numismatics
Diaries, Letters, and Memoirs
Dixie
Folk Narratives
Freedom of the Press
Handicrafts
Literature
  Literature in the Confederacy
Lost Cause
  Iconography of the Lost Cause
Magazines
Monuments and Memorials
Music
Newspapers
Photography
Printmaking
Theater
War Correspondents

SOCIETY AND CULTURE *(cont.)*

Other Supporting Topics

Arlington House
Beauvoir
Bread Riots
Conscription
Crime and Punishment
Davis Bend
Death and Mourning
Desertion
Dueling
Extortion
Farming
Fort Hill
Free Markets
Funerals
Guerrilla Warfare
Health and Medicine
Honor
Leisure
Northerners
Plain Folk
Planters
Poor Relief
Popular Culture
Poverty
Prostitution
Refugeeing
Soldiers' Aid Societies
Speculation
State Socialism
White House

Related Biographies

Alcorn, James L.
Berry, Harrison
Brock, Sallie A.
Cary, Hetty
Chapman, Conrad Wise
Chesnut, Mary Boykin
Clay-Clopton, Virginia
Clemens, Samuel Langhorne
Cooke, John Esten
Davis, Joseph E.
Davis, Varina Howell
Dorsey, Sarah Anne
Evans, Augusta Jane
Felton, Rebecca Latimer
Forsyth, John
Frietchie, Barbara
Gregg, William
Jones, J. B.
Julio, E. B. D.
Lanier, Sydney
Lynch, John Roy
Merrick, Caroline E.
Montgomery, Benjamin
Pearson, Richmond
Pollard, Edward A.
Rillieux, Norbert
Roudanez Brothers
Russell, William H.
Soulé, Pierre
Spencer, Cornelia Phillips
Stephens, Linton
Stone, Kate
Timrod, Henry
Trévigne, Paul
Turner, Joseph A.
Volck, Adalbert
Walls, Josiah
Wiley, Calvin H.
Wood, Fernando

VI. CONFEDERATE LEGACY

Principal Articles

Bibliography and Historiography
Lost Cause
An Overview
Iconography of the Lost Cause

Supporting Topics

Archaeology
Confederate Veteran
Diaries, Letters, and Memoirs
Discography
Film and Video
Lee Memorial Association
Lee Monument Association
Literature
The Confederacy in Literature
Memorial Day
Memorial Organizations
Monuments and Memorials
Museums and Archives
Oral History
Reenactments
Soldiers' Homes
Southern Historical Society

Appendix 1

South Carolina's Ordinance of Secession

Charleston, South Carolina, December 20, 1860

Reprinted from Frank Moore, ed., *The Rebellion Record,* vol. 1, New York, 1862, p. 2.

An Ordinance to Dissolve the Union between the State of South Carolina and other States united with her under the compact entitled the Constitution of the United States of America.

We, the people of the State of South Carolina, in Convention assembled, do declare and ordain, and it is hereby declared and ordained, that the ordinance adopted by us in Convention, on the 23d day of May, in the year of our Lord 1788, whereby the Constitution of the United States of America was ratified, and also all Acts and parts of Acts of the General Assembly of this State ratifying the amendments of the said Constitution, are hereby repealed, and that the union now subsisting between South Carolina and other States under the name of the United States of America is hereby dissolved.

Appendix 2

Declaration of the Immediate Causes of Secession

Charleston, South Carolina, December 24, 1860

Adopted by the South Carolina secession convention as the official explanation for the state's withdrawal from the Union, the declaration was drafted by a special committee chaired by Christopher G. Memminger. Reprinted from Frank Moore, ed., *The Rebellion Record,* vol. 1, New York, 1862, pp. 3–4.

The people of the State of South Carolina in Convention assembled, on the 2d day of April, A.D. 1852, declared that the frequent violations of the Constitution of the United States by the Federal Government, and its encroachments upon the reserved rights of the States, fully justified this State in their withdrawal from the Federal Union; but in deference to the opinions and wishes of the other Slaveholding States, she forbore at that time to exercise this right. Since that time these encroachments have continued to increase, and further forbearance ceases to be a virtue.

And now the State of South Carolina having resumed her separate and equal place among nations, deems it due to herself, to the remaining United States of America, and to the nations of the world, that she should declare the immediate causes which have led to this act.

In the year 1765, that portion of the British Empire embracing Great Britain undertook to make laws for the Government of that portion composed of the thirteen American Colonies. A struggle for the right of self-government ensued, which resulted, on the 4th of July, 1776, in a Declaration, by the Colonies, "that they are, and of right ought to be, FREE AND INDEPENDENT STATES; and that, as free and independent States, they have full power to levy war, conclude peace, contract alliances, establish commerce, and to do all other acts and things which independent States may of right do."

They further solemnly declared that whenever any "form of government becomes destructive of the ends for which it was established, it is the right of the people to alter or abolish it, and to institute a new government." Deeming the Government of Great Britain to have become destructive of these ends, they declared that the Colonies "are absolved from all allegiance to the British Crown, and that all political connection between them and the State of Great Britain is, and ought to be, totally dissolved."

In pursuance of this Declaration of Independence, each of the thirteen States proceeded to exercise its separate sovereignty; adopted for itself a Constitution, and appointed officers for the administration of government in all its departments—Legislative, Executive and Judicial. For purposes of defence they united their arms and their counsels; and, in 1778, they entered into a League known as the Articles of Confederation, whereby they agreed to intrust the administration of their external relations to a common agent, known as the Congress of the

United States, expressly declaring, in the first article, "that each State retains its sovereignty, freedom and independence, and every power, jurisdiction and right which is not, by this Confederation, expressly delegated to the United States in Congress assembled."

Under this Confederation the War of the Revolution was carried on; and on the 3d of September, 1783, the contest ended, and a definite Treaty was signed by Great Britain, in which she acknowledged the Independence of the Colonies in the following terms:

"ARTICLE 1. His Britannic Majesty acknowledges the said United States, viz.: New Hampshire, Massachusetts Bay, Rhode Island and Providence Plantations, Connecticut, New York, New Jersey, Pennsylvania, Delaware, Maryland, Virginia, North Carolina, South Carolina and Georgia, to be FREE, SOVEREIGN, AND INDEPENDENT STATES; that he treats with them as such; and, for himself, his heirs and successors, relinquishes all claims to the government, propriety, and territorial rights of the same and every part thereof."

Thus were established the two great principles asserted by the Colonies, namely, the right of a State to govern itself; and the right of a people to abolish a Government when it becomes destructive of the ends for which it was instituted. And concurrent with the establishment of these principles, was the fact, that each Colony became and was recognized by the mother country as a FREE, SOVEREIGN AND INDEPENDENT STATE.

In 1787, Deputies were appointed by the States to revise the articles of Confederation; and on 17th September, 1787, these Deputies recommended, for the adoption of the States, the Articles of Union, known as the Constitution of the United States.

The parties to whom this constitution was submitted were the several sovereign States; they were to agree or disagree, and when nine of them agreed, the compact was to take effect among those concurring; and the General Government, as the common agent, was then to be invested with their authority.

If only nine of the thirteen States had concurred, the other four would have remained as they then were—separate, sovereign States, independent of any of the provisions of the Constitution. In fact, two of the States did not accede to the Constitution until long after it had gone into operation among the other eleven; and during that interval, they each exercised the functions of an independent nation.

By this Constitution, certain duties were imposed upon the several States, and the exercise of certain of their powers was restrained, which necessarily impelled their continued existence as sovereign states. But, to remove all doubt, an amendment was added, which declared that the powers not delegated to the United States by the Constitution, nor prohibited by it to the States, are reserved to the States respectively, or to the people. On the 23d May, 1788, South Carolina, by a Convention of her people, passed an ordinance assenting to this Constitution, and afterwards altered her own Constitution to conform herself to the obligations she had undertaken.

Thus was established, by compact between the States, a Government with defined objects and powers, limited to the express words of the grant. This limitation left the whole remaining mass of power subject to the clause reserving it to the States or the people, and rendered unnecessary any specification of reserved rights. We hold that the Government thus established is subject to the two great principles asserted in the Declaration of Independence; and we hold further, that the mode of its formation subjects it to a third fundamental principle, namely, the law of compact. We maintain that in every compact between two or more parties, the obligation is mutual; that the failure of one of the contracting parties to perform a material part of the agreement, entirely releases the obligation of the other; and that, where no arbiter is provided, each party is remitted to his own judgment to determine the fact of failure, with all its consequences.

In the present case, that fact is established with certainty. We assert that fourteen of the States have deliberately refused for years past to fulfil their constitutional obligations, and we refer to their own statutes for the proof.

The Constitution of the United States, in its fourth Article, provides as follows:

"No person held to service or labor in one State under the laws thereof, escaping into another, shall, in consequence of any law or regulation therein, be discharged from such service or labor, but shall be delivered up, on claim of the party to whom such service or labor may be due."

This stipulation was so material to the compact that without it that compact would not have been made. The greater number of the contracting parties held slaves, and they had previously evinced their estimate of the value of such a stipulation by making it a condition in the Ordinance for the government of the territory ceded by Virginia, which obligations, and the laws of the General Government, have ceased to effect the objects of the Constitution. The States of Maine, New Hampshire, Vermont, Massachusetts, Connecticut, Rhode Island, New York, Pennsylvania, Illinois, Indiana, Michigan, Wisconsin, and Iowa, have enacted laws which either nullify the acts of Congress, or render useless any attempt to execute them. In many of these States the fugitive is discharged from the service of labor claimed, and in none of them has the State Government complied with the stipulation made in the Constitution. The State of New Jersey, at an early day, passed a law in conformity with her constitutional obligation; but the current of Anti-Slavery feeling has led her more recently to enact laws which render inoperative the remedies provided by her own laws and by the laws of Congress. In the State of New York even the right of transit for a slave has been denied by her tribunals; and the States of Ohio and Iowa have refused to surrender to justice fugitives charged with murder, and with inciting servile insurrection in the State of Virginia. Thus the constitutional compact has been deliberately broken and disregarded by the non-slaveholding States; and the consequence follows that South Carolina is released from her obligation.

The ends for which this Constitution was framed are declared by itself to be "to form a more perfect union, to establish justice, insure domestic tranquillity, provide for the common defence, promote the general welfare, and secure the blessings of liberty to ourselves and our posterity."

These ends it endeavored to accomplish by a Federal Government, in which each State was recognized as an equal, and had separate control over its own institutions. The right of property in slaves was recognized by giving to free persons distinct political rights; by giving them the right to represent, and burdening them with direct taxes for, three-fifths of their slaves; by authorizing the importation of slaves for twenty years; and by stipulating for the rendition of fugitives from labor.

We affirm that these ends for which this Government was instituted have been defeated, and the Government itself has been destructive of them by the action of the non-slaveholding States. Those States have assumed the right of deciding upon the propriety of our domestic institutions; and have denied the rights of property established in fifteen of the States and recognized by the Constitution; they have denounced as sinful the institution of Slavery; they have permitted the open establishment among them of societies, whose avowed object is to disturb the peace of and cloin the property of the citizens of other States. They have encouraged and assisted thousands of our slaves to leave their homes; and those who remain, have been incited by emissaries, books, and pictures, to servile insurrection.

For twenty-five years this agitation has been steadily increasing, until it has now secured to its aid the power of the common Government. Observing the *forms* of the Constitution, a sectional party has found within that article establishing the Executive Department, the means of subverting the Constitution itself. A geographical line has been drawn across the Union, and all the States north of that line have united in the election of a man to the high office of President of the United States whose opinions and purposes are hostile to Slavery. He is to be intrusted with the administration of the common Government, because he has declared that that "Government cannot endure permanently half slave, half free," and that the public mind must rest in the belief that Slavery is in the course of ultimate extinction.

This sectional combination for the subversion of the Constitution has been aided, in some of the States, by elevating to citizenship persons who, by the supreme law of the land, are incapable of becoming citizens; and their votes have been used to inaugurate a new policy, hostile to the South, and destructive of its peace and safety.

On the 4th of March next this party will take possession of the Government. It has announced that the South shall be excluded from the common territory, that the Judicial tribunal shall be made sectional, and that a war must be waged against Slavery until it shall cease throughout the United States.

The guarantees of the Constitution will then no longer exist; the equal rights of the States will be lost. The Slaveholding States will no longer have the power of self-government, or self-protection, and the Federal Government will have become their enemy.

Sectional interest and animosity will deepen the irritation; and all hope of remedy is rendered vain, by the fact that the public opinion at the North has invested a great political error with the sanctions of a more erroneous religious belief.

We, therefore, the people of South Carolina, by our delegates in Convention assembled, appealing to the Supreme Judge of the world for the rectitude of our intentions, have solemnly declared that the Union heretofore existing between this State and the other States of North America is dissolved, and that the State of South Carolina has resumed her position among the nations of the world, as separate and independent state, with full power to levy war, conclude peace, contract alliances, establish commerce, and to do all other acts and things which independent States may of right do.

Appendix 3

Constitution of the Confederate States of America

Montgomery, Alabama, March 11, 1861

Reprinted from Emory M. Thomas, *The Confederate Nation: 1861–1865.* New York, 1979, pp. 307–322.

We, the people of the Confederate States, each State acting in its sovereign and independent character, in order to form a permanent government, establish justice, insure domestic tranquillity, and secure the blessings of liberty to ourselves and our posterity—invoking the favor and guidance of Almighty God—do ordain and establish this Constitution for the Confederate States of America.

Art. I

Sec. 1.—All legislative powers herein delegated shall be vested in a Congress of the Confederate States, which shall consist of a Senate and House of Representatives.

Sec. 2. (1) The House of Representatives shall be . . . chosen every second year by the people of the several States; and the electors in each State shall be citizens of the Confederate States, and have the qualifications requisite for electors of the most numerous branch of the State Legislature; but no person of foreign birth, not a citizen of the Confederate States, shall be allowed to vote for any officer, civil or political, State or Federal.

(2) No person shall be a Representative who shall not have attained the age of twenty-five years, and be a citizen of the Confederate States, and who shall not, when elected, be an inhabitant of that State in which he shall be chosen.

(3) Representatives and direct taxes shall be apportioned among the several States which may be included within this Confederacy, according to their respective numbers, which shall be determined by adding to the whole number of free persons, including those bound to service for a term of years, and excluding Indians not taxed, three-fifths of all slaves. The actual enumeration shall be made within three years after the first meeting of the Congress of the Confederate States, and within every subsequent term of ten years, in such manner as they shall by law direct. The number of Representatives shall not exceed one for every fifty thousand, but each State shall have at least one Representative; and until such enumeration shall be made the State of South Carolina shall be entitled to choose six; the State of Georgia ten; the State of Alabama nine; the State of Florida two; the State of Mississippi seven; the State of Louisiana six; and the State of Texas six.

(4) When vacancies happen in the representation of any State, the Executive authority thereof shall issue writs of election to fill such vacancies.

(5) The House of Representatives shall choose their Speaker and other officers; and shall have

the sole power of impeachment; except that any judicial or other federal officer resident and acting solely within the limits of any State, may be impeached by a vote of two-thirds of both branches of the Legislature thereof.

Sec. 3. (1) The Senate of the Confederate States shall be composed of two Senators from each State, chosen for six years by the Legislature thereof, at the regular session next immediately preceding the commencement of the term of service; and each Senator shall have one vote.

(2) Immediately after they shall be assembled, in consequence of the first election, they shall be divided as equally as may be into three classes. The seats of the Senators of the first class shall be vacated at the expiration of the second year; of the second class at the expiration of the fourth year; and of the third class at the expiration of the sixth year; so that one-third may be chosen every second year; and if vacancies happen by resignation or otherwise during the recess of the Legislature of any State, the Executive thereof may make temporary appointments until the next meeting of the Legislature, which shall then fill such vacancies.

(3) No person shall be a Senator, who shall not have attained the age of thirty years, and be a citizen of the Confederate States; and who shall not, when elected, be an inhabitant of the State for which he shall be chosen.

(4) The Vice-President of the Confederate States shall be President of the Senate, but shall have no vote, unless they be equally divided.

(5) The Senate shall choose their other officers, and also a President pro tempore, in the absence of the Vice-President, or when he shall exercise the office of President of the Confederate States.

(6) The Senate shall have sole power to try all impeachments. When sitting for that purpose they shall be on oath or affirmation. When the President of the Confederate States is tried, the Chief Justice shall preside; and no person shall be convicted without the concurrence of two-thirds of the members present.

(7) Judgment in cases of impeachment shall not extend further than removal from office, and disqualification to hold and enjoy any office of honor, trust, or profit, under the Confederate States; but the party convicted shall, nevertheless, be liable and subject to indictment, trial, judgment, and punishment according to law.

Sec. 4. (1) The times, places, and manner of holding elections for Senators and Representatives, shall be prescribed in each State by the Legislature thereof, subject to the provisions of this Constitution; but the Congress may, at any time, by law, make or alter such regulations, except as to the times and places of choosing Senators.

(2) The Congress shall assemble at least once in every year; and such meeting shall be on the first Monday in December, unless they shall, by law, appoint a different day.

Sec. 5. (1) Each House shall be the judge of the elections, returns, and qualifications of its own members, and a majority of each shall constitute a quorum to do business; but a smaller number may adjourn from day to day, and may be authorized to compel the attendance of absent members, in such manner and under such penalties as each House may provide.

(2) Each House may determine the rules of its proceedings, punish its members for disorderly behavior, and, with the concurrence of two-thirds of the whole number, expel a member.

(3) Each House shall keep a journal of its proceedings, and from time to time publish the same, excepting such parts as may in their judgment require secrecy, and the ayes and nays of the members of either House, on any question, shall, at the desire of one-fifth of those present, be entered on the journal.

(4) Neither House, during the session of Congress, shall, without the consent of the other, adjourn for more than three days, nor to any other place than that in which the two Houses shall be sitting.

Sec. 6. (1) The Senators and Representatives shall receive a compensation for their services, to be ascertained by law, and paid out of the Treasury of the Confederate States. They shall, in all cases except treason and breach of the peace, be privileged from arrest during their attendance at the session of their respective Houses, and in going to and returning from the same; and for any speech or debate in either House, they shall not be questioned in any other place.

(2) No Senator or Representative shall, during the time for which he was elected, be appointed to any civil office under the authority of the Confederate States, which shall have been created, or the emoluments whereof shall have been increased during such time; and no person holding any office under the Confederate States shall be a member of either House during his

continuance in office. But Congress may, by law, grant to the principal officer in each of the Executive Departments a seat upon the floor of either House, with the privilege of discussing any measure appertaining to his department.

Sec. 7. (1) All bills for raising revenue shall originate in the House of Representatives; but the Senate may propose or concur with amendments as on other bills.

(2) Every bill which shall have passed both Houses shall, before it becomes a law, be presented to the President of the Confederate States; if he approve he shall sign it; but if not, he shall return it with his objections to that House in which it shall have originated, who shall enter the objections at large on their journal, and proceed to reconsider it. If, after such reconsideration, two-thirds of that House shall agree to pass the bill, it shall be sent, together with the objections, to the other House, by which it shall likewise be reconsidered, and if approved by two-thirds of that House, it shall become a law. But in all such cases, the votes of both Houses shall be determined by yeas and nays, and the names of the persons voting for and against the bill shall be entered on the journal of each House respectively. If any bill shall not be returned by the President within ten days (Sundays excepted) after it shall have been presented to him, the same shall be a law, in like manner as if he had signed it, unless the Congress, by their adjournment, prevent its return; in which case it shall not be a law. The President may approve any appropriation and disapprove any other appropriation in the same bill. In such case he shall, in signing the bill, designate the appropriations disapproved; and shall return a copy of such appropriations, with his objections, to the House in which the bill shall have originated; and the same proceedings shall then be had as in case of other bills disapproved by the President.

(3) Every order, resolution, or vote, to which the concurrence of both Houses may be necessary (except on a question of adjournment) shall be presented to the President of the Confederate States; and before the same shall take effect shall be approved by him; or being disapproved by him, shall be repassed by two-thirds of both Houses, according to the rules and limitations prescribed in case of a bill.

Sec. 8.—The Congress shall have power—(1) To lay and collect taxes, duties, imposts, and excises, for revenue necessary to pay the debts, provide for the common defence, and carry on the Government of the Confederate States; but no bounties shall be granted from the treasury; nor shall any duties or taxes on importations from foreign nations be laid to promote or foster any branch of industry; and all duties, imposts, and excises shall be uniform throughout the Confederate States.

(2) To borrow money on the credit of the Confederate States.

(3) To regulate commerce with foreign nations, and among the several States, and with the Indian tribes; but neither this nor any other clause contained in the Constitution shall be construed to delegate the power to Congress to appropriate money for any internal improvement intended to facilitate commerce; except for the purpose of furnishing lights, beacons, and buoys, and other aids to navigation upon the coasts, and the improvement of harbors, and the removing of obstructions in river navigation, in all which cases, such duties shall be laid on the navigation facilitated thereby, as may be necessary to pay the costs and expenses thereof.

(4) To establish uniform laws of naturalization, and uniform laws on the subject of bankruptcies throughout the Confederate States, but no law of Congress shall discharge any debt contracted before the passage of the same.

(5) To coin money, regulate the value thereof, and of foreign coin, and fix the standard of weights and measures.

(6) To provide for the punishment of counterfeiting the securities and current coin of the Confederate States.

(7) To establish post-offices and post-routes; but the expenses of the Post-office Department, after the first day of March, in the year of our Lord eighteen hundred and sixty-three, shall be paid out of its own revenues.

(8) To promote the progress of science and useful arts, by securing for limited times to authors and inventors the exclusive right to their respective writings and discoveries.

(9) To constitute tribunals inferior to the Supreme Court.

(10) To define and punish piracies and felonies committed on the high seas, and offences against the law of nations.

(11) To declare war, grant letters of marque and reprisal, and make rules concerning captures on land and water.

(12) To raise and support armies; but no appropriation of money to that use shall be for a longer term than two years.

(13) To provide and maintain a navy.

(14) To make rules for government and regulation of the land and naval forces.

(15) To provide for calling forth the militia to execute the laws of the Confederate States; suppress insurrections, and repel invasions.

(16) To provide for organizing, arming, and disciplining the militia, and for governing such part of them as may be employed in the service of the Confederate States; reserving to the States, respectively, the appointment of the officers, and the authority of training the militia according to the discipline prescribed by Congress.

(17) To exercise exclusive legislation, in all cases whatsoever, over such district (not exceeding ten miles square) as may, by cession of one or more States, and the acceptance of Congress, become the seat of the Government of the Confederate States; and to exercise a like authority over all places purchased by the consent of the Legislature of the State in which the same shall be, for the erection of forts, magazines, arsenals, dock-yards, and other needful buildings, and

(18) To make all laws which shall be necessary and proper for carrying into execution the foregoing powers, and all other powers vested by this Constitution in the Government of the Confederate States, or in any department or officer thereof.

Sec. 9. (1) The importation of negroes of the African race, from any foreign country, other than the slaveholding States or Territories of the United States of America, is hereby forbidden; and Congress is required to pass such laws as shall effectually prevent the same.

(2) Congress shall also have power to prohibit the introduction of slaves from any State not a member of, or Territory not belonging to, this Confederacy.

(3) The privilege of the writ of habeas corpus shall not be suspended, unless when in cases of rebellion or invasion the public safety may require it.

(4) No bill of attainder, ex post facto law, or law denying or impairing the right of property in negro slaves shall be passed.

(5) No capitation or other direct tax shall be laid unless in proportion to the census or enumeration hereinbefore directed to be taken.

(6) No tax or duty shall be laid on articles exported from any State, except by a vote of two-thirds of both Houses.

(7) No preference shall be given by any regulation of commerce or revenue to the ports of one State over those of another.

(8) No money shall be drawn from the treasury but in consequence of appropriations made by law; and a regular statement and account of the receipts and expenditures of all public money shall be published from time to time.

(9) Congress shall appropriate no money from the treasury except by a vote of two-thirds of both Houses, taken by yeas and nays, unless it be asked and estimated for by some one of the heads of departments, and submitted to Congress by the President; or for the purpose of paying its own expenses and contingencies; or for the payment of claims against the Confederate States, the justice of which shall have been judicially declared by a tribunal for the investigation of claims against the Government, which it is hereby made the duty of Congress to establish.

(10) All bills appropriating money shall specify in federal currency the exact amount of each appropriation and the purposes for which it is made; and Congress shall grant no extra compensation to any public contractor, officer, agent, or servant, after such contract shall have been made or such service rendered.

(11) No title of nobility shall be granted by the Confederate States; and no person holding any office of profit or trust under them shall, without the consent of the Congress, accept of any present, emolument, office, or title of any kind whatever, from any king, prince, or foreign state.

(12) Congress shall make no law respecting an establishment of religion, or prohibiting the free exercise thereof; or abridging the freedom of speech or of the press; or the right of the people peaceably to assemble and petition the Government for a redress of grievances.

(13) A well-regulated militia being necessary to the security of a free State, the right of the people to keep and bear arms shall not be infringed.

(14) No soldier shall, in time of peace, be quartered in any house without the consent of the owner; nor in time of war, but in a manner to be prescribed by law.

(15) The right of the people to be secure in their persons, houses, papers, and effects, against unreasonable searches and seizures, shall not be violated; and no warrant shall issue but upon probable cause, supported by oath or affirmation, and particularly describing the place to be searched, and the person or things to be seized.

(16) No person shall be held to answer for a capital or otherwise infamous crime, unless on a presentment or indictment of a grand jury, except in cases arising in the land or naval forces, or in the militia, when in actual service, in time of war, or public danger; nor shall any person be subject for the same offence to be twice put in jeopardy of life or limb; nor be compelled in any criminal case to be a witness against himself; nor be deprived of life, liberty, or property, without due process of law; nor shall private property be taken for public use without just compensation.

(17) In all criminal prosecutions the accused shall enjoy the right to a speedy and public trial, by an impartial jury of the State and district wherein the crime shall have been committed, which district shall have been previously ascertained by law, and to be informed of the nature and cause of the accusation; to be confronted with the witnesses against him; to have compulsory process for obtaining witnesses in his favor; and to have the assistance of counsel for his defence.

(18) In suits at common law, where the value in controversy shall exceed twenty dollars, the right of trial by jury shall be preserved; and no fact so tried by a jury shall be otherwise reexamined in any court of the Confederacy, than according to the rules of common law.

(19) Excessive bail shall not be required, nor excessive fines imposed, nor cruel and unusual punishment inflicted.

(20) Every law, or resolution having the force of law, shall relate to but one subject, and that shall be expressed in the title.

Sec. 10. (1) No State shall enter into any treaty, alliance, or confederation; grant letters of marque and reprisal; coin money; make any thing but gold and silver coin a tender in payment of debts; pass any bill of attainder, or ex post facto law, or law impairing the obligation of contracts; or grant any title of nobility.

(2) No State shall, without the consent of Congress, lay any imposts or duties on imports or exports, except what may be absolutely necessary for executing its inspection laws; and the net produce of all duties and imposts, laid by any State on imports or exports, shall be for the use of the Treasury of the Confederate States; and all such laws shall be subject to the revision and control of Congress.

(3) No State shall, without the consent of Congress, lay any duty on tonnage, except on sea-going vessels, for the improvement of its rivers and harbors navigated by the said vessels; but such duties shall not conflict with any treaties of the Confederate States with foreign nations; and any surplus revenue, thus derived, shall, after making such improvement, be paid into the common treasury; nor shall any State keep troops or ships of war in time of peace, enter into any agreement or compact with another State, or with a foreign power, or engage in war, unless actually invaded, or in such imminent danger as will not admit of delay. But when any river divides or flows through two or more States, they may enter into compacts with each other to improve the navigation thereof.

Art. II

Sec. 1. (1) The Executive power shall be vested in a President of the Confederate States of America. He and the Vice-President shall hold their offices for the term of six years; but the President shall not be reeligible. The President and Vice-President shall be elected as follows:

(2) Each State shall appoint, in such manner as the Legislature thereof may direct, a number of electors equal to the whole number of Senators and Representatives to which the State may be entitled in the Congress; but no Senator or Representative, or person holding an office of trust or profit under the Confederate States, shall be appointed an elector.

(3) The electors shall meet in their respective States and vote by ballot for President and Vice-President, one of whom, at least shall not be an inhabitant of the same State with

themselves; they shall name in their ballots the person voted for as President, and in distinct ballots the person voted for as Vice-President, and they shall make distinct lists of all persons voted for as President, and of all persons voted for as Vice-President, and of the number of votes for each; which list they shall sign, and certify, and transmit, sealed, to the . . . government of the Confederate States, directed to the President of the Senate. The President of the Senate shall, in the presence of the Senate and House of Representatives, open all the certificates, and the votes shall then be counted; the person having the greatest number of votes for President shall be the President, if such number be a majority of the whole number of electors appointed; and if no person shall have such a majority, then, from the persons having the highest numbers, not exceeding three, on the list of those voted for as President, the House of Representatives shall choose immediately, by ballot, the President. But, in choosing the President, the votes shall be taken by States, the representation from each State having one vote; a quorum for this purpose shall consist of a member or members from two-thirds of the States, and a majority of all the States shall be necessary to a choice. And if the House of Representatives shall not choose a President, whenever the right of choice shall devolve upon them, before the fourth day of March next following, then the Vice-President shall act as President, as in case of the death, or other constitutional disability of the President.

(4) The person having the greatest number of votes as Vice-President shall be the Vice-President, if such number be a majority of the whole number of electors appointed; and if no person have a majority, then from the two highest numbers on the list, the Senate shall choose the Vice-President; a quorum for the purpose shall consist of two-thirds of the whole number of Senators, and a majority of the whole number shall be necessary for a choice.

(5) But no person constitutionally ineligible to the office of President shall be eligible to that of Vice-President of the Confederate States.

(6) The Congress may determine the time of choosing the electors, and the day on which they shall give their votes; which day shall be the same throughout the Confederate States.

(7) No person except a natural born citizen of the Confederate States, or a citizen thereof, at the time of the adoption of this Constitution, or a citizen thereof born in the United States prior to the 20th of December, 1860, shall be eligible to the office of President; neither shall any person be eligible to that office who shall not have attained the age of thirty-five years, and been fourteen years a resident within the limits of the Confederate States, as they may exist at the time of his election.

(8) In case of the removal of the President from office, or of his death, resignation, or inability to discharge the powers and duties of the said office, the same shall devolve on the Vice-President; and the Congress may, by law, provide for the case of the removal, death, resignation, or inability both of the President and the Vice-President, declaring what officer shall then act as President, and such officer shall then act accordingly until the disability be removed or a President shall be elected.

(9) The President shall, at stated times, receive for his services a compensation, which shall neither be increased nor diminished during the period for which he shall have been elected; and he shall not receive within that period any other emolument from the Confederate States, or any of them.

(10) Before he enters on the execution [of the duties] of his office, he shall take the following oath or affirmation:

"I do solemnly swear (or affirm) that I will faithfully execute the office of President of the Confederate States, and will, to the best of my ability, preserve, protect, and defend the Constitution thereof."

Sec. 2. (1) The President shall be commander-in-chief of the army and navy of the Confederate States, and of the militia of the several States, when called into the actual service of the Confederate States; he may require the opinion, in writing, of the principal officer in each of the Executive Departments, upon any subject relating to the duties of their respective offices; and he shall have power to grant reprieves and pardons for offences against the Confederate States, except in cases of impeachment.

(2) He shall have power, by and with the advice and consent of the Senate, to make treaties, provided two-thirds of the Senators present concur; and he shall nominate, and, by and with

the advice and consent of the Senate, shall appoint ambassadors, other public ministers, and consuls, Judges of the Supreme Court, and all other officers of the Confederate States, whose appointments are not herein otherwise provided for, and which shall be established by law; but the Congress may by law vest the appointment of such inferior officers, as they think proper, in the President alone, in the courts of law, or in the heads of departments.

(3) The principal officer in each of the Executive Departments, and all persons connected with the diplomatic service, may be removed from office at the pleasure of the President. All other civil officers of the Executive Departments may be removed at any time by the President, or other appointing power, when their services are unnecessary, or for dishonesty, incapacity, inefficiency, misconduct, or neglect of duty; and when so removed, the removal shall be reported to the Senate, together with the reasons therefor.

(4) The President shall have power to fill all vacancies that may happen during the recess of the Senate, by granting commissions which shall expire at the end of the next session; but no person rejected by the Senate shall be reappointed to the same office during their ensuing recess.

Sec. 3. (1) The President shall, from time to time, give to the Congress information of the state of the Confederacy, and recommend to their consideration such measures as he shall judge necessary and expedient; he may, on extraordinary occasions, convene both Houses, or either of them; and, in case of disagreement between them, with respect to the time of adjournment he may adjourn them to such time as he shall think proper; he shall receive ambassadors and other public ministers; he shall take care that the laws be faithfully executed, and shall commission all the officers of the Confederate States.

Sec. 4. (1) The President and Vice-President, and all Civil officers of the Confederate States, shall be removed from office on impeachment for, or conviction of, treason, bribery, or other high crimes and misdemeanors.

Art. III

Sec. 1. (1) The judicial power of the Confederate States shall be vested in one Supreme Court, and in such inferior courts as the Congress may from time to time ordain and establish. The judges, both of the Supreme and inferior courts, shall hold their offices during good behavior, and shall, at stated times, receive for their services a compensation, which shall not be diminished during their continuance in office. . . .

Art. IV

Sec. 1. (1) Full faith and credit shall be given in each State to the public acts, records, and judicial proceedings of every other State. And the Congress may, by general laws, prescribe the manner in which such acts, records, and proceedings shall be proved, and the effect thereof.

Sec. 2. (1) The citizens of each State shall be entitled to all the privileges and immunities of citizens of the several States, and shall have the right of transit and sojourn in any State of this Confederacy, with their slaves and other property; and the right of property in said slaves shall not be thereby impaired.

(2) A person charged in any State with treason, felony, or other crime against the laws of such State, who shall flee from justice, and be found in another State, shall, on demand of the executive authority of the State from which he fled, be delivered up to be removed to the State having jurisdiction of the crime.

(3) No slave or other person held to service or labor in any State or Territory of the Confederate States, under the laws thereof, escaping or [un]lawfully carried into another, shall, in consequence of any law or regulation therein, be discharged from such service or labor; but shall be delivered up on claim of the party to whom such slave belongs, or to whom such service or labor may be due.

Sec. 3. (1) Other States may be admitted into this Confederacy by a vote of two-thirds of the whole House of Representatives, and two-thirds of the Senate, the Senate voting by States; but no new State shall be formed or erected within the jurisdiction of any other State; nor any State be formed by the junction of two or more States, or parts of States, without the consent of the Legislatures of the States concerned as well as of the Congress.

(2) The Congress shall have power to dispose of and make all needful rules and regulations concerning the property of the Confederate States, including the lands thereof.

(3) The Confederate States may acquire new territory; and Congress shall have power to legislate and provide governments for the inhabitants of all territory belonging to the Confederate States, lying without the limits of the several States, and may permit them, at such times, and in such manner as it may by law provide, to form States to be admitted into the Confederacy. In all such territory, the institution of negro slavery, as it now exists in the Confederate States, shall be recognized and protected by Congress and by the territorial government; and the inhabitants of the several Confederate States and Territories shall have the right to take to such territory any slaves lawfully held by them in any of the States or Territories of the Confederate States.

(4) The Confederate States shall guarantee to every State that now is or hereafter may become a member of this Confederacy, a Republican form of Government, and shall protect each of them against invasion; and on application of the Legislature, (or of the Executive when the Legislature is not in session,) against domestic violence.

Art. V

Sec. 1. (1) Upon the demand of any three States, legally assembled in their several Conventions, the Congress shall summon a Convention of all the States, to take into consideration such amendments to the Constitution as the said States shall concur in suggesting at the time when the said demand is made; and should any of the proposed amendments to the Constitution be agreed on by the said Convention—voting by States—and the same be ratified by the Legislatures of two-thirds thereof—as the one or the other mode of ratification may be proposed by the general convention—they shall thenceforward form a part of this Constitution. But no State shall, without its consent, be deprived of its equal representation in the Senate.

Art. VI

1.—The Government established by this Constitution is the successor of the Provisional Government of the Confederate States of America, and all the laws passed by the latter shall continue in force until the same shall be repealed or modified; and all the officers appointed by the same shall remain in office until their successors are appointed and qualified, or the offices abolished.

2. All debts contracted and engagements entered into before the adoption of this Constitution, shall be as valid against the Confederate States under this Constitution as under the Provisional Government.

3. This Constitution, and the laws of the Confederate States, made in pursuance thereof, and all treaties made, or which shall be made, under the authority of the Confederate States, shall be the supreme law of the land; and the judges in every State shall be bound thereby, any thing in the Constitution or laws of any State to the contrary notwithstanding.

4. The Senators and Representatives before mentioned, and the members of the several State Legislatures, and all executive and judicial officers, both of the Confederate States and of the several States, shall be bound, by oath or affirmation, to support this Constitution; but no religious test shall ever be required as a qualification to any office or public trust under the Confederate States.

5. The enumeration, in the Constitution, of certain rights, shall not be construed to deny or disparage others retained by the people of the several States.

6. The powers not delegated to the Confederate States by the Constitution, nor prohibited by it to the States, are reserved to the States, respectively, or to the people thereof.

Art. VII

1.—The ratification of the conventions of five States shall be sufficient for the establishment of this Constitution between the States so ratifying the same.

2. When five States shall have ratified this Constitution in the manner before specified, the Congress, under the provisional Constitution, shall prescribe the time for holding the election of President and Vice-President, and for the meeting of the electoral college, and for counting the votes and inaugurating the President. They shall also prescribe the time for holding the first

election of members of Congress under this Constitution, and the time for assembling the same. Until the assembling of such Congress, the Congress under the provisional Constitution shall continue to exercise the legislative powers granted them; not extending beyond the time limited by the Constitution of the Provisional Government.

Adopted unanimously by the Congress of the Confederate States of South Carolina, Georgia, Florida, Alabama, Mississippi, Louisiana, and Texas, sitting in convention at the capitol, in the city of Montgomery, Alabama, on the Eleventh day of March, in the year Eighteen Hundred and Sixty-One.

HOWELL COBB
President of the Congress

(Signatures)

Appendix 4

Cornerstone Speech

Savannah, Georgia, March 21, 1861

The Cornerstone Speech was delivered extemporaneously by Vice President Alexander H. Stephens, and no official printed version exists. The text below was taken from a newspaper article in the *Savannah Republican,* as reprinted in Henry Cleveland, *Alexander H. Stephens, in Public and Private: With Letters and Speeches, before, during, and since the War,* Philadelphia, 1886, pp. 717–729.

At half past seven o'clock on Thursday evening, the largest audience ever assembled at the Athenæum was in the house, waiting most impatiently for the appearance of the orator of the evening, Hon. A. H. Stephens, Vice-President of the Confederate States of America. The committee, with invited guests, were seated on the stage, when, at the appointed hour, the Hon. C. C. Jones, Mayor, and the speaker, entered, and were greeted by the immense assemblage with deafening rounds of applause.

The Mayor then, in a few pertinent remarks, introduced Mr. Stephens, stating that at the request of a number of the members of the convention, and citizens of Savannah and the State, now here, he had consented to address them upon the present state of public affairs.

Mr. Stephens rose and spoke as follows:

Mr. Mayor, and Gentlemen of the Committee, and Fellow-Citizens:—For this reception you will please accept my most profound and sincere thanks. The compliment is doubtless intended as much, or more, perhaps, in honor of the occasion, and my public position, in connection with the great events now crowding upon us, than to me personally and individually. It is however none the less appreciated by me on that account. We are in the midst of one of the greatest epochs in our history. The last ninety days will mark one of the most memorable eras in the history of modern civilization.

[There was a general call from the outside of the building for the speaker to go out, that there were more outside than in.]

The Mayor rose and requested silence at the doors, that Mr. Stephens' health would not permit him to speak in the open air.

Mr. Stephens said he would leave it to the audience whether he should proceed indoors or out. There was a general cry indoors, as the ladies, a large number of whom were present, could not hear outside.

Mr. Stephens said that the accommodation of the ladies would determine the question, and he would proceed where he was.

[At this point the uproar and clamor outside was greater still for the speaker to go out on the steps. This was quieted by Col. Lawton, Col. Freeman, Judge Jackson, and Mr. J. W. Owens going out and stating the facts of the case to the dense mass of men, women, and children who were outside, and entertaining them in brief speeches—Mr. Stephens all this while quietly sitting down until the furor subsided.]

Mr. Stephens rose and said: When perfect quiet is restored, I shall proceed. I cannot speak so long as there is any noise or confusion. I shall take my time—I feel quite prepared to spend the night with you if necessary. [Loud applause.] I very much regret that every one who desires cannot hear what I have to say. Not that I have any display to make, or any thing very entertaining to present, but such views as I have to give, I wish *all,* not only in this city, but in this State, and throughout our Confederate Republic, could hear, who have a desire to hear them.

I was remarking, that we are passing through one of the greatest revolutions in the annals of the world. Seven States have within the last three months thrown off an old government and formed a new. This revolution has been signally marked, up to this time, by the fact of its having been accomplished without the loss of a single drop of blood. [Applause.]

This new constitution, or form of government, constitutes the subject to which your attention will be partly invited. In reference to it, I make this first general remark. It amply secures all our ancient rights, franchises, and liberties. All the great principles of Magna Charta are retained in it. No citizen is deprived of life, liberty, or property, but by the judgment of his peers under the laws of the land. The great principle of religious liberty, which was the honor and pride of the old constitution, is still maintained and secured. All the essentials of the old constitution, which have endeared it to the hearts of the American people, have been preserved and perpetuated. [Applause.] Some changes have been made. Of these I shall speak presently. Some of these I should have preferred not to have seen made; but these, perhaps, meet the cordial approbation of a majority of this audience, if not an overwhelming majority of the people of the Confederacy. Of them, therefore, I will not speak. But other important changes do meet my cordial approbation. They form great improvements upon the old constitution. So, taking the whole new constitution, I have no hesitancy in giving it as my judgment that it is decidedly better than the old. [Applause.]

Allow me briefly to allude to some of these improvements. The question of building up class interests, or fostering one branch of industry to the prejudice of another under the exercise of the revenue power, which gave us so much trouble under the old constitution, is put at rest forever under the new. We allow the imposition of no duty with a view of giving advantage to one class of persons, in any trade or business, over those of another. All, under our system, stand upon the same broad principles of perfect equality. Honest labor and enterprise are left free and unrestricted in whatever pursuit they may be engaged. This subject came well nigh causing a rupture of the old Union, under the lead of the gallant Palmetto State, which lies on our border, in 1833. This old thorn of the tariff, which was the cause of so much irritation in the old body politic, is removed forever from the new. [Applause.]

Again, the subject of internal improvements, under the power of Congress to regulate commerce, is put at rest under our system. The power claimed by construction under the old constitution, was at least a doubtful one—it rested solely upon construction. We of the South, generally apart from considerations of constitutional principles, opposed its exercise upon grounds of its inexpediency and injustice. Notwithstanding this opposition, millions of money, from the common treasury had been drawn for such purposes. Our opposition sprang from no hostility to commerce, or all necessary aids for facilitating it. With us it was simply a question, upon *whom* the burden should fall. In Georgia, for instance, we have done as much for the cause of internal improvements as any other portion of the country according to population and means. We have stretched out lines of railroads from the seaboard to the mountains; dug down the hills, and filled up the valleys at a cost of not less than twenty-five millions of dollars. All this was done to open an outlet for our products of the interior, and those to the west of us, to reach the marts of the world. No State was in greater need of such facilities than Georgia, but we did not ask that these works should be made by appropriations out of the common treasury. The cost of the grading, the superstructure, and equipments of our roads, was borne by those who entered on the enterprise. Nay, more—not only the cost of the iron, no small item in the aggregate cost, was borne in the same way—but we were compelled to pay into the common treasury several millions of dollars for the privilege of importing the iron, after the price was paid for it abroad. What justice was there in taking this money, which our people paid into the common treasury on the importation of our iron, and applying it to the improvement of rivers and harbors elsewhere?

The true principle is to subject the commerce of every locality, to whatever burdens may be necessary to facilitate it. If Charleston harbor needs improvement, let the commerce of Charleston bear the burden. If the mouth of the Savannah river has to be cleared out, let the sea-going navigation which is benefitted by it, bear the burden. So with the mouths of the Alabama and Mississippi river. Just as the products of the interior, our cotton, wheat, corn, and other articles, have to bear the necessary rates of freight over our railroads to reach the seas. This is again the broad principle of perfect equality and justice. [Applause.] And it is especially set forth and established in our new constitution.

Another feature to which I will allude, is that the new constitution provides that cabinet ministers and heads of departments may have the privilege of seats upon the floor of the Senate and House of Representatives—may have the right to participate in the debates and discussions upon the various subjects of administration. I should have preferred that this provision should have gone further, and required the President to select his constitutional advisers from the Senate and House of Representatives. That would have conformed entirely to the practice in the British Parliament, which, in my judgment, is one of the wisest provisions in the British constitution. It is the only feature that saves that government. It is that which gives it stability in its facility to change its administration. Ours, as it is, is a great approximation to the right principle.

Under the old constitution, a secretary of the treasury for instance, had no opportunity, save by his annual reports, of presenting any scheme or plan of finance or other matter. He had no opportunity of explaining, expounding, inforcing, or defending his views of policy; his only resort was through the medium of an organ. In the British parliament, the premier brings in his budget and stands before the nation responsible for its every item. If it is indefensible, he falls before the attacks upon it, as he ought to. This will now be the case to a limited extent under our system. In the new constitution, provision has been made by which our heads of departments can speak for themselves and the administration, in behalf of its entire policy, without resorting to the indirect and highly objectionable medium of a newspaper. It is to be greatly hoped that under our system we shall never have what is known as a government organ. [Rapturous applause.]

[A noise again arose from the clamor of the crowd outside, who wished to hear Mr. Stephens, and for some moments interrupted him. The mayor rose and called on the police to preserve order. Quiet being restored, Mr. S. proceeded.]

Another change in the constitution relates to the length of the tenure of the presidential office. In the new constitution it is six years instead of four, and the President rendered ineligible for a re-election. This is certainly a decidedly conservative change. It will remove from the incumbent all temptation to use his office or exert the powers confided to him for any objects of personal ambition. The only incentive to that higher ambition which should move and actuate one holding such high trusts in his hands, will be the good of the people, the advancement, prosperity, happiness, safety, honor, and true glory of the confederacy. [Applause.]

But not to be tedious in enumerating the numerous changes for the better, allow me to allude to one other—though last, not least. The new constitution has put at rest, *forever,* all the agitating questions relating to our peculiar institution—African slavery as it exists amongst us—the proper *status* of the negro in our form of civilization. This was the immediate cause of the late rupture and present revolution. Jefferson in his forecast, had anticipated this, as the "rock upon which the old Union would split." He was right. What was conjecture with him, is now a realized fact. But whether he fully comprehended the great truth upon which that rock *stood* and *stands,* may be doubted. The prevailing ideas entertained by him and most of the leading statesmen at the time of the formation of the old constitution, were that the enslavement of the African was in violation of the laws of nature; that it was wrong in *principle,* socially, morally, and politically. It was an evil they knew not well how to deal with, but the general opinion of the men of that day was that, somehow or other in the order of Providence, the institution would be evanescent and pass away. This idea, though not incorporated in the constitution, was the prevailing idea at that time. The constitution, it is true, secured every essential guarantee to the institution while it should last, and hence no argument can be justly urged against the constitutional guarantees thus secured, because of the common sentiment of the day. Those ideas, however, were fundamentally wrong. They rested upon the assumption of the equality of races. This was an error. It was a sandy foundation, and the government built upon it fell when the "storm came and the wind blew."

Our new government is founded upon exactly the opposite idea; its foundations are laid, its corner-stone rests upon the great truth, that the negro is not equal to the white man; that slavery—subordination to the superior race—is his natural and normal condition. [Applause.]

This, our new government, is the first, in the history of the world, based upon this great physical, philosophical, and moral truth. This truth has been slow in the process of its development, like all other truths in the various departments of science. It has been so even amongst us. Many who hear me, perhaps, can recollect well, that this truth was not generally admitted, even within their day. The errors of the past generation still clung to many as late as twenty years ago. Those at the North, who still cling to these errors, with a zeal above knowledge, we justly denominate fanatics. All fanaticism springs from an aberration of the mind—from a defect in reasoning. It is a species of insanity. One of the most striking characteristics of insanity, in many instances, is forming correct conclusions from fancied or erroneous premises; so with the anti-slavery fanatics; their conclusions are right if their premises were. They assume that the negro is equal, and hence conclude that he is entitled to equal privileges and rights with the white man. If their premises were correct, their conclusions would be logical and just—but their premise being wrong, their whole argument fails. I recollect once of having heard a gentleman from one of the northern States, of great power and ability, announce in the House of Representatives, with imposing effect, that we of the South would be compelled, ultimately, to yield upon this subject of slavery, that it was as impossible to war successfully against a principle in politics, as it was in physics or mechanics. That the principle would ultimately prevail. That we, in maintaining slavery as it exists with us, were warring against a principle, a principle founded in nature, the principle of the equality of men. The reply I made to him was, that upon his own grounds, we should, ultimately, succeed, and that he and his associates, in this crusade against our institutions, would ultimately fail. The truth announced, that it was as impossible to war successfully against a principle in politics as it was in physics and mechanics, I admitted; but told him that it was he, and those acting with him, who were warring against a principle. They were attempting to make things equal which the Creator had made unequal.

In the conflict thus far, success has been on our side, complete throughout the length and breadth of the Confederate States. It is upon this, as I have stated, our social fabric is firmly planted; and I cannot permit myself to doubt the ultimate success of a full recognition of this principle throughout the civilized and enlightened world.

As I have stated, the truth of this principle may be slow in development, as all truths are and ever have been, in the various branches of science. It was so with the principles announced by Galileo—it was so with Adam Smith and his principles of political economy. It was so with Harvey, and his theory of the circulation of the blood. It is stated that not a single one of the medical profession, living at the time of the announcement of the truths made by him, admitted them. Now, they are universally acknowledged. May we not, therefore, look with confidence to the ultimate universal acknowledgment of the truths upon which our system rests? It is the first government ever instituted upon the principles in strict conformity to nature, and the ordination of Providence, in furnishing the materials of human society. Many governments have been founded upon the principle of the subordination and serfdom of certain classes of the same race; such were and are in violation of the laws of nature. Our system commits no such violation of nature's laws. With us, all of the white race, however high or low, rich or poor, are equal in the eye of the law. Not so with the negro. Subordination is his place. He, by nature, or by the curse against Canaan, is fitted for that condition which he occupies in our system. The architect, in the construction of buildings, lays the foundation with the proper material—the granite; then comes the brick or the marble. The substratum of our society is made of the material fitted by nature for it, and by experience we know that it is best, not only for the superior, but for the inferior race, that it should be so. It is, indeed, in conformity with the ordinance of the Creator. It is not for us to inquire into the wisdom of his ordinances, or to question them. For his own purposes, he has made one race to differ from another, as he has made "one star to differ from another star in glory."

The great objects of humanity are best attained when there is conformity to his laws and decrees, in the formation of governments as well as in all things else. Our confederacy is founded upon principles in strict conformity with these laws. This stone which was rejected by the first builders "is become the chief of the corner"—the real "corner-stone"—in our new edifice. [Applause.]

I have been asked, what of the future? It has been apprehended by some that we would have arrayed against us the civilized world. I care not who or how many they may be against us, when we stand upon the eternal principles of truth, *if we are true to ourselves and the principles for which we contend,* we are obliged to, and must triumph. [Immense applause.]

Thousands of people who begin to understand these truths are not yet completely out of the shell; they do not see them in their length and breadth. We hear much of the civilization and christianization of the barbarous tribes of Africa. In my judgment, those ends will never be attained, but by first teaching them the lesson taught to Adam, that "in the sweat of his brow he should eat his bread," [applause,] and teaching them to work, and feed, and clothe themselves.

But to pass on: Some have propounded the inquiry whether it is practicable for us to go on with the confederacy without further accessions? Have we the means and ability to maintain nationality among the powers of the earth? On this point I would barely say, that as anxiously as we all have been, and are, for the border States, with institutions similar to ours, to join us, still we are abundantly able to maintain our position, even if they should ultimately make up their minds not to cast their destiny with us. That they ultimately will join us—be compelled to do it—is my confident belief; but we can get on very well without them, even if they should not.

We have all the essential elements of a high national career. The idea has been given out at the North, and even in the border States, that we are too small and too weak to maintain a separate nationality. This is a great mistake. In extent of territory we embrace five hundred and sixty-four thousand square miles and upward. This is upward of two hundred thousand square miles more than was included within the limits of the original thirteen States. It is an area of country more than double the territory of France or the Austrian empire. France, in round numbers, has but two hundred and twelve thousand square miles. Austria, in round numbers, has two hundred and forty-eight thousand square miles. Ours is greater than both combined. It is greater than all France, Spain, Portugal, and Great Britain, including England, Ireland, and Scotland, together. In population we have upward of five millions, according to the census of 1860; this includes white and black. The entire population, including white and black, of the original thirteen States, was less than four millions in 1790, and still less in '76, when the independence of our fathers was achieved. If they, with a less population, dared maintain their independence against the greatest power on earth, shall we have any apprehension of maintaining ours now?

In point of material wealth and resources, we are greatly in advance of them. The taxable property of the Confederate States cannot be less than twenty-two hundred millions of dollars! This, I think I venture but little in saying, may be considered as five times more than the colonies possessed at the time they achieved their independence. Georgia, alone, possessed last year, according to the report of our comptroller-general, six hundred and seventy-two millions of taxable property. The debts of the seven confederate States sum up in the aggregate less than eighteen millions, while the existing debts of the other of the late United States sum up in the aggregate the enormous amount of one hundred and seventy-four millions of dollars. This is without taking into account the heavy city debts, corporation debts, and railroad debts, which press, and will continue to press, as a heavy incubus upon the resources of those States. These debts, added to others, make a sum total not much under five hundred millions of dollars. With such an area of territory as we have—with such an amount of population—with a climate and soil unsurpassed by any on the face of the earth—with such resources already at our command—with productions which control the commerce of the world—who can entertain any apprehensions as to our ability to succeed, whether others join us or not?

It is true, I believe I state but the common sentiment, when I declare my earnest desire that the border States should join us. The differences of opinion that existed among us anterior to secession, related more to the policy in securing that result by co-operation than from any difference upon the ultimate security we all looked to in common.

These differences of opinion were more in reference to policy than principle, and as Mr. Jefferson said in his inaugural, in 1801, after the heated contest preceding his election, there might be differences of opinion without differences on principle, and that all, to some extent, had been federalists and all republicans; so it may now be said of us, that whatever differences of opinion as to the best policy in having a co-operation with our border sister slave States, if the worst came to the worst, that as we were all co-operationists, we are now all for independence, whether they come or not. [Continued applause.]

In this connection I take this occasion to state, that I was not without grave and serious apprehensions, that if the worst came to the worst, and cutting loose from the old government should be the only remedy for our safety and security, it would be attended with much more serious ills than it has been as yet. Thus far we have seen none of those incidents which usually attend revolutions. No such material as such convulsions usually throw up has been seen. Wisdom, prudence, and patriotism, have marked every step of our progress thus far. This augurs well for the future, and it is a matter of sincere gratification to me, that I am enabled to make the declaration. Of the men I met in the Congress at Montgomery, I may be pardoned for saying this, an abler, wiser, a more conservative, deliberate, determined, resolute, and patriotic body of men, I never met in my life. [Great applause.] Their works speak for them; the provisional government speaks for them; the constitution of the permanent government will be a lasting monument of their worth, merit, and statesmanship. [Applause.]

But to return to the question of the future. What is to be the result of this revolution?

Will every thing, commenced so well, continue as it has begun? In reply to this anxious inquiry, I can only say it all depends upon ourselves. A young man starting out in life on his majority, with health, talent, and ability, under a favoring Providence, may be said to be the architect of his own fortunes. His destinies are in his own hands. He may make for himself a name, of honor or dishonor, according to his own acts. If he plants himself upon truth, integrity, honor and uprightness, with industry, patience and energy, he cannot fail of success. So it is with us. We are a young republic, just entering upon the arena of nations; we will be the architects of our own fortunes. Our destiny, under Providence, is in our own hands. With wisdom, prudence, and statesmanship on the part of our public men, and intelligence, virtue and patriotism on the part of the people, success, to the full measures of our most sanguine hopes, may be looked for. But if unwise counsels prevail—if we become divided—if schisms arise—if dissensions spring up—if factions are engendered—if party spirit, nourished by unholy personal ambition shall rear its hydra head, I have no good to prophesy for you. Without intelligence, virtue, integrity, and patriotism on the part of the people, no republic or representative government can be durable or stable.

We have intelligence, and virtue, and patriotism. All that is required is to cultivate and perpetuate these. Intelligence will not do without virtue. France was a nation of philosophers. These philosophers become Jacobins. They lacked that virtue, that devotion to moral principle, and that patriotism which is essential to good government. Organized upon principles of perfect justice and right—seeking amity and friendship with all other powers—I see no obstacle in the way of our upward and onward progress. Our growth, by accessions from other States, will depend greatly upon whether we present to the world, as I trust we shall, a better government than that to which neighboring States belong. If we do this, North Carolina, Tennessee, and Arkansas cannot hesitate long; neither can Virginia, Kentucky, and Missouri. They will necessarily gravitate to us by an imperious law. We made ample provision in our constitution for the admission of other States; it is more guarded, and wisely so, I think, than the old constitution on the same subject, but not too guarded to receive them as fast as it may be proper. Looking to the distant future, and, perhaps, not very far distant either, it is not beyond the range of possibility, and even probability, that all the great States of the north-west will gravitate this way, as well as Tennessee, Kentucky, Missouri, Arkansas, etc. Should they do so, our doors are wide enough to receive them, but not until they are ready to assimilate with us in principle.

The process of disintegration in the old Union may be expected to go on with almost absolute certainty if we pursue the right course. We are now the nucleus of a growing power which, if we are true to ourselves, our destiny, and high mission, will become the controlling power on this continent. To what extent accessions will go on in the process of time, or where it will end, the future will determine. So far as it concerns States of the old Union, this process will be upon no such principles of *reconstruction* as now spoken of, but upon *reorganization* and new assimilation. [Loud applause.] Such are some of the glimpses of the future as I catch them.

But at first we must necessarily meet with the inconveniences and difficulties and embarrassments incident to all changes of government. These will be felt in our postal affairs and changes in the channel of trade. These inconveniences, it is to be hoped, will be but temporary, and must be borne with patience and forbearance.

As to whether we shall have war with our late confederates, or whether all matters of differences between us shall be amicably settled, I can only say that the prospect for a peaceful adjustment is better, so far as I am informed, than it has been.

The prospect of war is, at least, not so threatening as it has been. The idea of coercion, shadowed forth in President Lincoln's inaugural, seems not to be followed up thus far so vigorously as was expected. Fort Sumter, it is believed, will soon be evacuated. What course will be pursued toward Fort Pickens, and the other forts on the gulf, is not so well understood. It is to be greatly desired that all of them should be surrendered. Our object is *peace,* not only with the North, but with the world. All matters relating to the public property, public liabilities of the Union when we were members of it, we are ready and willing to adjust and settle upon the principles of right, equity, and good faith. War can be of no more benefit to the North than to us. Whether the intention of evacuating Fort Sumter is to be received as an evidence of a desire for a peaceful solution of our difficulties with the United States, or the result of necessity, I will not undertake to say. I would fain hope the former. Rumors are afloat, however, that it is the result of necessity. All I can say to you, therefore, on that point is, keep your armor bright and your powder dry. [Enthusiastic cheering.]

The surest way to secure peace, is to show your ability to maintain your rights. The principles and position of the present administration of the United States—the republican party—present some puzzling questions. While it is a fixed principle with them never to allow the increase of a foot of slave territory, they seem to be equally determined not to part with an inch "of the accursed soil." Notwithstanding their clamor against the institution, they seemed to be equally opposed to getting more, or letting go what they have got. They were ready to fight on the accession of Texas, and are equally ready to fight now on her secession. Why is this? How can this strange paradox be accounted for? There seems to be but one rational solution—and that is, notwithstanding their professions of humanity, they are disinclined to give up the benefits they derive from slave labor. Their philanthropy yields to their interest. The idea of enforcing the laws, has but one object, and that is a collection of the taxes, raised by slave labor to swell the fund, necessary to meet their heavy appropriations. The spoils is what they are after—though they come from the labor of the slave. [Continued applause.]

Mr. Stephens reviewed at some length, the extravagance and profligacy of appropriations by the Congress of the United States for several years past, and in this connection took occasion to allude to another one of the great improvements in our new constitution, which is a clause prohibiting Congress from appropriating any money from the treasury, except by a two-third vote, unless it be for some object which the executive may say is necessary to carry on the government.

When it is thus asked for, and estimated for, he continued, the majority may appropriate. This was a new feature.

Our fathers had guarded the assessment of taxes by insisting that representation and taxation should go together. This was inherited from the mother country, England. It was one of the principles upon which the revolution had been fought. Our fathers also provided in the old constitution, that all appropriation bills should originate in the representative branch of Congress, but our new constitution went a step further, and guarded not only the pockets of the people, but also the public money, after it was taken from their pockets.

He alluded to the difficulties and embarrassments which seemed to surround the question of a peaceful solution of the controversy with the old government. How can it be done? is perplexing many minds. The President seems to think that he cannot recognize our independence, nor can he, with and by the advice of the Senate, do so. The constitution makes no such provision. A general convention of all the States has been suggested by some.

Without proposing to solve the difficulty, he barely made the following suggestion:

"That as the admission of States by Congress under the constitution was an act of legislation, and in the nature of a contract or compact between the States admitted and the others admitting, why should not this contract or compact be regarded as of like character with all other civil contracts—liable to be rescinded by mutual agreement of both parties? The seceding States have rescinded it on their part, they have resumed their sovereignty. Why cannot the whole question be settled, if the north desire peace, simply by the Congress, in both branches, with the concurrence of the President, giving their consent to the separation, and a recognition of our independence?" This he merely offered as a suggestion, as one of the ways in which it might be done with much less violence by constructions to the constitution than many other acts of that government. [Applause.] The difficulty has to be solved in some way or other—this may be regarded as a fixed fact.

Several other points were alluded to by Mr. Stephens, particularly as to the policy of the new government toward foreign nations, and our commercial relations with them. Free trade, as far as practicable, would be the policy of this government. No higher duties would be imposed on foreign importations than would be necessary to support the government upon the strictest economy.

In olden times the olive branch was considered the emblem of peace; we will send to the nations of the earth another and far more potential emblem of the same, the cotton plant. The present duties were levied with a view of meeting the present necessities and exigencies, in preparation for war, if need be; but if we have peace, and he hoped we might, and trade should resume its proper course, a duty of ten per cent. upon foreign importations it was thought might be sufficient to meet the expenditures of the government. If some articles should be left on the free list, as they now are, such as breadstuffs, etc., then, of course, duties upon others would have to be higher—but in no event to an extent to embarrass trade and commerce. He concluded in an earnest appeal for union and harmony, on part of all the people in support of the common cause, in which we were all enlisted, and upon the issues of which such great consequences depend.

If, said he, we are true to ourselves, true to our cause, true to our destiny, true to our high mission, in presenting to the world the highest type of civilization ever exhibited by man—there will be found in our lexicon no such word as fail.

Mr. Stephens took his seat, amid a burst of enthusiasm and applause, such as the Athenæum has never had displayed within its walls, within "the recollection of the oldest inhabitant."

[Reporter's Note.—Your reporter begs to state that the above is not a perfect report, but only such a sketch of the address of Mr. Stephens as embraces, in his judgment, the most important points presented by the orator.—G.]

Appendix 5

Parole of Robert E. Lee and Staff

Appomattox, Virginia, April 9, 1865

Reprinted from U.S. War Department, *War of the Rebellion: A Compilation of the Official Records of the Union and Confederate Armies,* Washington, D.C., 1880–1901, ser. 1, vol. 46, pt. 2, p. 667.

We, the undersigned prisoners of war belonging to the Army of Northern Virginia, having been this day surrendered by General Robert E. Lee, C. S. Army, commanding said army, to Lieut. Gen. U. S. Grant, commanding Armies of the United States, do hereby give our solemn parole of honor that we will not hereafter serve in the armies of the Confederate States, or in any military capacity whatever, against the United States of America, or render aid to the enemies of the latter, until properly exchanged, in such manner as shall be mutually approved by the respective authorities.

Done at Appomattox Court-House, Va., this 9th day of April, 1865.

R. E. LEE,
General.

W. H. TAYLOR,
Lieutenant-Colonel and Assistant Adjutant-General.

CHARLES S. VENABLE,
Lieutenant-Colonel and Assistant Adjutant-General.

CHARLES MARSHALL,
Lieutenant-Colonel and Assistant Adjutant-General.

H. E. PEYTON,
Lieutenant-Colonel, Adjutant and Inspector General.

GILES B. COOKE,
Major and Assistant Adjutant and Inspector General.

H. E. YOUNG,
Major, Assistant Adjutant-General, and Judge-Advocate-General.

[Indorsement.]

The within named officers will not be disturbed by the United States authorities so long as they observe their parole and the laws in force where they may reside.

GEORGE H. SHARPE,
Assistant Provost-Marshal-General.

Appendix 6

Robert E. Lee's Farewell to the Army of Northern Virginia

Reprinted from *Southern Historical Society Papers* 42 (1889): 373–374.

Headquarters Army of Northern Virginia,

Appomattox Courthouse, April 10, 1865.

(General Orders No. 9)

After four years' arduous service, marked by unsurpassed courage and fortitude, the Army of Northern Virginia has been compelled to yield to overwhelming numbers and resources.

I need not tell the survivors of so many hard fought battles who have remained steadfast to the last, that I have consented to this result from no distrust of them, but feeling that valor and devotion could accomplish nothing that could compensate for the loss which would have attended the continuation of the contest, I have determined to avoid the useless sacrifice of those whose past services have endeared them to their countrymen. You will take with you the satisfaction that proceeds from the consciousness of duty faithfully performed, and I earnestly pray that a merciful God may extend to you His blessing and protection. With an increasing admiration of your constancy and devotion to your country, and a grateful remembrance of your kind and generous consideration of myself, I bid you an affectionate farewell.

Robert E. Lee, *General.*

Appendix 7

Parole of Joseph E. Johnston and Troops

Durham Station, North Carolina, April 26, 1865

Reprinted from U.S. War Department, *War of the Rebellion: A Compilation of the Official Records of the Union and Confederate Armies*, Washington, D.C., 1880–1901, ser. 1, vol. 47, pt. 2, p. 313.

Terms of a military convention entered into this 26th day of April, 1865, at Bennett's house, near Durham's Station, N. C., between General Joseph E. Johnston, commanding the Confederate Army, and Maj. Gen. W. T. Sherman, commanding the United States Army in North Carolina.

1. All acts of war on the part of the troops under General Johnston's command to cease from this date.

2. All arms and public property to be deposited at Greensborough, and delivered to an ordnance officer of the United States Army.

3. Rolls of all the officers and men to be made in duplicate, one copy to be retained by the commander of the troops, and the other to be given to an officer to be designated by General Sherman, each officer and man to give his individual obligation in writing not to take up arms against the Government of the United States until properly released from this obligation.

4. The side-arms of officers and their private horses and baggage to be retained by them.

5. This being done, all the officers and men will be permitted to return to their homes, not to be disturbed by the United States authorities so long as they observe their obligation and the laws in force where they may reside.

W. T. SHERMAN,
Major-General, Commanding U. S. Forces in North Carolina.

J. E. JOHNSTON,
General, Commanding C. S. Forces in North Carolina.

RALEIGH, N. C., *APRIL 26, 1865.*

Approved:

U. S. GRANT,
Lieutenant-General.

Appendix 8

Parole of Richard Taylor and Troops

Citronelle, Alabama, May 4, 1865 (accepted May 8, 1865)

Reprinted from U.S. War Department, *War of the Rebellion: A Compilation of the Official Records of the Union and Confederate Armies,* Washington, D.C., 1880–1901, ser. 1, vol. 47, pt. 2, p. 609.

Memorandum of the conditions of the surrender of the forces, munitions of war, &c., in the Department of Alabama, Mississippi, and East Louisiana, commanded by Lieut. Gen. Richard Taylor, C. S. Army, to Maj. Gen. Edward R. S. Canby, U. S. Army, entered into on this 4th day of May, 1865, at Citronelle, Ala.

I. The officers and men to be paroled until duly exchanged, or otherwise released from the obligations of their parole by the authority of the Government of the United States. Duplicate rolls of all officers and men surrendered to be made, one copy of which will be delivered to the officer appointed by Major-General Canby and the other retained by the officer appointed by Lieutenant-General Taylor; officers giving their individual paroles and commanders of regiments, batteries, companies, or detachments signing a like parole for the men of their respective commands.

II. Artillery, small-arms, ammunition, and all other property of the Confederate Government to be turned over to the officers appointed for that purpose on the part of the Government of the United States. Duplicate inventories of the property surrendered to be prepared, one copy to be retained by the officer delivering and the other by the officer receiving it, for the information of their respective commanders.

III. The officers and men paroled under this agreement will be allowed to return to their homes, with the assurance that they will not be disturbed by the authorities of the United States so long as they continue to observe the conditions of their paroles and the laws in force where they reside, except that persons residents of Northern States will not be allowed to return without permission.

IV. The surrender of property will not include the side arms or private horses or baggage of officers.

V. All horses which are, in good faith, the private property of enlisted men will not be taken from them; the men will be permitted to take such with them to their homes, to be used for private purposes only.

VI. The time and place of surrender will be fixed by the respective commanders, and will be carried out by the commissioners appointed by them.

VII. The terms and conditions of the surrender to apply to officers and men belonging to the armies lately commanded by Generals Lee and Johnston, now in this department.

VIII. Transportation and subsistence to be furnished at public cost for the officers and men after surrender to the nearest practicable point to their homes.

R. Taylor,
Lieutenant-General.

Ed. R. S. Canby,
Major-General.

Appendix 9

Parole of E. Kirby Smith and Troops

New Orleans, Louisiana, May 26, 1865

Reprinted from U.S. War Department, *War of the Rebellion: A Compilation of the Official Records of the Union and Confederate Armies,* Washington, D.C., 1880–1901, ser. 1, vol. 48, pt. 2, pp. 600–602.

Terms of a military convention entered into this 26th day of May, 1865, at New Orleans, La., between General E. Kirby Smith, C. S. Army, commanding the Department of Trans-Mississippi, and Maj. Gen. E. R. S. Canby, U. S. Army, commanding the Army and Division of West Mississippi, for the surrender of the troops and public property under the control of the military and naval authorities of the Trans-Mississippi Department.

I. All acts of war and resistance against the United States on the part of the troops under General Smith shall cease from this date.

II. The officers and men to be paroled until duly exchanged or otherwise released from the obligation of their parole by the authority of the Government of the United States. Duplicate rolls of all officers and men paroled to be retained by such officers as may be designated by the parties hereto, officers giving their individual paroles and commanders of regiments, battalions, companies, or detachments signing a like parole for the men of their respective commands.

III. Artillery, small-arms, ammunition, and other property of the Confederate States Government, including gun-boats and transports, to be turned over to the officers appointed to receive the same on the part of the Government of the United States. Duplicate inventories of the property to be surrendered to be prepared, one copy to be retained by the officer delivering and the other by the officer receiving it, for the information of their respective commanders.

IV. The officers and men paroled under this agreement will be allowed to return to their homes, with the assurance that they will not be disturbed by the authorities of the United States as long as they continue to observe the conditions of their parole and the laws in force where they reside, except that persons resident in the Northern States, and not excepted in the amnesty proclamation of the President, may return to their homes on taking the oath of allegiance to the United States.

V. The surrender of property will not include the side-arms or private horses or baggage of officers.

VI. All horses which are in good faith the private property of enlisted men will not be taken from them. The men will be permitted to take such with them to their homes, to be used for private purposes only.

VII. The time, mode, and place of paroling and surrender of property will be fixed by the respective commanders, and it will be carried out by commissioners appointed by them.

VIII. The terms and conditions of this convention to extend to all officers and men of the Army and Navy of the Confederate States, or any of them being in or belonging to the Trans-Mississippi Department.

IX. Transportation and subsistence to be furnished at public cost for the officers and men (after being paroled) to the nearest practicable point to their homes.

S. B. BUCKNER,
Lieutenant-General and Chief of Staff.
(For General E. Kirby Smith.)

P. JOS. OSTERHAUS,
Major-General of Volunteers and Chief of Staff.
(For Maj. Gen. E. R. S. Canby, commanding Military Division of West Mississippi.)

Approved:

ED. R. S. CANBY
Major-General, Comdg. Army and Division of West Mississippi.

[First indorsement.]

GALVESTON HARBOR, *JUNE 2, 1865.*

Approved, understanding that by the provisions of this convention C. S. officers observing their paroles are permitted to make their homes either in or out of the United States.

E. KIRBY SMITH,
General.

[Second indorsement.]

This question was raised by General Smith's commissioners, but I declined to make any stipulation with regard to it, because I had no authority to determine the policy of the Government in any question of this kind.

ED. R. S. CANBY,
Major-General of Volunteers.

SUPPLEMENTAL ARTICLES.

I. The troops and property to be surrendered within the limits of the Division of the Missouri will be turned over to commissioners appointed by the commander of that division.

II. The men and material of the C. S. Navy will be surrendered to commissioners appointed by the commanders of the Mississippi and West Gulf Squadrons, respectively, according to the limits in which the said men and materials may be found.

III. If the U. S. troops designated for the garrisons of interior points should not reach their destination before the work of paroling is completed, suitable guards will be detailed for the protection of the public property. These guards, when relieved by U. S. troops, will surrender their arms and be paroled in accordance with the terms of this convention.

S. B. BUCKNER,
Lieutenant-General and Chief of Staff.
(FOR GENERAL E. K. SMITH.)

P. JOS. OSTERHAUS,
Major-General of Volunteers and Chief of Staff.
(For Maj. Gen. E. R. S. Canby, çommanding Military Division of West Mississippi.)

Approved:

ED. R. S. CANBY,
Major-General, Comdg. Army and Division of West Mississippi.

Approved:

E. KIRBY SMITH,
General.

Encyclopedia of the Confederacy

Index

Numbers in boldface refer to the main entry on the subject. Numbers in italic refer to illustrations.

A

"A" (pseudonym). *See* Alexander, Peter
Abatis, 619, 625, 1201
Abbott, Richard H., *as contributor*, 1560–1562
Abingdon, Virginia
  attack on saltworks, 1724
  bread riots, 213
Abingdon bloc, 859
Ableman v. Booth, 1534
Abolitionism. *See* Antislavery; Emancipation; Emancipation Proclamation
Abraham Africanus I (pamphlet), 934
A. B. Reading & Brother, 98
Absalom, Absalom! (novel by Faulkner), 939
Absentee Shawnees, 811, 813, 1408, 1409
Absent without leave. *See* Desertion
Absterdam projectiles, 102
Academy Hospital (Tennessee), 796
Accotink River, 1556
Acid. *See* Nitric acid; Sulfur and sulfuric acid production
Action at Aquila (Allen), 939
Actors. *See* Film and video; Theater
Act to protect the Confederate States against Frauds, 377
Act to Raise Money for the Government and to Provide for the Defence of the Confederate States of America, 509
Adair, George, 1144
Adair, Henrietta Buford, 31
Adair, William Penn, 305
Adams, Charles Francis, 19, 21, 349, 480, 484, 713, 904
Adams, Charles W., *52*
Adams, Daniel Weisiger, **1**, 2, 684, 754, 1197
Adams, Henry, 921
Adams, John (brigadier general), **1–2**, 960
Adams, William Wirt, 1, **2**, 837–838, 839, 1033, 1241
Adams Express Company, 1511
Address of Congress to the People of the Confederate States, 440
Address of the Southern Clergy to Christians, An (Hotze), 1271
Address to the Citizens of Alabama on the Constitution and Laws of the Confederate States of America, An (Smith), 1478
Address to the People of South Carolina, 463
Address to the People of West Virginia (Ruffner), 45, 1186
Address to the Slave-Holding States (Rhett), 1324
"Adieu to the Star Spangled Banner Forever" (song), 1232
Adultery, 1009, 1709
Advance (ship), **2–3**, 726, 1157, 1536
Advance and Retreat (Hood), 790
Advertisements, 1232
Adzuma (ship), 1548
African American forgeworkers, **3–4**, 96, 97, 315, 372, 1440, 1443
African Americans in the Confederacy, **4–9**
  education, 520, 521, 643, 941, 1030, 1150, 1450–1451, 1588, 1722
  family life, 563–565
  forgeworkers, **3–4**
  free blacks, **642–644**, 1487
  Freedmen's Bureau papers, 473
  fugitive slaves, 648–650
  handicrafts, 735
  horse stealing, 427
  hospital workers, 795
  literary portrayals, 938
  miscegenation, 1044–1046
  music, 1103–1104
  narrative tradition, 594
  naval enlistment, 1131, **1132**
  New Orleans, 1137
  population, 1233
  racism, *1044*, 1273
  selected bibliography, 170
  slave labor, 1442–1443
  slaves as troops proposal, 7, 8–9, 12, 27, 45, 54, 70, 75, 107, 124, 131, 141, 160, 230, 244, 256, 260, 311, 345, 362, 385, 394, 399, 401, 525, 532, 631, 654, 670, 684, 689, 694, 700, 708, 767, 887, 901, 912, 956, 1131, 1132, 1194, 1220, 1304, 1326, 1386, 1396, 1443, 1480, 1487, 1490, 1681, 1697
  women, 1741–1742
  see also Slave drivers; Slavery; particular states
African Americans in the Confederate Army. *See under* Army
African Americans in the Confederate Navy. *See under* Navy, Confederate
African Americans in the Union Navy, 441, 1132
African American troops in the Union Army, 6–7, **9–12**, 70, 75, 564, 887, 1420, 1444, 1480, 1668
  Alabama, 14
  Arkansas, 53, 57
  bombardment of Charleston, 287
  caricature, *335*
  casualties, 12
  Confederate retaliation policy, 1396
  contraband, **405–406**
  Dallas, Moses, 442

African American troops in the Union Army, *continued*
ex-slaves, 1446–1447, 1472
first engagement with Confederate forces, 11
Florida, 588, 590
Fort Pillow massacre, **614–616**
Fort Wagner, South Carolina, 630
Georgia, 670, 671
Kentucky, 888
Louisiana, 645, 956
as manpower resource, 339
North Carolina, 1152
Paducah, Kentucky, 1177
Port Hudson, Louisiana, 1239
prisoner of war status, 532, 779, 931, 1258, 1260–1261, 1263
prison guards, 1221–1222
racist attitudes, 1007
recruitment, 1217
response to Emancipation Proclamation, 532
Rivers, Prince, 1335
runaways, 648
Saltville massacre, 1362, 1363
South Carolina, 1509
Tennessee, 1579
treatment of, 1348
Tupelo, Mississippi, 1624, 1625
African Labor Supply Association, 985
African Methodist Episcopal (AME) Church, 535, 1035, 1321
African slave trade. *See* Slave traders
Agassiz, Louis, 1274
Agent, naval. *See* Anglo-Confederate purchasing
Agnew, J. P., 3
Agricultural and mechanical colleges, 520
Agriculture. *See* Farming
A. H. DeWitt Company, 514
Ahl, George W., 610
Aid associations. *See* Soldiers' aid societies; Women's aid societies
Aide-de-Campe (McCabe), 936
Ainsworth, Fred C., 1264
Ainsworth, William H., 1590
Akin, Warren, **13–14**, 138
Alabama, **14–19**
Army of. *See* Army of Alabama, Mississippi, and Eastern Louisiana
arsenal and armory, 1461, 1469
banks, 128
black-white population comparison, *1435*
bread riots, 596
class conflict, 1492
congressmen, 308–309, 347–350, 355–356, 431–432, 439–440, 444, 454, 479, 569, 630–631, 729–730, 841–842, 865, 927, 963, 979, 1203, 1286–1287, 1302, 1343, 1426, 1477–1478, 1482–1483, 1680, 1749–1750
conscription controversy, 345, 398, 873
Constitution ratification, 403
cooperationists, 411, 1379, 1380
cotton plantations, 1436
"Courthouse Legislature," 928
currency, 1279
debt, 462
Democratic party, 465
Department of. *See* Department of Alabama, Mississippi, and Eastern Louisiana
desertions and resistance, 1426
education, 516, 519, 520
election of 1860, 521, 522, 523
election of 1863, 524
farm acreage, *1484*
farming, 172–173
fire-eaters, 1376–1377
flag, 587
foreign population, 602
free people of color, 642, 644–645
governors, 14, 18–19, 524, 661, 701, 702, 703, 927–928, 1075, 1287, 1426–1427, 1695
guerrillas, 345, 1492
hospitals, 794, 1160
infantry, 817
iron production, 1148, 1387–1388, 1410
limestone cave, 1375
manufacturing, 514
mining, 1043
miscegenation, 1045
newspapers, 1144
niter production, 1147
population, 1233
railroads, 1294, 1295, 1296
Reconstruction, 927–928
salt making, 1362
secession. *See under* Secession
secession and Confederacy membership dates, *1379*
secession date correlated with total black population, *1486*
secession opponents, 720, 1477
Shelby Iron Company, 1410
Shorter, John G., 1425–1427
slaveholdings, *1485*
slavery, 551, 553
small arms manufacture, 16, 1458, 1470
soldiers' home, 1502
state navy, **1530**
taxes, 1283, 1284
Unionism. *See under* Unionism
Union occupation, 1426, 1640
urbanization, 1643
see also particular cities and place names
Alabama (Native American peoples), 812
Alabama (ship), **19–20**, 50, 240, 375, 484, 591, 712, *879*, 880, 904, 992, 1150, 1516, 1627, 1691
commerce raiding, 374, 385, 1123, 1129
ordnance, 374, 1120
Semmes (Raphael) command, 1392, 1393, 1394
sinking of, 1394
see also Alabama claims
Alabama and Mississippi Railroad, 1075
Alabama Arms Manufacturing Company, 16
Alabama claims, **21–22**, 374, 376, 484
Laird shipyards, 904
Alabama Equal Rights Association, 351
Alabama Platform of 1848, 1678, 1747, 1748
Alabama River, 1387, 1388, 1691
Alabama State Militia, 1389
Alar (ship), 375, 674
Albany Plan of 1754, 1531
Albatross (ship), 533
Albemarle (ship), **22**, 23, 407, 445, 528, 824, 984, 1124, 1126, 1130, 1151, 1236, 1303, 1425, 1603, 1689
Albert, prince consort of Great Britain, 1015
Albertson, Jonathan, 1684
Albright, James W., 1587–1588
Alcohol
distillation ban, 1426
prices, 591
soldiers' use of, 1498
see also Drunkeness; Prohibition movement
Alcorn, James L., **23–24**, 226, 411, 1215
Alcott, Louisa May, 742
Alden, James D., 700
Alert (ship), 1530
Alexander, Edward Porter, **24–25**, 503, 891, 946, 996, 1721
Confederate Signal Corps, **1428–1430**
memoirs, 25, 474–475
Alexander, G. W., 1590

Alexander, George, 519
Alexander, George W., 266
Alexander, Peter, 274, 1683
Alexander, Thomas G., and Tracy L. Alexander, *as contributors*, 1708–1709
Alexander, W. A., 1557, 1558
Alexander Collie and Company, 491, 1341
Alexander Denny & Company, 673
Alexander Stephen and Sons, 1411
Alexandra (ship), **25–26**, 240, 375, 903
Alexandria, Virginia
  antebellum population, *1642*
  barricades, *620*
  population and urban ranking, *1658*
  slave pen (Price, Birch, and Company), *1452*
  Union occupation, 1640, 1647
Alice (ship), 185
Alien and Sedition Acts, 1531–1532
Alien Enemies Act of 1861, 391
Allaire Works, 744
Allan, William, 797
Allatoona, Georgia, 1753
Allegheny (ship), 1236
Allegheny Mountains, 1413, 1415
Allen, Henry W., **26–27**, 701, 702, 703, 955–956, 1078, 1480
Allen, James W. F., 728
Allen, Robert T. P., 519
Allen, Thompson, 1614, 1615
Allen, W., *80*
Allen, William, 1104
Allen, William Wirt, **27–28**, 36
Allen and Wheelock, 1463
Allison, Abraham K., **28**, 702, 1567
Allston Association, 1673
All the King's Men (novel by Warren), 939
Alonzo Child (ship), 1580
Altamont. *See* Palmer, John
Alvarado (ship), 841
Amazon River, 1624
Ambrotype, 1230–1231
AME Church. *See* African Methodist Episcopal (AME) Church
Amelia (ship), 1567
Amelia Court House (Virginia), 45, 46, 1201
America (ship). *See Camilla* (ship)
American Bank Note Company, 436
American Bar Association, 1397
American Bible Society, 164, 165, 1722
American Colonization Society, 44, 164
American Disruption, The (Hope), 1271
American Diver (submarine), 777, 801, 1557
American Indians. *See* Indians; Indian Territory; particular peoples
American Jewry and the Civil War (Korn), 162
American party (Know-Nothing), **28**, 1224, 1562
  Bleeding Kansas, 175, 176
  Georgia, 137, 772, 786, 1146
  Gilmer, John A., 687
  Hatton, Robert, 751
  Kentucky, 234, 1011
  New Orleans, Louisiana, 675, 1395
  Smith, William Russell, 1482
  Texas, 1715, 1718
  see also Constitutional Union party
American Railroad Journal, 1294
American Revolution
  Confederate struggle seen paralleling, 1499
  inspiring slave emancipation, 1434, 1436, 1486
  state rivalries, 1531
American Society for Promoting National Unity, 1275
American System, 740, 1708
American Tobacco Company, 1332
American Union, The (Spence), 1271
Ames, Adelbert, 24, 226, 569, 800
AME Zion church, 1035
Ammunition. *See* Arms, weapons, and ammunition
Amnesty
  Confederate prisoners of war, 1263
  deserters, 398, 468
  presidential proclamation, 1081
A. M. Paxton Company, 98
Amputation, 139, 756–757, 795
  artificial limbs, 1052, 1181
  surgical kit, *756*
Anaconda Plan, 326
Anbinder, Tyler, *as contributor*, 1223–1226
Anderson, "Bloody Bill." *See* Anderson, William
Anderson, Clifford, **28–29**, 882
Anderson, Edward C., 116, 254, 1465, 1467
Anderson, George B., **29**, 1407–1408
Anderson, George Thomas ("Tige"), **30**, 1592
Anderson, George W., Jr., 1369
Anderson, James Patton, **30–33**, 1095, 1197, 1404, 1688
Anderson, John Q., 1546
Anderson, Josephine, 38
Anderson, Joseph R., **33–35**, 96, 907, 1330, 1592, 1616, 1617, 1647
  Gaines' Mill, Virginia, 653
  Mechanicsville, Virginia, 1020
Anderson, Margaret Adair, 30
Anderson, Patton. *See* Anderson, James Patton
Anderson, Richard (Revolutionary War colonel), 35
Anderson, Richard E., 880
Anderson, Richard Heron, **35–36**, 212, 1002, 1503
  Cold Harbor, Virginia, 366–367
  Gettysburg campaign, 679, 680
  Harpers Ferry, West Virginia, 742–743
  Mine Run campaign, 1043
  Sharpsburg campaign, 1406, 1407–1408
  Spotsylvania campaign, 1518, 1519
Anderson, Robert (brigadier general), 27, **36–37**
Anderson, Robert (major, U.S. Army), 146, 285, 298, 627, 629, 887
  Fort Sumter command, 1207–1208, 1381, 1507, 1508, 1526
Anderson, Samuel Read, **37–38**, 751
Anderson, Thomas, 116
Anderson, William, **38**, 839, 1289
  guerrilla activity, 274, 275, 724, 1599
Anderson, William Preston, 30
Andersonville (Kantor), 939, 1264
Andersonville Diary (recording), 488
Andersonville Prison, **38–40**, 155, 362, 385, 774, 866, 1258, 1264, 1267, 1353
  death rates, 39, 673
  Jones (Joseph) reports, 867
  photographs, 1206, *1263*
  ration issuing, *1263*
  Stoneman's raid, 1546–1547
  Winder, John H., 1734
  Wirz, Henry, 866, 1735
Andrew, John, 11
Andrews, Eliza Frances, 472
Andrews, James J., 41, 109; *see also* Andrews raid
Andrews, William, 1563
Andrews raid, **41**, 109, 674, 1298, 1574
Andrus, Michael J., *as contributor*, 441, 850–851
Anesthesia, 756
Angels of Destruction, 927
Anglicanism. *See* Episcopal Church
Anglo-Confederate purchasing, **41–43**
  Anglo-Confederate Trading Company, **43**, 129, 181

Anglo-Confederate purchasing, *continued*
artillery, **102–103**
blockade running, 180–181, 507
Bulloch, James D., 239–240, 992
commerce raiders, 375
cotton embargo, 507–508, 711–712
Laird shipyards, 903–904, 904
Maury, Matthew Fontaine, 1018
naval guns, 1119–1120
naval vessels, 19, **25–26**, 42, 484, 673, 1018, 1123, 1129
North, James H., 1150
overview article, **41–42**
small arms, 60, 232, 1465–1469, 1470
Anglo-Confederate Trading Company. *See under* Anglo-Confederate purchasing
Animated Weekly, 572, 573
Annie (ship), 184, 185
"Annie Laurie" (song), 1103, 1498
"Annie of the Vale" (song), 1103
Anniversary Oration (Harper), 1273
Antebellum expansionism. *See* Expansionism in the antebellum South
Antebellum slavery. *See under* Slavery
Anthem
"Dixie," 488
national, 1102
Anthropology, 1046
Anticipations of the Future (Ruffin), 1350
Antietam campaign. *See* Sharpsburg campaign
Antietam Bridge, Maryland, *1339*
Antietam Creek, *1405*, 1406, 1408
Antietam National Battlefield Site, 1072, 1073, 1074
Antifederalists, 1531
Anti-Semitism, 559, 599, 1157, 1320–1321, 1367, 1517
Antislavery, **43–45**
abolitionist extremism, 318, 319–320, 1374
abolitionist impact, 1374
Bleeding Kansas, **175–176**
caricature, *649*, *933*, *1044*
cornerstone speech, 415
and expansion of slavery, 552
Fugitive Slave Law, **648–650**
German Texans, 676
Great Britain, 44, 160, 553, 556, 1016, 1629
guerrillas, 647, 719, 1289, 1752
Helper, Hinton, 762
Indian missionaries, 297
John Brown's raid. *See under* Harpers Ferry, West Virginia
Lincoln, Abraham, 933, 934
Quakers, 1493
Republican party, *933*, *1044*, 1375, 1377, 1441, 1534
South Carolina, 370
Sumner (Charles) speech, 1560–1561
Thirteenth Amendment, **1590–1591**
Tubman, Harriet, 1623
U.S. congressional disposition, 9
view of slaveholders, 787
Wisconsin state rights argument, 1534
see also Compromise of 1850; Emancipation Proclamation; Wilmot Proviso
Apaches, 144, 983, 984
Apalachicola, Florida, U.S. arsenal seizure, 866, 1461, 1469
Apalachicola River, defenses, 1032
Appeal to the Christian Women of the South (Grimke), 44
Appomattox campaign, **45–48**
final volley, 422
Grimes, Bryan, 718
Lee (Robert E.) surrender, *47*, 212, *330*, 571, 920, 921, 975
map, 46
Stonewall Brigade, 1548, 1549
Archaeology, **48–50**
Alabama Association, 20
artifact collections, 1099–1100
projectile excavation, 103
Archer, James Jay, **50–51**, 968
Gaines' Mill, Virginia, 653
Mechanicsville, Virginia, 1020
Archer, Junius L., 96
Archer, Sally, 33
Archer (ship), 374, 375, 1309
Archer & Daly, 1242, 1523
Archer and Halpin, 436
Archer's Brigade, 816
Archive of Folk Culture, 487
Archives. *See* Museums and archives
Arctic (ship), 726
Argus (newspaper), 1143
Ariel (ship), 368
Arizona, **51**, 1538
congressional delegates, 391, 1174
established by Confederacy, 984
established by United States, 1136
governors, 143–144
railway routes, 983
slavery, 554
Arizona (ship), 1357
Arkadelphia, Arkansas, 56
Arkansas, **51–54**
arsenal and armory, 1461, 1469, 1470
black-white population comparison, *1435*
campaign. *See* Arkansas campaign of 1864
congressmen, 141, 262–263, 658–661, 662, 736, 856, 1056, 1349, 1355–1356, 1594, 1694
Constitution ratification, 403
cotton plantations, 1436
debt, 462
defense, 561
Democratic party, 465
education, 519
election of 1860, 521, 522, 523
farm acreage, *1484*
flag, 587
governors, 587, 588, 701, 702, 703, 961, 1097, 1313–1314
guerrilla activity, 721
Indian Territory, 811, 1390
infantry, 911
Juneteenth, 1446
mail delivery, 1312
martial law, 1349
niter production, 1147
population, 602, 642, 1233
Prairie Grove, 1427
railroads, 1293, 1295, 1296
Reconstruction, 54, 661, 736
Red River campaign. *See* Red River campaigns
Republican party, 1322
rice production, 1328
secession. *See under* Secession
secession and Confederacy membership, *1379*
secession date correlated with total black population, *1486*
slaveholdings, *1485*
slavery, 551, 553, 1484
social tensions, 1492
tories, 1602
Trans-Mississippi Department, 1606
Unionism. *See under* Unionism
Union occupation, 1640
see also particular cities and place names
Arkansas (ship), **54–55**, 141, 227, 685, 992, 1049, 1124, 1129, 1236, 1303, 1309, 1425, 1656
Arkansas campaign of 1864, 53, **55–57**, 1610
black regiments, 12
Gano, Richard, 657
Shelby, Joseph O., 1409

Arkansas Comedian. *See* Macarthy, Harry
Arkansas Gazette (newspaper), 940, 941, 1144
Arkansas Military Institute, 519
Arlington House, **58**, 916, 917
Arlington National Cemetery, 58
Arman, Lucien, 1303, 1547
Armant, Leopold, 426
Armistead, Lewis A., **58–59**, 136, 683, 1582
  as Gettysburg casualty, 1391
  Malvern Hill, Virginia, 996
Armistead, Mary Marot, 1628
Armories. *See* Arsenals and armories
Armor-plated ships. *See* Ironclads
Armstrong, Frank Crawford, **63**, 1679
Armstrong, William G., 102, 1119–1120
Armstrong gun, 93, 94, 103, 1119, *1120*
Arms, weapons, and ammunition, **59–63**
  Alabama, 16, 1388–1389, 1458, 1470
  ammunition and lead production, 90, 1469–1471
  Army ordnance, **59–62**, **1168–1170**
  artillery, **93–94**, 102
  captured, 1684
  deployment, 1352
  edged weapons, **512–515**
  explosive shells, 62, 93, 94, 95, 1300
  fortification armament, 623
  Gorgas (Josiah), 698–699
  infantry, 817, 818–819
  Joe Brown's pikes, 846
  lead, **913**
  Morgan's raiders, 1086
  museum collections, 1100
  naval ordnance, **62–63**
  Ordnance Bureau, **1168–1170**
  patents, 1181
  production. *See* Arsenals and armories; Niter and Mining Bureau; Ordnance Bureau; Powder works
  saltpeter, **1375**
  shortages, 1678
  slave labor, 48
  sources for, 1169, 1455–1471, 1469–1371
  South Carolina, 1179
  spar torpedoes, **1515–1516**
  war mobilization, 508–509
  see also Hand grenades and land mines; Naval guns; Small arms; Torpedoes and mines
Army, Confederate, **63–75**, 385, 1069, 1157
  African Americans, 4, 6, 14, **74–75**, 399, 643, 644, 645
  "Butternuts" nickname, 1495
  cavalry, **266–270**
  Confederate gray, 356
  conscription. *See* Conscription
  departments, **71–74**, 1386
  desertion, **467–469**
  edged weapons, 513–514
  flags, **585–586**
  foreign-born troops, 603–604
  generals. *See* Generals; particular names
  German volunteers, 676
  Indian volunteers, 812, 813, 815, 1290, 1390
  infantry, **815–820**
  Irish volunteers, 822, 823
  Jewish volunteers, 845, 846
  legion, 733, 816
  manpower, **69-71**, 385, 1131, 1151-1152; *see also* Soldiers
  naming of armies, 1691
  Ordnance Bureau, **1168–1170**
  organization, 737
  Orphan Brigade, **1180**
  overview article, **64–69**
  Provisional Army of the Confederate States, 64, 66
  Quartermaster Bureau, **1291–1292**
  Regular Army, 64
  rules of war, **1352–1353**
  Signal Corps, **1428–1430**
  small arms, **1455–1471**
  soldiers' aid societies, **1501–1502**
  soldiers' convalescent homes, **1502–1503**
  special units, **1516**
  surgeons, 1022
  uniforms, 817–818, **1633–1636**
  West Virginia troops, 1700
  see also Arms, weapons, and ammunition; Veterans; particular armies, campaigns, departments, and generals
Army, U.S.
  African American troops. *See* African American troops in the Union Army
  battle reenactments, 1317
  cotton for food exchanges, 1686
  documentary films, 572
  Gettysburg reunions, 1027
  military telegraph service, 1573
  oath of allegiance, 1163
  power to free slaves, 391
  West Virginia troops, 1700
  white Southern Unionist troops, 45, 53, 1574, 1576, **1602–1603**, *1637*, 1638, 1639
  see also particular armies, campaigns, and generals
Army and Navy Gazette (newspaper), 1354
Army and Navy Herald (newspaper), 1034, 1400
Army Life in a Black Regiment (Higginson), 10
Army of Alabama, Mississippi, and East Louisiana, 68, 74; *see also* Department of Alabama, Mississippi, and Eastern Louisiana
Army of Central Kentucky, 737
Army of East Louisiana, Mississippi, and Alabama. *See* Army of Alabama, Mississippi, and East Louisiana
Army of Kentucky, 67, 890
Army of Mississippi, 67, 84
  Allen, Henry W., 26
  Anderson, James Patton, 32
  Atlanta campaign, 113
  Dalton, Georgia, 442
  Wheeler, Joseph, 1707
  see also Department of Alabama, Mississippi, and Eastern Louisiana; Department of Mississippi and East Louisiana
Army of Missouri, 1252, 1253
Army of Northern Virginia, 66–67, **76–83**, 111
  Alexander, Edward Porter, 25
  Anderson, George Thomas ("Tige"), 30
  Anderson, Richard Heron, 35, 36
  Appomattox campaign, 45–48
  Armistead, Lewis A., 59
  artillery, 92, 94, 407, 1191
  Baker, Laurence Simmons, 122
  Barksdale's Mississippi Brigade, **132–133**
  battle flag, 585, *586*
  Benning, Henry L., 162
  Brockenbrough, John Mercer, 222–223
  Bryan, Goode, 235
  casualties, 1240–1241
  cavalry, 122, 209–211, 266, 267, 268, 270, 276–277
  Chancellorsville campaign, 67, 80, 279–282
  civilian background, 815
  Cold Harbor, Virginia, 366–367
  composition, 66

Army of Northern Virginia, *continued*
desertions, 95
Early, Jubal, 501–503
elite units, 1516
engineer regiment, 534, 1444
espionage support, 537
field fortifications, 626
foraging, 601
Fredericksburg campaign, 637–640
Gaines' Mill, Virginia, 653–654
Gettysburg campaign, 676–683, 918, 945–946
Grant, Ulysses S., 1198–1202
Heth, Henry, 769
Hill, A. P., 770–771
Hill, D. H., 775
Hood, John Bell, 789, 790
Hood's Texas Brigade, 716, 791
horses, 269, 792–793
Humphreys, Benjamin, 800
hunger, 152
infantry composition, 816
Jackson, Thomas J. ("Stonewall"), 834, 836
Jones, David Rumph ("Neighbor"), 864
Jones, John M., 866–867
Kelly's Ford, Virginia, 880–881
Lee, Robert E. *See under* Lee, Robert E.
Lee, William Henry Fitzhugh, 921
Longstreet, James. *See under* Longstreet, James
Louisiana Tigers, 957
Lynchburg, Virginia, 963
McLaws, Lafayette, 974
Malvern Hill, Virginia, 994–996
Manassas, First, 996–999
Manassas, Second, 999–1003
Mechanicsville, Virginia, 1020–1021
Mine Run campaign, 1043
Mosby's Rangers, 1091
naming, 66, 76, 918
officer corps, 693
Peck, William Raine, 1185
Pender, William Dorsey, 1190
Pettigrew, J. Johnston, 1202–1203
rations, 595
reconnaissance and mapmaking, 797
records, 1099
reorganization, 36, 51, 78, 80, 775, 834, 914, 918, 945, 1698
reputation, 1581–1582
retreat from Maryland, 1408
Richmond defenses, 1400, 1553
Rodes, Robert, 1344–1345
Sharpsburg campaign, 79, 918, 1404–1408
Smith, Gustavus W., 1474
Spotsylvania campaign, 1518–1520
staff, 77
Stoneman's raids, 1546
Stonewall Brigade, 850, 1549
Stuart (J. E. B.) raids, 1553
supplies, 963, 1094
surrender, 74, 920
uniforms and equipment, 817
Virginians, 1664
war correspondents, 274, 1683, 1684
Wickham, Williams Carter, 1713
Wilderness campaign, 1719–1721
Winchester, Virginia, 1732
Wise, Henry A., 1736
Wofford, William Tatum, 1738
Yellow Tavern, Virginia, 1750–1751
see also Department of Northern Virginia; Lee, Robert E.
Army of Southwest Virginia, 1011
Army of Tennessee, 67, 71, **83–88**, 361
Adams, John, 1
Anderson, James Patton, 32, 33
Anderson, Robert, 36–37
anti-Bragg faction, 85–86, 87, 88, 296, 775, 777, 946, 1011–1012, 1227–1228
artillery, 92, 93, 530
Atlanta campaign, 110–115
battle flag, 586
Bragg, Braxton. *See under* Bragg, Braxton; *subhead* anti-Bragg faction *above*
Brantly, William Felix, 211
Breckinridge, John C., 84, 87, 139, 214, 1706
Cantey, James, 258
Carter, John Carpenter, 264
cavalry, 266, 267, 1707–1708
Chattanooga campaign, 292–295
Chattanooga Rebel as mouthpiece of, 1143
Cheatham, B. Franklin, 295–296
Chickamauga campaign, 67, 72, 86, 204–205, 302–304
Cleburne, Patrick, 353–354
composition, 66
Dalton, Georgia, 442
Deshler, James, 469–470
division commands, 1475
engineers, 534–535, 913
formation, 1575
fortifications, 620, 626
Franklin and Nashville campaign, 260, 632–636
Hill, Benjamin Jefferson, 774
Hood, John Bell. *See under* Hood, John Bell
hunger, 595
internal politics, 354
Johnston, Albert Sidney. *See under* Johnston, Albert Sidney
Johnston, Joseph E. *See under* Johnston, Joseph E.
Lee, Stephen D., 921
Longstreet, James, 86, 87, 946, 1706
Lowrey, Mark Perrin, 959
Mackall, William W., 973
Manigault, Arthur Middleton, 1004
medical department, 1549, 1550
Murfreesboro, Tennessee, 1094–1096
naming, 891
Orphan Brigade, **1170**
Polk, Leonidas. *See under* Polk, Leonidas
Sherman's March to the Sea, 1005, 1006, 1007
Shoup, Francis, 1427
small arms, 1468
Smith, Thomas Benton, 1478
Stevenson, Carter, 1545
Stewart, Alexander P., 1545
Strahl, Otho French, 1550–1551
Taylor, Richard, 1572
Texans, 1584
war correspondents, 1683, 1684
Wharton, John Austin, 1706–1707
see also Department of East Tennessee; Department of Tennessee
Army of the Cumberland, 111, 891, 1708
Chattanooga campaign, 292–295
Chickamauga campaign, 302–304
Dalton, Georgia, 442
Army of the Frontier, 1246
Army of the James
Appomattox campaign, 46, 47, 48
Drewry's Bluff, 496
Army of the Kanawha, 1736
Army of the Northwest, 834
Army of the Ohio
Atlanta campaign, 111
Dalton, Georgia, 442
Knoxville campaign, 895
Nashville occupation, 1420
Stoneman, George, Jr., 1546, 1547
Army of the Peninsula, 360, 1191
Army of the Potomac, Confederate, 66, 266; *see also* Army of Northern Virginia

Army of the Potomac, U.S., 76, 81, 111, 815, 1331, 1750
advance on Richmond, 1400–1401, 1402–1403
Appomattox campaign, 46
casualties, 626
Chancellorsville campaign, 67, 80, 279–282
Chattanooga campaign, 293–295
Cold Harbor, Virginia, 366–367
espionage operations, 540
field fortifications, 626
Frayser's Farm, Virginia, 636–637
Fredericksburg campaign, 79, 637–640
Gaines' Mill, Virginia, 653–654
Gettysburg campaign, 676–683
Harpers Ferry, West Virginia, 742
Lynchburg, Virginia, 963
Malvern Hill, Virginia, 994–996
Mechanicsville, Virginia, 1020–1021
Mine Run campaign, 1043
Overland campaign, 1198
Peninsular campaign, 1191–1193
Petersburg campaign, 1198–1202
Seven Days' Battles, 1400–1401
Seven Pines, Virginia, 1402–1403
Spotsylvania campaign, 1518–1520
Stoneman's raids, 1546
Stuart's raids, 1553, 1554–1556
Wilderness campaign, 1719–1721
Army of the Shenandoah, 1413, 1417–1418
Army of the Southwest, 526
Army of the Tennessee, U. S.
Atlanta campaign, 111, 113
Port Gibson, Mississippi, 1237
Army of the Trans-Mississippi. *See* Trans-Mississippi Department
Army of the Valley, 66, 503, 504, 947, 1418
Cedar Creek, Virginia, 271
Fisher's Hill, Virginia, 582
Mechanicsville, Virginia, 1020
Peninsular campaign, 1193
Army of the West, 68, 970, 1017, 1251, 1515
battle flag, 586
Rust, Albert, 1355
Van Dorn, Earl, 1652
Wilson's Creek campaign, 1730
see also Department of the West; Trans-Mississippi Department
Army of Vicksburg. *See* Department of Mississippi and East Louisiana
Army of Virginia, U. S.
Manassas, Second, 999–1003
Pope (John) command, 549, 1134
Army of West Tennessee, 835
Arnold, Samuel, 935
Arrington, Archibald Hunter, **89**, 1626
Arsenal (Nashville Military Institute), 519
Arsenal, The (Columbia, South Carolina), 312
Arsenals and armories, **89–91**
altered U.S. small arms, 1464–1465
Apalachicola, Florida, 866, 1461, 1469
archaeological excavations, 48–49
cannon manufacture, 96–97
Charleston, South Carolina, 285, 287
Confederate-produced handguns, 1459–1461
Confederate-produced long arms, 1455–1458
De Lagnel, Julius, 464–465
Harpers Ferry, West Virginia, 104, **738–740**, 807
Missouri, 1053
Ordnance Bureau, 698, 1168, 1169
Palmetto Armory, **1179–1180**
Quaker guns, 95
St. Louis, Missouri, 647–648, 828, 1053
seizures of U.S., 386, 647–648, 866, 1461–1464, 1469–1470, 1507
Selma, Alabama, 1387–1388, 1458
Arson, 428
Art
engraving, 1231
Federal Civil War parks, 1073
lithographs, 1231, 1256
Lost Cause iconography, 460, 1554
museum collections, 1100
popular, 1231
selected bibliography, 168
see also Caricature; Monuments and memorials; particular artists and art works
Articles of Confederation (1781), 400, 1531
Articles of War, 468, 1038, 1039, 1277
Artifacts. *See* Archaeology
Artillery, **91–103**
acquisition, 61
Army of Northern Virginia, 92, 94, 407, 1191
companies, 816
Confederate-produced, **96–98**
edged weapons and, 513
elite units, 1516
English, imported, **102–103**
field, 91, 93, 94, 96
at Fredericksburg, 25
heavy, 91, 93, 513, *513*
insignia and colors, 1633
Ordnance Bureau, 698, 1168
overview article, **91–95**
Provisional Army, 66
reorganization, 80, 92
training, 1040
United States Colored Troops, 11
U.S., captured, **99–102**
Walker, Reuben Lindsay, 1679–1680
see also particular types
Artisans, 735, 900, 902
creole, 644
free black, 1486
see also Labor, skilled
Artists. *See* Art; particular names
Artist's Wife, The (Hewitt), 1590
Asboth, Alexander S., 526
Ash, Stephen V., *as contributor*, 1574–1579, 1640–1641
"Ashantee." *See* Linebaugh, John
Ashby, Richard, 104, 740
Ashby, Turner, **103–105**, 431, 834
elite unit, 1516
intelligence operations, 202, 543
seizure of Harpers Ferry, 144, 740
Ashby's Gap, Virginia, 1713
Ashe, Samuel A., 1627
Ashe, Thomas S., **105–107**, 1311
Ashe, William S., 1296–1297
Asheville, North Carolina, armory, 1457
Ashland, Tennessee, 1708
Ashmore, John D., *1505*
"Ashokan Farewell" (song), 488
Ashwood Plantation, 1194
Associate Reformed Presbyterians, 1247
Association of the Army of Northern Virginia, 503, 1027
Association of the Army of Tennessee, 1027
Atalanta (ship), 186, 376, 1727; *see also Tallahassee*
Atchison, David R., 829, 875, 1053
Athens, Georgia, 517
emancipatioon celebration, 924
hospitals, 796
small arms manufacture, 1458
Athens Manufacturing Company, 1458
Athens Southern Banner (newspaper), 1683
Atkins, J. D. C., **107–108**
Atlanta, Georgia, **108–115**
arsenal, 90
battle of, 114, 115, 163
bread riots, 109, 212, 1226
burning of, 111, 673, 1648

Atlanta, Georgia, *continued*
campaign, 27, 67, 87, 110, **111–115**, 139, 163, 336, 442, 512, 519, 672–673, 691, 738, 786, 790, 819, 859, 880, 885–886, 1032, 1087, 1180, 1314, 1404, 1427, 1475, 1478, 1544, 1546, 1573, 1707
city, **108–111**
defenses, *99*, 620
hospitals, 109, 110, 796
monuments and memorials, 951–952
railroads, 108, 109, 672, 1294, 1645
refugees, 110, 1318
small arms and munitions manufacture, 1121, 1460, 1470, 1471
Union occupation, 111, 672, 1640
Atlanta (ship), **116**, 441, 1126, 1130, 1303, *1303*, 1370, 1425, 1596
Atlanta Baptist College, 1321
Atlanta Daily Intelligencer (newspaper), 1082, 1245, 1587, 1683
Atlanta Journal (newspaper), 570
Atlanta Naval Works Ordnance, 1121
Atlanta Register (newspaper), 1144
Atlanta Rolling Mill, 508, 902, 1124
Atlanta Southern Confederacy (newspaper), 1144, 1619
Atlantic (ship), 1124
Atlantic and Gulf Railroad, 1094, 1297
Atlantic Blockading Squadron, 178
Atlantic cable, 223
Atlantic Dry Dock, 1562
Atlantic Iron Works, 1725
Atlantic Monthly (magazine), 476, 646
Atlas to Accompany the Official Records of the Union and Confederate Armies, 798
A. T. Patterson Company, 98
Atrocities
Confederate allegations of Union, 933–934
guerrilla activity, 719, 720, 722, 724
see also Massacres
Attack formation, 819
Attorney general, 251, 315
Benjamin, Judah P., 159, 206, 452
Bragg, Thomas, 206–207
Davis, George, 448
departmental status, 249
Keyes, Wade, 892
Patent Office, 1181
Sequestration Act, 389
Watts, Thomas H., 1695
Attorneys, 1489
Atzerodt, George A., *539*
Auburn Masonic Female College, 520
Aucaigne, Felix, 1271
Audio books, 488
Augusta, Georgia
antebellum population, *1642*
arsenal, 90, 96–97, 1461, 1469
bread riots, 212, 1226
clinch rifles, *672*
Irish immigrants, 822
lawlessness, 1744
manufacturing, 1168, 1645, 1647
population and urban ranking, *10*
powder works, 1245, 1246
railroads, 1297
roads, 1339
small arms manufacture, 1459, 1460, 1470, 1471
Southern Express Company, 1511
textile industry, 1645
Augusta Chronicle and Sentinel (newspaper), 273, 610, 774, 1144, 1744
Augusta Constitutionalist (newspaper), 1144
Augusta Machine Works, 1460
Augusta Powder Works, 508, 1168, 1245, 1246, 1470, 1604
Auman, William Thomas, *as contributor*, 341–342, 768–769, 854–855, 1183–1184, 1631–1632
Austin, Stephen F., 913
Austin, Texas, **116–117**
Austin Association for Maintaining Our Rights in the Union, 116
Austria
European Brigade, 603
ordnance imports, 102
small arms manufacture, 1468
Autobiography. *See* Diaries, letters, and memoirs
Autobiography (Adams), 921
Autobiography (Hunton), 805
Avalanche (newspaper), 1143
Avary, Myrta Lockett, 300
Averasboro, North Carolina, **117–118**, 262, 1152
Averell, William W., 277, 913, 915, 1702
Avery, William Waightstill, **118**
Avery Island, Louisiana, 955, 1362
AWOL. *See* Desertion
Axton, Hoyt, 487
Ayer, Lewis Malone, **118–119**, 1326
Ayres and Wade, 937
Azores Islands, 1393

B

B & O. *See* Baltimore and Ohio Railroad
Babits, L. E., *as contributor*, 48–50, 125
Bachelor's Button: A Monthly Museum of Southern Literature, The (magazine), 1482
Bachman, John, 1274
"Backdoor to the Confederacy" (Brownsville, Texas), 232
Badgett, Henry, 1453
Bagby, Arthur P., **121**
Bagby, George W., 193, 937, 985, 986, 1142
Bahama (ship), 375
Bahamas, 177
Bahnson, George F., 1084
Bailey, Anne J., *as contributor*, 173–174, 187, 249, 311, 343, 409, 525–527, 604–605, 656–657, 715, 753–754, 759–760, 776–777, 785, 932, 970–971, 973, 976, 990, 1145–1146, 1210–1211, 1246–1247, 1250, 1340, 1343, 1357, 1432, 1472–1474, 1605–1611, 1627–1628, 1651–1652, 1678–1679, 1706–1707
Bailey, Fred Arthur, *as contributor*, 55–57, 511–54, 685–686, 894–895, 939–941, 1573–1574
Bailey, Joseph, 1317
Bailey, R. A., 750
Bailey, William, 1021, 1639
Baird, Absolam, 295
Baird, W. David, *as contributor*, 810–812, 812–815, 1290, 1398, 1408–1409
Baker, Alpheus, **121–122**
Baker, Bolling, 1615
Baker, Edward D., 126, 127
Baker, James McNair, **122**
Baker, Lafayette C., 541–542, 601
Baker, Laurence Simmons, **122**
Baldwin, B. G., 77
Baldwin, John B., **122–125**, 1381
Baldwin, Joseph G., 172, 749
Baldwin, Philemon, 304
Baldwin, William Edwin, **125**, 1236, 1237, 1605
Baldwin Blues, 490
Ball, Douglas A., *as contributor*, 187–190, 433–438, 461–463, 485, 820–821, 1022–1026, 1140–1141, 1279–1286, 1614–1616, 1618–1619
Ballads, 487, 1104
Ballard, Michael B., *as contributor*, 1188–1189

Ballinger, W. P., 1716
Balloon, 24, **125**, *126*, 447
Ball's Bluff, Virginia, **126–127**, 569
  map, 127
Baltic (ship), 236, 420, 685, 1062
Baltimore, Lord, 1016
Baltimore, Maryland
  defenses, 1621
  Early's raid, 504–505
  emancipationist sentiment, 1378
  printmaking center, 1255
  riot, **127**
Baltimore and Ohio Railroad, 104, 504, 1295–1296, 1415, 1418, 1700, 1703, 1704, 1705, 1732, 1733
  attacks by Mosby's Rangers, 723, 725
Baltimore Association to Advise and Assist Friends in the Southern States, 1493
Baltimore riot, **127**
Bancroft, George, 235
Band music. *See* Music
Band Music of the Confederacy (recording), 487
Band of Angels (film), 580
Band of Angels (novel by Warren), 939
Banking, **128–129**
  bankers' convention, 1025
  Charleston, South Carolina, 1660
  currency issuance, 1279–1280
  factorage centers, 1644
  Lamar, Gazaway B., 905
  Morgan's raids, 1089
  small-change notes' depreciation, 1424
  specie payments, 18
Bank of the United States, 1629
Banks, Nathaniel P., 1357, 1372
  Arkansas campaign, 53, 55–57
  Cedar Mountain, Virginia, 272
  Front Royal, Virginia, 549, 647
  Louisiana command, 1419, 1473
  Louisiana Reconstruction, 956
  Mansfield, Louisiana, 1004–1005
  New Orleans occupation, 1138–1139
  Port Hudson, Louisiana, 1238, 1239
  Red River campaigns, 53, 151, 709, 713, 955, 961, 1223, 1314–1317, 1538, 1572, 1609–1610
  Republican party, 1322
  Shenandoah Valley invasion, 1415, 1416
  sugar plantation operations, 1560
  Texas, 232, 233, 1584, 1609
  Winchester, Virginia, 104, 549, 1732
Bannon, John, 1271
Banshee (ship), 43, **129**, 184, 185
Baptist Church, **130–131**, 1321
  Atlanta, Georgia, 108
  Bible societies, 164–165
  chaplains, 282
  Ford, Samuel Howard, 602
  Richmond, Virginia, 1330
  sermons, 1399
  slavery, 320
Baptist General Association of Virginia, 164–165
Barbara Frietchie (film), 574, *578*
Barbour, Alfred M., 740
Bardolph, Richard, *as contributor*, 118, 448, 467–469, 492–493, 961, 975, 1085–1086
Barges, 1692
Barksdale, Ethelbert, **131**, 727, 1051
Barksdale, William, **131–132**, 203, 800, *1050*
  Fredericksburg campaign, 638, 639
  as Gettysburg casualty, 1391
  Harpers Ferry, West Virginia, 743
  Mississippi Brigade, 132–133
Barksdale's Mississippi brigade, **132–133**
Barlow, Francis, 1072
Barnard, George N., 99, 108
Barnes, James, 1221
Barney, J. N., 592
Barney, William L., *as contributor*, 125, 199, 416, 582, 664, 713, 1323–1326, 1373–1383, 1476, 1479, 1653–1654, 1747–1750
Barnwell, Robert W., **133**, 309, 872, 1023–1024, 1171
Barr, Alwyn, *as contributor*, 207, 444, 655, 715–717, 1097–1098, 1583–1587, 1696, 1746
Barrett, John G., *as contributor*, 260–262, 1752–1753
Barrett, John G. (commissioner of patents), 768
Barrett, Joseph, 855
Barrett, Robert T., *as contributor*, 245–246, 613, 666, 730, 730–732
Barrett, Theodore H., 232, 234, 1611
Barrien, John M., 1708
Barringer, D. Moreau, 134
Barringer, Rufus, **133–134**, 1341
Barron, Samuel, 290, 1394
Barrow, R. F., 1556
Barrow, Robert Ruffin, 777
Barry, John Decatur, **134**, *135*
Barry, William Taylor Sullivan, **135**, 1047
Barteau, Clark S., 219
Barter, 1491, 1511
Barthelmess, Richard, 578
Barton, David, 224
Barton, Joseph, 721
Barton, Seth Maxwell, **135–136**
Barton, William S., 1039
Bartow, Francis S., **136–138**, 604, 665, 1366
  Manassas, First, 658, 997, 998
Baseball, 923, *1262*
Bass, Fredrick S., 791
Bass, Nathan, **138**
Bates, Edward, 390
Bate, William Brimage, 113, **138–139**, 600
  Chickamauga battle report, 1500
Bates, Edward, 390
Bath Paper Mills, 1470
Baton Rouge, Louisiana, **140–141**, 340, 1170
  arsenal, 90, 140, 648, 1053, 1461, 1469
  shelling of, 720
  Union occupation, 954, 1640
Batson, Felix I., **141**, 263, 1594
Battalion
  composition, 816
  system, 25
Battelle, Gordon, 1702
Batterson, J. G., 1073
Battery, 91, 665; *see also* Company
Battery Beauregard, 623
Battery Buchanan, 622
Battery Dupre. *See* Tower Dupre
Battery Gregg. *See* Fort Gregg, South Carolina
Battery Jones, 618
Battery Pegram, 620
Battery Robinett, 414, 415
Battery Wagner. *See* Fort Wagner, South Carolina
Battle, Amanda, 1146
Battle, Cullen Andrews, **141–142**
Battle, The (film), 575
Battle above the Clouds. *See* Lookout Mountain
Battle axes, 515
Battlefields
  archaeology, 48
  monuments and memorials, **1071–1074**
  ordnance recovery, 100, 513, 698, 913
Battlefields of Virginia, The (Allan), 797
Battle flags. *See* Flags, military
Battle-Ground, The (novel by Glasgow), 938
Battle injuries. *See under* Health and medicine

Battle of . . . . *See* particular battle names; *See also* Battles, naming of, *for discussion of battles with multiple names*
Battle of Chancellorsville, The (film), 573
Battle of Gettysburg, The (film), 575
Battle of Gettysburg, The (television program), 573–574
"Battle of Antietam Creek, The" (recording), 487
Battle-Pieces (Melville), 937
Battle reenactments. *See* Reenactments
Battles, naming of, **142–143**
Batty, Peter, 574
Beaufort (ship), 840, 1124, 1180
Baxley, Catherine Virginia, **143**, 543, 1090
Baxter, Elisha, 661
Baxter, John, 1563
Baxter Springs, Kansas, 722, 724
Bayard, James, 1454
Baylor, George W., 1707
Baylor, John R., 51, **143–144**, 705, 983, 1136, 1174, 1606
Baylor, William S. H., 1549
Bayne, Thomas L., 181–182, 1140, 1169, 1687
Bay of Pigs (Cuba), 557
Bayonets, 60, 513, 515, 817, 818, 1040
Bayou City (ship), 656, 744
Bayou LaFourche expedition, 954
Bayou Teche, 954–955, 956, 1314, 1315, 1572
Beale, Richard Lee Turberville, **144**
Beall, John Y., **144–145**, 258, 375, 538, 857
Beall, Lloyd J., 1007
Beall, William N. R., **145**, 1649
Bean's Station, Tennessee, 897
"Bear, The" (novella by Faulkner), 938
Beard, Charles A., 317, 318
Beard, John, 693
Bearss, Edwin C., *as contributor*, 624–627, 1071–1074
Bearss, Sara B., *as contributor*, 802–805, 1335–1338, 1628–1631
Beatty, Ellen Adair, 31
Beaufort, North Carolina, 1152
Beaufort, South Carolina, 1325, 1509
Beauregard, P. G. T., *65*, **146–150**, 474, 547, 549, 698, 889, 1251, 1427
  Army of Tennessee, 67, 84, 85, 88
  and Butler's Woman Order, 246
  Charleston defense, 191, 283, 285, 287–288, 1003, 1386, 1475, 1509, 1558
  congressional support, 1172
  creole heritage, 146, 426
  and Davis (Jefferson) view of, 336, 453, 1396, 1514–1515
  Drewry's Bluff, Virginia, 496, 780, 1736
  espionage, 542, 601, 714
  flag design, 148, 249, 585, 586
  fortifications development, 617
  Fort Sumter, South Carolina, negotiations, 146, 298, 324, 628, 629, 1066, 1333, 1381–1382, 1508
  Fort Wagner, South Carolina, 877–878
  Franklin and Nashville campaign, 633
  ironclads command, 1129–1130
  Manassas, First, 24, 76, 148, 150, 265, 530, 714, 832, 952, 996–999, 1573, 1716
  memoirs, 150, 331, 475–476
  Midwest confederacy, 413
  military departments, 71–72
  Military Division of the West, 74
  opinion of Benjamin (Judah P.), 159
  personality, 146, 148
  Petersburg campaign, 1198, 1199
  rifled guns use, 619
  Savannah defense, 1368
  Shiloh campaign, 148–149, 150, 204, 1420, 1421, 1423
  staff, 298, 300, 570, 776, 864, 868, 870, 871, 920, 1223, 1249, 1504, 1544, 1661
  strategy and tactics, 148, 327, 822, 862, 1248, 1659
  war correspondents, 274
  withdrawal from Columbus, Kentucky, 1420
"Beauregard Felix." *See* Beauregard, P. G. T.
Beauregard (ship), 1269
Beauvoir, **150**, 388, 453, 492, 1100, 1502
Beaver Dam Creek. *See* Mechanicsville, Virginia
Beckham, Robert F., 209
Bee, Barnard E., **150–151**, 548, 834, 1624
  Jackson (Thomas J. "Stonewall") nickname, 834
  Manassas, First, 997, 998
  staff, 1544
Bee, Hamilton P., **151**, 231, 233, 1037, 1608
Beechenbrook (Preston), 936
Beecher, Henry Ward, *1561*, 1673
Beefsteak raid, **151–152**, 1200, 1573
Beers, Augustus P., 152
Beers, Fannie, **152–153**, 795
Beirne, Betty, 1038
Beirne, George P., 348
Belgium, 603, 1004
  diplomacy, 479, 484, 1529
  small arms manufacture, 1468–1469
Bell, Caryn Cossé, *as contributor*, 644–645, 1348, 1621
Bell, Caspar Wistar, **153**
Bell, Hiram Parks, **153–154**
Bell, John, 264, *381*, *404*, 1575, 1708
  election of 1860, 14, 109, 122, 153, 213, 235, 403, 426, *494*, **521–524**, 588, 667, 687, 706, 763, 778, 786, 976–977, 1047, 1052, 1057, 1085, 1187, 1336, 1376, 1477, 1482, 1574, 1583, 1623, 1637, 1647, 1650, 1695, 1699, 1744, 1755
Bell, Joshua F., 987
Bell, Mary, and Mollie Bell, 1276
Bell, Tyree Harris, **154**
"Bell Brandon" (song), 1103
Belle Boyd, in Camp and Prison, 201
Bellechasse Plantation, 1333
Belle Grove, 271
Belle Isle Prison, **154–155**, 1266, 1268, 1353, 1667
  Kilpatrick-Dahlgren raid, 892–893
Belle of the Fifties, A (Clay-Clopton), 351
Bell family, 224
Bellona Iron Works (Richmond), 96, 98, 1117, 1122
Belmont, August, 1454
Belmont, Missouri, **155–157**, 438, 835, 1652–1653
Belvidere Baptist Church (Richmond), 212
Beman, Nathan S. S., 841
Benavides, Santos, **157**
Ben Bolt (Hewitt), 1590
Bench and the Bar of the South and Southwest, The (Foote), 600
Benedict, Michael Les, *as contributor*, 847–849
Benedict Arnold (Simms), 1590
Bent, Stephen Vincent, 136, 161
Benezet, Anthony, 43
Benjamin, Judah P., **157–162**, *250*, 273, 492, 911, 952, 1385, 1454
  as attorney general, 159, 206, 231, 251, 452
  on British neutrality, 1528–1529
  cabinet positions, 1248, 1528
  critics of, 599, 858, 872, 1157
  election to U.S. Senate, 709

Hampton Roads Conference, 804
likeness on Treasury note, 438, *445*
New Plan, 1140
persona, 1528
prominence in Confederacy, 383, 385, 845–846, 1157
retirement to England, 1529–1530
as secretary of state, 160, 251, 483, 485, 632, 689, 781, 884, 924, 980–981, 1004, 1016, 1354
as secretary of war, 90, 148, 159–160, 174, 245, 251, 410, 474, 640, 654, 834, 947, 979, 1075–1076, 1094, 1334, 1619, 1684, 1686, 1700
and slavery, 75, 160, 808
Benjamin, Ninnette, 159
Bennett, James, and Lucy Bennett, 1153
Bennett, Joseph, 1023
Bennett, Thomas H., 1023
Bennett and Lurges, 97–98
Benning, Henry L., **162–163**, 497
Bensel, Richard Franklin, *as contributor*, 249–252
Bentley, Lee M., 864
Benton, Samuel, **163**
Benton, Thomas Hart, 163, *381*, 597, 599, 802, 828, 1336
Bentonville, North Carolina, 117, **163–164**, 262, 715, 943, 1152, 1323
Bergeron, Arthur W., Jr., *as contributor*, 235–237, 991–994
Bergreen, Alan, 488
Beringer, Richard E., *as contributor*, 325–329, 524–525
Berkeley County, Virginia, 1413
Bermuda
blockade running, 177, 185
transshipment of supplies, 699
Bermuda (ship), 180, 184, 1242, 1469
Bermuda Hundred, Virginia, 496, 1209
Bernard, George N., 999
Bernard, Simon, 617
Berrien, John McPherson, 137
Berry, Harrison, **164**
Berry, Ike, 725
Berryville Canyon, Virginia, 1418
Bertonneau, E. Arnold, 1348
Bethune, Thomas ("Blind Tom"), 109, 307
Beulah (Evans), 547
Bible
British procurement, 165
Confederate parallels in, 568, 1399
publishing, 194
and slavery, 1449–1450
Bible societies, 130, **164–165**, 194, 1320
sermons, 1400
Bible Society of the Confederate States, 165
Biblical Recorder (newspaper), 130
Bibliography and historiography, **165–171**
Civil War causes, 317–318
Civil War interpretations, 949
contemporary histories, 1229
guides to archival collections, 1098
proslavery literature, 1273
selected bibliography, 167–171
Southern Historical Society, **1512**
themes of historical writing, 166–167
Bickley, George W. L., 411–412
Big Bethel, Virginia, **171–172**, 930, 989
Lane, James, 907
map, 172
Richmond Howitzers, 1306
Big Blue River, 1254
Big Chief, 1173
Biggs, Asa, 355
Big Kennesaw, 1683
Big Peck. *See* Peck, William Raine
Big Shanty, Georgia, 41, 109
Bilharz, Hall, and Company, 1456
Bill of Rights, 1531
Biloxi, Mississippi, 1502
Bindswanger, Nathan, 845
Birney, James G., 44, 1010
Birth of a Nation, The (film), 575–577, 938, 949
Bishop, John Peale, 939
Bisland, Louisiana, 1428
Black belt, **172–173**
Blackburn's Ford, Virginia, 945, 975, 996
Black Codes, 257, 1172, 1699
Black Diamonds (Pollard), 1228
Black Dog, 1173
Blackford's Ford. *See* Boteler's Ford
Black Hawk, 450
Black Horse Troop, 267
Blackmar, Henry Clay, 1101
Blackmar and Brother, 1101, 1103
Blacks. *See* African Americans in the Confederacy; African American troops in the Union Army; Army; Emancipation; Free people of color; Navy, Confederate; Slavery
Blacksmiths, 793, 902
Blackwood's Magazine, 479
Blada, V. *See* Volck, Adalbert
Bladenboro, North Carolina, bread riots, 213
Blaine, James G., 774
Blair, Francis P.
on Calhoun (John C.), 253
Hampton Roads Conference, 256, 733, 804, 1184
peace advocacy, 1063, 1386 1541
Blair, Francis P., Jr., 1321
Blair, Frank, 838, 1052, 1053, 1251, 1729
Blair, Montgomery, 1242, 1321
Blair, William Alan, *as contributor*, 26–27, 208, 501–505, 582–583, 775–776, 1304–1305, 1372, 1729–1731
Blair's Landing, Louisiana, 1316, 1317
Blakely, Alexander T., 102–103, 1120
Blakely guns, 49, 50, 93, 94, 102–103, 1119, 1120
Blakey, Arch Fredric, *as contributor*, 122, 458–459, 776, 1013, 1020, 1090, 1175–1176, 1345, 1364, 1688, 1734
Blanchard, Albert Gallatin, **173–174**
Blandford, Mark Hardin, **174**
Blandwood, 715
Blankets, 817
Blease, Coleman L., 372
Bledsoe, Albert T., **174–175**, 476, 583, 1035, 1082
Bledsoe family, 224
Bleeding Kansas, **175–176**
and caning of Sumner, 1560, 1561–1562
guerrilla warfare, 719
peacekeeping force, 1551
see also Kansas-Nebraska Act
Blelock & Co., 1256
"Blind Tom." *See* Bethune, Thomas ("Blind Tom")
Blockade, **176–186**
Anglo-Confederate Trading Company, **43**
announcement of, 480, 1353
British neutrality, 484, 711, 712, 1528, 1748, 1749
Brownsville, Texas, 231–232, 233
Confederate attack on, 822, 1125, 1129
Confederate substitute goods, **1558–1559**
cotton diplomacy, 418, 480–481, 507–508, 1687
Cuba, 432
damage to Savannah economy, 1366–1367
Davids, 445, 446
European cotton famine, 632–632, 1194

Blockade, *continued*
Florida, 590, 591
Fort Pulaski, Georgia, 616
Galveston, Texas, 655, 1586
growth, 980
inflation relationship, 820, 821
initiation, 1508
lead shortages, 90
legitimacy, 1527, 1528
luxury items, 287, 1727, 1741
Maffitt, John N., 984
minerals and metals shipments, 699, 913, 1147–1148
Mobile, Alabama, 1057–1058
New Orleans, Louisiana, 178, *1562*, 1563
New Plan, **1140–1141**
overview article, **176–179**
profiteers, 591
runners, 2–3, 42, 116, 129, 177–178, **183–186**, 240, 254, 256, 368, 685, 712, 726, 744, 757, 963, 1107, 1123, 1124, 1130, 1152, 1156, 1157, 1169, 1242, 1353, 1429, 1465, 1469, 1491, 1509, 1537, 1567, 1647, 1648, 1726, 1727
running, **179–183**, 507–508, 591–592, 711–712, 905, 992
Semmes (Raphael) strategy, 1393, 1563
ship bonding, 592
shortages caused by, 471–472
social impact, 1491
submarines, 1556, 1557
torpedo expeditions, 289, 1516
Wilkinson, John, 1723, 1727
Wilmington, North Carolina, 1726, 1727
see also Commerce raiders; Privateers; particular blockade runners
Bloody Angle (Spotsylvania), 82, 609, 746, 908, 1195, 1582
Daniel (Junius) at, 443
"Bloody Bill." *See* Anderson, William
Bloody Hill (Wilson's Creek campaign), 1730
Bloody Lane, battle for the (Sharpsburg), 29, 36, 1408
Blount County, Alabama, 516
Blue and the Gray, The (film), 573
Blue and the Gray, The (television program), 580
Blue Caps, 1215
Blue Ridge Mountains, 1415
Blue Springs, Tennessee, 761
Bluffton movement, **186**, 568
Blunt, James G., 305, 722, 814, 1254, 1255, 1607, 1609
Prairie Grove, Arkansas, 1246–1247
Boarding pikes, 515
Board of Relief (Columbia, South Carolina), 370
Boatwright, James, 1179
Bocock, Thomas S., **186–187**, 273, 361
Boetticher, Otto, 1262
Boggs, William Robertson, **187**, 753
Bogler's Creek, Alabama, 1389
"Bohemian." *See* Shepardson, William
Bold, Thomas, 674
Bold Hunter (ship), 674
Bolt projectiles, 61
Bonaparte, Napoleon. *See* Napoleon I, emperor of France
Bonding, ship ransom, 20, 592
Bonds, **187–190**, 1024, 1280
archival collections, 1099
banking, 128–129
cotton, 181, 980, 992, 1616
direct taxes, 1569
Erlanger loan, 536
foreign trade, 507
and inflation, 392–393, 509, 803
as legal tender, 499, 659, 660, 665
as military rail transport payment, 1296
produce loan, 1270
Provisional Congress, 1069
state issues, 18, 462, 590
unacceptability of Confederate, 1242
see also Debt; Treasury notes
Boney, F. N., *as contributor*, 228–230, 667–673, 925–926, 1479–1481
Bonham, Milledge L., **190–192**, 474, 701, 703, 891, 972, 1244–1245, 1431, *1505*, 1509, 1510
Bonner, Sherwood, 937
"Bonnie Blue Flag, The" (song), 487, 587, 735, 836, 1101, 1498, 1590
Bonnin, Patricia Dora, *as contributor*, 416–420
Bonsal, Louis, 222
Booby traps, 1300
Book publishing, **193–194**, 671, 1232
book mail rates, 1241
Mobile, Alabama, 1059
rare book collections, 1099
textbook, **1587–1588**
see also Literature
Boomerang, The (film), 574
Boone, North Carolina, 1152
Boone, William P., 1088
Boonsboro, Virginia. *See* South Mountain, Virginia
Boonville, Missouri, 1009, 1251, 1253, 1254, 1409
Booth, John Wilkes, **194–195**, 545
Lincoln (Abraham) assassination, 145, 538, 545, 934–935
Booth, Lionel F., 614, 615
Booth, Sherman, 1534
"Booth Killed Lincoln" (song), 487, 1104
Boots. *See* Shoes and boots
Border Rangers, 843
Border states, **195–197**, 333, 383
American party, 28
brothers of war, 224
election of 1860, 522, 523
Emancipation Proclamation, 530
manpower, 69
map, 384
Montgomery convention role, 1067, 1068
population, 339, 1233
Republican party, 1321–1322
slavery, 4, 6, 390, 551, 558, 1337
tobacco farming, 1598
U.S. Confiscation Act, 390
Washington Peace Conference, 1689
see also Delaware; Kentucky; Maryland; Missouri; West Virginia
Borglum, Gutzon, 573, 952, 1073
Borglum, Solon, 951, 952
Bormann fuze, 61
"Born again" soldiers, 1034
Bosserman, Alden, 314
Bossieux, Virginius, 154
Boston Club (New Orleans), 1397
Boston Post Road, 1338
Botany, medical, 757–758, 759
Boteler, Alexander R., **197–198**, 783, 864, 1700
Boteler, Helen, 198
Boteler's Ford (Potomac River), 1406, 1408
Botetourt Artillery, 1237, 1238
Bott, John M., 209
Botts, Henry Minor, 314
Botts, John Minor, 123
Botts Grays, 144
Botume, Elizabeth, 307
Boubalina (ship), 368
Boudinot, Elias C., **198–199**, 812, 983, 984, 1693
Bowen, John Stevens, **199**, 664, 713, 1236, 1237, 1605
Bowen & Co., 1245
Bowie, Walter, 546
Bowie knives, 16, 60, 817
Bowlegs, Billy (Sonaki Mikko), 1390
Bowser, Mary Elizabeth, 1652
Box and Cox (Morton), 1590

Boyce, W. W., **199–201**, 877, 878, 1172, 1184, *1505*
peace movement, 1224, 1225
Boycott, 1739
Boyd, Belle, **201–202**, 387, 543, 1680
Boyd, David F., 957
Boyd, James, 939
Boydton Plank Road. *See* Hatcher's Run, battle of
Boykin, Burwell, 979
Boyle, Gamble, and MacFee, *513*, 514
Boyles, J. R., 1190
Boynton, H. V., 1073
"Boys, Keep Your Powder Dry" (song), 1232
Bracken, Peter J., 41
Bradford, Alexander Blackburn, **202–203**
Bradford, William F., 615
Bradley, Benjamin Franklin, **203**
Brady, Allen G., 1221
Brady, Mathew, 577, 873, 1231; *see also* various photographs throughout encyclopedia
Bragg, Braxton, **203–206**, 211, 952, 1172, 1386, 1408, 1433, 1544, *1577*
anti-Bragg faction, 85-86, 87, 296, 775, 777, 946, 1011-1012, 1227-1228; *see also subhead* personality conflicts *below*
Army of Tennessee, 67, 72, 84, 85–87, 204–205, 296, 313, 361, 595, 775–776, 777, 790, 838, 1613, 1658, 1707, 1717
Army of the West, 1515
Averasboro, North Carolina, 117–118
battle flag, 586
Chattanooga campaign, 86–87, 292–295, 302, 738, 895, 897, 1386
Chickamauga campaign, 204–205, 214, 302–304, 327
conscription, 398, 399
criticism of, 239, 244, 475, 1661
Davis (Jefferson) view of, 453
hospital administration, 1549
intelligence operations, 544
Kentucky campaign. *See* Kentucky campaign of Bragg
Knoxville campaign, 895, 897, 1563
martial law imposition, 109, 599
Murfreesboro, Tennessee, 1094–1096
newspaper censorship, 1143
offensive in West, 1473
offer of volunteer to shoot, 1096
personality conflicts, 33, 67, 205-206, 214, 296, 353, 361, 607, 969-970, 1096, 1227-1228, 1679; *see also subhead* anti-Bragg faction *above*
and press, 273–274
railroad troop movement, 1298
recall, 72, 73, 1386
Santa Rosa Island, 613–614
Shiloh campaign, 149, 691, 830, 1420, 1421, 1422, 1423
staff, 35, 340, 498, 605, 648, 973, 1186
strategy, 1248
Wilmington, North Carolina, 611, 612, 1727
Yellow Tavern, Virginia, 1751
Bragg, John, 206
Bragg, Thomas, **206–207**, 251, 1152
Brain, John C., 375, 1269
Bramlette, Thomas Elliott, 216, 702, 887
Branch, Anthony Martin, **207**, 710
Branch, Lawrence O'Bryan, **207–208**, 907
death at Sharpsburg, 1408
Gaines' Mill, Virginia, 653
Branch banking, 128
Brandon, William Lindsay, **208**
Brandy Station, Virginia, 81, **208–211**, 269, 677, 1342
Barringer, Rufus, 134
Butler, Matthew Calbraith, 246
Hampton, Wade, 134, 731
Jones, William Edmondson ("Grumble"), 869
Lee, William Henry Fitzhugh, 921
map, 209
Stuart, J. E. B., 1553
Brannan, John, 302
Branson and Farrar, 1588
Brantley, William Felix. *See* Brantly, William Felix
Brantly, William Felix, **211**
Bratton, John, **211–212**
Bravay and Company, 903
Brazil, neutrality proclamation, 480
Brazos Santiago, Texas, 233, 234, 1611
Bread riots, **212–213**, 332, 346, 387, 461, 559, 566–567, 596, 900, 901, 1517, 1648, 1740
Atlanta, Georgia, 109, 212, 1226
Columbia, South Carolina, 371
free markets, 642
Macon, Georgia, 212, 978, 1226
Mobile, Alabama, 1058, 1226
Richmond, Virginia, 212–213, 346, 1226, 1306, 1331, 1669, 1740
Texas, 1586
Breaman, J. D., 777
Breastworks, 81, 325, 624, 626
Breckinridge, John (father of Robert J.), 215
Breckinridge, John C., 108, 196, **213–215**, 217, 519, 1355, 1363, 1673, 1743, 1748
Army of Tennessee, 84, 87, 139, 214, 1706
attack on Baton Rouge, 140–141
caricature, *335*
Chickamauga campaign, 214, 304
Democratic party, 465
election of 1860, 14, 109, 118, 131, 137, 138, 213–214, 276, *494*, **521–524**, 588, 655, 664, 667, 745, 753, 779, 802–803, 869, 907, 976–977, 1011, 1047, 1065, 1087, 1097, 1137, 1150, 1151, 1164, 1175, 1370, 1375, 1376, 1454, 1483, 1506, 1551, 1583, 1630, 1678, 1699, 1744
Lynchburg defense, 963
Marion, Virginia, 1547
Murfreesboro, Tennessee, 1094, 1096
New Market, Virginia, 1135–1136
New Orleans defense, 954
Orphan Brigade command, 1170
Port Hudson, Louisiana, 1238
press support, 1483
on secession, 1637
as secretary of war, 149, 214–215, 251, 256, 1684, 1687–1688
Shiloh campaign, 1420, 1421, 2022
staff, 779, 1210, 1250, 1622
surrender negotiations, 1313
Tennessee raids, 685–686
troop recruitment, 720
Breckinridge, Robert J., **215–217**, 887, 889, 1320
Oath of Allegiance, 1163
Breckinridge, Robert J., Jr., **217**
Brent, Joseph L., 1611, 1697
Br'er Rabbit stories, 1450
Brevard, Theodore Washington, **218**, 1566
Brewer, James H., 5
Brewer, Susan, 1034
Briarfield Arsenal, 98
Brice's Cross Roads, Mississippi, **218–219**, 239, 1051, 1624
map, 218
Bridgeford, D. B., *77*, *80*
Bridgers, Robert R., **219–220**
Bridges, Eloise, 1590
Bridges
Antietam, Maryland, *1339*
burning of, 263, 1340

Bridges, *continued*
construction, 534, 1340
James River, 1340
pontoon, 293, 295, *534*, 1007
Brief Enquiry into the True Nature and Character of our Federal Government (Upshur), 1395
Brierfield Plantation. *See* Davis Bend
Brigade, 66
attack formation, 819
Barksdale's Mississippi, **132–133**
European, 603–604
Gartrell's, 665
Hood's Texas, 81, 716, 751, 789, **791**, 816, 1343
infantry, 92
Irish, 823
Laurel, 459, 870, 1341–1342
McGowan's, 816
organization and nicknames, 816
Orphan, 508, 736, 816, 888, 929, 1170
Stonewall, 816, 836, 1190, **1548–1549**
Bright, John, 1454
"Brighton Camp" (song), 1103
Brisbane, William Henry, 44
Bristoe Station, Virginia, **220–221**, 880, 894
Cooke, John Rogers, 408
Hill, A. P., 81, 771
Lee, Robert E., 918–919
map, 220
Bristol, Tennessee, railroads, 1297
Britain. *See* Great Britain
British West Indies, proslavery, 1273
Broadhorns, 1692
Broadsides, **221–222**, 1232
Brock, R. A., 1512
Brock, Sallie A., **222**, 1330
Brockenbrough, John Mercer, **222–223**, 1676
Brockenbrough, John White, **223**, 1337
Brodine, Charles E., Jr., *as contributor*, 1017–1018
Bromly & Company, 1044
Bromwell, W. J., 193
Brooke, John M., **223**, 709, 863, 1127, 1236, 1725
ironclad design, 992
naval ordnance design, 96, 1117–1118, 1121, 1124
patents, 1181
Virginia design, 1670
Brooke, Walker, **223–224**
Brooke rifle, 93, 96, 97, 223, *1117*
Brooklyn (ship), 613, 1137, 1393, *1562*, 1563
Brooks, Cleanth, 938
Brooks, Joseph, 661
Brooks, Preston S., 175, 190, 322, 787, 876, 1310, 1715
caning of Sumner (Charles), 1560, 1561
Brooks, William, 1082–1083
Broome, James E., 1688
Brothels. *See* Prostitution
Brother against Brother (film), 574
Brothers of war, **224**
McIntosh brothers, 973
Terrill family, 1581
Broun, William, 913, 1471
Brown, Albert Gallatin, **224–226**, 557, 598, 808, 1047, *1050*, 1051
Brown, Benjamin Gratz, 1322
Brown, Charles A., 261
Brown, George, 127
Brown, Isaac Newton, **226–227**
Brown, Jacob, 231
Brown, John, 740, *741*, 832, 1112
guerrilla activity in Kansas, 175, 176, 322, 719
raid. *See under* Harpers Ferry, West Virginia
Stuart (J. E. B.) encounter with, 1551
Brown, John Calvin, **227–228**, 1179
Brown, Joseph E., **228–230**, 600, 909, 929, 1168, 1386, 1601
conscription opposition, 397, 474, 872, 1535
criticism of, 1625–1626
defense of Georgia, 1475
election campaign, 786
Fort Pulaski seizure, 1366
as Georgia governor, 13, 111, 137, 176, 314, 667–669, 670, 673, 674, 701, 702, 703–704, 772, 773, 845, 854, 1142, 1144, 1623
obstructionist policies, 331, 387, 1093, 1224, 1225, 1249
opposition to Davis (Jefferson), 29, 882, 1655
peace proposals, 1184, 1542, 1543
pike advocacy, **846**
rifle confiscation, 360
secession, 1377, 1536
speculation policy, 1517
state rights advocacy, 228–229, 346, 1535, 1536, 1539, 1540, 1541, 1551, 1679
state-supported schools, 515
Western and Atlantic Railroad, 1294
Brown, Josephine, 543
Brown, Joseph N., 1520
Brown, Kent Masterton, *as contributor*, 163, 533–535, 913–914
Brown, Lizinka Campbell, 549–550
Brown, Norman D., *as contributor*, 1523–1524
Brown, Richard H., *as contributor*, 1055–1056
Brown, William H., 254
Browne, William M., **230**, 251, 1528
Brown Fellowship Society of Charleston, 1486
Browning, Orville, 390
Browning, Robert S., III, *as contributor*, 22, 407, 605–606, 699–700, 839–841, 960, 1018–1019
Brownlow, "Parson." *See* Brownlow, William G.
Brownlow, William G., **230–231**, 273, 373, 746, 895, 1143, 1399, 1573–1574, 1638
clemency recommendations, 657
as Tennessee governor, 703, 1111, 1578–1579
Unionism, 640, 1576
Brown's Gap, Virginia, 1418, 1419
Brown's Hotel (Washington, D.C.), 1089
Brown's Island explosion, 316
Brownsville, Texas, **231–234**
as "backdoor to the Confederacy," 232
battles, **233–234**
city, **231–232**
Bruce, Charles, 1384, 1385
Bruce, Dickson, D., Jr., *as contributor*, 497
Bruce, Edward Caledon, 1231
Bruce, Eli M., **234**
Bruce, George B., 1105
Bruce, Horatio Washington, **234–235**
Brumby, Arnoldus, 519
Bruns, John, 1683
Brunswick rifle, 1467
Bryan, Charles F., Jr., *as contributor*, 291–292, 744–746, 750–751
Bryan, Goode, **235**
Bryan, Joseph, 604
Bryant's Minstrels, 488
Buchanan, Franklin, 31, **235–237**, 567, 605, 840, 863, 993, *1127*, 1568, 1670
Mobile Squadron, 1059, 1062, 1126, 1130, 1580–1581
Buchanan, James, *381*, *494*, 1375, 1380, 1395, 1454
appointments, 698, 975, 991
cabinet, 359, 410, 592, 1594

Fort Sumter negotiations, 133, 312, 589, 613, 627
Fort Sumter reinforcements, 1507, 1526
John Brown's raid, 741
Morrill Act veto, 348
as president, 213, 230, 322, 527, 529, 583, 617, 709, 1171, 1628, 1630
on secession, 324
and slavery issue, 176, 465, 557, 808
Buck, Lucy Rebecca, 471
Buckland, Ralph, 1422
Buckland Mills, Virginia, **237**
Buckner, Simon Bolivar, 86, 196, 214, **238–239**, 416, 637, 779, 850, 851, 887, 1611, 1744
Henry and Donelson campaign, 125, 593, 766, 767, 1211
Munfordville, Kentucky, 1093
Orphan Brigade command, 1170
Perryville, Kentucky, 1197
staff, 447
Buckner Hospital, 152
Budd, Captain, 1603
Buell, Don Carlos, 7, 328, 825, 1298, 1473, 1577
Kentucky campaign, 887, 888, 889, 890, 891, 1086
Mill Springs, Kentucky, 1041, 1042
Munfordville, Kentucky, 1093
Nashville occupation, 767, 1109, 1420, 1576
Perryville, Kentucky, 1196, 1197, 1198
Shiloh campaign, 327, 685, 1423
supply line, 1088
"Buffaloes" (Union sympathizers), 1152
Buffington Island, Ohio, 1089
Buford, Abraham, 219, **239**, 964, 1177, 1371, 1625
Buford, Jefferson, 175
Buford, John
Brandy Station, 209, 211, 269
Gettysburg campaign, 678, 679
Bugle, *1105*
Buie, Mary Ann, 1726
Bujac and Bennett, 97, 98
Bulletin (Memphis newspaper), 1143
Bullets. *See* Cartridges; Minié ball
Bulloch, James Dunwoody, 179, 180, **239–240**, 368, 903, 904, 1547, 1684, 1723
commerce raiding, 375
Shenandoah purchase, 1411
ship #290, 1393
ship procurement, 19, 26, 42, 116, 484, 992, 1129, 1130, 1150, 1303
twin-screw vessels, 186
Bullock, Robert, **241**
Bullock, Rufus, 774, 928, 1476, 1543
Bull Run, Virginia. *See* Manassas, First; Manassas, Second
Bummers, **241**, *242*, 260, 261, 601
Bumpass, Orville, 1277
Burbridge, John Q., 343
Burbridge, Stephen G., 216, 725, 888, 1089, 1363
Burch, John, 1143
Bureau for Colored Troops, U.S., 11, 12
Bureau of Conscription. *See* Conscription Bureau
Bureau of Foreign Supplies, 699, 1687
Bureau of Indian Affairs, 812, 1685
Bureau of Inspection, 308
Bureau of Medicine and Surgery
creation, 1123
Navy Department office, 1127–1128
Bureau of Military Information, U.S., 541
Bureau of Military Justice, U.S., 1264
Bureau of Orders and Detail
creation, 1123
Forrest, French, 605
Mitchell, John K., 1056, 1127
Navy Department, 1127
Rousseau, Lawrence, 1349
Bureau of Ordnance and Hydrography
Brooke, John M., 223
creation, 1123
duties, 1127
ordnance design, 96, 223, 1117–1118, 1121, 1124
Bureau of Provisions and Clothing
creation, 1123
Navy Department office, 1128
Bureau of War, 1685–1686
Burgess's Mill. *See* Hatcher's Run, battle of
Burgwyn, Henry King, Jr., 1650
Burial. *See* Funerals
Burial of Latané, The (painting), **242**, *243*, 459–460, 951, 1231, 1554
Burke, Boykin, and Company, 193, 937
Burnaby, Andrew, 1531
Burnett, Henry C., **243–244**
Burnett, Theodore Legrand, **244**
Burning, The (Shenandoah Valley), 583, 1733
Burns, Anthony, 650
Burns, Ken, and Ric Burns, 574
Burnside, Ambrose E., 79, 244–245, 279, 336, 544, 637, 1075, 1149, 1650, 1724, 1736
Chattanooga campaign, 293
Dumfries raid, 269
Fredericksburg campaign, 637, 638, 639, 640, 918
Manassas, First, 997, 998
Morgan's raids, 1089
in North Carolina. *See* Burnside's expedition to North Carolina
Petersburg campaign, 1199, 1200
Sharpsburg campaign, 1408
Spotsylvania campaign, 1518–1519
in Tennessee, 895–896
Burnside's expedition to North Carolina, **244–245**, 666, 1152
Burr, Aaron, 426
Burr, David J., 1460
Burrell, Isaac, 656
Burrison, John A., *as contributor*, 735
Burt, E. B., 226
Burton, James H., 90, 740, 1168, 1460
Burton, Orville Vernon, *as contributor*, 416–420, 562–565, 1483–1493, 1597–1599
Burton bullet. *See* Minié ball
Bushwhackers, 671, 1155, 1610, 1705; *see also* Guerrilla warfare
Business. *See* Economy
Busteed, Richard, 1478
Butler, Andrew P., 787, 1560, 1561
Butler, Benjamin F., 127, 254, 385, 804, 1419–1420, 1444, 1504, 1673, 1736
assault on Richmond, 149, 496, 850, 894, 1666
attack on Fort Fisher, 1152
Big Bethel, Virginia, 171, 172
black troops, 10, 11, 12
contraband, 405
enlistment of tories, 1602
and fugitive slaves, 7, 900
New Orleans occupation, 6, 159, 178, 645, 954, 956, 1101, 1138, 1139, 1140, 1163
Norfolk, Virginia, 1150
outlaw status, 1258
prisoner exchanges, 761, 1258, 1262
woman order. *See* Butler's woman order
Butler, Matthew Calbraith, 210, **245–246**, 267, 499
Butler, Pierce, 161
Butler's woman order, **246–247**, 1138
Butterfield Overland Mail, 983, 1339
Butternut. *See* Unionism
Buttons, Confederate uniform, *1635*
Bybee, J. N., 30
Bynum, Victoria E., *as contributor*, 222, 265, 1009–1010, 1188
Byrne, Edward, 1170

Byrne, Frank L., *as contributor*, 38–40, 154–155, 265–266, 610, 856–857, 1221–1222, 1256–1264, 1265–1268, 1734–1735

C

Cabaniss, E. G., 1623
Cabell, Mary Hopkins, 215
Cabell, William Lewis, **249**, 1254
Cabin Creek, Oklahoma, 12, 1694
Cabinet, **249–252**
  appointments, 892, 1126
  assassination plot, 893
  conflicts, 1024, 1243
  creation, 452
  flight from Richmond, 715, 993–994, 1130
  last meeting, 715
  prewar politics, 1225
  restructuring, 1687
  seats in Congress, 400
  selection, 1248
  state representation, 206, 250, 991, 1678
  term-limitation bill, 1396
  unpopular members, 1528
  see also particular departments and members
Cable, George Washington, 937, 938
Cache, battle of the, 1355
Caddos, 305, 811, 813
Cade, Edward W., 974
Cadet Rangers, 312
Cahaba Prison, 1267
Cahaba Rifles, 1087
Cailloux, André, 645, 1239
Caird and Company, 2
Caissons, 91
Caldwell, James Fitz, 1721
Caleb Cushing (ship), 592, 1309
Calhoon, Robert M., *as contributor*, 1247
Calhoun, James M., 109, 110
Calhoun, John C., 109, **252–253**, *381*, 497, 1167, 1171, 1285
  Fort Hill plantation, 613
  as leader of South, 186, 542, 802, 1014, 1024, 1629, 3450
  likeness on postal stamp, 1242, 1523, *1523*
  nullification doctrine, 730, 1113, 1160, 1207, 1324, 1374, 1377, 1533, 1715
  slavery defense, 319, 552, 555, 557, 803, 1533
  state rights advocacy, 253, 321, 347, 383, 439, 1399, 1532–1533, 1536
Calhoun, Ransom, 497
Calhoun (ship), 1269
California
  election of 1860, 521
  horses and mules supply, 791–793
  statehood and slavery issues, 321, 380, 381, 554, 555, 556, 557, 650, 1374, 1533
Calkins, Chris, *as contributor*, 45–48, 186–187, 218, 406–407, 627, 690, 728–729, 1186, 1591, 1711–1712
Callahan, Samuel Benton, 199, **253–254**, 812
Call certificates, 187, *188*, 189, 190
Camalier, Vincent, 547
Camanche (ship), 354
Cambridge (ship), 177
Camden, South Carolina, 1510
Camden Expedition. *See* Arkansas campaign of 1864
Camels, supply transport, 1697
Cameron, John, 731
Cameron, Paul, 1151
Cameron & Company, 98
Camilla (ship), **254**
Camp, Raleigh S., 75
Campaigns, election. *See entries titled* Election
Campaigns, military. *See* particular campaigns, e.g., Vicksburg campaign
Camp Asylum, South Carolina, 1268
Campbell, A. G., 243
Campbell, Alexander William, **254–255**
Campbell, Archibald, 1321
Campbell, Edward D. C., Jr., *as contributor*, 515–517, 572–580, 1230–1232, 1587–1588, 1589–1590
Campbell, James, 1587–1588
Campbell, John A., **255–256**, 410, 708, 872, 1080, 1338, 1385, 1387, 1541, 1684, 1685, 1687, 1688
  Hampton Roads Conference, 256, 733, 804
Campbell, Josiah A. Patterson, **257**
Campbell, William B., 264, 1578
Campbell and Co., 1169
Camp Chase, Ohio, 716
Camp Douglas, Illinois, 1261
  conspiracy, 1159, 1595
Camp followers. *See* Prostitution
Camp Ford, Texas, 1267, 1268
Camp [Francis T.] Nicholls Confederate Soldiers' Home of Louisiana, 1502
Camp Groce, Texas, 1267
Camp Hoffman, Maryland. *See* Point Lookout Prison
Camp Jackson, Missouri, 828
Camp Morton, 1261
Camp Sorghum, South Carolina, 370, 1268
Camp Sumter, Georgia. *See* Andersonville Prison
Canada, **257–258**
  annexation, 711
  clandestine operations, 160, 258, 348–350, 538–539, 543, 545, 546–547, 1261, 1271–1272, 1595
Canadian River, 1290
Canals, 259, 1612, 1692
Canard, Motey, 425
Canby, Edward R. S., 588, 1136, 1427, 1572, 1611, 1695
Cane River Crossing, Louisiana, 1316, 1317
Canister projectile, 61–62, 93, 94, 95, 101
Cannibals All! or, Slaves without Masters (Fitzhugh), 583
Cannon, Walker, 445
Cannons, 93, 96
  batteries, 625
  English imports, 102–103
  fort, 94, 623
  Gosport Navy Yard seizure, 62, 100
  iron field carriages, 49
  see also Rifled guns
Cantabro (ship), 491
Canteen, 817
Cantey, James, 113, **258–259**
Canton (ship), 375
Cantrell, Mark Lea ("Beau"), *as contributor*, 454
Cape Fear (ship), 1727
Cape Fear Minutemen, 1726
Cape Fear River, 1691
  Fort Fisher, North Carolina, 48, 611, 622
  Wilmington, North Carolina, 1726–1727
Capers, Ellison, **259**, 312
Capers, Francis Withers, 674
Capers, Henry, 315
Caperton, Allen T., **259–260**, 1700
Capitalism
  antebellum South and, 1112
  see also State socialism
Capital punishment. *See* Crime and punishment, executions; Hanging
Capitol (ship), 726
Capitol building (Richmond), *1331*

"Capitol Legislature" (Alabama), 928
Captain's Bride, The (Herrington), 1232
Capture of Courtland, Alabama, The (play), 1231
Captured Property Act of 1863, U.S., 390
Carbines. *See under* Long arms
Caribbean
  Confederate privateering, 1393
  expansion of slavery, 551, 555–556, 556, 557, 688
  slave labor, 1436
  U.S. sugar imports, 1560
  see also British West Indies; particular islands
Caricature
  abolitionists, *649*, *933*
  blockade, *177*
  collapse of Confederacy, *335*
  contraband, *405*
  Crittenden Compromise, *429*
  Davis, Jefferson, *335*, *412*, *732*, 951
  Dred Scott decision, *494*
  election of 1864, *412*
  Great Britain, *712*
  Jackson, Claiborne F., *1054*
  Lincoln, Abraham, *412*, *494*, *933*, *1044*, 1673
  miscegenation, *1044*
  quality, 1231
  Volck, Adalbert, 1673–1674
Carleton, Mark T., *as contributor*, 140–141, 957
Carlile, John S., 1699, 1700, 1702
Carlin, James, 183
Carlisle, James, 1566
Carlota, Mexico, 1252, 1409
Carlton, David L, *as contributor*, 1641–1648
Carmichael, Peter S., *as contributor*, 24–25, 150–151, 208–211, 271, 718, 944–947, 988–989, 1299–1300, 1706
"Carolina" (Timrod), 937
Carolina Art Association, 285
Carolinas campaign of Sherman, **260–262**
  Bentonville, North Carolina, 163
  map, 261
  North Carolina, 1152–1153
  Raleigh, North Carolina, 1301
  South Carolina, 1510
  strategic intent, 328–329
Carondelet (ship), 55, 264, *766*, 1134, *1135*
Carpenter, J. E., 1103
Carpenter brothers, 224
Carpenter, The; or, the Stranger in Gray (film), 574
Carr, Eugene A., 526
Carrigan, A. H., 1349
Carroll, David W., **262–263**
Carroll, William Henry, **263**, 428, 429
Carson, Kit, 51, 1136
Cartel (prisoner exchange), 1266
Carter, George Washington, 207
Carter, John Carpenter, **263–264**
Carter, Jonathan H., **264**, 1055
Cartes de visite, 1230, 1231
Cartland, Fernando, 1494
Cartoons. *See* Caricature
Cartridges
  box, 63, 817, *1495*
  bullet wounds, 756
  lead, 1470
  manufacture, 285, 1470, 1471
  output, 90
Caruthers, Robert Looney, **264–265**, 600, 703, 1576
Cary, Hetty, **265**
Case shot, 61, 93
Cash, W. J., 949
Cash crop system, 1214, 1215
Cashin, Joan E., *as contributor*, 456–457
Casket of Reminiscences (Foote), 600
Cass, Lewis, 380, *381*
Cassville Standard (newspaper), 1738
Castle Godwin, 265
Castleman, John B., 349
Castle Morgan Prison. *See* Cahaba Prison
Castle Pinckney, South Carolina, *1265*, 1266, 1507
Castle Thunder Prison, **265–266**, 1266
  civilian prisoners, 727
  investigation of conditions, 767
Casualties. *See* Civil War, losses and numbers; Death and mourning; Health and medicine; *under* Generals; *under* Strategy and tactics; *under* particular battles
Catawbas, 811, 1069
Catholicism. *See* Roman Catholic Church
Catlett's Station, Virginia, Stuart's raid, 269, 1553, 1554
Cattle-rustling. *See* Beefsteak raid
Catton, Bruce, and William Catton, 1293
Cavalry, **266–270**
  Ashby, Turner, 104–105
  Buckland Mills, Virginia, 237
  Butler, Matthew Calbraith, 246
  Chambliss, John Randolph, Jr., 277–278
  Chancellorsville campaign, 279
  congressional bill, 1714
  depredations, 1153–1154
  dismounted, 270
  Early, Jubal, 268, 276–277
  edged weapons, 513, *1462*
  Forrest, Nathan Bedford, 266, 267, 302, 606–607
  Hampton, Wade, 731
  horse supply, 792, 793
  insignia and colors, 1633
  Iron Brigade, 1409
  Jones, William Edmondson ("Grumble"), 869
  Lee, William Henry Fitzhugh, 921
  Provisional Army, 66
  raids, 17, 114, 151–152, 173, 268–269, 276–277, 279, 328, 386, 607, 608–609, 1029, 1053, 1086–1087, 1252–1255, 1267, 1546, 1702, 1705, 1707–1708
  saber, *513*, *1462*
  special units, 1516
  Stuart, J. E. B., 1552–1556
  tactics, 1552
  training, 1040
  Trans-Mississippi Department, 68
  United States, 269, 270
  United States Colored Troops, 11
  Wheeler, Joseph, 1707
  see also Infantry, mounted
Cavalry of the West, 234
Cavalry Tactics (Wheeler), 1707
Cavanah, G. W., 641
Cawthon, William Lamar, Jr., *as contributor*, 1202
Cazier, M. C., 671
Cecil (ship), 185
Cedar Creek, Virginia, **271**, 503, 694, 892, 1419
Cedar Mountain, Virginia, 78, 208, **272–273**, 834, 1549, 1734
Celtic thesis, 1112
Cemeteries
  Arlington National, 58
  National Park Service, 1072
Cemetery Hill (Gettysburg), 679, 681, 693, 918
Censorship, **273–274**, 314, 346
  of military data, 1141
  newspaper, 1143, 1144
  and press freedom, 273–274, 640
Census
  1860, 1232–1233
  tax collection, 486, 511, 1224, 1282–1283

Centennial, Civil War, 950
Central America, and Southern expansionism, 225, 688, 808, 1145
Central economy. *See* State socialism
Centralia massacre, 38, **274–275**, 724
Central of Georgia Railroad, 673, 976, 978, 1299
Centreville, Virginia, Quaker guns, *95*
Century magazine, 150, 354
"Cerro Gordo." *See* Williams, John S.
Certificates, cotton. *See* Cotton bonds
Cevor, Charles, 125
Chalmers, James Ronald, **275–276**, 1093, 1096, 1625, 1682
  Fort Pillow, 614
  Shiloh campaign, 1422
Chambers, Henry Cousins, **276**
Chambers, Thomas Jefferson, 1097
Chambersburg, Pennsylvania, **276–277**
  burning of, 277, 503, 849, 968, 1417
  McCausland's raid, 276, 277
  Stuart's raid, 269, 276–277, 1553, 1556
Chambliss, John Randolph, Jr., 144, **277–278**
Chambliss, John Randolph, Sr., **278–279**
Chameleon (ship), 1567, 1723, 1727
Champion's Hill, Mississippi, 664
Chancellorsville campaign, 222, **279–282**, 308
  Anderson, Richard Heron, 36
  Archer, James Jay, 51
  Barksdale, William, 132
  captured Union side arms, 1462
  casualties, 282, 338
  Colston, Raleigh Edward, 369
  Doles, George, 490
  field fortifications, 626
  films about, 573
  Godwin, Archibald, 693
  Gordon, John, 697
  Grimes, Bryan, 718
  high morale following, 1079
  Hill, A. P., 771
  intelligence operations, 541
  Iverson, Alfred, 826
  Jackson, Thomas J. ("Stonewall"). *See under* Jackson, Thomas J. ("Stonewall")
  Jones, J. R., 866
  Last Meeting of Lee and Jackson (painting), 873–874, *951*, 1100
  Lee, Fitzhugh, 915
  Lee (Robert E.) victory, 279–282, 918, 1553
  map, 280
  monument, *1071*
  Nicholls, Francis, 1145
  Rodes, Robert, 1344
  Scales, Alfred Moore, 1370
  Second Louisiana Brigade, 957
  Simms, James Phillip, 1430
  Stonewall Brigade, 1549
  Stuart's raids, 1553
  Wickham, Williams Carter, 1713
  Wilcox, Cadmus Marcellus, 1718
Chandler, Zachariah, 21
Chaplain Hills. *See* Perryville, Kentucky
Chaplains, **282–283**, 388, 1320, 1321, 1586
  Baptist, 282
  Episcopal, 535
  Methodist, 1034–1035
  and military morale, 283
  Presbyterian, 1247
  revivalist, 1247
Chapman, Conrad Wise, **283**, *284*, 778, 1231
Chapman, John Gadsby, 283
Charcoal, 1470
Charity. *See* Free markets; Poor relief; Soldiers' aid societies
Charleston, South Carolina, **284–288**
  arsenal, 90, 97, 1461, 1469
  banking, 1660
  blockade, 822
  blockade running, 1647, 1648
  bombardment of, **287–288**, 1386, 1475, 1509
  city, **284–287**, 1659, *1659*
  commercial atmosphere, 1644, 1659
  defenses, 48, 125, 227, *283*, 620, 622, 686, 988, 1003, 1300, 1302, 1303, 1333, 1479, 1509, 1510, 1558, 1675
  education, 516
  evacuation, 183, 191
  festive mood, 472
  Fort Wagner, 630
  free blacks, 642
  free markets, 641–642, 1229
  harbor torpedoes and mines, 993
  hospitals, 794, 795
  Irish immigrants, 822, 823
  as literary center, 193
  local currency, 462
  mayors, 1038
  munitions manufacture, 1470, 1509
  population and urban ranking, 1504, 1506, *1642*, 1643, 1644, *1658*, 1659
  prisons, 1267, 1268
  privateers, 1269
  secessionism, 1647
  shipyards, 1424, 1509
  slave trade, 1443
  slave uprising, 1440, 1453, 1647
  Union occupation, 1510, 1640, 1648
  wealth inequality, 1506
  weapons imports, 1469
  see also Morris Island, South Carolina
Charleston (ship), 287, 289, 709, 1119, 1124, 1130
Charleston Courier (newspaper), 308
Charleston Daily Carolinian (newspaper), 201
Charleston Importing and Exporting Company, 181
Charleston Mercury (newspaper), 176, 273, 314, 319, 711, 742, 892, 1081, 1324, 1325
Charleston Pilot Boat No. 7. See Savannah (ship)
Charleston Squadron, **289**, 1124, 1125, 1623
Charlotte, North Carolina, **289–290**
  railroads, 1297
Charlotte Naval Ordnance Works, 289
  output, 1121, 1122
Charlotte Navy Yard, **290**, 1178
Charlotte News (newspaper), 201
Charlottesville, Virginia, 796
Chase, Salmon P., 389–390, 1165, 1299
Chasseurs Pied, 140
Chatham (ship), 905
Chattahoochee (ship), **291**, 685, 726, 863, 1100, 1125, 1371
  ordnance, 1118
Chattahoochee River, 114, 1475, 1691
Chattanooga, Tennessee, **291–295**
  campaign, 86–87, **292–295**, 328, 738, 964, 1386
  city, **291–292**
  hospitals, 796, 1549
  map, 294
  National Military Park, 304, 1072, 1073, 1074
  railroads, 1294, 1297
Chattanooga Rebel (newspaper), 274, 1143
Chaudron, Adelaide de Vendel, 1059
Cheatham, B. Franklin, 88, 114, 115, 156, 228, **295–296**, 850, 886, 1179
  Chickamauga campaign, 304
  Franklin and Nashville campaign, 353–354, 632, 634
  Murfreesboro, Tennessee, 1094
  Perryville, Kentucky, 1197
  staff, 254
Cheat Mountain, 37, 1705
Cheops (ship), 1303
Cheraw, South Carolina, 1510

Cherokee Baptist College, 1738
Cherokee Reconstruction Treaty, 1694
Cherokees, 53, **296–297**, 391, 551, 810, 811, 812, 813, 815, 984, 1084, 1391
  Boudinot, Elias C., 198–199
  Thomas, William Holland, 1593–1594
  Watie, Stand, 1692–1694
Chesapeake (ship), 258, 375, 781, 1269
Chesapeake and Ohio Canal, 1677, 1692
Chesnut, James, 133, **298–299**, 400, 629, 877, 988, 1171, *1505*
Chesnut, Mary Boykin, 298, **299–300**, 387, 1066, 1080, 1330, 1739, 1740
  on Barnwell, Robert W., 133
  on Benjamin, Judah P., 161
  on Bonham, Milledge L., 190
  on Boteler, Alexander Robinson, 198
  on Boyce, W. W., 200, 201
  on cabinet appointments, 1023–1024, 1396
  on Campbell (John A.) resignation, 255
  on clothing, 923
  on Confederate White House atmosphere, 1710
  on conscription substitutes, 1083
  on Davis, Jefferson, 299, 300
  on de Jarnette, Daniel, 464
  diary, 298, 471, 472, 937, 1226
  on education, 517
  on Jordan, Thomas, 871
  on Keitt, Lawrence, 878
  on McCord, Louisa Cheves, 969
  on Magrath, Andrew G., 988
  on newspapers, 273
  on Northrop, Lucius, 1158
  on nursing, 1160, 1161
  on patriotic sermon, 1399
  on Pickens, Francis W., 1207, 1208
  on prostitutes, 1276
  on Richmond life, 1741
  on Russell, William, 1354
  on Seddon, James A., 1385
  on Semmes (Thomas and Mary) parties, 1397
  on slaves' strategy, 1442
  on social relations, 1488
  on South Carolina Executive Council, 299
  on war mobilization, 1215
Chesson, Michael B., *as contributor*, 212–213, 1329–1333
Chesterfield, South Carolina, 1510
Chevaux-de-frise, 619, *621*, 622
Cheves, Langdon, 125, 969
Chew's Battery, 104
Chicago conspiracy. *See* Northwestern Conspiracy
Chicago Times (newspaper), 411
Chicago Tribune (newspaper), 495
Chickahominy. *See* Gaines' Mill, Virginia
Chickahominy River, Peninsular campaign, 1400, 1402, 1403, 1554
Chickahominys (Native American peoples), 811
Chickamauga (ship), **301**, 374, 376, 1008, 1723, 1727
Chickamauga and Chattanooga National Military Park, 304, 1072, 1073, 1074
Chickamauga campaign, **302–304**, 327, 672, 830, 891, 1577, 1653
  Anderson, James Patton, 32
  Army of Tennessee, 67, 72, 86, 204–205
  artillery, 92
  Bate, William Brimage, 139, 1500
  Bragg, Braxton, 204–205, 214, 302–304, 327
  Breckinridge, John C., 214, 304
  Buckner, Simon Bolivar, 239
  captured Union small arms, 1461
  casualties, 338
  Clayton, Henry DeLamar, 352
  Deshler, James, 469–470
  Ector, Matthew Duncan, 512
  field fortifications, 626
  Forrest, Nathan Bedford, 607
  Govan, Daniel, 700
  Gregg, John, 716
  Hood, John Bell, 790
  Johnson, Bushrod, 850
  Kelly, John Herbert, 880
  Lewis, Joseph, 929
  Longstreet, James. *See under* Longstreet, James
  map, 303
  National Park. *See* Chickamauga and Chattanooga National Military Park
  Orphan Brigade, 1170
  rail travel to, 1297, 1298
  Sharp, Jacob Hunter, 1404
  Smith, Preston, 1477
  Stevens, Clement Hoffman, 1544
  Stewart, Alexander P., 1545
  Walker, W. H. T., 1681
  Walthall, Edward Cary, 1683
  Wilson, Claudius Charles, 1728–1729
  Wood, Sterling Alexander Martin, 1744
  Wright, Marcus Joseph, 1746
  Young, William Hugh, 1753
Chickamauga Memorial Association, 1073
Chickasaws, 254, **304–305**
  congressional delegates, 391
  Indian Territory, 810, 811, **812–815**
  Jones, Robert McDonald, 868
  military duty, 305, 310
  refugee camp, 1391
  treaty, Confederate, 1390
  treaty, U.S., 1339
Chicora (ship), 185, 287, *289*, 692, 778, 822, 1124, 1125, 1130, 1180, 1303, 1371, 1424, 1515, 1599, 1616, 1623, 1689
Chicora Importing and Exporting Company, 181
Chihuahua, Mexico, 808
Childbearing, 754, 1487
Childhood, **305–308**
  child labor, 1687
  diseases, 754
  free children, **305–307**, 562
  mixed-race children, 1045
  shoe shortages, 357
  slave children, **307–308**, 563
Children of the Confederacy (memorial organization), 307, 1027
Child's Index (magazine), 1232
Chilton, Robert Hall, **308**
Chilton, William P., **308–309**
Chimborazo Hospital (Alabama), 795
Chimborazo Hospital (Georgia), 795
Chimborazo Hospital (Raleigh), 795
Chimborazo Hospital (Richmond), 795–796, 1077, 1161, 1188, 1667
  food, 595–596
Chisolm, Alexander, 298
Chisolm, J. Julian, 755
Chivington, John, 693
Chloroform, 756
Choctaws, 254, **309–310**, 551
  congressional delegates, 391
  Cooper, Douglas Hancock, 409
  Indian Territory, 810, 811, 812–813, 815
  Jones, Robert McDonald, 868
  military duty, 305, 310
  treaty, Confederate, 1390
  treaty, U.S., 1339
Chrisman, James Stone, **311**
Christian, Letitia, 1628, 1629
Christian, Samuel H., 105, 106, 911
Christian Advocate (Methodist publication), 1035

Christianity
slaves' version of, 1450
see also Religion; particular denominations and sects
Christian Repository (Ford), 602
Christ in the Camp (anthology), 476
"Christmas" (Timrod), 937
Christy, David, 416
Churches. *See* Religion; Sermons; particular denominations and sects
Churchill, Thomas James, **311**, 1568
Churchill, Winston (American novelist), 938
Churchill, Winston (British statesman), 786
Church-state relations. *See* Religion; Sermons
Chustenahlah, battle of, 198, 409, 425, 813, 973, 1693
Chusto-Talasah, battle of, 305, 425, 813
Cimbala, Paul A., *as contributor*, 389–391
Cincinnati (ship), 1334
Cincinnati Gazette (newspaper), 411
Cinema. *See* Film and video
Cissell, John F., *as contributor*, 303–304, 469–470, 1476–1477, 1728–1729, 1744, 1746
Citadel, The, **311–312**, 518, 519, 520, 674
graduates, 259, 312, 519, 728, 909
Cities. *See* Urbanization; particular cities
Citizens' Bank and Trust Company of Louisiana, 488
Citizenship, **312–313**
City Point, Virginia, espionage operations, 538
City of Bath (ship), 674
City of Richmond (ship), 448
Civilians
bread riots, 109, **212–213**, 461, 559, 566–567, 596, 900, 901, 1648
Chambersburg, Pennsylvania, 277
clothing shortages, 356–357
community life, 378–379
courts-martial for, 728
diet, 596, 758
foraging effects on, 601
guerrilla action and retribution against, 722
hostage taking, 760
labor force, 900
land mine testing on, 725
malnutrition. *See subhead* diet *above*
military action against, 1352
military arrest of, 1278
prisoners, 265, 439, 543, 544, 640, 727, 728
Sherman's March to the Sea and, 1006
as victims of total war, 1213
see also Class conflicts; Home front; Morale; Society
Civil liberties, **313–314**
abridgments, 331, 427, 1224; *see also* Habeas corpus; Martial law
Davis (Jefferson) policies, 314, 452
free blacks, 643, 644
and Fugitive Slave Law, 650
Lincoln (Abraham) policies, 934, 1224
North Carolina, 707
opposition to wartime curbs, 331
slave restrictions, 1399, 1437, 1722
suspension, 427
see also Censorship; Freedom of speech; Freedom of the press
Civil Rights Act of 1875, 962
Civil service, Confederate, **314–316**
female, 1740
manpower shortage, 1686–1687
patronage elimination, 401
Treasury Department, 1614
Civil service, U.S., oath of allegiance, 1163
Civil War, **316–340**
bloodiest single day (1862), 918, *1407*, 1408
causes, 166–167, **317–324**, 452, 949, 1485–1486, 1533–1534, 1536
causes of defeat, 166, **329–337**, 463, 486, 511, 793, 1078, 1536
Centennial, 950
cities and, 1647–1648, 1669
class conflicts, **344–347**, 1490–1491
Confederate mobilization, 508–509
Confederate view of, 1499
confiscation, **388–391**
conflicting interpretations, 949
crumbling of Confederate Cause, 1386
film and video documentaries, **572–574**
film and video fictional portrayals, **574–580**
gubernatorial support for, 702–704
historiography and historical societies. *See* Museums and archives
last engagement of, 1433, 1473
losses and numbers, 12, 70, 312, 333, **337–340**, 460, 564, 590, 626, 754, 791, 918, 957, 958, 1052, 1264, 1353, *1407*, 1408, 1499, 1666, 1669, 1672, 1682, 1740
master-slave relationship and, 1433–1434
middle class and, 1490
names for, 253, **316–317**
naming of battles, **142–143**
naval war, **1124–1126**
opening shots of, 627–630, 1383, 1508
oral histories, **1167**
popular discontent, 1491–1492
religious support for, 832, 1398–1400
romanticization of. *See* Lost Cause
slavery during, **1441–1447**
slave trading during, 1453
social effects, **1483–1493**
soldiers, **1494–1501**
songs, 1498
Southern nationalism and, 1114–1116
Southern perceptions of, 1490–1491
strategy and tactics, **325-329**, 1385, 1386; *see also* Strategy and tactics
surrender at Appomattox, 212, *330*, 571, 921, 975
as total war, 601, 1352
turning point, 1408
see also Generals; Morale; Peace movements; Union occupation; particular battles and personal names; related subjects
Civil War, The (television documentary), 574
soundtrack, 488
Civil War, The: A Short History (recording), 488
Civil War Music Collector's Edition, The (recording), 488
Claiborne Machine Works. *See* T. M. Brennan & Company
Clandestine operations. *See* Espionage
Clansman, The (novel by Dixon), 575, 938
Clanton, James Holt, **340**
Clapp, J. W., 1173
Clapp, Gates, and Company, 1457
Clarence (ship), 374, 375, 592, 1309
Clarendon, George W. F., 21
Clarendon Foundry, 407
Clarion (Mississippi newspaper), 131
Clark, Amy, 421
Clark, Asia Booth, 545
Clark, Blue, *as contributor*, 304–305
Clark, Charles, 24, 141, **340–341**, 455, 701, 702, 703, 749, 837, 1051, 1204
Clark, Charlotte Moon. *See* Moon sisters
Clark, Edward, **341**, 703, 748, 961, 1585

Clark, Henry T., 159, **341–342**, 701, 702, 703, 781, 1156
Clark, Jessie, 1590
Clark, Jim, 1075
Clark, Joe, 643
Clark, John B., 153, **342–343**, 408–409, 762, 825
Clark, John B., Jr., **343**
Clark, R. K., 1088
Clark, Walter, 467
Clark, William W., **344**, 506
Clarke, Jerome, 888
Clarke, Marcellus, 725
Clarke County, Virginia, 1413
Clarkson, John, 843
Class conflicts, **344–347**
  Charleston, South Carolina, 285
  conscription, 332, 396, 397
  desertion, 468
  employment of slaves, 5–6
  farmers and planters, 379
  historiographical view of, 166
  leisure activities, 923
  Little Rock, Arkansas, 941
  Mississippi, 1051
  and morale decline, 1082–1083
  North Carolina, 1154, 1155
  Northern, 333
  plain folk, 1212, 1213, 1214, 1225–1226
  poverty exacerbating, 1244
  sources of, 1489–1492
  and Southern social hierarchies, 787
  theft, 427
  tobacco habits, 1599
  urban, 1647, 1648
  see also Society
Class structure. *See* Society
Clay, Cassius, 1321
Clay, Clement C., *15*, 300, **347–350**, 351, 872, 1009, *1272*, 1678, 1680
  as commissioner to Canada, 258, 538, 546–547, 781, 1271, 1595
  likeness on Treasury note, 438
Clay, Edward Williams, 649
Clay, Henry, *381*, 658, 763, 1336, 1629, 1708
  Missouri Compromise, 381–382, 665, 886, 1056
  nullification controversy, 1160
  slavery issue, 552, 554, 557
Clay, Susanna, 1218
Clay-Clopton, Virginia, **350–351**, 1009, 1739
Clay rifled guns, 1119
Clayton, Alexander M., 203, **351**
Clayton, Henry DeLamar, **351–352**, 786
Clayton, John, *381*, 1004
Clayton, Philip, 1614
Clayton, Powell, 56, 57
Cleary, William W., 349
Cleburne, Patrick, *52*, **352–354**, 700, 737, 823, 850, 886, 890, 894, 1228, 1476–1477, 1744
  Atlanta campaign, 111, 113
  battle flag, 586
  British background, 604
  Chattanooga campaign, 295
  Chickamauga campaign, 304
  death, 1475
  elite infantry division, 1516
  enlistment of slaves, 1386, 1681
  Jonesboro, Georgia, 33
  Murfreesboro, Tennessee, 1094, 1095
  Perryville, Kentucky, 1197
  response to Emancipation Proclamation, 532
  Shiloh campaign, 1422
Clemens, Jeremiah, 411
Clemens, Samuel Langhorne (Mark Twain), **354**
Clements, Archie, 275
Clemson, Thomas Green, 613
Clemson University, 613
Clergy Hall. *See* Fort Hill
Clergymen. *See* Chaplains; Religion; Sermons; particular denominations and sects
Cleveland, Grover, 28, 107, 527, 906, 910, 1073, 1341, 1581
Cleveland, Marshall, 719
Clifton, Elmer, *576*
Clifton (ship), 656, 1357, 1609
Clingman, Thomas Lanier, **354–355**, 926, 1747
Clingman's Dome, 355
Clinton, Catherine, *as contributor*, 173–174, 1214–1219, 1276–1277, 1623
Clisby, Joseph, 1144
Clitherall, Alexander B., 1614
Clopton, David, *15*, 351, **355–356**
Clothing, **356–357**
  for Georgia troops, 229, 668
  handicrafts, 735
  prisoners of war, 1259–1260
  shortages, 18, 508, 566, 1151, 1153, 1491, 1668
  soldiers' aid societies, 1501–1502
  speculation, 1517
  substitutes, 1558–1559
  textile industry, 443, 1151, 1589
  see also Shoes and boots; Uniforms
Cloverdale furnace, 96
Cloyds Mountain, Virginia, **357–358**, 844, 870
Cluskey, M. W., **358**
Clyde steamers, 185
Coal mining, 1043, 1044
Coastal fortifications. *See under* Forts and fortifications
Coates, James H., 1032, 1033
"Co. Aytch" Maury Grays (Watkin), 475
Cobb, Howell, 348, **358–362**, *381*, 665, 852, 1614
  army service, 364, 581, 673, 978, 1547
  bid for presidency, 200, 423, 424, 877
  Democratic party, 465, 675
  Montgomery convention, 363, 667, 1066, 1067
  personal papers, 1099
  on slavery, 8–9, 12, 75, 160
Cobb, Robert, 1170
Cobb, Thomas R. R., 358, 359, 360, **362–365**, 400, 423, 667, 1738
  Fredericksburg campaign, 640
  state-supported schools, 515
Cobb, Williamson R. W., *15*, 660
Cocke, John H., 1335
Cocke, Philip St. George, **365**, 997, 998
Cockrell, Francis Marion, **366**, 1061, 1236, 1237
Coclanis, Peter A., *as contributor*, 1327–1328
Code of honor. *See* Honor
Codes and code-breaking, 1429
Coding disk, *537*
Cofer, Thomas W., 1460
Coffee substitutes, 596, 1558
Coffin, Charles Carleton, 1453
Coffin, Levi, 44
Coffman, Samuel, 1031
Coffman, W. E., 728
Coggins' Point, 1573
Cohen, Gratz, 845
Cohen, Moses, 1106
Cohen, Solomon, 845
Coins. *See* Currency
Colbert, Winchester, 305
Cold Harbor, Virginia, **366–367**
  defenses, 534
  Finegan, Joseph, 581
  Keitt, Lawrence, 878
  Lee, Robert E., 920
  map, 366
  ordnance disposition, 25
Cole, R. G., *77*
Coleman. *See* Shaw, Henry
Coleman, Kenneth, *as contributor*, 1501–1502
Coles, Cowper, 903

College Hill Arsenal (Nashville), 514
College of Charleston, 518
College of South Carolina, 1023
Colleges and universities. *See* Higher education; Military education; particular institutions
Collie, Crenshaw, and Co., 1169
Collier, Charles Fenton, **367–368**, 684
Collins, Napoleon, 592
Collins, Robert, 1492
Collins, Wilkie, 193
Colonel Lamb (ship), 184, 185, **368**
Colored Methodist Episcopal Church. *See* African Methodist Episcopal (AME) Church
Colors, uniforms, 356, 1633, 1636
Colporters, 130, 165, 282
  Bible societies, 164
Colquitt, Alfred H., 281, **368**, 424, 1513, 1567
Colquitt's Salient, 627
Colston, Raleigh Edward, **368–369**
Colt-style revolvers. *See* Handguns, revolvers
Columbia, South Carolina, **369–372**
  burning of, 261, 371–372, 1510, 1648
  edged weapons manufacture, 514
  Hampton's Legion, 733
  hospitals, 794, 795
  Palmetto Armory, 1179–1180
  powder works, 1245, 1246
  prisons, 1259, 1262–1263, 1267
  refugees, 1318
Columbia, Texas, small arms manufacture, 1460
Columbia (ship), 372, 700, 824, 1124, 1236, 1469, 1580
Columbia Photograph Company, 572
Columbia Telescope (South Carolina newspaper), 1737
Columbia Zouaves, 733
Columbine (ship), 724
Columbus, Georgia, 673, 822, 1648
  arsenal. *See* Columbus Naval Iron Works
  bread riots, 212
  edged weapons manufacture, 514
  hospitals, 794
  Memorial Day observance, 1026, 1027
  Naval Museum, 291
  railroads, 1297
  small arms and munitions manufacture, 1458, 1460, 1470
  textile industry, 1645
Columbus, Kentucky
  Confederate withdrawal, 1420
  defenses, 226
  Union occupation, 1227
Columbus, Mississippi
  arsenal, 90
  small arms and munitions manufacture, 1459, 1470, 1471
Columbus (ship), 700
Columbus Fire Arms Manufacturing Company, 1460
Columbus Iron Works Company. *See* Columbus Naval Iron Works
Columbus Naval Iron Works, 90, 96, 97, **372**, 446
  output, 1121, 1122
Columbus Sun (Georgia newspaper), 201, 1144
Colyar, A. S., **372–373**, 598, 600
Comanches, 425, 749, 811, 813, 1608
Comedians and Tragedians of the North (Volck), 1673
Commentaries on the Constitution of the United States (Story), 1395
Commentary on the Campaign and Battle of Manassas, A (Beauregard), 150
Commerce. *See* Economy; Foreign trade
Commerce raiders, 186, **373–376**, 992, 1567
  British shipbuilding, 712
  Bulloch, James Dunwoody, 239–240, 375
  Confederate Navy, 1123–1124, 1129
  Marine Guards, 1008
  Maury, Matthew Fontaine, 1018
  privateers vs., 1269
  recruitment, 1131
  Semmes, Raphael, 1393–1394, 1563
  Slidell, John, 1454
  Waddell, James, 1675
  see also Privateers; particular ships
Commercial expansion. *See* Imperialism
Commissary Bureau, **376–378**, 1266, 1517, 1685
  Atlanta, Georgia, 109
  fraud, 876
  Northrop, Lucius B., 1158
  Pillow, Gideon, 1211
  prisons, 1268
  Subsistence Department, 595, 901, 1412
  Winder, John H., 1734
Committee of Fifteen (Louisiana), 1395
Committee of Nine (Virginia), 124
Committee of Public Safety (Texas), 1583
Committees of Safety, 1616
Committee of Thirteen (Senate), 429, 451, 803
Common School Journal, 1721
Communications. *See* Broadsides; Telegraph; Signal Corps
Community life, **378–380**
  plain folk, 1212
  scarcities, 1491
  social class and, 1489
  women's roles, 1488
  see also Family life: Home front; Society
Compact discs. *See* Discography
Company (basic artillery unit), 91, 92
Compendium of the Impending Crisis, The (Helper), 762
Compensation, for confiscated property, 388–391
Complete Grammar of the French Language, A, 1588
Complete Treatise on Field Fortification, A (Mahan), 617
Compromise of 1850, 31, 321, 359, **380–382**, 582
  Calhoun, John C., 253
  Foote, Henry S., 598
  Fugitive Slave Law, 650
  Georgia Platform, **675**
  Harris, Wiley Pope, 747
  Seddon, James A., 1383
  Stephens, Alexander H., 1539
  as step toward secession, 1374–1375, 1533
  see also Crittenden Compromise; Wilmot Proviso
Concentrations for the Battle of Gettysburg (film), 573
Concepción (ship), 1341
Concise History of Instruction and Regulation for the Militia and Volunteers of the United States, The (Cooper), 410
Concubinage, 1045–1046
Condor (ship), 1727
Confederacy, The (recording), 487
Confederacy of Jones. *See* Jones County, Mississippi
Confederate Army. *See* Army
Confederate Brigadiers, 1019
Confederate Camp, 3rd Kentucky Infantry, at Corinth, Miss. (Chapman), 283
Confederate Chaplaincy Association, 282
Confederate Congress. *See* Congress, Confederate
Confederate Constitution. *See* Constitution, Confederate

Confederate flag. *See under* Flags
Confederate Flag over Fort Sumter, October 20, 1863 (Chapman), *284*
Confederate gray, 356
"Confederate Guards" (Company E), 1364
Confederate Memorial Institute, Battle Abbey Shrine, 573
Confederate Memorial Ladies' Association, 1711
Confederate Military History, 548, 798
Confederate Museum (Charleston), 1100
Confederate Museum (New Orleans), 1100
Confederate Museum (Richmond), 1028, 1711
Confederate Naval Academy, 840
Confederate Naval Museum (Columbus), 291, 1100
Confederate Navy. *See* Navy, Confederate
Confederate Press Association, 1141
  war correspondents, 1683–1684
Confederate Primer, The (textbook), 1588
Confederate Receipt Book, The (cookbook), 597
Confederate Rolling Mill. *See* Atlanta Rolling Mill
Confederate Signal Corps. *See* Signal Corps
Confederate Southern Memorial Society, 388
Confederate Spelling Book (textbook), 307, 1588
Confederate Spirit and Knapsack of Fun (magazine), 1232
Confederate Spy, The (film), 574
Confederate State Department. *See* State Department
Confederate States Acid Works, 289–290
Confederate States Armory, 514
Confederate States Central Laboratory, 90, 1168
Confederate States Educational Association, 516
Confederate States Medical and Surgical Journal, 1077
Confederate States of America, **382–388**
  African Americans and. *See* African Americans in the Confederacy
  army. *See* Army
  artillery production, **96–98**
  cabinet. *See* Cabinet
  capitals, 109, 148, 360, 383, 444, 452, 453, 1064, 1065–1066, 1300–1301, 1329, 1331
  central government, 106, 389, 396, 400, 401, 452, 464, 466, 535, 701, 736, 753, 772, 872, 883, 1079, 1081, 1128, 1249, 1304
  cities, 1647-1648; *see also* particular names
  citizenship, 313
  conflicts with state governments, 1535–1536
  Congress. *See* Congress, Confederate
  currency. *See* Currency
  debt. *See* Debt
  departmental organization, 71–74
  diplomacy. *See* Diplomacy
  economy. *See* Economy
  education. *See* Education
  Emancipation Proclamation impact on, 532
  European nonrecognition, 1529; *see also* Diplomacy
  first secessionist states, 1373, 1441
  flag, **584–585**
  foreigners, **602–604**
  formation, 1441
  German contributions, 676
  German dissidents, 675
  governors, 701–704
  guerrilla warfare, 718–725
  historical papers, 1512
  ideological rift, 1749
  imperialism, 808–809
  Indian contributions, 812, 813, 815, 1390
  Indian dissidents, 1390–1391
  Indian treaties, 747, 811–812, 813, 1173, 1290, 1398, 1408
  Irish contributions, 822, 823
  Jewish contributions, 845–846
  loss of border states, 196–197
  map, 384
  membership by state and date, *1379*
  Montgomery Convention. *See* Montgomery Convention
  national anthem, 1102
  Navy. *See* Navy, Confederate
  Northerners prominent in, **1157**
  oral histories, **1167**
  policy on retaliation, 1395–1396
  politics, 391, 525, **1223–1226**
  population, **1232–1235**
  postal service, **1242–1244**
  presidency, **1247-1249**; *see also* Davis, Jefferson
  Provisional Constitution, 1380
  railroads, **1293–1299**
  religious support for, 1398–1400
  romanticization of. *See* Lost Cause
  seal, *436*, 864–865
  secession from, 870, 1536
  social structure, **1483–1493**
  soldiers' home, 1502
  Southern nationalism, **1114–1116**
  Southern Unionism, 1638–1640
  state rights in, 1535–1536
  telegraph wires, 1573
  theater, 1589–1590
  vice presidency, **1664-22-17**; *see also* Stephens, Alexander H.
Confederate States of America, The (Coulter), 333
Confederate States Ordnance Works, 1458
Confederate States Protestant Episcopal Church, 535
Confederate Subsistence Department. *See under* Commissary Bureau
Confederate Torpedo Bureau. *See* Torpedo Bureau
Confederate Veteran (magazine), **388**, 1027, 1035
Confederate Veterans (umbrella organization), 1027
Confederate Vivandiere; or, The Battle of Leesburg (Hodgson), 1589
Confederate War Papers (Smith), 1475
Confederate Women of Arkansas, 594
Confederate Women's Home (Richmond), 1600
Confiscation, **388–391**, 463
  Confederate, **388–389**
  contraband, **405–406**
  U.S., 388, **389–391**, 406
  War Department, 250
  see also Impressment; Sequestration Act of 1861
Confiscation Act of 1863, Confederate, 192
  see also Sequestration Act of 1861
Confiscation Acts of 1861 and 1862, U.S., 388, 389, 390, 406
Congaree Foundry, 98
Congress (ship), 236, 863, 1670–1671, *1671*
Congress, Confederate, 383, **391–394**
  absence of political parties, 1225
  Arizona Territory, 51, 391, 983, 984, 1174
  arming of slaves, 9, 345, 394, 1194
  authority over slavery, 884
  bill, *393*
  bond issues, 187, 189, 190

Congress, Confederate, *continued*
cavalry bill, 1714
censorship, 273
confiscation, 388, 389, 391
conscription law. *See* Conscription
constitutionally outlined powers, 1534
copyright act, 193
cotton purchase authorizations, 419, 1616
currency policy, 434, 1280, 1385
election of 1863. *See* Election of 1863
Finance Committee, 659
First, 392–393
foreign relations, 1325
franking privilege, 1242
fraud act, 377
guerrilla warfare authorization, 1086
hospital legislation, 795
impressment bill, 1426
Indian representatives, 198–199, 253–254, 812, 868
Indian treaty ratification, 812
investigation of prison conditions, 266
investigation of Quartermaster Bureau, 1292
ironclad appropriations, 992
laissez-faire attitude, 452
legislative powers, 401
loan legislation, 509
member states, 1373
money bills, 434
naval appointments, 1128, 1131
naval appropriations, 42, 1018
New Plan, 1140
ommission of general welfare clause, 1285
opposition to Davis. *See under* Davis, Jefferson
peace advocates. *See* Peace movements, congressional advocates
proceedings transcripts, 1512
produce loan, 1270
Provisional, 360–361, 363, 383, 391–392, 1068–1069, 1085
railroad legislation, 1297, 1612
Second, 393–394
sedition act, 640
state rights debate, 348
Stephens (Alexander H.) and, 1540, 1541–1542
suspension of habeas corpus. *See under* Habeas corpus
tax bills, 485, 510–511, 1282, 1283, 1287, 1569, 1571
tobacco planting restrictions, 1598
Tredegar loans, 1617
Unionism. *See under* Unionism
see also particular acts and members
Congress, U.S.
African slave trade ban, 552
Alabama delegation, *15*
Calhoun-Webster state rights debate, 1533
caning of Sumner (Charles), 1560–1562
compensation for Southern Unionists, 1639
"Confederate Brigadiers," 1019
confiscation of property, 388, 389, 390
Crittenden Compromise. *See* Crittenden Compromise
enlistment of blacks, 9
gag rule, 186, 321
Mississippi delegation, *1050*
Missouri Compromise. *See* Missouri Compromise
oath of allegiance legislation, 1163, 1164
peace movement, 1183
policies toward territories, 1534
prison inquiry, 1261, 1264
reaction to secession movement, 1379
slave confiscation, 7
slavery prohibition powers, 1375
South Carolina delegation, *1505*
Speaker of the House contest (1859–1860), 322
Tennessee delegation, *1576*
territorial expansion, 380
Thirteenth Amendment, 1590–1591
Wilmot Proviso, 320, 354, **1728**
see also particular acts and members
Conical projectiles, 98
Conner, James, **394–395**, *1634*
Conover, Sanford, 935
"Conquered Banner, The" (poem by Ryan), 938
"Conquered Banner, The" (song), *948*
Conrad, Charles M., **395–396**
Conrad, James Lee, *as contributor*, 674–675
Conrad, Robert Young, 1337
Conrad, Thomas, 544, 545
Conrad (ship). *See Tuscaloosa*
Conrad's Store, Virginia, 1415, 1416
Conrow, Aaron H., **396**
Conscientious objectors. *See* Pacifism
Conscription, 385, **396–399**
Alabama, 1695
civil liberties, 313, 314
class diversity, 1495, 1509
class-related resentments, 345, 1492
congressional debate, 396–398, 439, 667, 694, 705, 707, 727, 736, 747, 750, 767, 772–773, 779, 864, 982, 1030–1031, 1172, 1194, 1250, 1287, 1482, 1535, 1717, 1749, 1750
congressional enactment, 392
constitutionality, 402, 872–873, 1535
controversy. *See subhead* congressional debate *above*; *subhead* opposition *below*; *subhead* substitution issue *below*
exemptions, 5, 70, 106, 107, 174, 226, 315, 345, 367, 385, 394, 396-398, 399, 464, 508-509, 516, 532, 589, 596, 640, 760, 900, 902, 911, 924, 942, 988, 1038, 1076, 1083, 1205, 1243, 1298, 1312, 1511, 1686; *see also subheads below for particular exemptions*
Florida, 1042
foreign-born, avoidance by, 655, 1367
Georgia, 229, 230, 872, 1367
habeas corpus and, 402, 1184, 1535
impact on farming, 566
legislation. *See* Conscription Acts of 1862 and 1864
Mississippi, 208, 1698
and morale, 1079, 1080, 1083
North Carolina, 715, 1012, 1152, 1153, 1155, 1184, 1650
opposition, 105-106, 122, 229, 279, 331-332, 446, 525, 662, 667, 670, 1184, 1535, 1539, 1540, 1542-1543, 1623, 1650; *see also subhead* congressional debate *above*
overseer exemption, 89, 107, 191, 279, 345, 392, 397, 398–399, 532, 776, 884, 902, 1083, 1155, 1174–1175, 1230, 1395, 1514
planters and 1215-1216, 1219, 1220, 1491-1492; *see also* Twenty-Slave Law
as political issue, 1223
of Quakers, 1493
resisters, 385, 398, 715, 1392
South Carolina, 191–192, 872, 988, 1509
state officials' exemption, 229, 1156, 1536
substitution issue, 332, 345, 385, 397–398, 671, 1083, 1155, 1184, 1216, 1492, 1698
Virginia, 1480
see also Desertion

Conscription Acts of 1862 and 1864, 70, 191, 396–399, 662, 772–773, 878, 1131, 1219, 1278, 1306, 1686, 1749, 1750
  antigovernment violence, 720
  first, 396–397
  naval enlistment, 1131
  North Carolina, 1155, 1156
  second, 397–380
  Semmes (Thomas) amendment, 1395
  supporters, 710, 1326, 1349
  third, 380–381
Conscription Bureau
  Anderson, Samuel Read, 37–38
  civil service, 315–316
  dissolution, 399, 1687
  establishment, 398
  Preston, John Smith, 1249
  War Department, 1685
Conservative (Raleigh newspaper), 1142
Conservative party, North Carolina, 106, 1224, 1626
Constitution (periodical), 230
Constitution (ship), 674
Constitution, Confederate, **399–403**
  central government role, 716
  citizenship provision, 313
  civil liberties, 313
  Clayton, Alexander M., 351
  Davis (Jefferson) strict construction of, 1536
  drafting, 392, 423, 464, 667, 1023, 1067, 1067–1068, 1090, 1146, 1325, 1478
  freedom of the press, 640
  habeas corpus, 727–728
  internal improvements provision, 1612
  judicial clauses, 871, 872
  military justice, 1038
  overseas slave trade ban, 1451
  Permanent, 400–403
  presidency provisions, 1247–1248
  Provisional, 391, 399–400, 1380
  ratification, 133, 360, 402–403, 877, *1379*
  secession justification, 1534–1535
  similarity to U.S. Constitution, 400
  on slavery, 253, 415, 808, 884, 1194, 1696
  on state rights, 1534–1535
  Stephens, Alexander H., 1539
  taxation provisions, 486, 511
  text of, 1774–1782
  vice presidency provisions, 1654–1655
Constitution, U.S.
  citizenship, 312–313
  Confederate borrowing from, 400
  Crittenden Compromise plan, 429, 803
  Fourteenth Amendment, 124, 312–313, 434, 1010, 1081, 1699
  slavery justification, 253
  slave trade ban, 1437
  strict vs. broad interpretation, 1531–1532
  Thirteenth Amendment, 1434, 1446, **1590–1591**
Constitutional Union party, **403**, *404*, 1224, 1477, 1482
  Alabama, 340
  cooperationists, 411
  election of 1860, 14, 105, 123, 153, 227, 235, 403, 448, 497, 521–524, 658, 667, 687, 706, 763, 786, 907, 1187, 1224, 1295, 1574, 1623, 1637, 1647, 1688, 1699
  formation, 403, 675, 1336, 1601
  Missouri, 1052
  Tennessee, 372
  Virginia, 1187
Constitutional View of the Late War between the States, A (Stephens), 253, 316, 317, 586, 1536, 1542
Continental Vocalists, 1103
Continuous voyage doctrine, 178
Contraband, 332, **405–406**
  Butler (Benjamin F.) declaration, 1103
  camps, 956, 1579
  confiscation, 390
  slave children, 307
  slaves as, 7, 405–406, 540, 900, 1444–1446
Conway, Kate Cashman, 1167
Cook, Enoch Hooper, 224
Cook, Ferdinand W., 1458
Cook, Francis, 1458
Cook, George, 1206, 1207
Cook, Phillip, **406–407**
Cook and Brother, 515, 1458
Cooke, Flora. *See* Stuart, Flora Cooke
Cooke, James W., 22, **407**, 1151
Cooke, John Esten, 193, **407–408**, 798, 936, 937, 938, 985, 1553, 1669, 1683
Cooke, John Rogers, 220–221, **408**
Cooke, Philip St. George, 408, 1551, 1553, 1554
Cooke, William Mordecai, **408–409**
Cooley, Samuel A., 100
Cooling, B. Franklin, *as contributor*, 592–593, 764–767, 1211
Cooper, Douglas Hancock, 297, 305, 310, **409**, 425, 812, 813, 814, 1167, 1211, 1390, 1391
Cooper, Samuel, 64, 136, 149, 256, **409–410**, 860, 1157, 1191, 1385, 1658, 1685, 1688
Cooper, Thomas, 1113
Cooperationists, **411**
  Alabama, 1057
  Louisiana, 426
  Mississippi, 1203–1204, 1594
  and secessionist movement, 1379, 1380
  Smith, William Russell, 1482
  South Carolina, 988, 1207, 1506, 1507
  and Unionism, 1637–1638, 1639
  Withers, Thomas, 1737
Copperheads, 297, 332, 333, 335, 349, **411-413**, 538, 715, 808, 813, 1159, 1595, 1693; *see also* Northwestern Conspiracy
Copper mining, 1043, 1147
Copper tokens, 1424
Copyright Act, 193
Coquette (ship), 185
Corbell, LaSalle, 1208
Corinth, Mississippi, 84, **413–415**, 835, 858, 889, 891, 908, 1049, 1355, 1596
  Confederate line, 1420
  Gladden, Adley, 691
  Lovell, Mansfield, 958
  map, 414
  Union capture, 1423
  Van Dorn, Earl, 825, 1652, 1656, 1661
  see also Shiloh campaign
Corlew, Robert E., *as contributor*, 264–265, 597–600, 666–667, 763–764, 868–869, 1098, 1592–1593, 1595–1596
Corley, J. L., *77*
Cormany, Samuel E., 278
Cornell, David, 1166
Cornerstone speech, 383, 402, **415**, 1220, 1275
  text of, 1783–1790
Cornish, Dudley T., *as contributor*, 9–12
Corn prices, 566
Corns, James M., 843
Cornubia (ship), 182, 185
Corn women, 18
Coronet International Films, 574
Corps
  composition, 816
  organization, 66, 84

Corps d'Afrique, 1138
Corpus Christi, Texas, forts, 623
Correspondence. *See* Diaries, letters, and memoirs
Corruption charges
  Butler, Benjamin, 1138
  Commissary Bureau, 377–378
  Quartermaster Bureau, 377, 876, 1292
Corse, Montgomery Dent, **415–416**
Cortada, James W., *as contributor*, 432
Cortina, Juan N., 157
Corwin, Thomas, *381*, 1209
Corwin (ship), 1722
Corypheus (ship), 656
Cosby, George Blake, **416**
Coski, John M., *as contributor*, 439–440
Cotton, **416–420**, 1443–1444, 1537
  in agricultural economy, 506
  Alabama production restrictions, 1426
  in antebellum period, 416–418, 1643–1644, 1645
  black belt, 172, 173
  bonds, 181, 980, 992, 1616
  certificates, 510
  crop value and slave population, 1436–1437, *1436*
  economic value. *See* "Cotton diplomacy"
  embargo, 507–508, 711–712, 1366–1367
  Erlanger loan, 510, 536
  European dependency, 483, 631, 1270
  Georgia, 976, 1364, 1365, 1366–1367
  government purchase, 509, 604, 1025
  impressment, 1586, 1608
  Mississippi, 1047, 1051
  Mobile market, 1057
  munitions exchanges, 980, 1140–1141, 1169, 1686, 1687
  plantation overseers, 1174
  prices, 554
  produce loan, 1270
  production curtailment, 1215
  Red River Valley, 1314, 1317
  role in Confederacy, 418–420
  sales to Northerners, 419
  Savannah port trade, 1364, 1365
  slave labor, 319, 417, 552, 1214–1215, 1439, 1449–1450
  smuggling, 420
  South Carolina, 1504, 1506
  speculation, 1517
  Tennessee, 1028
  Texas, 233, 1097, 1232, 1583, 1585–1586, 1586
  textile industry, 717, **1588–1589**
  trade, 232, 233, 432, 1169, 1215, 1364, 1365, 1586, 1608, 1659
  and urbanization, 1659
"Cotton Boll, The" (Timrod), 936, 937, 1597
Cotton bonds, 181, 980, 992, 1616
Cottonclads, **420**, 744, 1302
  Galveston Bay, 656
  River Defense Fleet, 1334
"Cotton diplomacy," 179–181, 392, 416, 418, 480–481, 483, 507–508, 711, 1025, 1194, 1325
Cotton gin, 417, 552, 1436
Cotton Is King (Christy), 416
Cotton Planters' Association, 138
Coulter, E. Merton, 26, 327, 333, 597
Counterfeiting, 109, **421**, 427, 428, 436
Counterintelligence, 541
Countryman (magazine), 1232, 1625, 1626
Country music, Lost Cause link, 949
Courier (Charleston newspaper), 1143, 1144, 1683
Courier (Natchez newspaper), 870
Courier, The; or, The Siege of Lexington (Hewitt), 1590
Courier service, *537*
Courtenay, William, 1683
Courtney & Tennant, 515
Courtship, **421–422**
  abandonment of traditional, 1009–1010
  soldiers' love letters, 1496
  see also Marriage and divorce
Courts-martial
  Alexander, George W., 266
  Barksdale, William, 132
  civilian, 728
  Crawford, Martin J., 424
  Crittenden, George B., 429
  desertion, 469
  drum-head, 1039
  Evans, Nathan G. ("Shanks"), 549
  general, 1039
  McCown, John P., 969–970
  regimental, 1039
  soldier insubordination, 1497
  Tattnall, Josiah, 1568–1569
  Thomas, William Holland, 1594
  Twiggs, David E., 1627–1628
  Wright, Ambrose Ransom ("Rans"), 1744
Courts of inquiry, military, 1039
Court system. *See* Judiciary
Cousin marriage, 562
Cowardin, James, 1141
Cowell, D. T., 873
Cox, Jacob Dolson, 163, 1011, 1700, 1705
Cox, Merlin G., *as contributor*, 588–591, 1166, 1196
Cox, William Ruffin, **422**
Coxe, Robert, 546–547
Coxetter, Louis M., 183, 841, 1269
Crabb, George W., 1482
Crabb, Henry, 1174
Cracker Line (Chattanooga campaign), 293
Crafts and craftsmen. *See* Artisans; Handicrafts; Labor, skilled
Craige, Francis Burton, **422–423**
Craig v. Missouri, 1279
Crampton's Gap, Maryland, 361, 364, 1513
Cramton, Louis C., 58
Crane, Stephen, 938
Crania Americana (Morton), 1274
Crater, battle of the, 82, 528, 990, 1200, 1682, 1698
Craven, Avery, 318
Craven, Braxton, 1232
Crawford, George W., 423
Crawford, John, 812
Crawford, Martin J., 174, **423–424**, 628, *669*, 822, 1345, *1382*
Crawford, Nathaniel Macon, 130
Crawford, Samuel J., 11
Crawford, William H., 423, 1532
"Crazy Bet." *See* Van Lew, Elizabeth
Credit. *See* Banking; Bonds; Debt
Creeks, 253–254, 391, **424–425**, 551, 810, 811, 812–813, 1084, 1607
  Confederate treaty, 1390
  Opothleyahola as leader, 297, 1166–1167
Crehen, Ernest, 1102, 1231, 1256
Crenshaw and Collie and Company, 181, 301
Creoles, **425–426**, 644–645, 956, 957, 1621
Crew, Charles C., 27
"Crime against Kansas" speech, 175, 176
Crime and punishment, **427–428**
  abolitionists, 44, 370
  Andrews' raiders, 41, 109
  Atlanta, Georgia, 109, 110, 673
  bank robberies, 1089
  bushwhackers and looters, 110, 117, 671, 1155
  civilian courts-martial, 728
  counterfeiting, 109, **421**, 427, 428, 436
  deserters, 398, 468–469, 1039, 1190, 1209

dueling, 427
executions, 11, 145, *539*, 724, 941, 1149, 1209, 1258, 1353, *1735*
guerrilla activity, 719, 720, 722, 724–725
military punishments, 788
prisoners, 39, 266
Richmond, Virginia, 212
runaway slaves, 253
spies, 941
tories, 1602–1603
war criminals, 1158
see also Corruption charges; Courts-martial; Military justice
Crimean War, 823, 1752
Crisis (Ohio publication), 411
Crisis, The (novel by Churchill), 938
Crisp, Cecilia, 1590
Crisp, W. H., 1589
Crist, Lynda Lasswell, *as contributor*, 458
Crittenden, George B., 224, 263, **428–429**, 887, 1755
Mill Springs, Kentucky, 1041
Crittenden, John J., 28, 196, 224, *381*, 403, 428, 429, 688, 886, 1380, 1431, *1561*, 1689, 1708
see also Crittenden Compromise
Crittenden, Thomas, 224, 428, 492, 1737
Crittenden family, 272, 428
Crittenden Compromise, 220, **429**, 659, 688, 762–763, 809, 1601
Hunter, Robert M. T., 803
Republican rejection, 1380, 1381
see also Washington Peace Conference
Crockett, Davy, 970, 1709
Crockett, John Watkins, **430**
Crofts, Daniel W., *as contributor*, 122–125, 687–690, 705–708
Cronauer, Adrian, 488
Cronin, John R., *as contributor*, 1352–1353
Crook, George, 582, 725, 843, 1702, 1733
Cloyds Mountain, Virginia, 357–358
Shenandoah campaign, 1417, 1418, 1419
Crooks, Adam, 44
Cross, Charlotte, 1715
Cross Keys and Port Republic, Virginia, **430–431**, 834, 1417, 1521
Crossland, Edward, 1389
Cross of Honor medal, 1028
Cross of Military Service medal, 1028
Crowther, Edward Riley, *as contributor*, 130–131
Croxton, John, 17, 1389
Crozet, Claudius, 1672
Cruft, Charles, 294
Cruger, Louis, 1614–1615
Cruikshank, Marcus H., **431–432**, 439
Crump, William W., 1600, 1614
Crump Landing, Mississippi, 1420
Crutchfield, Stapleton, 1673
"Cry to Arms, A" (Timrod), 937
Cuba, **432**
expansion of slavery, 554, 555, 556, 557, 558, 808, 1715
Havana blockade running, 177, 185
Spanish interests, 1513
transshipment of supplies, 699
Trent affair, 1015
Cullop, Charles P., *as contributor*, 810, 1270–1272
Culture
of Lost Cause, 949–950
male versus female, 923
miscegenation, 1046
popular, **1230–1232**
selected bibliography, 170
see also Art; Literature; Music; Theater
Cumberland (ship), 62, 235–236, 700, 863, 1670–1671
Cumberland Gap, 637
Cumberland River, 1420, 1691, 1707–1708
defenses, 226
gunboat patrols, 1110
Henry and Donelson campaign, 765–766
Cumberland University, 264
Cumberland Valley Railroad, 1555
Cumming, Alfred, **432**
Cumming, Kate, 795, 1161
Cunningham, Anne Pamela, 1202
Cunningham, Sumner A., 388, 1027
Currency, **433–438**
archival collections, 1099
barter replacing, 1491, 1511
in circulation, 1279–1280
congressional money bills, **434**, 1280, 1385
counterfeit, 109, **421**, 427, 428, 436
inflation effects, 234, 386, 511, 820–821, 1284, 1686
interest on specie, 189
legal tender controversy, 599, 659, 660, 1024, 1280
New Plan, 1140–1141
numismatics, **434–338**
overview article, **433–434**
printing expertise, 436, 438, 1231
redundant, 392, 1280
shinplasters (generic term), **1424**
signatures, 315, 1614
speculation, 1517
state government, 462, 1280–1281
suspension of specie payments, 18, 128, 1137, 1395
Current, Richard N.
on causes of Confederate defeat, 330–331
as contributor, 142–144, 252–253, 382–388, 530–532, 627–630, 791–793, 1526, 1531–1536, 1602–1603
as editor in chief, vii-viii
Currier & Ives, Lost Cause iconography, 950–951
Currin, David M., 358, **438–439**
Curry, Jabez L. M., *15*, 19, 309, 432, **439–440**, 547, 1741
Curtis, Benjamin Robbins, 495
Curtis, Moses Ashley, 1274
Curtis, Samuel R., 141, 526, 829, 1053, 1097, 1254, 1255, 1340, 1355, 1606
Cushing, William B., 22, 445, 1130, 1603, 1689
Custer, George Armstrong, 237, 1419
Custis, George Washington Parks, 916, 917
Custis, Mary. *See* Lee, Mary Custis
Custis, Mary Fitzhugh, 916
Cutlasses, naval, 1469
Cutshaw, Wilfred E., 1418

D

Dabney, Robert Lewis, *80*, 788, 1320, 1398
Dabney, Thomas, 1742
Dacotah (ship), 1177
Dahlgren, John, 445, 630, 863, 892
Dahlgren, Ulric
burial, 1652
Dahlgren papers, **441**, 893, 1386
Fredericksburg raid, 637
Kilpatrick-Dahlgren raid, 441, **892–893**, 931
Dahlgren design. *See* Dahlgren-system guns
Dahlgren papers, **441**, 893, 1386
Dahlgren-system guns, 62, 1117, *1118*, 1119
boat howitzer, 101
Gosport Navy Yard storage, 699–700
Daily Enquirer (Richmond newspaper), 1142

Daily Intelligencer (Atlanta newspapere), 108
Daily North Carolinian (newspaper), 1143
Dallas, Moses, **441–442**
Dallas, Georgia, 113
Dallas County, Alabama, 1387
Dalton, Edmond R., 1231, 1590
Dalton, Georgia, **442**, 861
"Damnesty oath," 231, 1110
Dan (film), 574
Dana, Napoleon J. T., 232, 233
Dance and Park. *See* J. H. Dance and Bros.
Daniel, John Moncure, 213, 1142, 1229
Daniel, Junius, **442–443**
Daniel, W. Harrison, *as contributor*, 164–165, 1398–1400
Daniells, Mrs., 1161
Danmark (Ship), 1303
Danville, Virginia, **443–444**, 796, 1648
  long arms manufacture, 1456, 1457
  prisons, 1267, 1268
  railroads, 1294, 1297
  refugee government, 453
Danville Female Academy, 516
Danville Review (journal), 216
Danville Theological Seminary, 216
Darden, Stephen Heard, **444**
Dargan, E. S., **444**, 599
Darien, Georgia, destruction of, 672
Dark Command (film), 580
Daughters of the Confederacy. *See* United Daughters of the Confederacy
David (torpedo boat), 287, 289, 445, 692, 1124, 1515, 1599–1600
Davids, **445–446**, 993, 1515–1516
Davidson, Allen Turner, **446–447**, 942
Davidson, Donald, 938, 939
Davidson, Henry Brevard, **447**
Davidson, Hunter, 445–446, **447–448**, 538, 1603
Davidson County, North Carolina, peace movement, 1183
Davies, Henry E., 237
Davies, Marion, 578
Davies, Thomas, 414
Davis, Alexander Jackson, 1672
Davis, Charles, 55, 227, 1655
Davis, Edmund J., 157, 1585
Davis, Garrett, 972
Davis, George, 251, **448**, 892
Davis, Hector, 1453
Davis, Henry Winter, 687, 1322
Davis, Jefferson, *65*, *250*, **448–453**, 596, *1050*, 1354, 1554, 1563
  advisers and staff, 299, 749, 915, 917, 918, 961
  appointments, 25, 26, 27, 110, 133, 203, 205, 230, 252, 499, 698, 709–710, 775–776, 788, 858, 860–861, 908, 1126, 1140, 1158, 1189, 1312, 1324–1325, 1355, 1356, 1527, 1566, 1748; *see also subhead* cabinet *below*
  army organization, 64, 66, 71–72, 86
  Beauvoir estate, **150**, 388, 453, 458, 492, 1100, 1502
  Benjamin (Judah P.) relationship, 1528
  Bragg (Braxton) controversy, 85, 86, 87
  bread riots, 212
  and Butler (Benjamin F.) woman order, 247
  cabinet 2, 206, 249-252, 255, 448, 1023-1024, 1225, 1243, 1248, 1385, 1527, 1528, 1678, 1686, 1687; *see also subhead* appointments *above*
  capture and imprisonment of, 453, 673, 1244
  caricatures, *335*, *412*, *732*, 951
  and central government role, 387, 872–873
  charges of Union atrocities, 933–934
  civil liberties policies, 314, 452
  command arrangements, 74, 85, 86, 146, 149, 672, 714, 1656, 1716
  and Confederate state rights extremism, 1536
  congressional opponents, 106, 153, 154, 200, 260, 363, 446, 455, 597–598, 599, 651, 689, 733, 782, 858, 910–911, 911–912, 929, 942, 1164, 1171, 1172, 1173, 1176, 1325, 1396, 1481, 1482, 1514–1515, 1626, 1651, 1661, 1749
  congressional supporters. *See subhead* support for *below*
  conscription policies, 872–873, 1535, 1536
  criticism of, 273, 391–392, 393, 475, 1142, 1143–1144, 1229
  currency policies, 1395
  Dahlgren papers, 441, 893
  Davis Bend, Mississippi, 458
  Democratic party, 465, 466
  departmental system, 71, 72, 73, 74, 84
  on deserters, 398, 467
  despotism charges against, 1543
  education policy, 516
  election handbill, *1667*
  election as president, 383, 391, 400, 451, 1066, 1068, 1324, 1380, 1539
  emancipation policies, 9, 160, 530, 532, 934, 1487
  engravings, 1231
  family, 453–454, 456–457, 1572, 1743
  flight from Richmond, 215, 235, 256, 290, 453, 478, 506, 570, 666, 715, 961, 993–994, 1130, 1313, 1654, 1688
  foreign policy, 348, 452, 479, 507
  Fort Sumter bombardment, 324, 628–629, 1381–1382, 1508
  government finances, 1140–1141
  guerrilla warfare advocacy, 725
  image in South, 130, 934, 951
  inauguration, 109, 130, 309, 313, 360, 488, 1068, 1248, 1287
  Indian policies, 198, 749, 811, 812
  lack of unified opposition party, 1225
  legends, 1167
  likeness on postage stamps, *1521*, *1522*, 1523, *1524*
  martial law, 1396
  memoirs, 161, 166, 453, 476, 1264
  Mexican War service, 203
  monuments, 1028, 1069, *1070*, 1074
  munitions manufacture, 1470
  nationalism, 1079
  naval policies, 42, 1128, 1131
  opinion of generals, 336, 453, 1251, 1608
  peace initiatives, 387, 733, 804, 1184
  personality, 336, 1248–1249, 1679
  personal papers, 1099
  portraits and likenesses, *436*, 438, *451*, 1230, 1242, 1256; *see also subhead* caricatures *above*
  press criticism, 1510
  privateering policy, 373, 1269, 1369
  and quartermasters, 1292
  religion, 535
  retaliation policy, 1396
  reward for arrest of, 934
  on Sabine Pass battle, 1357
  and secessionist movement, 1381, 1383
  siege of Vicksburg, 1659
  slave emancipation proposal. *See subhead* emancipation policies *above*
  and slavery, 8, 317, 321, 451, 742, 747, 808, 1132
  soldiers' home veto, 1502
  and southernized Northerners, 1157
  and state boards of commissioners, 809

state political opponents, 23, 191, 229, 668, 707, 871, 877, 878, 1142, 1156, 1650, 1651
state rights' broadside, *221*
state rights' stance, 1536
support for, 13, 29, 105, 131, 133, 141, 235, 244, 265, 276, 279, 311, 344, 358, 395, 396, 430, 439, 444, 458, 550, 610, 630, 641, 662, 665, 684, 710, 727, 736, 753, 761, 763–764, 767, 772, 773, 804, 853–854, 856, 882, 883, 884, 906, 907, 925, 926, 928, 964, 965, 967, 971, 1038, 1075, 1093, 1205, 1250, 1287, 1302, 1426–1427, 1431, 1432, 1563, 1595–1596
trial preparations, 748, 965, 1081
Unionism, 225
as U.S. secretary of war, 321, 377, 409, 450, 737, 983
as U.S. senator, 31, 321, 450–451, 802
vice president, 1539, 1540, 1541, 1542
vice-president's relationship with, 668, 1225, 1655
view of press, 640
War Department involvement, 1385, 1386
war strategy, 148, 326–328, 329, 386, 394, 452–453, 508–509, 632, 708, 713, 862, 894, 934, 1020, 1127, 1191, 1248–1249, 1326, 1601, 1700, 1717
Whig party, 1709
wife. *See* Davis, Varina Howell

Davis, Jefferson C. (brigadier general)
Chickamauga campaign, 304
Elkhorn Tavern, Arkansas, 526
Murfreesboro, Tennessee, 1095
Sherman's March through Georgia, 1007

Davis, Joseph E. (brother of Jefferson Davis), 450, **453–454**, 456, 1064, 1347
Davis Bend, 458

Davis, Joseph Evan (son of Jefferson Davis), 453, 457, 1710
Davis, Joseph Robert, **454**
Davis, Lewis, 1408
Davis, Margaret, 453
Davis, Nicholas, **454**
Davis, Reuben, 340, **455–456**, 747, 782, 982
Davis, Sam, 541, 544–545
Davis, Samuel, and Jane Cook Davis, 448
Davis, Sarah Knox Taylor, 450, 456
Davis, Stephen, *as contributor*, 1544, 1631
Davis, S. W., 290
Davis, Varina Anne ("Winnie," daughter of Jefferson Davis), 150, 422, 453
monument, 1028

Davis, Varina Howell (wife of Jefferson Davis), 150, 159, 299, 300, 348, 450, 453, **456–457**, 492, 1066, 1143, 1301, 1739
criticism of, 596, 910, 1106
marriage, 1009
White House, 1710

Davis, William C., *as contributor*, 64–69, 539–542, 738, 929, 1170, 1205–1207, 1363
Davis, William George Mackey, **458**
Davis, Winnie. *See* Davis, Varina Anne
Davis and Bozeman, 1458
Davis Bend, 451, 453–454, **458**, 1064
Davis Guards ("Fighting Irishmen"), 823, 1357, 1516
Medal, *1021*, 1022

Dawkins, James Baird, **458–459**
Dawson, John, 1726
"Day-Star Circular" (Tyson), 1632
Dead Angle (Kennesaw Mountain, Georgia), 886
Dean, Horace, 768–769
Deane, Francis B., 1616
Dearing, James, 47, **459**, 1341
"Dear Mother, I'll Come Home Again" (song), 1232
Deas, Zachariah Cantey, **459**
Death and mourning, **459–461**
atmosphere in Richmond, 1667
funerals, **651**
mass grave, *40*
see also Civil War, losses and numbers; *subhead* casualties *under particular battles and campaigns*

Death penalty. *See* Crime and punishment, execution; Hanging
DeBar, Clementina, 1590
De Bow, James D. B., 506, 509, 583, 584, 985, 1615, 1630
De Bow's Review (magazine), 583, 717, 985, 987, 1232, 1350, 1739
on blockade, 480
textbooks, 516

DeBray, Xavier B., **461**
De Bree, John, 1128
Debt, 403, **461–463**, 511
bonds, **187–190**, 418
certificates, *1282*
government accounts, 509
loans, 418–419, 509–510, 536
public, 1281–1282
specie payment, 1280
state, 665–666
Tredegar Iron Works, 1617

Decie, Henry, 254
Declaration of Immediate Causes, 133, **463**, 1534
text of, 1770–1773

Declaration of Independence, 1274
Declaration of Paris (1856). *See* Treaty of Paris
Declaration of the Causes of Secession. *See* Declaration of Immediate Causes
De Clouet, Alexandre, **464**
Decorations. *See* Medals and decorations
DeCredico, Mary A., *as contributor*, 388–389, 506–512, 717, 809–810, 1517–1518, 1538, 1559, 1571, 1588–1589
Deerhound (ship), 20, 1394
Defection. *See* Desertion; Tories
Defense of the South against the Reproaches and Encroachments of the North, A (pamphlet), 319
Defense of Virginia (Dubney), 1275
Defenses, field. *See* Field fortifications
Defiance (ship), 1334
De Fontaine, Felix Gregory, 1683
DeForest, John W., 938
De-ga-ta-ga. *See* Watie, Stand
Degler, Carl N., *as contributor*, 1636–1640
De Gobineau, Joseph Arthur, 583
De Jarnette, Daniel C., **464**, 1063
De Lagnel, Julius Adolph, 90, **464–465**
Delaney, Norman C., *as contributor*, 879–880, 1269, 1627
De La Rue & Co., 1523
Delaware
black-white population comparison, *1435*
as border state, 195–196
election of 1860, 196, 521, 522, 523
population, 1233
secession date correlated with total black population, *1486*
slavery in, 1437
Unionism, 1380, 1441

Delaware (ship), 700
Delawares (Native American peoples), 425
Delchamps, J. J., 937, 1590
De Leon, David Camden, 845, 1022, 1685
De Leon, Edwin. *See* Leon, Edwin de

De Leon, Thomas Cooper, 472, 1330, 1686
De Lhuys, Édouard Drouyn, 484, 632
Dell, Bess, 1218
Delta Rifles, 140
DeMille, Cecil B., *575*, 577
DeMille, William C., *575*
Democrat (Mississippi newspaper), 131
Democratic party, 335, 387, **465–467**, 1708, 1709
  Alabama, 18, 1286
  attempts to paralyze Lincoln administration, 333
  Bluffton movement, 186, 568
  Compromise of 1850, 381
  Dred Scott decision, 494, 495
  election of 1844, 1629
  election of 1860, 285, 403, 521–524, 1375–1376, 1630
  election of 1864, 349, 1080
  farmers' support, 344
  Florida, 1013
  Georgia, 228
  Kentucky, 972
  last antebellum president, 1375
  Mississippi, 225, 1047
  Montgomery convention, 1067
  national convention, 322, 1047, 1595
  North Carolina, 1626, 1627
  Orr, James L., 1171
  peace movement, 1183, 1184
  and secessionism, 14, 1150, 1377, 1640
  Semmes, Thomas, 1395
  slavery issue, 320, 321, 553, 554, 557
  Smith, Robert Hardy, 1477
  Stephens, Alexander H., 1539
  Tennessee, 1574, 1575
  Texas, 1097, 1715
  Wilmot Proviso, 1728
  see also Copperheads
Democratic-Republican party, 1373
  constitutional interpretation, 1531–1532
Demographics. *See* Population
De Morny, Count, 480
Denbigh (ship), 184, 185
Deneale, George, 310
Denmark, ram sales, 1303
Department of Alabama, Mississippi, and Eastern Louisiana, 416, 1572
  surrender, 237
  see also Army of Alabama, Mississippi, and Eastern Louisiana
Department of East Tennessee
  Buckner, Simon Bolivar, 238–239
  Donelson, Daniel Smith, 492
  Frazer, John Wesley, 637
  see also Army of Tennessee; Department of Tennessee
Department of Inspection and Censorship, 273
Department of Middle and Eastern Florida, 1613
Department of Mississippi and East Louisiana, 68, 72; *see also* Army of Alabama, Mississippi, and Eastern Louisiana; Department of Alabama, Mississippi, and Eastern Louisiana
Department of North Carolina and Southern Virginia, 72, 149, 1582
Department of Northern Georgia, 1738
Department of Northern Virginia, 71, 72; *see also* Army of Northern Virginia
Department of South Carolina, Georgia, and Florida, 72, 149, 917, 1189, 1681
Department of Southwest Virginia, 214, 869
Department of Tennessee, 72, 74; *see also* Army of Tennessee; Department of East Tennessee
Department of the Gulf, 238, 952, 1314
Department of the Ohio, U.S., 1703
Department of the Trans-Mississippi. *See* Trans-Mississippi Department
Department of the West, 72, 74, 410
  Johnston (Joseph E.) command, 1386
  see also Army of the West; Trans-Mississippi Department
Departments, military, 71–74
  map, 73
  see also particular armies and departments
Depositories, 1615–1616
Derry, Joseph T., 1592
De Saligny, Dubois, 631
Desertion, 329, **467–469**
  Alabama, 17, 18, 1426
  by blacks, 7
  bushwhackers, 671, 1155, 1610, 1705
  as disaffection sign, 346, 398, 468–469
  disciplinary procedures, 398, 468–469, 1039, 1190, 1209
  and family honor, 562
  Galvanized Yankees, 654
  Georgia, 670, 671
  Greensboro as haven, 714
  guerrillas, 671, 720, 722, 1155
  haven in Jones County, Miss., 870
  Heroes of America, 768, 1154
  impact on war effort, 70–71, 332, 385, 1116, 1246–1247, 1686, 1687
  Jackman's brigade, 827
  Mississippi, 341, 864, 1051
  newspaper listings, 831
  North Carolina, 715, 1154, 1155
  pardons proposal, 876
  plain folk, 1213
  Price's Missouri raid, 1255
  prisoners, 265
  provost duty, 1278
  punishment. *See subhead* disciplinary procedures *above*
  rates, 385, 1080, 1386, 1492
  reasons for, 66, 421, 467, 563, 901, 903, 1025, 1230, 1426
  Salisbury Prison, 1361
  South Carolina, 192, 1510
  by substitute conscriptees, 397
  Texas, 1586
  tories, 441, 469, 1602
  Trans-Mississippi, 1608, 1610
  Union soldiers, 467
Deshler, James, **469–470**
De Stoeckl, Édouard. *See* Stoeckl, Édouard de
Destruction and Reconstruction (Taylor), 1572
Destructives (North Carolina), 1155
De Vauban, Marquis, 617
Devereux, Frances Anne, 1227
Devil, slave conception of, 1450
Devil in Paris, The (Selby), 1590
DeVilliers, Charles A, 843
D-guard side knife, *513*
Dew, Thomas R., 1273
DeWitt, William H., **470**
Dial, Jonathan, 735
Diana (ship), 491
Diaries, letters, and memoirs, **470–477**
  Alexander, Edward Porter, 25
  apologias, 166
  Beauregard, P. G. T., 150, 331, 475–476
  Beers, Fannie, 153
  Boyd, Belle, 201
  Bragg, Thomas, 207
  Brock, Sallie A., 222
  Campbell, John A., 256
  chaplains, 282
  Chesnut, Mary Boykin, 298, 299–300
  Clay-Clopton, Virginia, 351
  condolence letters, 460–461
  Confederate Veteran magazine, 388
  Davis, Jefferson, 161, 166, 452, 453, 1264
  Davis, Reuben, 455–456

Davis, Varina Howell, 161, *457*
desertion explanations, 467, 1230
Duke, Basil Wilson, 498
Early, Jubal, 503
expressing determination, 333
film documentaries, 574
Freedmen Bureau papers, 473
Fremantle, Arthur J. L., 193
Gorgas, Josiah, 508
Grant, Ulysses S., 354
home front letters, 1244, 1245
Hotchkiss, Jedediah, 797–798
Hunter, Robert M. T., 804
Johnston, Joseph E., 331, 475
Jones, J. B., 333, 865–866
Kean, Robert Garlick Hill, 1686
as leisure activities, 923
Liddell, St. John, 932
love letters, 421
mail service, 1312
Manigault, Arthur Middleton, 1004
mention of fast days, 568
mention of prostitution, 1276, 1277
Merrick, Caroline E., 1034
military memoirs and diaries, 474–475
Moon, Virginia B., 1075
Pember, Phoebe Yates, 1188
prisoners of war, 1264
Sheridan, Philip, 266
soldiers, 307, 398, 421, 470, 474–476, 524, 1103, 1496, 1497–1498, 1500
Stephens, Alexander H., 166
Stone, Kate, 307, 1546
Taylor, Richard, 1572
Taylor, Thomas, 129
women, 307, 387, 422, 471–472, 1009, 1226, 1739, 1741
Wright, D. Giraud, Mrs., 265
Diarrhea, 39, 460
occurrence and treatment, 754, 758
prisoners of war, 1260
Diary from Dixie, A (Chesnut), 300
Dibrell, George Gibbs, **478**
Dickens, Charles, 1330
Dickens, D. Augustus, 891
Dickey, Theophilus L., 784
Dickinson, Andrew B., 1145
Dickinson, Daniel S., *381*
Dickinson, Jack L., *as contributor*, 842–844
Dickinson, James Shelton, **479**
Dickison, John Jackson, 590, 724, 1516
Dickson, Nelson, and Company, 1458
Dictator (ship), 674
Diet. *See* Food
Digest of the Military and Naval Laws of the Confederate States, A (Lester and Bromwell), 193
Digest of the Statute Laws of the State of Georgia (Cobb), 363
Dill, Benjamin, 1143
Dinwiddie Court House, Virginia, 45, 1201
Diplomacy, **479–485**
Alabama claims, 21–22
Alexandra controversy, 25–26
attempt for European recognition, 479–480, 483
bibliography, 170–171
Confederate hopes and failures, 385
cotton, 179–181, 392, 416, 418, 480–481, 483, 507–508, 711, 1025, 1194, 1325, 1687
Davis (Jefferson) view of, 452
Foote (Henry S.) mission, 599
foreign trade and, 507–508
France. *See under* France
Great Britain. *See under* Great Britain
Greenhow (Rose O'Neal) mission, 714
Laird rams, 903–904
Lamar (L. Q. C.) mission, 906
Leon (Edwin de) mission, 924
Mann (A. Dudley) mission, 1004
Mexico. *See under* Mexico
Pickett (John T.) mission, 1209–1210
Rhett (Robert Barnwell, Jr.) mission, 1325
Rost (Pierre A.) mission, 1347–1348
Russia. *See under* Russia
Soulé (Pierre) mission, 1504
Spain. *See under* Spain
State Department, **1527–1530**
state ventures into foreign, 704
Trent affair, 481–482, **1619–1621**
Direct tax, 486, 511, 1025, 1282
Direct Tax Act, **486**
Dirtdiggers, 619, 625, 626
Disciples of Christ, 1320
Discography, **487–488**
Discourse on the Character and Services of John Hampden (Rives), 1336
Discourse on the Constitution and Government of the United States (Calhoun), 253
Discourse on the Uses and Importance of History (Rives), 1336
Disease. *See* Health and medicine, sickness and disease; particular diseases
Dispatch (Richmond newspaper), 1141–1142, 1330
Displaced persons. *See* Refugeeing
Dissolving Views of Richmond (lithographs), 1231
District of Columbia. *See* Washington, D.C.
District of Florida, 32
District of South Mississippi and East Louisiana, 1572
District of Texas, New Mexico, and Arizona, 1677
District of Western Louisiana, 1572, 1677
Disunion. *See* Secession
Divided Union, The (television program), 574
Division
attack formation, 819
composition, 816
Divorce. *See* Marriage and divorce
Dix, John A., 258, 1257
Dixie, **488–489**
Mason-Dixon Line, 1016
Dixie (ship), 1269
"Dixie" (song), 488, *489*, 940, 950, 1027, 1101, 1103, 1498
Dixieland (film), 573
Dixie Land Songster, The, 1104
Dixie Primer for the Little Folks (textbook), 1588
Dixie's Land (recording), 487
"Dixie's Nurse" (song), *712*
Dixon, George E., 778, 1557, 1558
Dixon, Jeremiah, 1016
Dixon, Thomas, 575, 938
Doaksville Constitution, 309
Dobbins, A. S., *52*
Dockery, Thomas Pleasant, **490**
Dockstader, Lew, 574
Doctors. *See* Health and medicine; Hospitals; Medical Department; particular names
Documentary films. *See under* Film and video
Dodd, David, 941
Dodd, Harrison H., 412, 1159
Dodge, Grenville M., 540–541, 542
Doggett, D. S., 1035
Doles, George Pierce, 407, **490**
Dolphin (ship), 700
Don (ship), **491**
Donald, David, 331, 934, 1218
Donaldsville, Louisiana, 720
Donelson, Daniel Smith, **491–492**, 828, 1096
Doniphan, Alexander, 1337
Dorn, A. J., 812, 1290, 1398, 1408
Dorsey, Samuel Worthington, 492

Dorsey, Sarah Anne, 150, **492**
Dorson, Richard M., 593
Dortch, William Theophilus, 107, 118, **492–493**, 1749–1750
Doss, Harriet E. Amos, *as contributor*, 1057–1059
Doubleday, Abner, 1406
Douglas, Henry Kyd, *80*, 502
Douglas, Stephen A., *381*, 451, 1293, *1375*, *1561*
  election of 1860, 14, 109, 138, 225, 321, 426, 454, *494*, 521–524, 588, 667, 851, 852, 907, 925, 1047, 1052, 1057, 1065, 1171, 1355, 1374, 1375, 1477, 1483, 1506, 1539, 1637, 1647, 1654, 1698, 1699, 1709, 1745
  Kansas-Nebraska Act, 175, 176, 852, 875–876, 1375
  repeal of Missouri Compromise, 465
  territorial expansion, 381–382
Douglass, Frederick, 320, 649, 1440, 1450
Dove Creek, Texas, 1584
Dover (ship), 904
Dowling, Richard W. ("Dick"), 623, 1357, 1584, 1609
Downs, Alan C., *as contributor*, 89, 263, 422–423, 512, 835, 1304, 1652–1653, 1654, 1655–1660, 1680–1681, 1754
Draffin, John, 641
Draft. *See* Conscription
Drama. *See* Theater
Drayton, Percival, 493, 1240
Drayton, Thomas F., **493**, 1240
Dred Scott decision, **493–495**
  and causes of Civil War, 322
  Confederate Constitution on, 402
  impact on secessionists, 1375, 1377
  and Missouri Compromise, 255, 1056, 1534
  as state sovereignty endorsement, 1534
Dred Scott v. Sandford. *See* Dred Scott decision
Drew, John, 297, 813
Drewry (ship), 840, 841
Drewry's Bluff, Virginia, **496**, 567, 620, 780, 850, 863, 930, 1182, 1193, 1675, 1736
  naval academy, 1131
Drill units, 1040
Drought. *See* Weather
Dr. Sevier (Cable), 938
Drugs. *See* Pharmaceuticals
"Drummer Boy of Shiloh, The" (song), 487, 1101, 1103
Drummers, 1105
Drummers and Fifers Guide, The (Bruce and Emmett), 1105
Drum-Taps (Whitman), 937
Drunkenness
  Barksdale, William, 132
  Breckinridge, John C., 214
  Carroll, William Henry, 263, 429
  Cheatham, B. Franklin, 296
  Clark, John B., 343
  criminality, 427
  Crittenden, George B., 428–429
  disciplinary procedures, 1039
  Evans, Nathan ("Shanks"), 549
  Hooker, Joseph, 281
  Magruder, John B., 360, 989
  Pickett, John T., 1036, 1209
  soldiers, 1498
  Toombs, Robert, 1068, 1601
  Whiting, W. H. C., 1712
  Wigfall, Louis T., 1714, 1716
  see also Prohibition movement
Dublin and Glasgow Sailing and Steam Packet Company, 2
Dubney, Robert L., 1275
DuBose, Dudley McIver, **497**
Dubose, Julia Ann, 1600
Dubuque Herald (newspaper), 411
Ductown, Tennessee, mines closure, 1471
Dudgeon, John, and William Dudgeon. *See* John & William Dudgeon
Dudley, Thomas Haines, 240, 484, 1308, 1567
Dueling, **497**
  Adams, Daniel Weisiger, 1
  Barksdale, William, 131
  Breckinridge (John C.) and Bragg (Braxton), 214
  Chambers (Henry Cousins) and Lake (William A.), 276
  Conrad, Charles M., 395
  criminality, 427
  Davis (Jefferson) and Benjamin (Judah P.), 159
  Foote, Henry S., 598
  Jackson, Thomas J. ("Stonewall"), 831, 1677
  personal honor and, 787
  Pike (Albert) and Roane (John Selden), 1211, 1340
  Toombs (Robert) and Hill (D. H.), 1601
  Waddell, James, 1675
  Walker, James Alexander, 1677
  Walker (Lucius Marshall) and Marmaduke (John Sappington), 1009, 1679
  Wigfall, Louis T., 1715
Duff, Walter, 126
Duffie, Alfred N., 210, 211
Dufilho, Aguider, 514
Duke, Basil C., **497–498**
Duke, Basil Wilson, 214, **498**, 1180, 1547
Duke, James B., 1332
Duke University Library, Clay (Clement C.) papers, 350
Dumbarton Avenue Methodist Church, 544
Dumfries raid, 269
Duncan, Blanton, 1231
Duncan, Johnson K., **498**, 1140
Duncan, Richard R., *as contributor*, 127
Duncan, Russell, *as contributor*, 1511, 1565–1566
Dunham, Cyrus L., 608, 1093
Dunker church, Maryland, 1406
Dunn, George, 438
Dunn, R. W., 777
Dunovant, John, **498–499**
DuPont, Alfred I., Mrs., 922
Du Pont, Samuel F.
  attack on Charleston Harbor, 1180
  attack on Port Royal, 1129, 1239–1240, 1370
  praise for Smalls (Robert), 1472
Du Pont, Samuel L., 1509
Dupre, Louis, 1144
Dupré, Lucien Jacques, **499**
Durbec, F. W., 1205
Durham, Walter T., *as contributor*, 1028–1030, 1107–1111
Durrill, Wayne K., *as contributor*, 565–567, 762
Duval, Thomas H., 116
Dwight, William, 1239
Dykes, Charles, 1566
Dysentery, 39, 199, 460
  occurrence and treatment, 754, 758

E

Eads ironclads, 993
Eagle and Enquirer (Memphis newspaper), 1143
Eagle Orator. *See* Henry, Gustavus Adolphus
Earle, Robinson, 1747
Early, Jubal, 36, 82, 150, **501–503**, 550, 780, 920, 1581
  cavalry, 268, 276–277
  Cedar Creek, Virginia, 271

Chambersburg, Pennsylvania, 276–277, 1417
Chancellorsville campaign, 279, 280, 281, 282
Cold Harbor, Virginia, 366–367
criticism of Longstreet (James), 946
Fisher's Hill, Virginia, 582–583, 1418
Fredericksburg campaign, 638, 639
Gettysburg campaign, 677, 678, 679, 680, 681, 682
as Hill (A. P.) replacement, 1518
Kelly's Ford, Virginia, 880, 881
Lee Monument, 922
Lynchburg defense, 963, 1413
Manassas, First, 997, 998, 1552
Manassas, Second, 1000, 1002
Maryland raids, 1222
Mine Run campaign, 502–503, 1043
Mosby's Rangers, 723
personality, 501, 502
personal papers, 1099
Shenandoah campaign. *See under* Shenandoah Valley
Southern Historical Society, 948–949, 1512
Spotsylvania campaign, 1519
staff, 694, 797, 867
Washington raid. *See* Early's Washington raid
Williamsburg, Virginia, 1725
Early County, Georgia, 1424
Early's Washington raid, 214, 386, 503, **504–505**, 505–506, 836, 849, 963, 968, 1413, 1417, 1602, 1676, 1752
Earthenware, 735
Earthworks, 619–622
Andersonville Prison, 39
archaeology, 48
artillery, 94
Austin, Texas, 117
Fort Fisher, North Carolina, 611, 1152, *1153*
Paducah, Kentucky, *888*
Port Hudson, Louisiana, 1238
Spotsylvania campaign, 82
Williamsburg, Virginia, 1724
Winchester, Virginia, 1732
see also Trenches
Eason, James, 1424
East, E. H., 703
East Alabama Female College, 1196
Eastern Clarion (newspaper), 982
Eastern Shawnees, 811, 812, 1408–1409
Eastport (ship), **505**
East Tennessee and the Civil War (Temple), 1574
East Tennessee and Virginia Railroad, 1547
East Tennessee Relief Association, 1574
East Tennessee University, 517
Eaton, Clement, 597
Eaton, John, 1709
Ebenezer Church, Alabama, battle of, 1389
Echo (ship), 841, 1269
Echols, Harriet, 259
Echols, John, **505–506**, 694, 1702
Echols, Joseph Hubbard, 344, **506**
Eclipse (ship), 1692
Economic warfare. *See* Counterfeiting
Economy, 386–387, 419, **506–512**
antebellum urbanization, 1107–1108, 1643–1645
bonds, 187–190
currency. *See* Currency
debt. *See* Debt
effect on morale, 1081–1082
extortion, 559–560
farming, 565–567
Georgia, 670
impressment burden, 809–810
inflation, **820–821**, 1367, 1648
Kentucky, 888–889
legal tender controversy, 659, 660, 665
New Plan, 419, 1140
nullification controversy, 1374
public finance. *See* Public finance
as secession factor, 1376
selected bibliography, 170
sermons on, 1399
slavery role, 4–5, 1435–1437, 1439–1441, 1443
Southern nationalism and, 1112, 1113
speculation, 1517–1518
state socialism, 1537–1538
Texas, 1586
Virginia's contributions, 1663–1664
war mobilization, 508–509
see also Blockade; Cotton; Foreign trade; Manufacturing; particular industries
Ector, Matthew Duncan, **512**
Edenton, North Carolina, 1152
Edgar, Walter B., *as contributor*, 133, 199–201, 876–878
Edged weapons, 60, **512–515**
army, **513–514**
Joe Brown's pikes, **846**
museum collections, 1100
navy, 63, **515**, 1469
Palmetto Armory, 1179
Edgefield Advertiser (South Carolina newspaper), 1082, 1598, 1714–1715
Edgefield Hussars, 245, 733
Edgeworth Female Seminary (Greensboro), 715
Ed Howard (ship), 264
Edison Company (documentary films), 573
Edith (ship), 186, 301, 376, 1723, 1727
Edmonston, Catherine Ann Devereux, 387, 470, 472, 788
Education, 305, 307, **515–521**
African Americans, 520, 521, 643, 941, 1030, 1150, 1450–1451, 1588, 1722
Charleston, South Carolina, 1023
Georgia, 108–109, 671–672
higher, **517–518**, 1108
Kentucky, 216, 519
literacy percentages, 1490
Little Rock, Arkansas, 940
medical, 1108, 1110
military, 311–312, **518–520**, 674–675, 957, 1671–1673
Mobile, Alabama, 1059
naval, 1131, 1182
North Carolina, 216, 516, 519, 520, 1518, 1721–1722
plain folk, 1212
plantation, 1214
primary and secondary, **515–517**
Quaker, 1494
Raleigh, North Carolina, 1301
Richmond, Virginia, 1330
slaves. *See subhead* African Americans *above*
social advancement link, 1490
textbooks, 307, 516, 714, 1587–1588
women, 516, **520–521**, 1108
yeomen, 1440
see also Teachers; particular institutions
Edward, Armand, 1101
Edward Lawrence and Company, 43
Edwards, J. D., 1205, 1206
Edwards, John N., 1289
Edwards Ferry, North Carolina, 1425
Eelman, Bruce W., *as contributor*, 403, 429
Egypt, Mississippi, 683
E. I. du Pont Nemours (film documentaries), 573
E. J. Johnston Company, 514
Elder, John, 1231
Elder, William H., 1346

Eleanor S. Brockenbrough Library (Richmond), 1099
Election of 1844, 554, 1629
Election of 1852, 381
Election of 1856, 28, 322, 772, 1321, 1454
Election of 1860, **521–524**
Alabama, 14, 1057, 1065, 1605, 1678, 1695
Bell, John. *See under* Bell, John
Bleeding Kansas, 176
border states, 195
Breckinridge, John C. *See under* Breckinridge, John C.
campaign banner, *404*
caricature, *494*
chart of vote totals by Confederate state, 522
Constitutional Union party. *See under* Constitutional Union party
creoles, 426
Democratic party. *See under* Democratic party
Douglas, Stephen A. *See under* Douglas, Stephen A.
expansion of slavery issue, 554
Florida, 122, 588, 1688
Georgia, 109, 137, 667, 786, 976–977, 1744
Hunter, Robert M. T., 802–803
Johnson, Herschel V., 852–853
Kentucky, 886, 1011
Lincoln, Abraham. *See under* Lincoln, Abraham
Louisiana, 140, 1698
Mississippi, 131, 276, 1047
Missouri, 828, 1052
North Carolina, 118, 133, 1150, 1151
overview, 1375–1376
Republican party. *See under* Republican party
Richmond, Virginia, 1329
and secession, 522, 524, 1171, 1373, 1376, 1377, 1379, 1384, 1506, 1507, 1562
South Carolina, 1506
Southern Unionism during, 687, 706, 1637, 1638, 1650
Tennessee, 138, 598, 745, 753, 763, 798, 1574–1575
Texas, 655, 1583, 1715–1716
urban voters, 1137, 1647
Venable, Abraham Watkins, 1654
Virginia, 925, 1187, 1630
West Virginia, 1699
Election of 1861, 392
Alabama, 16
handbill, *1667*
Tennessee, 1576
Virginia, 279, 1630
Election of 1862, 337
Election of 1863, 393, **524–525**
Alabama, 18–19
Mississippi, 1051
North Carolina, 1156–1157
political issues, 1224
Tennessee, 1576
Virginia, 1714
Election of 1864
campaign banner, *466*, *1322*
caricatures, *412*
Confederate sabotage plots, 1595
Democratic party, 349, 1080
effect of Shenandoah Valley campaign, 503
Johnson, Andrew, 848, 1638
Kentucky, 217, 887
Lincoln, Abraham, 336, 349
and Lincoln war strategy, 1165, 1166
McClellan, George B., 217, *412*, *466*, 887, 1252, 1272, 1632
propaganda efforts, 1271–1272
Radical Republicans, 1632
Republican party, 1044
Tennessee, 1578
war's effect on, 327–328, 336, 632, 1198, 1252, 1253, 1610, 1733
Electoral college system, 1068
Elements of Military Art and Science (Halleck), 862
Elite, 1490, 1491, 1506
see also Planters; Society
Elizabeth City, North Carolina
Burnside (Ambrose) raids, 1152
shipyards, 1424
Elkhorn Tavern, Arkansas, 84, **525–527**, 813, 829, 858, 908, 930, 973, 1017, 1053, 1323, 1607, 1652, 1693
Cherokees, 297
Choctaws, 310
Creeks, 425
Garland, Rufus, 653
Green, Martin Edward, 713
Greer, Elkanah, 715
Hébert, Louis, 759
Little, Lewis, 939
McCulloch, Ben, 970
map, 525
Pike, Albert, 53
Slack, William Yarnel, 1432
Elkin, North Carolina, 1152
Elkridge Plantation, Louisiana, 492
Ella and Anna (ship), 185
Ella Warley (ship), 1469
Ellerbrock, Charles, 1103
Ellerson's Mill, Virginia. *See* Mechanicsville, Virginia
Ellet, Henry T., 251, **527**, 1241
Elliot, Stephen, Jr., **527–528**, 1200
Elliott, Gilbert, 22, **528**, 1425
Elliott, John Milton, **528–529**
Elliott, Stephen (Episcopal bishop), 535
Elliott Richie (ship), 744
Elliott's Brigade, 1682
Ellis, Eliza Brooks, 203
Ellis, Ellizah W., 1133
Ellis, John W., 342, **529**, 701, 702, 703, 781, 1142, 1151, 1156, 1626
Ellis, Richard E., *as contributor*, 1159–1160
Ellis (ship), 407
Ellison family, 643
Ellmore, Edward C., 1614
Elmira, New York, 1258
El Monassir (ship), 903
Elting, John R., *as contributor*, 91–95, 815–820, 1428–1430
El Tousson (ship), 903
Elzey, Arnold, 213, **529–530**, 997, 998, 1544
Emancipation
border states, 1322
Breckinridge, Robert J., 215–216
celebrations, 924
church support, 1399
compensated, 44, 215, 887
as Confederate bid for diplomatic recognition (1865), 485, 1529
as Confederate wartime measure, 564, 884
Davis (Jefferson) support, 9, 160, 530, 532, 934
gradual, 1217
Juneteenth (Texas), 655, **874**, 874, 924, 950, 1586
Kentucky, 889
slave-owner response to, 472
Tennessee, 848
uncompensated, 391, 762
Union occupation and, 1138, 1640–1641
voluntary. *See* Manumission
see also Free people of color; Thirteenth Amendment
Emancipation Proclamation, 4, 6–7, 9, 216, 337, 387, 390, **530–532**, 934
conditions, 1434
Davis (Jefferson) on, 9
Georgia, 670

Hampton Roads Conference, 733
impact on Southern banking, 1424
and increased contraband, 406
Kentucky, 887
Louisiana, 956
North Carolina, 1151
planters' reaction to, 1220
Preliminary (1862), 1408, 1447
slave children, 307–308
symbolic importance, 1446
Tennessee exclusion, 1110, 1574, 1578, 1579
Embalming, 651
Emerson, John, 493
Emerson, Ralph Waldo, 742
Emile Erlanger and Company, 510, 536, 980, 1248
Emmett, Dan, 488, 1105
Emory, William H., 505, 582, 1417
Emory University, 518
Empire Hospital, 796
Employees. *See* Civil Service; Labor
Enchantress affair, **533**, 841, 1269
Encyclopedia Britannica, 574
Encyclopedia of the Social Sciences, 786
Enfield navy cutlass bayonet, 515
Enfield rifles, 63, 90, 182, 232, 1169
Engineer Bureau, **533–535**
employees, 1687
Gilmer, Jeremy Francis, 686
Leadbetter, Danville, 913
Smith, Martin Luther, 1476
Stevens, Walter Husted, 1544
Whiting, W. H. C., 1712
England. *See* Great Britain
Engraving. *See* Printmaking
Engs, Robert Francis, *as contributor*, 1437–1441, 1441–1447, 1448–1451
Enlistees. *See* Soldiers
Enloe, Abraham, 1167
Enoch Train (ship), 1302
Enrica (ship), 19, 1120
Entertainment. *See* Leisure; Popular culture
Entrenchment. *See* Trenches
Epidemics. *See* Health and medicine; particular diseases
Episcopal Church, 259, **535**, 1190, 1320
chaplains, 282
Polk, Leonidas, 1227
Southern sermonists, 1399
Epistle to the Clergy of the Southern States (Grimke), 44
Equipment. *See* Small arms; Supplies; Uniforms; particular kinds
Era No. 5 (ship), 420
Erlanger, Frederick Emile, 536
Erlanger, Raphael, 536
Erlanger loan, 234, 418, 510, **536**, 980, 1026, 1169, 1248, 1454, 1687
Erwin, Marcus, 447
Erysipelas, 795
Escape from Fort Bravo (film), 580
Escott, Paul D., *as contributor*, 117–118, 206–207, 380–382, 611–612, 871–873, 882, 892, 906–907, 910–913, 942, 1078–1083, 1150–1157, 1229–1230, 1244–1245
on bread riots, 559
on preservation of white liberty, 934
Espionage, **536–547**
Alcorn, James L., 24
Beall, John Y., 145, 375
Canadian operations, 160, 258, 538–539, 543, 545, 546–547, 1595
curtailment efforts, 314
Dodd (David) hanging, 941
by free blacks, 643
Gettysburg campaign, 677
Greenhow, Rose O'Newal, 714
guerrilla partisans, 721
Harrison, Henry Thomas, 748
Holcombe, James P., 780–781
military spies, Confederate, 195, **542–547**, 1574
Moon sisters, 1074–1075
Morgan, John Hunt, 1086
Morris, Augusta Hewitt, 1089–1090
prisoners, 265
provost duties, 1278
saboteurs, 538
Secret Service, Confederate, **537–539**, 870–871, 1429–1430
Secret Service, U.S., **539–542**
Slater, Sarah, 1432
Stuart's raids, 1552, 1553, **1554–1556**
war correspondents, 1683
by women, 143, 201–202, 387, 540, 542–544, 601, 714, 750, 1074–1075, 1089–1090, 1432, 1623, 1652, 1740
Essay on Calcareous Manures, An (Ruffin), 1349
Essay on Liberty and Slavery (Bledsoe), 175
Essex (ship), 55
Essex Junto, 1532
Estell, Dick, 488
Ether anesthesia, 756
Ethnicity
Southern, 1112
see also Foreigners; particular groups
"Ethnogenesis" (Timrod), 222, 936, 937, 1597
Ethnology, racial doctrines, 583
Etowah Manufacturing and Mining Company, 1475
Eubank, Cordelia Gay, 1063
Eufaula Rifles, 1286, 1287
Eugénie, empress of France, 1454
Eugenie (ship), 182
Europe. *See* Diplomacy; particular countries, e.g., Great Britain
European Brigade, 603–604
Eustis, George, 481, 482
Evangelicalism. *See* Revivalism
Evangelical Tract Society of Petersburg, Virginia, 1400
Evans, Augusta Jane, **547**, 936, 1058, 1059, 1741
Evans, Clement A., 271, 504, **548**, 798
Evans, David, *as contributor*, 41, 490, 752, 981, 1546–1547, 1707–1708
Evans, Eli N., *as contributor*, 157–162
Evans, Matt, and Sarah Howard Evans, 547
Evans, Nathan ("Shanks"), 528, **548–549**, 996, 998, 1544, 1681
Ball's Bluff, 126–127
Manassas, Second, 1002
Secessionville defense, 1479
Evans, William E., 1019
Evans and Cogswell, 165, 193, 937
"Evelyn." *See* Shepardson, William
Evening Gun of Sumter (Chapman), 283
Everett, Edward, 403, *404*
Everglade (ship), 1530
Ewbank, Thomas, 1274
Ewell, Richard S., 36, 81, 501, 502, **549–550**, 1572, 1621
Brandy Station, Virginia, 209
Fort Harrison, Virginia, 612
Gettysburg campaign, 550, 677, 678, 679, 680, 681, 682, 693, 918
Harpers Ferry, West Virginia, 743
Manassas, Second, 1001
Port Republic, Virginia, 431
on quartermasters, 1292
Sharpsburg division, 1406, 1407
Shenandoah division, 1416, 1417
Spotsylvania campaign, 1518, 1519–1520
staff, 395, 797, 867, 915
Wilderness campaign, 1719
Winchester, Virginia, 1732
Ewing, George Washington, **550–551**
Ewing, Thomas, 721, 1054, 1252
Examiner (Richmond newspaper), 1142
Exchange Hotel (Montgomery), 1066

Exchange of prisoners. *See under* Prisoners of war
Executions. *See under* Crime and punishment; Hanging
Executive branch. *See* Cabinet; Davis, Jefferson; Presidency; Vice Presidency
Executive Council (Kentucky), 1075
Executive Council (South Carolina), 1208
Exemption Act of 1862, 1172
Exemption Act of 1863, 1230
Exemptions. *See under* Conscription
Exercices de Cacographie (textbook), 1588
"Expand or perish" (motto), 551
Expansionism in the antebellum South, **551–558**, 688, 1047, 1209, 1715
  Brown, Albert Gallatin, 225
  Fugitive Slave Law and, 556, 558, 640, 649
  Mexico, 1036
  Nicaragua, 1145
  slavery, 320–321, 1380, 1383, 1384, 1437–1441
  soil exhaustion, 417
  Southern nationalism, 1114
  Texas, 1629
  Wilmot Proviso, **1728**
  see also Compromise of 1850; Crittenden Compromise; Filibustering expeditions; Kansas-Nebraska Act
Ex parte Garland, 661
Ex parte Merryman, 934
Ex parte Milligan, 728
Explosive shells, 62, 93, 94, 95
  booby traps, 1300
Express mail service, 1242, 1243, 1511
Extortion, **559–560**, 1082, 1244
Ezell, Frank, 1498
Ezra Church, Georgia, 87, 110, 112, 114, 1404, 1545

F

Factorage system, 1644, 1646
Factories. *See* Manufacturing; Textile industry
Facts of Reconstruction, The (Lynch), 962
Fagan, James F., 57, 145, **561**, 1610
  Price's Missouri raid, 1252, 1254, 1255
Fairfax, Virginia, 722
Fair Oaks battle. *See* Seven Pines, Virginia
Fallen Timbers, Tennessee, 1423
Falling Waters, Maryland, 222, 771
Falling Waters, Virginia, 832
Falls of Richmond (recording), 487
Family life, **562–565**
  absence of men, 1491
  brothers of war, **224**
  childhood, **305–308**
  concubinage and, 1045–1046
  effect of food shortages, 596
  farming, 565–566
  gender roles, 1487–1488
  marriage and divorce, **1009–1010**
  miscegenation, 1045–1046
  plain folk, 1213
  refugees, 1319
  slave, *5*, 563–565, 1448–1449, 1451
  soldiers' homesickness, 1496
  Southern reverence for, 1488
  yeomen honor, 1490
"Famous knitter," 923
Fannie (ship), 185
Farmer's Bank of Kentucky, 1089
Farmers Exchange Bank (Charleston), 1024
Farmers' Register (journal), 1349
Farming, **565–567**
  acreage by states, *1484*
  as basis of economy, 506
  black belt, **172–173**
  cash crop system, 1214, 1215
  cotton, **416–420**
  demographics, 1484–1485
  effects of conscription, 1244–1245
  expansion of slavery, 551–552
  free blacks, 1486
  impressment of produce. *See under* Impressment
  Kentucky price index, 888
  labor, 901
  manpower losses, 1413
  negative impact of slavery, 1440–1441
  plain folk, 1212
  produce loan, 1270
  reform, 1349
  rice, **1327–1328**
  self-sustaining, 1660
  Shenandoah Valley, 1412–1413, 1415, 1418–1419
  tariffs, 1114
  taxes, 1570
  tax-in-kind, 345, 1571
  tobacco, **1597–1599**
  Trans-Mississippi, 1606
  women, 900, 1739
  yeomanry, 1378, 1380–1381, 1440–1441, 1490
  see also Plantation; Planters; Yeomanry
Farragut, David, 55, 227, 611, 1124, 1314, 1357, 1504, 1655–1656, 1691
  caricature, *732*
  Galveston, Texas, 656
  Mobile Bay, 179, 236–237, 1059, 1062, 1126, 1130, 1581, 1695
  Mobile blockade, 1058
  New Orleans, 178, 246, 645, 954, 993, 1049, 1137, 1138, 1139
  response to guerrilla activity, 720
  Sabine Pass, 1609
  shelling of Baton Rouge, 140
Farrand, Ebenezer, **567–568**, 1062
Farrow, James, **568**
Fascines, *624*, *625*
Fast days, **568–569**, 1275, 1320
  Methodist Church, 1034
  sermons, 1399
Father of Booms. *See* Hotchkiss, Jedediah
Father of West Virginia. *See* Peirpoint, Francis H.
Fathers, The (Tate), 939
Faulkner, William, 788, 939, 949
Fauntleroy, Charles M., 1055, 1308
Fauquier County, Virginia, 1090, 1091
Faust, Drew Gilpin, 1115, 1116
Fawcett and Preston, 591
Fay, Edwin Hedge, 475
Fayetteville, North Carolina
  arsenal, 48–49, 90, 262, 465, 1461, 1469
  newspapers, 1143
  small arms manufacture, 1455, 1457, 1462, 1470
  textile industry, 1645
Fayetteville pistol-carbine, 1461
Fearn, Mary Walker, 1058
Fearn, Thomas, 454, **569**
Featherston, Winfield Scott, **569**
Federalist Papers (The Federalist), 1531
Federalist party, 1373
  constitutional interpretation, 1531, 1532
Federal occupation. *See* Union occupation
Fehrenbacher, Don, 495
Fellman, Michael, *as contributor*, 38, 839, 1289, 1599, 1754
Felton, Rebecca Latimer, **570**, 1742
Felton, William Harrell, 570
Fencibles, 140
Fendall, Philip R., 1338
Ferguson, Champ, 724, 1363
Ferguson, Samuel Wragg, **570**
Ferguson, William, 735

Ferrero, Edward, 1200
Ferries, 1340
Fetzer, Dale, Jr., *as contributor*, 1318
Ficklin, Ben, 1723
Fiction
 after Civil War, 938–939
 during Civil War, 936–937
 film, **574–580**
 popular, 1232
 publishing, 193–194
Field, Charles W., 30, **570–571**, 612
 Gaines' Mill, Virginia, 653
 Mechanicsville, Virginia, 1020
Field fortifications, **624–627**
 archaeology, 48
 Army of North Virginia, 81–82
 artillery, 91, 93, 94, 96
 guns, *995*
 hasty entrenchments, 819–820
 Lee, Robert E., 76, 78, 625, 917, 920
 Longstreet, James, 945
 tactics, 325–326
 see also Earthworks; Trenches
Fife and drum, 1105
Fifth Company, Washington Artillery of New Orleans. *See* Slocum's Battery
Fifth U.S. Colored Cavalry, 1363
Fifty-fourth Massachusetts Infantry, 11, 12, 1074, 1259
"Fighting Joe." *See* Wheeler, Joseph
Fighting for the Confederacy (Alexander), 25, 474–475
"Fighting Irishmen." *See* Davis Guards
File closers, **571**, 572
 to prevent desertion, 468
Filibustering expeditions, 557, 648, 808, 1036, 1145, 1174, 1209, 1384, 1504, 1631, 1715
Fillmore, Millard, 28, *381*, 706, 772, 1011, 1224
Film and video, **572–580**
 documentary, **572–574**
 fictional presentations, **574–580**
Film Associates of California, 574
Finance. *See* Banking; Bonds; Currency; Economy; Public finance
Financial Failure and Confederate Defeat (Ball), 1248
Findlay Iron Works, 97
Finegan, Joseph, **581**, 590, 823, 1567
 Olustee battle, 1165–1166
Fingal (ship), 116, 180, 184, 240, 1126, 1370, 1465, 1596, 1684; *see also* *Atlanta* (ship)
Finkelman, Paul, *as contributor*, 399–403, 493–495, 1728
Finley, Jesse Johnson, **581**, 1682
Finn, Bernard S., *as contributor*, 1573
Finns Point National Cemetery, 610
Fire
 Atlanta, Georgia, 111, 673, 1648
 Chambersburg, Pennsylvania, 277, 503, 849, 968, 1417
 Charleston, South Carolina, 285, 288
 Cloyds Mountain, Virginia, 358
 Columbia, South Carolina, 261, 371–372, 1510, 1648
 Jackson (ship), 839
 Randolph, Tennessee, 1030
 Richmond, Virginia, 1331–1332
 St. Albans, Vermont, 350, 538
 Salisbury Prison, 1152, 1362
 scorched-earth policy, 200, 361, 1006, 1217, 1352
 Shenandoah Valley, 583, 1733
 wooden bridges, 263, 1340
Fire-eaters, 14, 16, 318, **582**, 1065
 Barksdale, William, 131
 Barry, William Taylor Sullivan, 135
 black belt, 173
 Davis, Jefferson, 225, 1716
 Davis, Reuben, 455
 election of 1860, 176, 1441
 Georgia, 423, 675
 Gregg, Maxcy, 717
 Mississippi, 1051
 Montgomery convention, 1067
 Pickens, Francis W., 1207
 Rhett, Robert Barnwell, Sr., 582, 1323, 1350
 Ruffin, Edmund, 1350
 secession leadership, 1376–1377, 1383, 1507, 1639–1640, 1647
 sense of honor, 787, 788
 Toombs, Robert, 1601
 Wigfall, Louis T., 1715
Firmin & Sons, 515
First Dixie Reader (textbook), 307
First Kentucky Brigade. *See* Orphan Brigade
First Manassas. *See* Manassas, First
First Missouri Brigade, 1516
First Presbyterian Church of Lexington, Kentucky, 216
First South Carolina Volunteers, 1447
First Virginia Infantry Regiment, 1516
First Volunteer Regiment of Georgia, 1366
First Wheeling Convention. *See* Wheeling Convention
First Year of the War, The (Pollard), 475, 1229
Firth, Pond and Company, 488
Fish, Hamilton, 21
Fish Boat (submarine), 777, 801
Fisher, Sidney George, 1274
Fisher's Hill, Virginia, 268, **582–583**
 Early (Jubal) defeat at, 1418
Fishing Creek, Kentucky, 761
Fisk, John F., 988
Fisk Jubilee Singers, 1104
Fitch, Clyde, 578
Fitzgerald, F. Scott, 578
Fitzgerald, Michael W., *as contributor*, 344–347
Fitzgerald, Oscar, 1035
Fitzhugh, George, **583–584**
Fitzmorris, Terrence W., *as contributor*, 729, 883–885
Fitzpatrick, Benjamin, *15*, 411
Fitzsimons, Catherine Elizabeth, 730
Five Civilized Tribes, 172, 526, 748-749, 810, 811, 812, 813, 1607; *see also* Cherokees; Chickasaws; Choctaws; Creeks; Indians; Indian Territory; Seminoles
Five Forks, Virginia, 45, 83, 1201
 shad bake, 915, 1209
Five Southern Tribes. *See* Five Civilized Tribes
Flag Act of 1818, 587
Flagg, Benjamin, 1179
Flag of His Country, The (film), 574
Flag of the Union (newspaper), 1205
Flag over Sumter, 1863 (Chapman), 283
Flags, **584–587**
 adoption of Stars and Bars, 1068
 Confederate, 148, 249, *436*, **584–585**, 950
 Confederate design, 1038
 Confederate Signal Corps, 1428–1429
 first flag of independence, *668*
 military, **585–586**
 museum collections, 1100
 North Carolina, 1301
 return of captured, 573
 state, **587**, 1507
Flamingo (ship), 185
Flanagin, Harris, 53, **587–588**, 661, 701, 702, 703, 1314
Flash, Henry, 985
Flatboat, 1691–1692
Fleming, Robert, 1588
Fletcher, Thomas, **588**, 702
Flight from the flag, 20, 21
Flintlock musket, 60, 819, 1461–1465, 1467
Flora (ship), 1727
Florence Gazette (newspaper), 1744
Florence Museum, South Carolina, 1185

"Florence Nightingale of the Confederacy." *See* Newsom, Ella King
Florence Prison, South Carolina, 1268
Florida, **588–591**
  arsenal and armory, 866, 1461, 1469
  black-white population comparison, *1435*
  congressmen, 30–33, 122, 241, 458, 776, 1013, 1020, 1090, 1175–1176, 1345, 1364, 1682, 1688
  conscription, 392, 873
  Constitution ratification, 403
  currency, 1279
  debt, 462
  Democratic party, 465
  Department of. *See* Department of Middle and Eastern Florida; Department of South Carolina, Georgia, and Florida
  education, 516
  election of 1860, 521, 522, 523
  farm acreage, *1484*
  flag, 587
  foreign population, 602
  Fort Pickens, 1381
  free people of color, 642, 644–645
  governors, 28, 701, 702, 703, 704, 1042, 1195, 1196, 1688
  guerrilla activity, 724
  hospitals, 794, 796
  niter production, 1147
  Olustee battle, 1165–1166
  Owens, James B., 1175–1176
  Pensacola Navy Yard, 1424
  population, 1233
  railroads, 1294, 1295, 1296, 1297
  Reconstruction, 1682
  rice production, 1327, 1328
  roads, 1339
  salt-making industry, 1362
  secession. *See under* Secession
  secession and Confederacy membership dates, *1379*
  secession date correlated with total black population, *1486*
  slaveholdings, *1485*
  slavery, 551, 552, 557
  state navy, 1530
  state rights, 1535
  sugar industry, 1559, 1560
  Unionism. *See under* Unionism
Florida (ship), 21, 22, 183, 240, 375, 484, **591–592**, 712, 984, 992, 1062, 1150, 1309
  Blakely rifle, 1120
  commerce raiding, 374, 376, 1123, 1129
Florida Agricultural and Mechanical University, 1682
Florida Sentinel (newspaper), 1566
Floridian and Journal (newspaper), 1566
Flour mills (Richmond), 1330
Floyd, John B., 238, 474, **592–593**, 843, 1322, 1464, 1700, 1736
  Henry and Donelson campaign, 765, 766, 767, 1211
  staff, 447
Floyd's Rifles, 29
Flush Times in Alabama and Mississippi (Baldwin), 172, 749
Flusser, Charles W., 22
Flying artillery. *See* Horse artillery
Foard Hospital (Tennessee), 796
Foch, Marshall, 573
Folkes, John, 1143
Folk music, 487, 1104
Folk narratives, **593–594**
  Free State of Jones, 870
  Frietchie, Barbara, 646
  Harris, Joel Chandler, 671, 938
  Hart, Nancy, 750
  and oral histories, 1167
  slave, 1450
Folsom, Simpson N., 310
Fontenot, Kevin S., *as contributor*, 395–396, 464, 499, 778, 1345–1346
Food, **594–597**
  antebellum Southern imports, 1441
  Army of Northern Virginia malnutrition, 79
  Beefsteak raid, 151–152
  civilian malnutrition, 596, 758
  cotton exchanges, 420
  distribution to needy. *See* Poor relief; State socialism
  foraging, **600–601**
  free markets, **641–642**, 1058, 1229
  high prices, 419, 566, 591, 641, 1367, 1517
  hoarding, 1082, 1244
  hospital, 795, 1161
  impressment, 377, 393, 463, 596, 1244, 1571
  morale, 1082
  nutritional deficiencies, 595, 754, 758
  poor relief, 1229, 1230; *see also subhead* free markets *above*
  poverty, 1154, 1244–1245
  prison rations, 38, 610, 1158, 1260, 1261, *1263*
  production, 419
  riots. *See* Bread riots
  sailors' rations, 1360
  Salisbury Prison, 1362
  salt preservation, 1362
  Savannah shortages, 1367
  scavenging, 597
  Shenandoah Valley destruction, 1413, 1418–1419
  Shenandoah Valley supplies, 1412, 1415
  shortages, 467–228, 559, 563, 689, 758, 1082, 1154, 1244–1245, 1367, 1426, 1491, 1686
  slave diet, 597
  soldiers' hunger, 378, 1239
  soldiers' rations, 595, 1495–1496
  starvation parties, 597, 1330
  starvation rations, 595, 1686
  substitutes, 1558
  see also Commissary Bureau; Farming; Fast days
Fool's Errand, A (Tourge), 938
Foot artillery. *See* Heavy artillery
Football, 923
"Foot Cavalry," 78
Foote, Andrew H., 887
  Henry and Donelson campaign, 327, 764, 765, 766, 1596
  New Madrid and Island Number 10, 1133
Foote, Henry S., 153, 314, 373, *381*, 444, 559, **597–600**, 736, 864, 872, 942, 1047, 1063, 1338
  dismissal of Mallory (Stephen R.), 438
  gubernatorial election, 450
  peace proposal, 786
  resignation, 1203
Foote, Shelby, 331, 939
Footwear. *See* Shoes and boots
Foraging, 17, 328, 595, **600–601**
  accounts, 475
  Arkansas campaign, 57
  Army of Northern Virginia, 45
  bummers, **241**, *242*
  horses and mules, 793
  Sherman's troops, 117, 260, 601, 793, 901
Force Act of 1833, 1160, 1336
Forced Funding Act of 1864, 820
Ford, Antonia, 543, **601**
Ford, John, 580
Ford, John S. ("Rip"), 231, 232, 233, 234, 1583, 1585, 1611
Ford, Sallie Rochester, 193, 1232
Ford, Samuel Howard, **602**
Ford, Tennessee Ernie, 487

Ford Motor Company (film documentaries), 573
Ford's Theatre (Washington, D.C.), *935*
Foreign Enlistment Act (Great Britain), 25, 240, 1271
Foreigners, **602–604**
American party, 28
Arkansas, 52
Charleston, South Carolina, 285, 1506
citizenship, 313
as Confederate officers, 353
conscription, 348, 900, 1076
extortion accusations, 559
Germans. *See* Germans
Irish. *See* Irish
Little Rock, Arkansas, 940
Louisiana Tigers, 957
Memphis, Tennessee, 1028
population, 602, 1234
recruitment, 339, 980–981, 1261
small percentage in military, 1494
in Stonewall Brigade, 1549
Tallahassee, Florida, 1566
Texas, 1583, 1585
Unionism, 346
urban immigrants, 1137, 1646–1647
Foreign relations. *See* Diplomacy; particular countries
Foreign trade, 507–508
advocacy of free, 511, 1114, 1287; *see also* Nullification controversy
African slave. *See* Slave traders
and antebellum urbanization, 1643–1645
bonds, 507
Confederate government controls, 1537
cotton, 232, 233, 418–420, 432, 1169, 1215, 1364, 1365, 1586, 1608, 1659
diplomacy, 507–508
France and England, 507–508, 1184
luxury item imports, 50, 174, 1140
Mexican agreements, 1037
Savannah port, 1364, 1365
see also Anglo-American purchasing; Blockade; Commerce raiders; Privateering; particular commodities
Forge, The (Stribling), 939
Forgeworkers, African American. *See* African American forgeworkers
Forgie, George B., *as contributor*, 116–117, 231–232
Forman, Thomas Marsh, **604**
Forney, John Horace, **604–605**, 893, 894, 974, 1478
Forney, William Henry, 604, **605**
Forrer, Daniel, 797
Forrest, French, **605–606**, 840, 1127
Forrest, Nathan Bedford, 17, 238, **606–607**, 839, 846, 871, 921, 1173, 1386, 1622, 1708
Atlanta campaign, 114
Brice's Cross Roads, 218–219
cavalry, 266, 267, 302
elite units, 1516
Fallen Timbers, Tennessee, 1423
Fort Pillow Massacre, 614, 615, 616, 1603
Franklin and Nashville campaign, 633
Henry and Donelson campaign, 765, 767
Ku Klux Klan, 607
Meridian campaign objective, 1032, 1033
Mississippi, 1049, 1051, 1624, 1625
personal honor, 787
raids. *See* Forrest's raids
recklessness of, 788
Selma, Alabama, 18, 440, 1388, 1389–1390
staff, 255, 1525
Tennessee, 275–276, 328, 447, 779, 835, 1577, 1656
Forrest's raids, 154, 239, 269, 328, 478, 607, **608–609**, 1186, 1329, 1343
Memphis, Tennessee, *609*, 1029
Mississippi, 1032
Paducah, Kentucky, **1177**
Forsyth, John, 424, **609–610**, 628, 1142, 1144, 1345, *1382*, 1683
Forsyth, Georgia, bread riots, 213
Fort Alafia, Florida, 617
Fort Alexis, Alabama, 622
Fort Anderson, Kentucky, 1177
Fort Ann, Mississippi, 621
Fort Arbuckle, Indian Territory, 813
Fort Baldwin, Virginia, 621
Fort Barrancas, Florida, 589, 613, 618, 1205
Fort Beaulieu, Georgia, 618
Fort Beauregard, South Carolina, 1240
Fort Bisland, Texas, 713
Fort Blakely, Alabama, 622, 1061
Fort Bliss, Texas, 623
Fort Blunt, Indian Territory, 814
Fort Boggs, Georgia, 618
Fort Brown, Texas, 231, 233, 618, 1611
Fort Caswell, North Carolina, 179, 529, 1726–1727
Fort Clark, North Carolina, 178
Fort Clinch, Florida, 590
Fort Cobb, Indian Territory, 813
Fort Cobb, North Carolina, 623
Fort Darling, Virginia. *See* Drewry's Bluff, Virginia
Fort Davidson, Missouri, 1252
Fort Davis, Texas, 623
Fort Delaware Prison, **610**
Fort DeRussy, Louisiana, 1315
Fort DeSoto, Florida, 617
Fort Donelson (ship), 1341
Fort Donelson, Tennessee. *See* Henry and Donelson campaign
Fort Fisher, North Carolina, 129, 179, 205, 301, **611–612**, 622, 623, 759, 894, 1152, *1153*, 1712, 1727
Fort Forrest, North Carolina, 622
Fort Gaines, Alabama, 618
Fort Garrott. *See* Square Fort, Mississippi
Fort Gibson. *See* Fort Blunt
Fort Gregg, South Carolina, *100*, 622, 630
Fort Gregg, Virginia, 45, 621, 746
Fort Harrison, Virginia, **612**, 621, 894
Fort Haskell, Virginia, 627
Fort Hatteras, North Carolina, 178, 666, 1152, 1678
Fort Heiman, Tennessee, 764, 1596
Fort Henry, Alabama, 1426
Fort Henry, Tennessee. *See* Henry and Donelson campaign
Fort Hill, Mississippi, 621
Fort Hill (South Carolina plantation), **613**
Fort Hindman, Arkansas, 311, 981
Fort Hoke, Virginia, 621
Fort Jackson, Georgia, 1366
Fort Jackson, Louisiana, 618, 619, 769, 954, 1334
Fort Johnson, Virginia, 621
Fort Johnston, North Carolina, 529, 1726
Fort Larned, Kansas, 1390
Fort Lee, Georgia, 618
Fort LeFlore, Mississippi, 621
Fort McAllister, Georgia, 618, 619, 672, 1366, 1368
Fort Macon, Georgia, *977*
Fort Macon, North Carolina, 1152
Fort McRee, Florida, 613, 618, 1205, 1661
Fort Magruder, Virginia, 1725
Fort Mahone, Virginia, 45, 620
Fort Mercer, Georgia, 618
Fort Mill, South Carolina, 1069
Fort Monroe, Virginia, 405, 453, 1149, 1191, 1192, 1229, 1623
as sanctuary for escaped slaves, 1444
Fort Moore, Mississippi, 621

Fort Morgan, Alabama, 17, 617, 618, 1059, 1178
Fort Moultrie, South Carolina, 622, 1333, 1507; *see also* Fort Sumter, South Carolina
Fort Negley, Tennessee, 1110
Fort Pemberton, Mississippi, 227, 621, 1696
Fort Pickens, Florida, *589*, **613–614**, 617, 618, 628, 991, 1205, 1381
Fort Pillow, Tennessee
  command, 1661
  field fortifications, 226, 626
Fort Pillow Massacre, 11, 276, 564, **614–616**
  Forrest, Nathan Bedford, 607
  tories, 1603
Fort Powell, Alabama, 619
Fort Pulaski, Georgia, 256, **616**, 617, *618*, 672, 909, 1125, 1259, 1366
  guns, 619, 623
  slave escapes, 1367
Fort Rose Dew, Georgia, 618
Fort Sabine, Texas, 623
Fort St. Philip, Louisiana, 619, 769, 1334
Fort Sanders, Tennessee, 896–897, 914
Fort Scott, Kansas, 11
Forts and fortifications, **616–627**
  African American labor, 75, 399
  armament, 623
  artillery, 94
  Atlanta, Georgia, 109, *110*
  coastal, 617–619, 1678
  engineer regiments, 534–535
  field, **624-627**; *see also* Field fortifications
  French, Samuel G., 646
  Grant, Ulysses S., 1198
  impressed slave, 192, 899, 900
  Lee, Robert E., 367
  North Carolina, *1152*
  overview article, **616–623**
  Port Hudson, Louisiana, 1238
  rampart grenades, 734
  Texas, 1583
  see also Earthworks; Trenches
Fort Smith, Arkansas, 1290
Fort Smith peace treaty (1865), 1398, 1409
Fort Stedman, Virginia, **627**, 697, 1201
Fort Stephens, Virginia, 621
Fort Sumter, South Carolina, **627–630**, 689, 1333
  Citadel cadets, 312, 519
  Confederate firing on, 285, 324, 1382, 1508
  as Confederate sovereignty symbol, 324
  construction, 619
  defenses, 146, 622
  design, 617
  first shot fired, 1350
  fortification, 1544
  guns, 623
  Harriet Lane, 744
  negotiations, 298–299, 383, 424, 1038, 1066, 1381–1382, 1678
  photographs, 1205, *1207*
  pulling down U.S. flag over, 864
  and secession, 1373, 1507–1508
  Star of the West, **1526**
  Union attack on, 1509
  Wigfall (Louis T.) at, 1716
Fort Taylor, Florida, 589
Fort Texas, Mississippi, 621
Fort Tyler, Georgia, 623
Fort Wagner, South Carolina, 179, 622, **630**, 877–878, 1333–1334, 1509
Fort Walker, South Carolina, 1240
Fort Walker, Virginia, 621
Fort Warren, Massachusetts, 447, 716, 1015, 1179, 1619, 1622
  prisoners, *1260*
Fort Washita, Indian Territory, 813
Fort Whitworth, Virginia, 620
.45 Whitworth rifle, 818
Foster, Ephraim, 1708
Foster, Gaines M., *as contributor*, 922–923, 948–950, 1026–1027, 1069–1071, 1512
Foster, Kevin J., *as contributor*, 116, 129, 254, 368, 373–376, 491, 674, 744, 777–778, 801, 841, 1302–1304, 1308–1310, 1340–1341, 1369, 1411–1412, 1530, 1567, 1599–1600, 1675
Foster, Thomas J., **630–631**
Foundries, 96–98
  African American forgeworkers, **3–4**, 96
  artillery, 96
  locations, 3
  naval ordnance works, 1121–1122
  skilled labor, 96, 97, 902
Fourier, Charles, 645
Four Seasons of the Confederacy (painting), 1100
Fourteenth Amendment, 124, 312–313, 1081, 1699
  legalization of slave marriages, 1010
  payment of Confederate Treasury notes, 434
Fowler, William M., Jr., *as contributor*, 1126–1130
Fox, Gustavus, 334
Fox, John, Jr., 578
Fox (ship), 185
Fox-Genovese, Elizabeth, *as contributor*, 470–477, 520–521, 547
Fox's Gap (South Mountain, Maryland), 1513
Fraise, 1201
France, **631–632**
  commerce raiders, 374, 376
  cotton, 1270
  diplomatic missions to, 9, 385, 479, 482, 485, 631–632, 712, 714, 803, 884, 924, 1347, 1454–1455, 1487, 1527, 1529
  intelligence operations, 542
  Mexican interests, 232, 464, 479, 485, 631, 1036, 1063, 1314
  naval vessel sales and construction, 1123, 1150, 1547
  neutrality, 480
  ordnance imports, 102, 513
  propaganda, 1271
  small arms manufacture, 1469
  trade, 507, 1194
Franking privilege, congressional, 1242
Frank Leslie's Illustrated (magazine), 722, 986, 987
Franklin, Benjamin, 1531
Franklin, Jimmie Lewis, *as contributor*, 962
Franklin, William B., 1357, 1609
  Fredericksburg campaign, 638, 639
  South Mountain, Maryland, 1513
Franklin and Nashville campaign, 88, **632–636**, 700, 835, 1111, 1291
  Adams, John, 1–2
  Bate, William Brimage, 139
  Carter, John Carpenter, 264
  Cheatham , B. Franklin, 296
  Deas, Zachariah, 459
  Gist, States Rights, 691
  Gordon, George, 695
  Granbury, Hiram, 708
  Hood, John Bell, 149, 790
  Lowry, Robert, 960
  map, 633, 635
  Smith, James Argyle, 1475
  Strahl, Otho French, 1551
  Walthall, Edward Cary, 1683
Franks, Kenny A., *as contributor*, 340, 347–350, 497–498, 527, 684–685, 736, 750, 841–842, 862, 927–928, 979–981, 1019, 1692–1694
Fraser, Walter J., Jr., *as contributor*, 284–288, 641–642, 1333–1334, 1364–1369, 1504–1510

Fraser, Trenholm, and Company, 179, 180, 368, 511, 1107, 1169, 1616, 1619, 1687
Frayser's Farm, Virginia, 78, **636–637**, 654, 834, 918, 1192, 1193, 1400
  Hill, A. P., 770
  map, 1401
  Sanders, John Caldwell Calhoun, 1364
Frazee, P. F., 370
Frazer, John Wesley, **637**
Frazier, Donald S.
  as cartographer, x
  as contributor, 233–234, 337–340, 518–520, 655–656, 692–693, 749, 791, 889–891, 1041–1042, 1174, 1196–1198, 1346–1347, 1707
Frederick, Maryland, 1404–1406
Frederick County, Virginia, 1413
Fredericksburg (ship), 692, 840, 841, 1124, 1126, 1303, 1424
Fredericksburg campaign, 79, **637–640**, 826, 835, 1386, 1556
  artillery, 93
  captured Union small arms, 1462
  Cobb's brigade, 364–365
  drummer boy, 1105
  Early, Jubal, 502
  field fortifications, 626
  First Louisiana Brigade, 957
  Godwin, Archibald, 693
  Gregg, Maxcy, 717
  Hill, A. P., 771
  Hoke, Robert, 780
  Jones, J. R., 866
  Kershaw, Joseph, 891
  Lee, Robert E., 637, 638, 639, 819, 918, 1386
  Longstreet, James, 638, 945
  McDowell (Irvin) Union forces, 1415, 1416
  McLaws, Lafayette, 974
  McRae, William, 983
  map, 638
  Scales, Alfred Moore, 1370
  tactics, 25, 819
Free blacks. *See under* Free people of color
Free Church of Glasgow, 730
Freedman's Village, Arlington House, 58
Freedmen's Bureau, 292, 1064, 1446
  Davis Bend, 453–454, 458
  New Bern, North Carolina, 1152
  papers, 473
Freedom of speech, 313, 314
Freedom of the press, 313, 314, **640–641**
  censorship, 273–274, 640
Freehling, William W., *as contributor*, 551–558, 648–650, 875–876
Freeman, Douglas Southall, 167, 663, 810, 1512
Freeman, Thomas W., **641**
Free markets, **641–642**, 1058, 1229
Free people of color, **642–645**
  Alabama, 1057, 1065
  blacks, 6, 75, 369, 564, 620, **642–644**, 886, 887, 956, 976, 1137, 1138, 1172, 1646, 1647
  border states, 195
  Charleston, South Carolina, 285, 1504, 1506
  Civil War loyalties, 1486
  creoles, **425–426**, **644–645**, 956, 1621
  demographics, 1484, 1486–1487
  Dred Scott decision, 493–495
  education, 643, 941, 1030, 1150
  impressment of, 38, 75, 704, 1148, 1217
  metalworkers, 902
  miscegenation, 1045, 1046
  Missouri, 1052
  population, 1233
  Port Royal and Sea Islands communities, 1240
  Reconstruction leadership, 962
  religion, 1321
  Richmond, Virginia, 1330
  social mobility, 1490
  sugar plantation work, 1560
  in Union Army, 10, 779
  urban, 1484, 1506
Free-Soil party, 175–176, 321, 1375, 1728
  platform, 495
Free State of Jones. *See* Jones County, Mississippi
Free State party, 956, 1138
Fregonese, Hugo, 580
Fremantle, Arthur J., 193, 232
Frémont, John C., 105, 155, *381*, 549, 1251, 1702, 1705, 1730
  Cross Keys and Port Republic, Virginia, 430, 431
  Shenandoah Valley campaign, *1414*, 1415, 1416, 1417
French, Daniel Chester, 1073
French, S. B., 1080
French, Samuel G., **645–646**, 886, 1157, 1373
French, William H., 831, 1408
Friedman Memorial Library (Alabama), 842
Friendly fire, 93, 94, 817
  Cobb, Thomas R. R., 1364
  Jackson, Thomas J. ("Stonewall"), 80, 279, 835, 908, 918
  Jenkins, Micah, 93, 844
  Lee, Robert E., 93
  Longstreet, James, 93, 946
  Wilderness campaign, 891–892
Friends. *See* Society of Friends
Frietchie, Barbara, **646**
Fripp, John Edwin, 1217
Froelich, Louis, 514
Frolic (ship). *See Advance*
Frontier forts, 622–623
Front Royal, Virginia, 202, 549, **647**, 957, 1732
  Shenandoah Valley campaigns, 1416, 1418
Frost, Daniel Marsh, 199, 343, **647–88**, 1053
Fry, Birkett Davenport, **648**, 816
Fry, Joseph, 182, 183
Frye, Dennis E., *as contributor*, 103–105, 738–744, 807–808, 1404–1408, 1417–1419, 1512–1513, 1556, 1677
Fugitive Slave Law of 1793, 1533
Fugitive Slave Law of 1850, 130, 321, 322, 381, 382, 390, 521, 556–557, **648–650**, 675, 787, 802, 1014, 1337, 1690
  impact on secessionists, 1375, 1377
  Union Army enforcement, 7, 9, 1442
  Wisconsin unconstitutionality argument, 1534
Fugitive slaves, 7–8, 564, **648–650**, 670, 720, 721, 724, 836–837, 901, 1220, 1623
  Constitution, Confederate, 402
  as "contraband of war," 405–406, 1444–1446
  family as impediment, 1448
  fomenting slave insurgencies, 552
  New Bern, North Carolina, 1152
  reward poster, *1439*
  Southern expansionism and, 556, 558, 649, 650
  as Union soldiers, 648, 1447
Fuller, Thomas C., **650–651**
Fuller, William A., 41
Fulton, James, 1142–1143
Fulton, Leonard, 1658
Fulton, Robert, 1515, 1556
Fulton (ship), 1123, 1530
Funerals, **651**
  as community event, 1489
  see also Death and mourning

Funsten, David, **651–652**
Furman, James C., 1399
Fuse, torpedo, 1604
F. W. Dana (ship), 1530

G

Gabions, *624*
Gable, Clark, 580
Gadsden Purchase (1853), 558, 808
Gaines (ship), 236, 685, 1062, 1118, 1125, 1126, 1388, 1581
Gaines' Mill, Virginia, 78, **653–654**, 805, 826, 918, 1192, 1193, 1208, 1400, 1676
  Archer, James Jay, 50–51
  battle description, 1500
  Elzey, Arnold, 530
  field fortifications, 625
  Hale, Stephen, 730
  Hill, A. P., 770
  Hood's Brigade, 791
  Jackson, Thomas J. ("Stonewall"), 834
  map, 1401
  see also Cold Harbor, Virginia
Gaither, Burgess S., **654**
Galena (ship), 496
Gallego mill, 1330
Galphin, George, 1045–1046
Galvanized rebels, 654; *see also* Tories
Galvanized Yankees, **654**, 1261
  prisoner recruits, 1222
  see also Tories
Galveston, Texas, **655–656**
  battle, 461, **655–656**, 1372, 1386
  forts, 623
  Green, Thomas, 713
  hospitals, 796
  Irish immigrants, 823
Gamble, Hamilton R., 702, 1606
Gander-pulling, 923
Gangrene, 39, 795, 867
  fatalities, 757
  hospital service, 796
Gano, Richard Montgomery, **656–657**, 815
Gano's Brigade, 1584–1585
GAR. *See* Army, U.S.
Gardenhire, E. L., **657**
Gardiner, David, 1629
Gardiner, Julia, 1629
Gardner, Alexander, 5, 539
Gardner, Charles, 657
Gardner, Franklin, 145, **657–658**, 955, 1239
Gardner, Frederick J., 1471
Gardner, James, 1144
Gardner, W. M., **658**, 1267
Garsche, P. Baudery, 1246
Garfield, James A., 1011
Garland, Augustus Hill, 263, **658–662**, 1088, 1396
Garland, Rufus K., 659, **662**, 1349
Garland, Samuel, Jr., **662–663**, 826, 1513
Garlington, A. C., 988
Garnett, Muscoe Russell Hunter, **663**
Garnett, Richard Brooke, 364, **663–664**, 834, 1734
  as Gettysburg casualty, 1391
  Stonewall Brigade command, 1549
Garnett, Robert S., 465, 663, **664**, 797, 836, 1186, 1700, 1703, 1704
  staff, 1526
Garrard, Kenner Dudley, 1546
Garrett, J., and F. Garrett, 1461
Garrett, John W., 1295
Garrett, T. Elwood, 1103
Garrett and Company, 1457
Garrison, Wendell Phillips, 1104
Garrison, William Lloyd, 44, 319, *649*
Garrott, Isham Warren, **664**, 1236, 1237, 1477
Gartrell, Lucius Jeremiah, 138, **665**, *669*
Gartrell's Brigade, 665
Gary, Martin Witherspoon, 246, **666**
Gaston, C. A., 1430, 1573
Gate City Guardian (Atlanta newspaper), 108
Gatlin, Richard Caswell, **666**
Gauges, railroad track, 1294, 1297
Gay, Edwin Scott, 212
Gayarr, Charles, 426
Gayle, Amelia, 698, 1168
Gayle, Richard N., 182, 183
GBMA. *See* Gettysburg Battlefield Memorial Association
Geary, John W., 294, 442
Gee, John Henry, 1264, 1361, 1362
Gemsbok (ship), 177
Genealogy, miscegenation, 1046
General (locomotive), 41, 109, 674, 1298, 1574
General, The (film), 577, *579*
General A. P. Hill: The Story of a Confederate Warrior (recording), 488
General Bragg (ship), 1334
General Breckenridge (ship), 1334
General Conscription Law of 1862. *See* Conscription Acts of 1862 and 1864
General Hospital Number 24 (Richmond), 796
General Jackson's Military Road, 1339
General Lovell (ship), 1334
General Orders, Confederate
  No. 4, 571
  No. 5, 601
  No. 9, 83
  No. 39, 1607
  No. 77, 508
  No. 100 (Lieber Code), 1352
  see also Special Order No. 191, Confederate
General Orders, U.S.
  No. 11, 722
  No. 28. *See* Butler's woman order
  see also Special Field Order No. 26, U.S.
General Polk (ship), 264
General Price (ship), 1334
General Removal Act of 1830, 811
Generals
  Arkansas, *52*
  attitudes toward press, 273–274, 314
  casualties, 664, 1240
  Confederate losses at Spotsylvania, 1520
  full, 148
  group photograph, *65*
  Indian, 1694
  inexperience, 94
  last surviving, 968, 1342, 1474
  leadership abilities, 334, 336
  North Carolina, 1151
  Northern-born Confederate, 1157
  personality conflicts, 33, 67, 68, 76, 85–86, 87, 88, 149, 206, 214, 239, 272, 275–276, 296, 308, 353, 361, 413–414, 438, 501, 549, 607, 947, 969–970, 974, 1096, 1227, 1606, 1610, 1679, 1700, 1707, 1708
  political, 10, 214, 361, 364, 1211, 1600, 1609
  postwar benevolence activity, 1502
  ranking controversy, 1716
  strategy and tactics. *See* Strategy and tactics
  Texas, 1472–1474
  Virginia, 1664
  see also particular generals
General Sumter (ship), 1334
General Synod, Lutheran Church, 961
General Tract Agency of Raleigh, North Carolina, 1400
General Van Dorn (ship), 1334
Geneva Arbitration Tribunal, *Alabama* claims, 904

Gen. Lee Songster, The, 1104
Gen. Rob't E. Lee's Favorite 26th N.C. Band (recording), 487
Gentleman's Decision (television program), 573
Gentry, Judith Fenner, *as contributor*, 536
Gentry, Meredith Poindexter, **666–667**
Geographical Reader for the Dixie Children (textbook), 1588
Geography for Beginners (textbook), 1588
George Dunn and Company, 1231
George Griswold (ship), 674
George Peabody Fund, 440
Georgia, **667–673**
  agriculture, 172–173
  arsenals and armories, 1461, 1469
  Atlanta campaign. *See under* Atlanta, Georgia
  black-white population comparison, *1435*, 1460
  bread riots, 596
  Chickamauga campaign. *See* Chickamauga campaign
  congressmen, 13–14, 28–29, 136–138, 153–154, 174, 344, 358–362, 363–364, 506, 604, 665, 750, 771–774, 785–786, 881–882, 924–925, 928, 929, 1093–1094, 1146, 1420, 1475–1476, 1479, 1539, 1542, 1551, 1601, 1622–1623; 1738, 1745
  conscription controversy, 872–873, 1686
  cooperationists, 411, 1379, 1380
  currency, 1281
  debt, 462
  Department of. *See* Department of Northern Georgia; Department of South Carolina, Georgia, and Florida
  education, 519, 520, 523
  election of 1860, 521, 522
  farm acreage, *1484*
  flag, 587
  fortifications, 1475
  free blacks, 642, 643
  governors, 13, 368, 696–697, 701, 702, 703–704, 772, 1476, 1542
  habeas corpus controversy, 727–728
  hospitals, 794, 796
  Ingram, Porter, 822
  iron production, 1148
  Kennesaw Mountain battle. *See* Kennesaw Mountain, Georgia
  limestone cave, 1375
  manufacturing, 514, 1647
  military events, 672–673
  mining, 1043
  morale, 1286
  munitions arsenals, 1168
  music publishing, 1101
  newspapers, 671, 1144
  niter production, 1147
  pike production, 846
  population, 602, 642, 1233
  prisons, 38–40
  Quakers, 1493, 1494
  railroads, 1293, 1294, 1295, 1296, 1297
  Reconstruction, 230, 750, 773–774
  rice production, 1327, 1328
  Savannah campaign. *See under* Savannah, Georgia
  Savannah Squadron, 1370
  secession. *See under* Secession
  secession and Confederacy membership dates, *1379*
  secession date correlated with total black population, *1486*
  separate peace proposal, 1536, 1541, 1543
  Sherman's march through. *See* March to the Sea, Sherman's
  slaveholdings, *1485*
  slavery, 552, 675
  small arms imports, 1465
  small arms manufacture, 1458, 1459, 1470, 1471
  state navy, 1530
  state rights extremism, 1535, 1536, 1540
  Stephens, Alexander H., 1538–1542
  Stephens, Linton, 1542–1543
  sugar industry, 1559, 1560
  taxation, 1283, 1284, 1570
  textbook publishing, 1587
  textile industry, 1645
  tories, 1602
  Unionism. *See under* Unionism
  Whig party, 1708
  see also particular cities and place names
Georgia (ship), 21, 22, 49, 374, 375, **673–674**, 1008, 1018, 1019, 1124, 1125–1126, 1370, 1691
Georgia Armory, 1458
Georgia Hussars, 1366
Georgia Military Institute, 519, **674–675**
Georgian (ship), 145
Georgia Platform, **675**
Georgia Railroad, 1294, 1295
Georgia Railroad and Banking Company, 344
Georgia Reserve Force, 362, 424
Georgia Scenes (Longstreet), 172
Georgia Sketches (Johnston), 671, 937
Georgia State Guard, 361, 362
German edged weapons, 513
Germans, 602, **675–676**
  border states, 195
  Charleston, South Carolina, 285
  conscription exemptions, 900
  European Brigade, 603
  Little Rock, Arkansas, 940, 941
  Mississippi, 1047
  Missouri, 1052, 1053
  Mobile, Alabama, 1057
  recruitment, 1271
  Richmond, Virginia, 1330
  Roman Catholics, 1346
  Savannah tensions, 1367
  Texas, 1321, 1583, 1585
Germantown (ship), 700
Gery, George T., ironclad design, *1117*
Getty, George W., 1719
Getty brass-framed Sharps carbine, 1456, 1457
Gettysburg Battlefield Memorial Association, 943, 1071, 1072-1073; *see also* Gettysburg National Military Park
Gettysburg campaign, 67, 81, 337, 524, **676–683**, 826, 850, 862, 866–867, 894, 1732
  Alexander, Edward, 25
  Anderson, George Thomas ("Tige"), 30
  Anderson, Richard Heron, 36
  Archer, James Jay, 51
  Barksdale, William, 132
  battlefield park, 943
  Brockenbrough, John Mercer, 222
  casualties, 338, 1151, 1391
  Confederate infantry, 816, 819
  Confederate officer casualties, 1391
  Confederate prisoners, *1499*
  Daniel, Junius, 443
  Davis, Joseph Robert, 454
  dead Confederate sharpshooter, *1501*
  Doles, George, 490
  Early, Jubal, 502
  espionage operations, 537, 748
  Ewell, Richard, 550, 693, 918
  field fortifications, 626
  film depictions, 575
  Fry, Birkett, 648
  Godwin, Archibald, 693
  Gordon, James, 696

Gettysburg campaign, *continued*
  Gordon, John, 697
  Hampton, Wade, 731
  Heth, Henry, 769
  Hill, A. P. *See under* Hill, A. P.
  Hood, John, 789
  Humphreys, Benjamin, 800
  impact on morale, 1079–1080
  inexperience of officers, 94
  Jones, John M., 867
  Kemper, James, 881
  Kershaw, Joseph, 891
  Lee, Robert E., 328, 676–683, 918, 945–946, 1553
  Leventhorpe, Collett, 926–927
  Longstreet, James. *See under* Longstreet, James
  Louisiana Tigers, 958
  maps, 678, 680, 682
  Pender, William Dorsey, 1190
  Perrin, Abner Monroe, 1195
  Pickett's Charge. *See* Pickett's Charge
  reunions and reenactments, 572, 573, 1027, 1318
  Rodes, Robert, 1345
  Sanders, John Caldwell Calhoun, 1364
  Scales, Alfred Moore, 1370
  Semmes, Paul J., 1391
  Shenandoah Valley link to, 1412
  Stonewall Brigade, 1549
  Stuart's charge, 1553
  telegraph use, 1573
  Wright, Ambrose Ransom ("Rans"), 1744
  see also Brandy Station, Virginia; Winchester, Virginia
Gettysburg National Military Park, 1072, 1073, 1074
Gholson, Cary Ann, 684
Gholson, Samuel Jameson, **683–684**
Gholson, Thomas Saunders, 367, **684**
Ghost of Dismal Swamp, The (play), 1231
Gibbes, Lewis R., 285
Gibbon, Israel, 1683
Gibbon, John, 571, 1001
"Gibraltar" (Fisher's Hill, Virginia), 582
Gibralter (ship), 1563
Gibraltar of the Confederacy. *See* Vicksburg
Gibson, James F., 99, 999
Gibson, Randall Lee, **684–685**
Gienapp, William E., *as contributor*, 28, 1321–1322
Gift, George W., 291, **685**, 1371
Gilbert, Charles C., 1197
Gildersleeve, Basil, 476, 1142
Giles, Valerius Cincinnatus, 475
Gillam and Miller Company, 1457
Gillem, Alvan C., **685–686**, 1087
Gillespie, Finley, 760
Gillmore, Quincy A., 287, 496, 616, 619, 630, 988, 1509
Gilmer, George R., 928
Gilmer, Jeremy Francis, 533, **686**, 1544, 1685
Gilmer, John A., **687–690**, 706
Gilmer, William P., Mrs., 795
Gilmer Hospital (Tennessee), 796, 1685
Giraffe (ship), 1723
Girard, Charles, 1469
Girardey, Victor Jean Baptiste, **690**
Girardy percussion fuze, 98
"Girl I Left Behind Me, The" (song), 1103, 1498
Gist, States Rights, 259, **691**
Gist, William H., 1378, 1506, 1507
Gladden, Adley Hogan, **691**, 1342
Gladstone, William E., 484
Glasgow, Ellen, 938
Glassell, William T., 289, 445, **692**, 1515, 1599
Glatthaar, Joseph, 11
Glaze, William, 1179–1180, 1464, 1465
Glendale, Virginia. *See* Frayser's Farm, Virginia
Glenwood, 1745
Globe Tavern, Virginia, 1200
Glorieta Pass, New Mexico, **692–693**, 1136, 1428, 1584
GMI. *See* Georgia Military Institute
Godbold, E. Stanley, *as contributor*, 1593–1594
Goddin, O., 1154, 1155
Goddin Hall (Richmond), Post Office Department, 1242
Godey's Lady Book (magazine), 986, 987
Go Down, Moses (short story collection by Faulkner), 939
"Go Down, Moses" (song), 1103–1104
Godwin, Archibald Campbell, **693**, 880
Goebel, William, 217
Goetzel, S. H., 1587; *see also* S. H. Goetzel and Company
Goggin, James Monroe, **693–694**
Goings, Henderson, 643
Gold
  final supply, 841
  mining, 1043
  prices, 820
  -to-paper currency ratio, 821
Golden Rocket (ship), 1393, 1563
Goldsboro, North Carolina, 117, 163, 262, 1152, 1153
Goldsborough, Louis, 244, 245
  on Confederate ordnance, 1118–1119
Gone with the Wind (film), 318, 574, 578, 580, 949, 1103
Gone with the Wind (novel by Mitchell), 318, 787, 939, 1103, 1218
Gonorrhea, 770, 771, 1276
Gonzales, John Edmond, 597
"Goober Peas" (song), 1104
Goode, John, Jr., **694–695**
Good Hope (ship), 674
Goodloe, Daniel Reeves, 44–45, 768, 855
Goodman, Thomas, 275
Goodrich, James W., *as contributor*, 153, 274–275, 342–343, 396, 408–409, 641, 747, 1159, 1204, 1722
Goodrich, Ralph L., 940
Goodrich, Thomas, *as contributor*, 718–725
Goodwin, John N., 51
Goodwyn, Thomas J., 371
Goose Creek, Kentucky, 1362
Gorchakov, Alexander M., 1354
Gordon, Augustus, 696
Gordon, B. Frank, **695**
Gordon, Caroline, 939
Gordon, George Washington, **695**
Gordon, James Byron, **695–696**
Gordon, John B., 36, 47–48, 67, 82, 214, 271, 503, 504, 548, **696–697**, 983, 1185, 1721, 1733
  Cedar Creek, Virginia, 1419
  Confederate Veterans, 1027
  Fisher's Hill, Virginia, 582
  Fort Stedman, Virginia, 83, 627
  Petersburg campaign, 1201
  statue, 951–952
Gordon, Martin, 1453
Gordon (ship), 185, 1014–1015, 1269
Gordon-Burr, Lesley Jill, *as contributor*, 151–152, 366, 529–530, 613–614, 653–654, 662–663, 710, 769–770, 892–893, 1017, 1059–1062, 1076, 1191–1193, 1474–1475, 1592, 1660–1661
Gordon Hospital (Nashville), 794, 1549
Goree, Thomas Jewett, 475
Gorgas, Josiah, 174, 256, 337, **698–699**, 1361
  blockade running, 181, 1726
  diary, 1080
  Engineer Bureau, 533
  foreign procurement, 179
  governmental economic controls, 1537
  influence on Davis (Jefferson), 1249

munitions sources, 1469–1470, 1471
Northern background, 1157
Ordnance Bureau. *See under* Ordnance Bureau
personal papers, 1099
powder works, 1245–1246
resourcefulness, 336
Whitworth rifles, 1467
Gorgas, William Crawford, 698
Gorman, Willis, 126
Gorsuch, Edward, 650
Gosport Navy Yard, 290, **699–700**, 1149, 1664, 1725
captured ordnance, 62, 99–100, 515, 1119
Confederate seizure of, 990, 1424
output, 94, 1121
"Go in the Wilderness" (song), 1104
Gottchalk, Charles, 1021
Govan, Daniel Chevilette, *52*, **700**
Government, state and local. *See* State and local government
Government girls, 370
Government House (Montgomery), 1684
Government workers. *See* Civil service
Governors, **701–704**
chart, 702–703
correspondence, 1226
military, 685–686, 848, 1151
obstructionist, 331, 387, 446, 1093, 1106, 1156–1157, 1184, 1224, 1225, 1249
state rights policies, 452, 1249
see also particular names; *under* particular states
Gracie, Archibald, Jr., **704–705**, 897
Grady, Henry, 774
Graebner, Norman A., *as contributor*, 257–258, 479–485, 631–632, 1004, 1354–1355, 1513–1514, 1527–1530
Graham, Malcolm D., **705**
Graham, William A., 200, 689, **705–708**, 781, 804, 1338
coup attempt, 1651
Granbury, Hiram Bronson, **708–709**
Grand Army of the Republic. *See* Army, U.S.
Grand Divisions, Army of Tennessee, 66, 84
Granger, Gordon, 304, 874
Granite City (ship), 1357
Graniteville, South Carolina, 717
Granny Lee (Robert E. Lee nickname), 917
Grant, L. P., 109
Grant, Ulysses S., *329*
Alabama claims, 21
appointments, 1172, 1652
Appomattox campaign, 45–48, 920
Belmont, Missouri, 155–156
caricature, *732*
Chattanooga campaign, 293–294, 295
Cold Harbor, Virginia, 366–267
cotton for food exchanges, 420
foraging, 601
guerrilla activities against, 723
Hampton Roads Conference, 733
Henry and Donelson campaign, 238, 764–767, 1576
Heroes of America, 768–769, 855
Holly Springs raid, 783–784, 785, 835
Hotchkiss maps, 797
intelligence operations, 540, 541
Iuka, Mississippi, 825
Jackson, Mississippi, 837
Kentucky campaign, 887, 889, 890, 891
Lynchburg, Virginia, 963
nickname, 887
offensives, 81–82
Petersburg campaign, 1198–1202
Port Gibson, Mississippi, 1236, 1237, 1238
presidency, 226, 600
prisoner exchanges, 1258, 1259, 1261, 1262–1263, 1353
Red River campaign, 1314, 1315
Shenandoah Valley campaign, 503, 963, 1413, 1417, 1418, 1419
Shiloh campaign, 327, 1420–1421, 1422, 1423, 1576, 1584
Spotsylvania campaign, 1518, 1519
Stoneman's raids, 1547
strategy and tactics, 56, 111, 156, 326, 328–329, 334, 357, 537, 546, 626, 837, 963, 1177, 1314, 1413, 1417, 1418, 1419, 1625
Tennessee advances, 1420
Vicksburg campaign, 53, 328, 608, 837, 838, 1189, 1476, 1656–1660
Virginia battles, 149, 919–920, 1666
Wilderness campaign, 550, 919, 1719–1721
wiretaps, 1573
Grapeshot, 61, 94
archaeological excavations, 49
Graphic arts. *See* Art; Lithography; Printmaking
Graves, James R., 130
Graves, John, 952
Graves, Rice E., 1170
Graves, William A., **709**, 1515
Gray, Henry, **709–710**
Gray, Peter W., **710**
Gray, Virginia Davis, 472
Gray Ghost. *See* Mosby, John S.
Grayson, John Breckinridge, **710**
Great Bazaar (Columbia, South Carolina), 371
Great Britain, **710–713**
Alabama claims, 21–22
antislavery, 44, 160, 553, 556, 1016, 1629
arms shipments, 60, 102–103, 232, 1465–1468, 1470
Bible procurement, 165
Confederate propaganda in, 798, 810, 1270–1271
Confederate recognition. *See subhead* diplomatic missions *below*; *subhead* neutrality *below*
Confederate stamps contract, 1523
cotton shortages, 483, 1014–1016
diplomatic missions to, 9, 385, 479–480, 482–485, 632, 711–712, 714, 803, 884, 924, 1014–1016, 1347, 1487, 1527, 1619, 1748–1749
edged weapons manufacture, 515
Foreign Enlistment Act, 26
intelligence operations, 542
Laird rams, 903–904
London Convention, 631
naval ordnance manufacture, 1119–1120
neutrality, 178, 180, 240, 257–258, 374, 375, 385, 480, 483, 632, 711, 1325, 1353, 1528, 1620, 1627, 1748
proslavery, 1273
Scottish ship construction, 484, 673, 1150
trade, 507–508, 1194
Trent affair. *See Trent* affair
U.S. history of strained relations, 1619–1622
see also Anglo-Confederate purchasing; Russell, John, Lord
Great Creole. *See* Beauregard, P. G. T.
Great Kanawha River, West Virginia, salt making, 1362
Great Locomotive Chase. *See* Andrews raid
"Great panic" (Nashville, Tennessee), 1109
Great Raid, Morgan, John Hunt, 1089
Great Smoky Mountains, 355
Great Valley Road, 1338
Greeley, Horace, 349, 495, 762, 781, 1279, 1689
caricatures, *933*, *1044*
Green, Bruce, 487
Green, Daniel, 210

Green, Donald E., *as contributor*, 424–425, 1166–1167
Green, Harriet, 1623
Green, J. U., 1329
Green, James S., 713, 858
Green, Martin Edwin, 414, 490, **713**, 1236, 1237
Green, Philip, 1528
Green, Thomas, 117, 461, 543, 544, **713** 749, 961, 990, 1317, 1538, 1585, 1609
Greene, George, 1406
Greene, Israel, 741
Greene, Nathaniel, 1365
Greeneville Convention. *See* Knoxville and Greeneville conventions
Greenhow, Rose O'Neal, 143, 387, 537, 540, 542–543, 544, 546, **714**, 870–871, 1089, 1090, 1430, 1727
Greenhow Prison (Washington, D.C.), 143
Greensboro, Georgia, small arms manufacture, 1459
Greensboro, North Carolina, **714–715**, 1648
 ordnance complex, 1457
 railroads, 714, 1294
 small arms manufacture, 1457, 1461
 Stoneman's raid, 1152
Greensboro College, 715
Greensborough Patriot (newspaper), 715
Green's Brigade, 1584
Greenville, South Carolina, 1457, 1510
Greenville and Columbia Railroad, 395, 1172
Greenwood, Mississippi, 621
Greenwood and Gray, 1458
Greer, Elkanah Brackin, 512, **715**, 908, 1145
Gregg, Alexander, 1399
Gregg, David M., 209, 210, 211, 278
Gregg, John, 269, **715–717**, 1658
 Hood's Texas Brigade, 791
 Jackson, Mississippi, 838
Gregg, Maxcy, 463, **717**, 972
 Fredericksburg campaign, 638, 639
 Gaines' Mill, Virginia, 653
 Manassas, Second, 1001, 1002
Gregg, William, 506, **717**
Grenades. *See* Hand grenades and land mines
Gretna, Louisiana, powder works, 1245
Greyhound (ship), 543
Grice, Charles, 22
Grierson, Benjamin H., 219, 1624, 1625
 Mississippi raids, 837, 1658
Griffe, 1045
Griffen gun, 101
Griffin, Charles, 997, 998
Griffin, Georgia, hospitals, 794
Griffith, D. W., 574, 575, 578, 938
Griffith, John, 784, 785
Griffith, Richard, 132, **717–718**
Grimball, Meta Morris, 472
Grimes, Bryan, **718**
Grimke, Sarah, and Angelina Grimke, 44
Griswold, Samuel, 1459
Griswold and Gunnison, 1459, 1461
Griswoldville, Georgia, 1459
Groce, W. Todd, *as contributor*, 195–197, 752–753
Groene, Bertram Hawthorne, *as contributor*, 1567
Grover, Cuvier, 141
Groveton, Virginia, 1526, 1549
Guadalupe (ship), 904
Guadalupe Hidalgo, Treaty of, 232
Guard for Home Defense (North Carolina), 1184–1185
Guerre de course. *See* Commerce raiders
Guerrillas, The (McCabe), 937, 1590
Guerrilla warfare, 68–69, **718–725**
 Alabama, 345
 Anderson, William, 38
 Andrews raid, **41**, 109, 674, 1298. 1574
 Angels of Destruction, 927
 Arkansas, 53
 Bowie, Walter, 546
 Centralia massacre, 38, **274–275**, 724
 Chickasaws, 305
 class conflict and, 1492
 Indian troops, 1390
 James brothers, 721, 724, 839
 Johnson, Adam Rankin ("Stovepipe"), 846–847
 Kentucky raids, 888
 Louisiana, 140, 955
 Missouri, 11, 719–720, 722, 724, 725, 1053–1054
 Morgan, John Hunt, 1086–1087
 Mosby's Rangers, 1090, **1091–1092**, 1516
 North Carolina, 379–380, 1492
 oral history, 1167
 Price's Missouri raid, **1254**
 Quantrill, William Clarke, 1289
 rivers as target, 1692
 rules of war and, 1352
 by Southern Unionists, 1638–1639
 special units, 1516
 as subject of legends, 594
 Tennessee, 1030, 1576
 Todd, George, 1599
 at war's end, 215, 993
 West Virginia, 1705–1706
 Younger brothers, 1754
 see also Commerce raiders
Guild, L., *77*
Guilford County, North Carolina
 Greensboro as seat of, 714–715
 Quakers, 715, 1493, 1494
Guilford College, 1494
Guilford Grays (North Carolina), 715
Guirot, Anthony J., 1615
Gum opium, 757
Gunboats
 Confederate purchasing, 1150
 construction, 991–992
 defense of Memphis, Tennessee, 1029
 Henry and Donelson campaign, 764, 765, 766
 steam powered, 1018
"Gun Deck of the *Merrimack*, The" (engraving), *1120*
Gunnison, A. W., 1459
Gunpowder. *See* Powder works
Guns. *See* Arms, weapons, and ammunition; Rifled guns; Small arms; particular kinds
Gunter family, 562
Guntown. *See* Brice's Cross Roads, Mississippi
Gustavus Adolphus, king of Sweden, 571
Gutheim, James, 845
Guthrie, James, 1295, 1337, 1630
Guthrie, John J., 291, **725–726**
Gwynn, Walter, 1154

H

Habeas corpus, **727–728**
 peace movement and, 1184, 1185
 as political issue, 393, 394, 431, 525, 1223–1224
 suspension advocacy, 105, 652, 657, 665, 684, 705, 760, 761, 773, 862, 882, 884, 1337, 1717
 suspension by Davis (Jefferson), 313–314, 452, 768
 suspension by Lincoln (Abraham), 332, 728
 suspension for civilian prisoners, 640
 suspension for draft evaders, 398, 1184
 suspension in Kentucky, 1177

suspension opposition, 106, 107, 119, 122, 124, 229, 260, 446, 599, 651, 654, 660–661, 662, 689, 911, 912, 967, 1038, 1156, 1304, 1349, 1535, 1540, 1543, 1745
suspension-related fears of despotism, 707
see also Martial law
Hadfield, George, 58
Hagan, John, 1499
Hagerstown Pike, 1406, *1407*
Hagood, Johnson, 312, **728–729**
Hague, Parthenia, 471–472, 1215
Hahn, Michael, 702, **729**, 956, 1322, 1348
Haiman, Louis, and Elias Haiman, 845, 1460
Haines, Bert, 577
Hale, Edward J., 1143
Hale, John P., 382
Hale, Stephen Fowler, **729–730**
Half-breed, 1045
Hall, James O., *as contributor*, 748
Hall, John (North Carolina judge), 206
Hall, John H. (rifle manufacturer), 739–740
Hall, Willard Preble, 702
Hall breechloading rifles, 1465
Halleck, Henry W.
Chattanooga campaign, 293, 1086
Corinth, Mississippi, 1049
Henry and Donelson campaign, 327, 764, 767
Jomini (Henry) influence on, 862
Red River campaign, 1314
Shenandoah Valley campaign of Sheridan, 1417
Shiloh campaign, 1420
strategy, 326
on Stuart's raids, 1556
Hallock, Judith Lee, *as contributor*, 203–206, 973, 1613–1614
Hall rifles. *See* Rifles; Hall breechloading rifles
Halltown, Virginia, 1418
Halpin, Frederick W., 873, 951
Hamer, Fritz P., *as contributor*, 394–395, 548–549
Hamilton, Alexander, 1285, 1373, 1531, 1626
Hamilton, Andrew J., 232, 1585
Hamilton, Charles, 414
Hamilton, James, 1159, 1160
Hammer, Mark, 488
Hammersley, John, 1141
Hammond, Charles, 1698
Hammond, James H., 200, 411, 416, 555, 583, **730**, 1273, 1349, *1505*, 1714
Hammond, John Swainston, 202
Hampt, Herman, 620
Hampton, Frank, 731
Hampton, Preston, 731–732
Hampton, Wade, 82, 117, 134, 144, 163, 246, 262, 267, 278, 299, 300, 695, **730–732**, 747, 816, 1172, 1431, 1707, 1753
Beefsteak raid, 151–152, 1200
Brandy Station, Virginia, 209, 210, 731
Buckland Mills, Virginia, 237
Cadet Rangers, 312
cavalry, 266
Columbia, South Carolina, 371, 372
Kilpatrick-Dahlgren raid, 893
Lee Monument unveiling, *922*
Legion, 666, 731–732, 733–734, 816, 1516, 1753
Manassas, First, 548, 731
Petersburg campaign, 731–732, 1199
Hampton (ship), 840, 1125
Hampton Roads, Virginia
blockade, 178
Buchanan, Franklin, 235–236
naval battle, 1149, 1181, 1424, 1670–1671, *1671*, 1743
Union fleet, 1556
Hampton Roads Conference, **732–733**
Campbell, John A., 256, 733, 804
disappointment in failure of, 201, 506, 924
Emancipation Proclamation issue, 532
Gilmer, John, 689
Graham, William A., 708
Hill, Benjamin, 773
Hunter, Robert M. T., 256, 730, 804
initiative controversy, 804
Orr, Jehu Amaziah, 1173
Stephens, Alexander H., 256, 532, 730, 731, 773, 804, 1541–1542, 1655
Hampton-Rosser cattle raid. *See* Beefsteak raid
Hampton's Legion, 666, 731–732, **733–734**, 816, 1614
casualties, 734
Hanckel, Charles F., 1614
Hancock, Winfield Scott
Gettysburg campaign, 59, 679
Petersburg campaign, 1198, 1199, 1201
Spotsylvania campaign, 1519, 1520
Wilderness campaign, 1503, 1719, 1721
Williamsburg, Virginia, 1725
Hand grenades and land mines, **734–735**
booby traps, 1300
rules of war, 1352
see also Torpedoes and mines
Handguns
ammunition, 1470–1471
captured U.S., 1463–108
Confederate-manufactured, **1459–1461**
imports, *1466*, 1467, 1469
naval, 1469
revolvers, 63, 93
Handicrafts, **735**
artisan labor, 900
creole artisans, 644
free black and slave artisans, 902, 1486
Hanes, Lewis, 1183
Hanging
desertion, 1209
Dodd, David, 941
Lincoln conspirators, 145, *539*
Wirz, Henry, *1735*
see also Crime and punishment
Hanly, Thomas B., 263, **736**
Hanson, Roger, **736**, 1096
Orphan Brigade command, 1170
Harbin, Thomas, 547
Harby, Levy Myers, 845
Hardcastle, Aaron, 1422
Hardee, William J., 32, 149, 193, 194, 238, 263, 353, 428, 691, **737–738**, 885, 890, 1544, 1744
Army of Tennessee, 84, 85, 86, 87, 296
artillery command, 1427
Atlanta campaign, 111, 112, 139
Averasboro, North Carolina, 117–118, 262
battle flag, 586
Charleston defense, 287, 288, 1510
Chattanooga campaign, 295
Dalton, Georgia, 442
March to the Sea, 1006, 1007
Munfordville, Kentucky, 1093
Murfreesboro, Tennessee, 1095
on Orphan Brigade, 1170
Perryville, Kentucky, 1197
refusal to replace Bragg (Braxton), 1386
Savannah defense, 665, 674–675, 1368, 1369
Shiloh campaign, 1420, 1421, 1422

Hardee, William J., *continued*
staff, 880, 932
strategy and tactics, 193, *194*, 737, 1040, 1059
Hardee's Tactics. See Rifle and Infantry Tactics
Hardeman, Thomas, *669*
Hardeman, William Polk, **738**
Hardin, Elizabeth, 472
Harding, Sidney, 1319
Hardinge, Samuel, 202, 543
Hardison, Keith Anderson, *as contributor*, 150
Hardtack, 109
Hard Tack (magazine), 1232
Harlan and Hollingsworth, 184
Harleston, John, 1369
Harmon, J. L., 812
Harney, Thomas F. ("Frank"), 545
Harney, William S., 7, 829, 1251
Harper, William, 1273
Harpers Ferry, West Virginia, **738–744**, *1701*
archaeological excavations, 48–49
arsenal and armory, 90, **738–740**, 1455, 1457, 1461, 1700
battle of 1862, **742–744**, 836, 883, 891, 1404, 1406, 1526, 1552
captured artillery, 100–101
Confederate plot to capture (1861), 104, 807
John Brown's raid, 103–104, 198, 322, **740–742**, 917, 1295, 1375, 1376, 1465, 1506, 1552, 1715, 1736
and Sharpsburg campaign, 1408
as Shenandoah Valley boundary, 1415
South Mountain, Maryland, 1513
Stuart, J. E. B., 1552
Union command, 1417–1418
see also under Jackson, Thomas J. ("Stonewall")
Harper's Monthly (magazine), 986, 987
Harper's Weekly (magazine), 985, 987
Harriet Lane (ship), 63, 656, **744**, 1689
Harris, David Golightly, 568
Harris, Emily Lyles, 1739
Harris, Isham G., **744–746**
alliance with Confederacy, *1379*
secession advocacy, 173, 894, 1593
as Tennessee governor, 83, 295, 598, 703, 751, 763, 1028, 1211, 1575–1576, 1755
Harris, Joel Chandler, 671, 937, 938, 1232, 1625
Harris, Nathaniel Harrison, **746**, 1520
Harris, Thomas A., **747**, 1159
Harris, Wiley Pope, 400, **747–748**
Harris, William C., *as contributor*, 781–782, 1184–1185, 1678–1679
Harrison, Benjamin, 1073
Harrison, Henry Thomas, 537, 544, **748**
Harrison, James (Union spy), 677
Harrison, James Edward, **748–749**
Harrison, James Thomas, **749**
Harrison, Lowell H., *as contributor*, 213–217, 851, 886–889, 987–988
Harrison, Thomas, 748, **749**
Harrison, William Henry, 1628, 1709
Harrisburg, Pennsylvania, 550
Harrisonburg, Virginia, 1415, 1416, 1418
Harrison's Landing, Virginia, map, 1401
Hart, Edwin, 1566
Hart, Nancy, **750**
Harter, Dale F., *as contributor*, 866
Hartford, John, 487
Hartford (ship), 692
Hartford Convention (1814-1815), 1532
Hartranft, John F., 627
Hartridge, Julian, **750**, 1365
Hart's South Carolina Battery, 734
Hartstene, H. J., 289
Hartsville, Tennessee, 736
Hartwig, D. Scott, *as contributor*, 630, 676–683
Harvey Birch (ship), 374, 1107
Hatcher, John, 1684
Hatcher, Richard W., III, *as contributor*, 1729–1731
Hatcher's Run, Virginia, 83, 1201
Hattaway, Herman, *as contributor*, 144–145, 920–921
Hatteras, North Carolina, privateering, 1269
Hatteras (ship), 20, 375, 1392, 1393
Hatton, Raymond, *575*
Hatton, Robert Hopkins, 50, **750–751**
Haupt, Herman, 334
Havana, Cuba, blockade running, 177, 185
Havana (ship). *See Sumter* (ship)
Havas, Auguste, 1271
Haversack, 817
Hawes, J. M., **751**, 1696
Hawes, Richard, 701, 702, 703, **752**, 887
Hawks, W. J., *80*
Hawthorn, Alexander Travis, **752**
Hay, Charles C., 1495
Hay, John, 1165
Haya Maru (ship), 1567
Hayes, Rutherford B., 107, 358, 582, 600, 685, 1395, 1699
Haygood, Atticus, 1035
Hayne, Paul Hamilton, 936, 937, 985
Haynes, Daniel, 578
Haynes, Landon Carter, **752–753**, 761
Hays, Harry Thompson, 187, **753–754**, 880, 957, 1406, 1751
Hays, Will S., 487, 1101, 1103
Hazen, William B., 293, 1007, 1096, 1368
H. C. Lamb and Company, 1457
Health and medicine, **754–759**
artificial limbs, 1052
Atlanta epidemics, 110
battle injuries, 338, **755–757**
death rates, 37, 110, 337–338, 460
herbal and home remedies, 757–758, 759, 1559
hospitals. *See* Hospitals
Jones (Joseph) studies, 867–868
medical manufacturing, 370, 757–758
medical training, **758–759**, 1108, 1110
medical treatments, **757–758**
Navy Bureau of Medicine and Surgery, 1123, 1127–1128
nursing. *See* Nursing
nutritional deficiencies, 595, 754, 758
Port Hudson, Louisiana, 1238
prison conditions, 38, 39, 610, 1259, 1262, 1362
research, 867
sailors, 1358, 1359
sickness and disease, 595, 610, **754–755**, 867, 1498
soldiers' convalescent homes, 1501–1502
venereal diseases, 1276–1277
see also Medical Department
Heart of the Confederacy (film), 573
Hearts and Flags (film), 574
Heath, James Ewell, 986
Heaven and Hell (Jake), 939
Heavy artillery, 91
edged weapons, 513
infantry, 93
short sword, *513*
Hébert, Louis, **759**, 1544
Corinth, Mississippi, 413, 414
Elkhorn Tavern, Arkansas, 526
Iuka, Mississippi, 825
Hébert, Paul O., 426, **759–760**, 990, 1584, 1606
Hedrick, Benjamin Sherwood, 768, 855
Heintzelman, Samuel P., 1402, 1403
Heiskell, Carrick W., 761
Heiskell, Frederick, 761
Heiskell, J. B., **760–761**
Heiss, John P., 1145
Helena, Arkansas, 785, 1609, 1679

"Hell Broke Loose in Georgia" (song), 1104
Helm, Benjamin Hardin, 234, **761–762**, 929, 1170, 1622
Helm, Charles J., 180
Helper, Hinton Rowan, 44, 45, **762**
Hemp, 1214
Hemphill, John, **762–763**
Hempstead Hornets (Arkansas), 662
Henderson, G. F. R., 798, 1669
Hendren, John N., 1614
Hennen, Anne Marie, 790
Hennessy, John J., *as contributor*, 863–864, 996–1003
Henry, Alexander, 1468
Henry, Gustavus Adolphus, **763–764**
Henry and Donelson campaign, 83, 84, 125, 244, **764–767**, 850, 858, 887, 1420, 1596, 1691, 1706
  Buckner, Simon Bolivar, 238, 1211
  casualties, 765
  defenses, 71, 621–622, 686, 1576, 1596, 1597
  field fortifications, 626
  Floyd, John, 592–593, 1211
  Forrest, Nathan Bedford, 606
  Gholson, Samuel, 683
  Gregg, John, 716
  Johnson, Bushrod Rust, 593, 765, 767, 1211
  Johnston, Albert Sidney. *See under* Johnston, Albert Sidney
  map, 765
  Pillow, Gideon, 1211
  Quarles, William, 1290–1291
  starvation rations, 595
  surrender of forts, 1108
Henry Dodge (ship), 1530
Herald (ship), 184, 185
Herald (Wilmington newspaper), 1142
Herbal medicines, 757–758, 759, 1559
Herbert, Caleb C., **767**
"Her Bright Eyes Haunt Me Still" (song), 1498
Heritage Military Music Foundation, 487
Hermann, Janet Sharp, *as contributor*, 453–454
Herndon, Thomas H., 51, 928
Heroes of America, 387, **768–769**, 1183, 1226, 1492, 1638, 1639, 1650
  Johnson, John Lewis, 854–855
  Logan, George Washington, 942
  in North Carolina, 768, 1154–1155, 1183
Herold, David E., execution of, *539*
Herrington, W. D., 1232
Herron, Francis J., 232, 1246–1247, 1607
Hesper, and Other Poems (Hill), 936, 1232
Hesseltine, William B., prison study, 1264
"He stands." *See* Watie, Stand
Hester, Joseph Goodwin, 1563
Heth, Henry, 51, **769**, 968, 1200, 1702, 1744
  Department of East Tennessee command, 720
  Gettysburg campaign, 678, 679, 680, 683
Hetty, Jennie, 265
Hewitt, John Hill, 193, 936, 1101, 1590
Hewitt, Lawrence L., *as contributor*, 145, 264, 420, 498, 505, 783, 958–959, 1055, 1133–1134, 1139–1140, 1238–1239, 1697, 1712
Heyliger, Louis, 180–181
Heyward, DuBose, 939
Heyward, James Barnwell, 1174–1175, 1216
Hibbard, Frederick, 1074
Hibbard, Walter R., Jr., *as contributor*, 1043–1044
Hickey, Damon D., *as contributor*, 1493–1494
Hicks, Stephen G., 1177
Hicks, Thomas, 127, 196
Higgins, Edward, **769–770**
Higginson, Thomas Wentworth, 5, 10, 11, 12, 1104, 1335
High, Nathaniel Rue, Jr., 202
Higher education, 517-518, 1108; *see also* Military education; particular institutions
High Point, North Carolina, 1152
  small arms manufacture, 1457
Hildebrand, Jessie, 1422
Hildebrand, Sam, 724
Hill, A. P., 36, 45, 50, *65*, 81, 82, 272, **770–771**, 834, 864, 972, 1406
  artillery, 1679–1680
  Ashby's Gap, 1713
  Bristoe Station, 220–221
  Cold Harbor, Virginia, 366–367
  death, 1201
  dispute with Longstreet (James), 1503
  Early (Jubal) replacement of, 1518
  Frayser's Farm, Virginia, 636
  Gaines' Mill, Virginia, 653
  Gettysburg campaign, 677, 678, 679, 680, 682, 771
  Harpers Ferry, West Virginia, 743, 744
  Light Division, 1516
  Malvern Hill, Virginia, 994, 996
  Manassas, Second, 770, 1000, 1001
  Mechanicsville, Virginia, 78, 770, 1020, 1021
  personal papers, 1099
  Petersburg campaign, 1199, 1200–1201
  Seven Days' Battles, 571, 1190, 1400
  Sharpsburg campaign, 771, 817, 1408
  Tennessee Brigade, 50
  Wilderness campaign, 1719, 1720
  Williamsburg, Virginia, 1725
Hill, Benjamin H., 348, 368, **771–774**, 853, 872, 873, 994, 1541, 1745, 1750
Hill, Benjamin Jefferson, **774**
Hill, Charles W., 856
Hill, D. H., 289, 490, 663, 697, **775–776**, 780, 844, 850, 1151, 1193, 1229, 1342
  Army of Tennessee, 86, 214
  battle names, 142
  Big Bethel, Virginia, 171, 172
  espionage operations, 537
  family, 134
  Fredericksburg campaign, 638, 639
  Lynchburg defense, 963
  Malvern Hill, Virginia, 994, 995, 996
  Mechanicsville, Virginia, 1020
  North Carolina Military Institute, 519
  prisoner exchanges, 1257
  Seven Days' Battles, 1400
  Seven Pines, Virginia, 990
  Sharpsburg campaign, 1406
  Williamsburg, Virginia, 1725
Hill, Hunter, 1232
Hill, Joshua, *669*
Hill, Louise B., 1537
Hill, Theophilus Hunter, 936
Hills Run Red, The (film), 580
Hillyev, Lambert, 578
Hilton, John, 768
Hilton, Robert B., **776**
Hilton, Winthrop E., 421
Hilton Head, South Carolina, 1240, 1509
Hindman, Thomas C., 32, *52*, 648, **776–777**, 785, 941, 1211, 1355, 1404, 1427
  appointments, 1133
  martial law and habeas corpus suspension, 141, 660, 1314, 1349
  Prairie Grove, Arkansas, 1246, 1247
  strategy and tactics, 1246, 1247
  Trans-Mississippi Department, 53, 68, 1340, 1607

Hine, William C., *as contributor*, 1335, 1471–1472
Hines, Thomas H., 349
Hiniha Mikko. *See* Jumper, John
Historical societies. *See* Museums and archives
Historic buildings. *See* Museums and archives
Histories of the North Carolina Regiments (Clark), 467
Historiography. *See* Bibliography and historiography; Museums and archives
History and Debates of the Convention of the People of Alabama (Smith), 1482
History of Morgan's Cavalry, A (Duke), 498
History of Rome Hanks, The (Pennell), 939
History of the Confederate States Navy from Its Organization to the Surrender of Its Last Vessel (Scharf), 1371
History of the Life and Times of James Madison (Rives), 1338
His Trust (film), 574
His Trust Fulfilled (film), 574
Hitchcock, Ethan Allen, 11
H. L. Hunley (submarine), 178, 287, 289, 588, **777–778**, 801, 993, 1124, 1130, 1556, 1557–1558, 1623
  Chapman (Conrad Wise) painting, 283
  spar torpedo, 1516
HOA. *See* Heroes of America
Hoarding, 1082, 1244
Hobart-Hampden, Augustus Charles, 184, 491
Hobdy Plantation, 1286
Hobson, Edward H., 1089
Hodge, Benjamin Louis, **778**
Hodge, George Baird, **778–779**
Hodgson, Joseph, 1589
Hoe ridge cultivation, 417
Hoffbauer, Charles, 1100
Hoffman, William, 856, 1221, 1256
Hogg, Ima, 780
Hogg, Joseph Lewis, **779–780**
Hoke, Robert Frederick, 36, 355, 496, 612, 693, **780**, 880
Holcombe, A. Robert, Jr., *as contributor*, 290, 291, 372, 515, 528, 567–568, 709, 725–726, 823–824, 839, 1121, 1122, 1133, 1185, 1235–1236, 1469, 1515–1516, 1580–1581, 1596, 1669–1671, 1725
Holcombe, James P., 258, 348, 349, **780–781**
Holcombe, Thomas, 1367
Holden, William W., 207, 273, 690, 707, **781–782**, 912, 1304
  denunciation of Confederacy, 1142
  gubernatorial election, 346, 387, 1157, 1185
  impeachment defense, 1481
  peace movement, 106, 447, 768, 855, 1156, 1157, 1183–1184, 1224, 1301, 1626–1627, 1640, 1650, 1651
Holder, William Dunbar, **782**
Holidays
  celebrations, 1319–1320
  Juneteenth, 655, **874**, 924, 950, 1446, 1586
  Memorial Day, **1026–1027**
Holien, Kim Bernard, *as contributor*, 126–127, 1516
Holliday, Frederick William Mackey, **782–783**
Hollins, George N., 264, 290, **783**, 993, *1127*
  New Madrid operation, 1134
Holly Springs, Mississippi, 328, **783–785**, 835, 1049, 1652, 1656
  arsenal, *89*
  map, 784
Hollywood Cemetery (Richmond), 1069, 1331
Holmes, Amy J., 1546
Holmes, Barbara Galphin, 1046
Holmes, Emma, 472
Holmes, George F., 583
Holmes, Michael E., *as contributor*, 1361, 1361–1362
Holmes, Oliver Wendell, Jr., 337
Holmes, Theophilus H., **785**, 941, 1151, 1208
  Arkansas, 53, 1314
  charges against McRae (Dandridge), 981
  Manassas, First, 1573
  martial law and suspension of habeas corpus, 660, 662, 1314
  staff, 408
  Trans-Mississippi Department, 68, 961, 1133, 1356, 1473, 1607, 1609
Holston River, 1547
Holt, Caroline E., 771–772
Holt, Hines, 174, **785–786**, 822
Holt, Joseph, 412, 610, 1263–1264
Holtzclaw, James Thadeus, **786**
Holy Scripture. *See* Bible
Holzer, Harold, *as contributor*, 242, 950–952, 1521–1524, 1673–1674, 1710–1711
Home for Confederate Women, 1332–1333
Home front
  archaeological excavations, 48
  blacks, 5, 670–671
  children, 305–308
  community life, 379
  crime, 563
  desertion reasons, 346, 467, 563
  Florida, 590–591
  folk legends and jokes, 594
  Georgia, 668, 670–672
  labor, 900
  leisure activities, 923
  Mississippi, 1051–1052
  morale erosion, 260, 314, 443–444, 461, 524, 591, 670, 714, 902–903, 1229, 1623, 1686
  North Carolina, 1153–1154
  South Carolina, 1510
  Texas, 1585–1587
  Virginia, 1667–1669
  women's diaries, 471–472
  see also Bread riots; Civilians; Class conflicts; Food; Society
Home guard. *See* State militia
Home Missionary Societies, 1320
Homespun, 357
"Homespun Dress, The" (song), 357, 735
Homestead Act, 1715
"Home, Sweet Home" (song), 923, 1498
Honduras, 982, 1081
Honey Springs, Oklahoma, 12, 305, 310, 425, 814, 1609
Honor, 206, 319, 606, **786–788**
  as battle motivation, 1499, 1500
  Civil War seen in terms of, 1491
  dueling, **497**
  elite, 1490
  as enlistment motivation, 1494
  and expansion of slavery, 558
  family life, 562
  fire-eaters, 582
  of Lost Cause, 330, 422, 949
  and morale, 1080–1081
  plain folk, 1212
  yeomen, 1490
Honor of His Family, The (film), 574
Honor roll. *See* Roll of Honor
Hood, John Bell, 30, 36, *65*, 173, 277, 300, **789–790**, 861, 959, 1343, 1373, 1386, 1753
  Army of Tennessee, 67, 74, 87–88, 296, 327–328, 790, 973, 1005, 1006, 1007, 1427, 1572, 1577, 1584, 1717

Atlanta campaign, 110–111, 112, 114, 672–673, 819
brigade. *See* Hood's Texas Brigade
Dalton, Georgia, 442
Franklin and Nashville campaign, 149, 386, 632, 633, 634, 636, 1683
Gaines' Mill, Virginia, 653
Gettysburg campaign, 679, 680, 682, 909
Kennesaw Mountain, Georgia, 886
Manassas, Second, 1000, 1002
memoirs, 475
Sharpsburg divisions, 1406, 1407
Tennessee campaign, 154, 276, 607, 685, 835, 947, 964, 1110–1111, 1323, 1577
Hood's Texas Brigade, 81, 716, 751, 789, **791**, 816, 1033, 1343, 1516, 1584
Hampton's Legion, 734
Wilderness campaign, 1721
Hooe, Richardetta, 1351
Hooker, Joseph, 80, 336, 501, 835
Atlanta campaign, 111
Brandy Station, Virginia, 209
Chancellorsville campaign, 279–282, 918, 1553
Chattanooga campaign, 293–295
Chickamauga campaign, 1683
command relief, 1573
field fortifications, 626
Frayser's Farm, Virginia, 637
Gettysburg campaign, 677
intelligence operations, 541
Mechanicsville, Virginia, 1020
Sharpsburg campaign, 1406
South Mountain, Maryland, 1513
Stoneman's raids, 1546
Williamsburg, Virginia, 1725
Hope, Alexander James Beresford, 1271
Hope (ship), 368
Hopkins, Edward, 1042
Hopkins, Juliet Ann Opie, 795, 1160
Hopkins' New Orleans 5 Cent Song-Book, 1104
Hopley, Catherine Cooper, 591
Horace Waters Company, 1104
Horgan, James J., *as contributor*, 314–316, 798, 1347–1348, 1504
Hornet (ship), 445, 840
Hornet's Nest (Shiloh), 26, 32, 204, 1422, 1423
Horses and mules, 386, **791–793**
Arkansas campaign, 56
artillery, 91, 95, 104
border states, 196
cavalry, 267, 268, 270
as food, 1239
government supply, 1714
Morgan's raids, 1086
Paducah (Kentucky) raid, 1177
as plunder, 955
theft of, 427, 428
Trans-Mississippi, 1606
as transportation, 1612
Horse Soldiers, The (film), 580
Horsman, Reginald, *as contributor*, 176–179
Horst, Samuel L., *as contributor*, 1031
Horton, Bobby, 487
Hospitals, **793–796**
administrative districts, 1022
Atlanta, Georgia, 109, 110
Beers, Fannie, 152–153
Columbia, South Carolina, 371
doctors' conduct, 344
Florida, 591
food, 595–596
Georgia Military Institute, 674
inspection of, 344, 1161
Little Rock, Arkansas, 941
McCord, Louisa Cheves, 969
Mobile, Alabama, 1058
Nashville, Tennessee, *8*, 1110
naval, 1128
nursing. *See* Nursing
patient-surgeon ratio, 1022
Pember, Phoebe Yates, 472, 1188
prison, 796
statistics, 867
Stout, Samuel Hollingsworth, 1549
for U.S. prisoners, 1353
Virginia, 222, 1188, 1667
wayside, 371, 795, 1022
women's role, 152–153, 671, 795, 796, 1141, 1160–1161, 1740
Hostages, civilian, 760
Hotchkiss, Jedediah, *80*, 271, 601, **797–798**, 944
Shenandoah Valley mapmaking, 1416
Hotchkiss projectiles, 98, 102
Hotze, Henry, 174, 482, **798**, 1142, 1144, 1270, 1271
Houmas, 811
Housatonic (ship), 588, 778, 801, 993, 1130
sinking of, 1516, 1556, 1558
House, John F., **798–799**
House, T. W., 744
House Divided (Williams), 939
Houston, George S., *15*, 1287
Houston, Mark, 244
Houston, Sam, 28, 116, 341, *381*, 1311, *1583*, 1585, 1629, 1715
Unionism, 1378
Houston, Texas, 823
Howard, Oliver Otis, 114, 117, 261, 371, 502, 1006, 1368, 1551
Chancellorsville campaign, 281–282
Gettysburg campaign, 678, 679
Manassas, First, 997, 998
Howard, Thomas S., 1133
Howard's Grove Hospital (Richmond), 591, 796
Howard-Tilton Memorial Library (Tulane University), 1099
Howe, Thomas J., *as contributor*, 1198–1202
Howell, Augustus, 547
Howell, Becket K., 1008
Howell, R. H., 1231, 1256
Howell, William B., 456
Howie, J. M., 290
Howitzer, 49, 61, 93, 94, 96, 98, 99, 101
Hoyer & Ludwig Printers, 436, *445*, 1231, 1242, 1255, 1256, 1522–1523, 1524
Hubbard, David, 812
Hubbard, Thomas, 658
Hudson, George, 310
Hudson, Robert S., 1083
Huey, C. A., *as contributor*, 102–103, 1465–1467, 1467–1468
Huff, A. V., Jr., *as contributor*, 118–119, 371–372, 568, 978–979, 988, 1038, 1172, 1207–1208, 1431, 1737
Huger, Benjamin, 35, 173, 245, **799**, 945, 989
Frayser's Farm, Virginia, 636
Malvern Hill, Virginia, 994, 995
Mechanicsville, Virginia, 1020
Seven Pines, Virginia, 1402
Hughes, Henry, 1275
Hughes, John, 215
Hughes, Nathaniel Cheairs, Jr., *as contributor*, 737–738, 1300, 1427
Hugo, Victor, 193, 1232
Humes, William Young Conn, **799–800**
Humor. *See* Jokes
Humphreys, Andrew A., 45
Humphreys, Benjamin Grubb, 133, **800–801**
Humphries, Solomon, 976
Hungary, 1004
Hunger. *See* Food
Hunley, Horace, 777, **801**
submarine development, 1516, 1556, 1557, 1558
Hunley (submarine). *See H. L. Hunley*

Hunt, Gilbert, 643
Hunt, Washington, 403
Hunter, David, 776, 1335, 1366, 1623, 1673
 foraging, 601
 Lynchburg, Virginia, 963
 Piedmont, Virginia, 1210
 Shenandoah Valley, 503, 504, 697, 968, 1413
 slave regiments, 6, 9–10, 11
Hunter, John, 277
Hunter, Robert M. T., 300, 348, 466, 663, **801–805**, 1014, 1225, 1270, 1338, 1384, 1387, 1541, 1687, 1700
 Hampton Roads Conference, 256, 733, 804
 likeness on Treasury note, 438
 presidential candidacy, 1068
 proslavery argument, 1485
 as secretary of state, 251, 481, 482, 1527, 1528
 Spanish diplomacy, 1513
 tax-in-kind bill, 1395
Hunter, William H., 709
Huntington Library (San Marino, California), 1099
Hunton, Eppa, 127, **805**
Huntress (ship), 1530
Huntsville, Alabama, 98, 516
Huntsville, Missouri, guerrilla warfare, 724
Huntsville (ship), 236, 1062, 1124, 1126, 1303
Huntsville Democrat (Alabama newspaper), 347, 1205
Hurlbut, Stephen A., 713, 1029, 1030, 1032, 1422
Hurricane Plantation, 453, 458
Huse, Caleb, 179, 180, 181, 507, 757, 1169, 1368, 1465, 1467, 1684
Huston, James A., *as contributor*, 1338–1340, 1612, 1691–1692
Hutchinson Family, 1103
Hutchinson Island, Georgia, 1369
Hygiene. *See* Sanitation
Hyman, John D., 447

I

Iconography. *See under* Lost Cause
Ida (ship), 1530
Illinois
 Copperheads, 411
 slavery, 875
 withdrawal from war, 599
Illinois Central Railroad, 157, 1293
Illness. *See* Health and medicine, sickness and disease; particular illnesses
I'll Take My Stand, 318, 938, 949
Imboden, John D., **807**, 932, 1135
 civilian courts-martial, 728
 guerrilla activity, 721, 1702, 1705
 seizure of Harpers Ferry, West Virginia, 740
Immigrants. *See* Foreigners; Germans; Irish; Jews
Immortal Six Hundred, 1259
Impending Crisis of the South: How to Meet It (Helper), 44, 45, 762
Imperialism, **808–809**, 1174
 antebellum Southern expansionism, 551–558
Importing and Exporting Company of Georgia, 905
Importing and Exporting Company of South Carolina, 181
Imports. *See* Anglo-Confederate purchasing; Blockade; Foreign trade; *under* Luxury items
Impressment, 17, 106, 510, 760, 763, 804, **809–810**, 862, 926, 1749
 controversy, 107, 124, 207, 229, 750, 1686, 1695
 of cotton, 1586, 1608
 of crops and food, 377, 393, 463, 596, 1571
 Davis (Jefferson) support for, 452
 as desertion reason, 467
 extortion accusations, 559
 of firearms, 342
 as food shortage cause, 1244
 of free blacks, 38, 75, 704, 1148, 1487
 of horses and mules, 793
 inequities, 1153
 inflation relationship, 377, 820, 821
 legislation, 192
 Mississippi, 1051
 morale effects, 1081
 as political issue, 444, 667, 670, 1224, 1304
 by Quartermaster Bureau, 1291–1292
 railroads, 1717
 reliance on, 1571
 of slaves. *See under* Slavery
 South Carolina, 192
 support for, 1480
 Texas, 1097
 unpopularity, 596, 1080, 1153
 see also Confiscation
Impressment Act of 1863, 510, 590, 809, 810, 1426
 price setting, 567
Ince, Thomas H., 574, 575
Income tax, 1248
Indentured servants, 1598
Index (newspaper), 174, 482, **810**, 1016, 1142, 1144, 1270, 1271, 1272
 Hotze, Henry, 798
 response to Emancipation Proclamation, 532
India, 418
Indiana
 Copperheads, 411
 election of 1860, 522
 guerrilla activity, 720
 Morgan's raids, 1089
 Northwestern Conspiracy, 1158–1159
 withdrawal from war, 599
Indian Affairs Bureau. *See* Bureau of Indian Affairs
Indianapolis State Sentinel (newspaper), 1159
Indian Home Guard Regiments, USA, 1290, 1398, 1409
Indianola (ship), 420, 1697
Indians, **810–812**
 Arizona, 51
 Cherokees. *See* Cherokees
 Chickasaws. *See* Chickasaws
 Choctaws. *See* Choctaws
 Confederate treaties, 1390, 1398, 1408; *see also* particular peoples
 contributions to Confederacy, 812, 1173
 Creeks. *See* Creeks
 expansion of slavery, 551, 552, 553
 losses from Civil War, 815
 miscegenation, 1045
 Osages. *See* Osages
 Quapaws. *See* Quapaws
 Seminoles. *See* Seminoles
 Senecas. *See* Senecas
 Shawnees. *See* Shawnees
 Texas, 143, 961, 1583, 1584
 tobacco, 1597
 Trans-Mississippi, 1606, 1608
 Union allies, 1409
Indian Territory, 810, **812–815**, 1609
 Boudinot, Elias C., 198–199
 Confederate sympathizers, 1390, 1398
 Cooper, Douglas Hancock, 409
 Five Civilized Tribes, 172, 526, 747, 810, 811, 812, 813, 1607; *see also* Cherokees; Chickasaws; Choctaws; Creeks; Indians; Seminoles
 Gano, Richard Montgomery, 657
 Harrison, James Edward, 748–749
 Lane, Walter Paye, 908
 map, 814

Maxey, Samuel Bell, 1019
military contribution, 815, 1173
missionaries, 1247
Oklahoma, 296, 305, 309, 812–815, 1289, 1584
payment for seized materials, 984
Pike, Albert, 1211
population, 1605
Steele (William) command, 1538
Union invasions, 813–814, 1391
Union loyalists, 1166
Watie, Stand, 1607, 1693–1694
Indigent. *See* Poor relief; Poverty
Individual rights. *See* Civil liberties
Industrialization. *See* Manufacturing
Inez, A Tale of the Alamo (Evans), 547
Infantry, **815–820**
artillery, 93, 94
brigade, 92
cavalry as mounted, 270
combat efficiency, 815–816
desertions, 95
equipment, 817–818
"Foot Cavalry" term, 78
Indian division, 813
insignia colors, 1633
linear formations, 624
mounted, 816
organization, 816
Orphan Brigade, **1170**
Provisional Army, 66
special units, 1516, 1548–1549
tactics, 25, 94–95, 737, 819–820
uniforms, 817–818, 1633–1636
United States Colored Troops, 11
weapons, 59–60, 817, 818–819
Zouave units, 1137
Infantry Tactics (Casey), 1040
Infantry Tactics (Scott), 1040
Inflation, 386, 393, 511, 803, **820–821**, 865, 1648, 1668
Alabama, 18
bond interest rate, 434
bread riots, 212
cities, 346
class conflict, 1491, 1492
cotton smuggling, 420
currency and, 234, 386, 511, 820–821, 1284, 1686
by end of war, 345
factors influencing, 234, 377, 820, 821
farming and, 379, 566
Florida, 591
food prices, 419, 566, 641, 1367, 1517
general price index, 510
Georgia, 109–110, 229, 670, 671
government and loans. *See subhead* bond interest rate *above*; *subhead* public finance *below*
Jackson, Mississippi, 837
Jews as scapegoats, 1367, 1517
morale and, 434, 1081–1082
North Carolina, 1153
protests, 900
public finance and, 510, 1284, 1570; *see also subhead* currency *above*
Quartermaster Bureau and, 1291–1292
railway operations and, 1295
Richmond , Virginia, 1331
of slave prices, 1443, 1453
soldiers' pay and, 1495
speculation and, 1517–1518
tax rates, 1570
Texas, 1586
Virginian countermeasures, 1480
wages and, 821, 902–903, 1306
Informer, The (film), 574
Ingersoll, Robert G., 608
Ingraham, Duncan N., 289, **821–822**
Ingram, Porter, **822**
Injuries, battle. *See under* Health and medicine
"In Martial Manner" (Palmer), 936
In Old Kentucky (film), 574
In Ole Virginia (novel by Page), 938
Inquiry into the Causes Which Have Retarded the Accumulation of Wealth and Increase of Population in the Southern States (Goodloe), 44–45
Inquiry into the Law of Negro Slavery in the United States of America to which is Prefixed an Historical Sketch of Slavery, An (Cobb), 363, 400
Inscoe, John C., *as contributor*, 13–14, 28–29, 137–138, 153–154, 174, 344, 354–355, 423–424, 506, 604, 750, 771–774, 785–786, 822, 851–854, 881–882, 924–925, 928, 929, 1093–1094, 1146, 1420, 1475–1476, 1479, 1551, 1623, 1745
Inside the Confederate Government (Kean), 865
Insignia, 1633–1634, *1635*, 1636
Institution of Slavery in the Southern States, Religiously and Morally Considered in Connection with Our Sectional Troubles (Tyson), 1632
Instruments, musical, 1104–1105
Intelligence services. *See* Espionage; Signal Corps
Interior lines, 326
Intermarriage
within families, 562
see also Miscegenation
Internal improvements, appropriations for, 401, 1068
International News (film series), 572
Interracial unions. *See* Creoles; Miscegenation; Mulattoes
Intrepid (balloon), *126*
Inventions. *See* Cotton gin; Patent Office
Iowa
slavery, 875
statehood, 555
Irene (ship), 129
Irish, 602, **822–823**, 1646, 1647
border states, 195
Charleston, South Carolina, 285
conscription exemptions, 900
defense of Sabine Pass, Texas, 1357
Little Rock, Arkansas, 940
Mississippi, 1047
Missouri, 1052
Mobile, Alabama, 1057
nativist attacks on, 1395
recruiting, 1271
Richmond, Virginia, 1330
Roman Catholicism, 1346
Savannah, Georgia, 1364, 1367
Stonewall Brigade, 1549
see also Celtic thesis
Irish Bend, Texas, 713, 1314
"Irish Jaunting Car, The" (song), 1101
Iron
Alabama production, 1138, 1387–1388, 1410
Georgia production, 670
manufacturing, 372
mining, 1043, 1044
resources, 508, 1147
rolling, 508
shortages, 49, 96, 1147
skilled labor, 902
slave labor, 3–4, 96, 97, 315, 372, 1440, 1443
see also Foundries; particular foundries
Iron Age (ship), 1341
"Iron Battery" (fortification), 1544
Iron Brigade, 1409
Iron-Clad Ethiopian Troupe, 1231
Ironclads, 250, 799, **823–824**
Albemarle. See Albemarle
Arkansas. See Arkansas
Atlanta. See Atlanta
attack on Fort Sumter, 287
attack on *New Ironsides*, 445

Ironclads, *continued*
battles, 1059, 1124, 1126, 1130
blockade breaking, 178
Brooke, John M., 223
Brooke double-banded rifle, *1117*
Buchanan, Franklin, 235–236
Charleston, South Carolina, 289
Chickamauga. See Chickamauga
construction, 226–227, 264, 285, 438, 960, 963, 991–992, 1018, 1060, 1124
Cooke, James W., 407
Davidson, Hunter, 447
as defensive ships, 992
design, 1235–1236
Eads, 993
Eastport, **505**
elite units, 1516
Elliott, Gilbert, 528
foreign purchase of, 484, 1123, 1150
Georgia. See Georgia
Graves, William A., 709
Henry and Donelson campaign, 766
inactivity of, 1129
Jackson. See Jackson
James River Squadron, 840–841, 1124
Laird shipyards, 903–904
Louisiana. See Louisiana
Mallory, Stephen R., 991
Missouri. See Missouri
Neuse. See Neuse
New Orleans, Louisiana, 1139
ordnance, 62, 1117–1118
patents, 1181
photographs, 1206
rams, **1302–1304**
Randolph, Victor M., 1307
role in war, 1124
sailors' duties, 1358, 1359, 1360
Selma Naval Foundry, 1387–1388
shipyards, 1424–1425
Stonewall. See Stonewall
Tattnall, Josiah, 567
Tennessee. See Tennessee
Tift brothers, 1596
torpedoes, 1515
Tredegar Iron Works, 1617
Virginia. See Virginia
Warley, Alexander Frazer, 1688
Wilmington, North Carolina, 1727
see also Gunboats
Ironclad Test Oath of Loyalty. *See* Oath of allegiance
Iron Commission, 1297
Ironmonger Captain. *See* Cooke, James W.
Iroquois (ship), 1393, 1563
Irregular warfare. *See* Guerrilla warfare
Irving Prison (Memphis), *609*
Isaac, Saul, 1169
Isaacs, Samuel M., 845
Isabella (ship), 1269, 1341
Is Davis a Traitor; or, Was Secession a Constitutional Right Previous to 1861? (Bledsoe), 175, 476
Isherwood, Benjamin F., 700
Island Number 10. *See* New Madrid and Island Number 10
Island Queen (ship), 145, 375
Isondiga (ship), 1126
Isturiz, Francisco de, 1514
Iuka, Mississippi, 414, **825**, 891
Crittenden, George B., 428–429
Hébert, Louis, 759
Little, Lewis, 939
Iverson, Alfred, *669*, **825–826**, 1547
Ives, J. C., Mrs., 1589
"I Wish I Was in Dixie's Land" (song). *See* Dixie

J

Jackass artillery. *See* Pack artillery
Jackknives, 515
Jackman, John, 294
Jackman, Sidney D., **827**, 1254
Jack Sheppard (Ainsworth), 1590
Jackson, Alfred Eugene, **827–828**, 1594
Jackson, Andrew, 253, 552, 553, 557, 598, 811, 1285, 1335, 1336, 1453, 1593, 1708, 1709
appointments, 1062
likeness on stamp, 1242, *1522*, *1523*, 1524
martial law imposition, 727
nullification controversy, 1159–1160, 1533, 1637
slavery question, 1056
Jackson, Claiborne F., 196, 408, 641, 647, 701, 702, 703, 719, **828–829**, 1052, 1180, 1251, 1323, 1409, 1432, 1606
press support, 1483
Wilson's Creek campaign, 1729–1730
Jackson, Henry Rootes, 826, **829–830**, 1355
Jackson, Howell E., 438
Jackson, James (Georgia congressman), *669*
Jackson, James S. (U.S. general), 1197
Jackson, John J., 1699–1700
Jackson, John King, **830**, 1422
Jackson, Mary, 212
Jackson, Thomas J. ("Stonewall"), *65*, *80*, 136, 387, 519, 549, 775, **830–835**, 925, 985, 1191, 1526, 1734
appointments, 866
brigade. *See* Stonewall Brigade
Cedar Mountain, Virginia, 272–273
Chancellorsville campaign, 36, 80, 279–282, 908, 915, 918, *1071*
death, 80, 279, 282, 798, 835, 908, 918
fake postal stamp, 1524
family, 134
flag, *585*
Frayser's Farm, Virginia, 636
Fredericksburg campaign, 638, 639
Frietchie, Barbara, 646
Front Royal, Virginia, 647
Gaines' Mill, Virginia, 653, 1193
guides, 750
Harpers Ferry, West Virginia, 79, 104, 740, 742, 743, 744, 832, 834, 1295–1296, 1404, 1406, 1552, 1700
as hero of Lost Cause, 948–949, 951
intelligence operations, 543
Kernstown, Virginia, 663–664
likeness on Treasury note, *436*, 438
literary portrayals, 936, 937, 938, 939
Loring (W. W.) controversy, 836, 947, 1565, 1700, 1702
Malvern Hill, Virginia, 731, 733, 994, 995
Manassas, First, 832, 834, 997, 998, 1548, 1549
Manassas, Second, 78–79, 834, 999–1003, 1549
Mechanicsville, Virginia, 834, 1020
monuments, 1028, 1069, *1071*, 1074
newspaper portrayals, 1683
nickname, 151, 815, 832, 834, 998, 1548
opinion of Benjamin (Judah P.), 159
painting of, 873–874, *951*
personal papers, 1099
pike advocacy, 846
recklessness of, 788
relationship with Early (Jubal), 502
relationship with Hill (A. P.), 770–771
religion, 1247
removal of railroad tracks, 1297
service sword, 513
Seven Days' Battles, 834, 1400, 1526
Sharpsburg campaign, 834, 883, 1406, 1407
Shenandoah Valley campaign. *See* Shenandoah Valley, campaign of Jackson

songs about, 1232
staff, *80*, 197–198, 797, 836, 849, 914, 1182
strategy and tactics, 830, 834, 835, 1001, 1002
Stuart (J. E. B.) command takeover, 1493
Virginia Military Institute, 369, 831–832, 1672–1673, 1676–1677
and war correspondents, 274
White Oak Swamp, Virginia, 731
Jackson, William Hicks, 573, **835–836**
Franklin and Nashville campaign, 632
Holly Springs, Mississippi, 784
Selma campaign, 1389
Jackson, William Lowther ("Mudwall"), 828, **836**
Jackson, Mississippi, 172, **836–839**, 1033
antebellum population, 831
battle, **837–839**, 837
casualties, 838
city, **836–837**
map, 838
Jackson (ship), 685, **839**, 1100, 1124, 1599, 1722
ordnance, 1118
Jackson Clarion (Mississippi newspaper), 226, 1591
Jackson flag, *585*
Jackson Hospital (Richmond), 796
Jackson Mississippian (newspaper), 837
Jacksonville, Florida, 590, 1424
Jacob Bell (ship), *592*
Jaffa, Harry, 495
Jakes, John, 939
James, Charles Tillingham, 101
James brothers (Frank and Jesse), 725, **839**, 1054, 1289, 1753
Centralia, Missouri, raid, 724
Kansas raids, 721
James Adger (ship), 129, 1341
James and Kanawha Canal, 259
James City, North Carolina, 1152
James Conning Company, 514
James Gray (ship), 1530
James Island, South Carolina, 1479, 1509
James Jack and Company, 368
James rifle, 93, 100, 101
James River, 1193, 1691, 1692
Belle Isle prison, *155*
bridge, 1340
defenses, 235, 1018, 1178, 1623
Drewry's Bluff, Virginia, 496
Fort Harrison, Virginia, 612
fortifications, 621
naval academy, 1131
Peninsular campaign, 1400, 1401, 1402, 1554
submarine development, 1556
Tattnall, Josiah, 1568
James River Squadron, **839–841**, 960, 993, 1008, 1056–1057, 1124, 1126, 1181, 1359
Davidson, Hunter, 447
Forrest, French, 605
personnel, 692
Read, Charles W., 1309
Semmes, Raphael, 1392, 1394
ships, 1124, 1302, 1303
torpedo launches, 1515
Virginia II (ship), 709
Jamestown, North Carolina, 1457
Jamestown (ship), 840, 1124, *1671*
Jamison, David F., 119
Jamison, Sanders G., 1614
J. & G. Thomson. *See* Thomson brothers
Japan (ship), 375, 1019
Jasper, Tennessee, *268*
Jasper Greens (Irish militia), 1367
Jayhawkers. *See* Kansas Jayhawkers
J. E. Coffee (ship), 1530
Jefferson, Thomas, 1335, 1626
alleged miscegenation, 1045
confiscation of home, 389
constitutional interpretation, 1531, 1532
grandson, 1305
likeness on postal stamps, 1242, *1521*, *1523*, 1524
Louisiana Purchase, 552, 1532
slavery issues, 552, 553, 1056, 1274, 1378
state rights, 1373, 1532, 1533
Virginia and Kentucky Resolutions of 1798, 1374
Jefferson College (Mississippi), 519
Jefferson College (Pennsylvania), 216
Jefferson County, Virginia, 1413
Jefferson Davis (ship), 533, **841**, 1269
Jefferson Davis Declares Secession (film), 573
Jefferson Davis Memorial Home for Confederate Soldiers and Sailors. *See* Beauvoir
Jeffrey, Thomas E., *as contributor*, 107, 219–220, 411, 446–447, 650–651, 654, 971, 1288, 1310–1311, 1351, 1481, 1626–1627
"Jeff Wants to Get Away" (song), 335
Jemison, Robert, 19, **841–842**
Jenkins, Albert Gallatin, 267, **842–844**, 1040, 1700, 1702, 1705
Cloyds Mountain, Virginia, 357
Gettysburg campaign, 677
Jenkins, Charles J., 852
Jenkins, Micah, 212, 312, **844**, 891, 892, 896, 1721
feud with Law (Evander), 909
Jenkins' Ferry, Arkansas, 53, 57, 1252, 1316, 1696
Jennifer, Walter, 126
Jennings, Devereaux, 577
Jennings, Waylon, 487
Jennison, Charles, 719, 1053–1054
Jensen, Les, *as contributor*, 1021–1022, 1633–1636
Jerusalem Plank Road, 1200
Jesse scouts, 134
Jesuit Alumni Association, 1397
Jewish Messenger (publication), 845
Jews, **845–846**
anti-Semitism, 559, 599, 1157, 1320–1321, 1367, 1517
Benjamin (Judah P.) and Judaism, 157, 160, 161–162
Northern-born Confederates, 1157
Richmond, Virginia, 1330
urban, 1647
J. H. Dance and Bros., 1460
J. L. Smallwood (ship), 129
Joe Brown's pikes, **846**
John & William Dudgeon, 184, 301, 491, 1567
John Brown's Body (Bent), 161
John Brown's Raid. *See under* Harpers Ferry, West Virginia
John Caver (ship), 841
John Clark and Company, 97, 98
John F. Carr (ship), 656
John Fraser and Company, 179, 180, 1618
John F. Slater Fund, 440
John Laird and Sons, 903, 1303
John March, Southerner (Cable), 938
John Randolph (ship), 905
John Reid and Company, 184
John Russell (publishing co.), 193
Johns, John, 535
John Schreiner and Sons, 1101
Johnson, A. V. E., 275
Johnson, Adam Rankin ("Stovepipe"), 95, 720, **846–847**
Johnson, "Allegheny." *See* Johnson, Edward
Johnson, Andrew, 545, **847–849**, 1098, 1313, 1573, *1578*
Alabama claims, 21

Johnson, Andrew, *continued*
amnesties and pardons. *See subhead* pardons *below*
appointments, 341, 685, 686, 745, 1172
Breckinridge (John C.) support, 1575
Knoxville Convention, 895, 1575
and Lincoln (Abraham) assassination, 160, 934, 1595
military governorship, 703, 1029, 1109, 1110, 1577–1578
pardons, 29, 35, 215, 230, 362, 503, 600, 657, 661, 690, 753, 758, 761, 773, 800, 865, 869, 882, 967, 988, 1016, 1185, 1205, 1397, 1617, 1695
Reconstruction policies, 848–849, 956, 1699
response to Emancipation Proclamation, 532
as Tennessee governor, 667, 763, 1086
Thirteenth Amendment, 1591
and Unionism, 1638
Johnson, Benjamin J., 734
Johnson, Bradley Tyler, 196, 276, 277, **849**, 1361
Johnson, Bushrod Rust, 36, **849–850**, 897, 968, 1682
Henry and Donelson campaign, 593, 765, 767, 1211
Murfreesboro, Tennessee, 1095
Perryville, Kentucky, 1197
Petersburg campaign, 1198
University of Nashville, 519
Johnson, Chapman, 855
Johnson, Edward, **850–851**
Gettysburg campaign, 677, 680, 681, 682
Mine Run campaign, 1043
Shenandoah Valley, 1416
Spotsylvania campaign, 1520
on Stafford (Leroy), 1521
Winchester, Virginia, 1732–1733
Johnson, George W., 702, 703, 752, 779, **851**, 887
Johnson, Gerald W., 690
Johnson, Herschel V., 138, 200, 411, 772, 773, **851–854**, 1080, 1655
Johnson, Jilson P., 659, 660
Johnson, John Lewis, 768, **854–856**
Johnson, Richard Mentor, 1045, 1046, 1336
Johnson, Richard W., 295, 1086
Johnson, Robert W., 52, 263, 659, 660, **856**
Johnson, Thomas, **857**
Johnson, Waldo, **857–858**, 1396
Johnson, William, 1650
Johnson and Reconstruction (film), 573
Johnson's Island Prison, 51, 705, **856–857**, 1256, 1258, 1259
prisoners, 930, 964, 1622
raid, 144–145, 258, 349, 538, 545, 855, 960, 1595, 1723
Johnsonville, Tennessee, Forrest's raid, 607, 608, 609
Johnston, Albert Sidney, 107, 156, 196, 238, 328, 353, **858**, 860, 932, 1250, 1396
Army of Tennessee, 67, 83–85, 1227, 1607
death at Shiloh, 1422
Department No. 2 command, 71
Henry and Donelson campaign, 71, 148, 592–593, 764, 765, 767, 1576
Kentucky, 326, 455, 887, 1744
Mississippi, 428
Nashville armory, 1168
Nashville evacuation, 1420
on prostitution, 1276
Shiloh campaign. *See under* Shiloh campaign
strategy and tactics, 1249
Johnston, David S., 291
Johnston, George Doherty, **858–859**
Johnston, James D., 237, 1580
Johnston, John, 475
Johnston, Joseph E., *65*, 86, 104, 300, 474, 663, 786, 832, **859–861**, 1433, 1589, 1656
Army of Northern Virginia, 67, 76, 917
Army of Tennessee, 32, 67, 68, 72, 74, 87–88, 107, 117, 118, 205, 206, 296, 361, 442, 738, 790, 861, 947, 973, 1228, 1386, 1427, 1717
Army of the West, 1386
Atlanta campaign, 110, 111–115
in Carolinas, 163–164, 261, 262, 729, 1152–1153
congressional supporters, 1172
Davis (Jefferson) relationship, 336, 453, 917, 1225
Department of the West, 410
end of war, 149, 694, 959
field fortifications, 626
flag design, 249, 585, 586
Georgia, 110, **111–115**, 674, 1314
Harpers Ferry, West Virginia, 1552
Jackson, Mississippi, 838
Kennesaw Mountain, Georgia, 672, 885, 886
Lee Monument unveiling, *922*
Lee (Robert E.) as replacement, 917, 1400
Longstreet (James) support, 945
Manassas, First, 148, 714, 860, 996, 997, 998, 1716
memoirs and papers, 331, 475, 1099
on Orphan Brigade, 1170
pardon of, 1394
parole, text of, 1793
Peninsular campaign, 1191–1193
Petersburg campaign, 1201
placement on generals list, 788
praise for Smith (Gustavus W.), 1474
Seven Pines, Virginia, 1402, *1403*
staff, 24, 440, 459, 871, 914, 943, 1191, 1472–1473
strategy and tactics, 163, 862, 1189, 1248
Stuart (J. E. B.) cavalry support, 1552
surrender, 1152–1153, 1313
Vicksburg campaign, 716, 835, 1049, 1291, 1658, 1659, 1660, 1753
and war correspondents, 274
Williamsburg, Virginia, 1191, 1193, 1724–1725
Yorktown, Virginia, 496, 1752
Johnston, Mary, 938
Johnston, Oscar F., 1185
Johnston, Richard Malcolm, 671, 937
Johnston, Robert (congressman), **861–862**
Johnston, Robert Daniel (general), **862**
Johnston, William J., 1155
John Watt (ship), 674
Jokes, 593–594
Jomini, Henry, 146, 267, 325, 326, **862–863**
Jones, Archer, 328, 329
Jones, Arnold Elzey. *See* Elzey, Arnold
Jones, Catesby, 236, 290, 291, **863**, 1387, 1388, 1670
Jones, Charles, 932
Jones, Charles Colcock, Jr., 568–569
Jones, Charles T., 1614
Jones, David Rumph ("Neighbor"), **863–864**
Manassas, Second, 1000, 1002
Sharpsburg campaign, 1406, 1408
Jones, George Washington, **864–865**
Jones, Henry Cox, **865**
Jones, J. B., **865–866**, 1080, 1330, 1668, 1684, 1686
diary, 333
family life, 305
on Northrop (Lucius), 1158
Jones, J. R., 849, **866**, 1526
Jones, J. William, 130, 476, 1512
Jones, John, and Evan Jones, 297
Jones, John J., *669*

Jones, John M., **866–867**, 866, 1719
Jones, Joseph, **867**
Jones, Mary Sharp, 472
Jones, Robert McDonald, 309, 812, 813, **868**
Jones, Roger, 740, 1455
Jones, "Rum." *See* Jones, John M.
Jones, Sam (Georgia evangelist), 1035
Jones, Samuel (major general), 288, 843, **868**, 1268, 1567
Jones, Samuel J. (Kansas sheriff), 175
Jones, Terry L., *as contributor*, 957–958, 1004–1005, 1521, 1751–1752
Jones, Thomas A., 935
Jones, Thomas McKissick, **868–869**
Jones, V. C., 441
Jones, William Edmondson ("Grumble"), 267, 849, **869**, 1702, 1705
  Brandy Station, Virginia, 209–210, 269
  march through northwestern Virginia, 807
  Piedmont, Virginia, 1210
Jones, William Louis, 517
Jonesboro, Georgia, 32–33, 88, 110–111, 112, 114, 352
Jones County, Mississippi, **870**
Jones Field, Tennessee, 1526, 2022
Jones, Quiggin, and Company, 129, 184, 368
J. O. Nixon (ship), 1269
Jordan, Ervin L., Jr., *as contributor*, 642–644
Jordan, Thomas, 542, 544, 714, **870–871**, 1089, 1421
Joseph (ship), 1369
Joseph R. Anderson and Company. *See* Tredegar Iron Works
Joubert de la Ferte, Jean Ferdinand, 1523
Journal (Wilmington newspaper), 1142
Journalism. *See* Censorship; Freedom of the press; Magazines; Newspapers; War correspondents
Journal of Commerce (publication), 230, 494, 495
Journal of Music (publication), 1104
Journals. *See* Diaries, letters, and memoirs
J. R. Anderson and Co. *See* Tredegar Iron Works
J. R. Williams (ship), 815, 1694
J. R. Young & Company, 98
Juárez, Benito, 631, *1036*, 1037, 1209, 1586
Judah, Henry M., 1089
Judah (ship), 1530
Judaism. *See* Jews
Judd, H. O., 937
Judiciary, **871–873**
  Benjamin, Judah P., 159, 452
  conscription issue, 402, 727
  Constitution, 401–402
  constitutionality decisions, 1535–1536
  judge advocates, 1039
  Keyes, Wade, 892
  Magrath, Andrew G., 988
  Sequestration Act enforcement, 389
  see also Military justice; Supreme Court, Confederate
Judiciary Act of 1861, 661
Judson College, 520
Juge, Paul, 604
Julio, E. B. D., **873–874**, 951, 1100
Jumper, John (Hiniha Mikko), 1390
Juneteenth, 655, **874**, 924, 950, 1446, 1586
Junkin, Elinor, 832
Juno (ship), 185, 1599
Justice. *See* Crime and punishment; Courts-martial; Judiciary; Military justice
Justice Department, 249
  civil service, 314, 315
  secretaries, 252
  see also Attorney general; Judiciary
J. W. Seaver (ship), 674
J. W. Young & Co., 372

K

Kabat, Ric A., *as contributor*, 172–173, 1387–1388
Kalem studio, 574, 575, 577
Kamerling, Henry, *as contributor*, 1597–1599
Kanawha. *See* West Virginia
Kanawha Salt Company, 1040
Kansas
  African American troops, 9, 10–11
  congressional delegates, 1711
  guerrilla warfare, 719, 721–722, 724
  Indian loyalists, 1167
  Indian refugees, 1398, 1409
  proslavery riots, 1561
  Quantrill (William) raid, 1289
  slavery issue, 554, 556–557, 558, 1375
  statehood, 687, 1375
  Unionism, 719
  see also Bleeding Kansas; Kansas-Nebraska Act
Kansas Aid Meeting, 138
Kansas Jayhawkers, 647, 719, 1289, 1754
Kansas-Nebraska Act, 321, 322, 451, 556–557, 558, 852, **875–876**, 1056, 1321, 1715
  Bleeding Kansas, 175
  congressional passage, 1539
  Dred Scott decision, 494
  repeal of Missouri Compromise restrictions, 1375, 1534
  secessionism and, 1375
Kantor, MacKinlay, 939
Kate (ship), 184, 185, 1726
Kean, Robert Garlick, 410, 793, 865, 1306, 1685–1686
Kearny, Philip, 637, 1002
Kearsarge (ship), 20, 375, 592, 880, 1394
Keatinge, Edward, 436, 438
Keatinge and Ball, 436
Keaton, Buster, 577, *579*
Keats of the Confederacy. *See* Lanier, Sidney
Keeble, Edwin A., **876**
Keeble, Walter, 1231, 1590
Keen, W. S., 1245
Keen, Walker, and Company, 1456, 1457
Keetoowaha, 813
Keetowahs, 297
Keitt, Lawrence, 133, 200, **876–879**, 1310, *1505*, *1561*
Kell, John McIntosh, **879–880**, 1393, 1394, 1530
Kelley, Benjamin F., 725, 1700, 1702
Kelly, Dennis, *as contributor*, 259, 432, 616, 885–886
Kelly, James C., *as contributor*, 231
Kelly, John Herbert, **880**
Kelly's Ford, Virginia, **880–881**, 915, 1556, 1713
Kemper, James Lawson, **881**, 1000, 1002, 1076, 1582
Kenan, Augustus Holmes, **881–882**
Kenan, Owen Rand, **882**
Kenansville, North Carolina, 514
Kenedy, Mifflin, 232
Kennedy, John Doby, **882–883**
Kennedy, John F., 557
Kennedy, Joseph C. G., 688
Kenner, Duncan F., 485, **883–885**, 1529
Kennesaw Mountain, Georgia, 112, 114, 296, **885–886**, 1683
  field fortifications, 626
  Johnston, Joseph E., 672, 885, 886
  Vaughan, Alfred, 1653
Kennesaw Mountain National Battlefield Site, 1072, 1073

Kennington, John, Jr., *as contributor*, 1358–1361
Kentucky, **886–889**
Army of. *See* Army of Central Kentucky; Army of Kentucky; Army of Tennessee
black-white population comparison, *1435*
as border state, 195–196
Bragg (Braxton) campaign. *See* Kentucky campaign of Bragg
congressmen, 203, 217, 234–235, 243–244, 311, 391, 430, 528–529, 550–551, 602, 778–779, 972–973, 1011, 1012, 1062–1063, 1075–1076, 1310, 1431, 1593, 1622, 1709, 1724
Constitution ratification, 403
cotton plantations, 1436
currency, 1279
education, 216, 519
election of 1860, 521, 522, 523
election of 1863, 524
flag, 587
governors, 239, 677, 701, 702, 703, 752, 987–988
guerrilla warfare, 720, 725
habeas corpus suspension, 1177
Johnson, George W., 851
Johnson, Thomas, 857
livestock breeding, 791–792
Orphan Brigade, 736, 816, **1170**, 1516
population, 886, 1233
railroads, 1293
refugees, 1318
salt making, 1362
secession. *See under* Secession
secession date correlated with total black population, *1486*
slavery, 554
tobacco farming, 1598
Unionism, 85, 216, 720, 886–887, 1380, 1441
Union occupation, 1709
Whig party, 1708
see also particular city and place names
Kentucky and Virginia Resolutions (1798-1799)
and state rights arguments, 1532, 1533, 1534
and nullification controversy, 1374
Kentucky campaign of Bragg, 27, 72, 154, 196, 204, 239, 275, 491–492, 609, 752, 815, 887–888, **889–891**, 1011, 1041, 1074, 1323, 1576–1577, 1707
Anderson, James Patton, 32
Buckner, Simon Bolivar, 238–239
Cleburne, Patrick, 353
Gardner, Franklin, 657
guerrilla activity, 720
initiative for invasion, 1088
map, 889
Munfordville, Kentucky, 1093
Perryville, Kentucky, **1196–1198**
Kentucky Military Institute, 519, 780
Kenzer, Robert C., *as contributor*, 378–380
Keokuk (ship), 1472
Kernstown, Virginia, 104, 663–664, 866, 1415, 1549
Kerr, James, 1467, 1468
Kerr revolver, 1467
Kerr rifles, 918; *see also* Enfield rifles
Kershaw, Joseph B., 271, 882, 883, **891–892**, 1733
brigade, 878
Fredericksburg campaign, 640
Harpers Ferry, West Virginia, 743
Shenandoah Valley, 1418, 1419
staff, 693, 694
Ketchum, William F., 734
Key, Francis Scott, 1231
Key, John, 3
Key, John R., 1231
Keyes, Erasmus D., 1402, *1403*
Keyes, Frances Parkinson, 58
Keyes, Wade, 251, **892**
Keystone State (ship), *289*, 1125
Khedive's Egypt, The (Leon), 924
Kickapoos, 425
Ki-he-cah-te-da, 1290
Killian's Mills Prison, 1268
Kilpatrick, Hugh Judson
Brandy Station, Virginia, 210
Buckland Mills, Virginia, 237
in Carolinas, 118, 261, 262
Dahlgren Papers, 441
Dalton, Georgia, 442
raids. *See* Kilpatrick-Dahlgren raid
Sherman's March to the Sea, 1006
Kilpatrick-Dahlgren raid, 144, **892–893**
Dahlgren Papers, **441**
effect on Libby Prison, 931
map, 893
"Kilpatrick's Shirt-tail Skedaddle," 262
Kimball, Fiske, 922
Kin. *See* Family life
King, Alvy L., *as contributor*, 1714–1717
King, Francis T., 1494
King, Grace, 937
King, John P., 1295
King, Josephine S., *as contributor*, 388
King, Richard, 232, 1586
King, Rufus, 1001
King, William H., **893–894**
King, William R., *381*, 1293
King, Wilma, *as contributor*, 307–308
King Cotton. *See* Cotton; Diplomacy; Textile industry
Kingdom of Jones. *See* Jones County, Mississippi
King of Spades (Robert E. Lee nickname), 78, 625, 917, 920
Kingsbury, Mary Jane, 238
King's School House, Virginia, 690, 918, 1192, 1193, 1479
Kingston, Georgia, venereal disease hospital, 796
Kingsville, Missouri, guerrilla warfare, 724
Kinship networks. *See* Family life
Kiowas, 1608
Kirk, Edward, 1094
Kirkland, William Whedbee, 220–221, **894**, 983
Klement, Frank L., *as contributor*, 411–413, 1158–1159
Knights of the Golden Circle. *See* Copperheads
Knives, 16, 60, 515, 817
Knowledge of God, Objectively Considered, The (Breckinridge), 216
Knowledge of God, Subjectively Considered, The (Breckinridge), 216
Know-Nothing party. *See* American party
Knox, Myra. *See* Semmes, Myra Knox
Knoxville, Tennessee, 1013
campaign. *See* Knoxville campaign
martial law, 263
railroads, 1297
roads, 1338
Knoxville and Greeneville Conventions, **894–895**, 1574, 1575
Knoxville campaign, 30, 705, 870, 891, **895–897**, 1563
map, 896
Knoxville Register (newspaper), 760
Knoxville Whig (newspaper), 230, 231, 273, 640, 895, 1574
Koasati, 812
Kolb's Farm, Georgia, 112, 114
Korn, Bertram, 162
Kossuth, Louis, 1209
Koste, Jodi, *as contributor*, 793–796
Kotetsu (ship), 1548
Kraft, Goldschmidt, and Kraft, 514

Kreyling, Michael, *as contributor*, 908–909
Krick, Robert E. L., *as contributor*, 222–223, 769, 1676, 1679–1680
Krick, Robert K., *as contributor*, 29, 76–83, 131–132, 142, 207–208, 235, 272–273, 279–282, 308, 362–365, 430–431, 459, 637–640, 647, 717, 746, 805, 866–867, 947–948, 974, 1189–1190, 1344–1345, 1347, 1718, 1719–1721
Ku Klux Klan, 967, 1437, 1483
  Alabama, 928
  Arkansas, 54
  fictional depictions, 575, *576*, 938, 949
  Forrest, Nathan Bedford, 607
  opposition, 942
Kurtz, Wilbur G., 578

L

Labor, **899–903**
  African American forgeworkers, **3–4**, 96, 97, 372
  agricultural, 901
  artisans, 644, 735, 900, 902, 1486
  children, 307
  cotton-related, 418
  free blacks, 399, 642, 643, 1220, 1487
  indentured servants, 1598
  industrial, 1234
  overview article, **899–901**
  poor whites, 1489
  postal workers, 1242
  prisoners of war, 1261
  proslavery argument, 1273
  railroad shortages, 1298
  rice production, 1327
  shortages, 379, 1082, 1298, 1491
  skilled, 96, 97, 98, 356, 900, **902–903**, 1235, 1245, 1261
  slave, 4, 34, 70, 74–75, 96, 192, 320, 344–345, 372, 399, 533, 899–900, 901, 902, 903, 1235, 1434–1451, 1616, 1687
  textile industry, 1589
  Tredegar Iron Works, 1616
  urban, 1489
  women in work force, 315, 547, 900–901, 903, 1057, 1614, 1687, 1740–1741
  see also Civil service; Strikes; Wages and salaries
Ladies' aid societies, 596
Ladies' Hospital (Columbia, South Carolina), 371
Ladies' Hospital (Montgomery, Alabama), 794
Ladies' Hospital Association (Mecklenburg County, North Carolina), 290
Ladies' Lee Memorial Association, 922
Ladies' Memorial Association of Wilmington, 1027
Ladies' Relief Society (Wilmington, North Carolina), 1726
Lady Davis (ship), 1530
Lady's Clothing Association (Columbia, South Carolina), 969
Lafayette, Alabama, bread riots, 213
LaFlore, Mitchell, 305
LaGrange, Georgia, 794
Laird, John, Jr., 904
Laird, William, 904
Laird Rams, 240, 484, **903–904**, 1019, 1124, 1150, 1303, 1727
Laird Shipyards, 19, 129, 184, 484, **904**
Laissez-faire doctrine, 1024, 1285
Lake, William A., 276
Lake Pontchartrain, 1556
Lamar, C. A. L., 808
Lamar, Gazaway B., 485, **905**
Lamar, John B., 359
Lamar, L. Q. C., 23, 226, 761, **905–906**, 1047, *1050*, 1141, 1354, 1529
Lamar, Mary Ann, 358
Lamb, William, 368, 611, 612, 1149, 1152, 1727
Lambert, Paul F., *as contributor*, 1–2, 498, 983–984, 1286–1287, 1290–1291, 1477–1478, 1481–1483, 1546, 1695, 1721–1722
La Mesilla, Arizona, 983, 984
Lamkin, John Tillman, **906**
Lancaster, South Carolina, 1510
Lancaster (ship), 55
Lander, William, 882, **906–907**
Land mines. *See* Hand grenades and land mines
L & N. *See* Louisville and Nashville Railroad
Land's End Plantation, 1010
Land We Love, The (periodical), 776
Lane, Alexander G., 796
Lane, James, 80, 134, 719, 721, 722, **907–908**
Lane, James Henry, 10–11
Lane, Joseph, 1630
Lane, Walter Paye, 823, **908**
Lang, David, 476
Lang Syne Plantation, 969
Lanier, Charles D., Mrs., 922
Lanier, Robert S., 29
Lanier, Sydney, 29, **908–909**, 938, 976, 977
Lankford, Nelson D., *as contributor*, 197–198, 223, 259–260, 279, 367–368, 464, 651–652, 663, 684, 694–695, 780–781, 782–783, 861–862, 964–965, 971–972, 975–976, 1014–1016, 1040, 1063–1064, 1250, 1353–1354, 1371, 1711
La Plata (ship), 1620
Lapwing (ship), 592
La Renaissance Louisianaise (publication), 426
Last Meeting of Lee and Jackson, The (painting), 873–874, *951*, 1100
Last Ninety Days of the War in North Carolina, The (Spencer), 1518
Latané, John, 459–460
Latané, William. *See Burial of Latané, The*
Latin America. *See* Central America, and Southern expansionism; South America, and Southern expansionism
Latrines. *See* Sanitation
Laundresses, and prostitution, 1276
Laurel (ship), 1411, 1675
Laurel Brigade, 152, 459, 869, 1341–1342, 1516
La vérité sur les Etats Confédérés d'Amérique (brochure), 1271
Lavinia (ship), 744
Law, Evander McIvor, 312, **909**, 1196
  Gaines' Mill, Virginia, 653
  Sharpsburg campaign, 1406
Lawley, Francis, 161
Lawrence, John T., 129
Lawrence, Kansas
  proslavery riots, 1561
  raid, 38, 721–722, 1054, 1289, 1599
Lawrence Republican (newspaper), 742
Lawton, Alexander R., **909–910**, 1106, 1267, 1685
  defense of Savannah, Georgia, 1366
  Manassas, Second, 1000, 1001
  Quartermaster Bureau, 508, 509, 1291, 1292
Lawyers. *See* Legal profession
Lay, John, 299
Lazarus, Nathan, 845
Leach, James Madison, 524, **910–911**
Leach, James T., 524, 689, 910, **911–913**
  peace resolutions, 942, 1183
Lead, **913**
  blockade running, 1147–1148

Lead, *continued*
bullets, 1470
mining, 1147
production, 90
shortages, 90
Leadbetter, Danville, 533, **913–914**
League of United Southerners, 1350
Lebetter, M. T., 51
Lecompton constitution, 176, 322, 348, 465, 687, 875, 1539
LeConte, Emma, 472, 1217
LeConte, John, 517, 1148
LeConte, Joseph, 369, 370, 517, 1148, 1363
Ledlie, James, 1200
Lee, Ann Hill Carter, 916, 922
Lee, Charles H., 1039
Lee, Custis. *See* Lee, George Washington Custis
Lee, Edwin Gray, 538–539, 544, **914**, 1190, 1595
Lee, Fitzhugh, 82, **914–915**, 1183, 1209, 1713
Brandy Station, Virginia, 209
Buckland Mills, Virginia, 237
cavalry, 270
Lee Monument, 922, *923*
Shenandoah Valley, 1418
Spotsylvania campaign, 1519
Lee, Francis D., 1515, 1516
Lee, Francis Lightfoot, 922
Lee, George Washington Custis, 136, 893, **915–916**, 1331, 1551
Lee, Henry ("Light Horse Harry"), 914, 916, 922
Lee, Mary Custis, 58, 915, 917–918, 921
Lee, Richard Henry, 922
Lee, Robert E., *65*, 223, 285, 769, **916–920**, 1503
appointments, 686, 867
Appomattox campaign, 45–48
Arlington House, **58**, 916, 917
arming slaves as soldiers proposal, 8, 45, 75, 708, 1386, 1480, 1487, 1687
Army of Northern Virginia, 36, 66, 76–83, 220, 775, 917–920, 925, 981, 1664
biographers, 408, 944
caricature, *731*
cavalry raids, 152
Chancellorsville campaign, 279–282, 918, 1553
children, **915–916**, **922–923**
Cold Harbor, Virginia, 366–367
cotton for food exchanges, 420
criticism of, 364
Dahlgren Papers, 441
decision to fight for Confederacy, 1663
desertion curbs, 346, 467, 468
eating habits, 595
entrenchment, 367, 1193
exemption complaints, 1243
farewell address, 330
farewell address text, 1792
fort design, 617
Fort Pulaski, Georgia, 616
Fredericksburg campaign, 637, 638, 639, 819, 918, 1386
Gaines' Mill, Virginia, 653–654
Gettysburg campaign, 328, 676–683, 918, 945–946, 1553
Harpers Ferry, West Virginia, 742; *see also subhead* John Brown's raid *below*
as hero of Lost Cause, 503, 535, 920, 922, 948–949, 951
historical papers, 1512
and Hood's Brigade, 789
ill health, 918, 920
on irregular warfare, 722–723, 725
John Brown's raid, 740, 741, 917, 1295, 1552
Kelly's Ford, Virginia, 880–881
Kilpatrick-Dahlgren raid, 892
legends, 1721
literary portrayals, 936, 938, 939
Lynchburg, Virginia, defense, 963, 1413
Malvern Hill, Virginia, 994–996
Manassas, Second, 834, 918, 919, 999–1003
Mechanicsville, Virginia, 1020–1021
on military justice, 1039
Mine Run campaign, 1043
monuments and memorials, 58, 159, 922–923, 951, 952, 1028, 1069, 1074
on Mosby (John S.), 1090
newspaper portrayals, 1683
nicknames, 625, 917, 1401
parole, text of, 1791
peace initiatives, 912
personal and military papers, 476, 1099
personality, 67, 474, 788
Petersburg campaign, 920, 1198–1202
pike use, 846
portraits and paintings of, 873–874, *951*, 1230, 1231, 1256
rail system, 1294, 1297, 1299
on reasons for Civil War, 1485
relationship with subordinates, 221, 502, 770, 771, 859, 860, 861
response to Emancipation Proclamation, 532
Richmond, Virginia, defense, 834, 1400–1401, 1403, 1412
Savannah, Georgia, defense, 1366
service sword, 513
Seven Days' Battles, 918, 1400
Sharpsburg campaign, 864, 919, 1404–1408
Shenandoah Valley campaign reinforcements, 1416, 1418, 1419
on Smith (E. Kirby), 1473
on Smith (Gustavus W.), 1474
soldiers' home, 1502
South Carolina, Georgia, and Florida Military Department command, 1509
South Mountain, Maryland, 1512–1513
Spotsylvania campaign, 80, 697, 920, 1518–1520
staff, 25, *77*, 308, 664, 944, 1552
and Stoneman's raids, 1546
strategy and tactics. *See under* Strategy and tactics
Stratford Hall Plantation, 916, 922
and Stuart's raids, 1552, 1553, 1554–1556
supplies, 1727
surrender decision, *47*, 212, 262, 330, 571, 694, 920, 946, 975, 1338
telegraph operator, 1430
torpedo demonstration, 1515
and war correspondents, 274
Wilderness campaign, 716, 920, 1719–1721
Lee, R. W. (Indian affairs commissioner), 812
Lee, "Rooney." *See* Lee, William Henry Fitzhugh
Lee, Stephen D., 25, 32, 298, **920–921**, 1002, 1173, 1572, 1657
Brice's Cross Roads, Mississippi, 218, 219
Franklin and Nashville campaign, 632
Meridian campaign, 835, 1032, 1033
Tupelo, Mississippi, 1624, 1625
Vicksburg campaign, 1017
Lee, Thomas, 922
Lee, William Henry Fitzhugh ("Rooney"), 134, 144, 266, 278, **921**
Brandy Station, Virginia, 209, 210–211
hostage, 1258
Lee and His Lieutenants (Pollard), 1229
Lee Camp, 922

Leech, Thomas, 1459
Leech and Rigdon, 514, 1459–1460
Leeds and Company, 97, 98
Leeds Foundry, 1556
"Lee in the Mountains" (Davidson), 939
Lee Memorial Association, **922**, 1027
Lee Monument Association, **922–923**, 951
Leesburg, Virginia. *See* Ball's Bluff, Virginia
Lee's Legion, 144
Lee's Lieutenants (Freeman), 878
Lee's Light Horse, 144
Leeson, Elizabeth, 1082
Lee's Retreat. *See* Appomattox campaign
Lee's War Horse (James Longstreet nickname), 945
Leflore, Greenwood, 310
Legal profession, 1489
Legal system. *See* Judiciary
Legends. *See* Folk narratives
Legg, Thomas J., *as contributor*, 151, 709–710, 713, 748–749, 1092, 1222–1223, 1314–1317, 1538, 1690
Leggett, William, 436
Legion, 733, 816; *see also* Hampton's legion
Legislative branch. *See* Congress, Confederate
Leiberson, Goddard, 487
Leisure, **923–924**
  prisoners of war, 1260, *1262*
  slave children, 307
  soldiers, 1497
  sports, 923
LeMat, Jean A. F., 1469
LeMat revolvers, 63
Lent, John A., *as contributor*, 985–987
Leo Dragoons, 590
Leon, Edwin de, 482, 798, **924**, 1270–1271
Leopold, king of Belgium, 1004
Leovy, Henry, 777, 1556
Les Misérables (Hugo), 193, 194, 936–937, 1232
Lester, George N., **924–925**
  on quartermasters' ethics, 377, 1292
Lester, Richard I., *as contributor*, 41–42
Lester, W. W., 193
Letcher, John, **925–926**
  appointments, 198, 1017, 1063
  bread riots, 212
  gubernatorial successor, 124, 1479, 1480
  Harpers Ferry arsenal seizure, 104, 740
  Loring-Jackson incident, 834, 947, 1702
  Seddon-Tyler report to, 1384
  as Virginia governor, 174, 703, 1662, 1663, 1667–1668
Letter from the Hon. William C. Rives to a Friend, on the Important Questions of the Day (Rives), 1336
Letters. *See* Diaries, letters, and memoirs; Love letters; Post Office Department
Letters and Other Writings of James Madison (Rives), 1338
Letters of marque and reprisal, 373, 480, 979, 1269
Letters of Mozis Addums to Billy Ivvins (Bagby), 937
Leventhorpe, Collett, **926–927**
Leverett, Charles E., 1588
Leverett, Rudy, *as contributor*, 870
Le Vert, Octavia Walton, 1058
Levy, Lionel, 845
Lewis, Angela, 395
Lewis, David Peter, **927–928**, 1287
Lewis, David W., **928**
Lewis, John W., 853, **929**
Lewis, Joseph Horace, **929**, 1170
Lewis, Levin M., **930**
Lewis, William Gaston, **930**
Lewisburg, Virginia, 769, 1245
Lewis Cass (ship), 1530
Lexington, Virginia
  as Shenandoah Valley boundary, 1415
  Union occupation, 963
Lexington Rifles, 1086
L. Haiman and Brother, 514, 515, 1460
Lhuys, Édouard Drouyn de, 1529
Libby and Son, 1266
Libby Prison, 256, **930–932**, 1258, *1266*, 1353, 1387
  federal prisoners, 1652, 1667
  Kilpatrick-Dahlgren raid, 892–893
  photographs, 1206
Liberator (newspaper), 44
Liberia, 164, 215, 216
Liberty, Virginia, 796
Liberty party, 1728
Libraries, research. *See* Museums and archives
Library of Congress (Washington, D.C.)
  Confederate archival collection, 1098
  folk songs, 487
  War Department papers, 1688
License tax, 1569
Liddell, St. John Richardson, 700, **932**
Lieber Code (Confederate General Orders No. 100), 1352
Liège, Belgium, 1468–1469
Life of General Robert E. Lee, A (Cooke), 408
Life of Jefferson Davis, and Secret History of the Southern Confederacy (Pollard), 1229
Life of Johnny Reb, The (Wiley), 1103
Life of Stonewall Jackson, The (Cooke), 193, 408, 937
Life on the Mississippi (Twain), 354
Light artillery. *See* Artillery, field
Lightburn, Joseph A. J., 1702, 1705
Light Division, 1516
Lighthouse Bureau, 1392, 1615
Lightwood Knot Springs, 370
Ligon's Warehouse and Tobacco Factory, 1265
Lilley, Robert Doak, **932**
"Lily Dale," 1103
Limbs, artificial. *See* Prosthetics
Limestone caves and mining, 1043, 1375
Lincoln, Abraham, **932–936**
  African Americans in the Union Army, 1138, 1335, 1447, 1472
  assassination, 145, 160, 195, 341, 350, 351, 538, 539, 540, **934–936**, 1016, 1204, 1432, 1595
  attitudes toward, 332, 645, 1212; *see also* Copperheads
  Baldwin (John B.) interview, 123, 124
  Barringer (Rufus) meeting, 134
  Blair (Francis P.) initiative, 1541
  blockade declaration, 176, 374
  on Burnside (Ambrose E.) expedition, 244
  cabinet, 411, 687, 688, 706, 1310
  caricatures, *412*, *494*, *934*, *1044*, 1673
  civil liberties policies, 934, 1224
  confiscation policy, 390
  election of 1860, 213–214, 521–524, 706, 933, 1322, 1373, 1375–1376, *1376*, 1377, 1379, 1384, 1441, 1506, 1507, 1562, 1637, 1638, 1699
  election of 1864, 217, 332, 336, 349, *412*, 503, 887, 1080, 1165, 1166, *1322*, 1638
  electoral college vote, 1441
  Emancipation Proclamation, 6–7, 9, 530–532, 1408, 1434, 1446
  family members in Confederacy, 224
  Fort Sumter strategy, 324, 629, 1381–1383, 1508
  habeas corpus suspension, 332, 728
  Hampton Roads Conference, 733, 1541
  Heroes of America initiation, 768–769, 855

Lincoln, Abraham, *continued*
"house-divided" speech, 319, 495
image in Confederacy, 522, **933–934**
on importance of Kentucky, 216, 886
kidnap plot, 195, 537, 538, 544, 545, 935
law practice, 174
legends about, 593, 1167
military governorships, 1419, 1525
mobilization order, 383, 788
oath of allegiance, 1163
peace overtures, 123, 256, 349, 387, 733, 804, 1184, 1272, 1305–1306, 1337, 1745
personality, 336
photographic portrait, *1376*
prisoner of war exchanges, 1261
privateering policy, 1269, 1369
Reconstruction policies, 729, 956, 1097
religious belief, 1498
response to secessionists, 324, 613, 689, 1380–1381, 1384, 1638, 1663
rules of war, 1352
Sharpsburg victory, 1408
Shenandoah Valley campaign of Sheridan, 1417
slavery policies, 320, 429, 558, 809, 887, 1275; *see also subhead* Emancipation proclamation *above*
telegraph use, 326, 1573
Thirteenth Amendment, 1590
Trent affair, 1015, 1528, 1619, 1620
Union generals, 279, 685, 1134, 1752
vice president, 848
war strategy, 56, 326, 764, 892, 1165, 1314, 1609, 1752
Lincoln, Mary Todd, 761
Lincolnton, North Carolina, 1152
Lindgren, James M., *as contributor*, 58
Lindheimer, Ferdinand, 676
Lindsay, Robert B., 309, 928
Lindsay, William S., 483, 631
Linebaugh, John, 274, 1683
Line of battle formation, 819
Lipscomb, David, 1320
Liquor. *See* Alcohol; Drunkenness; Prohibition movement
"Listen to the Mocking Bird" (song), 1103
Literacy. *See* Education
Literary Fund (North Carolina), 1722
Literature, **936–939**
Berry, Harrison, 164
Charleston, South Carolina, 193, 284–285
Confederate soldiers' letters, 1496
Cooke, John Esten, 407–408
Dorsey, Sarah Anne, 492
Hunton's *Autobiography*, 805
Jones, J. B., 865–866
Lanier, Sidney, 908–909
literary magazines, 985–986
portrayals of Confederacy, **938–939**, 1264
produced in Confederacy, 193–194, 547, **936–937**
proslavery, **1272–1274**
Turner, Joseph A., 1625–1626
see also Bibliography and historiography; Book publishing; Diaries, letters, and memoirs; Popular culture; particular titles
Lithography, 1231, 1256
Little, Lewis Henry, 917, **939**
"Little Griffin" (Ticknor), 825
Little Ogeechee River, 1368
Littlepage, William, 441
Little Rebel (ship), 1334
Little Rock, Arkansas, 695, **939–942**, 1568, 1609, 1696
arsenal, 90, 1314, 1461, 1469
hospitals, 796, 941
Roane, John, 1340
Union occupation, 53, 941
Little Rose Is Gone (recording), 487
Little Shepherd of Kingdom Come, The (film), 578
Littlest Rebel, The (film), 578
Little Town Spicer (Seneca leader), 1398
Liverpool, England, Southern Bazaar, 1262
Livingston, David, 1524
Livingston, T. R., 11
Loans. *See* Debt; Erlanger loan
Local governments. *See* State and local governments
Loch Willow School (Churchville), 797
Lockett, Samuel H., 620
Lockwood, Lewis C., 1103–1104
Lockwood, Robert, 183
Lockwood, Thomas, 183, 185, 368
Locomotive chase. *See* Andrews raid
Lodge, Henry Cabot, 1338
Logan, George Washington, 447, 689, **942**
Logan, John A., 33, 1658
Logan, Thomas Muldrup, **942–943**
Logan's Cross Roads, Kentucky. *See* Mill Springs, Kentucky
Lomax, Lunsford Lindsay, 582, 583, **943**, 1418, 1751
London Armory Company, 1468
London Convention, 631
London Herald (newspaper), 482
London Post (newspaper), 482
London Times (newspaper), 1271
Long, Armistead Lindsay, **944**
Long, Eli, 1389
Long, Jesse Bradford, 735
Long arms
altered U.S., 1464–1465
ammunition, 1469–1471
captured and purchased U.S., 1461–1462
carbines, 60, 62–63
Confederate-manufactured, **1455–1458**
imported, 1465–1469
see also Flintlock musket; Rifle; Rifle-musket
Longmare, Emile, 547
Long Night, The (novel by Lytle), 939
Long Riders, The (film), 580
Long Roll, The (novel by Johnston), 938
Longstreet, Augustus B., 172, 905, 936, 937, 944, 1093–1094
Longstreet, James, *65*, **944–947**
Army of Northern Virginia, 80, 213, 274, 571, 864, 894, 909, 945–946
Army of Tennessee. *See under* Army of Tennessee
Brandy Station, Virginia, 209
charges against McLaws (Lafayette), 974
Chattanooga campaign, 293
Chickamauga campaign, 86, 204–205, 239, 303, 304, 327, 946, 1297, 1298, 1342, 1343, 1386, 1577
dispute with Hill (A. P.), 770, 1503
Early (Jubal) relationship, 502
Frayser's Farm, Virginia, 636
Fredericksburg campaign, 638, 945
Gaines' Mill, Virginia, 653
Gettysburg campaign, 36, 81, 677, 680, 681, 682, 918, 945–946, 949, 1512
Hampton's Legion, 734
historical papers on, 1512
intelligence operations, 537, 544, 748
Knoxville campaign, 895–896, 897, 914, 1013, 1563, 1577
Malvern Hill, Virginia, 994, 995
Manassas, First, 996, 997
Manassas, Second, 78, 79, 918, 945, 990, 1000, 1001, 1002–1003
Mechanicsville, Virginia, 1020
memoirs, 476
nickname, 945
Seven Days' Battles, 1400
Seven Pines, Virginia, 76, 1402

staff, 25, 1076, 1503
Wilderness campaign, 82, 817, 891, 892, 946, 1418, 1518, 1719, 1720, 1721
Williamsburg, Virginia, 35, 1191, 1193, 1725
Lookout Mountain, 293, 294–295
Look within for Fact and Fiction (Judd), 937
López, Albino, 1037
López, Narciso, 1209
Lord Clyde (ship), 2–3
"Lorena" (song), 1103, 1498
Lorenz rifle-muskets, 1468
Loring, W. W., 113, 569, 588, 834, 921, 944, **947**, 960, 968, 1658, 1700, 1702, 1705
fortifications, 621
incident with Jackson (Thomas J. "Stonewall"). *See* Loring-Jackson incident
Loring-Jackson incident, 834, **947–948**, 1565, 1700, 1702
Losses. *See under* Civil War; *subhead* casualties *under particular battles*
Losson, Christopher, *as contributor*, 295–296
Lost Cause, **948–952**
archaeology, 48–50
Atkins, J. D. C., 108
Baptist Church, 130
Beall, John Y., 145
Beers, Fannie, 153
Boteler, Helen, 198
Burial of Latané (painting), 460, 1554
Cary, Hetty, 265
Confederate Veteran (magazine), **388**
creole adherence, 426
Davis, Sam, 541
development, 1069–1071
"Dixie" (song), 488
Early, Jubal, 501, 503
Episcopal clergy, 535
film and video, 572–580
heroes of, 453, 920, 923
honor and, 330, 422, 788
iconography, 221–222, 242, *243*, 460, 873–874, **950–952**, 1028, 1099–1100, 1554, 1673–1674
inception, 1035
influencing postwar courtship, 422
literature, 936–939, 1229
March to the Sea legacy, 1007
Memorial Day observance, 1027
overview article, **948–950**
Protestantism and, 130, 535, 1035, 1321
Quaker rejection of, 1494
Richmond, Virginia, as shrine to, 917, 1332
romantic legends, 1218
selected bibliography, 171
Southern Historical Society Papers, 1512
Southern Methodists, 1035
Lost Cause, The (lithograph), 950–951
Lost Cause, The (Pollard), 166, 329, 948, 1229
Lost Cause Regained, The (Pollard), 1229
Loudoun County, Virginia, 1090, 1091
Loudoun Heights (Harpers Ferry), 1677
Louisa Court House, Virginia, 1546
Louis Haiman & Brothers. *See* L. Haiman and Brother
Louisiana, **952–956**
African American troops, 9, 10, 644
American party, 28
Army of. *See* Army of Alabama, Mississippi, and Eastern Louisiana
arsenals and armories, 1461, 1469
banks, 128
black-white population comparison, *1435*
congressmen, 395, 464, 499, 709, 778, 883–885, 1010, 1194, 1394–1397, 1504, 1514–1515, 1661
Constitution ratification, 403
cooperationists, 411, 1379
cotton plantations, 1436
creoles, 425–426, 644–645
currency issues, 433, 1281
debt, 462
Department of. *See* Department of Alabama, Mississippi, and Eastern Louisiana; Department of Mississippi and East Louisiana
education, 515, 516, 519
election of 1860, 521, 522, 523
farm acreage, *1484*
flag, 587
free blacks, 643, 1484
free black soldiers. *See subhead* African American troops *above*
freedom of the press, 641
government and politics, 955–956
governors, 26–27, 701, 702, 703, 729, 759, 952, 954, 955–956, 961, 1077–1078, 1145–1146, 1345, 1348, 1698–1699
guerrilla activity, 720–721
Indian soldiers, 812
Irish soldiers, 822, 823
Juneteenth celebration, 1446
livestock breeding, 792
manufacturing, 514, 515
military action, 954–955
politics, 1453–1454, 1504
population, 140, 602, 642, 1137, 1233, 1605
powder works, 1245
railroads, 1294, 1295, 1296
Reconstruction, 952, 956, 1138, 1348, 1698–1699
Red River campaigns. *See* Red River campaigns
religion, 1346
Republican party, 1322, 1348
rice production, 1328
salt making, 1362
secession. *See under* Secession
secession and Confederacy membership dates, *1379*
secession date correlated with total black population, *1486*
Semmes, Thomas, 1394–1397
slaveholdings, *1485*
slavery, 551, 553, 557, 558, 1436
Slidell, John, 1453–1455
small arms imports, 1465
small arms manufacture, 1458, 1469, 1470
soldiers' home, 1502
state navy, 1530
sugar plantations, 1436, 1559–1560
Tiger Brigade. *See* Louisiana Tigers
Trans-Mississippi Department, 1606
Unionism. *See under* Unionism
Union occupation, **1419–1420**, 1640, 1647
urbanization, 1643
U.S. acquisition. *See* Louisiana Purchase
see also particular cities and place names
Louisiana (ship), 685, 823, 992, 993, 1124, 1139, 1303, 1425, 1599, 1688, 1722–1723
Louisiana Brigade, 684–685
Louisiana Historical Society, 1194
Louisiana Hospital (Richmond, Virginia), 796
Louisiana Lottery Company, 1397
Louisiana Purchase, 320, 425, 426
Jefferson (Thomas) constitutional rationale, 1532
Missouri statehood and, 1055, 1533
slavery status and, 553, 1373–1374, 1533, 1534
Louisiana State Lottery, 150, 503

Louisiana State Seminary and Military Academy, 519, **957**
Louisiana State University, 957
Louisiana Tigers, *603*, 823, **957–958**, 1137, 1516
Louis Napoleon. *See* Napoleon III, emperor of France
Louis Napoleon (counterfeiter). *See* Richardson, John
Louis Philippe, king of France, 1335, 1336
Louisville, Kentucky
  prostitutes, 1277
  tobacco manufacturing center, 1598
Louisville and Nashville Railroad, 888, 889, 1088, 1089, 1092, 1295, 1682
Love, Peter E., *669*
Love and War (Jake), 939
Lovejoy's Station, Georgia, 1546
Love letters, 421, 1496
Lovell, Mansfield, **958–959**, 1334, 1697
  Corinth, Mississippi, 413, 414
  defense of New Orleans, 954, 1138, 1139, 1140
  Northern background, 1157
Love's Ambuscade; or, The Sergeant's Stratagem (Delchamps), 937, 1590
Lovett, Leslie A., *as contributor*, 1010, 1194, 1514–1515, 1661
Low, John, 1627
Lowe, Seth, 1286
Lowe, Thaddeus S. C., 125
Lower Fort, Mississippi, 621
Lowrey, Mark Perrin, **959–960**
Lowry, Robert, **960**
Loyalists. *See* Unionism; Tories
Loyall, Benjamin P., **960**
Loyalty oaths. *See* Oath of allegiance
Lubbock, Francis R., 341, 461, 701, 703, **960–961**, 1585, 1608
Lubin Company (film documentaries), 573
Lucas, Daniel, 544
Lucas, Marion B., 372
Lucy (ship), 185
Lucy Gwinn (ship), 656
Lukeman, Augustus, 573
Lumbees, 811
Lumber River, 262
Lumber trade, 1364, 1365
Lumpkin, Robert, 1453
Lunardini, Christine A., *as contributor*, 570, 1033–1034, 1141, 1518
Lund, Jennifer. *See* Smith, Jennifer Lund
L'Union (New Orleans newspaper), 645, 1348, 1621
Luray Valley, Virginia, 1416
Lutheran Church, **961**, 1320
  chaplains, 282
  Richmond, Virginia, 1330
Luxury items
  blockade runners, 287, 1727, 1741
  clothing, 357
  imports, 50, 174, 1140, 1285
  shortages, 222, 1219
Lynch, John Roy, **962**
Lynch, P. N., 1271
Lynch, Patrick, 1346
Lynch, William F., 245, **962**, 1019, 1727
  North Carolina naval forces, 960, 962, 1126
Lynchburg, Virginia, 83, **962–963**
  Confederate defense, 963, 1413
  hospitals, 794, 796, 1667
  McCausland, John, 967
  munitions manufacture, 1470
  railroads, 962, 1297
  roads, 1338
  tobacco, 1645
Lynchburg Virginian (newspaper), 201
Lyon, Francis Strother, **963–964**
Lyon, Hylan Benton, **964**, 1170
Lyon, James A., 1399
Lyon, Nathaniel, 53, 196, 648, 1009, 1053, 1180, 1251, 1323, 1606
  caricature, *1054*
  St. Louis arsenal defense, 828
  Wilson's Creek campaign, 1729, 1730, 1731
Lyons, James, **964–965**, 1630
Lyons, Richard Bickerton Pemell (Lord Lyons), 479, 480, 483, 484, 1528, *1620*
Lyons, Thomas B., 777
Lytle, A. D., 1206

M

Mabie, Hamilton Wright, 909
Mabry, Hinchie P., 1625
McAllister, William T., 152
Macaria; or, Altars of Sacrifice (Evans), 193, 547, 936, 937, 1059, 1232
McArthur, John, Shiloh campaign, 1422
Macarthy, Harry, 836, 1101, 1231, 1590
McArver, Charles, *as contributor*, 273–274, 609–610, 1141–1144, 1354, 1524, 1625–1626, 1683–1684
McBride, Jesse, 44
McCabe, James Dabney, Jr., 193, 936, 937, 1590
McCall, George, 126, 636
McCallum, Daniel C., 1298
McCallum, James, **967**
McCardell, John, *as contributor*, 186, 675
McCarthy, Harry. *See* Macarthy, Harry
McCauley, Charles S., 700
McCausland, John, 358, 504, 844, 849, **967–968**, 1673, 1702
  Chambersburg raid, 276, 277
McCaw, James Brown, 795–796
McClanahan, John, 1143
McClellan, George B., 336, 1556
  campaign song, 1103
  Cedar Mountain, Virginia, 272
  election of 1864, 217, *412*, *466*, 887, 1252, 1272, 1632
  espionage arrests, 1090
  espionage operations, 540
  Frayser's Farm, Virginia, 636
  fugitive slaves, 7
  Gaines' Mill, Virginia, 549, 653, 654
  Harpers Ferry, West Virginia, 742, 743, 744
  Malvern Hill, Virginia, 994–996
  Mechanicsville, Virginia, 1020–1021
  offer of medical supplies, 1353
  Ohio River control, 1691
  Peninsular campaign, 76, 989, 1191–1193, 1231, 1331, 1716
  Richmond, Virginia, 625, 1732
  Seven Days' Battles, 619–620, 836, 918, 1400, 1401
  Seven Pines, Virginia, 1402–1403
  Sharpsburg campaign, 79, 918, 1404, *1405*, 1406, 1407, 1408
  Shenandoah Valley, 834, 1412, 1415, 1416
  South Mountain, Maryland, 1513
  strategy, 126, 270, 327
  Stuart (J. E. B.) ride around, 78, 268–269, 276, 915, 918, 921, 1013, 1193, 1231, 1553, 1554, *1555*
  West Virginia, 1700, 1703, 1704
  Williamsburg, Virginia, 1724, 1725
  Yorktown, Virginia, 1752
McClellan, Henry B., 210
McClellan, W. C., 1277
McClernand, Alexander, 764–766
McClernand, John, 837, 1422, 1423, 1658, 1659
McClintock, James R., 777, 1556, 1557
McClung, Kitty Morgan, 770
McComb, William, 51, **968**
McCook, Alexander, 890–891, 1197, 1198
  Chickamauga campaign, 302
  Murfreesboro, Tennessee, 1094, 1095

McCook, Edward Moody, 591, 1389, 1546, 1547, 1567
McCook, "Fighting Dan," 1073
McCord, David James, 969
McCord, Louisa Cheves, 300, 795, **969**, 1740
McCord, Mary, 988
McCown, John P., 512, 800, 889, **969–970**, 1300, 1593, 1605, 1649
  Murfreesboro, Tennessee, 1094
  New Madrid operation, 1133, 1134
McCoy's Ferry, 1556
McCrady, Edward, 1038
McCulloch, Ben, 53, 908, **970**, 1053, 1583, 1584, *1585*, 1606, 1628, 1652, 1718
  Elkhorn Tavern, Arkansas, 526
  Missouri, 1251
  staff, 63, 943
  Wilson's Creek campaign, 1730, 1731
McCulloch, Henry Eustace, 893, **970–971**, 1472, 1583, 1606, 1608, 1690
McCulloch, Robert, 784, 785
McCurtain, Jackson, 310
McDaniel, Charles A., 924
McDaniel, Henry D., 1364
McDonald, Angus W., 104
McDonald, Cornelia Peake, 1218–1219
McDonald, James, 1142
McDowell, Irvin, 148, 537, 540, 542, 800, 1193, 1331, 1402, 1415, 1416, 1752
  Manassas, First, 714, 996, 997, 998
McDowell, James, *381*
McDowell, John, 1422
McDowell, Thomas David Smith, **971**
McDowell, Virginia, 174, 1416
McEvoy fuze ignitor, 98
Macfarland, James, 481
MacFarland, William H., 965, **971–972**, 1630
McGee v. Mathis, 661
McGhee, James, 721
McGill, Robert, 1499
McGowan, Samuel, 395, **972**, 988
  brigade, 816, 1520
McGraw-Hill, film documentaries, 573
McGuire, Hunter, *80*, 798, 1622
McGuire, Judith, 1218
Machen, Willis Benson, **972–973**
McIntosh, Chilly, 425
McIntosh, Daniel N., 425, 813, 1167
McIntosh, James McQueen, 526, **973**, 1606
McIntosh, James S., 908, 973
McIntosh, John Baillie, 973
McIntosh, William, 424, 425
Mackall, William W., **973**, 1433, 1503
  New Madrid and Island Number 10, 1134
  staff, 447
McKean, Thomas, 414
McKee, John, 1471
McKenzie, Robert H., *as contributor*, 3–4, 1121–1122, 1388–1389, 1410
McKim, Lucy, 1104
McKinney, Gordon B., *as contributor*, 1649–1651
McKinney, John A., 760
McLaughlin, Augustus, 839
McLaughlin, Napoleon B., 627
McLaws, Lafayette, 118, 361, 883, 891, 895–896, 946, **974**, 1725
  Chancellorsville campaign, 36, 282
  Gettysburg campaign, 679, 680, 682
  Harpers Ferry, West Virginia, 742
  Savannah defense, 1368
  Sharpsburg campaign, 1406, 1407
Maclay, Robert P., **974**
McLean, Alexander, 335
McLean, James Robert, **975**
McLean, John, *381*
McLean, Wilmer, 48, **975**
  house as Appomattox surrender site, *47*, *330*
McMahan, James P., 367
McMillen, Sally G., *as contributor*, 356–357, 594–597
McMullen, Fayette, **975–976**, 1250
McMurry, Richard M., *as contributor*, 36–37, 83–88, 138–139, 211, 227–228, 230, 241, 254–255, 263–264, 351–354, 366–367, 413–415, 458, 459, 570, 581, 632–636, 645–646, 691, 695, 704–705, 708–709, 760–761, 774, 829–830, 858–861, 959–960, 1003–1004, 1135–1136, 1178–1179, 1203, 1226–1228, 1371–1372, 1410, 1475, 1478, 1545, 1550, 1550–1551
McNair, Evander, **976**
McNeal Monument Company, 1071
McNeil, W. K., *as contributor*, 593–594, 1167
McNeill, Jesse, 1702
McNeill, John, 721, 723, 1702
Macon, Nathanial, 321
Macon, Georgia, **976–978**
  arsenal and armory, 90, 1461
  bread riots, 212, 978, 1226
  capture of, 673
  Confederate troop surrender, 1475
  Confederate victory, 826
  hospitals, 794, 796
  prison, 1267
  small arms and munitions manufacture, 97, 514, 1168, 1459, 1460, 1470, 1471
  Union prisoners, 1546–1547
Macon (ship), 1126, 1370
Macon and Western Railroad, 976, 1546
Macon German Artillery, 845
Macon Intelligencer (newspaper), 1144
Macon Ladies Soldiers' Relief Society, 977
Macon Telegraph (newspaper), 977, 1144, 1157
McPherson, James B., 1032, 1658, 1659
  Atlanta campaign, 111, 112, 113, 114, 115
  Dalton, Georgia, 442
  Jackson, Mississippi, 837–838
McPherson, James M., *as contributor*, 317–324, 329–337
McQueen, John, **978–979**, *1505*, 1737
McRae, Alexander, 982
McRae, Colin J., 183, 507, **979–981**, 982, 1169, 1687
  New Plan, 419, 1140
  Selma Naval Ordnance Works, 1388
McRae, Dandridge, **981**
McRae, John Jones, 905–906, 979, **981–982**, 1047, *1050*
McRae, William, **982–983**
McRae (ship), 685, 783, 1309, 1599
McWhiney, Grady, 788
Macwillie, Malcolm. *See* Macwillie, Marcus H.
Macwillie, Marcus H., **983–984**, 1174
Madaus, Howard Michael, *as contributor*, 59–62, 584–587, 1464–1465, 1468–1469
Maddex, Jack P., Jr., *as contributor*, 1228–1229
Madison, James
  antislavery, 44
  coastal defenses, 617
  constitutional interpretation, 1532, 1533
  currency proposal, 1279
  descendants, 662, 1433
  Federalist Papers, 1531
  Rives (William C.) biography, 1335, 1338
  Virginia and Kentucky Resolutions of 1798, 1374
Madison, Virginia. *See* Brock, Sallie A.
Madison County, North Carolina, 379–380

Maffitt, John N., 22, 183, 591, 592, **984**, 992, 1723
Magazines, **985–987**
De Bow's Review, 480, 516, 583, 717, **985**, 987, 1232, 1350, 1739
Georgia, 671
literary, 936, 937, 985–986
Northern magazines in the South, **986–987**
popular culture, 1232
selected bibliography, 168
Southern Illustrated News, 937, **985–986**, 1207, 1232, 1255, 1256
Southern Literary Messenger, 193, 460, 481, 985, **986**, 1230, 1330
Turner, Joseph A., 1625–1626
see also Newspapers; other particular publications
Magnolia Cadets, 1215
Magnolia Weekly (magazine), 1232, 1330, 1590
Magnum, Willie P., *381*
Magoffin, Beriah, 196, 216, 702, 886, 887, **987–988**
Magrath, Andrew G., 27, **988**, 1208
as governor of South Carolina, 702, 703, 1510
on legality of confiscation, 389
Magruder, John B., 76, 308, 360, 361, 461, 718, 961, **988–989**, 1190, 1252, 1356, 1361, 1364, 1372, 1433, 1610
Army of the Peninsula, 1191, 1192
capture of *Harriet Lane*, 744
Frayser's Farm, Virginia, 636
Galveston recapture, 655, 656, 1386, 1584
Malvern Hill, Virginia, 994, 995, 996
Mechanicsville, Virginia, 1020
recklessness, 788
Red River campaign, 1315
staff, 867, 1718
Texas, 1097
Trans-Mississippi Department, 1607–1608, 1609
Williamsburg, Virginia, 1724
Yorktown, Virginia, 268, 1306, 1752
Mahan, Dennis Hart, 325, 617
Mahon, Michael G., *as contributor*, 365, 443–444, 447, 686, 700, 786, 894, 932, 963, 975, 1013, 1087, 1195, 1370, 1412–1413, 1430, 1602, 1696–1697
Mahone, William, 82, 771, **989–990**, 1199, 1200, 1364, 1503, 1698, 1721
staff, 690
Mahony, Dennis A., 411
Mail service. *See* Post Office Department
Maine, statehood, 1373
Major, James Patrick, **990**, 1609
Major Dundee (film), 580
Malaria, 31, 460, 754
occurrence and treatment, 755, 758
Male culture, 923
see also Honor
"Male gap" (demographics), 563
Mallard, Mary Sharp Jones, 472
Mallet, John W., 90, 866, 1168, 1471
Mallet polygonal cavity shell, 98
Mallory, Charles, 7
Mallory, Stephen R., *250*, 300, 376, 599, **991–994**, 1385
accomplishments, 1130
appointments, 709, 963
arrest of, 773
calls for dismissal, 438
congressional inquiry, 1129
Fort Pickens, Florida, 613
impressment of railroad track, 1297
ironclad program, 22, 823, 824, 1123–1124, 1128–1129, 1596, 1669–1670
James River Squadron, 840
law partner, 1020
naval purchasing agent, 1150
as navy secretary, 4, 223, 235, 239, 250, 251, 290, 395, 452, 484, 588, 1017, 1126, 1127–1128, 1131, 1236, 1248, 1307, 1661
New Orleans defense, 783
Northern background, 1157
relationship with army, 1129–1130
resourcefulness, 336
on Selma Naval Ordance Works capacity, 1388
Semmes (Raphael) appointment, 1392, 1393, 1394
warship construction. *See subhead* ironclad program *above*
Malnutrition. *See* Food; Health and medicine, nutritional deficiencies
Malvern Hill, Virginia, 78, 167, 637, 654, 918, 983, **994–996**, 1192, 1193, 1400
Hampton, Wade, 731
Magruder, John B., 989
Mahone, William, 990
map, 994, 1401
Vance, Zebulon, 1650
Manassas (novel by Sinclair), 938
Manassas (ship), *824*, 1124, 1139, 1269, 1302, 1688
Manassas, First, 66, 76, 299, 410, 475, 540, 696, 844, 849, 864, 891, 894, **996–999**, 1354, 1716
Bartow, Francis, 137, 1366
Beauregard, P. G. T. *See under* Beauregard, P. G. T.
Bee, Barnard E., 151
Butler, Matthew Calbraith, 246
captured artilley, 100
captured small arms, 1461–1462
casualties, 734, 999–1000
cavalry, 267
Cocke, Philip St. George, 365
Confederate heroes, 998
Conner, James, 395
drummer boy, 1105
Early, Jubal, 501
Elzey, Arnold, 529–530
espionage, 537, 542, 713
Evans, Nathan, 548
flag confusion, 585
Forney, John Horace, 605
fortifications, 619–620
Gardner, W. M., 658
Gartrell, Lucius, 665
Gary, Martin, 666
Gist, States Rights, 691
Hampton, Wade, 548, 731, 733
Hampton's Legion, 731, 733–734
Jackson, Thomas J. ("Stonewall"), 832, 834, 997, 998, 1548, 1549
Johnston, Joseph E., 148, 714, 860, 996, 997, 998, 1716
Jones, Samuel, 868
Kennedy, John Doby, 882
Louisiana Tigers, 957
map, 997
monument, 1072
as morale-raiser, 1079
reenactments, 1317
Ruffin, Edmund, 1350
Signal Corps, 24, 1428
South Carolina units, 1508–1509
Stevens, Clement Hoffman, 1544
Stevens, Walter Husted, 1544
Stonewall Brigade, 1548, 1549
Stuart, J. E. B., 1552
telegraph use, 1573
Manassas, Second, 78–79, 836, 849, **999–1003**
battle conditions, 1500
casualties, 338, 1003
effect on foreign diplomacy, 483
Ewell, Richard, 549
Field, Charles, 571
Hill, A. P., 770, 1000–1001
infantry, 817

Jackson, Thomas J. ("Stonewall"), 78–79, 834, 999–1003, 1549
Jenkins, Micah, 844
Jones, David Rumph "Neighbor," 864
Kemper, James, 881
Lee, Robert E., 834, 918, 919, 999–1003
Longstreet, James. *See under* Longstreet, James
Louisiana Tigers, 957
Mahone, William, 990
map, 1000
Pope, John. *See under* Pope, John
Stafford, Leroy, 1521
Starke, William Edwin, 1526
Stonewall Brigade, 1549
Manassas Gap Railroad, 103, 723
Manassas Junction, Virginia, naval battery, *1125*
Manchester, Tennessee, powder works, 1245
Manchester, Virginia, contraband camp, *406*
Maney, George Earl, 799, **1003**
Manifest Destiny doctrine, 1728
Manigault, Arthur Middleton, **1003–1004**
Manigault, Louis, 867
Manly, Basil, 130, 1399
Manly, Charles, 1151
Mann, A. Dudley, 418, 479, 480, *481*–482, 484, 803, **1004**, 1271, 1347, 1748, 1749
diplomatic mission, 1527, 1529
Manpower
army, **69-71**, 385, 1131; *see also* Soldiers
military strength, 339
navy, 1128, **1130-1131**, 1358-1361; *see also* Sailors
population, 1233
prisoners, 1261
shortages, 330–331, 385, 532, 533, 1292, 1570, 1686
slave. *See* Army, Confederate, African Americans
Union military, 70, 71, 83, 346
see also Civil War, losses and numbers; Conscription
Mansfield, Joseph, 1406
Mansfield, Louisiana, 143, 426, **1004–1005**, 1315, 1316, 1317, 1572, 1610, 1696
Green, Thomas, 713
Mouton, Alfred, 1092
Polignac, Camille J., 1223
Manual of Military Surgery for the Use of Surgeons in the Confederate States Army, A (Chisolm), 755
Manufacturing
ammunition, 1469-1471; *see also* Arms, weapons, and ammunition
antebellum growth, 507
archaeological excavations, 48–49
arms, 623, 739-740, 1179, 1455-1461, 1469; *see also* Arms, weapons, and ammunition
artillery production, 96–98
Atlanta, Georgia, 108
Charleston, South Carolina, 285
Charlotte, North Carolina, 290
Confederate government controls, 1537–1538
cotton, 717
Danville, Virginia, 443
edged weapons, 513–514, 1179
employment, 1234
Georgia, 670
Greensboro, North Carolina, 714
handicrafts, 735
inflation, 1517
infrastructure, 902
Jewish wartime production, 845
locomotive factories, 1294
mill families, 1489
naval ordnance, 1117, 1121–1122, 1168, 1169
naval small arms, 1469
ordnance, 116, 513–514, 698, 977
powder works, **1245–1246**
raw material substitutes, 1559
Selma, Alabama, 1387–1388
Shelby Iron Company, **1410**
slave work force, 1440, 1443, 1646
small arms. *See subhead* arms *above*
South Carolina, 370, 1179
Texas, 655, 1586
textile industry, **1588–1589**
torpedoes, 1604
Tredegar Iron Works, 34–35
urban, 1108, 1644, 1645, 1647, 1648
and urban middle class growth, 1490
Virginia, 1659, 1663, 1664
war mobilization, 508–509
see also Arsenals and armories
Manufacturing and Direct Trade Association of the Confederate States, 717
Manumission, 44, 334, 1437, 1493
see also Emancipation Proclamation; Free people of color
Many Thousands Gone (Bishop), 939
Mapmaker of the Confederacy. *See* Hotchkiss, Jedediah
Maps and mapmaking
archival collections, 1099
Engineer Bureau, 533–534
Hotchkiss, Jedediah, 797–798
intelligence operations, 540–541
selected bibliography, 168
see also subhead map *under particular battle sites and campaigns*
Marais des Cygnes River, 176, 1009, 1255
Marching On (Boyd), 939
March to the Sea, Sherman's, 673, 674, 800, **1005–1007**, 1638, 1648
Allen, William Wirt, 27
Beauregard (P. G. T.) response, 149
black belt, 173
bummers, **241**, *242*
burning of Atlanta, 111, 673, 1648
Cobb (Howell) reaction, 362
culmination in Savannah, 260, 1369
diary accounts, 472
farm destruction, 567
foraging, 117, 260, 601, 793, 901
Georgia Military Institute cadets, 674
Georgia militia defenses, 2475
Hood, John Bell, 790
impact on hospitals, 1549
manufacturing disruption, 1459
map, 1005
railroad troop movement, 1298–1299
refugees, 1318
Southern Unionists and, 1638
strategic intent, 328–329
as total war, 260, 1352
treatment of women, 1741
Marcy, William, 556–557, 698
Margaret and Jessie (ship), 184, 185
Marietta, Georgia
bread riots, 213
hospitals, 794
Marine Corps, **1007–1008**
manpower, 1131
ordnance, 63
size, 1123
uniforms, 1636
Marine Police (Florida), 1530
Mariner (ship), 1269
Marion, Virginia, 1547
Marion (ship), 1530
Maritime law, 1353
Mark's Mill, Arkansas, 490
Marlboro (Confederate Army slave), *75*
Marlbourne (Virginia estate), 1349
Marmaduke, John Sappington, 56–57, 343, 695, **1008–1009**, 1246, 1409, 1609, 1610

Marmaduke, John Sappington, *continued*
duel with Walker (Lucius Marshall), 1009, 1679
raids, 1053, 1252, 1254, 1255
Maroon communities, 1390
Marque and reprisal, letters of. *See* Letters of marque and reprisal
Marriage and divorce, **1009–1010**
courtship, **421–422**, 1009–1010, 1496
divorce patterns, 1009
effects of war, 1739
family life, 562–563
free blacks, 1487
patriarchical structure, 1487–1488
shortage of men, 379, 422
slave marriages, 563–565, 1010
wartime marriages, 421, 671
Marriage of Pocahontas (Chapman), 283
Mars Bluff, South Carolina, shipyards, 1424
Marschall, Nichola, flag design, *584*
Marshall, Charles, *77*, 159, 874
Marshall, Henry, **1010**
Marshall, Humphrey, 203, 497, **1010–1012**, 1724
Marshall, J. K., 816
Marshall, John, 44, 1010, 1279, 1532
Marshall cavalry saber, *513*
Marsilly carriage, 62
Marston, Gilman, 1221
Marszalek, John F., *as contributor*, 836–837, 1005–1007
Marteau, the Guerrilla (play), 1231
Martello towers, 622
Marten, James, *as contributor*, 305–307, 1698–1699
Martial law
Arkansas, 141, 1314, 1340, 1349
Atlanta, Georgia, 229
civil liberties and, 313–314
crime as imposition reason, 427
Davis (Jefferson) request, 439, 1396
Florida, 28
gubernatorial imposition, 704
Kentucky, 1177
limitations bill, 1396
New Orleans, Louisiana, 1419
opponents, 331, 660, 667, 1404, 1482, 1539
provost enforcement, 1278
Richmond, Virginia, 314, 761, 1734
Tennessee, 263, 292, 401, 1576
Union occupation imposition, 1640
Van Dorn (Earl) imposition, 640
Virginia, 1188; *see also subhead* Richmond, Virginia *above*
see also Habeas corpus
Martin, H. Newell, 265
Martin, Isabella, 300
Martin, James Green, 528, **1012**, 1562
Martin, John (colonel), 825
Martin, John Marshall, **1013**
Martin, Joseph H., 936
Martin, Natalie S., 157
Martin, P. C., 545
Martin, Robert M., 350
Martin, Samuel J., *as contributor*, 549–550
Martin, William F., 22, 528
Martin, William M., 936
Martin, William Thompson, 27, 267, **1013**
Martinéz, Tomás, 1145
Marvin, William, 991
Marx, Karl, 1015
Mary Barker (Craven), 1232
Mary Chesnut's Civil War (Chesnut), 299, 300
Mary E. Thompson (ship), 841
Mary Goodell (ship), 841
Maryland
Army of Northern Virginia, 79
black-white population comparison, *1435*
as border state, 195–196
election of 1860, 521, 522, 523
flag, 587
free black population, 642
Point Lookout Prison, 1221–1222
population, 1233
religion, 1346
Republican party, 1322
secession date correlated with total black population, *1486*
Sharpsburg campaign. *See* Sharpsburg campaign
slavery, 402, 554, 1438–1439
South Mountain battle, 1512–1513
Stuart's raids, 1554, 1555, 1556
tobacco farming, 1598
Unionism, 127, 1441
"Maryland, My Maryland" (song), 265, 937, 985, 1103, 1498
Maryland-Steuart Collection (firearms), 1100
Mason, Charles, 1016
Mason, Emily, 795
Mason, George, 410, 914, 1014
Mason, James M., 798, 884, **1014–1016**, 1271, 1616, 1700, 1748–1749
diplomatic missions, 9, *481*–482, 483, 484, 485, 631, 711–712, 803, 1015–1016, 1354, 1453–1455, 1527, 1528, 1529
ship *No. 61*, 1150
Trent affair, 177, 385, 1015, 1619, 1620
Mason, John Francis, 1089
Mason, Mrs. *See* Morris, Augusta Hewitt
Mason, Sarah Maria, 410
Mason Arsenal and Armory, 1168
Mason-Dixon Line, **1016**
origin of term Dixie, 488
Massachusetts (ship), 1309
Massachusetts Arms Company, 1463
Massacres
Baxter Springs, Kansas, 722, 724
Centralia, 38, **274–275**, 724
Fort Pillow, 11, 276, 564, 607, **614–616**, 1603
Saltville, 1362, **1363**, 1547
Massanutten Mountain, Virginia, 1416, 1419
Matagorda (ship), 184, 185
Matamoros, Mexico, cotton trade, 232, 233
Material culture. *See* Archaeology
Matériel. *See* Arms, weapons, and ammunition
Mathews, John, 1173
Mathews, L. H., 274
Matrons, hospital staff, 1161
Mattea, Kathy, 487
Matter, William D., *as contributor*, 1518–1520
Matteson, Thomas H., 381
Matthews, Asa C., 310
Matthews, Brander, 1103
Matthews, Joseph W., 203
Maurer, Louis, 933
Maury, D. H., 17, **1017**, 1058
Corinth, Mississippi, 413, 414
Mobile campaign, 1060–1062
Maury, Matthew Fontaine, 226–227, 375, 447, 538, 925, 991, 992, **1017–1018**, *1127*
commerce raiding, 1675
as foreign purchasing agent, 673, 1308
gunboats, 528, 1125
monuments, 1069, 1074
naval warfare innovations, 1385
Southern expansionism, 808
torpedoes, 1603
Maury, R. H., 1465
Maury, William L., 375, 674, **1018–1019**, 1603–1604
Maxey, Samuel Bell, 151, 310, 813, **1019**, 1391, 1607

Maximilian, emperor of Mexico, 232, 1036, 1037, 1063, 1098, 1210, 1250, 1252, 1455, 1586
Maxwell, Augustus Emmett, **1020**
Maxwell, Grace Rushing, *as contributor*, 1682
May, Robert E., *as contributor*, 808–809
Maynard, Horace, 1563
Mayo, Joseph, 212, 1740
Mc-. *Headings beginning* Mc *are alphabetized as if spelled* Mac
Meade, George G.
  Bristoe Station, Virginia, 220–221
  Chancellorsville campaign, 279, 280
  Dahlgren papers, 441
  Fredericksburg campaign, 638, 639
  Gettysburg campaign, 81, 550, 677, 679, 680, 681, 682, 683, 918, 1553
  Kelly's Ford, Virginia, 880, 881
  Mine Run campaign, 1043
  Overland campaign, 1198
  Petersburg campaign, 1199
  Sharpsburg campaign, 1406
  Spotsylvania campaign, 1518, 1519
  and telegraph, 1573
  Wilderness campaign, 1719, 1720
  Yellow Tavern, Virginia, 1750
  see also Army of the Potomac
Meade, Robert Douthat, 161
Means, Harriet, 889
Measles, 360, 754
Mechanicsville, Virginia, 50, 625, 653, 918, **1020–1021**, 1192, 1193, 1400, 1548, 1751
  Hill, A. P., 78, 770
  Jackson, Thomas J. ("Stonewall"), 834, 1020
  map, 1401
Mechum's River Station, Virginia, 1416
Mecklenburg County, North Carolina. *See* Charlotte, North Carolina
Mecklenburg Iron Works. *See* Charlotte Naval Ordnance Works
MECS (Methodist Episcopal Church, South). *See* Methodist Church
Medals and decorations, **1021–1022**
  black troops, 12
  Medal of Honor, 41, 1021
  memorial organizations, 1028
Medary, Samuel, 411
Medical College of Virginia, 759
Medical Corps, 316
Medical Department, **1022**, 1685
  Army insignia and colors, 1633
  hospital system, 794, 795
  slave labor, 901
  Stout, Samuel Hollingsworth, 1549–1550
  surgeon general, 755, 757, 794, 867, 1022, 1077, 1685
Medical training. *See under* Health and medicine
Medical treatments. *See under* Health and medicine
Medicine. *See* Health and medicine; Hospitals
Meier, P. Neal, *as contributor*, 376–378, 571, 600–601, 654, 909–910, 1106, 1163–1164, 1291–1292
Meigs, Montgomery, 58, 334
Mejía, Tomás, 1037
Melton, Maurice K., *as contributor*, 289, 692, 821–822, 1056–1057, 1245–1246, 1424–1425
Melton, Samuel, 996
Melville, Herman, 937
Memminger, Christopher G., 107, 128, 133, *250*, 452, 509, 858, 911, 972, **1022–1026**, 1517, 1661
  caricature, *335*
  confiscation of property, 388, 389
  conscription exemptions, 1514
  cooperationism, 1506, 1507
  copper token coinage, 1424
  Declaration of Immediate Causes, 463
  direct taxes, 485
  likeness on Treasury note, 438
  monetary policy, 434
  Montgomery convention, 1067
  personality, 1024
  state-supported schools, 515
  tax policies, 485, 510, 1287
  as treasury secretary, 190, 251, 252, 315, 345, 360, 392–393, 418, 436, 1248, 1280, 1282, 1285, 1571, 1614, 1616, 1618
Memoirs. *See* Diaries, letters, and memoirs; particular titles
Memoirs of Service Afloat during the War between the States (Semmes), 1394
Memorial Day, **1026–1027**, 1070
Memorial organizations, **1027–1028**
Memorial Reminiscences (Confederate Women of Arkansas), 594
Memorials. *See* Memorial Day; Memorial organizations; Monuments and memorials
Memories: A Record of Personal Experience and Adventure during Four Years of War (Beers), 153
Memphis, Tennessee, **1028–1030**
  antebellum population, *1642*, 1643, 1645
  arsenal, 90
  battle, 1334
  cotton trade, 1659
  edged weapons manufacture, 514
  Forrest's raid, *609*, 1029
  Irish immigrants, 823
  newspapers, 1143
  ordnance manufacture, 98
  population and urban ranking, *1658*
  small arms manufacture, 1459, 1460, 1461
  Union occupation, 1423, 1640, 1647
Memphis (ship), 446, 1469
Memphis and Charleston Railroad, 1294
Memphis and Little Rock Railroad, 940, 941
Memphis Appeal (newspaper), 274, 871, 937, 1030, 1143, 1683
Memphis Avalanche (publication), 358
Memphis, El Paso, and Pacific Railroad, 1088
Memphis Novelty Works. *See* Leech and Rigdon
Menawa, 424
Mendenhall, Nereus, 1493
Mendenhall, Jones, and Company (Mendenhall, Jones, and Gardner), 49, 1457
Menees, Thomas, **1030–1031**
Mennonites, **1031**
Mental illness hospital, 796
Mercedita (ship), *289*, 822, 1125, 1180, 1242
Mercer, George, 1367, 1368
Mercer, Hugh Weedon, **1031–1032**
Merchant Marine, U.S., 19, 20, 21, 376
Merchant shipping. *See* Blockade; Commerce raiders; Foreign trade; Privateers
Mercié, Jean Antoine, 922–923, 951
Mercier, Henri, 479, 480, 483, 631, 632
Mercier, Robert, 395
Mercury (Charleston newspaper), 1143–1144, 1506, 1510, 1683
Mercury, fulminate of, 289
Meredith, Sol, 1177
Meridian campaign, **1032–1033**
  Jackson, William Hicks, 835
  map, 1032
  Starke, Peter Burwell, 1525
Meriwether, Anne Blythe, *as contributor*, 969
Merli, Frank J., *as contributor*, 26, 239–240, 903–904
Merrick, Caroline E., **1033–1034**, 1742
Merrick, Edwin Thomas, 1034
Merrimack (ship). *Virginia*

Merritt, Wesley, 1419
Mestizo, 1045
Metalworkers, 902
Methodist Church, **1034–1036**, 1320, 1321
 Akin, Warren, 13
 Atlanta, Georgia, 108
 Brownlow, William G., 230
 chaplains, 282
 Echols, Joseph Hubbard, 506
 Richmond, Virginia, 1330
 slavery, 320
 Southern sermonists, 1399
 women's education, 520
 see also African Methodist Episcopal (AME) Church
Methodist Episcopal Church, South. *See* Methodist Church
Metro-Goldwyn-Mayer, 573, 578
Metropolitan Gallery, 1230–1231
Metropolitan Theater (Richmond), 1231
Mexican Gulf Railroad, 622
Mexican Times (newspaper), 27
Mexican War, 1374, 1408, 1533
Mexico, **1036–1037**
 Benavides, Santos, 157
 blockade evasion, 178, 1586
 cotton smuggling, 1215
 cotton traffic, 232, 233, 1609
 diplomacy, 1209–1210, 1250
 ex-Confederates in, 1409, 1433, 1504, 1544
 and expansion of slavery, 320, 554, 555, 556, 558, 808, 1715
 French involvement in, 56, 385, 464, 479, 485, 631, 1314
 horses and mules supply, 791–793
 proposed war with, 733, 804, 1063, 1541
 see also Maximilian
Miami (ship), 22, 407
Michigan (ship), 145, 258, 857, 1723
Mid-Continent (magazine), 498
Middle class
 rural plain folk, **1212–1214**
 urban, 1489–1490, 1506
Middle Fort, Mississippi, 621
Middleton Place Plantation, 1214
Midge (ship), 446
Midlen, Erwin, 1216
Mikell, Emma C., 988
Mikko, Hiniha. *See* Jumper, John
Mikko, Sonaki. *See* Bowlegs, Billy
Miles, Dixon S., 743, 744
Miles, William Porcher, 193, **1038**, 1143, 1172, 1479, *1505*
 flag design, 585–586
Military departments. *See* Departments, military; particular armies and departments
Military Dictionary (Scott), foraging definition, 600
Military District of Georgia, 1032
Military Division of the West, 74, 149
Military education, 518–520
 Citadel, The, 311–312
 Georgia Military Institute, 674–675
 Louisiana State Seminary and Military Academy, 957
 naval academy, 1131, 1182
 soldiers' training, 1040, 1497
 Virginia Military Institute, 1671–1673
Military justice, **1038–1039**
 Alabama, 1679
 Brooke, Walter, 224
 desertion, 398, 468–469, 1039, 1190, 1209
 provost marshal, **1277–1278**
 Randolph, Victor M., 1307
 soldiers, 1497
 Wirz, Henry, 1735
 see also Courts-martial; Crime and punishment; Prisons
Military Memoirs of a Confederate (Alexander), 25, 474
Military occupation, U.S. *See* Union occupation
Military Operations of General Beauregard, The (Roman), 150
Military Reconstruction Acts of 1867, 708
Military service. *See* Army, Confederate; Conscription; Navy, Confederate; Sailors; Soldiers; particular armies
Military training, **1040**, 1497
 naval, 1131
 see also Military education
Militia. *See* State militia
Militia Act of 1808, 60, 61, 96, 99, 1179, 1463, 1464, 1465
Milledge, John, 1046
Milledgeville (ship), 1425
Milledgeville Southern Recorder (newspaper), 1625
Millen, Georgia, prison, 1267
Miller, D. R., 1406
Miller, Mary Boykin. *See* Chesnut, Mary Boykin
Miller, Randall M., *as contributor*, 1034–1036, 1433–1434
Miller, Samuel Augustine, **1040**
Miller, Stephen Decatur, and Mary Boykin, 299
Miller, William, **1040–1041**
Miller v. U.S., 390
Milliken's Bend, 971
Mills, Gary B., *as contributor*, 1044–1046
Mills, Joseph, 6
Mills, Robert, 1710
Mills, Roger Q., 469
Mills, cotton. *See* Textile industry
Mill Springs, Kentucky, 263, 887, **1041–1042**, 1682
 Crittenden, George B., 428
 Zollicoffer, Felix, 1755
Milroy, Robert H., 502, 1416
 Gettysburg campaign, 677
 Winchester, Virginia, 550, 1732, 1733
Milton, John, 28, 581, 589–590, 591, 702, 703, **1042**, 1196, 1566, 1567
Mims, W. J., 1276
Mineral production. *See* Mining
Mine Run campaign, 81, 850, 867, **1043**
 Early, Jubal, 502–503, 1043
 field fortifications, 626
 Gordon, James, 696
 Lee, Robert E., 918–919
Mines, land. *See* Hand grenades and land mines
Mines, naval. *See* Torpedoes and mines
Mingos. *See* Senecas
Minié ball, 60, 740, 818
 wounds from, 756
Mining, **1043–1044**
 lead, 913
Mining Bureau. *See* Niter and Mining Bureau
Minnesota, statehood, 555
Minnesota (ship), 445–446, 448, 1670, *1671*
Minnis and Cowell, 1230–1231
Minor, Benjamin B., 986
Minor, John, 1639
Minor, Robert D., 863
Minstrels, 1231
Mints, 434, 436, 438, 1615
Miscegenation, **1044–1046**
 see also Creoles; Mulattoes
Miscegenation; or, A Virginia Negro in Washington (play), 1231
Missionary Ridge, Tennessee, 32, 72, 139, 205, 241, 291, 294, 295, 626, 672, 700, 708, 830, 914, 1683
Mississippi, **1046–1052**
 agriculture, 172–173
 Army of. *See* Army of Alabama, Mississippi, and Eastern Louisiana; Army of Mississippi
 battles, 1049, 1051; *see also* particular place names

black-white population comparison, *1435*
congressmen, 131, 135, 202–203, 223–224, 226, 257, 276, 351, 455, 569, 747–748, 749, 782, 905, 906, 962, 982, 1173, 1204–1205, 1431–1432, 1594, 1683, 1694, 1698, 1729
conscription controversy, 398, 873
Constitution ratification, 403
cooperationists, 411
cotton plantations, 1436
currency, 1279
debt, 462
Democratic party, 465
Department of. *See* Department of Alabama, Mississippi, and Eastern Louisiana; Department of Mississippi and East Louisiana
election of 1860, 521, 522, 523
farm acreage, *1484*
flag, 587
foreign population, 602
free black employment, 643
free black population, 642
governors, 23, 24, 203, 225–226, 341, 450, 455, 701, 702, 703, 800–801, 960, 982, 1047, 1203–1204
habeas corpus issue, 1535
home front, 1051–1052
hospitals, 794
Indians, 310, 812
iron production, 1148
Iuka battle. *See* Iuka, Mississippi
map, 1048
Orr, Jehu Amaziah, 1173
population, 836, 1233
railroads, 1294, 1295, 1296
Reconstruction. *See under* Reconstruction
roads, 1339
secession. *See under* Secession
secession and Confederacy membership dates, *1379*
secession date correlated with total black population, *1486*
secession opposition, 720, 1694
slaveholdings, *1485*
slavery, 551, 553, 1439, 1484
small arms and munitions manufacture, 1459, 1470, 1471
soldiers' home, 1502
taxation, 485, 1284
Unionism. *See under* Unionism
Union occupation, 1640
Vicksburg. *See* Vicksburg campaign
see also Trans-Mississippi Department; particular cities and place names
Mississippi (ship), 823, 903, 993, 1124, 1139, 1303, 1424, 1596, 1675, 1688; *see also* Laird Rams
Mississippian (journal), 131
Mississippi Central Railroad, 351
Holly Springs raid, 783, 784, 785
"Mississippi Nightingales," 516
Mississippi River, 1612, 1691
control, 1238
New Madrid and Island Number 10, 1133–1134, 1420
River Defense Fleet, 1158, 1334
Missouri, **1052–1055**
Army of. *See* Army of Missouri
Army of Tennessee, 84
black-white population comparison, *1435*
as border state, 195–196
Centralia massacre, 38, 274–275, 724
Confederate militia, 828–829, 1053
Confederate raids, 1409
congressmen, 153, 342–343, 391, 396, 408–409, 641, 747, 857–858, 1159, 1204, 1483, 1654, 1722
Constitution ratification, 403
debt, 462
election of 1860, 521, 522, 523
election of 1863, 524
expansion of slavery, 557
First Brigade, 1516
governors, 701, 702, 703, 828–829, 1009, *1054*, 1323, 1606
guerrilla warfare, 11, 719–720, 722, 724, 725, 1053–1054
invasion of, 827, 1609
livestock breeding, 791–792
population, 1233
Price's raid. *See* Price's Missouri raid
Republican party, 1322
secession. *See under* Secession
secession date correlated with total black population, *1486*
slavery, 553, 875
statehood, 1373-1374; *see also* Missouri Compromise
tobacco farming, 1598
Trans-Mississippi Department, 1606
Unionism. *See under* Unionism
Wilson's Creek campaign. *See* Wilson's Creek campaign
see also particular cities and place names
Missouri (ship), 264, **1055**, 1124, 1125
Missouri Battery, 825
Missouri Brigade, battle flag, 586
Missouri Compromise, **1055–1056**
Crittenden Compromise and, 429, 809
Dred Scott decision and, 255, 493, 494, 495, 1056, 1534
extension, 1337
as first major sectional confrontation, 1373–1374
Kansas-Nebraska Act and, 875–876, 1375, 1534
Louisiana Purchase and, 1055, 1533
repeal, 465
Supreme Court decision, 1534
Missouri State Guard, flag, 587
Miss Ravenel's Conversion from Secession to Loyalty (novel by DeForest), 938
Mitchel, Charles Burton, **1056**
Mitchel, John, 1563
Mitchel, Ormsby M., 41
Mitchell, Elisha, 355
Mitchell, John K., 605, 840–841, **1056–1057**
James River Squadron, 993, 1056–1057
Office of Orders and Detail, 1056, 1127
Mitchell, Margaret, 574, 787, 939, 1218
Mitchell, O. M., 16
Mitchell, Reid, *as contributor*, 1111–1116
Mitchell and Tyler, 514
Mobile, Alabama, **1056–1062**
antebellum urbanization, 1643, 1644
banks, 128
battle of Mobile Bay, 993, **1059–1060**, 1580–1581
blockade, 178, 1647, 1648
bread riots, 1058, 1226
campaign, **1060–1062**
capture, 179, 183
city, **1057–1059**, *1658*, 1659
creole population, 644
defenses, 17, 48, 236, 620, 914, 979, 993, 1017, 1178, 1302, 1610
edged weapons manufacturing, 514
education, 516
food shortages, 18
foreign companies, 603
Forsyth, John, 609
free black population, 642, 644
free markets, 641, 1229
guardianship for free people of color, 645
harbor defenses, 1300, 1303, 1307
hospitals, 794
immigrants, 822

Mobile, Alabama, *continued*
importation site, 182
impressed slave labor, 1426
population and urban ranking, *1658*, 1659
shipyards, 1424–1425
submarine construction, 1557, 1558
Mobile Advertiser and Register (newspaper), 609–610, 798, 1057, 1059, 1144, 1683
Mobile and Ohio Railroad, 979, 1032, 1293, 1625
Holly Springs raid, 784
Mobile Bay, Alabama, battle of. *See under* Mobile, Alabama
Mobile Military Aid Society, 1058
Mobile Register (newspaper). *See Mobile Advertiser and Register*
Mobile Squadron, **1062**, 1124, 1126, 1580
Mobile Supply Association, 1058
Mobile Theatre, 1058
Mobile Tribune (newspaper), 201, 1737
Mobley, Benjamin L., 1364
Moccasin Point, 293, 295
Mogen, William, 1090
Mohawk, Joseph (Shawnee leader), 1408
Mohr, Clarence L., *as contributor*, 164, 441–442
Mohun (Cooke), 408
Moir, James, 1619
Mole, Robert, 513
Monarch (ship), 1334
Monck, Charles Stanley, Lord, 258
Money. *See* Currency; Inflation; Public finance
Moneyhon, Carl H., *as contributor*, 141, 262–263, 662, 705, 710, 762–763, 767, 856, 960–961, 1056, 1097, 1164–1165, 1311–1314, 1349, 1355–1356, 1404, 1594, 1694, 1718–1719
Monitor (ship), 178, 236, 496, 567, 840, 863, 1124, 1149, 1302, 1424, 1568, 1670, *1671*
Monocacy, Maryland. *See* Early's Washington raid
Monocacy River, 1677
Monroe, James, 44, 552, 1062, 1063, 1630
Monroe, John T., 247, 604, 954, 1138, 1139, 1504
Monroe, Thomas Bell, **1062–1063**
Monroe Doctrine, 1037, **1063**
French defiance of, 385, 631
U.S. and Confederate enforcement of, 464
Monroe's Crossroads, 262
Montague, A. J., 1063
Montague, Robert Latane, 663, **1063–1064**
Montauk (ship), 1107
Montevallo Female Institute, 520
Montevideo Plantation, 472
Montgomeries (currency), 436, 438
Montgomery, Benjamin, 458, **1064**
Montgomery, Horace, *as contributor*, 358–362
Montgomery, Isaiah, 1064
Montgomery, James, 11, 719, 1623
Montgomery, James Edward, 1334
Montgomery, Louis M., 1231
Montgomery, Mary Lewis, 1064
Montgomery, Thornton, 1064
Montgomery, William, 1585
Montgomery, Alabama, 172, **1064–1066**, 1329
as Confederate capital, 360, 383, 1064, 1065–1066, 1684
hospitals, 794
railroads, 1297
surrender, 18
Montgomery and Atlanta Railroad, 114
Montgomery & Sons, 1064
Montgomery convention, **1067–1069**
Chilton, William P., 309
Confederate Constitution, 383, 399–400, 401, 402
fire-eaters, 1079
functions, 383
Kenner, Duncan F., 883–884
Perkins, John, Jr., 1194
presidency, 359, 383
Provisional Constitution, 399–400, 1380
South Carolina delegation, 1507–1508
and Washington Peace Conference, 1689
Watts, Thomas H., 1695
Waul, Thomas Neville, 1696
Wilson, William Sydney, 1729
see also Congress, Confederate, Provisional
Montgomery Daily Advertiser (newspaper), 1144
Montgomery Mail (newspaper), 201
Monticello, confiscation, 389
Monument Avenue (Richmond), 923, 1069, 1074
Monuments and memorials, 949, 952, **1069–1074**
Arlington House, **58**
Atlanta, Georgia, 951–952
battlefields, 922, **1071–1074**
Chickamauga and Chattanooga National Military Park, 304
controversy, 1071
film documentaries, 573
Jefferson Davis Memorial, 388
Lee Memorial Association, **922**
Lee Monument Association, **922–923**
organizations, 1028
overview article, **1069–1071**
Richmond, Virginia, 917, 951, 1332, 1714
Wirz, Henry, 1735
Mooching through Georgia (film), 577
Moody, Young Marshall, **1074**
Moon, Virginia B. (Ginnie), and Charlotte (Lottie) Moon Clark. *See* Moon sisters
Moon sisters, 543, **1074–1075**
Moore, Absalom B., 1088
Moore, Andrew B., 14, 16, 18, 701, 702, 703, **1075**, 1426
denunciation of speculators, 1517
secessionism, 1378
Moore, Bartholomew, 492
Moore, David, 1422
Moore, James William, **1075–1076**
Moore, John Creed, **1076**
Moore, Joseph A., 825
Moore, Merrill, 938
Moore, Patrick Theodore, 823, **1076–1077**
Moore, Rayburn S., *as contributor*, 193–194, 936–937, 1597
Moore, Samuel Preston, **1077**, 1685
as surgeon general, 755, 757, 794, 867, 1022
Moore, Sydenham, *15*
Moore, Thomas O., 1, 617–618, 645, 684, 702, 703, 822, 952, 1055, **1077–1078**
Moore, William Preston, 1037, 1063
Moore, Winfred B., Jr., *as contributor*, 311–312
Moorefield, West Virginia, 849
Moore's Kentucky Reports, 1062
Morale, **1078–1083**
Army of Northern Virginia, 67
Army of Tennessee, 86
Atlanta, 110
Bible societies, 164
Confederate soldiers, 283, 398, 1666
Davis (Jefferson) efforts to promote, 452
declining, 378
effect of Averasboro battle, 118
effect of conscription exemptions, 70, 397

effect of criticism of Davis (Jefferson), 1325
effect of Galveston recapture, 656
effect of inflation, 434, 1081–1082
effect of Morgan's raids, 1089
effect of peace overtures, 1184, 1224
effect of political dissension, 380
effect of Roanoke Island loss, 245
effect of Sherman's March to the Sea, 1007
effect of slavery, 333–334
effect of speculation, 1517–1518
efforts to increase, 468
election of 1864, 271
erosion of home front, 260, 314, 443–444, 461, 524, 591, 670, 715, 902–903, 1229, 1623, 1686
fast days, 568–569
and field fortifications construction, 625
forces affecting, 1080-1083, *see also particular subheads above*
honor code aiding, 788
letters aiding, 1312
newspapers aiding, 1144
phases, 1079–1080
plain folk, 1213
planter, 1217
popular culture aiding, 1231
slave, 1220
soldier, 1496
soldiers' aid societies, 1501–1502
Tennessee, 1579
Trans-Mississippi Department, 1607, 1610
Union, 269, 271, 279, 328, 329, 336, 337, 503, 767, 781, 1609, 1733
Moran, Benjamin, 482
Moravian Church, **1084**
Mordecai, J. Randolph, 845
Morehead, Charles, 1337
Morehead, John Motley, 714, 715 **1085–1086**
Morehead City, North Carolina, 516, 1152
Morehouse College, 1321
Moreno, Angela, 991
Morgan, A. Glawson, 1088
Morgan, Bob. *See* Bell, Mary, and Mollie Bell
Morgan, George, 890
Morgan, Henrietta Hunt, 498
Morgan, James F., *as contributor*, 421
Morgan, John Hunt, 196, 214, 498, 847, 890, 913, **1086–1087**, 1708, 1743
cavalry, 266, 267
death of, 685
elite unit, 1516
Orphan Brigade, 1170
raids. *See* Morgan's raids
in Tennessee, 1577
Morgan, John Tyler, 17, **1087**
Morgan, Laura A., 1088
Morgan, Mark, *as contributor*, 616–623
Morgan, Martha Ready, 421
Morgan, Sarah, 1219
Morgan, Simpson Harris, **1087–1088**
Morgan (ship), 236, 1062, 1125, 1126, 1388, 1581
ordnance, 1118
Morgan's raids, 193, 269, 656, 793, 888, 1086–1087, **1088–1089**
raiders as elite unit, 1516
use of telegraph, 1086, 1430, 1573
Morganton, North Carolina, 1152
Morning Courier and Enquirer (New York City newspaper), 547
Morocco, naval incident, 674
Morphine, 757
Morrill, Dan L., *as contributor*, 289–290
Morrill, Justin S., 348
Morrill Land Grant Act, 348, 520
Morris, Augusta Hewitt, 143, **543**, 544, **1089–1090**
Morris, Charles M., 592
Morris, Thomas A. (general), 1704
Morris, Tom (minstrel), 1231
Morris Island, South Carolina, 287, 288, 630, 1334
firing on *Star of the West*, 1526
prison, 1259
Union captured Whitworth guns, 1120
Union occupation, 1509
Morrison, Eugenia, 134
Morrison, J. G., *80*
Morrison, Mary Anna, 832, 835
Morse, George W., 1457
Morse, Nathaniel, 273, 610, 1144
Morse, Samuel F. B., 1273, 1275, 1573
Mortar, 94
Morton, Charles, 1231, 1590
Morton, Jackson, **1090**
Morton, John (captain), 1516
Morton, John Maddison, 1590
Morton, Oliver P., Northwestern Conspiracy, 1158–1159
Morton, Richard, 1148
Morton, Samuel George, 1274
Mosby, John S., 543, **1090**, 1553
capture of Stoughton (Edwin H.), 601
guerrilla activity, 546, **722–724**, 725, 1352
see also Mosby's Rangers
Mosby's Confederacy, 1090, 1091
Mosby's Rangers, 722, *723*, 725, 1090, **1091–1092**, 1516
Moseley, John, 1500
Mosely, Alexander, 1142
Moses, Raphael, 845
Mosquito Fleet (North Carolina), 1530
Moss, William, *as contributor*, 221–222, 354
Mossbacks, 17
Mossy Creek Academy, 797
Mother's Parting Words to Her Soldier Boy (revivalist tract), 459–461
Motion pictures. *See* Film and video
Mott, C. H., 906
Motto, Confederate seal, 864–865
Mound City (ship), 1334
Mountain Department, U.S., 1705
Mountain Island Woolen Mills, 290
Mountain Rangers, 103
Mount Jackson, Virginia, 1415
Mount Vernon Arsenal, Alabama, 90, 705, 1461, 1469
Mount Vernon Ladies' Association, 1202
Mourning. *See* Death and mourning
Mouton, Alexandre, 426, 1092
Mouton, Alfred, 709, 1005, **1092**, 1223, 1317
Movies. *See* Film and video
Movietone News (documentary films), 573
Mower, Joseph A., 1254
Mud March, 279
"Mud-sill" speech, 730
Mudwell. *See* Jackson, William Lowther
Muhlenfeld, Elisabeth
as contributor, 299–300
Chesnut (Mary Boykin) diary scholarship, 471
Mulattoes, 285, 642, 1045, 1046, 1486, 1506
Mulberry Plantation, 299
Mules. *See* Horses and mules
Mule Shoe Salient, 82, 1305
Mumford, William, 1138, 1258
Mumps, 360
Mundy, Sue. *See* Clarke, Jerome
Munford, Thomas T., 211, 1713
Munfordville, Kentucky, 204, 890, **1092–1093**, 1682
Munitions. *See* Arms, weapons, and ammunition; Artillery; Naval guns; Niter and Mining Bureau; Ordnance; Ordnance Bureau; Naval guns; Small arms; particular types
Munnerlyn, Charles James, **1093–1094**, 1479

Munson, H. H., 1143
Murfree, Mary, 937
Murfreesboro, Tennessee, 1041, **1094–1096**, 1577
 Allen, William Wirt, 27
 Anderson, James Patton, 32
 Army of Tennessee, 67, 86
 Bragg, Braxton, 204
 casualties, 338, 1096
 Clayton, Henry DeLamar, 352
 Donelson, Daniel, 491–492
 Ector, Matthew Duncan, 512
 field fortifications, 626
 Hanson, Roger, 736
 Hardee, William, 737
 McCown, John P., 970
 map, 1094
 monument, 1072
 Orphan Brigade assault, 1170
 Palmer, Joseph Benjamin, 1179
 raid, 606–607, 608, 1707
 Smith, Thomas Benton, 1478
 Vance, Robert, 1649
 Vaughan, Alfred, 1652
 Withers, Jones Mitchell, 1737
 Young, William Hugh, 1753
"Murmur of the Shell, The" (song), 1232
Murphy, Anthony, 41
Murphy, Isaac, 52, 54, 661, 702, **1097**
Murphy, Robert C., 784, 785
Murphy, Terrence V., *as contributor*, 736, 789–790, 1671–1673, 1724
Murrah, Pendleton, 117, 702, 703, 974, **1097–1098**, 1585, 1586, 1608
Murray, E. C., 1425
Murray, John Porry, 1063, **1098**, 1458
Murrow, J. (Indian agent), 812, 1391
Muscle Shoals, Alabama, 1420
Muscogee (ship). *See Jackson*
Muscogee Foundry and Machinery Company, 1460
Muscogees. *See* Creeks
Museum of the Confederacy (Richmond), *1100*
 Brockenbrough Library, 1099
 Chapman (Conrad Wise) paintings, 283
 Davis (Jefferson) portrait, 451
 edged weapons collection, 513, 514
Museums and archives, **1098–1100**
 Anglo-Confederate purchasing records, 42
 Beauvoir, 150
 Benjamin (Judah P.) personal papers, 160
 Chapman (Conrad Wise) paintings, 283
 Clay (Clement C.) papers, 350
 Confederate war records, 1746
 court records study, 1009
 Dahlgren papers, 441
 desertion records, 467, 469
 Freedmen's Bureau papers, 473
 guerrilla units records, 68
 historic buildings, 1100
 medical department records, 1077
 military records, 215
 National Archives, 410
 Naval Museum, 291
 Official Records of the Union and Confederate Armies, 943
 primary sources bibliography, 167–168
 Provisional Army records, 66
 research libraries, 1099
 Southern Historical Society, 1512
 State Department records, 1210
 Tyler (John) papers, 1630–1631
 War Department records, 410, 1688
 see also Diaries, letters, and memoirs; particular museums and archives
Music, **1100–1105**
 country, 949
 discography, **487–488**
 Dixie, **488–489**
 folk, 487, 1104
 instrumental, 1104
 Lost Cause, 949
 military, 1104–1105
 popular songs, 836, 1231–1232
 publishing, 1101, 1103
 secession-related, *1507*
 sheet music, *335*, *712*, *948*, 1101–1103, *1102*
 soldiers' songs, 1498
 song broadsides, 222
 spirituals, 1103–1104
Music (ship), 1269
Music of the Civil War (recording), 487
Musket. *See* Flintlock musket; Rifle-musket
Musketoons, 60
Mutual Film Corporation (documentary films), 573
Mutual Weekly (documentary films), 572
Muzzle-loaders, 62, 93
Myer, Albert James, 538, 1428
Myers, Abraham C., 845, **1106**, 1628, 1685
 Northern background, 1157
 Quartermaster Bureau, 508, 910, 1291, 1292
 railroad rate structure, 1295–1296
Myers, Robert Manson, Jones family letters, 472
My Imprisonment and the First Year of Abolition Rule at Washington (Greenhow), 714
Myrtle Grove Plantation (New Orleans), 1034, 1333
Myths. *See* Folk narratives

N

Nagle, James, 1001
Nahant (ship), 116
Names of battles. *See* Battles, naming of
Namozine Church, Virginia, 46
Nance, Joseph Milton, *as contributor*, 1087–1088
Nanih Waiya, 309
Nansemond (ship), 840, 1125
Napoleon I, emperor of France
 disciples, 146
 tactics, 267, 325, 338, 624
Napoleon III, emperor of France, 385, 479, 480, 484, 485, 536, 631, 632, 712, 733, 804, 1037, 1063, 1354, 1454–1455, 1529, 1609, 1748
Napoleon Club, 325
Napoleon rifled gun, 61, 93, 94, 96, *97*, 98, *99*, 101
Narrative of Military Operations (Johnston), 475
Narrative tradition. *See* Folk narratives
Nashville, Tennessee, **1107–1110**
 antebellum population, 1107, *1642*
 arsenal, 90, 1168
 battle of, 1110, 1478
 diary account, 472
 fall of, 746, 767
 hospitals, *8*, 794, 1549
 ordnance manufacture, 98
 population and urban ranking, *1658*
 powder works, 1245
 prostitution, 1277
 shipyards, 1424
 Union occupation, 1109–1110, 1420, 1576, 1640, 1647
 see also Franklin and Nashville campaign
Nashville (ship), 177, 183, 236, 374, 1014, 1062, **1110–1111**, *1111*, 1124, 1126, 1303
 ordnance, 1118
Nashville American (newspaper), 373, 516
Nashville and Chattanooga Railroad, 492, 1096, 1624, 1737

Nashville and Northwestern Railroad, 1110
Nashville Convention, 255, 276, 380, 527, 1375
Nashville Daily Republican Banner (newspaper), 1300
Nashville Fugitives, 318, 949
Nashville Hospital Association, 794
Nashville Military Institute, 519
Nashville Plow Works, 514
Nassau
  blockade running, 177, 185
  collection of medical supplies, 757
  transshipment of supplies, 699
Natchez, Mississippi
  free markets, 641
  Union occupation, 1049, 1640
Natchez Trace, 1339
National anthem, 1102
National Archives (Washington, D.C.), 1098
  Confederate War Records, 410
  courts-martial records, 469
  "Rebel War Archives," 1688
National Bank Note Company, 434, 436
National debt. *See* Debt
National Detective Police, 541
National Era (newspaper), 44
Nationalism, 382, 387, **1111–1116**
  Confederate lack-of-will thesis, 333
  Davis, George, 448
  Davis, Jefferson, 452
  Fort Hill Address, 613
  Hammond, James H., 730
  regional loyalty vs., 1078–1079
  Ruffin, Edmund, 1349, 1350
  see also Sectionalism; State rights
Nationalized economy. *See* State socialism
National Park Service, U.S.
  battlefields and monuments, 1072
  cemeteries, 1072
National Portrait Gallery (Washington, D.C.), 1098–1099
National Union Convention, 690, 708
Nationwide Insurance (documentary films), 573
Native Americans. *See* Indians; Indian Territory; particular peoples
Native Guards (Louisiana), 75, 645, 1239
Nativism
  anti-Irish Catholics, 602
  extortion accusations, 559
  Semmes (Thomas) condemnation speech, 1395
  and Whig party decline, 175, 1395
  see also American party
Natural Bridge, Florida, 1567
Naturalization laws, 313
Navahos, 1136
Naval Coast Guard (Georgia), 1530
Naval guns, **1116–1121**
  captured U.S., **1119**
  European, **1119–1120**
  munitions, **1121**
Naval Ordnance Works. *See under* Selma, Alabama
Naval Submarine Battery Service, 447
Naval training, 1131, 1182
Navy, Confederate, 709, **1122–1132**
  African Americans, 7, 441–442, **1132**
  Brooke, John M., 223
  Brown, Isaac Newton, 226–227
  Buchanan, Franklin, 235–237
  Bulloch, James Dunwoody, 239–240
  Carter, Jonathan H., 264
  Charlotte Navy Yard, **290**
  Cooke, James W., 407
  creation, 991–992
  Davids, 445–446
  Davidson, Hunter, 447–448
  Department. *See* Navy Department
  edged weapons, 63, 515, 1469
  Elliott, Gilbert, 528
  engineers, 1725
  Gift, George W., 685
  Gosport Navy Yard, 290, **699–700**, 990, 1149, 1664, 1725
  guns, **1116–1121**, 1360, 1469
  historian, 962, 1371
  Hollins, George N., 783
  Ingraham, Duncan N., 821–822
  James River Squadron, **839–841**
  Jones, Catesby, 863
  Lynch, William F., 962
  manpower, 1128, **1130–1131**, **1358–1361**
  Marine Corps, **1007–1008**
  maritime law, 1353
  Maury, Matthew Fontaine, 1017–1018
  Mitchell, John K., 1056–1057
  naval academy, 1131, 1182
  naval stations, **1122**
  North Carolina, 1151
  ordnance works, 62–63, **1121–1122**, 1388–1389
  organization, 1131
  outfitting, 1128–1129
  overview article, **1123–1126**
  Page, Richard L., 1178
  Parker, William, 1180
  Patrick Henry floating campus, 1131, 1182
  Porter, John L., 1235–1236
  rams, **1302–1304**
  recruitment poster, *1123*
  River Defense Fleet, **1334**
  Savannah Squadron reinforcement, 1370
  special units, 1516
  state navies, **1530**
  submarines, **1556–1558**
  surgeons, 1022
  Tattnall, Josiah, 1568–1569
  torpedoes and mines, 1509, 1515–1516, **1603–1605**
  Tucker, John Randolph, 1623–1624
  uniforms, 1359, 1636
  warfare innovations, 1385; *see also subhead* submarines *above*; *subhead* torpedoes and mines *above*
  Warley, Alexander Frazer, 1688–1689
  Whittle, William C., 1712
  Wilkinson, John, 1722–1723
  Williamson, William P., 1725
  Wood, John Taylor, 1743
  see also Commerce raiders; Cottonclads; Ironclads; Navy Department; Shipyards; particular battles and ship names
Navy, U.S.
  blockade, 177
  Confederate seizure of guns, 1119
  Confederate seizure of shipyards, 1424
  Henry and Donelson campaign, 764, 765, 766
  old-system guns, *1119*
Navy Department, **1126–1130**
  civil service, 314–315
  investigation, 993
  New Plan, 419, 980, 1140–1141, 1285, 1286
  purchasing, 1150
  Savannah Squadron, 1370
  secretaryship, 249, *250*, 251
  shipyards, 1424
  see also Mallory, Stephen R.
Neely, Mark E., Jr., *as contributor*, 194–195, 521–524, 640–641, 727–728, 932–936
Neff, John F., 914
Negley, James, 32, 1095, 1096
Negro Soldier Law of 1865, 644
Nelson, Allison, **1132–1133**
Nelson, Larry E., *as contributor*, 1594–1595
Nelson, Thomas A. R., 532, 752, 760, 895, 1575
Nelson, William ("Bull"), 890

Neosho, Missouri, 1409
legislature, 1052
Neptune (ship), 656, 744
Netherlands, neutrality proclamation, 480
Neu-Braunfelser Zeitung (publication), 676
Neuces, Texas, German Unionists, 676
Neuse (ship), *49*, 960, 1124, 1126, **1133**, *1134*
ordnance, 49, 1133
Neutrality Law of 1818, 557
"New Ballad of Lord Lovell" (song), 958–959
New Bern, North Carolina, 1209, 1582, 1626, 1743
attack on Federal flotilla, 960
free black population, 642, 1152
surrender, 666, 1152
Newburgh, Indiana
arsenal seizure, 95, 720
raid on, 847
New Echota, Treaty of (1835), 1693
New England, state rights sentiment, 1532
New England Emigrant Company, 175
New Era (ship), 615
New Hope Church, Georgia, 113
New Ironsides (ship), 289, 445, 692, 1515, 1600
New Lost City Ramblers, 487
New Madrid and Island Number 10, 621, 800, 1028, **1133–1135**, 1420, 1576
field fortifications, 626
New Market, Virginia, **1135–1136**, 1416, 1673
Union retreat, 1413
Virginia Military Institute cadets, 214, 519, 1516
New Mexico, 51, **1136**
Confederate expansionism, 692–693, 1372, 1374–1375, 1427–1428, 1538
frontier forts, 622–623
Glorieta Pass, New Mexico, 692–693, 1428
horses and mules supply, 791–793
railway routes, 983
Sibley, Henry Hopkins, 121, 692–693, 713, 1136
slavery, 321, 554
statehood, 381
Newnan, Georgia
battle of, 1547
hospitals, 794
New Orleans, Louisiana, **1136–1140**
antebellum growth and population, *1642*, 1643, 1645
arsenal, 1461
banks, 128
blockade, 178, *1562*, 1563
Butler's woman order, 246–247
capture, 603–604, 954, 1129, **1139–1140**
city, **1136–1139**, *1658*, 1659
credit, 462
creole population, 644
defenses, 420, 498, 622, 769, 783, 958, 993, 1056, 1349, 1688
education, 516, 1621
foreign companies, 603
free blacks, 642, 643, 644, 645, 1484
free markets, 641, 1229
home guards, 4
Irish immigrants, 823, 1647
liberation plan, 1306
merchants, 555–556
mint, 1615
as music publishing center, 1101
newspapers, 645, 1144
ordnance production, 90, 97–98, 1121
political and social climate, 956, 1395, 1504
population and urban ranking, *1658*, 1659
powder works, 1245
printmaking, 1255
privateers, 1269
Roudanez brothers, 1348
shipyards, 1424, 1562
slave market, 1453
small arms and munitions manufacture, 514, 515, 1245, 1458, 1469, 1470
social events, 1397
submarine development, 1556–1557
theaters, 1589
Trévigne, Paul, 1621
Union occupation, 1163, 1419–1420, 1640, 1647
Washington Artillery, 1516
New Orleans (ship), 685, 726, 1692
New Orleans and Opelousas Railroad, 1092
New Orleans Daily Delta (newspaper), 823, 1144
New Orleans Daily Picayune (newspaper), 870, 1144
New-Orleans 5 Cent Song-Book, 1231
New Orleans Foundry and Ornamental Works. *See* Bennett and Lurges
New Orleans Naval Ordnance Works, 90, 1121
New Orleans Southern Rights Association, 1395
New Orleans Tribune (newspaper), 1348, 1621
New Plan, 419, 980, **1140–1141**, 1285, 1286
Newport News, Virginia, 1442
Newport News (ship), *1671*
New Regime (Norfolk newspaper), 1150
New Richmond theater, 1231, 1589, 1590
New River, 1691
New School United Synod (Presbyterian Church), 1247
Newsom, Ella King, 795, **1141**, 1161, 1740
Newsom, William Frank, 1141
Newsom Hospital (Tennessee), 796
"New South, The" (essay), 909
New South and the Episcopal Church, The (Newton), 1035
Newspapers, **1141–1145**
Atlanta, Georgia, 108
bans, 1030
Boyce (W. W.) letter, 201
censorship. *See* Censorship; Freedom of the press
crime reports, 428
deserters, 467, 468
dislike of amateur politicians, 1225
editorials, 50
editors' conscription exemption, 640
Felton, Rebecca Latimer, 570
Georgia, 671, 1144
Index, 810
on Irish support, 823
Jones, J. B., 865
literary contributions, 936
Louisiana, 1348
mail rates, 1241
morale building, 1081
New Orleans, 645
Norfolk, Virginia, 1150
North Carolina, 714, 1142–1143
paper shortages, 937
and peace movement, 1640
Pollard, Edward A., 1228–1229
postal service, 1242, 1243
reaction to *Trent* affair, 1619
recipes, 597
Russell, William H., 1354
secession movement, 322
Snead, Thomas L., 1483
South Carolina, 1143–1144
Southern religious, 1400
Stanley, Henry Morton, 1524
Tallahassee, Florida, 1566
Tennessee, 1143
Texas, 117

Virginia, 1141–1142, 1330
war correspondents, **1683–1684**
see also particular newspapers
Newsreels, 573
Newton, John C. Calhoun, 1035, 1567
New York (ship), 700
New York and Old Dominion Steamship Line, 1181
New York City
insurrection schemes, 1595
tobacco manufacturing, 1598
Wood, Fernando, 1743
New York Daily News (newspaper), 411, 1271–1272, 1743
New York Daily Tribune (newspaper), 924, 1271
New York Evening Post (newspaper), 466
New York Herald (newspaper), 1066
New York Ledger (magazine), 986, 987
New York Mercury (magazine), 987
New York Saturday Press, 354
New York Times (newspaper), 1354
New York Tribune (newspaper), 544, 762, 933, 1103–1104, 1272, 1689
Niagara (ship), 674, 1547
Niblack, Silas, 1682
Nicaragua, **1145**
filibustering expeditions, 554, 557, 558, 648, 808, 1228, 1395, 1631
Nicholls, Francis, **1145–1146**, 1397
Chancellorsville campaign, 957
soldiers' home, 1502
Nickajack (nonslave commonwealth), 720
Night attack. *See* Nocturnal attack
Nightingale (ship), 726
"N' Importe." *See* Street, Albert
Nina (ship), 905
Nisbet, Eugenius Aristides, 138, 853, 977, **1146**
Niter. *See* Saltpeter; Niter and Mining Bureau
Niter and Mining Bureau, 698, **1146–1148**, 1168, 1361, 1363, 1685
conscription exemptions, 509
employees, 1687
lead mining, 913
slave labor, 901, 1687
Nitric acid, 289
Noble, Andrew, 1066
Noble Brothers & Company, 98
Nocturnal attack, 880–881
No Name (Collins), 193
None Shall Look Back (novel by Gordon), 939
Norfolk, Virginia, **1148–1150**
antebellum population, *1642*, 1645
Forrest, French, 605
free black population, 642
martial law, 314, 727
newspapers, 1149
population and urban ranking, *1658*
Union occupation, 962, 1640, 1647
yellow fever epidemic, 1038
see also Gosport Navy Yard
Norfolk and Petersburg Railroad, 990
Norfolk Navy Yard. *See* Gosport Navy Yard
Norris, William, 1685
North, James H., 254, 484, 992, **1150**, 1303
North and South (Jakes), 580, 939
North Atlantic Blockading Squadron, 3, 129, 244, 1118–1119
North Carolina, 654, 882, 909–912, **1150–1157**, 1654
arsenal and armory, 1455, 1457, 1461, 1464, 1469, 1470
Averasboro, 117–118
banks, 128
black-white population comparison, *1435*
blockade, 178
blockade running, 1152, 1157
bread riots, 596
Burnside expedition, 244–245, 666, 1151
casualties, 1151–1152
Cherokees, 296, 812
class war, 346, 1154, 1155, 1492
community life, 379–380
congressmen, 89, 105–107, 118, 207–208, 219–220, 354–355, 422, 423, 446–447, 448, 492–493, 650–651, 906–907, 910–911, 911–913, 942, 971, 975, 1085, 1288, 1304, 1310–1311, 1351, 1481, 1626–1627
conscription resistance, 398
Constitution ratification, 403
currency, 1279
death toll, 1152
debt, 462
Department of. *See* Department of North Carolina and Southern Virginia
deserters, 1155
desertion study, 469
education, 216, 516, 519, 520, 1518, 1721–1722
election of 1860, 521, 522, 523
election of 1863, 524
farm acreage, *1484*
first Republican governor, 1640
flag, 587, 1301
food shortages, 689, 1153–1154
free blacks, 643, 1484
governors, 1–7, 206–207, 341–342, 529, 701, 702, 703, 705–708, 768, 781, 782, 1085–1086, 1370, 1649–1651
habeas corpus controversy, 727, 728
Heroes of America, 768, 1154–1155, 1183
home front burdens, 1153–1154
hospitals, 794, 796
infantry, 817
iron production, 1148
manufacturing, 514
manumission societies, 44, 1493
military governor, 702, 1152, 1524–1525
military operations, 260–262, 1152–1153
mining, 1043
morale, 1286
naval defense, 960, 962, 1126, 1152
newspapers, 714, 1142–1143
niter production, 1147
peace movements. *See under* Peace movements
poor relief, 1229, 1245
population, 602, 642, 1233
prisons, 1361–1362
Quakers, 1493
railroads, 714, 715, 1293, 1294, 1295, 1296, 1297
Reconstruction. *See under* Reconstruction
resolution against habeas corpus suspension, 1535
rice production, 1327, 1328
secession. *See under* Secession
secession and Confederacy membership dates, *1379*
secession date correlated with total black population, *1486*
slaveholdings, *1485*
slavery, 554
small arms imports, 1465
state navy, 1530
state rights extremism, 720, 1535–1536
Stoneman's raids, 1547
tax system, 1570
textbook publishing, 1587
textile industry, 1645
tobacco farming, 1598
troops supplies, 342

North Carolina, *continued*
Unionism. *See under* Unionism
Union occupation, 1524–1525, 1640
Vance, Zebulon. *See* Vance, Zebulon
Venable, Abraham Watkins, 1654
war contributions, 1151
Whig party, 1708
see also particular cities and place names
North Carolina (ship), 903, 1019, 1303, 1727
North Carolina Bible Society, 164
North Carolina Central Railroad, 290
North Carolina Institution for the Deaf and Dumb and the Blind, 516
North Carolina Journal of Education, 1721
North Carolina Manumission Society, 1493
North Carolina Military Institute, 519, 775
North Carolina Powder Manufacturing Company, 290
North Carolina Railroad, 687, 714, 715, 1085, 1295, 1297, 1298, 1627
North Carolina Reader (Wiley), 1587
North Carolina Standard (newspaper), 768, 781, 855, 1183, 1304, 1640
Northerners, **1157–1158**
Confederate sympathizers, *413*
confiscation of property, 388–389
cotton sales to, 419
depiction in South, 1081
investments in South, 463
Methodists, 1035
peace movement, 258, 537, 538
in Raleigh, North Carolina, 1301
view of honor, 787
see also Copperheads; particular personal names
Northern Methodist Church, 1321
Northern Missouri Railroad, 275
North Fork Town, Creek Nation, 811
North Georgia Agricultural College, 928
North Mountain, Virginia, 1418
Northrop, Claudian B., 1232
Northrop, Lucius B., 148, 376–378, 1148, **1158**, 1248, 1361, 1685, 1716
Davis (Jefferson) view of, 453
on salt supply, 1362
Northwestern Conspiracy, 349-350, 413, **1158-1159**, 1271, 1272, 1595; *see also* Copperheads
Northwest Ordinance of 1787 and 1789, 1533
Norton, Charles Eliot, 1274
Norton, Nimrod Lindsay, 747, **1159**
Notable Men of Tennessee from 1833 to 1875 (Temple), 1574
Nott, Josiah C., 1273, 1274
Novels. *See* Fiction
Nullification controversy, 401, 1067, **1159–1160**, 1202, 1207, 1324, 1637, 1737
Calhoun, John C., 253, 1533
Fort Hill Address, 613
Hammond, James H., 730
and secession, 1374, 1377
and Southern nationalism, 1113
Nulty, William H., *as contributor*, 1042
No. 61 (ship), 1150, 1303
Numismatics. *See under* Currency
Nursing, **1160–1161**
Brock, Sallie A., 222
Newsom, Ella King, 1141
Pember, Phoebe Yates, 1188
Roman Catholic Church, 795, 1160, 1346
shortages, 591
Tompkins, Sally L., 1600
women, 547, 671, 795, 1740
see also Hospitals
Nutrition. *See* Food

O

O. A. K. *See* Order of American Knights
Oak Alley Plantation, 1345
Oakes, Ziba, 1453
Oak Grove, battle of. *See* King's School House, Virginia
Oak Hills, Missouri, battle of. *See* Wilson's Creek campaign
Oakland Cemetery (Atlanta), 1069
Oates, William C., 293
Oath, amnesty, Union-occupied Tennessee, 1110, 1578
Oath of allegiance, 23, 1029, **1163–1164**
Ex parte Garland decision, 661
Norfolk, Virginia, 1149
Obenchain, Francis G., 1237
Object of the Administration in Prosecuting the War (Tyson), 1632
O'Brien, John, *as contributor*, 255–256, 283, 409–410, 865–866, 873–874, 1684–1688, 1754–1755
Observer (Fayetteville newspaper), 1143
"Occasional Address of the Supreme Commander," 412
Occupation, U.S. military. *See* Union occupation
"Occurrence at Owl Creek Bridge" (Bierce), 488
Oceanus (ship), 1472
Ochiltree, William B., **1164**, 1477
Ocmulgee River, 1547
Octorara (ship), 446
Octoroon, 1045
"Ode" (Timrod), 937, 1597
"Ode to the Confederate Dead" (Tate), 939
Offensive strategy. *See* Strategy and tactics; particular battles
Office of Medicine and Surgery. *See* Bureau of Medicine and Surgery
Office of Orders and Detail. *See* Bureau of Orders and Detail
Office of Ordnance and Hydrography. *See* Bureau of Ordnance and Hydrography
Office of Provisions and Clothing. *See* Bureau of Provisions and Clothing
Office of the Register (Treasury Department), 1614
Official Records of the Union and Confederate Armies. See War of the Rebellion: A Compilation of the Official Records of the Union and Confederate Armies
Ogden, Richard D'Orsay, 1231, 1590
Ogeechee River, 1368
Oglethorpe Light Infantry, 137
Ohio
Johnson's Island Prison, 856–857
Morgan's raids, 1089
withdrawal from war, 599
Ohio River, 1691
Oil Springs Indian refugee camp, 1391
Oklahoma (Indian Territory), 296, 305, 309, 812-815, 1289, 1584; *see also* particular place names
Okolona, Mississippi, 1051, 1624–1625
Oktarharsars Harjo, 425
O'Laughlin, Michael, 935
Old Bory. *See* Beauregard, P. G. T.
Old Capitol Prison (Washington, D.C.), 143, 202, 1090
"Old Dan Tucker" (song), 488
Old Duke. *See* Wickliffe, Robert
Old Gentlemen's Convention. *See* Washington Peace Conference
Old Granny General. *See* Holmes, Theophilus H.
Oldham, Williamson S., 763, **1164–1165**
Old Iron Sides. *See* Harrison, Thomas
Old Jack. *See* Jackson, Thomas J. ("Stonewall")

Old Jube. *See* Early, Jubal
Old Jubilee. *See* Early, Jubal
Old Natchez Road, 1339
Old One Wing. *See* Martin, James Green
Old Pap. *See* Price, Sterling
Old Pete. *See* Longstreet, James
Old Reliable. *See* Hardee, William J.
Old Rock. *See* Benning, Henry L.
"Old Sergeant, The" (song), 1103
Old Swet. *See* Featherston, Winfield Scott
Old Times in Dixie Land: A Southern Matron's Memories (Merrick), 1034
Olinde (ship), 1547
Olmstead, Charles H., 616 1366
Olmsted, Frederick Law, 44
Olson, John E., *as contributor*, 849
Olustee, Florida, 581, 590, **1165–1166**, 1567
Olustee (ship), 376, 1727; *see also Tallahassee* (ship)
O'Neal, Edward Asbury, **1166**
O'Neal, James, 722
Onward (ship), 1472
Opequon Creek, Virginia. *See* Winchester, Virginia, Third Battle of
Operator 13 (film), 578
Ophthalmic Hospital (Athens, Georgia), 796
Opium, 757
Opothleyahola, 297, 305, 310, 425, 813, **1166–1167**, 1390, 1693
Opposition (Virginia political faction), 1187
"Ora." *See* Reid, Samuel
Oral Catechism, 1588
Oral history, **1167**; *see also* Folk narratives
Orange and Alexandria Railroad, 209, 210, 220, 722, 963, 990, 996, 1001, 1556
Orange County, North Carolina, 379, 380
Orchards, battle of. *See* King's School House, Virginia
Ord, E. O. C., 46, 686, 825
Order of American Knights, 411, 412, 1252, 1253; *see also* Copperheads
Order of the Sons of Liberty. *See* Copperheads
Ordnance
  accomplishments, 336
  Anglo-Confederate purchasing, 42
  arsenals and armories, **89–91**
  commerce raiders, 374
  innovations, 94, 98, 734, 991, 1603–1605
  Macon, Georgia, 977
  naval, 62–63, 991, 992–993, 1018, 1121–1122
  rifled, 616
  technical innovations, 537, 1018
  Tredegar Iron Works, 1616–1617
  see also Arms, weapons, and ammunition; Artillery; Ordnance Bureau
Ordnance Bureau, 60, **1168–1170**
  Alexander, Edward Porter, 24–25
  blockade runners, 181–182, 185, 1169, 1726
  civil service, 315
  conscription exemptions, 509
  De Lagnel, Julius, 465
  Gorgas, Josiah, 34, 90–91, 465, 508, 698–699, 902, 913, 1146, 1168–1170, 1306, 1685, 1687
  laborers, 900
  McRae, Colin J., 979–980
  munitions sources, 1469–1471
  niter corps, 1146, 1147, 1361
  operation, 1687
  private enterprise controls, 1537
  slave labor, 901
  small arms imports, 1465, 1469
  small arms manufacture, 1455, 1456, 1458, 1460
  Tredegar Iron Works, 34
  war mobilization, 508
  weapons production, 60
Ordnance Instruction for the Confederate Navy, 63
Ordnance rifle, 61, 93, 94, 101, 102
Oregon
  election of 1860, 521
  statehood, 555
O'Reilly, Thomas, 111
Oreto (ship), 484, 591, 984
Organic Act for Arizona Territory, 984
Original Songs of the Atlanta Amateurs, 1231–1232
Orleans Guard, 426
Orphan Brigade, 736, 816, 888, 1096, **1170**, 1516
  Lewis, Joseph, 929
Orr, James L., 133, 200, 568, 804, 988, **1171–1172**, 1338
Orr, Jehu Amaziah, 524, **1173**, 1729
Orr, Sample, 1052
Osages, 811, 812, 813, **1173**
Osband, E. D., 341, 1051
Osborn, James M., 1205
Ostend Manifesto, 557
Ostendorff, J. M., 1245
Osterhaus, Peter J., 294, 526
O'Sullivan, Timothy, 5
Otey, James, 535
Ould, Robert, prisoner exchanges, 1257–1258, 1262
"Our National Confederate Anthem" (song), *1102*
Oury, Granville H., 983, 984, **1174**
Outlaw Josie Wales, The (film), 580
Outliers (army deserters), 1155
Outlines from the Outpost (Cooke), 408
Oven Bluff, Alabama, 1425
Overland campaign, 1198
Overseers, 5, 901, **1174–1175**, 1739
  archaeological excavations, 48
  conscription exemption, 89, 107, 191, 279, 345, 392, 397, 398–399, 532, 776, 884, 902, 1083, 1155, 1174–1175, 1230, 1395, 1514
  cotton plantation, 1439
  of impressed slaves, 900
  mining, 1043
  North Carolina plantation, 706
  and slave drivers, 1433–1434
  study, 1214
Owasco (ship), 656
Owen, Thomas, 237
Owens, James B., **1175–1176**
Owl (ship), 984
Ownby, Ted, *as contributor*, 559–560, 568–569, 923–924
Owsley, Frank L. (the elder)
  on habeas corpus controversy, 728
  on state rights, 331, 1115
Owsley, Frank L. (the younger), *as contributor*, 591–592, 984, 1062, 1178
Owsley, William, 216
Oxen, 791
Oxford Mercury, 1721

P

Pace, Robert F.
  as cartographer, x
  as contributor, 27–28, 778–779, 799–800, 825–826, 1010–1012
Pacific Mail Company, 1675
Pacifism
  Mennonites, 1031
  military exemptions, 397
  Quaker, 1493
Pack artillery, 91
PACS. *See* Provisional Army of the Confederate States
Paddy McGann (Simms), 937
Paducah, Kentucky, **1177**
  earthworks, *888*

Page, Richard L., 290, **1178**
Page, Thomas J., 1547
Page, Thomas Nelson, 937, 938
Paine, E. A., 1177
Paine, Halbert E., 1239
Painting. *See* Art; particular artists and art works
Palisades. *See* Chevaux-de-frise
Palmer, Benjamin M., 1137, 1275, 1399
Palmer, John (spy), 544
Palmer, John M. (general), 888, 1096
Palmer, John Williamson, 936, 937
Palmer, Joseph Benjamin, 1096, **1178–1179**
Palmer's Factory, prisoners, 265
Palmerston, Henry John Temple, 3d Viscount, 247, 483, 485, 1016, 1354, 1529
Palmetto (ship). *See Palmetto State*
Palmetto Armory, **1179–1180**
Palmetto Battery, 91, *92*
Palmetto Guard, 1350
Palmetto Iron Works, 1179
Palmetto Ranch, Texas, 1433
Palmetto Republic. *See* South Carolina
Palmetto Sharpshooters, 844
Palmetto State (ship), 287, *289*, 778, 822, 1124, 1125, 1130, 1180, 1303, 1515
"Palmetto State Song," *1507*
Palmito Ranch, Texas, 234, 1611
Pampero (ship), 375
Pamunkey raid, 1553
Paper
  cartridge, 1470
  shortages for music publishing, 1101
  shortages for printmaking, 1255
  shortages for stamp printing, 1242
Paper money. *See* Currency; Shinplasters
Papers. See Southern Historical Society Papers
Parapet, 619, 625
Pardo, 1045
Paris of the Confederacy. *See* Mobile, Alabama
Paris Patrie (journal), 1271
Parke, John G., Fort Stedman, 627
Parker, Foxhall, 1180
Parker, Sandra V., *as contributor*, 693, 1160–1161, 1600
Parker, Tom. *See* Bell, Mary, and Mollie Bell
Parker, William, 650, **1180**
Parker's Crossroads, Tennessee, 607, 608
Park Hill, Cherokee Nation, 811, 813
Parks, Thomas W., 777, 1558
Parks and Lyon's Foundry, 1557
Paroles, text of
  Johnston (Joseph E.) and troops, 1793
  Lee (Robert E.) and staff, 1791
  Smith (E. Kirby) and troops, 1795–1796
  Taylor (Richard) and troops, 1794
Parrish, William E., *as contributor*, 28, 190–192, 341, 529, 587–588, 752, 828–829, 1323, 1425–1427
Parrott, Robert Parker, 101
Parrott projectiles, 98, 102
Parrott rifle, 61, 93, 96, 99, *100*, 287
Parson Brownlow's Book (Brownlow), 231
Parsons, Lewis E., 928
Parsons, Mosby Monroe, 343, 396, 930, **1180**
Parsons, William Henry, 207
Parsons' Brigade, 1584
Partington, Mary, 1231
Partisan Leader (Tucker), 936
Partisan Ranger Act of 1862, 720, 722–723, 1086
Partisans. *See* Guerrilla warfare
Passport system, 1277, 1278
Patent Office, 864, **1181**
Paterson, Robert, 266
Pathe Weekly (documentary films), 572, 573
Patin, Marie Louise, 1345
Patriarchy, Southern, 562, 1487–1488, 1491
Patrick, Rembert, 589–590, 1166
Patrick Henry (ship), 840, 841, 960, 1124, 1126, 1180, **1181–1182**, 1371, 1623
  naval training, 1131, 1182
Patronage, 401, 1225
Patterson, E. D., 1500
Patterson, Robert, 996
Patterson, Rufus Lenoir, 1151
Paul, F. M., 1143
Paulding, Hiram, 700
Pawnee (ship), 700
Paw Paw (ship), 1177
Paxton, Elisha Franklin, **1182**, 1549
Payne, John A., 778
Payne, Lewis, 935
Payne, William Henry Fitzhugh, 943, **1182–1183**
Peabody, Everett, 1421–1422
Peace and Constitution Society, 1183, 1226
Peace Convention (1861). *See* Washington Peace Conference
Peace Democrats, 1224
Peace movements, 387, **1183–1184**
  Alabama, 1183, 1184
  Arkansas, 1183
  Boyce, W. W., 200–201
  caricature, *732*
  and civil liberties curtailment, 314
  Clay, Clement C., 349
  congressional advocates, 200, 201, 394, 731, 786, 854, 1172, 1173, 1184, 1476
  as desertion cause, 468
  Foote, Henry S., 599–600
  Forsyth, John, 609
  Georgia, 387, 423–424, 670, 773, 1080, 1183, 1184
  Gettysburg campaign and, 683
  Hampton Roads Conference. *See* Hampton Roads Conference
  newspaper support, 1142, 1144
  North Carolina, 106, 207, 387, 446–447, 448, 524, 654, 689, 707, 768, 782, 855, 911, 912, 942, 1080, 1154, 1155, 1156–1157, 1183–1184, 1185, 1224, 1301, 1311, 1326, 1626–1627, 1632, 1640, 1650–1651
  as political issue, 1224
  Secret Service efforts in North, 258, 537, 538
  Stephens, Alexander H., 1655
  Tennessee, 1183
  Washington Conference. *See* Washington Peace Conference
  Wickham, Williams Carter, 1714
  Wright, Augustus Romaldus, 1745
Peace Society, 1183, 1226
Peachtree Creek, Georgia, 87, 110, 114, 738
Peachtree Street (Atlanta), *99*, *108*
Peacock, George, 1388
Peake, Mary, 307, 1742
Peale, Charles Wilson, 197
Pearce, J. W., 310
Pearce, N. Bart, 1730
Pea Ridge, Arkansas. *See* Elkhorn Tavern, Arkansas
Pearl River, 1691
Pearse and Lockwood, 184
Pearson, Richmond, 873, **1184–1185**, 1650
  Conscription Act decision, 1155
Pease, Elisha M., 116, 1585
Peck, William Raine, **1185**
Peckinpah, Sam, 580
Peeble's Farm, Virginia, 1200
Pee Dee River, 1691

Pee Dee (ship), 1125, **1185**
ordnance, 1118
Peery, Charles V., *as contributor*, 515, 1150
Pegram, John, 83, 265, 271, 582, **1186**, 1703
elite unit, 1516
Pegram, Robert B., 374, 1107
Peirpoint, Francis H., **1186–1188**, 1700
command of Norfolk, Virginia, 1149–1150
as governor of Virginia, 703, 1702
Pelham, John
elite unit, 1516
Fredericksburg campaign, 639
horse artillery, 95
Pember, Phoebe Yates, 795, 1161, **1188**, 1740
diary, 472
Pemberton, John C., 501, 617, 620, 877, 878, **1188–1189**, 1237, 1248, 1366, 1386, 1479, 1652, 1656
Army of Vicksburg, 68, 72
Charleston, South Carolina, defense, 1333
flag design, 586
Holly Springs, Mississippi, raid, 784
Jackson, Mississippi, defense, 837
Northern background, 1157
Vicksburg campaign, 623, 664, 837, 838, 1049, 1322, 1658, 1659, 1660
Penateka Comanche, 811
Pender, William Dorsey, 1151, **1189–1190**, 1370, 1718
Gaines' Mill, Virginia, 653
Gettysburg campaign, 678, 679, 680, 681, 683, 1391
Mechanicsville, Virginia, 1020
on North Carolina desertion rate, 1155
Pendleton, Alexander S., *80*, 874, 914, 1190
Pendleton, George H., election of 1864, *466*
Pendleton, William N., 24, *77*, 535, 912, **1190–1191**, 1680
death of, 1418
Pendleton, South Carolina, 1245
Peninsular campaign, 917, 1181, **1191–1193**, 1231, 1666, 1716, 1736
Butler, Matthew Calbraith, 246
Hampton's Legion, 734
King's School House, Virginia, 690, 918, 1192, 1193, 1479
Magruder, John B., 989
map, 1192
Martin, William Thompson, 1013
Seven Days' Battles, **1400–1401**
Seven Pines, Virginia, **1402–1403**
Stuart (J. E. B.) ride around McClellan, 78, 268–269, 276, 915, 919, 922, 1013, 1193, 1231, 1553, 1554, *1555*
see also particular battles
Penn, Imogen Bradfute, 964
Penn, William, 1016
Pennell, Joseph Stanley, 939
Pennsylvania
Chambersburg, 269, 276–277, 503, 849, 968, 1417, 1553, 1556
election of 1860, 522
Gettysburg campaign. *See* Gettysburg campaign
Stuart's raids, 1553, 1554–1556
Pennsylvania (ship), 700
Pensacola, Florida, *1206*
bombardment of, 1433
Confederate camp, *1497*
Confederate evacuation plans, 1426
Fort Pickens, 613
free blacks, 644, 645
shipyards, 1424
strategic significance, 16, 589
Pensacola Harbor. *See* Fort Pickens
Pensacola Navy Yard, Confederate seizure of, 1424
Pensacola Observer (newspaper), 274
Pequot (ship), 491
Percussion cap machinery, 1471
Percussion rifles. *See* Rifles
Perdue, Theda, *as contributor*, 296–297
Periodicals. *See* Magazines; particular titles
"Peripatetic coffin." *See* Submarines
Perkins, John, Jr., **1194**
Perrin, Abner Monroe, **1195**, 1364
Perry, Benjamin, 1171, 1507, 1747
South Carolina governorship, 1172
Unionism, 1637
Perry, Edward Aylesworth, 581, **1195**
Perry, Madison S., 32, 589, 702, 703, 1042, **1196**
Perry, Matthew C., 235
Perry, Oliver Hazard, 235
Perry, Percival, *as contributor*, 1016
Perry, William Flank, **1196**
Perry (ship), 1369
Perryville, Kentucky, 85, 143, 310, 888, 890–891, 1041, **1196–1198**, 1737, 1744
Buckner, Simon Bolivar, 238
Donelson, Daniel, 491
Hardee, William, 737
Lester, George, 924
map, 1197
Personal Memoirs (Grant), 354
"Personne." *See* De Fontaine, Felix Gregory
Peru, Hydrographic Commission of the Amazon, 1624
Pessou and Simon lithogrpahs, 1231
Peter Ashley (Heyward), 939
Peters, George B., 1652
Peters, W. E., 277
Petersburg, Virginia
antebellum population, *1642*, 1643, 1645
bread riots, 212
campaign. *See* Petersburg campaign
hospitals, 794, 796
manufacturing, 1659
population and urban ranking, *1658*
railroads, 1297
siege of. *See under* Petersburg campaign
surrender, 367
Petersburg campaign, 82, 612, 805, **1198–1202**
artillery, 93
Beauregard, P. G. T., 149
defenses, 25, 94, 620, 646, 920
fascines, *625*
Fort Stedman, Virginia, **627**
Girardey, Victor, 690
Hampton, Wade, 731–732, 1199
Hill, A. P., 771
hungry soldiers, 901
map, 1199
prostitution, 1277
Sanders, John Caldwell Calhoun, 1364
siege, 686, 920, 1648
Sorrel, Gilbert Moxley, 1503
Petersburg Railroad, 1294
Petigru, James L., 298, 749, **1202**, 1507, 1597
Unionism, 1637
Pettigrew, J. Johnston, 926, **1202–1203**
brigades, 816
Gettysburg campaign, 51, 81, 681, 682, 683, 881, 1152, 1391
see also Pickett's Charge
Pettigrew, Mary, 795
Pettus, Edmund Winston, 664, **1203**
Pettus, J. J., 226, 1047, **1203–1204**
as governor of Mississippi, 701, 702, 703, 837, 1051
secessionism, 1377
war preparations, 836
Petty, J. W. (artist), 1205

Peyton, H. E., *77*
Peyton, Robert Ludwell Yates, **1204**
Pharmaceuticals
  Confederate laboratories, 757–758, 759
  substitutes, 1559
Phelan, James, 1083, 1172, **1204–1205**, 1216, 1694
Phelan, John D., 1205
Phelps, Samuel Ludyard, 505, 765
Philadelphia Sunday Dispatch (newspaper), 1619
Philadelphia Weekly Times (newspaper), 946
Phillips, Christopher, *as contributor*, 647–648, 657–658, 830, 969–970, 1008–1009, 1040–1041, 1252–1255, 1409, 1605
Phillips, Ulrich B., 1113
Phillips, Wendell, 320
Phillips, William A., 310, 814, 1391
Philo Parsons (ship), 145, 375
Phoenix (ship), 1303
Photography, **1205–1207**
  archival collections, 1098–1099
  as basis of Julio painting, 873–874
  cartes de visite, 1230, 1231
  popular culture, 1230–1231
  selected bibliography, 168
  slave depictions, *5*
  see also particular photographers
Physicians. *See* Health and medicine; Hospitals; Medical Department; particular names
Picacho Pass, Arizona, 51
Pickens, Andrew, 1207
Pickens, Francis W., 191, 245, 499, 628, 733, **1207–1208**, 1354
  critics, 1509
  Fort Sumter policy, 1507, 1508, 1526
  as governor of South Carolina, 701, 703
  military units, 731, 1508–1509
Pickens, Lucy Holcombe, *436*, 438
Pickett, George E., 45, **1208–1209**
  burial, 1331
  charge at Gettysburg. *See* Pickett's Charge
  Fort Stedman, 1201
  treatment of tories, 1602
Pickett, Jane, 1217
Pickett, John T., **1209–1210**
  mission to Mexico, 1036–1037, 1063
Pickett's Charge, 81, 664, 681, 682, 819, 881, 918, 946, 1151, 1208–1209, 1516, 1553, 1582, 1622
  Armistead, Lewis A., 59
  Cooke, John Rogers, 408
  Davis, Joseph Robert, 454
  Dearing, James, 459
  Fry, Birkett, 648
  Pettigrew, J. Johnston, 1203
  playing of "Dixie," 488
Pickett's Mill (Georgia), 112, 113
Piedmont, North Carolina, recruiting agents, 566
Piedmont, Virginia, 870, **1210**
Piedmont Railroad, 714, 1297
Pierce, Ebenezer, 171, 172
Pierce, Franklin, 31, 255, 359, 382, 450, 556, 557, 598, 852, 875, 1534
  Gadsden Purchase, 808
Pierce, George Foster, 1034, 1399
Pierce, Joseph, 1580
Pierpont, Francis H. *See* Peirpoint, Francis H.
Pierson, William S., 856
Pigott, Jennings, 1525
Pike, Albert, 52, 297, 409, 488, 940, **1210–1211**, 1340, 1607
  Elkhorn Tavern, 526
  Indian treaties, 53, 305, 425, 811–812, 813, 1173, 1290, 1390, 1398, 1408
  Indian troop command, 1390
Pikes (weapons), 16, **846**, 1350, 1594
Pillow, Gideon, 238, 835, **1211**, 1268, 1329
  Belmont, Missouri, 156, 438, 737
  Henry and Donelson campaign, 83, 593, 765, 766, 767
  Mississippi River operations, 887, 1133
  Murfreesboro, Tennessee, 83
  Polk (Leonidas) controversy, 438
  recruiting activity, 398
  staff, 254
Pilot Knob, Missouri, 1252, 1253, 1254
Pinkerton, Allan, 540, 541, 714, 1752
Pins. *See* Keetowahs
Pioneer (submarine), 777, 801, 993, 1269, 1556, *1557*
Piracy. *See* Privateers
Pirogues, 1692
Pistols. *See* Handguns
Piston, William Garrett, *as contributor*, 1402–1403
Pitchlynn, Peter P., 310
Pitt-Rivers, Julian, 787
Pittsburg (ship), 1134
Pittsburg Landing, Tennessee. *See* Shiloh campaign
Pius IX, Pope, 1004, 1271
Plain folk, **1212–1214**
  Charleston immigrants, 1506
  fast days, 568
  inflation effects, 566–567
  political influence, 1225–1226
  poor whites, 1489
  slavery, 1235
  soldiers, 1494–1495
  see also Yeomanry
Plains Comanches, 811
Plains Indians, 811, 812, 813; *see also* particular peoples
"Plan of a Provisional Government for the Southern Confederacy" (Memminger), 1023
Plane, Helen, 952
Plant, Henry B., 1514
Plantation, 5, **1214–1218**
  abandonment, 1051
  agricultural decline, 1216
  archaeological excavations, 48
  black belt, 172–173
  conscription exemptions, 397
  cotton. *See* Cotton
  Davis Bend, 458
  dependency on world markets, 1112
  Fort Hill, 613
  government interference, 1081
  miscegenation, 1045, 1046
  mistress. *See* Plantation mistress
  overseers. *See* Overseers
  Perkins, John, Jr., 1194
  planters. *See* Planters
  slave drivers' functions, **1433–1434**
  slave labor, 901, 1435–1437, 1439
  slave life, *5*, 1448–1451
  slave population, 1235
  slave resistance, 1443–1444
  slave women, 1741
  slave work habits, 1451
  sugar, 1174–1175, 1214, 1215, 1559, 1560
  taxes, 345
  tobacco, 1174–1175, 1214, 1598
  and urbanization, 1644
  see also Slavery
Plantation: A Southern Quarterly Journal, 1625
Plantation mistress, 5, **1218–1219**, 1738–1739
  Merrick, Caroline E., 1034
  relationship with slave women, 1741
  shortages, 1217
  wartime adjustment, 1220
  wartime responsibilities, 1433, 1487–1488
Planter (ship), 7, 1471–1472

Planters, 387, 565, **1219–1221**
Alabama, 1057
alienation from Confederate cause, 1081
and capitalist system, 1112
children, 305, 306
class conflicts, 344–345, 379, 1212
conscription issue, 392, 397, 1215–1216, 1491
creole, 644
as elite, 1490
factors, 1660
leadership in antebellum South, 1112–1113
Mississippi, 1047, 1051
mobilization, 1219
morale, 1079
postwar, 1221
produce loan, 1270
protection of slavery, 1234–1235
resentment of, 1492
slave insurrection fears, 1217
social mobility, 1490
taxes, 419, 1283, 1570
theft complaints, 427
tobacco, 1598
Unionists, 1639
women. *See* Plantation mistress
see also Plantation
Planters' House Hotel (St. Louis), 1251, 1483, 1729
Plaquemines Frauds, 1454
Platoon, artillery, 91
Pleasant Hill, Louisiana, 1223, 1315, 1316, 1317, 1610, 1696
Green (Thomas) death at, 713
Pleasonton, Alfred, 209, 1252, 1254, 1553
Brandy Station, Virginia, 211, 269
Gettysburg campaign, 677
Plessy v. Ferguson, 1621
Plummer, Joseph, 1730
Plymouth (ship), 62, 700
Pneumonia, occurrence and treatment, 755
Poague, William T., elite unit, 1516
Poe, Edgar Allan, 986, 1101, 1330
Poe, Orlando, 896
Poems (Timrod), 1597
Poesta (ship), 1177
Poetry, 1232
war-inspired, 936, 937, 938
see also particular poems and poets
Point Lookout Prison, 504, 849, 1008, **1221–1222**, 1258, 1261, 1723
Poison Springs, Arkansas, 11, 53, 57, 305, 310, 815, 1009, 1316, 1610
Poland, recruitment mission, 980–981
Police force, Irish in, 823
Polignac, Camille J., 573, 1005, **1222–1223**, 1317, 1591
brigade, 1585
French background, 604
Political prisoners, 1261–1263
Salisbury Prison, 1361
Political Text-book, or Encyclopedia (Cluskey), 358
Politics, **1223–1226**
absence of political parties, 387, 1224–1225
American party, **28**
Bluffton movement, **186**
Boyce party, 200, 201
Confederate government, 387, 391, 525
Democratic party, **465–467**
effect of raids on, 327–328
elections, 1223
Louisiana, 955–956
Mississippi, 1047
North Carolina, 707, 1156–1157
prisoners of war, 1261–1263, 1361
Republican party, **1321–1322**
sectional, 382–383
selected bibliography, 169
Wilmot Proviso response, 1728
see also Copperheads; entries titled Elections; particular states
Polk, Ann F., 852
Polk, James K., 186, 554, 598, 685, 802, 852, 1453, 1454, 1593, 1629, 1679
Democratic party, 465
law partner, 1211
territorial expansion, 380, 868
Polk, Leonidas, 204, 491, 569, 830, 852, 885, 890, **1226–1228**, 1475, 1545
Army of Tennessee, 67, 84, 85, 86, 87, 263, 1227–1228
Atlanta campaign, 111, 112, 113
battle flag, 586
Belmont, Missouri, 155–157, 438
Chickamauga campaign, 303, 304
Dalton, Georgia, 442
as Episcopal bishop, 518, 535
Kentucky, 1011, 1679
Meridian campaign, 1032, 1033
Munfordville, Kentucky, 1093
Murfreesboro, Tennessee, 1094, 1096
Perryville, Kentucky, 204, 1197
Pillow (Gideon) controversy, 438
Shiloh campaign, 1420, 1421, 1422
staff, 254, 340
Polk, Lucius Eugene, *52*, **1228**
Polk, William H., 1576
Polk Hospital (Macon, Georgia), 796
Pollard, Edward A., 193, 329, 444, 948, 1142, **1228–1229**, 1495
memoirs, 166, 475
Pollard, H. Rives, 1228, 1229
Poll tax, Georgia, 1570
"Polygonal shell," 1168
Pontoon bridges, 293, 295, *534*, 1007
Poor relief, **1229–1230**, 1245, 1285, 1310, 1320
aid societies. *See subhead* women's aid societies *below*
Alabama, 18, 1426
breakdown in system, 1491, 1492
Columbia, South Carolina, 370
Florida, 28
free markets, **641–642**
Galveston, Texas, 655
Georgia, 109, 229, 668, 670, 704
legislation, 566, 596
Louisiana, 1078
McCord, Louisa Cheves, 969
North Carolina, 1154
poorhouses, 1489
for Quakers, 1493–1494
Savannah, Georgia, 1367
soldiers' aid societies, 1502
soldiers' families, 379
South Carolina, 717
urban, 1137, 1647, 1648
women's aid societies, 378–379, 671, 1647
see also Free markets
Pope, John, 35, 78, 272, 336, 549, 713, 1666
counterfeiting, 421
General Order No. 5, 601
Manassas, Second, 269, 273, 834, 918, 999–1003
New Madrid operation, 1133–1134
and Stuart's raids, 1553, 1554
Pope, Joseph Daniel, 1614
Poplar Springs Church. *See* Peeble's Farm, Virginia
Popular culture, **1230–1232**
Dixie, **488–489**
Lost Cause, 949–950
Popular sovereignty, 380, 1534
Popular View of the American War, A (Hope), 1271
Population, **1232–1235**
African Americans, 4, 319, 642, 1045, 1438, 1486; *see also subhead* slave *below*
African Americans in Union army, 12
Alabama, 14, 1057, 1059, 1064–1065
Arizona, 51

Population, *continued*
Arkansas, 52, 939–940, 941, 1605
black belt counties, 172
border states, 195, 339
children, 305
Choctaws, 309
Confederate States, 69, 386, 506, 563
Cuba, 432
distribution of Southern black (1790–1860), 1438
1860 census, 1232–1233
Florida, 588, 1566
foreigners, 602, 1234
free creoles, 644–645
Georgia, 108, 110, 552, 667, 976, 978
German, 675
growth, 1234
Indian Territory, 1605
Kentucky, 886, 1233
literacy rate, 1490
Louisiana, 140, 602, 642, 1137, 1233, 1605
"male gap," 563
manpower, 339
Mississippi, 836, 837, 1047
Missouri, 1052, 1605–1606
New Mexico, 1136
North Carolina, 290, 714, 1151, 1152, 1300, 1726
Northern, 563, 1045
Northerners in Confederacy, 1157, 1301
planters, 1219
prison, 39, 154, 610, 1267
refugee, 1318
slave, 307, 552, 1047, 1052, 1233; *see also subhead* African Americans *above*
slave percentages, 1486
South Carolina, 285, 369, 1504, 1506
Southern black-white proportion, 1434–1435, *1435*
Southern demographics, 1483–1485
Southern homogeneity, 1112
tax census, 486, 511, 1224, 1282–1283
Tennessee, 291, 1028, 1107, 1574
Texas, 116, 231, 655, 1583, 1586, 1605
Trans-Mississippi, 1605
Unionist, 1115–1116
urban percentage, 1489
Virginia, 443, 1148–1149, 1150, 1329–1330, 1333, 1663
wealthy, 1215
West Virginia, 1699
see also particular cities
Porcher, Francis P., 193, 757, 758, 759
Porter, Andrew, 997, 998
Porter, David Dixon, 224, 611, 863, 1004, 1049, 1064, 1371, 1655, 1657, 1658, 1659, 2022
attack on Fort Fisher, North Carolina, 1152
capture of New Orleans, 1138, 1139
Red River campaign, 1315, 1316, 1317, 1610
Porter, Felicia Grundy, 1160–1161
Porter, Fitz John, 995, 1400
Gaines' Mill, Virginia, 653
Manassas, Second, 1000, 1002
Mechanicsville, Virginia, 1020
Porter, John L., 22, 1185, **1235–1236**, 1580, 1670, 1725
ironclad design, 223, 992
Porter, Joseph, 719, 1053
Porterfield, George A., 1700
Portfolio (magazine), 1232
Port Gibson, Mississippi, **1236–1238**, 1605
Bowen, John Stevens, 199, 713
casualties, 1238
Garrott, Isham, 664
Lowry, Robert, 960
map, 1236
Port Hudson, Louisiana, 145, **1238–1239**, 1314, 1609
assault, 955, 956
field fortifications, 626
Gardner, Franklin, 657
map, 1238
Native Guards, 645
Portia Club, 1034
Port Republic, Virginia. *See* Cross Keys and Port Republic, Virginia
Port Royal, South Carolina, 178, 191, 527, 1129, **1239–1240**, 1568
casualties, 1240
fall to Union forces, 1370, 1433, 1509
see also Sea Islands, South Carolina
Port St. Marks, Florida, 1566, 1567
Portsmouth, Virginia
martial law, 314, 727
small arms manufacture, 1460
Union occupation, 1647
Posey, Carnot, **1240–1241**
Postmaster general, 251
Post Office Department, 2, 249, 250, 383, 527, **1241–1244**
Butterfield Overland Mail, 983, 1339
civil service, 315
employee conscription exemption, 1243
express mail service, 1243
Indian routes, 812
Reagan, John H., 1312–1313
Southern Express Company, 1511
stamps, **1521–1524**
Potens, Aime, 1348
Potomac River, 1415, 1691
Boteler's Ford, 1406, 1408
Stuart's raids, 1556
Potomac Squadron, 129
Potter, David, 336, 1111
Pottery production, 735
Poverty, **1244–1245**
class conflicts, 1155, 1244
eroding morale, 1229
North Carolina, 1154, 1155, 1229
plain folk, 1213
"respectable" vs. destitute, 1489
soldiers' homes, 1502
urban, 1648
Virginia, 1668
war-related, 1155, 1491
see also Poor relief
Powder works, 116, 336, 993, 1168, **1245–1246**
Georgia, 670
gunpowder, 62, 1470
saltpeter. *See* Saltpeter
shortages, 90
see also Cartridges; Niter and Mining Bureau
Powell, Jennie, 1231, 1590
Powell, Lawrence N., *as contributor*, 246–247, 952–956, 1077–1078, 1136–1139, 1394–1397
Powell, Lewis T., execution, *539*
Powell, Robert H., 791
Powell, Samuel, 1197
Powell, William S., *as contributor*, 1084, 1300–1301
Power, J. Tracy, *as contributor*, 30, 122, 497, 605, 648, 658, 693–694, 799, 862, 909, 947, 1166, 1196, 1202–1203, 1240–1241, 1307–1308, 1391, 1525–1526
Powers Studio, 573
Powhatan (ship), 629, 1515
P. P. Werlein and Halsey, 1101
Prairie Grove, Arkansas, 53, 561, **1246–1247**, 1427
Pratt, Daniel, 506
Pratt, Nathaniel A., 1148
Preachers. *See* Chaplains; Sermons
Prentiss, Joseph, Shiloh campaign, 1420, 1422, 1423, 1427
Prepare for Battle (revivalist tract), 459–461

Presbyterian Church, **1247**, 1320, 1321
Breckinridge, Robert J., 215, 216
Richmond, Virginia, 1330
Southern sermons, 1398, 1399
Presidency, Confederate, 251, 400–401, **1247–1249**
Davis, Jefferson. *See* Davis, Jefferson
First Lady, 456–457
term of office, 383, 400, 1068, 1146
White House, 1710
see also Politics
Presidency, U.S.
Johnson, Andrew. *See* Johnson, Andrew
Lincoln, Abraham. *See* Lincoln, Abraham
Presidential elections. *See entries titled* Election
Presidios, Confederate utilization, 623
Press. *See* Censorship; Freedom of the press; Newspapers; War correspondents; particular publications
Press Association of the Confederate States, 641, 671
Preston, John Smith, 300, 398, 467, 790, **1249–1250**
Preston, John Thomas Lewis, 741, 1671
Preston, Margaret Junkin, 936
Preston, Sally ("Buck"), 790
Preston, Walter, 975, **1250**
Preston, William, **1250**
on legal profession, 1489
Preston, William Ballard, 260, 1096, **1250–1251**, 1305
Price, Giles, 643
Price, Sterling, 196, 474, 747, 800, 890, **1251–1252**, 1323, 1356
Arkansas campaign, 55–57, 141, 274, 1568, 1696
arrest of Marmaduke (John Sappington), 1679
battle flag, 586
caricature, *1054*
Corinth, Mississippi, 413
Elkhorn Tavern, Arkansas, 526, 713
Iuka, Mississippi, 825, 891
Missouri expedition inquiry, 493
Missouri raid. *See* Price's Missouri raid
Missouri State Guard, 829, 1053
politics, 412
Red River campaign, 490, 1315, 1317, 1610
scouts, 38, 1599
staff, 408, 683, 1159, 1483
sword, 514
Wilson's Creek campaign, 1606, 1729, 1730, 1731
Price, Birch and Company, slave pen, *1452*
Prices
cotton fluctuation, 417
extortion, 559–560
salt, 18, 566
of slaves, 554, 1234, 1413, *1436*, 1437, 1443, 1453
see also Impressment; Inflation; Speculation
Price's Missouri raid, 53, 57, 68, 343, 561, 695, 827, 829, 1009, 1053, 1055, **1252–1255**, 1323, 1409, 1610, 1652
map, 1253
Prigg v. Pennsylvania, 649–650
Primary sources. *See* Museums and archives
Primogeniture, 1437–1438
"Prince John." *See* Magruder, John B.
Prince of Wales (ship), 674
Princess Royal (ship), 1120
Princeton, Arkansas, 1409
Princeton (ship), 62, 1629
Pringle, Jane, 1318
Printmaking, 1231, **1255–1256**
Burial of Latané, 242, *243*
paper money, 436
stamps, 1242
Treasury notes and bonds, 1024–1025, 1614
Prioleau, Charles K., 180
Prisoners of war, 941, **1256–1264**
African American guards, 1259
African American Union soldiers, 564, 779, 1278, 1353
civilian, 265, 439, 543, 544, 640, 727, 728; *see also subhead* political *below*
commissary general, 1351
conditions, 1222, 1258–1261
congressional inquiry, 1250
Danville, Georgia, 444
deaths, 338
escape attempts, 144–145, 504, 931, 1222, 1259, 1723
exchanges, 1, 11, 121, 125, 135, 136, 144, 202, 227–228, 238, 254, 311, 361, 385, 465, 498, 610, 648, 692, 695, 700, 705, 708, 716, 736, 759, 761, 769, 800, 921, 931, 1076, 1177, 1179, 1183, 1203, 1229, 1256–1258, 1262–1263, 1266, 1268, 1309, 1322, 1353, 1540, 1572, 1596, 1599, 1681, 1688, 1696, 1713, 1723
executions, 11, 724, 1353
Fort Pillow massacre, 616
Gettysburg, *1499*
Grimes (Bryan) opinion of Northern, 718
Harpers Ferry, West Virginia, 742, 744
land mine testing on, 725
officers, 1258–1259
political, 1261-1263, 1361; *see also subhead* civilian *above*
privateers, 533, 1269
rations, 38, 610, 1158, 1260, 1261, *1263*
recruitment of, 654
Spotsylvania, 1520
tories, 1602
treatment, 51, 203, 1259, 1353
women spies, 714
see also particular prisons
Prisons, **1265–1268**
Andersonville, **38–40**
Belle Isle, **154–155**
Castle Pinckney, *1265*, 1266, 1507
Castle Thunder, **265–266**, 727, 767, 1266
conditions, 38, 39, 610, 1258–1261, 1262, 1362
deaths, 338
Fort Delaware, **610**
Fort Warren, Massachusetts, 447
Gardner, W. M., 658
Godwin, Archibald, 693
Harpers Ferry, West Virginia, 740
hospitals, 796
Irving, *609*
Johnson's Island, **856–857**
Kilpatrick-Dahlgren raid, **892–893**
Libby, **930–932**
Point Lookout, 504, **1221–1222**
religious services, 283
Richmond, Virginia, 1598; *see also subhead* Castle Thunder *above*
Salisbury, 342, **1361–1362**
sites, 1256
Stoneman's raid, 1546–1547
Union, 447, 716, 1353
Virginia, 1666–1667
Winder, John H., 1734
Wirz, Henry, 1735
Pritchard, Russ A., *as contributor*, 96–102, 464–465, 513–514, 734–735, 1179–1180, 1455–1458, 1459–1461, 1461–1464
Privateers, 979, **1269**
Beall, John Y., 144–145
captured, 1256–1257

Privateers, *continued*
Chesapeake (ship), 258
commerce raiders versus, 373
Enchantress affair, **533**, 841, 1269
Jefferson Davis, 533, 831, 841, 1269
letters of marque and reprisal, 373, 480, 979, 1269
prosecution, 1353
Savannah, 1369
Webb, 1697
"Private History of a Campaign that Failed, The" (Twain), 354
Private property. *See* Confiscation; Impressment
Proclamation of Amnesty and Reconstruction, 1578
Procurement
decentralized distribution, 698–699
foreign supplies, 1140
horses and mules, 793
impressment, **809–810**
see also Anglo-Confederate purchasing; Quartermaster Bureau; Supplies
Produce loan, 392, 509–510, 1248, **1269–1270**, 1285, 1385, 1615, 1616
Provisional Congress, 1069
Produce Loan Bureau, 419, 1615
Progressive school, historiography, 317–318
Prohibition movement, 596, 1034, 1285–1286, 1488
Projectiles
canister, 61–62, 93, 94, 95, 101
conical, 98, 101, 102
excavation, 103
Propaganda, **1270–1272**
Charleston Mercury (newspaper), 1326
Copperheads, 412
Fitzhugh, George, 583–584
Hotze, Henry, 798
Index (newspaper), **810**
Lincoln, Abraham, 934
Macaria; or, Altars of Sacrifice (Evans), 547
Palmer, John, 544
postwar anti-Confederate, 1735
printmaking, 1255
response to Emancipation Proclamation, 532
Southern Unionist, 688
Tyson, Bryan, 1631
Volck (Adalbert) etchings, 1673
Proslavery, **1272–1275**
Alabama Platform, 1678
Bleeding Kansas, 175–176
Brownlow, William G., 230
Calhoun, John C., 252–253
doctrine, 1221
Dred Scott decision, 493–495
fire-eaters. *See* Fire-eaters
Fitzhugh, George, 583–584
Hammond, James H., 730
Kansas riots, 1561
Lecompton constitution, 176, 322, 348, 465, 687, 875
magazines, 985, 986
Ruffin, Edmund, 1349, 1350
South Carolina, 403
and Southern nationalism, 1113
state rights defense, 1533–1535
see also Antislavery; Racism; Secession; Slavery
Prosser, Gabriel, 1440
Prosthetics, 1052, 1181
Prostitution, 428, 562, 923, **1276–1277**, 1740
Butler's woman order, 246–247
Charleston, South Carolina, 285
increase in, 671
Little Rock, Arkansas, 941
Macon, Georgia, 978
Nashville, Tennessee, 1110
Wilmington, North Carolina, 1726
Protestant churches, 1321, 1709
Bible societies, 164
see also Chaplains; Religion; Sermons; particular denominations and sects
Protestant Episcopal Church. *See* Episcopal Church
Provisional Army of the Confederate States, 64, 66; *see also* Army, Confederate
Provisional Congress. *See under* Congress, Confederate
Provisional Constitution. *See under* Constitution, Confederate
Provost marshal, 1039, **1277–1278**
prisoners, 265
Taylor, Thomas Hart, 1572
Winder, John H., 1734
Pruitt, Paul M., Jr., *as contributor*, 14–19
Pryne, Abraham, 230
Pryor, Roger A., 367, 629, 808, **1278–1279**
Psychological trauma of war, 460
Public debt. *See* Debt
Public finance, 509–511, 1025, **1279–1286**
confiscation of Northern property, 388–389
see also Bonds; Currency; Debt; Produce loan; Taxation
Public health. *See* Health and medicine
Public schools. *See* Education, primary and secondary
Publishing
Bible societies, 165
broadsides, **221–222**
journals and diaries, 471, 472
music, 1101, 1103
textbooks, 516
Turner, Joseph A., 1625–1626
see also Book publishing; Literature; Magazines; Newspapers
Puerperal fever, 754
Pugh, James Lawrence, *15*, **1286–1287**
Pulaski Gun Factory, 1458
Pulmonary tuberculosis, occurrence and treatment, 755
Puncheon Creek, Kentucky, 857
Punishment. *See* Crime and punishment; Hanging
Purchasing. *See* Anglo-Confederate purchasing; Erlanger loan; New Plan; Procurement; Quartermaster Bureau
Puryear, Richard C., **1288**
Putnam, H. S., 630
Putnam, Richard, 222
Putnam, Sallie A. *See* Brock, Sallie A.
Putnam (ship), 841
Putnam's Monthly (magazine), 987
"P. W. A" (pseudonym). *See* Alexander, Peter
Pyemia, fatalities, 757
Pyron, Charles, 692

Q

Quadroon, 1045, 1046
Quaker guns, *95*, 619
Quakers. *See* Society of Friends
Quantrill, William Clarke, 38, 68, 719, 720, 721–722, 724, 725, 815, 839, 888, 1053–1054, **1289**, *1290*, 1599, 1608, 1754
raiders, 68–69, *719*
Quapaws, 811, 812, 813, **1290**
Quarles, William Andrew, **1290–1291**
Quartermaster Bureau, **1291–1292**, 1685
Atlanta, Georgia, 109, 110
bill, *393*
frauds, 377, 876, 1292
horse shortage, 792
infantry equipment, 817

Jackson, Alfred Eugene, 827
Lawton, Alexander R., 910
Myers, Abraham C., 1106
slave labor, 901
Southern Express Company, 1514
textile production, 717
uniform issuance, 1634
war mobilization, 508–509
Queen of the West (ship), 55, 420
"Quel Qu' Un" (pseudonym), 1683
Quids (state rights advocates), 1532
Quinby & Robinson, 98
Quinine
malaria treatment, 591, 755, 758
substitutes, 1559
Quintard, Charles T., 1320
Quintero, José Augustín, 1037
Quitman, John A., 31, 173, 454, 458, 557, 808, 1047
Quitman Guard, 1052

R

Rable, George C., *as contributor*, 1318–1320
"Raccoon Roughs" (Georgia), 696
Racism
antebellum, 1113
British, 1273
literature, 938
miscegenation fears, *1044*
Union Army, 1007
urban, 1647
see also Proslavery
Radcliffe, Thomas W., 1179
Radicalism, Southern. *See* Fire-eaters; Secession
Radical Republicans, election of 1864, 1632
Radley, Kenneth, *as contributor*, 1038–1039, 1277–1278
Raid, The (film), 580
Raiders. *See* Commerce raiders
Raids and Romance of Morgan and His Men (Ford), 193, 1232
Railroad Raiders, The (film), 577
Railroad Redoubt, 621
Railroads, 386, **1293–1299**, 1612
Andrews raid, 41, 109, 674, 1298, 1574
and antebellum urbanization, 52, 1645–1646
black laborers, 74
centralization, 1326, 1617
Confederate-built, 714, 1297, 1648
cotton transportation, 417
engineer regiments, 534–535
Georgia, 108, 109, 670, 673
Greensboro, North Carolina, 714–715, 1294
guerrilla raids, 328, 607, 608, 722, 723, 725, 783-784, 1049, 1051, 1298-1299; *see also subhead* Stoneman's raids *below*; *subhead* Stuart's raids *below*; *subhead* Andrews raid *above*
Holly Springs, Mississippi, raid, 783–785
impact on agriculture, 565
impressed slave labor, 1426
increased mileage, 506
Jackson, Mississippi, 837
Lynchburg, Virginia, 962, 963, 1297
mail-hauling rates, 1242
Nashville, Tennessee, 1107
nationalization, 452, 667–668, 1538
New Mexico Territory, 983
Norfolk, Virginia, 1149
North Carolina, 714–715, 1085, 1294
seaport competition, 1612
Selma, Alabama, 1387, 1388
Shenandoah Valley, 1412, 1413, 1415, 1416
Stoneman's raids, 1546, 1547
strategic significance, 109, 156, 289, 326, 685, 698, 714, 962, 1110, 1655, 1659
Stuart's raids, 1556
supply substitutes, 1559
Tallahassee, Florida, 1566
track gauges, 1294, 1297
transcontinental military, 450
U.S. military, 1298, 1299
Virginia, 962, 1330, 1332, 1546, 1547, 1556, 1664
War Department control, 1285
Wilmington, North Carolina, 1726
see also particular railroads
Rains, Gabriel J., 336, 734, **1299–1300**, 1685
Rains, George W., 90, 336, 1168, 1246, 1363, 1388, 1470
Rains, James Edwards, 1095, **1300**, 1649
Raleigh, North Carolina, **1300–1301**
hospitals, 794
newspapers, 1142
powder works, 1245
refugees, 1318
Union occupation, 1153
Raleigh (ship), 840, 1124, 1126, 1727
Raleigh Bayonet Factory, 514
socket bayonet, *513*
Raleigh Register (newspaper), 421, 1142
Raleigh Sentinel (newspaper), 1142, 1627
Raleigh Standard (newspaper), 201, 207, 273, 314, 1142, 1156
Ralls, John Perkins, **1302**
Ramage, James A., *as contributor*, 238–239, 846–847, 880, 1086–1087, 1088–1089
Rams, **1302–1304**
Laird, 240, 484, **903–904**, 1124, 1157, 1303
see also Ironclads
Ramsay, Henry Ashton ("Harry"), 289, 290
Ramsay, James Graham, **1304**
Ramsdell, Charles W., 386–387
Ramseur, Dodson, 271, 504, 582, 583, 1151, **1304–1305**, 1733
Chancellorsville campaign, 422, 718
Shenandoah division, 1418, 1419
Randal, Horace, 974, **1305**
Randall, James G., 318
Randall, James Ryder, 936, 937, 985, 1103
Randolph, George Wythe, 171, 174, 907, 1083, 1188, 1300, **1305–1306**
likeness on Treasury note, *436*, 438
resignation, 1385, 1474
as secretary of war, 251, 255, 273, 396, 410, 1191, 1297, 1684, 1686
Randolph, John, 44, 1532
Randolph, Victor M., 236, 1062, **1307**
Randolph County, North Carolina, peace movement, 1183
Ranger (ship), 685
Ransom, John Crowe, 938
Ransom, Matt Whitaker, **1307**
Ransom, Robert, Jr., 288, 496, **1307–1308**
on Smith (Gustavus W.), 1474
Ransom, Roger L., *as contributor*, 69–71, 1232–1235
Rape, 427
Raphall, Morris Jacob, 1275
Rapidan River, 1001, 1520
Mine Run campaign, 1043
Stoneman's raids, 1546
Rapier, John, 643
Rappahannock River
bridge, 502
Fredericksburg campaign, 918
Stoneman's raids, 1546
Stuart's raids, 1556
Rappahannock (ship), 375, **1308**, *1309*
Rappahannock Military Academy, 990
Raritan (ship), 700

Rations. *See* Commissary Bureau; Food
Rattlesnake (ship), 1107, 1269; *see also* *Nashville* (ship)
Rattlesnakes (Georgia unit), 1215
Ravenel, St. Julien, 969
Raymond, Henry J., caricature, *933*
Rayner, Kenneth, 28, 1154, 1668
Ray of Light, A; or, A Treatise on the Sectional Troubles Religiously and Morally Considered (Tyson), 1183, 1631
Read, Charles W., 592, **1308–1310**, 1697
Read, Henry English, **1310**
Read, Theodore, 47
Read and Watson, 1456, 1457, 1465
Reade, Edwin G., 107, 687, **1310–1311**
Readjuster party, 990
Reagan, John H., *250*, 812, 911, 991, 1164, **1311–1313**, 1523, 1585
as postmaster general, 252, 315, *1241*–1242
as secretary of treasury, 1024
Reams' Station, 983, 1200, 1341
Reaves, George A., III, *as contributor*, 691, 779–780, 783–785, 825, 1420–1423
Rebel War Archives (National Archives), 1688
Rebel War Clerk's Diary, A (Jones), 865, 866, 1684
Recollections of Henry Watkins Allen (Dorsey), 492
Recollections of Mississippi and Mississippians (Davis), 455–456
Reconstructed Rebel, A (film), 574
Reconstruction
Alabama, 610, 927–928, 1059, 1287
Arkansas, 54, 661, 736
class conflict, 346
Florida, 1682
Georgia, 230, 750, 773–774
Johnson (Andrew) policies, 848–849, 956, 1699
Lincoln (Abraham) policies, 729, 956, 1097
Louisiana, 685, 952, 956, 1138, 1348, 1698–1699
Mississippi, 24, 226, 455, 748, 800–801, 960, 962, 1694
North Carolina, 107, 690, 708, 782, 911, 912, 1627, 1651
Sea Islands (South Carolina), 1104, 1240, 1741
seen as antiwhite conspiracy, 788
severity of, 725
South Carolina, 133, 732, 1026, 1240, 1741
Tennessee, 139, 231, 686, 1138, 1577–1579
Virginia, 124, 187, 1187–1188, 1332
and women, 1742
Recordings. *See* Discography
Recreation. *See* Leisure
Recruitment
black troops in Union Army, 1217
of foreigners, 339, 980–981, 1261
naval, 1131
Provisional Army, 64, 66
see also Conscription; Soldiers
Rector, Henry M., 52, 588, 659, 701, 702, 703, **1313–1314**
Recusant conscripts. *See* Desertion
Redans, 619, 625
Red Badge of Courage, The (novel by Crane), 938
Red dogs. *See* Shinplasters
Rede, William Lemon, 1590
Red Fort, Alabama, 622
Red Legs, 721, 722
Redmoor, 1350
Redoubts, 619, 620, 625
Red River campaigns, 893, 955, 961, 1238, **1314–1317**, 1585
Arkansas, 12
Debray, Xavier, 461
Dockery, Thomas, 490
Gray, Henry, 709
Green, Thomas, 713
Lane, Walter, 908
Mansfield, Louisiana, 1004–1005
maps, 1315, 1316
Missouri (ship), 1055
Mouton, Alfred, 1092
Price, Sterling, 1252
Randal, Horace, 1305
Steele, William, 1538
Taylor, Richard, 121, 461, 713, 955, 1305, 1315, 1316, 1317, 1572, 1610, 1696
Terrell, Alexander W., 1581
Trans-Mississippi, 1223, 1609–1610
see also Arkansas campaign of 1864
Red Rover (ship), 726
Red Shirt movement, 246
Red Strings. *See* Heroes of America
Redwood, Alan Christian, 1231
Reel Life, documentaries, 572
Reenactments, battle, 572, 573, **1317–1318**
Rees, David, 1206
Refugeeing, **1318–1320**
African American, 1235
Atlanta, Georgia, 110, 1318
Baton Rouge, Louisiana, 141
Chattanooga, Tennessee, 292
children, 307
Columbia, South Carolina, 370
Indian, 310, 425
Little Rock, Arkansas, 941
Louisiana, 956
Macon, Georgia, 978
Memphis, Tennessee, 1030
plain folk, 1213
social class and, 1491
Stone (Kate) diary description, 1546
Trans-Mississippi, 1608–1609
undermining traditional authority, 6
urban, 346, 596, 1235, 1318, 1491
women, 1741
Regiment
common formation, 819
organization of, 816
see also particular regiments
Regionalism. *See* Sectionalism
Regular Army, 64
Rehm, Karen G., *as contributor*, 914–915
Reid, Samuel, 1683
Reid, Whitelaw, 411, 1299
Reidenbaugh, Lowell, *as contributor*, 35–36, 50–51, 134, 135–136, 144, 211–212, 277–278, 368, 422, 490, 493, 569, 581, 696–697, 780, 844, 849–850, 882–883, 891–892, 907–908, 914, 926–927, 968, 972, 982–983, 989–990, 1190–1191, 1341, 1432–1433, 1503–1504, 1544, 1592, 1738, 1744
Reidy, Joseph P., *as contributor*, 405–406, 899–903
R. E. Lee: A Biography (Freeman), 167
R. E. Lee Camp Soldiers' Home of Virginia, 1502
Relic rooms, 1028
Relief. *See* Free markets; Poor relief; State socialism
Religion **1320–1321**
Bible societies. *See* Bible Societies
chaplains, **282–283**, 1320, 1321, 1586
clergymen's social role, 1489
death and mourning, 460
doubts and defeatism, 334
fast days, 568–569
Georgia churches, 108, 672
Indian missionaries, 297
Little Rock, Arkansas, 940–941
mill families, 1489
Nashville, Tennessee, 1108
patriotism equated with, 1399

peace church tax, 1031
plain folk, 1212
prisoner ministrations, 1259
refugees, 1319
revivalism, 460, 535, 1034, 1490
righteousness of cause, 476, 832; *see also subhead* sermons *below*
Sabbath-breaking, 363–364
sermons, **1398–1400**
slave, 1449–1450
slave marriages, 564
slavery issue, 476, 535, 551, 961, 1247, 1320, 1399
slavery justification, 1274, 1275
soldiers' beliefs, 1498–1499
and Southern homogeneity, 1112
women, 520, 923, 1741
yeomen, 1490
see also Bible; particular denominations and sects
Relyea, C. J., 1472
Remington revolvers. *See* Handguns
Reminiscences. *See* Diaries, letters, and memoirs
Reminiscences of an Active Life (Lynch), 962
Reminiscences of General Basil W. Duke, C. S. A. (Duke), 498
Renaiscence. *See* Southern Renaiscence
Reneau, Sallie Eola, 516
Rennie, William, 1411
Reno, Jesse L, 1513
Renshaw, William B., 656
Reorganized Government of Virginia, 1700, 1702
Reporters. *See* Freedom of the press; Newspapers; War correspondents
Repressible Conflict, The (Craven), 318
Republican Banner (Nashville newspaper), 1143
Republican party, 1225, **1321–1322**
antislavery caricature, *933*, *1044*
as antislavery party, 1375, 1377, 1441, 1534
Arkansas, 54
caning of Sumner (Charles), 1560–1562
Crittenden Compromise, 429
Dred Scott decision, 494, 495
election of 1856, 322, 1321
election of 1860, 285, 521–524, 1322, 1375–1376
election of 1864, 1044
emergence, 451
and expansion of slavery, 321–322, 558
formation, 1375
growth, 466
Kansas-Nebraska Act, 176
Louisiana, 956, 1348, 1699
North Carolina governorship, 1640
Radical, 411
and secessionist movement, 1379, 1380, 1381
views on slavery, 4, 320
see also Democratic-Republican party; Lincoln, Abraham; Reconstruction
Republic of Jones. *See* Jones County, Mississippi
Resaca, Georgia, 112, 113, 519, 674
Resolute (ship), 1334, 1370, 1603
Resources of the Southern Fields and Forests, Medial, Economical, and Agricultural (Porcher), 193, 757, 758
Restored Government of Virginia, 1187
"Reveille" (song), 1105
Review in the Debate of the Virginia Legislature of 1831 and 1832 (Dew), 1273
Revisionism, historiograpic, 318
Revivalism, 460, 535, 1034, 1490, 1709
Revolvers. *See under* Handguns
Reynolds, Alexander Welch, **1322**
Reynolds, Daniel Harris, **1323**
Reynolds, John E., 1073
Reynolds, John F., 678, 679, 1001
Reynolds, Joseph J., 57, 661
Reynolds, Thomas C., 305, 701, 702, 703, 828, 1052, 1054, 1055, 1252, 1254, **1323**
Rhett, Alfred, 497
Rhett, Robert Barnwell, Jr., 1067, 1143, 1326
Rhett, Robert Barnwell, Sr., 119, 133, 309, 400, 423, 463, 497, 568, 876, 877, 1225, 1297, **1323–1326**, 1716, 1748, 1749
Bluffton movement, 186
criticism of Davis (Jefferson), 1510
editorials, 1143
fire-eater label, 582, 1323, 1350, 1376–1377, 1383, 1506, 1507
Montgomery convention, 1507
nullification controversy, 1159
Rheumatism, treatment for, 755
Rhodes, James Ford, 317, 336, 1264
Rhodes, Rufus, 1181
Rice, 1214, **1327–1328**
crop value, 554–555
plantation overseers, 1174–1175
slave labor, 552
South Carolina, 1504
Rice, Otis K., *as contributor*, 1699–1703, 1705–1706
Richards, Adolphus, 724, 725
Richardson, Israel, 1408
Richardson, John, 421, 1714, 1715
Richardson, Lucien W., 266
Richardson, Robert Vinkler, **1328–1329**
Richmond, Virginia, **1329–1333**
antebellum population, *1642*, 1643, 1645
arsenal and armory, 90, 1455–1456, 1458, 1464, 1470, 1471
bread riots, 212–213, 346, 1226, 1306, 1331, 1669, 1740
as capital of Confederacy, 148, 360, 383, 452, 1066, 1069, *1379*, 1647, 1663, 1684
Capitol building, *1331*
crime, 428
defenses, 25, 45, 76, 82, 149, 299, 326, 534, 550, 619–620, 621, 625, 646, 686, 690, 696, 716–717, 775, 834, 1191, 1306
emancipationist sentiment, 1378
free black population, 642
free markets, 641, 1229
hospitals, 222, 794, 795–796, 1160, 1161, 1600
Irish immigrants, 822
Lee-Jackson defense, 1412
Libby Prison, 930–932
life in, 1741
manufacturing, 1659, 1664; *see also* Tredegar Iron Works
maps, 1329, *1665*
martial law imposition, 727, 761
military governorship, 314
mining, 1043, 1044
Monument Avenue, 923, 1069, 1074
monuments, 922–923, 951, 1069, *1070*
munitions manufacture, 1470, 1471
newspapers, 1141–1142, 1330
plot to burn, 441
population and urban ranking, *1658*
printmaking, 1255
prisons, 265–266, 693, 1266, 1268, 1598
prostitution, 1276, 1277
railroads, 1294, 1297
refugees in, 1491
roads, 1338
Rocketts Ship Yard, 1424
ruins, *1668*
siege, 1268, 1648
slave price drop, 1453
slave resistance, 1440

Richmond, Virginia, *continued*
slave trade, 1453
social events, 1397
spy ring, 1652
theaters, 1589
torpedo launches, 1515–1516
Union advance on (1862), 1400–1401, 1402–1403, 1416, 1553, 1554
Union advance on (1864), 1553
Union occupation, 1420
White House, 1710–1711
Yellow Tavern, Virginia, 1751
Richmond (ship), 840, 841, 960, 1124, 1126, 1236, 1303, 1424, 1697
Richmond and Danville Railroad, 45–48, 239, 1085, 1547
Richmond and York River Railroad, 1330
Richmond-class ironclads, 824
Richmond Dispatch (newspaper), 274, 529–530, 1683
Richmond during the War: Four Years of Personal Observations by a Richmond Lady (Brock), 222
Richmond Enquirer (newspaper), 712, 742, 965, 1081, 1244, 1276, 1277, 1330, 1619
Richmond Examiner (newspaper), 153, 213, 273, 314, 345, 532, 911, 1078, 1082, 1083, 1228–1229, 1243, 1330, 1662
Richmond, Fredericksburg, and Potomac Railroad, 541, 1330, 1546, 1751
Richmond Gas Works, 125
Richmond Howitzers, 91, 407, 1305, 1306, 1516
Richmond Naval Ordnance Works, output, 1121
Richmond Naval Squadron, 1126
Richmond under Three Flags (film), 573
Richmond Whig (newspaper), 148
Rich Mountain, West Virginia, 465
Ricketts, James B., 504, 998, 1406
Riddle, A. J., 1206, *1263*
Ride around McClellan. *See under* Stuart, J. E. B.
Ridge, John, 1693
Ridgely, J. V., *as contributor*, 938–939
Ridgway, Robert, 1142
Ridman method, 1117
Rifle
ammunition, 1470–1471
Blakely, 49, 50, 93, 94, 103
Brooke, 93, 96, 97, 223, *1117*
Brooke double- and triple-banded, 223, *1117*
Continental imports, 1468–1469
Enfield, 63, 90, 182, 232, 918, 1169
English imports, 918, 1465, 1466, 1467
infantry, 818, 819
naval ordnance design, 1117–1118
ordnance, 61, 93, 94, 101, 102
Parrott, 61, 93, 96, 99, *100*, 287
production at Harpers Ferry, 739–740
Whitworth, 49, 50, 93, *103*, 192, 918, 1467
see also Rifle-musket
Rifle and Infantry Tactics (Hardee), 193, *194*, 737, 1040, 1059
Rifled guns, 61, 62, 93, 992
English manufacture, 1119–1120
Fort Pulaski, Georgia, 616, 619
Rifle-musket, 60, 62, 63, 94
Austrian imports, 918
Belgian imports, 919
captured U.S., 1462
English imports, 915, 916, 917
infantry use, 60, 624, 818, 819
Springfield, 62
tactics, 325
Rifle pits, 624, 626
Rigdon, Charles H., 1459; *see also* Leech and Rigdon
Rigdon, Ansley, and Company, 1459, 1460
Rillieux, Norbert, **1333**, 1559–1560
Rillieux, Vincent, 1333
Rinaldo (ship), 1620
Ring-and-lance tournaments, 923
Ringgold Gap, 708
Riordan, Bartholomew, 1684
Riots. *See* Baltimore riot; Bread riots
Ripley, Roswell Sabine, 1020, **1333–1334**
Rise and Fall of the Confederate Government, The (Davis), 150, 166, 201, 317, 453, 476, 629, 1536
Ritchie, Thomas, 465
River Defense Fleet, 420, **1334**
River Queen (ship), 732, 804
Rivers, Prince, **1335**
Rivers. *See* Waterways; particular rivers
Rives, Alfred L., 1685
Rives, William C., 403, 804, 1215, **1335–1338**, 1690
Roads, 94, **1338–1340**, 1612, *1613*
Alabama, 18
Valley Turnpike, 1732
Roane, Archibald, 1615
Roane, John Selden, 1211, **1340**
Roane, Spencer, 1532
Roanoke (ship), 375, 1269
Roanoke Island, North Carolina, 178, 962, 1691
Burnside (Ambrose) expedition, 244, 245, 1152
Roanoke River, 1691
Roark, James L., *as contributor*, 1219–1221
Robert E. Lee (ship), 182, 184, **1340–1341**, 1723
Robert E. Lee Memorial Association. *See* Lee Memorial Association
Robert Gilfillan (ship), 1107
Robert McClelland (ship), 1530
Robert Mole Company, 515
Robert Napier & Sons, 184
Roberts, Charles, *as contributor*, 309–310
Roberts, John, 1495
Roberts, William Paul, **1341**
Robertson, Beverly Holcombe, 209, 210, 211, 267, 269, **1341–1342**
Robertson, Felix Huston, 968, **1342–1343**, 1363
Robertson, James I., Jr., *as contributor*, 58–59, 134, 171–172, 220–221, 224, 316–317, 357–358, 369, 408, 454, 505–506, 570–571, 651, 663–664, 733–734, 770–771, 830–835, 836, 868, 870–871, 881, 913, 943, 944, 1158, 1182, 1351–1352, 1413–1417, 1494–1501, 1543, 1548–1549, 1581–1582, 1621–1622, 1661–1669, 1676–1677, 1733–1734
Robertson, Jerome Bonaparte, 791, **1343**
Robertson, John, 794, 1600
portrait of Davis (Jefferson), 451
Robertson, William Glenn, *as contributor*, 71–74
Robertson & Company, 1411
Robertson Hospital (Richmond), 1160, 1600
Robinson, Charles, 175
Robinson, Cornelius, **1343**
Robinson, James F., 702, 887, 988
Robinson, Julia Augusta, 1186
Robinson, S. C., 1456
Robinson, Stuart, 216, 543
Robinson, W. Stitt, *as contributor*, 175–176
Robinson Revolver Factory, 1460
Rockbridge Artillery, 91, 93, 1190, 1516
Rocketts Navy Yard (Richmond), 1236, 1424
Rock Island, Illinois, 1258
Roddey, Philip Dale, 17, 440, **1343**, 1344

Rodes, Robert, 142, 369, 422, 504, 880, 1168, 1305, **1344–1345**, 1673, 1719
Chancellorsville campaign, 281
death of, 1418
Gettysburg campaign, 443, 677, 678, 679, 680, 682
Mine Run campaign, 1043
Seven Pines, Virginia, 696–697
Sharpsburg campaign, 1407–1408
Shenandoah campaign, 1418
South Mountain, Maryland, 1513
Winchester, Virginia, 1186, 1733
Rodman, I. P., 1408
Rodman gun, 62, 101
Rogers, Arthur L., 585
Rogers, Samuel St. George, **1345**
Rogers, William Warren, *as contributor*, 308–309
Rogers, William Warren, Jr., *as contributor*, 1064–1066
Roland, Charles P., *as contributor*, 858
Rolfe, John, 1597
"Roll Jordan Roll" (song), 1104
Roll of Honor, 1021
Roman, Alfred, 150
Roman, André Bienvenu, 424, 426, 628, **1345–1346**, *1382*
Roman, Jacques Etienne, 1345
Roman Catholic Church, 515, **1346**
American party. *See subhead* nativist prejudice *below*
Atlanta, Georgia, 108
chaplains, 282
free creoles, 644–645
nativist prejudice, 28, 602
nursing, 795, 1160, 1346
Richmond, Virginia, 1330
Semmes, Thomas, 1397
support for Confederate cause, 1320
urban, 1647
Romance. *See* Courtship; Lost Cause
Romantic Richmond (film), 573
Rome, Georgia, ordnance manufacture, 98
Roosevelt, Theodore, 239
Rootes, Thomas Reade, 362
Roper, John Lonsdale, 1150
Roper Hospital (Charleston), 1267
Rosecrans, William S., 204, 328, 475, 825, 857, 891, 1186, 1652, 1659–1660, 1700, 1703
Army of the Cumberland, 736
Chickamauga campaign, 302–304, 327
Corinth, Mississippi, 414, 415, 1049
Murfreesboro, Tennessee, 1094–1096
Price's Missouri raid, 1254, 1255
prostitutes, 1277
Tennessee, 291, 292–293, 676, 1577
Rosenburg, R. B., *as contributor*, 107–108, 358, 372–373, 438–439, 470, 657, 760–761, 798–799, 864–865, 876, 967, 1030–1031, 1502–1503, 1563, 1745–1746
Rose of the South, A (film), 574
Ross, Benjamin, 1623
Ross, Erasmus, 931
Ross, John, 297, 811, 813, 1693
Ross, Lawrence Sullivan, 1033, **1346–1347**
brigade, 1584
Rosser, Thomas Lafayette, 152, 271, 1183, 1209, **1347**
Hampton's Legion cavalry unit command, 732
harassment of Sheridan (Philip H.), 1419
Ross's Brigade, 1584
Rossville, Tennessee, 294
Rost, Pierre A., **1347–1348**
English mission, 418, 480, 803, 1347, 1748, 1749
French mission, 479, 480, 1347
Spanish mission, 1347–1348, 1513–1514, 1527
on *Trent* affair, 482
Roudanez brothers (Jean-Baptiste and Louis Charles), 1138, **1348**, 1621
Roughing It (Twain), 354
Round Mountain, 813, 1390
Rousseau, Lawrence, **1348–1349**
Rousseau, Lovell, 17, 1066, 1095
Rowan County Bible Society, 164
Royal Ape, The (Smith), 937
Royston, Grandison D., 662, **1349**
R. P. Parrott foundry, 96
Rudisell Gold Mine, 290
Ruffin, Edmund, **1349–1351**
filibustering expeditions, 808
fire-eater label, 582, 1324, 1376–1377
Fort Sumter attack, 1662
Ruffin, Thomas, 1154, **1351**, 1668
Ruffner, Henry, 45, 1186
Ruggles, Daniel, **1351–1352**
Baton Rouge, Louisiana, 141
Northern background, 1157
prison command, 1268
as provost marshal, 1277
Shiloh campaign, 1423
Rules of war, **1352–1353**
black soldiers, 11
Confederate purchasing agents, 42
torpedo use, 1603
Runnels, Ran, 176, 1145
Running the Blockade (Taylor), 129
Runyan, Morris C., 290
Rural life. *See* Community life; Farming; Plain folk; Yeomanry
Rush-Bagot agreement, 258
Russell, Charles Wells, **1353–1354**, 1700
Russell, David, 1418
Russell, John (Lord Russell)
Confederate diplomatic mission, 418, 480, 483, 712, 1016, 1748, 1749
Laird rams issue, 904
naval sales policy, 26, 240, 485
response to blockade of Confederate ports, 484, 631, 1353, 1454, 1528–1529, 1748
Trent affair, 481–482, 1620
Russell, William H., **1354**
Russellville, Kentucky, convention, 243, 311, 430, 851, 1075
Russia, **1354–1355**
diplomatic missions to, 385, 479, 484, 906, 1529
and Louis Napoleon tripartite proposal, 632
Rust, Albert, **1355–1356**
Ruth, David R., *as contributor*, 298–299
Ruth, Samuel, 541, 1331
Rutherfordton Enquirer (North Carolina newspaper), 942
Ryan, Abram, 388, 936, 1320
Ryan, William, 184

S

Saber bayonet, 60, *513*
Sabers, 60, 93, *1462*
Sabine Cross Roads, Louisiana. *See* Mansfield, Louisiana
Sabine Pass, Texas, 232, 823, **1357**, *1358*, 1609
Davis Guards, 1516
Sabotage. *See* Espionage; Guerrilla warfare
Sachem (ship), 656, 1357, *1358*, 1609
Sacramento, Kentucky, 606
Sacramento (ship), 1547
Sacramento Union (newspaper), 354
Sadd, Henry S., 381
Saddles, 793
Saffold, Georgia, shipyards, 1424
Sailors, **1358–1361**
St. Albans, Vermont, raid, 350, 538
St. Charles, Arkansas, amphibious operation, 1133
St. Elmo (Evans), 547

St. Gaudens, Augustus, 1073
St. John, Isaac M., 376, 378, **1361**, 1363, 1685
  Niter and Mining Bureau, 1147, 1148, 1168
St. Louis, Missouri
  arsenal, 647–648, 828, 1053
  emancipationist sentiment, 1378
  free black population, 1052
St. Louis Bulletin (newspaper), 1483
St. Mary's (ship), 375, 1269
St. Nicholas (ship), 783
St. Patrick (ship), 446
Saint Philip's Hospital and Aid Society (Atlanta), 109
Salaries. *See* Wages and salaries
Salem, North Carolina, 1084
Salem College, 520
Salient Works, 621
Salisbury, North Carolina
  food riots, 567
  hospitals, 794
  Stoneman's raid, 1152
Salisbury Prison, 155, 342, 693, 1152, 1259, *1262*, 1264, 1266, 1268, **1361–1362**
Sallie (ship), 1269
"Sallust." *See* Alexander, Peter
Salt, **1362**
  African American laborers, 74
  Alabama, 1426
  extraction process, 49
  Florida, 361, 588–589
  Georgia, 929
  impressment, 1480
  Louisiana, 955
  North Carolina, 1726
  prices, 18, 566
  shortages, 229, 596, 1082, 1244
  speculation, 1517
  Virginia, 596, 925, 929, 1724; *see also* Saltville Massacre
Saltpeter, 698, 699, **1363**
  artificial beds, 1470–1471
  manufacture, 370
  Niter and Mining Bureau, 1146–1147, **1361**
Saltville Massacre, Virginia, 1362, **1363**, 1547
Saluda Factory, 370
Sampson (ship), 1370, 1371
San Antonio, Texas, arsenal seizure, 1461, 1469
Sanborn, John B., 825
Sanders, Elizabeth Willis Boddie, 912
Sanders, George N., 349, 934
Sanders, John Caldwell Calhoun, **1364**
Sanders, Simon T., 658
Sanders, William, 896
Sanderson, John Pease, 412, **1364**
Sands. *See* Oktarharsars Harjo
Sandy Rangers, 843
Sanford, John, 493
San Francisco (ship), 1675
San Francisco Call (newspaper), 354
Sanitation
  army camp, 1496
  disease and, 754
  hospital, 795
  prison, 1259, 1268
San Jacinto (ship), 360, 481, 1015, 1454, 1619; *see also Trent* affair; Wilkes, Charles
Santa Anna, Antonio López de, 450, 1210
Santa Clara (ship), 841
Santa Rosa Island, Florida, 32, 613–614
Santee River, 1691
Santiago de Cuba (ship), 3
Santos, Refugio, and Cristobal Santos, 157
Sappers, 878
Sassacus (ship), 407
Satire. *See* Caricature; Jokes
Sattler, Richard A., *as contributor*, 1391
Saturday Evening Post (magazine), 300
Sauta Cave, Alabama, 1375
Savage's Station, Virginia, 654, 1192, 1193, 1400, *1401*
  Griffith, Richard, 718
  Magruder, John B., 989
Savannah, Georgia, *668*, **1364–1369**
  antebellum population, *1642*, 1645
  arsenal, 90
  blockade, 1647
  bread riots, 213
  campaign, 820, **1368–1369**, 1475
  city, **1364–1368**, *1365*
  evacuation of, *1368*, 1369
  free black population, 642, 643
  harbor defenses, 48, 685, 1300, 1302, 1681
  Irish immigrants, 822, 823
  population and urban ranking, *1658*
  prisons, 1267
  railroads, 1297
  Savannah Squadron defense. *See* Savannah Squadron
  shipyards, 1424, 1425
  slave trade, 1453
  surrender, 673
  Union occupation, 1367, 1640, 1648
  see also Fort Pulaski, Georgia
Savannah (ship), 372, 685, 879, 984, 1124, 1126, 1130, 1178, 1269, **1369**, 1370, 1425, 1530
Savannah Morning News (newspaper), 1683
Savannah Republican (newspaper), 853, 1144, 1683
Savannah Rifles, 1215
Savannah River, 1368, 1369, 1370, 1691
Savannah Squadron, 1369, **1370**, 1425
  Dallas, Moses, 441
  ships, 1124, 1303
  Tombs, James H., 1600
Saxton, Rufus, 10, 1335
Sayler's Creek (Virginia), 36, 46, 83, 694, 850, 916, 1008, 1624
Scalawags, 927
Scales, Alfred Moore, **1370**
Scantlon, David, 1105, 1495
Scarborough, William K., *as contributor*, 1174–1175, 1350–1351
Scarlet fever, 110, 945
Scary Creek, West Virginia, 843
Scavenging. *See* Foraging
Scharf, John Thomas, 434, **1371**
Schenkl projectiles, 98, 102
Schiller, Herbert M., *as contributor*, 754–759, 1022
Schmier, Louis E., *as contributor*, 845–846
Schneider and Glassick, 1460, 1461
Schoenmakers, Father, 1173
Schoepf, Albin Francisco, 610
Schofield, John M., 163, 173, 262, 296, 633, 634, 790, 1006, 1007, 1188
  Atlanta campaign, 111
  Dalton, Georgia, 442
  Greensboro, North Carolina, 715
Schools. *See* Education; Teachers; particular institutions
Schoonover, Thomas, *as contributor*, 1063, 1145, 1209–1210
Schott, Thomas E., *as contributor*, 415, 730–732, 1067–1069, 1538–1542, 1542–1543, 1654–1655
Schreiner, Herman L., 1101
Schroeder-Lein, Glenna R., *as contributor*, 152–153, 867, 1077, 1146–1148, 1361, 1363, 1549–1550
Schult, Frederick, *as contributor*, 33–35, 561, 1150, 1616–1617
Schultz, Marvin, *as contributor*, 1, 1342–1343, 1624
Schweikart, Larry, *as contributor*, 128–129, 1424
Schweninger, Loren, *as contributor*, 1590–1591
Scofield and Markham Iron Works, 108, 1122

Scorched-earth policy, 200, 361, 1006, 1217, 1352
Scorpion (ship), 445, 840, 903, 904
Scotland, ship construction, 484, 673, 1150
Scott, Anne Firor, *as contributor*, 1738–1742
Scott, George W., 1567
Scott, H. L., 600
Scott, J. K., 1556
Scott, J. L., *as contributor*, 967–968, 1210
Scott, John S., 1093
Scott, Robert Eden, **1371**
Scott, S. S., 812
Scott, Thomas, **1371–1372**
Scott, Walter, 354
Scott, Winfield, 146, *381*, 382, 450, 605, 706, 916–917, 945, 1628, 1663, 1709
  Fort Sumter protection, 1526
  strategy and tactics, 326, 1040
Scows, 1692
Screen Telegram (documentary films), 572
Sculpture. *See* Art; Monuments and memorials
Scurry, William R., 692, **1372**, 1690
Scurvy, 39, 755, 1260
  treatment, 758
Sea Hawk (ship), 1269
Sea Islands, South Carolina
  cotton production, 1504
  music study, 1104
  Reconstruction community, 1240, 1741
  slave defectors, 1445
  slave drivers, 1433
Sea King (ship). *See Shenandoah*
Seal, Confederate States of America, *436*, 865
Searcy and Moore Company, 1457
Sears, Claudius Wistar, **1372–1373**
Seay, William A., 957
Secession, **1373–1383**
  Alabama, 14, 16, 141, 352, 444, 569, 664, 927, 963–964, 1057, 1065, 1302, 1343, 1378, *1379*, 1380, 1441, 1477, *1486*, 1678
  Alabama opposition, 720, 1477
  Arizona Territory, 983, 1174
  Arkansas, 52, 262, 629, 659, 662, 736, 776, 1056, 1313–1314, 1355, 1373, *1379*, 1382, 1441, *1486*, 1594, 1694
  banking effects, 128
  Baptist Church, 130
  border states, 195–196
  Calhoun, John C., 252, 253
  Charleston, South Carolina, 285
  cities and, 1647
  as Civil War cause, 322, 324
  Compromise of 1850 and, 1374–1375, 1383
  from Confederacy, 870, 1536
  constitutional grounds, 1067, 1534–1535
  cooperationist view, 411, 1379, 1380
  Crittenden Compromise, 429, 803
  Davis (Varina) concerns, 456–457
  Democratic party, 466
  drawbacks, 1114
  economic factors, 1376, 1377
  election of 1860 and, 522, 524, 1171, 1373, 1376, 1377, 1379, 1384, 1506, 1507, 1562
  fire-eaters, **582**, 788, 1376–1377, 1747–1748, 1749
  Florida, 28, 32, 581, 589, 776, 991, 1013, 1196, 1345, 1378, 1380, 1441
  Fort Sumter attack and, 629, 1382–1383
  Georgia, 29, 109, 153, 162, 228, 362, 363, 665, 667, 675, 772, 851–852, 853, 882, 909, 928, 929, 977, 1146, 1365–1366, 1378, 1380, 1441, 1551, 1601, 1623, 1744, 1745
  guerrilla activity, 720
  Harpers Ferry raid igniting, 742, 1506
  historical interpretations, 166, 1485
  imperialism and, 808
  Jones County, Mississippi, 870
  Kentucky, 216, 383, 528, 779, 851, 972, 987, 1011, 1062, 1709
  Louisiana, 2, 140, 464, 720, 778, 952–954, 1010, 1077, 1137, 1194, 1378, 1380, 1395, 1441, 1454
  in lower South, 1378–1382
  Mississippi, 23, 131, 135, 226, 351, 455, 527, 569, 598, 747–748, 836, 905–906, 979, 1047, 1203–1204, 1375, 1377, 1378, 1380, 1431, 1441, 1594, 1694, 1698, 1729
  Missouri, 383, 719, 1323, 1722
  Missouri Compromise and, 1373–1374
  New Mexico Territory, 983
  newspaper support, 1142, 1143
  nonslaveholders and, 344, 1485
  North Carolina, 45, 89, 206, 355, 423, 492, 529, 650, 654, 688–689, 706, 781, 906–907, 911, 975, 1085, 1151, 1156, 1184, 1373, 1441, 1626, 1726
  nullification controversy and, 1374
  plain folk and, 1212
  planters and, 1219
  radical leadership. *See subhead* fire-eaters *above*
  "Resistance or submission" rally, 1377
  sectionalism and, 360–361, 382–383
  selected bibliography, 169
  Semmes, Thomas, 1395
  sermon justifications, 1399
  slavery factor, 1441
  South Carolina, 133, 199–200, 245, 285, 298, 463, 666, 717, 876–877, 1171, 1249, 1324, 1350, 1373, 1375, 1377, 1378, 1379, 1441, 1506–1507, 1534, 1681, 1769
  Southern honor factor, 1375, 1377
  and Southern nationalism, 1111–1114
  Southern Unionist opposition, 1637–1638
  state rights basis, 1531, 1536
  Stephens (Alexander H.) position, 1539, 1542
  Tennessee, 138, 264, 291, 372, 491, 666, 667, 688, 745, 752–753, 847–848, 869, 894–895, 1098, 1373, 1382, 1441, 1574–1576, 1593, 1595
  Texas, 116, 231, 655, 705, 716, 720, 762–763, 961, 1133, 1311, 1378, 1380, 1441, 1583, 1637, 1706, 1715
  in upper South, 1380–1381, 1382–1383, 1384
  Virginia, 123, 443, 464, 663, 694, 780–781, 964, 1040, 1186–1187, 1250, 1278, 1350, 1354, 1373, 1382, 1384, 1441, 1506, 1662–1664, 1690, 1703
  Washington Peace Conference, 1689–1690
  see also Constitutional Union party; Declaration of Immediate Causes; Wilmot Proviso
Secession, Coercion and Civil War (Jones), 865
Secessionville, South Carolina, 1479
Second Confiscation Act, U.S., 9
Second Great Awakening, 1709
Second Manassas. *See* Manassas, Second
Second Texas Lunette, 621
Second U.S. Cavalry, 1472
Second Wheeling Convention. *See* Wheeling Convention
Secretaries of Confederate executive departments. *For discussion of duties and functions, see* Cabinet; Judiciary; Navy Department; Post Office Department; State Department; Treasury Department; War Department

Secret Order of the Star-Spangled Banner, 28
Secret Service. *See under* Espionage
Secret Service (film), *577–578*
Sectionalism
and future of slavery, 1377, 1378
rise of political, 1114
and secession, 360–361, 382–383
slavery causing, 319–320
see also Nationalism
Seddon, James A., 612, 1337, **1383–1387**, 1474, 1630, 1650
cotton exports, 1140–1141
on impressment, 1153, 1244
rules of war, 1352
as secretary of war, 114, 183, 187, 192, 212, 251, 252, 255–256, 274, 410, 723, 972, 1079, 1082, 1243, 1249, 1312, 1385–1387, 1607, 1684, 1685, 1686, 1687
Seddon, John, 1386
Sedgwick, John, 282, 501, 502, 637, 881, 1407, 1519
Sedition legislation, 273
See America First (film series), 573
Seeger, Pete, 487
Seibles, John J., 1477
Selby, Charles, 1590
Selcer, Richard, *as contributor*, 1208–1209, 1582
Selma, Alabama, **1387–1390**
arsenal, 90
city, **1387–1388**
ironworks. *See* Selma Iron Works
Naval Ordnance Works, 17, 97, 734, 863, 977, 979–980, 992, 1117, 1118, 1121, 1122, 1124, **1388–1389**, 1580
small arms and munitions manufacture, 1458, 1470
war industry, 1647, 1648
Wilson's raid, 17–18, 19, 173, 362, 607, 658, 673, 1066, 1388, **1389–1390**, 1410, 1648
Selma (ship), 236, 1062, 1126, 1387, 1581
ordnance, 1118
Selma Iron Works, 980, 1617
Selma Manufacturing Company, 979
Selma, Marion, and Memphis Railroad, 607
Selma Naval Foundry, 1387–1388
Selznick, David O., 574, 578
Seminole (ship), 1236
Seminoles, 253–254, 391, 425, 551, 810, 811, 812–813, **1390–1391**
Semmes, Myra Knox, 1397
Semmes, Paul J., 235, **1391**
Semmes, Raphael, 374, 375, 841, *879*, 992, 993, *1018*, 1057, *1127*, **1392–1394**, 1627, 1684
Alabama, 19, 904
Sumter, 1562
Semmes, Thomas, **1394–1397**, 1514
Semple, Henry, 1395
Semple, Letitia Tyler, 1160
Senate. *See* Congress
Seneca-Shawnees. *See* Eastern Shawnees
Senecas (Mingos), 811, 812, 813, **1398**
Sener, James B., 1683
Sentinel (Richmond newspaper), 1142
Sequatchie Valley, Tennessee, raid, 1087
Sequestration. *See* Confiscation
Sequestration Act of 1861, 388, 389, 391, 658, 659, 1202, 1385
Sequoyah syllabary, 810
Serious Address to the Rulers of America, on the Inconsistency of Their Conduct Respecting Slavery, A (Benezet), 43
Sermons, **1398–1400**
chaplains, 283
Methodist, 1034
see also Bible societies; Fast days
Service Afloat and Ashore during the War with Mexico (Semmes), 1392
Settle, Thomas, 1651
Seven Days' Battles, 361, 785, 849, 864, 891, 918, **1400–1401**
Army of Northern Virginia, 78
Baldwin Blues, 490
balloon use, 24, 126
captured Union small arms, 1461
casualties, 338, 1400–1401
defenses, 620
Field, Charles, 571
field fortifications, 625
Frayser's Farm, Virginia. *See* Frayser's Farm, Virginia
Gaines' Mill, Virginia. *See* Gaines' Mill, Virginia
Gregg, Maxcy, 717
Hill, A. P., 770
Holliday, Frederick, 783
Jackson, Thomas J. ("Stonewall"), 834, 1400, 1526
King's School House, Virginia. *See* King's School House, Virginia
Magruder, John B., 989
Malvern Hill, Virginia. *See* Malvern Hill, Virginia
map, 1401
Mechanicsville, Virginia. *See* Mechanicsville, Virginia
Pender, William Dorsey, 1190
railroad troop movement, 1298
Savage's Station, Virginia. *See* Savage's Station, Virginia
Scales, Alfred Moore, 1370
Seven Pines, Virginia. *See* Seven Pines, Virginia
Smith, Gustavus W., 1474
Stafford, Leroy, 1521
Starke, William Edwin, 1526
Stonewall Brigade, 1548–1549
Stuart, J. E. B., 1553
Thomas, Edward Lloyd, 1592
White Oaks Swamp, Virginia. *See* White Oaks Swamp, Virginia
Wise, Henry A., 1736
Wofford, William Tatum, 1738
Seven Pines, Virginia, 76, 212, 751, 844, 860, 862, 1192, 1193, **1402–1403**
Anderson, George B., 29
casualties, 1403
field fortifications, 625
Gordon, John, 696–697
Hampton, Wade, 731
Hopkins, Juliet, 1160
Johnston, Joseph E., 917
Longstreet, James, 945
Mahone, William, 990
map, 1403
Wirz, Henry, 1735
Seward, William H., 258, 319, 416, 687, 688
as Booth (John Wilkes) conspiracy target, 538, 545, 935
caricature, *933*
diplomacy, 480, 482, 485, 631, 632
Fort Sumter policy, 1381
and Great Britain, 21, 711, 1620
Hampton Roads Conference, 387, 733, 773, 804, 1184, 1541
Mexican scheme, 1210
peace negotiations, 123, 424, 628, 1345
Trent affair, 177, 1015, 1528, 1619
Sewing groups, 923
Sexias, James M., 181, 1726
Sexton, Francis B., **1404**
Sexually transmitted diseases. *See* Venereal diseases
Seymour, Horatio, 411
Seymour, Thomas, 411
Seymour, Truman A., 590, 1165, 1166, 1567
Shackelford, George Green, *as contributor*, 174–175, 1305–1306
Shackleford, Eugenia, 1093
Shadbourne, George D., 152

"Shadow" (pseudonym), 1683
Shadrack (fugitive slave), 650
Shaftesbury, Earl of, 483
Shaifer, A. K., 1237
Shakanoosa Arms Company, 1458
Shannaon, Wilson, 175
Sharkey, William, 341, 1639
Sharp, Jacob Hunter, **1404**
Sharp and Hamilton. *See* Nashville Plow Works
Sharpe, George H., 541, 542
Sharps, Christian, 1456
Sharpsburg campaign, 361, **1404–1408**
  Anderson, George B., 29
  Anderson, Richard Heron, 36
  Army of Northern Virginia, 79
  Barksdale, William, 132
  Bloody Lane, 29, 36
  casualties, 338, 918, 1407, 1408
  Cooke, John Rogers, 408
  desertion, 467
  Early, Jubal, 501–502
  and Emancipation Proclamation, 1446
  file closers, *572*
  First Louisiana Brigade, 957
  Garnett, Richard, 664
  Gordon, John, 697
  Hill, A. P., 771, 817
  Hill, D. H., 775
  infantry, 817
  Iverson, Alfred, 826
  Jackson, Thomas J. ("Stonewall"), 834, 883, 1406, 1407
  Johnson, Bradley Tyler, 849
  Johnston, Robert, 862
  Jones, David Rumph ("Neighbor"), 864
  Jones, J. R., 866
  Kemper, James, 881
  Kennedy, John Doby, 883
  Lee, Robert E., 864, 918, 1404–1408
  Longstreet, James, 945
  map, 1405
  national battlefield site, 1072, 1073, 1074
  Pendleton, William N., 1191
  Sorrel, Gilbert Moxley, 1503
  Stafford, Leroy, 1521
  Starke, William Edwin, 1526
  strategy, 328
  Toombs, Robert, 1601
  see also Harpers Ferry, West Virginia, battle of 1862; South Mountain, Maryland
Sharpshooters, 816, 818
Shaw, Henry, 245, 544, 545
Shaw, Robert Gould, 630, 1074
Shawnees, 425, 811, 813, **1404–1408**
Sheath knives, 515
Sheet music, 1101–1103
  covers, *335*, *712*, *948*, *1102*
Shelby, Joseph O., 56, 396, 695, 827, **1409**, 1610
  Iron Brigade, 1409
  raids, 1053, 1252, 1254, 1255
  scouts, 38, 1599
Shelby Iron Company, 4, 1124, 1388, **1410**
  government contractor, 1121, 1122
  records, 1099
Shelley, Charles Miller, **1410**
Shell guns, 62
Shelton Laurel region, North Carolina, 720
Shenandoah (film), 575, 580
Shenandoah (ship), 21, 22, 240, 376, 712, 1008, 1151, **1411–1412**, *1411*, 1516, 1675, 1691, 1712
  commerce raiding, 374, 1123
Shenandoah River, 1415, 1416, 1417
Shenandoah Valley, **1412–1419**
  agriculture, 1664
  campaign of Jackson, 76, 78, 104–105, 124, 174, 201–202, 258, 386, 430–431, 530, 549, 647, 663–664, 832, 834, 849, 866, 894, 909, 947, 957, 1298, 1402, 1412, **1413–1417**, 1548, 1565, 1702, 1705, 1732, 1734
  campaign of Sheridan, 214, 268, 271, 336, 337, 503, **582–583**, 601, 723, 740, 815, 836, 958, 1092, 1262, 1352, 1413, **1417–1419**, 1733
  casualties, 1417, 1418, 1419
  Cedar Creek, Virginia, 271, 503, 694, 892, 1419
  Confederate defeat, 1417–1419
  destruction, 1413, 1418–1419
  Early, Jubal, 82, 503, 504, 505, 506, 697, 807, 882, 921, 932, 943, 963, 1186, 1345, 1347, *1417*, 1418, 1419, 1706, 1713, 1733
  map, 1414, 1417
  Mennonites, 1031
  mining, 1043, 1044
  New Market, Virginia, 1135–1136, 1413, 1416, 1673
  overview article, **1412–1413**
  Piedmont, Virginia, 870, 1210
  prisoners, *1257*
  Stonewall Brigade, 1548–1549
  strategic importance, 1415
  West Virginia operations, 1703–1706
  see also Cross Keys and Port Republic, Virginia; Early's Washington Raid; Fisher's Hill, Virginia; Front Royal, Virginia; Lynchburg, Virginia; New Market, Virginia; Winchester, Virginia
Shepardson, William, 274, 1683
Shepherd, Heyward, 741, 1028
Shepherd, Oliver, 1095
Shepley, George F., 702, **1419–1420**
Sheppard, William Ludwell, 1231
Sheridan, Philip H., 277, 501, 1666, 1699
  Appomattox campaign, 45, 47
  caricature, *732*
  cavalry, 266, 268, 270
  Chattanooga campaign, 294
  Fisher's Hill, Virginia, 582
  foraging, 601
  Lynchburg, Virginia, 963
  Murfreesboro, Tennessee, 1095
  Perryville, Kentucky, 891, 1197
  Petersburg campaign, 1201
  Shenandoah Valley campaign. *See under* Shenandoah Valley
  Spotsylvania campaign, 1519, 1553
  Yellow Tavern, Virginia, 1713, 1750–1751
Sherman, John, 762
Sherman, William Tecumseh, 287, 887, *1006*
  Atlanta campaign. *See under* Atlanta, Georgia
  Averasboro, North Carolina, 117
  caricature, *732*
  Carolinas campaign. *See* Carolinas campaign of Sherman
  Chattanooga campaign, 293–294
  Columbia, South Carolina, 371, 372, 1262–1263
  field fortifications, 626
  foraging, 601, 901
  on Forrest (Nathan Bedford), 219
  Franklin and Nashville campaign, 633
  image in South, 934
  intelligence network, 541
  Jackson, Mississippi, 2, 837, 838, 839
  Kennesaw Mountain, Georgia, 885, 886
  Louisiana State Seminary, 519, 957
  march through Georgia. *See* March to the Sea, Sherman's
  Meridian campaign, 835, 1032–1033, 1051
  on Morgan, John Hunt, 1086
  pardons, 1394
  peace overtures, 773, 854, 1536, 1745

Sherman, William Tecumseh, *continued*
  Petersburg campaign, 1201
  response to guerrilla warfare, 724–725
  Savannah campaign, 1368–1369, 1370
  Savannah occupation policies, 1367, 1368
  scorched-earth policy, 1217
  Shiloh campaign, 1422–1423
  South Carolina invasion, 1510
  and Stoneman's raids, 1546
  strategy and tactics, 260, 325, 326, 328–329, 334, 886
  supply lines, 291–292, 1006, 1032, 1087, 1624, 1707, 1708
  surrender terms, 1153, 1313
  Tennessee, 1030
  treatment of slaves, 391
  Vicksburg campaign, 1049, 1476, 1656, 1657, 1658–1659
Sherman, Texas, bread riots, 213
Sherman's March to the Sea. *See* March to the Sea, Sherman's
Shewmake, John Troupe, 928, **1420**
S. H. Goetzel and Company, 193, 194, 937, 1059, 1232
Shields, James, 104, 430, 431, 549
  Shenandoah Valley campaign, 1415, 1416, 1417
Shields, J. H., 1563
Shiloh (Foote), 938
Shiloh campaign, 327, 340, 887, **1420–1423**, 1426, 1576, 1605
  Allen, Henry W., 26
  Anderson, James Patton, 32
  Army of Tennessee, 67
  Bate, William Brimage, 139
  Beauregard, P. G. T., 148–149, 150, 1514
  Bragg, Braxton, 203–204
  casualties, 338, 1423
  Cleburne, Patrick, 353
  Confederate infantry tactics, 819
  Fagan, James, 561
  Forrest, Nathan Bedford, 606
  Gibson, Randall, 684
  Gillem, Alvan, 685
  Hardee, William, 737
  Jackson, John, 830
  Johnson, Bushrod Rust, 850
  Johnson, George, 851
  Johnston, Albert Sidney, 148, 150, 691, 751, 819, 858, 1049, 1420, 1421, 1422–1423, 1426, 1584
  Kelly, John Herbert, 880
  map, 1421
  Moore, John Creed, 1076
  Mouton, Alfred, 1092
  naming of battle, 143
  Orphan Brigade, 1170
  Ruggles, Daniel, 1351
  Shoup, Francis, 1427
  Withers, Jones Mitchell, 1736
  Young, William Hugh, 1753
Shiloh National Military Park, 1072, 1073, 1074
Shingles. *See* Shinplasters
Shingleton, Royce, *as contributor*, 1743–1744
Shinplasters, **1424**
Ship #290, 1393
Shipp, Scott, 1673
Shipbuilding. *See* Ironclads; Shipyards; Submarines; particular ships
Shipping. *See* Blockade; Commerce traders; Foreign trade; Privateers; Transportation
Ships. *See* Commerce raiders; Davids; Ironclads; Navy, Confederate; Privateers; Rams; Shipyards; Submarines; particular names
Shipyards, **1424–1425**
  Charleston, South Carolina, 1509
  New Orleans, Louisiana, 1424, 1562
  Savannah, Georgia, 1366
  Williamson, William P., 1725
  see also Charlotte Navy Yard; Gosport Navy Yard; Laird Shipyards; Tift brothers
Shirley, John, 54, 1425
Shirley Plantation (Richmond), 1668
Shockhoe Foundry. *See* Richmond Naval Ordnance Works
Shoemaker, Edward M., *as contributor*, 1364–1368
Shoes and boots
  infantry, 817
  Quartermaster Bureau, 1291
  sailors, 1359
  shortages, 356, 357
  substitutes, 1559
Shooting Star (ship), 301
Short, Beanie, 594, 1167
Shortages. *See* Bread riots; Clothing; Food; Salt; Substitutes
Shorter, John G., 16, 17, 18–19, 701, 702, 703, 927, 1075, 1343, **1425–1427**, 1695
Short History of the Confederate States (Davis), 453
Shotguns, 63
Shoup, Francis, **1427**
Shoupade redoubt, 620
Shrapnel, 61, 93, 94
Shreveport, Louisiana
  hospitals, 796
  Smith (E. Kirby) headquarters, 2473
  Union threat, 1473
Shropshire, R. D., 135
SHS. *See* Southern Historical Society
Shun pikes, 1339
Sibley, Henry Hopkins, 144, 1372, **1427–1428**, 1584, 1606
  New Mexico campaign, 121, 692–693, 1136
  staff, 713, 1538
Sibling exchange, 562
Sickles, Daniel E.
  Chancellorsville campaign, 281
  Gettysburg campaign, 680, 681
Sickness and disease. *See under* Health and medicine
"Side" knife. *See* Bowie knife
Sigel, Franz, 1180
  Elkhorn Tavern, 526
  Manassas, Second, 1001
  New Market, Virginia, 214, 1135–1136, 1210, 1673
  Shenandoah Valley strategy, 1413
  Wilson's Creek campaign, 1729–1731
Signal Corps, **1428–1430**
  Alexander, Edward Porter, 24
  secret courier line, 537–538
  stations, *1428*, 1429–1430, *1429*
  structure, 1685
  see also Balloon
Silber, Irwin, 487
Silber, Nina, *as contributor*, 646
Silbey, Joel H., *as contributor*, 465–467
Silver Hill Mines, North Carolina, 1147
Silverman, Jason H., *as contributor*, 603–604, 675–676, 822–823, 1157
Simhi, Kohava, *as contributor*, 985–987
Simms, James Phillip, **1430**
Simms, William E., **1430–1431**
Simms, William Gilmore, 193, 284, 372, 936, 937, 985, 1590
Simons, Thomas, 1144
Simpson, William Dunlap, **1431**
Sims, Frederick W., 1297
Simultaneous advances, 326, 328
Sinclair, Upton, 938
Singer, E. C., 777
Singer, Ralph B., Jr., *as contributor*, 108–111, 976–978
Singleton, Otho Robards, *1050*, **1431–1432**
Sitterson, J. Carlyle, *as contributor*, 1560
Sivley, Eliza Burleson, 516
6-pound gun, 61

Sixteen String Jack, the Gallant Highwayman (Rede), 1590
S. J. Waring (ship), 841, 1269
Skates, Ray, *as contributor*, 23–24, 131, 135, 202–203, 223–224, **224–226**, 257, 276, 340–341, 351, 455–456, 747–748, 782, 800–801, 837–839, 905–906, 924, 981–982, 1032–1033, 1046–1052, 1173, 1203–1204, 1204–1205, 1431–1432, 1624–1625, 1694, 1698, 1729
Skates & Company, 98
Sketches from the Civil War in North America (Volck), 1673
Sketches of the Rise, Progress, and Decline of Secession (Brownlow), 231
Skilled labor. *See* Artisans; *under* Labor
Skirmishers, 819
Slack, William Yarnel, **1432**
Slasher and Crasher (Morton), 1590
Slater, Sarah, 543, **1432**
Slaughter, James Edwin, 1037, **1432–1433**, 1608, 1748
Slaughter Mountain. *See* Cedar Mountain, Virginia
Slave drivers, **1433-1434**; *see also* Overseers
Slave patrols, 1437, 1444
Slave pens, *1452*
Slave resistance, 1367, 1433, 1440, 1442, 1443–1446, 1487
- Emancipation Proclamation and, 530
- fugitive slaves, 552
- Georgia, 70, 670, 671
- North Carolina, 379
- plantation mistress and, 1218
- planters' fears, 1217
- preventive codes, 427, 1333
- South Carolina, 285, 1333, 1647
- Tubman, Harriet, 1623
- Union policies, 9

Slavery, **1434–1451**
- abolitionism, 1374
- African American syncretic culture, 1448
- African trade. *See* Slave traders
- antebellum, **1434–1441**
- archaeological excavations, 48
- Arkansas, 1484
- as basis of Southern society, 1485–1486
- black belt, 172–173
- black churches, 1321
- black women, 1741
- Bleeding Kansas, **175–176**
- border states, 195
- Brownsville, Texas, 231
- caricatures, *405*
- as central Civil War issue, 317–324, 949, 1536
- children, 307–308, 563
- during Civil War, **1441–1447**
- colonization issue, 44, 45, 164
- confiscation of slaves, 388, 390–391, 733
- constitutional issues, 252, 253, 402, 884, 1067, 1068, 1325
- conversions, 1399
- Cornerstone speech, 383, 402, **415**, 1220, 1275
- cotton and entrenchment of, 417
- cotton gin impact on, 1436–1437
- Crittenden Compromise, **429**
- Davis (Jefferson) view of, 451
- diffusion of, 552, 553, 554
- Dred Scott decision, **493–495**
- education. *See subhead* slave education *below*
- emancipation. *See* Emancipation; Emancipation Proclamation; Juneteenth; Thirteenth Amendment
- Emancipation Proclamation and, 532
- enslavement of free blacks, 642
- escapes. *See* Fugitive Slave Law; Fugitive slaves
- expansion. *See* Expansion of slavery in the antebellum South
- family life, *5*, 563–565, 1448–1449, 1451
- film representations, 574–575
- free black slaveholders, 643, 1506
- Georgia, 670, 675, 1367
- "house-divided" speech, 495
- immigrant opposition to, 676
- impact on Civil War, 332, 344–345
- impressment, 34, 35, 38, 39, 75, 192, 229, 290, 315, 405, 564, 619, 620, 625, 643, 655, 667, 670, 704, 763, 809–810, 862, 899–900, 913, 926, 1029, 1110, 1148, 1217, 1220, 1297, 1426
- Indian slaveholders, 296–297, 309, 813, 1166, 1390
- innovative management techniques, 453
- justifications, 363
- Kansas-Nebraska Act, **875–876**
- legal end to (1865), 1434
- in lower South, 1439
- manumission, 44, 334, 1437
- Mason-Dixon Line, 1016
- miners, 1043–1044
- Mississippi, 1484
- Missouri, 1052
- Missouri Compromise, 465, **1055–1056**, 1373–1374
- morality issue, 130, 333–334, 558
- Moravian Church, 1084
- myth of slave loyalty, 242
- negative economic effects, 883, 1440–1441
- Nicaragua, 1145
- plain folk support for, 1213–1214
- planters' dedication to, 1214–1215, 1219
- price of slaves, 554, 1234, 1413, *1436*, 1437, 1443, 1453
- punishments, 427, *1439*, 1448
- Quaker system, 1493
- railroad workers, 1297, 1298
- reform advocates, 1399, 1722
- religion of slaves. *See subhead* slave religion *below*
- as religious issue, 476, 535, 551, 961, 1247, 1320, 1399
- relocation of slaves, 552
- Republican party, 1321
- restrictions on criticism of, 641
- restrictive codes, 1399, 1437, 1722
- rice production, 1327
- Roman Catholic Church and, 1346
- runaways. *See* Fugitive Slave Law; Fugitive slaves
- Second Wheeling Convention, 1702
- Sherman's March to the Sea and, 1006–1007
- slave diet, 597
- slave education, 520, 521, 1450–1451, 1588, 1722
- slaveholdings by states, *1485*
- slave intermediaries, 1433–1434
- slave laborers, 34, 899-900, 901
- slave life, 563–564, 1438, 1439, **1448–1451**
- slave marriages, 563–565, 1010
- slave marts, 1330
- slave religion, 1399, 1449–1450
- slave resistance. *See* Slave resistance
- slave reunions, 572
- slaves as contraband, 7, **405–406**, 540, 900, 1444–1446
- slave skilled labor, 902, 903
- South Carolina, 1484, 1504
- Southern nationalism and, 1112, 1113, 1114, 1116
- Southern sectionalism and, 1377, 1378
- Southern Unionism and, 687–688, 706, 848, 1116, 1638, 1639

Slavery, *continued*
spirituals, 1103–1104
state rights defense of, 1533–1535
task system, 1327–1328, 1438
taxation, 1283
Tennessee, 1574
Texas, 1586
Twenty-Slave Law. *See* Twenty-Slave Law
in upper South, 1438–1439
urban, 1646, 1647
Washington Peace Conference, 1689–1690
West Virginia, 1705
Wilmot Proviso, **1728**
work habits, 1451
see also African Americans in the Confederacy; African Americans in the Union Army; Antislavery; Cotton; Emancipation Proclamation; Overseers; Plantation; Proslavery; Slave drivers; Slave resistance; Slave traders; Sugar; Tobacco
Slavery and Abolitionism as Viewed by a Georgia Slave (Berry), 164
Slave Songs of the United States, 1104
Slave traders, **1451–1453**
Confederate ban on international, 402, 1481
interstate, 1377, 1437–1438, 1443, 1451–1453
marts, 1330
Southern movement to reopen international, 554, 1228, 1715
U.S. ban on international, 552, 1436, 1437
Slayback, Alonzo, 1254
Sledd, R. N., 1034
Sledge, James, 1683
Slemmer, Adam, 589, 618
Slidell, Conrad, and Benjamin Slidell, 395
Slidell, John, 146, 613, 883, 924, 952, 954, **1453–1455**, 1504, 1514, 1616
Democratic party, 465
diplomatic missions, 9, *481*–482, 484, 485, 631, 632, 711–712, 803, 884, 1014, 1271, 1303, 1354, 1527, 1528, 1529
Erlanger loan, 510, 536
foreign procurement, 1140
ship *No. 61*, 1150
and slavery, 808
Trent affair, 177, 385, 1014–1016, 1619, 1620
Sloan, John M., 1495
Slocum, Henry W., 117, 163, 261, 839, 1006, 1152, 1368
Slocum's Battery, 1516
Slough, John, 692
Small arms, **1455–1471**
altered, U.S., **1464–1465**
army ordnance, 59–60
arsenals and armories, 90
captured and purchased U.S., 62, 513, 515, 744, 1169, **1461–1464**
filed gun, *995*
handguns, **1459–1461**
imported, 1169, **1465–1469**, 1470
imported, Austrian, 102, 1468
imported, Belgian, 1468–1469
imported, English, 60, 102–103, 232, 1465–1468, 1470
imported, French, 102, 513, 1469
impressment, 342
munitions, **1469–1471**
naval, 62–63, **1469**
Ordnance Bureau, 223, 698, 1168
production at Harpers Ferry, 739
rifles and muskets, 817, 818–819, 1168, 1169, **1455–1458**, **1464–1465**
see also Arms, weapons, and ammunition; Edged weapons; Handguns; Niter and Mining Bureau; Ordnance Bureau; particular kinds
Smallpox, 110, 754, 796
prison epidemics, 39, 610
Smalls, Robert, 7, **1471–1472**
Small Town Spicer (Seneca chief), 1398
Smallwood and Company, 129
Smith, A. J., 276, 1051, 1252, 1624, 1625
Franklin and Nashville campaign, 633, 634
Red River campaign, 1314, 1315, 1316
Smith, Channing, 547
Smith, Charles F., 1177
Henry and Donelson campaign, 764–767
Smith, Charles H., Bill Arp stories, 671
Smith, E. Kirby, 85, 588, 941, 1186, 1427, **1472–1474**, 1545, 1572, 1690
anti-Bragg faction, 1011
appointments, 343
cotton impressment, 1586
department command, 72
Kentucky campaign, 187, 458, 887, 888, 889, 890, 891
Knoxville campaign, 1093, 1322
parole, text of, 1795–1796
Perryville, Kentucky, 1197, 1198
Red River campaign, 1223, 1315, 1316, 1317
surrender of Indian Territory command, 815
surrender of last Confederate armies, 1446, 1473
Trans-Mississippi Department, 7, 187, 207, 234, 461, 695, 738, 827, 908, 956, 974, 1004, 1097, 1145, 1180, 1607–1610, 1611
Smith, Franklin, 1431
Smith, G. Clay, 1088
Smith, Gustavus W., 251, 1191, 1193, **1474–1475**, 1684
Savannah, Georgia, defense, 1368
Seven Pines, Virginia, command, 1402, 1403
Sherman's March to the Sea, 1006
Smith, J. J., 5
Smith, James Argyle, 708, **1475**
Smith, James Milton, **1475–1476**, 1623
Smith, Jennifer Lund, *as contributor*, 37–38, 163–164, 258–259, 396–399, 499, 612, 695–696, 827–828, 880–881, 942–943, 1043, 1249–1250, 1323, 1750–1751
Smith, John David, *as contributor*, 203, 234–235, 243–244, 311, 430, 528–529, 550–551, 602, 857, 972–973, 1062–1063, 1075–1076, 1310, 1430–1431, 1593, 1622, 1709
Smith, John Preston, 988
Smith, Martin Luther, **1476**, 1655, 1656
Smith, P. E., and W. H. Smith, 528
Smith, P. J., *80*
Smith, Persifor, 63
Smith, Preston, 304, 358, **1476–1477**, 1653
Smith, Richard M., 1142
Smith, Robert (blockade runner), 183, 185
Smith, Robert Hardy, **1477–1478**
Smith, S. P., 654
Smith, Thomas Benton, **1478**
Smith, Watson, 1658
Smith, William Duncan, **1478–1479**
Smith, William Ephraim, **1479**
Smith, William ("Extra Billy"), 75, 198, 651, 701, 703, 1371, **1479–1481**
Smith, William F., 293, 496, 1725
Smith, William N. H., **1481**
Smith, William Russell, **1481–1483**
literary accomplishments, 1482
Smith, William Sooy, 1032, 1033, 1051
Smith and Pocahontas: A Poem (Martin), 936

Smith and Wesson, 1463
Smithsonian Institution, 450, 573
Smith's Revised English Grammar, 1588
Smoker, John, 1055
Smyrna, Georgia, 114
Smyth, Thomas, 1274
Smythe, Charles W., 1588
Snare drum, *1105*
Snead, Thomas L., 828, **1483**
Sneden, Samuel, 184
Snuff, 1598
Sober View of the Slavery Question, A (Wiley), 44
Social benevolence. *See* Free markets; Poor relief; Soldiers' aid societies; Women's aid societies
Social class. *See* Class conflicts; Middle class; Plain folk; Planters; Society; Yeomanry
Socialism. *See* State socialism
Social tensions. *See* Class conflicts
Social welfare. *See* Poor relief
Society, **1483–1493**
  African American families, 563–565
  Alabama, 1058
  Charleston, South Carolina, 1506
  class conflict, **344–347**, 1488–1492, 1510
  class origins of soldiers, 1495
  conflict sources, 1489–1492
  domination and subordination divisions, 1488
  elite, 1490
  family life, **562–565**
  free blacks, 642–643, 1487–1488
  Galveston, Texas, 655
  gender roles, 1487-1488; *see also* Women
  hierarchies, 787
  historiographical view, 166–167
  honor, 786–788
  leisure, **923–924**
  Little Rock, Arkansas, 940, 941
  miscegenation, 1046
  mobility, 1490
  poor whites, 1489
  proslavery arguments, 1273–1274
  refugees, 1319
  rural, 565
  selected bibliography, 170
  slavery shaping, 1485–1486
  South Carolinian secessionist unity, 1506–1507
  Texas, 1586
  urban, 1646–1647
  view of Irish, 823
  war-related discontent. *See subhead* class conflicts *above*
  wartime changes, 332, 387, 1235
  white families, 562–563
  see also African Americans in the Confederacy; Community life; Desertion; Education; Family life; Foreigners; Indians; Nationalism; Peace movements; Plain folk; Planters; Popular culture; Population; Poverty; Religion; Slavery; Soldiers' aid societies; Urbanization; Women
Society for Cessation of Hostilities, 1271
Society for the Diffusion of Political Knowledge, 1275
Society of Friends, 707, **1493–1494**
  antislavery, 43, 44
  Guilford County, North Carolina, 687, 715
  Heroes of America, 1154
  Quaker guns, *95*, 619
Sociology for the South; or, The Failure of Free Society (Fitzhugh), 583
Socket bayonets, 60
Soldiers, **1494–1501**
  aid societies for. *See* Soldiers' aid societies
  alcohol use, 1498
  battle motivation and conduct, 1499–1500
  Bible societies, 164, 165
  boot and shoe shortages, 356
  cadets used as, 519, 674–675, 1672–1673
  camaraderie, 378
  camp life, 1496–1498
  characteristics, 1494–1495
  clothing shortages, 356
  condolence letters, 460–461
  courts-martial, 1497
  death and mourning, 459–461
  desertion, **467–469**
  discipline. *See* Military justice
  employment of disabled, 783
  enlistment form, *306*
  entrenchment, 626
  file closers, 571
  food rations, 595, 1495–1496
  free black, 643, 644
  Galvanized Yankees, **654**
  home front effect on, 1213
  illness. *See subhead* sickness and disease *below*
  Jesse scouts, 134
  labor, 899
  legends and jokes by, 593–594
  leisure activities, 923, 1497–1498
  letters and diaries, 307, 398, 421, 470, 474–476, 524, 1103, 1496, 1497–1498, 1500
  monuments and memorials, 1069–1074
  morale, 1496
  narrative traditions, 593–594
  North Carolina, 1012, 1151–1152
  pay, 7, 89, 345, 566, 670, 902, 912, 967, 1495
  photographic portraits, 1206, 1230
  postage privileges, 1243
  rations. *See subhead* food rations *above*
  recreation. *See subhead* leisure activities *above*
  religion, 1320, 1498–1499
  revivals, 1034
  rural roots, 378
  sickness and disease, 141, 754–755, 1498
  side switchers, 63
  songs, 1103
  South Carolinian recruitment, 1509
  standard firearms, 624
  supplies, 1495–1496
  tobacco use, 1599
  tories, **1602–1603**
  training, 1040, 1497
  uniforms, 356, 1495
  women in male disguise, 265, 421, 1740
  see also Brothers of war; Cavalry; Conscription; Infantry; Military justice; Prisoners of war; Veterans
Soldiers' aid societies, 977, 979, 1027, 1229, 1488, **1501–1502**, 1570, 1740
Soldiers' Aid Society of Wilmington, 1027
Soldiers' homes, **1502–1503**
  Beauvoir, 150, 1502
  Montgomery, Alabama, 794
Soldiers' National Cemetery (Gettysburg), 1073
Soldiers' Paper, The (publication), 1034, 1400
Soldiers' relief associations. *See* Soldiers' aid societies
Soldier's Rest Hospital (Richmond), 152
Soligen, Germany, edged weapons, 513
Somerset Plantation, 1194
Sonaki Mikko. *See* Bowlegs, Billy
"Song of the Contrabands: O Let My People Go" (song), 1104
Songs. *See* Music; particular collections and titles

Songs and Ballads of American History and the Assassinaiton of Presidents (recording), 487
Songs of the Civil War (recording), 487
Songs of the CSA (recording), 487
"Songs of the Freedmen of Port Royal," 1104
Songster music books, 1104
Sonora, Mexico, 808, 1174
Sons of Confederate Veterans, 307, 388, 949, 950, 1317
Sons of Liberty. *See* Copperheads
Sons of the Confederacy, 1027
Sons of Union Veterans, 1317
So Red the Rose (film), 574, 578, *580*
So Red the Rose (novel by Young), 939
SoRelle, James M., *as contributor*, 874
Sorrel, Gilbert Moxley, 502, 748, **1503–1504**
Soulé, Pierre, 1454, **1504**
Southall, Valentine W., 1337
South America, and Southern expansionism, 808
"South Americans," 687
South Carolina, **1504–1511**
  African American majority, 1504
  African American troops, 9–10
  arsenal and armory, 1461, 1469, 1507
  banking, 1644
  battlefield casualty rate, 1510
  black-white population comparison, 1434–1435, *1435*
  Bluffton movement, 186
  bread riots, 596
  class-related guerrilla warfare, 1492
  congressmen, 118, 133, 190, 191, 199–201, 212, 298–299, 568, 978–979, 1038, 1207, 1323–1326, 1431, *1505*, 1560–1562, 1737
  conscription controversy, 872
  Constitution ratification, 403
  cooperationists, 411
  cotton, 1504, 1506
  currency, 1281
  debt, 462
  Declaration of the Causes of Secession, 1534
  Department of. *See* Department of South Carolina, Georgia, and Florida
  devastation of, 1510
  election of 1860, 521, 522, 523
  Executive Council, 1208
  farm acreage, *1484*
  fire-eaters, 1376–1377
  flag, 587
  foreign population, 602
  Fort Hill plantation, 613
  Fort Sumter. *See* Fort Sumter, South Carolina
  free blacks, 642, 643
  German troops, 676
  governors, 191–192, 322, 701, 702, 703, 704, 728–729, 730–732, 988, 1207–1208, 1507, 1510, 1714
  Hampton, Wade, 730–732
  Hampton's Legion, 731–732, 733–734, 816, 866, 1516
  hospitals, 794, 795, 796, 969
  iron production, 1148
  manufacturing, 514
  military command, 1479
  military operations, 260–262, 917
  military units, 1508–1509
  mining, 1043
  newspapers, 1143–1144, 1683
  niter production, 1147
  nullification controversy, 1159–1160, 1374, 1377
  Orr, James L., 1171–1172
  Palmetto Armory, 1179–1180
  political system, 465
  population, 1233
  railroads, 1293, 1294, 1295, 1296
  Reconstruction, 133, 734, 1026, 1240, 1741
  rice production, 1327, 1328, 1504
  Sea Island slave drivers, 1433
  secession. *See under* Secession
  secession and Confederacy membership dates, *1379*
  secession date correlated with total black population, *1486*
  secession leadership. *See under* Secession
  secession ordinance, text of, 1769
  Simpson, William Dunlap, 1431
  slaveholdings, *1485*
  slave population, 1437, 1484, 1504
  small arms and munitions manufacture, 1457, 1470
  state navy, 1530
  sugar industry, 1559, 1560
  Sumner (Charles) speech against, 1560–1561
  taxation, 485, 1283, 1284
  tories, 1602
  Union invasion, 1509, 1510
  Unionism, 1202, 1637
  war-weariness, 1510
  wealth inequality, 1506
  see also Carolinas campaign of Sherman; particular cities and place names
South Carolina College, 517, 518
South Carolina Executive Council, 299
South Carolina Historical Society, 285
South Carolina Military Academy. *See* Citadel, The
South Carolina Railroad, 290, 371, 1645
  wayside hospitals, 795
South Carolina Tract Society, 193
Southern (magazine), 498
Southern Alliance, 567
Southern Baptist Convention, 165, 1320
Southern Baptists. *See* Baptist Church
Southern Bivouac (periodical), 153
Southern Boy of '61 (film), 574
Southern Cinderella, A (film), 574
Southern Claims Commission, 1217, 1639
Southern code of honor. *See* Honor
Southern Commercial Convention, 808, 1350
Southern Confederacy (newspaper), 108, 1143
Southern Confederacy Arithmetic (Leverett), 307, 1588
Southern Convention, 985
Southern Cross of Honor, 1022
Southerner, The (novel by Dixon), 938
Southern Express Company, 1242, **1511**
Southern Heroes (Cartland), 1494
Southern Historical Collection, 1099
Southern Historical Society, 358, 1017, 1027, 1099, 1100, **1512**, 1512
Southern Historical Society Papers, 804, 1512
  Long, Armistead, 944
Southern History of the War (Pollard), 1229
Southern Home, The (newspaper), 776
Southern Hotel (New York City), 234
Southern Illustrated News (magazine), 937, **985–986**, 1207, 1232, 1255, 1256, 1330, 1590
Southern Literary Companion, The (magazine), 1232
Southern Literary Magazine, The (magazine), 1232
Southern Literary Messenger (magazine), 193, 460, 481, 985, **986**, 1230, 1330
Southern Manifesto, 1716
Southern Methodist Publishing House, 165
Southern Methodists. *See* Methodist Church
Southern Monitor (journal), 865
Southern Monthly (magazine), 1232
Southern Mothers' Society, 794

"Southern Moving Dioramic Panorama," 1231
Southern nationalism. *See* Nationalism
Southern Negroes, 1861-1865 (Wiley), 1722
Southern Odes (Northrop), 1232
Southern Opposition, 687
Southern Pacific Railroad, 1715
Southern Pictorial Primer, 1588
Southern Press (publication), 924
Southern Punch (magazine), 1232, 1330, 1589, 1590
Southern Quarterly (magazine), 987
Southern Railroad, 1032
Southern Renaiscence, 938–939
Southern Review (Methodist publication), 174, 1035
"Southern Rights" broadside, *221*
Southern Rights resolutions, 665
"Southern Soldier, The" (recording), 487
Southern Star (ship), 1722
Southern Telegraph Company, 1685
Southern Times (publication), 730
Southern Torpedo Company, 445
"Southern Triumvirate," 802
Southern Watchman (publication), 735
Southern Woman's Story, A (Pember), 1188
Southfield (ship), 22, 407
South Fort, 621
South Mountain, Maryland, 549, 826, **1512–1513**
  Gordon, John, 696
  Lee (Robert E.) retreat from, 1404, 1406
South Side Railroad, 45, 46, 47, 1200
Southwestern Publishing House, 165
Sovereign states. *See* State rights
Spafford (ship), 375
Spain, **1513–1514**
  diplomatic missions to, 1347–1348
  expansion of slavery and, 557
  London Convention, 631
  neutrality proclamation, 432, 480
  territorial acquisitions, 553
Spanish-American War, 1408
Spanish Fort, Alabama, 622
Sparrow, Edward, **1514–1515**
  anti-administration policies, 1396
  overseer draft exemptions, 1395
"Sparta." *See* Reid, Samuel
Spar torpedoes, 445, 447–448, 993, 1303, **1515–1516**, 1604
Spaulding, James Reed, 547
Spearman, Charles M., *as contributor*, 428–429, 491–492, 1094–1096, 1649, 1736–1737
Special Field Orders No. 26, U.S., 371
Special Order No. 191, Confederate, 79, 742, 743, 775, 1404, 1406, 1512, 1513, 1677
Special Service Department (Navy), 993
Special units, **1516**; *see also* particular elite units
Speculation (financial), 434, 1020, 1082, 1244, 1491, **1517–1518**
  Charleston, South Carolina, 288
  Columbia, South Carolina, 370
  see also Bread riots; Extortion; Inflation
Speech freedom. *See* Freedom of speech
Spence, James, 1271, 1272
Spencer, Cornelia Phillips, **1518**, 1742
Spencer, Warren F., *as contributor*, 904, 1392–1394, 1548, 1563
Sphinx (ship), 1303, 1547
Spies. *See* Espionage
Spiller, Edward N., 1460
Spiller and Burr, 1459
Spindel, Donna J., *as contributor*, 427–428
Spirituals, 1103–1104
  recordings, 487
"Spontaneous People's Convention" (Virginia), 1384
Sports, 923
Spotswood, W. A. W., 1127–1128
Spotsylvania campaign, 81–82, 534, 850, 851, **1518–1520**
  casualties, 338, 1520, 1549
  Early, Jubal, 503
  Ewell, Richard, 550
  Gordon, James, 696
  Gordon, John, 697
  Grimes, Bryan, 718
  Lee, Robert E., 80, 697, 920, 1518–1520
  map, 1519
  Steuart, George Hume, 1543
  Stonewall Brigade decimation, 1549
  Wilcox, Cadmus Marcellus, 1718
  see also Yellow Tavern, Virginia
Spotsylvania Court House, 270, 1721
Spratt, Leonidas, 1275, 1683
"Spring" (Timrod), 937
Springfield Advertiser (Missouri newspaper), 1722
Springfield rifle-musket, 62
Spring Hill, Tennessee, 88, 296, 634
Spying. *See* Espionage
Square Fort, Mississippi, 620
"Squatter sovereignty." *See* Popular sovereignty
Squib (submarine), 445, 447–448, 1515
St. *Headings beginning* St. *are alphabetized as if spelled* Saint
Staerkodder (ship), 1547
Stafford, Leroy A., 958, 1185, **1521**, 1719
Stainless Banner, *585*
Stallworth, James A., *15*
Stampp, Kenneth M., 334
Stamps, **1521–1524**
  availability, 1241, 1242
  counterfeit, 421
  non-recognition by foreign countries, 1243
  postal operation, 1312
  postwar fakes, 1524
  printing, 1231, 1242
Standard (London newspaper), 482
Stanley, C. Vaughan, *as contributor*, 922
Stanley, David, 414, 634, 825
Stanley, Henry Morton, **1524**
Stanly, Edward, **1524–1525**
  military governorship of North Carolina, 702, 1152
Stanton, Edwin M., 11, 58, 134, 160, 545, 1020, 1335, 1687
  African American troops policy, 1472
  characterization of Stoneman (George, Jr.), 1547
  on Lincoln assassination plot, 1016
  Methodist Church decree, 1035
  prisoner of war exchanges, 1261
  Shenandoah policy, 1417, 1418
  as U.S. secretary of war, 334
Staples, Waller R., **1525**
Starke, Peter Burwell, 839, **1525–1526**
Starke, William Edwin, 957, 1000, 1001, 1002, 1525, **1526**
  death at Sharpsburg, 1407
  Manassas, Second, 1521
Starling, A. M., 886
Star of the West (ship), 255, 285, 312, 627–628, 1507, **1526**, *1527*, 1594
Starr, James H., 1243
Starr, Joseph B., 651
Starr, William C., 750
Starry, John W., 741
Stars and Bars, *584*, 1068
Starvation. *See* Food
Starvation parties, 597, 1330
State and local governments
  archival collections, 1099
  bond sales, 1283–1284
  currency issues, 433, *434*, 1279, 1280–1281
  food production, 1220
  free markets, 641
  indebtedness, 462

State and local governments, *continued*
poor relief, 379, 1229–1230
socialism, 1285–1286
state debt, 1281–1282
state officials' exemptions, 229, 1156, 1536
taxation, 1283–1284, 1569–1571
see also Civil service; Governors; particular cities and states
State Department, 249, 250, **1527–1530**
Barnwell, Robert W., 133
Benjamin, Judah P., 160, 483, 485, 632, 781, 924, 1354
Browne, William M., 230
civil service, 314
diplomacy, **479–485**
Hunter, Robert M. T., 803–804
records, 1210
secretaries, 251, 252; *see also* particular names
staff, 1528
Toombs, Robert, 1601
State House (Columbia, South Carolina), 369, *370*
State Journal (Raleigh newspaper), 1142
State Military Works (South Carolina), 1457
State militia, 69, 315, 529
Alabama, 17, 1695
Florida, 1042
Georgia, 109, 229, 387, 1697
Mississippi, 1204
Missouri, 1053
mustering, 1684
North Carolina, 342, 1155, 1184–1185
recruitment, 385
slave resistance, 345
Texas, 1097
State navies, **1530**
State rights, 387, **1531–1536**
as antislavery argument, 1534
as basis of secession, 1373
blockade running, 1140
Brown, Albert Gallatin, 225
Brown, Joseph E., 228–229, 346, 1535, 1536, 1539, 1540, 1541, 1551, 1679
Calhoun, John C., 253, 321, 347, 383, 439, 1399, 1532–1533, 1536
citizenship, 312–313
as Civil War cause, 317, 318
Clayton, Alexander M., 351
and Confederate nationalism, 670, 1115
congressional supporters, 663, 736, 1172, 1176
conscription issue, 1535
constitutional guarantees, 1067
Constitution, Confederate, and, 401–402
Curry, Jabez L. M., 439
Davis (Jefferson) view of, 451
Declaration of Immediate Causes, 463
and extension of slavery, 1533–1534
as factor in Confederate defeat, 1536
fire-eaters, 582, 1324
Georgia, 346, 423
habeas corpus suspension and, 1223–1224
historical background, 1531–1532
of individual Confederate states, 1535–1536
Mississippi, 982
navy department decentralization, 1128
North Carolina, 245, 1156
nullification controversy, 1159–1160
politics, 1223
and prosecution of war, 331
as proslavery argument, 1533
railroads, 1299, 1326
role of central government, 1081
role of judiciary, 871–873
role of president, 1249
secession and, 1373, 1531, 1536
Semmes, Thomas, 1395
sermons espousing, 1399
slavery and, 321–322
Southern Rights resolutions, 665
state socialism versus, 1536
Stephens, Alexander H., 387, 1535, 1536, 1539
Stephens, Linton, 1542–1543
Toombs, Robert, 1601
Watts, Thomas H., 1695
Wigfall, Louis T., 1714, 1715
State Rights in the Confederacy (Owsley), 331
State socialism, 379, **1537–1538**, 1570
North Carolina, 1245
public finance, 1284–1286
Texas, 1586
State-supported schools. *See* Education, primary and secondary
Statesville, North Carolina, 1152
Statues. *See* Monuments and memorials
Staunton, Virginia
currency, *445*
Shenandoah campaign, 1416
Steamboats, 326, 1692
blockade running, 182, 184, 185
Stedman, Griffin A., 627
Steele, Frederick, 343, 561, 941, 1097, 1314–1315, 1316, 1317, 1372, 1409, 1568, 1610
Arkansas campaign, 53, 55–57, 1609, 1696
march toward Shreveport, Louisiana, 1473
Steele, Johnathon, 184, 185
Steele, William, 813, **1538**, 1607, 1609
Indian command, 1391, 1538
Stephens, Alexander H., 229, *250*, 253, 363, 673, 772, 852, 853, 877, **1538–1542**, 1601, 1680, 1708, 1709, 1745
as cooperationist, 411
Hampton Roads Conference, 256, 532, 733, 773, 804, 1541–1542, 1655
likeness on Treasury note, 438
memoirs, 166
Montgomery convention, 1067–1068
opposition to conscription, 314, 1535, 1540
opposition to Davis (Jefferson) administration, 314, 331, 401, 1224, 1225, 1396
opposition to habeas corpus suspension, 314, 331, 653–654, 1535, 1540
peace resolutions, 1184
proslavery argument, 1485–1486
slavery views, 9, 317, 383, 402, 415, 665, 808, 1068, 1220, 1275, 1485–1486
state rights advocacy, 387, 1535, 1536, 1539
Unionism, 360, 411
vice presidency, 109, 111, 391, 401, 667, 668, 1066, 1068, 1146, **1654–1655**
writings, 166, 1536, 1542
see also Cornerstone speech
Stephens, Linton, 229, 668, 773, 1081, 1184, 1535, 1539, 1540, 1541, **1542–1543**, 1709
Stephenson, Roy R., *as contributor*, 63, 121, 461, 695, 827, 893–894, 908, 939, 974, 1132–1133, 1180, 1305, 1322, 1373, 1568, 1581, 1596–1597
Stereoscopic views, 1205–1206
Sterling, Richard, 1587–1588
Stetar, Joseph M., *as contributor*, 517–518
Steuart, George Hume ("Maryland"), 1043, **1543**, 1544, 1732
Stevens, Clement Hoffman, 259, **1544**
Stevens, Isaac, 1002
Stevens, John, 1658

Stevens, Walter Husted, *77*, 759, **1544**
Stevenson, Adlai, 1073
Stevenson, Carter, 113, 115, 228, 1300, 1322, **1545**, 1605, 1649
  Murfreesboro, Tennessee, 1094
Stevenson, Thomas G., 630
Stewart, Alexander P., 33, 87, 113, 139, 228, 850, 883, 959, **1545**
  Chickamauga campaign, 302, 304
  Franklin and Nashville campaign, 632, 634
  staff, 1550, 1551
Stewart, Peter C., *as contributor*, 1148–1150
Stewart, William M., 600
Stickney, Lyman P., 1165
Stiles, Kenneth L., *as contributor*, 237, 266–270, 276–277, 1012, 1182–1183, 1341–1342, 1364, 1681–1682, 1712–1714
Stiles, Robert, 503
Still, William N., Jr., *as contributor*, 54–55, 226–227, 533, 863, 1107, 1123–1126, 1370, 1568–1569
Stillman, Charles, 232
Stillwell, Joseph, 659
Stockade, *620*
Stockton, Missouri, 1409
Stoeckl, Édouard de, 479
Stoesen, Alexander R., *as contributor*, 714–715
Stokes, E. H., 1453
Stone, Charles, 126, 127
Stone, Dudley Marvin, 306
Stone, John M., 257
Stone, Kate, 307, 461, 471, **1546**, 1740
Stone Bridge (Manassas), 997, 998, *999*
Stoneman, George. *See* Stoneman's raids
Stoneman's raids, 27, 114, 290, 362, 715, 826, 913, **1546–1547**
  casualties, 1546
  North Carolina, 1152
  Salisbury Prison capture and burning, 1152, 1362
Stone Mountain, Georgia, 573, 952, 1069
Stone Mountain Monumental Association, 952
Stones River, Tennessee. *See* Murfreesboro, Tennessee
Stonewall (ship), 448, 824, 992, 1008, 1123, 1303, 1334, **1547–1548**
  ordnance, 1120
Stonewall Brigade, 1190, **1548–1549**
  command successors, 1549
  drummer boy, 1105
  as elite unit, 1516
  Manassas, First, 832, 834
  medals, 1022
  name, 816
  Paxton, Elisha Franklin, 1182
  Shenandoah Valley, 834
  socioeconomic makeup, 1549
  Walker, James Alexander, 1549, 1677
  Williams, Terry, 1582
  Winder, Charles S., 1734
"Stonewall Jackson's Way" (poem by Palmer), 936, 937
"Stonewall Jackson's Way" (song), 487, 1103
Stonewall Songbook, The, 1104
Store, The (Stribling), 939
Storey, Wilbur F., 411
Story, Joseph, 1395
Stoughton, Edwin H., 601, 722
Stout, Samuel Hollingsworth, 796, **1549–1550**
Stovall, Marcellus Augustus, **1550**
Stover, John F., *as contributor*, 1293–1299
Stowe, Harriet Beecher, 45
Strahl, Otho French, **1550–1551**
Strange Story, A (Bulwer-Lytton), 193
Strasburg, Virginia, 1415, 1416
Strategic Corps, 538
Strategy and tactics, **325–329**, 334, 386
  Alexander, Edward Porter, 25
  artillery, 94–95
  balloon, 125
  Beauregard, P. G. T., 148
  Bragg, Braxton, 890
  casualties, 338–339
  cavalry, 266, 267–270, 270
  coastal defense, 1302–1304
  control of Mississippi River, 1238
  Cooper, Samuel, 410
  Cumming, Alfred, 432
  espionage, 537
  field fortifications, 624–627
  file closers, 571, *572*
  Forrest, Nathan Bedford, 218–219, 606, 607
  forts and fortifications, 616–627
  gap between technology and tactics, 338
  Grant, Ulysses S., 56, 111, 156, 328–329, 357, 537, 546, 626, 962, 1177, 1198, 1200, 1314
  Hardee, William J., 193, 194, 737, 1040, 1059
  Hindman, Thomas C., 1246, 1247
  infantry, 819–820
  intelligence gathering, 542–547
  Jackson, Thomas J. ("Stonewall"), 830, 834, 835, 1001, 1002
  Johnston, Albert Sidney, 1249
  Johnston, Joseph E., 163, 862, 1189, 1248
  Jomini, Henry, 267, **862**
  Lee, Robert E., 24, 76, 78, 79, 163, 271, 272, 281, 328, 334, 410, 537, 571, 624, 625, 636, 637, 742, 917, 918, 920, 945–946, 962, 1002, 1020, 1043, 1165, 1191, 1700, 1721
  Lincoln, Abraham, 56, 326, 764, 892, 1165, 1314, 1609, 1752
  Longstreet, James, 945
  Lynchburg as strategic location, 962
  mapmaking, 797
  naval weaknesses, 685
  nocturnal attack, 880–881
  "offensive-defensive" war plan, 326–327, 1248
  offensive in West, 1473
  railroads, 289
  rules of war, 1352–1353
  Seddon, James A., 1385, 1386
  Sherman, William Tecumseh, 260, 886
  small arms, 60
  Smith, E. Kirby, 1473
  Stuart, J. E. B., 95, 862, 1552
  telegraph, 1573
  Van Dorn, Earl, 140
  waterways, 764, 1691, 1692
  Wheeler, Joseph, 1707
  see also particular battles and campaigns
Stratford Hall Plantation, 916, 922
Street, Albert, 1683
Street, Hungerford & Company, 98
Streight, Abel D., 17, 607, 720, 1343, 1602
Stribling, T. S., 939
Strickland, Hardy, **1551**
Strickland, William, 720
Strikes
  civil service, 315
  Richmond postal employees, 1243
  wage, 316
Stringer, Pembroke, and Company, 1567
Stringfellow, Benjamin Franklin, 547
Strong, George C., 630
Strother and Marcom, 1232
Stuart, Alexander H. H., 124, 1305
Stuart, David, 1422
Stuart, Flora Cooke, 1551
Stuart, Henry Carter, 573
Stuart, J. E. B., *65*, 122, 144, 278, 604, 663, 695–696, 1331, 1347, **1551–1554**

Stuart, J. E. B., *continued*
Ashby's Gap, Virginia, 1713
Brandy Station, Virginia, 209–210, 211
Buckland Mills, Virginia, 237
cavalry, 266–267, 731, 869
Chancellorsville campaign, 282, 918
death of, 82, 1519, 1553, 1750, 1751
elite unit, 1516
espionage, 601
Gettysburg campaign, 677, 682, 683, 1553
irregular operations, 722
John Brown's raid, 741
in literature, 936, 938
Manassas, Second, 78, 79
Mechanicsville, Virginia, 1020
monuments and memorials, 951, 1069, 1074
personal papers, 1099
portrait, 1256
raids. *See* Stuart's raids
recklessness of, 788
ride around McClellan, 78, 268–269, 276, 915, 918, 921, 1013, 1193, 1231, 1553, 1554, *1555*
saber, 513
scouts, 544, 1090
Seven Days' Battles, 1400
Sharpsburg campaign, 1406
Spotsylvania campaign, 1519
staff, 198, 407, 733, 985, 1190
tactics, 95, 862, 1552
telegraph operator, 1430
Wilderness campaign, 270
Williamsburg, Virginia, 1724
Yellow Tavern, Virginia, 1519, 1553, 1554, 1750–1751
see also Stuart's raids
Stuart, James Ewell Brown, Jr., 1551, 1553
Stuart, Phillip St. George Cooke. *See* Stuart, James Ewell Brown, Jr.
Stuart, W. H., 990
Stuart, Buchanan & Co. saltworks, 1362
Stuart General Hospital (Richmond), 796
Stuart Horse Artillery, 1516
Stuart's raids, 1516, 1552, **1554–1556**
Chambersburg, Pennsylvania, 268–269, 276–277, 1553, 1556
see also Brandy Station, Virginia; Gettysburg campaign
Stump tails. *See* Shinplasters
Sturgis, Samuel D., 218–219, 1051, 1624, 1730, 1731
Submarine Boat H. L. Hunley (Chapman), 283
Submarines, 993, **1556–1558**
American Diver, 777, 801, 1557
blockade breaking, 178
Davids, **445–446**, 993, 1515–1516
elite unit, 1516
Fish Boat, 777, 801
H. L. Hunley, **777–778**, 1124, 1130
Hunley, Horace, 801
Pioneer, 777, 801, 993, 1269, 1556, *1557*
privateering, 1269
spar torpedoes, 1515, 1516
Tredegar Iron Works, 1617
Subsistence Department. *See under* Commissary Bureau
Substitutes, conscription. *See under* Conscription
Substitutes, raw materials and consumer goods, 370, 472, 596, 1244, **1558–1559**, 1560, 1740
Suffrage
black, 1698
Merrick, Caroline E., 1034
Roudanez brothers, 1348
see also entries titled Election
Sugar, 808, **1559–1560**
plantations, 1174–1175, 1214, 1215, 1559, 1560
produce loan, 1270
refining, 1333
Rillieux, Norbert, 1333
slave labor, 1436
slave resistance, 1433
substitutes, 596, 1558, 1560
Sulfur and sulfuric acid production, 289, 698, 1147, 1470
Sullavan, Margaret, *580*
Sullins, David, 1399
Sullivan, Betsy, 1161
Sullivan, David M., *as contributor*, 1007–1008
Sullivan, James, 445
Sullivan, Jeremiah, 608, 825
Sullivan's Island, South Carolina, 877–878
Sulphuret lead, 913
Sulphur and sulphuric acid. *See* Sulfur and sulfuric acid production
Sultana (ship), 1267
Summary of the Art of War (Jomini), 862
Summers, George W., 123, 1337
Summerville, West Virginia, 750
Sumner, Charles, 175, 300, 322, *323*, 1590
Alabama claims, 21
caning of. *See* Sumner, caning of
caricatures, *1044*
Sumner, Edward, 1402, *1403*
Sumner, Edwin V., 637, 944
Sumner, caning of, 175, 322, 787, 876, 1310, **1560–1562**, 1715
Sumter, Francis, 555
Sumter (ship), 183, 374, 879, 1008, **1562–1563**
Semmes (Raphael) command, 1392, 1393
Sumter, Fort. *See* Fort Sumter, South Carolina
Sumter Light Guards, *818*
Sunshine Church, Georgia, 1547
Supplies
Danville, Virginia, 443
Florida, 590–591
foraging, **600–601**
Georgia, 109, 1286
horses and mules, 791–793
impressment, 393, **809–810**
infantry, 817–818
inflation, 1517
Lynchburg, Virginia, 962–963
medical, 757–758
naval, 1128
North Carolina, 1152, 1157, 1286
Quartermaster Bureau, **1291–1292**
soldiers', 1495–1496
state contributions, 704
substitutes, **1558–1559**
Union management of, 334, 336
see also Anglo-Confederate purchasing; Food; Ordnance Bureau; Small arms; Uniforms
Supply Service, 316
Supreme Court, Confederate, 207, 249, 348, 660, 661, 772, 871, 872; *see also* Judiciary
Supreme Court, U.S.
Campbell, John A., 255
constitutional interpretation, 1532
Dred Scott decision, 494–495, 1375, 1377, 1534
Miller v. U.S., 390
Semmes (Thomas) and, 1397
state sovereignty decision, 1534
Supreme Court Manual, The (Cobb), 362
Supreme courts, state, 1535
Surgeon general, 1685
De Leon, David Camden, 845, 1022, 1685
Moore, Samuel Preston, 755, 757, 794, 867, 1022, 1077, 1685

Surgeons. *See* Health and medicine; Hospitals; Medical Department; Surgeon general
Surgery. *See* Health and medicine, battle injuries
Surratt, John H., 935, 1432
Surratt, Mary Elizabeth, *539*, 1432
Surry of Eagle's-Nest (novel by Cooke), 408, 938
Sutherland, Daniel E., *as contributor*, 1212–1214
Sutherland Station, 45
Suttler, Bernard, 1744
Sutton, Elijah H., 1364
Swain, David, 1010
Swain, Eleanor, 1010
Swan, William G., **1563**
Swanson, Guy R., *as contributor*, 1098–1100
Sweeny, Thomas, 1730
"Sweet Evelina" (song), 1103
Swell's Point (ship), *1671*
Swift Run Gap, Virginia, 1415
Swinton, William, 83
S. Wolff & Company, 97, 98
Swords, 63, 513
Sydnor, Charles S., 597
Symonds, Craig L., *as contributor*, 111–115, 241, 1180
Synod, Lutheran Church, 961
Syphillis, 1276, 1277
Syren (ship), 184, 185

T

Taastanaki, Ahalak, 1390
Tacony (ship), 374, 375, 592, 1260, 1309
Tactics. *See* Strategy and tactics; particular battles
Tadman, Michael, *as contributor*, 1451–1453
Taft, William Howard, 572
Taglicher Anzeiger (Richmond newspaper), 1330
Tales of the Home Folk in Peace and War (Harris), 938
Taliaferro, H. B., 957
Taliaferro, William Booth, 33, 118, 630, 1526, **1565–1566**
Tall, Micah, 373
Talladega Alabama Reporter (newspaper), 431
Talladega Reporter and Watchtower (newspaper), 432
Tallahassee, Alabama, long arms manufacture, 1456, 1458
Tallahassee, Florida, 590, **1566–1567**
Tallahassee (ship), 374, 375, 685, 1008, **1567**, 1723, 1727, 1743
Tallahassee Floridian (newspaper), 776
Tallmadge, James, 1055, 1373
Tammany Hall, 1743
Taney, Roger B., 402, 494–495, 934, 1534
Tapp, Catharine, 1719
Tappan, James Camp, *52*, **1568**
Tap Roots (film), 580
"Taps" (song), 1105
Tariff of Abominations, 1114, 1159; *see also* Nullification controversy
Tariffs of 1828, 1832, and 1833, 1374, 1533; *see also* Nullification controversy
Tarpley, Jere H., 1457
Tarpley carbine, 1457, 1461
Tarpley rifle, 1232
Task system, 1327
Tate, Allen, 938, 939
Tattnall, Josiah, 1018, *1127*, 1178, 1370, 1530, **1568–1569**, 1670
  court-martial, 567
  Port Royal, South Carolina, 1129, 1240
  Savannah Squadron, 984
Taxation, 510–511, 529, 862, **1569–1571**
  Alabama, 18
  collection, 316, 1616
  constitutional provisions, 401
  cotton sales, 419
  difficulties, 1248
  direct tax, 486, 511, 1025, 1282
  inflation relationship, 821
  legislation, 1025
  peace churches, 1031
  poll tax, 7
  property tax, 858
  Provisional Congress, 1069
  public finance, 1282–1284
  Pugh, James Lawrence, 1287
  real estate tax, 1282
  social inequities, 1492
  value-added tax, 1248
  see also Tax-in-kind
Tax Collection Bureau, 316
Tax-in-kind, 18, 89, 106, 124, 345, 452, 506, 510, 803, 901, 911, 912, 942, 1081, 1194, 1248, **1571**, 1746
  farm products, 379
  and food shortages, 1244
  hunger relief, 1230
  North Carolina, 1154
  opposition, 1224
  Semmes, Thomas, 1395
Tax-in-Kind Acts of 1863, 510
Taylor, George B., 1588
Taylor, James B. (clergyman), 1400
Taylor, Jim, 487
Taylor, John, 1532
Taylor, Richard, 151, 173, 426, 658, 786, 952, 961, 990, 1185, 1372, 1538, **1571–1572**, 1591, 1690, 1695, 1746
  army commands, 67, 1607
  Army of Tennessee, 88
  Cross Keys and Port Republic, Virginia, 431
  Front Royal, Virginia, 647
  Irish Bend, Texas, 715, 1314
  on Irish fighting spirit, 823
  Louisiana Tigers, 957
  Mansfield, Louisiana, 1004–1005
  military appointments, 1389
  parole, text of, 1794
  praise for Green (Thomas), 713
  Red River campaign, 121, 461, 713, 955, 1305, 1315, 1316, 1317, 1572, 1610, 1696
  staff, 1521
  strategy disagreement, 1473
  Trans-Mississippi Department, 1607, 1608, 1609, 1610
  Vicksburg campaign, 709
  Winchester, Virginia, 549, 1732
Taylor, Sarah Knox, 450, 456, 1743
Taylor, Thomas E., 43, 129
Taylor, Thomas Hart, **1572**
Taylor, Walter, *77*, 874, 1615
Taylor, Zachary, 450, 501, 864, 945, 952, 1336, 1572, 1695, 1709, 1743
  cabinet, 1250
  presidential election, 380
Taylor's Southern Songster, 1232
Teachers, 307, 516, 520
  feminization of teaching, 521, 1488
  North Carolina, 1722
  textbooks, 1587–1588
  women, 520, 521, 1488, 1740
  see also Education
Teaser (ship), 125, 447, 840, 1124
Tea shortage, 596
Tebbel, John, 194
Tec-Tac Disjoint, 338
Tecumseh (ship), 17, 1581
Tehuantepec Company, 808
Telegraph, 289–290, 1066, 1086, **1573**
  Signal Corps, 1429, 1430
  strategic use, 326, 328
  wiretaps, 1430
Telescopes, 1429

Television
  documentaries, 573–574
  dramatized documentaries, 573
  fictional presentations, 580
Temperance. *See* Prohibition
Temple, Oliver Perry, 895, **1573–1574**
Temple, Shirley, 578
Ten Islands, 340
Tennessee, **1574–1579**
  agriculture, 172–173
  Army of. *See* Army of Tennessee; Army of West Tennessee
  arsenal and armory, 1458, 1464
  black-white population comparison, *1435*
  Chattanooga campaign. *See under* Chattanooga
  class-related guerrilla warfare, 1492
  congressmen, 107, 264–265, 358, 372–373, 438–439, 478, 597–600, 657, 666–667, 752–753, 760–761, 763–764, 798–799, 864, 868–869, 876, 967, 1030–1031, 1098, 1563, 1592–1593, 1595–1596, 1745
  conscription resistance, 398
  Constitution ratification, 403
  cotton plantations, 1436
  criminal gangs, 428
  currency, 1281
  debt, 462
  Department of. *See* Department of East Tennessee; Department of Tennessee
  education, 519
  election of 1860, 521, 522, 523
  election of 1863, 524
  exclusion from Emancipation Proclamation provisions, 1110
  farm acreage, *1484*
  flag, 587
  foreign population, 602
  Forrest's raids, 607, 608–609
  free black soldiers, 643, 644
  governors, 139, 228, 231, 255, 265, 597–600, 685, 701, 703, 744–746, 1576
  Heroes of America, 768
  hospitals, 794, 1549
  iron production, 1148
  Jones, Thomas McKissick, 869–870
  Knoxville and Greeneville conventions, 894–895
  Knoxville campaign, 870, 891, 895–897
  livestock breeding, 792
  manufacturing, 514
  manumission societies, 44
  military action, 1576–1577
  newspapers, 1143
  niter production, 1147
  population, 642, 1233
  railroads, 1293, 1294, 1295, 1296
  readmission to Union, 231
  Reconstruction. *See under* Reconstruction
  refugees, 1318
  Republican party, 1322
  secession. *See under* Secession
  secession and Confederacy membership dates, *1379*
  secession date correlated with total black population, *1486*
  Shiloh campaign, 1420–1423
  slaveholdings, *1485*
  slavery, 554
  tobacco farming, 1598
  tories, 346, 1602
  Unionism. *See under* Unionism
  Union occupation, 1423, 1577–1579, 1640, 1647
  Whig party, 1708
  see also particular cities and place names
Tennessee (ship), 17, 236, 237, 372, 992, 1062, 1124, 1126, 1130, 1236, 1303, 1387, 1516, **1580–1581**
  battle of Mobile Bay, 1059, 1062
  ordnance, 97, 1118
Tennessee II (ship), 1124
Tennessee Baptist (newspaper), 130
Tennessee Ernie Ford Sings Songs of the Civil War (recording), 487
Tennessee Johnson (film), 573
Tennessee River, 293, 1227, 1420, 1612, 1691, 1692
  Henry and Donelson Campaign, 764–765
Ten Percent Plan, 1097
  New Orleans, 1138
  Tennessee, 1578
Ten-Slave Law, 1444
Terrapin from Franklin. *See* Early, Jubal
Terrell, Alexander W., **1581**
Terrett, George H., 415
Terrill, James Barbour, 224, **1581–1582**
Terrill, William R., 224, 1197
Territorial expansion. *See* Expansionism in the antebellum South; Imperialism
Terry, Alfred H., 611, 1152
Terry, Benjamin Franklin, 1706
Terry, Henry D., 856
Terry, William, 504, 1185, 1549, **1582**
Terry, William Richard, **1582**
Terry's Texas Rangers, 749, 1584
Texas, **1583–1587**
  annexation, 320, 553, 1374, 1629, 1715
  arsenal and armory, 1461, 1469
  battles, 1372
  black-white population comparison, *1435*
  bread riots, 1586
  Confederate commands, 713, 1433
  congressmen, 143–144, 207, 444, 705, 710, 715–717, 762–763, 767, 1088, 1164, 1311–1312, 1404, 1696, 1715–1717, 1718, 1746
  conscription controversy, 873
  Constitution ratification, 403
  cotton trade, 1169, 1215, 1586, 1608
  currency issues, 433, 1279, 1281
  debt, 462
  Democratic party, 465
  education, 516, 519
  election of 1860, 521, 522, 523
  emancipation, 874
  enslavement of free blacks, 642
  farm acreage, *1484*
  flag, 587
  foreign population, 602, 675, 676, 1346
  free black population, 642
  frontier forts, 622–623
  governors, 143–144, 341, 701, 702, 703, 704, 960–961, 1097–1098, 1346–1347, 1716
  Hood's Brigade, 791
  invasion of, 1314
  Irish regiment, 823
  Juneteenth celebration, 874, 1446
  last Civil War engagement, 1433, 1473
  livestock breeding, 792
  mail delivery, 1312
  military actions, 1584–1585
  neutral border, 1606
  niter production, 1147
  population, 1233
  railroads, 1293, 1295, 1296, 1297
  refugees, 1318, 1608–1609
  rice production, 1328
  roads, 1339
  Roman Catholics, 1346
  Sabine Pass battle, 1357
  secession. *See under* Secession
  secession and Confederacy membership dates, *1379*
  secession date correlated with total black population, *1486*

slaveholdings, *1485*
slavery, 551, 557
small arms and munitions manufacture, 1458, 1470
statehood, 381, 555
state navy, 1530
sugar industry, 1559, 1560
taxation, 485
Trans-Mississippi Department, 1606
Unionism, 56, 116, 655, 676, 1583, 1585
see also particular cities and place names
Texas (locomotive), 41, 109
Texas (ship), 1303, 1580
Texas and Pacific Railroad, 1088
Texas and the Texans (Foote), 598
Texas Brigade. *See* Hood's Texas Brigade
Texas Marine Department, 1128
Texas Military Institute, 519
Texas Rangers, 1498
Texas State Military Board, 1585–1586
Textbooks, 516, **1587–1588**
patriotic, 307
publishing, 194, 715
readers, 1059
Textile industry, **1588–1589**
clothing, 356–357
Europe, 418
flag manufacture, 586
Georgia, 670
Great Britain, 180, 418, 711
handicrafts, 735
Mississippi, 1051
and urbanization, 1645
war efforts, 566, 1152
Thalian Association (Wilmington), 1726
Thalian Hall (Wilmington), 1589
Thanksgiving days, 1275
Thayer, John M., 56
Theater, 1231, **1589–1590**
Macon, Georgia, 978
music, 1101
popular Southern actors, 1231
Theft prosecutions, 427
Theodora (ship), 1619
They Met at Gettysburg (film), 573
Third Louisiana Redan, 621
Third System, fort construction, 617
Thirteenth Amendment, 7, 532, 708, 733, 1434, 1446, **1590–1591**
Thirty Years of Life in Three Continents (Leon), 924
Thirty Years' View (Benton), 597
Thoburn, Joseph, 583
Thomas, Allen, **1591**
Thomas, Bryan Morel, **1592**
Thomas, Dean S., *as contributor*, 1469–1471
Thomas, Edward Lloyd, 1001, **1592**
Thomas, Ella Gertrude Clanton, 472, 476, 520, 1009
Thomas, Emory M.
on blacks in Confederate Army, 4
on bread riots, 213
as contributor, 167–171, 915–916, 916–920, 921, 1181, 1554, 1600–1602
on Southern nationalism, 1114–1115
Thomas, George H., 111, 205, 260, 263, 304, 547, 674, 790, 887, 1006, 1007, 1755
Army of the Cumberland, 293, 294, 295
Chickamauga campaign, 302
Dalton, Georgia, 442
field fortifications, 626
Franklin and Nashville campaign, 633, 634–636, 1111, 1577
Mill Springs, Kentucky, 428, 1041, 1042
Thomas, J. Jefferson, 1009
Thomas, James Houston, **1592–1593**
Thomas, Jerry Bruce, *as contributor*, 797–798, 1186–1188
Thomas, John J., **1593**
Thomas, Lorenzo, 11–12
Thomas, William Holland, 297, **1593–1594**
Thomas, William T., 1061
Thomas de la Rue & Company, 1242
Thomas, Griswold & Company, 514, 515
Thomas L. Wragg (ship), 1107
Thomason, Hugh French, 659, **1594**
Thomasville, Georgia, bread riots, 213
Thompson, Albert P., 1177
Thompson, George, 215
Thompson, H. S., 1103
Thompson, Jacob, 258, 348, 538, 934, 1271, 1272, 1526, **1594–1595**
Thompson, Jerry, *as contributor*, 143–144, 157, 1427–1428
Thompson, John R., 459–460, 936, 937, 985, 986, 1142
Thompson, M. Jeff, 1053, 1254, 1334
guerrilla warfare, 720
New Madrid and Island N. 10, 1133
Thompson, Waddy, 554, 555
Thompson, William T., 1683
Thompson's Station, Tennessee, 416, 835
Thomson, James, and George Thompson. *See* Thomson brothers
Thomson, M. S., 977
Thomson brothers (James and George)
blockade runners, 116, 184
Fingal (ship), 116, 184
Giraffe (ship), 1340
ironclad construction, 484, 1150
rams, 1303
Thoreau, Henry David, 742
Thorington, Jack, 309
Thornwell, James Henley, 1247
Thornwell, Thomas H., 1398
Thouvenel, Antoine Édouard, 482, 631, 632, 1620
Thrailkill, John, 274, 275, 725, 1599
Three Months in the Southern States (Fremantle), 193
Throckmorton, James, 1585
Tibbs, William Henry, 373, **1595–1596**
Ticket-of-Leave Man, The (play), 1231
Ticknor, Francis Orray, 936, 937
Tidball, E. M., 1127
Tidwell, William A., *as contributor*, 537–539, 542–547
Tift brothers (Asa and Nelson), 116, 1424, **1596**
Tiger Brigade. *See* Louisiana Tigers
Tiger-Lilies (novel by Lanier), 938
T. I. K. men, 510, 1571
Tilden, Samuel, 107
Tilghman, Lloyd, 764–765, **1596–1597**
Timberlake brothers, 224
Time-Life Company, 574
Times (London newspaper), 160, 161, 483, 1354
Timocas, 811
Timrod, Henry, 222, 936, 937, 985, **1597**, 1683
Tinclads, 1302
Tinsely, Elizabeth, 1346
Tipton, Missouri, 1409
Tise, Larry E., *as contributor*, 43–45, 583–584, 1272–1275
Tishomingo Creek. *See* Brice's Cross Roads, Mississippi
Tithing law. *See* Tax-in-kind
T. M. Brennan & Company, 98
Tobacco, **1597–1599**
consumption, 1598
Danville, Virginia, 443, 1598
and expansion of slavery, 552
plantation, 1174–1175, 1214
produce loan, 1270
rations, 1599
Virginia, 1330, 1643, 1645
Todd, Emily, 761
Todd, George, 274, 275, 725, 1289, **1599**

Todd's Tavern, 270
Tombigbee River, 1425
Tombs, James H., 445, 446, **1599–1600**
Tompkins, Sally L., 794, 1160, 1161, **1600**, 1740
Tom's Brooks, Virginia, 1347, 1419
Tonkawas, 1409
Toombs, Robert, 137, 229, *250*, 359, 400–401, 452, 474, 480, 497, 665, 668, *669*, 673, 675, 772, 773, 802, 803, 929, 1068, 1297, 1326, 1542, *1561*, **1600–1602**
  opposition to Davis (Jefferson), 1225
  as secretary of state, 251, 315, 479, 1023–1024, 1527, 1601
  Sharpsburg campaign, 1408
  voicing secessionists' fears, 1377–1378
Toon, Thomas Fentress, **1602**
Topography. *See* Mapmaking
Toppin, Edgar A., *as contributor*, 4–9, 1333
Torbert, Alfred T. A., 1418
Torch (ship), 446
Torches, Signal Corps, 1429
Tories, 385, **1602–1603**
  Alabama, 345–346
  Dallas, Moses, 441
  drain on manpower, 346
  Missouri, 1055
  see also Galvanized Yankees
Torpedo (ship), 447, 840
Torpedo Battery Service, 1360
Torpedo boats. *See* Davids
Torpedo Bureau, 287, 538, 734
  Rains, Gabriel, 1300
Torpedoes and mines, 336, 725, 1509, 1558, **1603–1605**
  Beauregard (P. G. T.) advocacy, 1130
  Brown, Isaac Newton, 226, 227
  Charleston as experimentation center, 289
  Davids, 445–446
  Davidson, Hunter, 447–448
  development, 993
  espionage operations, 538
  Glassell, William T., 692
  ironclad attack on Fort Sumter, 287
  Maury, Matthew Fontaine, 1017–1018
  naval use of, 777–778, 1126
  Rains, Gabriel, 1300
  Savannah harbor, 685
  spar, **1515–1516**
  Tombs, James H., 1599–1600
  Tredegar Iron Works, 1617
  see also Hand grenades and land mines
Torrence, Leonidas, 475
Torture, guerrilla warfare, 719, 720, 722, 724
Total war, 260, 277, 334, 348, 390, 601, 1007, 1213, 1352
Totten, Joseph G., 617
Touchstone, Blake, *as contributor*, 313–314, 1419–1420
Tourge, Albion W., 938
Tower defense, 622
Tower Dupre, 622
Towns, George W., 162, 675, 852
Townsend, James H., 1334
Tracts, religious, 1400
Tracy, Edward Dorr, 1236, 1237, **1605**
Trade. *See* Anglo-American purchasing; Blockade; Commerce raiders; Foreign trade; Nullification controversy; Privateers
Trader, Ella K. *See* Newsom, Ella King
Trader, William H., 1141
Trans-Mississippi Department, 68, 72, 1340, **1605–1611**
  Arkansas campaign, 56, 57
  Bagby, Arthur P., 121
  battle flags, 586
  command, 785
  composition, 66
  early military operations, 1606–1607
  Elkhorn Tavern, Arkansas, 526, 527
  Forney, John Horace, 605
  founding, 72
  Hardeman, William, 738
  Hays, Harry, 753
  headquarters, 941
  Hindman, Thomas C., 776–777
  Holmes, Theophilus H., 785, 961, 1133
  Louisiana, 955
  Marmaduke, John Sappington, 1009
  Maury, D. H., 1017
  Nicholls, Francis, 1145
  ordnance, 799
  Parsons, Mosby Monroe, 1180
  Polignac, Camille J., 1223
  Prairie Grove, Arkansas, 1246
  Price, Sterling, 1251–1252
  quartermaster, 249
  Smith, E. Kirby, 7, 207, 461, 695, 738, 827, 908, 956, 1145, 1473, 1607–1610
  soldiers' pay, 345
  surrender, 74, 234, 956, 1515
  Texas, 1097
  Walker, Lucius Marshall, 1679
  Waterhouse, Richard, 1690
Transportation, 386, **1612**, *1613*
  camels, 1697
  Confederate regulation, 1172
  cotton, 417, 418
  engineer regiments, 534–535
  horses and mules, **791–793**
  inflation effects, 820
  mail, 1242
  Quartermaster Bureau function, 1291
  refugees, 1318
  Richmond, Virginia, 1330
  roads, **1338–1340**
  and urbanization, 1644
  war mobilization, 509
  see also Railroads; Waterways
Trapier, James H., **1613–1614**
Treasury Department, 249, 250, **1614–1616**
  civil service, 315, 370
  currency, 433–438
  debt, 461–463, 1618
  evacuation, 1180
  fiscal policy, 509–511
  Macon depository, 978
  Memminger, Christopher G. *See* Memminger, Christopher G.
  New Plan, 1140
  printing contest, 436, 438
  produce loan, 1269–1270
  public finance, 509–510, 1025, 1279–1286
  secretaries, 251, 252
  strains on, 64
  Trenholm, George. *See* Trenholm, George
Treasury notes, 433, *435*, *436*, *437*
  banking, 128
  Bureau, 1614
  circulation, 1248
  to finance war, 105, 392
  fundable into bonds, 434, 1024, 1025
  and inflation, 820, 821, 1270
  interest-bearing, 1280
  as legal tender, 392–393, 430, 1194, 1618
  mobilization funds, 1280
  as payment for impressed goods, 810
  Provisional Congress, 1069
  see also Bonds
Treaties, Indian, 811–812, 813, 815, 1173, 1290
Treatise on the Law of Sale of Personal Property (Benjamin), 160
Treatise on Therapeutics and Pharmacology, or Materia Medica (Wood), 758
Treaty of Paris (1856), 373, 418, 1527, 1528
  blockade legality, 481, 484, 631, 1353

Treaty of Washington, *Alabama* claims, 21–22
Tredegar Battalion, 34–35, 1617
Tredegar Iron Works, 34, 386, 407, 508, 902, 1043, 1044, 1124, 1330, 1332, **1616–1617**, 1645, 1647, 1648
  Anderson, Joseph R., 33–35, 96
  archaeological excavations, 49
  artillery manufacture, 96, 98
  cannons, 992
  Confederate government takeover, 1537
  government contractor, 1121, 1122
  labor, 3–4, 5, 74, 903
  locomotive production, 1294
  naval ordnance, 1117, 1118, 1604
  slave labor, 1440, 1443
  submarine development, 1556
Tregle, Joseph G., Jr., *as contributor*, 146–150, 425–426, 1453–1455
Tremblett, F. W., 1271
Trenches
  Army of Northern Virginia, 81, 82
  artillery, 94
  casualties, 338
  digging, 619
  field fortifications, 624, 919, 921
  hastily made, 819–820
  Mine Run campaign, 1043
  Petersburg campaign, 920, 1198, 1201
  see also Earthworks
Trenholm, George, 181, 511, 1025, 1026, 1248, **1618–1619**
  as secretary of treasury, 183, 251, 1614
Trenholm, William, 1616
Trenholm Brothers, 1616
Trent affair, 177, 360, 385, 631, 711–712, 803, 1015, **1619–1621**, 1749
  British reaction, 1528
  diplomacy, 481–482
  effect on U.S.-Canadian relations, 257
  Mason, James E., 1014–1016
  Slidell, John, 1014–1016, 1454–1455
Trévigne, Paul, 1138, **1621**
Trigg, Robert, 304
Trimble, Isaac, 196, 431, **1621–1622**
  Gettysburg campaign, 681, 682
  Sharpsburg campaign, 1406
Triplett, George Washington, **1622**
Trippe, Robert Pleasant, 1476, **1622–1623**
Triracial groups, 1046
Triumph (ship), 116
Tropic (ship), 1530
Trowbridge, Charles, 10
Trumbull, Lyman, 390
Tuberculosis, 754, 806
Tubman, Harriet, 1450, **1623**
Tubman, John, 1623
Tucker, Beverly, 934
Tucker, John, 475
Tucker, John Randolph, 289, 840, 1008, 1181, **1623–1624**
Tucker, Nathaniel Beverly, 936
Tucker, St. George, 1532
Tucker, Spencer C., *as contributor*, 62–63, 223, 1117–1120
Tucker, William Feimster, 1404, **1624**
Tucker and Perkins lithographs, 1231
Tulane University, 957
Tulifinny Creek, South Carolina, 312
Tullahoma campaign, 86, 302, 373, 524, 657, 700, 1577
Tunstall, Peyton Randolph, and Ann Arrington Tunstall, 350
Tunstall, Virginia. *See* Clay-Clopton, Virginia
Tupelo, Mississippi, **1624–1625**
Turchin, John B., 293
Turner, Joseph A., **1625–1626**
Turner, Josiah, 89, **1626–1627**
Turner, Maxine, *as contributor*, 445–446, 447–448, 685, 962, 1307, 1334, 1348–1349, 1371, 1556–1558, 1603–1605, 1688–1689
Turner, Nat, 989, 1350
Turner, Richard R., 931, 932
Turner, Thomas (weapons manufacture), 1468
Turner, Thomas P. (Libby Prison commandant), 930–931
Turner's Gap (South Mountain, Maryland), 1513
Turnpikes, 1339
Tuscaloosa (ship), 20, 236, 374, 1124, 1126, 1303, 1393–1394, **1627**
Tuscarora (ship), 1107
Tuscumbia and Decatur Railroad, 1692
Tuscumbia Female Academy, 520
Twain, Mark. *See* Clemens, Samuel Langhorne
Twenty-Slave Law of 1862, 89, 345, 392, 397, 532, 884, 1083, 1216, 1219, 1395, 1444
  social conflict, 1491–1492
Twiggs, David E., 432, 623, 769, 970, 1138, 1583, 1596, **1627–1628**
Twin-screw vessels, 182, 186
"290." *See* Reid, Samuel
Two Roads to Sumter (Catton and Catton), 1293
Tybee Island, Georgia, 1366
Tyler, John, 383, 553, 964–965, 1336, 1337, 1384, **1628–1631**, 1662
  congressional election, 972
  Washington Peace Conference, 1630, 1689, 1690
Tyler, Lyon G., *as contributor*, 1689–1690
Tyler, Robert Charles, 623, 1478, 1614, 1630, **1631**
Tyler, Texas
  arsenal, 90
  long arms manufacture, 1458
Tyler (ship), 55
Typhoid fever, 755, 867, 1195
  prison epidemic, 39, 610
Typhus fever, 755
Tyson, Aaron, 1631
Tyson, Bryan, 1183, **1631–1632**

U

UDC. *See* United Daughters of the Confederacy
Ullman, Daniel, 11
Uncle Tom's Cabin (Stowe), 45
Unconditional surrender, 765, 767
Unconditional Union party, 217
Underground Railroad, 44, 1493, 1623
Under Southern Stars (film), 573
Undertakers, 651
Under the Stars and Crescent (Leon), 924
Underwater archaeology, 48, 49
Underwood, John W. H., *669*
Underwood convention, 804
Underwriter (ship), 685, 960, 1008, 1126, 1371, 1743
Undine (ship), 609
Unfinished Cathedral (Stribling), 939
Unicoy Road, 1339
Uniforms, **1633–1636**
  African American Union regiment, 1447
  army, 1495, 1501–1502, **1633–1636**
  artillery, 92–93
  Confederate gray, 137, 356
  Hill, A. P., 770
  Hindman, Thomas C., 776
  infantry, 817–818
  Louisiana Tigers, *958*
  McCulloch, Ben, 970
  manufacture, 290
  medical officers, 1022
  Mosby's Rangers, 722
  museum collections, 1100
  navy and marines, 1359

Uniforms, *continued*
North Carolina troops, 1152, 1636
Quartermaster function, 508, 1291
shortages, 356
textile industry, 1589
Trans-Mississippi, 1608
Zouaves, 603
Union
debate over legal nature of, 1373
see also Northerners; Secession; State rights; Union occupation
Union Army. *See* Army, U.S.
Union Benevolent Society (Richmond), 641, 1229
Union Burial Ground Society, 643
Union First Corps, 826
Union Indian Brigade, 309
Unionism, 387, 1078, 1079, **1636–1640**
Alabama, 14, 17, 308–309, 431, 454, 842, 927, 1482, 1637, 1638, 1639, 1679, 1695
Arkansas, 54, 57, 659, 660, 662, 1097, 1349, 1380, 1594, 1638, 1639, 1640, 1694
Compromise of 1850, 1375
Confederate Congress, 393, 525
cooperationists and, 1637–1638
craftsmen, 902
Crittenden Compromise, 429
Democratic party and, 466–467
election of 1860, 522
expansion of slavery, 555–556
farmers, 1226
Florida, 1637, 1639
foreign-born, 346
Fort Sumter and, 1382–1383
Frietchie, Barbara, 646
Georgia, 29, 138, 359, 670, 772, 786, 882, 1375, 1637, 1745
German immigrant, 676
and guerrilla activity, 720–725
Heroes of America, **768–769**
Indian loyalists, 1166–1167
Jones County, Mississippi, 863–864
Kansas, 719
Kentucky, 216, 720, 886–887, 987
and legal right to secession, 1375
Louisiana, 141, 729, 952, 1419–1420, 1637, 1639, 1640, 1698–1699
Maryland, 127
Mississippi, 224, 450, 1047, 1639
Missouri, 1251, 1380, 1441, 1606
North Carolina, 105, 134, 342, 379–380, 446, 654, 687–689, 705–708, 781, 855, 912, 942, 971, 1150, 1151, 1154–1155, 1288, 1301, 1304, 1380, 1631, 1650–1651
opposition to secession, 324, 788, 1637–1638
Peace Convention (1861). *See* Washington Peace Conference
peace movements, 1183, 1640
plain folk, 1213
planters, 1217, 1219
population, 1115–1116
Quaker, 1493
Republican party, 1322
Second Congress, 525
South Carolina, 1202, 1637
suppression of, 332
Tennessee, 230–231, 263, 291, 292, 332, 372, 387, 470, 532, 598, 640, 705–707, 745–746, 750–751, 798, 848, 894–895, 1380, 1573–1574, 1575–1576, 1578, 1638, 1639, 1640
Texas, 56, 116, 655, 676, 1583, 1585
tories, **1602–1603**
and Union occupation, 1138, 1163, 1640, 1641
victories in upper South, 1380–1381
Virginia, 123, 197, 260, 278, 332, 387, 443, 501, 926, 971, 1186–1187, 1250, 1331, 1337, 1380, 1381, 1638, 1640, 1662, 1699, 1711, 1712
"Waving the Bloody Shirt" of, 467
West Virginia, 1638
Wickham, Williams Carter, 1714
Unionist Creek Indians. *See* Creeks
Union Lead Mines (Virginia), 1147
Union occupation, **1640–1641**, 1647
Alabama, 1426
border states, 196
Charleston, South Carolina, 1510
free black labor experiments, 1220
Jackson, Mississippi, 837, 838, 839
Louisiana, 869–870
Nashville, Tennessee, 1420
Norfolk, Virginia, 1149–1150
North Carolina, 1524–1525
political clout of poor whites, 1226
Richmond, Virginia, 1420
Savannah, Georgia, 1367, 1368
Tennessee valley, 16–17
see also Reconstruction; particular cities and states
Union party, 123, 359
Union, Past and Future, The (publication), 663
Union Rangers, 720
United Confederate Veterans, 259, 388, 548, 695, 697, 909, 949, 1027
battle reenactments, 1317
documentaries, 572
founders, 921
United Daughters of the Confederacy, 160–161, 307, 388, 949, 950, 952, 1027–1028, 1333, 1600
Andersonville memorial, 1735
archaeology of Lost Cause, 48
documentaries, 573
Memorial Day observance, 1026
monuments, 1069, 1071
Southern Cross of Honor, 1022
United Sons of Confederate Veterans, 150
United States Colored Troops
regiments, 11, 12
see also African American troops in the Union Army
United States Military Academy
curriculum, 325
Jackson, Thomas J. ("Stonewall"), 830
Lee, Robert E., 916, 917
Virginia graduates, 84
United States Military Railroad, 1201, 1298, 1299
Universal Film (documentary films), 572, 573
Universalists, 215
Universities and colleges. *See* Higher education; Military education; particular institutions
University of Alabama, 518, 519, 1389, 1482–1483
archival collections, 1099
University of Georgia, 518
archival collections, 1099
University of Louisiana, 957
University of Mississippi, 517, 518, 1047
University of Nashville, 519
University of North Carolina, 517, 518, 1518
University of South Carolina, 517
University of Tennessee, 517–518
University of the South, 373, 518
University of Virginia, 518, 1336
"Unknown Dead, The" (Timrod), 937
Unvanquished, The (novel by Faulkner), 788, 939
Upham, Samuel C., 421
Upshur, Abel P., 1395, 1629
Upton, Emory, 1389, 1519
Urbanization, **1641–1648**
African American population, 1484, 1504, 1506
antebellum, 1633–1646
archaeology, 48
crime, 427
Danville, Virginia, 443
demographics, 1646–1647

and disease, 754
food riots, 1517
foreign-born population, 602
free black population, 1486
free-born population, 642
free markets, 641
German immigrants, 675
index of relative, *1642*, 1643
inflation, 346, 1517
Irish immigrants, 822–823
labor, 1489
Little Rock, Arkansas, 940–941
middle class, 1489–1490
populations, 1234
principle cities, *1658*
refugees, 346, 596, 1235, 1318, 1491
secession and Confederacy, 1137, 1647–1648
slave markets, 1453
and slavery, 1440, 1644, 1646
and transportation, 1645–1646
working women, 900–901
see also particular cities
USCT. *See* United States Colored Troops
Utah
slavery, 321
statehood, 381
as territory, 346, 1374–1375

V

Vaccination, 754
Vail, Alfred, 1573
Valentine Museum (Richmond), 283
Vallandigham, Clement L., 411, 412, 1183, 1271, 1595, 1743
Valley campaigns. *See* Shenandoah Valley
Valley Turnpike, Virginia, 1338, 1339, 1416, 1418, 1732
Value-added tax, 1248
Valuska, David L., *as contributor*, 1130–1131
Valverde, New Mexico, 1136, 1428
Van Buren, Martin, 802, 1336, 1629
Vance, Robert Brank, **1649**
Vance, Zebulon, 3, 192, 273, 314, 492, 768, 781, 782, 1142, 1386, 1594, **1649–1651**
blockade runners, 1152
on Confederate cavalry depredations, 1153–1154
on conscription, 1156–1157, 1244–1245
debate with Lander (William), 907
denunciation of speculators, 1517
as governor of North Carolina, 106, 342, 446, 447, 689, 690, 701, 702, 704, 707, 708, 1151, 1153–1157, 1297, 1301, 1307, 1311
gubernatorial election, 1156, 1157
joke-telling skills, 594
obstructionist policies, 331, 387, 1157, 1184, 1224, 1225, 1249
peace movement, 1626
state rights extremism, 1535–1536
Van Cleve, H. P., 302, 1095, 1096
Vanderbilt University, 318
Van Derveer, Ferdinand, 1073
Vandiver, Frank E.
as contributor, 89–91, 448–453, 698–699, 1170, 1247–1249
on Confederate strategy, 327, 386
Van Dorn, Earl, 68, 891, 930, 1472, 1584, **1651–1652**
Army of the West, 1251
battle flag, 586
Corinth, Mississippi, 413–415
Elkhorn Tavern, Arkansas, 526–527, 1693
Holly Springs, Mississippi, raid, 328, 783–785
martial law imposition, 640
in Mississippi, 662, 825, 835
staff, 943, 990, 1622
strategy and tactics, 140
suspension of habeas corpus, 599
Trans-Mississippi Department, 970, 1606–1607
Vicksburg campaign, 890, 1656
and war correspondents, 274
Van Dyke, Henry J., 1275
Van Evrie, John H., 583, 1274, 1275
Van Lew, Elizabeth, 541, 1331, **1652**
Varieties Theater (Richmond), 1231
Varon, Elizabeth R., *as contributor*, 143, 201–202, 601, 714, 1074–1075, 1089–1090, 1432, 1652
Varuna (ship), 1139, 1334
Vaughan, Alfred Jefferson, Jr., 695, **1652–1653**, 1753
Vaughn, John Crawford, 1210, 1547, **1653–1654**
Vaughn and Lynn Company, 1562
Venable, Abraham Watkins, **1654**
Venable, Charles S., *77*, 546
Venereal diseases, 1276–1277
Hill, A. P., 770, 771
hospital, 796
treatment, 755
see also particular diseases
Venus (ship), 609
Vernon, Ida, 1231, 1590
Verot, Augustin, 1346
Vesey, Denmark, 311, 1333, 1440, 1647
"Vesper" (pseudonym), 1683
Vest, George C., **1654**
Vest Resolutions, 1654
Veteran Reserve Corps, 1221
Veterans
battle reenactments, 1317
Lee Monument Association, 922–923
Memorial Day, 1026–1027
memorial organizations, 1027–1028
monuments and memorials, 1069–1074
oral histories, 1167
preservation of Lost Cause, 949
reunion documentaries, 572, 573
reunions, 1027, 1035, 1074
soldiers' homes, 1501–1502
see also particular organizations
Veto, single-item, 400, 1068
V. H. Ivy (ship), 1269
Vice presidency, 251, 383, **1654–1655**
selection, 1068
Stephens, Alexander H., 1539–1542
term of office, 1068
Vicksburg, Mississippi
defenses, 620
ordnance manufacture, 98
Vicksburg (ship), 1580
Vicksburg campaign, 53, 125, 337, 524, 608, 623, 676, 838, 860, 1049, 1572, 1605, 1609, **1655–1660**, *1656*
Chocktaw unit, 812
Ector, Matthew Duncan, 512
Featherston, Winfield Scott, 569
field fortifications, 626
Green, Martin Edwin, 713
Gregg, John, 716
Hawes, J. M., 751, 835
Higgins, Edward, 769
impact on morale, 1079–1080
intelligence operations, 541
Jackson, Mississippi, 837–839
Johnston, Joseph E., 716, 835, 1049, 1291, 1658, 1659, 1660, 1753
map, 1657
monument, 1072
Orphan Brigade, 1170
Pemberton, John C., 1189
Port Gibson, Mississippi, 1236–1238
Quarles, William Andrew, 1291
Seddon, James A., 1386
Shoup, Francis, 1427
siege, 1659–1660
Smith, Martin Luther, 1476

Vicksburg campaign, *continued*
starvation rations, 595
Stevenson, Carter, 1545
Stone (Kate) diary description, 1546
strategic significance, 328, 1655, 1659
and supply cutoffs, 1165
Union occupation, 1640
Waul, Thomas Neville, 1696
Young, William Hugh, 1753
Vicksburg Evening Post (newspaper), 1167
Vicksburg National Military Park, 921, 1072, 1073, 1074
Vicksburg Sharpshooters, 1052
Vicksburg Whig (newspaper), 1144
Victor (ship), 375, 1308
Victoria, queen of Great Britain, 180, 711, 1015
neutrality proclamation, 19, 385, 480, 1620
Vidaurri, Santiago, 1586
Video. *See* Film and video
Video History of the Civil War, The, 574
Vidor, Florence, *578*
Vidor, King, 578
Viele, Egbert, 1149
Vignaud, Charles, 426
Villepigue, John Bordenave, 145, **1660–1661**
Villeré, Charles Jacques, **1661**
Viper (ship), 446
Virginia, **1661–1669**
antebellum population, 1663
Appomattox campaign. *See* Appomattox campaign
Army of. *See* Army of Northern Virginia; Army of Southwest Virginia
arsenals and armories, 1455–1456, 1458, 1464, 1465
Ball's Bluff, 126–127, 569
as battleground, 1347, 1664-1666; *see also* particular sites and battles
black-white population comparison, 1434, *1435*
blockade, 177–178
Buckland Mills, 237
Chancellorsville campaign. *See* Chancellorsville
Confederate march through northwestern, 807
congressmen, 124–125, 144, 186–187, 197–198, 223, 259–260, 278–279, 367, 464, 651–652, 663, 684, 694–695, 780–781, 782–783, 802–804, 805, 842–844, 861–862, 964–965, 971–972, 975–976, 1014, 1040, 1063–1064, 1250–1251, 1278, 1337–1338, 1353–1354, 1371, 1385, 1479, 1480, 1525, 1582, 1628, 1677, 1711, 1712, 1714
conscription controversy, 873
Constitution ratification, 403
currency issues, 433, 1279, 1281
debt, 462
Department of. *See* Department of North Carolina and Southern Virginia; Department of Northern Virginia; Department of Southwest Virginia
education, 515, 516
election of 1860, 521, 522, 523
employment of free blacks, 643
farm acreage, *1484*
fire-eaters, 1376–1377, 1547
First Brigade. *See subhead* Stonewall Brigade *below*
First Infantry Regiment, 1516
flag, 587
foreign population, 602
Fredericksburg campaign. *See* Fredericksburg campaign
free black population, 642, 643, 644, 1484, 1646
free black volunteers, 643
freedom of the press, 641
freeing of surplus slaves, 1436
Gosport Navy Yard. *See* Gosport Navy Yard
government, 1187
government reorganization, 1700, 1702
governors, 701, 703, 782–783, 925–926, 1187–1188, 1479, 1480–1481, 1736
guerrilla warfare, 722, 725
Heroes of America, 768, 769
historical societies, 1512
hospitals, 794
Imboden, John D., 807
iron production, 1148
livestock breeding, 792
mining, 1043
Mosby's Confederacy, 1090
motto, 587
newspapers, 1141–1142
niter production, 1147
peace movements, 1336–1337
Peninsular campaign. *See* Peninsular campaign
population, 1233
prisons, 1667
railroads, 1293, 1294, 1295, 1296, 1297, 1546, 1556
Reconstruction. *See under* Reconstruction
Republican party, 1322
roads, 1339
Saltville Massacre, 1362, 1363, 1547
secession. *See under* Secession
secession and Confederacy membership dates, *1379*
secession date correlated with total black population, *1486*
Seddon, James A., 1383–1387
Seven Days' Battles. *See* Seven Days' Battles
Seven Pines. *See* Seven Pines
Shenandoah campaigns. *See* Shenandoah Valley
slave conditions, 1438–1439
slave escapes, 1444
slaveholdings, *1485*
slavery, 402, 554
small arms and munitions manufacture, 1455–1457, 1460, 1464, 1470, 1471
small arms imports, 1465
Smith, William ("Extra Billy"), 1479–1481
soldiers' home, 1502, 1503
Spotsylvania campaign. *See* Spotsylvania campaign
Stoneman's raids, 1547
Stonewall Brigade, 1548–1549
taxes, 1283, 1284, 1570
tobacco farming, 1598
tories, 346, 1602
Underwood convention, 804
Unionism. *See under* Unionism
Union occupation, 1640, 1647
urbanization, 1643, 1645, 1646
Washington Peace Conference, 1381, 1384, 1689–1690
West Point graduates, 84
Whig party, 1708
Wilderness campaign. *See* Wilderness campaign
Wilmot Proviso response, 1728
Yorktown siege, 1752
see also West Virginia; West Virginia operations; particular cities and place names
Virginia (ship), 22, 178, 223, 235–236, 289, 447, 496, 567, 823, 840, 863, 992, 993, 1018, 1124, 1129, 1149, 1193, 1302, 1516, **1669–1671**, 1725
battle with *Monitor*, 700, 1149, 1181, 1424, 1670–1671, *1671*, 1743
conversion at Gosport Navy Yard, 1424

design, 1235, 1236
Norfolk, Virginia, 605
ordnance, 96, *1118*, 1119, *1120*
scuttling of, 1018, 1568–1569
Virginia II (ship), 824, 840, 841, 1124, 1126, 1303, 1424
design and construction, 709
Virginia and Kentucky Resolutions. *See* Kentucky and Virginia Resolutions
Virginia and Tennessee Railroad, 357, 913, 1702, 1704, 1705
Virginia Armory. *See* Richmond, Virginia, arsenal and armory
Virginia Bible Society, 165
Virginia Brigade. *See* Stonewall Brigade
Virginia Cavalier, The (Alexander), 1590
Virginia Central Railroad, 1001, 1330, 1412, 1413, 1416, 1546, 1714
Virginia City (film), 580
Virginia City Territorial Enterprise, 354
Virginia Company (London), 1598
Virginia Conservation Commission, 573
Virginia Educational Association, 1587
Virginia Historical Society. *See* Southern Historical Society
Virginia Military Institute, 223, 506, 518, 519, 520, 674, 741, 916, 957, 1018, **1671–1673**
elite unit, 1516
Garland, Samuel, 663
graduates, 222, 224, 369, 519, 799, 907, 967, 990, 1182, 1344, 1581, 1582, 1676–1677, 1679, 1706
Jackson, Thomas J. ("Stonewall"), 369, 831–832, 1672–1673, 1676–1677
Kemper, James Lawson, 881
Lynchburg, Virginia, defense, 963
New Market, Virginia, 1135, 1136
Ruffin, Edmund, 1350
Walker, James Alexander, 1676–1677
Virginia School (state rights), 1532
Virginia State Agricultural Society, 1349
Virginia State Armory, 174
Virginia State Line, 925
Vitagraph Studios, 574
Vivant, Constance, 1333
VMI. *See* Virginia Military Institute
Volck, Adalbert, 1231, 1255, **1673–1674**
Volunteer Relief Committee (Mobile), 1058
Von Borcke, Heros, 604
Voorhees, Daniel W., 411
Vore, Israel G., 812
Voting rights. *See* Suffrage
Vowles, D. W., 1267
Vulcan Iron Works, 1725

W

Wabash (ship), 446, 1240, 1269
Wachusetts (ship), 375, 592
Waddell, A. M., 1142
Waddell, James, 376, 1151, 1500, **1675**
Shenandoah commission, 1411–1412
Wade, Benjamin F., 159, 1702
Wade, John, 258
Wadley, William M., 1297
Wadsworth, James, 678, 679
Wagener, John A., 676
Wages and salaries
African American Union soldiers, 12
civil service, 315
congressmen, 373
female clerks, 1740
inflation effects, 821, 902–903, 1306
postal workers, 1243
railroad, 1298
soldiers, 7, 89, 345, 566, 670, 902, 912, 967, 1495
strike, 316
teachers, 1722
Waggaman, Eugene, 958
Wagner, A. J., 1684
Wagons, 791, *792*, 793
Waite, C. A., 1628
Wakarusa War, 175
Wake Forest College, 517, 518
Wakelyn, Jon L., *as contributor*, 282–283, 535, 1320–1321, 1346
Walhalla, South Carolina, powder works, 1245
Walker, David, 1333
Walker, Francis, 1095
Walker, Gilbert C., 124
Walker, Henry H., 222–223, **1676**
Walker, James Alexander, **1676–1677**
Stonewall Brigade command, 1549
Walker, John George, 586, 605, 971, 974, 1372, 1610, 1660, **1677**, 1696
Harpers Ferry, West Virginia, 742, 743
Mansfield, Louisiana, 1005
Sharpsburg campaign, 1406
Walker, John H., 893
Walker, John Williams, 1678
Walker, Judith Page, 1335
Walker, Leroy P., 159, 206, *250*, 452, 628, 629, 710, **1678–1679**, 1680
as secretary of war, 251, 273, 348, 410, 1248, 1528, 1684, 1686, 1716
Walker, Lucius Marshall, 1475, **1679**
Walker, Mary, 266
Walker, "Mud." *See* Walker, Henry H.
Walker, Norman Stewart, 181, 684
Walker, "Old Rube." *See* Walker, Reuben Lindsay
Walker, "Old Shot Pouch." *See* Walker, W. H. T.
Walker, Reuben Lindsay, **1679–1680**
Walker, Richard Wilde, 19, 348, **1680**
Walker, Robert J., 1681
Walker, "Stonewall Jim." *See* Walker, James Alexander
Walker, Tandy, 305, 310, 813, 815
Walker, W. H. T., 86, 829, 1544, **1680–1681**, 1728
Walker, William (brigadier general), **1681**
Walker, William (filibusterer), 255, 557, 808, 1145, 1209, 1228, 1631
prosecution of, 1395, 1504
Seddon (James A.) praise, 1384
Walker Legion, 138
Walker, Richards, and Company, 193
Walker's Appeal (Walker), 1333
Wallace, Lee A., Jr., *as contributor*, 407–408, 415–416, 1278–1279, 1697–1698
Wallace, Lew, 503, 504, 505, 697
Henry and Donelson campaign, 766
Shiloh campaign, 1420, 1422, 1423
Wallace, William Henry, **1681–1682**
Wallace, William H. L. (Union general), 1422
Wallenstein, Peter, *as contributor*, 51, 74–75, 1136, 1269–1270, 1525, 1569–1571
Wallpaper, 1232
Walls, Josiah, **1682**
Walthall, Edward Cary, 163, **1682–1683**
Walthall, Henry B., *576*
Walthall, William T., 150
Walton, James B., 25
Wanderer (ship), 394
War. *See* Civil War; Guerrilla warfare; Rules of war; Total war; other particular wars
War: A Poem with Copious Notes, Founded on the Revolution of 1861–1862 (Hewitt), 936
War between the States. *See* Civil War, names for
War between the States, The (television program), 573
War correspondents, 273–274, 985, **1683–1684**
Clemens, Samuel Langhorne, 354

War Department, **1684–1688**
agents, 547
army organization, 66
Benjamin, Judah P., 90, 148, 159–160, 252, 474, 640, 654, 836, 947, 1334, 1528
bill payment, 1614
Bledsoe, Albert T., 174
Breckinridge, John C., 214–215
bureaus, 1685
and cabinet, 249, 250, 251, 252
Campbell, John A., 255–256
censorship, 273
civil service, 315, 316
Clay, Clement C., 348
confiscation, 250
conscription exemption, 397
Cooper, Samuel, 410
desertion estimates, 467
letters from soldiers' families, 1244, 1245
New Plan, 1140
Niter and Mining Bureau, 1147
organization, 1684–1686
Randolph, George Wythe, 1306, 1385, 1475
Regular Army, 64
secretaries, *251*, 252; *see also* particular names
Seddon, James A., 1385–1387
Smith, Gustavus W., 1475
state contributions, 704
Trans-Mississippi Department, 68
Walker, Leroy P., *250*, 1678–1679
war matériels policies, 1537–1538
see also particular bureaus
Ward, Geoffrey C., 574
Ward, George Taliaferro, 1364, 1566, **1688**
Ward, John Quincy Adams, 1073
Ward, William H., 1567
Ware, Charles Pickard, 1104
Ware, Horace, 1410
Ware Bottom Church, 1681
Warley, Alexander Frazer, 22, 407, **1688–1689**
War matériels. *See* Arms, weapons, and ammunition; State socialism
Warmoth, Henry Clay, 1348
Warner Brothers (documentary films), 573
War of 1812, 1408, 1532
War of Secession. *See* Civil War, names for
War of the Rebellion. *See* Civil War, names for
War of the Rebellion (Foote), 600
War of the Rebellion: A Compilation of the Official Records of the Union and Confederate Armies, 102, 125, 943, 1746
Warren, G. K., 45, 1199, 1200, 1719
Gettysburg campaign, 681
Manassas, Second, 1002
Mine Run campaign, 1043
Warren, Robert Penn, 938–939
Warrens of Virginia, The (film), *575*, 577
Warrington Navy Yard (Florida), *1497*
Warrior (ship), 1334
War's Aftermath, The (television program), 573
Warsaw, Missouri, 1409
Warships. *See* particular ships
War Songs of the South, 1232
War-te-she, 1290
Wartime Papers (Lee), 476
Washburn, Cadwallader C., 1029, 1030
Washington, George, 395, 741, 747, 916, 1516
constitutional interpretation, 1531
establishment of armories and arsenals, 738
likeness on postal stamp, *1523*
slave manumission, 44
Washington, Lewis, 741
Washington, Lucius Quinton, 1528
Washington, William D., *Burial of Latané*, 242, 243, 459, 460, 951, 1231, 1554
Washington, D.C.
bordellos, 1276
Confederate signal station plan, 1429–1430
Early's raid. *See* Early's Washington raid
Heroes of America, 768
peace conference. *See* Washington Peace Conference
population, 339
slavery, 381, 429
slave trade abolishment, 1374
Washington, North Carolina, 379, 380
civil order breakdown, 1492
shipyards, 1424
Washington (ship), 1530
Washington and Lee University, 45, 223, 505
Lee, George Washington Custis, 916
Lee, Robert E., 920
Lee statue, 922, 951, 1069
Washington Artillery, 952, 1205, 1347, 1516
uniforms, 93
Washington Battalion, 91
Washington College. *See* Washington and Lee University
Washington Peace Conference, 223, 1085, 1336–1337, 1345–1346, 1381, 1630, 1662, **1689–1690**
Wasp (ship), 445, 840
Watchman (publication), 1518
Waterhouse, Richard, **1690**
Waterhouse & Bowes, 1245
Water Oaks Pond, Tennessee, 1423
Waterways, 767, 1612, **1691-1692**; *see also* particular waterways
Water Witch (ship), 441, 1008, 1360, 1371
Watie, Buck. *See* Boudinot, Elias C.
Watie, Isaac S. *See* Watie, Stand
Watie, Stand, 198, 199, 297, 813, 814–815, 1607, **1692–1694**
Indian troop command, 1390, 1391
surrender to Union, 1391
Watie, Thomas, 1693
Watkin, Sam, 475
Watkins, Beverly, *as contributor*, 658–662
Watkins, Henningham, 964
Watkins, William W., 659, **1694**
Watson, Baxter, 777, 1556, 1557
Watson, John W. C., 200, 1205, **1694**
Watson, Thomas E., 570
Watterson, Henry, 274, 1143, 1683
Watts, Ann Selden, 780
Watts, Gordon, *as contributor*, 2–3, 19–20, 21–22, 710–713, 1619–1621, 1722–1723
Watts, Kate, 1492
Watts, Thomas H., 14, 16, 17, 18–19, 207, 348, 701, 702, 703, 892, 1075, **1695**
Alabama gubernatorial contest, 1426, 1427
as attorney general, 251, 252
Waul, Thomas Neville, 893, **1696**
Waul's Legion, 1696
Wayne, Henry Constantine, **1696–1697**
Waynesboro, Georgia, 27
Wayside hospitals, 795, 1022, 1089
Weapons. *See* Arms, weapons, and ammunition; Artillery; Edged weapons; Hand grenades and land mines; Naval guns; Ordnance Bureau; Small arms; Torpedoes and mines; particular weapons
Wearing of the Gray (Cooke), 408
Weather, effects on farming, 566, 596, 1412–1413
Webb, Isaac, 744

Webb, James Watson, caricature, *933*
Webb, Ross A., *as contributor*, 1177
Webb, Thomas, 1298
Webb, William A., 116, 441
Webb (ship), 1309, **1697**
Webster, Daniel, *381*, *649*, 1532, 1533, 1626, 1629
Webster, H. D. L., 1103
Webster, Timothy, 540
Wedderburn and Alfriend, 985–986
Weed, Thurlow, 687, 688
Weehawken (ship), 116
Weekly Courier (Rome, Georgia, newspaper), 1082
Weekly Standard (Raleigh newspaper), 1183
Weems, Charles Force, 1518
Weer, William, Indian Expedition, 97
Weichmann, Louis J., 1432
Weigley, Russell F., 328
Weiner, Marli F., *as contributor*, 1027–1028
Weisiger, David Addison, **1697–1698**
Weitzel, Godfrey, 954, 1239, 1420
Welch, Israel Victor, **1698**
Weld, Theodore, 319
Weldon Railroad. *See* Globe Tavern, Virginia; Wilmington and Weldon Railroad
Welfare. *See* Free markets; Poor relief; State socialism
Welles, Gideon, 178, 588, 611, 700, 934, 1353, 1394
  caricature, *177*
Wells, James Madison, 702, 885, 1639, **1698–1699**
Wells, Robert W., 494
Werlich, David P., *as contributor*, 1181–1182, 1623–1624
Wert, Jeffry D., *as contributor*, 1090, 1091–1092
Wesleyan College, 520
West, A. L., 734
West, A. M., 455
West and Johnston, 193, 194, 937, 1232
Western and Atlantic Railroad, 41, 109, 112, 113, 229, 447, 607, 672, 929, 1294, 1297, 1298, 1697, 1708
Western Carolinian (newspaper), 422
Western concentration bloc, 196
Western Military Institute, 519
Western Sanitary Fair, 1064
Westfield (ship), 656
West Florida Commercial (newspaper), 994
West India Squadron, 179
West Indies. *See* Caribbean; particular islands
West Point, New York. *See* United States Military Academy
West Point, Ohio, capture of Morgan (John Hunt), 1089
"West Point of the South." *See* Virginia Military Institute
Westport, Missouri, 1252, 1255
West Virginia, 387, 551, **1699–1703**
  formation, 6, 522, 1187, 1663, 1702–1703, 1704–1705
  governors, 1700
  Harpers Ferry. *See* Harpers Ferry
  Heroes of America, 768
  military actions, 1700-1702; *see also* Harpers Ferry, West Virginia; West Virginia operations
  Peirpoint, Francis H., 1187
  Republican party, 1322
  Rich Mountain, 465
  salt making, 1362
  tax system, 1570
  tories, 1602
  Unionism, 1638
West Virginia operations, **1703–1706**
  of 1861, 1700–1701, **1703–1706**
  of 1862 and 1863, **1705–1706**
  map, *1704*
  see also Harpers Ferry, West Virginia
Wet plate photographic process, 1205, 1206
W. G. Clark and Company, 1059
Wharton, Gabriel Colvin, 271, 582, **1706**
Wharton, John Austin, 151, 961, 1197, 1317, 1538, **1706–1707**, 1708
  cavalry, 266
  Murfreesboro, Tennessee, 1095
W. H. Crisp troupe, 1231
Wheat, Roberdeau, 952, 957
Wheeler, Joseph, 27, 37, 440, 736, 779, 800, 826, 880, 1547, **1707**
  Army of Tennessee, 85, 87, 88, 1013
  Atlanta campaign, 111, 112, 113
  cavalry, 266, 267, 749
  Chattanooga campaign, 293
  Dalton, Georgia, 442
  Fayetteville, North Carolina, 262
  Franklin and Nashville campaign, 632, 633
  Knoxville campaign, 895
  Murfreesboro, Tennessee, 1094
  Perryville, Kentucky, 1196–1197
  raids. *See* Wheeler's raids
  Savannah line of retreat, 1369
  Sherman's March to the Sea, 1006, 1007
Wheeler's raids, **1707–1708**
Wheeling Convention
  first, 1187, 1699–1700, 1704–1705
  second, 1187, 1700, 1702
"When Johnny Comes Marching Home Again" (song), 1498
Whig and Public Advertiser (Richmond newspaper), 1142, 1330
Whig and Rebel Ventilator (Knoxville newspaper), 1143
Whiggamore, 1708
Whig party, 387, 456, **1708–1709**, 1728
  Alabama, 16, 18, 308, 524, 1286, 1477, 1482
  Arkansas, 587
  in cities, 1647
  Compromise of 1850, 381
  Confederate Congress, 391–392, 393
  Constitutional Union party formation, 403
  creoles, 426
  demise, 451, 464, 1224
  Democratic party relationship, 387, 465
  election of 1860, 521, 1376
  expansion of slavery, 320, 553, 554, 557
  Florida, 122, 1688
  Georgia, 13, 1623
  Kansas-Nebraska Act, 175, 176
  Kentucky, 1011, 1075, 1724
  Louisiana, 395, 1698
  Mississippi, 23, 203, 224, 1047, 1694
  Montgomery convention, 1067
  North Carolina, 105, 106, 448, 781, 1085, 1184, 1288, 1593, 1626, 1631
  opposition to secession, 333
  peace movements, 1183
  and Southern Unionists, 654, 842, 1637, 1638, 1639, 1640
  Stephens, Alexander H., 1539
  Tennessee, 264, 666, 667, 763, 895, 1300, 1573, 1574, 1575, 1595
  territorial expansion, 380, 381
  Virginia, 33, 34, 123, 197, 259, 278, 802, 1186, 1250, 1329, 1336, 1628–1629
  see also Know-Nothing party
Whiskey. *See* Alcohol
Whisper (ship), 1723
White, Daniel Price, **1709**
White, Hugh L., 1628
White, James L., 1387
White, John, 3
White, Thomas W., 986
White House, Confederate, 1028, 1100, 1332, **1710–1711**
  prisoners of war display, 1262

White House, U.S., plot to blow up, 538
"White Knight of the Valley." *See* Ashby, Turner
White Man, The (newspaper), 143
White Oak Road, Virginia, 45
White Oaks Swamp, Virginia, 78, 731, 834, 918
  map, 1401
White Point Battery, South Carolina, 622
Whites, LeeAnn, *as contributor*, 350–351
White's Ford, 1556
White supremacy
  urban, 1647
  see also Proslavery; Racism; Slavery
White Supremacy and Negro Subordination (Van Evrie), 1275
Whitfield, John Wilkins, **1711**
Whitfield, Robert Henry, 1083, **1711**
Whiting, W. H. C., 611, 612, **1711–1712**, 1727
Whitlock's Warehouse, 265
Whitman, Walt, 937
Whitney, B. A., 777
Whitney, Eli, 417, 552, 1436
Whitney-style revolver. *See* Handguns
Whittier, John Greenleaf, 646
Whittle, William C., 993, **1712**
Whittle, William C., Jr., 1712
Whitworth, Joseph, 1467
  ordnance manufacture, 102, 1120
Whitworth guns, 49, 50, 93, 102–103, *103*, 917, 1119, 1120
Who Shall Rule This Nation (Songs of Henry Clay Work) (recording), 487
Why the South Lost the Civil War (Beringer, Hattaway, Jones, and Still), 333, 334
Wichitas, 425, 811, 813
Wickham, Williams Carter, **1712–1714**
Wickliffe, Charles A., 887
Wickliffe, Robert, 215
Wiener, Jonathan, 172
Wigfall, Halsey, 1717
Wigfall, Levi Durand, and Eliza Wigfall, 1714
Wigfall, Louis T., 300, 861, 872, 878, 1171, 1585, **1714–1717**, 1749
  Hood's Texas Brigade, 791
  opposition to Davis (Jefferson), 1225, 1716–1717
Wiggins, Sarah Woolfolk, *as contributor*, 355–356, 431–432, 444, 479, 569, 630–631, 729–730, 865, 963–964, 1075, 1302, 1343, 1680
Wilcox, Cadmus Marcellus, 1002, 1043, **1718**
Wilcox, John A., 444, **1718–1719**
Wild, Edward A., 1630
Wildcat currency. *See* Shinplasters
Wilder, John, 238, 304, 1093
Wilderness (novel by Warren), 939
Wilderness campaign, 25, 81, 850, **1719–1721**
  casualties, 338, 1721
  cavalry, 270
  Early, Jubal, 503
  Ewell, Richard, 550
  field fortifications, 626
  Gregg, John, 716
  Hampton, Wade, 731
  Hill, A. P., 771
  Hood's Texas Brigade, 791
  infantry, 817
  Jackson, Thomas J. ("Stonewall"), 835
  Jenkins, Micah, 844
  Jones, John M., 867
  Lee, Robert E., 716, 920, 1719–1721
  Longstreet, James, 82, 817, 891, 892, 946, 1418, 1518, 1719, 1720, 1721
  Louisiana Tigers, 958
  map, 1720
  Pegram, John, 1186
  Sanders, John Caldwell Calhoun, 1364
  Sorrel, Gilbert Moxley, 1503
  and Spotsylvania campaign, 1520
  Stafford, Leroy, 1521
  Stuart, J. E. B., 1554
  telegraph use, 1573
  Wilcox, Cadmus Marcellus, 1718
Wildway plantation, 187
Wildwood plantation, 347
Wiley, Bell Irwin, 4, 11, 74, 1103
Wiley, Calvin H., 44, 515, 1587, **1721–1722**
Wilkes, Charles, 481, 711, 1015, 1454, 1528, 1619, 1620
Wilkes, Peter Singleton, 641, **1722**
Wilkesboro, North Carolina, 1152
Wilkinson, John, 182, 301, 1341, 1567, **1722–1723**, 1727
Wilkinson, Susan, 1207
Wilkinson, Warren, *as contributor*, 30–33, 292–295, 442, 637, 664, 895–897, 1092–1093, 1703–1705, 1736
Willard Hotel (Washington, D.C.), 1689
Willey, Waitman T., 1699–1700, 1702
William Aiken (ship), 1530
William C. Miller and Sons, 25, 591
William G. Hewes (ship), 185
William Glaze & Co., 1464
William H. Webb (ship). *See Webb* (ship)
William J. McElroy Company, 514
William Laird and Sons Company. *See* Laird shipyards
William L. Smith (engine), 41
William Mitten (Longstreet), 936, 937
William Penny & Co., 372
Williams, Alpheus, 1406
Williams, Ben Ames, 939
Williams, James, 10–11
Williams, John (captain), 310
Williams, John S. ("Cerro Gordo"), 244, 497, 761, 1363, 1593, **1724**
Williams, T. Harry, 327, 797
Williams, Thomas, 140, 141
Williamsburg, Virginia, **1724–1725**
  field fortifications, 625
  Garland, Samuel, 663
  Hill, A. P., 770
  Lamar, L. Q. C., 906
  Longstreet, James, 35, 1191, 1193, 1725
  Peninsular campaign, 1191, *1192*, 1193
  Wickham, Williams Carter, 1712
Williamson, William P., 1236, 1670, **1725**
Willich, August, 1094
Willington, Aaron, 1144
Willink, Henry F., 1366, 1422
Wills, Brian S., *as contributor*, 2, 154, 218–219, 239, 244–245, 275–276, 478, 496, 606–609, 614–616, 636–637, 666, 683–684, 717–718, 846, 964, 994–996, 1020–1021, 1074, 1195, 1239–1240, 1328–1329, 1343, 1389–1390, 1400–1401, 1711, 1724–1725, 1752
Willy, A. B., 572, 573
Wilmington, North Carolina, 179, **1726–1727**
  blockade of, 1648
  blockade running, 1152, 1647, 1648
  capture, 1152
  defenses, 48, 205
  entry port, 182
  Fort Fisher, 611
  hospitals, 794
  newspapers, 1142–1143
  port closing, 183
  railroads, 1297
  Union occupation, 1640
Wilmington (ship), 1727
Wilmington and Manchester Railroad, 1726
Wilmington and Weldon Railroad, 729, 1200, 1294–1295, 1296, 1297, 1330, 1364, 1726

Wilmington, Charlotte, and Rutherford, 1726
Wilmington Squadron, ships, 1124, 1302
Wilmot, David, 380, 1374, 1728
Wilmot Proviso, 320, 321-322, 354, 380, 675, 1374, 1533, 1678, 1715, **1728**; *see also* Compromise of 1850
Wilson, Augusta Evans. *See* Evans, Augusta Jane
Wilson, Charles Henry, 290
Wilson, Charles Reagan, *as contributor*, 459–461
Wilson, Claudius Charles, **1728–1729**
Wilson, Henry, 542
Wilson, James H.
  burning of *Jackson* (ship), 839
  Columbus Naval Iron Works capture, 372
  raid on Selma, Alabama, 17–18, 19, 173, 362, 607, 658, 673, 1066, 1388, 1389–1390, 1410, 1648
  surrender of Macon, Georgia, 978
Wilson, Lorenzo Madison, 547
Wilson, Terry P., *as contributor*, 198–199, 253–254, 868, 1173
Wilson, Thomas Ruggles, 1247
Wilson, William Sydney, 1173, **1729**
Wilson, Woodrow, 572, 1247
Wilson's Creek campaign, 53, 343, 490, 695, 811, 973, 981, 1053, 1180, 1251, 1606, 1693, **1729–1731**
  map, 1729
Wilson Zouaves, 35
Winchester, Virginia, 81, 549, 582, 647, 693, 850, 894, 957, 1145, 1418, 1555, **1731–1733**
  Ashby, Turner, 104
  captured artillery, 101
  Early, Jubal, 502
  Jackson, Thomas J. ("Stonewall"), 834, 1415, 1416
  map, 1732
  Peck, William Raine, 1185
  in Sheridan (Philip H.) strategy, 1418
  Smith, E. Kirby, 1473
  Stafford, Leroy A., 1521
Winchester and Potomac Railroad, 1732
Winder, Charles S., 272, 834, 914, 1565, **1733–1734**
  Stonewall Brigade command, 1549
Winder, John H., 38, 213, 266, 1142, 1256, 1257, 1261, 1262, 1265, 1267–1268, **1734**, 1735
  as provost marshal, 1277
  Richmond command, 314, 727
  and Salisbury Prison conditions, 1362
Winder, Richard B., 38
Winder, William Henry, 1734
Winder, William Sidney, 38, 39
Winder Hospital (Richmond), 795, 796, 1667
Windward (ship), 841
Wings (army divisions), 66
Winkler, C. M., 791
Winner, Septimus, 1103
Winnsboro, South Carolina, 1510
Winschel, Terrence J., *as contributor*, 1236–1238
Winslow, John A., 20, 1394
Winslow (ship), 1530
Winston, John A., 598, 808
Winston County, Alabama, 720
Winthrop, Theodore, 172
Wiretaps. *See* Telegraph
Wirz, Henry, **1734–1735**
  Andersonville Prison, 38–39, 40
  hanging of, *1735*
  monument, 1028
  trial, 1264
  trial re-creation, 574
  trial reportage, 866
  trial testimony, 867
Wisconsin
  statehood, 555
  state rights, 1534
Wise, Henry A., 159, 245, 474, 544, 907, 1142, 1150, 1629, 1630, 1662, 1700, **1736**, 1743
  Petersburg campaign, 1198
  seizure of Harpers Ferry, 104, 740
Wise, O. J., 245, 1142
Wise, Stephen R., *as contributor*, 43, 179–186, 905, 1726–1727, 1742–1743
Wise Legion Cavalry, 843, 1736
Wise's Fork, 894
Withers, Jones Mitchell, 32, 664, 1592, 1613, **1736–1737**
  Murfreesboro, Tennessee, 1094, 1096
Withers, Thomas, **1737**
Witherspoon, James Hervey, **1737**
Wivern (ship), 903, 904
Wm. R. King (ship), 801
Wofford, William Tatum, 791, **1738**
Wofford College, 517, 518
Wolfe, Charles K., *as contributor*, 487–488, 488–489, 1100–1105
Wolford, Frank L., 887
Women, **1738–1742**
  abolitionism, 44, 1623
  African American, 520, 521, 900, 1439, 1741–1742
  aid societies, 378–379, 671, 1488, 1502, 1647
  bread riots, 212, 566–567, 596, 978, 1058, 1226, 1517
  Burial of Latané, 242, *243*
  Butler's woman order, **246–247**, 1138
  Castle Thunder prisoners, 265–266
  changing role of, 387, 461, 470–471, 563, 591, 671, 1487–1488, 1586
  Chesnut (Mary Boykin) on, 300
  concern over subscription, 1216
  courtship, 421–422
  diaries and letters, 307, 387, 422, 471–472, 1009, 1226, 1739, 1741
  disguised as men, 265, 421, 1740
  education, 516, **520–521**, 1108
  first U.S. Army surgeon, 266
  food riots. *See subhead* bread riots *above*
  food scavenging, 597
  handicrafts, 735
  hospital work, 152–153, 222, 671, 795, 796, 1141, 1160–1161, 1740
  increased political power, 1226
  Lost Cause romanticization, 422
  and male code of honor, 786
  marriage and divorce, 1009–1010
  memorial associations, 922, 1027
  memorials to, 1028, 1069
  nursing, 547, 671, 795, 1188, 1740; *see also subhead* hospital work *above*
  patriotism, 421, 1215
  plain folk, 1213
  plantation mistress, **1218–1219**, 1738
  preachers, 1320
  prostitution, 1276–1277
  purity ideal, 1277
  refugees, 1319
  religious culture, 923
  role of Davis (Varina Howell), 457
  selected bibliography, 170
  slave. *See subhead* African American *above*
  soldiers' aid societies, 1502
  spies, 143, 201–202, 387, 540, 542–544, 601, 714, 750, 1074–1075, 1432, 1487, 1623, 1652, 1740
  teachers, 520, 521, 1488, 1740
  Treasury clerks, 315, 370, 1614
  urban social benevolence, 378–379, 1647
  violence against, 427, 719, 720
  War Department, 316
  wartime class conflict, 1492
  white, 1738–1741

Women, *continued*
women's rights advocates, 1034
in work force, 315, 547, 900–901, 903, 1057, 1614, 1687, 1740–1741
Women's aid societies, 378–379, 671, 1488, 1502, 1647
Women's Christian Temperance Union, 1488
Women's Relief Society, 1160
Wood, Benjamin, 411, 1271–1272, 1743
Wood, Fernando, 905, **1742–1743**
Wood, George B., 758
Wood, John Taylor, 375, 376, 1567, **1743–1744**
underwriter raid, 1371
Wood, Robert C., Jr., 1743
Wood, Sterling Alexander Martin, 263, 1422, **1744**
Wood, Thomas, 294, 295, 1095
Woodard, John R., *as contributor*, 121–122, 442–443, 527–528, 665, 930, 1404
Woodclads, 1302
Woodfin, Nicholas W., 446
Woodruff, William, Sr., 940, 941
Woodruff, William E. (colonel), 843
Woodson, W. O., 1684
Woodstock, Virginia, 1419
"Woodstock Races," 1419
Woodward, C. Vann, 300, 471, 949
Woodward, George W., 411
Woodward, Thomas S., 1046
Woodworth, Steven E., *as contributor*, 155–157, 857–858, 1483, 1654
Wool, John, 1149
Woolcott, Francis, 1103
Wooster, Ralph A., *as contributor*, 463
Word of Warning for the Sick Soldier, A (revivalist tract), 459–461
Work, Henry Clay, 487
Workers. *See* Labor
World in Miniatures, The (book), 1588
Worth, Daniel, 44
Worth, Jonathan, 44, 428, 690, 912, 1151, 1154, 1157, 1638
Worth, Joseph A., 1154, 1668
Wrenn, Ella, 1231, 1590
Wright, Ambrose Ransom ("Rans"), 13, 29, 281, 690, 1503, **1744**
Savannah defense, 1368
Wright, Augustus Romaldus, **1745**
Wright, D. Giraud, Mrs., 265
Wright, David, 1149
Wright, Horatio G., 45, 504, 582, 890, 1201, 1520
Shenandoah campaign, 1417, 1419
Wright, John C., 1337
Wright, John V., **1745–1746**
Wright, Marcus Joseph, 1745, **1746**
Wright, Phineas C., 412
Wright, William Bacon, 1088, **1746**
Wrighton, W. T., 1103
Wright's Boys, 1745
Wyatt-Brown, Bertram, *as contributor*, 492, 786–788
Wyllie, Joannes, 184
Wyndham, Sir Percy, 105
Wyoming (ship), 1393
Wytheville Mines (Virginia), 913, 1147
Wytheville Telegraph (Virginia newspaper), 1582

Y

Yager, Richard, 721
Yahola, Opothle. *See* Opothleyahola
Yalobusha Rifles, 1682
Yancey, William Lowndes, 14, 16, 173, 308, 348, 423, 803, 841, 842, 964, 1065, 1066, 1068, 1324, 1678, 1695, **1747–1750**
conflict with Hill (Benjamin), 772
diplomatic missions, 418, 479, 480, 482, 1347, 1527
filibustering expeditions, 808
fire-eater label, 582, 1376–1377
influence, 1151, 1350
opponents, 1477
views on proposed supreme court, 872
Yazoo City, Mississippi, 1033, 1681
Yazoo River, 227, 1425
Yeardon, Richard, 1144
Yearns, W. Buck, *as contributor*, 312–313, 391–394, 434, 701–704
Ye Exploits of Ye Distinguished Attorney and General B. F. B. (Bombastes Furioso Buncombe) (Volck), 1673
Yell, Archibald, 1340
Yellow Bayou, Louisiana, 1316, 1317
Yellow fever, 754
Florida (ship) epidemic, 591
Galveston, Texas, 655
New Orleans epidemic, 790
Norfolk epidemic, 1038
North Carolina, 926, 1726
Yellowley, Edward C., 220
"Yellow Rose of Texas, The" (song), 1103
Yellow Tavern, Virginia, **1750–1751**
Stuart (J. E. B.) mortally wounded at, 1519, 1553
Yell Rifles, 352–353
Yeomanry
conscription and, 1155, 1492
impact of slave system on, 1440–1441
as plain folk, **1212–1214**
refugees and, 1491
secessionist movement and, 1378, 1380–1381
social class, 1490
war-created poverty, 1155, 1491, 1492
Yonah (engine), 41
York, Zebulon, 504, 958, **1751–1752**
York (ship), 1269
York River
defense, 1712
Peninsular campaign, 1400, 1402
Yorktown, Virginia, 496, 540, 1191, 1192, 1306, **1752**
use of land mines, 734
Yorktown (ship), *1671*
see also Patrick Henry
Yorktown-Warwick line, 625
You Are There (television program), 573
Young, Bennett H., 258, 350, 538
Young, H. E., *77*
Young, Henry C., 1431
Young, Pierce Manning Butler, 364, 674, **1752–1753**
Young, Stark, 578, 939
Young, William Hugh, **1753–1754**
Younger, Bob. *See* Younger brothers
Younger, Coleman. *See* Younger brothers
Younger, Henry W. (father of Bob). *See* Younger brothers
Younger, James ("Jim"). *See* Younger brothers
Younger, John. *See* Younger brothers
Younger, Thomas Coleman ("Cole"). *See* Younger brothers
Younger brothers, 721, 1054, 1289, **1754**
Youths. *See* Childhood
Yulee, David Levy, 581, 845, 1090

Z

Zamacona, Manuel Mara, 1209
Zollicoffer, Felix K., 263, 428, 827, 887, **1755**
Mill Springs, Kentucky, 1041, 1042
Zouaves, Confederate, 35, 957, 1137
Columbia, South Carolina, 733
Louisiana, 603